FOUNDATIONS
OF EVOLUTIONARY
PSYCHOLOGY

FOUNDATIONS OF EVOLUTIONARY PSYCHOLOGY

EDITED BY

CHARLES CRAWFORD
DENNIS KREBS

 Lawrence Erlbaum Associates
Taylor & Francis Group

New York   London

Lawrence Erlbaum Associates
Taylor & Francis Group
270 Madison Avenue
New York, NY 10016

Lawrence Erlbaum Associates
Taylor & Francis Group
2 Park Square
Milton Park, Abingdon
Oxon OX14 4RN

© 2008 by Taylor & Francis Group, LLC
Lawrence Erlbaum Associates is an imprint of Taylor & Francis Group, an Informa business

Printed in the United States of America on acid-free paper
10 9 8 7 6 5 4 3 2 1

International Standard Book Number-13: 978-0-8058-5957-7 (Softcover) 978-0-8058-5956-0 (Hardcover)

Library of Congress Cataloging-in-Publication Data

Foundations of evolutionary psychology / [edited by] Charles Crawford and Dennis Krebs.
   p. cm.
   Includes bibliographical references and index.
   ISBN-13: 978-0-8058-5957-7 (alk. paper)
   ISBN-10: 0-8058-5957-8 (alk. paper)
   1. Evolutionary psychology. I. Crawford, Charles (Charles B.) II.
   Krebs, Dennis. III. Title.

BF698.95.F68 2007
155.7--dc22   2007016577

Visit the Taylor & Francis Web site at
http://www.taylorandfrancis.com

and the LEA and Routledge Web site at
http://www.routledge.com

Contents

Preface   ix

About the Editors   xiii

Contributors   xv

1   Evolutionary Psychology: The Historical Context 1
Catherine Salmon and Charles Crawford

PART I   Biological Foundations of Evolutionary Psychology

2   Evolutionary Questions for Evolutionary Psychologists 25
John Alcock and Charles Crawford

3   Life History Theory and Human Development 47
Stephen C. Stearns, Nadine Allal, and Ruth Mace

4   Sex and Sexual Selection 71
Anders Pape Møller

5   Kinship and Social Behavior 91
Stuart A. West, Andy Gardner, and Ashleigh S. Griffin

PART II   Development: The Bridge from Evolutionary Theory to Evolutionary Psychology

6   Sociogenomics for the Cognitive Adaptationist 117
William M. Brown

7   Selfish Genes, Developmental Systems, and the Evolution of Development 137

Michele K. Surbey

PART III *Evolved Mental Mechanisms: The Essence of Evolutionary Psychology*

8   Biological Adaptations and Human Behavior 153

Steven W. Gangestad

9   Evolved Cognitive Mechanisms and Human Behavior 173

H. Clark Barrett

10   Adaptations, Environments, and Behavior: Then and Now 191

Charles Crawford

11   Evolutionary Psychology Research Methods 215

David P. Schmitt

PART IV *The Evolutionary Psychology of Sex Differences*

12   Physical Attractiveness: Signals of Phenotypic Quality and Beyond 239

Glenn J. Scheyd, Christine E. Garver-Apgar, and Steven W. Gangestad

13   Two Human Natures: How Men and Women Evolved Different Psychologies 261

Alastair P. C. Davies and Todd K. Shackelford

14   Heroes and Hos: Reflections of Male and Female Sexual Natures 281

Catherine Salmon

PART V *The Evolutionary Psychology of Prosocial Behavior*

15   How Selfish by Nature? 293

Dennis Krebs

16   Gene-Culture Coevolution and the Emergence of Altruistic Behavior
      in Humans 313

      Herbert Gintis, Samuel Bowles, Robert Boyd, and Ernst Fehr

17   Renaissance of the Individual: Reciprocity, Positive Assortment,
      and the Puzzle of Human Cooperation 331

      Dominic D. P. Johnson, Michael E. Price, and Masanori Takezawa

18   Cooperation and Conflict between Kith, Kin, and Strangers:
      Game Theory by Domains 353

      Douglas T. Kenrick, Jill M. Sundie, and Robert Kurzban

19   On the Evolution of Moral Sentiments 371

      Robert H. Frank

PART VI The Evolutionary Psychology of Antisocial Behavior and Psychopathology

20   Is the "Cinderella Effect" Controversial?: A Case Study of
      Evolution-Minded Research and Critiques Thereof 383

      Martin Daly and Margo Wilson

21   Intergroup Prejudices and Intergroup Conflicts 401

      Mark Schaller and Steven L. Neuberg

22   The Evolution of Brain Mechanisms for Social Behavior 415

      Simon Baron-Cohen

23   An Evolutionary Theory of Mind and Mental Illness:
      Genetic Conflict and the Mentalistic Continuum 433

      Christopher Badcock

24   Psychopathology and Mental Illness 453

      Alfonso Troisi

PART VII Exploring the Explanatory Power of Evolutionary Psychology

25   The Evolutionary Psychology of Religion 477

Scott Atran

Author Index   499

Subject Index   511

Preface

This is the third version of books we have edited that are designed to help integrate evolutionary theory into psychology and the other human behavioral sciences. The first version, *Psychology and Sociobiology: Ideas, Issues and Applications*, appeared in 1987. At that time, evolutionary psychology, as we now know it, was just coming into being. In the preface to the 1987 book, we argued, "Sophisticated explanations of behavior require an understanding of both its adaptive significance and the proximate mechanisms producing it." Our goal was to produce a book that "would facilitate the integration of evolutionary theory into psychology and the other social sciences by communicating some of the major ideas, issues and applications of sociobiology that are relevant to psychology."

The second version, titled *Handbook of Evolutionary Psychology: Idea, Issues and Applications,* appeared 10 years later. By that time, evolutionary psychology, the study of the naturally selected design of innate psychological mechanisms, had replaced sociobiology as the venue for integrating evolutionary thinking into psychology and the other human behavioral sciences. An important feature of the second version of our book was its emphasis on evolutionary theory. Four of the 21 chapters were devoted to basic ideas in evolutionary theory. The remaining 17 chapters focused on issues and applications of the theory of evolution to the study of human behavior.

Evolutionary psychology has flourished since the publication of the second version of our book in 1998. Many mainstream psychology journals, such as *Psychological Bulletin, Psychological Review,* and the *Journal of Personality and Social Psychology,* regularly publish articles by researchers using evolutionary psychology as their theoretical orientation. Each year, a dozen or more academic books on evolutionary psychology are published. The trade shelves in bookstores contain a wide variety of books purporting to use evolutionary theory to help with a wide variety of personal, social, and political problems. The days when a mainstream psychology journal would publish a review of a book applying evolutionary thinking to human behavior under a title like "Sociobiology: The psychology of sex, violence and oppression," as *Contemporary Psychology* did in 1990, are gone.

Nevertheless, evolutionary psychology, in its present form, remains a newcomer to the field of psychology. Is it a separate area of psychology, such as behavioral neuroscience, social psychology, or developmental psychology? Or does it belong within one of these areas of psychology; and if it does, which one will it inhabit? Is it a perspective that should infuse all areas of psychology? Is it a methodology like statistics and research design? Is it both a perspective and a methodology? How and when should be it taught? These are some of the questions that must be answered if evolutionary psychology is to continue growing.

Foundations of Evolutionary Psychology is not a book advocating the application of evolutionary theory to psychology. Those who read it will already be interested in at least exploring the application of Darwinian thinking to the study of human behavior. The book is designed for 4th-year undergraduates, graduate students, and interested professionals who wish to either learn evolutionary psychology from the ground up or wish to advance their understanding of basic issues and applications. Hence, it is both a textbook and a handbook.

Foundations begins with a chapter on the history of attempts to apply evolutionary theory to psychology since Darwin's suggestion in the *Origin of the Species* that "psychology will be based on a new foundation, that of the necessary acquirement of each mental power and capacity by gradation. Light will be thrown on the origin of man and his history." This chapter is followed by seven sections.

The first section, *The Biological Foundations of Evolutionary Psychology*, contains four chapters. It begins with "Evolutionary questions for evolutionary psychologists," is coauthored by a biologist and an evolutionary psychologist, and includes chapters on life history theory, sex and sexual selection, and kinship and social behavior. These four chapters provide a thorough introduction to those aspects of evolutionary theory that we believe are essential for developing rigorous evolutionary explanations for human behaviors. However, the chapters on history and evolutionary theory provide a good introduction to the study of evolution and human behavior. Some readers may wish to begin with the these two chapters and treat the life history theory, sexual selection, and kinship chapters as reference material to be consulted as needed when reading the other chapters.

The goal of part II, *Development: The Bridge from Evolutionary Theory to Evolutionary Psychology*, is to develop the relation between ultimate evolutionary explanations considered in part I to the proximate psychological explanations considered in the remainder of the book. The primary focus is on developmental genetics and their role in developing proximate explanations for psychological phenomena. The issue of developmental systems theory, the notion that hierarchical gene-environment interactions at many levels provides a preferred alternative to evolutionary psychology for developing an evolutionary approach to psychology, is considered in these chapters.

Evolutionary psychology has become the study of how evolved, innate specialized psychological mechanisms are involved in the production of human behavior. Part III, *Evolved Mental Mechanisms: The Essence of Evolutionary Psychology*, contains four chapters that are necessary to understand current thinking in evolutionary psychology. The first deals with the nature of evolved adaptations, and the second considers the nature of specialized cognitive mechanisms, which are the focus of much research in evolutionary psychology. The third considers how adaptations that evolved in ancestral environments function in the environments where we now live. The fourth discusses research methods that can be used by evolutionary psychologists to study how psychological adaptations function.

One of the most fascinating aspects of evolutionary psychology is how it explains gender differences in behavior. The three chapters in part IV, *The Evolutionary Psychology of Sex Differences*, apply some ideas from sexual selection theory, explained in chapter 4, to gender differences in behavior. The first two chapters focus on aspects of mate choice, while the third deals with gender differences in pornography. These three chapters provide an entry into the extensive literature on gender differences in mate choice and the management of interactions with mates that has developed in the last 15 years.

We humans have been struggling with problems of how to live together in more or less harmonious ways since the beginning of recorded time. The first chapter in part V, *The Evolutionary Psychology of Prosocial Behavior*, explores the age-old question of how selfish we are by nature. The section continues with three chapters that consider recent research on how cooperation, altruism, and morality can be understood from an evolutionary perspective. An important theme in these chapters is the role of moral emotions, empathy, and ethnic identity in the moderation of self-directed and other-directed behaviors.

Part VI, *The Evolutionary Psychology of Antisocial Behavior and Psychopathology*, begins with a chapter by two of the founders of evolutionary psychology, whose work on homicide, child abuse, and child neglect has recently been criticized by those who claim that its deficiencies cast doubt on the whole enterprise of evolutionary psychology. Marin Daly and Margo Wilson defend their theory and research, and they identify glaring problems in the evidence adduced against them by critics. The following chapter deals with an issue of considerable practical importance in the modern world, prejudice and conflict between groups. The next two chapters deal with a set of similar issues pertaining to sex differences in empathy, theory of mind, mechanistic abilities, and systematizing. In addition, both of these chapters deal with autism, a topic that is currently of considerable theoretical and practical significance.

Part VII, *Exploring the Explanatory Power of Evolutionary Psychology*, contains only one chapter, which focuses on one of the great challenges for evolutionary psychologists: religion. Religion is universal. It has great costs. It is the source of good and evil. Using evolutionary psychology to account for religion is a challenging enterprise that is explored fully in the final chapter.

As we see it, this book can be used in a number of ways. First, a through reading of all chapters would offer a great introduction to evolutionary psychology for advanced undergraduate students and all graduate students. The material is organized in a way that lends itself to use in both seminar and lecture courses. If it is used in a seminar course, the instructor may need to assist students who do not have a background in biology to understand the material in part I, *Biological Foundations of Evolutionary Psychology*, and part 2, *Development: The Bridge from Evolutionary Theory to Evolutionary Psychology*. A less demanding course would use chapters 1 and 2, and then move to part III, *Evolved Mental Mechanisms: The Essence of Evolutionary Psychology*. In this case, the material in chapters three through seven can be used as supplementary resource material. *Foundations of Evolutionary Psychology* can also be used as a resource for researchers and other professionals who would profit from a thorough introduction to the theory and methods of evolutionary psychology.

About the Editors

Charles Crawford is an emeritus professor of psychology at Simon Fraser University, Burnaby, British Columbia, Canada. He earned a B.A. (Honors) and M.Sc. from the University of Alberta, and a Ph.D. from McGill University. Dr. Crawford is a fellow of the Canadian Psychological Association and the Association of Psychological Science and winner of the Sterling Prize for Controversy. He was a visiting professor of psychology at Tianjin Normal University, Tianjin, PR China during 2004 and is returning there this fall to teach evolutionary psychology to senior undergraduates and graduate students.

He began his academic career in multivariate statistical analysis. During the late 1970s he worked in behavior genetics for several years. Since the early 1980s Dr. Crawford has devoted all of his academic energies to the application of evolutionary theory to psychology. As he sees it, evolutionary psychology is concerned with the stresses and problems our primate and hominin ancestors encountered in their environments, the specialized psychological mechanisms that natural selection shaped to help them deal with these problems and stresses, and the way the specialized psychological mechanisms that evolved enable us to function in the moments of evolutionary time where we live. Hence, he sees evolutionary psychology as an environmentalist discipline because it focuses on understanding psychological adaptations that helped our human and primate ancestors deal with the stress and strains of their environment. Dr. Crawford's current research focuses on the relation between ancestral environments, ancestral adaptations and current behavior; the reproductive suppression model of anorexic behavior; and integrating evolutionary theory into psychology.

He is a hard core evolutionary psychologist who takes every opportunity to fight crypto creationism--the notion that natural selection made us humans so special a being that if God did not create us, then we must have created ourselves.

Dr. Crawford lives on the Fraser River in New Westminster, British Columbia, with his wife, Carol. When he is not doing evolutionary psychology he "visits" his grandchildren using web cameras, tries his hand at cooking, and plays his Roland Digital accordion.

Dennis Krebs is a colleague of Charles Crawford at Simon Fraser University. He grew up in Vancouver, Canada, received his B.A. degree from the University of British Columbia, and won a Woodrow Wilson Fellowship. He was awarded M.A. and Ph.D. degrees from Harvard University. Dr. Krebs taught at Harvard for several years before returning to Canada. He spent a year at (and is a Fellow of) The Center for Advanced Study in the Behavioral Sciences. He has won an Excellence in Teaching award from Simon Fraser University, and was selected as one of the top 10 educational leaders in Canada by the 3M selection committee. Dr. Krebs has published more than 80 articles and has edited or co-edited several books. His recent publications advance an integrative model of the evolution of morality.

Contributors

John Alcock
School of Life Sciences
Arizona State University
Tempe, Arizona

Nadine Allal
Department of Anthropology
University College London
London, United Kingdom

Scott Atran
Institut Jean Nichod
CNRS
Paris, France
Institute for Social Research
The University of Michigan
Ann Arbor, Michigan
John Jay College of Criminal Justice
New York, New York

Christopher Badcock
University of London
London, United Kingdom

Simon Baron-Cohen
Autism Research Centre
Department of Psychiatry
University of Cambridge
Cambridge, United Kingdom

H. Clark Barrett
Department of Anthropology
University of California, Los Angeles
Los Angeles, California

Samuel Bowles
Santa Fe Institute
Santa Fe, New Mexico
Department of Economics
University of Siena
Siena, Italy
Department of Economics
University of Massachusetts Amherst
Amherst, Massachusetts

Robert Boyd
Department of Anthropology
University of California, Los Angeles
Los Angeles, California

William M. Brown
Department of Psychology
Brunel University West London
Uxbridge, Middlesex, United Kingdom

Charles Crawford
Department of Psychology
Simon Fraser University
Burnaby, British Columbia, Canada

Martin Daly
Department of Psychology, Neuroscience &
  Behaviour
McMaster University
Hamilton, Ontario, Canada

Alastair P. C. Davies
Department of Psychology
Florida Atlantic University
Davie, Florida

Ernst Fehr
Institute for Empirical Research in Economics
University of Zurich
Zurich, Switzerland
Department of Economics
Massachusetts Institute of Technology
Cambridge, Massachusetts

Robert H. Frank
Johnson Graduate School of Management
Cornell University
Ithaca, New York

Steven W. Gangestad
Department of Psychology
University of New Mexico
Albuquerque, New Mexico

Andy Gardner
Institute of Evolutionary Biology
School of Biological Sciences
The University of Edinburgh
Edinburgh, Scotland

Christine E. Garver-Apgar
Department of Psychology
University of New Mexico
Albuquerque, New Mexico

Herbert Gintis
Santa Fe Institute
Santa Fe, New Mexico
Department of Economics
Central European University
Budapest, Hungry

Ashleigh S. Griffin
Institute of Evolutionary Biology
School of Biological Sciences
The University of Edinburgh
Edinburgh, Scotland

Dominic D. P. Johnson
Department of Politics
School of Social and Political Studies
The University of Edinburgh
Edinburgh, Scotland

Douglas T. Kenrick
Department of Psychology
Arizona State University
Tempe, Arizona

Dennis Krebs
Psychology Department
Simon Fraser University
Burnaby, British Columbia, Canada

Robert Kurzban
Department of Psychology
University of Pennsylvania
Philadelphia, Pennsylvania

Ruth Mace
Department of Anthropology
University College London
London, United Kingdom

Anders Pape Møller
Laboratoire de Parasitologie Evolutive
Université Pierre et Marie Curie
Paris, France

Steven L. Neuberg
Department of Psychology
Arizona State University
Tempe, Arizona

Michael E. Price
Department of Psychology
Centre for Culture and Evolutionary Psychology
School of Social Sciences
Brunel University, West London
Uxbridge, Middlesex, United Kingdom

Catherine Salmon
Department of Psychology
University of Redlands
Redlands, California

Mark Schaller
Department of Psychology
University of British Columbia
Vancouver, British Columbia, Canada

Glenn J. Scheyd
Division of Social and Behavioral Sciences
Nova Southeastern University
Davie, Florida

David P. Schmitt
Department of Psychology
Bradley University
Peoria, Illinois

Todd K. Shackelford
Department of Psychology
Florida Atlantic University
Davie, Florida

Stephen C. Stearns
Department of Ecology and Evolutionary
    Biology
Yale University
New Haven, Connecticut

Jill M. Sundie
Department of Marketing & Entrepreneurship
C.T. Bauer College of Business
University of Houston
Houston, Texas

Michele K. Surbey
Department of Psychology
School of Arts and Social Sciences
James Cook University
Townsville, QLD, Australia

Masanori Takezawa
Tilburg Institute for Behavioral Economic
    Research
Department of Social Psychology
Tilburg University
Tilburg, The Netherlands

Alfonso Troisi
Department of Neurosciences
School of Medicine
University of Rome Tor Vergata
Rome, Italy

Stuart A. West
Institute of Evolutionary Biology
School of Biological Sciences
The University of Edinburgh
Edinburgh, Scotland

Margo Wilson
Department of Psychology, Neuroscience &
    Behaviour
McMaster University
Hamilton, Ontario, Canada

1

Evolutionary Psychology
The Historical Context

CATHERINE SALMON AND
CHARLES CRAWFORD

"In the distant future I see open fields for far more important researchers. Psychology will be based on a new foundation, that of the necessary acquirement of each mental power and capacity by gradation. Light will be thrown on the origin of man and his history."

Charles Darwin, 1859, *On the Origin of Species*

One such new field is Evolutionary Psychology. This discipline focuses on the study of human behavior from an adaptationist perspective, examining the mental mechanisms that evolved to solve problems faced in our ancestral past and how those mechanisms continue to produce behavior today. There are several peer review journals that focus specifically on this field, including Evolution and Human Behavior and Human Nature; ones that focus mainly on this field, including Evolution and Cognition and Politics and the Life Sciences; and many others that regularly publish articles from this perspective including Behavioral and Brain Sciences, Journal of Personality and Social Psychology, Animal Behavior, Quarterly Review of Biology, and Cognition. This chapter will describe the historical antecedents of the evolutionarily informed study of human behavior.

EVOLUTIONARY THINKING BEFORE DARWIN

For much of our recorded history, and perhaps long before, people have been fascinated with the natural world and our place in it. The complexity of our own nature, both physical and mental, has been a source of particular interest. How could something as complex as a person come into existence if not by the hand of God? In the eyes of many, such complexity (epitomized by the

1

human eye) seemed to require special design, which implies a designer. The idea that all of nature, including man, was created as it is by an omnipotent power has been a wide-ranging belief, formalized in religious doctrine. Aristotle contributed to this belief with "The Great Chain of Being," the idea being that each species had its own particular place in a hierarchical progression. God was at the top of the ladder (true perfection), followed by angels, men, women, animals, plants, and inanimate objects. The implication is that there is a natural order to things, something or someone cannot move from one rung of the ladder to another.

But not all pre-Darwin thinking about human origins was quite so creationist. Plato (as cited in Davis, 1849), for example, suggested, in discussing the ideal society, that

> It necessarily follows ... from what has been acknowledged that the best men should as often as possible form alliances with the best women, and the most depraved men, on the contrary, with the most depraved women; and the offspring of the former is to be educated, but not of the latter, if the flock is to be of the most perfect kind ... As for those youths, who distinguish themselves, either in war or other pursuits, they ought to have rewards and prizes given them, and the most ample liberty of lying with women, that so, under this pretext, the greatest number of children may spring from such parentage. (p. 144)

Plato was making not only moral statements but genetic ones as well. Of course, animal domestication and breeding had been going on among early hunter-gatherers. As far back as 15,000 BC, dogs and sheep were shaped through a combination of natural selection and selective breeding by humans. Plato applied the same thinking to humans, suggesting that moral qualities could also be bred for selectively in order to produce a more ideal society.

The 1700s were a century in which many ideas about evolution were proposed, most characterized by a belief in progress. Condorcet argued that man's history illustrated movement from lower to higher states. Humans developed from primitive savages through increasing enlightenment, and ultimately, they would reach perfection. Lyell, focusing on the earth rather than people, claimed that the land and seas acquired their current form gradually through a series of causes or events that continue to operate and can be observed. German philosopher Immanuel Kant (1798/1998) suggested that other primates might develop the mechanisms for walking and speech, to evolve the capacities of man including reason. Erasmus Darwin proposed that all living things could have emerged from a common ancestor, with competition the driving force. Lamarck argued for the inheritance of acquired characteristics as a mechanism of evolution. And, Thomas Malthus, an Anglican clergyman, published an essay on population that helped set Charles Darwin on the road to developing his theory of evolution by natural selection. Malthus wrote that populations of organisms grow exponentially, while natural resources increase arithmetically. What this means is that population growth exceeds the growth of resources required to maintain the entire population. Thus, individuals will inevitably compete for survival.

Malthus used his theory to argue for a variety of measures to keep the human population under control. It took Darwin and Wallace to realize that Malthus had provided a basis for understanding how species are formed and how they change. Their insights led to the reading of *On the Tendency of Species to Form Varieties* and *On the Perpetuation of Varieties and Species by Natural Means of Selection* at the Linnaean Society and the publication of Darwin's book, *On the Origin of Species by Means of Natural Selection,* in 1859.

DARWIN'S INSIGHTS

In 1858, Darwin and Wallace's ideas were proposed at a meeting of the Linnaean Society. The paper that was read claimed that evolution occurs because of "natural selection." As evidence, they offered studies of comparative morphology and fossil records. They proposed a mechanism for evolution, natural selection. They used as an analogy the artificial selection used in the breeding of domestic animals, except that in the case of natural selection, it was the environment that shaped species, not the individuals doing the breeding. The two components that are essential to the process of natural selection are (a) heritable variation (i.e., individuals in a population differ from each other and some of that difference is heritable) and (b) differential reproductive success (i.e., some individuals, because of their differences, are better able to survive and reproduce than others are). In the world Malthus described, of individuals in competition for available resources, it is easy to see how heritable variation that improved one's chances to utilize such resources, in comparison with other individuals, would increase in the next generation. Those variations that were helpful would spread, and those that were not, would die out.

This was the essential nature of the argument. To use the giraffe as an example, if giraffes with longer necks than the average were slightly more successful at feeding from the tops of trees than giraffes with average necks, they would grow and survive better than other giraffes and be more successful at reproducing as well. Their offspring, who would share their slightly longer necks, would increase proportionately in the population of giraffes. Over time, the distribution of neck lengths would shift due to the reproductive advantage held by those with longer necks.

It is important to remember that natural selection is not just about the differential ability to survive. If traits are to be passed on, reproduction must also occur. All species overproduce offspring, not all of which can survive to reproduce themselves. There is, as a result, competition within a species for the means to survive and to reproduce, and any advantage at either task will be naturally selected.

Because most traits are passed on from parent to offspring and are modified over time based on their ability to help their possessors deal with the environment, there is an emphasis on descent in Darwin's writing. Each species has descended from earlier species, and its characteristics (e.g., opposable thumbs) must be understood in the context of their origin in earlier species. When we consider the evolution of humans, we ask how the hominid line has descended from earlier primates and how the hominids in our direct line, such as *Homo habilis* and *Homo erectus*, gave rise to *Homo sapiens*. Because the great apes are descended from a primate ancestor that also gave rise to the hominid line, their anatomy, physiology, and behavior is of value for understanding our human characteristics. *The Descent of Man* closes with the following:

> Man with all his noble qualities, with sympathy that feels for the most debased, with benevolence which extends not only to other men but to the humblest of living creatures, with his god-like intellect which has penetrated into the movements and constitution of the solar system—with all these exalted powers—still bears in his bodily frame the indelible stamp of his lowly origin. (p. 405)

The outraged response to Darwin's theory is well known. In what is probably the most famous account, during a debate at Oxford, Bishop Samuel Wilberforce asked Huxley whether he claimed descent from monkeys on his mother's and father's side. Huxley (1900) replied that he would rather be descended from an ape than to have as an ancestor a man who would debate such a serious matter with such mockery.

Darwin believed that his theory could account for all aspects of human evolution. Wallace, the codiscoverer of natural selection, could not accept that the evolution of the human brain, in all of its complexity, could be explained by natural selection or that the same principles that explained the evolution of human anatomy could also explain human mental evolution. For some, this is still a controversial issue. Wallace eventually turned to spiritualism and religion for his answer to the design of the human brain.

One thing that puzzled Darwin, was the presence of structures that seemed unrelated to survival, the most famous being the brilliant plumage of the peacock's tail. There is obviously a metabolic cost to producing such a tail, and it is a walking advertisement of a meal for predators. If there is no survival benefit, how could natural selection explain it? Darwin also noted that in some species males and females are dramatically different in size and possess quite different features (e.g., the peacock's tail). Why such differences when males and females face the same problems of avoiding predation and finding food?

Darwin's answer was his theory of sexual selection, which he envisioned as a second theory of evolution. Darwin saw natural selection as focusing on adaptations that came about because of competition to survive while sexual selection focused on adaptations that were the result of competition for reproductive opportunities. He suggested that sexual selection could take two forms: (a) intrasexual competition and (b) intersexual selection. Intersexual competition is competition between members of the same sex where the outcome contributes to matings with the other sex (to the victor go the spoils). Typically, a male will gain sexual access to females directly as a result or by controlling territory or resources that females desire. The loser in the competition will typically fail to mate. Whatever traits lead to victory (e.g., size, strength, etc.) will be passed on through the mating success of the winners while the losers' qualities will fail to be transmitted.

The second method of sexual selection is intersexual selection or mate choice. If there are qualities that are valued by one sex in a mate, then individuals of the opposite sex possessing those qualities will be preferentially chosen as mates. Those that lack those qualities will not get mating opportunities. Over time, those qualities desired in a mate will increase in frequency. Darwin called this female choice because he had noticed that in a majority of animal species, the females are choosy about the males with whom they mate. Though Darwin believed natural and sexual selection were two different evolutionary processes, we now know they are part of the same basic process of differential reproductive success because of heritable differences in design. But keeping both terms reminds us of the usefulness of distinguishing between adaptations that are the result of survival advantages and those that are the result of advantages in attracting a mate.

In *The Descent of Man and Selection in Relation to Sex*, Darwin (1883) not only applied his theory of natural selection to human evolution and detailed his theory of sexual selection; he also discussed his thoughts on human faculties such as love, sympathy, beauty, and morality. He argued against making a distinction between mind and body and suggested that we shared many aspects of our human faculties with other animals. He stated, "[N]evertheless the difference in mind between man and the higher animals, great as it is, certainly is one of degree and not of kind" (Darwin, 1883).

Darwin (1980) elaborated on his ideas about the evolution of human and animal emotions in *The Expression of Emotion in Man and Animals*. In it, he suggested that the process of evolution by natural selection applies not only to anatomic structures but also to the "mind" of an animal and to expressive behavior. He believed that facial expression developed as a mechanism of communication and that there are specific inborn emotions with a specific pattern of activation of facial muscles and behavior in response to each emotion. Today, emotion researchers, such as Paul Ekman (Ekman & Davidson, 1994), continue in this tradition, exploring the cross-cultural functions and expression of various emotions,

THE EARLY ENTHUSIASTS
(DARWIN'S INFLUENCE ON NONPSYCHOLOGISTS)

While much attention has been paid to early opposition to Darwin's views, there were many who took inspiration from them. Throughout history, people have sought explanations and justifications for moral order in the world. We mentioned Plato's views on this earlier. Since the theory of evolution by natural selection provided an explanation for the origin and shape of life on earth, some wondered if it might help provide an explanation for the nature of society and even a blueprint for the type of society that human beings should strive to create.

British philosopher Herbert Spencer was an important advocate of using evolutionary theory to understand human social organization. He coined the phrase "survival of the fittest," which is often attributed to Darwin, and he wrote many articles and books on how evolutionary theory could help create an ideal society. He saw evolution as a moral force that would bring human society from the primitive to a modern democratic industrialized state. For this to happen, he argued, free competition between individuals must be allowed and encouraged, and interference from outside sources (e.g., government) should be avoided. Those individuals or businesses unable to cope, should be allowed to fail, propping them up would weaken society. Nature must be allowed free rein to select the strongest, the result being a continuously improving society. This type of thought was typical of what became known as "Social Darwinism." It can, one can imagine, can be taken to unpleasant extremes. It has been used to argue for the support of imperialism, the subordination of women, and the existence of the social class system. In an address to a children's Sunday school, John D. Rockerfeller said, as cited in Crawford, 1979, p. 260, "The growth of a large business is merely a survival of the fittest ... it is merely the working out of a law of nature and a law of God." Of course, it has also been taken to greater extremes by individuals such as Adolf Hitler, using such a model to justify the extermination of those he considered unfit in his quest to purify the German people and create his own ideal society.

McDougall in the United Kingdom and William James in the United States both studied what are referred to as instincts, defined as the inherent disposition of an organism to behave in a particular way. The idea was that instincts are unlearned inherited patterns of response or reaction to certain kinds of stimuli. An example would be an infant sucking at a nipple. James is often referred to as the father of U.S. psychology, publishing his *Principles of Psychology* in 1890. In particular, he outlined instincts such as fear, love, and curiosity as driving forces of human behavior, suggesting that humans may possess more instincts than other animals do.

Another early psychologist, James Mark Baldwin (1896), was fascinated by the question of how a process like natural selection could produce an organism with the creative capacities of the human mind. His answer was called the Baldwin Effect, though ethologist Morgan and paleontologist Osborn presented the same basic idea in the same year (Depew, 2003). The core of the theory is that the human capacity to learn can guide the evolutionary process in ways other than Lamarckian inheritance (which had already been discredited among scientists). The Baldwin Effect suggests that if a subset of the population possesses a unique, inherent advantage in the capacity to learn, and this advantage enhances their survival, this feature will be under significant selection pressure. As a result, it will spread though the population until it is widespread and effective enough to have the same properties as an inherent trait. In other words, it claims specific selection for general learning ability with the result that offspring would have an increased capacity for learning new skills. It also implies that abilities that initially require learning can eventually be replaced by the evolution of genetically determined systems that do not require learning. What was previously learned may become instinctive without any direct transfer of learned abilities from one generation to the next. Gene frequencies change in a way that supports the behavior (Dennett, 1995).

Why did the ideas of the early enthusiasts fade?

Of course, there are several obvious problems with a Social Darwinist approach. The first was that many Social Darwinists were Lamarckians, believing in the inheritance of acquired characteristics. They argued that if, during the course of free competition, some individuals developed greater intelligence or a finer morality, and such traits were passed on to their children, that such free competition would lead to a better society for all. The German biologist Weismann demonstrated that acquired characteristics could not be inherited with an elegant experiment in which he cut off the tails of mice and observed their descendents over several generations. The acquired trait of taillessness was not passed on to offspring. Another problem was that some early enthusiasts believed that natural selection favored traits that were for the good of the group. We now know that the gene is the proper unit of selection. As well, Spencer believed that as long as nothing interfered with the natural order and free competition, human perfection would eventually be reached. This belief implies that natural selection is a process driven by an ultimate goal. This is not the case; natural selection can have no ultimate goal, and it merely selects traits that are most adaptive in a particular environment at a particular time.

Instinct theory faded within psychology for several reasons. For one, the term instinct itself was seen as being imprecise (Bateson, 2000). There was also the fact that many behaviors called instincts can be modified by experience, which makes the boundary between instincts and learning rather fuzzy. The final blow was the rise of a new school of thought in the social sciences that denied the existence of instincts and saw culture as responsible for human behavior.

There are two main reasons the Baldwin Effect has fallen out of favor in terms of evolutionary thought. The first is that, like Lamarkian theory, it assumes that learned material can enter the germ line. The other reason is that it imposes directionality on the evolutionary process, which is directly counter to the Darwinian model of evolution (Silverman, personal communication, July 8, 2006). But it should be noted that aspects of the Baldwin Effect have been considered in more recent evolutionary thinking (Depew, 2003).

The eminent child psychologist, Jean Piaget, began his career as a biologist. While many aspects of Piaget's (1929) theories have stood the test of time, particularly that children think differently from adults and that their schemata change over time, more recent research has challenged his assumptions about what children know and when (Feldman, 2003). The evidence suggests that Piaget underestimated the mental abilities of young children and infants, in particular, and studies have shown that they are considerable more sophisticated in their thinking than previously assumed (Baillargeon, 2004; Hofstadter & Reznick, 1996; Mandler, 1992). The biological aspects of Piaget's work have been largely ignored. Discussions of schemata and stages of development occur in contemporary articles and textbooks without any consideration of why they occur in a particular order, why children attend to some things more than others, or why such schemata might be important to have. Piaget explained these issues, attributing them to "invariant functions" such as adaptation and organization, assimilation, and accommodation, but their importance seemed to fade for the majority of others interested in the development of thought.

EUGENICS, BEHAVIORISM, AND ENVIRONMENTALISM

During Darwin's time, no one knew anything about genetics, except for Gregor Mendel. Mendel was an Austrian Monk, now famous for the series of breeding experiments he conducted on hybrid pea plants. One of Mendel's great insights was that inheritance is particular. Darwin had assumed that offspring traits were a blend of their parents' traits, a reasonable assumption at the time. In many animal species, the mating of a large male and a small female produces offspring that are somewhere in between in size. But Mendel noted that if a white flowered pea plant was crossed with a red flowered one, the offspring were red or white, not the pink that a blended model would predict. However, scientists were slow to recognize the significance of this finding, and it was not until the 20th century when Mendel's work was rediscovered. The conclusions Mendel came to after his experiments are known as Mendel's Laws of Genetics. It is important to note that Mendel never saw a gene; he conducted his experiments in the 1800s. He reasoned that they must exist based on results of his experiments. A summary of his laws would include the following:

1. Inheritance is particulate, with each parent contributing equally to the offspring.
2. Characteristics are influenced by the fact that genes occur in pairs. The complete set of genes in an individual is called the genotype.
3. Genes exist in two or more alternate forms, or alleles. When an individual has identical alleles at a specific locus, it is said to be homozygous for that characteristic. When

an individual has different alleles at the same locus, it is said to be heterozygous. The complete description of characteristics produced by genes is called the phenotype.

4. Dominant alleles override recessive alleles in their expression in the phenotype. Recessive genes can be expressed in the phenotype only when they occur in a double dose.

5. Only one allele from each parent is passed on to each of their offspring. Genes for different characteristics are passed on individually rather than attached. They are segregated.

6. Phenotypic features that occur together in an adult will not necessarily appear together in their offspring. This is independent assortment, the result of segregation (Mendel, 1967).

The fusion of modern genetics and evolutionary theory led to what is known in biology as "The Modern Synthesis."

Two new approaches to human behavior emerged in the aftermath of the rediscovery of Mendel's work: (a) eugenics and (b) environmentalism. Eugenics is concerned with improving the human race through selective breeding. Animal and plant breeders have been improving their stock for thousands of years using selective breeding, or artificial selection.

Darwin's cousin, Francis Galton, intrigued by the theory of evolution, founded the eugenics movement in the late 19th century. He proposed that moral character and intelligence were inherited traits. Galton developed some of the first intelligence tests. With an interest in improving society by improving those living in it, he attempted to apply evolutionary theory to the problem via selective breeding. The idea was to encourage those who traits might benefit society to produce many offspring and discourage those with traits seen as less desirable from having any offspring at all. The following quote is a good summary of Galton's (1864) philosophy:

> If a twentieth part of the cost and pains were spent in measures for the improvement of the human race that is spent on the improvement of the breed of horses and cattle, what a galaxy of genius might we not create! (pp. 165–166)

In the early part of the 20th century, sterilization was performed on those considered psychologically unfit. Hundreds of thousands were sterilized worldwide. By 1960 in the United States, 60,000 involuntary sterilizations had occurred (Reilly, 1991). The largest and most systematic application of eugenics, however, was the elimination in Nazi Germany of millions of those considered "unfit," including Jews, homosexuals, and the mentally handicapped.

The eugenics movement fell out of favor for several reasons. As scientists learned more about population genetics, they realized that the time span needed for genetic change was much longer than previously thought. The harm that resulted from the extreme misuse of eugenics in Adolf Hitler's Nazi Germany turned public opinion against its study and use. In addition, a better understanding of the evolutionary process led to the realization that there are no ideal traits. Natural selection merely selects traits that are best suited to a particular environment.

The other approach to human behavior was to suggest that genes were not involved at all in producing differences in higher mental functions between people. This environmentalist perspective gave rise to the behavioralist movement. The belief was that a few general principles of learning could account for the complexity of human behavior. The behaviorist movement gave scientific credibility to the tabula rasa, or blank slate, view of the mind. This view, that the human mind is an empty canvas on which experience writes, has dominated the Western intellectual community since the early 1920s. Along with it comes the view that culture (environment) is the only major factor shaping behavior. This view is often referred to as the Standard Social Science Model (SSSM). Anthropologist Franz Boas, who in many ways was the founder of what became the SSSM, argued that most differences between individuals were due to their different cultures and that, to understand people, you must understand their culture. In many ways, that is a reasonable assumption. Think about language. Why does one person speak French and another Mandarin? Because one grew up in a French speaking culture and the other in a particular Chinese culture. The language difference is due to cultural differences not biological ones.

The problem with this view is in the way it came to dominate all thinking in the social sciences, to the exclusion of even considering other ways of thought. And along with it came an almost pathological fear of any kind of biological or evolutionary explanation for behavior. Instead, the blank slate view, that human nature was infinitely malleable (by culture) came to dominate. Margaret Mead (1935), a student of Boaz, wrote, "We are forced to conclude that human nature is almost unbelievably malleable, responding accurately and contrastingly to contrasting cultural conditions" (p. 280).

REDISCOVERING DARWIN (THE BIOLOGISTS)

Despite the resistance of psychologists and other social scientists, Darwinian thought remained alive and well in other disciplines. Ethology was the first major field to develop around the study of behavior from an evolutionary perspective. Konrad Lorenz, who shared the Nobel Prize in Medicine in 1973 with Tinbergen and von Frisch, focused on the early social interactions of animals. He is perhaps best known for his work on imprinting; pictures abound of him walking along, followed by a group of goslings. What Lorenz observed was that early interactions, usually with parents, lead to the learning of appropriate behavior. Goslings imprint on the first moving object they see, usually a parent. Goslings exposed to humans rather than adult geese at an early age, will imprint on people, follow them around, and learn "appropriate" behavior from them. For example, male goslings that imprint on a person rather than a goose might prefer a human as a mate rather than another goose. Lorenz's insight was that this learning could not occur without a prepared brain, whose genetically influenced development enabled it to respond to special kinds of information from the social environment. In Lorenz's (1966) book *On Aggression*, he emphasized that aggressive behavior has evolved because of its adaptive value to the aggressor. What he failed to see was that it is sensitive to early experience. Like the goslings who imprint on whatever animal they see first, humans and other animals are sensitive to the levels of aggression they are exposed to early in life.

Niko Tinbergen was also interested in the behavior of young animals. He was particularly interested in instincts, behavior patterns that appear in fully functional form the first time they are performed, even though the animal may have no previous experience with the eliciting cue. Tinbergen studied begging behavior in chicks (Tinbergen, 1951). When gull chicks are hungry, they peck at the parent's bill, and the parent responds by regurgitating partially digested food for their offspring to eat. Interestingly, it is not the parent per se that elicits the pecking behavior on the part of the chick. Very young chicks attend almost exclusively to the shape and red color of the bill. Tinbergen (1960; Tinbergen & Perdeck, 1951) believed that when a chick sees certain simple stimuli, sensory signals are transmitted to the brain where motor neurons generate the response of pecking at the stimulus, whether that stimulus is the red spot on their parent's bill or a red stick.

Tinbergen, Lorenz, and von Frisch (1967) were awarded their Nobel Prize for developing an understanding of the proximate causes of behavior. In fact, Tinbergen suggested that four causes or explanations can be used in developing an understanding of an animal's behavior: (a) immediate or proximate causation, (b) function, (c) development, and (d) evolution. A complete science of behavior should be able to accommodate explanations at all levels. If one were to use aggression as an example, proximate explanations might involve a specific stimulus, for example, a man being insulted in a bar. A functional explanation would involve an analysis of the survival or reproductive benefit of his response. A developmental one would consider how his environment might contribute to his response, while an evolutionary one might examine aggression in related species. In general, the field of evolutionary psychology is focused more strongly on ultimate causation and functional explanations than on proximate causation, though both are often taken into account.

One of the necessary steps on the road to rediscovering the power of Darwinian thought was dealing with the issue of group selection. When individuals like Herbert Spencer argued for the survival of the fittest and how society would benefit, they were talking about a form of group selection, traits being favored because they were for the good of the group. In Spencer's case, the group was society or the human species. Wynne-Edwards' (1962) book, *Animal Dispersion in Relation to Social Behavior*, argued that most animals restrain their reproduction for the good of their group so that the group does not become too large (and run out of resources). But Mendel and modern genetics point out that the gene is the proper unit of selection, not the group.

An elegant response to the idea of group selection can be found in the work of ornithologist David Lack. He suggested that, even though in some bird species it appeared as though birds restrained their breeding (laid less eggs than they could) for the good of the species, a female bird, on average, would not increase her individual reproductive success by laying more eggs. He demonstrated this in European swifts, which usually lay a clutch of two eggs, and rarely three or four. He pointed out that in a poor year for obtaining food, parents with three chicks might lose them all and that in such a year fewer chicks are fledged successfully from a brood of three or four chicks than from ones with only two (Lack, 1954, 1968). Typically, the most common clutch size is the most productive one. Natural selection will tend to eliminate genotypes that produce less productive clutches. There are some exceptions to the Lack effect; sometimes the most common size is smaller than the most productive. This can occur if some birds are able to vary clutch size to some degree based on food availability. In such cases, one should see larger broods raised by those best able to do so successfully (Ward, 1965). It is also the case that parents may sometimes conserve their own resources (in the goal of lifetime reproductive success, not just this season's reproductive success), especially if their survival to the next season might be jeopardized (Goodman, 1974).

Kinship is an important concept in evolutionary theory because it helped to solve the puzzle of altruism. Altruism can generally be defined as a behavior that benefits a recipient at a cost to the donor. It has been a puzzle because, by definition, it entails a fitness cost, and thus, it should be eliminated by natural selection. But there are many examples of altruistic behavior in animals, including humans, such as alarm calling in Belding's ground squirrels. Before kinship theory, group selection was the usual explanation for the evolution of altruistic behavior. Evolutionary biologist W. D. Hamilton provided an alternative. Hamilton (1964) demonstrated that altruistic behavior (behavior performed at a cost to oneself and a benefit to others) could evolve if the individuals involved were related. Even though the direct reproductive fitness of the donor is reduced, if his actions aid his own genetic kin, then he receives an indirect fitness benefit. Typically, this idea is expressed by the equation $br > c$, where b = the benefit to the recipient, r = the genetic correlation between the donor and the recipient, and c = the cost to the donor (Crawford & Salmon, 2004). In the equation, r represents the probability that the two individuals each have an allele that is a copy of one in a common ancestor ($r = 0.5$ for parent and offspring or between siblings, half-siblings 0.25). Such an allele is called identical by common descent and the probability of such is called a genetic correlation or a coefficient of relatedness between individuals. *Br* is the indirect benefit to the donor through the recipient's fitness, and *C* is the direct cost to the helper. Both sides of the equation refer to changes in donors' fitness because of their actions. This was a revolutionary concept. No longer were organisms simply reproductive strategists; they were also nepotistic strategists. Organisms can be seen as designed by natural selection to contribute to the replication of their genes whether those genes are in their offspring or other relatives.

Another evolutionist who did not buy into Wynne-Edwards use of group selection to explain altruism was George Williams. In 1966, he wrote *Adaptation and Natural Selection: A Critique of Some Current Evolutionary Thought*. Williams argued that when animals do cooperate, it is usually cooperation between close relatives, which means benefiting copies of their own genes in their kin. Thus from the point of view of the gene, it is not altruistic, but selfish. A point emphasized years later by Richard Dawkins (1977) in his book *The Selfish Gene*. As Tooby and Cosmides (2005) noted,

> Williams provided the first fully modern statement of the relationship between selection and adaptive design; clarified that selection operates at the genic level; developed strict evidentiary standards for deciding what aspects of a species' phenotype were adaptations, by-products of adaptations, or noise, and usefully distinguished the present usefulness of traits from their evolved functions (if any). (p. 9)

In the 1970s, Robert Trivers, a student of Hamilton's, forged ahead with the ideas proposed by Hamilton and Williams, contributing three theories that revolutionized evolutionary studies: (a) parental investment, (b) parent-offspring conflict, and (c) reciprocal altruism. Hamilton's kinship theory helped a great deal in developing an understanding of helping behavior among kin. Trivers elaborated on this theory with regard to parental investment as well as conflict between parent and offspring. From the parental perspective, each individual's overall reproductive effort is a combination of mating effort (e.g., courtship, etc.) and parental effort or investment. Trivers (1972) defined parental investment as any investment by the parent in an individual offspring that increases the offspring's chance of surviving (and hence reproductive potential) at the cost of the parent's ability to invest in other offspring (either current or future). In many species, this involves food provisioning and protection from predators. In humans, it can involve much more, from providing food and shelter to supporting education, hockey practice, and iPods. As Trivers pointed out, Hamilton's rule can shed light on how parents and offspring treat one another. The inequality that sums up the conditions under which a particular behavior would be expected to spread is $Br > C$, and in the parent-offspring case $r = 0.5$. Obviously, a parent's investment in its offspring provides a benefit to the offspring, which increases the parent's inclusive fitness. As long as the cost of parental investment does not begin to outweigh the benefit to the offspring times the degree of relatedness, it should continue. This is also where Trivers' ideas on parent-offspring conflict come into play.

Conflict over weaning in mammals (Trivers, 1974) is a very clear example of parent-offspring conflict. Parents are selected to continue to invest in their offspring up to the point when the cost in terms of reduced reproductive success (the more parents invest in a current offspring, the less they have to invest in future ones) begins to outweigh the benefits of increased survival (or success) for the current offspring. Or, as soon as the costs begin to exceed the benefits ($b/c < 1$), parents should stop investing in the current offspring and start to work on the next (Trivers, 1974).

At this point, the offspring would still like investment to continue, being more closely related to itself than to any future siblings; it has been selected to demand investment until the cost-benefit ratio drops below 0.5. After that point, continued demands for investment would lead to a reduction in indirect fitness because the parent would produce fewer siblings with whom the offspring would share genes. But until that point is reached, offspring should attempt to obtain as much parental investment as possible, enhancing its own reproductive fitness in the process. As a result, weaning conflict tends to involve a gradual shift in parental investment.

Trivers also developed a theory of reciprocal altruism in an effort to explain how altruistic behavior directed toward individuals other than kin could have evolved. Reciprocity based altruism occurs when individuals cooperate by trading helpful acts. Following the format of Hamilton's rule, Trivers (1971) suggested that when the benefit to the recipient of an altruistic act is greater than the cost to the actor, both participants will benefit so long as the act is reciprocated sometime in the future. In order for reciprocity to evolve and continue being beneficial to the individual engaging in it, certain conditions must be met. Since reciprocity involves delayed repayment, there is always the possibility of not being repaid. Trivers developed his theory to deal with these issues and the following conditions are considered necessary for the evolution of reciprocal altruism. First, the initial act must be of low cost to the donor and a high benefit to the recipient. Second, there must be a reasonably high probability that the roles will be reversed. Third, individuals that are interacting must be able to recognize each other (so the original beneficiary can return the favor and individuals can discriminate against those that do not reciprocate). Tied to Trivers' theory of reciprocal altruism is his perspective on emotion. He suggests that emotions such as gratitude, sympathy, and guilt evolved to regulate systems of reciprocity (Trivers, 1985). .

Another one of the early figures in the revitalization of Darwinian thinking was Harvard zoologist E. O. Wilson. His book *Sociobiology: The New Synthesis* set out a platform for the modern evolutionary approach to studying behavior (E. O. Wilson, 1975/2000). This approach became known as sociobiology, the study of the biological basis of social behavior. In terms of animal research, the book was uncontroversial, E. O. Wilson was well known for his research on the social behavior of ants. But while most of the content of *Sociobiology* focused on animals studies, the last chapter focused on human behavior, and it was this that generated a storm of controversy. Critics, including some of E. O. Wilson's Harvard colleagues, such as Stephen Jay Gould and Richard Lewontin, accused him of promoting eugenics, racist, and sexism, focusing on the social harm they felt would arise from his theoretical perspective on humans. He was accused of being right wing even though he held many left leaning views on social policy and was an early environmentalist. Much of the debate even occurred outside of a scientific forum and included not only written and verbal attacks but physical ones as well. At the 1978 meeting of the American Association for the Advancement of Science, E. O. Wilson was not only met with vocal opposition, a pitcher of water was dumped over his head. Within the academic community, the Sociobiology Study Group (of which Gould and Lewontin were members) criticized sociobiology on scientific and moral grounds, suggesting that seeking a biological basis to behavior was akin to supporting the Nazis! E. O. Wilson (1976) and others refuted these charges successfully, but to this day, criticisms rising largely from misunderstandings of the evolutionary approach to human behavior exist. But along with opposition came support, and more and more individuals thinking about human behavior from a Darwinian perspective.

Biologist Richard Alexander was another significant figure in the application of evolutionary theory to human behavior. He studied a wide range of species, from crickets and cicadas to the social behavior of naked mole rats and horses. He has also applied evolutionary theory to questions of human behavior, publishing *Darwinism and Human Affairs* in 1979 and *The Biology of Moral Systems* in 1987. Alexander (1990) suggested, "[H]umans obviously began to cooperate to compete, specifically against groups of conspecifics, this intergroup competition becoming increasingly elaborate, direct, and continuous" (p. 4). Our human brain (the generator of our behavior in response to the environment) evolved in this context of social cooperation and competition. Alexander (1987) focused a great deal on the evolution of reciprocity, particularly indirect reciprocity. Alexander viewed moral systems as systems of indirect reciprocity. The moral rules or ideals exist to control the tendencies of individuals to behave selfishly (e.g., to cheat on a social exchange). Moral rules exist to keep a group of individuals together and as such, may only apply to members of the group, not to outsiders. It is also important to remember what Alexander was not claiming that biology can tell us what is right and what is wrong in terms of our behavior. What it can do is explain the origins of our behavior and how we tend to use it. Right or wrong labels are most frequently imposed by a particular society at a particular time.

HERALDS OF MODERN EVOLUTIONARY THINKING

John Bowlby is a figure who, outside of the field itself, is not often associated with evolutionary psychology. He was a psychoanalyst interested in the impact of early childhood experiences on emotional and social development. Bowlby (1969) believed that early experience, especially mother-infant interaction, had a significant effect on adult personality and behavior. Bowlby's theory of attachment developed from his observations of children orphaned during World War II. Those children who had been well fed as infants were still more likely to be depressed and to develop other emotional or behavioral problems than children who had not experienced maternal deprivation. In the 1950s, Harry Harlow (1958) reported similar results in his studies of infant monkeys deprived of maternal comfort. Harlow found that normal social and emotional development in rhesus monkeys required physical contact with their mother (or a suitable substitute), not just being fed. Since humans infants are so helpless for so long, Bowlby believed their chances for avoiding predators in the "environment of evolutionary adaptedness" would be enhanced by a strong motivation to remain close to their mother. From this perspective, natural selection shaped in infants the goal of remaining close to mother because infant survival was increased by keeping infants close to their main source of safety. This capacity for attachment is universal and innate, developing from history of mother-infant interactions. The infants develop a working model of relationships with others because of these early experiences with their mother; a model to help guide future behavior. Bowlby's ideas have continued to be elaborated by those interested in development and life history theory. Current attachment theory suggests that individual differences in the quality of parent-infant attachment are largely shaped by the quality of care provided to the child and that a secure relationship early in life influences future development (Belsky, 1997, 2000). It has been suggested that variation in attachment security evolved to increase reproductive fitness under variable conditions and that environmentally modified life history traits generally serve our reproductive fitness (Belsky, Steinberg, & Draper, 1991; Bjorklund & Pellegrini, 2002; Chisholm, 1996).

One of the most influential figures of the early days of evolutionary psychology was Don Symons. Symons (1978) trained as an anthropologist, writing *Play and Aggression: A Study of Rhesus Monkeys* that focused on the functional nature of play. He is perhaps best known for his 1979 book *The Evolution of Human Sexuality,* which not only inspired a generation of researchers to go out and test his theories, but also is still in print today and an essential read for anyone interested in an evolutionary perspective on human sexuality. He was one of the first to emphatically point out the essential nature of sex differences:

> Men and women differ in their sexual natures because throughout the immensely long hunting and gathering phase of human evolutionary history, the sexual desires and dispositions that were adaptive for either sex were for the other tickets to reproductive oblivion. (Symons, 1979, preface)

Symons was also an early critic of the view that human behavior will be reproduction maximizing and that a science of human behavior can be based on analyses of the reproductive consequences of human action. Symons (1992) emphasized that reproductive success in the EEA, not the current environment, is relevant. He suggested that the study of human behavior needs to attend to our ancestral history and to the design of the behavior—its functionality, not "counting babies." He suggests two main approaches to the study of adaptations: design analysis and the comparative method.

Symons (1992) also emphasized that it was unlikely that a general-purpose mechanism of the mind could solve the wide range of problems faced by an organism. The human brain clearly has many functions, designed to solve very different sorts of problems, which are likely to require very different solutions. In fact, he suggested that our behavior is more complex than that of other species because we have more psychological mechanisms than other organisms. "There is no such thing as a general problem solver because there is no such thing as a general problem" (p. 142).

EVOLUTIONARY PSYCHOLOGY

The modern field of evolutionary psychology is sometimes characterized as the study of the evolved cognitive structure of the mind. The focus is on the workings of the mental mechanisms that evolved in ancestral populations to solve the problems faced in those environments. Such workings include the constraints on their operation and the effects or influence of environmental inputs, including not only the immediate social or physical environment but also experience and learning. There are perhaps six main assumptions made by the majority of people in the field. They are

1. human behavior can (and should) be explained at both a proximate and ultimate level of analysis;
2. domain specificity, that adaptive problems are solved through specific designated physical and behavioral structures or mental modules;
3. these mental mechanisms are innate; there is no genetic variation in them between people (except for those differences between the sexes related to differences in the ancestral problems they faced);
4. human nature is explained best as the product of genes and environment;
5. the workings of most mental mechanisms are not available to consciousness; and
6. there are differences between the current and ancestral environment that may influence the functioning or outcome of evolved mechanisms (some Darwinian anthropologists discount this difference).

Far too many figures currently play an important role in the field of evolutionary psychology to discuss here, but five need to be mentioned, not only for their discipline-defining work but also because they illustrate the three main methodological types of approaches to evolutionary psychology typically seen today.

John Tooby and Leda Cosmides have brought an information processing cognitive-experimental perspective to what has become evolutionary psychology, emphasizing that it is the mechanisms that produce behavior that evolve, not the behavior per se. From this perspective, the causal link between evolution and behavior is made through the psychological mechanism. As they write, "[T]he evolutionary function of the human brain is to process information in ways that lead to adaptive behavior" (Cosmides & Tooby, 1987). Tooby and Cosmides, unlike many cognitive psychologists who view the mind as a general-purpose computer with domain general processes, emphasize the necessity for domain-specific information processing. They write, "Behavior is a transaction between organism and environment; to be adaptive, specific behaviors must be elicited by evolutionarily appropriate environmental cues. Only specialized domain specific Darwinian algorithms can ensure that this will happen" (Cosmides & Tooby, 1987, p. 300).

One of Tooby and Cosmides' other contributions to the development of evolutionary psychology is social contract theory, through which they explain the evolution of cooperative exchange and, in particular, how humans have solved the problem of detecting cheaters. Social exchange relationships are vulnerable to cheating in that many exchanges do not occur simultaneously. The opportunity to take a benefit without paying the cost later can be tempting; anyone who can get away with it is at an evolutionary advantage over noncheaters (Cosmides & Tooby, 1992). For reciprocal altruism to evolve, a mechanism must exist in individuals for detecting and avoiding cheaters. Cosmides and Tooby set out five cognitive abilities that would be necessary for the detection and avoidance of cheaters:

1. the ability to recognize individuals;
2. the ability to remember your interactions with others;
3. the ability to communicate your values to others;

4.   the ability to model the values of others; and

5.   the ability to represent costs and benefits independent of the particular items/favors exchanged.

These abilities would allow individuals to engage in successful social exchange.

Cosmides and Tooby (1992) tested their theory with the Wason selection task, examining people's responses to if … then logic problems. They noted that people are not good at solving this kind of abstract logical problem. However, if the problem is given in the context of a social contract, if you take the benefit, you must pay the cost, people are much better at solving the problem correctly. Some cross-cultural data also confirm that their results (Sugiyama, Tooby, & Cosmides, 2002) are not unique to North American undergraduates. These data suggest that our mechanism for detecting violations of conditional rules is not domain general, but specific to detecting violations of conditional rules in the context of social exchange and contracts.

Martin Daly and Margo Wilson were trained in the behavioral ecology tradition, starting their careers with the study of desert rodents and monkeys. There is an emphasis in their approach on the use of cross-cultural and demographic data, with a focus on ecological validity. They are well known for their epidemiological studies of homicide, in which they view homicide as an assay of interpersonal conflict. They have drawn attention to the mechanisms of discriminative solicitude, emphasizing that, under natural selection, parental psychology will be a discriminative psychology and as such, will allocate parental effort so as to yield the greatest return (Daly & Wilson, 1988). Studies examining this solicitude have investigated attempts by the mother and female kin to assure the father of the baby's resemblance to him based on the hypothesis that if paternity certainty increases the intensity of paternal investment mothers should be highly motivated to perceive paternal resemblance and point it out (Daly & Wilson, 1988). Daly and M. Wilson (1982) found exactly that when they looked at the remarks made by mothers in the immediate aftermath of their baby's birth. It was the baby's resemblance to the father that was remarked upon by the mother and her family.

Their other area of inquiry into parental solicitude (or lack of) is their work on stepparenthood and the risk of child abuse. Because a stepparent is not genetically related to their stepchild, one might expect that from the stepparental perspective, the child is seen as a cost, rather than a benefit in this new marital relationship. Starting with the cross culturally ubiquitous image of the evil stepmother, Daly and M. Wilson (1984, 1985, 1988; M. Wilson, Daly, & Weghorst, 1980) examined demographic data in the United States and Canada on the number of stepparent households and the incidence of child abuse, concluding that living with a stepparent is a major risk factor for child abuse. Daly and M. Wilson's 1998 book *The Truth About Cinderella* nicely sums up this work.

Daly and M. Wilson have also drawn attention to the proprietary view that men have of their partner's sexual and reproductive capacity. They looked for evidence of sexually proprietary behavior in other species that share the human features of internal fertilization and paternal care and then compared the results to human behavior. They also looked at uxoricide cross-culturally, finding the same basic pattern; women who have left their husbands are at a substantially higher risk of being killed that those that remain (Daly & M. Wilson, 1996). They have noted that the "major source of conflict in the great majority of spousal killings is the husband's knowledge or suspicion that his wife is either unfaithful or intending to leave him" (Daly & M. Wilson, 1992, p. 305). The idea that a discovery of infidelity could drive a man to murder and that this is a reasonable response is one that has been at times legally acceptable over time and across cultures (Daly & M. Wilson, 1988).

David Buss (1992, 2000, 2005) trained as a personality psychologist and has focused on studies of mate preferences and sexual strategies for the most part with some recent work looking into homicide as an adaptation. Many of Buss' studies have involved the use of questionnaires to collect data, such as his cross-cultural study of mate preferences (Buss, 1989). In that study, he noted that females valued cues to resource acquisition in a mate more than males did, whereas males valued characteristics indicating reproductive capacity more than females did, providing cross-cultural evidence of sex differences in reproductive strategies. Buss has also elaborated on differences in long-term versus short-term mating strategies and on how each sex has distinct psychological mechanisms to solve the problems inherent in these different mating contexts (Buss & Schmitt, 1993).

Like Daly and M. Wilson, Buss is also interested in the functional nature of sexual jealousy, examining sex differences in this trait. Buss tested the hypothesis that women would be more upset by emotional infidelity and men would be more upset by sexual infidelity with questionnaires and physiological measures and did indeed find a sex difference (Buss, Larsen, Westen, & Semmelroth, 1992). Buss has also found sex differences in a variety of other aspects of the mating arena. In looking at intrasexual competition, he has documented different tactics of attraction and derogation, pointing out that what individuals choose to derogate in their competitors is exactly what the other sex attends to in their mate preferences. Females tend to impugn their competitors' appearance and promiscuity while males tend to impugn their competitors' resources or achievements (Buss, 1988; Buss & Dedden, 1990; Buss & Shackelford, 1997). Buss' work emphasizes that males and females have faced different adaptive problems over our evolutionary history in the mating arena, and as a result, they have evolved different sexual strategies to deal with them.

CURRENT ISSUES IN EVOLUTIONARY PSYCHOLOGY

As evolutionary psychology has developed as a discipline, certain topics have continued to be topics of debate. Several chapters in this book will touch on issues such as modularity, the importance of the EEA, research methods, reproductive success, life history theory and development, altruism and morality, mating, emotions, and theory of mind.

The majority of evolutionary psychologists assume that psychological mechanisms are relatively specialized and that these mechanisms generate mind, behavior, and culture as they respond to the varying conditions in the human environment. But if mechanisms evolved in the ancestral environment and they are very specialized, how are humans able to adjust to current environments? Sperber's and Barrett's (this volume) chapter addresses this issue, reviewing current views on the degree of specialization of physiological and psychological mechanisms, while Crawford's (this volume) chapter "Adaptations, Environments and Behavior: Then and Now" addresses how ancestral adaptations function in the modern environment.

How important is the concept of the EEA and our understanding of what it was like to conducting evolutionary psychological research? Many would argue that to understand an evolved psychological mechanism one must understand the features of the environment in which that particular psychological mechanism evolved. The Pleistocene, which began 1.8 million years ago and ended about 12,000 years ago, is often pointed out as a likely environment for a majority of our adaptations; during this period, the genus *Homo* arose. However, many critics claim we have too little information about the EEA. While it is true that our information is not complete, there is no shortage of anthropological evidence, as well as comparative studies of other primates such as the chimpanzee and bonobo. No doubt, we lived in small groups of related individuals and engaged in hunting and gathering as well as conflict with other groups (Dunbar, 1993; Tooby & DeVore, 1987).

What are appropriate research methods for the Darwinian study of human behavioral adaptations? Such methods are outlined in detail by Schmitt (this volume) in his chapter. Empirical evidence of a psychological adaptation needs to include a demonstration of special design for a specific function and that there would have been a reproductive or survival advantage to such a function in our ancestral past. Andrews, Gangestad, and Matthews (2002) suggested six standards of evidence for testing whether a trait is an adaptation: (a) comparative standards, (b) fitness maximization standards, (c) beneficial effects standards, (d) optimal design standards, (e) tight fit standards, and (f) special design standards. The first five standards provide indirect evidence, while special design is more rigorous. Ideally, one would collect evidence from all these types of standard, but a special focus should be on evidence of special design. It is when this is not done, that many accusations of "just so stories" are leveled. One needs to study the mechanism, not just the output.

Related in a sense to the issue of research methods is the topic of reproductive success. Some researchers (in the past this view has been referred to as Darwinian anthropology) have suggested that "modern Darwinian theory predicts that human behavior will be adaptive, that is, designed to promote maximum reproductive success through available descendent and nondescendent relatives" (Turke & Betzig, 1985, p. 79). Its method for locating adaptation in humans is in the reproductive outcome of their behavior and, as a result, emphasizes the measurement of reproductive success. However, others have pointed out,

> Darwin's theory of natural selection is a theory of adaptation, a *historical* account of the origin and maintenance of phenotypic design ... the key issue is whether differential reproductive success historically influenced the design of a given trait, not whether the trait currently influences differential reproductive success. (Symons, 1992, p. 150)

This focus on reproductive data tends to emphasize the hypothesis testing nature of science at the expense of examining phenotypic design. The mechanism underlying behavior is the adaptation, not the behavior per se.

The role of natural and sexual selection in the developmental timetable of people's lives is the focus of life history theory (Chisholm, 1999; Ellis & Garber, 2000; Gangestad & Simpson, 2000; Kaplan, Hill, Lancaster, & Hurtado, 2000). Stearns, Allal, and Mace (this volume) discuss the basic theory of life history and how it applies to humans while Ellis's (this volume) chapter focuses on specific ways this perspective can inform us about family relations and mate choice. Daly and M. Wilson (this volume) discuss the Cinderella effect and stepparenting, as well as many of the typical critiques that are raised with regard to evolutionarily inspired research in the area. Our adaptations for dealing with the problem of mate choice are also addressed in chapters by Grammer and Fink (this volume) as well as Alastair and Shackelford (this volume), while the basic issues of sexual selection itself are discussed in Moller's (this volume) chapter.

Altruistic and helping behavior has long been a topic of interest in studies of animal and human behavior (Alexander, 1987; Andreoni & Petrie, 2004; Boyd & Richerson, 1988; Burnham, 2003; Kurzban & Leary, 2001; Perreault & Bourhis, 1999). West's (this volume) chapter addresses the role of kinship in explaining helping behavior. Johnson and Price (this volume) examine reciprocity theory and its role in explaining altruism between unrelated individuals while Krebs (this volume) criticizes the popular idea that all species are selfish by nature.

WHY THE WARINESS?

Why is there still a certain reluctance with regard to the application of a Darwinian perspective to the study of human behavior? Don Symons (1992) suggested that one day there would be no need for evolutionary psychology because all psychology would take into account a Darwinian perspective. That day is clearly not yet here. And from outside psychology, there is still concern and at times suspicion. We suspect several issues are in play.

The first has to do with methodology. In many ways, the standards that are expected of evolutionary psychology are higher than those of other areas of psychology are. Even within the field, there have been disagreements about the utility of measuring reproductive success, as discussed previously. The design analysis required and the converging evidence from indirect sources are all necessary and until all the data are in, many individuals are skeptical, indeed, even hostile, claiming that the evidence is merely a "just so story."

Some of this reaction also comes from a fear of change in scientific paradigms. Becoming a successful scientist or scholar takes a very long time. Individuals that have invested a great deal in one way of thinking are often very resistant to changes that threaten their way of thinking (Kuhn, 1962). Social psychology has been one of the areas where this has been most apparent with a great deal of friction developing between those social and personality psychologists who have embraced the Darwinian perspective and those that are strongly resistant.

Others are concerned about the possible risks to personal or political agency. Some of this rises from a belief in the naturalistic fallacy, which entails deriving conclusions about what ought to be from what is. Or, if it is natural, then that is the way it should be. However, from a logical perspective, it does not make sense to reason from what is to what ought to be. Empirical and moral (or social justice, etc.) realms are not the same. Acknowledging that under some circumstances one can predict from a cost-benefit equation that a mother would abandon her infant does not make it morally right or wrong, it just helps to explain why the behavior occurs. This information can also help us to understand how to change the behavior, if "we" decide it is a behavior we would like to reduce (Crawford & Salmon, 2004).

There is also the old nature-nurture fallacy implying that if you say a behavior evolved, then it cannot be changed. This is clearly a mistaken idea. Buss (2004) explains this with an example from social psychology. Studies indicate that men tend to have a lower threshold for inferring sexual intent than women do. So, when a woman smiles at a man, he assumes (as do other men) that she is interested in him (Abbey, 1982). Women do not make the same assumption. The presumed explanation for this sex difference is that men have an adaptation that motivates them to seek out novel women for the chance of a sexual encounter (Buss, 2003). A better understanding of this phenomenon might actually help men to be less likely to make unwanted and harassing advances toward women who are not interested. It might also help women to be aware of this and react accordingly, which is not to say that changing evolved behavior is easy; but the better we understand our evolved nature, the better equipped we are to try.

There are still also accusations of genetic determinism. Genetic determinism is the idea that behavior is controlled entirely by genes, with little input from the environment. Such a view would indicate that behavior cannot be changed without genetic change. This is a misperception in that evolutionary psychology posits that human behavior requires evolved adaptations (the structure of which is created by genes) and input from the environment into the mechanism to produce behavior. However, for those who only understand the misperception, this can make evolutionary psychology appear a threat to political agency. Many individuals and organizations want to be able to sell their political philosophies and agendas to others. If people's minds were a blank slate, this would be much easier to do, regardless of whether the views being sold belong to the far left or right. As a result, some feel that evolutionary psychology restricts their political agency. One example of this is Alice Eagly's work on human reproductive strategies where she argues that social structure (or society) causes psychological sex differences, "Because men and women tend to occupy different social roles, they become psychologically different in ways that adjust them to these roles" (Eagly & Wood, 1999, p. 408). If this is true, men and women can be happy in any social role. Their psychology will be shaped by the role they are given rather than their psychology shaping the roles they desire. This is handy if you want to create any type of society that pops into your head and believe people will be happy and the society will last. History has suggested that this is unlikely because the mind is not a blank slate. Our psychology does shape our social lives (Crawford & Salmon, 2004).

SUMMARY

The path from philosophy to ethology, biology to psychology, has been a long and convoluted one for Darwin's dangerous idea. Many figures made important contributions along the way, some recognized at the time, some only after the fact. This volume is designed to give the reader a solid grounding in evolutionary theory, how it is applied to animal and human behavior, and the application of evolutionary theory to the study of the psychological mechanisms that make up the human mind. As all good evolutionary psychologists know, nature and nurture interact. Over time, the acceptance of evolutionary theory has been influenced by the social environment. In Darwin's day and up until relatively recently, religion, scientific inertia, and numerous other factors clouded the development of an evolutionary science of human nature. The efforts, both public and academic, of many researchers are introducing the field to many, recruiting young people of various disciplines, and encouraging the spread of an evolutionary perspective. Their research results demonstrate the utility of such a perspective, how it suggests questions that might not otherwise be asked. Darwin's "distant future" seems, finally, to be coming to light.

REFERENCES

Abbey, A. (1982). Sex differences in attributions for friendly behavior: Do males misperceive females' friendliness? *Journal of Personality and Social Psychology, 42*, 830–838.

Alexander, R. D. (1987). *The biology of moral systems.* New York: Aldine.

Alexander, R. D. (1990). *How did humans evolve? Reflections on the uniquely unique species.* Ann Arbor: University of Michigan, Museum of Zoology.

Allen, L., Beckwith, B., Beckwith, J., Chorover, S., Culver, D., et al. (1975). Against "sociobiology." *New York Review of Books, 22*, 43–44.

Andreoni, J., & Petrie, R. (2004). Public goods experiments without confidentiality: A glimpse into fundraising. *Journal of Public Economics, 88*, 1605–1623.

Andrews, P. W., Gangestad, S. W., & Matthews, D. (2002). Adaptationism—How to carry out an exaptationist program. *Behavioral and Brain Sciences, 25*, 489–553.

Baillargeon, R. (2004). Infants' physical world. *Current Directions in Psychological Science, 13*, 89–94.

Bateson, P. (2000). Taking the stink out of instinct. In H. Rose & S. Rose (Eds.), *Alas poor Darwin: Arguments against evolutionary psychology* (pp. 157–173). London: Jonathan Cape.

Belsky, J. (1997). Attachment, mating, and parenting: An evolutionary interpretation. *Human Nature, 8*, 361–381.

Belsky, J. (2000). Conditional and alternative reproductive strategies: Individual differences in susceptibility to rearing experience. In J. Rodgers & D. Rowe (Eds.), *Genetic influences on fertility and sexuality* (pp. 127–146). Boston: Kluwer Academic.

Belsky, J., Steinberg, L., & Draper, P. (1991). Childhood experience, interpersonal development, and reproductive strategy: An evolutionary theory of socialization. *Child Development, 62*, 647–670.

Bjorklund, D. F., & Pellegrini, A. D. (2002). *The origins of human nature: Evolutionary developmental psychology.* Washington, DC: American Psychological Association.

Bowlby, J. (1969). *Attachment and loss* (Vol. 1). New York: Basic Books.

Boyd, R., & Richerson, P. J. (1988). The evolution of reciprocity in sizable groups. *Journal of Theoretical Biology, 132*, 337–356.

Burnham, T. C. (2003). Engineering altruism: A theoretical and experimental investigation of anonymity and gift giving. *Journal of Economic Behavior and Organization, 50*, 133–144.

Buss, D. M. (1988). From vigilance to violence: Mate retention tactics in American undergraduates. *Ethology and Sociobiology, 9*, 291–317.

Buss, D. M. (1989). Sex differences in human mate preferences. *Behavioral and Brain Sciences, 12*, 1–49.

Buss, D. M. (1992). Mate preference mechanisms: Consequences for partner choice and intrasexual competition. In J. Barkow, L. Cosmides, & J. Tooby (Eds.), *The adapted mind: Evolutionary psychology and the generation of culture* (pp. 556–579). New York: Oxford University Press.

Buss, D. M. (2000). *The dangerous passion: Why jealousy is as necessary as love and sex.* New York: Free Press.

Buss, D. M. (2003). *The evolution of desire: Strategies of human mating* (Rev. ed.). New York: Free Press.

Buss, D. M. (2004). *Evolutionary psychology: The new science of the mind.* Boston: Allyn & Bacon.

Buss, D. M. (2005). *The murderer next door: Why the mind is designed to kill.* New York: Penguin Press.

Buss, D. M., & Dedden, L. A. (1990). Derogation of competitors. *Journal of Social and Personal Relationships, 7,* 395–422.

Buss, D. M., Larsen, R. J., Westen, D., & Semmelroth, J. (1992). Sex differences in jealousy: Evolution, physiology, and psychology. *Psychological Science, 3,* 251–255.

Buss, D. M., & Schmitt, D. P. (1993). Sexual strategies theory: An evolutionary perspective on human mating. *Psychological Review, 100,* 204–232.

Buss, D. M., & Shackelford, T. K. (1997). From vigilance to violence: Mate retention tactics in married couples. *Journal of Personality and Social Psychology, 72,* 346–361.

Chisholm, J. S. (1996). The evolutionary ecology of attachment organization. *Human Nature, 7,* 1–38.

Chisholm, J. S. (1999). *Death, hope, and sex: Steps to an evolutionary ecology of mind and morality.* Cambridge, U.K.: Cambridge University Press.

Cosmides, L., & Tooby, J. (1987). From evolution to behavior: Evolutionary psychology as the missing link. In J. Dupre (Ed.), *The latest on the best: Essays on evolution and optimality* (pp. 277–306). Cambridge, MA: MIT Press.

Cosmides, L., & Tooby, J. (1992). Cognitive adaptations for social exchange. In J. H. Barkow, L. Cosmides, & J. Tooby (Eds.), *The adapted mind: Evolutionary psychology and the generation of culture* (pp. 163–228). Oxford, U.K.: Oxford University Press.

Crawford, C. (1979). George Washington, Abraham Lincoln, and Arthur Jensen: Are the compatible? *American Psychologist, 34,* 664–672.

Crawford, C., & Salmon, C. (2004). The essence of evolutionary psychology: An introduction. In C. Crawford & C. Salmon (Eds.), *Evolutionary psychology, public policy, and personal decisions* (pp. 23–49). Mahwah, NJ: Lawrence Erlbaum Associates.

Daly, M., & Wilson, M. (1982). Whom are newborn babies said to resemble? *Ethology and Sociobiology, 3,* 69–78.

Daly, M., & Wilson. M. (1984). A sociobiological analysis of human infanticide. In G. Hausfater & S. Hrdy (Eds.), *Infanticide: Comparative and evolutionary perspectives* (pp. 487–505). New York: Aldine.

Daly, M., & Wilson, M. (1985). Child abuse and other risks of not living with both parents. *Ethology and Sociobiology, 6,* 197–210.

Daly, M., & Wilson, M. (1988). The Darwinian psychology of discriminative parental solicitude. *Nebraska Symposium on Motivation, 35,* 91–144.

Daly, M., & Wilson, M. (1988). *Homicide.* Hawthorne, NY: Aldine.

Daly, M., & Wilson, M. (1996). Evolutionary psychology and marital conflict: The relevance of stepchildren. In D. M. Buss & N. Malamuth (Eds.), *Sex, power, conflict: Feminist and evolutionary perspectives* (pp. 9–28). New York: Oxford University Press.

Daly, M., & Wilson, M. (1998). *The truth about Cinderella: A Darwinian view of parental love.* New Haven, CT: Yale University Press.

Darwin, C. R. (1859). *On the origin of species.* London: John Murray.

Darwin, C. R. (1980). *Expression of emotions in man and animals.* London: St. Martins Press. (Original work published 1872.)

Darwin, C. R. (1981). *The descent of man, and selection in relation to sex.* Princeton, NJ: Princeton University Press. (Original work published 1871.)

Davis, H. (1849). *The works of Plato* (Vol. 2). London: Bohn.

Dawkins, R. (1977). *The selfish gene.* New York: Oxford University Press.

Dennett, D. (1995). *Darwin's dangerous idea: Evolution and the meanings of life.* New York: Simon & Schuster.

Depew, D. J. (2003). Baldwin and his many effects. In B. H. Weber & D. J. Depew (Eds.), *Evolution and learning: The Baldwin Effect reconsidered* (pp. 3–31). Cambridge, MA: MIT Press.

Dunbar, R. I. M. (1993). The co-evolution of neocortical size, group size, and language in humans. *Behavioral and Brain Sciences, 16,* 681–735.

Eagly, A., & Wood, W. (1999). The origins of sex differences in human behavior: Evolved dispositions versus social roles. *American Psychologist, 54,* 408–423.

Ekman, P., & Davidson, R. J. (1994). *The nature of emotion.* New York: Oxford University Press.

Ellis, B. J., & Garber, J. (2000). Psychosocial antecedents of variation in girls' pubertal timing: Maternal depression, stepfather presence, and marital and family stress. *Child Development, 71,* 485–501.

Feldman, D. H. (2003). Cognitive development in childhood. In R. M. Lerner, M. A. Easterbrooks, & J. Mistry (Eds.), *Handbook of psychology*: Vol. 6.: *Developmental psychology* (pp. 195–210). New York: Wiley.

Galton, F. (1864). Hereditary talent and character. *MacMillan's Magazine, 11,* 157–166.

Gangestad, S. W., & Simpson, J. A. (2000). The evolution of human mating: The role of trade-offs and strategic pluralism. *Behavioral and Brain Sciences, 23,* 675–687.

Goodman, D. (1974). Natural selection and a cost ceiling on reproductive effort. *American Naturalist, 108,* 247–268.

Hamilton, W. D. (1964). The genetical evolution of social behavior, I. *Journal of Theoretical Biology, 7,* 1–16.

Harlow, H. (1958). The nature of love. *American Psychologist, 3,* 673–685.

Hofstadter, M. C., & Reznick, J. S. (1996). Response modality affects human infant delayed-response performance. *Child Development, 67,* 646–658.

Huxley, L. (1900). *The life and letters of Thomas Henry Huxley* (Vol. 1). London: Macmillan.

Kant, I. (1998). *Anthropology from a pragmatic point of view.* Carbondale: Southern Illinois University Press. (Original work published 1798)

Kaplan, H. S., Hill, K., Lancaster, J. B., & Hurtado, A. M. (2000). A theory of human life history evolution: Diet, intelligence, and longevity. *Evolutionary Anthropology, 9,* 156–185.

Kuhn, T. S. (1962). *The structure of scientific revolutions.* Chicago: University of Chicago Press.

Kurzban, R., & Leary, M. R. (2001). Evolutionary origins of stigmatization: The functions of social exclusion. *Psychological Bulletin, 127,* 187–208.

Lack, D. (1954). *The natural regulation of animal numbers.* Oxford, U.K.: Oxford University Press.

Lack, D. (1968). *Ecological adaptations for breeding in birds.* London: Methuen.

Lorenz, K. Z. (1966). *On aggression.* New York: Harcourt Brace.

Mandler, J. M. (1992). How to build a baby: II. Conceptual primitives. *Psychological Review, 99,* 587–604.

Mead, M. (1935). *Sex and temperament in three primitive societies.* New York: William Morrow.

Mendel, G. (1967). *Experiments in plant hybridization* (Royal Horticultural Society of London, Trans.). Cambridge, MA: Harvard University Press.

Perreault, S., & Bourhis, R. Y. (1999). Ethnocentrism, social identification, and discrimination. *Personality and Social Psychology Bulletin, 25,* 92–103.

Piaget, J. (1929). *The child's conception of the world.* New York: Harcourt Brace.

Reilly, P. (1991). *The surgical solution: A history of involuntary sterilization in the United States.* Baltimore: Johns Hopkins University Press.

Sugiyama, L., Tooby, J., & Cosmides, L. (2002). Cross-cultural evidence of cognitive adaptations for social exchange among the Shiwiar of Ecuadorian Amazonia. *Proceedings of the National Academy of Sciences, 99,* 11537–11542.

Symons, D. (1978). *Play and aggression: A study of rhesus monkeys.* New York: Columbia University Press.

Symons, D. (1979). *The evolution of human sexuality.* New York: Oxford University Press.

Symons, D. (1992). On the use and misuse of Darwinism in the study of human behavior. In J. H. Barkow, L. Cosmides, & J. Tooby (Eds.), *The adapted mind: Evolutionary psychology and the generation of culture* (pp. 137–159). New York: Oxford University Press.

Tinbergen, N. (1951). *The study of instinct.* New York: Oxford University Press.

Tinbergen, N. (1960). *The herring gull's world.* Garden City, NY: Doubleday.

Tinbergen, N., & Perdeck, A. C. (1951). On the stimulus situations releasing the begging response in the newly hatched herring gull (Larus argentatus). *Behaviour, 3,* 1–39.

Tooby, J., & Cosmides, L. (2005). Conceptual foundations of evolutionary psychology. In D. M. Buss (Ed.), *The handbook of evolutionary psychology* (pp. 5–67). Hoboken, NJ: Wiley.

Tooby, J., & DeVore, I. (1987). The reconstruction of hominid behavioral evolution through strategic modeling. In W. Kinzey (Ed.), *Primate models of hominid behavior* (pp. 183–237). New York: SUNY Press.

Trivers, R. L. (1971). The evolution of reciprocal altruism. *Quarterly Review of Biology, 46,* 35–57.

Trivers, R. L. (1972). Parental investment and sexual selection. In B. Campbell (Ed.), *Sexual selection and the descent of man: 1871–1971* (pp. 136–179). Chicago: Aldine.

Trivers, R. L. (1974). Parent-offspring conflict. *American Zoologist, 14,* 249–264.

Trivers, R. L. (1985). *Social evolution.* Menlo Park, CA: Benjamin-Cummings.

Turke, P., & Betzig, L. (1985). Those who can do: Wealth, status, and reproductive success on Ifaluk. *Ethology and Sociobiology, 6,* 79–87.

von Frisch, K. (1967). *The dance language and orientation of bees.* Cambridge, MA: Harvard University Press.

Ward, P. (1965). The breeding biology of the black-faced dioch Quelea quelea in Nigeria. *Ibis, 107,* 326–349.

Williams, G. C. (1966). *Adaptation and natural selection.* Princeton, NJ: Princeton University Press.

Wilson, E. O. (1976). Academic vigilantism and the political significance of sociobiology. *BioScience, 26,* 187–190.

Wilson, E. O. (2000). *Sociobiology, the new synthesis.* Cambridge, MA: Harvard University Press. (Original work published 1975)

Wilson, M., & Daly, M. (1992). The man who mistook his wife for a chattel. In J. Barlow, L. Cosmides, & J. Tooby (Eds.), *The adapted mind: Evolutionary psychology and the generation of culture* (pp. 289–322). New York: Oxford University Press.

Wilson, M., Daly, M., & Weghorst, S. J. (1980). Household composition and the risk of child abuse and neglect. *Journal of Biosocial Science, 12,* 333–340.

Wynne-Edwards, V. C. (1962). *Animal dispersion in relation to social behaviour.* Edinburgh: Oliver & Boyd.

Part I
BIOLOGICAL FOUNDATIONS OF EVOLUTIONARY PSYCHOLOGY

The theory of evolution is complex and multifaceted. This section covers the essentials of evolutionary theory necessary for the study of human behavior.

2

Evolutionary Questions for Evolutionary Psychologists

JOHN ALCOCK AND
CHARLES CRAWFORD

Evolutionary theory has stimulated debate ever since Darwin presented his ideas in 1859. Some disputes have been driven by the antievolutionary zeal of religious fundamentalists, whose dismay with Darwinian thought continues to this day—as witness the intelligent design movement (Forrest & Gross, 2003; Jones, 2005). But attempts to understand evolutionary theory have generated plenty of genuine scientific questions and controversies (Dawkins & Coyne, 2005). This chapter will review several of these issues as a way to organize some of the major ideas underpinning modern evolutionary psychology (see also Hagen, 2005).

WHAT THEORY PROVIDES THE FOUNDATION
FOR EVOLUTIONARY PSYCHOLOGY?

We begin by examining the intellectual origins of evolutionary psychology, a relatively recent subdiscipline of psychology—the label having first surfaced in the late 1980s in articles that championed the approach as fundamentally new (Barkow, Cosmides, & Tooby, 1992; Griffiths, 2006; Symons, 1989). The key features of the field were said to be its focus on the adaptive design of the human brain and our cognitive abilities, attributes that were believed to have evolved in the past in the environment of evolutionary adaptedness (EEA).

There is no question that this approach differs from that of another, older kind of evolutionary psychology, which went under the title of comparative animal psychology (Cartwright, 2000; Dewsbury, 2000). A main goal of comparative animal psychologists was to track down the antecedents of human behavior by identifying commonalities in the behavior exhibited by different animal species. Any shared features were thought to be derived from a common ancestor of the modern species under study, an ancestral animal that had provided its descendants with a particular ability or attribute. Darwin (1872) himself was a comparative psychologist of this sort, most notably in the book *The Expression of the Emotions in Man and Animals*, which traced human facial expressions to our mammalian ancestors.

Comparative animal psychology rested on Darwin's theory of evolution by descent with modification, a theory designed to trace the sequence of changes that occurred as a given species or trait was gradually modified over evolutionary time. This aspect of evolutionary theory has had great success in explaining why certain groups of modern species exhibit certain similarities; the theory can also help identify the probable evolutionary predecessors of certain complex characteristics of living things (Brooks & McLennan, 1991).

So, for example, we can ask why all ant species exhibit an intensely cooperative lifestyle in which most individuals in any given colony are sterile workers whose actions benefit the relatively few reproductive members of the group. An evolutionary answer to this question is that all modern ants have descended from a single ancestral eusocial (caste-forming) species. Going back farther in time, we can deduce that this ancestral ant must have been derived from a wasp ancestor. Ants and wasps belong to the same order (the Hymenoptera) because they share some important structural similarities inherited from their common ancestor, which surely had a stinger. If an ancestral wasp gave rise to the ants, we can predict that in this lineage there must have been a now extinct ant-wasp or wasp-ant with a blend of wasp and ant characteristics. Such a creature has been found in 90-million-year-old amber (Wilson, Carpenter, & Brown, 1967). This species had the predicted mixture of wasp and ant characters, including a wasp-like thorax endowed with a special gland that is now possessed only by ants.

Because many wasps are not social at all, as is true for the large majority of Hymenoptera, it seems highly likely that somewhere in the wasp lineage leading to ants was a solitary species. From one such ancestor, which did not form colonies or have sterile workers, came one or more wasp species that exhibited some simple social attributes that led individuals to form small colonies of family members, a lifestyle still practiced by some modern descendants of these ancient wasps. A modestly social wasp ancestor eventually gave rise to a eusocial wasp-ant, which gave rise to a richly branched evolutionary tree of ants, all of which have retained the complex eusociality of their common ancestor (Hunt, 1999).

Thus, the theory of descent with modification can provide us with hypotheses on the evolutionary history of attributes of interest. What the theory does *not* explain is the evolved function, or the adaptive value, of the traits of living things, whether these functions are biochemical, physiological, structural, psychological, or behavioral. So, for example, having outlined the possible history behind the evolution of eusocial ant colonies populated by masses of sterile workers, we can still ask what caused eusociality to spread through an ancestral ant or wasp-ant species. For this kind of problem, Darwin offered his theory of evolution by natural selection that, in modified form, has been used to tackle the problem of adaptive eusociality. Darwin (1859) realized that if the individuals of a species differed in their hereditary attributes and if these differences affected the reproductive success of individuals, then those members of the species that generated more surviving descendants would reshape the species in their image over generations.

One can readily envision this process by reference to any of the thousands upon thousands of cases of superb camouflage that exist in the animal kingdom (Figure 2.1). The classic example, of course, is that of the peppered moth, *Biston betularia*, which exists in a number of hereditarily different forms or morphs. In unpolluted woodlands in England and North America, the whitish salt and pepper form of the moth predominate, but in polluted woodlands the melanic mutant takes precedence (Grant, Cook, Clarke, & Owen, 1998). This evolutionary result is related to the color of the bark of trees on which this species rests during the daytime. Tree trunks and limbs in unpolluted areas tend to be light in color, often because they are adorned with whitish lichens. Against this background, blackish adult moths tend to stand out, making them more vulnerable to avian

Figure 2.1 An extraordinarily well camouflaged grasshopper whose pale green coloration and hairy cuticle closely match the color of the hairy leaves of its food plant. Selection acting on genetic variation within this grasshopper species could easily have been responsible for the evolution of the color and structure of the insect, which currently help conceal it from predators.

predators (Howlett & Majerus, 1987). To the extent that birds preferentially capture, kill, and eat the melanic morphs, these peppered moths tend to produce fewer descendants on average than the whitish forms. This statistical outcome insures that black forms become progressively rarer while whitish forms take over the population in natural woodlands.

But in polluted woodlands in which lichens are scarce and darker backgrounds common, the situation is reversed. The greater survivability of the melanic types relative to the salt and pepper types translates into greater reproductive success or fitness for the melanics. This in turn leads to an increase in the proportion of blackish moths in the population from generation to generation. Given enough time under the appropriate conditions, entire populations will consist almost exclusively of melanics; under other conditions, differential reproduction over time will transform a largely melanic population into one composed of mostly salt and pepper types. When conditions change, as has occurred via the introduction of pollution controls in Europe and North America, the frequencies of the two forms of *B. betularia* can change dramatically in a matter of decades (Cook, 2003; Grant et al., 1998). Similarly rapid evolution in response to changed selection pressures has been recorded in other species, such as Australian black snakes, which now refuse to attack the exotic and highly lethal cane toad, a behavioral change that has occurred in less than 25 snake generations following the introduction of the toad to Australia (Phillips & Shine, 2006).

Any hereditary form, whether we are talking about a color pattern, a metabolic pathway, a neural network, a behavior, or a developmental or life history attribute (see Stearns, this volume), will spread at the expense of competing alternatives if the "favored" form confers higher reproductive success to individuals on average than any of the competing alternatives. The inexorable logic of this argument leads to a sweeping prediction: the process of natural selection should create organisms with reproductive adaptations, that is, attributes that help individuals leave more surviving descendants (and thus, more surviving copies of their genes) than individuals that happen to have alternative forms of these characteristics. One of the more famous passages from *On the Origin* presents a key prediction derived from this logic:

> If it could be proved that any part of the structure of any one species had been formed for the exclusive good of another species, it would annihilate my theory, for such could not have been produced through natural selection. (Darwin, 1859, p. 201)

Darwin (1859) realized that in a population in which individuals did things only to help others reproduce, any hereditary variation that caused individuals to act for their own advantage would spread through the species by natural selection. If selection shaped the attributes of living things, traits that only benefit members of another species should not exist.

IS EVOLUTIONARY PSYCHOLOGY FUNDAMENTALLY DIFFERENT FROM SOCIOBIOLOGY?

We may now ask just how novel evolutionary psychology is. This new discipline clearly relies heavily on an old theory, Darwinian natural selection (Buss, 1999; Gaulin & McBurney, 2001; Kenrick, 1995). The theory comes into play when evolutionary psychologists try to determine whether operational elements of the human brain have "design features" that reflect an evolutionary history shaped by natural selection. This approach is not novel in that other disciplines also use natural selection theory as a foundation for research. Paramount among these disciplines is sociobiology, with its focus on the evolution by natural selection of social behavior, broadly defined, especially cooperative behaviors and self-sacrificing altruism. Behaviors of this sort pose a challenge to the adaptationist when they appear to reduce the reproductive success of individuals. The adaptive puzzles associated with social behavior were featured in E. O. Wilson's (1975) sweeping review of behavioral research in his *Sociobiology: The New Synthesis*.

The publication of this book gave sociobiology its name. Subsequently, those persons who accepted the label "sociobiologist" have used natural selection theory to ask how such and such a behavioral trait might boost individual fitness (i.e., individual reproductive success, or descendant-leaving success, or genetic success as measured in the number of copies of the individual's genes that it contributes to the next generation). The sociobiological focus has been on behavior, rather than psychological mechanisms, and on nonhuman animals, especially the social insects, birds, and mammals, rather than on humans. But the approach of the field has been adaptationist, which is to say that researchers have been interested primarily in hypotheses on the possible adaptive value of social traits.

As previously noted, evolutionary psychology emerged as a subdiscipline within academic psychology not long after the birth of sociobiology. Although some evolutionary psychologists have detected a fundamental similarity between sociobiology and their new field (e.g., Crawford, 1987), others have drawn a distinction between the two enterprises (e.g., Buss, 1995). Buss argued that sociobiologists, unlike evolutionary psychologists, were victims of a "sociobiological fallacy," which was to view humans as fitness maximizers when in reality the psychological mechanisms that control human behavior do not always maximize the genetic success of individuals. He argued that only evolutionary psychologists realized that the mechanisms underlying human behavior can misfire, actually reducing individual fitness, as for example when male sexual psychology induces men to spend time and money on pornographic material rather than engaging in other activities more likely to raise reproductive success.

Sociobiologists, however, like evolutionary biologists in general, fully recognize that not every action of every human being is adaptive for a variety of reasons (see the section called "Is Everything an Adaptation?"). Selection cannot guarantee that a psychological mechanism or the behavior that it controls will always be employed in a fitness-raising manner, especially if an individual is operating in a novel environment. Selection results in the spread of traits that are *better* than other alternatives at promoting fitness, not traits that are perfect in some idealized sense. Joint acceptance of this view means that both sociobiologists and evolutionary psychologists consider the possibility that our behavioral abilities and the psychological mechanisms that underlie these behaviors are the products of reproductive competition among individuals in the past. This principle is the foundation for both disciplines and, indeed, for all evolutionists who focus on adaptation. Both evolutionary psychologists and sociobiologists share the goal of determining whether a given trait has enabled individuals to leave more copies of their genes in the past and if so, how. As a result, researchers in both camps devise and test hypotheses on the possible adaptive value of traits of interest to them. In fact, the similarities between sociobiologists and evolutionary psychologists are far greater than their differences (Lopreato & Crippen, 1999).

IS NATURAL SELECTION THEORY A CIRCULAR ARGUMENT?

Given the importance of natural selection theory to evolutionary psychology it would be devastating to learn that the theory was a vacuous circularity. Some persons, however, have made just this claim by arguing that Darwinian theory can in effect be reduced to the survival of the fittest, which leads to the assertion that only the fittest survive (Peters, 1976). If the theory were no more than this statement in a nutshell, one would be justified in thinking that the argument was circular and of little use to scientists or anyone else. But, as previously noted, natural selection theory is a logical claim about what must happen if, and only if, certain conditions apply: If hereditary variation exists within a species that affects the reproductive or genetic success of individuals, then hereditary attributes that happen to help individuals have the greatest chance of reproducing or passing on their genes will spread through the species. The validity of the theory is therefore open to test, which rescues it from empty circularity (Caplan, 1977).

Natural selection theory has been tested repeatedly, and these tests have demonstrated that not only is the theory logical but it is almost certainly correct (Endler, 1986). Darwin himself contributed to this end by testing the prediction that humans could cause animal species to evolve if they "experimentally" regulated the reproductive success of different hereditary variants. He showed that humans have indeed had the predicted effect in their domesticated companions, such as dogs, pigeons, and the like (see Darwin, 1859, chapter 1).

All adaptationists currently accept that natural selection theory is both logical and correct. They therefore do not seek to test the theory itself again, but to use it. And as previously indicated, they do so by putting the theory to work when producing their hypotheses. For example, adaptationists have used Darwinian theory when trying to explain why human infants cry loudly and often. If the ability of babies to wail has been shaped by natural selection, then the ability must confer a reproductive benefit of some sort that generally overcomes the obvious disadvantages of the behavior, such as the energy expended by the crying child, the risk that an exasperated caretaker will attack the vocal baby rather than help it, or the chance that a predator would use the cries of the infant to locate it. One adaptationist hypothesis for crying is that it enables infants to convey both their need for assistance from a parental caretaker and their capacity for survival should they receive the additional care that they are in effect requesting (Zeifman, 2001).

This hypothesis generates many predictions, such as the expectation that infants carried everywhere by their mothers and nursed on demand, as is the custom in most traditional societies, will cry less often than those left more often to their own devices, as is the custom in modern western society. In addition, we can expect that infants unable to cry loudly and robustly will tend to suffer from developmental defects that are correlated with a low probability of long-term survival and reproductive success. Parents of babies of this sort could potentially boost their lifetime reproductive success by abandoning these low-quality children in favor of investing in other offspring with a better chance of reaching the age of reproduction. Evidence that is supportive of some predictions, but not all, derived from adaptationist hypotheses on crying has been assembled by Zeifman (2001).

Darwinian selectionist theory has been greatly admired by scientists ever since 1859 because it can be applied productively to a vast array of topics. And the application of the theory has helped adaptationists make sense of things that cannot be explained otherwise. Note, for example, that the selectionist dimension is essential if we are to acquire a complete set of causes for infant crying. To see why, imagine that we possessed total understanding of how an infant's brain worked and how this organ had developed. This kind of information would enable us to identify how certain kinds of stimuli triggered crying in response. But this *proximate* accounting, useful though it would be in determining the immediate causes of crying, would not tell us why the baby's developmental and psychological mechanisms have persisted over time. For this, we need evolutionary theory. We will have more to say later on the complementarity of proximate and evolutionary explanations.

IS SEXUAL SELECTION FUNDAMENTALLY DIFFERENT FROM NATURAL SELECTION?

Darwin (1871) devised sexual selection theory in response to the observation that certain attributes of animals appeared to reduce the survival chances of individuals while at the same time increasing the ability of those individuals to acquire mates. Given the importance to the process of natural selection of differences among individuals in their survival abilities, Darwin felt that he needed an adjunct theory to account for the persistence of survival-reducing traits (Figure 2.2), such as the elaborate ornaments of male birds such as the cock-of-the-rock, the immense jaws and horns of certain male scarab beetles, and the display courts of male bowerbirds. He realized that these male attributes could potentially spread through species if males with relatively elaborate ornaments, weapons, or displays either attracted more females or defeated rival males more effectively in the competition for mates, even if these traits carried with them a survival handicap.

Note, however, that any naturally selected traits that promote the survival of individuals will spread only if these individuals also reproduce more than those competitors less capable of surviving do. In other words, whether we are talking of natural selection or sexual selection, evolutionary change occurs only when individuals differ in their reproductive success, which affects their ability to transmit their hereditary information to the next generation. Thus, sexual selection is really a subset of natural selection, namely that component that is caused by differences among individuals in their access to mates. Nonetheless, sexual selection theory has been retained as a distinct concept because of its usefulness in understanding the often conspicuous and puzzling traits employed in

Figure 2.2 Sexual selection is responsible for an immense array of animal attributes. For example, in Dawson's burrowing bee, the male (the upper bee in the left hand photo) is often as large as or larger than his mate, an unusual situation among bees, perhaps because large body size comes at a cost. In Dawson's burrowing bees, however, the disadvantages of being large and aggressive can be outweighed by the benefits of these traits in the violent fights that occur among males over access to receptive females, which often happen when an emerging female (center of right hand photo) is surrounded by males.

reproductive competition (Andersson, 1994). Indeed, much research in evolutionary psychology deals exclusively with sexually selected traits (Hagen, 2005).

WHAT IS MORE IMPORTANT TO THE HISTORY OF A SPECIES: SELECTION FOR INDIVIDUAL REPRODUCTIVE SUCCESS OR SELECTION FOR GROUP SURVIVAL?

As we have seen, the logic of Darwinian natural selection and sexual selection requires that hereditary traits will spread only if they are better than other alternatives at helping individuals leave copies of the genes associated with these traits. Nothing in these theories suggests that traits benefiting entire groups will automatically spread by natural selection. Yet, as George C. Williams (1966) explained in his great book *Adaptation and Natural Selection*, many biologists in the first two-thirds of the 20th century had apparently concluded that natural selection could act to preserve species from extinction or even to protect entire ecosystems.

Williams' (1966) book debunked these claims, which were based on what is now labeled group selection theory, the theory that selection occurs when groups differ in their hereditary features in ways that affect the relative survival chances (or productivity) of these groups. Williams asked his readers to consider what would happen over evolutionary time if two hereditary traits, one group benefiting and the other helping only the actor, were in competition with one another. Let Trait A advance the reproductive success of individuals, even if the spread of this trait increases the likelihood of the eventual extinction of the group or species to which these individuals belong. Let the alternative Trait B increase the odds that the group or species as a whole would survive but at the expense of these individuals who sacrifice for the benefit of their group. Under these circumstances, the greater reproductive success of individuals exhibiting the A phenotype should result in the gradual elimination of their genetically distinct B competitors, whose actions have the effect of removing their genes from the gene pool (Williams, 1966).

The logic of Williams' (1966) thought experiment convinced biologists to be skeptical of casual claims that such and such a characteristic had evolved in order to promote the welfare of a group, a species, or a community of species, especially if the characteristic required some individuals to engage in personally costly activities for the benefit of others. For example, earthworms expend much energy burrowing through soil. Do they do so to aerate the soil, increasing its capacity to absorb water and thereby improving its quality for the local plant community? Or did this behavior evolve solely because of certain benefits to the worms themselves? Williams (1966) argued that the food collected by burrowing earthworms was sufficient in and of itself to account for the evolution of their behavior. As he pointed out, any worm that did some extra burrowing to aerate the soil exclusively for some other species would surely be selected against. Therefore, any gains enjoyed by plant communities from earthworm activity must be an incidental side effect of a trait that evolved for entirely different reasons having to do with the reproductive success of individual earthworms.

Williams (1966) noted that the temptation to offer naïve group benefit explanations is particularly great when discussing animal social behavior. When two animals cooperate, it is easy to view the helpful actions of one to be designed primarily to assist the other. However, if there were no gain for the helper (or its relatives—see the following section), then selection would surely act against any tendency to engage in unrewarded cooperation. In evolutionary terms, the reproductive benefit enjoyed by the receiver of help can usually be considered an incidental effect of a trait whose evolved function is to secure fitness for the helper.

The distinction between *evolved function* and *incidental effect* is always important if we wish to know why in evolutionary terms a particular trait has been retained in the face of natural selection. When traits provide net reproductive benefits for individuals, they can be selected for—that is, they can become more common in a species over time; however, when individuals work strictly for the benefit of others, selection can be expected to favor other individuals with different, more self-benefiting attributes.

There is one exception to the general rule that we can ignore the effects of individuals on the survival of the groups to which they belong. It is possible for individuals to sacrifice themselves for others in an adaptive manner, when the group in question is a cluster of related individuals. Darwin (1859) illustrated this point by reference to domestic cattle, noting that animals slaughtered by farmers for their beef could nevertheless perpetuate their family lineage if the dead animals' qualities as food was such that their fathers or mothers were permitted to sire still more offspring, some of whom would be retained as breeding stock for the next generation (see pp. 237–238 in Darwin, 1859).

More than a century later, W. D. Hamilton (1964) formalized this explanation for adaptive altruism and Williams (1966) reported this advance in his book. As a result, what is now known as kin selection or indirect selection theory is a major part of evolutionary theory (Brown, 1987; Dawkins, 1976). Note that both natural selection and kin selection are processes that occur when individuals differ in their ability to propagate their genes. Natural selection increases the frequency of individuals with hereditary traits that enable their possessors to reproduce successfully, so that they pass on their genes *directly* to the next generation in the bodies of their offspring. Kin selection leads to an increase in the frequency of individuals with hereditary traits that cause those individuals to help their relatives reproduce; because relatives share some proportion of their genes in common, a helper can make copies of its genes *indirectly* by increasing the reproductive success of genetically similar individuals. Because gene contributions, whether direct or indirect, can be measured in the same units (genes copied and transmitted to the next generation), it is possible to speak of an individual's *inclusive fitness,* his or her total genetic contribution that arises from his or her actions.

WHAT IS THE UNIT OF SELECTION: THE GENE OR THE INDIVIDUAL?

By 1970 or thereabouts, the differences, and similarities, between natural selection, the naïve form of group selection, and kin selection had been largely worked out. Ever since then, selection among groups has been rarely invoked as an explanation for behavior of any sort (but see Sober & Wilson, 1998; Wilson & Hölldobler, 2005), except in those special cases in which the group is a family. Thus, groups (species or populations) are rarely considered fundamental units of selection. Both genes and individuals, however, have been nominated for this role.

Given that Williams (1966) championed inclusive fitness theory, it is not surprising that he promoted the gene as the essential unit of selection. Indeed, he gave Darwinian natural selection a new name, "genic selection," to emphasize that in the last analysis genes are in competition with one another, with winners persisting in gene pools to influence the attributes of the members of the next generation (Williams, 1966). Dawkins (1976) accepted and popularized the gene thinking or inclusive fitness perspective of Hamilton and Williams in his book *The Selfish Gene.* Although the adjective "selfish" was clearly metaphorical, some readers insisted on taking Dawkins literally, apparently believing, for example, that he was saying that genes have a near-conscious capacity to act in their self-interest. In reality, Dawkins was simply using "selfish gene" as a synonym for the kind of gene that would be likely to replicate sufficiently to persist in populations in the face of natural or kin selection.

Not everyone, however, accepted the gene-centered view of evolution. Among others, Stephen Jay Gould (1977) and Ernst Mayr (1982) noted that selection cannot act on individual genes *directly* but instead must focus on complete individuals, whose development and operation require the integrated action of entire genotypes. In this vein, Gould (1977) wrote, "Selection simply cannot see genes and pick among them directly. It must use bodies as an intermediary" (p. 24).

Moreover, the complexity of interactions among the multitude of genes within individuals is such that a particular gene can potentially have either a positive or a negative effect on fitness, depending on the context provided by its fellow genes. According to Mayr (1982), the context-dependent nature of a gene's developmental effect makes it impossible to calculate the fitness consequences of any single gene taken in isolation from its fellow genes.

However, although it is true that gene interactions are the norm and that selection does not act directly on genes themselves but only on phenotypic differences among individuals, nonetheless, selection has evolutionary significance only when it affects the frequency of genes in gene pools, which it is perfectly capable of doing. Some genes do affect the developmental process. These developmentally influential genes sometimes occur in different forms (alleles) in populations where they generate phenotypic variation. Under these circumstances, a change in allele frequencies is all but inevitable given the very low probability that different hereditary phenotypes will have exactly the same fitness on average. As Williams (1966) points out,

> No matter how functionally dependent a gene may be, and no matter how complicated its interactions with other genes and environmental factors, it must always be true that a given gene substitution [allele] will have an arithmetic mean effect on fitness in any population. (p. 57)

An allele that has the highest arithmetic mean effect on fitness will spread at the expense of alternative forms of that gene. Therefore, it is appropriate to focus on selection on allelic differences, an emphasis that does not prevent one from acknowledging that the competitive performance of genetically different phenotypes usually establishes which alleles persist and which do not.

Another way to make this point is to claim that although alleles are the fundamental *units* of selection, because only alleles can persist from one generation to the next, selection can act on different entities or *levels,* usually on the level of the individual, but potentially also at the level of the group or the gene (Crespi, 2000). Table 2.1 provides a summary of the conditions (assumptions) required for selection to occur at these different levels as a result of competition among groups, individuals, or alleles. Note the similarities between the assumptions underlying group, individual, and allelic selection. As Table 2.1 makes clear, essentially the same kind of logic that underlies individual and genic selection can also be applied to selection at the level of the group, showing that there is nothing inherently illogical about group selection. If the various assumptions are met, one can legitimately infer that selection will occur, resulting in the evolutionary spread of traits (i.e., *adaptations*) that tend to enhance the replicating success of groups, individuals, or alleles relative to other entities with different attributes.

By emphasizing the similarities between the three levels of selection, we can also illuminate the differences between them. "Individual" selection can be treated as the reference point for all comparisons of this sort inasmuch as Darwin (1859) presented the argument for this kind of selection in *On the Origin of Species*. Mayr (1977) helped make Darwin's logic clear to a modern audience. Selection at the level of the gene is, as has been noted, a post-Darwinian development associated with the work of Hamilton (1964) and Williams (1966), whose contributions were popularized and expanded by Dawkins (1976, 1982). Selection at the level of the group was first formally proposed by Wynne-Edwards (1962), which stimulated a critical response from defenders of individual and genic selection. As noted, the problem with group selection theory is not that its premises are impossible or illogical but that individuals *within groups* would inevitably compete reproductively among themselves. Therefore, if a group-benefiting attribute usually led to lower fitness within the group, that trait would tend to be replaced by an alternative that enhanced individual fitness.

Likewise, if an allele had a developmental effect that tended to promote its replicating chances at the expense of the individual and the other genes in its genome (as in those alleles that distort meiosis so that they are disproportionately represented in the individual's sperm or eggs), then selection might well favor individuals whose genomes were composed of cooperating genes at other

Table 2.1 Logic of Natural Selection for Groups, Individuals and Alleles

Kind of Selection	Group	Individual	Allelic
Definitions			
Natural Selection	The differential contribution of groups to the next generation by genetically different groups of a population.	The differential contribution of offspring to the next generation by genetically different members of a population.	The differential contribution of alleles to the next generation by different alleles of a population.
Assumptions & Inferences			
Assumption 1 Population growth	The number (or size) of groups that descend from ancestral groups can grow exponentially.	The number of descendents of organisms in a population can grow exponentially.	The number of copies of alleles in a gene pool can grow exponentially.
Assumption 2 Limited resources	Resources enabling individuals in a population to exist can expand only arithmetically.	Resources enabling individuals in a population to exist can expand only arithmetically.	Resources enabling individuals in a population to exist can expand only arithmetically.
Assumption 3 Population size	The number (or size) of groups in a population remains relatively constant across time.	The size of a population of individuals remains relatively stable across time.	The size of the gene pool of a population remains relatively constant across time.
Inference 1	Competition between groups in a population for existence or group growth (or group propagation) ensues.	Competition between individuals in a population for existence and reproduction ensues.	Competition between alleles in a gene pool for existence and replication ensues.
Assumption 4 Differences between competing entities	Groups differ in traits that enable them to survive and reproduce.	Individuals differ on traits that enable them to survive and reproduce.	Alleles differ in the production of traits that enable them to replicate.
Assumption 5 Heritability	Some of the variation in these traits is genetic.	Some of the variation in these traits is genetic.	Some of the variation in these traits is genetic.
Inference 2	If assumptions 4 and 5 apply, there will be differential propagation by or survival of genetically different groups within a population—and then by definition group selection will have occurred.	If assumptions 4 and 5 apply, there will be differential contribution of offspring to the next generation by genetically different members of a population"—and then by definition Darwinian natural selection will have occurred.	If assumptions 4 and 5 apply, there will be "differential replication of different alleles in the next generation of a population"—and then by definition genic selection will have occurred.
Inference 3	Over many generations groups with individuals whose anatomical structures, physiological process, or behavior patterns contributed most to groups' ability to survive and reproduce (grow in size) will become more common relative to alternative traits. These "winning" traits can be labeled *group-benefiting adaptations*.	Over many generations, anatomical structures, physiological process, or behavior patterns that contributed most to individuals' ability to survive, and reproduce will become more common relative to other alternative traits. These "winning" traits can be labeled *Darwinian adaptations*.	Over many generations, anatomical structures, physiological process, or behavior patterns that contributed most to alleles' ability to replicate[1] will become more common relative to other alternative traits. These "winning" traits can be labeled *genic adaptations*.

[1] Here, replicatation requires the survival, growth, and reproduction of the bodies that carry the alleles in question.

loci that suppressed any self-promoting alleles in their midst (Crow, 1979). As predicted, meiosis is rarely subverted by "outlaw" genes that act in their own narrow self-interest.

DOES NATURAL SELECTION LEAD TO EVOLUTIONARY PROGRESS?

The processes of evolutionary change, whether caused by differences among groups, individuals or alleles, lead to products, namely living things with their generally adaptive features. Our species with its bundle of special attributes is one such product. Many persons who accept the reality of evolution believe that the human species constitutes an end or goal toward which selection was aiming all along. Deeply embedded in this widespread view is the notion of a *scala naturae* with single-celled organisms at the base of a ladder, which has intermediate rungs for fish, amphibians, and reptiles, then mammals, culminating in a top rung reserved for human beings. This scenario is highly problematic. For one thing, evolution does not generate a linear series of species, some of which are lower and more primitive while others are higher and more advanced. Instead, all modern organisms have an evolutionary history of equal duration, forming an extraordinarily branched evolutionary tree with living species arrayed on the twigs at the end of those branches (Gould, 1986).

Moreover, because natural selection is a blind process, not a guiding force, it cannot generate the kind of anthropocentric "progress" imagined by the average person (Gould, 1996b). Selection cannot have been "trying" to produce our species because natural selection cannot anticipate future needs or control evolution so that a particular species is formed at a particular time. Indeed, the role of selection in speciation itself is probably secondary to other factors that result in the splitting of one ancestral population into two geographically isolated units, which may then undergo the kind of genetic divergence that results in the formation of two descendant species from the ancestral one (Mayr, 1963). Speciation may be facilitated by differences in selection within the two separated populations, but Darwinian selection has the primary effect of producing adaptations, not new species (Williams, 1966).

If, however, we focus strictly on the spread and accumulation of adaptations within a species, we may be able to rescue the concept of progress in evolution (Dawkins, 1997). The changes that are produced by selection increase the proportion of individuals in a population that possess those attributes that were most effective in helping individuals pass on their genes in a certain environment. To the extent that we equate progress with the cumulative spread of new fitness-enhancing traits within populations, then we are on firmer ground when claiming that selection generates progress.

Dawkins (1997) is an exponent of this view, noting that the effect of selection is to increase the match, or "fit," between the members of a species and the environment in which they operate. Improvements of this sort can be seen, for example, in the highly complex set of defensive devices employed by a prey species (e.g., Figure 2.1) that has been subject to repeated rounds of coevolutionary interactions with its predators. But adaptive improvement is also seen in the body plan of a parasite that has lost its digestive tract as result of the selective advantages gained by foregoing an expensive-to-produce organ system that is redundant for a creature with access to a supply of predigested food. Thus, it is not increases in complexity per se that constitute progress in a Dawkinsian view but rather changes that produce a better fit between an organism and the elements of the environment with which it interacts.

This kind of evolutionary progress is actually dependent upon a highly conservative aspect of selection, which is the elimination of most mutations because of their deleterious effect on individual reproductive success. *Stabilizing selection* (selection in favor of the mean or average form of a given attribute) results in the maintenance of a currently advantageous hereditary phenotype. Although natural selection is strongly associated in the popular mind with evolutionary *change,* in many respects selection acts primarily to maintain current adaptations, rather than to cause the spread of novel attributes (Williams, 1966). The stabilizing removal of fitness-reducing alleles from populations means that adaptive traits are not compromised simply by the passage of time but instead are available for improvement upon the rare occurrence of a mutant allele that happens to have the unusual effect of producing a superior form of a current trait.

IS EVERYTHING AN ADAPTATION?

Given the consequences of natural selection, we can expect that any alleles that manage to persist in populations will have proximate developmental and physiological effects that help propagate those very alleles. As already noted, this logic underlies the attempts of adaptationists, whether they are called sociobiologists, behavioral ecologists, or evolutionary psychologists, to understand why living things, including human beings, have certain proximate mechanisms within their bodies and not other forms of those mechanisms with different properties and somewhat different functions.

This approach was attacked by Gould (1978, 2002; Gould & Lewontin, 1979) from the 1970s right through to the publication of his final book. He argued consistently and influentially that adaptationists foolishly believed that all the traits of living things were in fact adaptations and that, furthermore, these persons were prepared to accept any speculative adaptive explanation for a given trait, no matter how implausible. In one of Gould's (1984) more temperate comments on the supposed failure of the adaptationist approach, he wrote, "[W]e have become overzealous about the power and range of selection by trying to attribute every significant form and behavior to its direct action" (p. 18).

Gould's efforts to depreciate sociobiologists in particular and adaptationists in general found a receptive audience composed in part of academics, such as cultural anthropologists, social psychologists, and sociologists, for whom human sociobiology represented a disciplinary threat (Kenrick, 1995; Lopreato & Crippen, 1999). Needless to say, adaptationists were not part of this audience but instead disputed Gould's assertions (Alexander, 1979; Barash, 2002; Borgia, 1994; Dawkins, 1985; Queller, 1995). Many of these defenders of adaptationism noted that evolutionary biologists have long recognized that not every phenotypic characteristic is adaptive. Indeed, this was a central point of Williams (1966), who emphasized the need for caution in assigning adaptive value to a given trait. For example, because modern traits are the products of selection that has occurred in the past, some attributes are likely to be maladaptive holdovers from a time when selection pressures were different from those in current environments (Crespi, 2000). This is particularly true of course for the human species, which to a considerable extent has created its own rapidly changing cultural environment.

Another very common class of maladaptive phenotypes includes those traits that arise as by-products or side effects of developmental processes that underlie the production of other traits that truly do promote fitness, that is, traits that qualify as adaptations (Crespi, 2000). At a proximate level, nonadaptive side effects can occur because a biochemical reaction may contribute to the building of more than one part of an organism. Since each reaction is dependent upon a particular enzyme, which in turn requires genetic information for its production, a single gene, in theory, can have several phenotypic effects; some may be adaptive, others may not be.

ARE ADAPTATIONISTS JUST-SO STORY TELLERS?

Because evolutionary biologists have long known that some traits may be neutral or maladaptive, they have long known that hypotheses about the possible adaptive value of such and such a trait require testing. This leads us to Gould's ancillary claim, also false, that adaptationists skip the testing phase of science and simply accept just-so stories about the supposed adaptive value of such and such a trait. Gould and Lewontin (1979) write, "We fault the adaptationist programme ... for its reliance upon plausibility alone as a criterion for accepting speculative tales" (p. 581).

In reality, adaptationists are no different from any other scientists in testing their working hypotheses in the traditional manner. The market for untested evolutionary hypotheses is, and always has been, remarkably small, thanks to the peer review process that precedes publication in research journals. So, for example, articles dealing with the evolutionary reasons why babies cry have used selectionist theory in the manner outlined earlier, namely to generate hypotheses consistent with theory on the possible adaptive value of the behavior (Lummaa, Vuorisalo, Barr, & Lehtonen, 1998; Zeifman, 2001). These articles often have considered several different tentative hypotheses on the phenomenon, a reflection of the fact that adaptationist researchers can often think of multiple explanations for this or that trait. When there is more than one hypothesis to consider, the need for testing in order to reject incorrect ideas is obvious. And indeed, published work on infant crying never stops at the point of hypothesis presentation but instead proceeds to hypothesis testing via the presentation of evidence relevant to the supposed "just-so story" or "stories" in question. At least one hypothesis on the possible function of crying has been rejected by Soltis (2004). He rules against the possibility that infants cry manipulatively to secure more care and feeding than is advantageous for their caregivers. This hypothesis leads to the prediction that "excessive" crying should be associated with relatively older babies, who could consume and benefit from extra milk in amounts that mothers might be unwilling to provide unless pushed into doing so by a noisy, manipulative infant. In reality, however, crying peaks very early in life when infants are too small to consume large quantities of milk (Soltis, 2004).

IS IT TRUE, HOWEVER, THAT ADAPTATIONISTS GREATLY OVERESTIMATE THE PREVALENCE OF ADAPTATION?

Gould attempted to elevate his criticism of adaptationism by making some additional arguments, both semantic and theoretical, that require additional analysis here. In his famous paper on the spandrels of San Marco written with Richard Lewontin (Gould & Lewontin, 1979; see the following section) and in several of his later papers (e.g., Gould, 1997; Gould & Vrba, 1982), Gould defined adaptation in such a way as to greatly narrow the use of the term in evolutionary biology. For Gould and others of like mind, *adaptation* is a word that must be restricted to traits that had originally been selected for because of a particular function and that had retained this function over evolutionary time to the present. According to this definition, any phenotype that had taken on a novel function during evolution could not be labeled an adaptation. To distinguish between traits with unaltered functions (adaptations in the narrow Gouldian sense) and those characteristics that had been co-opted for a new function, Gould and Vrba proposed the term *exaptation* for the latter category. They furthermore distinguished between the two classes of traits by stating that "[a]daptations have functions; exaptations have effects" (p. 6), a pronouncement that leaves the impression that the two classes of traits are fundamentally different.

The effect of accepting the restrictive definition of adaptation proposed by Gould and his coauthors would be to reduce the number of characteristics of living things that qualified as adaptations, thereby presumably reducing the number of traits that could be studied by adaptationists. However, as Darwin (1862) noted long ago, "When this or that part has been spoken of as contrived for some special purpose, it must not be supposed that it was originally always formed for this sole purpose" (p. 346). Darwin added, "The regular course of events seems to be, that a part which originally served for one purpose by slow changes, becomes adapted for widely different purposes" (p. 346).

Many modern adaptationists have agreed with Darwin, noting that if one goes back far enough in time no modern trait would have the same function as its distant predecessors (Dennett, 1995; Reeve & Sherman, 1993). So, for example, the wing feathers of flying birds clearly possess structural features that have the function of facilitating flight. Yet we can be all but certain that the original feathers on the forelimbs of a dinosaurian prebird had some other function, perhaps thermoregulatory in nature or perhaps related to courtship or aggressive display. These nonflight feathers in turn were probably derived from quill like projections from the skin that almost certainly had a defensive function (Figure 2.3; Prum, 1999). Given that selection must have been as involved in the process that produced wing primaries as in changing a body scale into a defensive shaft, one wonders what analytical benefit is gained by calling wing feathers exaptations, particularly if this label misleads one into thinking that flight feathers were produced by evolutionary mechanisms other than natural selection.

Gould and Lewontin (1979) also introduced the term *spandrels* into the evolutionary literature as part of their antiadaptationist campaign. They argued that many of the features of living things were analogous to architectural spandrels, namely structures that are created as by-products of building the necessary, functional components of an edifice or an organism. Thus, the adjoining arches in the cathedral at San Marco provided critical support for the dome of the building (their "true" function), but the conjunction of these arches also created open surfaces that could then be ornamented with religious art (as they were). Gould noted that although the spandrels have been secondarily taken advantage of by the cathedral's builders for ornamental purposes, the arches were obviously not built to provide surface area for these ornaments. In this sense, spandrels and all that has been put on them are mere by-products of the truly functional (adaptive) element of the cathedral, its supporting arches. As Gould (1997) put it, "[We] borrowed the architectural term 'spandrel' … to designate the class of forms and spaces that arise as necessary byproducts of another decision in design, and not as adaptations for direct utility in themselves" (p. 10750).

Most sociobiologists and evolutionary biologists reject this semantic argument on the grounds that the essential point is whether or not the particular genes that contribute to a given by-product of development are selected for or against. To the extent that it can be demonstrated that an inherited organic spandrel contributes to the genetic success of the individuals that possess this form of the spandrel, then we can say that natural selection has resulted in the spread or maintenance of this hereditary phenotype. Understanding the adaptive value of the spandrel provides an explanation for its existence as opposed to some other alternative. As Darwin (1862) put it, "Although an organ may not have been originally formed for some special purpose, if it now serves for this end, we are justified in saying that it is specially contrived for it" (p. 348).

BUT ARE ADAPTATIONS OFTEN LESS THAN OPTIMAL BECAUSE OF THE CONSTRAINTS PLACED ON THEM BY THE EVOLUTIONARY PROCESS?

The constraints argument is yet another line of attack that Gould developed as part of his dismissal of the adaptationist approach. Gould (1986; Gould & Lewontin, 1979) claimed that constraints on adaptation would arise because the functional genetic and developmental systems already in place would limit the kinds of hereditary modifications that the organism could possibly accommodate. Thus, to take a crude example, pigs and humans are unlikely to evolve wings because there just is not the bodily infrastructure needed to accommodate mutant incipient wings in these species. Limits of this sort could prevent potential improvements in an existing trait from taking hold, thereby eliminating options that would offer greater reproductive success for individuals if these individuals could only be redesigned without having to use the current phenotype as a starting point. Therefore, what has happened in the past can constrain the kinds of changes that are possible in the present.

Evolutionary biologists of all stripes fully accept that natural selection acts only on what is available, not on all imaginable variants. Dawkins (1982) illustrated this point with the following analogy. He asked us to imagine that human aeronautic engineers had to construct a jet airplane, not by starting from scratch but through a series of small modifications of a propeller-driven plane with the requirement that each change produce an entirely functional and at least slightly

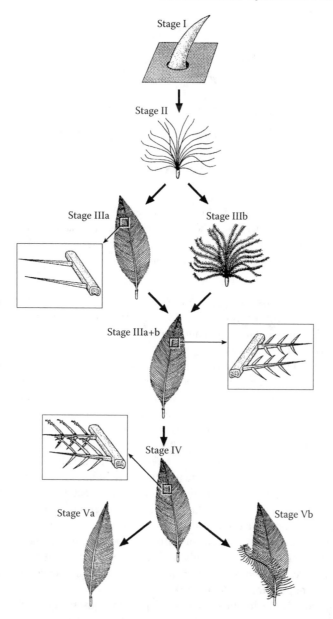

Figure 2.3 At each stage during the evolution of the flight feathers of modern birds, selection would have been required as defensive scales gave rise to projections with a different function, which in turn became modified over time as the basis for adaptive flight (from Prum, 1999).

improved aircraft. Needless to say, this is not how human engineers do things, but natural selection can only act on variants of preexisting phenotypes, with the result that organisms often have at least some jury-rigged characteristics that bear the obvious imprint of the past (Darwin, 1871; Gould, 1986).

For example, humans have a blind spot in their eyes caused by the fact that the nerve fibers project outward from the retina, so that when they coalesce into an optic nerve that carries this information to the brain behind the eye, the nerve must pass through the retina to reach its goal (Figure 2.4). The retinal area sacrificed for the passage of the optic nerve obviously lacks receptors, so we

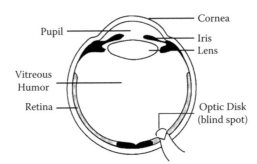

Figure 2.4 The human retina has a blind spot because the photoreceptors on the outer surface of the retina have to relay their information back through the eye's receiving surface via the optic nerve to the brain. This feature stems from the origin of human eyes from far simpler visual systems that consisted of a thin patch of photoreceptors lying on the surface of the ancestral organism.

cannot see light that strikes this spot (Williams & Nesse, 1991). This imperfection in design can be traced to the fact that we evolved from a tiny, transparent ancestor that had a small patch of light-sensitive cells near its surface. Our retina and those of all vertebrates evolved from this creature's "retina" with its outward projecting cells.

Gould (1986) argued that many of the traits of living things are rather like the human retina, a suboptimal device trapped by the rigidity of developmental systems, which in turn are the historical legacy of evolution. In this light, he pointed to evidence from the distribution of the so-called *Hox* genes, which speaks to the extraordinarily conservative nature of the evolutionary process. These genes play critical roles in the development of the bodies of fruit flies, mice, and men, to name a few (Gould, 2002). The genes in question have clearly been retained from a very distant common ancestor of insects, vertebrates and others, presumably because of their value in organizing and integrating the development of body components whether the body in question is destined to become a fly, a mouse, or a person (Holland & Garcia-Fernandez, 1996; Maconochie, Nonchev, Morrison, & Krumlauf, 1996). One could take, as Gould did, the *Hox* genes story to indicate that evolutionary change is blocked by reliance on a critical set of highly conserved genes that have been employed in a great diversity of organisms for hundreds of millions of years. On the other hand, the fact that the bodies of humans and fruit flies are strikingly different would seem to suggest that whatever developmental constraints are imposed by evolutionary conservatism are not so great after all, provided natural selection has enough time to do its work.

Even more importantly, the implication that "adaptation" must be reserved for attributes that are perfect in a developmentally and phylogenetically unconstrained sense completely misses the point. Ever since Williams's (1966) *Adaptation and Natural Selection*, evolutionists have understood that adaptation, like fitness, is a relative term. Adaptations are traits that confer *higher* fitness than other existing alternatives, not traits that confer the highest absolute fitness against all imaginable alternatives, no matter how unrealistic (Williams, 1966). If a modification does spread through a population through the process of natural selection, despite all the restrictions, limitations, and constraints surrounding the change, then it must be better at promoting individual fitness than any other alternative form of the trait with which it coexists for some time. A demonstration that a current trait enhances the fitness of individuals relative to others (or would have done so under conditions of the recent past) suggests that the trait spread or is being maintained by natural selection, which gives us an evolutionary cause for this characteristic's persistence to the present.

IN THE CASE OF HUMANS, SHOULD SOCIOCULTURAL EXPLANATIONS FOR OUR BEHAVIOR TAKE PRECEDENCE OVER EVOLUTIONARY ONES?

In order to understand the selectionist history of elements of human behavior and human psychology, evolutionary psychologists ask whether these traits do (or did) a better job of raising individual reproductive success than other variants that are (or were) present in our species do (or did). But given the obvious influence of culture on human behavior, some persons have argued that when offered a choice between a sociocultural hypothesis and an adaptationist hypothesis for human phenotypes, one should give the nod to the sociocultural, or "nonbiological," alternative (Gould, 1974, 1996a). Pinker (2002) provides a full account of the pervasiveness of this argument in the social sciences.

The fundamental problem with this dichotomy is that it puts proximate hypotheses about human behavior in conflict with evolutionary or ultimate hypotheses, confounding two complementary levels of analysis. We noted earlier, when discussing why babies cry, that one can differentiate between the immediate or proximate causes of crying, such as the genetic factors that contribute to brain development or the hunger or pain stimuli that elicit crying, and the evolutionary or ultimate causes of this behavior, such as the survival (and thus, reproductive) advantages gained by being able to signal certain needs to a caregiver. Every biological trait has both proximate and ultimate causes. Treating proximate and ultimate hypotheses as conflicting alternatives is misguided because both are needed for a full understanding of any phenotype. On the proximate hand, we need to know how traits develop and how they operate while in ultimate terms, we need to learn why selection has retained certain internal devices, structures, and behaviors in living things. Mayr (1961) made this point by noting the difference between questions like "how does it work" and "why is it advantageous to work that way." This message is ignored in the claim that human behavior is best understood in terms of its sociocultural (proximate) causes rather than its adaptive value or selectionist (ultimate) causes.

At the heart of the eagerness of many to insist that culturally influenced, socially learned human behaviors are somehow immune to evolutionary analysis is the belief that learning is "environmentally determined" and, therefore, exists without an evolvable genetic-physiological foundation. A moment's reflection reveals the failings of this position, given that no one seriously disputes that learning is based on specific biochemical reactions in particular brain cells. These reactions, which occur as the human brain is being built and later as it responds to certain environmental stimuli, require enzymes, which in turn cannot be produced without the appropriate genetic information. Thus, learning is every bit as "biological" as instinct, every bit as dependent upon heredity, every bit as likely to vary in response to mutations, and thus, every bit as capable of evolving (Hagen, 2005). Likewise, no one doubts that there have been highly significant genetic changes within the human brain during our evolution (Preuss, Caceres, Oldham, & Geschwind, 2004). To think that these changes were irrelevant to our capacity to learn makes very little sense, especially since, for example, specific portions of the cerebral cortex that are essential for language learning have been identified, named, and distinguished from other neighboring regions of the brain. Therefore, to insist that learning is purely "environmental" leads to proximate hypotheses that are incompatible with the genetic-physiological evidence. Hypotheses of this sort cannot be integrated with complementary evolutionary explanations of human behavior, an outcome that is highly undesirable.

Even if one accepts that human learning relies on remarkably open-ended brain mechanisms for the undifferentiated acquisition of all culturally supplied data rather than on specific modules dedicated to particular kinds of learning tasks, one would still have to posit the evolution of clusters of neurons capable of all-purpose learning. In other words, if we are to understand the human capacity for culture, we cannot sweep evolutionary hypotheses under the rug. The fact that human behavior is dependent on cultural traditions and is unusually flexible does not mean that we alone of all species have been unaffected by standard evolutionary processes (Alexander, 1987; Hagen, 2005).

GIVEN THAT WE KNOW SO LITTLE ABOUT THE ANCESTRAL ENVIRONMENT OF HUMANS, HOW CAN WE KNOW ANYTHING ABOUT THE SELECTION PRESSURES OPERATING ON OUR ANCESTORS?

Evolution is an historical process, which is to say that the attributes of today's organisms were shaped by previous episodes of natural selection. In order to understand existing phenotypic attributes, therefore, it would be helpful to know something about past environments, and thus past selection pressures. If we knew these things, then we could match current traits with the features for which they were adapted. A prominent approach of evolutionary psychologists has therefore been to try to define the environment in which our ancestors were evolving in order to better understand the evolved function of assorted human abilities. So, for example, people who live today in environments with few or no poisonous snakes nevertheless often exhibit an intense fear of these creatures, poisonous or not. This irrational element of human psychology can potentially be explained as the product of past selection operating over millennia during which time our ancestors generally lived with and were subject to attack by highly poisonous snakes.

The attempt to describe the past EEA for the purpose of explaining modern human psychology and behavior has been greeted with intense resistance, even ridicule, by some critics of evolutionary psychology. Thus, David Buller (2005) wrote, "There is no reason to think that contemporary humans are, like Fred and Wilma Flintstone, just Pleistocene hunter-gatherers struggling to survive and reproduce in evolutionarily novel suburban habitats" (p. 112).

This kind of flat rejection of the EEA approach is based on the claim that too little information exists for an accurate description of the EEA. Moreover, modern cultural diversity is said to be so great that past selection cannot have exerted much constraint on human behavioral phenotypes, and so it can be ignored. For a rebuttal to this critique, we need only return to the snake phobia example. Abundant evidence tells us that the human species and its immediate predecessors evolved initially in sub-Saharan Africa, a region that is still home to many dangerous, even lethal snakes. Thus, it is entirely reasonable to propose that the long history of human-snake interactions would select for psychological mechanisms that encouraged our ancestors to have a healthy respect for snakes, thereby reducing the likelihood of snakebite (Tooby & Cosmides, 1990). One way to test this idea would be to predict that humans should not be so fearful when faced with modern, evolutionarily novel risks. It is well known that despite the substantial dangers associated with automobiles, most of us do not become fearful when observing motor vehicles.

In fact, we can also be highly confident about many other elements present in the EEA, thanks to abundant paleontological and anthropological evidence as well as comparative data from our fellow primates, especially the common chimpanzee. Our ancestors surely lived in small groups composed largely of closely related individuals, people in these groups engaged in hunting and gathering with the potential for conflicts over resources with members of other groups, adult female fertility declined with age, and so on. All of these components of the ancestral environmental could be expected to have major selective consequences for our species. For example, the simple but profound fact that, in the past (as in the present), older women surely tended to be less likely to become pregnant than younger women can be expected to have shaped the evolution of both male and female sexual psychologies (Geary, 1998; Hagen, 2005). Men can be predicted to be highly sensitive to cues associated with female age and to use this information, consciously or otherwise, to motivate their sexual preferences. Women should be sensitive to their declining reproductive value with age and should modify their mate preferences and standards accordingly. Many predictions of this sort, based on the likely parameters of the EEA, have been generated by evolutionary psychologists and sociobiologists and form the basis of a considerable body of research into human psychology and behavior (Buss, 1999; Gaulin & McBurney, 2001).

SUMMARY

Evolutionary psychology is part of the branch of evolutionary biology that relies on the adaptationist approach. This research approach is founded on the Darwinian theory of evolution by natural selection. In modern terms, the theory states that the evolution of living things has been shaped by an unconscious competition among alternative alleles with different developmental effects. Those alleles that in the past have on average helped produce phenotypes with superior fitness have spread through populations over time. Once having replaced competing alternative alleles, these "winning" genes may persist in populations indefinitely provided that any new mutations reduce the gene-copying success of individuals relative to others that carry the established genes. The hereditary effects of alleles that survive this kind of competition are likely to help individuals develop fitness-enhancing attributes (i.e., adaptations).

As is true for sociobiology and behavioral ecology as well, evolutionary psychologists use natural selection theory to identify interesting evolutionary problems, namely characteristics that initially seem unlikely to advance individual inclusive fitness or gene-copying success, which is achieved either directly through the production of surviving offspring or indirectly by helping close relatives reproduce more than they would have otherwise. Adaptationists then propose and test explanations for these traits consistent with theory, a task requiring either that these traits are adaptations after all (inclusive fitness promoters) or that they arise as nonadaptive or even maladaptive by-products of other traits that are adaptive. Evolutionary psychologists have employed this kind of thinking to good effect in their research into the psychological mechanisms that underlie human behavior. The number of evolutionary psychologists and the sophistication of their research have increased dramatically over the last 25 or so years, during which time psychology and the adaptationist approach have been united.

REFERENCES

Alexander, R. D. (1979). *Darwinism and human affairs.* Seattle: University of Washington Press.
Alexander, R. D. (1987). *The biology of moral systems.* Hawthorne, NY: Aldine de Gruyter.
Andersson, M. (1994). *Sexual selection.* Princeton, NJ: Princeton University Press.
Barash, D. P. (2002). Grappling with the ghost of Gould. *Human Nature Review, 2,* 283–292.
Barkow, J. H., Cosmides, L., & Tooby, J. (Eds.). (1992). *The adapted mind: Evolutionary psychology and the generation of culture.* New York: Oxford University Press.
Borgia, G. (1994). The scandals of San Marco. *Quarterly Review of Biology, 69,* 373–375.
Brooks, D. R., & McLennan, D. A. (1991). *Phylogeny, ecology, and behavior.* Chicago: University of Chicago Press.
Brown, J. L. (1987). *Helping and communal breeding in birds: Ecology and evolution.* Princeton, NJ: Princeton University Press.
Buller, D. J. (2005). *Adapting minds: Evolutionary psychology and the persistent quest for human nature.* Cambridge, MA: MIT Press.
Buss, D. M. (1995). Evolutionary psychology: A new paradigm for psychological science. *Psychological Inquiry, 6,* 1–30.
Buss, D. M. (1999). *Evolutionary psychology, the new science of the mind.* Boston: Allyn and Bacon.
Caplan, A. L. (1977). Tautology, circularity, and biological theory. *American Naturalist, 111,* 390–393.
Cartwright, J. (2000). *Evolution and human behavior.* Cambridge, MA: MIT Press.
Cook, L. M. (2003). The rise and fall of the *carbonaria* form of the peppered moth. *Quarterly Review of Biology, 78,* 399–417.

Crawford, C. (1987). Sociobiology: Of what value to psychology? In C. Crawford (Ed.), *Sociobiology and psychology: Ideas, issues, and applications* (pp. 3–30). Hillsdale, NJ: Lawrence Erlbaum Associates.

Crespi, B. J. (2000). The evolution of maladaptation. *Heredity, 84,* 623–629.

Crow, J. (1979). Genes that violate Mendel's rules. *Scientific American, 240,* 134–146.

Darwin, C. (1859). *On the origin of species.* London: Murray.

Darwin, C. (1871). *The descent of man and selection in relation to sex.* London: Murray.

Darwin, C. (1872). *The expression of the emotions in man and animals.* London: John Murray.

Darwin, C. (1862). *The various contrivances by which orchids are fertilised by insects.* New York: D. Appleton.

Dawkins, R. (1976). *The selfish gene.* New York: Oxford University Press.

Dawkins, R. (1982). *The extended phenotype: The gene as the unit of selection.* San Francisco: W. H. Freeman.

Dawkins, R. (1985). Sociobiology: The debate continues. *New Scientist,* 59–60.

Dawkins, R. (1997). Human chauvinism: Review of Full House. *Evolution, 51,* 1015–1020.

Dawkins, R., & Coyne, J. (2005, September 1). One side can be wrong. *The Guardian,* www.guardian.co.uk/science/sep/01/schools.research.

Dennett, D. C. (1995). *Darwin's dangerous idea.* New York: Simon & Schuster.

Dewsbury, D. A. (2000). Issues in comparative psychology at the dawn of the 20th century. *American Psychologist, 55,* 750–753.

Endler, J. A. (1986). *Natural selection in the wild.* Princeton, NJ: Princeton University Press.

Forrest, B. C., & Gross, P. R. (2003). *Creationism's Trojan horse: The wedge of intelligent design.* New York: Oxford University Press.

Gaulin, S. J. C., & McBurney, D. H. (2001). *Psychology, an evolutionary approach.* Upper Saddle River, NJ: Prentice Hall.

Geary, D. C. (1998). *Male, female: The evolution of human sex differences.* Washington, DC: American Psychological Association.

Gould, S. J. (1974). The nonscience of human nature. *Natural History, 83,* 21–25.

Gould, S. J. (1977). Caring groups and selfish genes. *Natural History, 86,* 20–24.

Gould, S. J. (1978). Sociobiology: The art of storytelling. *New Scientist, 80,* 530–533.

Gould, S. J. (1984). Only his wings remained. *Natural History, 93,* 10–18.

Gould, S. J. (1986). Evolution and the triumph of homology, or why history matters. *American Scientist, 74,* 60–69.

Gould, S. J. (1996a). The diet of worms and the defenestration of Prague. *Natural History, 105,* 18–24.

Gould, S. J. (1996b). *Full house: The spread of excellence from Plato to Darwin.* New York: Three Rivers Press.

Gould, S. J. (1997, June 12). The pleasures of pluralism. *The New York Review,* pp. 47–52.

Gould, S. J. (2002). *The structure of evolutionary theory.* Cambridge, MA: Harvard University Press.

Gould, S. J., & Lewontin, R. C. (1979). The spandrels of San Marco and the panglossian paradigm: A critique of the adaptationist programme. *Proceedings of the Royal Society of London B, 205,* 581–598.

Gould, S. J., & Vrba, E. S. (1982). Exaptation—A missing term in the science of form. *Paleobiology, 8,* 4–15.

Grant, B. S., Cook, A. D., Clarke, C. A., & Owen, D. F. (1998). Geographic and temporal variation in the incidence in melanism in peppered moth population in America and Britain. *Journal of Heredity, 89,* 465–471.

Griffiths, P. E. (2006). Evolutionary psychology. In S. Sarkar (Ed.), *The philosophy of science: An encyclopedia* (pp. 263–268). New York: Routledge.

Hagen, E. H. (2005). Controversies surrounding evolutionary psychology. In D. M. Buss (Ed.), *The handbook of evolutionary psychology* (pp. 145–173). Hoboken, NJ: John Wiley & Sons.

Hamilton, W. D. (1964). The genetical theory of social behaviour, I, II. *Journal of Theoretical Biology, 7,* 1–52.

Holland, P. W. H., & Garcia-Fernandez, J. (1996). Hox genes and chordate evolution. *Developmental Biology, 173,* 382–395.

Howlett, R. J., & Majerus, M. E. N. (1987). The understanding of industrial melanism in the peppered moth (*Biston betularia*; Lepidoptera: Geometridae). *Biological Journal of the Linnean Society, 30,* 31–44.

Hunt, J. H. (1999). Trait mapping and salience in the evolution of eusocial vespid wasps. *Evolution, 53,* 225–237.

Jones, J. J. E., III. (2005). *Kitzmiller vs. Dover area school board, memorandum opinion.* Case No. 04cv2688.

Kenrick, D. (1995). Evolutionary theory versus the confederacy of dunces. *Psychological Inquiry, 6,* 56–61.

Lopreato, J., & Crippen, T. (1999). *Crisis in sociology: The need for Darwin.* New Brunswick, NJ: Transaction Publishers.

Lummaa, V., Vuorisalo, T., Barr, R. G., & Lehtonen, L. (1998). Why cry? Adaptive significance of intensive crying in human infants. *Evolution and Human Behavior, 19,* 193–202.

Maconochie, M., Nonchev, S., Morrison, A., & Krumlauf, R. (1996). Paralogous Hox genes: Function and regulation. *Annual Review of Genetics, 30,* 529–556.

Mayr, E. (1961). Cause and effect in biology. *Science, 134,* 1501–1506.

Mayr, E. (1963). *Animal species and evolution.* Cambridge, MA: Harvard University Press.

Mayr, E. (1977). Darwin and natural selection. *American Scientist, 65,* 321–327.

Mayr, E. (1982). *The growth of biological thought.* Cambridge, MA: Harvard University Press.

Peters, R. H. (1976). Tautology in evolution and ecology. *American Naturalist, 110,* 1–12.

Phillips, B. L., & Shine, R. (2006). *An invasive species induced rapid adaptive change in a native predator: Cane toads and black snakes in Australia.* Proceedings of the Royal Society B, *273,* 1545–1550.

Pinker, S. (2002). *The blank slate: The modern denial of human nature.* New York: Viking.

Preuss, T. M., Caceres, M., Oldham, M. C., & Geschwind, D. H. (2004). Human brain evolution. *Nature Reviews Genetics, 5,* 850–860.

Prum, R. O. (1999). Development and evolutionary origin of feathers. *Journal of Experimental Zoology, 285,* 291–306.

Queller, D. C. (1995). The spaniels of St. Marx and the panglossian paradox: A critique of a rhetorical programme. *Quarterly Review of Biology, 70,* 485–490.

Reeve, H. K., & Sherman, P. W. (1993). Adaptation and the goals of evolutionary research. *Quarterly Review of Biology, 68,* 1–32.

Sober, E., & Wilson, D. S. (1998). *Unto others: The evolution and psychology of unselfish behavior.* Cambridge, MA: Harvard University Press.

Soltis, J. (2004). The signal functions of early infant crying. *Behavioral and Brain Sciences, 27,* 443–490.

Symons, D. (1989). A critique of Darwinian anthropology. *Ethology and Sociobiology, 10,* 131–144.

Tooby, J., & Cosmides, L. (1990). The past explains the present: Emotional adaptations and the structure of past environments. *Ethology and Sociobiology, 11,* 375–424.

Williams, G. C. (1966). *Adaptation and natural selection.* Princeton, NJ: Princeton University Press.

Williams, G. C., & Nesse, R. M. (1991). The dawn of Darwinian medicine. *Quarterly Review of Biology, 66,* 1–22.

Wilson, E. O. (1975). *Sociobiology: The new synthesis.* Cambridge, MA: Harvard University Press.

Wilson, E. O., Carpenter, F. M., & Brown, W. L. (1967). The first mesozoic ants. *Science, 157,* 1038–1040.

Wilson, E. O., & Hölldobler, B. (2005). Eusociality: Origin and consequences. *Proceedings of the National Academy of Science, 102,* 13367–13371.

Wynne-Edwards, V. C. (1962). *Animal dispersion in relation to social behaviour.* Edinburgh, U.K.: Oliver & Boyd.

Zeifman, D. M. (2001). An ethological analysis of human infant crying: Answering Tinbergen's four questions. *Developmental Psychobiology, 39,* 265–285.

3

Life History Theory and Human Development

STEPHEN C. STEARNS,
NADINE ALLAL, AND RUTH MACE

INTRODUCTION

The field of life history evolution studies how the entire life cycle from conception to death is designed by natural selection to ensure reproductive success despite problems posed by the environment in the forms of mortality and scarce resources. The design occurs within a framework of constraints and trade-offs shaped by past evolution working on the materials out of which organisms are built and the developmental and physiological mechanisms organisms have inherited from ancestors.

The field focuses on these traits: age and size at maturity, number and size of offspring, investment in offspring, sex-specific growth and mortality rates of offspring, interval between births, number of births per lifetime, length of the reproductive portion of the lifetime, and length and function of the postreproductive period, if any. Humans differ from their primate relatives in several ways: They have slow physical development during which their brains grow and mental capacities are gradually acquired, hence an extended childhood prior to the juvenile period shared with other mammals; they have relatively short intervals between births, hence a reproductive rate higher than that of their closest relatives of similar size; although they usually bear one offspring, they can bear twins; females have a postreproductive period—menopause; and they have a relatively long life span. In the following section, we discuss how natural selection shaped these features of the human life cycle as well as others.

Why should an evolutionary psychologist care about life history evolution? Because this is the framework within which our mental processes develop, mature, support our behavior, and then senesce and diminish. Developmental state at birth and length of childhood combine with learning from particular environmental experiences to determine brain capacity and content at adulthood. Our stage in life influences the costs and benefits of many serious decisions, including when to mate, with whom to mate, and how much risk to take in producing offspring. Every generation must learn a great deal to live a successful life; life history evolution has given humans 15 to 20 years in which to do that. Every individual must attempt to produce offspring that survive to produce grandchildren; life history evolution has given humans about 25 years in which to do that. And the evolution of senescence, in the human case, has limited the fully rational period of our life span to about 60 years; we do not have any longer than that in which to acquire and exercise understanding and wisdom. Thus, life history evolution created the framework within which psychology is expressed and by which psychology is constrained.

THE COMPARATIVE EVIDENCE: HUMANS AMONG PRIMATES

Compared to their closest relatives, the bonobos, chimpanzees, and gorillas, humans are average in some life history traits and unusual in others (Table 3.1). We are about the same size as chimpanzees and bonobos, much smaller than gorillas, and about as sexually dimorphic as bonobos, less so than chimpanzees and gorillas. Our gestation length is slightly longer than that of bonobos and gorillas and significantly longer than that of chimpanzees. Our offspring are nearly twice as heavy at birth as bonobo and chimpanzee offspring and one and one-half times heavier than those of gorillas, despite our lighter body weight. Although our offspring develop more slowly than those of other apes do, we wean them 2 years earlier than do bonobos, chimpanzees, and gorillas. The length of our estrus cycle is the same as that of gorillas and a bit shorter than that of bonobos and chimpanzees, and the age at which human females first give birth is nearly twice that of these three close relatives. Our interbirth intervals are one and one-half years shorter than those of chimpanzees and bonobos, and half a year shorter than those of gorillas. Our average maximum life span is 20 years longer than bonobos, 25 years longer than chimpanzees, and 30 years longer than that of gorillas.

Table 3.1 Comparison of the Life Histories of Humans and Their Closest Relatives

	Humans Homo sapiens	Bonobos Pongo pygmaeus	Chimpanzees Pan troglodytes	Gorillas Gorilla gorilla
Female weight (kg)	40.1	37.0	31.1	93.0
Male weight (kg)	47.9	42.5	41.6	160.0
Ratio male/female wt	1.19	1.15	1.34	1.72
Gestation length (d)	267	260	228	256
Birth weight (kg)	3.30	1.73	1.76	2.11
Age at weaning (y)	2.0	3.9	4.0	4.3
Estrus cycle length (d)	28	30	36	28
Female age at first breeding (y)	19.3	10.7	11.5	9.9
Mean age of reproduction	28.2	—	22.4	—
Average maximum life span (y)	70	50	45	39
Rate of increase of senescent mortality with age	0.095	—	0.147	—
Interbirth interval (y)	3.5	4.8	5.0	4.0

Source: From Harvey and Clutton-Brock (1985). Interbirth intervals for humans from Hill and Hurtado (1996; for bonobos from Furuichi et al., 1998). Mean age of reproduction and rate of increase of senescent mortality with age from Gage (1998).

Much intraspecific variation (e.g., see Ruff, 2002) is buried in the averages reported in Table 3.1, but this much is clear: Humans give birth to larger, less developed offspring that grow and mature more slowly (Aiello & Wells, 2002) and need parental care for a longer period of time than do the offspring of other apes, but we manage to wean them earlier and to give birth at shorter intervals than do all three of our closest relatives. We mature a decade later and live 2 to 3 decades longer, and our females therefore have a longer period of postreproductive life than they do. We do so because we experience lower adult mortality rates, especially after the age of 50, when the mortality rates of chimpanzees in particular rise dramatically (Gage, 1998).

HOW TO CONSTRUCT AN EVOLUTIONARY EXPLANATION OF A LIFE HISTORY

The study of evolution is divided into two subdisciplines, microevolution and macroevolution. Microevolution deals with short-term evolutionary dynamics occurring within populations and species, and macroevolution deals with deep time, broad relationships, and big patterns. Microevolution thus occurs within a framework of constraints created by macroevolution.

The Historical Explanations of Macroevolution

The type of explanation provided by macroevolution is historical: Things are so because they had a particular history whose consequences have been inherited. To understand that history, evolutionary biologists can use one or both of two approaches—paleontology and the comparative method. Because life histories do not fossilize, those taking a macroevolutionary approach to life histories have concentrated on the comparative method. To use that method, one must reliably reconstruct the phylogenetic tree expressing the relationships of the species of interest with their closest relatives. In recent decades, phylogenetic reconstruction has been made more rigorous and reliable by improvements to logic and to data collection. In combination, those methods applied to such data yield the most reliable hypotheses of relationships currently available. Given a phylogenetic tree, one can then use comparative methods to infer some of the sequence of events that resulted in the observed life history. By mapping the states of the traits in each species onto the tips of the branches of the tree, one can infer ancestral states and search for correlated changes among traits (e.g., Felsenstein, 1985; Pagel, 1994).

The Selection Explanations of Microevolution

Two processes in microevolution affect the current state of the life history of a species or population: natural selection and genetic drift. Drift results in random differences among lineages; it can be used as the null hypothesis in testing other explanations. Deviations from random expectation are analyzed with approaches that assume that natural selection has designed the phenotype to improve reproductive success; these include optimization (Roff, 2001; Stearns, 1992), game theory, and adaptive dynamics, often incorporating risk reduction (Stearns, 2000) and conflicts among relatives mediated by kin selection (Griffin & West, 2002). The object explained is sometimes a single phenotypic state and sometimes, more powerfully, a reaction norm that expresses the range of phenotypes that a single genotype can express when confronted with a range of environments. For example, one can predict how age and size at maturity should evolve to change across a range of growth conditions in a specific manner described as the norm of reaction to that change in conditions (Berrigan & Koella, 1994; Kawecki & Stearns, 1993; Stearns & Koella, 1986).

Because the strength of natural selection is limited by the amount of variation in reproductive success in a population, selection explanations are couched in terms of the means and variances of mortality rates and birth rates acting on populations whose responses are constrained by trade-offs. Trade-offs occur when an evolutionary change in one trait that increases fitness is linked through physiological or developmental mechanisms to changes in other traits that decrease fitness (Stearns, 1989; van Noordwijk & de Jong, 1986). Often added insight is gained by analyzing the proximate mechanisms of development and physiology that cause trade-offs and, therefore, constrain the response to selection (Drent & Daan, 1980).

The Mechanistic Explanations of Development and Physiology

Proximate mechanisms are important because they determine the set of possible responses, a set that may include responses unanticipated by any theory. For life history evolution, proximate mechanisms are particularly important when they determine the possible rates and types of resources acquired and how those resources are allocated to growth, reproduction, and maintenance: when they mediate trade-offs among those functions. Our phylogenetic history has given us particular proximate mechanisms. We are mammals with internal fertilization and a 9-month pregnancy, giving birth to helpless young that require intense parental care for many years before they have good chances of surviving to reproduce. We are subject to infectious disease, which we counter with an adaptive but costly immune system. Our females store fat prior to and during pregnancy to finance the costs of pregnancy and nursing. Because we have determinate growth and stop increasing in height at maturation, our allocations switch at that point from growth to reproduction, always also involving fat storage, disease resistance, and other types of maintenance. Hormones produced in the brain and in other endocrine glands control the mechanisms that mediate those allocations. They determine how genetic variation will be expressed in the population and how trade-offs are realized in the whole organisms that we can observe and measure.

Evolutionary Explanations of the Major Life History Traits

Four types of approaches have been taken in explaining the evolution of life history traits: (a) optimization (including invariants), (b) adaptive dynamics (including its precursor, game theory), (c) genetic transmission of quantitative traits, and (d) comparative methods based on phylogenetics. Each makes its own assumptions in representing the process and history of evolution. The data used to test these explanations are estimated with the methods of demography.

Optimality models assume that natural selection has shaped life history traits within a framework of trade-offs to maximize some fitness measure, usually reproductive success per time unit or per lifetime. They ignore genetic details, assume that the optimal state is somehow attainable, look for equilibrium solutions, neglect dynamics (Stearns, 1992), and thus, assume that evolution has gone on in large populations that encounter stable ecological conditions for long periods. In such populations, their predictions are consistent with those of quantitative genetics (Charlesworth, 1990). Authors using optimality models to understand human life histories include Hill and Hurtado (1996), Voland (1998), Hill and Kaplan (1999), Mace (2000), Strassman and Gillespie (2002), and Ellison (2003a).

Life history invariants are the ratios (usually log-log) of life history traits that broadly characterize clades, such as birds, fish, or mammals (Charnov, 1993; e.g., the ratio of the log of age at maturity to the log of life span). The derivation of invariants usually assumes stationary populations in which lifetime reproductive success measures fitness. They are useful in posing both a puzzle—why these values and why the differences among groups?—and an expectation—why does this species deviate from the value for the clade?

Adaptive dynamics compares the performance of alternative phenotypes competing over many generations. The evolving population is modeled by studying the invasion of alternative strategies. The issues include the following: What strategies are stable against invasion by all conceivable alternatives? What strategies are not only stable but also actually attainable? How does the dynamic itself change selection? The method, particularly appropriate when frequency- and density-dependent effects are strong (e.g., De Mazancourt & Dieckmann, 2004; Dercole, Ferriere, & Rinaldi, 2002), predicts a diversity of evolutionary outcomes not perceived by other approaches.

Evolutionary quantitative genetics deals with traits that vary continuously, such as weights at birth and reproductive investments, in contrast to traits that fall clearly into distinct classes. It makes a plausible assumption, convenient for statistical analysis, about the genetics of traits influenced by many genes. To infer the genetic and environmental contributions to variation, it measures the phenotype, the final product of the assumed causes, not the mechanisms—the physiology and development—that produce the phenotype. Its fundamental measures are the heritabilities of and genetic covariances among traits and the gradient of selection pressures operating on traits, all estimated empirically. By multiplying the heritabilities and genetic covariances by the selection gradient, one can predict evolutionary change from one generation to the next (Roff, 1997, 2001). Quantitative genetics is a useful framework in which to examine generation-to-generation microevolutionary change (e.g., Käär, Jokela, Helle, & Kojola, 1996).

Phylogenetic methods are described previously. As an example of the insights they can yield, Holden and Mace (1999) used a cultural phylogeny based on language to understand how the division of labor between males and females affects sexual dimorphism in human body size. They found that in cultures where women do more work to acquire food, there is less difference in stature between the sexes.

We now step through the human life history from gamete production and conception to aging and death.

CRITICAL EARLY EVENTS INVOLVING GAMETES AND EMBRYOS

Selection Arenas, Oocytic Atresia, and Menopause

A selection arena is a process based on the principle of natural selection that occurs inside an entity, such as a reproductive female, that has been designed by natural selection at a higher level. Oocytic atresia is a selection arena operating in humans and other mammals. Atresia means degeneration or loss. All oocytes are lost by menopause in humans (Finch & Sapolsky, 1999). The process starts in the third month of pregnancy, when about 7 million oocytes are present in the newly formed ovaries. By the time the child is born, that number has fallen to about a million, by menarche to less than 1,000, and by menopause to near zero. Such dramatic destruction of a key resource demands an explanation.

The explanation appears to be that atresia eliminates oocytes that contain genetic defects in either the nuclear or the mitochondrial genome. The rate of mutation in the nuclear genome is between 0.1 and 100 mutations in each genome per generation. Mitochondria are a special issue because they usually reproduce asexually, pass regularly through population bottlenecks, and therefore cannot avoid accumulating deleterious mutations (Muller, 1964). This problem is solved if only a small number of mitochondria are introduced into each of many oocytes and if the oocytes with defective mitochondria advertise that fact in their biochemical profile, giving maternal tissue capable of action a signal used to decide from which oocytes nourishment should be withdrawn (Jansen & de Boer, 1998; Krakauer & Mira, 1999). There is some support for this idea. The probability of oocyte destruction is affected by the state of the mitochondrial genome in rodents (Perez, Trbovich, Gosden, & Tilly, 2000), and the number of mitochondria in a primordial oocyte is small, less than 10 (Jansen & de Boer, 1998). The nature of the signal that elicits destruction is yet unknown.

Sperm Selection

Human males have a higher mutation rate than human females because there are many more cell divisions between zygote and sperm than between zygote and egg (Crow, 1993). That children with new dominant mutations tend to have older fathers (Haldane, 1947) suggests that older males have a higher proportion of genetically defective sperm than younger males do. To the extent that genetic defects erode the performance of sperm in finding oocytes in a female reproductive tract designed to detect and eliminate defective sperm, sperm also pass through a selection arena that improves zygote quality. While sperm selection is well documented in other species, selection against genetically defective sperm is not yet well demonstrated in humans. Doctors working in reproductive medicine assume that it occurs and are concerned about the potential consequences of bypassing it when they perform in vitro fertilizations.

Spontaneous Abortion

Spontaneous abortions occur more frequently than is often assumed. The rate is difficult to determine precisely, for most aborted zygotes and embryos pass out with the next menses. Estimates of the proportion of pregnancies that end in early, unrecognized abortion range from 30% to 75% (Haig, 1998). Clinically recognized pregnancies miscarry in 10–20% of cases, most of which have chromosomal abnormalities. Twins are another situation in which spontaneous abortion is frequent: Up to 71% of gestations diagnosed as twins were singletons when delivered (Levi, 1976). This suggests that spontaneous abortion functions both to eliminate defective embryos and to halve the reproductive investment implied by twins.

Evidence for one important reason for recurrent spontaneous abortions comes from Ober, Elias, Kostyu, and Hauck's (1992) work on Hutterite communities in South Dakota. The Hutterites, who moved to North America from Switzerland in the 19th century, are a small community that has become relatively inbred. Some Hutterite women suffer from recurrent spontaneous abortions. Ober et al. discovered that women whose husbands had similar combinations of immune genes were more likely to suffer spontaneous abortions than women who had married men with combinations different from their own. The vertebrate immune system relies on diversity in the immune genes to generate through recombination the broad spectrum of antibodies needed to fight novel infections. Offspring unable to generate that broad spectrum would have been likely to die young of infectious disease in premodern societies. Ober's work suggests that the female human reproductive tract evolved to detect and discard immunologically deficient embryos early in development before they cost very much in either time or energy, giving the mother another chance to conceive a healthy embryo, a chance that would be better with a different father.

The screening system that eliminates genetically deficient embryos probably suffers from the general decline in performance that accompanies aging. If it does, that would explain the increased incidence of birth defects in children born to older women, notably Down's syndrome (Forbes, 1997). At the other end of life, the strikingly higher rate of spontaneous abortions in women who reach menarche at age 12 or less, as compared with those who do so at age 14 or more (Liestøl, 1980), might be the result of less previous screening through oocytic atresia in the younger group, which would allow more defective genomes to be conceived and thus elicit compensatory screening through spontaneous abortion at the zygote stage.

Conflicts over Intrauterine Growth

Once a zygote has survived the gauntlets of atresia and spontaneous abortion and has settled into the uterus to grow, it does not relax into a supportive environment, for its interest in nutrition can exceed what its mother has been selected to transfer (Haig, 1993; Trivers, 1974). The fetus can win part of this conflict by remodeling the endometrium to gain direct access to the maternal blood supply with vessels that do not constrict, rendering the mother incapable of limiting nutrition to the fetus without also limiting it to her own tissues, and by turning the placenta into an endocrine gland with direct access to maternal blood. Placental hormones manipulate maternal physiology for fetal benefit and are countered by increased maternal insulin production; if this countermeasure is not sufficient, gestational diabetes results in the mother. If the fetus is poorly nourished, it may increase its blood supply by increasing the resistance of its mother's peripheral circulation, resulting in pre-eclampsia (dangerously high maternal blood pressure).

Conflicts also exist within fetal cells among genes that are only expressed when derived from the mother and genes that are expressed only when derived from the father. Such differential gene expression is programmed in the germ lines of the parents through selective methylation, or imprinting, of specific genes; imprinted genes are silenced during the development of the embryo. Most genes imprinted in humans affect embryonic growth through their control of insulin-like grown factors (IGFs). The genes that are turned off in the paternal germ line are those that would restrict fetal growth; those turned off in the maternal germ line are those that would accelerate fetal growth. Thus, the father's imprinting acts to remove more resources from the mother than she has been selected to provide, and the mother's imprinting acts to counter the paternal effect. The effects of imprinting are revealed by mutations in humans and genetic manipulations in mice that prevent imprinting from occurring in one sex or the other. When the father's genes are not imprinted, the maternal genes have the upper hand, and the embryo is about 10% lighter at birth. When the mother's genes are not imprinted, paternal genes have the upper hand, and the embryo is about 10% heavier at birth (Haig, 1992).

The duration of pregnancy and the weight of the child at birth are thus determined both by the mutual interests of mother, father, and child in the health of the child and by subtle conflicts between child and mother and mother and father over the level of investment actually given.

Size at Birth

Human birth weight correlates well with human age at maturity (Harvey & Clutton Brock, 1985), but as age at maturity is rather late in humans compared with other primates, babies are heavier than would be expected based on the weights of their parents alone. The extra weight is due to larger brain size and more adipose tissue than in other primate offspring. In fact, brain size should be even bigger at birth when compared to the brain size of adult humans (Leakey, 1994), but human pelvises, which have to remain narrow for our upright gait, limit the size of a baby's head. Human babies are thus particularly altricial, with brain development continuing outside the womb, leaving more scope for environmental interactions than in other primates. Why human babies are so much fatter than their primate relatives is not yet clear: Arguments range from "pretty baby" runaway selection processes (with mothers favoring their plumper children) to the fact that humans may be the only primates with enough surplus food (thanks to cooperative feeding) to produce fat babies (Haig, 1998; Pond, 1997).

Human birth length ranges from 40 to 57 cm and birth weight from 1 to 4.5 kg (Tanner, 1990), with extreme values for viable infants having increased with advances in modern medicine. Average birth weight is consistently 0.5 kg lower than the weight that would produce optimal survival of newborn babies (Karn & Penrose, 1952). Blurton Jones (1978) suggested that this is due to parent-offspring conflict. Because the range of birth weights at which babies can survive is broader under modern medical care than in the past, stabilizing selection for optimal birth weights is now relaxed (Ulizzi & Manzotti, 1988; Ulizzi & Terrenato, 1992).

The 50th percentile healthy baby in the United States measures 51 cm and weighs 3.2 kg. Birth weight averages range from 2.4 kg in poor regions to 3.6 kg in affluent ones (Eveleth & Tanner, 1976). Low birth weight can have several causes, each with differing consequences: Low birth weight due to mild prematurity with adequate weight for age may have few long-term consequences if adequate care is provided. However, stunted babies, who are small for their gestational age, usually suffer more long-term consequences, which vary depending on shape. Light babies may either be normal and short or long and thin, depending on the timing of food restriction during pregnancy. Overall, low birth weight is associated with increased infant mortality and morbidity and adversely affects long-term physical growth, immune response, and mental development (Hokkenkoelaga et al., 1995; McCormick, 1997). It can also affect the timing of maturation (Adair, 2001): Long, thin baby girls achieve menarche 6 months earlier than do normal short ones. But weight is not the whole story: For various reasons, and despite lower birth weights, females and firstborns suffer less mortality than males and late born offspring (Cogswell & Yip, 1995).

GROWTH AND MATURATION

Human Growth Patterns

Population means for height range from 136 to 152 cm for adult females and from 164 to 183 cm for adult males (Eveleth & Tanner, 1976). Population means for weight range from 38 kg to 72 kg for females and from 46 kg to 76 kg for males. Secular trends have been influencing these means for decades, with humans in developed countries gaining 1–2 cm in height per decade. In addition, worldwide obesity is increasing and accelerating. In the United States in particular, height has reached a plateau but weight still is growing (Bogin, 1999; Harrison, Tanner, Pilbeam, & Baker, 1977; Malina, Zavaleta, & Little, 1987; Tanner, 1990), while in Mexico and India obesity and diabetes are spreading at a striking rate. The energy in food places stronger restrictions on human growth than does the limitation of specific nutrients (Calow, 1979). And stress interacts with available energy to affect growth and age at menarche in girls, including stress caused by father absence: Girls whose fathers are absent mature earlier, for reasons still under debate (cf. Hulanicka, Gronkiewicz, & Koniarek, 2001; Kanazawa, 2001; Macintyre, 1992; Maclure, Travis, Willett, & MacMahon, 1991; Quinlan, 2003).

Following years studying children whose catch-up growth rates vary to compensate for periods of food restriction or other stress, Tanner (1963) portrayed human growth as target seeking and self-stabilizing. But as Bogin (1999) points out, such a descriptive approach does nothing to explain why human growth has this pattern, nor how it differs from our primate relatives. Human growth can be divided into five periods: (a) *infancy* (from birth to weaning, traditionally around age 2), (b) *childhood* (from weaning to full brain growth, around age 7—Bogin argues this is a uniquely human stage), (c) the *juvenile* period (from age 7 to the beginning of puberty, around age 10 in girls and age 12 in boys), (d) *adolescence* (from the beginning of puberty to full sexual maturity around age 14 in girls and 16 in boys—Bogin argues that the length of adolescence is special in humans), and (e) *adulthood,* when growth has normally stopped, although in cases of stunting catch-up growth can be observed until age 25 in both sexes (but not if the young women are pregnant).

Bogin (1999) sees childhood as a feeding adaptation: Human babies can be weaned earlier than expected, freeing the mother to get pregnant again, because child food can be provided by group members other than the mother (grandmother, father, older sister, or neighbor depending on social arrangements). This unique adaptation enables humans to rear large costly offspring much more rapidly than can our primate relatives. Children still depend on adult care during this period, being unable to survive on their own or to gather their own food to any significant degree. In contrast, juveniles have some ability to fend for themselves and might survive if orphaned or abandoned, despite their lack of adult size, skills, and experience. Juveniles learn to be independent while benefiting from group support without the stress of competition for adult status and reproductive opportunities. Adolescence follows and is especially marked in humans. Other species put on weight at adolescence, but the human height growth spurt is unique in magnitude (Watts, 1986). It appears advantageous to shorten the transition from protected childhood to exposed adulthood, possibly to avoid sexual competition before one is ready to mate. Because girls usually appear to be adult and even start menses before they are completely fertile, they can start to engage in adult roles without immediately becoming pregnant. In males, the opposite is true: Boys start to produce functional sperm before growing tall and exhibiting adult male characteristics. Some have speculated that this could be to enable covert paternities while avoiding aggression from competing adult males. Both patterns reduce the initial costs of adulthood.

Growth yields adult women smaller than it yields adult men—human sexual dimorphism. Why should women be smaller than men? One reason might be that there is greater sexual dimorphism in polygynous species than there is in monogamous species, mostly due to increased male-male competition in a polygynous environment. Compared to their primate relatives, human males are only slightly larger than human females, implying mild polygyny (cf. Diamond, 1991; Trivers, 1985). Nettle (2002) confirmed in Britain that tall men generally had high reproductive success but found that both very short and very tall women had lower reproductive success: In that environment, selection favors a stable sex dimorphism. However, in a natural-fertility/natural-mortality environment, Sear, Allal, Mace, and McGregor (2004) found that tall Gambian women enjoyed a significant reproductive advantage via lower offspring mortality.

Women also differ from men in storing more fat, especially in the buttocks, thighs, and breasts. Men tend to be more muscular. This difference is thought to reflect women's greater need for fat reserves for reproduction and men's greater need for muscular tissue for competition. The exact patterning of tissue in the body, in particular the waist-to-hip ratio in women and the obviousness of their breasts, is probably the result of sexual selection (Bailey, 1982; Bailey & Katch, 1981; Bogin, 1999; Lieberman, 1982; Pond, 1997; Singh, 1993; Stini, 1969).

Optimal Age and Size at Maturity

Optimal age and size at maturity is determined by the trade-off between maturing early at a smaller size and later at a larger size. The advantages of early maturity are mainly short generation lengths, whose benefits are compounded across generations, and the security of having reproduced before random mortality may strike. The advantages of later maturity are increased size, knowledge, experience, and acquisition of goods or shelter, which may all contribute to more successful reproduction in the longer term, particularly to the survival and reproductive success of offspring.

The timing of puberty is hormonally controlled from the brain (Bogin, 1999; Cameron, 1991, 1996; Knobil, 1990), but hormone production is influenced by environmental cues (e.g., nutrition and paternal presence). Walker et al. (2006) review 22 hunter-gatherer life histories and provide average age and size at first birth for 16 populations. Reproductive maturity ranges from 16 to 20 years in females, with a mean of 19.2 years. Adult height ranges from 136 to 166 cm, with a mean of 149 cm. Males mature later at larger size.

The first formal models of optimal age and size at first birth focused on maternal weight gain: Fatter women are more fertile and later maturity allows more time to accumulate fat before starting a long cycle of pregnancies and breastfeeding. Stearns and Koella (1986) drew on historical data to illustrate this trade-off, and Hill and Hurtado (1996) developed a detailed population-level model for Aché hunter-gatherers on the same assumptions. Both models predicted optimal age at first birth accurately and were consistent with observations that puberty is completed earlier under better nutritional conditions and with increasing obesity (Herman-Giddens et al., 1997). In general, age at puberty is positively correlated with age at first reproduction (Udry, 1979).

The growing discrepancy between biological puberty, which arrives earlier and earlier as nutrition improves, and psychosocial maturation and socially accepted age at first birth, increasingly delayed in Western societies, affects the evolutionary psychology of adolescents, for their bodies and their cultures are sending them conflicting messages concerning appropriate behavior (Gluckman & Hanson, 2006).

THE PATTERNING OF REPRODUCTIVE INVESTMENT AFTER PUBERTY

Distinguishing the proximate and ultimate determinants of human reproductive rate and parental investment is helpful. Demographers are brought up on Bongaart's (1980) proximate determinants of fertility: He argued that marriage patterns, postpartum subfecundity, contraceptive use, and venereal disease explain most of the variation in birth rates among populations. An evolutionary perspective shifts the emphasis toward explaining both population level and individual differences. Evolutionary ecology and life history theory draw attention to factors affecting fertility not in Bongaart's list by considering the ultimate causes of that variation. In particular evolutionary demographers have investigated how access to resources influences individual variation in marriage patterns (e.g., Josephson, 2002) and—given the unusual life history pattern of humans compared to other apes—how grandmother presence (e.g., Sear, Mace, & McGregor, 2000) and father absence (e.g., Waynforth, 2002) affect reproductive scheduling. In general one expects a combination of cultural, social, and economic conditions affecting marriage patterns, hormone levels mediating postpartum subfecundity (Bribiescas, 2001; Ellison, 1994), and conscious decisions about birth rate to explain how population and individual variation in fertility maximize reproductive success in given environments, while sexually transmitted infections may lead to maladaptive outcomes.

Interbirth Intervals

There is a trade-off between infant survival and mother's fertility, for children compete for her investment. Several studies show that short birth intervals can endanger the life of the children that open and close that interval (Alam, 1995; Bøhler & Bergström, 1995; Hobcraft, McDonald, & Rutstein, 1985). It appears that large families also impose costs on 2- to 4-year-old children (LeGrand & Phillips, 1996). Mothers usually maximize their lifetime reproductive success by having more children than would maximize offspring survival, a central tenet of parent-offspring conflict (Trivers, 1985).

Blurton Jones (1986) showed that hunter-gatherer Kung mothers with shorter interbirth intervals experienced higher infant mortality, with the optimal balance between the birth interval and infant survival at around 4 year intervals. He argued that this interval, which is longer than the average in developed countries, results from hunter-gatherers having to carry both infant and food supply: More closely spaced offspring would be impossible to transport. It should be noted, however, that another forager group, the Aché, who also carry their young everywhere, manage a three-year interbirth interval (Hill & Hurtado, 1996). Some attribute the long Kung interbirth intervals to the prevalence of sexually transmitted infections in that population.

In a natural fertility population of farmers in Mali, Strassmann & Gillespie (2002) found that most mothers in fact achieved reproductive success far below the population maximum. The reason is that individuals vary in condition and experience: Some mothers are better than others at producing viable offspring, and mothers reproduce according to their individual optima.

Single Versus Multiple Births

Most human births are singleton, but enough births (around 4%) are twins for this to be more than a developmental accident. Twinning provides a clear example of the "supermum" effect. Mothers of twins experience higher lifetime reproductive success and longer reproductive spans in some environments but not others (Sear, Shanley, McGregor, & Mace, 2001). Some studies of natural fertility societies have shown that if both twins are girls the twins can be successful (Lummaa, Jokela, & Haukioja, 2001). Overall, there is much evidence that twinning may be costly for the twins themselves. In the Gambia, twin mortality is double that of singleton mortality, suggesting that the process is inefficient to the point of maladaptation (Sear et al., 2001). Twinning could be a by-product of polyovulation that allows high quality women to maintain short interbirth intervals; the down side is that twinning sometimes occurs and then infant mortality is high. Infanticide is more frequent in twin than in singleton births in societies like the Aché and may be a facultative option exercised in times of food stress (Hill & Hurtado, 1996).

Sex Allocation

There is rather mixed evidence that human mothers influence the sex ratio of their offspring at birth in direct response to body condition, as Trivers and Willard (1973) predicted for polygynous species. Many studies have failed to find any effect, but some studies have found local effects. For example, Ethiopian women with higher body mass indices were more likely to have sons after a drought year, suggesting that male fetuses were less likely to be carried to term in more food-stressed women (Gibson & Mace, 2003). However, humans are not seasonal breeders. We have the option of altering the birth interval in response to the state of nutrition or workload (e.g., Gibson & Mace, 2006; Jasienska & Ellison, 1998; Wood, 1994), and this may well be a more common response to environmental conditions than is the sex ratio manipulation seen in more seasonal breeders like red deer. Far more common in humans is sex biasing of parental investment after the child is born.

Parental investment in humans is not just about nutrition. Intergenerational transfers of resources, such as territory, skills, or wealth, are key to reproductive success in many social species, including humans. In wealth-inheriting societies, parents may have to show the color of their money, in the form of bride-price or dowry, to marry off their children. Bride-price is a payment from the groom or his family to the parents of the bride and is typically found in polygynous societies (Hartung, 1982), where males use resources to monopolize several females if they can afford to. Poorer males in such societies are unable to acquire mates. Dowry, where money is paid from the family of the bride to the newlyweds or their family, occurs when it is females that are in competition for mates (Gaulin & Boster, 1990). Such female-female competition is most likely to arise in societies with socially imposed monogamy. In contrast to polygynous societies, in which the benefits of wealth are likely to be diluted among many wives, in monogamous societies a women who marries a wealthy man has sole access to his wealth for the benefit of her offspring alone, and hence, female-female competition for wealthy men becomes intense. The costs of bride-price and dowry influence parental reproductive scheduling. A father who already has sons does not want too many more in bride-price societies where the groom or his family provide the main costs of marriage and setting up home (Mace, 1996), whereas in dowry societies, female infants with a large number of elder sisters can be at increased risk of infanticide for the same reason (Das Gupta, 1987).

The economic framework of reproductive decisions is also important in Western societies, as exemplified in the following three studies. First, in babies born in Philadelphia over a 6-month period with parental investment measured by the amount of breast feeding and the length of the subsequent birth interval, families with incomes over $60,000 per year invested more heavily in sons than in daughters, whereas the reverse was true in families earning less than $10,000 per year (Gaulin & Robbins, 1991). Second, whereas contemporary Hungarian gypsies invest significantly more heavily in daughters than in sons, as measured by the duration of breast-feeding, the length of the subsequent birth interval, and the length of secondary education, the relatively wealthier native Hungarians exhibit the opposite pattern. The investment patterns closely matched the relative numbers of grandchildren gained through each sex of offspring (Bereczkei & Dunbar, 1997). Third, such reproductive decisions may change with the economic circumstances of the parents from one generation to the next. In six north German peasant communities in the mid-19th century, the preference for sons over daughters as measured by their respective mortality rates during the first year of life varied with economic circumstances. When populations were able to expand into virgin land, sons were preferred because they could acquire farms, but when populations were at saturation levels and there was little opportunity to acquire new land, daughters were preferred because they could still marry into higher socioeconomic classes. There appeared to be about a 30-year, or one generation, lag between the environmental stimulus and the corresponding behavioral response (Voland, Dunbar, Engel, & Stephan, 1997).

Biased investment by parents does not necessarily involve deliberate killing, although it is clear that sometimes it does. Often the children die from neglect, cryptic physical abuse, or the consequences of psychological or economic discrimination. Whatever the mechanisms, it is striking that humans in both traditional and contemporary societies sometimes display precisely the kinds of differential investment in offspring of the two sexes that have been so creatively predicted and strikingly confirmed in other species.

Bet-Hedging and Risk Minimization

Humans reduce the risk of reproductive failure in several ways. Some females have the opportunity to mate several times; the resulting higher level of genetic variation among their half-sib offspring increases the probability that some of their offspring will resist disease and be more attractive to potential mates. Whether these theoretical benefits of multiple paternity outweigh the potential costs in not clear. An increase in offspring number is itself a method of spreading the risk of reproductive failure, an effect reflected in the royal reproductive strategy "an heir and a spare." In The Gambia mothers are explicit about wanting many children in the hope that one will be lucky and successful (Allal, personal communication, 2006).

Infanticide

Deliberate infanticide by mothers may have been common in hunter-gatherer and other traditional populations. Child abandonment (tantamount to infanticide) appears to have reached epidemic proportions in some parts of historical Europe, particularly during urbanization or when natural mortality was declining, birth rates were high, and contraceptive practices were not well developed (Hrdy, 2000). In hunter-gatherer societies, female infanticide appears to be more common than male infanticide, possibly because males have additional value to families as hunters and warriors.

There is more female infanticide in the Inuit at more northerly latitudes (E. A. Smith & S. A. Smith, 1994): This group is highly reliant on food hunted by males, who must use dangerous hunting strategies, and polygyny is hardly possible for males, for the costs of supporting even one wife are great in this harsh environment (where mothers may be so constrained by the need to keep young children out of the cold that they may not be able to leave their houses for much of the year). In other groups, such as the Aché, the fitness benefits, if any, of female-biased infanticide is not clear (Hill & Hurtado, 1996). However children who lost one of their parents were at high risk of infanticide—few Aché were prepared to pay the high costs of raising any child that is not their own. In farming societies, the chances of surviving orphanhood appear to be much higher (e.g., Mace & Sear, 2005; Pavard, Gagnon, Desjardins, & Heyer, 2005). But there is clear evidence of a small but measurable mortality risk associated with a mother's remarriage to a new male in most societies in which this has been investigated, including contemporary settings such as Canada (Daly & Wilson, 1988). The adverse effect of human stepparents is certainly not equivalent to the normative infanticide practiced by incoming males in such species as langurs or lions. A recent study of accidental child deaths in Australia (Tooley, Karakis, Stokes, & Ozanne-Smith, 2006) found a significant increased mortality risk in stepparent households in cases where no foul play was suspected, suggesting that it is the distraction of a mother's efforts from parental investment in existing children to investment in a new mate that is likely to be a major effect in the fitness costs experienced by stepchildren.

Menopause

The existence of several postreproductive decades in human females has triggered much debate about how such a long section of women's lives could persist without immediate Darwinian benefits. Two questions focus this debate. First, is menopause unique in human females, or does it exist in other mammals, perhaps to a lesser extent? Second, have the existence and duration of menopause been the direct objects of selection, or are they the neutral or deleterious by-products of selection of some other trait? Menopause may also have originated as a by-product that then experienced mild positive selection.

Menopause around age 50 is universal in human populations (Wood, 1994), whereas in the wild it has been observed only in pilot whales and in captivity it has been reported only in few very old primate females (one bonobo, one pigtail macaque) both very near death (Austad, 1994; Pavelka & Fedigan, 1991). Although the captive animals showed similar hormonal profiles and oocyte depletion as do humans, their "menopause" was in step with their general senescence and not decades earlier as in women. Note that even with the relatively low life expectancies found in natural mortality populations, survival rates after cessation of childbearing are good, with many women reaching 60 or 70 years of age (Hill & Hurtado, 1991).

One proximate reason for the sudden cessation of reproduction is oocyte depletion: Menopause may be a by-product of atresia (Cresswell et al., 1997; Faddy & Gosden, 1996; Gosden et al., 1998). Under this view, selection is seen as having adjusted the stringency of the oocytic atresia filter in human ancestors to the level currently found in chimpanzees and bonobos, where females run out of oocytes at about the time they have their last offspring. Changes in other traits—in humans many of them social—then lead to improved survival late in life. Because selection pressures late in life are not strong, they cannot rapidly readjust the stringency of the atresia filter, whose advantage is strong and comes early in life. Both females and males live longer, but females have run out of oocytes. Menopause is then not a selected adaptation but a by-product of selection on the stringency of the atresia filter. A significant period of postreproductive survival would be expected in species in which there has been a relatively recent drop in late life mortality. In the end, weak selection for further reproduction will reduce the stringency of the atresia filter and lengthen reproductive life span. This atresia by-product hypothesis for menopause is certainly not yet established, but it does have one attractive feature not shared by the grandmother hypothesis: It explains the striking variation in age of onset of menopause (45–54 years; cf. Faddy & Gosden, 1996, figure 2) as the by-product of slight random variations in the long atresia process. If menopause were a primary adaptation rather than a by-product of something else, it should be much less variable in age of onset than it in fact is. This explanation neatly connects processes at the beginning and the end of life.

While the atresia hypothesis is good at explaining why female reproduction must decline in an abrupt manner when compared with males, there remain two aspects of menopause that need further discussion:

1. Women often stop having children a decade before menopause takes place, even accounting for declining fecundity rates. This suggests that optimal family size may often be reached before atresia is completed (Bogin, 1999). There are at least two reasons why this might be the case. First, the rate of death of mothers in childbirth increases with maternal age and number of prior pregnancies and is probably linked to lower muscle tone and decreased immunological performance (Bergsjø, 1997; Fikree, Midhet, Sadruddin, & Berendes, 1997). Second, as families grow larger, the costs linked to sibling rivalry and divided inheritances rise. For at least these reasons, the optimal number of children each woman should have may be selected to be fewer than the maximum possible. There would then be no selection pressure for reproduction after a certain age.

2. What thus needs to be explained are the selection pressures keeping women fit and functional two or more decades after the end of childbearing. Two important ideas are the "mother" and "grandmother" hypotheses, which argue that investment in current offspring or grand-offspring can bring enough inclusive fitness gains to compensate for losses in direct reproduction. The grandmother hypothesis has been repeatedly modeled and tested in several natural fertility populations, both historic and contemporary (Alvarez, 2000; Hawkes, O'Connell, Blurton Jones, Alvarez, & Charnov, 2000; Mace & Sear, 2005; Rogers, 1993; Sear et al., 2000; Shanley & Kirkwood, 2001; Voland & Engel, 1986). The benefits of grandmothering for the survival and reproductive success

of their children and grandchildren are usually significant but not often large enough to compensate for the lack of direct childbearing, if it is assumed that additional childbearing would have the same benefits in older as in younger women, which can be questioned by the arguments previously mentioned. The benefits of grandmothering have probably contributed to selection for longer female lives, despite earlier cessation of direct reproduction, in interaction with conditions imposed by atresia, childbearing risks that increase with age, and indirect costs of large families.

LIFE SPAN AND AGING

Age-specific selection pressures adjust the length of life to an intermediate optimum determined by the interaction of selection with trade-offs intrinsic to the organism. The conditions that select for longer life are those that decrease the value of offspring and increase the value of adults. These include lower adult mortality rates, higher juvenile mortality rates, increased variation in juvenile mortality rates from one reproductive event to the next, and increases in the ability of adults to transfer fitness-increasing support to the next generation (i.e., parental and group care of offspring). Superimposed on the adaptive pattern determined by optimal allocation of resources to maintenance and reproduction are the maladaptive effects of aging. The effects of aging increase mortality rates and decrease fecundity rates in late life beyond the levels predicted from optimal allocation.

Aging evolves because the strength of selection declines with age (Fisher, 1930; Haldane, 1941; Hamilton, 1966). Because there is always some mortality, as individuals age their continued survival contributes less and less to their reproductive success. This fact causes the strength of selection to decline with age and permits genes that have negative effects only late in life but positive (Williams, 1957) or neutral (Medawar, 1952) effects early in life to spread through the population to fixation. Aging follows the onset of reproduction with widespread, diffuse erosion of physiological and biochemical functions caused by many genes of small effect that produce aging as a by-product of selection for reproductive performance—including parental and group care—earlier in life. Aging is not itself an adaptation.

We age more slowly than do our closest relatives, living 2 to 3 decades longer than chimpanzees, bonobos, or gorillas. One reason for the evolution of our longer life is that we have encountered lower extrinsic adult mortality rates because of our cooperative social organization and effective group defense against predators and enemies. However, the drop in adult mortality rates is not itself sufficient to explain our longer life. As Kaplan and Robson (2002) and Lee (2003) have shown, the effects of intergenerational transfers—parental investment and cooperative child care—are needed to explain the long life, low fertility, and high investment in offspring that have evolved in humans and other species. Such effects appear to have been stronger in humans than in our closest relatives.

Evidence is mixed on whether intergenerational transfers impose costs on those who make them: whether a cost of reproduction exists in humans. Three studies illustrate the variety of effects found. In one, Friedlander (1996) documented significantly poorer survival in women who had children than in those who did not, and poorer maternal survival per child ever born, in women born 1880–1904 in Southern California. Those effects were not significant in the cohorts born 1905–1929. Her results suggest that having children increases women's risk of mortality from late-life diseases, that such risks increase with maternal age, and that they have been decreased by modern hygiene and medicine. In a second study, Lycett, Dunbar, and Voland (2000) saw a different pattern in farmers in northwest Germany followed from 1720 to 1870. They found no relation between number of children and longevity in their total sample, but when they broke it down by economic class, they found an increasingly strong negative relation between number of children and longevity in poorer and poorer women. Thus, human females do appear to suffer a cost of reproduction whose expression depends on socioeconomic environment. In the third, Doblhammer and Oeppen (2003) controlled for the effects of differences in health and of mortality occurring within the reproductive age classes in a genealogy of the British peerage and then found a significant trade-off between reproduction and longevity for females—but not for males. Whether or not humans experience a cost of reproduction thus appears to depend on their sex, nutritional status, economic well-being, and social class.

DEVELOPMENT AND PHYSIOLOGY

Developmental Determinants of Adult Survival and Reproduction

Barker (1998; Barker, Winter, Osmond, Margetts, & Simmonds, 1989) discovered that women who are nutritionally stressed during pregnancy give birth to underweight children who later in life are more likely to develop insulin resistance, obesity, high blood pressure, and cardiovascular disease. This observation stimulated a large literature reviewed in Lummaa (2003), Gluckman, Hanson, and Spencer (2005), and Kuzawa and Pike (2005). The pattern has been confirmed experimentally in rats (Desai & Hales, 1997) and in human populations in Europe and India, and the definition of the inducing stimulus has been broadened from events occurring during pregnancy to include postnatal stresses with long-term consequences. While the original observations were made on populations encountering severe famine, later work has shown that smaller babies run higher risks of late-life diabetes, hypertension, and cardiovascular disease whether their mothers were undernourished or not (Gluckman, Hanson, Spencer, & Bateson, 2005).

One interpretation is that the developing embryo perceives its undernutrition as a signal predicting the nutritional conditions it will encounter later in life and sets its metabolism to anticipate nutritional stress throughout life. If this prediction is wrong—if late-life nutrition is actually adequate—then the mismatch between physiology and environment produces a maladaptive response involving obesity, diabetes, and heart disease. Another interpretation is that the embryo's development and physiology is simply irrevocably disrupted by undernutrition and that it is stuck for the rest of its life making the best of a bad job. Both interpretations remain plausible and the subjects of ongoing research.

This connection between early-life environments and late-life susceptibility to disease helps to explain the global epidemic of obesity, diabetes, and heart disease, especially in India, Mexico, and Africa, where the adult level of nutrition may be poor but improving and still better than that of Paleolithic environments, and where the stress of starvation falls especially heavily on pregnant women.

The early life events that induce late life responses extend from prenatal development into early childhood. Girls who are stunted by poor nutrition as children attain menarche about a year later than those with good nutrition (Khan, Schoeder, Martorell, Haas, & Rivera, 1996) and have reduced output of ovarian hormones throughout their adult life (Ellison, 1996).

These plastic life history responses have profound implications for medicine, epidemiology, and public health, especially in the Third World.

Sex Hormones: Trade-offs, Morphology, and Buffering

Within an individual, trade-offs among traits are often mediated by energy allocations controlled by hormones (Calow, 1978, 1979; Ellison, 2003b; Wade, Schneider, & Li, 1996). Hormones elicit responses on the scale of seconds to hours and coordinate both the development and the activity of many tissues with a single signal. The difference in response of various tissues is often a function of the density of receptors on their cell surfaces, not of local variation in the concentration of the hormone, which is well mixed in the blood. Sex hormones play important roles in trade-offs between reproduction, disease resistance, and fat storage. Testosterone and leptin are two of the hormones that mediate human life history trade-offs.

Testosterone is a steroid secreted primarily from testes and ovaries but also from the adrenal glands and placenta. Males produce about 20 times as much as females do and that difference in circulating testosterone concentration accounts for many of the differences between the sexes in morphology, physiology, and behavior. In most tissues, testosterone activates androgen receptors on the cell surface directly; it can also be converted to estradiol and activate estradiol receptors, primarily in bones and brain. In embryonic development, testosterone induces the formation of the male genitals and the development of the prostate gland and the seminal vesicles. At puberty, increasing testosterone levels accompany the appearance in both sexes of adult body odor, increased skin oil, acne, pubic and axillary hair, the adolescent growth spurt, bone maturation, and fine hair on the upper lip and sideburns. Late-puberty testosterone effects are normal only in males but may cause changes in females with hormone imbalance. They include penis enlargement, increased libido, growth of hair on face, chest, and thighs, decreased subcutaneous fat, increased muscle mass, increased aggression, spermatogenesis, remodeling of face, chest, and shoulders, and completion of bone growth. In adults of both sexes testosterone maintains muscle mass and strength, bone mass and strength, and mental and physical energy. It is thus a key hormone coordinating the expression of many traits throughout the life cycle.

Two traits thus coordinated are survival and reproductive effort; they are tied together through the effects of testosterone on the immune system and on secondary sexual characters and fat storage. Substantial evidence from other vertebrates, somewhat less from humans and nonhuman primates, suggests that testosterone and other androgens regulate the allocation of energy between reproduction and immune functions. During infections, energy is switched from maintaining skeletal muscle mass, red blood cells, and bone density to increasing the immune response, much more so in males than in females. In uninfected males, the normal maintenance of secondary sexual characters by androgens diverts energy away from immune function and increases susceptibility to disease (Muehlenbein & Bribiescas, 2005): The more macho the male, the greater his risk of infection.

In females another hormone, leptin, mediates the trade-offs between reproduction and survival. Leptin is a protein that regulates energy intake and expenditure through effects on appetite and metabolism. It is secreted by fat cells and its concentration in the blood reflects overall fat storage in the body. It binds to the part of the hypothalamus known as the "satiety center," where it signals to the brain that the body has eaten enough. It works by inhibiting neurons that stimulate eating and stimulating neurons that inhibit eating by giving the feeling of satiation. Insulin is the only other hormone functioning as a signal of adiposity; together with leptin, it regulates body fat levels. Obese people have high levels of leptin circulating in their blood, but their bodies are resistant to its effects, just as people with type 2 diabetes are resistant to the effects of insulin. Leptin also plays a role in angiogenesis, the growth of new blood vessels. Because angiogenesis must occur to feed growing cancers, leptin plays a role in regulating the conditions necessary for the growth of metastatic cancers. Therefore obese women experience two effects mediated by leptin that increase their risk of metastatic cancers. They cycle dependably, not experiencing stress-induced amenorrhea, and thus, undergo the frequent episodes of cell differentiation that make possible the mutations that lead to cancer (Strassmann, 1996); when cancer does occur, their bodies are ready to respond by growing the arteries needed to feed it.

The human ovary responds adaptively to stress and nutrition as signals of the probability of a positive reproductive outcome as affected by age, maturation, energy balance, and activity level (Ellison, 1990, 1996). The stress of agricultural work and of poor nutrition appear to be related through effects on ovarian function to seasonal variation in conceptions and spatial and temporal variation in lactation and in the ability of lactation to suppress reproductive function (Ellison, 1994). Even without changing fat stores, the stress of physical work can itself suppress female reproductive function (Jasienska & Ellison, 1998). When women come under nutritional stress, some reproductive traits respond sensitively, and some do not. Ovarian function, duration of gestation, and final birth weight are sensitive to energy balance, but the rate at which energy is supplied to the embryo by the mother is less sensitive. Energy balance does not have strong effects on the volume of milk produced during lactation, but it does affect the duration of lactational amenorrhea (Ellison, 2003a). Thus pregnant and nursing mothers are strongly stressed by poor nutrition, which causes early births of underweight infants and increases the interbirth intervals of their mothers. Leptin is perhaps the most important signal mediating interactions of stress, fat stores, and female reproduction.

DISCUSSION

The causes of variation in life histories among and within human populations are diverse and hierarchical. Phylogenetic history creates one framework within which other effects are expressed: The life histories of the Dobe ! Kung and Northern Europeans differ in part because they have been reproductively isolated from each other for roughly 100,000 years. Natural selection causes local adaptation: Life span decreases where externally imposed mortality rates are high, and it increases where such rates are low. Genes and culture probably coevolve to produce effects on life histories, but this has not yet been demonstrated conclusively. Nutrition plays a key role: Well-nourished humans mature earlier and have shorter interbirth intervals than nutritionally stressed humans. Conflicts within the family, between parents and offspring and among sibs, also affect performance through impacts on growth, mating opportunities, and other traits. The way in which genetic differences interact with the local environment to produce phenotypic differences is mediated by physiological mechanisms, many of them controlled by hormones. Thus understanding human life history evolution requires a broad view across many academic specialties and an ability to synthesize the effects of diverse causes.

Human evolution did not stop in the Pleistocene. Human life histories can still be evolving, for many human life history traits are heritable and there is abundant variation in reproductive success in contemporary human populations. The key issue is whether variation in life history traits currently correlates strongly with variation in reproductive success. In some environments, it probably does; in others, it probably does not; the issue thus remains open. If, as seems likely, human life histories are evolving, they are doing so at a rate that is very slow compared to the rate of cultural change. It is thus virtually certain that contemporary human life histories are increasingly becoming poorly matched to rapidly changing cultural environments.

The human life history constrains both cognition and cultural dynamics. It implies that it will take humans 15–20 years to complete the physiological development and cultural learning required for adult function. Because this must be done by every individual in every generation, the rate of cultural change is constrained by both the evolved rate of brain development and the rate at which culture can be acquired by learning. Every population consists of a mixture of the young, who are still involved in doing this, and the older, who might form a different culture if they were not both constrained and stimulated by the young. After 5–6 decades of functional adulthood, aging erodes cognitive capacity. Thus, the window available for fully realized cultural transmission is framed by the portion of the population roughly between 20 and 80 years of age. This is a fundamental constraint on cultural evolution.

REFERENCES

Adair, L. S. (2001). Size at birth predicts age at menarche. *Pediatrics, 107*, E59.
Aiello, L. C., & Wells, J. C. K. (2002). Energetics and the evolution of the Genus *Homo. Annual Review of Anthropology, 31*, 323–338.

Alam, N. (1995). Birth spacing and infant and early childhood mortality in a high fertility area of Bangladesh: Age-dependent and interactive effects. *Journal of Biosocial Science, 27*, 393–404.

Alvarez, H. P. (2000). Grandmother hypothesis and primate life histories. *American Journal of Physical Anthropology, 113*, 435–450.

Austad, S. N. (1994). Menopause: An evolutionary perspective. *Experimental Gerontology, 29*, 255–263.

Bailey, S. M. (1982). Absolute and relative sex differences in body composition. In L. Hall (Ed.), *Sexual dimorphism in Homo sapiens. A question of size* (pp. 363–390). New York: Praeger.

Bailey, S. M., & Katch, V. L. (1981). The effects of body size on sexual dimorphism in fatness, volume and muscularity. *Human Biology, 53*, 337–349.

Barker, D. J. P. (1998). *Mothers, babies and health in later life* (2nd ed.). Edinburgh, U.K.: Churchill Livingstone.

Barker, D. J. P., Winter, P. D., Osmond, C., Margetts, B., & Simmonds, S. J. (1989). Weight in infancy and death from ischemic heart-disease. *Lancet, 2*(8663), 577–580.

Bereczkei, T., & Dunbar, R. I. M. (1997). Female-biased reproductive strategies in a Hungarian Gypsy population. *Proceedings of the Royal Society of London B, 264*, 17–22.

Bergsjø, P. (1997). Recent evolution within obstetrics. Nordic experience since the 70s, as evidenced by statistics. *Acta Obstetrica et Gynecologia Scandinavica, 76*, 613–618.

Berrigan, D., & Koella, J. (1994). The evolution of reaction norms: Simple models for age and size at maturity. *Journal of Evolutionary Biology, 7*, 549–566.

Blurton Jones, N. G. (1978). Natural selection and birth weight. *Annals of Human Biology, 5*, 487–489.

Blurton Jones, N. G. (1986). Bushman birth spacing: A test for optimal inter-birth intervals. *Ethnology and Sociobiology, 7*, 91–105.

Bogin, B. (1999). *Patterns of human growth* (2nd ed.). Cambridge, U.K.: Cambridge University Press.

Bøhler, E., & Bergström, S. (1995). Subsequent pregnancy affects morbidity of previous child. *Journal of Biosocial Science, 27*, 431–442.

Bongaart, J. (1980). Does malnutrition affect fecundity? A summary of evidence. *Science, 208*, 564–568.

Bribiescas, R. G. (2001). Reproductive ecology and life history of the human male. *Yearbook of Physical Anthropology, 44*, 148–176.

Calow, P. (1978). *Life cycles: An evolutionary approach to the physiology of development, reproduction, and ageing.* New York: Halsted.

Calow, P. (1979) The cost of reproduction—A physiological approach. *Biological Reviews, 54*, 23–40.

Cameron, J. L. (1991). Metabolic cues for the onset of puberty. *Hormone Research, 36*, 97–103.

Cameron, J. L. (1996). Nutritional determinants of puberty. *Nutrition Reviews, 54*, S17–22.

Charlesworth, B. (1990). Optimization models, quantitative genetics, and mutation. *Evolution, 44*, 520–538.

Charnov, E. L. (1993). *Life history invariants.* Oxford, U.K.: Oxford University Press.

Cogswell, M. E., & Yip, R. (1995). The influence of fetal and maternal factors on the distribution of birthweight. *Seminars in Perinatalogy, 19*, 222–240.

Cresswell, J. L., Egger, P., Fall, C. H. D., Osmond, C., Fraser, R. B., & Barker, D. J. P. (1997). Is the age of menopause determined in utero? *Early Human Development, 49*,143–148.

Crow, J. F. (1993). How much do we know about spontaneous human mutation rates? *Environmental and Molecular Mutagenesis, 21*, 122–129.

Daly, M., & Wilson, M. (1988). *Homicide.* New York: Aldine de Gruyter.

Das Gupta, M. (1987). Selective discrimination against female children in rural Punjab, India. *Population and Development Review, 13*, 77–100.

De Mazancourt, C., & Dieckmann, U. (2004). Trade-off geometries and frequency-dependent selection. *American Naturalist, 164*, 765–778.

Dercole, F., Ferrier, R., & Rinaldi, S. (2002). Ecological bistability and evolutionary reversals under asymmetrical competition. *Evolution, 56*, 1081–1090.

Desai, M., & Hales, C. N. (1997). Role of fetal and infant growth in programming metabolism in later life. *Biological Reviews, 72*, 329–348.

Diamond, J. (1991). *The rise and fall of the third chimpanzee.* London: Vintage.

Doblhammer, G., & Oeppen, J. (2003). Reproduction and longevity among the British peerage: the effect of frailty and health selection. *Proceedings of the Royal Society of London B, 270,* 1541–1547.

Drent, R. H., & Daan, S. (1980). The prudent parent: Energetic adjustments in avian breeding. In H. Klomp & J. W. Woldendorp (Eds.), *The integrated study of bird populations* (pp. 225–252). Amsterdam: North-Holland Publishers.

Ellison, P. T. (1990). Human ovarian function and reproductive ecology: new hypotheses. *American Anthropologist, 92,* 933–952.

Ellison, P. T. (1994). Advances in human reproductive ecology. *Annual Review of Anthropology, 23,* 255–275.

Ellison, P. T. (1996). Developmental influences on adult ovarian hormonal function. *American Journal of Human Biology, 8,* 725–734.

Ellison, P. T. (2003a). Energetics and reproductive effort. *American Journal of Human Biology, 15,* 342–351.

Ellison, P. T. (2003b). *On fertile ground: A natural history of human reproduction.* Cambridge, MA: Harvard University Press.

Eveleth, P. B., & Tanner, J. M. (1976). *Worldwide variation in human growth. International Biological Programme 8.* Cambridge, U.K.: Cambridge University Press.

Faddy, M. J., & Gosden, R. G. (1996). A model conforming the decline in follicle numbers to the age of menopause in women. *Human Reproduction, 11,* 1484–1486.

Felsenstein, J. (1985). Phylogenies and the comparative method. *American Naturalist, 125,* 1–15.

Fikree, F. F., Midhet, F., Sadruddin, S., & Berendes, H. W. (1997). Maternal mortality in different Pakistani sites: Ratios, clinical causes and determinants. *Acta Obstetrica et Gynecologia Scandinavica, 76,* 637–645.

Finch, C. E., & Sapolsky, R. M. (1999). The evolution of Alzheimer disease, the reproductive schedule, and apoE isoforms. *Neurobiology of Aging, 20,* 407–428.

Fisher, R. (1930). *The genetic theory of natural selection.* Oxford, U.K.: Clarendon Press.

Forbes, L. S. (1997). The evolutionary biology of spontaneous abortion in humans. *Trends in Ecology and Evolution, 12,* 446–450.

Friedlander, N. J. (1996). The relation of lifetime reproduction to survivorship in women and men: A prospective study. *American Journal of Human Biology, 8,* 771–783.

Furuichi, T., Idani, G., Ihobe, H., Kuroda, S., Kitamura, K., Mori, A., et al. (1998). Population dynamics of wild bonobos (*Pan paniscus*) at Wamba. *International Journal of Primatology, 19,* 1029–1043.

Gage, T. B. (1998). The comparative demography of primates: With some comments on the evolution of life histories. *Annual Review of Anthropology, 27,* 197–221.

Gaulin, S. J. C., & Boster, J. S. (1990). Dowry as female competition. *American Anthropologist, 92,* 994–1005.

Gaulin, S. J. C., & Robbins, C. J. (1991). Trivers-Willard effect in contemporary North American society. *American Journal of Physical Anthropology, 85,* 61–69.

Gibson, M. A., & Mace, R. (2003). Strong mother bear more sons in rural Ethiopia. *Proceedings of the Royal Society B, 270,* S108–S109.

Gibson, M. A., & Mace, R. (2006). An energy-saving development initiative increases birth rate and childhood malnutrition in rural Ethiopia. *PLoS Medicine, 3,* 476–484.

Gluckman, P. D., & Hanson, M. A. (2006). Evolution, development and timing of puberty. *Trends in Endocrinology and Metabolism, 17,* 7–12.

Gluckman, P. D., Hanson, M. A., & Spencer, H. G. (2005). Predictive adaptive responses and human evolution. *Trends in Ecology and Evolution, 20,* 527–533.

Gluckman, P. D., Hanson, M. A., Spencer, H. G., & Bateson, P. (2005). Environmental influences during development and their later consequences for health and disease: Implications for the interpretation of empirical studies. *Proceedings of the Royal Society B, 272,* 671–677.

Gosden, R. G., Dunbar, R. I. M., Haig, D., Heyer, E., Mace, R., Milinski, M., et al. (1998). Evolutionary interpretations of the diversity of reproductive health and disease. In S. C. Stearns (Ed.), *Evolution in health and disease* (pp. 108–120). Oxford, U.K.: Oxford University Press.

Griffin, A. S., & West, S. A. (2002). Kin selection: Fact and fiction. *Trends in Ecology and Evolution, 17,* 15–21.

Haig, D. (1992). Genomic imprinting and the theory of parent-offspring conflict. *Seminars in Developmental Biology, 3*, 153–160.

Haig, D. (1993). Genetic conflicts in human pregnancy. *Quarterly Review of Biology, 68*, 495–532.

Haig, D. (1998). Genetic conflicts of pregnancy and childhood. In S. C. Stearns (Ed.), *Evolution in health and disease* (pp. 77–90). Oxford, U.K.: Oxford University Press.

Haldane, J. B. S. (1941). *New paths in genetics.* London: Allen and Unwin.

Haldane, J. B. S. (1947). The mutation rate of the gene for haemophilia, and its segregation ratios in males and females. *Annals of Eugenics, 13*, 262.

Hamilton, W. D. (1966). The moulding of senescence by natural selection. *Journal of Theoretical Biology, 12*, 12–45.

Harrison, G. A., Tanner, J. M., Pilbeam, D. R., & Baker, P. T. (1977). *Human Biology: An introduction to human evolution, variation, growth and ecology.* Oxford, U.K.: Oxford University Press.

Hartung, J. (1982). Polygyny and inheritance of wealth. *Current Anthropology, 23*, 1–11.

Harvey, P. H., & Clutton Brock, T. H. (1985). Life history variation in primates. *Evolution, 39*, 559–581.

Hawkes, K., O'Connell, J. F., Blurton Jones, N. G., Alvarez, H., & Charnov, E. L. (2000). The 'grandmother hypothesis' and human evolution. In L. Cronk, N. Chagnon, & W. Irons (Eds.), *Adaptation and human behavior* (pp. 237–260). New York: Aldine de Gruyter.

Herman-Giddens, M. E., Slora, E. J., Wasserman, R. C., Bourdony, C. J., Bhapkar, M. V., Koch, G. G., et al. (1997). Secondary sexual characteristics and menses in young girls seen in office practice: A study from the pediatric research in office settings network. *Pediatrics, 99*, 505–512.

Hill, K., & Hurtado, A. M. (1991). The evolution of premature reproductive senescence and menopause in human females: An evaluation of the 'grandmother hypothesis.' *Human Nature, 2*, 313–350.

Hill, K., & Hurtado, A. M. (1996). *Aché life history: The ecology and demography of a foraging people.* New York: Aldine de Gruyter.

Hill, K., & Kaplan, H. (1999). Life history traits in humans: Theory and empirical studies. *Annual Review of Anthropology, 28*, 397–430.

Hobcraft, J. N., McDonald, J. W., & Rutstein, S. O. (1985) Demographic determinants of infant and early childhood mortality: A comparative analysis. *Population Studies, 39*, 363–85.

Hokkenkoelaga, A. C. S., Deridder, M. A. J., Lemmen, R. J., Denhartog, H., DeKeizershrama, S. M. P. F., & Drop, S. L. S. (1995). Children born small for gestational age: do they catch up? *Pediatric Research, 38*, 267–271.

Holden, C., & Mace, R. (1999). The sexual division of labour and dimorphism in stature: A phylogenetic cross-cultural analysis. *American Journal of Physical Anthropology, 110*, 27–45.

Hrdy, S. B. (2000). *Mother nature: Maternal instincts and how they shape the human species.* New York: Ballantine.

Hulanicka, B., Gronkiewicz, L., & Koniarek, J. (2001). Effect of familial distress on growth and maturation of girls: A longitudinal study. *American Journal of Human Biology, 13*, 771–776.

Jansen, R. P. S., & de Boer, K. (1998). The bottleneck: Mitochondrial imperatives in oogenesis and ovarian follicular fate. *Molecular and Cellular Endocrinology, 145*, 81–88.

Jasienska, G., & Ellison, P. T. (1998). Physical work causes suppression of ovarian function in women. *Proceedings of the Royal Society of London B, 265*, 1847–1851.

Josephson, S. C. (2002). Does polygyny reduce fertility? *American Journal of Human Biology, 14*, 222–232.

Käär, P., Jokela, J., Helle, T., & Kojola, I. (1996). Direct and correlative phenotypic selection on life-history traits in three pre-industrial human populations. *Proceedings of the Royal Society of London B, 263*, 1475–1480.

Kanazawa, S. (2001). Why father absence might precipitate early menarche. *Evolution and Human Behavior, 329*, 334.

Kaplan, H. S., & Robson, A. J. (2002). The emergence of humans: The coevolution of intelligence and longevity with intergenerational transfers. *Proceedings of the National Academy of Sciences USA, 99*, 10221–10226.

Karn, M. N., & Penrose, L. S. (1952). Birth weight and gestation time in relation to maternal age, parity and infant survival. *Annals of Eugenics, 16*, 147–164.

Kawecki, T. J., & Stearns, S. C. (1993). The evolution of life histories in spatially heterogeneous environments: Optimal reaction norms revisited. *Evolutionary Ecology, 7*, 155–174.

Khan, A. D., Schroeder, D. G., Martorell, R., Haas, J. F., & Rivera, J. (1996). Early childhood determinants of age at menarche in rural Guatemala. *American Journal of Human Biology, 8,* 717–723.

Knobil, E. (1990). Concluding remarks. In M. M. Grumbach, P. C. Sizonenko, & M. C. Aubert (Eds.), *Control of the onset of puberty* (pp. 690–693). Baltimore: Williams and Wilkins.

Krakauer, D. C., & Mira, A. (1999). Mitochondria and germ-cell death. *Nature, 400,* 125–126.

Kuzawa, C. W., & Pike, I. L. (2005). Introduction. *American Journal of Human Biology, 17,* 1–4.

Leakey, R. (1994). *The origin of humankind.* New York: Harper Collins.

Lee, R. D. (2003). Rethinking the evolutionary theory of aging: Transfers, not births, shape social species. *Proceedings of the National Academy of Science USA, 16,* 9637–9642.

Legrand, T. K., & Phillips, J. F. (1996). The effect of fertility reductions on infant and child mortality: Evidence from Matlab in rural Bangladesh. *Population Studies—A Journal of Demography, 50,* 51.

Levi, S. (1976). Ultrasonic assessment of the high rate of human multiple pregnancy in the first trimester. *Journal of Clinical Ultrasound, 4,* 3–5.

Lieberman, L. S. (1982). Normal and abnormal sexual dimorphic patterns of growth and development. In R. L. Hall (Ed.), *Sexual dimorphism in Homo sapiens: A question of size* (pp. 263–316). New York: Praeger.

Liestøl, K. (1980). Menarcheal age and spontaneous abortion: a causal connection? *American Journal of Epidemiology, 111,* 753–758.

Lummaa, V. (2003). Early developmental conditions and reproductive success in humans: Downstream effects of prenatal famine, birthweight, and timing of birth. *American Journal of Human Biology, 15,* 370–379.

Lummaa, V., Jokela, J., & Haukioja, E. (2001). Gender difference in benefits of twinning in pre-industrial humans: Boys did not pay. *Journal of Animal Ecology, 70,* 739–746.

Lycett, J. E., Dunbar, R. I. M., & Voland, E. (2000). Longevity and the costs of reproduction in a historical human population. *Proceedings of the Royal Society of London B, 267,* 31–35.

Mace, R. (1996). Biased parental investment and reproductive success in Gabbra pastoralists. *Behavioral Ecology and Sociobiology, 38,* 75–81.

Mace, R. (2000). The evolutionary ecology of human life history. *Animal Behaviour, 59,* 1–10.

Mace, R., & Sear, R. (2005). Are humans cooperative breeders? In E. Voland, A. Chasiotis, & W. Schiefenhoevel (Eds.), *Grandmotherhood: The evolutionary significance of the second half of female life* (pp. 143–159). Piscataway, NJ: Rutgers University Press.

Macintyre, S. (1992). The effects of family position and status on health. *Social Science and Medicine, 35,* 453–464.

Maclure, M., Travis, L. B., Willett, W., & MacMahon, B. (1991). A prospective cohort study of nutrient intake and age at menarche. *American Journal of Clinical Nutrition, 54,* 649–656.

Malina, R. M., Zavaleta, A. N., & Little, B. B. (1987). Secular changes in the stature and weight of Mexican American schoolchildren in Brownsville, Texas, between 1928 and 1983. *Human Biology, 59,* 509–522.

McCormick, M. C. (1997). The outcomes of very low birth weight infants: Are we asking the right questions? *Pediatrics, 99,* 869–876.

Medawar, P. B. (1952). *An unsolved problem of biology.* London: H. K. Lewis.

Muehlenbein, M. P., & Bribiescas, R. G. (2005). Testosterone-mediated immune functions and male life histories. *American Journal of Human Biology, 17,* 527–558.

Muller, H. J. (1964). The relation of recombination to mutational advance. *Mutation Research, 1,* 2–9.

Nettle, D. (2002). Women's height, reproductive success and the evolution of sexual dimorphism in modern humans. *Proceedings of the Royal Society of London B, 269,* 1919–1923.

Ober, C., Elias, S., Kostyu, D. D., & Hauck, W. W. (1992). Decreased fecundability in Hutterite couples sharing HLA-DR. *American Journal of Human Genetics, 50,* 6–14.

Pagel, M. (1994). Detecting correlated evolution on phylogenies: A general method for the comparative analysis of discrete characters. *Proceedings of the Royal Society of London B, 225,* 37–45.

Pavard, S., Gagnon, A., Desjardins, B., & Heyer, E. (2005). Mother's death and child survival: the case of early Quebec. *Journal of Biosocial Science, 37,* 209–227.

Pavelka, M. S. M., & Fedigan, L. M. (1991). Menopause: A comparative life history perspective. *Yearbook of Physical Anthropology, 34,* 13–38

Perez, G. I., Trbovich, A. M., Gosden, R. G., & Tilly, J. L. (2000). Reproductive biology—Mitochondria and the death of oocytes. *Nature, 403,* 500–501.

Pond, C. M. (1997). The biological origins of adipose tissue in humans. In M. E. Morbeck, A. Galloway, & A. L. Zihlman (Eds.), *The evolving female* (pp. 147–162). Princeton, NJ: Princeton University Press.

Quinlan, R. J. (2003). Father absence, parental care and female reproductive development. *Ecology and Human Behavior, 24,* 376–390.

Roff, D. A. (1997). *Evolutionary quantitative genetics.* New York: Springer.

Roff, D. A. (2001). *Life history evolution.* Sunderland, U.K.: Sinauer.

Rogers, A. R. (1993). Why menopause? *Evolutionary Ecology, 7,* 406–420.

Ruff, C. (2002). Variation in human body size and shape. *Annual Review of Anthropology, 31,* 211–232.

Sear, R., Allal, N., Mace, R., & McGregor, I. A. (2004). Height and reproductive success among Gambian women. *American Journal of Human Biology, 16,* 223.

Sear, R., Mace, R., & McGregor, I. A. (2000). Maternal grandmothers improve nutritional status and survival of children in rural Gambia. *Proceedings of the Royal Society of London B, 267,* 461–467.

Sear, R., Shanley, D., McGregor, I. A., & Mace, R. (2001). The fitness of twin mothers: Evidence from rural Gambia. *Journal of Evolutionary Biology, 14,* 433–443.

Shanley, D. P., & Kirkwood, T. B. L. (2001). Evolution of the human menopause. *BioEssays, 23,* 282–287.

Singh, D. (1993). Body shape and female attractiveness: The critical role of waist-to-hip ratio. *Human Nature, 4,* 297–331.

Smith, E. A., & Smith, S. A. (1994). Inuit sex-ratio variation—Population control, ethnographic error, or parental manipulation? *Current Anthropology, 35,* 595–624.

Stearns, S. C. (1989). Tradeoffs in life-history evolution. *Functional Ecology, 3,* 259–268.

Stearns, S. C. (1992). *The evolution of life histories.* Oxford, U.K.: Oxford University Press.

Stearns, S. C. (2000). Daniel Bernoulli (1738): Evolution and economics under risk. *Journal of Biosciences, 25,* 221–228.

Stearns, S. C., & Koella, J. (1986). The evolution of phenotypic plasticity in life-history traits: Predictions of norms of reaction for age- and size-at-maturity. *Evolution, 40,* 893–913.

Stini, W. A. (1969). Nutritional stress and growth: Sex difference in adaptive response. *American Journal of Physical Anthropology, 31,* 417–426.

Strassmann, B. I. (1996). The evolution of endometrial cycles and menstruation. *Quarterly Review of Biology, 71,* 181–220.

Strassmann, B. I., & Gillespie, B. (2002). Life-history theory, fertility and reproductive success in humans. *Proceedings of the Royal Society of London B, 269,* 553–562.

Tanner, J. M. (1963). Regulation of growth in size in mammals. *Nature, 199,* 845–850.

Tanner, J. M. (1990). *Fetus into man: Physical growth from conception to maturity, revised and enlarged.* Cambridge, MA: Harvard University Press.

Tooley, G. A., Karakis, M., Stokes, M., & Ozanne-Smith, J. (2006). Generalising the Cinderella Effect to unintentional childhood fatalities. *Evolution and Human Behavior, 27,* 224–230.

Trivers, R. (1974). Parent-offspring conflict. *American Zoologist, 14,* 249–264.

Trivers, R. (1985). *Social evolution.* Menlo Park, CA: Benjamin/Cummings.

Trivers, R. L., & Willard, D. E. (1973). Natural selection of parental ability to vary the sex ratio of offspring. *Science, 179,* 90–92.

Udry, J. R. (1979). Age at menarche, at first intercourse and at first pregnancy. *Journal of Biosocial Science, 11,* 433–441.

Ulizzi, L., & Manzotti, C. (1988). Birth weight and natural selection. An example of selection relaxation in man. *Human Heredity, 38,* 129–135.

Ulizzi, L., & Terrenato, I. (1992). Natural selection associated with birth weight. VI. Towards the end of the stabilizing component. *Annals of Human Genetics, 56,* 113–118.

van Noordwijk, A. J., & de Jong, G. (1986). Acquisition and allocation of resources: Their influence on variation in life history tactics. *American Naturalist, 128,* 137–142.

Voland, E. (1998). Evolutionary ecology of human reproduction. *Annual Review of Anthropology, 27,* 347–374.

Voland, E., Dunbar, R. I. M., Engel, C., & Stephan, P. (1997). Population increase and sex-biased parental investment in humans: Evidence from 18th- and 19th-century Germany. *Current Anthropology, 38,* 129–135.

Voland, E., & Engel, C. (1986). Is the postmenopausal age at death a function of a fitness maximizing strategy? [English translation]. *Anthropologisches Anzeiger, 44,* 19–34.

Wade, G. N., Schneider, J. E., & Li, H.-Y. (1996). Control of fertility by metabolic cues. *American Journal of Physiology, 270,* 1–19.

Walker, R., Gurven, M., Hill, K., Migiliano, H., Chagnon, N., De Souza, R., et al. (2006). Growth rates and life histories in twenty-two small scale societies. *American Journal of Human Biology, 18,* 295–311.

Watts, E. S. (1986). Evolution of the human growth curve. In F. Falkner & J. M. Tanner (Eds.), *Human growth* (2nd ed., Vol. 1, pp. 153–166). New York: Springer.

Waynforth, D. (2002). Evolutionary theory and reproductive responses to father absence: Implications of kin selection and the reproductive returns to mating and parenting effort. In C. S. Tamis-LeMonda & N. Cabrera (Eds.), *Handbook of father involvement: Multidisciplinary perspectives* (pp. 337–359). Mahwah, NJ: Lawrence Erlbaum Associates.

Williams, G. C. (1957). Pleiotropy, natural selection and the evolution of senescence. *Evolution, 11,* 398–411.

Wood, J. W. (1994). *Dynamics of human reproduction: Biology, biometry, demography.* New York: Aldine de Gruyter.

4

Sex and Sexual Selection

ANDERS PAPE MØLLER

THE EVOLUTION OF SEX AND ITS IMPLICATIONS

Why do males and females look so different in many species? Why are members of one sex colored in gaudy ways in some species, while members of the other sex are not? How can such exaggerated traits that apparently hamper survival evolve? And why are there different sexes in the first place?

These questions posed a puzzle for Charles Darwin. He invoked sexual selection to answer the first three questions. The last question, about how different sexes evolved in the first place, was largely neglected by Darwin and was only addressed later on. Intensive research effort leading to new theoretical developments and empirical tests has clarified several of these issues in recent decades.

This chapter starts by defining sex, followed by a review of the evolution of sex. Then follows a section on the crucial differences between males and females. These differences provide the basis for sexual selection, a process that has played an important role in producing the anatomy, physiology, behavior, and psychology of all sexually reproducing organisms. The chapter ends with a brief review of the literature on sex, sex differences, and sexual selection in humans. Figure 4.1 provides a guide to the sequence of events that led to the evolution of sex, the evolution of gametes of different size (anisogamy), sperm competition, sexual selection, and parental effort.

DEFINITION OF SEX

Sex produces genetic diversity by the mixing and exchange of genetic material by two individuals with different genomes. The mixing and exchange occurs during two different processes, during which the number of chromosomes is first halved by division of the nucleus (meiosis), following by the fusion of two such reduced nuclei (i.e., the process of fertilization). Features of sexually reproducing organisms such as production of gametes, differentiation of males and females, or production of offspring are not necessary conditions for sexuality. These features are best considered by-products of the initial evolution of sex.

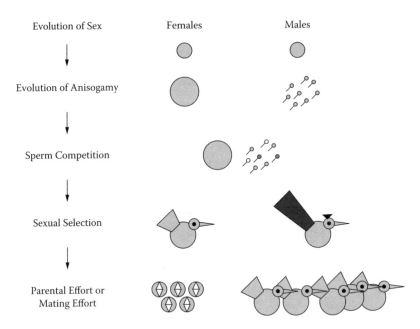

Figure 4.1 Evolutionary scenario for the order of evolution of sex, anisogamy, sperm competition, sexual selection, and parental investment by males and females.

CURRENT THEORIES OF EVOLUTION OF SEX

The enigmatic nature of sex can best be understood by considering the twofold advantage of asexual reproduction. Any asexually reproducing individual will enjoy a twofold advantage over a sexually reproducing individual by producing twice as many replicas of itself. Hence, it is the presence of males that do not themselves produce eggs that is the puzzle that needs to be explained.

Sexual reproduction can be advantageous because of immediate benefits, or because of delayed benefits caused by the genetic processes of sex. The immediate benefits of sexual reproduction are of three different kinds (Kondrashov, 1993). First, selection of mates may provide an advantage due to the production of offspring that are more fit, either because a high quality mate has been chosen, or because a high quality gamete without genetic defects has fertilized an egg. Second, deleterious mutations may be repaired during the process of sexual reproduction when the two copies of pairs of otherwise identical chromosomes become aligned during meiosis, potentially allowing for recognition and repair of deletions, inversions, and deleterious mutations. However, this would require a "knowledge" of which copy of the genetic information is the original one, a process for which there is no known mechanism. Third, offspring may be more fit due to the efforts of two parents rather than one. Such an advantage could arise from biparental care or defense of offspring, processes that did not evolve until late compared to the evolution of sex.

The delayed advantages of sexual reproduction arise from the fact that sex results in the production of offspring that differ in genetic constitution. First, sex results in chromosomal reassortment with exchange of chromosomes of the two parental origins. There is a second benefit of chromosomal admixture from the two parental copies linked to recombination, whereby parts of chromosomes are exchanged. This results in novel associations between loci. A consequence of such exchange is that it allows for different mutations to end up in the same individual, hence, speeding up the beneficial association of different mutations that have occurred in different individuals. These benefits of genetic rearrangements will favor sexual individuals over asexual ones because elevated genetic variation among progeny in sexual species will enhance the probability of any two individuals that disperse to a habitat patch being able to succeed in the presence of sibling competition (Williams, 1975). In contrast, offspring of an asexual species entering a patch are genetically similar, making it unlikely that any of them will succeed, and if they do, then enhanced sib competition will reduce this benefit because everybody will succeed. A slightly different tack on this theme is the tangled bank hypothesis arguing that offspring of a sexual organism will be slightly different, allowing for the use of slightly different niches in a given environment (Bell, 1982). In contrast, progeny of asexual organisms are genetically identical, increasing the level of competition and reducing the range of niches exploited in a given environment.

Parasites have been suggested to provide a sufficiently common and strong selection pressure to account for the evolution and the maintenance of sex. Parasites are ubiquitous, and they impose strong selection pressures on their hosts. Host resistance to parasites and parasite virulence has a genetic basis, and, therefore, the optimal host genotype varies temporally (Hamilton, Axelrod, & Tanese, 1990). Coevolutionary interactions between hosts and parasites can change what is the most beneficial host genotype, with currently beneficial alleles being disadvantageous at a later stage. Sex may be advantageous in such a situation because it allows recovery of rare alleles in the population through the process of recombination, allowing for the production of individuals that become selectively favored through their rare alleles that parasites are unable or less likely to attack.

Empirical evidence consistent with the parasite theory of evolution of sex was provided by Curt Lively (1987), who in New Zealand studied natural variation in sex in the partially hermaphroditic freshwater snail *Potamopyrgus antipodarum* infected with a trematode parasite. He found a positive correlation between the proportion of males and the level of parasitism across sites. Such a positive correlation could be interpreted as implying that parasitism promotes sex, although the alternative line of causation, that sex promotes parasitism, is equally likely. If sex was an efficient way of combating parasitism, then one could perhaps even expect a negative rather than a positive correlation. Tests of the parasite hypothesis require careful experiments that allow causation to be inferred. No such tests have been conducted to date.

Mutations have different effects on organisms with asexual and sexual reproduction. To gain the benefits of two beneficial mutant alleles, an asexual organism must await the occurrence of both in the same lineage, whereas sexual reproduction through recombination will produce individuals with both alleles at a much more rapid pace (Fisher, 1930). Mutations may also be important for the evolution of sex in another way. Mutations with slightly deleterious effects are common and accumulate constantly, causing individuals with the fewest mutations to enjoy a selective advantage. In an asexual organism, the number of mutations will invariably increase by a process that has been termed "Muller's ratchet" (with each new mutation representing another notch having been reached in the unidirectional turning of the ratchet), while recombination of different genomes can produce a novel combination with few mutations that will then be favored by selection (Muller, 1964). Muller originally assumed accumulation of mutations with similar effects, but it was later realized that having a new mutation may in fact cause a greater reduction in fitness in the presence of several other mutations rather than in their absence (Kondrashov, 1988). Such contamination of the genome with mutations due to Muller's ratchet can be ameliorated by sexual reproduction because some individuals, through recombination, will have very few mutations, while others will have a lot.

The two sexes generally differ in mutation rate, with males having much higher rates than females, as we shall see later. Sexual selection may be a cause of this difference, because males, by producing an increasingly large number of gametes to win at fertilization over other males, increase the number of cell divisions in their gametes and, hence, the mutation rate. If there is a sufficiently large variance in mating success among males, with females choosing males with relatively few mutations as mates and thereby eliminating individuals with a high mutational load each generation, then mutations may play an important role in the maintenance of sex. This hypothesis rests on the assumptions that so-called "good genes" sexual selection due to female mate preference for genetic benefits is important (see later), that selection against mutants is intense due to an extreme skew in male mating success, as is commonly observed, and that a considerable portion of the variance in fitness is due to mutations (Agrawal, 2001; Siller, 2001).

HOW MANY SEXES

Primitive isogamous organisms (organisms with gametes that are indistinguishable), with mating types of different kinds only mating with each other, preceded the evolution of sex. This raises the question why there are only two mating types and only two sexes. In fact, more than two mating types have been reported for a number of organisms (Hurst & Hamilton, 1992).

Two sexes are ubiquitous in sexually reproducing organisms. Although males and females are distinct in a number of ways, as described below, the characteristics of males and females are themselves continuous characters, with some individuals being more "male-like" and others more "female-like." In other words, males and females differ phenotypically from each other (i.e., there is sexual dimorphism), and such differences are selectively advantageous. This implies that individuals that are more male-like enjoy an advantage in terms of fitness, and likewise for females that are more female-like, while intermediates are at a selective disadvantage (disruptive selection). There are many examples of gynandrous individuals (individuals of mixed sex) with both male and female characteristics. For example, humans can have a mixture of male and female reproductive characters. Studies of rare gynandrous birds have shown an absence of reproductive success by such individuals, therefore effectively selecting against intermediate phenotypes and, hence, convergence of the two sexes.

Not all organisms have separate sexes. Numerous plants and animals (such as sea urchins, mollusks, worms and many others) are simultaneous hermaphrodites, with the same individual having both male and female functions, while others, such as for example many fishes, are sequential hermaphrodites, first being males when small and later females when large.

CHARACTERISTICS OF MALES AND FEMALES

A number of different features characterize males and females, including size of gametes, parental investment, potential rates of reproduction, sex-specific mutation rates, and sex-specific inheritance of organelles. We will briefly go through these features and discuss how they arose as a consequence of the evolution of sex (see also Figure 4.1).

GAMETE SIZE AND NUMBERS

Sexual organisms were originally of a similar size, and such isogamous organisms could fuse, allowing exchange of genetic material and formation of two new individuals. Cell fusion occurred between individuals of different mating types.

Anisogamy, the condition of individuals of one sex producing many small gametes (sperm) and the other few large gametes (eggs), is believed to have evolved through the benefits from producing a large zygote by fusion between a small and a large gamete from two individuals and the benefits in terms of fertilization from producing many small gametes.

Parker, Baker, and Smith (1972) developed a now-classical theoretical model that accounted for this transition caused by disruptive selection for gametes of different size (disruptive selection favors extreme phenotypes like small and large gametes over gametes of intermediate size). Two selection pressures would account for anisogamy: Selection for increased zygote size due to the survival advantages of large size, and selection for an increased number of small gametes due to the increased probability of fertilization. Under this scenario, small gametes that fused with large gametes would be favored over small gametes that fused with other small gametes (such zygotes would be small and, hence, have low survival prospects). Likewise, large gametes that only fused with other large gametes would have very low success because of the overall scarcity of large gametes. This would cause disruptive selection on gamete size and would effectively maintain two sexes with differently sized gametes. Empirical studies of gamete dimorphism and cellular organization in algae and protozoa are consistent with this model (e.g., Knowlton, 1974).

There are alternative hypotheses accounting for the evolution of small sperm that stem from the idea that small gamete size may prevent transmission of cytoplasmic organelles and parasites to the zygote. Many organisms have intracellular parasites that transmit during fusion of gametes. If one gamete type was small, preventing it from having intracellular parasites, or reducing their number, this could enhance the swimming speed of this type of gamete, but it could also cause such gametes to be preferred fusion partners by large gametes, because the resulting zygote would have relatively few parasitic elements (Hurst, 1990).

If the size of sperm and eggs are subject to selection, we should expect sperm size relative to the size of eggs to vary among species due to evolutionary change. In particular, we should expect that large sperm would be selectively advantageous in species where there is little competition for fertilization. In fact, several species of fruit flies have sperm that, at several millimeters, are even longer than the body of a male, with the total number of sperm produced by a male being only a few tens, similar to the number of eggs produced by the average female (Pitnick, Spicer, & Markow, 1995). These exceptions to the rule are as expected from the evolutionary scenario proposed by Parker et al. (1972).

PARENTAL INVESTMENT AND POTENTIAL RATES OF REPRODUCTION

Darwin (1871) found that males generally have a greater degree of weaponry, adornment, and other kinds of exaggerated secondary sexual characters than females, while females and young individuals often look the same. The evolutionary basis for these differences is intense male competition for access to females and their rare gametes, relative low male parental investment and higher female investment.

Females are generally limited in their reproduction by their ability to produce eggs, while males are limited by access to females. Bateman (1948), in a classical study of *Drosophila* fruit flies, showed that while male reproductive success increased linearly with the number of females mated, female success did not increase further after mating with one or two males. Thus, the factors that determine reproductive success of the two sexes differ significantly, and these limiting factors have dramatic consequences for the intensity of sexual selection in the two sexes.

Females generally provide greater parental investment than males, mainly because females produce few, large eggs, while males produce many, small sperm. In contrast, males generally invest more in displays and fights (Darwin, 1871). Trivers (1972) emphasized that sexual selection was stronger in males than in females because of the relatively greater contribution of females to rearing of offspring. He defined parental investment as the effort to raise the survival prospects of offspring at the expense of that of raising other offspring. The crux of this definition is that the residual reproductive value of parents (the survival and fecundity prospects of an individual during the rest of its life) is reduced, as defined by life history theory, with the sex making the least parental investment (usually males) competing the most for access to individuals of the sex making the most parental investment. Trivers' ideas helped explain phenomena such as mutual sexual selection in species with similar parental investment in the two sexes, and female competition over choosy males in species where males invest heavily in offspring production. Differences in parental investment by males and females may arise from sex differences in intensity of sexual selection and, hence, may be associated with sex differences in external phenotypes.

Parental investment theory is not, however, equipped to explain variations in male and female competition for mates in species with male uniparental care. Many fish, such as three-spined sticklebacks *Gasterosteus aculeatus*, have males that provide all care for their offspring, but such males have brighter color and display more intensely than females. A possible explanation for this sex difference is that males of such species generally are territorial, allowing them to provide paternal care (fanning eggs, removing addled eggs, protecting eggs) while in their territories. The sex that has the higher potential reproductive rate will be subject to more intense sexual selection, as evidenced by the bright coloration of males and the drab coloration of females. To explain this idea, male sticklebacks may be able to care for more clutches of eggs than females are able to produce, for example, because males can care for several broods at a time, thereby causing females to be a limiting resource. Consistent with this effect of potential reproductive rates, Clutton-Brock and Vincent (1991) showed for all cases of uniparental male care in fishes, frogs, and birds that competition was more intense in males in 13 of 14 species in which the observed male rate of reproduction exceeded that of females, while in all 14 species with more intense competition in females, observed female reproductive rates were greater than those of males. In species with more intense male competition, males are more brightly colored, while females of species with more intense female competition display the most extravagant colors. These differences among species also apply to spatial and temporal variation in sex roles within species. For example, fish embryos develop faster when seawater is warm than when it is cold. Therefore, males should be able to care for eggs faster at the end than at the beginning of the summer, changing the intensity of competition from mainly being due to female competition early during the season to male competition late during summer. In a study of marine gobies, there was more intense female competition for males early in the season, but more intense male competition later in the season, as predicted by the theory (Forsgren, Amundsen, Borg, & Bjelvenmark, 2004).

SEX DIFFERENCES IN RATE OF MUTATION AND THEIR CONSEQUENCES

Errors in DNA replication are the main source of point mutations (changes in a single "letter" of a DNA sequence). Mutations accumulate in the male germline at a higher rate than they do in the female germline due to a larger number of cell divisions during the production of sperm (spermatogenesis) than during the production of eggs (oogenesis). A greater male than female mutation rate has been recorded in numerous taxa such as plants, fish, birds, and mammals, including humans (Hurst & Ellegren, 1998). Sex-bias in mutations should reflect sex-bias in number of cell divisions. For example, in humans, female germ cells undergo 24 divisions in total, while male germ cells undergo 150 cell divisions by age 20 years and 600 by age 40 years (Hurst & Ellegren, 1998). Hence, we would expect the sex difference in mutation rates in humans to be roughly six (150 divided by 24 = 6.25), and that is actually the case (Makova & Li, 2002). Sex-bias in mutation rate is generally caused by the mutation rate being higher in males than in females, even in species with males having similar and females different sex chromosomes (Hurst & Ellegren, 1998). Hence, it is "maleness" rather than heterogamety (which sex has different sex chromosomes) that accounts for sex-bias in mutation.

Sex-bias in mutation rates is an important characteristic of sexually reproducing species, because it can generate genetic variation on which sexual selection can act. Sex-bias in mutation rates can evolve because life history can affect the relative rate of cell divisions in the two sexes. Sex-bias in mutation rates can be estimated from rates of sequence evolution in genes shared between sex chromosomes if sex-linked sequences have evolved independently since the cessation of recombination between sex chromosomes. Bartosch-Härlid, Berlin, Smith, Møller, and Ellegren (2003) analyzed such sex specific sequence evolution in 31 species of birds to test the prediction that intensity of sexual selection was related to sex-bias in mutation rates. Species with intense sperm competition (competition between the sperm of two or more males for fertilization of the eggs of a single clutch produced by one female) should have elevated sperm production and, hence, an increase in the number of male cell divisions over female cell divisions. Using the frequency of extrapair paternity (paternity by males other than the partner) in socially monogamous bird species as a measure of the intensity of sexual selection, Bartosch-Härlid et al. found a significant increase in male-biased mutation with extrapair paternity.

A major conundrum in the theory of sexual selection is how mate choice by females for males with exaggerated displays that reflect genetic fitness benefits can be maintained, when the fitness advantages of beneficial alleles are so large, making all such beneficial alleles go to fixation (all individuals having the same beneficial alleles). This is the so-called lek paradox questioning why females apparently choose partners for genetic benefits when no such benefits are to be had (see below). Sex-bias in mutation rates, and lineage differences in mutation rates, could potentially resolve this problem, if mutational input to genetic variation increased with increasing intensity of sexual selection. Indeed, a comparative study of germline mutation rates for minisatellites (particular repeated short sequences of DNA) in birds revealed that mutation rates increased in species with a higher frequency of extrapair paternity and, hence, more intense sexual selection (Møller & Cuervo, 2003). Therefore, genetic benefits from mate choice may be maintained or may even increase in lineages with intense sexual selection, because novel genetic variants are produced due to increased sex-bias in mutation rates. This mechanism will work as long as females eliminate most mutants (that by definition are likely to be inferior in one or more respects) every generation by choosing individuals without mutations or with rare beneficial mutations as mates. Females could potentially identify such males if mutations reduced the quality of male displays.

SEX-SPECIFIC TRANSMISSION OF ORGANELLES

Most living organisms have intracellular organelles such as mitochondria and chloroplasts with their own genomes. Such organelles play key roles in the normal functioning of cells, but their selfish genetic interests may be at conflict with those of the nucleus of the cell. While nuclear genes from both parents are required for normal functioning of a cell, that is not the case for organelles. If organelles of different parental origin meet, this would allow organelles to exchange genetic material and, hence, potentially increase their rate of evolution and their power in the genetic conflict between the nucleus and organelles (Cosmides & Tooby, 1981). If sperm do not have cytoplasm or organelles, the resulting zygote will suffer less from conflict between genomes of different origin than would a zygote produced by sperm with such extranuclear genetic material.

Typically, organelles such as mitochondria are inherited through the female line, and such unisexual inheritance of organelles is a defining feature of the two sexes. However, there is evidence of rare cases of mitochondrial inheritance through the male line in *Drosophila* and mice, usually with disastrous consequences for the organism concerned. Likewise, there is evidence of mitochondrial recombination, suggesting that mitochondria of different parental origin sometimes meet and exchange genetic material. These exceptions tend to support the general rule, showing that there is still selection for unisexual inheritance of organelles.

These four different mechanisms may each, or in combination, contribute to the maintenance of sex, all having arisen as a consequence of the initial evolution of sex followed by evolution of anisogamy.

SEXUAL SELECTION

Sexual selection is the process that promotes the evolution of characters that provide individuals with a competitive advantage in gaining mating success, mates with high fecundity, and ultimately, fertilization success (Darwin, 1871). Sexual selection differs from natural selection because the latter is the process involved in the evolution of traits that promote fecundity and survival. Charles Darwin was puzzled by the presence of a range of traits, most often in adult males, such as exuberant coloration, extravagant vocalizations and displays, exaggerated size, and adornments such as horns, tusks, and antlers. These traits seemed to have a deleterious effect on male survival prospects, raising the issue how they could have evolved and be maintained in the face of viability costs. The solution to this problem was that such traits might have evolved either through mate choice, usually by females, and/or through competition among individuals of the same sex, usually males, for access to and control of fertilization of individuals of the other sex. Typically, male traits related to the presence of weaponry, or sheer size, have evolved and are being maintained by male-male competition, while visual and vocal displays are involved in mate choice, although exceptions occur.

As an example, let us consider the blue peacock *Pavo cristatus*, a pheasant. This bird is almost the archetypical product of sexual selection. In males, the upper tail coverts are exaggerated to such a degree that these feathers are longer than the body. Males aggregate during spring at communal display grounds, so-called leks, raising their trains of feathers with eyespots, and shaking them while giving a display call. The dull-colored females arrive at the lek and inspect a number of males before choosing a single male for copulation, later leaving to lay her eggs elsewhere. The offspring may never encounter their father. Male mating success in the peacock increases linearly with the number of eyespots (Figure 4.2a; Petrie, Halliday, & Sanders, 1991). Other characters are also exaggerated in the peacock, such as their spurs, their coloration, and length of their feathers, and any of these traits could potentially account for male mating success. Therefore, it is crucial to manipulate male traits to determine which ones are affecting female choice. Removal of twenty eyespots from a group of males reduced their average mating success compared to that of a control group, showing a direct effect of eyespot number on mate choice (Figure 4.2b; Petrie & Halliday, 1994).

By definition, each offspring of a sexually reproducing species has a mother and a father, so average mating success of the two sexes must be identical. However, the variance in mating success between the sexes may differ to the extent that only a small share of individuals of one sex monopolizes most individuals of the other sex. It is this sex-difference in variation in mating success that

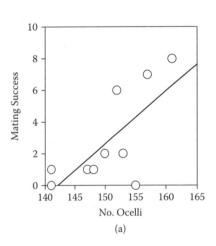

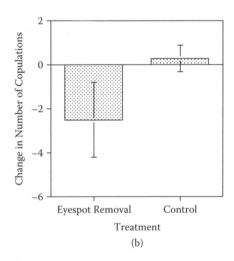

(a)   (b)

Figure 4.2 (a) Mating success of peacocks in relation to number of eyespots in their train. The line is the linear regression line. Adapted from Petrie et al. (1991). (b) Mating success of peacocks with twenty eyespots removed and a control group of males with their eyespots left intact. Values are means (SE). Adapted from Petrie and Halliday (1994).

fuels sexual selection: The greater the variance in mating success, the greater the intensity of sexual selection.

If males and females are similar in appearance and behavior, as is the case in many monogamous species, this may arise from the fact that natural selection is so strong that it has prevented the evolution of elaborate traits. That may be the case in species in which adults of both sexes resemble juveniles (that, by definition, are not reproducing) in phenotype. However, males and females of many species have elaborate coloration or other traits that appear exaggerated. If males and females provide similar amounts of parental investment, individuals of the two sexes should be subject to a similar intensity of sexual selection, with appearance of adults being similar. Such mutual sexual selection may be common in monogamous species, where males and females often have similar parental roles. Consistent with this idea, several experimental studies have shown evidence of mutual mate preferences in the two sexes, with both males and females preferring individuals as mates when they have exaggerated coloration or plumage (e.g., Jones & Hunter, 1993).

The intensity of sexual selection as reflected by the social mating system has been shown to predict exaggeration of male body size, evolution of weaponry and exaggerated coloration and other kinds of displays. For example, sexual size dimorphism in such diverse taxa as pinnipeds, ungulates and primates increase from monogamous species over multimale polygyny to single-male polygyny (Alexander, Hoogland, Howard, Noonan, & Sherman, 1979). Numerous studies of other groups of animals have shown similar patterns.

SEXUAL SIGNALS AND THEIR RELIABILITY

Whether females choose mates in order to obtain more resources, genes to enhance viability of their offspring, or genes for offspring ornamentation, females must glean this information from the ornaments and the displays of males. Hence, females must indirectly use the expression of signals to obtain the required information. The evolution of sexual signals as predictors of any feature of male quality has been the topic of intense theoretical debate and empirical research, because reliability of sexual signals is a prerequisite for their evolution.

The magnitude of costs of secondary sexual characters—and, hence, their degree of exaggeration—must be considered relative to the benefits in terms of mating success and the environment in which a given species lives. As long as the benefits are so large that they outweigh the costs, male survival rate may be reduced to the extent that males effectively become semelparous (have only one opportunity to reproduce during their lifetime). Extensive studies of survival prospects of males in relation to the expression of their sexual signals have shown that males with the largest traits on average survive the best (Jennions, Møller, & Petrie, 2001). This implies that such males, on average, must have been in better condition both before producing their secondary sexual characters, as revealed by their larger secondary sex traits, but also after, as shown by their greater survival prospects.

Secondary sexual characters generally have a high degree of heritability, with over 60% of the variance in their expression being accounted for by additive genetic variation (Pomiankowski & Møller, 1995). Thus, the size of sexual traits will reflect underlying genetic variation to some extent. Signaling of material and genetic benefits would require that male traits reflect these underlying benefits. A mechanism that can account for reliability of such signals is the handicap principle (Zahavi, 1975), according to which signals maintain reliability due to their costs, with individuals in poor condition suffering relatively greater costs. It is this latter condition that prevents males in poor condition from cheating by signaling at a higher level than their condition would allow (Figure 4.3a). Several models and empirical tests have provided evidence consistent with this mechanism. For example, manipulation of the length of the outermost tail feathers of the sexually size dimorphic barn swallow *Hirundo rustica* revealed that tail feather elongation reduced survival rate, while tail shortening improved survival (Figure 4.3b; Møller & de Lope, 1994). This demonstrates that natural tails in males are longer than the natural selection optimum. Furthermore, the viability costs of experimentally long and short tails depended on original tail length, with tail elongation being less costly for males with originally short rather than long tails (Figure 4.3c). In addition, tail shortening benefited males with originally short tails the most because such males enjoyed a greater boost to their survival than males with long tails due to the poor condition of such individuals. These three results are consistent with the predictions of the handicap principle.

A number of alternative mechanisms may maintain reliability of sexual signals (Getty, 2006). For example, sensory bias due to the way in which the sensory system works in other contexts such as foraging or predator avoidance may set the scene for the evolution of reliable signals (Garcia & Ramirez, 2005).

BENEFITS OF MATE CHOICE

Given the extreme directional mate preferences for males with larger and more elaborate traits expressed by females in species ranging from mites and insects to fish, anurans, and reptiles, as well as to birds and mammals, there must be very large benefits associated with such preferences. Alternatively, if the costs of the traits were small, strong preferences could also be maintained. Clearly, females would reproduce much more rapidly—and, hence, avoid the fitness costs of waiting to reproduce—if they just mated with the first male that they encountered. Two different types of benefit, which are not necessarily mutually exclusive, may account for these benefits of mate choice: (a) material benefits and (b) genetic benefits (the latter of which may stem from good genes or from compatible genes).

Material benefits are the most obvious basis for mate choice and sexual selection because choosy females gain such benefits directly from choice of an attractive male, and their presence is not based on specific requirements concerning maintenance of genetic variation. If male display or coloration reflects the magnitude of one or more of these kinds of benefits, a directional female preference for such a male character could be perpetually maintained, as long as males with exaggerated traits on average had access to more of the given resource. Material benefits come in many different forms, such as resources provided by males (territory, protection, nuptial gifts), male parental care, sperm quality, and many others. Møller and Jennions (2001) reviewed over 160 studies of direct benefits. In 26 studies of fertility (ability to fertilize eggs) in relation to expression of male sexually selected traits, the male trait on average explained 6.3% of the variation in fertility. In contrast, in 76 studies of female fecundity (production of eggs) in relation to expression of male sexually selected traits, the male trait on average explained 2.3% of the variation in fecundity, which is an exceeding small amount. Likewise, female preference for male sexually selected traits only explained 1.3% of variation in male care for offspring in 39 studies of birds, an amount that was not significantly different from zero. Finally, 23.6% of hatching success of eggs in species with male guarding of offspring was explained by the expression of male sexually selected traits in 26 studies of ectotherms. Thus, females may obtain direct material benefits in terms of fertility in a wide range of taxa and hatching success of eggs in male guarding ectotherms, while it seems unlikely that female fecundity and male parental care related to the expression of male sexually selected traits can sustain female mate preferences. In those taxa, other benefits have to be invoked.

Genetic benefits of female mate preferences may arise from the effects of "good" genes, such as parasite resistance genes (Hamilton & Zuk, 1982) or general viability genes (Andersson, 1994), genes for attractiveness of sons (the self-reinforcing process of Fisher, 1930, and the sexy son hypothesis of Weatherhead & Robertson, 1979), or compatible genes that result in offspring with an optimal mix of maternal and paternal genes. Good genes mechanisms have been demonstrated several times, using correlational data or breeding experiments. Møller and Alatalo (1999) reviewed 22 studies of offspring viability in relation to the expression of male secondary sexual characters.

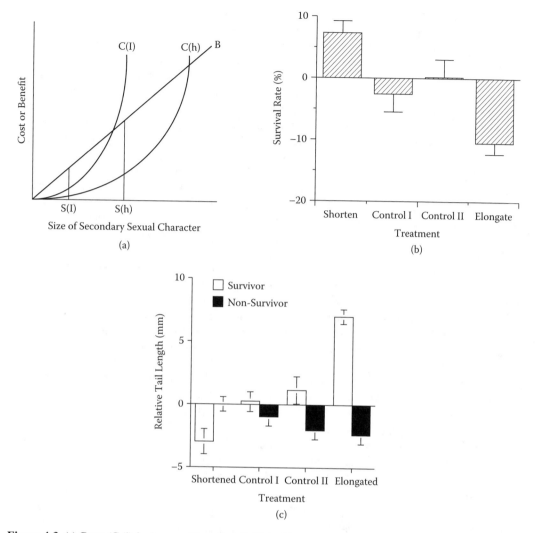

Figure 4.3 (a) Costs (C (l) for low-quality males, C (h) for high-quality males), benefits (B) and optimal levels of sexual signaling (the difference between the benefit and the cost curves) in a hypothetical animal with two categories of males. Males of low quality have a smaller optimal size of their sexual signal (S(l)) than males of high quality (S9(h)) because the rate of increase of the cost function is greater for low than for high-quality males. (b) Annual survival rate (%) of adult male barn swallows that had their outermost tail feathers shortened, elongated, cut and glued (control I), or just captured and handled (control II). Average survival is set to zero. Values are means (SE) for four different experiments. (c) Relative tail length (mm) of male barn swallow survivors and nonsurvivors during the year following the manipulation and, hence, after the annual molt in relation to experimental tail manipulation. Survivors with elongated tails had much longer pretreatment tails than nonsurvivors, whereas survivors with shortened tails had much shorter pre-treatment tails than nonsurvivors. Relative tail length (mm) was set to zero for the average male. Values are means (SE) for four different experiments. (b) and (c) adapted from Møller and de Lope (1994).

The overall effect accounted for 1.5% of the variance in offspring viability, with considerable variation among species, and stronger viability effects in species with greater skew in mating success among males (hence, the effects of good genes seemed to be greater in species with more intense sexual selection).

Parasite-mediated sexual selection with male secondary sexual characters reliably reflecting the level of infection by debilitating parasites may account for some of this variation in viability. Parasites are significant agents of natural selection, imposing considerable mortality on their hosts. In addition, parasites can maintain continuous variation in genetically based resistance because selection for host resistance subsequently selects for genetically based parasite virulence (reduction in fitness of hosts due to the presence or the actions of parasites; Hamilton & Zuk, 1982). A large number of studies have shown that males with the most elaborate secondary sexual characters generally have fewer parasites than the average male (Møller, Christe, & Lux, 1999). Furthermore, such males have considerably stronger immune responses than the average male, implying that females may obtain paternal resistance genes for their offspring through mate choice (Møller et al., 1999).

The lek paradox arises from the empirical observation that females on leks (communal displays by males) often make stringent choices of a particular male as a sire, with no obvious benefits from their mate choice other than genetic benefits, causing extreme skew in male mating success, that eventually should result in all beneficial alleles having gone to fixation (Borgia, 1979). In such a situation, females would benefit from random mating, but that is not what females do. They prefer one or a few males as sires. How can this paradox be explained? This is a question that goes way beyond leks, pertaining to the maintenance of female preferences for genetic benefits when such variation eventually should disappear because all individuals have the beneficial genes. Several possibilities have been proposed. First, Pomiankowski and Møller (1995) noted that additive genetic variation was greater for secondary sexual characters than for ordinary characters, and for life history traits closely associated with fitness, while there was no difference in the amount of environmental and nonadditive genetic variance. Therefore, they suggested that intense directional selection that is greater than linear selects for greater phenotypic variation. Such selection will favor genetic modifiers that increase the number of genes and the average contribution of a locus to phenotypic variance in sexual traits and in viability. Second, Rowe and Houle (1996) noted that most secondary sexual characters are condition-dependent, implying that many different physiological pathways—and, hence, many different genes—contribute to their expression. Therefore, they suggested that when a trait becomes the target of sexual selection, an increasing number of genes will affect its expression, with more genes and interactions among such genes maintaining genetic variation in the trait. Third, Møller and Cuervo (2003) noted that sex-bias in mutation rates will be affected by sperm competition through the effects of extra sperm production on the number of cell divisions. Therefore, an increase in the intensity of competition for fertilizations actually will increase mutational input and, hence, the amount of additive genetic variation. Indeed, the amount of genetic variation was greater in bird species with a higher frequency of extrapair paternity, as predicted (Petrie, Doums, & Møller, 1998). In addition, germline mutation rates increased with frequency of extrapair paternity in birds (Møller & Cuervo, 2003). Any of these three mechanisms—either alone or in combination with one or both of the others—could potentially solve the lek paradox.

Genetic compatibility occurs when an individual benefits from having two (or more) different alleles rather than a single allele. If females choose mates with a different genetic composition for specific genes, offspring resulting from such mate choice will have two different alleles per locus and, therefore, will enjoy a selective advantage by being able to produce a more diverse subset of proteins. An example of this mechanism is the major histocompatibility complex (MHC), a complex of genes that accounts for parasite resistance in vertebrates due to production of antibodies and other mechanisms. An individual with two different alleles at a locus of this genetic complex will be able to produce a more diverse array of antibodies than an individual with two copies of the same allele is able to do. The presence of numerous loci for the MHC, each with two alleles, allows for the possibility of a high degree of genetic diversity. In fact, female three-spined sticklebacks prefer males with a large number of MHC alleles, thereby being able to produce offspring that are genetically diverse. However, female sticklebacks do not prefer males with dissimilar alleles, suggesting that mate choice in this species is not caused by genetic compatibility (Reusch, Häberli,

Aeschlimann, & Milinski, 2001). In contrast, women prefer the smell of T-shirts worn by men with dissimilar MHC-genotypes (Wedekind, Seebeck, Bettens, & Paepke, 1995). There is no current overview of the relative importance of genetic compatibility for sexual selection, although the mechanism is potentially important.

Discussions about the origins and the maintenance of intense directional sexual selection boil down to discussions about the relative importance of material and genetic benefits. As we have seen, different species differ in the importance of material and genetic benefits of mate choice. Interestingly, while material benefits are substantial in some groups of animals, they seem to be negligible in others. For example, direct benefits of male parental care only account for 1.3% of the variance in expression of male secondary sexual characters, while male traits accounted for 1.5% of variation in offspring viability. Why are direct benefits important in some species and indirect genetic benefits in others? In a comparative study of birds, Møller and Thornhill (1998) showed that in species in which the most elaborately adorned males provided most paternal care, extrapair paternity was absent or rare, while species in which the most ornamented males provided least paternal care had high levels of extrapair paternity. If extrapair paternity arises from socially monogamous females copulating with males other than their social mates in order to obtain genetic benefits for their offspring (because there are few potential direct benefits arising from sperm alone), then we would expect such extrapair copulations to be particularly common in species in which the most adorned males spend most reproductive effort on mating and the least on parental investment, as actually observed.

SEXUAL CONFLICT

Once sex and anisogamy (differences in size of gametes produced by the two sexes) had arisen, sexual conflict within and between the sexes was a ubiquitous outcome. Due to the production of different numbers and sizes of gametes by the two sexes, males generally compete intensely for fertilization of many or more fecund females. In contrast, because females produce few large gametes and invest more in reproduction, they maximize their reproductive success by showing greater care in their choice of sexual partners (Parker, 1979).

Sexual conflict can occur over mating frequency, female remating behavior, fertilization, relative parental effort by the two sexes, female reproductive rate, and sex ratio (Arnqvist & Rowe, 2005).

An example of sexual conflict pertains to different interests in parental care provided by males and females. Given that parental investment is costly, it generally pays to mate with a partner that works harder, but because such behavior is costly, there will be evolution of resistance to manipulation by individuals of one sex of individuals of the other. Offspring of the two sexes may also experience a conflict through genomic imprinting and its effects on parental care. An allele may be expressed differently depending on the parental origin of the allele (so-called genomic imprinting), because it is not in the genetic interest of alleles from mothers in an offspring generally to overexploit maternal resources and diminish the future reproductive success of the mother. In contrast, an allele with a paternal origin may benefit from demanding excessive amounts of parental care from the mother, especially when certainty of paternity is low. Numerous examples of physiological interactions between mothers and embryos in mice and humans are consistent with expectations from such conflict due to excessive demands by offspring caused by alleles of paternal origin and resistance to such exploitation provided by alleles of maternal origin (Haig, 1993).

In the following three sections, we will see how sexual conflict has affected competition for fertilization (sperm competition), parental investment, and sex ratio of progeny.

SPERM COMPETITION

Sperm competition arises from competition among gametes of different males over fertilization of the eggs of a single clutch of a female (Parker, 1970). Fertilization will ultimately determine fitness of an individual; that is, mating success does not matter unless it results in fertilization. Females may allow copulations by more than a single male during a single reproductive event, causing uncertainty about paternity. Cryptic mate choice of sperm within the body of a female may allow females extraordinary control over fertilization, leading to sexual conflict over fertilization (Thornhill, 1983).

Sperm competition has proven to be taxonomically widespread, with numerous studies showing evidence of male-male competition over fertilization and multiple or extrapair paternity. Not surprisingly, a number of different mechanisms have evolved as a consequence of sexual conflict over fertilization, with the evolutionary dynamics arising from conflicts between a male partner, other males, and a female (Birkhead & Møller, 1992, 1998). First, production of many, small sperm is a defining feature of anisogamy, leading to male-male competition over fertilization. Not surprisingly, males have been selected to produce even more and smaller sperm in such situations, with males investing differentially in mating competition rather than parental investment when certainty of paternity is low. Second, sperm precedence describes the phenomena by which probability of paternity is related to copulation order. First or last male mating advantages may evolve through female sperm storage, female patterns of copulation, or male attempts to block further copulations by or enforce additional copulations on a female. Third, seminal fluid and other ejaculate components may provide males with a mating advantage during sperm competition, but such components may also evolve under the influence of selection from females, because ejaculate components may damage females as a way of reducing propensity for female remating. Fourth, females of species with internal fertilization release vast numbers of phagocytes immediately following copulation, with such white blood cells eliminating a large fraction of all sperm, potentially producing a conflict between the female and the male that produced the sperm. Finally, male mate guarding is a widespread behavioral mechanism that ensures paternity by preventing other males from gaining access to a female.

The consequences of sperm competition for animal behavior are numerous (Birkhead & Møller, 1992, 1998). Lower certainty of paternity may render males more likely to engage in mating effort and less likely to provide parental effort (Low, 1978). Even when individuals of the two sexes invest similarly in gametes, by definition, males will compete much more intensely for the much rarer eggs. This eventually leads to selection for optimal timing and allocation of sperm, but also for sperm that accurately locate and penetrate eggs. Sperm competition will have consequences for certainty of paternity, thereby reducing the fitness gains from paternal care (Queller, 1997). Consistently, males of bird species with elaborate coloration provide less parental care than males of species with less sexual dichromatism, and this effect is mediated by sperm competition as revealed by males of species with high levels of extrapair paternity, providing little or no costly food provisioning (Møller & Cuervo, 2000). In addition, environmental conditions that only allow successful reproduction in the presence of both a male and a female may constrain the intensity of sperm competition, because males of such species are indispensable for any reproductive success, thus biasing males against mating effort and toward parental effort (Møller, 2000).

The second mechanism associated with reduced male parental care in species with intense sperm competition stems from the disproportionately large mating success of particular males in such species (Queller, 1997). Such attractive males have a greater reproductive rate than the average female, making it more beneficial for attractive males to invest their reproductive effort in mating rather than parental effort. Hence, it is anisogamy that gives rise to sperm competition, thereby producing the initial conditions for an increase in the intensity of sexual selection, and it is sexual selection (differential mating success of attractive males) that subsequently results in such males searching for additional mates rather than providing paternal care.

DIFFERENTIAL PARENTAL INVESTMENT

Sexual conflict arises from the relative investment by the two sexes in reproduction. This is implicit in the evolution of anisogamy, but also later on in parental investment. In species with biparental care, how much should a female invest in its offspring depending on the phenotype of its partner, and how much should males and females invest relative to the investment of individuals of the other sex? *Differential parental investment* refers to investment by a female in reproduction being dependent on the phenotype of the partner. A classical example of this form of investment is the response of female zebra finches *Taeniopygia guttata* (a socially monogamous bird species with a red beak) to the phenotype of the male. Females prefer males with red coloration, for example, in the form of red plastic leg bands. If a female has a mate with red leg bands, she will lay more eggs, produce more broods, and provide a relatively greater share of parental care than when exactly the same female is mated to the same male wearing green leg bands (Burley, 1986). Two different mechanisms account for differential parental investment. First, females of superior condition will have differential access to attractive males, with such males mating earlier and, hence, enjoying a reproductive advantage due to their early start of reproduction (e.g., Fisher, 1930; Møller, 1988). Second, females will put more effort into reproduction when mated to an attractive male (i.e., differential parental investment; Burley, 1986). Numerous studies have shown effects of differential parental investment, and this mechanism may even account for elevated reproductive success of preferred males in species with uniparental care such as lekking species.

Interestingly, it is the "willingness" of females to carry the extra burden of providing the parental care that their mates are "unwilling" to provide that is the basis for differential parental investment. Females gain from copulating with attractive males through the effects of good genes, even in the presence of direct fitness costs for females of providing parental care. Attractive males gain from searching for additional females, this mate search being facilitated by differential parental investment by females.

SEX RATIO AND SEX RATIO MANIPULATION

The evolution of sex also affects the optimal level of investment in offspring of the two sexes. Fisher (1930) realized that the optimal sex ratio depends on the frequency of the two sexes in the population, with frequency-dependent selection always favoring production of offspring of the less common sex. Therefore, females should always produce a sex ratio among their offspring that favors the less common sex in the population. These arguments only apply to the special case where sons and daughters are equally costly to produce. However, sons are often more costly to produce than daughters, because sons are larger and, hence, require more resources. Therefore, Fisher's sex ratio theory requires that parents are paid back for their parental investment by equal investment in sons and daughters, and this reduces to equally as many sons and daughters when these are equally costly to produce. Parents cannot improve the return on investment when investment into sons and daughters is equal, causing this investment to be the evolutionary equilibrium (Charnov, 1982).

Given the fact that sons and daughters often require different parental investment, this should also cause the sex ratio of offspring produced by females to depend on the mothers' condition. The reason is that the return on investment in a son will be greater if this son is in prime condition, something that is facilitated by parental investment. Because the returns from a son produced by a mother in poor condition will be small, such mothers would be expected to produce more daughters than mothers in prime condition, who would be expected to produce more sons (Trivers & Willard,

1973). This theory was developed to account for sex ratio variation among mammals with a single offspring, but a similar mechanism can account for sex ratio variation in relation to other factors, such as parental condition of both the father and the mother, local ecological conditions such as size of hosts in parasitoids, and the presence of helpers in cooperatively breeding birds and mammals (e.g., Charnov, 1982; Trivers, 1985).

There are numerous studies of sex ratio variation, and although it superficially seems obvious how to tally the number of sons and daughters, this is often not the case. Arguments about adaptive variation in sex ratio only apply to the primary sex ratio at conception, while the secondary sex ratio (the sex ratio at birth) and the tertiary sex ratio (the sex ratio among adults) are irrelevant in this context. Given that it is exceedingly difficult to estimate primary sex ratios at the moment of fertilization due to elimination of embryos at early stages of development, many empirical studies of sex ratio variation may be biased. The literature on sex ratio adjustment suggests that there is evidence consistent with theory, explaining 4–15% of variation in sex ratio adjustment both in insects and birds (West & Sheldon, 2002). However, a recent review of all bird studies showed no deviation in sex ratio from the null expectation of no effect (Ewen, Cassey, & Möller, 2004), implying that current knowledge may be based on biased information.

The mechanisms underlying sex ratio manipulation by parents are diverse, varying greatly among taxa (Charnov, 1982). First, chromosomal sex determination is widespread in birds and mammals, with the potential for an additional hormonal basis of sex allocation due to androgens and corticosterone having been hypothesized. Second, environmental sex determination in reptiles depends on temperature at the start of embryonic development. Third, bacteria of the genus *Wolbachia* cause sex ratio distortion in many invertebrates (Skinner, 1982). Finally, in haplo-diploid organisms males develop from unfertilized eggs, while females derive from fertilized eggs, providing the egg-laying female with almost complete control over the sex ratio.

HUMANS AS A SEXUALLY SELECTED SPECIES

Humans are primates with a tendency for monogamy, a rare mating system in mammals, but a common one in birds. Therefore, humans share many more similarities with birds than they do with mammals. Sexual selection permeates all aspects of the life of sexually reproducing species, and the following contains a brief summary of the literature on humans as a sexually selected species. Dixon (1998) and Low (2000) provide a general overview of this theme.

Men generally have much greater variance in mating success than women have, and the same applies to fertilizations (Trivers, 1985). The man with the largest number of children, Sultan Moulay Ismael of Morocco, had 888 children, while the woman with most children "only" had 69 in 27 pregnancies.

Human females from different cultures generally have strong preferences for males who possess resources, while males prefer female beauty (Buss, 1989), particularly in parts of the world where parasite-mediated mortality is frequent (Gangestad & Buss, 1993). Women are inclined to engage in extrapair matings with men who possess different (attractive) characteristics from those possessed by their stable partners (e.g., Gangestad, Thornhill, & Garver, 2002).

Human males are larger than females, particularly in adulthood, and such size dimorphism has evolved as a consequence of male-male competition. Sexual size dimorphism is greater in more polygynous human cultures, as expected from their more intense sexual selection (Alexander et al., 1979). Intense competition among men is the basis of sex differences in risk taking, with men taking much greater risks during puberty and the following decade (Wilson, Daly, & Gordon, 1998). This leads to sex differences in longevity, with men on average living for shorter periods of time than women live (Trivers, 1985). Recent changes in the competitive environment in Russia and Eastern Europe are associated with a dramatic reduction in longevity, especially among men, as expected from sexual selection theory.

Men and women show a number of physiological differences relating to differences in physical strength and greater competition among men. These differences are most pronounced during early adulthood. For example, men have a dramatic peak in circulating testosterone levels during late teens and early twenties, being closely associated with pronounced male excess mortality among these age classes (Daly & Wilson, 1983).

Many anatomical and physiological features of men and women have recently been interpreted from a sexual selection perspective (Baker & Bellis, 1995). For example, sperm production and sperm allocation in humans appear to be adaptations to an environment of sperm competition. Likewise, male and female reproductive tracts show features consistent with expectations based on sperm competition theory.

A unique feature of humans is the enlarged brain, and sexual size dimorphism in brain size. Brain size evolution in humans has been attributed to sexual selection, with the human brain being the anatomical basis for an exaggerated mental peacock's tail (Miller, 2000). Recent comparative studies of birds have shown that brains are relatively larger in females in species with a high frequency of extrapair paternity (Garamszegi, Eens, Erritzøe, & Møller, 2005), suggesting a role for sexual selection in evolution of sexually size dimorphic brains.

Humans show great variation in sex ratio related to maternal body condition, paternal phenotype, and environmental factors such as food abundance (Trivers, 1985). Human parental investment is biased toward mothers, with evidence for differential parental investment by women mated to attractive men. Uncertainty of paternity is associated with reduced male parental investment, increased risk of child abuse and death, and increased risk of divorce.

SUMMARY

Sex—the production of genetic diversity caused by mixing and exchange of genetic material by two individuals with different genomes—may have evolved due to the advantages of coping with a heterogeneous environment, including a biotic environment that imposes continuous natural selection due to parasitism. Once sex had evolved, disruptive selection on gamete size, and the advantage of producing a large zygote, resulted in the evolution of anisogamy, the production of few, large gametes by individuals of one sex and of many, small gametes by the other. Few, large gametes caused intense competition for fertilization in males, resulting in sperm competition, but also setting the stage for sex differences in the intensity of sexual selection and, hence, sex differences in parental investment.

Males and females differ in size of gametes, parental investment, potential rates of reproduction, mutation rates, and transmission of organelles, all features having evolved as a consequence of the evolution of sex and anisogamy.

Sexual selection—and its two component processes, (a) sexual competition and (b) mate choice—evolved as a consequence of anisogamy. Sexual signals may provide reliable information about the state of the signaler, allowing individuals of the choosy sex, usually females, to gain fitness advantages from their mate choice. Such advantages may be based on direct material benefits, or indirect genetic benefits in terms of viability of offspring, attractiveness of sons, or compatible genes that enhance the viability of offspring.

Sexual conflict is at the base of all male-female interactions, because male and female genetic interests diverged ever since the evolution of aniogamy. Sperm competition is an important mechanism of sexual selection arising from competition over fertilization of eggs, and a whole range of behavioral, physiological, and anatomical mechanisms have evolved as a consequence of evolutionary conflicts between male partners, other males and females. Sex ratio of progeny is a specific area of sexual conflict, with the optimal sex ratio for parents of the two sexes depending on the return on investment from specific sex ratios for parents of the two sexes.

Humans are just like all other vertebrate sexual organisms, with all the resultant consequences for conflicts between and within the sexes over mating and fertilization. Not surprisingly, patterns of sexual behavior, physiology, and anatomy resemble those of other animals with a mating system biased from polygyny toward monogamy, mainly birds rather than mammals.

REFERENCES

Agrawal, A. F. (2001). Sexual selection and the maintenance of sex. *Nature, 411,* 692–695.

Alexander, R. D., Hoogland, J. D., Howard, R. D., Noonan, K. M., & Sherman, P. W. (1979). Sexual dimorphism and breeding systems in pinnipeds, ungulates, primates, and humans. In N. A. Chagnon & W. Irons (Eds.), *Evolutionary biology and human social behavior: An anthropological perspective* (pp. 402–435). North Scituate, MA: Duxbury Press.

Andersson, M. (1994). *Sexual selection.* Princeton, NJ: Princeton University Press.

Arnqvist, G., & Rowe, L. (2005). *Sexual conflict.* Princeton, NJ: Princeton University Press.

Baker, R. R., & Bellis, M. A. (1995). *Sperm competition: Copulation, masturbation, and infidelity.* London: Chapman and Hall.

Bartosch-Härlid, A., Berlin, S., Smith, N. G. C., Møller, A. P., & Ellegren, H. (2003). Life history and the male mutation bias. *Evolution, 57,* 2398–2406.

Bateman, A. J. (1948). Intra-sexual selection in *Drosophila. Heredity,* 2, 349–368.

Bell, G. (1982). *The masterpiece of nature: The evolution and genetics of sexuality.* San Francisco: University of California Press.

Birkhead, T. R., & Møller, A. P. (1992). *Sperm competition in birds: Evolutionary causes and consequences.* London: Academic Press.

Birkhead, T. R., & Møller, A. P. (Ed.). (1998). *Sperm competition and sexual selection.* London: Academic Press.

Borgia, G. (1979). Sexual selection and the evolution of mating systems. In M. S. Blum & N. A. Blum (Eds.), *Sexual selection and reproductive competition in insects* (pp. 19–80). New York: Academic Press.

Burley, N. (1986). Sexual selection for aesthetic traits in species with biparental care. *American Naturalist, 127,* 415–445.

Buss, D. M. (1989). Sex differences in human mate preferences: Evolutionary hypotheses tested in 37 cultures. *Behavioral and Brain Sciences,* 12, 1–49.

Charnov, E. L. (1982). *The theory of sex allocation.* Princeton, NJ: Princeton University Press.

Clutton-Brock, T. H., & Vincent, A. C. J. (1991). Sexual selection and the potential reproductive rates of males and females. *Nature, 351,* 58–60.

Cosmides, L. M., & Tooby, J. (1981). Cytoplasmic inheritance and intragenomic conflict. *Journal of Theoretical Biology, 89,* 83–129.

Daly, M., & Wilson, M. (1983). *Sex, evolution, and behavior.* Boston: Willard Grant.

Darwin, C. (1871). *The descent of man, and selection in relation to sex.* London: John Murray.

Dixon, A. F. (1998). *Primate sexuality.* San Diego: Oxford University Press.

Ewen, J., Cassey, P., & Møller, A. P. (2004). Facultative primary sex ratio variation: A lack of evidence in birds? *Proceedings of the Royal Society of London B, 271,* 1277–1282.

Fisher, R. A. (1930). *The genetical theory of natural selection.* Oxford, U.K.: Clarendon.

Forsgren, E., Amundsen, T., Borg, Å. A., & Bjelvenmark, J. (2004). Unusually dynamics sex roles in a fish. *Nature, 429,* 551–554.

Gangestad, S. W., & Buss, D. M. (1993). Pathogen prevalence and human mate preference. *Ethology and Sociobiology, 14,* 89–96.

Gangestad, S. W., Thornhill, R., & Garver, C. E. (2002). Changes in women's sexual interests and their partners' mate-retention tactics across the menstrual cycle: Evidence for shifting conflicts of interest. *Proceedings of the Royal Society of London B, 269,* 975–982.

Garamszegi, L. Z., Eens, M., Erritzøe, J., & Møller, A. P. (2005). Sperm competition and sexually size dimorphic brains in birds. *Proceedings of the Royal Society of London B, 272,* 159–166.

Garcia, C. M., & Ramirez, E. (2005). Evidence that sensory traps can evolve into honest signals. *Nature, 434,* 501–505.

Getty, T. (2006). Sexually selected signals are not sports handicaps. *Trends in Ecology and Evolution, 21,* 83–88.

Haig, D. (1993). Genetic conflicts in human pregnancy. *Quarterly Review of Biology, 68,* 495–532.

Hamilton, W. D., Axelrod, R., & Tanese, R. (1990). Sexual reproduction as an adaptation to resist parasites (a review). *Proceedings of the National Academy of Science USA, 87,* 3566–3573.

Hamilton, W. D., & Zuk, M. (1982). Heritable true fitness and bright birds: A role for parasites? *Science, 218,* 384–387.

Hurst, L. D. (1990). Parasite diversity and the evolution of diploidy, multicellularity and anisogamy. *Journal of Theoretical Biology, 144,* 429–443.

Hurst, L. D., & Ellegren, H. (1998). Sex biases in the mutation rates. *Trends in Genetics, 14,* 446–452.

Hurst, L. D., & Hamilton, W. D. (1992). Cytoplasmic fusion and the nature of sexes. *Proceedings of the Royal Society of London B, 247,* 189–194.

Jennions, M. D., Møller, A. P., & Petrie, M. (2001). Sexually selected traits and adult survival: A meta-analysis of the phenotypic relationship. *Quarterly Review of Biology, 76,* 3–36.

Jones, I. L., & Hunter, F. M. (1993). Mutual sexual selection in a monogamous seabird. *Nature, 362,* 238–239.

Knowlton, N. (1974). A note on the evolution of gamete dimorphism. *Journal of Theoretical Biology, 46,* 283–285.

Kondrashov, A. S. (1988). Deleterious mutations and the evolution of sexual reproduction. *Nature, 336,* 435–440.

Kondrashov, A. S. (1993). Classification of hypotheses on the advantage of amphimixis. *Journal of Heredity, 84,* 372–387.

Lively, C. M. (1987). Evidence of a New Zealand snail for the maintenance of sex by parasitism. *Nature, 328,* 519–521.

Low, B. S. (1978). Environmental uncertainty and the parental strategies of marsupials and placentals. *American Naturalist, 112,* 197–213.

Low, B. S. (2000). *Why sex matters.* Princeton, NJ: Princeton University Press.

Makova, K. D., & Li, W. H. (2002). Strong male-driven evolution of DNA sequences in humans and apes. *Nature, 416,* 624–626.

Miller, G. (2000). *The mating mind.* New York: Doubleday.

Møller, A. P. (1988). Female choice selects for male sexual tail ornaments in the monogamous swallow. *Nature, 322,* 640–642.

Møller, A. P. (2000). Male parental care, female reproductive success and extra-pair paternity. *Behavioral Ecology, 11,* 161–168.

Møller, A. P., & Alatalo, R. V. (1999). Good genes effects in sexual selection. *Proceedings of the Royal Society of London B, 266,* 85–91.

Møller, A. P., Christe, P., & Lux, E. (1999). Parasite-mediated sexual selection: Effects of parasites and host immune function. *Quarterly Review of Biology, 74,* 3–20.

Møller, A. P., & Cuervo, J. J. (2000). The evolution of paternity and paternal care. *Behavioral Ecology, 11,* 472–485.

Møller, A. P., & Cuervo, J. J. (2003). Sexual selection, germline mutation rate and sperm competition. *BMC Evolutionary Biology, 3*(6), 1–11.

Møller, A. P., & de Lope, F. (1994). Differential costs of a secondary sexual character: An experimental test of the handicap principle. *Evolution, 48,* 1676–1683.

Møller, A. P., & Jennions, M. D. (2001). How important are direct fitness benefits of sexual selection? *Naturwissenschaften, 88,* 401–415.

Møller, A. P., & Thornhill, R. (1998) Male parental care, differential parental investment by females, and sexual selection. *Animal Behaviour, 55,* 1507–1515.

Muller, H. J. (1964). The relation of recombination to mutational advance. *Mutation Research, 1,* 2–9.

Parker, G. A. (1970). Sperm competition and its evolutionary consequences in the insects. *Biological Reviews, 45,* 525–567.

Parker, G. A. (1979). Sexual selection and sexual conflict. In M. S. Blum & N. A. Blum (Ed.), *Sexual selection and reproductive competition in insects* (pp. 123–166). New York: Academic Press.

Parker, G. A., Baker, R. R., & Smith, V. G. F. (1972). The origin and evolution of gamete dimorphism and the male-female phenomenon. *Journal of Theoretical Biology, 36,* 529–533.

Petrie, M., Doums, C., & Møller, A. P. (1998). The degree of extra-pair paternity increases with genetic variability. *Proceedings of the National Academy of Science of the USA, 95*, 9390–9395.

Petrie, M., & Halliday, T. (1994). Experimental and natural changes in the peacock's train can affect mating success. *Behavioral Ecology and Sociobiology, 35*, 213–217.

Petrie, M., Halliday, T., & Sanders, C. (1991). Peahens prefer peacocks with elaborate trains. *Animal Behaviour, 41*, 323–331.

Pitnick, S., Spicer, G. S., & Markow, T. A. (1995). How long is a giant sperm? *Nature, 375*, 109.

Pomiankowski, A., & Møller, A. P. (1995). A resolution of the lek paradox. *Proceedings of the Royal Society of London B, 260*, 21–29.

Queller, D. C. (1997). Why do females care more than males? *Proceedings of the Royal Society of London B, 264*, 1555–1557.

Reusch, T. B. H., Häberli, M. A., Aeschlimann, P. B., & Milinski, M. (2001). Female sticklebacks count alleles in a strategy of sexual selection explaining MHC polymorphism. *Nature, 414*, 300–302.

Rowe, L., & Houle, D. (1996). The lek paradox and the capture of genetic variance by condition dependent traits. *Proceedings of the Royal Society of London B, 263*, 1415–1421.

Siller, S. (2001). Sexual selection and the maintenance of sex. *Nature, 411*, 689–692.

Skinner, S. W. (1982). Maternally inherited sex ratio in the parasitoid wasp *Nasonia vitripennis. Science, 215*, 1133–1134.

Thornhill, R. (1983). Cryptic female choice and its implications in the scorpionfly *Harpobittacus nigriceps. American Naturalist, 122*, 765–788.

Trivers, R. L. (1972). Parental investment and sexual selection. In B. Campbell (Ed.), *Sexual selection and the descent of man, 1871–1971* (pp. 136–179). Chicago: Aldine.

Trivers, R. L. (1985). *Social evolution.* Menlo Park, CA: Benjamin/Cummings.

Trivers, R. L., & Willard, D. E. (1973). Natural selection of parental ability to vary the sex ratio of offspring. *Science, 179*, 90–92.

Weatherhead, P. J., & Robertson, R. J. (1979). Offspring quality and the polygyny threshold: "The sexy son hypothesis." *American Naturalist, 113*, 201–208.

Wedekind, C., Seebeck, T., Bettens, F., & Paepke, A. J. (1995). MHC-dependent mate preferences in humans. *Proceedings of the Royal Society of London B, 260*, 245–249.

West, S. A., & Sheldon, B. C. (2002). Constraints in the evolution of sex ratio adjustment. *Science, 295*, 1685–1688.

Williams, G. C. (1975). *Sex and evolution.* Princeton, NJ: Princeton University Press.

Wilson, M., Daly, M., & Gordon, S. (1998). The evolved psychological apparatus of human decision-making is one source of environmental problems. In T. Caro (Ed.), *Behavioral ecology and conservation biology* (pp. 501–523). Oxford, U.K.: Oxford University Press.

Zahavi, A. (1975). Mate selection—A selection for a handicap. *Journal of Theoretical Biology, 53*, 205–214.

5

Kinship and Social Behavior

STUART A. WEST, ANDY GARDNER, AND ASHLEIGH S. GRIFFIN

Hamilton's theory of kin selection (inclusive fitness) provides a framework for understanding social interactions between relatives. It suggests that individuals should show greater selfish restraint, less aggression and greater altruism toward closer relatives. Kin selection theory predicts when conflicts as well as cooperation should occur. In this chapter, we summarize the basic principles of kin selection and how they can be applied to specific areas. We provide a very general discussion, using the best examples available, which are often from nonhuman animals.

SOCIAL BEHAVIORS

A behavior is social if it has consequences for both the actor and another individual (recipient). These can be categorized according to the consequences they entail for the actor and recipient (Hamilton, 1964, 1970, 1971; West, Griffin, & Gardner, 2007; Table 5.1). A behavior increasing the direct fitness of the actor is mutually beneficial if the recipient also benefits, and selfish if the recipient suffers a loss. A behavior that reduces the fitness of the actor is altruistic if the recipient benefits, and spiteful if the recipient suffers a loss. It is easy to see how natural selection favors mutually beneficial or selfish behavior, whereas altruism and spite are more difficult to explain. We use cooperation to refer to a behavior that (a) increases the fitness of the recipient and (b) is selected for, at least partially, because of its benefit for the recipient (West, Griffin, & Gardner, 2007). Cooperation can therefore be mutually beneficial or altruistic depending upon the effect on the actor.

LANGUAGE

Before we discuss specific examples, it is necessary to clarify our use of language. As is done by most workers in our field, we will use informal shorthand, and write things such as "individuals are selected to maximize their reproductive success." This does not mean that we think animals are

Table 5.1 A Classification of Social Behaviors

		Effect on recipient	
		+	−
Effect on actor	+	Mutual Benefit	Selfishness
	−	Altruism	Spite

consciously maximizing their reproductive success or that they are consciously aware of the links between various behaviors and reproductive success, and the consequences of natural selection. We use such phrases to avoid the constant repetition of long and tedious sentences detailing precisely how natural selection works, for example, individuals who have a greater reproduce success provide a greater genetic contribution to the next generation and hence natural selection will favor genes that lead to individuals behaving in a way that maximizes their reproductive success. Formal links between the process of natural selection and the analogy of fitness-maximizing individuals are given by Grafen (2002, 2006a).

KIN SELECTION, COOPERATION, AND ALTRUISM

Hamilton's (1963, 1964) theory of kin selection was developed to solve the problem of altruistic cooperation. Natural selection favors individuals with the highest reproductive success. The problem of cooperation, therefore, is why should an individual carry out a costly behavior that benefits other individuals? Humans cooperate over numerous activities, such as hunting, food sharing, conserving common property resources, and warfare. Furthermore, cooperation can be found throughout the animal kingdom. For example, why should an individual forgo reproduction and instead help another to breed, as occurs in cooperatively breeding mammals such as meerkats and some primates, or social insects such as ants, bees, wasps, and termites?

These examples of cooperation seem to go completely against the Darwinian idea of "survival of the fittest." More specifically, populations of altruists are vulnerable to invasion by cheaters who do not cooperate, but gain the benefit from others cooperating (Hamilton, 1963, 1964). Cheaters will spread through a population, regardless of the detrimental consequences at the level of the population or species. This problem is well known in the fields of economics and human morality, where it is termed the tragedy of the commons (Hardin, 1968): The tragedy is that as a group, individuals would benefit from cooperation, but cooperation is not sustainable because each individual can gain by selfishly pursuing their own short-term interests. Consequently, we would not expect cooperative behaviors to be maintained in a population—put formally, cooperation should not be evolutionarily stable.

William D. Hamilton's (1963, 1964) theory of kin selection provides an explanation for cooperation by looking at the problem from the point of view of the gene, not the individual (Dawkins, 1976). By helping a close relative reproduce, an individual is still passing on its own genes to the next generation, albeit indirectly. It does not matter from the gene's point of view which copy of itself is passed on, just that as many copies as possible are passed on to the next generation. So from the point of view of the gene, an altruistic cooperative behavior can actually be selfish.

This theory is encapsulated in a pleasingly simple form by Hamilton's (1963) rule, which states that altruism is favored when $rb\text{-}c$ where c is the fitness cost to the altruist, b is the fitness benefit to the recipient and r is their genetic relatedness. This predicts that altruism is favored when r or b are higher and c lower. An alternative way of writing Hamilton's rule that can be useful in some cases is $br_r > cr_a$, where r_r is the relatedness of the actor to the offspring that are produced by the recipient as a result of the helping behavior, and r_a is the relatedness of the actor to the offspring that it would have been able to produce as a result of not helping. The specific application of this equation to real data is discussed in a later section.

Hamilton's theory is referred to in many ways. Hamilton (1963, 1964) called it "inclusive fitness theory," but it is more often referred to as "kin selection," a term coined by Maynard Smith (1964). J. L. Brown and E. R. Brown (1981) pointed out that the inclusive fitness of an individual is divided into two components: "direct fitness" and "indirect fitness." An individual accrues direct fitness through the production of offspring, and indirect fitness by increasing the reproduction of relatives. By definition, a behavior is only altruistic if it leads to a decrease in direct fitness, and hence, altruism can be favored only when there is an indirect benefit that outweighs this direct cost, as shown by Hamilton's rule. Cooperative behaviors can also be favored if they lead to a direct fitness benefit (i.e., negative c in Hamilton's rule), but then they are mutually beneficial, not altruistic (Table 5.1).

It is less well appreciated that Hamilton's (1964) rule also predicts selfish (or competitive) restraint. Put simply, behaviors that involve taking too much from close relatives will not be selected for. This can be shown with Hamilton's rule by considering a selfish behavior that provides a benefit to the actor (negative c), and a cost to the recipient (negative b). This will be favored when $rb - c > 0$, which is more likely to occur with a higher benefit to the actor (more negative c), lower cost to the recipient (less negative b), and a lower relatedness (r).

KIN SELECTION MORE GENERALLY

The true power of kin selection theory is its generality—as previously mentioned, kin selection can help explain a huge range of social interactions and not just altruistic cooperation (Hamilton, 1963, 1964, 1967, 1970, 1971. 1972, 1975, 1979). The simplest cases are that when interacting individuals are more closely related, they should be more likely to cooperate, show more selfish restraint, and show less aggression (Hamilton, 1964). A range of more subtle possibilities arises whenever there is the potential for cooperation or conflict between relatives. A few examples of these are

- individuals are expected to be more likely to give warning calls about the presence of predators, if they are in the presence of close relatives, as occurs in ground squirrels (Sherman, 1977);
- in species where cannibalism occurs in response to food limitation, individuals should prefer to eat nonrelatives, as occurs in tiger salamanders (Pfennig, Collins, & Ziemba, 1999) and ladybirds (Joseph, Snyder, & Moore, 1999);
- in social insects, such as wasps and bees, workers remove eggs laid by other workers (policing), because they are more related to the queen's eggs, than are the worker-laid eggs (Ratnieks, Foster, & Wenseleers, 2006);
- in many insects, related males (brothers) compete with each other for mates (often their sisters), before these females disperse to lay eggs elsewhere; when this happens, mothers produce a female-biased offspring sex ratio, to reduce this competition between brothers (Hamilton, 1967; West, Shuker, & Sheldon, 2005); and
- if the relatedness between the parasites infecting a host is high, they are expected to be more prudent in their exploitation of that host, causing less damage and mortality (virulence; Frank, 1996; Hamilton, 1972).

In other words, kin selection theory describes when individuals should behave altruistically and also when they should curtail their selfishness (Hamilton, 1964). Furthermore, kin selection theory also predicts the existence of spiteful behaviors, where an individual suffers a personal cost ($c > 0$) in order to inflict harm upon a social partner ($b < 0$). Such behaviors are favored when $rb > c$ is satisfied, which requires a negative relatedness ($r < 0$) between spiteful actor and victim (Gardner & West, 2004a; Hamilton, 1970). Examples of spiteful behaviors include bacteria-producing chemicals that kill nonrelatives, or wasp larvae preferentially attacking and killing individuals to whom they are less closely related (Gardner & West, 2004a, 2004b; Gardner, West, & Buckling, 2004; Gardner, Hardy, Taylor, & West, 2007).

A general caveat here is that we have emphasized the use of Hamilton's rule because it is an excellent conceptual tool. However, modern theoretical analyses of specific problems do not usually use Hamilton's rule as a starting point. While we do not have space to go into details here, if the aim is to construct theory for a specific situation, it is usually conceptually and technically easier to start with an equation for fitness based upon the relevant biology, and then derive predictions using modern kin selection methodology (Frank, 1998; Taylor & Frank, 1996; Taylor, Wild, & Gardner, 2007). Hamilton's rule in some form will appear from this, and can be very useful for interpreting the results. Taylor and Frank (1996) provide an excellent introduction to this methodology.

What is relatedness?

The most basic form of giving aid to a relative is parental care. From a selfish gene's perspective, we are not surprised to see a parent hard at work feeding its offspring, because natural selection favors individuals who maximize their genetic contributions to future generations. The young will have copies of their parent's genes and so parental care is not selfish from a genetic perspective. From this, it is a small step to appreciate that we also share genes with other relatives. However, in order to make clear theoretical predictions, we need to be able to weight the relative importance of different individuals from a gene's perspective. For example, how much more is a sibling worth than a cousin is? This is formalized by the coefficient of relatedness, r.

The coefficient of relatedness is a statistical concept, describing the genetic association between social partners (Grafen, 1985; Hamilton, 1970; Queller, 1994). It is given by $r = (p_{AR} - p_{AX})/(p_{AA} - p_{AX})$ where p_{AR} is the probability that a gene drawn at random from the focal locus in the perpetrator of the social behavior (actor) is identical in state (IIS) to a gene drawn at random from the focal locus in the individual who is affected by the social act (recipient), p_{AA} is the probability that a gene drawn at random from the focal locus in the actor is IIS with the gene obtained in a further draw (with replacement) from the focal locus in the actor, and p_{AX} is the probability that a gene drawn from the actor is IIS to a gene drawn from a random population member (Grafen, 1985). In other words, the coefficient of relatedness describes how similar two individuals are over and above the average similarity of all individuals in the population (i.e., it is a regression coefficient). By definition, two individuals picked randomly from the population will be related to each other by zero, on average. And since there are individuals who will be more similar than average, there must also be individuals who are less similar than average, and the latter are said to be negatively related.

Often it is of interest, and technically easier, to follow the progress of a rare genetic variant, so that p_{AX} is very small, and when identity in state will be due to coancestry (i.e., identity by descent, IBD). Because of the importance of IBD as a cause of genetic similarity, the p terms are often referred to as coefficients of consanguinity—literally, "shared blood." Here, the expression for relatedness simplifies to $r \rightarrow p_{AR}/p_{AA}$ as $p_{AX} \rightarrow 0$. In eukaryotes this gives the classic results such as relatedness between full-sibs is $r = 0.5$, and between half-sibs is $r = 0.25$, in the absence of inbreeding (Grafen, 1985; see Figure 5.1). Interestingly, if genealogical closeness is the cause of genetic similarity between social partners, then the ratio of coefficients of consanguinity accurately recovers the coefficient of relatedness even for genes that are segregating at appreciable frequency in the population. This means that the relatedness of $r = 0.5$ to full-sibs and $r = 0.25$ to half-sibs is a robust result.

We have described the kin selection coefficient of relatedness as providing a measure of how much a focal actor values other individuals according to relative genetic similarity. This has assumed

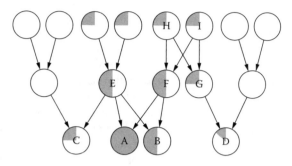

Figure 5.1 A family tree tracing the ancestry of four individuals (A, B, C, and D) back two generations, in a sexual, diploid population. Individual A is the focal actor contemplating an act of altruism. What is his relatedness to each of the other three individuals in his generation? Individual B is the full sibling of A, as they both share the same two parents (E and F). Picking a gene from A, the probability that a gene that is identical by descent is picked from B is $p_{AB} = \frac{1}{4}$. Picking two genes at random from A, with replacement, the probability of identity by descent is $p_{AA} = \frac{1}{2}$; in other words, the probability of picking the same gene twice from A. The relatedness between A and B describes how much A values B relative to how much A values itself, and is therefore $r_{AB} = p_{AB}/p_{AA} = \frac{1}{2}$. Individual C is a half-sibling of A, as they share only one common parent (E). The probability of identity by descent for two genes picked from A and C is $p_{AC} = \frac{1}{8}$, and so the relatedness between these two half-siblings is $r_{AC} = p_{AC}/p_{AA} = \frac{1}{4}$. Individual D is the cousin of A, because they have parents who are full siblings (F and G). The probability of identity by descent for two genes picked at random from A and D is $p_{AD} = \frac{1}{16}$, and so the relatedness of these two cousins is $r_{AD} = p_{AD}/p_{AA} = \frac{1}{8}$. A quick way to calculate relatedness in such a tree is to trace each route through which the two individuals can share genes identical by descent, multiplying by $\frac{1}{2}$ for each connecting arrow, and summing over all possible routes. For example, there are two ways for a gene in A and a gene in D to be identical by descent, through the route A-F-H-G-D ($\frac{1}{2} \times \frac{1}{2} \times \frac{1}{2} \times \frac{1}{2} = \frac{1}{16}$) and the route A-F-I-G-D ($\frac{1}{2} \times \frac{1}{2} \times \frac{1}{2} \times \frac{1}{2} = \frac{1}{16}$) giving a relatedness of $r_{AD} = \frac{1}{16} + \frac{1}{16} = \frac{1}{8}$.

that individuals are otherwise equivalent. More generally, different individuals may fall into different classes—according to their age, sex, size, and so forth—and individuals in different classes might have different reproductive successes. For example, a small offspring may be less likely to reproduce than a large offspring is, and so a focal actor should take size as well as relatedness into account when deciding on the most profitable course of action. In general, the different valuation of individuals in different classes is handled by the concept of reproductive value (Fisher, 1930; Grafen, 2006b; Taylor, 1990, 1996). Reproductive value represents the long-term genetic legacy of an individual, although this simple definition hides a lot of complexity, and so we will not pursue this complication further in this chapter.

How does kin selection work?

Kin selection requires a sufficiently high degree of relatedness between cooperating individuals. More specifically, the relatedness (r) term needs to be high enough for Hamilton's rule to be met (for a given b and c). Hamilton (1964) suggested two possible mechanisms for this. First, kin discrimination would allow cooperation to be preferentially directed toward relatives (Hamilton, 1964). Second, limited dispersal (population viscosity) would tend to keep relatives together (Hamilton, 1964, 1971). In this case, altruism directed indiscriminately toward all neighbors will be favored, as those neighbors tend to be relatives.

Kin Discrimination

Kin discrimination has been observed in many vertebrate species (Griffin & West, 2003; Komdeur & Hatchwell, 1999). The prediction here is that you would be more likely to help individuals who are perceived as close kin. This has been the focus of considerable study in cooperatively breeding vertebrates, where a dominant pair usually produces the majority of the offspring, but the cost of caring for offspring is shared by nonbreeding subordinates. Typical examples of this lifestyle make for popular nature documentaries, with species such as meerkats and African wild dogs. In many of these species, it has been shown that helpers provide closer kin with preferential care (kin discrimination), as would be predicted by kin selection theory (Griffin & West, 2003). One of the best-studied cases of this is the long-tailed tit, where the mechanistic basis of this kin discrimination has also been uncovered (Russell & Hatchwell, 2001; Sharp, McGowan, Wood, & Hatchwell, 2005). In this species, when an individual has failed to breed independently, they preferentially go and help at the nest of closer relatives (Figure 5.2). Individuals distinguish between relatives and nonrelatives on the basis of vocal contact cues, which are learned from adults during the nesting period (associative learning). This leads to the situation where individuals tend to help relatives with whom they have been associated with during the nestling phase (Sharp et al., 2005).

Several studies have investigated the extent to which humans can discriminate kin from nonkin. We would predict psychological mechanisms that lead to behaviors being adjusted in response to relatedness (or at least did so in ancestral conditions). A variety of behaviors has been examined from mother-baby interactions to mate choice. One line of work has been suggested that individuals can discriminate kin from nonkin on the basis of odor (Porter, 1999; Weisfeld, Czilli, Phillips, Gall, & Lichtman, 2003). This could potentially occur through learning odor cues via repeated interactions (as with the long-tailed tits), or genetic determined odor cues such as the major histocompatability complex (MHC; J. L. Brown & Eklund, 1994; Wedekind & Füri, 1997). Work on incest avoidance in humans has provided clear evidence for kin discrimination. Mating with close relatives is costly because this leads to homozygous offspring that express recessive deleterious mutations. Several studies have shown that individuals will avoid marrying or mating with close relatives, and that the underlying cue used to assess relatedness is the time of coresidence during childhood (Lieberman, Tooby, & Cosmides, 2003; Shepher, 1971; Wolf, 1995).

The evidence for a learned basis to kin discrimination in humans just discussed is analogous to the long-tailed tit example given previously. It supports the general idea that kin discrimination will usually occur via mechanisms such as learning rather than direct kin recognition (Grafen, 1990). The reason for this is that there can be genetic conflicts over kin recognition. If cooperation were

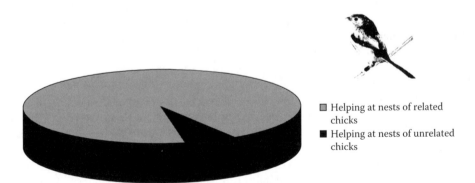

■ Helping at nests of related
   chicks
■ Helping at nests of unrelated
   chicks

Figure 5.2 Kin discrimination in long-tailed tits. 96% of long-tailed tit helpers prefer to help at nests containing related chicks when they have the choice of where to invest their efforts (Russell & Hatchwell 2001). Data are from the helping decisions of 17 nonbreeders.

preferentially directed toward closer relatives, then possible recipients of a helping behavior would always benefit from appearing more closely related to potential helpers. Consequently, any gene that was able to signal close relatedness would quickly spread through a population (Crozier, 1986). Learned cues, especially when based on direct recognition, can allow ways around this problem. For example, if you were raised in the same nest as me you are a sibling, with an average relatedness of $r = 0.5$.

Another area in humans where the influence of relatedness has been investigated is family violence (Daly & M. Wilson, 1982, 1988, 1997). Homicide is an extreme manifestation of interpersonal conflict, and so kin selection theory would predict that it occurs less frequently between closer relatives. Within family groups, homicide victims are 11 times more likely to have been killed by nonrelatives (e.g., spouse or stepparent) than by relatives. Many further analyses provide similar conclusions. For example, abusive stepparents discriminate, being less likely to assault or abuse their own children. There seems to be a lack of analogous studies examining whether cooperative behaviors are influenced by kin discrimination in humans (Jones, 2000). Although exceptions to this include a preference for adoption of relatives in islands throughout Oceania (Silk, 1980), and evidence that relatedness predicts the remittances that South African migrant workers send to their families (Bowles & Posel, 2005).

Kin discrimination will not always be expected, even if it is possible. We have already discussed how genetic conflicts and selection for manipulation can make kin discrimination unstable. Another possibility is that kin discrimination may be unnecessary. If individuals tend to interact with only, or almost only, close relatives, then there is no need for kin discrimination. Instead, indiscriminate altruism will be favored, as discussed in the following section. This could explain the lack of kin discrimination in some cooperative breeding vertebrates such as the stripe-backed wren (Griffin & West, 2003). The other possible reason is that it may not be worthwhile, if kin selection is not sufficiently important. For example, in cooperative breeding vertebrates, as the benefit of helping becomes lower, the level of kin discrimination becomes weaker (Griffin & West, 2003; Figure 5.3). In the extreme, if helping provides no real benefit, then there is no point preferentially directing it toward relatives. In these studies, the benefit of helping was measured by examining how the number of helpers influenced the number of young that groups were able to rear successfully. The point here is that kin selection theory and Hamilton's rule, predict when kin discrimination will be favored, but also when it will not. The importance of helping behaviors

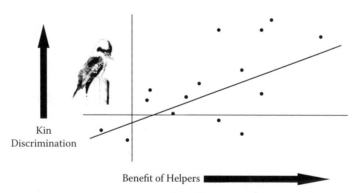

Figure 5.3 Kin discrimination and the benefit of helping. Helpers are more likely to discriminate in favor of relatives when the amount of help they provide increases the survival of offspring to the following year. The extent to which individuals preferentially help closer relatives (kin discrimination) is plotted against the benefit of helping. The significant positive relationship between these two variables is predicted by kin selection theory. The figure is taken from Griffin and West (2003), with two additional data points added from studies on the bell miner (*Manorina melanophrys*) and the red-cockaded woodpecker (*Picoides borealis*).

in humans is predicted to depend upon the benefit that they provide (i.e., their position on the *x*-axis of Figure 5.3).

Limited Dispersal

Limited dispersal has been suggested to be an important force in generating high relatedness, and hence kin selection for cooperation, in a wide range of cases from bacteria to humans (West, Pen, & Griffin, 2002b). This is likely to be important in contexts such as cooperative foraging in microbes, where kin discrimination faculties are expected to be lacking (West, Griffin, Gardner, & Diggle (2006). Unfortunately, it is difficult to verify this mechanism empirically. Kin discrimination makes the clear prediction that individuals adjust their behavior in response to with whom they interact, and this is readily tested. In contrast, limited dispersal predicts that cooperation should be more likely in populations where the average relatedness between interacting individuals tends to be higher (i.e., a response over evolutionary time). Suggestive evidence for this would be if relatedness tended to be high between cooperating individuals (but how high is high enough?), or if there were higher levels of cooperation in species where relatedness tended to be higher. However, it is often hard to rule out alternative explanations, such as correlated variation in the direct benefit of a behavior (Griffin & West, 2002).

Experimental evidence for this predicted effect of limited dispersal has come from an experimental evolution study in bacteria (Griffin, West, & Buckling, 2004). Bacterial growth is often limited by the availability of iron, and so many bacteria produce iron-scavenging molecules termed *siderophores*. This is a cooperative trait, with siderophore production being costly to the individual that produces them, but providing a local benefit, because neighbors can take up these siderophores. Griffin et al. initiated populations with a mixture of a cooperative strain that produced siderophores, and a cheater that did not produce siderophores. They then manipulated relatedness experimentally, by allowing the bacteria to grow and interact in groups derived from a single clone (relatively high relatedness) or from two clones (relatively low relatedness). As predicted by kin selection theory, it was observed that a wild type strain that produced siderophores outcompeted a selfish mutant strain when cultured under conditions of high relatedness but not when relatedness was lower (Figure 5.4).

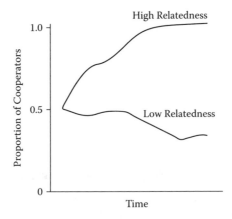

Figure 5.4 Cooperation is favored by higher relatedness. The figure shows the results from an experimental evolution study on the bacterial pathogen *Pseudomonas aeruginosa* (Griffin et al., 2004). The proportion of cooperative individual cells that produce iron-scavenging siderophores is plotted against time. The different lines represent relatively high and low relatedness.

MEASURING RELATEDNESS

Relatedness (r) is a measure of the proportion of genes identical by descent between individuals, so between a pair of full-sibs $r = 0.5$, for a pair of half-sibs $r = 0.25$, and so on. Measuring relatedness by the extent to which individuals share common alleles in molecular marker loci (or band sharing) can provide information about the relationship between individuals about which no pedigree history is known. However, measures of band sharing do not provide information about the nature of the relationship between individuals; for example, a parent-offspring pair will be indistinguishable from a full-sib pair as both have r-values of 0.5. A widely used measure is simply the correlation of the frequency of an allele in a potential actor with that in a potential beneficiary—Wright's correlation coefficient (Wright, 1969). Further subtleties are involved, however, when measuring inclusive fitness with Hamilton's inequality which states that an animal should provide benefit for another individual if $rb - c > 0$. Genetic similarity can be caused by factors besides the sharing of a common ancestor (e.g., if a population is inbred) and it is this similarity and not common ancestry that is often most relevant in evolutionary terms (Hamilton, 1970, 1972, 1975).

Grafen (1991) defines "the relatedness of a potential actor A to the potential recipient R [as] the extent to which A helping R is like A helping itself." In other words, the important measure of genetic similarity when considering the "r" in Hamilton's inequality is the genetic similarity between two individuals relative to that between random individuals in the population as a whole. Queller and Goodnight (1989) have provided a method of estimating Grafen's (1985) "identity by descent" relatedness measure from single-locus genotypic data. This method has several advantages over other methods as it allows information from multiple loci with multiple alleles to be amalgamated to provide a single estimate. Also, crucial to the study social interactions, estimates can be made for the relatedness between as few as two individuals.

TESTING KIN SELECTION THEORY: QUANTITATIVE HAMILTON'S RULES

One way to test kin selection theory is to try to examine if Hamilton's rule holds for a certain behavior (Grafen, 1982, 1984). So, for example, does an altruistic helping behavior satisfy the condition $rb - c > 0$? This requires measuring relatedness between individuals, the cost of a behavior, and the benefit of a behavior. This can be an extremely nontrivial task, with many potential pitfalls (Grafen, 1984).

An early example of this is provided by Grafen's (1984) analysis of superb fairy wren data. In this species, pairs sometimes breed alone, and sometimes with a helper. Can helping behavior in superb fairy-wrens be explained by kin selection? To answer this question the number of young successfully raised in a nest each year was compared in nests with and without helpers. It turns out that, on average, pairs with helpers produced 2.83 offspring and pairs without helpers produced 1.50 offspring. The benefit of helping can be estimated as the difference in productivity due to having a helper, giving $b = 2.83 - 1.50 = 1.33$ offspring. The cost of helping will depend upon whether or not a potential helper is able to find a mate and breed on own, or if this is prevented by some constraint, such as lack of breeding territories or lack of mates. If they could potentially breed then the cost is the productivity if they had bred themselves, which gives $c = 1.50$ offspring. If they could not have bred, then $c = 0$ offspring.

We can now proceed in two ways. Firstly, we can weight the cost of helping by the number of offspring that would have been produced by the helper if it had bred instead of helped (by multiplying the cost term by the relatedness to the offspring that would have been produced if the potential helper bred itself, $r = 0.5$). Helpers produce full siblings ($r = 0.5$), which gives us the following values for Hamilton's rule $r_{siblingB} - r_{offspringC} > 0$. If potential helpers can find a mate and breed on their own, this gives $(0.5 \times 1.33) - (0.5 \times 1.50) = -0.09$. This gives a net negative inclusive fitness effect, and so, it would not be explained by kin selection. In this case, possible explanations would be poor estimates of b and c, due to factors such as direct fitness benefits to helping (see the following section). If potential helpers cannot find a mate and breed independently, then we obtain $(0.5 \times 1.33) - (0.50 \times 0) = 0.67$, which gives a value > 0 and so can be explained by kin selection. So if individuals can breed independently we should expect them to do so, and if not, we would expect them to help.

The alternate way to proceed is to say that the value of r is 1.0, because the choice is between creating siblings and creating offspring, which are equally related. Another way of looking at this is that the helper helps both his parents increase their number of offspring, and the sum of his relatedness to his parents is one. This gives $rb - c = (1.0 \times 1.33) - 1.50 = -0.17$ when individuals can breed independently (< 0), and $(1 \times 1.33) - 0 = 1.33$ when individuals cannot breed independently (> 0). Identical conclusions are given by both methods.

The previous example used observational data, which can be confounded by other factors such as territory quality. Often, it is not possible to do the correct experiments (e.g., helper-removal) for ethical or conservation reasons. For example, are helping individuals of lower quality than the breeders that they help are? In this case, the cost of breeding could have been lower, as they would not have been able to rear 1.50 offspring. Does the likelihood of obtaining a helper vary with breeder quality? Does the effort involved with helping lead to cost in terms of reduced independent breeding success the following year, in which case we would be underestimating c? Experimental data can avoid these problems and allow the costs and benefits to be estimated more accurately (Heinsohn & Legge, 1999; Mumme, 1992).

The previous discussion is focused on the most simple possible data analysis. Recently, an improved method has been developed for calculating inclusive fitness, and how it is partitioned between direct and indirect fitness, utilizing matrix algebra (Oli, 2003). MacColl and Hatchwell (2004) applied this method to a long-term data set from long-tailed tits, providing one of the most impressive and comprehensive measurements of inclusive fitness in a natural population. They found that (a) on average, the direct component of fitness was more important than the indirect component and (b) about one fifth of individuals who accrued fitness did so only through helping (MacColl & Hatchwell, 2004). Birds tended to gain fitness either directly through breeding successfully or indirectly through helping if they could not breed successfully. This suggests that helping is a "best-of-a-bad-job" tactic favored by kin selection. Helping appears to have no direct benefit in this species because individuals that help do not tend to also accrue direct fitness. However, it should be noted, that while a similar pattern may occur in other species, we also expect there to be some cooperative breeding vertebrates, where cooperation and helping is explained primarily by direct benefits and not kin selection (Griffin & West, 2002, 2003; Clutton-Brock, 2002).

TESTING KIN SELECTION THEORY: COMPARATIVE STATICS

An alternative way of testing kin selection theory is to make predictions for how a behavior should vary with some other parameter. In this case, the aim is to make qualitative predictions for trends, not quantitative predictions for a single case. We have already discussed an example of this, when considering kin discrimination in cooperative breeding vertebrates. Specifically, individuals should be more likely to help, or give higher levels of help to closer relatives—for example, there should be a correlation between amount of helping and relatedness (Griffin & West, 2003). Another example that we have already discussed is the experimental evolution study on the production of cooperative iron-scavenging siderophore molecules in bacteria, where we expected (and observed) greater levels of cooperation when relatedness was higher (Griffin et al., 2004). This approach is sometimes termed *comparative statics* (Frank, 1998). Formally, statics is analysis of equilibriums and distinguished from dynamics, which is the analysis of change.

Numerous other examples could be given with this method. Much attention has been given to predicting (and observing) how behaviors should vary with relatedness. For example, we would expect (a) the level of aggression between individuals to be negatively correlated with relatedness (Hamilton 1964, 1979), (b) the likelihood of cannibalism to be negatively correlated with relatedness (Pfennig et al., 1999), and (c) parasite virulence to be negatively correlated with relatedness (Frank, 1996). In contrast, it is perhaps less often appreciated that predictions can also be made for how behaviors should vary with the benefit (b) and cost (c) of performing that behavior. For example, (a) higher levels of aggression are expected when a greater resource is being contested (West, Murray, Machado, Griffin, & Herre, 2001), (b) cannibalism should be more common when alternate food resources are more limiting, (c) higher levels of kin discrimination are expected when the benefits of helping are greater (Griffin & West, 2003), and (d) higher levels of helping when the cost (c) of helping is lower.

Frank (1998) has argued that this comparative approach is the most powerful way to test theory. He pointed out that we should not expect theory to be met quantitatively because theory is only ever a hugely simplified abstraction of the real world. Plus, even if the quantitative predictions of a theory were met, it would presumably be possible to come up multiple theories that make the same prediction. Comparative predictions avoid these problems. Another advantage of the comparative approach is that in cases where it is difficult or impossible to collect sufficient data to predict what should happen in one population, it can still be possible to make predictions for variation across populations or species (Griffin et al., 2005). The point here is that by focusing on variation in one variable, such as r, many complications can be swept under the table.

KIN SELECTION AND CONFLICT BETWEEN INDIVIDUALS

The ability of kin selection to explain cooperation is well accepted. However, outside of the evolutionary and ecological literature, it is less well appreciated that kin selection has also been remarkably successful in predicting when conflict will occur. Even when individuals live in cooperative groups, there is still plenty of scope for conflict within the group, and this conflict is predicted by kin selection theory. The point here is that when $r > 0$ kin selection can favor cooperation, but when $r < 1$ individuals will have different interests—so, when $0 < r < 1$, there will be potential for both cooperation and conflict. While individuals will be selected to cooperate with relatives, they are also selected to exploit their own selfish interests whenever they can.

PARENT-OFFSPRING CONFLICT

In a hugely influential paper, Trivers (1974) used Hamilton's rule to show that there can be conflict over the amount of investment that a parent should give to its offspring. This has been termed *parent-offspring conflict*. Trivers showed that offspring will be selected to get more resources from their parents, when from the parents point of view, it would be better to put those resources to other uses, such as producing other offspring (Trivers, 1974). This idea was criticized by Alexander (1974), who argued that parent-offspring conflict would not be important because the parent would always win. Specifically, he argued that a gene leading to relatively selfish behavior by offspring would be eliminated by selection because these selfish offspring would produce similarly selfish offspring. The problem with this argument is that looking at it from the point of view of offspring, the opposite conclusion can be reached—a gene leading to more selfish and successful offspring would lead to parent who produced more successful offspring. In the 1970s, a number of population genetic models were developed to address this problem more formally. These models showed that genes that caused an offspring to take more than the parental optimum could spread and that Triver's argument was correct (Godfray, 1995; Mock & Parker, 1997).

Since then, research has moved from discussing whether conflict could exist, to examining cases where it does and how it is resolved. One topic that has attracted much attention in this area is whether begging represents an honest signal of need from offspring to parents (Kilner & Johnstone, 1997). Begging can be costly through energetic expenditure or attracting predation. If begging is costly, then offspring with greater needs are predicted to beg (or signal) at greater rates, and their parents are expected to adjust their feeding rates depending upon the begging rate (Godfray, 1995; Godfray & Parker, 1991; Mock & Parker, 1997; Royle, Hartley, & Parker, 2002). Support for these predictions has been found, primarily in birds, but also in other taxa such as some insects where begging occurs (Clutton-Brock, 1991; Kilner & Johnstone, 1997; Kilner, Noble, & Davies, 1999; Smiseth, 2003).

Possibly the clearest support for parent-offspring conflict has been provided by conflicts between the queen and workers over the sex ratio in the social hymenoptera (e.g., ants, bees, and wasps). The relevant sex ratio here is that of sexual brood (reproductives)—workers are all female. The potential for conflict here was first realized by Hamilton (1972), but it was Trivers who formally developed and tested the idea (Trivers & Hare, 1976). Queens are equally related to sons and daughters ($r = 0.5$), and so would prefer to invest equal resources in sons and daughters. In contrast, when the queen is singly mated, the haplodiploid genetic system means that female workers are more related to their sisters ($r = 0.75$) than their brothers ($r = 0.25$). Consequently, workers would rather invest a greater proportion of resources in sisters. The workers could be in a good position to do this because, although the queen lays the eggs, it is the workers who feed, care for, and raise the young. Trivers and Hare compiled an impressive data set in favor of this argument, showing that the investment tended to be biased toward females, as would be expected if workers were in control and winning the conflict.

Since then, far greater support for worker control of the sex ratio has been found from detailed within species studies. The relative relatedness between workers and the male and female sexual brood varies with a number of factors, such as queen mating frequency and the number of queens in the colony. Boomsma and Grafen (1990, 1991; Boomsma, 1991) showed that this should lead to split sex ratios with the workers favoring the production of only males in some colonies and only females in the others. For example, as queen mating frequency goes up, workers are still more related to their sisters than their brothers but the difference gets smaller. This means that, in colonies where the queen has mated relatively few times, the workers are relatively more related to sisters and so should rear only females, whereas in colonies where the queen has mated many times, the workers are relatively less related to sisters and so should rear only males. There is considerable evidence from both observational and experimental work that such sex ratio adjustment occurs in a number of species, providing clear evidence for worker control of the sex ratio (Chapuisat & Keller, 1999). In some cases, the precision of sex ratio adjustment can be incredible. In *Formica truncorum*, workers in a single colony even adjust the sex ratio from year to year, in response to how mixed up the queen's sperm is that year (Boomsma et al., 2003; Sundstrom & Boomsma, 2000). Sperm mixing will determine the effective mating frequency—for example, if the sperm is poorly mixed, then even though a queen has mated multiple males, she can end up using the sperm of only one male and so effectively is singly mated. However, workers do not always win. In some species, the queens are in control of the sex ratio and a more even allocation of resources to sons and daughters occurs (Passera, Aron, Vargo, & Keller, 2001; Rosset & Chapuisat, 2006). The next level of research in this area will be to determine how the conflict between queens and workers is resolved, and explain the variation in who wins (Mehdiabadi, Reeve, & Mueller, 2003).

SIBLING CONFLICT

Kin selection theory also predicts conflict between siblings. While individuals are related to their siblings ($r = 0.5$ for full siblings, $r = 0.25$ for half siblings), they are more related to themselves

($r = 1.0$). Consequently, when there is a pool of resources to be shared between a number of siblings, each individual is expected to try and get a greater share. The extent to which this can lead to conflicts within broods of animals such as birds and mammals has attracted much attention (Clutton-Brock, 1991; Mock & Parker, 1997). This conflict can manifest itself in many ways, from competitive begging, to fatal attacks on siblings, to cannibalism.

The potential for conflict between siblings in hymenopteran social insects (e.g., ants, bees, and wasps) has allowed some particularly nice tests of kin selection theory. In these species, when the queens have mated many times, workers are more related to their own sons ($r = 0.5$) than those laid by the queen ($r = 0.25$), and so workers are predicted to lay sons (Ratnieks et al., 2006). However, other workers are more related to the sons laid by the queen ($r = 0.25$) than they are to the sons produced by the laying workers ($r = 0.125$), and so they are predicted to remove eggs laid by other workers (worker policing). This leads to wasteful situations where workers can lay a large number of eggs, but these eggs are almost all removed. Furthermore, there is good support for predictions of how the level of egg laying and policing should vary with the number of times that a queen mates, as this influences the relatedness structure within the colony (Ratnieks et al., 2006). The work on worker control of sex ratio and worker policing described in this section has provided some of the clearest support for kin selection theory—it is ironic that this comes from its ability to predict conflicts.

KIN SELECTION AND GENOMIC IMPRINTING

Kin selection theory also predicts conflict within individuals. It has been found that in some mammals and plants, including humans, maternally and paternally derived alleles have different patterns of expression (Burt & Trivers, 2006). This phenomenon where gene expression depends upon which parent they came from is termed genomic imprinting. Usually, one allele is silent and the other active, although the difference can be more subtle. Kin selection theory can explain this, because paternal and maternal genes in one individual have different probabilities of also being present in that individual's siblings (e.g., if siblings have different fathers), and hence, these genes will "disagree" over how the focal individual should behave toward its siblings (Haig, 2002).

One area where kin selection theory predicts that genomic imprinting will be important is in genes involved in parental investment (Haig, 2002). Assuming a large outbred population, a gene derived from the father will have relatedness $r = 0$ to the mother, whereas a gene derived from the mother will have relatedness $r = 1$ to the mother. Consequently, paternal genes will be selected to maximize the amount of resources obtained from the mother. In contrast, maternal genes have a kin-selected (indirect) interest in the mother's survival and production of further (related) offspring.

The existing data, which is mainly derived from mice and humans, support this prediction (Burt & Trivers, 2006). Approximately 100 genes are imprinted in the mammalian genome, out of 30,000. Of these, a high proportion is involved in fetal growth, with paternal imprinting leading to greater growth and hence greater resource acquisition from the mother. In addition, it has been suggested that an imbalance in imprinting, due to factors such as the absence of a paternal or maternal copy of a gene, or the breakdown of the genomic imprinting mechanism, can explain conditions such as Prader-Willi syndrome, Angelman syndrome, and autism (Badcock & Crespi, 2006; Haig & Wharton, 2003). The idea here is that maternal and paternal genes are each pulling in different directions, and that this usually leads to a balance somewhere in between. However, if one parent wins too much, then it can lead to problems such as these conditions.

COMPETITION AND COOPERATION

We have stated previously that limited dispersal is one of the two ways to obtain a high relatedness and hence make kin selection important—the other is kin discrimination. Although this is true, limited dispersal will not always lead to selection for cooperation and reduced conflict. The reason for this is that it can also lead to increased competition between relatives (reviewed by Queller, 1992a; West et al., 2002b). This reduces the advantage of cooperation because the increased fitness of the relative who receives the altruism is increasingly paid for by other relatives. Put simply, there is no point helping a brother if his increase in fitness comes at a cost to another brother.

There is a huge theoretical literature on this topic, showing that the extent to which limited dispersal favors the evolution of cooperation will often depend upon biological details. A pair of highly influential papers by Taylor (1992a, 1992b) showed that, in the simplest possible scenario, limited dispersal increases relatedness and increases local competition, such that these exactly cancel out—consequently, limited dispersal has no influence on the evolution of cooperation. However, it has since been shown that there a number of ways around this problem. For example, limited dispersal will increase selection for altruism if (a) altruism occurs before dispersal and competition occurs after dispersal (Queller, 1992a; Taylor, 1992a, 1992b); (b) altruism allows groups to be maintained at higher densities (elasticity; Taylor, 1992a, 1992b); (c) relatives disperse in groups (budding; Gardner & West, 2006); and (d) cooperation occurs between generations (Taylor & Irwin, 2000).

Experimental support for this idea was provided by the experimental evolution work on cooperative iron scavenging molecules (siderophores) in bacteria (Griffin et al., 2004). We have already described how relatedness was manipulated in that experiment. However, the extent of cooperation between relatives was also manipulated, by allowing competition to occur locally (within groups) or more globally. As predicted, when competition was more local and, hence, there was greater competition between relatives, cooperative siderophore production was selected against.

Local competition between relatives is also able to explain instances in nature where aggressive and violent conflict occurs between close relatives (Griffin & West, 2002; West et al., 2001). For example, fig wasp brothers routinely chop off each others' heads in conflict over mates, because competition for mates occurs on a very local scale within fig fruits (West et al., 2001). Indeed, across fig wasp species, the average relatedness between competing males shows no correlation with the level of aggression, which would be expected when competition is completely local (Figure 5.5).

The problem of local competition selecting against cooperation also occurs in interactions between nonrelatives (West et al., 2006b). As competition becomes more local, the fitness of an individual becomes more dependent upon how they do relative to the partners with whom they interact and potentially cooperate. In this case, cooperation is selected against because it never leads to an increase in payoff relative to the beneficiary of cooperation. Support for this prediction comes from experimental work on humans, where individuals were shown to be more likely to cooperate when competition was more global (West et al., 2006b; Figure 5.6). In this experiment, the scale of competition was manipulated by making people play games where they could cooperate (the prisoner's dilemma) in small groups, and giving out cash prizes to the highest score in each group (relatively local competition) or the highest scores in the room (relatively global competition). Manipulation of the scale of competition, or at least perception of it, provides a means for altering the level of cooperation amongst humans (Crespi, 2006; West et al., 2006a).

OLD GROUP SELECTION

It is sometimes thought that if a behavior cannot be explained by kin selection, then an alternative possibility is group selection. In order to explain why this is incorrect, it is useful to distinguish between two different types of group selection (Grafen, 1984). Wynne-Edwards (1962) first coined the term *group selection* in the 1960s. He thought that the relative success of cooperative groups over groups of selfish individuals could explain the evolution of altruistic behavior, such as reproductive restraint. In groups consisting of selfish individuals (who reproduce at the maximum rate),

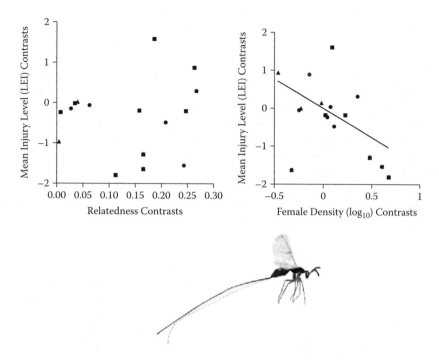

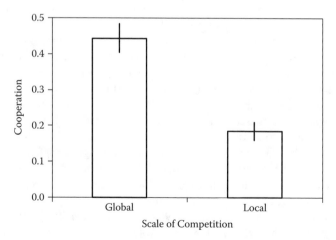

Figure 5.5 The mean injury level in male fig wasps shows no significant relationship with relatedness, but is negatively correlated to female density. Data points are phylogenetically independent contrasts across species (West et al., 2001).

Figure 5.6 Human cooperation and the scale of competition. The mean proportion of cooperative decisions made by individuals with respect to the scale of competition. Individuals were less likely to cooperate when competition was relatively local (prizes awarded within groups), compared with relatively global (prizes awarded within the class), as predicted by theory (West et al., 2006b).

resources would be over exploited, and the group would go extinct. In contrast, groups consisting of altruistic individuals who restricted their birth rate would not over exploit their resources and not go extinct. Hence, by a process of differential survival of groups, behavior evolved that was for the good of the group.

During the 1960s and 1970s, a large body of theoretical and empirical work revealed the flaw in Wynne-Edward's (1962) logic. Theory showed that this type of group selection would only work under extremely restrictive conditions, and so its importance would be rare or nonexistent (Leigh, 1983; Levin & Kilmer, 1974; Maynard Smith, 1964, 1976; Williams, 1966). For example, Maynard Smith (1976) showed that group selection would not work if the number of successful migrants produced per group is greater then one—successful migrants are individuals who leave a patch and reproduce in a different patch. Empirical work showed that individuals were reproducing at the rate that maximized their lifetime reproductive success and were not practicing reproductive restraint (Krebs & Davies, 1993; Lack, 1966; Perrins, 1964). Unfortunately, there is still widespread confusion about group selection, which leads people to the false conclusion that individuals will do something because it is "for the good of the species."

NEW GROUP SELECTION

In the 1970s and 1980s, a new form of group selection was developed, based on a different conception of the group (D. S. Wilson, 1975, 1977). The idea here was that at a certain stages of an organism's life cycle, interactions take place between only a small number of individuals. Although not initially developed with this, the Price (1970, 1972; see also Frank, 1995; Hamilton, 1975) equation can be useful for formalizing such theory. These kinds of new group selection are sometimes referred to as trait-group or demic selection. One way of conceptualizing the difference between the old and new group selection models is that the new group selection models rely on within-population group selection, whereas old group selection theory worked on between-population group selection (Reeve & Keller, 1999). Another key difference is that the old group selection approach argued that selection at that level was the driving force of natural selection, whereas the new group selection emphasizes that there are multiple levels of selection, and these can vary in their importance.

It has since been shown that kin selection and new group selection are just different ways of conceptualizing the same evolutionary process. They are mathematically identical, and hence are both valid (Bourke & Franks, 1995; Frank, 1986b, 1998; Grafen, 1984; Hamilton, 1975; Queller, 1992b; Taylor, 1990; Wade, 1985). New group selection models show that cooperation is favored when the response to between-group selection outweighs the response to within-group selection, but it is straightforward to recover Hamilton's rule from this. Both approaches tell us that increasing the group benefits and reducing the individual cost favors cooperation. Similarly, group selection tells us that cooperation is favored if we increase the proportion of genetic variance that is between-group as opposed to within-group, but that is exactly equivalent to saying that the kin selection coefficient of relatedness is increased. In all cases where both methods have been used to look at the same problem, they give identical results (Frank, 1986b; Wenseleers, Helantera, Hart, & Ratnieks, 2004). More generally, the partitioning of selection into within-group and between-group components can be done for any arbitrarily defined group (Wade, 1985).

Although the equivalence of the kin selection and new group selection approaches has long been appreciated (Grafen, 1984; Hamilton, 1975), there has been a huge amount of fruitless debate in this area, mainly due to semantics (Frank, 1998; Reeve & Keller, 1999). While this debate was solved conclusively during the 1960s to 1980s by evolutionary biologists, it seems to reoccur and lead to confusion as new fields embrace the relevant aspects of social evolution (Reeve & Keller, 1999). Recent examples include the parasitology literature (Toft, Aeschlimann, & Bolis, 1991), the agricultural literature (Denison, Kiers, & West, 2003), the microbial literature (West et al., 2006b), and the human cooperation literature (West et al., 2007).

While both approaches are valid, most evolutionary biologists focus on kin selection methodology. Kin selection is focused upon because it is usually easier to construct models, interpret the predictions of theory, and then apply these to real biological cases. For example, (a) recent advances in kin selection methodology mean that models can be constructed much more simply and for much more general cases (Frank, 1998; Taylor & Frank, 1996; Taylor et al., 2007); (b) in some of the most successful areas of social evolution, predictions arise elegantly from kin selection models, whereas the corresponding group selection models would be either unfeasible or so complex that they have not been developed (Frank, 1986a, 1998; Queller, 2004); (c) kin selection methodologies can usually be linked more clearly to empirical research, both empirically (through modern genetic marker-based methodologies; Queller & Goodnight, 1989) and conceptually—"knowing that $r = 0.22$ gives many biologists an understanding of the genetic closeness described; the knowledge that $n = 10$ and $v/v_b = 2.98$ is (at least for the present) less illuminating" (Grafen, 1984); (d) the kin selection approach recovers a single evolutionary maximand for Darwinian individuals, Hamilton's inclusive fitness (Grafen, 2006a)—it is easier to ask whether a strategy increases or decreases an individual's inclusive fitness than it is to mentally partition and quantify within and between group fitness components for a group selection analysis; and (e) the group selection methodology seems to increase the potential for semantic confusion to arise, by using several fundamental terms in ways that were different from their established (valuable and clear) meanings (Dawkins, 1979; Foster, Wenseleers, & Ratnieks, 2006; Grafen, 1984; Maynard Smith, 1983; Trivers, 1998; West et al., 2007).

KIN SELECTION, COOPERATION AND ALTRUISM—REVISITED

We opened this chapter by discussing how selection can solve the problem of cooperation, and then, we discussed several examples in later sections. In this section, we provide some generalizations on the importance of kin selection in explaining cooperation across the animal kingdom. Before doing so, it is useful to clarify the alternative to kin selection—direct fitness benefits.

There are a number of ways in which cooperation could provide a direct fitness benefit to the individual that performs the behavior, which outweighs the cost of performing the behavior (Sachs, Mueller, Wilcox, & Bull, 2004; West et al., 2006b; Lehmann & Keller, 2006). One possibility is that individuals have a shared interest in cooperation. For example, in many cooperative breeding species, larger group size may provide a benefit to all the members of the group through factors such as greater survival or higher foraging success—in this case, individuals can be selected to help rear offspring that are not their own, in order to increase group size (Kokko, Johnstone, & Clutton-Brock, 2001). Another possibility is that there is some mechanism for enforcing cooperation, by rewarding cooperators or punishing cheaters (Frank, 2003; Trivers, 1971). This could happen in a variety of ways, which have been termed punishment, policing, sanctions, reciprocal altruism, indirect reciprocity, and strong reciprocity (see the following section). There are a growing number of studies suggesting that cooperation in humans provides direct fitness benefits through such mechanisms (Fehr & Fischbacher, 2003; Fehr & Rockenbach, 2003).

If cooperation is explained by direct fitness benefits, then it is mutually beneficial and not altruistic (Table 5.1). One problem here is that the term reciprocal altruism is a bit misleading, as it does not involve altruism as defined by Hamilton (Table 5.1 and Table 5.2). This may help explain the common and incorrect assumption that kin selection and reciprocal altruism are the two leading explanations for altruism or cooperation (West et al., 2007). In fact, reciprocal altruism is just one of many possible ways in which cooperation can lead to direct fitness benefits, and it would be better termed reciprocity. Furthermore, reciprocity is thought to be of extremely limited importance outside of humans. There are many semantic problems with how altruism is used in the literature, and we discuss these in detail elsewhere (West et al., 2007). If cooperation is truly altruistic (Table 5.1; a direct cost), then kin selection (indirect benefits) is the only possible explanation. Consequently, determining the importance of kin selection in explaining cooperation, requires a determination

Table 5.2 Glossary

Actor: focal individual who performs a behavior

Altruism: a behavior that is costly to the actor and beneficial to the recipient

Cheaters: individuals who do not cooperate (or cooperate less than their fair share), but are potentially able to gain the benefit of others cooperating.

Cooperation: a behavior that provides a benefit to another individual (recipient) and that is selected for because of its beneficial effect on the recipient

Direct fitness: the component of fitness gained from aiding the reproduction of descendant relatives

Hamilton's Rule: condition *(rb–c > 0)* which predicts when a trait is favored by kin selection, where *c* is the cost to the actor of performing the behavior, *b* is the benefit to the individual who the behavior is directed toward (recipient), and *r* is the genetic relatedness between those individuals.

Indirect fitness: the component of fitness gained from aiding the reproduction of nondescendant relatives

Kin discrimination: when behaviors are preferentially directed toward individuals depending upon their relatedness to the actor

Kin selection: process by which traits are favored because of their beneficial effects on the fitness of relatives

Mutual benefit: a behavior that is beneficial to both the actor and the recipient

Public Goods: something that is costly to the individual to produce, but provides a benefit to all of the individuals in the local group or population

Relatedness: a measure of genetic similarity

Selfishness: a behavior that is beneficial to the actor and costly to the recipient

Spite: a behavior that is costly to both the actor and the recipient

Tragedy of the Commons: situation when individuals would do better by cooperation, but this is not stable, because each individual gains by selfishly pursuing its own short-term interests

of the relative importance of direct (mutually beneficial) and indirect (altruistic) benefits (Clutton-Brock et al., 2002; Griffin & West, 2002).

The classic example of kin selection explaining cooperation is the eusocial insects, the ants, bees and wasps (Hamilton, 1964, 1972). In these, kin selection is the only possible explanation for the existence of the sterile worker cast. Consequently, kin selection explains cooperation within colonies and, as we have previously discussed, is able to explain the conflicts within colonies. Suggestions that kin selection is not important in the eusocial insects (E. O. Wilson, 2005; E. O. Wilson & Hölldobler, 2005) are based upon some serious misunderstandings of evolutionary theory (Foster et al., 2006). In more primitively social wasps and bees, kin selection is also thought to often be important (Langer, Hogendoorn, & Keller, 2004). However, because subordinate individuals are still able to reproduce, direct fitness consequences of cooperation can be important in some cases. For example, individuals will help unrelated individuals if it increases their chance of attaining dominance in a group (Queller et al., 2000) or are less likely to help when they have a greater opportunity to obtain dominance in a group (Field, Cronin, & Bridge, 2006).

In cooperative breeding vertebrates the relative importance of direct benefits and kin selection are likely to vary across species (Griffin & West, 2003). Some evidence for this is shown in Figure 5.3, which illustrates how the benefit of helping and the extent of kin discrimination vary across species (Griffin & West, 2003). To examine this question in detail, it would also be necessary to examine the importance of direct fitness benefits to helping, which can be much harder, as they can accrue more subtly and over a longer time span. Nonetheless, there seem to be examples at both ends of the continuum. For example, in the long-tailed tit, individuals that help do not breed (Mac-Coll & Hatchwell, 2004), and so there can be no direct benefits to cooperation. At the other end of the continuum, direct fitness benefits have been argued to be the main driving force of cooperation in species such as meerkats (Clutton-Brock et al., 2002). Although even in meerkats, there are complications, such as the potential for the importance of kin selection to vary between the sexes (Griffin et al., 2003).

It has recently been realized that many micro-organisms such as bacteria perform cooperative behaviors (Crespi, 2001). In many of these cases, kin selection is likely to be the primary driving force (West et al., 2006b). Kin selection has the potential to be very important in these species because their life history will often lead to the potential for kin selection via limited dispersal. This is because single (or small numbers of) cells colonize and grow asexually in a local area. In this case, the individuals interacting over a small area will be clonal, corresponding to r = 1, which can be very conducive to the evolution of cooperation. In an earlier section, we discussed the production of public goods molecules such as iron-scavenging siderophores, where we believe kin selection to be important (Griffin et al., 2004; West & Buckling, 2003; Figure 5.4). However, there are also examples of altruistic behaviors where kin selection must be key. One of the clearest cases of this is in the social amoebae or slime moulds, when forming fruiting bodies (Queller et al., 2003; Strassmann, Zhu, & Queller, 2000). Under harsh conditions, species such as *Dictyostelium discoideum* form fruiting bodies to disperse. Within these fruiting bodies, some cells become spores, whereas others sacrifice themselves and become nonviable stalk cells. The altruistic stalk raises the spores off the ground, aiding in their dispersal to more favorable environments.

One area where kin selection would be expected to be unimportant is explaining cooperation between species, termed *mutualisms*—for example, fig wasps pollinating fig fruits or rhizobia bacteria providing nitrogen to their legume plant hosts. In this case, there is clearly no relatedness between cooperators, so cooperation can be explained only if it provides some beneficial feedback (or avoidance of punishment; West, Kiers, Simms, & Denison, 2002a). However, kin selection can still play a role, because the beneficial feedback may go to the individual that performed the cooperation (direct benefit) or their relatives (indirect benefit; Foster & Wenseleers, 2006; West et al., 2002a).

CONCLUSIONS

Kin selection theory is the only true theoretical advance in the understanding of natural selection since Darwin (Trivers, 2000). In Darwin's formulation, natural selection is expected to mould individuals so that their behavior maximizes their own reproductive success (Grafen, 1996b). Hamilton's contribution was to show that more generally individuals maximize their inclusive fitness, which includes the effects of their behaviors on their relatives' reproductive success as well as on their own (Grafen, 2006a).

Kin selection theory has acquired a huge amount of empirical support from both observational and experimental data, and even experimental evolution. Furthermore, this support has come from an incredibly diverse range of topics, such as cooperation, sex ratios, aggression, conflict, cannibalism, and kin discrimination. However, this should not be taken to mean that kin selection is the only mechanism driving the evolution of social interactions. It is important to take care before dismissing the direct fitness benefits of a behavior (Griffin & West, 2002).

ACKNOWLEDGMENTS

We thank Andy Russell for providing the long-tailed tit figure; Charles Crawford for inviting the chapter and useful comments; and the Royal Society, NERC, and the BBSRC for funding.

REFERENCES

Alexander, R. D. (1974). The evolution of social behavior. *Annual Review of Ecology and Systematics, 5,* 325–383.

Badcock, C., & Crespi, B. J. (2006). Imbalanced genomic imprinting in brain development: An evolutionary basis for the etiology of autism. *Journal of Evolutionary Biology, 19,* 1007–1032.

Boomsma, J. J. (1991). Adaptive colony sex ratios in primitively eusocial bees. *Trends in Ecology and Evolution, 6,* 92–95.

Boomsma, J. J., & Grafen, A. (1990). Intraspecific variation in ant sex ratios and the Trivers-Hare hypothesis. *Evolution, 44,* 1026–1034.

Boomsma, J. J., & Grafen, A. (1991). Colony-level sex ratio selection in the eusocial Hymenoptera. *Journal of Evolutionary Biology, 3,* 383–407.

Boomsma, J. J., Nielsen, J., Sundstrom, L., Oldham, N. J., Tentschert, J., Petersen, H. C., et al. (2003). Informational constraints on optimal sex allocation in ants. *Proceedings of the National Academy of Sciences of the United States of America, 100,* 8799–8804.

Bourke, A. F. G., & Franks, N. R. (1995). *Social evolution in ants.* Princeton, NJ: Princeton University Press.

Bowles, S., & Posel, D. (2005). Genetic relatedness predicts South African migrant workers' remittances to their families. *Nature, 434,* 380–383.

Brown, J. L., & Brown, E. R. (1981). Kin selection and individual selection in babblers. In R. D. Alexander & D. W. Tinkle (Eds.), *Natural selection and social behavior: Recent research and new theory* (pp. 244–256). New York: Chiron Press.

Brown, J. L., & Eklund, A. (1994). Kin recognition and the major histocompatability complex: An integrative review. *American Naturalist, 143,* 435–461.

Burt, A., & Trivers, R. (2006). *Genes in conflict: The biology of selfish genetic elements.* Cambridge, MA: Harvard University Press.

Chapuisat, M., & Keller, L. (1999). Testing kin selection with sex allocation data in eusocial Hymenoptera. *Heredity, 82,* 473–478.

Clutton-Brock, T. H. (1991). *The evolution of parental care.* Princeton, NJ: Princeton University Press.

Clutton-Brock, T. H. (2002). Breeding together: Kin selection, reciprocity and mutualism in cooperative animal societies. *Science, 296,* 69–72.

Clutton-Brock, T. H., Russell, A. F., Sharpe, L. L., Young, A. J., Balmforth, Z., & McIlrath, G. M. (2002). Evolution and development of sex differences in cooperative behavior in meerkats. *Science, 297,* 253–256.

Crespi, B. J. (2001). The evolution of social behavior in microorganisms. *Trends in Ecology and Evolution, 16,* 178–183.

Crespi, B. J. (2006). Cooperation: Close friends and common enemies. *Current Biology, 16,* R414–R415.

Crozier, R. H. (1986). Genetic clonal recognition abilities in marine invertebrates must be maintained by selection for something else. *Evolution, 40,* 1100–1101.

Daly, M., & Wilson, M. (1982). Homicide and kinship. *American Anthropologist, 84,* 372–378.

Daly, M., & Wilson, M. (1988). Evolutionary social-psychology and family homicide. *Science, 242,* 519–524.

Daly, M., & Wilson, M. (1997). Crime and conflict: Homicide in evolutionary psychological perspective. *Crime and Justice, 22,* 51–100.

Dawkins, R. (1976). *The selfish gene.* Oxford, U.K.: Oxford University Press.

Dawkins, R. (1979). Twelve misunderstandings of kin selection. *Zeitschrift für Tierpsychol, 51,* 184–200.

Denison, R. F., Kiers, E. T., & West, S. A. (2003). Darwinian agriculture: When can humans find solutions beyond the reach of natural selection. *The Quarterly Review of Biology, 78,* 145–168.

Fehr, E., & Fischbacher, U. (2003). The nature of human altruism. *Nature, 425,* 785–791.

Fehr, E., & Rockenbach, B. (2003). Detrimental effects of sanctions on human altruism. *Nature, 422,* 137–140.

Field, J., Cronin, A., & Bridge, C. (2006). Future fitness and helping in social queues. *Nature, 441,* 214–217.

Fisher, R. A. (1930). *The genetical theory of natural selection.* Oxford, U.K.: Clarendon.

Foster, K. R., & Wenseleers, T. (2006). A general model for the evolution of mutualisms. *Journal of Evolutionary Biology, 19,* 1283–1293.

Foster, K. R., Wenseleers, T., & Ratnieks, F. L. W. (2006). Kin selection is the key to altruism. *Trends in Ecology and Evolution, 21,* 57–60.

Frank, S. A. (1986a). The genetic value of sons and daughters. *Heredity, 56*, 351–354.

Frank, S. A. (1986b). Hierarchical selection theory and sex ratios. I. General solutions for structured populations. *Theoretical Population Biology, 29*, 312–342.

Frank, S. A. (1995). George Price's contributions to evolutionary genetics. *Journal of Theoretical Biology, 175*, 373–388.

Frank, S. A. (1996). Models of parasite virulence. *Quarterly Review of Biology, 71*, 37–78.

Frank, S. A. (1998). *Foundations of social evolution.* Princeton, NJ: Princeton University Press.

Frank, S. A. (2003). Repression of competition and the evolution of cooperation. *Evolution, 57*, 693–705.

Gardner, A., & West, S. A. (2004a). Spite and the scale of competition. *Journal of Evolutionary Biology, 17*, 1195–1203.

Gardner, A., & West, S. A. (2004b). Spite among siblings. *Science, 305*, 1413–1414.

Gardner, A., & West, S. A. (2006). Demography, altruism, and the benefits of budding. *Journal of Evolutionary Biology, 19*, 1707–1716.

Gardner, A., West, S. A., & Buckling, A. (2004). Bacteriocins, spite and virulence. *Proceedings of the Royal Society of London Series B, 271*, 1529–2535.

Gardner, A., Hardy, I. C. W., Taylor, P. D., & West, S. A. (2007). Spiteful soldiers and sex ratio conflict in polyembryonic parasitoid wasps. *American Naturalist, 169*, 519–533.

Godfray, H. C. J. (1995). Evolutionary theory of parent-offspring conflict. *Nature, 376*, 133–138.

Godfray, H. C. J., & Parker, G. A. (1991). Clutch size, fecundity and parent-offspring conflict. *Philosophical Transactions of the Royal Society of London Series B, 322*, 67–79.

Grafen, A. (1982). How not to measure inclusive fitness. *Nature, 298*, 425–426.

Grafen, A. (1984). Natural selection, kin selection and group selection. In J. R. Krebs & N. B. Davies (Eds.), *Behavioural ecology: An evolutionary approach* (pp. 62–84). Oxford, U.K.: Blackwell Scientific Publications.

Grafen, A. (1985). A geometric view of relatedness. *Oxford Surveys in Evolutionary Biology, 2*, 28–89.

Grafen, A. (1990). Do animals really recognise kin? *Animal Behaviour, 39*, 42–54.

Grafen, A. (1991). Modelling in behavioural ecology. In J. R. Krebs & N. B. Davies (Eds.), *Behavioural ecology: An evolutionary approach* (pp. 5–31). Oxford, U.K.: Blackwell.

Grafen, A. (2002). A first formal link between the Price equation and an optimisation program. *Journal of Theoretical Biology, 217*, 75–91.

Grafen, A. (2006a) Optimisation of inclusive fitness. *Journal of Theoretical Biology, 238*, 541–563.

Grafen, A. (2006b). A theory of Fisher's reproductive value. *Journal of Mathematical Biology, 53*, 15–60.

Griffin, A. S., Pemberton, J. M., Brotherton, P. N. M., McIlrath, G., Gaynor, D., Kansky, R., et al. (2003). A genetic analysis of breeding success in the cooperative meerkat (Suricata suricatta). *Behavioral Ecology, 14*, 472–480.

Griffin, A. S., Sheldon, B. C., & West, S. A. (2005). Cooperative breeders adjust offspring sex ratios to produce helpful helpers. *American Naturalist, 166*, 628–632.

Griffin, A. S., & West, S. A. (2002). Kin selection: Fact and fiction. *Trends in Ecology and Evolution, 17*, 15–21.

Griffin, A. S., & West, S. A. (2003). Kin discrimination and the benefit of helping in cooperatively breeding vertebrates. Science, 302, 634–636.

Griffin, A. S., West, S. A., & Buckling, A. (2004). Cooperation and competition in pathogenic bacteria. *Nature, 430*, 1024–1027.

Haig, D. (2002). *Genomic imprinting and kinship.* New Brunswick, NJ: Rutgers University.

Haig, D., & Wharton, R. (2003). Prader-Willi syndrome and the evolution of human childhood. *American Journal of Human Biology, 15*, 1–10.

Hamilton, W. D. (1963). The evolution of altruistic behaviour. *American Naturalist, 97*, 354–356.

Hamilton, W. D. (1964). The genetical evolution of social behaviour, I & II. *Journal of Theoretical Biology, 7*, 1–52.

Hamilton, W. D. (1967). Extraordinary sex ratios. *Science, 156*, 477–488.

Hamilton, W. D. (1970). Selfish and spiteful behaviour in an evolutionary model. *Nature, 228*, 1218–1220.

Hamilton, W. D. (1971). Selection of selfish and altruistic behaviour in some extreme models. In J. F. Eisenberg & W. S. Dillon (Eds.), *Man and beast: Comparative social behavior* (pp. 57–91). Washington, DC: Smithsonian Press.

Hamilton, W. D. (1972). Altruism and related phenomena, mainly in social insects. *Annual Review of Ecology and Systematics, 3*, 193–232.

Hamilton, W. D. (1975). Innate social aptitudes of man: An approach from evolutionary genetics. In R. Fox (Ed.), *Biosocial anthropology* (pp. 133–155). New York: Wiley.

Hamilton, W. D. (1979). Wingless and fighting males in fig wasps and other insects. In M. S. Blum & N. A. Blum (Eds.), *Reproductive competition and sexual selection in insects* (pp. 167–220). New York: Academic Press.

Hardin, G. (1968). The tragedy of the commons. *Science, 162*, 1243–1248.

Heinsohn, R., & Legge, S. (1999). The cost of helping. *Trends in Ecology and Evolution, 14*, 53–77.

Jones, D. (2000). Group nepotism and human kinship. *Current Anthropology, 41*, 779–800.

Joseph, S. B., Snyder, W. E., & Moore, A. J. (1999). Cannibalizing harmonia axyridis (coleoptera: coccinellidae) larvae use endogenous cues to avoid eating relatives. *Journal of Evolutionary Biology, 12*, 792–797.

Kilner, R. M., & Johnstone, R. A. (1997). Begging the question: Are offspring solicitation behaviours signals of need. *Trends in Ecology and Evolution, 12*, 11–15.

Kilner, R. M., Noble, D. G., & Davies, N. B. (1999). Signals of need in parent-offspring communication and their exploitation by the common cuckoo. *Nature, 397*, 667–672.

Kokko, H., Johnstone, R. A., & Clutton-Brock, T. H. (2001). The evolution of cooperative breeding through group augmentation. *Proceedings of the Royal Society of London Series B, 268*, 187–196.

Komdeur, J., & Hatchwell, B. J. (1999). Kin recognition: Function and mechanism in avian societies. *Trends in Ecology and Evolution, 14*, 237–241.

Krebs, J. R., & Davies, N. B. (1993). *An introduction to behavioural ecology* (3rd ed.). Oxford, U.K.: Blackwell Scientific Publications.

Lack, D. (1966). *Population studies of birds*. Oxford, U.K.: Clarendon Press.

Langer, P., Hogendoorn, K., & Keller, L. (2004). Tug-of-war over reproduction in a social bee. *Nature, 428*, 844–847.

Lehmann, L., & Keller, L. (2006). The evolution of cooperation and altruism. A general framework and classification of models. *Journal of Evolutionary Biology, 19*, 1365–1378.

Leigh, E. (1983). When does the good of the group override the advantage of the individual? *Proceedings of the National Academy of Sciences of the United States of America, 80*, 2985–2989.

Levin, B. R., & Kilmer, W. L. (1974). Interdemic selection and the evolution of altruism: A computer simulation study. *Evolution, 28*, 527–545.

Lieberman, D., Tooby, J., & Cosmides, L. (2003). Does morality have a biological basis? An empirical test of the factors governing moral sentiments relating to incest. *Proceedings of the Royal Society of London Series B, 270*, 819–826.

MacColl, A. D. C., & Hatchwell, B. J. (2004). Determinants of lifetime fitness in a cooperative breeder, the long tailed tit Aegithalos caudatus. *Journal of Animal Ecology, 73*, 1137–1148.

Maynard Smith, J. (1964). Group selection and kin selection. *Nature, 201*, 1145–1147.

Maynard Smith, J. (1976). Group selection. *Quarterly Review of Biology, 51*, 277–283.

Maynard Smith, J. (1983). Models of evolution. *Proceedings of the Royal Society of London Series B, 219*, 315–325.

Mehdiabadi, N. J., Reeve, H. K., & Mueller, U. G. (2003). Queens versus workers: Sex-ratio conflict in eusocial Hymenoptera. *Trends in Ecology and Evolution, 18*, 88–93.

Mock, D. W., & Parker, G. A. (1997). *The evolution of sibling rivalry*. Oxford, U.K.: Oxford University Press.

Mumme, R. L. (1992). Do helpers increase reproductive success: An experimental analysis in the Florida scrub jay. *Behavioral Ecology and Sociobiology, 31*, 319–328.

Oli, M. K. (2003). Hamilton goes empirical: Estimation of inclusive fitness from life-history data. *Proceedings of the Royal Society of London Series B, 270*, 307–311.

Passera, L., Aron, S., Vargo, E. L., & Keller, L. (2001). Queen control of sex ratio in fire ants. *Science, 293*, 1308–1310.

Perrins, C. M. (1964). Survival of young swifts in relation to brood size. *Nature, 201*, 1147–1149.

Pfennig, D. W., Collins, J. P., & Ziemba, R. E. (1999). A test of alternative hypotheses for kin recognition in cannibalistic tiger salamanders. *Behavioral Ecology, 10*, 436–443.

Porter, R. H. (1999). Olfaction and human kin recognition. *Genetica, 104*, 259–263.

Price, G. R. (1970). Selection and covariance. *Nature, 227*, 520–521.

Price, G. R. (1972). Extension of covariance selection mathematics. *Annals of Human Genetics, 35*, 485–490.

Queller, D. C. (1992a). Does population viscosity promote kin selection? *Trends in Ecology and Evolution, 7*, 322–324.

Queller, D. C. (1992b). Quantitative genetics, inclusive fitness, and group selection. *American Naturalist, 139*, 540–558.

Queller, D. C. (1994). Genetic relatedness in viscous populations. *Evolutionary Ecology, 8*, 70–73.

Queller, D. C. (2004). Kinship is relative. *Nature, 430*, 975–976.

Queller, D. C., & Goodnight, K. F. (1989). Estimating relatedness using genetic markers. *Evolution, 43*, 258–275.

Queller, D. C., Ponte, E., Bozzaro, S., & Strassmann, J. E. (2003). Single-gene greenbeard effects in the social amoeba dictostelium discoideum. *Science, 299*, 105–106.

Queller, D. C., Zacchi, F., Cervo, R., Turillazzi, S., Henshaw, M. T., Santorelli, L. A., et al. (2000). Unrelated helpers in a social insect. *Nature, 405*, 784–787.

Ratnieks, F. L. W., Foster, K. R., & Wenseleers, T. (2006). Conflict resolution in insect societies. *Annual Review of Entomology, 51*, 581–608.

Reeve, H. K., & Keller, L. (1999). Levels of selection: Burying the units-of-selection debate and unearthing the crucial new issues. In L. Keller (Ed.), *Levels of selection in evolution* (pp. 3–14). Princeton, NJ: Princeton University Press.

Rosset, H., & Chapuisat, M. (2006). *Sex allocation conflict in ants: When the queen rules.* Manuscript submitted for publication.

Royle, N. J., Hartley, I. R., & Parker, G. A. (2002). Begging for control: When are offspring solicitation behaviours honest. *Trends in Ecology and Evolution, 17*, 434–440.

Russell, A. F., & Hatchwell, B. J. (2001). Experimental evidence for kin-biased helping in a cooperatively breeding vertebrate. *Proceedings of the Royal Society of London Series B, 268*, 2169–2174.

Sachs, J. L., Mueller, U. G., Wilcox, T. P., & Bull, J. J. (2004). The evolution of cooperation. *Quarterly Review of Biology, 79*, 135–160.

Sharp, S. P., McGowan, A., Wood, M. J., & Hatchwell, B. J. (2005). Learned kin recognition cues in a social bird. *Nature, 434*, 1127–1130.

Shepher, J. (1971). Mate selection among second generation kibbutz adolescents and adults: Incest avoidance and negative imprinting. *Archives of Sexual Behavior, 1*, 293–307.

Sherman, P. W. (1977). Nepotism and the evolution of alarm calls. *Science, 197*, 1246–1253.

Silk, J. B. (1980). Adoption and kinship in Oceania. *American Anthropology, 82*, 799–820.

Smiseth, P. T. (2003). Partial begging: An empirical model for the early evolution of offspring signalling. *Proceedings of the Royal Society of London Series B, 270*, 1773–1777.

Strassmann, J. E., Zhu, Y., & Queller, D. C. (2000). Altruism and social cheating in the social amoeba dictyostelium discoideum. *Nature, 408*, 965–967.

Sundstrom, L., & Boomsma, J. J. (2000). Reproductive alliances and posthumous fitness enhancement in male ants. *Proceedings of the Royal Society of London Series B, 267*, 1439–1444.

Taylor, P. D. (1990). Allele-frequency change in a class structured population. *American Naturalist, 135*, 95–106.

Taylor, P. D. (1992a). Altruism in viscous populations—An inclusive fitness model. *Evolutionary Ecology, 6*, 352–356.

Taylor, P. D. (1992b). Inclusive fitness in a homogeneous environment. *Proceedings of the Royal Society of London Series B, 249*, 299–302.

Taylor, P. D. (1996). Inclusive fitness arguments in genetic models of behaviour. *Journal of Mathematical Biology, 34*, 654–674.

Taylor, P. D., & Frank, S. A. (1996). How to make a kin selection model. *Journal of Theoretical Biology, 180*, 27–37.

Taylor, P. D., & Irwin, A. J. (2000). Overlapping generations can promote altruistic behaviour. *Evolution, 54*, 1135–1141.

Taylor, P. D., Wild, G., & Gardner, A. (2007). Direct fitness or inclusive fitness: How shall we model kin selection. *Journal of Evolutionary Biology, 20*, 301–309.

Toft, C. A., Aeschlimann, A., & Bolis, L. (1991). *Parasite-host associations coexistence or conflict?* Oxford, U.K.: Oxford Scientific Publications.

Trivers, R. (1971). The evolution of reciprocal altruism. *Quarterly Review of Biology, 46,* 35–57.

Trivers, R. (1974). Parent-offspring conflict. *American Zoologist, 14,* 249–264.

Trivers, R. (1998). As they would do to you. *Skeptic, 6,* 81–83.

Trivers, R. (2000). William Donald Hamilton (1936–2000). *Nature, 404,* 828.

Trivers, R., & Hare, H. (1976). Haplodiploidy and the evolution of the social insects. *Science, 191,* 249–263.

Wade, M. J. (1985). Soft selection, hard selection, kin selection, and group selection. *American Naturalist, 125,* 61–73.

Wedekind, C., & Füri, S. (1997). Body odour preferences in men and women: Do they aim for specific MHC combinations or simply heterozygosity? *Proceedings of the Royal Society of London Series B, 264,* 1471–1479.

Weisfeld, G. E., Czilli, T., Phillips, K. A., Gall, J. A., & Lichtman, C. M. (2003). Possible olfaction-based mechanisms in human kin recognition and inbreeding avoidance. *Journal of Experimental Child Psychology, 85,* 279–295.

Wenseleers, T., Helantera, H., Hart, A., & Ratnieks, F. L. W. (2004). Worker reproduction and policing in insect societies: An ESS analysis. *Journal of Evolutionary Biology, 17,* 1035–1047.

West, S. A., & Buckling, A. (2003). Cooperation, virulence and siderophore production in bacterial parasites. *Proceedings of the Royal Society of London Series B, 270,* 37–44.

West, S. A., Gardner, A., Shuker, D. M., Reynolds, T., Burton-Chellow, M., Sykes, E. M., et al. (2006a). Cooperation and the scale of competition in humans. *Current Biology, 16,* 1103–1106.

West, S. A., Griffin, A. S., & Gardner, A. (2007). Social semantics: Altruism, cooperation, mutualism, strong reciprocity, and group selection. *Journal of Evolutionary Biology, 20,* 415–432.

West, S. A., Griffin, A. S., Gardner, A., & Diggle, S. P. (2006b). Social evolution theory for microbes. *Nature Reviews Microbiology, 4,* 597–607.

West, S. A., Kiers, E. T., Simms, E. L., & Denison, R. F. (2002a). Sanctions and mutualism stability: Why do rhizobia fix nitrogen? *Proceedings of the Royal Society of London Series B, 269,* 685–694.

West, S. A., Murray, M. G., Machado, C. A., Griffin, A. S., & Herre, E. A. (2001). Testing Hamilton's rule with competition between relatives. *Nature, 409,* 510–513.

West, S. A., Pen, I., & Griffin, A. S. (2002b). Cooperation and competition between relatives. *Science, 296,* 72–75.

West, S. A., Shuker, D. M., & Sheldon, B. C. (2005). Sex ratio adjustment when relatives interact: A test of constraints on adaptation. *Evolution, 59,* 1211–1228.

Williams, G. C. (1966). *Adaptation and natural selection.* Princeton, NJ: Princeton University Press.

Wilson, D. S. (1975). A theory of group selection. *Proceedings of the National Academy of Sciences of the United States of America, 72,* 143–146.

Wilson, D. S. (1977). Structured demes and the evolution of group advantageous traits. *American Naturalist, 111,* 157–185.

Wilson, E. O. (2005). Kin selection as the key to altruism: Its rise and fall. *Social Research, 72,* 159–168.

Wilson, E. O., & Hölldobler, B. (2005). Eusociality: Origin and consequences. *Proceedings of the National Academy of Sciences of the United States of America, 102,* 13367–13371.

Wolf, A. P. (1995). *Sexual attraction and childhood association: A Chinese brief for Edward Westermarck.* Stanford, CA: Stanford University Press.

Wright, S. (1969). *The theory of gene frequencies.* Chicago: University of Chicago Press.

Wynne-Edwards, V. C. (1962). *Animal dispersion in relation to social behaviour.* Edinburgh, U.K.: Oliver and Boyd.

Part II

DEVELOPMENT: THE BRIDGE FROM EVOLUTIONARY THEORY TO EVOLUTIONARY PSYCHOLOGY

The chapters in the previous section focused on the aspects of evolutionary theory that are concerned with the ultimate causes of behavior. The two chapters in this section focus on the role evolution has played in shaping the ways in which animals develop. The chapters provide a bridge between the section dealing with evolutionary theory and the section dealing with psychological mechanisms.

6

Sociogenomics for the Cognitive Adaptationist

WILLIAM M. BROWN

"Perhaps the most interesting thing to come out of the realization of possible conflict within the genome is a philosophical one. We see that we are not even in principle the consistent wholes that some schools of philosophy would have us be."

W. D. Hamilton (2001)

BACKGROUND

We are all a product of a long line of successful ancestors. Evolutionary approaches to behavior are concerned with adaptive behavior given an organism's ecology. Behavior can evolve[1] by means of natural selection provided there were: (a) past behavioral alternatives in an ancestral population; (b) the phenotypic differences were heritable. Specifically variation in the behavior or underlying cognitive mechanisms was based on genetic variation; and; (c) some of these behaviors and underlying cognitive mechanisms conferred a fitness advantage whereas others did not. In the following, I review some basic concepts from genetics for the introductory reader before presenting more recent developments in the study of genes and behavior.

Mendelian Fairness

Gregor Mendel was an Augustinian monk who presented the principles of heredity in 1865. Mendel did a number of experiments on pea plant inheritance patterns. Mendel did not know about genes,

---

[1] It should be pointed out that evolution is a population concept. Specifically the genetic make-up of a population changes over time. Therefore only populations evolve not individuals.

117

chromosomes,[2] mitosis, and meiosis.[3] However, his work on peapod size and color revealed the principles of heredity that facilitated the field of genetics, Crick and Watson's discoveries, and the human genome project.

Mendel's First Law is called the *"Law of Segregation."* It states the phenotype of the individual (e.g., blue and brown eye color) is influenced by a pair of hereditary factors (i.e., genes) inherited from your parents. These genes remain unaltered throughout your lifetime and, when you reach reproductive age, only one can be present in a gamete (i.e., the egg or the sperm). The law of segregation is a probability concept. Specifically imagine that *B* symbolizes the gene for brown eyes and *b* is the gene for blue eyes—this hypothetical individual would have a *Bb* genotype. The law tells us that a person with the *Bb* genotype *on average* will produce five offspring with a brown eye gene and five offspring with a blue eye gene. Because the concept is probabilistic, in any given 10 offspring there may be, for example, three or seven offspring with a particular version of gene. Mendel's first law tells that life is fair in that each gene of a pair has on average a 50% chance of being passed on (Ridley, 2001). Unfortunately, life is not always fair. Outlaw genes[4] are genes that defy Mendel's first law—there are several genes that fit this category. Perhaps the most famous is a gene in fruit flies called the segregation distorter (SD), a rare gene in wild populations. A normal gene has a 50% chance of entering the gametes, however the SD gene has a higher probability of entering because it indirectly kills the normal version of the gene to guarantee its entry in the gamete (Ridley, 2001).

Mendel's first law refers to any one gene pair, however Mendel's second law refers to more than one gene pair. It is called the law of independent assortment. For example, we may be interested in height and eye color (*B* or *b*). Imagine that some people are very tall (*H*) whereas others are very short (*h*). Therefore a tall person with brown eyes could have a genotype *BbHh* if we assume that the brown eye variant is dominant (i.e., expressed in homozygotic and heterozygotic condition) and not recessive (i.e., only expressed when homozygous). Mendel's second law states that for two characteristics genes are inherited independently. Therefore, if you had the genotype *BbHh* you would make four kinds of gametes: they would contain the combinations of either *BH*, *bH*, *Bh* or *bh*. If your mother had the genotype *BBHH* then you would have inherited *BH* from her. Suppose also that your dad had the genotype *bbhh* then you would have inherited *bh* from him. The combinations of *BH* and *bh* are the parental genotypes. Your genotype is *BbHh* and some of your children will inherit these *parental* types, either *BH* or *bh*, from you. Color and height genes in this hypothetical example are inherited independently. This is because of recombination, which is the mechanism that shuffles genes during sexual reproduction. Recombination makes it possible for some of your children to inherit *novel combinations*, called recombinants. These are *bH* and *Bh* in this hypothetical example.

It has been argued that recombination evolved to suppress outlaw genes and ensure fair meiosis (Mendel's first law; see Ridley, 2001). One mechanism for recombination is that maternal and

---

[2] Chromosomes are the containers for genes—there are two types, diploid and haploid. A diploid cell has one chromosome from each parental set. The sex chromosomes can be haploid, which describes a nucleus, cell, or organism possessing a single set of unpaired chromosomes.

[3] Mitosis is a method of cell division building the somatic tissue of the organism and critical for development of phenotype. Mitosis is characterized by the separation of chromosomes into two parts, one part of each chromosome being retained in each of two new daughter cells resulting from the original cell. Meiosis differs from mitosis because there are two cell divisions in meiosis, resulting in cells with a haploid number of chromosomes. Meiosis is the type of cell division by which germ cells (i.e., eggs and sperm) are produced. Meiosis involves a reduction in the amount of genetic material where one parent cell produces four daughter cells. Daughter cells have half the number of chromosomes found in the original parent cell and, with crossing over, become genetically different.

[4] The term *outlaw gene* is adopted from Dawkins (1989) and will be discussed later in the chapter under the rubric of selfish genetic elements.

paternal genes on each chromosome swap physical fragments between themselves. The DNA[5] of the parental chromsomes break and the paternal end joins the maternal end. However due to linkage between genes—especially at the centers of the chromosomes—Mendel's second law can be violated. Linked genes are genes that share the same region of the chromosome and are inherited together unless recombination separates them (Ridley, 2001).

Gene frequency and evolutionary change

Gene frequency refers to the proportion of alleles (i.e., alternative versions of the same gene) that are of a particular type. For example, if 60% of the alleles in a population are b and 40% are B, then the gene frequency of b is 0.6 and the gene frequency of B is 0.4. Over small time scales, evolution involves changes in gene frequencies in a population. Godfrey Harold Hardy, an English mathematician, and Wilhelm Weinberg, a German physician, stated that Mendelian inheritance leads to a maintenance of genetic diversity under random mating in sexually reproducing organisms—this is the Hardy-Weinberg Law. The Hardy-Weinberg is useful for demonstrating evolutionary change because when there are significant deviations from the expected allele frequencies under random conditions (i.e., Hardy-Weinberg Equilibrium) there may be evidence for the action of natural selection (or perhaps mutation, migration or inbreeding).

Evolutionarily the effects of genes influence their representation in a population. One way this occurs is via the alteration of the behavioral strategies of the genes themselves.[6] The following section provides a general background on how we get from genes to behavior is described. After this section, the view that genes are strategists in an evolutionary sense is presented.

FROM DNA TO BEHAVIOR

DNA is a storage medium of all the information necessary to help build an organism given its particular environment. DNA is a relatively stable molecule residing in the nucleus of most cells.[7] DNA is like a library where information is sheltered in a stable form so that it can be passed from one generation to the next. However unlike a library "opening hours" are much more flexible. Gene expression involves a particular pathway depicted in Figure 6.1.

When necessary, information in the DNA can be unlocked and transcribed into RNA[8] ("transcription" in Figure 6.1). RNA takes several forms, but often messenger RNA or mRNA is studied. Messenger RNA runs the genetic information from the DNA in the nucleus out into the cytoplasm where ribosomes are located. Ribosomes are large assemblies that are designed to translate the

---

[5] DNA or *Deoxyribonucleic Acid* is the molecule of heredity and therefore the informational basis for development and evolution. In a cell's chromosomes, DNA occurs as a spiral coil of fine threads, resembling a twisted ladder. To gain a sense of exactly how long an uncoiled DNA molecule is we can magnify the cell 1,000 times. When we do this, the length of DNA in the cell's nucleus would be 3 km. The genetic information of DNA is encoded in the sequence of bases and is transcribed as the strands unwind and replicate. As pointed out by others, DNA is not a blueprint for life, but more like a recipe that critically depends on the environment in order to build phenotype. Specifically, just like if you had a wonderful dish at a French restaurant you would be unable to determine exactly what the recipe was. This same holds for determining the underlying DNA information that contributed to a person's outward characteristics. That is, if DNA was a blueprint, then you could simply inspect an individual's outward phenotype and reconstruct the exact blueprint. A blueprint metaphor for DNA *incorrectly* suggests that just like a house you could take measurements of ourselves and reconstruct the blueprint (Dawkins, 1996).

[6] It is the premise of this chapter that genes have phenotypes (i.e., their expression patterns) within individuals. Genes can be difficult to define and in some cases constitute multiple functional components derived from a common source (Plagge & Kelsey, 2006).

[7] Mammalian erythrocytes (red blood cells) have no nucleus but contain mitochondrial DNA.

[8] Ribonucleic acid or RNA is a class of single-stranded molecules transcribed from DNA.

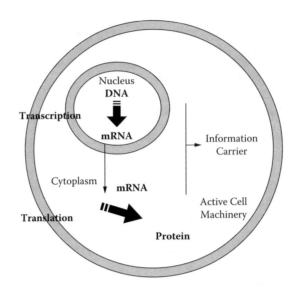

Figure 6.1 A diagram depicting how we get from DNA to protein via transcription and translation processes in the cell. The adaptor molecule is transfer RNA (tRNA) that facilitates recognition of the codon sequence in mRNA allowing for translation into the appropriate amino acid.

mRNA into protein. When mRNA binds to a ribosome, the information in the genetic recipe is decoded and proteins[9] with the proper sequence are synthesised. Ribosomes help decode the genetic information and make proteins. In general genes exert their actions in a dynamic fashion, interacting with many other genes in the genome and in response to complex interactions with the environment. When genes interact with other genes to influence trait expression it is called *epistasis*.[10] Genes underlie variation in behavior in several ways. Some genes exhibit allelic variation that affects behavior (de Bono & Bargmann, 1998; Osborne et al., 1997; Robinson, 1999). Others do not vary genetically, but change their expression within an individual over time, resulting in changes in behavior (e.g., plasticity). Some studies begin with observations of protein expression differences between individuals that differ in behavior.

GENES AS STRATEGISTS

Genes are catalysts whereby the reactions they catalyse influence their representation in a population (Dawkins, 1976; Doolittle & Sapienza, 1980; Haig, 2000; Hamilton, 1964; Orgel & Crick, 1980; Trivers, 1971; Williams, 1966). Evolutionary psychology[11]—the study of the evolutionary basis of information-processing mechanisms mediating behavior—has much to gain from recent advancements in behavioral genomics because the effects of strategic genes are critical for the developmental implementation of neurocognitive adaptations. For evolutionary psychologists genes are strategists in an evolutionary game where replicator representation depends on the development of effective vehicles for genic transmission. However, it is critical to keep in mind that there are

---

[9] Polypeptide proteins are folded polypeptides with quaternary structure—one of the big challenges for molecular biology is to learn how a protein sequence defines its 3D structure (Bowie, 2005).

[10] Most geneticists refer to inhibition of one gene by another when they refer to epitasis.

[11] For the purpose of this chapter "evolutionary psychology" includes ethology, behavioral ecology, human behavioral ecology, sociobiology and all other evolutionary approaches to behavior in humans and other animals (e.g., cognitive ecology, cognitive ethology, neuroethology and so on). Granted these areas emphasize different aspects of the organism (e.g., brain, cognition and/or behavior) or often study different species / model organisms. Nonetheless the underlying evolutionary logic is identical.

also "selfish genetic elements" (SGEs[12]), which are different from Dawkins' (1976) concept of the "selfish gene" (Burt & Trivers, 2006). Dawkins' (1976) selfish gene could be more aptly called a strategic gene because it can be either cooperative or selfish as long as there are higher level benefits to the vehicle (i.e., host organism). In contrast, a SGE's replication strategies can be in conflict with the interests of the organism[13] itself due to different transmission rules (e.g., when some genes evade fair meiosis) or relatedness asymmetries[14] (Burt & Trivers, 2006; Haig, 2000; Ridley, 2001; Stearns & Hoekstra, 2000). Different transmission rules between sex chromosomes (X, Y) and the autosomes could cause intragenomic conflicts over behavioral choices[15] (Brown, 2001a; Haig, 2000; Haig, 2006; Trivers, 2000). The idea that genes can be parasitic in the sense that they have detrimental effects on the individual organism was first raised by Lewis (1941) and Östergren (1945) in a discussion of B Chromosomes.

Compared to previous reviews on this topic that compared and contrasted genetics with evolutionary psychology (Bailey, 1998; Barendregt & Van Hexewijk, 2005), the assumption of this chapter is that the two approaches are necessarily complementary—despite misconceptions and debates—because both are branches of zoology and critical for elucidating phenotypic design. Further, rather than being a historical summary of work on genes and behavior, this chapter will present recent developments and future directions.[16]

---

[12] Whether a selfish genetic element (SGE) has deleterious effects on the individual is an empirical question. There would be at least three conditions suggesting the existence of a true SGE: (a) there is very low horizontal transmission of the putative SGE (Hurst, 1996); (b) the presence of other genes suppressing effect of the putative SGE; and (c) there are no benefits to the host so selection is operating below the individual level. For example, a commonly studied SGE (i.e., transposable element) could have benefits. Specifically cultures of bacteria with transposable elements are more successful than bacterial cultures without them under artificial conditions (Charlesworth, 1987). However, it must be acknowledged that artificial conditions of the laboratory do not definitively show that transposable elements are beneficial to individuals, but it does suggest that selection could convert a SGE to a strategic gene. I imagine a series of arms races between SGEs and suppressors. But this arms race does not prevent mutations occurring where the suppressor must always be a suppressor or the SGE must always be deleterious. Specifically a suppressor could mutate into a converter whereby it converts the SGE into a beneficial contributor to the public good (i.e., the organism itself). The SGE could oscillate between beneficial and detrimental states over evolutionary time scales or perhaps within the life-course of the individual. For a review of the evidence and importance of selfish genetic elements, the most authoritative source is Burt and Trivers (2006).

[13] SGEs bypass interests of the organism in a way that is either neutral or deleterious.

[14] Relatedness asymmetries are defined as the differences between coefficients of relatedness for parental genomes (Haig, 1997). Specifically an individual's kin can be categorized as *symmetric* relatives (with *equal* probabilities of sharing copies of an individual's maternally and paternally derived genes) and *asymmetric* relatives (with *unequal* probabilities of sharing maternally and paternally derived genes). Relatedness asymmetries influence the chances of intragenomic conflicts (Haig, 1997, 2000). A pathway to relatedness asymmetry is multiple paternity. For example if mother produces several offspring with different males, paternal genetic relatedness decreases between siblings, increasing the potential for intragenomic conflict.

[15] For example, let us consider an example of increased inclusive fitness for the acceptance of religious celibacy. The celibates' family (e.g., sibs) could receive social benefits (trust, mating opportunities) from others by having a celibate sibling. However if there is multiple paternity within the family matrilineal coefficients of relatedness will be higher (all sibs share the same mother) compared to patrilineal coefficients (i.e., $r_{pat} = 0$) because sibs were sired by different fathers. An intragenomic conflict approach predicts a divided mind in this situation even though religious celibacy may be socially desirable in some societies (Brown, 2001a). Specifically it is predicted that the paternal genome within self will reject the celibacy norm whereas the maternal genome will favor its acceptance. An escalation of conflicting parental gene expression within self is expected when there are relatedness asymmetries either due to sex-biased dispersal or multiple paternity.

[16] The first Gordon Research Conference on Genes and Behavior (February, 2004, Ventura, CA) was a partial source for the diverse work on behavioral genomics presented in this chapter. The preponderance of evidence shows that gene expression influences behavior and behavior influences gene expression. However, much of this work is based on a handful of model organisms. This is unfortunate considering 99.9% of extant species are not studied even though their diversity could reveal unforeseen associations between genes and behavior.

THEORETICAL GENETICS

The modern synthesis

Linking genetics to evolutionary theory[17] was probably the most significant development that led to the underlying foundations of evolutionary psychology (EP). This is partially why EP resembles ethology and sociobiology in fundamental ways. Granted EP departs from ethology and sociobiology in that it deals with information-processing mechanisms that are hypothesized to have been selected in their own right.[18] Some developmentalists[19] who criticize EP are largely critical of this intellectual ancestry, questioning whether the modern synthesis between genetics and evolution missed something, namely the whole organism. Why is this case? The often-cited developmental alternative to EP is that organisms are flexible and/or greater than the sum of their parts, and this is solely caused by developmental pathways unique to each individual. These facts are inconsequential and tell us only limited information about adaptive evolution at the behavioral level because it only focuses on one part of the story. Furthermore, this holistic observation could render empirical hypothesis testing difficult or worse impossible. Nonetheless it is clear that evolutionary researchers study evolved flexibility in a variety of organisms despite claims to the contrary. This area is largely influenced by the work on reaction norms. A gene–environment interaction occurs when the actions of a gene are different in one environment than in another environment. For example, in some fish species individuals with the same genotype look so different from one another that early researchers thought they were members of different species. In humans we can view language differences as a prime example of gene-by-environment interaction. We have particular genes that allow us to learn language (e.g., genes involved in vocal chord development, the neural areas for production and reception of linguistic information, etc.). However the exact language we learn (e.g., Chinese or English) depends critically on the environment in which we are raised. Most individuals have the genetic predisposition to learn language but the particular form of the language we learn is the product of gene–environment interactions.

Phenotypic plasticity[20]

Richard Woltereck (1928) defined a reaction norm as the range of phenotypes exhibited over all environments. His insight was: "Genotypus = Reaktionsnorm" or the idea that the genotype contains the information for developmental plasticity. It is important to note as de Jong (2003) has, that

---

[17] The architects of the modern synthesis between genetics and evolution were Dobzhansky, Fisher, Haldane, J Huxley, Morgan, Simpson, Stebbins, and Wright. From around 1910 to 1932, a mathematical theory of population and quantitative genetics was established that attempted to explain the effects of natural selection, mutation, inbreeding, and genetic drift in small and large populations. The success with these issues promoted genetics to be at the core of evolutionary biology (Grafen, 2004; Stearns & Hoekstra, 2000).

[18] Many evolutionary psychologists credit Robert Trivers' classic papers (2002) on the evolution of cooperation, parental investment, and parent–offspring conflict as the key foundations of evolutionary psychology because of his explicit discussion of psychology in conjunction with underlying evolutionary principles—a clear departure from much of the previous work from evolutionary biology before the 1970s.

[19] Developmental Systems Theorists (DST) erroneously argue that advocates of the modern synthesis ignore development and treat the organism as a black box. The black box criticism is surprising considering that much empirical work on behavioral evolution because the modern synthesis ranges across Tinbergen's levels of causation (i.e., life history biology, neuroethology, adaptationist, and phylogenetic analyses).

[20] There is little evidence that developmental plasticity is an initiating factor of adaptive novelty that precedes genetic change despite expectations to the contrary (West-Eberhard, 2003). In fairness to West-Eberhard's (2003) position that plasticity drives evolutionary change before genetic accommodation an absence of evidence is not absence of fact. Nonetheless the more general point made by West-Eberhard (2003) is that developmentally plastic phenotypes evolved in a context of varying ecological conditions is on firmer ground.

when Woltereck transplanted water fleas *Daphnia* from Denmark to Italy the environment did not modify the reaction norm. Genes respond to the environment and this is one way that cognitive adaptations are executed and selected for during the course of evolution (Crawford & Anderson, 1989). The current evidence shows that developmental plasticity is taxonomically widespread and has a genetic basis (de Jong, 2003). In part, the evidence supporting this is that different genotypes display different reaction norms. I will return to development and evolution later in the chapter.

Population genetics and game theory

Two approaches to understanding the evolutionary origins and maintenance of genes in populations exist: (a) population genetics, which investigates allelic variation and spread of adaptive novelties in a background of constraints; and (b) game theory, which looks at genes as strategists against rival versions in an evolutionary game where the best strategy depends on the strategies of other genes in the population. Constraints can also be included in game theoretic modeling (e.g., what strategies are available). Kin selection is largely a population genetics model focusing on the conditions for the spread of a novel altruistic allele (Hamilton, 1964), although Evolutionarily Stable Strategies (ESS) approaches are game theoretic in the sense that strategy success depends on the behavior of others in the population (Hamilton, 1967; Maynard Smith, 1984; Maynard Smith & Price, 1973; Nowak, 2006; Trivers, 1971). Trivers and Haig have combined these two approaches to investigate parent–offspring conflict and intragenomic conflicts due to asymmetries in relatedness. In the following section, the kinship or conflict theory of genomic imprinting is introduced.

Sociogenomics I: Genomic imprinting

Most genes have identical effects regardless of whether they were passed on matrilineally or patrilineally. However, for a small group of genes, parent of origin influences gene expression, a phenomenon known as "genomic imprinting" (Murphy & Jirtle, 2003). Genomic imprinting is the inactivation of a particular allele depending on parent of origin (Figure 6.2).

The kinship theory (also referred to as the genomic conflict hypothesis) of imprinting proposes that asymmetries in relatedness (e.g., due to multiple paternity and/or sex-biased dispersal; see Figure 6.3) favors the differential expression of maternal and paternal alleles so that (a) paternal alleles increase the cost to the offspring's mother (at some benefit to themselves); and (b) the maternal alleles reduce these costs (Haig, 2002).

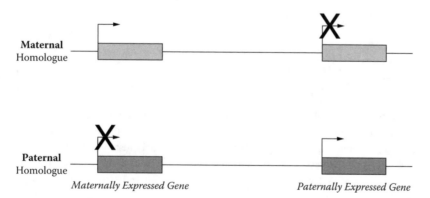

Figure 6.2 The simplest case of imprinted gene expression. The gene on the left is only expressed from the maternal allele and expression is silenced (bold x) from the paternal allele. The gene on the right has the opposite pattern of expression and is paternally expressed/maternally silenced. The imprint is erased in the gametes and new imprints are made that indicate whether the gene was transmitted from an egg or a sperm. Courtesy of Dr. Ben Dickins.

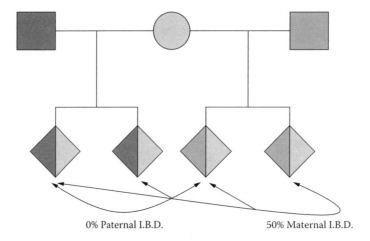

Figure 6.3 Asymmetric relations in a family using standard pedigree symbols. If the mother mates with more than one male, maternally and paternally derived alleles in her offspring will show asymmetric patterns of relatedness within the family group. For autosomal genes maternal alleles in half sibs will be related to each other by descent with a probability of 50% ($r = .50$), but paternal alleles will not be shared. This can be seen by the arrows in the diagram. Due to multiple paternity during mammalian evolutionary history the average relatedness of paternal alleles between siblings would have been less than .50. This asymmetry is the basis of intragenomic conflict. IBD stands for identical-by-descent. Courtesy of Dr. Ben Dickins.

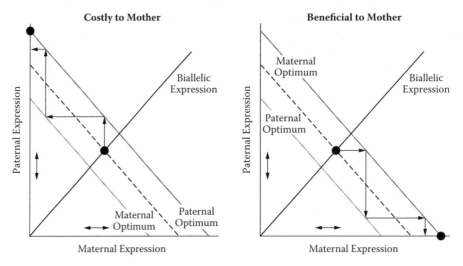

Figure 6.4 A hypothetical evolutionary arms race for maternally costly versus beneficial genes. Diagonal line represents biallelic expression (solid black). Blue and red diagonal lines represent the optimal levels of paternal and maternal expression, respectively, whereas the dotted diagonal line represents the family optimum (for unimprinted genes). Allelic expression for unimprinted genes is the black dot. Changes in the expression of the parental alleles will lead to fixed expression from one or the other allele. Courtesy of Dr. Ben Dickins.

The kinship theory of genomic imprinting suggests that imprinting evolves at a locus when the gene expression levels that maximise matrilineal inclusive fitness differ from the gene expression levels that maximise patrilineal inclusive fitness (Haig, 1999a; Haig & Wharton, 2003; see Figure 6.4). Kinship theory predicts that paternal genes within children will lead to behaviors that increase a mother's costs of child rearing and, conversely, maternal genes within the child will be selected to *reduce* these costs. One can think of this as an intrapersonal conflict (i.e., within-child) between unrelated genetic elements over securing parental investment. Parental investment is defined (Trivers, 1972) as all care delivered by a parent to an offspring that increases the likelihood that the offspring survives at the expense of that parent's capacity to care for any other offspring (alive or yet to be born). Examples of parental investment include but are not limited to gamete size, lactation, feeding, protection, and teaching.

To this point, imprinting researchers have focused primarily on prenatal nourishment/growth (Haig, 1999b) and neonatal investment (Haig & Wharton, 2003). For an extreme example of growth enhancer paternal genes versus growth suppression maternal genes, see Figure 6.5.

Throughout childhood, there may be further opportunities for intragenomic conflict. For example, it may be that paternally expressed genes influence infant wakefulness during co-sleeping that increases maternal costs (McNamara, 2004). Corroborating this conjecture is a recent review of REM sleep patterns and the neural areas mediating milk let-down in humans (McNamara, Dowdall, & Auerbach, 2002; McNamara, 2004; Messinger et al., 2002). McNamara and colleagues have suggested that infant REM facilitates positive attachment to mother (to gain resources from her) and may be regulated via paternal genes.

There are other reasons to expect that intragenomic conflicts persist after birth and shape cognitive mechanisms. In experiments with chimeric mice, maternal genes are overexpressed in cells found in the neocortex (involved in flexible decision-making) and paternal genes are overexpressed in the cells of the hypothalamus, involved in homeostasis, emotion, hunger, and sex (Allen et al., 1995; Keverne Fundele, Narasimha, Barton, & Surani,, 1996). Considering the potential involvement of paternal genes in the limbic system it may be that the hyperactive and fearful behavioral phenotype may reflect an underlying intragenomic conflict (Brown, 2004). This possibility is further explored in the section on epigenetic maternal effects on offspring development.

Nonfeeding costs to mother are recognized by kinship theorists as being important but are just starting to be explored from a kinship theory perspective (Brown & Consedine, 2004; Haig & Wharton, 2003; McNamara, 2004). Ethologists and psychologists have long been aware that mammalian mothers provide more than nourishment; they provide social learning opportunities and bonding that are crucial for child development (Ainsworth, 1979; Altmann, 1980; Bowlby, 1969; Brown, 2001a; Harlow, 1958; Hinde, 1976). One strategy for securing investment from mother lies in the process of forming an emotional attachment and eliciting maternal investment through

Figure 6.5 Mouse pups with uniparental duplications of chromosome 11. Pup X is paternally disomic and significantly larger than Pup Y that is maternally disomic. Figure from Cattanach and Kirk (1985).

nonverbal signals. Brown and Consedine (2004) suggested that the emotion signals produced by infants (and young children more generally) are best understood within an intragenomic conflict framework. Specifically, paternal genes may have designed emotion signals in children to increase the costs on matrilineal inclusive fitness. Lack of such care-eliciting signals would suggest overexpression of maternal genes within the child designed to reduce these costs. Empirical studies based on this theoretical approach are yielding novel insights into human cognitive development (Crespi, 2007; Isles & Wilkinson, 2000; Oliver et al., 2007).

Even if an evolutionary psychologist is not convinced by the intragenomic conflict approach to the mind, there is much to be gained from understanding (and continually updating one's knowledge) on genes, brain and behavior (Robinson, 1999). More generally, because all fundamental cognitive mechanisms must have a neurobiological and genetic basis a clear ally to evolutionary psychology is the burgeoning field of neurogenetics. In the following section, some of the key findings from neurogenetics with relevance to evolutionary psychology are presented.

NEUROGENETICS AND THE CANDIDATE GENE APPROACH

Neurogenetics is a field that studies how genetical systems influence brain development, morphology, and neural activation. Genetic technologies have lead to the development of animal models for aspects of human psychology, even if the respective behavioral phenotypes do not naturally occur in these animals (Pulst, 2003). In principle, these technologies can be applied to any animal, but unfortunately only mouse (*Mus musculus*), zebra fish (*Danio rerio*), fruit fly (*Drosophila melanogaster*), and nematode (*Caenorhabditis elegans*) are most often investigated. For phenotypes involving cognitive function, there is a reliance on rats as model organisms. Two main approaches are used to alter the genetic constitution of animals. The first involves insertion of a novel, often mutated gene into the germline; the second, an alteration of endogenous genes by gene targeting or random mutagenesis.

Importantly the conservation of gene function across distantly related species means that genes known to influence behavior in one organism are likely to influence similar behaviors in other organisms. The Candidate Gene Approach (CGA) offers methodological tools to greatly expand evolutionary psychological research. Expression of candidate genes reveals their contribution to behavioral variation and/or phenotypic plasticity. For example, learning evolves in laboratory populations (Mery & Kawecki, 2002) and retaining learning capacities could have fitness costs (Mery & Kawecki, 2003; Vet, Lewis, & Cardé, 1995). The cellular and genetic mechanisms responsible for learning and memory are evolutionarily conserved (Mery & Kawecki, 2002). Zebra finch *Taeniopygia guttata* songs are learned (Doupe & Kuhl, 1999; Marler, 1990) much like human language acquisition (Doupe & Kuhl, 1999). *FOXP2* mutations are associated with severe abnormalities in human speech and language (Lai, Fisher, Hurst, Vargha-Khadem, & Monaco, 2001). Interestingly Haesler et al. (2004) have found greater *FOXP2* expression in the basal ganglia vocal nucleus of vocal-learning birds when song is acquired. The basal ganglia nucleus is required for song learning. *FOXP2* expression is not found in nonvocal basal ganglia areas or in nonvocal-learning birds. These results indicate that *FOXP2* is a vocal learning candidate gene. The candidate gene approach to the study of behavioral ecology (Fitzpatrick et al., 2005) will likely bolster the theoretical foundations of evolutionary psychology.

In summary, neurogenetics and the CGA contribute to the evolutionary psychology paradigm by providing evidence that genetic variation influences the neuroarchitecture of psychological mechanisms. It could be suggested that little or no genetic variation would be expected in psychological adaptations, which would be the case if there were only directional selection (as opposed to frequency-dependent selection or adaptive phenotypic plasticity). However, genetic variation in pathological populations can also be a window into normally functioning phenotypes. Therefore, it is useful for evolutionary psychologists to consider and incorporate the work of neurogenetics.

The work on brain and behavior has generally adopted the stance that neural tissue is sensitive to environmental factors. Because a key aspect of human ecology is the social domain we may also expect that social forces are a determinant of gene expression. A social organism insensitive to the social environment would likely be an unfit individual indeed.

Sociogenomics II: Indirect genetic effects

Quantitative genetics has modeled the phenotype as the product of two components: genes, and the environment in which these genes experience during development. However, when social interactions occur, one individual provides the "environment" for another, meaning that the environment can have a genetic component and therefore the environment itself can evolve (Wolf, Brodie, Cheverud, Moore & Wade, 1998) and quite possibly in an antagonistic fashion (Rice & Holland, 1997). This complexity introduces a new component that may affect an individual's phenotype: Indirect genetic effects (IGEs). IGEs occur whenever the genes of one individual, through their effect on that individual's phenotype, influence the phenotypic expression of a trait in an interacting individual (Wolf et al., 1998). IGEs cause reliable cross-generational phenotypes in other individuals. For example, in Australian fruit flies Drosophila serrata there is some evidence for IGE's in male display traits; D. serrata males use contact pheromones to attract females (Chenoweth & Blows, 2006; Petfield Chenoweth, Rundle, & Blows, 2005). Petfield et al. (2005) conducted a multivariate quantitative genetic analysis to uncover IGEs on male sexual displays. The researchers wished to determine how genes underlying female condition influence male sexual displays. The authors found that in D. serrata the genetic variation in female body condition accounted for approximately 20% of the indirect genetic variation in male pheromone production (Petfield et al., 2005). The demonstration of indirect genetic effects in Petfield et al. (2005) suggests that D. serrata males consider female body condition (which is likely partially mediated by resource availability) an important fitness indicator.

Sociogenomics III: Maternal epigenetics

Epigenetic inheritance is when there is reversible and heritable nongenetic variation in phenotype. When environmental information from a previous generation influences gene expression in the current generation, this can also be referred to as epigenetic. Imprinted genes are an example whereby the source of environmental information is whether the gene was present in a sperm or egg in the previous generation. Interestingly in mammals there are maternal environmental effects on fear behavior (e.g., defensive responses) in adult offspring (Higley Hasert, Suomi, & Linnoila 1991; Meaney, 2001). For example, in rats, fear is influenced by variations in maternal parental investment. Specifically maternal behavior stably alters the development of behavioral and endocrine responses to stress in the offspring through tissue-specific effects on gene expression (Francis, Diorio, Liu, & Meaney, M. J., 1999; Liu et al., 1997). Adult offspring of mothers that showed increased pup "Licking Grooming and Arched-Back Nursing" (High LG-ABN mothers) over the first week of postnatal life exhibit reduced fearfulness and lower hypothalamic-pituitary-adrenal (HPA) responses to stress.

In rats increased fear responses to stress are associated with decreased hippocampal neurogenesis and synaptic density (Liu et al., 1997). These findings suggest an influence of maternal investment on hippocampal gene expression. Cross-fostering experiments provide support for a relationship between maternal care and measures of hippocampal gene expression, behavioral responses to stress, and hippocampal development. Importantly offspring of low LG-ABN mothers reared by high LG-ABN mothers resemble the normal offspring of high LG-ABN mothers (Francis et al., 1999).

These findings suggest that variations in maternal behavior can directly influence defensive responses to stress and serve as a mechanism for the development of individual differences in stress reactivity across generations (Francis et al., 1999; Meaney, 2001; Weaver, Meaney, & Szyf, 2006). Previous studies suggest that maternal programming of individual differences in gene expression and stress responses in the rat involve modifications of epigenetic mechanisms, including DNA methylation (Weaver et al., 2006).

Sociogenomics bolsters evolutionary psychology because it demonstrates that gene expression is influenced by family dynamics, a key element to behavioral adaptations from a gene's eye view (e.g., inclusive fitness). Perhaps successful attachment between mother and offspring is a consequence of increased maternal investment and in reciprocated exchange a reduction of paternal gene expression within the offspring—this could facilitate *intrapersonal* reciprocity (Haig, 2003). However the increased stress response in offspring raised by low-investing mothers could be a product of retaliatory strategies by the paternal genome—this could escalate *intrapersonal* conflict. The hypothesis of intrapersonal reciprocity may seem far-fetched, but surely reciprocity is easier to evolve between genes within a genome than between genes in different genomes (Haig, 2003). Now that some of the major findings from sociogenomics have been presented, I return to the issue of development and evolution raised earlier in the chapter.

DEVELOPMENT

Developmental Systems Theory has adopted the stance that development constrains morphological evolution. Constraints arguments are largely a reaction to the neo-Darwinian hypothesis that all small variations are possible and selection is the main factor explaining morphological evolution. However, to make the claim that there is a constraint implies that it is known what an organism's phenotype would be without the constraint and this is difficult or perhaps impossible (Salazar-Ciudad, 2006). Nonetheless, some DST advocates regard developmental constraints as an alternative to selection for explaining the distribution of phenotypes. This is an unreasonable position if one considers that all morphological variation is dependent on developmental dynamics caused by genetic and/or environmental variation (including conspecifics—see previous sections on sociogenomics). Studying constraints and selection would be more empirically useful than arguing about the relative importance of either. Finally, the very reactivity of developmental systems is itself a product of natural selection (Pigliucci, Murren, & Schlichting, 2006), thus, arguments based on development as constraining evolution are largely misleading in principle (Salazar-Ciudad, 2006).

It is assumed that neo-Darwinists treat development as a black box[21] despite serious treatments of development and evolution (Brown, 2002; Hall, 2003; Klingenberg & Leamy, 2001; Maynard Smith et al., 1985; Salazar-Ciudad, 2006). DST enthusiasts have tried to extend this criticism to evolutionary psychology without empirical success. However one area that has received much empirical attention is the debate between developmentalists and evolutionary biologists regarding the evolution of neural anatomy.

Developmental constraints

According to the developmental constraints hypothesis of comparative mammalian neuroanatomy, brain components increased predictably in size, both ontogenetically and phylogenetically, in concert with the entire brain. On the adaptationist side of the debate are those who hypothesize that brain components were shaped independently by natural selection. This adaptationist view also called mosaic brain evolution contrasts sharply with the belief that the whole brain increased in size for nonadaptive reasons via concerted evolution (Finlay & Darlington, 1995; Gould, 1977). The

---

[21] Some experimentalists feel that we can treat development as a black box to see how far we get. The remaining variation (i.e., not explicable in terms of selection) must then be explored. This view would be similar to testing for main effects and interactions and the elucidation of the remaining variation must be left to future studies.

argument has been used by developmental systems theorists to dispute the power of natural selection in shaping neural architecture.

There is a large literature from independent research groups suggesting that mosaic evolution of brain structure is common across taxa (Barton & Harvey, 2000; de Winter & Oxnard, 2001; Rilling & Insel, 1998). It is unlikely that a uniform developmental constraint was an overriding influence on brain evolution. Internal reorganizations of the brain are not simply size-related. Increases in functionally related brain components occur along different axes in separate orders. For example, frugivorous species of bats and primates are highly encephalized compared with insectivores, but this is due to a proportional expansion of different neural systems in each of these orders (Brown, 2001b). This suggests that brain structures with functional and anatomical links evolved independently of other structures. Mosaic brain evolution has been investigated in cetaceans. One study of bottlenose dolphins *Turiops truncates* and common dolphins *Delphinus delphis* found that the cerebellum (important for balance) was larger than in primates (including humans) in spite of the fact that dolphins and primates have similarly sized brains (Marino Rilling, Lin, & Ridgway, 2000). Overall, the findings across taxa suggest that mosaic brain evolution is caused by specialized behavioral adaptations to a particular ecological niche (de Winter & Oxnard, 2001).

Mosaic brain evolution may be related to social transmission capacities (Reader & Laland, 2002). Timmermans et al. (2000) found that in 17 avian taxa, the neostriatum–hyperstriatum ventrale complex may have a similar role as that of the primate neocortex in behavioral flexibility. Future comparative research in birds, cetaceans and primates should be performed with attempts to correlate social transmission capacities, underlying neural architecture and gene expression. Candidate genes have now been discovered that are involved in ongoing adaptive evolution of brain size in humans (Evans et al., 2005; Mekel-Bobrov et al., 2005). The candidate gene approach discussed earlier in the chapter could provide further description of the underlying mechanisms and ecological correlates (Fitzpatrick et al., 2005).

EVOLUTIONARY PSYCHOLOGY: DOMAINS, LEVELS AND CHALLENGES[22]

Is evolutionary psychology necessarily a form of nativism?

Clearly when nativism[23] is used as a sole explanation for phenotype it is intellectually vacuous, much like socialization theory. Empirically motivated evolutionary scientists spend their time studying phenotype and the mechanisms producing adaptations as opposed to making nativism claims. Even when they study genes they really are interested in the phenotypic effects. We know that phenotypes are produced by genes, environments,[24] and interactions between the two. Nativism claims are analogous to socialization theory in reverse that states "people behave this way because they were socialized"—nativism simply argues the "people behave this way because they were born that way." The reason both these arguments are impoverished is because they do not explain why

---

[22]This is a reference to George C. Williams' (1992) classic book on the major challenges facing evolutionary biology. Some of these challenges could be easily extended to evolutionary psychology.

[23]When I am using the term *nativism*, I am not questioning the importance of universal grammar or a language acquisition device. Neither am I disputing the fact that genes are important for the development of cognitive adaptations. Nativism or general genetic determinism as the sole explanatory tool is the target discussed here. Specifically we are interested in how traits develop, evolve or are implemented at the neurocognitive/behavioral levels. Despite an apparent pop-cultural allure, statements such as men and women are innately different tell us very little.

[24]Environments can include genotypes in other individuals known as indirect genetic effects. Maternal care is the most studied indirect genetic effect but recent work investigates mate choice.

we were born that way or socialized that way (as opposed to some other way). It is the evolutionary approach that attempts to unravel the causal forces producing adaptations and non-adaptations. Simply describing the phenomenon is not an explanation of it. Therefore socialization and nativism as theories should be rejected. If they were, theories they would make specific predictions. I would suggest evolutionary psychologists avoid the term nativism much like instinct has been avoided because it adheres to a debate that is now over in principle. All phenotypes are produced by 100% genes and 100% environment via biochemical cascades. Selection shapes the catalytic reactions of genes to increase their replication success given their *environmental context*. Therefore, this chapter strongly discourages the endorsement of nativism—unless it can be shown that it brings something empirically useful beyond the banal statement that genes determine human nature.

Are evolutionary psychologists only interested in universals?

It is an important observation if a trait is not variable across diverse environments. Unfortunately determining the causes of such variation is difficult. Human universals can be a product of shared environment, shared genes or shared developmental pathways (including cultural inheritance). Therefore a universal cannot in and of itself be evidence of a psychological adaptation. Evidence of special design and further elucidation of the underlying mechanisms would be required to suggest psychological adaptation. There are many examples from plants to nonhuman animals suggesting that one genotype can produce multiple adaptive phenotypes[25] so if we find differences between populations, there is no good reason to assume that these traits have no evolutionary relevance or that they are merely quirks of cultural inheritance.

Is the gene the sole unit of selection?

We cannot state that the gene is the sole unit of selection, according to the late W. D. Hamilton (Hamilton, 1996) a pioneer of strategic gene approach to social behavior. Rather the gene is the "atom of selection," and a catalyst of reactions that affect its own replication success. There are multiple levels of vehicles such as individual, group, species, and ecosystem. Indeed, there may even be conflict between levels (e.g., gene versus individual or individual versus group). The gene-level *must* be included in all levels of selection paradigms because it is the atom of selection. It is known that group selection is mathematically possible (Williams, 1966) and has been experimentally demonstrated using artificial selection regimes in laboratory settings (Swenson, Wilson, & Elias, 2000; Wade, 1980). One problem with the multilevel approach is that we have little to no evidence that such processes occur naturally outside artificial selection experiments (Williams, 1992). More importantly, from the point of view of this chapter, it is unclear how empirical psychology would be different based on a multilevel selection approach. From an empirical perspective of human psychology, a multilevel selection approach would be unprofitable if group level benefits are an _epiphenomenon_ of the benefits to individuals. What is needed is a clear demonstration that the between- and within-group forces of natural selection have independently shaped neurocognitive mechanisms *differently*. Beyond this demonstration multilevel selection theory will be little more than an interesting thought experiment for the study of behavior.

GENE TO ORGANISM DOMAIN-SPECIFICITY?

Theoretical controversies aside it should be clear from this chapter and volume that evolutionary psychology is based on solid theoretical and empirical grounds. Notions of reverse engineering adaptation and game theoretic logic allow for ample predictions to be tested in the field or lab. The fact that genes influence and are influenced by behavior is exactly what an evolutionary psychologist

---

[25]For a discussion of genetic variation underlying evolutionary psychology see Nettle (2006).

would expect if information-processing bundles are the products of a mosaic evolution at different levels (genes, cells, neurons, structure, cognitive mechanisms, and outward behavior).

Ironically perhaps cooperation within individuals may be a challenge to explain evolutionarily. That is there may be a coordination problem—such as a public goods dilemma among members of the collective whose free-riding members threaten the success of the whole group. When cooperation is observed within the genome it must be explained rather than taken for granted. Because the same evolutionary logic applies, evolutionary psychologists may have important insights to make regarding cooperation within the genome, just as they have made contributions to the study of cooperation between individual organisms.

Many details of how gene expression influences (and is influenced by) human ontogeny still need to be worked out, but there is no reason to believe that the underlying principle of adaptation by natural selection will be violated or subsumed by the largely philosophically oriented Developmental Systems Theory.

It is the premise of this chapter that organisms are not necessarily cohesive wholes but rather bundles of interests with common and conflicting goals. These bundles are subject to selection and include catalytic reactions, biochemical cascades, neuronal firing, structural components, neuro-cognitive activation, behavior, and learning (individual to social). Gene to organism developmental modules are most likely to be explicated with neo-Darwinian principles and empirically driven science. There is much more to come for evolutionary psychology in the age of genomics but this will require further interdisciplinary synthesis among various fields (e.g., Burt & Trivers, 2006, Frank, 1998; Keller, 1999; Maynard Smith & Szathmary, 1995; Michod, 1999; Nowak, 2006).

ACKNOWLEDGMENTS

I am thankful to Charles Crawford, Ben Dickins, David Haig, Michael Price, and Nicole Sutherland for their comments and referencing assistance.

REFERENCES

Ainsworth, M. D. S. (1979). Attachment as related to mother–infant interaction. *Advances in the Study of Behavior, 9,* 2–52.

Allen, N. D., Logan, K., Lally, G., Drage, D. J., Norris, M. L., & Keverne, E. B. (1995). Distribution of parthenogenetic cells in the mouse brain and their influence on brain development and behavior. *Proceedings of the National Academy of Sciences USA , 92,* 10782–10786.

Altmann, J. (1980). *Baboon mothers and infants.* Cambridge, MA Harvard University Press.

Bailey, J. M. (1998). Can behavior genetics contribute to evolutionary behavioral science? In C. B.Crawford, & D. L. Krebs (Eds.), *Handbook of Evolutionary Psychology: Ideas, Issues, and Applications* (pp. 211–233). Mahwah, NJ: Erlbaum.

Barendregt, M., & Hezewijk, R. (2005). Adaptive and genomic explanations of human behavior: Might evolutionary psychology contribute to behavioral genomics? *Biology and Philosophy, 20,* 57–78.

Barton, R. A., & Harvey, P. H. (2000) Mosaic evolution of brain structure in mammals. *Nature, 405,* 1055–1058.

Bowie, J. U. (2005). Solving the membrane protein folding problem. *Nature, 438,* 581–589.

Bowlby, J. (1969). *Attachment and loss* (Vol. 1). New York: Basic.

Brown, W. M. (2001a). Genomic imprinting and the cognitive architecture mediating human culture. *Journal of Cognition and Culture, 1,* 251–258.

Brown, W. M. (2001b). Natural selection of mammalian brain components. *Trends in Ecology and Evolution, 16,* 471–473.

Brown, W. M. (2002). Development: The missing link between exaptationist and adaptationist accounts of organismal design. *Behavioral and Brain Sciences, 25,* 509–510.

Brown, W. M. (2004). Evolved cognitive architecture mediating fear: A genomic conflict approach. In P. L. Gower (Ed.), *The Psychology of Fear* (pp. 171–182). New York: Nova Science Publishers.

Brown, W. M., & Consedine, N. S. (2004). Just how happy is the Happy Puppet? An emotion signaling and kinship theory perspective on the behavioral phenotype of children with Angelman syndrome. *Medical Hypotheses, 63,* 377–385.

Burt, A., & Trivers, R. (2006). *Genes in conflict.* Cambridge, MA: Belknap Press of Harvard University.

Cattanach, B. M., & Kirk, M. (1985). Differential activity of maternally and paternally derived chromosome regions in mice. *Nature, 315,* 496–498.

Charlesworth, B. (1987). The population biology of transposable elements. *Trends in Ecology and Evolution, 2,* 21–23.

Chenoweth, S. F., & Blows, M. W. (2006). Dissecting the complex genetic basis of mate choice. *Nature Reviews Genetics, 7,* 681–692

Crawford, C., & Anderson, J. (1989). Sociobiology: An environmentalist discipline? *American Psychologist, 44,* 1449–1459.

Crespi, B. J. (2007). Sly *FOXP2*: genomic conflict in the evolution of language. *Trends in Ecology and Evolution, 22,* 174–175.

Dawkins, R. (1976). *The selfish gene.* Oxford, U.K.: Oxford University Press.

Dawkins, R. (1989). *The extended phenotype.* Oxford, U.K.: W. H. Freeman.

Dawkins, R. (1996). Video Interview from M. Ridley *Evolution 2nd Edition* (CD-ROM). Oxford, U.K.: Blackwell Science.

de Bono, M., & Bargmann, C. I. (1998). Natural variation in a neuropeptide Y receptor homolog modifies social behavior and food response in *C. elegans. Cell, 94,* 679–689.

de Jong, G. (2003). A flexible theory of evolution. *Nature, 424,* 16–17.

de Winter, W., & Oxnard, C. E. (2001). Evolutionary radiations and convergences in the structural organization of mammalian brains. *Nature, 409,* 710–714.

Doolittle, W. F., & Sapienza, C. (1980). Selfish genes, the phenotype paradigm and genome evolution. *Nature, 284,* 601–603.

Doupe, A. J., & Kuhl, P. K. (1999) Birdsong and human speech: Common themes and mechanisms. *Annual Review of Neuroscience, 22,* 567–631.

Evans, P. D., Gilbert, S. L., Mekel-Bobrov, N., Vallender, E. J., Anderson, J. R., & Vaez-Azizi, L. M., et al. (2005). Microcephalin, a gene regulating brain size, continues to evolve in humans. *Science, 309,* 1717–1720.

Finlay, B. L. & Darlington, R. B. (1995) Linked regularities in the development and evolution of mammalian brains. *Science, 268,* 1578–1584

Fitzpatrick, M. J., Ben-Shahar, Y, Smid, H. M., Vet, L. E. M., Robinson, G. E., & Sokolowski, M. B. (2005). Candidate genes for behavioral ecology. *Trends in Ecology and Evolution, 20,* 97–103.

Francis, D., Diorio, J., Liu, D., & Meaney, M. J. (1999). Nongenetic transmission across generations of maternal behavior and stress responses in the rat. *Science, 286,* 1155–1158.

Frank, S. (1998). *Foundations of social evolution.* Princeton, NJ: Princeton University Press.

Gould, S. J. (1977). *Ontogeny and phylogeny.* Cambridge, MA: Harvard University Press.

Grafen, A. (2004). William Donald Hamilton (1 August 1936–7 March 2000). *Biographical Memoirs of Fellows of the Royal Society, 50,* 109–132.

Haesler, S., Wada, K., Nshdejan, A., Morrisey, E. E., Lints, T., & Jarvis, E. D., et al. (2004). *FOXP2* expression in avian vocal learners and non learners. *Journal of Neuroscience, 24,* 3164–3175.

Haig, D. (1999a). Multiple paternity and genomic imprinting. *Genetics, 151,* 1229–1231.

Haig, D. (1999b). Genetic conflicts of pregnancy and childhood. In S. C. Stearns, (Ed.), *Evolution in Health and Disease* (pp. 77–90). Oxford, U.K.: Oxford University Press.

Haig, D. (1997). Parental antagonism, relatedness asymmetries, and genomic imprinting. *Proceedings of the Royal Society B Biological Sciences, 264,* 1657–1662.

Haig, D. (2000). Genomic imprinting, sex-biased dispersal, and social behavior. *Annals of the New York Academy of Sciences, 907,* 149–163.

Haig, D. (2002). *Genomic imprinting and kinship.* Piscataway, NJ: Rutgers University Press.

Haig, D. (2003). On intrapersonal reciprocity. *Evolution and Human Behavior, 24,* 418–425.

Haig, D. (2006). Intrapersonal conflict. In M. K. Jones & A. Fabian (Eds), *Conflict* (pp 8–22). Cambridge, U.K.: Cambridge University Press.

Haig, D., & Wharton, R. (2003). Prader–Willi syndrome and the evolution of human childhood. *American Journal of Human Biology, 15,* 320–329.

Hall, B.K. (2003). Evo-devo: Evolutionary developmental mechanisms. *International Journal of Developmental Biology, 47,* 491–495.

Hamilton, W. D. (1964). The genetical evolution of social behavior I and II. *Journal of Theoretical Biology, 7,* 1–52.

Hamilton, W. D. (1967). *Extraordinary sex ratios. Science, 156,* 477–488.

Hamilton, W. D. (1996). Video Interview from M. Ridley. On *Evolution 2nd Edition* (CD-ROM). Oxfprd, U.K.: Blackwell.

Hamilton, W. D. (2001). *Narrow roads of gene land vol. 2: Evolution of Sex..* Oxford, U.K.: Oxford University Press.

Harlow, H. F. (1958). The nature of love. *American Psychologist, 13,* 673–685.

Higley, J. D., Hasert, M. F., Suomi, S. J., & Linnoila, M. (1991). Nonhuman primate model of alcohol abuse: Effects of early experience, personality, and stress on alcohol consumption. *Proceedings of the National Academy of Science USA , 88,* 7261–7265.

Hinde, R. A. (1976). On describing relationships. *Journal of Child Psychology and Psychiatry,17,* 1–19.

Hurst, L. D. (1996). Adaptation and selection at the sub-individual level. In M. R Rose & G. V. Lauder (Eds), *Adaptation* (pp. 407–449). San Diego: Academic Press.

Isles, A. R., & Wilkinson, L. S. (2000). Imprinted genes, cognition and behavior. *Trends in Cognitive Sciences, 4,* 309–318.

Keller, L. (Ed.). (1999). *Levels of selection in evolution.* Princeton, NJ: Princeton University Press.

Keverne, E. B., Fundele, R., Narasimha, M., Barton, S. C, & Surani, M. A. (1996). Genomic imprinting and the differential roles of parental genomes in brain development. *Development and Brain Research, 92,* 91–100.

Klingenberg, C. P., & Leamy, L. J. (2001). Quantitative genetics of geometric shape in the mouse mandible. *Evolution, 55,* 2342–2352.

Lai, C. S. L., Fisher, S. E., Hurst, J. A., Vargha-Khadem, F., & Monaco, A. P. (2001) A forkhead-domain gene is mutated in a severe speech and language disorder. *Nature, 413,* 519–523.

Lewis, D. (1941). Male sterility in natural populations of hermaphrodite plants. *New Phytologist, 40,* 56–63.

Liu, D., Diorio, J., Tannenbaum, B., Caldji, C., Francis, D., & Freedman, A. (1997). Maternal care, hippocampal glucocorticoid receptors, and hypothalamic-pituitary adrenal responses to stress. *Science, 277,* 1659–1662.

Marino, L., Rilling, J. K., Lin, S. K., & Ridgway, S. H. (2000). Relative volume of the cerebellum in dolphins and comparison with anthropoid primates. *Brain Behavior and Evolution, 56,* 204–211.

Marler, P. (1990) Song learning: the interface between behavior and neuroethology. *Philosophical Transactions of the Royal Society B Biological Sciences, 329,* 109–114.

Maynard Smith, J. (1984). Game theory and the evolution of behavior. *Behavioral and Brain Sciences 7,* 95–125.

Maynard Smith, J., Burian, R., Kauffman, S., Alberch, P., Campbell J., & Goodwin, B., et al. Developmental constraints and evolution. *Quarterly Review of Biology, 60,* 265–287.

Maynard Smith, J., & Price, G. (1973). Logic of animal conflict. *Nature, 246,* 15–18.

Maynard Smith, J., & Szathmary, E. (1995). *The major transitions in evolution.* Oxford, U.K.: W.H. Freeman.

McNamara, P. (2004). Genomic imprinting and neurodevelopmental disorders of sleep. *Sleep and Hypnosis, 6,* 82–90.

McNamara, P., Dowdall, J., & Auerbach, S. (2002). REM sleep, early experience, and the development of reproductive strategies. *Human Nature, 13,* 405–435.

Meaney, M. J. (2001). Maternal care, gene expression, and the transmission of individual differences in stress reactivity across generations. *Annual Review of Neuroscience, 24,* 1161–1192.

Mekel-Bobrov, N., Gilbert,S. L., Evans, P. D., Vallender, E. J., Anderson, J. R., & Hudson, R. R., et al. (2005). Ongoing adaptive evolution of ASPM, a brain size determinant in *Homo sapiens. Science, 309,* 1720–1722.

Mery, F., & Kawecki, T. J. (2002). Experimental evolution of learning ability in fruit flies. *Proceedings of the National Academy of Sciences USA, 99,* 14274–14279.

Mery, F., & Kawecki, T. J. (2003). A fitness cost of learning ability in *Drosophila melanogaster. Proceedings of the Royal Society B Biological Sciences, 270*, 2465–2469.

Messinger, D., Dondi, M., Nelson-Goens, G. C., Beghi, A., Fogel, A., & Simion, F. (2002). How sleeping neonates smile. *Developmental Science, 5*, 48–54.

Michod, R. E. (1999). *Darwinian dynamics: Evolutionary transitions in fitness and individuality.* Princeton, NJ: Princeton University Press.

Murphy, S. K., & Jirtle, R. L. (2003). Imprinting evolution and the price of silence. *BioEssays, 25*, 577–588.

Nettle, D. (2006). The evolution of personality variation in humans and other animals. *American Psychologist, 61*, 622–631.

Nowak, M. (2006). *Evolutionary dynamics.* Cambridge, MA: Belknap Press of Harvard University.

Oliver, C., Horsler, K., Berg, K., Bellamy, G., Dick, K., & Griffiths, E. (2007). Genomic imprinting and the expression of affect in Angelman syndrome: what's in the smile? *Journal of Child Psychology and Psychiatry, 48*, 571–579.

Orgel, L. E., & Crick, F. H. C. (1980). Selfish DNA: The ultimate parasite. *Nature, 284*, 604–607.

Osborne, K. A., Robichon, A., Burgess, E., Butland, S., Shaw, R. A., & Coulthardet A., et al. (1997). Natural behavior polymorphism due to a cGMP dependent protein kinase of *Drosophila, Science, 277*, 834–836.

Östergren, G. (1945). Parasitic nature of extra fragment chromosomes. *Botaniska Notiser, 2*, 157–163.

Petfield, D., Chenoweth, S. F., Rundle, H. D., & Blows, M. W. (2005). Genetic variance in female condition predicts indirect genetic variance in male sexual display traits. *Proceedings of the National Academy of Science USA , 102*, 6045–6050.

Pigliucci, M., Murren, C. J., & Schlichting, C.D. (2006). Phenotypic plasticity and evolution by genetic assimilation. *The Journal of Experimental Biology, 209*, 2362–2367.

Plagge, A, & Kelsey, G. (2006). Imprinting the Gnas locus. *Cytogenetic and Genome Research, 113*, 178–187.

Pulst, S. M. (2003). Neurogenetics: Single gene disorders. *Journal of Neurosurgery and Psychiatry, 64*, 1608–1614.

Reader, S., & Laland, K. (2002). Social intelligence, innovation, and enhanced brain size in primates. *Proceedings of the National Academy of Science USA, 99*, 4436–4441.

Rice, W. R., & Holland, B. (1997). The enemies within: Intergenomic conflict, interlocus contest evolution (ICE), and the intraspecific Red Queen. *Behavioral Ecology and Sociobiology, 41*, 1–10.

Ridley, M. (2001). *The cooperative gene: How Mendel's demon explains the evolution of complex beings.* New York: The Free Press.

Rilling, J. K., & Insel, T. R. (1998). Evolution of the cerebellum in primates: differences in relative volume among monkeys, apes and humans. *Brain Behavior and Evolution, 52*, 308–314.

Robinson, G. (1999). Integrating animal behavior and sociogenomics. *Trends in Ecology and Evolution, 14*, 202–205.

Salazar-Ciudad, I. (2006). Developmental constraints vs. variational properties: how pattern formation can help to understand evolution and development. *Journal of Experimental Zoology Part B Molecular and Developmental Evolution, 306b*, 107–125.

Stearns, S. C., & Hoekstra, R. F. (2000). *Evolution: An introduction.* Oxford, U.K.: Oxford University Press.

Swenson, W., Wilson, D. S., & Elias, R. (2000). Artificial ecosystem selection. *Proceedings of the National Academy of Science USA, 97*, 9110–9114.

Timmermans, S. et al. (2000) Relative size of the hyperstriatum ventrale is the best predictor of feeding innovation rate in birds. *Brain Behavior and Evolution, 56*, 196–203.

Trivers, R. (1971). The evolution of reciprocal altruism. *Quarterly Review of Biology, 46*, 35–57.

Trivers, R. (1972). Parental investment and sexual selection. In B. Campbell (Ed.), *Sexual selection and the descent of man 1871–1971*(pp. 139–179). Chicago: Aldine Press.

Trivers, R. (2000). The elements of a scientific theory of self deception. *Annals of the New York Academy of Sciences, 907*, 114–131.

Trivers, R. (2002). *Natural Selection and Social Theory: Selected Papers of Robert Trivers.* Oxford, U.K.: Oxford University Press.

Vet, L. E. M., Lewis, W. J., & Cardé, R. T. (1995) Parasitoid foraging and learning. In R. T.Cardé & W. J. Bell (Eds.), *Chemical Ecology of Insects* (pp. 65–101). Chapman & Hall.

Wade, M. J. (1980). Group selection, population growth rate, and competitive ability in the flour beetles, *Tribolium spp. Ecology, 61,* 1056–1064.

Weaver, I. C. G., Meaney, M. J., & Szyf, M. (2006). Maternal care effects on the hippocampal transcriptome and anxiety-mediated behaviors in the offspring that are reversible in adulthood. *Proceedings of the National Academy of Science USA, 103,* 3480–3485.

Wolf, J. B., Brodie E.D. III, Cheverud, J. M., Moore, A. J., & Wade, M. J. (1998). Evolutionary consequences of indirect genetic effects. *Trends in Ecology and Evolution,* 13, 64–69.

Woltereck, R. (1928). *Bemerkungen uber die Begriffre "Reaktions-Norm" und "Klon"* [Remarks about the concepts "norm-of-reaction" and "clone"]. *Biologisches Zentralblatt, 48,* 167–172.

Williams, G. C. (1966). *Adaptation and Natural Selection.* Princeton, NJ: Princeton University Press.

Williams, G. C. (1992). *Natural Selection: Domains, Levels and Challenges.* Oxford, U.K.: Oxford University Press.

7

Selfish Genes, Developmental Systems, and the Evolution of Development

MICHELE K. SURBEY

Development is a gene's chosen route to perpetuity. By building and developing phenotypes, genes have been able to exploit uncharted niches that a simple naked replicator could not. An organism's *life history* is an evolved solution for inhabiting a niche more successfully than any other competing organism. Niches are not constant, but have opened up through geological time, providing organisms opportunities to infiltrate them. Some niches have become extinct, trapping species and leaving their embalmed remains in the paleontological record. Others have been modified over time, drawing along with them species that have managed to keep up with the changes. At any one point in history, even established, well-functioning niches are not static—they change, as with the seasons. In order to fully exploit a niche, organisms must not only evolve to infiltrate them, but they must change over time within them. Thus, natural selection has created a unique complement of genes for each species whose expression necessarily varies over time. Hence, capsules of inert selfish genes are not the ultimate focus of selection, but developmental patterns of gene expression entrenched in dynamic life cycles. Moreover, organisms do not just track or respond to changes within the environment; they act on niches, altering them and pushing their boundaries as an outcome of their own developmental processes. In this sense, organisms are not solely products of selective forces in the environment; rather, they forge their own niches from the inside out, constrained by characteristics in the physical world in which niches are necessarily embedded. Like balloons self-expanding in confined spaces of different shapes, phylogeny involves the creation of organisms that exist at the boundaries of internal and external pressures. Phylogeny is simultaneously an inside-out and outside-in process of development—and so is ontogeny. If organisms are conglomerates of adaptive solutions to developmental problems, some of these have been of their own making as they pushed forward the frontiers of their niches.

The human ontogeny, or life cycle, is the latest rendition of those in the hominid lineage. It is a continuation, yet a variation, of past cycles. Its features bear witness to the problems surmounted by our ancestors, but include unique developmental solutions that have made us who we are and distinguish us from our nearest extinct and current relatives. Each stage of the life cycle resolves some problems, foreshadows others, and creates new problems in the next stage. It is not enough to infiltrate a mother's tissues and take hold in the womb; we must then have a means to escape the womb, to succor parental investment outside the womb, and to learn the necessary skills and find helpful companions in our adventure through the external world, until we reach the point at which we are ready to create replacements for ourselves to continue the cycle of life. The evolution of the human species and its life history is a story gradually unfolding. Of course, it all would have been a simpler story to tell, and we would not be here to tell it, had simple naked replicators not evolved to develop.

RELATIONSHIPS BETWEEN EVOLUTIONARY AND DEVELOPMENTAL THEORY IN THE 19TH AND EARLY 20TH CENTURIES

The application of an evolutionary perspective to development, and developmental psychology, in particular, has seen several attempts and false starts. Long before psychology emerged as an independent discipline in the late 1800s, both philosophers and scientists assumed that the processes of ontogeny (individual development) and phylogeny (development of species) somehow inform one another. Darwin suggested that the study of individual development could lend insight into the phylogenetic development of species and he devised methods for the careful documentation of growth and development in children. However, Darwin's theoretical impact on developmental psychology in terms of his greatest conceptual advance, natural selection theory, was relatively small (Charlesworth, 1992). A number of early developmentalists were captivated with evolutionary theory, but adopted evolutionary notions that were generally non-Darwinian.

For example, the biogenetic law or recapitulation theory (Haeckel, 1866) that suggested "ontogeny recapitulates phylogeny" had an enormous impact on biology that extended to the newly found discipline of psychology (Gould, 1977). The notion lent itself particularly well to the stage theories of Freud, Hall, and Piaget. Freud's (1967) thesis that human history is "recapitulated" during personality development was revealed in a discussion of the regressive nature of dreams when he stated that "in so far as each individual repeats in some abbreviated fashion during childhood the whole course of development of the human race, the reference is phylogenetic" (p. 209). Similarly, Hall (1904) described how individuals retrace the psychological history of humanity by passing through the developmental stages of animal-like primitivism, savagery, and barbarism, finally entering maturity, a stage akin to modern civilization. Piaget's exposure to the biogenetic law during his early training as a biologist likely influenced his concept of genetic epistemology (see Piaget, 1971).

Like many of their contemporaries, Freud and Piaget were additionally influenced by Lamarck's (1809) theory of the inheritance of acquired characteristics. The notion that species' characteristics could be altered through their use or disuse created a type of feedback between ontogeny and phylogeny that was compelling even to Darwin, although he never fully accepted the notion (see Darwin, 1888, p. 108; Darwin, 1871, Vol. 1, p. 112). Lamarckism and the biogenetic law were eventually discredited with advances in embryology and the discovery of the particulate nature of inheritance through Mendel's work. With their fall, most psychologists turned away from biological and evolutionary explanations of human behavior and embraced Watson's new behaviorism. A few developmentalists, such as Baldwin (1902), continued formulating theories relating developmental and evolutionary processes, but none of these achieved the impact of Lamarckism or the biogenetic law. A general theory of the relationship between evolution and development remained elusive.

THE MODERN SYNTHESIS, THE RISE OF "SELFISH GENES," AND EVOLUTIONARY VIEWS OF HUMAN DEVELOPMENT EMERGING IN THE LATE 20TH CENTURY

The modern synthetic theory of evolution arose in the 1930s when the work of the population geneticists, R. A. Fisher, J. B. S. Haldane, and Sewell Wright was amalgamated with natural selection theory. Evolution had become defined as a permanent change in gene frequencies, and natural selection was considered the primary agent of that change. Three decades later, by redefining fitness in terms of the number of copies of one's genes passed on through surviving offspring as well as those in descendant collateral kin, *inclusive fitness theory* (W. D. Hamilton, 1964) extended the synthetic theory further, taking a gene's-eye view of the process. The focus on the gene as the unit of selection was expanded by Williams (1966) and made popular by Dawkin's (1976) notion of the *selfish gene*. That competition between genes for greater representation in the next generation underlies not only the evolution of morphology but of psychological processes and behavior formed the basis for the discipline of sociobiology (Wilson, 1975) and its offshoot, evolutionary psychology (Barkow, Cosmides, & Tooby, 1992; Buss, 1995; Daly & Wilson, 1988; Symons, 1979; Tooby & Cosmides, 1992).

The rise of sociobiology and evolutionary psychology offered developmentalists a number of theoretical notions with which to reexamine aspects of human development. For example, the concepts of *life history strategies* (Stearns, 1992), *parental investment* (Trivers, 1972), *discriminative parental solicitude* (Daly & Wilson, 1980), *parent-offspring conflict* (Trivers, 1974), *parental manipulation* (Alexander, 1974), and *intragenomic conflict* and *genomic imprinting* (Bartolomei & Tilghman, 1997; Cosmides & Tooby, 1981; Eberhard, 1980; Haig, 1993; Trivers & Burt, 1999) began to be applied to our understanding of aspects of human development from prenatal events through dying and death. Over the last two and a half decades a series of volumes focusing on aspects of human development from an evolutionary perspective were published (e.g., Bjorklund & Pelligrini, 2002; Burgess & MacDonald, 2005; Butterworth, Rutkowska, & Scaife, 1985; Chisholm, 1999; Ellis & Bjorklund, 2005; Fishbein, 1976; MacDonald, 1988a, 1988b; Segal, G. E. Weisfeld, & C. C. Weisfeld, 1997; G. Weisfeld, 1999). In addition, articles with this same focus have been regularly accepted by and published in mainstream academic journals, including *Developmental Psychology* and *Child Development*, in greater and greater numbers. This growing literature now represents the collected ideas and research results of individuals from many fields, including anthropologists; human ethologists; biologists; archaeologists; psychiatrists; and developmental, cognitive, educational, and evolutionary psychologists. Emerging from this interdisciplinary work over the last two decades are a number of themes concerning the evolution of human development.

Theme 1

The human life history is a result of natural selection operating on human ontogenies over the evolutionary history of the hominid lineage. The result is a human life history that shares some aspects with other species, yet possesses some unique characteristics. We are a long-living, large bodied, big-brained species, with an extended juvenile period and a relatively late onset of reproduction, which produces few offspring iteroparously, investing considerably in each one. The selective forces that have shaped and produced this particular life history have been the focus of investigation. For example, such a life history may be the type required for a generalist species that survives through social affiliation, cognitive skills, and the use of technology, rather than through specialization, and physical agility or weaponry.

Illustration. Comparisons of the human life history with those of our closest primate relatives show that humans have an extended juvenile phase of development that is in turn related to increased brain size and life in larger social groups (see Bogin, 1999; Joffe, 1997). Large brain size itself does not distinguish *Homo sapiens*, as Neanderthals also had large brains. Recent archaeological findings have suggested that Neanderthals matured faster than *Homo sapiens*. Mithen (1996) suggested that the slower brain growth of *Homo sapiens* relative to Neanderthals resulted in cognitive differences. In particular, while Mithen believed that the Neanderthal mind consisted of domain-specific cognitive modules, he suggested that these modules were not well integrated or connected because of more rapid brain growth. Whereas the Neanderthals became extinct, *Homo sapiens* survived and experienced a creative explosion in art and technology in the Upper Paleolithic. Mithen, along with others (Chiappe & MacDonald, 2005; Geary, 2004) have argued that humans possess both domain-general and domain-specific mechanisms. The operation of domain-general mechanisms, or other superordinate processes, insofar as they facilitated the coordination of domain-specific modules, may have played a role in the success of early *Homo sapiens*.

The current constellation of correlated traits in the human life history (slow development, large brains, domain-general and specific brain processes, increased sociality and technology) may best be seen as a "package deal" that was accumulated over time as newly acquired adaptations became both the source of new hurdles and preadaptations for later traits. That an increase in brain size occurred over the hominid lineage, potentially as a result of selection for greater social and technological intelligence, is well documented. This increase would have likely been constrained by the size of the birth canal, limited in turn by bipedalism. One possible way around the constraint on further encephalization was for much of brain development to occur after birth. Postnatal brain development would then become subject to selection forces, with aspects of brain development, other than size, undergoing further modification depending on their long-term consequences. Finally, an extended juvenile period would have produced selection pressures for heightened parental care (see discussion in Bjorklund & Pelligrini, 2002).

Theme 2

Because the human life history has been selected as a whole, ontogeny is not simply a preparation for adulthood, but instead involves the passage of individuals through a series of stages that are adapted, in some sense, to the environmental circumstances at that point in the lifespan. In order for individuals to become adults and reproduce, they must, for example, survive the challenges of prenatal development, infancy, childhood, and adolescence. Hence, adulthood is not the only competent stage of the species, but rather each stage displays its own forms of competence and this is witnessed in the psychology, behavior, and physiology displayed at each stage.

Illustration. One of the most fascinating avenues of research illustrating this theme concerns adaptations arising in the prenatal environment. The study of prenatal development is typically limited to medicine, and has not been a great focus of interest in developmental psychology or psychology generally. Yet the characteristics of adaptations invoked at this early stage in the lifespan may have profound implications in the development and evolution of the human brain and mental mechanisms. How it was possible for the conceptus, essentially a foreign cell containing only one half of the maternal genotype, to infiltrate the mother's tissues, manipulate her physiology to its own benefit, and extract resources was not well understood in the medical community for many years. These phenomena are now explained by the concepts of intragenomic conflict and genomic imprinting (Haig, 1993). Intragenomic conflict refers to competition between different portions of the genome, including mitochondrial DNA, and DNA of maternal and paternal origin (Cosmides & Tooby, 1981; Eberhard, 1980). Some alleles of maternal and paternal origin appear to be imprinted and are only expressed in individuals if they are of a particular parental origin, a phenomenon referred to as "genomic imprinting" or "parent-specific-gene expression" (Ohlsson, 1999).

Paternally imprinted genes appear to be active in the trophoblastic cells that eventually become the placenta and it is under their influence that the conceptus infiltrates maternal tissues (Haig, 1993). Paternal genes have an interest in promoting the welfare of their bearers, even if it occurs at the expense of the mother. For example, in mice, a paternally imprinted gene is responsible for the heightened growth of pups, but its effects are counteracted by the effects of a maternally imprinted gene (see Haig, 1993). These types of prenatal "battles of the sexes" may also be manifested in the development of the brain. For example, the neocortex appears to derive largely from the expression of maternal genes, whereas the limbic system, especially the hypothalamus, appears to be under paternal control (Haig, 2000; Trivers, 2000). The limbic system controls emotions, drives, and appetites, and is involved in memory and learning, whereas the neocortex is the center of higher reasoning and serves as an interface between environmental conditions and individual needs. The differential expression of paternal and maternal genes in these different brain tissues may produce a divided mind or "multiple selves," or a "parliament of the mind" (Haig, 2000). In particular, the neocortex, largely under the influence of maternally imprinted genes, likely moderates kin social interactions and altruism, in part by suppressing the demands of the limbic system whose appetites and interests are largely driven by paternally derived genes (Badcock, 2000; Haig, 2000; Trivers, 2000). It is even possible that the evolution of greater brain size and complexity in hominids is the result of an arms race between maternally and paternally imprinted genes, with the cortex expanding to suppress the interests of subcortical systems (Badcock, 2000). Thus, genomic conflict and genomic imprinting may have far-reaching implications in understanding both human development and evolution.

Theme 3

That specific adaptations have arisen to solve specific problems faced by our ancestors in the Environment of Evolutionary Adaptedness (EEA; Bowlby, 1969) is a basic premise of evolutionary psychologists. In a similar vein, a developmental perspective suggests that specific adaptations have arisen to solve problems continually faced in the Developmental Environment of Evolutionary Adaptedness, or the DEEA. Presumably such adaptations solve both continuous and discontinuous developmental problems. These adaptations include dedicated and specialized morphological and physiological mechanisms as well as domain-specific mental modules. Domain-specific mental modules refer to processes based on specialized neural circuitry that respond to evolutionary-relevant information in adaptive and predictable ways. In modern environments their effects may be manifested in either currently adaptive, maladaptive, or unique ways. Therefore "current adaptiveness" does not reliably signify that a developmental solution evolved in the DEEA.

Illustration. Perhaps one of the areas of study showing the most growth in the last fifteen years concerns the identification of domain-specific modules activated through the course of development, presumably in the service of different developmental needs. Although an advocate for the role of both domain-general and domain-specific processes, Geary (1998) described a hierarchy of domain-specific modules that develop or are engaged as children negotiate their social and physical environments. Although young children are egocentric, and this selfish behavior may serve them well in the first few years of life, childhood involves the acquisition of social cognitive skills useful in social relationships and the formation of alliances with others. A crucial step in social cognition is the achievement of "theory of mind" (Premack & Woodruff, 1978). Theory of mind, or the ability to make inferences about the beliefs and desires of others, develops at about the time prototypical children are weaned, around 3–4 years of age. Baron-Cohen and his colleagues (e.g., Baron-Cohen, 1989; Baron-Cohen et al., 1999) have provided convincing evidence that theory of mind is part of a specialized mental mechanism that operates independently from other cognitive processes. For example, while many cognitive processes, such as memory and spatial abilities, remain intact and high functioning in this condition, Baron-Cohen has shown that autism appears to involve the specific impairment of theory of mind. Moreover, neurological studies employing *f*MRI show circuitry in the prefrontal cortex, and in areas designated as part of the "social brain," are activated by theory of mind tasks (Baron-Cohen et al., 1999). The identification and exploration of other domain-specific modules activated during development, such as those described by Geary, will continue to be a productive area.

THE INTRODUCTION OF DEVELOPMENTAL SYSTEMS THEORY

At the beginning of the current millennium the interest in an evolutionary approach to developmental psychology gathered even more momentum. Along with this increased momentum came attempts to redefine and structure its theory and scope. For example, in synthesizing and building upon previous work, Bjorklund and Pelligrini (2000, 2002) identified a number of principles of the field they define as Evolutionary Developmental Psychology (EDP) (see overview and summaries in Bjorklund & Pelligrini, 2000, 2002; Blasi & Bjorklund, 2003; Geary & Bjorklund, 2000). Most of these principles, having been built upon the previous work in human ethology, psychology and evolutionary psychology, anthropology, archaeology, sociobiology, and related fields, are well supported and in accord with an evolutionary psychology perspective. However, some the proponents of EDP distinguish their approach from mainstream evolutionary psychology in a number of ways. The primary distinction arises from their contention that, although evolutionary psychologists acknowledge the role of the environment in development, they don't offer any well-developed models in support of this position (Bjorklund & Pelligrini, 2000, 2002; Blasi & Bjorklund, 2003). Hence, some proponents of EDP have advocated employing Developmental Systems Theory (DST) as an adjunct or as a broad theoretical basis for EDP, as a means of addressing this apparent deficit.

Developmental Systems Theory is based on the concept of epigenesis (Gottlieb, 1998, 2000; Oyama, 1985, 2000; Oyama, Griffiths, & Gray, 2001). DST describes how two-way transactions between biological and environmental factors, nested at different levels of organization, produce a particular pattern of ontogeny. According to Oyama (1985), genes do not "control" development of the organism in the classical gene-centered (e.g., selfish gene) way; rather, genes are one source of "information" that is drawn upon in developmental systems. The same DNA in one developmental system may be expressed very differently or lead to very different products in another developmental system. According to DST, species differences arise because not only is a species-typical genome inherited, but also a species-typical environment. Their typical co-occurrence accounts for the production of universal features among members of lineages or species. Individual differences, however, can arise when developmental systems are exposed to novel environments or those that deviate from the species-typical environment. According to Griffiths and Gray (2001), heritable variants of developmental systems can be selected by natural selection. As a result, evolution involves a change in the composition of populations of developmental systems over time. Developmental Systems Theory, therefore, attempts to bring developmental processes back into an account of evolution.

Furthermore, at her most radical, Oyama (1985) suggests that to fully embrace DST we must give up outmoded ideas such as the dichotomy between nature and nurture, the distinction between internal versus external causes, a focus on the adaptation of species to their environments, the notion of DNA as a genetic "blueprint," and the view of selfish genes or replicators "directing" organisms and their development. Oyama's transcendence of artificial boundaries and her focus on the multilayered interactions between genes and influences, internal and external, to organisms provide useful changes of perspective. There is certainly value in turning strongly held views and dogmas on their heads to appreciate their strengths and structural deficits more clearly. However, were some of these notions to be completely abandoned, evolutionary approaches to developmental psychology, specifically EDP, would surely become isolated from mainstream evolutionary psychology and biology. This would not be a productive divide. Evolutionary psychologists and biologists are not yet prepared to give up theoretical concepts that have so far been very useful in advancing research, for others of questionable utility. To do so may be quite foolhardy (see Crawford, 2003).

Lickliter and Honeycutt (2003) promote an even broader application of DST by suggesting that a developmental dynamics approach (an alternative term for DST) should replace the theoretical assumptions of evolutionary psychology as *a whole*, not just conceptions of the relationship between evolution and development. They (wrongly) suggest that the synthetic theory ignores interactions between genes and external factors. That genes interact with one another as well as with other factors internal and external to organisms is intrinsic to modern evolutionary accounts. For example, decades ago, in summing up the current position of the "synthetic theory" at that time, Mayr (1963) stated

> Our ideas on the relation between gene and character have been totally revised and the phenotype is more and more considered not as a mosaic of individual gene-controlled characters but as the joint product of a complex interacting system, the total epigenotype. (p. 6)

In addition, Lickliter and Honeycutt argue for the necessity of a developmental dynamics approach to explain the generation of variability because "natural selection has no formative or creative power but is instead best viewed primarily as a filter for unsuccessful phenotypes generated by developmental processes" (p. 827). Somehow they have missed another core assumption of the modern synthesis: that development generates variation in phenotypes on which natural selection acts (see Krebs, 2003). As Mayr clearly stated, "It is not the 'naked gene' that is exposed to natural selection, but rather the phenotype, the manifestation of the entire genotype" (p. 178). The assumption that natural selection acts on phenotypes (generated by development) whereas evolution involves the differential survival of genotypes is a cornerstone of the modern synthetic theory of evolution.

If both DST and the synthetic theory assume interactionism and that development provides the variety in phenotypes acted upon by natural selection, then what more does DST have to offer? Buss and Reeve (2003) argue that the developmental dynamics approach may have something to add, but it could never replace the theoretical bases of evolutionary psychology. This is because developmental dynamics lack the crucial aspects of a good theory (e.g., theoretical cogency and predictive ability, thus the ability to generate empirical study), and hence cannot be a successful alternative theory of development or human psychology in general. As noted by Egeth (2003), Oyama (2000) herself admits that DST does not furnish empirical predictions. Rather than being a true *theory* of development, DST appears to be predominantly a *description* of the complex developmental processes occurring at multiple levels of organization, as revealed by molecular and developmental biology over the last century. In summarizing their argument that DST could not satisfactorily replace evolutionary psychology's theoretical basis Buss and Reeve state:

> How does Lickliter and Honeycutt's proposed replacement of the current principles of evolutionary psychology by developmental dynamics fare when evaluated by scientific standards? Does it lead investigators to new domains of inquiry about the evolution of behavior? Does it propose specific, testable, and falsifiable evolutionary predictions? Does it better account for existing findings discovered by evolutionary psychologists in the domains of mating, altruism, cooperation, aggression, parent-offspring conflict, dominance hierarchies, and so on? Does if offer more parsimonious explanations? The answer to all of these questions appears to be a resounding "no" (p. 851).

Therefore, the wholehearted adoption of DST, as a theory, by developmentalists needs to be carefully and critically contemplated. DST, however, may be useful as a means of organizing and examining the complex interactions between genes and environments, internal and external to the individual, and their effects within the broader tenets of the synthetic theory. DST intersects evolutionary theory by proposing that developmental systems, or life cycles, have evolved and that, in a sense, phylogeny is the accumulation of evolved ontogenies. This idea is surely correct, but it is not unique to the proponents of DST and has been around at least since the beginning of the 20th century (see Castall, 1985). However, the suggestion that developmental systems or life cycles have evolved begs the question as to why they exist in the first place. From whence came developmental systems? Why do we have developmental systems—or, more specifically, why do most forms of life develop? Why don't naked unchanging replicators rule the biotic world? These are the crucial questions at the heart of the evolutionary and developmental juncture.

THE SEARCH FOR A GENERAL THEORY OF THE RELATIONSHIP BETWEEN EVOLUTION AND DEVELOPMENT

The promotion of Developmental Systems Theory may be construed as the most recent attempt to find an overarching theory of the relationship between ontogeny and phylogeny. To the extent that the current theorizing in evolutionary psychology in examinations of development largely involves the application of midrange evolutionary theories (e.g., parental investment theory and sexual strategies theory) it could be said such a central theory is still not available. However, a successful evolutionary theory of human development (including psychological development) must be situated in a workable theory of the relationship between evolution and development in general. The lack of such a general thesis has necessitated the reliance on partially satisfying notions at best, and wholly unsatisfying notions at worst. However, many of the elements of such a general theory are now at hand and widely available.

To use one of Oyama's practices of integration instead of dichotomization (see Oyama, 1985), perhaps we should not be talking about a theory of the relationship *between* evolution *and* development, but rather about a theory *of the evolution of development*. Once we agree on a general theory of the evolution of development, it may serve as a backdrop for more specific theories of the evolution of human development, especially psychological development. Below, I draw together ideas from many common, and a few less common, sources, to begin to sketch out such a theory. To some, the ideas may appear obvious or simplistic. To others, they may seem speculative. At the very least they are in accord with known, tested, and testable principles of evolutionary thought.

A General Theory of the Evolution of Development

Development is an adaptive strategy of genes, whose origin traces back to the original replicators. The general function of development was to enable individual replicators or genes or whole genomes to explore, mold, and utilize new niches, while avoiding risk. The entry into new niches involved the surmounting of static as well as developmental problems. Those aspects of development best suited for solving these types of problems have been retained by natural selection, whereas others became extinct. In the history of life the strategy of development takes many alternative forms, but their ultimate purposes are the same. Life history theory describes how alternative forms of a general strategy of development arise as a function of history and varying ecological contingencies.

Development is not a separate process, divorced from that of natural selection. Development is both an outcome of natural selection, with only the most successful (i.e., fit) life cycles retained over generations, and an instigator of natural selection by providing variation in phenotypes. Particular developmental features in lineages were selected to the extent that they were productively embedded in evolutionarily successful life cycles.

Developmental problems both across and within life histories are solved by the combined and contingent actions of gene expression and physiological processes occurring in a given external milieu. The most successful solutions endure in lineages to the point at which a buildup of internal or external changes makes them no longer viable and new solutions must be adopted. A reservoir of solutions to developmental problems exists in the unexpressed genes found in all genomes, in processes that moderate gene expression, the occurrence of mutation, and in the varied responses elicited by changes in the world external to individual genes.

This view, therefore, brings us back to the idea expressed at the very beginning of this chapter: *development is a gene's chosen route to perpetuity.* It has been speculated that in the early days of organic life on earth, simple replicators arose (see Dawkins, 1976; Rollo, 1995; Weisman, 1889, 1893). Those most efficient at replicating themselves simply out-competed the rest. The most efficient way for a replicator to duplicate itself and ensure its immortality was to put all resources into replication. Instead, some replicators banded together and harnessed the use of RNA to build proteins, hence somas. Somas offered protection from the environment, but, more importantly, a means of reading, filtering, and negotiating the environment. Once replicators produced somas—thus phenotypes—the strategy of developing, as opposed to simply replicating, had been chosen.

From this perspective, Bjorklund and Pellegrini's (2002) statement, "The modern synthesis' emphasis on the separation of the somatic and germ line essentially afforded no role for development in evolution" (p. 48), seems to miss the point. Lickliter and Honeycutt (2003) similarly noted that

> Weismann claimed that only changes in the germ line could contribute to evolutionary changes and that these changes were distinct from what happens to the organism during its lifetime. The adoption of this view in the first half of the 20th century effectively divorced issues of development from those of evolution. (p. 824)

Ironically, distinguishing the germ and somatic lines was not just important in advancing evolutionary theory in the late 1880s, but, in retrospect, it likely spoke directly to the "role for development in evolution." That, at some point in the history of life, germ lines (replicators) began to build somas is the very reason why development is an important process in evolution and vice versa. Building somas and phenotypes that, by their very nature, *imply* development is an evolutionary strategy of genes.

Building a soma presumably involved a cost/benefit analysis and not all replicators followed that route. While naked replicators no longer exist, single-celled prokaryotes such as bacteria and viruses are the nearest approximation, with their short lifecycles primarily devoted to the process of replication. Not surprisingly, they typically inhabit relatively stable niches provided by the soma of larger, slower-developing species. Frequency-dependent selection may have maintained a steady proportion of large developers versus single-celled replicators creating a tenuous equilibrium in the animal kingdom, part of which was that between parasites and hosts (Hamilton & Zuk, 1982).

Phenotypes are capable of filtering and responding to environmental information (Rollo, 1995). Behavioral change is likely the main means of shifting and constructing niches. "A shift into a new niche or adaptive zone is, almost without exception, initiated by a change in behavior" (Mayr, 1963, p. 604). According to Mayr (1958), structural and other adaptations to a new niche are acquired only secondarily. In choosing the long-lived phenotype route, resources are freed up and can be devoted to endeavors other than reproduction. Thus we arrive at a basic postulate of life history theory, that life histories involve a trade-off in investing resources into growth, maintenance, and reproduction (Stearns, 1992). In the long-lived phenotype, resources are shifted into growth and maintenance. In humans, one of the largest consumers of resources devoted to growth is the brain. It uses 20% of the calories, but comprises only 2% of total body weight. The expansion of the brain in the hominid line had implications for our current abilities and capabilities. With a relatively frail physique and no real weaponry (e.g., the canines disappeared millions of years ago) individuals in the hominid line survived on ingenuity, by collaborating with conspecifics, and using technology. These skills served to push the boundaries of their niches further and further.

Intrinsic to the strategy of development is the production of variability. We generally think about evolution occurring because of natural selection "selecting out" particular alleles. As a rule, the editing of genes from a genome has a much higher cost associated with it than the altering of gene expression and interactions (Rollo, 1995). Once an allele is extinct, it may not be easy to return it to the genome, especially if it is not due to a commonly occurring spontaneous mutation. From both the gene and genome's point of view it may be better to silence some genes or alter their expression, but preserve them. This way, should the environment change, they could eventually become active and employed again (Kimura, 1983). Ultimately, natural selection has operated to preserve genes and genomes, but to diversify their expression. Gene expression is diversified, for example, through alterations in timing (heterochrony), the actions of suppressors or inactivation, cytoplasmic manipulation, genomic imprinting, pleiotropy, mutations, the dominance-recessive system, hormonal factors, and other environmental influences (see Davidson, 2001; Lewin, 1974; McKinney & McNamara, 1991; Maclean, 1976; Rollo, 1995). Development, therefore, is the result of contingent gene expression. Evolution, in the present millennium, may best be defined as a permanent change in gene frequencies and in developmental or contingent gene expression.

SUMMARY AND CONCLUDING REMARKS

In the last 25 years interest in applying an evolutionary perspective to the study of human development, particularly psychological development, has grown enormously. The literature has developed around a number of themes, including the uniqueness of the human life history, and the idea that entire lifespans have evolved, resulting in individuals exhibiting adaptations appropriate for the conditions typically encountered at each stage. Although much of the theorizing and research generated in this area is based on modern concepts in evolutionary theory, there have been calls to adopt Developmental Systems Theory as an adjunct or in their place. As a descriptive system, DST may be useful in organizing the wealth of information concerning interactions between genes and other levels of organization. Insofar as DST is not a theory per se, by itself it is unlikely to fully explain the nature of the interface between evolution and development. Theories of human development need to be situated in a broader, workable, and testable theoretical framework that considers the development of all species. In the chapter I provided to the previous edition of this *Handbook* (Surbey, 1998), I suggested that, in applying evolutionary notions to human development, "Some caution and skepticism is warranted, however, to avoid both panglossian adaptationism or the inappropriate use of evolutionary concepts, such as that resulting in a backlash against adaptationist approaches in the early part of this century" (p. 399).

This statement now seems ironically prophetic—ironic because not only has Panglossian adaptationism been avoided in some newer conceptualizations of development, but adaptation per se has been apparently eliminated; and prophetic because, in the place of well-supported notions in evolutionary psychology compatible with the synthetic theory, alternative "theories" of evolution, that are really not theories at all, have been prescribed. Although it is the nature of science that all theories undergo challenge and refinement, some challenges are more facund than others. It is important to develop and choose reasonably well-tested, rigorous, and workable evolutionary notions compatible with greater theoretical frameworks in examinations of developmental phenomena from an ultimate perspective. This is what is needed to move evolutionary accounts of human psychology and development steadily forward.

AUTHOR NOTE

Correspondence should be sent to M. K. Surbey, Department of Psychology, School of Arts and Social Sciences, James Cook University, Townsville, QLD, Australia 4811; e-mail: Michele.Surbey@jcu.edu.au.

ACKNOWLEDGMENTS

I thank B. Slugoski for timely and very helpful comments on the manuscript.

REFERENCES

Alexander, R. D. (1974). The evolution of social behavior. *Annual Review of Ecology and Systematics, 5,* 325–383.

Badcock, C. (2000). *Evolutionary psychology: A critical introduction.* Oxford, U.K.: Polity Press.

Baldwin, J. M. (1902). *Development and evolution.* New York: McMillan.

Barkow, J., Cosmides, L., & Tooby, J. (Eds.). (1992). *The adapted mind.* New York: Oxford University Press.

Baron-Cohen, S. (1989). The autistic child's theory of mind: A case of a specific developmental delay. *Journal of Child Psychology and Psychiatry, 30,* 285–298.

Baron-Cohen, S., Ring, H. A., Wheelright, S., Bullmore, E. T., Brammer, M. J., Simmons, A., et al. (1999). Social intelligence in the normal and autistic brain: An *f*MRI study. *European Journal of Neuroscience, 11,* 1891–1898.

Bartolomei, M. S., & Tilghman, S. M. (1997). Genomic imprinting in mammals. *Annual Review of Genetics, 31,* 493–525.

Bjorklund, D. F., & Pelligrini, A. D. (2000). Child development and evolutionary psychology. *Child Development, 71,* 1687–1708.

Bjorklund, D. F., & Pelligrini, A. D. (2002). *The origins of human nature: Evolutionary developmental psychology.* Washington, DC: American Psychological Association.

Blasi, C. H., & Bjorklund, D. F. (2003). Evolutionary developmental psychology: A new tool for better understanding human ontogeny. *Human Development, 46,* 259–281.

Bogin, B. (1999). *Patterns of human growth* (2nd ed.). Cambridge, U.K.: Cambridge University Press.

Bowlby, J. (1969). *Attachment and loss* (Vol. 1). New York: Basic Books.

Burgess, R. L., & MacDonald, K. (2005). *Evolutionary perspectives on human development* (2nd ed.). Thousand Oaks, CA: Sage.

Buss, D. M. (1995). Evolutionary psychology: A new paradigm for psychological science. *Psychological Inquiry, 6,* 1–49.

Buss, D. M., & Reeve, H. K. (2003). Evolutionary psychology and developmental dynamics: Comment on Lickliter and Honeycutt. *Psychological Bulletin, 129,* 848–853.

Butterworth, G., Rutkowska, J., & Scaife, M. (Eds.). (1985). *Evolution and developmental psychology.* Brighton, Sussex, U.K.: Harvester Press.

Castell, A. (1985). Specious origins? Darwinism and developmental theory. In G. Butterworth, J. Rutkowska, & M. Scaife (Eds.), *Evolution and developmental psychology* (pp. 30–41). Brighton, Sussex, U.K.: Harvester Press.

Charlesworth, W. R. (1992). Darwin and developmental psychology: Past and present. *Developmental Psychology, 28,* 5–16.

Chiappe, D., & MacDonald, K. (2005). The evolution of domain-general mechanisms in intelligence and learning. *Journal of General Psychology, 132*(1), 5–40.

Chisholm, J. S. (1999). *Death, hope and sex: Steps to an evolutionary ecology of mind and morality.* Cambridge, U.K.: Cambridge University Press.

Cosmides, L., & Tooby, J. (1981). Cytoplasmic inheritance and intragenomic conflict. *Journal of Theoretical Biology, 89,* 83–129.

Crawford, C. B. (2003). A prolegomenon for a viable evolutionary psychology—The myth and the reality: Commentary on Lickliter and Honeycutt (2003). *Psychological Bulletin, 129,* 854–857.

Daly, M., & Wilson, M. (1980). Discriminative parental solicitude: A biological perspective. *Journal of Marriage and the Family, 42*, 277–288.

Daly, M., & Wilson, M. (1988). *Homicide*. Hawthorne, NY: Aldine

Darwin, C. (1871). *The descent of man* (Vols. 1–2). New York: Appleton.

Darwin, C. (1888). *The origin of species* (6th ed.). London: John Murray.

Davidson, E. H. (2001). *Genomic regulatory systems: Development and evolution*. New York: Academic Press.

Dawkins, R. (1976). *The selfish gene*. London: Oxford University Press.

Eberhard, W. G. (1980). Evolutionary consequences of intracellular organelle competition. *Quarterly Review of Biology, 55*, 231–249.

Egeth, M. (2003). Evolution and ontogeny. *Theory & Psychology, 13*, 716–718.

Ellis, B. J., & Bjorklund, D. F. (Eds.). (2005). *Origins of the social mind: Evolutionary psychology and child development*. New York: Guilford Press.

Fishbein, H. D. (1976). *Evolution, development, and children's learning*. Santa Monica, CA: Goodyear.

Freud, S. (1967). *A general introduction to psychoanalysis*. New York: Washington Square. (Original work published 1924)

Geary, D. C. (1998). *Male female: The evolution of human sex differences*. Washington, DC: American Psychological Association.

Geary, D. C. (2004). *The origin of mind: Evolution of brain, cognition, and general intelligence*. Washington, DC: American Psychological Association.

Geary, D. C., & Bjorklund, D. F. (2000). Evolutionary developmental psychology. *Child Development, 71*, 57–65.

Gottlieb, G. (1998). Normally occurring environmental and behavioral influences on gene activity: From central dogma to probabilistic epigenesis. *Psychological Review, 105*, 792–802.

Gottlieb, G. (2000). Environmental and behavioral influences on gene activity. *Current Directions in Psychological Science, 9*, 93–102.

Gould, S. J. (1977). *Ontogeny and phylogeny*. Cambridge, MA: Harvard University Press.

Griffiths, P. E., & Gray, R. D. (2001). Darwinism and developmental systems. In S. Oyama, P. E. Griffiths, & R. D. Gray (Eds.), *Cycles of contingency: Developmental systems and evolution* (pp. 195–218). Cambridge, MA: MIT Press.

Haeckel, E. (1866). *Generelle morphologie der organismen: Allgemeine Grundzuge der organischen Formen-Weissenschaft, mechanisch bergrundet durche die von Charles Darwin reformirte Descendenz-Theorie*. Berlin, Germany: George Reimer

Haig, D. (1993). Genetic conflicts in human pregnancy. *The Quarterly Review of Biology, 68*(4), 495–532.

Haig, D. (2000). Genomic imprinting, sex-biased dispersal and social behavior. In D. LeCroy & P. Moller (Eds.), *Annals of the New York Academy of Sciences: Evolutionary perspectives on human reproductive behavior* (Vol. 907, pp. 149–163). New York: New York Academy of Sciences.

Hall, G. S. (1904). *Adolescence* (Vols. 1–2). New York: Appleton.

Hamilton, W. D. (1964). The genetical evolution of social behavior: I and II. *Journal of Theoretical Biology, 7*, 1–52.

Hamilton, W. D., & Zuk, M. (1982). Heritable true fitness and bright birds: A role for parasites? *Science, 218*, 384–387.

Joffe, T. H. (1997). Social pressures have selected for an extended juvenile period in primates. *Journal of Human Evolution, 32*, 593–605.

Kimura, M. (1983). *The neutral theory of molecular evolution*. Cambridge, U.K.: Cambridge University Press.

Krebs, D. L. (2003). Fictions and facts about evolutionary approaches to human behavior: Comment on Lickliter and Honeycutt. *Psychological Bulletin, 129*, 842–847.

Lamarck, J.-B. (1809). *Philosophie zoologique* (Vol. 2). Paris: Dentu.

Lewin, B. (1974). *Gene expression* (Vol. 1). London: John Wiley & Sons.

Lickliter, R., & Honeycutt, H. (2003). Developmental dynamics: Toward a biologically plausible evolutionary psychology. *Psychological Bulletin, 129*, 819–835.

MacDonald, K. B. (1988a). *Social and personality development*. New York: Plenum

MacDonald, K. B. (Ed.). (1988b). *Sociobiological perspectives on human development*. New York: Springer-Verlag.

Maclean, N. (1976). *Control of gene expression*. London: Academic Press.

Mayr, E. (1958). Behavior and systematics. In A. Roe & G. G. Simpson (Eds.), *Behavior and evolution* (pp. 341–362). New Haven, CT: Yale University Press.

Mayr, E. (1963). *Animal species and evolution*. Cambridge, MA: Belknap.

McKinney, M. L., & McNamara, K. J. (1991). *Heterochrony: The evolution of ontogeny*. New York: Plenum.

Mithen, S. (1996). *The prehistory of the mind*. London: Thames & Hudson.

Ohlsson, R. (Ed.). (1999). *Genomic imprinting: An interdisciplinary approach*. Heidelberg, Germany: Springer.

Oyama, S. (1985). *The ontogeny of information: Developmental systems and evolution*. Cambridge, U.K.: Cambridge University Press.

Oyama, S. (2000). *The ontogeny of information: Developmental systems and evolution* (2nd ed.). Durham, NC: Duke University Press.

Oyama, S., Griffiths, P. E., & Gray, R. D. (2001). *Cycles of contingency: Developmental systems and evolution*. Cambridge, MA: MIT Press.

Piaget, J. (1971). *Biology and knowledge*. Chicago: University of Chicago Press.

Premack, D., & Woodruff, G. (1978). Does the chimpanzee have a theory of mind? *Behavioral and Brain Sciences, 1*(4), 515–526.

Rollo, C. D. (1995). *Phenotypes: Their epigenetics, ecology, and evolution*. London: Chapman & Hall.

Segal, N. L., Weisfeld, G. E., & Weisfeld, C. C. (1997). *Uniting psychology and biology: Integrative perspectives on human development*. Washington, DC: American Psychological Association.

Stearns, S. C. (1992). *The evolution of life histories*. Oxford, U.K.: Oxford University Press.

Surbey, M. K. (1998). Developmental psychology and modern Darwinism. In C. B. Crawford & D. Krebs (Eds.), *Handbook of evolutionary psychology: Ideas, issues and applications* (pp. 369–404). Hillsdale, NJ: Erlbaum.

Symons, D. (1979). *The evolution of human sexuality*. New York: Oxford.

Tooby, J., & Cosmides, L. (1992). The psychological foundations of culture. In J. Barkow, L. Cosmides, & J. Tooby (Eds.), *The adapted mind: Evolutionary psychology and the generation of culture* (pp. 19–136). New York: Oxford University Press.

Trivers, R. L. (1972). Parental investment and sexual selection. In B. Campbell (Ed.), *Sexual selection and the descent of man 1871–1971* (pp. 136–179). Chicago: Aldine.

Trivers, R. L. (1974). Parent-offspring conflict. *American Zoologist, 14*, 247–262.

Trivers, R. L. (2000). The elements of a scientific theory of self-deception. In D. LeCroy & P. Moller (Eds.), *Annals of the New York Academy of Sciences: Evolutionary perspectives on human reproductive behavior* (Vol. 907, pp. 114–131). New York: New York Academy of Sciences.

Trivers, R. L., & Burt, A. (1999). Kinship and genomic imprinting. In R. Ohlsson (Ed.), *Genomic imprinting* (pp. 1–21). New York: Springer Verlag.

Weisfeld, G. (1999). *Evolutionary principles of human adolescence*. Boulder, CO: Westview Press.

Weismann, A. (1889). *Essays upon heredity*. Oxford, U.K.: Clarendon Press.

Weismann, A. (1893). *The germ-plasm: A theory of heredity* (W. N. Parker & H. Ronnfeldt, Trans.). London: Walter Scott. (Original work published 1889)

Williams, G. C. (1966). *Adaptation and natural selection*. Princeton, NJ: Princeton University Press.

Wilson, E. O. (1975). *Sociobiology: The new synthesis*. Cambridge, MA: Harvard University Press.

Part *III*

EVOLVED MENTAL MECHANISMS: THE ESSENCE OF EVOLUTIONARY PSYCHOLOGY

The chapters in this section deal with ideas and evidence specific to the application of evolutionary theory to psychology. A thorough understanding of the subject requires reading all four chapters.

8

Biological Adaptations and Human Behavior

STEVEN W. GANGESTAD

Darwin's theory of evolution through natural selection is an explanation of biological adaptation. At the time that Darwin was developing his ideas, natural theologians (e.g., Paley, 1836) emphasized that organisms are eminently well designed for habitats they occupy. They reasoned that the existence of design required a conscious designer and, hence, inferred the existence of a Creator. Darwin's (1859) theory explains how organisms can become adapted to their environments over evolutionary timescales through a material process involving no conscious designer, one he named natural selection.

A key element in Darwin's theory is a material basis for heritability of traits contained within germ cells, which could account for similarity of parental and offspring traits. At the time Darwin wrote, of course, the nature of that material basis was unknown. The rediscovery of Mendel's laws in 1900 led biologists to conclude that it was passed on as particulate units, which were named genes several years later. Though Darwinism and Mendelian genetics were not obviously compatible at first, within a few decades these frameworks were fused—a "second Darwinian revolution" (Mayr, 1991, p. 132). Within the synthesis, evolution consists of changes in frequencies of genes within populations. New variations in genes are introduced through mutation. Gene frequencies can change due to migration of individuals into and out of a population. They can also fluctuate due to mere chance, a process known as random drift. Finally, gene frequencies can change because of selection. Occasionally, a mutation produces an effect on an individual's traits that gives that organism a reproductive advantage over other individuals in the population. Because individuals carrying the advantaged gene outreproduce those not carrying it, the gene becomes more frequent in the population over time, until nearly all individuals carry the gene. Evolution—a change in which genes exist in a population—has occurred. And because it occurred through differential reproduction of individuals due to effects of the gene on individuals' reproductive success, evolution was produced through natural selection on individuals.

The years from 1900–1960 were a triumph for evolutionary genetic theory. Quantitative models of basic processes through which gene frequencies may change as a function of selection, change, mutation, and so on were introduced and developed by geneticists such as Fisher (1930/1958), Wright (1968), and Haldane (1932). To work out these models, theorists did not need to specify *why* a particular gene in the model was advantaged over alternatives. They only needed to assume that it *was* advantaged and by how much. Though much was learned about the power of selection on evolution, much about selection was not investigated: Typically, phenotypes were left out of the modeling. Why are some traits advantaged over others? What aspects of environments lead some traits to be selected? How do environments thereby shape organisms to function more adaptively within their environments? How do we identify which traits have evolved through selection (as opposed to, for instance, drift)? Biologists had not yet systematically addressed these questions in deep, principled ways and, hence, had yet to develop powerful theories and methodologies to understand the broader phenomenon of biological adaptation to environments.

At the close of this period, biologists increasingly offered insights into how theories of adaptation might be profitably developed. Pittendrigh (1958) called for a new subfield of evolutionary biology he named *teleonomy*, one that seeks to understand the biological function of traits. Williams's (1966) classic book, *Adaptation and Natural Selection*, attempted to explicate clearly the meaning and relations between core concepts such as adaptation and function and to develop empirical criteria for identifying the effects of natural selection. At the same time, biologists began developing quantitative models of selection pressures that environments imposed on individuals, ones expressed in terms of costs and benefits (e.g., Lack, 1954). An approach for understanding adaptation through evolutionary economic analysis emerged. By the early 1970s, a new approach within evolutionary biology, *adaptationism*, was crystallizing. Adaptationism, as a research strategy, seeks to identify outcomes of selection and to elucidate the specific selection pressures that forged them in an organism's evolutionary past.

Today, probably no biologist doubts that the concept of biological adaptation is fundamental to evolutionary biology. Most would agree that many of the most important theoretical advances in evolutionary biology over the past four decades pertain to adaptation. Nonetheless, important disagreements about how to think about biological adaptations persist. In the 1970s, the adaptationist approach was attacked by paleontologist Stephen Jay Gould and geneticist Richard Lewontin (e.g., Gould & Lewontin, 1979; Lewontin, 1978, 1979). Perhaps their most prominent criticism was that the explanations that adaptationists gave for traits were analogous to Rudyard Kipling's "just-so" stories, fanciful children's stories about how the world came to be (e.g., "How the Camel Got Its Hump"). But they and others also questioned adaptationists' fundamental assumptions of both the processes and outcomes of adaptation. Some ensuing debates have not been resolved to the satisfaction of all.

In this chapter, I discuss the conceptual status of biological adaptations. I draw basic distinctions that adaptationists make, describe criteria used to identify adaptations, and discuss the methodological and theoretical tools adaptationists bring to bear on understanding adaptation. Criticisms, as well as adaptationist defenses, of these approaches, are introduced. Specific issues pertaining to behavioral and psychological adaptations are discussed. Finally, I discuss a few outstanding issues.

FUNDAMENTAL CONCEPTS

Traits and Effects

Biologists use the term *trait* to refer to an aspect of an organism's phenotype. Liberally defined, a trait is any relatively stable aspect of the phenotype that can be discriminated based on any criterion—its causes, its effects, its appearance, and so forth. They include dispositional traits (e.g., the disposition to develop callouses with friction, the disposition to learn a behavior under some specified conditions). The subset of such traits that could *potentially* qualify as adaptations are those that have *effects* (e.g., Williams, 1966; see also Gould & Vrba, 1982). An effect refers to the way (or ways) in which an aspect of the phenotype interacts with the environment: Wings can produce flight under normal conditions; callouses are less penetrable or easily abraded than uncalloused skin; peacocks' tails affect reactions of peahens. All of these traits have effects. Traits need not be completely genetically distinct from each other, as two traits with very different effects may have common genetic underpinnings.

Traits develop within an individual's lifetimes through epigenetic processes. The systems that give rise to developmental outcomes and organismic features involve genes as well as other elements, including products of previous developmental events and experiences the developing organism encounters. Traits are not products of genes alone. It is not precisely accurate to say that a trait is "encoded" in the genes. Even a gene "for" a simple trait such as brown eyes has its effects in the context of complex physiological processes. And most traits are affected by many genes. As Williams (1966) stressed, to say that a gene "affects" a trait is merely to say that, given background conditions (the developmental system in which the gene is an important interactant), the gene has a net mean impact on trait expression.

Behaviors and psychological phenomena regulate an organism's interactions with the environment. They are perhaps not best thought of as traits in and of themselves, as they are too transient to be considered a stable feature of an organism. Behaviors nonetheless *reflect* traits of organisms. At one level of analysis, these traits are aspects or components, properties, or networks within the nervous systems of organisms, which yield particular behavioral outcomes (e.g., motor movements, perceptions, emotional experiences, thoughts) in the context of particular environmental contexts. At another level, these traits may be described in terms of underlying decision-rules and information-processing algorithms represented in the structure of the nervous system through an epigenetic process. Psychological theory (whether learning, cognitive, or socioemotional theory, just to name a few) aims to describe the nature, properties, and regularities ("traits") of these underlying processes.

ADAPTATIONS AND FUNCTIONS

Effects, Selection, and Evolution

Traits evolve as the genes that affect their development evolve. Again, genes evolve (change in relative frequency within a population) due to any one of four evolutionary forces: (a) mutation, (b) migration, (c) drift, and (d) selection. Selection can operate at multiple levels (the genetic level, the individual level, the group level), but is most often conceived of as occurring at the level of the individual organism. By definition, selection on individuals is a process that operates on traits. It can operate only by virtue of a trait's effects. *Selection* occurs when a trait (or particular trait level—e.g., a particular bird's beak size, relative too all alternative beak sizes) has an effect such that individuals possessing the trait have a propensity to possess greater or lesser fitness than individuals possessing alternative traits. Selection affects genetic evolution if the trait variants that are favored by selection are affected by different genes than those trait variants disfavored by selection. Under those circumstances, selection enhances the replicative success of the genes contributing to the favored trait's development. Selection thereby also results in changes in representation of phenotypes in the population: If selection results in increased representation of genes contributing to a favored trait within a population, then over time the population will increasingly be populated by individuals possessing the favored trait. These statements are simply Darwin's theory of evolution by natural selection couched in the language of genetics.

The Concepts of Adaptation and Function

The word *adaptation* has two meanings in evolutionary biology (Gould & Vrba, 1982). It refers to the process by which natural selection modifies phenotypes in favor of traits whose effects facilitate the propagation of genes. It also refers to the products of that process—that is, the traits that have come to characterize organisms through a process of phenotypic modification by natural selection for traits' gene-propagating effects. Put otherwise, an adaptation is a trait that evolved because it was favored by selection for its effects. The effect that causes the trait to evolve is referred to as the *function* of the trait.

Simple examples illustrate adaptations and their functions. Simply put, bird wings are adaptations *for* the function of flight. Eyes are adaptations *for* the function of seeing. Release of gonadotropins by human fetuses into the bloodstream of their mothers appears to be an adaptation *for* the function of increasing the likelihood fetuses will be retained by the mother (Haig, 1993).

By definition, the concepts of an adaptation and its function are *historical* in nature. An adaptation arose *in the past* due to selection in favor of it. Its function was the benefit that *led to* the adaptation being favored by selection. For this reason, the concepts of adaptation and *adaptiveness* are distinct (Sober, 1984). A trait is currently adaptive if it is presently favored by selection. Current adaptiveness is neither a necessary nor a sufficient feature of an adaptation. A trait that evolved in the past may no longer be adaptive if the current environment contains novelties that render it no longer beneficial. Preferences for sweet and fatty foods may have been adaptive for hominid (or prehominid) ancestors living in conditions in which their next meal required effort to obtain and thereby evolved through selection. In modern conditions, in which heart disease and other metabolic disorders (e.g., diabetes) are major causes of middle-aged death, these same preferences may not be adaptive (see Crawford, 1998, on "pseudopathologies"). By definition, however, the (currently maladaptive) preferences are adaptations: They evolved through modification of the phenotype due to selection for particular gene-propagating effects.

Conversely, a trait that is beneficial now need not have evolved through natural selection for its beneficial effects in the past. Reading is beneficial to modern humans. But reading did not evolve because of the beneficial effects *of reading*. Reading is a modern practice that likely relies upon various adaptations for specific cognitive functions. But there is no adaptation (or set of adaptations) *for* the function of reading.

An Alternative Concept of Function

Medical science has made its gains through an understanding of function (e.g., Symons, 1987). Four centuries ago, William Harvey concluded that the function of the heart is to pump blood. Since his discovery, hundreds of components of human physiology (e.g., the liver, kidneys, lymph nodes, intestinal villae, macrophages, cytokines, etc.) have been profitably investigated through functional analysis. Is the medical definition of function the same as the evolutionary one? No. Harvey knew nothing of the phenomenon of natural selection. He did not claim that hearts evolved through selection for the benefits of blood circulation. Yet the evolutionary concept of function cannot be disentangled from historical natural selection; the evolutionary biologists' definition of function contains explicit reference to selection. The functional analysis Harvey engaged in was causal role functional analysis (e.g., Godfrey-Smith, 1993). Causal role functional analysis examines how an organism can perform various activities. Sometimes, the causal role function of a feature corresponds to its evolutionary function. The heart presumably *was* selected in the past to pump blood, which is its causal role function. But some causal role functional analysis does not yield evolutionary function. Some psychologists address the interesting question of how people manage to read by examining the roles of various psychological capacities. They are thereby doing causal role functional analysis. But that functional analysis does not reveal evolutionary functions. Though psychological processes function, in a causal role sense, in reading, their *evolutionary functions* do not have to do with reading.

Put otherwise, the evolutionary definition of function is not a conceptual definition; it is a *scientific definition* (Millikan, 1989). The meanings of many terms scientists use are embedded within scientific theory. The meaning of the physicist's term *proton,* for instance, cannot be separated from particular scientific theory about the nature of matter. Similarly, the meaning of the evolutionary notion of function cannot be separated from the scientific theory of evolution by natural selection.

BY-PRODUCTS

When selection occurs due to the beneficial effect of a particular trait, it inevitably modifies the phenotype in many ways. The trait that has the beneficial effect leading to modification through selection is an adaptation. Many other traits also modified but with no beneficial effects themselves are *by-products* of selection. They are also referred to as *incidental effects* or *spandrels* (Gould & Lewontin, 1979). Vertebrate bones are composed of calcium phosphate. Bones are adaptations that enable effective movement. Calcium phosphate is white and, hence, so too are bones. The whiteness of bones has no beneficial effect itself, however; this trait is a by-product of selection.

Selection for a single adaptation may potentially lead to many by-products. For instance, the precise distance between the eyes in humans may be partly due to selection for effective binocular vision. But this distance also affects the precise distance between each eye and any other physiological structure (e.g., the right and left kneecaps, each metatarsal bone, the appendix, etc.). In all likelihood, virtually all of these distances are mere by-products of selection; they have no gene-propagating effects themselves. More generally, most traits are not adaptations but rather have no functional significance whatsoever. As an understanding of adaptation requires that adaptations be identified, which come with no labels, a key methodological question concerns how adaptations can be picked out and distinguished from a myriad of by-products. Adaptationism proposes methodologies for doing so (see the section on Adaptationist Methodology).

EXAPTATION AND FORTUITOUS EFFECTS

The Concept of Exaptation

Gould and Vrba (1982) introduced the concept of exaptation. An *exaptation* is a preexisting trait (i.e., one that has already evolved) that acquires a new beneficial effect without being modified by selection for this effect (i.e., it takes on a new role but was not designed for it by selection). Because the beneficial effect did not contribute to the trait's evolution, the effect the trait is "exapted to" cannot qualify as a function but instead is merely an effect: "Adaptations have functions; exaptations have effects" (Gould & Vrba, 1982, p. 6).

Exaptation can be defined in terms of adaptiveness and adaptation: An exaptation is a trait that is currently adaptive without being an adaptation for that adaptive effect. As previously emphasized, modification of the phenotype is essential to the concept of adaptation. Natural selection cannot bring about adaptation without the changes that evolved genes make to the phenotype. For a trait to become exapted to a new beneficial effect, it must have acquired it without being modified by selection for the effect.

Gould and Vrba (1982) discuss a variety of examples of exaptation. One is the way the black heron uses its wing to shade water. When foraging for fish, the heron may raise its wing to reduce glare of the sun's light off the water and increase visibility of prey under the water's surface. The wing itself evolved through selection for flight. There is no evidence that the wing's structural properties were modified through selection for water shading. The wing is therefore an adaptation for flight, and has been exapted to adaptive effects of water shading. In this instance, water shading may have involved adaptation, as selection may have favored variations in the heron's *brain* that led it to use its wing for shading. But the *wing itself* is not an adaptation *for water shading*.

A trait may become an exaptation through one of two scenarios. First, the trait initially evolves as an adaptation for a particular effect, and then subsequently becomes exapted to another effect (Gould & Vrba, 1982). The black heron's wing being used for shading is an example. Second, the exapted trait is a by-product of selection for another trait. For example, some species of snails have a space in their shell that they use to brood eggs (Gould, 1997). The space exists even for snails that do not use the space. It presumably is an incidental outcome of a plan for shell development that was selected, later exapted to brooding eggs.

Secondary Adaptation

If a trait that has been exapted undergoes a process of structural modification to facilitate the new beneficial effect, it has undergone a process of adaptation and the resultant structural changes are adaptations. Gould and Vrba (1982) refer to an initially exapted trait as a *primary exaptation*. Subsequent adaptive structural modifications are *secondary adaptations*. For example, feathers may have evolved initially for their insulation properties rather than for flight (Gould & Vrba, 1982). Many of the feathers on a bird (e.g., wing and tail feathers) became useful for flight. Prior to any modification, they were pure primary exaptations to flight. Subsequently, however, some have been modified specifically for flight, and hence, they represent secondary adaptation for flight. This example is not an isolated one. The sequence in the evolution of a trait of exaptation and subsequent adaptation may nearly always apply whenever we see adaptation. Most any adaptation had to exist in some form prior to being shaped for a particular function. If it was to be shaped for that function, it must have been beneficial (even in a very diminished way) prior to that shaping process.

Is the Concept of Exaptation Useful?

Biologists have long recognized that adaptations had to be useful, in some small way, for them to be selected for their ultimate function. Again, bird feathers, though evolved for insulation, must have been able to provide some degree of lift for feathers to be subsequently modified for flight. And some sweat glands, in ancestral mammals, must have provided some nutritional benefits to offspring licking them for them to be subsequently modified to be mammary glands (Cowen, 1990). In older literature, biologists spoke of the preexisting utility of adaptations for what became their functions as *preadaptation*. Because this terminology was already available, not all biologists believe that Gould and Vrba's (1982) new terminology is particularly useful.

Gould and Vrba (1982) argued for new terminology in two ways. First, the concept of preadaptation is deceptive, as it implies that selection can be forward looking. Of course, no biologist who uses the term preadaptation actually believes that selection "put it there" so that it could evolve into an adaptation. Still, Gould and Vrba argued, if the term does have connotations that hinder its proper understanding, a new term is desirable.

Second, and more substantively, the concept of preadaptation implies that a fortuitously beneficial trait *will* indeed be modified through selection into an adaptation. Gould and Vrba's (1982) conceptualization allows that *some* fortuitously beneficial traits are not modified for new purposes (e.g., the heron's wing has not been modified for water shading). They remain, in their terminology, primary exaptations. It makes little sense to say that these traits remain "preadaptations."

Even when a trait or complex of traits has been modified by selection for a new effect, some components may remain unchanged. The hand is a complex trait, one that has particular effects (e.g., grasping) by virtue of the organization of subtraits (e.g., fingers, bone structure, musculature that permit grasping). Complex features such as the hand are probably mixtures of exaptations and secondary adaptations. With regard to the skeletal structure and musculature of land-living vertebrates, "The order and arrangement of tetrapod limb bones is an exaptation for walking on land;

many modifications of shape and musculature are secondary adaptations for terrestrial life" (Gould & Vrba, 1982, p. 12). Naturally, one expects that the finer details of a complex feature that are most subject to secondary modification are those that do not serve the new exapted effect well: "Any coopted effect (an exaptation) will probably not arise perfected for its new effect. It will therefore develop secondary adaptation for the new role. The primary exaptations and secondary adaptations can, in principle, be distinguished" (p. 13).

The point that some beneficial traits were not selected for that benefit has, according to Gould and Vrba (1982), important methodological implications. Namely, the mere fact that a trait has beneficial effects cannot be taken by itself as evidence that selection has modified that trait to provide that benefit. One must apply criteria that discriminate adaptations and primary exaptations. This point was fully appreciated by Williams (1966). As he noted, a fox's paws may be beneficial for purposes of stamping down snow. But that need not imply that the fox's paws have a function of stamping down snow; the beneficial effect could be merely fortuitous. The criterion Williams proposed for separating adaptations from exaptations, functional design, is discussed in the section called Adaptationist Methodology (see also The Role of Comparative and Phylogenetic Analyses for Establishing Adaptation).

CONSTRAINTS

The Costs of Traits

Selection is limited in what it favors. A *constraint* opposes the modifying influence of a selective force on the phenotype. Physical laws are examples of constraints that limit the possible outcomes that alleles could produce. No allele could ever arise that will allow an organism to have zero mass or violate the law of conservation of energy. Hence, organisms cannot spend energy that they have not captured from the environment. And what energy an organism spends on developing a trait (i.e., a large brain) cannot be allocated to the development of other traits. Accordingly, all traits, even when favored, also have costs, namely the opportunity costs lost because resources (e.g., energy) allocated to the trait cannot be used otherwise. Selection should favor an outcome in which net benefits—benefits minus costs—are maximized.

A selective force on a trait may constrain other selective forces on the same trait if they have opposing effects. For example, selection favors large clutch size in birds because larger clutch size will increase fitness in the absence of an opposing selective force. But because parents find it difficult to raise all offspring from a large clutch to weaning, there is an opposing selective force favoring smaller clutch sizes. Optimal clutch size should be an intermediate value, a function of these two selection forces (e.g., see Seger & Stubblefield, 1996). Another way to put this point is to say that increased clutch size has a cost as well as a benefit.

Recognition that all traits, even when favored, have costs, led theorists in the 1950s and 1960s to begin developing explicit cost-benefit models to understand outcomes selection should favor. Indeed, analysis of clutch size (Lack, 1954) and trait evolution in light of energetic constraints (the idea that every trait has opportunity costs; e.g., Cole, 1954) were early examples of this kind of modeling. Evolutionary economic modeling of costs and benefits to understand selection forces is now a major theoretical tool in evolutionary biology (e.g., see Parker & Maynard Smith, 1990).

Genetic and Developmental Constraints

A selective force on one trait may also indirectly constrain a selective force on another trait if the traits are inextricably tied to each other, given the particular makeup of the organism. For instance, when a new mutation arises, it arises in a genome that has been subject to a long history of selection. As such, much of the genome will be highly conserved because it results in advantageous phenotypic effects. Possibly, the only new mutation that could result in a given beneficial trait also interacts with the existing genome to produce costly effects that outweigh the beneficial effects. Selection will then disfavor the evolution of the new trait and the design of the organism will be constrained. This *genetic constraint* should be understood as a selective trade-off between the new mutation and the existing genome. Because the advantages afforded by the preexisting genome outweigh the beneficial effects of the new mutant, the new mutant cannot evolve, and the trait is constrained from reaching optimal design for its function.

A particular form of a genetic constraint is *developmental constraint*. The construction of an organism through the developmental process depends on the coordinated action of many different genes. Possibly, a new mutation could code for a beneficial new trait only by interfering with the developmental process, thereby disrupting development of the rest of the organism. If the costs of disruption outweigh the advantages provided by the new mutant, the new mutant will be disfavored and the trait's design constrained.

In humans (and most other vertebrates), the esophagus and the bronchial tubes converge and share common openings, the mouth and nose; eating and breathing are performed through some shared pathways. If there is some advantage for these two actions to be performed through completely independent tracts, that outcome is nonetheless very unlikely to evolve. The cost of disrupting the developmental plan leading to the current design would almost certainly outweigh the benefits.

Another example of developmental constraint is the existence of the foveal blind spot of the vertebrate eye. The blind spot is due to the fact that the wirings carrying information from the individual photoreceptors of the eye run along the inner surface of the eye and converge at the optic nerve, where they exit and lead to the brain. At the point of convergence, the wirings are so dense that no photoreceptors can capture light, accounting for the blind spot. A simple design alteration would eliminate the blind spot: Change the wirings so that they lead from the photoreceptors out the *back* of the eye, run along its *outer* surface, and converge to form the optic nerve (i.e., reverse the order of the layers of the retina so that the layer of photoreceptors is on the inside). The likely reason why this change has not been achieved is developmental constraint. The wirings cannot be changed (via mutation) to lead out the back of the eye without costly disruption of the existing developmental plan.

These examples illustrate how genetic constraints can maintain imperfections in design. Historically, constraints have been used to argue in favor of Darwin's theory over the natural theologians' claims that a designer accounted for design. A designer with forethought should not have designed the eye to have an obvious flaw. Blind selection can only tinker with what exists, based on immediate gains; it cannot foresee flaws that might arise down the road.

Because it is difficult to know the costs that lead to developmental constraints, these kinds of costs are typically left out of explicit cost-benefit models of how selection acts used by adaptationists. For instance, we simply do not know the cost of disrupting development to change the direction photoreceptor wirings exit the cells in the vertebrate eye and, indeed, infer that it must be considerable only a posteriori, based on the observation that an imperfect design persists.

ADAPTATIONIST METHODOLOGY

How to Identify Adaptation

Evolutionary biologists are interested in understanding the selective forces that shaped an organism. Of the many specifiable traits that individual organisms possess, only a small subset are adaptations—traits that evolved because historically they had effects favored by natural selection. Adaptationism has been described as a methodology for "carving" the organism into those aspects of its phenotype that have evolved due to net fitness benefits historically and nonfunctional by-products (e.g., Thornhill, 1997). In doing so, the researcher not only understands what aspects of the phenotype are indeed functional. The researcher also infers the specific nature of important selective forces that shaped the organism and thereby understands some important evolutionary events that led to the organism we now observe. That is, a researcher not only identifies adaptations but also identifies biological function (what those adaptations are *for*).

Williams (1966), often credited with offering the first systematic statements that gave direction to the modern approach of adaptationism, noted that two criteria are inadequate for claiming that a trait is an adaptation. First, as already noted, it is not sufficient to show that a trait is beneficial currently. Second, it is not sufficient to argue that a trait had past utility. Exaptations have utility but need not have evolved because of selection for those beneficial effects. Williams argued that the biological concept of adaptation is an onerous one and required stringent standards of evidence. Those standards are captured by the concept of *functional* or *special design*.

SPECIAL DESIGN

Arguments of Design

A trait or constellation of traits exhibits special design for a particular function if it performs a particular function effectively and, furthermore, it is difficult to imagine another scenario that would have led to the evolution of the trait or constellation of traits. The classic example is the vertebrate eye (e.g., see Williams, 1992). The eye and its detailed features are effective for seeing. Furthermore, it is difficult to imagine an evolutionary scenario under which the eye would have evolved other than one in which its details were selected for their optical properties and thereby the function of sight. Thus, for instance, it is unimaginable that the eye evolved through pure mutation pressure or random drift. And it is very difficult to fathom that the eye is nonfunctional by-product of selection. The only plausible evolutionary scenario is one in which features of the eye were favored by selection for the function of sight.

An argument of special design is an argument to the best explanation (e.g., see Sterelny & Griffiths, 1999). In this form of argument, it is considered reasonable to accept (at least provisionally) one explanation over competing explanations if the preferred explanation explains the facts better than competitors do. The theory that the features of the eye evolved through selection for sight explains the exceptionally good fit between their properties and the function of sight. Any other theory leaves these details completely unexplained.

How Is "Good Design" Assessed?

As previously noted, a special design argument states that a feature or set of features exhibits special design for a particular function because it performs that function proficiently and, in addition, it is difficult to imagine it arising through an alternative evolutionary process. In Williams's (1966) terms, design is recognized when a feature performs a function with sufficient *specificity*, *precision*, *efficiency*, and *economy* to rule out chance. Or, as he later put it, "Adaptation is demonstrated by observed conformity to *a priori* design specifications" (Williams, 1992, p. 40). As implied by this passage, a special design argument has two components: a priori design specifications and an assessment of fit to those specifications.

A priori design specifications and engineering analyses. A special design argument claims that a feature or complex of features performs a particular task well. That claim implies an understanding of what it means to perform the task well. In some instances, it can be useful to have an *engineering analysis* that reveals the kinds of devices that would be good for the function our trait is claimed to exhibit.

Evaluation of wing design illustrates how engineering analysis can shed light on biological function. Bird wings vary in shape and other characteristics—along dimensions of breadth, width, degree of camber, rigidity, and so on. One can do engineering analyses on the characteristics of flight different kinds of wing designs facilitate (e.g., speed, soaring, hovering, diving, maneuverability, and at what flight speeds). Good designs for particular kinds of flight can then be compared with actual wing designs of different species in light of the flight characteristics their foraging patterns might demand. And, in fact, different species of birds tend to possess wings appropriate to the flight demands of their foraging niche (e.g., Norberg, 2002).

Fit to design specifications. The second component of a special design argument is an evaluation of how well the actual feature of a set of features an organism possesses satisfies the a priori specifications of good design. As Williams (1992) noted, "Unfortunately those who wish to ascertain whether some attribute of an organism does or does not conform to design specifications are left largely to their own intuitions, with little help from established methodology" (p. 41). There simply are no formal rules by which to evaluate claims of fit. Ultimately, a special design argument is one about probabilities: "[W]hether a presumed function is served with sufficient precision, economy, efficiency, etc., to rule out pure chance [i.e., any possibility other than adaptation for a particular effect] as an adequate explanation" (Williams, 1966, p. 10; see also Thornhill, 1990, 1997). But the means by which investigators evaluate the possibility that pure chance is an adequate explanation are informal.

An argument from design need not claim that fit to specification is perfect. Indeed, as Williams (1992) observed, the vertebrate eye is simultaneously a superb example of a feature exhibiting design for function and a feature that is "stupidly designed" (p. 73). Were the eye intelligently designed, the retinal layers would not be inverted, with nerves and blood vessels on the inner surface of the eye, in front of the photoreceptors (giving rise to the blind spot). Despite the obvious flaws of the eye's design, it nonetheless contains many telltale signs of having been shaped through selection as an optical device. The probability that it would have the details permitting sight without selection for its optical properties cannot be estimated precisely but it strikes the intuitions of most biologists to be minute.

Though formal criteria for evaluating functional design fit may be desired, they are probably too much to hope for. Does that mean that adaptationist arguments lack scientific rigor? Not at all. Indeed, as theoretical claims in science go, special design arguments are in no way exceptional. Scientific hypotheses are often accepted based on similar kinds of informal arguments of probabilities (e.g., Salmon, 1984). Thus, for instance, the physicist Perrin (1913) claimed that atoms truly exist (despite not being observable) based on the observation that Avogadro's number (the number of molecules in a mole, which assumes "countable" entities) can be estimated to be approximately the same value using over 10 different, independent methods to do so (e.g., features of Brownian motion, the thickness of soap bubbles, the color of the sky, rates of radioactive decay). This claim, in fact, is based on an informal assessment of the probability that the independent methods would provide approximately the same estimated value *if*, in fact, atoms did not exist. In philosopher of science Wesley Salmon's terms, it would be a very "strange coincidence" if atoms did not exist, in light of the converging estimates. Adaptationists' arguments for special design rely on this same form of logic: They claim that exceptional fits between a trait's forms and purported functions would have to be extraordinarily "strange coincidences" *if* selection had not shaped the traits for their purported functions.

The Nature of Psychological Adaptations

I have illustrated design arguments using morphological traits such as eyes and wings. In these instances, engineering analyses on design for sight or flight can be performed and the resulting specifications of design can be compared with the structure of eyes or wings. Evolutionary psychologists, however, are faced with inferring psychological adaptations, not morphological ones. How should special design arguments about *psychological adaptation* be constructed?

Behaviors and psychological phenomena are often responses of the organism to aspects of the environment. They are effects of components of the nervous system interacting with each other or effects of the nervous system interacting with the muscular-skeletal system. Behaviors and psychological processes are like traits in that they produce effects of their own (e.g., the movement of a hand that shapes the environment to create a tool), and these effects are often functional. Psychological processes can qualify as adaptations—features of an organism shaped by selection because of their beneficial effects on the organism's fitness. To evaluate special design of psychological processes as adaptations, we need (a) a description of the psychological adaptation and (b) specifications of design of a psychological adaptation that would be good for producing a particular function.

Psychological adaptations are properties of nervous systems, and in theory, it might one day be possible to describe them in terms of brain processes. (Indeed, some can probably be described at that level today.) But they can be described at a different level as well, at the information processing, cognitive, or decision-rule level. Psychological processes act on information in the external or internal environment of an organism and produce behavioral responses (e.g., ones that qualify as thinking, feeling, sensing, perceiving, preferring, etc., as well as overt behaviors observable to others). One can describe an organism's responses or behavioral adjustments to information within its environment in terms of information processing algorithms or decision rules. Psychological theories generally try to describe psychological processes in this manner.

In the simplest of terms, a psychological adaptation might "look like" a rule of the following sort: "If environmental feature A is encountered, do X" (e.g., "if a snake is encountered, orient to it"). More complex rules add additional conditional statements (e.g., "if you are a child and you live with another child, be averse to sex with that person"). Some psychological adaptations lead to changes in behavioral responses over time (learning; e.g., "if behavior X is followed by reinforcer R in situation A, do X when in situation A again"; e.g., see Crawford, 1998, for more discussion of the structure of psychological adaptations). Psychological adaptations are not observed directly. They are typically what philosophers of science refer to as "dispositional" traits, and they must be inferred from repeated observations of individuals in relevant circumstances.

A special design argument about psychological adaptation is an argument about whether the decision rule or information-processing algorithm of the alleged adaptation fits specifications of design of a psychological process that would perform a particular function well. Hence, an argument of design requires a specification of good design in addition to a description of adaptation.

Tooby and Cosmides (1992) proposed that researchers perform a *task analysis* to identify good design. This term is borrowed from Marr's (1980) usage of the term in perceptual psychology. In that context, a task analysis identifies what kinds of information available in the environment can solve a particular perceptual problem (e.g., object identification, depth perception, and color constancy). Tooby and Cosmides generalized the term to refer to identification of what kinds of information would be needed to solve any adaptive problem. Hence, individuals must solve the problem of identifying siblings to avoid incest and know who to invest in relatively altruistically as one would a sibling. One possible cue is given by the Westermarck hypothesis: coresidence with another child during early life. Another possible cue is seeing one's mother (primary caretaker) breast-feed another child (though that cue would be available only to older siblings). Based on a task analysis, one can build hypotheses specifically about what kin discrimination adaptations might look like and then test those hypotheses. If one finds that individuals do indeed avoid sex with individuals with whom they coreside during childhood, it seems reasonable to infer, based on a design argument, that this effect is due to psychological adaptations that evolved for the function of discriminating kin and avoiding incest (e.g., Lieberman, Tooby, & Cosmides, 2003).

In some cases, a priori design specification is aided through optimality or game theoretic analyses—the kinds of cost-benefit analyses described earlier. An optimization model quantitatively models the selection pressures on a particular trait or suite of traits (Seger & Stubblefield, 1996; Winterhalder & Smith, 2000). The model has one or more actors expressing the phenotypes that the theoretician is trying to understand. The payoffs of the model are expressed in a currency, such as actual fitness units or some correlate of fitness (e.g., units of energy). The decision set is the suite of phenotypic or behavioral options available for pursuing the goal, and the selective constraints delineate how these options are translated into costs and benefits. The optimal phenotypic or behavioral option is the one that satisfies the benefits expressed in the currency (see Parker & Maynard Smith, 1990, for more discussion).

Consider an example. One might be interested in knowing what the optimum interbirth interval is within a foraging group. Delaying reproduction has the costs of reducing the number of live births a woman can achieve in her lifetime. But reproducing too soon after the birth of one child has the costs of reducing the likelihood of survival of that child. If one can estimate the costs as well as the benefits of delay, as a function of the delay period, one can build a model that can specify the optimum interbirth interval. Blurton Jones (1986) did so using Kung San bushman data, and found that an interval of approximately 48 months was optimal. As it happens, that value matched the actual modal interbirth interval in this group.

Optimality analyses, it should be emphasized, do not provide a model of psychological (or physiological) processes sufficient to solve a problem in the same way that a task analysis does. Rather, an optimality analysis is a model of ancestral selection pressures. It addresses what strategy would have been favored by selection (under assumptions of the model). In some cases, an optimality analysis will suggest a favored strategy that would not have been obvious based on verbal reasoning about the problem.

Though not offering models of psychological processes, optimality analyses can aid generation of hypotheses about psychological adaptation. Once a favored strategy has been suggested by an optimality analysis, one can do a task analysis and ask what kinds of psychological process would lead to that outcome. What environmental features must be identified to achieve the outcome? What kinds of conditions that modify optimal response must be discriminated? More generally, what kinds of information-processing algorithms and decision rules would achieve the favored outcome?

The Problem of Exapted Learning Mechanisms

A special design argument claims that there is a sufficiently tight fit between a feature and specifications of design to solve an adaptive problem to rule out all explanations aside from natural selection for a purported function. In the case of psychological adaptation, a special problem of inference can arise, one due to learning. Learning is a process in which feedback from the environment modifies the neurological structures that give rise to behavior and cognition. Learning mechanisms are themselves adaptations that allow the organism to adaptively modulate behavior with changing environments (e.g., Crawford & Anderson, 1989). As adaptations, they have functions (e.g., to learn a language, to fear a predator, etc.). However, by their very nature, learning mechanisms are somewhat flexible with respect to outcome. A learning mechanism can be so flexible that it can develop behavioral and cognitive traits that perform tasks that are not the function of the adaptation. For instance, being able to drive a car or play the stock market in some sense must represent the output of learning mechanisms that evolved for other purposes. Learning mechanisms have been exapted to new problems. Andrews, Gangestad, and Matthews (2003) referred to these outcomes as outputs of an *exapted learning mechanism* (ELM).

ELMs pose a problem for special design arguments because they can lead an individual to behave in ways very consistent with specifications of good design for performing a task without any natural selection for the specific function of performing that task. Again, the ability to drive a car is a good example—so too is the ability to read. (In some sense, selection has been involved in shaping these task performances, but it is not natural selection on genes. As Skinner, 1981, argued, both natural selection on gene frequencies over phylogenetic timescales and selection on behavior shaped ontogenetically through consequences involve selection; see Gould & Lewontin, 1979, for a similar point).

How can we discriminate cases in which proficiency for solving a task is due to selection, over phylogenetic time, for solving the task, and cases in which proficiency is due to an ELM? In some instances, we can rule out selection over phylogenetic time, as we know that the task was not performed ancestrally. People cannot have adaptations for the functions of driving or reading because they have not been doing those tasks long enough for selection to produce adaptations for them. This criterion is not enough, however. First, our knowledge of ancestral environments is imperfect; we cannot always know whether a particular task was performed ancestrally. Second, we cannot rule out the possibility that our ancestors solved tasks relevant to them through ELMs. (After all, if humans still inhabit Earth 10,000 years from now and still read, they still, in all likelihood, will not have adaptations *for* the function of reading. Reading will still be achieved through an ELM.)

Andrews et al. (2002) proposed a provisional list of additional criteria that might be applied to demonstrate special design for a particular function, recognizing that not all criteria will be suitable for all adaptations:

Developmental specificity and biased learning. If a performance is achieved early, easily, and prior to other learned outcomes, special design for the performance is more likely. Children learn to speak words more readily and earlier than they learn to read (e.g., Pinker, 1994). Children learn "intuitive physics," expectations about the physical world, in ways that suggest they have not built up these expectations from repeated instances (e.g., Spelke, 1990). Individuals learn fears to specific stimuli (e.g., snakes, spiders) more readily than they learn fears to other and, currently, equally dangerous stimuli (e.g., electrical outlets; Öhman & Mineka, 2001).

Mismatches with the current environment. Some outcomes do not appear to be particularly useful in a current environment, though they may have been adaptive in an ancestral environment. Hence, people, particularly children, exhibit cravings for foods high in sugar or fat content (e.g., Drewnowski, 1997). Eating these foods is now associated with poor health, and indeed, children are regularly exposed to models encouraging them to eat the "right" foods. Their adaptive utility in energy-constrained ancestral populations, however, is understandable. These cravings may hence be likely to be outcomes of adaptations that evolved in ancestral environments.

Empirical evidence difficult for an ELM to explain. In general, any evidence that is difficult for an ELM to explain can bolster a special design argument. Developmental specificity is one kind of such evidence. But other kinds are possible. For instance, research has shown that women's mate preferences change across the ovulatory cycle. It is not at all obvious how these changes would be due to an ELM. Moreover, the constellation of preference shifts is broad. When in the fertile phase of their cycles, women prefer more masculine faces, more masculine voices, more arrogant behavioral displays, and the scents of more socially dominant men and symmetrical men than when in the nonfertile, luteal phase of their cycles (for a review, see Gangestad, Thornhill, & Garver-Apgar, 2005). These preference shifts fit a hypothesis that women have a suite of adaptations that function to increase the chances that sires of their offspring have genes that enhance offspring success (whether or not they do *in contemporary environments*). It is not obvious how this range of preference shifts would be the output of an ELM.

As should be evident from this discussion, demonstrating that a feature exhibits special design for a particular effect, thereby ruling out all alternative to selection *for that effect*, requires evidence that goes beyond evidence for design per se. One must demonstrate design and reasonably argue that the fit of the psychological process to the purported function did not arise through a broad-based learning mechanism (ELM).

The Role of Comparative and Phylogenetic Analyses for Establishing Adaptation

Williams (1966), Symons (1979, 1987, 1992), Thornhill (1990, 1997), and Crawford (1993) stress criteria of special design for establishing adaptation, evidence that pertains to particular, individual species. As Symons (1979) argued, if one wants to understand adaptations in humans, one must study human features for evidence of design.

Undoubtedly, however, comparative or phylogenetic analyses can be useful for understanding adaptation, particularly when design evidence is, by itself, not compelling. Andrews et al. (2003) discussed one example. Vertebrate skeletons are composed largely of calcium phosphate. This compound dissolves slightly in the presence of lactic acid, which is produced when vertebrates quickly mobilize energy through anaerobic metabolism. Invertebrates do not possess capacities for anaerobic metabolism. From design features alone, one cannot infer that vertebrates possess adaptation for resistance to the dissolving effects of lactic acid. The skeletal systems of invertebrates, however, are composed largely of calcium carbonate. Calcium carbonate is even more susceptible to dissolution in the presence of lactic acid than calcium phosphate. Based on this comparative evidence, it is reasonable to postulate that, in fact, vertebrate skeletal systems do possess adaptation for resisting the detrimental effects of lactic acid.

More generally, phylogenetic comparisons can be very useful for suggesting function in instances in which design has not been fully explored. Exploration of associations between evolution of a trait and an environmental feature or other trait through the use phylogenetic comparisons has become a popular method within comparative biology (e.g., Harvey & Pagel, 1991). Thus, for instance, relative size of the visual cortex in primates is positively associated, within a phylogenetic tree, with fruit eating, which suggests that fruit eating coevolved with neural adaptations for discriminating fruit and its ripeness (e.g., Barton, 1999).

Some researchers, however, have made stronger claims: that comparative or phylogenetic analyses are necessary to understand adaptation. Such claims are based on the difference between adaptation and exaptation. If a trait is an adaptation, it evolved because of a particular function. If it is an exaptation, it evolved because it served a different function or was a by-product prior to acquiring a new benefit. Hence, some argue, it is not sufficient to demonstrate that a trait is beneficial in one species to claim that a trait is an adaptation. One must also demonstrate that a homologous trait (one with a common evolutionary origin) in an ancestor with a different function or qualifying as a by-product did *not* exist—that is, one must demonstrate that the trait is not a pure exaptation. That demonstration requires phylogenetic analyses. By comparing the traits of extant species or based on the fossil record, one can make inferences about the traits of ancestral species. According to some scholars, one must do so to distinguish adaptations from exaptations (e.g., Dannemiller, 2002).

In principle, adaptations are distinguishable from primary exaptations in terms of history. Organisms themselves are historical documents, however, and therefore, in principle, can provide the basis for discriminating adaptation from exaptation. The evidence is to be found, once again, in design. Bird wings simply show too close a fit to specifications of design for flight to be a primary exaptation for flight. That is, it simply is unreasonable to think that wings were co-opted, without modification, for flight. In Williams's (1992) view, "[D]emonstration of conformity to design specifications is superior to phylogenetic comparison as a way of demonstrating adaptation" (p. 104).

Again, however, phylogenetic comparisons can be very useful. In addition to adding information where information pertaining to conformity to design is not fully convincing, phylogenetic information provides insight into questions of origin, as opposed to function, which evidence pertaining to design cannot do (Thornhill, 2007). Hence, from design evidence, we can know that wings were shaped by selection for flight and that mammary glands evolved for the function of feeding offspring. Design evidence cannot tell us that wings were initially exapted to a function of facilitating flight from features that previously functioned to provide thermoregulation or that mammary glands first appeared in very early mammals, having been evolved from modified sweat glands. Phylogenetic comparisons, however, can tell us so.

SOME OUTSTANDING ISSUES PERTAINING TO ADAPTATION

In this last section, I visit several issues debated over the years with perhaps no firm resolution. By no means is this list exhaustive. Rather, the section provides some appreciation of the fact that, similar to other methodologies, adaptationist methodology is subject to continual critical analysis and open to modification.

Issue 1. The Problem of Atomizing Traits

Gould and Lewontin (1979) criticized adaptationists for weak epistemological standards for demonstrating adaptation. I have discussed their claim that adaptationists told "just-so stories" and adaptationists' reply that, in fact, adaptation is an "onerous" concept (Williams, 1966) reserved for features that show clear evidence of special design for function. In a section entitled "What is a trait?" Gould and Lewontin identified a separate *ontological* problem, which Dupré (2002) has argued remains unresolved: Adaptationists atomize the organism into distinct parts, each of which is then assumed to be optimally designed for a specific function. In fact, however, organisms are integrated phenotypes and it is not possible to merely "carve" the organism into component parts, interpreted in isolation from the rest of the organism. Selection cannot operate on individual features in isolation. Due to ubiquitous pleiotropy (effects of genes on multiple traits) and patterns of correlated growth (e.g., increases in size of certain regions can perhaps only be achieved through increases in size of other regions; Finlay, Darlington, & Nicastro, 2001), the phenotypic space through which selection can move the evolution of an organism is not the entire n-dimensional space defined by all variation in all n measurable features; as noted earlier, it is constrained. Many of the basic "traits" that adaptationists speak of, let alone the adaptations, do not exist.

Andrews et al. (2002) responded to Dupré by arguing that, in fact, special design evidence can address the question of what a trait is as well as whether the trait qualifies as an adaptation. That is, an adaptationist claim that a particular feature has been honed by selection to serve a particular function typically entails two subclaims: first, that selection was able to operate on that feature with sufficiently low costs arising from developmental constraints to yield telltale design, and second, that the benefits responsible for its evolution correspond to those of the claimed function. The first of these claims is that which Gould and Lewontin (1979) argued cannot be assumed casually. While Andrews et al. agreed, they went on to note that, in fact, the claim is not immune to empirical evaluation. Evidence for the special design of the feature for the putative function is evidence *not only* of the claim that the function drove the evolution of the feature; it is evidence that the feature was not so developmentally constrained that it was could not be modified by selection. Behavioral ecologists and evolutionary psychologists, in fact, have identified design in many aspects of animal and human behavior to possess special design, which implies that these features, at least, can reasonably be treated as "traits."

Issue 2. Is Current Fitness Relevant After All?

Adaptations, again, need not be currently adaptive. To demonstrate that a trait (e.g., preferences for sweets) is an adaptation, showing that the trait is currently adaptive is neither sufficient nor necessary.

Borgerhoff Mulder (2007) and Reeve and Sherman (2007) argue that examination of current adaptiveness is nonetheless a useful adaptationist tool. Reeve and Sherman discuss two different methods for inferring past selection for adaptations. One is the forward method, typically preferred by evolutionary psychologists. Use of this method involves identifying a past selection pressure (or adaptive problem; e.g., detecting cheaters) and then hypothesizing the existence of an adaptation that evolved in response to that selection pressure (e.g., a cheater detection mechanism; e.g., Cosmides, 1990). Demonstration of adaptation requires examination of design of the purported adaptation.

Reeve and Sherman (2007) argue that one problem with this method is that we often do not know what the ancestral environment was like. The backward method is an alternative that they argue does not require knowledge of ancestral environments. Here, a researcher identifies what traits are associated with success in current environments. The researcher assumes that the current environment is sufficiently like ancestral environments, such that past selection can be inferred from present fitness differentials. Because one may not be able to assume that offspring production meaningfully taps fitness in the sense of capacity to outreproduce others, however, Reeve and Sherman suggest that researchers measure current success in terms of "fitness tokens" such as acquisition of status or access to sexual partners, outcomes that would have led to offspring production in past environments.

Borgerhoff Mulder (2007) argues that, while traits adaptive in past environments need not be adaptive now, studies of current fitness are useful for addressing a range of important questions relevant to understanding human adaptation (e.g., what environments favor particular traits, whether hypotheses about selection fit relevant data, particularly when evaluated in environments presumed similar to ancestral ones, e.g., in traditional foraging societies, questions about conflicting selection pressures). As she explains, the key is to interpret results within a sophisticated adaptationist framework, not simplistically, and in concert with other kinds of evidence (e.g., considerations of design). Indeed, behavioral ecologists studying animals have undeniably made many important discoveries by examining what predicts success in animal populations. Though modern humans may be unusual in that modern Western environments might be quite unlike ancestral environments, in some respects and in some populations, modern environments may be quite like ancestral ones.

Issue 3. Reverse Engineering Versus Reverse Tinkering

A simple description of the task analysis of evolutionary psychology is that it answers the question, "What design features (e.g., information processing capabilities) would have solved adaptive problem X (where X could be any purported adaptive problem) in ancestral environments, and therefore possibly evolved?" In addressing this question, one must keep in mind that humans were not constructed anew for their particular niche. Humans were the outcome of eons of evolutionary process, appearing 400 million years or more since the appearance of the first vertebrates and perhaps 200 million years since the origin of mammals. Never across these vast timescales were ancestral species formed anew as a set of solutions for their environments. Rather, in each generation, selection operated on variations on a preexisting design. "Reverse engineering" is an approach for trying to understand the biological function of something designed for a particular purpose, and sometimes compared to attempts to understand the function of objects that were designed by humans. Unlike human artifacts, however, biological "design features" were not constructed from scratch. The evolution of adaptations probably involves "tinkering" more than "engineering" (e.g., Jacob, 1977). Hence, evolutionary psychologists should perhaps be trying to "reverse tinker" rather than "reverse engineer." A challenge of this task is that we do not always know the preexisting design that was tinkered with at any point in evolution (see also Andrews et al., 2002).

A response to these complications is that one need not always know the full history of a biological feature to reverse engineer it effectively. Mammary glands originally were "tinkered" sweat glands. But they too contain telltale signs of selection for a particular function, feeding young (Thornhill, 2007). Features of psychological processes may also possess telltale signs of selection, despite being outcomes of "tinkering" with prior features.

Still, some features surely do possess "mixed designs"—mixtures of features reflecting design for a phylogenetically older function as well as design for a more recent function. This point was one of Gould and Vrba's (1982) key arguments for the importance of the concept of exaptation (see also Andrews et al., 2002). But if a trait possesses mixed design, with no special design for any one specific function, it may not appear to have been designed for either. In these cases, phylogenetic methods may be useful. By examining the distribution of individual features across phylogenetically related species, researchers may be able to identify an older design separately, including how it was altered by recent function. Once again, though design considerations are important, evolutionary psychologists can also learn much about adaptation from phylogenetic data (Sterelny & Griffiths, 1999; Thornhill, 2007).

Issue 4: Organisms Create Environments

The concept of adaptation may imply that organisms "adapt" to something—namely, an environment—and, in so doing, "solve" a problem that the environment "poses." Indeed, the task analysis of evolutionary psychology assumes a preexisting environment that poses problems for organisms to solve. As Lewontin (1983) argued, this view of the relation between organisms and their environments is overly simplistic. Organisms create as well as respond to their environments. Perhaps more profoundly, however, neither organisms nor their environments can be fully defined without reference to the other. They are part of a coevolved system in which neither element can be separated from the other.

The coevolved nature of organisms and their environments is illustrated by work on niche construction (e.g., Laland, Odling-Smee, & Feldman, 2000). Organisms are adapted to their environments partly because they find niches for which they possess adaptive features. Did humans *adapt to* the hunter-gatherer lifestyle? Or did they develop a hunter-gatherer lifestyle because they *already possessed features* (evolved for other reasons, either for other functions or as by-products) that rendered hunting and gathering successful? In all likelihood, the answer to both questions is yes. The adaptationist methods of evolutionary psychology (e.g., task analysis, reverse engineering) may ignore the latter possibility (indeed, the latter possibility illustrates why exaptation may be common; organisms that enter a niche to which they are already adapted thereby exapt preexisting traits).

Of course, task analysis and reverse engineering *have* proven useful. Many organismic features evolved in response to features of the environment (e.g., immune systems to pathogen stress, means of kin detection to the problem of discriminating kin, and mate choice criteria to the problem of identifying suitable mates) and standard adaptationist methods have successfully identified evolved function in many such cases. For some questions, however, perhaps a broader approach is called for. Richerson and Boyd (2005), for instance, argue that a key human "trick" allowing people to rapidly spread across the globe was the invention of culture, which permitted much useful information to be stored in and transmitted through the minds of people. Is it useful to think of the invention of culture as a solution to a particular problem the environment posed? Perhaps, but another possibility is that human intellectual capacities and social predilections that evolved for other reasons permitted humans to transmit information horizontally and *create* a component of culture, to which preexisting traits were exapted.

Are organism-environment coevolutionary phenomena of this sort readily incorporated into the standard framework of evolutionary psychology, one that gives priority to evolutionary task analysis and reverse engineering? Or is a new metatheory for evolutionary psychology called for (e.g., Sterelny, 2007)? This issue will no doubt continue to be debated.

SUMMARY

The concept of adaptation is fundamental to evolutionary biology and evolutionary psychology. The key adaptationist tools of task analysis and reverse engineering have led to many discoveries about the nature of ancestral selection acting on nonhuman species and humans, despite us not being able to directly observe ancestral environments. These methods remain somewhat informal in nature, guided by Williams' basic idea that, through examination of design, we attempt to find evidence that renders a very small probability that anything other than specific selection pressures led to the evolution of a purported adaptation. Useful attempts to make clear the relevant criteria, however, continue. Some critical issues about adaptation and the criteria used to identify it remain. No doubt, the future holds progress toward a more complete understanding of adaptation.

REFERENCES

Andrews, P. A., Gangestad, S. W., & Matthews, D. (2002). Adaptationism—How to carry out an exaptationist program. *Behavioral and Brain Sciences, 25*, 489–504.

Barton, R. A. (1999). The evolutionary ecology of the primate brain. In P. C. Lee (Ed.), *Primate socioecology* (pp. 167–184). Cambridge, U.K.: Cambridge University Press.

Blurton Jones, N. G. (1986). Bushman birth spacing: A test of optimal interbirth intervals. *Ethology and Sociobiology, 7*, 91–105.

Borgerhoff Mulder, M. (2007). On the utility, not the necessity, of tracking current fitness. In S. W. Gangestad & J. A. Simpson (Eds.), *The evolution of mind: Fundamental questions and controversies* (pp. 78–85). New York: Guilford.

Cole, L. C. (1954). The population consequences of life history phenomena. *Quarterly Review of Biology, 29*, 103–137.

Cosmides, L. (1990). The logic of social exchange: Has natural selection shaped how humans reason? Studies with the Wason selection task. *Cognition, 31*, 187–276.

Cowen, R. (1990). *History of life.* Boston: Blackwell Scientific Publications.

Crawford, C. B. (1993). The future of sociobiology: Counting babies or studying proximate mechanisms? *Trends in Ecology and Evolution, 8*, 183–186.

Crawford, C. B. (1998). The theory of evolution in the study of human behavior: An introduction and overview. In C. B. Crawford & D. L. Krebs (Eds.), *Handbook of evolutionary psychology* (pp. 3–41). Mahwah, NJ: Lawrence Erlbaum.

Crawford, C. B., & Anderson, J. L. (1989). Sociobiology: An environmentalist discipline? *American Psychologist, 12*, 1449–1459.

Dannemiller, J. L. (2002). Lack of evidentiary criteria for exaptations? *Behavioral and Brain Sciences, 25*, 512–513.

Darwin, C. (1859). *On the origin of species by means of natural selection or the preservation of favored races in the struggle for life.* London: Murray.

Drewnowski, A. (1997). Taste preferences and food intake. *Annual Review of Nutrition, 17*, 237–253.

Dupré, J. (2002). Ontogeny *is* the problem. *Behavioral and Brain Sciences, 25*, 516–517.

Finlay, B. L., Darlington, R. B., & Nicastro, N. (2001). Developmental structure in brain evolution. *Behavioral and Brain Sciences, 24*, 263–307.

Fisher, R. A. (1958). *The genetical theory of natural selection.* New York: Oxford University Press. (Original work published 1930)

Gangestad, S. W., Thornhill, R., & Garver-Apgar, C. E. (2005). Adaptations to ovulation: Implications for sexual and social behavior. *Current Directions in Psychological Science, 14*, 312–316.

Godfrey-Smith, P. (1993). Functions: Consensus without unity. *Pacific Philosophical Quarterly, 74*, 196–208.

Gould, S. J. (1997). The exaptive excellence of spandrels as a term and prototype. *Proceedings of the National Academy of Science USA, 94*, 10750–10755.

Gould, S. J., & Lewontin, R. C. (1979). The spandrels of San Marco: A critique of the adaptationist programme. *Proceedings of the Royal Society of London* B, *205*, 581–598.

Gould, S. J., & Vrba, E. S. (1982). Exaptation: A missing term in the science of form. *Paleobiology, 8*, 4–15.

Haig, D. (1993). Genetic conflicts in human pregnancy. *Quarterly Review of Biology, 68*, 495–532.

Haldane, J. B. S. (1932). *The causes of evolution.* New York: Harper.

Harvey, P. H., & Pagel, M. D. (1991). *The comparative method in evolutionary biology. Oxford Series in Ecology and Evolution*. Oxford, U.K.: Oxford University Press.

Jacob, F. (1977). Evolution and tinkering. *Science, 196*, 1161–1166.

Lack, D. (1954). *The natural regulation of animal numbers*. Oxford, U.K.: Oxford University Press.

Laland, K. N., Odling-Smee, J., & Feldman, M. W. (2000). Niche construction, biological evolution, and cultural change. *Behavioral and Brain Sciences, 23*, 131–175.

Lewontin, R. C. (1978). Adaptation. *Scientific American, 239*, 212–230.

Lewontin, R. C. (1979). Sociobiology as an adaptationist program. *Behavioral Science, 24*, 5–14.

Lewontin, R. C. (1983). Gene, organism and environment. In D. S. Bendall (Ed.), *Evolution from molecules to men* (pp. 273–285) . Cambridge, U.K.: Cambridge University Press.

Lieberman, D., Tooby, J., & Cosmides, L. (2003). Does morality have a biological basis? *Proceedings of the Royal Society of London* B, *270*, 819–826.

Marr, D. (1980). *Vision*. New York: Freeman.

Mayr, E. (1991). *One long argument: Charles Darwin and the genesis of modern evolutionary thought*. Cambridge, MA: Harvard University Press.

Millikan, R. (1989). In defense of proper functions. *Philosophy of Science, 56*, 288–302.

Norberg, U. M. L. (2002). Structure, form, and function of flight in engineering and the living world. *Journal of Morphology, 252*, 52–81.

Öhman, A., & Mineka, S. (2001). Fear, phobias and preparedness: Toward an evolved module of fear and fear learning. *Psychological Review, 108*, 483–522.

Paley, W. (1836). *Natural theology* (Vol. 1). London: Charles Knight.

Parker, G. A., & Maynard Smith, J. (1990). Optimality theory in evolutionary biology. *Nature, 348*, 27–33.

Perrin, J. (1913). *Les atom*. Paris: Gallimard.

Pinker, S. (1994). *The language instinct*. New York: Harper Collins.

Pittendrigh, C. S. (1958). Adaptation, natural selection, and behavior. In A. Roe & G. G. Simpson (Eds.), *Behavior and evolution* (pp. 390–416). New Haven, CT: Yale University Press.

Reeve, H. K., & Sherman, P. W. (2007). Why measuring reproductive success in current populations is valuable: Moving forward by going backward. In S. W. Gangestad & J. A. Simpson (Eds.), *The evolution of mind: Fundamental questions and controversies* (pp. 86–94). New York: Guilford.

Richerson, P. J., & Boyd, R. (2005). *Not by genes alone: How culture transformed human evolution*. Chicago: University of Chicago Press.

Salmon, W. C. (1984). *Scientific explanation and the causal structure of the world*. Princeton, NJ: Princeton University Press.

Seger, J., & Stubblefield, J. W. (1996). Optimization and adaptation. In M. R. Rose & G. V. Lauder (Eds.), *Adaptation* (pp. 93–123). New York: Academic Press.

Skinner, B. F. (1981). Selection by consequences. *Science, 213*, 501–156.

Sober, E. (1984). *The nature of selection: Evolutionary theory in philosophical focus*. Cambridge, MA: MIT Press.

Spelke, E. S. (1990). Principles of object perception. *Cognitive Science, 14*, 25–56.

Sterelny, K. (2007). An alternative evolutionary psychology? In S. W. Gangestad & J. A. Simpson (Eds.), *The evolution of mind: Fundamental questions and controversies* (pp. 178–185). New York: Guilford.

Sterelny, K., & Griffiths, P. E. (1999). *Sex and death: An introduction to the philosophy of biology*. Chicago: University of Chicago Press.

Symons, D. (1979). *The evolution of human sexuality*. New York: Oxford University Press.

Symons, D. (1987). If we're all Darwinians, what's the fuss about? In C. Crawford, M. Smith, & D. Krebs (Eds.), *Sociobiology and psychology: Ideas, issues, and applications* (pp. 121–146). Hillsdale, NJ: Erlbaum.

Symons, D. (1992). On the use and misuse of Darwinism. In J. H. Barkow, L. Cosmides, & J. Tooby (Eds.), *The adapted mind: Evolutionary psychology and the generation of culture* (pp. 137–159). New York: Oxford University Press.

Thornhill, R. (1990). The study of adaptation. In M. Bekoff & D. Jamieson (Eds.), *Interpretation and explanation in the study of behavior: Explanation, evolution, and adaptation* (Vol. 2, pp. 31–62). Boulder, CO: Westview.

Thornhill, R. (1997). The concept of an evolved adaptation. In M. Daly (Ed.), *Characterizing human psychological adaptations* (pp. 4–13). New York: Wiley.

Thornhill, R. (2007). Comprehensive knowledge of human evolutionary history requires both adaptationism and phylogenetics. In S. W. Gangestad & J. A. Simpson (Eds.), *The evolution of mind: Fundamental questions and controversies* (pp. 31–37). New York: Guilford.

Tooby, J., & Cosmides, L. (1992). Psychological foundations of culture. In J. Barkow, L. Cosmides, & J. Tooby (Eds.), *The adapted mind* (pp. 19–136). New York: Oxford University Press.

Williams, G. C. (1966). *Adaptation and natural selection.* Princeton, NJ: Princeton University Press.

Williams, G. C. (1992). *Natural selection: Domains, levels and challenges.* New York: Oxford University Press.

Winterhalder, B., & Smith, E. A. (2000). Analyzing adaptive strategies: Human behavioral ecology at twenty-five. *Evolutionary Anthropology, 9,* 51–72.

Wright, S. (1968). *Evolution and genetics of populations.* Chicago: Chicago University Press.

9

Evolved Cognitive Mechanisms and Human Behavior

H. CLARK BARRETT

THE EXPLANATORY ROLE OF MECHANISMS IN EVOLUTIONARY PSYCHOLOGY

The goal of the behavioral sciences is to explain behavior in causal terms. This is one of the most difficult problems in science because the causes of human behavior are complex and operate interactively over many scales of space and time. Some approaches to human behavior attempt to gloss this problem by treating humans like elementary particles whose behavior is governed by relatively simple laws. Economic theories, for example, sometimes treat humans as utility maximizers, assuming that humans will act as if they are maximizing utility when viewed in the aggregate, even though the proximate mechanisms that cause this behavior are unspecified.

Evolutionary psychology attempts to move past "as if" models by identifying the proximate causal mechanisms of human behavior in the brain and linking these to ultimate evolutionary causes. The principle that guides evolutionary psychology research is that evolutionary processes shape brain mechanisms and brain mechanisms shape behavior. Evolved mechanisms are the units of explanation that distinguish evolutionary psychological accounts from other approaches, which tend either to attempt to link ultimate causes directly to behavior or to focus on only proximate causes (Cosmides & Tooby, 1987).

Because of their ambitious nature, evolutionary psychological approaches have been criticized on several grounds, including that ultimate causal events occurred in the past and so cannot be directly observed (Buller, 2005). This reflects a misunderstanding of the role of evolutionary theorizing in evolutionary psychology. Evolutionary principles rarely lead to deductive certainties. Instead, they are a heuristic for the generation of hypotheses about the possible design features of mechanisms. These hypotheses are then tested empirically, and ultimately, the combination of data and theory weigh for or against a particular evolutionary hypothesis, as illustrated in the following examples.

Critics have also attacked the notion that the mind contains many specialized mechanisms that are closely linked to adaptive problems that recurred over evolutionary time, as opposed to a few general mechanisms that are not specialized to solve specific problems (for a review, see Barrett & Kurzban, 2006). This debate is largely unnecessary. Few would argue that no mechanisms can solve a wide range of problems. However, the explanatory burden faced by theories of "general-purpose" mechanisms is the same as that faced by theories of specialized mechanisms: Namely, what are the information-processing features that allow the mechanism to perform the tasks that it is invoked to account for, and what are the evolutionary processes that shaped those features? Presumably, few would postulate mechanisms that have no function at all or that solve problems without any particular features that allow them to do so. Moreover, arguments about the degree to which the mind contains many, as opposed to few, specialized mechanisms cannot be resolved a priori. That question is an empirical one.

Here, I will review research on evolved cognitive mechanisms to show that the evidence for specialized mechanisms is in fact substantial. This research shows how evolutionary reasoning can play a useful heuristic role in the search for the design features of cognitive mechanisms.

THE FORM-FUNCTION FIT, DESIGN FEATURES, AND DOMAIN SPECIFICITY

A cognitive mechanism is anything that plays a causal role in guiding behavior on the basis of neurally coded information. Evolutionary psychologists view specialized cognitive mechanisms as synonymous with cognitive *modules*, but the notion of modules in evolutionary psychology differs substantially from the conventional view in cognitive psychology (Fodor, 1983, 2000). For example, while evolutionary psychologists expect the mind to be multimodular, the modularity that evolutionary psychologists have in mind is interactive, not rigid and isolated as many psychologists suggest (Barrett, 2005b). Evolved cognitive modules are not expected to operate in isolation from other systems because a key value of specialization is that it leads to flexibility and computational power when modules interact. Nor are features such as automaticity or other features suggested by Fodor (1983) necessary features of evolved modules (Barrett, Frederick, Haselton, & Kurzban, 2006). Instead, evolutionary psychologists regard the key feature of modularity to be *functional specialization* (Barrett, 2005b; Barrett & Kurzban, 2006; Carruthers, 2005; Sperber, 1994, 2002, 2005).

Functional specialization refers to the fit between form and function that is characteristic of biological adaptations. For morphological adaptations like fins or wings, the meaning of *form* is clear. In the case of cognitive mechanisms, form refers to information-processing features of the mechanism. These can be thought of as the mechanism's *design features* (where "design" refers not to design by an intelligent agent but to design by evolutionary processes). Typically, a list of a mechanism's design features would include a specification of the kinds of inputs the mechanism accepts, and the operations that it performs on those inputs. Of necessity, all mechanisms will operate on information only of a particular format. The format requirements of a mechanism delineate the mechanism's *domain* (Barrett & Kurzban, 2006; Sperber, 1994).

Many authors use the term *domain* in a more narrow sense to refer to *content* or *meaning* domains. However, from an evolutionary perspective, there is no reason to restrict the concept of domain specificity to only content domains (Barrett & Kurzban, 2006). For example, the hypothesized phonological loop in working memory (Baddeley, 2002) has a clear input domain in that it accepts only representations of sound, yet the content of the sounds it handles is not restricted. Nevertheless, the set of inputs handled by the phonological loop and the visuospatial sketchpad, another hypothesized component of working memory (Baddeley, 2002) are well defined and distinct. The domains of these information-processing mechanisms are specific and do not overlap.

A useful distinction can be made between a mechanism's *proper domain*—the range of inputs that the mechanism evolved to process—and its *actual domain*—the range of inputs that the mechanism actually accepts, whether or not they influenced the evolution of the mechanism (Sperber, 1994). For example, a mechanism for detecting biological motion might be triggered by computer-generated animations of dinosaurs, even though these animations clearly played no role in the evolution of the mechanism. Together, the notions of specialized function, input conditions, operations on inputs, and the distinction between proper and actual domains provide the theoretical basis for the study of evolved information-processing mechanisms.

THE EMPIRICAL STUDY OF SPECIALIZED COGNITIVE MECHANISMS

Evidence for specialized mechanisms comes in the form of signatures of specialization that can be observed empirically. For example, evidence that information of one kind is processed differently from information of another kind suggests either that multiple mechanisms are involved or a single mechanism that is structured to handle particular information types differently. Another kind of signature can be observed in neuropsychological dissociations: the differential loss of information processing abilities following brain damage or developmental disruption (Shallice, 1988).

However, just as it is the case that no single set of features is general to all specialized mechanisms, it is also the case that no single method or set of methods can be used across the board to diagnose the presence of specialized mechanisms. For example, mechanisms will vary in the extent to which their operations share resources with, or are influenced by, other systems. Therefore, although evidence that manipulating one system or mechanism (e.g., occupying working memory with a string of digits) affects some other mechanism might bear on hypotheses about how such systems interact, it does not falsify that specialized systems are operating (Barrett, Frederick, Haselton, & Kurzban, 2006). The same goes for neuropsychological dissociations. Brain damage will not necessarily affect all of and only one mechanism and neither will developmental damage necessarily affect all of and only one system because development is interactive (Shallice, 1988). Because causation in the brain is complex, it can be difficult to disentangle the effects of distinct mechanisms, and multiple sources of evidence are usually necessary.

A general heuristic for empirical studies of cognitive mechanisms is that the methods should fit the hypotheses about the design feature under investigation. If rapid speed is an expected design feature of the system in question based on evolutionary reasoning—as in the case, for example, of a perceptual mechanism for detecting snakes—then methods such as reaction time might be appropriate. For other systems, such as mate choice, for which there is reason to expect slow processing integrating much information, rather than speed, such methods might reveal little.

With these principles in mind, I will now review a few examples of specialized information-processing mechanisms, focusing on evidence of functional specialization and how it relates to hypotheses about evolved function.

FACE RECOGNITION

One of the best studied examples of a specialized cognitive system in humans is the face recognition system. There are evolutionary reasons to think that it would be advantageous not only to detect the presence of conspecifics but also to identify them individually, which could be useful in regulating behavior in both antagonistic and friendly contexts, for kin recognition, and in social contexts in which individual reputation is important. Because individual identity is so important in social interaction, we would expect the evolution of a dedicated system for face recognition. Because faces have specific properties that make recognizing them a different matter from recognizing other kinds of objects, one might expect such a system to have specialized design features specifically for processing faces, including mechanisms for detecting identity, mood, gender, and age.

There is substantial evidence that information about faces is processed differently from information about other kinds of objects. The overall arrangement of the parts, rather than just the parts themselves, is more important in face recognition than for other objects (Young, Hellawell, & Hay, 1987). Turning faces upside down makes them much more difficult to recognize than other kinds of objects (Farah, K. D. Wilson, Drain, & Tanaka, 1995). Faces are attended to more quickly than other stimuli in infants (Morton & Johnson, 1991). Specific brain regions are involved in face processing: in particular, the fusiform gyrus in the inferior right temporal lobe (Barton, Press, Keenan, & O'Connor, 2002; Kanwisher, McDermott, & Chun, 1997).

Perhaps the best evidence for specialized, evolved face recognition mechanisms is a disorder known as *prosopagnosia*, in which face recognition is selectively impaired, leaving other abilities intact (Duchaine, 2000; Duchaine, Yovel, Butterworth, & Nakayama, 2006; Farah, 1990, 1996). Prosopagnosia can occur developmentally: For example, impairment of visual input to the right hemisphere in early childhood due to infantile cataracts can result in prosopagnosia later in life, even if the cataracts are later corrected, suggesting that particular inputs are required for the mechanism to develop normally (Le Grand, Mondloch, Maurer, & Brent, 2003). Prosopagnosia can also be acquired following brain trauma (Barton et al., 2002). Several sources of evidence suggest that the deficit in prosopagnosia is specific to faces. For example, face and object recognition can dissociate even when differences in task difficulty are accounted for (Duchaine & Nakayama, 2005; Farah, 1996), and there are inverse dissociations, in which patients show normal face recognition while recognition of other objects is impaired (Moscovitch, Winocur, & Behrmann, 1997).

The principle debate in the study of face recognition and prosopagnosia is whether the underlying mechanisms are specialized for processing faces in particular, or whether they have a broader function. Because the alternative hypotheses have been fairly well specified, and because there is a substantial literature attempting to test them, face recognition presents an excellent case study of how empirical evidence can be used to test hypotheses about evolved cognitive mechanisms and, in particular, to distinguish between different hypotheses about evolved function.

Duchaine et al. (2006) list the alternative explanations of prosopagnosia that have been proposed to date. These include the hypothesis that prosopagnosia results from damage to a mechanism specifically designed to recognize faces (Moscovitch et al., 1997). Alternative explanations propose different, broader functions of the mechanism that is damaged. These include that the mechanism is designed to distinguish objects within a class (the individuation explanation; A. R. Damasio, H. Damasio, & Van Hoesen, 1982), that it is designed to process objects that cannot be decomposed into individual parts and therefore must be processed as a complex whole (the holistic explanation; Farah, 1990), that it is specialized to represent the spacing of parts within an object (the configural processing explanation; Freire, Lee, & Symons, 2000), that it is designed to represent curved surfaces (the curvature explanation; Kosslyn, Hamilton, & Bernstein, 1995), and that is designed to distinguish members within a class that are visually homogeneous and share a first-order configuration (the expertise explanation; Diamond & Carey, 1986; Gauthier & Tarr, 1997). In each of these cases, evidence has been offered in favor of the alternative hypothesis, often in the form of showing impairments for objects other than faces (e.g., curved objects).

Duchaine et al. (2006) point out that most studies of prosopagnosics address only one or a few of the possible explanations for prosopagnosia, and therefore do not narrow the possible explanations down to a single one. To remedy this, they tested a prosopagnosic individual, "Edward" (a 53-year-old developmental prosopagnosic), using tasks designed to test the predictions of all of the available hypotheses. They found that Edward's face-recognition abilities were indeed severely impaired, using a "famous faces" recognition task and a task requiring him to remember novel faces. He was able to identify the presence of faces normally, but he was impaired at identifying individuals, emotional expressions, and gender (suggesting that detecting that a face is present relies on different mechanisms from those involved in recognizing individual faces and their features). However, Edward was normal at recognizing other kinds of objects, even within classes (e.g., tools) and even objects requiring holistic or configural processing (e.g., animals). His identification of upright faces was impaired with respect to controls, but his identification of inverted faces was not, which is inconsistent with curvature, holistic, configural, and individuation explanations. His performance on a "visual closure" task in which parts are obscured, forcing configural processing, was normal. In a task in which the spacing of parts was changed, his performance was normal for objects (e.g., spacing of windows in a house) but not for faces (e.g., spacing of eyes and nose). Finally, Edward was trained in expertise on "greebles," an artificial class of visually homogenous objects that share first-order configuration, which is sometimes used to test the expertise explanation (Gauthier & Tarr, 1997). He performed normally. He also performed normally on a task testing long-term expertise, matching upright bodies, but not on a task involving matching upright faces. These data rule out all available explanations except for the face-specific explanation, yielding perhaps the strongest evidence yet that prosopagnosia results from an impairments of mechanisms specific to faces and not to broader classes of objects.

These and other data suggest that humans possess a mechanism specialized for recognizing faces. In fact, evidence suggests that there may be multiple mechanisms, including not just mechanisms for recognizing individuals, but also for recognizing features such as gender, gaze, and emotion expression (Haxby, Hoffman, & Gobbini, 2002). Moreover, face-processing systems must certainly interact with social decision-making systems. A variety of studies suggest that this is a promising area for future work, including several recent studies showing that facial cues (eye gaze) increase prosocial behavior (Bateson, Nettle, & Roberts, 2006; Burnham & Hare, in press; Haley & Fessler, 2005; Kurzban, 2001).

MECHANISMS FOR INFERRING THE INTENTIONS OF OTHERS

The ability to infer the internal states of others, including intentions, knowledge, goals, and desires, is likely to have significant fitness benefits, including advantages in predicting others' behavior and in adjusting one's own behavior accordingly. However, the internal states of others cannot be directly observed. Thus, natural selection might have favored the evolution of mechanisms that use perceptual cues to generate inferences about the goals and intentions that underlie others' behavior. Such cues include motion (Is the individual approaching or running away?), gaze (Where is the individual looking?), posture (Is the individual relaxed or tense?), and cues to the identity of the individual (Is it a conspecific? male or female? adult or child? stranger or friend?). Some of these mechanisms facilitate inferences about beliefs and desires, a capacity known as "theory of mind" (Baron-Cohen, 1995; Leslie, 1994), which is reviewed in another chapter in this volume. Another more basic set of mechanisms support inference about goal-directed behavior more generally, which is sometimes called *agency* (Barrett, 2005b; Leslie, 1994). These include, for example, mechanisms for discriminating living from nonliving things and for inferring attention from eye gaze (for reviews, see Johnson, 2000; Rakison & Poulin-Dubois, 2001; Scholl & Tremoulet, 2000), which are probably phylogenetically widespread.

The ability to distinguish between animate and inanimate objects has clear fitness benefits in contexts ranging from predation to social interaction (Barrett, 2005a). There is evidence for specialized perceptual mechanisms that take as their input particular patterns of motion and produce an interpretation of the motion as animate (Michotte, 1963; Tremoulet & Feldman, 2000). These mechanisms appear to develop early in infancy (Rochat, Morgan, & Carpenter, 1997). They use cues that reliably indicate that the motion is animate and goal directed, such as contingency. For example, when a predator pursues a prey the motion of the prey responds contingently to the motion of the predator. Johnson, Slaughter, and Carey (1998) and Johnson, Booth, and O'Hearn (2001) have shown that infants will construe even a virtually featureless blob as an agent if the object first interacts contingently with the infant, beeping in response to noises the infant makes but not when the beeping of the object is random with respect to the infant's own vocalizations. The mechanism that guides infants' attention toward animate objects in the environment probably evolved because of benefits to both learning about animate objects, including people, and being vigilant with respect to them.

Beyond distinguishing animates from inanimates, there could be important fitness benefits to inferring the specific goals of animate behavior. There is evidence that a mechanism for inferring specific goals from animate motion develops as early as 9 months. For example, a display of one object trying to reach another triggers an inference of the goal of approach, and infants are surprised when observed behavior appears inconsistent with this goal (Csibra, Bíró, Koós, & Gergely, 2003; Gergely, Nádasdy, Csibra, & Bíró, 1995). Additionally, the type of motion matters: Different motion signatures can trigger different inferences about the intentions of the agents involved, for example, triggering an interpretation of intentions such as pursuit and evasion, leading and following, or play (Barrett, Todd, Miller, & Blythe, 2005). Specific brain regions are involved, and the underlying mechanisms can be selectively impaired (Abell, Happé, & U. Frith, 2000; Castelli, Happé, U. Frith, & C. D. Frith, 2000). This evidence suggests that there are early developing mechanisms that take as inputs perceived patterns of motion and output inferences of goals and intentions. These may have evolved due to the benefits of predicting others' behavior, both friendly and antagonistic, in a variety of behavioral contexts.

These basic mechanisms are likely to be only the tip of the iceberg of a complex cognitive system for inferring intentions, which involves many mechanisms still waiting to be discovered. The human capacity to infer intentions plays an important role in contexts ranging from cooperation to language learning, and there is substantial evidence that even very young children are skilled at making such inferences. For example, young children imitate successful rather than unsuccessful actions in the handling of tools (Want & Harris, 2001) and are even able to choose the intentional (vs. accidental) parts of an action to imitate even when they did not observe the outcome (Meltzoff, 1995). They attend to the emotions of the actor to determine whether the outcome matched the actor's goals (Phillips, Wellman, & Spelke, 2002). At 12 months old, infants can infer the goal of a complex set of actions and, when imitating, go straight to the desired end state, skipping the intermediate steps (Carpenter, Call, & Tomasello, 2005). Infants as young as 9 months old react impatiently when an actor appears unwilling to perform an action, but not when the actor appears unable to do so, indicating an understanding of intentions even when outcomes are held constant (Behne, Carpenter, Call, & Tomasello, 2005). These skills are not present in other species that have been tested, and probably involve mechanisms that have been crucial in the evolution of the unique forms of human sociality including culture, language, and the ability to cooperate in large groups (Povinelli, 2000; Tomasello, Carpenter, Call, Behne, & Moll, 2005).

KIN RECOGNITION AND MECHANISMS REGULATING INTERACTIONS WITH KIN

Since the advent of evolutionary theory, the question of why organisms should provide benefits to others has presented a puzzle. If individuals compete for resources and differential fitness is the engine of natural selection, why help others? One reason, originally proposed by Hamilton (1964), is that natural selection can act at the level of the gene, and genes can increase in frequency if they cause organisms to preferentially direct assistance toward others to a degree moderated by the likelihood that those others share genes. This is the fundamental reason why organisms interact differently with kin than with nonkin (for a more detailed discussion, chapter 5, this volume). In addition, because the increased probability of shared genes among kin includes the possibility of sharing deleterious recessive alleles, we would expect natural selection to have favored mechanisms that induce individuals to exclude kin from mating interactions (Bittles & Neel, 1994). Evolutionary theory does not predict that cues to kinship should trigger affiliation across the board, but rather, it predicts domain specificity in affiliation: In particular, individuals should seek to help kin but avoid mating with them. This is a source of hypotheses about the design of cognitive mechanisms regulating kin interactions.

There are many studies demonstrating that people are nicer to kin than to nonkin (for reviews, see Burnstein, 2005; Kurland & Gaulin, 2005). A variety of ethnographic studies in small-scale traditional societies show that genetic kinship plays a role in food sharing (Betzig & Turke, 1986; Kaplan & Hill, 1985) as well as other forms of helping (Chagnon & Bugos, 1979; Hames, 1987; Kaplan & Hill, 1985). This is true in large-scale societies as well (Jankowiak & Diderich, 2000; Judge & Hrdy, 1992; Smith, Kish, & Crawford, 1987). A particularly telling source of evidence is the difference in how children are treated by genetic parents and stepparents. For example, children suffer higher risks of abuse by stepparents (Daly & M. Wilson, 1988).

What information-processing mechanisms are involved in regulating this behavior? What are the cues that are used to detect kinship, and how are these cues integrated to compute a subjective (and perhaps subconscious) estimate of degree of kinship with another individual? How does this internal representation of kinship then enter into computations that regulate attitudes toward those individuals?

Perhaps the first proposal of a psychological mechanism for kin recognition was Westermarck's (1921) suggestion that being raised with another individual during childhood might inhibit sexual attraction toward that individual. This would have fitness benefits because, in ancestral environments, individuals reared together were often likely to have been genetic kin and, therefore, faced health and mortality risks associated with inbreeding. There now exist several sources of evidence for the existence of a mechanism that takes as input cues about coresidence during childhood, and outputs representations of kinship, adjusts attitudes toward kin (sexual attraction, familial sentiments), and regulates behavior toward them. This mechanism is hypothesized to use coresidence as a cue because it correlated with kinship in ancestral environments, even though this means that the mechanism can generate subjective estimates of kinship that are incorrect (e.g., for unrelated children raised together). Systematic errors such as this can be useful evidence for design features, especially because they show that a proximal observable cue rather than kinship itself, which cannot be directly detected, is being used by the mechanism.

Shepher (1971) studied individuals raised together in kibbutzim in Israel and found that sexual attraction between individuals raised together in childhood, even unrelated individuals, was low. Wolf (1995) studied a Taiwanese marriage practice of adopting future brides for their sons into the family at an early age. These marriages were substantially less successful than marriages among noncoresident spouses in, for example, number of children produced. Measures of marriage success were strongly, inversely correlated with how young the bride was when she was adopted into the family, suggesting that the mechanism either has a sensitive period in early childhood (Bevc & Silverman, 2000; Shepher, 1971; Wolf, 1995) or modulates kinship estimates and sexual attraction based on length of coresidence or both. In addition to Shepher's and Wolf's studies, there exist several other studies consistent with Westermarck's hypothesis (Bevc & Silverman, 2000; Fessler & Navarrete, 2004; Fox, 1962; Lieberman, Tooby, & Cosmides, 2003; Walter & Buyske, 2003).

Lieberman et al. (2003) investigated third-party attitudes toward incest as a methodological technique to avoid the difficulties of investigating individuals' own preferences with regard to incest. In their sample of California undergraduates, they found that kinship was correlated with length of coresidence. Whereas previous studies such as those by Shepher (1971) and Wolf (1995) examined coresidence among people who were not actually related, this study had the advantage of studying kin recognition among actual kin. As expected, Lieberman et al. found that length of coresidence predicted third-party moral judgments about sibling incest. Judgments of moral wrongness were stronger among those who had spent more time coresiding with siblings. Interestingly, coresidence predicted attitudes toward sibling incest better than actual degree of relatedness, consistent with the hypothesis that people use coresidence, not actual kinship, as a cue to relatedness. This result also suggests that coresidence might be a stronger cue than other cues to kinship such as phenotype matching (see the following section). Fessler and Navarrete (2004) also investigated third-party attitudes toward sibling incest and found similar effects of coresidence: Coresidence predicted moral attitudes better than actual kinship.

Other cues have been suggested to act as inputs to a kin detection system. Some of these proposed cues involve phenotype matching. Phenotype matching can operate when similarity on some phenotypic dimension (e.g., smell, appearance) correlates with genetic relatedness. Phenotype matching is known to occur in other animals and often involves the individual "imprinting" on a close relative as a source of information about the self. For example, mice use the major histocompatibility complex (MHC) to compute kinship via phenotype matching, imprinting on the MHC haplotypes of coreared individuals. Interestingly, coresidence is ultimately the cue to kinship in this system as well, but it is used to tune the MHC phenotype matching system (Penn & Potts, 1999; Yamazaki et al., 1988). There is also evidence that MHC might play a role in human phenotype matching. For example, Ober et al. (1997) documented MHC-dissimilar mating preferences in a Hutterite community (though some studies have shown preferences for MHC similarity rather than dissimilarity; e.g., Jacob, McClintock, Zelano, & Ober, 2002; for a discussion, see Potts, 2002). More generally, there is evidence that humans can recognize kin through olfactory cues (Porter & Moore, 1981).

Another cue that might be used for phenotype matching is appearance. Again, this raises a chicken-and-egg issue: Given that it might have been rare to see a well-resolved image of oneself in ancestral environments (except for reflections in water), familial imprinting might be the only available mechanism for forming a representation of "self" against which to gauge similarity. However, there is evidence that facial appearance is a cue used by a phenotype-matching-based kin-recognition mechanism.

DeBruine (2002) conducted an experiment in which participants played an economic game designed to measure trust of others. Using computer software, she morphed participants' facial features with those of their game partners, to create a degree of self-resemblance in photos of the partner. This process increased trust relative to non-self-resembling individuals. In a follow-up study, DeBruine (2005) found that, while resemblance to self increased trust, it decreased sexual attraction. This is consistent with the double-edged aspect of kinship discussed previously: Investing in kin can increase fitness, but mating with them can decrease it.

Because humans can increase their fitness by investing in their own offspring, mechanisms regulating parental investment are expected to be sensitive to cues of relatedness. Because women give birth to their offspring, they can be certain of relatedness, whereas for men, there is paternity uncertainty. Therefore, investment mechanisms in men might use phenotypic matching to assess relatedness. Platek, Burch, Panyavin, Wasserman, and Gallup (2002) morphed faces of adult male and female participants with faces of babies, and found that men preferentially selected self-resembling babies as targets of investment, whereas women did not. Interestingly, both sexes were able to detect resemblance, but the resemblance affected hypothetical investment decisions only in males (Platek et al., 2003). This sex difference reveals a possible design feature that makes little sense except in the light of evolutionary theory.

THE SOCIAL EXCHANGE SYSTEM

In addition to kinship, other reasons for sociality have been proposed. Because we engage in diverse kinds of social interaction with nonkin, many involving coordination and cooperation for mutual gain, we might expect that humans would possess evolved specialized cognitive mechanisms for regulating such behavior. I will briefly review the evidence for one such specialized system in humans—the social exchange system.

Evolutionary biologists have identified a relatively small number of reasons why organisms might systematically provide benefits to others. One is genetic kinship. Another is what Trivers (1971) termed *reciprocal altruism*: the exchange of benefits for mutual gain, which can also be called social exchange. While this form of cooperation can be highly beneficial to all parties involved, biologists have found it to be relatively rare in the animal kingdom, although it is present in humans (Cosmides & Tooby, 2005). Game theoretic models have shown that specific conditions are necessary for this form of cooperation to evolve, including the ability to recognize individuals and to remember their past actions in social exchange contexts. In addition, there is the possibility of cheating: accepting benefits from others, but withholding benefits in turn. Game theoretic models have shown that cheaters must be identifiable and excludable from interaction if social exchange is to remain stable in the end.

Cosmides (1989) proposed that humans must have evolved a means of detecting cheaters, given that social exchange exists in our species. To test this idea she used a reasoning task, the Wason selection task, originally developed to examine people's ability to identify the conditions that would falsify particular kinds of logical statements, "if-then" statements. Participants are given an if-then rule and a set of four cards, each of which represents a state of affairs in the world to which the rule might apply. For example, the rule might be, "If there is a vowel on one side of the card, then there must be an even number on the other side." Each card has a letter on one side and a number on the other, but participants initially see only one side of each card. They might be shown, for example, four cards showing "E," "D," "2," and "7." Participants are then asked to indicate which cards they would have to turn over to determine whether the rule had been violated. Logically, for a rule of the form "If P, then Q," subjects should turn over only those cards showing "P" and "not Q" ("E" and "7" in this case). Many studies have shown that people are not able to detect rule violation conditions across the board, suggesting that they do not possess a general logical ability to identify falsifying conditions for if-then statements (Cosmides, 1989).

However, Cosmides (1989) found that participants are very good at solving such problems when they are framed in terms of social contracts of the general form "If [person A gives a benefit to person B], then [person B gives a benefit to person A]." The reason for this, she suggested, was that the mind contains a mechanism for detecting cases of cheating on social contracts. Cosmides suggested that framing an if-then rule as a social contract rule serves as input to a cheater detection mechanism that generates, as output, an inference about the situations that would constitute cheating. On the standard Wason tasks she used, these are the same as the situations that falsify the logical rule "if P then Q:" namely, "P" (benefit taken) and "not Q" (reciprocal benefit not transferred).

Since the publication of Cosmides' early research, a controversy ensued about whether the results were specific to social contracts per se, or to some broader class of contexts, including moral rules involving permission (what one *may* do; Cheng & Holyoak, 1985), deontic rules more generally (rules involving obligation and entitlement; Almor & Sloman, 1996; Manktelow & Over, 1987), relevance of the information on the card to the rule (Sperber, Cara, & Girotto, 1995), and even considerations of general utility of obtaining new information (Oaksford & Chater, 1994). In this sense, the debate has been parallel to the debate over face recognition described previously: Do the results implicate a mechanism *specific* to the domain in question (faces, social contracts), or are they a by-product of more domain-general mechanisms (holistic processing, deontic reasoning)?

This controversy has generated a large literature involving many studies that attempt to test between proposed explanations for content effects (effects of rule type) on performance in social contract reasoning. Several kinds of evidence exist to support the claim that humans have a specialized mechanism for detecting cheaters on social contracts. In addition to Cosmides' (1989) finding that social contract content elicited better performance on the Wason task than abstract rules, she found that this is not merely a familiarity effect: Performance was also high for unfamiliar social contracts. Moreover, this performance does not generalize to broader classes of rules. For example, Cheng and Holyoak (1985) proposed another broader class of rules, permission rules, of the form "if one is to take action A, then one must satisfy precondition B." All social contract rules are permission rules, but not all permission rules are social contract rules. Cosmides and Tooby (1992) constructed permission rules that were not social contract rules, and found poor performance on these rules. The evidence is also inconsistent with another more domain-general proposal regarding deontic rules, which involve obligations and entitlements more generally (Manktelow & Over, 1987). Additionally, Sugiyama, Tooby, and Cosmides (2002) found that Shiwiar hunter-horticulturalists and American university students show similar performance on social contract rules, suggesting that the result is not merely an effect of education or familiarity with logic tasks. Finally, Gigerenzer and Hug (1992) demonstrated that the classic result in the Wason task—selection of "P" and "not Q" cards—can be reversed in cases where both parties in the contract have the potential to cheat, and subjects are cued to looking for cheating on the part of the second party.

Fiddick (2004) proposed that in addition to a mechanism for detecting cheaters on social contracts, there might be a mechanism for detecting violations of precaution rules. A precaution rule specifies a condition for avoiding hazards: For example, "If you drive, then you wear a seatbelt." Because breaking such rules entails fitness costs, Fiddick suggested that a mechanism might have evolved that detects violations. Fiddick found that performance in detecting violations of precaution rules was indeed high. Stone, Cosmides, Tooby, Kroll, and Knight (2002) found that reasoning on social exchange and precaution rules can be dissociated. In a patient who had suffered brain trauma, social contract reasoning was impaired while precaution reasoning remained intact.

There is evidence for an additional design feature that distinguishes social contract from precautionary reasoning. Game theorists have found that cooperation in social exchanges can be stabilized if people distinguish between intentional and accidental violations, and forgive mistakes. For hazards, however, unintentional violations of the rule could be just as detrimental to fitness as intentional ones. Cues to intentional violation should therefore affect the cheater-detection mechanism but not the precaution mechanism. Fiddick (2004), Barrett (1999), and Cosmides and Tooby (2005) found that cueing subjects to the possibility of intentional cheating increases performance on social-contract violation-detection tasks, but not for precautions.

OTHER MECHANISMS: LEARNING, REGULATORY, AND INTERFACE MECHANISMS

Space has precluded an exhaustive review of all specialized mechanisms that are known in psychology. Instead, I have focused on a few examples that demonstrate principles of specialization that make sense in the light of evolutionary theory, and how they are illuminated by data. I would briefly like to mention a few more types of mechanism that are often not considered under the rubric of specialized information-processing mechanisms, though they should be.

Perhaps because of the tendency to focus on the "innateness" of evolved capacities, learning is sometimes viewed as inconsistent with evolved specialization. However, learning is only possible because of mechanisms evolved specifically for learning. No learning mechanism is entirely domain general because all learning mechanisms depend in particular ways on the structure of the input in their learning algorithms, which have been shaped by natural selection (Gallistel, 1990). In humans, there are likely to be a variety of learning mechanisms, including mechanisms specialized for learning in domains such as dangers (Öhman & Mineka, 2001), food preferences and food aversions (Cashdan, 1988), and language (Pinker, 1984).

Emotion mechanisms are another important class of evolved mechanisms that influence information processing in fitness-promoting ways. There is evidence for a specialized fear system that regulates other cognitive systems, such as attentional and learning systems (Öhman & Mineka, 2001). Disgust is another such system, probably composed of multiple evolved mechanisms, which plays a regulatory role in learning, decision making, and social behavior (Rozin, Haidt, & McCauley, 2000). Many other specialized emotion mechanisms probably exist as well.

Finally, a class of mechanisms that is often overlooked is what might be called interface mechanisms. These mechanisms serve to coordinate the interaction of other systems, to pass information between them, and to make information available in a common format so that other systems can operate on it (Barrett, 2005b). The mechanisms of working memory would be one such system (Baddeley, 2002). Language might be another (Carruthers, 2002; Jackendoff, 2002), along with mechanisms involved in analogical reasoning and metaphor (Gentner, 1999). It is important to bring such mechanisms under the rubric of specialized evolved mechanisms, even though they are often considered "domain general" and therefore outside the purview of evolutionary psychology. Such mechanisms, if they do exist, constitute an important part of our evolved multimodular mind, and a complete explanation of behavior would be impossible without them.

GENERAL PRINCIPLES

These examples illustrate a few general principles about specialized mechanisms. One principle is that evolved cognitive mechanisms operate on inputs in specialized, domain-specific ways, and often have multiple effects on different systems. DeBruine's (2002) result, for example, shows that if there is a system for recognizing kin via phenotype matching, then it does not produce a general desire to "affiliate" with that individual: It increases trust as measured in a trust game but decreases attractiveness, suggesting that one class of affiliative behaviors (mating) is downregulated by detection of phenotypic similarity, while another class of affiliative behaviors (trust) is upregulated. This is consistent with the hypothesis that a phenotype-based kin-detection mechanism exists, and that when activated, it has multiple psychological and behavioral effects.

Another principle is that multiple sources of evidence can shed light on the design features of mechanisms. For example, the mechanisms underlying face recognition can be studied using behavioral experiments on normal individuals (e.g., the inverted faces effect), brain scan techniques (which show different patterns of activation for faces vs. other objects), and experiments with developmental or acquired prosopagnosia. Experiments can be carefully tailored to tease apart different possible explanations for face recognition, as shown in Duchaine et al.'s (2006) series of studies with Edward.

A third principle is that evolved specialization does not mean that developmental processes play no role in shaping the phenotypic features of mechanisms. Although this seems obvious, prominent developmentalists have accused evolutionary psychological approaches to specialized mechanisms of being "preformationist" and have implied that evolutionary and developmental accounts are mutually exclusive (for a review, see Barrett & Kurzban, 2006). This is not the case. Specialized mechanisms can be shaped by the developmental process. For example, visual input to the right hemisphere in infancy is crucial for face recognition mechanisms to develop normally (Le Grand et al., 2003). Evolved specialized mechanisms also can guide development, as in the case of mechanisms that help infants orient toward faces (Johnson & Morton, 1991) or to discriminate agents from nonagents (Johnson, 2000).

A final principle is that mechanisms do not operate in isolation but, rather, interact. Face recognition mechanisms probably interact with a host of social cognition mechanisms, including those involved in inferences about agency, kin interactions, and social exchange. Moreover, these interactions are not merely random but coordinated as a matter of design. For example, gaze detection mechanisms appear to influence social decision making in systematic ways. Schematic eyes increase donation behavior in anonymous situations (Bateson et al., 2006; Burnham & Hare, in press; Haley & Fessler, 2005; Kurzban, 2001). This suggests that not only are perceptual and decision-making mechanisms linked, they are linked in principled ways that make sense in the light of evolutionary theories, but not other theories. Eyes were reliable cues to being observed in ancestral environments, and so might regulate social behavior in principled ways even when it is "irrational" in the context of the experiment, because nobody is actually looking. In general, an evolutionary view suggests that evolved cognitive mechanisms should be linked richly and causally in their regulation of behavior.

EXPLAINING THE SEAMLESS WHOLE OF BEHAVIOR

The common theme in each of the previous sections is that what looks like a complicated but seamless cognitive capacity, such as inferring intentions or interacting with others, is actually composed of many specialized mechanisms that interact in coordinated ways to produce observed behavior. It is important to stress this latter point: Specialized cognitive mechanisms *interact* with each other in adaptively coordinated ways, and they have been designed by natural selection to do so. It is important to stress this because it is widely held that a mind composed of specialized mechanisms entails a lack of interaction between those mechanisms. Indeed, it is widely but incorrectly considered to be a hallmark of modularity that modules are isolated from one another, operate independently, and can neither influence nor be influenced by other systems (Fodor, 1983, 2000).

Evolutionary psychologists have argued that this is exactly the opposite of what one would expect of modular systems, which derive their power precisely from the coordination of specialized activities (Barrett, 2005b; Barrett & Kurzban, 2006; Carruthers, 2002, 2005; Sperber, 2005). In organismal development, for example, one sees massive modularity of developmental mechanisms and components, but it is the interaction of these mechanisms in a causal cascade that results in the complex and finely tuned structure of the whole organism (West-Eberhard, 2003). If developmental processes were not interactive, the exquisitely orchestrated complexity of organisms would not be possible. The same applies to cognition, which has as its outcome the equally exquisitely orchestrated complexity of thought and behavior. Modularity is not inconsistent with flexibility and complexity but, rather, is a source of it (Sperber, 2005).

That said, it is important to recognize that there remains a vast gap between what we know of individual specialized cognitive mechanisms, or modules, and how they interact to produce observed behavior. The interactions between mechanism described previously and other kinds of specialized mechanisms, such as attentional mechanisms (Leonards, Sunaert, Van Hecke, & Orban, 2000), working memory (Baddeley, 2002), and language (Jackendoff, 2002), are still poorly understood. What is clear, however, is that such interactions must exist. A theory of mind system, for example, would be of little use unless it interfaced with attentional systems for gathering information, motor systems for guiding behavior, and others.

A case can be made that the future of psychology lies not in the insistence upon capturing generalities about cognition using mathematical redescriptions of observed data but, rather, in aiming to discover the causal mechanisms of thought and to understand how these mechanisms interact to produce the seamless whole of thought. Although the research reviewed here suggests that substantial progress is being made, we have likely only scratched the surface of the complex web of specialized evolved mechanisms that comprise the human mind. This is good news for those who are just beginning their research careers.

REFERENCES

Abell, F., Happé, F., & Frith, U. (2000). Do triangles play tricks? Attribution of mental states to animated shapes in normal and abnormal development. *Journal of Cognitive Development, 15*, 1–20.
Almor, A., & Sloman, S. (1996). Is deontic reasoning special? *Psychological Review, 103*, 374–380.
Baddeley, A. D. (2002). Is working memory still working? *European Psychologist, 7*, 85–97.

Baron-Cohen, S. (1995). *Mind blindness.* Cambridge, MA: MIT Press.

Barrett, H. C. (1999). *Guilty minds: How perceived intent, incentive, and ability to cheat influence social contract reasoning.* Paper presented at the 11th annual meeting of the Human Behavior and Evolution Society, Salt Lake City, UT.

Barrett, H. C. (2005a). Adaptations to predators and prey. In D. M. Buss (Ed.), *The handbook of evolutionary psychology* (pp. 200–223). New York: Wiley.

Barrett, H. C. (2005b). Enzymatic computation and cognitive modularity. *Mind and Language, 20*, 259–287.

Barrett, H. C., Frederick, D., Haselton, M., & Kurzban, R. (2006). Can manipulations of cognitive load be used to test evolutionary hypotheses? *Journal of Personality and Social Psychology, 91*, 513–518.

Barrett, H. C., & Kurzban, R. (2006). Modularity in cognition: Framing the debate. *Psychological Review, 113*, 628–647.

Barrett, H. C., Todd, P. M., Miller, G. F., & Blythe, P. (2005). Accurate judgments of intention from motion alone: A cross-cultural study. *Evolution and Human Behavior, 26*, 313–331.

Barton, J. J., Press, D. Z., Keenan, J. P., & O'Connor, M. (2002). Lesions of the fusiform face area impair perception of facial configuration in prosopagnosia. *Neurology, 58*, 71–78.

Bateson, M., Nettle, D., & Roberts, G. (2006). Cues of being watched enhance cooperation in a real-world setting. *Biology Letters, 2*, 412–414.

Behne, T., Carpenter, M., Call, J., & Tomasello, M. (2005). Unwilling versus unable: Infants' understanding of intentional action. *Developmental Psychology, 41*, 328–337.

Betzig, L., & Turke, P. (1986). Food sharing on Ifaluk. *Current Anthropology, 27*, 397–400.

Bevc, I., & Silverman, I. (2000). Early separation and sibling incest: A test of the revised Westermarck theory. *Evolution and Human Behavior, 21*, 151–161.

Bittles, A. H., & Neel, J. V. (1994). The costs of human inbreeding and their implications for variation at the DNA level. *Nature Genetics, 8*, 117–121.

Buller, D. (2005). *Adapting minds: Evolutionary psychology and the persistent quest for human nature.* Cambridge, MA: MIT Press/Bradford Books.

Burnham, T., & Hare, B. (in press). Engineering human cooperation: Does involuntary neural activation increase public goods contributions? *Human Nature.*

Burnstein, E. (2005). Altruism and genetic relatedness. In D. M. Buss (Ed.), *The handbook of evolutionary psychology* (pp. 528–551). New York: Wiley.

Carpenter, M., Call, J., & Tomasello, M. (2005). Twelve- and 18-month-olds copy actions in terms of goals. *Developmental Science, 8*, F13–F20.

Carruthers, P. (2002). Modularity, language, and the flexibility of thought. *Behavioral and Brain Sciences, 25*, 705–719.

Carruthers, P. (2005). The case for massively modular models of mind. In R. Stainton (Ed.), *Contemporary debates in cognitive science* (pp. 205–225). Oxford, U.K.: Blackwell.

Cashdan, E. (1988). Adaptiveness of food learning and food aversions in children. *Social Science Information, 37*, 613–632.

Castelli, F., Happé, F., Frith, U., & Frith, C. D. (2000). Movement and mind: A functional imaging study of perception and interpretation of complex intentional movement patterns. *NeuroImage, 12*, 314–325.

Chagnon, N., & Bugos, P. E. (1979). Kin selection and conflict: An analysis of a Yanomamö ax fight. In N. Chagnon & W. Irons (Eds.), *Evolutionary biology and human social behavior* (pp. 213–237). North Scituate, MA: Duxbury Press.

Cheng, P., & Holyoak, K. (1985). Pragmatic reasoning schemas. *Cognitive Psychology, 17*, 391–416.

Cosmides, L. (1989). The logic of social exchange: Has natural selection shaped how humans reason? Studies with the Wason selection task. *Cognition, 31*, 187–278.

Cosmides, L., & Tooby, J. (1987). From evolution to behavior: Evolutionary psychology as the missing link. In J. Dupre (Ed.), *The latest on the best: Essays on evolution and optimality* (pp. 277–306). Cambridge, MA: MIT Press.

Cosmides, L., & Tooby, J. (1992). Cognitive adaptations for social exchange. In J. Barkow, L. Cosmides, & J. Tooby (Eds.), *The adapted mind* (pp. 163–228). New York: Oxford University Press.

Cosmides, L., & Tooby, J. (2005). Social exchange: The evolutionary design of a neurocognitive system. In M. S. Gazzaniga (Ed.), *The new cognitive neurosciences* (Vol. 3, pp. 1295–1308). Cambridge, MA: MIT press.

Csibra, G., Bíró, S., Koós, O., & Gergely, G. (2003). One-year-old infants use teleological representations of actions productively. *Cognitive Psychology, 27*, 111–133.

Daly, M., & Wilson, M. (1988). *Homicide*. New York: Aldine de Gruyter.

Damasio, A. R., Damasio, H., & Van Hoesen, G. W. (1982). Prosopagnosia: Anatomic basis and behavioral mechanisms. *Neurology, 32*, 331–341.

DeBruine, L. M. (2002). Facial resemblance enhances trust. *Proceedings of the Royal Society of London B, 269*, 1307–1312.

DeBruine, L. M. (2005). Trustworthy but not lust-worthy: Context-specific effects of facial resemblance. *Proceedings of the Royal Society of London B, 272*, 919–922.

Diamond, R., & Carey, S. (1986). Why faces are and are not special: An effect of expertise. *Journal of Experimental Psychology, 115*, 107–117.

Duchaine, B. (2000). Developmental prosopagnosia with normal configural processing. *Neuroreport, 11*, 79–83.

Duchaine, B., & Nakayama, K. (2005). Dissociations of face and object recognition in developmental prosopagnosia. *Journal of Cognitive Neuroscience, 17*, 249–261.

Duchaine, B., Yovel, G., Butterworth, E., & Nakayama, K. (2006). Prosopagnosia as an impairment to face-specific mechanisms: Elimination of the alternative hypotheses in a developmental case. *Cognitive Neuropsychology, 23*, 714–747.

Farah, M. J. (1990). *Visual agnosia*. Cambridge, MA: MIT Press.

Farah, M. J. (1996). Is face recognition "special?" Evidence from neuropsychology. *Behavioural Brain Research, 76*, 181–189.

Farah, M. J., Wilson, K. D., Drain, H. M., & Tanaka, J. R. (1995). The inverted face inversion effect in prosopagnosia: Evidence for mandatory, face-specific perceptual mechanisms. *Vision Research, 35*, 2089–2093.

Fessler, D. M. T., & Navarrete, C. D. (2004). Third-party attitudes toward sibling incest: Evidence for Westermarck's hypotheses. *Evolution & Human Behavior, 25*, 277–294.

Fiddick, L. (2004). Domains of deontic reasoning: Resolving the discrepancy between the cognitive and moral reasoning literatures. *Quarterly Journal of Experimental Psychology, 57A*(4), 447–474.

Fodor, J. (1983). *The modularity of mind*. Cambridge, MA: MIT Press.

Fodor, J. (2000). *The mind doesn't work that way: The scope and limits of computational psychology*. Cambridge, MA: MIT Press.

Fox, J. R. (1962). Sibling incest. *British Journal of Sociology, 13*, 128–150.

Freire, A., Lee, K., & Symons, L. A. (2000). The face-inversion effect as a deficit in encoding of configural information: Direct evidence. *Perception, 29*, 159–170.

Gallistel, C. R. (1990). *The organization of learning*. Cambridge, MA: MIT Press.

Gauthier, I., & Tarr, M. J. (1997). Becoming a "greeble" expert: Exploring mechanisms for face recognition. *Vision Research, 37*, 1673–1682.

Gentner, D. (1999). Analogy. In R. A. Wilson & F. C. Keil (Eds.), *The MIT encyclopedia of the cognitive sciences* (pp. 17–20). Cambridge, MA: MIT Press.

Gergely, G., Nádasdy, Z., Csibra, G., & Bíró, S. (1995). Taking the intentional stance at 12 months of age. *Cognition, 56*, 165–193.

Gigerenzer, G., & Hug, K. (1992). Domain specific reasoning: Social contracts, cheating, and perspective change. *Cognition, 43*, 127–171.

Haley, K. J., & Fessler, D. M. T. (2005). Nobody's watching?: Subtle cues affect generosity in an anonymous economic game. *Evolution and Human Behavior, 26*, 245–256.

Hames, R. (1987). Relatedness and garden labor exchange among the Ye'kwana. *Ethology and Sociobiology, 8*, 354–392.

Hamilton, W. D. (1964). The genetical evolution of social behaviour I and II. *Journal of Theoretical Biology, 7*, 1–16, 17–52.

Haxby, J. V., Hoffman, E. A., & Gobbini, M. I. (2002). Human neural systems for face recognition and social communication. *Biological Psychiatry, 51*(1), 59–67.

Jackendoff, R. (2002). *Foundations of language*. New York: Oxford University Press.

Jacob, S., McClintock, M. K., Zelano, B., & Ober, C. (2002). Paternally inherited HLA alleles are associated with women's choice of male odor. *Nature Genetics, 30*, 175–179.

Jankowiak, W., & Diderich, M. (2000). Sibling solidarity in a polygamous community in the USA: Unpacking inclusive fitness. *Evolution and Human Behavior, 21*, 125–139.

Johnson, M. H., & Morton, J. (1991). *Biology and cognitive development: The case of face recognition.* Cambridge, MA: Blackwell.

Johnson, S., Slaughter, V., & Carey, S. (1998). Whose gaze will infants follow? The elicitation of gaze-following in 12-month-olds. *Developmental Science, 1*, 233–238.

Johnson, S. C. (2000). The recognition of mentalistic agents in infancy. *Trends in Cognitive Science, 4*(1), 22–28.

Johnson, S. C., Booth, A., & O'Hearn, K. (2001). Inferring the unseen goals of a non-human agent. *Cognitive Development, 16*, 637–656.

Judge, D. S., & Hrdy, S. B. (1992). Allocation of accumulated resources among close kin: Inheritance in Sacramento, California, 1890–1984. *Ethology and Sociobiology, 13*, 495–522.

Kanwisher, N., McDermott, J., & Chun, M. M. (1997). The fusiform face area: A module in human extrastriate cortex specialized for face perception. *Journal of Neuroscience, 17*, 4302–4311.

Kaplan, H., & Hill, K. (1985). Food sharing among Ache foragers: Tests of explanatory hypotheses. *Current Anthropology, 26*, 223–246.

Kosslyn, S., Hamilton, S., & Bernstein, J. (1995). The perception of curvature can be selectively disrupted in prosopagnosia. *Brain and Cognition, 27*, 36–58.

Kurland, J. A., & Gaulin, S. J. C. (2005). Cooperation and conflict among kin. In D. M. Buss (Ed.), *The handbook of evolutionary psychology* (pp. 447–482). New York: Wiley.

Kurzban, R. (2001). The social psychophysics of cooperation: Nonverbal communication in a public goods game. *Journal of Nonverbal Behavior, 25*, 241–259.

Le Grand, R., Mondloch, C. J., Maurer, D., & Brent, H. P. (2003). Expert face processing requires visual input to the right hemisphere during infancy. *Nature Neuroscience, 6*, 1108–1112.

Leonards, U., Sunaert, S., Van Hecke, P., & Orban, G. A. (2000). Attention mechanisms in visual search: An fMRI study. *Journal of Cognitive Neuroscience, 12*, 61–75.

Leslie, A. M. (1994). ToMM, ToBy, and agency: Core architecture and domain specificity. In L. A. Hirschfeld & S. A. Gelman (Eds.), *Mapping the mind: Domain specificity in cognition and culture* (pp. 119–148). Cambridge, U.K.: Cambridge University Press.

Lieberman, D., Tooby, J., & Cosmides, L. (2003). Does morality have a biological basis? An empirical test of the factors governing moral sentiments relating to incest. *Proceedings of the Royal Society: Biological Sciences, 270*, 819–826.

Manktelow, K., & Over, D. (1987). Reasoning and rationality. *Mind and Language, 2*, 199–219.

Meltzoff, A. N. (1995). Understanding the intentions of others: Re-enactment of intended acts by 18-month-old children. *Developmental Psychology, 31*(5), 838–850.

Michotte, A. (1963). *The perception of causality.* New York: Basic Books.

Morton, J., & Johnson, M. H. (1991). CONSPEC and CONLERN: A two-process theory of infant face recognition. *Psychological Review, 98*, 164–181.

Moscovitch, M., Winocur, G., & Behrmann, M. (1997). What is special about face recognition? Nineteen experiments on a person with visual object agnosia and dyslexia but normal face recognition. *Journal of Cognitive Neuroscience, 9*, 555–604.

Oaksford, M., & Chater, N. (1994). A rational analysis of the selection task as optimal data selection. *Psychological Review, 101*, 608–631.

Ober, C., Weitkamp, L. R., Cox, N., Dytch, H., Kostyu, D., & Elias, S. (1997). HLA and mate choice in humans. *American Journal of Human Genetics, 61*, 497–504.

Öhman, A., & Mineka, S. (2001). Fear, phobias and preparedness: Toward an evolved module of fear and fear learning. *Psychological Review, 108*, 483–522.

Penn, D. J., & Potts, W. K. (1999). The evolution of mating preferences and major histocompatibility complex genes. *American Naturalist, 153*, 145–164.

Phillips, A. T., Wellman, H. M., & Spelke, E. S. (2002). Infants' ability to connect gaze and emotional expression to intentional action. *Cognition, 85*, 53–78.

Pinker, S. (1984). *Language learnability and language development.* Cambridge, MA: Harvard University Press.

Platek, S. M., Burch, R. L., Panyavin, I. S., Wasserman, B. H., & Gallup, G. G., Jr. (2002). Reactions to children's faces: Resemblance matters more for males than females. *Evolution and Human Behavior, 23*, 159–166.

Platek, S. M., Critton, S. R., Burch, R. L., Frederick, D. A., Myers, T. E., & Gallup, G. G., Jr. (2003). How much resemblance is enough? Sex difference in reactions to resemblance, but not the ability to detect resemblance. *Evolution and Human Behavior, 24*, 81–87.

Porter, R. H., & Moore, J. D. (1981). Human kin recognition by olfactory cues. *Physiology and Behavior, 27*, 493–495.

Potts, W. K. (2002). Wisdom through immunogenetics. *Nature Genetics, 30*, 130–131.

Povinelli, D. J. (2000). *Folk physics for apes: The chimpanzee's theory of how the world works*. New York: Oxford University Press.

Rakison, D. H., & Poulin-Dubois, D. (2001). Developmental origin of the animate-inanimate distinction. *Psychological Bulletin, 127*, 209–228.

Rochat, P., Morgan, R., & Carpenter, M. (1997). Young infants' sensitivity to movement information specifying social causality. *Cognitive Development, 12*, 441–465.

Rozin, P., Haidt, J., & McCauley, C. R. (2000). Disgust. In M. Lewis & J. Haviland (Eds.), *Handbook of emotions* (2nd ed., pp. 637–653). New York: Guilford Press.

Scholl, B., & Tremoulet, P. (2000). Perceptual causality and animacy. *Trends in Cognitive Sciences, 4*, 299–308.

Shallice, T. (1988). *From neuropsychology to mental structure*. Cambridge, U.K.: Cambridge University Press.

Shepher, J. (1971). Mate selection among second-generation kibbutz adolescents: Incest avoidance and negative imprinting. *Archives of Sexual Behavior, 1*, 293–307.

Smith, M. S., Kish, B. L., & Crawford, C. B. (1987). Inheritance of wealth as human kin investment. *Ethology and Sociobiology, 8*, 171–182.

Sperber, D. (1994). The modularity of thought and the epidemiology of representations. In L. A. Hirschfeld & S. A. Gelman (Eds.), *Mapping the mind: Domain specificity in cognition and culture* (pp. 39–67). New York: Cambridge University Press.

Sperber, D. (2002). In defense of massive modularity. In E. Dupoux (Ed.), *Language, brain and cognitive development: Essays in honor of Jacques Mehler* (pp. 47–57). Cambridge, MA: MIT Press.

Sperber, D. (2005). Modularity and relevance: How can a massively modular mind be flexible and context-sensitive? In P. Carruthers, S. Laurence, & S. Stich (Eds.), *The innate mind: Structure and content* (pp. 53–68). Oxford, U.K.: Oxford University Press.

Sperber, D., Cara, F., & Girotto, V. (1995). Relevance theory explains the selection task. *Cognition, 57*, 31–95.

Stone, V., Cosmides, L., Tooby, J., Kroll, N., & Knight, R. (2002). Selective impairment of reasoning about social exchange in a patient with bilateral limbic system damage. *Proceedings of the National Academy of Sciences, 99*(17), 11531–11536.

Sugiyama, L., Tooby, J., & Cosmides, L. (2002). Cross-cultural evidence of cognitive adaptations for social exchange among the Shiwiar of Ecuadorian Amazonia. *Proceedings of the National Academy of Sciences, 99*(17), 11537–11542.

Tomasello, M., Carpenter, M., Call, J., Behne, T., & Moll, H. (2005). Understanding and sharing intentions: The origins of cultural cognition. *Behavioral and Brain Sciences, 28*, 675–735.

Tremoulet, P. D., & Feldman, J. (2000). Perception of animacy from the motion of a single object. *Perception, 29*, 943–951.

Trivers, R. (1971). The evolution of reciprocal altruism. *Quarterly Review of Biology, 46*, 35–57.

Walter, A., & Buyske, S. (2003). The Westermarck effect and early childhood co-socialization: Sex differences in inbreeding-avoidance. *British Journal of Developmental Psychology, 21*, 353–365.

Want, S. C., & Harris, P. L. (2001). Learning from other people's mistakes: Causal understanding in learning to use a tool. *Child Development, 72*(2), 431–443.

West-Eberhard, M. J. (2003). *Developmental plasticity and evolution*. Oxford, U.K.: Oxford University Press.

Westermarck, E. A. (1921). *The history of human marriage*. London: Macmillan.

Wolf, A. P. (1995) *Sexual attraction and childhood association: A Chinese brief for Edward Westermarck*. Stanford, CA: Stanford University Press.

Yamazaki, K., Beauchamp, G. K., Kupniewski, D., Bard, J., Thomas, L., & Boyse E. A. (1988). Familial imprinting determines H-2 selective mating preferences. *Science, 240*, 1331–1332.

Young, A. W., Hellawell, D., & Hay, D. (1987). Configurational information in face perception. *Perception, 16*, 747–759.

10

Adaptations, Environments, and Behavior
Then and Now

CHARLES CRAWFORD

As I see it, evolutionary psychology is concerned with the problems and stresses our hominin and primate ancestors encountered in their environments, the psychological adaptations natural selection shaped to deal with these problems and stresses, and the way these adaptations function in the infinitesimal slices of evolutionary time in which we now live (Crawford & Anderson, 1989). Consider some examples. Obtaining sugar and fat were beneficial for our ancestors. Therefore, natural selection shaped psychological mechanisms in ways that rendered them tasty, and these adaptations, in turn, motivated our ancestors to take the risks and do the work needed to obtain them (Nesse & Williams, 1994). Adaptations designed to detect and punish cheaters evolved to help uphold the fitness-enhancing social contracts formed by early humans (Cosmides, 1989). Incest produced defective children. In response, natural selection designed mate-selection mechanisms that disposed humans to avoid mating with close kin (Shepher, 1983; Westermarck, 1891). The process was slow, but it shaped beings with a vast organization of interacting cognitive, emotional, and motivational mechanisms for interacting with each other and the physical and social environments in which their ancestors evolved. However, mechanisms that evolved to deal with ancestral problems may be produce unusual and possibly even maladaptive behaviors in some current environments (Crawford, 1998).

I claim that if it could be shown that natural selection had created the human mind as a *tabula rasa*, then evolutionary theory would be of little or no value in the study of human mind and behavior. The value of evolutionary theory to psychology is that it gives us a framework for investigating the functioning of the specialized psychological adaptations that evolutionary theorists claim natural selection creates. I assume that our genes provide information about the ancestral history of our species and contain information about the problems our ancestors encountered and the solutions that natural selection shaped to help deal with them. Evolutionary psychology is concerned with understanding how this information is involved in the development of the specialized mechanisms that produce current behavior. Hence, the central purpose of this chapter is to describe the role that evolutionary psychologists assume ancestral genes and ancestral environments play in the production of current behavior. It begins with a definition of innate developmental organization. It then considers possible social and political outcomes for low and high levels of innate developmental organization paired with different beliefs about these levels. The notion of psychological mechanisms as evolved adaptations is considered in some detail. Then the ways in which evolutionary psychologists claim that genes are involved in the development of adaptations is considered. The chapter concludes with a framework for considering how ancestral adaptations function in current environments and outlines some ways studying them.

INNATE GENETIC SPECIALIZED GENETIC ORGANIZATION

Most psychologists agree that actual behavior is produced by highly specialized, peripheral behavior-producing mechanisms. Eye blinks, blushes, smiles, frowns, foraging for food, finding a mate, managing a mate once it is found, developing cooperative relationships, adjusting one's level of aggression to external circumstances, scheming for advantage—all require specialized peripheral information-processing mechanisms. However, evolutionary and nonevolutionary psychologists often disagree sharply on the degree of the specialization of genetic predispositions involved in their development. Consider explanations of sexual strategies as an example.

Eagly and Wood (1999) argue that although natural selection does have a role in the functioning of the sexual strategies we use in finding and managing mates, it is indirect. These theorists accept that physical differences between males and females, especially man's greater size and strength and woman's ability to bear children and to lactate, are evolved differences between men and women. However, these theorists argue, they produce behavioral differences between men and women because they interact with shared cultural beliefs, social organization, and demands of the economy, all of which influence the role assignments that are constitutive of the division of labor within a society. In these theorists' view, humans do not possess specific genetic predispositions for the development and functioning of psychological mechanisms that produce gender differences in behavior. Finally, they claim that changing the cultural beliefs and social organization of a culture can produce major and long-lasting changes in the sexual strategies that men and women use for dealing with each other and with their wider society. Moreover, these changes can persist even though the evolved physical differences between men and women also persist.

In contrast to explanations such as those advanced by Eagly and Wood (1999), evolutionary psychologists argue that men and women from all cultures inherit evolved dispositions to employ mating strategies that were adaptive in ancestral environments. Additionally, they argue that both sexes have a variety of tactics they can employ for acquiring and managing mates, depending on the situation. They argue that many sex differences in mating behavior have their basis in ancestral differences in relative male and female parental investment and competition for mates (Buss, 2004). This perspective leads to the expectation that it will be more difficult than theorists such as Eagly and Wood assume to induce men and women to change the strategies they invoke. It also leads to the expectation that male and female sexual strategies may generalize to nonreproductive contexts and situations in modern environments (Walters & Crawford, 1994), and that there will be a tendency for men's and women's strategies to revert to their ancestral form under some circumstances (Crawford, 1998).

Innate genetic developmental organization is concerned with how ancestral genetic predispositions are involved in the development of the specialized mechanisms that produce behavior. It may vary from relatively weak and indirect influences, as in the case of political and religious attitudes, to relatively strong and direct influence, as in the case of eye color and height. Modern liberal thinkers, such as B. F. Skinner, Franz Boas, and Alfred Krober, as well as Alice Eagly and Wendy Wood, have convinced most reform-minded individuals that a high degree of genetic involvement in the development of the human psyche "is one of the chief hindrances to the rational treatment of great social questions, and one of the greatest stumbling blocks to human improvement" (Mill & Stillinger, 1969, p. 162). Table 10.1 is designed to explore the consequences of this view.

The possible states of nature for the degree of genetic involvement in the development of the specialized peripheral mechanisms that produce behavior are shown in the columns of the table. Only two of the many possible states of nature are shown: low and high degrees of genetic involvement. The rows represent the possible beliefs about these states. Again, only two of the many possible beliefs are shown. Franz Boas (1966), Alfred Kroeber (1952), and B. F. Skinner (1972, 1976) are shown as examples of theorists who assume little genetic involvement in development. Konrad Lorenz (1965), Irenäus Eibl-Eibesfeldt (1989), Donald Symons (1979), Leda Cosmides, and John Tooby (1992), as well as Steven Pinker (2002) and David Buss (2004), are indicated as theorists who assume a considerable degree of genetic involvement in development of specialized mechanisms. Finally, although research can increase our knowledge of the true state of nature, it is, in principle, an unknown.

The cells in the table enumerate some of the consequences for the beliefs about the development of the specialized psychological mechanisms that produce behavior that might be expected when the possible states of nature are paired with possible beliefs in them. Two cells contain valid outcomes: (a) low genetic involvement paired with a belief in low genetic involvement, and (b) high genetic involvement paired with a belief in it. The other two cells contain invalid outcomes: (a) belief in little genetic involvement paired with a high degree of genetic involvement, and (b) belief in a high degree of genetic involvement paired with a low degree of genetic involvement.

Inspecting the cells of the table can help us think about the consequences of the intersection of the possible states of nature with possible beliefs in them. Consider the first row of the table, labeled "Small role for genetic involvement." It reflects the thinking of theorists such as B. F. Skinner, Franz Boas, and Alice Eagly, who postulate little role for genetic involvement in the development of specialized mechanisms that produce behavior. Its intersection with the state of nature column for low genetic involvement produces the first cell in the body of the table. It is a valid outcome and is labeled "Anything is possible." Some implications of this position are that sex role differences can be eliminated through education, homosexuality can be remediated through educational psychotherapy, people are capable in living in the harmonious ways described by Skinner's (1976) *Waldon II* and *Beyond Freedom and Dignity* (Skinner, 1972), all political systems can be equally satisfying, capitalism and communism can work, and the American Dream is valid for most people. Finally, gene therapy is of little relevance for treating psychological problems. Many liberal thinkers assume the situation described in this cell will lead to the rational treatment of great social questions.

Some of the possible consequences of incorrectly believing in low genetic involvement in development are shown in the next cell in this row of the table. It is labeled "Realization difficult." If genes do, in fact, play a significant role in the outcomes described, attempts to equalize sex roles through education will not work very well because biological differences between men and women are not recognized. Laws regulating commercial behavior may not be optimally effective because they are based on an inadequate understanding of the psychological mechanisms producing reciprocal interactions. Attempts to change people's sexual orientation through psychotherapy will not succeed. Attempts to create utopian communities based on principles of reinforcement are destined to fail. Moreover, both communism and free enterprise capitalism will end up producing suffering and disillusionment for many people, and the American Dream will remain just that—a dream—for most people. Because ancestral genetic predispositions affect behavior, there will be a tendency for behavior to ancestralize—to return to ancestral ways of functioning when economic and political conditions liberalize. For example, since the human ancestral mating system is likely

Table 10.1 Outcomes of the Debate about the Role of Ancestrally Evolved Innate Genetic Factors in the Development of Psychological Mechanisms

Possible Beliefs about Degree of Genetic Involvement in Developmental Organization	Possible States of Nature: Degree of Genetic Involvement in Developmental Organization of Behavior-Producing Psychological Mechanism(s)	
	Low	High
Small role for genetic involvement in development of psychological mechanisms: • Tabula rasa (Locke et al., 1794) • Cultural anthropology (Boas, 1966), (Kroeber, 1952) • Classic behaviorism (Skinner, 1948, 1971), (Watson, 1919)	**Correct decision:** explanations that work—anything is possible • Sex role differences eliminated through education • Remediating homosexuality through "education" works • Waldon II produces harmonious society • All religions/political systems can be equally satisfying • Effective laws for regulating sexual/reproductive/commercial behavior • Communism workable • Capitalism workable • Valid American dream • Gene therapy of no use • Ancestralization does not occur	**Incorrect decision:** Inadequate explanations—realization difficult • Sex roles differences NOT eliminated through education • Remediating homosexuality through "education" fails • Waldon II produces oppressive society • Some religions/political systems can be oppressive • Ineffective laws for regulating sexual/reproductive/commercial behavior • Communism unworkable • Capitalism produces suffering • Limited American dream • Gene therapy not tried • Ancestralization can be problematic • Moralistic fallacies
Large role for genetic involvement in development of psychological mechanisms: • Evolutionary psychology (Barkow et al., 1992) • Classic ethology (Lorenz, 1966), (Eibl-Eibesfeldt, 1989) • Behavior genetics (Fuller & Thompson, 1960), (Plomin et al., 1997) • Sociobiology (Wilson, 1975), (Lumsden & Wilson, 1981)	**Incorrect decision:** Explanations that fail—missed opportunities • Inappropriate special schools, jobs for males/females/social classes • Ineffective laws for regulating sexual/reproductive/commercial behavior • Communism not tried • American dream not tried • Inappropriate drug/physical psychotherapy • Ancestralization does not occur • Naturalistic fallacies	**Correct decision:** Explanations that work—limits on policy options • Appropriate special schools, jobs for males/females/social classes • Effective laws for regulating sexual/reproductive/commercial behavior • Communism unworkable • American dream limited • Gene/drug/physical psychotherapy may be useful • Ancestralization attenuated

Sources: Barkow, J., Cosmides, L., & Tooby, J. (1992). *The adapted mind: Evolutionary psychology and the generation of culture.* New York: Oxford University Press.

Fuller, J. K., & Thompson, W. R. (1960). *Behavior genetics.* New York: Wiley.

Locke, J., Wynne, J., Locke, J., & Locke, J. (1794). *An abridgment of Mr. Locke's essay concerning human understanding.* Boston (Printed by Manning & Loring for J. White Thomas & Andrews D. West, E. Larkin, J. West and the proprietor i.e., William Pynson Blake of the Boston Bookstore.)

Lorenz, K. Z. (1966). *On aggression.* New York: Harcourt Brace Jovanovich.

Lumsden, C., & Wilson, E. O. (1981). *Genes, mind, and culture.* Cambridge: Harvard University Press.

Plomin, R., DeFries, J. C., & McClearn, G. E. (1997). *Behavioral genetics* (3rd ed.). New York: W. H. Freeman.

Skinner, B. F. (1948). *Waldon II.* New York: Macmillan.

Skinner, B. F. (1971). *Beyond freedom and dignity.* Toronto: Bantam Books.

Watson, J. B. (1919). *Psychology from the standpoint of a behaviorist.* Philadelphia: J.B. Lippincott.

polygynous (Daly & Wilson, 1983), a monogamous society will gravitate toward forms of polygyny, such as sequential monogamy and concubinage, when political and economic conditions make them possible.

The consequences of underestimating the role of genetic involvement in the development and functioning of psychological mechanisms claimed for this cell elicit many social conservatives' worst fears: aggressive, but ineffective, social interventions and manipulations designed to make people into what the liberal environmentalists think they ought to be. Much of the suffering and distress postulated for this cell would be the result of the *moralistic fallacy*: claiming that *What ought to be can be* (Crawford, 2004).

Now consider the bottom row in Table 10.1, labeled "Significant role for genetic involvement in development." The thinking of most evolutionary psychologists belongs in this row. It intersects with the first column, labeled "Low genetic involvement in development," to produce the second invalid outcome. It is labeled "Missed opportunities" because many current social activists focus on the impediments to "the rational treatment of great social questions" that they believe this outcome must produce. Some of the hypothesized negative consequences listed in this cell are inappropriately designed special educational institutions for males/females and social classes as well as a dearth of educational procedures for changing behavior because of the invalid assumption about the importance of genes in behavioral development. Moreover, communism will likely not be tried because people are assumed to be innately selfish. The American dream may be unattractive because the assumed genetic limitations on ability and motivation restrict it to only a few. Laws for regulating sexual/reproductive behavior may be ineffective because they are based on incorrect assumptions about the role of genetic factors in the development of gender differences in sexual and reproductive behaviors. Laws regulating commercial behavior may not be optimally effective because they are based on an inadequate understanding of the psychology of trading favors. Although ancestralization is expected, it will not occur. The outcomes in this cell are liberal environmentalists' worst fears: social, educational, and occupational policies based on invalid assumptions about the role of genetic predispositions in behavioral development. Much of the injustice and suffering that could occur because of the policies adopted could be the result of the *naturalistic fallacy*: claiming that *What is, is what ought to be.*

Finally, consider the last cell—the most controversial one—in the table: believing in a significant degree of genetic involvement in the development of specialized behavior-producing mechanisms when this is the true state of nature. It is the second valid outcome and is the cell where many evolutionary psychologists, sometimes uncomfortably, find themselves. It can be characterized by outcomes such as appropriate special jobs, education, for males/females, social classes that are based on genetic propensities of individuals. Communism does not work very well because of the importance of genetic predispositions to selfishness. The American dream is illusory for some, but not for others, because of genetic involvement in the development of abilities and motivations. Gene and drug therapies are useful for treating many illnesses because the role of biological factors in the development of disease and other noxious conditions is recognized. Laws for regulating sexual and reproductive behavior are effectible because they are based on the recognition of biological differences between men and women. Laws for encouraging economic interactions are effective because they can be based on an understanding of the evolved mechanisms mediating cooperation and helping behavior. To the extent that evolutionary psychologists are interested in public policy that makes societies better places to live, they are interested in developing the positive outcomes in this cell and minimizing the negative ones. See Crawford and Salmon (Crawford, 2004) for a discussion of evolutionary psychology and public policy issues. The remainder of this chapter explores the last cell in the table—correctly believing that biological predispositions affect many behaviors. Explicating it requires a discussion of evolved adaptations and how they function.

ADAPTATIONS AND THEIR FUNCTIONING

The concept of evolved adaptation is the fulcrum on which the application of evolutionary theory revolves and must provide the basis of any consideration of how evolutionary theory is used in the study of human behavior. Wilson's (1975) definition of an adaptation as "any structure, physiological process, or behavior pattern that makes an organism more fit to survive and reproduce in comparison with other members of the same species" (p. 577) provides an excellent beginning for the discussion of psychological adaptations. Before considering how this definition might be modified to make it more useful for psychologists, consider several instructive examples of adaptations.

Scorpionfly Mating Illustrates Concurrently Contingent Tactics

Scorpionflies are insects that feed upon decaying vegetation and dead or dying insects. The mating behavior of the males illustrates how natural selection has produced behaviors enabling organisms to adjust to the varying conditions in their environments. The male's mating strategy has three tactics for obtaining a mating. Males may obtain a dead insect, present it to a female, and copulate with her as she eats it. They may generate a proteinaceous salivary mass, present it to the female, and copulate with her as she eats it. If they cannot obtain a dead insect or generate the salivary mass for a nuptial gift, they may attempt to force a mating with a female (Thornhill, 1980). These behavioral tactics evolved because: (a) there was competition between alleles for a place on the loci for the mating strategy of ancestral males, (b) these alleles differed in the production of strategies that enabled them to replicate, (c) some of the variation in these strategies was genetic, hence, (d) there was differential contribution of alleles for the different mating strategies to the scorpionfly gene pool, and finally, (e) across many generations, the mating strategy of the male scorpionfly evolved by natural selection.

Thornhill (1980) has shown that all three tactics are available to all adult males and that success in male-male competition determines the mating tactic employed. The tactics of the strategy respond to both current external and internal environmental contingencies. External conditions refer to the availability in the male's environment of dead insects or other resources required to generate the salivary masses. Internal conditions refer to the characteristics of the male—such as his size, strength, and health—that enable him to compete with other males for the environmental resources. The tactics are said to be *concurrently contingent* on the environment because they are always available to all adult males (Crawford & Anderson, 1989).

Figure 10.1 diagrams the operation of these three tactics. Part (a) shows how the tactics depend on male competitive ability. Part (b) shows how the tactics are related to reproductive success across evolutionary time. For example, the dead insect tactic is most successful when males have high competitive ability, and the forced mating tactics is most successful when males have low competitive ability. Note also that at the point where the three lines intersect, all tactics have the same expected success. Finally, note that the heritability, h2, the amount of genetic variation in the adaptation, is shown as 0.0 because all males are capable of using all tactics: the one used depending on the male's ability in male-male competition.

The Bluegill Sunfish

Bluegill sunfish are small freshwater fish found in the lakes and ponds of southern Ontario, New York State, and down to the Gulf States and the Carolinas. Male bluegills provide the parental care. The males have two different tactics for acquiring matings: (a) parental and (b) cuckoldry. The parental males grow slowly, mature later than cuckolders mature, build nests, court females, and provide paternal care once the eggs are fertilized. The smaller cuckolders grow rapidly and never provide parental care. When they are small, they attempt to sneak matings by darting in and releasing sperm just before the parental male releases his sperm. When they grow larger, sneaking matings becomes difficult, so they mimic females in order to approach a male courting a true

(a) Male Competitive Ability and Male-Male Competition

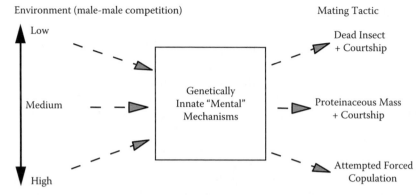

(b) Expected Life Time Reproductive Success of Males Differing in Competitive Ability

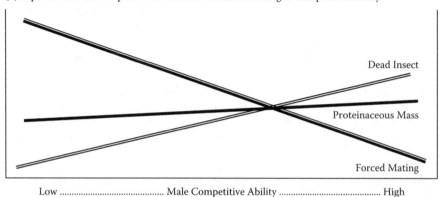

Figure 10.1 The mating strategy of the male scorpionfly. Part (a) shows the three mating tactics—dead insect, proteinaceous mass, and forced mating—of the mating strategy of the male scorpionfly. The male's ability in male-male competition determines the tactics used. The heritability is shown as 0 since all males are capable of all tactics. In part (b), the contribution of each tactic to the males' expected lifetime reproductive success is shown as a function of his ability to compete. Note that the dead insect tactic is the best for highly competitive males, while the forced mating tactics is the best for low-competitive males. Finally, males with intermediate competitive ability do best with the proteinaceous mass tactic. The graphs are heuristic and are not based on experimental data.

female and attempt to release sperm before the parental male can release his sperm (Gross, 1996). The tactics are said to be developmentally contingent on environmental circumstances (Crawford & Anderson, 1989) since the tactic employed depends on conditions during the male's development. In the case of bluegill sunfish, natural selection shaped the mating strategy so that information on which tactic to use is acquired during the male's growth. Hence, male bluegills do not have as much flexibility in choosing their adult mating tactics as do scorpionflies. A diagram for the male bluegill sunfish would look similar to that for male scorpionflies. However, the abscissa would be calibrated in terms of the males' growth rate. The determinants of male bluegill growth rate and male scorpionfly competitive ability are not known. They could be a complex function of both genetic and environmental factors.

Fever

Fever appears to be the result of a specific regulatory mechanism that adjusts body temperature in response to the toxins of some bacteria. When drugs, such as aspirin, block fever, resistance to infection may be decreased. (Nesse & Williams, 1994). Fever, like the mating tactics of male scorpionflies, is concurrently dependent on environmental conditions because the body adjusts temperature in response to current invasions of pathogens. If a diagram of the fever adaptation were made, it would resemble the one for scorpionflies. However, there would be a continuous distribution of tactics rather than the discrete tactics of the male scorpionfly and bluegill sunfish.

Incest Avoidance

Close inbreeding is detrimental to reproduction and survival because it brings deleterious recessive alleles, such as those causing phenylketonuria, albinism, and color blindness together in the same individuals. At least four sources of evidence support Westermarck's (1891) argument that natural selection has produced an adaptation that produces an aversion to adult sexual contact with childhood intimates of the opposite sex. Boys and girls reared in the same children's houses in Israeli kibbutzim rarely find each other sexually attractive as adults (Shepher, 1983). There is reduced reproductive success and marriage stability of the Chinese *shim pau* marriages, in which a genetically unrelated baby girl is adopted into a family at birth with the expectation that she will marry a son of the family at their sexual maturity (Wolf, 1995). The third-party reactions to fictional cases of sibling incest (Lieberman, Tooby, & Cosmides, 2003) also support Westermarck's claim. Finally, adult genetic siblings who were separated at birth have been found to become sexually attracted to one another (Bevc & Silverman, 2000).

There are many other examples of evolved adaptations in humans that interest evolutionary psychologists. Some examples are evolved mechanisms for detecting cheaters on social obligations (Cosmides, 1989), dealing with threats and dangers (Fiddick, Spampinato, & Grafman, 2005), mating strategies (Buss, 2004), and recognizing faces (Boyer & Barrett, 2005). In all these cases, the logic of natural selection explains how the adaptation evolved. Although evolutionary psychologists often focus on the functioning of particular mechanisms in their research programs, they understand that all ongoing behaviors are produced by the interaction and cooperation of a variety of evolved mechanisms. For example, waist-to-hip ratio (Singh, 1993), fluctuating body asymmetry (Thornhill & Gangestad, 1993), detectors of cheaters on social obligations (Cosmides & Tooby, 1992), detecting and avoiding threats (Fiddick et al., 2005), recognizing genetic relatives (Alexander, 1979), and facial recognition (Duchaine, 2000) are all likely involved in mate attraction and choice.

Characteristics of Adaptations

Ancestral. Biologists who study animals in their natural habitat may not need to emphasize differences between ancestral and current environments unless they have reason to believe that the environment of the species has been disturbed in some way. However, when the focus is on human adaptations, the definition must be modified to consider the possibility of differences between Then and Now. Since the development of antibiotics, the fever adaptation does not contribute to fitness to the same extent that it did in the past. Male scorpionfly mating tactics may not have the same relative success when males are reared under laboratory conditions as they do in the natural habitat. For example, if male-male competition were reduced in the laboratory, the forced copulation tactic would not be seen. However, if male-male competition were very intense, it would be the only tactic seen. Human mate attraction and choice mechanisms, such as the attractiveness of women with good waist-to-hip ratios (Singh, 1993) and men with symmetrical bodies (Thornhill & Gangestad, 1993), may not now be as useful in indicating mate quality as they once were. Therefore, the phrase "makes an organism more fit" in Wilson's definition of adaptation, must be replaced with the phrase "made an ancestral organism more fit" to emphasize that although adaptations are being expressed in a current environment, they came into being in an ancestral environment.

Adaptations and Behavior

Are behavior patterns adaptations as indicated in Wilson's (1975) definition? In some organisms, such as bees, wasps, and ants, development of behavior patterns is highly canalized. In such instances, it may be possible to speak of feeding behavior, defensive behavior, care-giving behavior, and so forth as though the behaviors themselves are adaptations. However, this perspective does not imply that it is either desirable or possible to have an evolutionary science of human behavior without a science of the mechanisms producing it (Symons, 1989). Evolutionary psychologists assume that it is outputs of psychological adaptations—sensations, perceptions, cognitions, intentions, emotions, preferences, and motivations—that produce behavior. Moreover, few, if any, human behaviors depend on the functioning of a single adaptation.

Decision Makers

The development and/or functioning of all adaptations require decision making. By "decision making" I do not mean conscious decision making, I mean the selection of alternatives by some evolved mechanism. The fever adaptation, for example, can be considered as a set of decision processes for dealing with certain kinds of invading bacteria. Its operation might be described by a rule such as, "If bacteria A, B, or C are invading the body, raise body temperature X degrees." Similarly, the mating strategy of the male scorpionfly can be described by a set of decision rules. Some of these might be, "If strong and dominant, and resources are available, compete vigorously for them. If a dead insect is obtained, produce courtship pheromones." Many other rules would be needed for a complete description of the adaptation's functioning. An even more complex set would be required to describe a human male's response to an attractive woman in a particular situation. Finally, even anatomical adaptations, such as the beaks of Darwin's finches, involve decision making. As the finch's beak grows, for example, its size must be coordinated with the growth of other anatomical structures and physiological process. The coordination requires decision making.

Specialized. Evolutionary psychologists assume that because adaptations evolved in response to specific ancestral conditions, they must be specialized in design. Upright walking depends on complex set of specified adaptations for coordinating balance and movement (Boyd & Silk, 2006). The functioning of the human digestion system depends on a complex set of specialized mechanisms for transforming ingested substances into nutrients. The specialization refers to design. Evolved adaptations may appear to be general in the way they function in the sense that they may be involved in different processes. As an example, consider the wheel and axel. The design is specialized. The wheel must be round. The axel must be in the middle of the wheel. Hence, it is specialized. However, it is general in that the wheel and axel can become part of many different complex machines. In a similar way, the apparent generality of the human locomotion and digestive systems is the result of the integrative functioning of a large number of highly specialized mechanisms. From this perspective, most evolutionary psychologists would assume that male scorpionflies have at least one specialized mechanism for choosing and implementing the appropriate courtship tactic, and that human males have at least one specialized psychological mechanism for responding to an attractive woman. Finally, the human psyche could not have evolved to be a general problem solver because there were no general mental problems to which natural selection could respond. Its apparent generality results from the integrative functioning of a large number of specialized information-processing and decision-making adaptations (Cosmides & Tooby, 1992).

Cost-Benefit Structure

The functioning of all adaptations has costs and benefits. A benefit of the fever adaptation is that it may destroy harmful bacteria, but it also has costs. Energy is required to raise body temperature and maintain it at the appropriate level. Moreover, the rise in body temperature can damage other systems of the body if it is excessive and prolonged. Similarly, the three mating tactics of male scorpionflies have associated costs and benefits. Even the strong, dominant male scorpionflies that obtain mates by presenting dead insects to females risk broken legs and torn wings in competition with other males (Thornhill, 1980). The functioning of any adaptation can always be translated into measures of reproductive success. For example, the energy used to produce the fever an organism uses in fighting pathogens could produce additional offspring if it were not expended fighting pathogens. However, if is needed to fight pathogens, it enables the organisms to produce additional offspring that it would not have produced without it. Similarly, the tactics male scorpionflies use in competing for mates and the benefits they obtain from using them can be calibrated in terms of offspring produced. I use the term *cost-benefit structure* of an adaptation to refer to the set of decision rules and their associated ancestral costs and benefits that can be used to describe its functioning. If humans have adaptations for detecting cheaters on social obligations, taking precautions to avoid threats and dangers, choosing mates, or avoiding incest, they will have costs as well as benefits.

Moreover, the functioning of an adaptation must reflect the evolutionary forces that shaped it, rather than those in any particular time interval where it is expressed. If organisms could make local adjustments to the cost-benefit structures of their adaptations, they could be perfectly adapted to any environment. The fever adaptation, for example, cannot "know" that antibiotics have altered its cost-benefit structure. If it did, it could avoid the costs of fever by "refusing" to raise body temperature in response to invading pathogens. This would imply that information can flow backward in time to redesign the adaptation in terms of current needs (Crawford, 2003).

Finally, the costs of adaptations can be pathological, especially if the effects of the adaptation are expressed in a novel environment. Although fever may have a role in fighting parasites, physicians have often considered it a condition to be treated. Once antibiotics or other treatments for the conditions that fever evolved to respond to become available, fever may indeed be pathological because its benefits are eliminated and only its costs remain.

The Unit of Selection

Wilson's (1975) definition includes the notion that adaptations evolved because they contribute to the reproductive success of individuals. In theory, natural selection can act at the level of the species, the group, the individual, or the gene (Sober & Wilson, 1998). Though the issue is controversial, most evolutionary psychologists claim that the unit of selection is the lowest level at which selection can act—the gene. See Williams (1966), Crespi (2001), and Sober and Wilson for discussions of the level at which natural selection operates.

Adaptation Defined

Wilson's (1975) definition of an adaptation refers to the aspect of the adaptation that operates on the environment. However, the definition must focus on genes, since it is genes that are passed from generation to generation and that natural selection ultimately acts on. Finally, I define an adaptation as "a set of genes that code for development of decision processes that embody the costs and benefits of the functioning of the decision processes across evolutionary time, and that organized the development of the effector processes for dealing with those contingencies in such a way that the gene(s) producing the decision processes were reproduced better than alternate gene(s)" (modified from Crawford, 1998). Explicating this definition requires distinguishing between innate (the genotype) and operational (the phenotype) adaptations, between ancestral and current developmental environments, between ancestral and current immediate environments, and between ancestral and current reproductive success.

The genotype of an adaptation contains information about an environmental problem that members of species encountered, as well as its solution, which was encoded in genes by natural selection. At conception, this information becomes available to a developing organism. During development, it cooperates with information from the current developmental environment to produce the phenotype of the adaptation. In particular episodes of behavior the phenotype responds to information in the immediate environment to produce the behavioral responses. However, the phenotype of an adaptation may not contribute to reproductive success in particular moments of evolutionary time where an organism actually lives. In the past, I have used the term *innate adaptation* for the genotype of an adaptation, and the term *operational adaptation* for the phenotype of an adaptation to distinguish these two meanings of adaptation (Crawford, 1993).

The Incest Avoidance Adaptation: Then and Now

Figure 10.2 shows how adaptations are assumed to function in ancestral and current environments. In the upper panel, the assumption is that brothers and sisters who avoided incest had greater expected lifetime reproductive success across evolutionary time than those who did not. Studies of incest have shown that, in most cases, there is a detrimental effect of close inbreeding on reproductive success (Cavalli-Sforza, 1977). Hence, natural selection selected genes for producing one or more mechanisms for avoiding it. Here, we are concerned with a mechanism for avoiding sexual contact between siblings through adult sexual aversion to childhood intimates, who in an ancestral environment would likely have been genetic siblings.

The ancestral developmental environment, being intimately reared with genetic siblings, produces the ancestral operational adaptation, which, in turn, produces the adult aversion to sexual contact with adult childhood intimates. Note the assumption that natural selection designed the avoidance mechanism(s) for a specific purpose—reducing the likelihood of mating between genetic siblings. Its operation can be described in terms of decision rules, such as, "If you had close contact with a member of the opposite sex during your first few years of life, store information about the phenotypic features of that individual," and "Use this information as a factor in choosing the objects of adult sexual attraction." The ancestral immediate environment refers to particular instances of contact with sexually mature, ancestral, opposite-sex individuals. The functioning of the ancestral operational adaptation reduced the likelihood of brothers and sisters mating and contributed to their reproductive success across evolutionary time.

Reproductive Success

However, note also that in any particular short segment of evolutionary time, the adaptation may not have contributed to the actual lifetime reproductive success of brothers and sisters. For example, there may have been times in our evolutionary history—say, when group size was very small or groups were widely dispersed—when avoiding mating between brothers and sisters would have been detrimental to their lifetime reproductive success. Hence, it is necessary to distinguish between *expected lifetime reproductive success* measured across many lifetimes in evolutionary time *and realized lifetime reproductive success* measured on the lifetimes of individuals in one or possibly a few generations. We are concerned with expected reproductive success when considering the evolution of adaptations.

Now consider the bottom panel of the figure. It represents a moment of evolutionary time—a few years in an Israeli kibbutz or a Chinese *shim pau* marriage or the meeting of an adult brother and sister who were separated at birth and reared in different homes. In all three cases, the putative adaptation continues to function as it evolved to function with respect to childhood intimates. However, because it is functioning in novel environments, its decision processes produces consequences that do not serve its original function and that are detrimental to current reproductive success. In the case of the Israeli kibbutzniks, its malfunction likely has little effect on reproductive

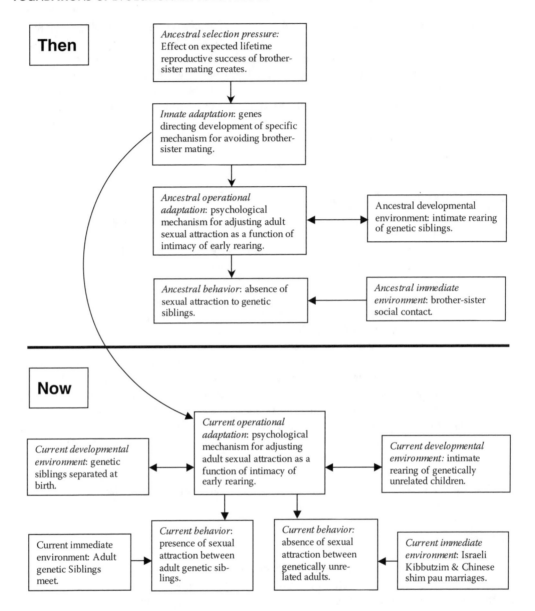

Figure 10.2 Adaptation functioning: Then and Now. The evolutionary psychologist's perspective on how an evolved adaptation in conjunction with ancestral and current developmental and immediate environments can produce different behaviors in ancestral and current environments. Note that the adaptation that evolved to prevent brother-sister incest in ancestral environments can produce either sexual attraction between genetic siblings or absence of sexual attraction between genetically unrelated individuals, depending on the conditions of rearing in the current environment. Because there is a clear distinction between ancestral and current environments and between ancestral and current operational adaptations (although not between ancestral and current innate adaptations), ancestral and current behavior may differ considerably. Although ancestral behavior contributed to ancestral fitness and, hence, to the evolution of the innate adaptation, current behavior need not contribute to current fitness. Finally, note that although the behaviors produced in the current environment would not have been seen ancestrally and are maladaptive, the psychological mechanism procuring them functions as they have always functioned. Hence, they can be studied by the methods of experimental psychology. Note also, that the current behaviors are maladaptative. Hence, across evolutionary time natural selection would modify the innate adaptation producing them.

success, as there are many opportunities for finding mates in modern Israel. In the case of the *shim pau* marriages, Wolf (1995) has shown that these marriages have lower than average reproductive success. These examples illustrate that it is not easy to see how studies of reproductive success in current environments, whether they are of current hunter-gatherer environments or modern urban environments, can tell us much about what evolutionary psychologists are interested in—namely, the functioning of evolved psychological adaptations. Similar reasoning has led many evolutionary psychologists to conclude that studies of reproductive success in current environments are not useful in elucidating the functioning of psychological adaptations (Symons, 1989). However, see Crawford (2007) for a somewhat different interpretation.

Note, also, that the two current behaviors—"Sexual attraction between adult siblings" and "Absence of sexual attraction between genetically unrelated individuals"—shown at the bottom of Figure 10.2 detract from current reproductive success. If these behaviors persisted, natural selection would modify this particular incest avoidance mechanism. However, it could take a very long time.

As a final point, note that the incest avoidance mechanism(s) are functioning as they evolved to function—even when they develop in novel environments and have maladaptive consequences. This has important implications for evolutionary psychology research. It indicates that the basic functioning of the avoidance mechanisms is not affected greatly by rearing circumstances—its basic information-processing, cost-benefit structure functions as it has always functioned. Hence, its functioning can be studied by the usual methods of modern experimental psychology, just as psychological mechanisms hypotheses from other perspectives can be studied. Since evolved psychological mechanisms are assumed to have a basis in genetics, we now turn to the role of genetics in the development and functioning of psychological mechanisms.

THE GENETICS OF ADAPTATIONS

The most heuristic approach to the genetics of adaptations is through evolutionary life history theory. Genes have evolved to produce adaptations that acquire resources from their environment and convert them into progeny that carry them. However, time and energy are limited; hence, organisms have evolved to make decisions about how they invest. An organism can replicate many of its alleles if it produces a very large number of offspring and invests heavily in each of them. Since time and energy are limited, it cannot do both. An organism can replicate many alleles if it spends a great deal of time in finding a mate. However, if it does this, it then has fewer resources for rearing the offspring that result from the mating. Again, if an organism invests heavily in infant care, it has less time and energy for adolescent care. Therefore, natural selection shapes various types of adaptations for trade-offs during the organism's life. Life history theory and research are concerned with the timing and intensity of reproduction; with age span and size at maturity; with trade-offs between somatic growth, maintenance, and repair versus reproduction; with decisions about the number and size of offspring; and with investment in current versus future reproduction. Since the characteristics of the life history evolved by natural selection, they are genetic traits. However, the trade-offs of the life history enable organisms to respond to internal and external environmental circumstances, as, for example, do male scorpionflies and bluegill sunfish. Hence, life history theory provides a framework for considering genetic and environmental interactions in the development and functioning of adaptations.

A *life history* is a genetically organized life course that describes how resources are allocated to survival, growth, and reproduction at each age throughout a typical individual's life (Wittenberger, 1981). It is implemented through strategies and tactics. Here I have adopted Gross's (1996) terminology. However, I identify his strategy (decision rule) with my innate adaptation. His tactics are equivalent to my tactics. A strategy is an adaptation that mediates the life history trade-offs. It is a set of decision rules encoded in genes that organizes how somatic development and behavior are used to implement the life history. Tactics are the somatic developments and/or psychological mechanisms that implement the strategy. They come into existence when information about the solution of ancestral problems, encoded in the genes of the strategy, cooperates with information from the current environment to produce the phenotype tactics. In the terminology of Figure 10.2, strategies are the innate adaptations (the genotype) and tactics are the operational adaptations (the phenotype). Tactics may be concurrently contingent on environmental circumstances, as is the case for scorpionfly mating tactics, or developmentally contingent, as is the case for bluegill sunfish mating tactics. Often, both types of tactics are associated with a strategy, as is likely the case with human mating strategies (Buss, 2004). Within a population, life histories compete with each other across evolutionary time. Strategies, with their associated tactics, are how they compete. Figure 10.1, which describes male scorpionfly mating, shows a single genetic strategy with three concurrently contingent environmental tactics for obtaining matings. In the past, there may have been other strategies, but they have been eliminated by natural selection, leaving a single strategy with its three tactics.

Sex Differences in Life History

There is one major exception to the rule that there is little or no genetic variation in life history traits within a species: It is the genetic organized life differences associated with sex. In humans, a single genetic locus, the TDF locus, seems to provide a genetic switch that determines sex and thus organizes the development of sexual dimorphism in a number of traits ranging from anatomy of the sex organs to body size and proportion, brain anatomy and physiology, and age at sexual maturity. This same switch may also be involved in the development of gender differences in personality and intellectual abilities. The existence of sexual dimorphism provides the best, and possibly the only, example of genetic life history differences in humans.

There is evidence that there are gender differences in a variety of behaviors, including empathy, altruism, and aggression (Mealey, 2000). Human males and females may be viewed as having two slightly different genetic life histories, each with developmentally and concurrently contingent tactics for negotiating the problems experienced from birth to death. Some gender differences may be a reflection of different strategies and tactics. Consider sensation seeking and impulsiveness, for example (Zuckerman, Buchsbaum, & Murphy, 1980). Both traits are more characteristic of men than of women and have relatively high heritability, which suggests that they could reflect different ancestral male and female life histories that may be affecting current behavior.

GENETIC VARIATION AND NATURAL SELECTION

Suppose that identical twins that were separated at conception were reared in different environments, and that because of the different environments, their adult personalities and abilities differ greatly. One twin is extroverted while the other is introverted. One is aggressive and the other submissive. One is better at verbal reasoning while the other is better at quantitative reasoning. A common interpretation is that because the twins are genetically identical, making the heritability of the tactics zero, genes are not involved in the production of these differences.

Let us return to Figure 10.1, which describes scorpionfly mating, to help with the logic of this issue. Suppose that identical triplet scorpionflies reside in environments differing in male-male competition. Triplet A resides in an environment high in male-male competition. Triplet B resides in one with moderate competition. Finally, triplet C resides in an environment where male-male competition is absent. How will their behaviors differ? Attempted forced copulation will be absent in the environment of triplet C, which is free from competition. However, it will be the usual tactic in the high competition environment of triplet A. The proteinaceous mass tactic will be a frequent mating tactic in the moderate competition environment of triplet B. Finally, the dead insect tactic will be the one seen in environment of triplet C.

Because the three male scorpionflies are genetically identical, gene differences between them cannot be contributing to the differences in courtship behavior. Hence, the heritability of the tactics is zero. However, the genes that all three males have—and, indeed, the genes that every male scorpionfly has—contribute to the development of the behaviors that are seen. While it is true that the environmental differences are producing the behavioral differences, and that genetic differences are not involved, the environmental differences are acting through the genetically innate information-processing mechanisms that all male scorpionflies possess (Crawford & Anderson, 1989). Hence, the genes that every male scorpionfly possesses are deeply involved in producing all these different behaviors. Zero heritability does not imply that genes do not affect development!

Since the mating tactics of the scorpionfly are concurrently contingent on environmental circumstances, the behavior of our three triples could be changed by changing the current living conditions of each of the triplets. However, it could not produce tactics, such as singing a fine courtship song that females might "prefer" and that males might "like" to perform. The reason is that males have the genetically innate capacity for only the three tactics described above. The tactics for the bluegill sunfish are developmentally contingent on the environment. Hence, changing their adult reproductive behaviors would require changing their rearing conditions during development. Finally, changing their rearing conditions could not enable them to sing a fine courtship song or affect the female sunfish's ability to appreciate it.

Although genetic variation is necessary for an adaptation to evolve by natural selection, from an evolutionary perspective, genetic variation is not the main focus in the study of adaptation. What is of interest is the correlation of the behavioral differences with fitness in the environment in which the trait evolved, as well as the ways in which it functions in contemporary environments. Although the different tactics of male scorpionflies do not depend on genetic differences, variation in the tactics is correlated with environmental differences, and with fitness differences in those environments.

Figure 10.3 illustrates the role of genetic variation in the study of adaptation. At the left of the figure, we see that natural selection acts on ancestral genetic variation to produce an adaptation.

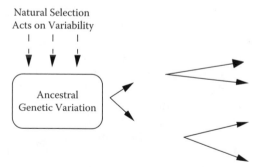

Figure 10.3 The possible effects of natural selection on ancestral genetic variation. Natural selection impacts on ancestral genetic variation in the formation of an adaptation as shown in the left of the figure. In the top path, natural selection has eliminated genetic variation. In the upper branch of this path, the effects of genes on the adaptation's functioning have been eliminated. Some of those who argue that the mind is a blank slate apparently take such a view. In the lower branch of this pathway, the effects of genes remains, although they affect everyone in the same way. Genetic variation remains for the bottom path. In the upper branch of this path, the genetic variation contributes to individual differences in the adaptation's functioning. This view is taken by many behavior geneticists. The lower branch of this path shows the view held by many evolutionary psychologists. There is no genetic variation in the design of the adaptation. The observed genetic variation is caused by genetic variation at the protein level of organs. Hence, the observed genetic variation in the functioning of an adaptation is a fortuitous effect of this variation.

There are two possible pathways, each with two branches. First, as shown in the upper pathway, genetic variation with respect to the adaptation has been eliminated by natural selection, and the heritability for behavioral differences for both branches is zero. Here, there are two possible interpretations of the absence of genetic variation. The first is that because genetic variation has been eliminated—the heritability of current behaviors is zero—current behavior is not influenced by genes. This view of the human psyche is apparently held by many social scientists, such as those in the first row of Table 10.1. The discussion of the role of genetics in producing differences in mating behavior in identical triplet scorpionflies given shows its inadequacy.

The second interpretation is that although natural selection has eliminated genetic variation with respect to the design of the adaptation, thus making the genetic basis of the adaptation identical for all individuals, the genes that all members of the species now possess still contribute to the behaviors produced by the adaptation. The second interpretation is more congenial to evolutionary psychologists. It is possible to make Eagly and Wood's (1999) thinking compatible with this view. To do so, they would have to assume the human psyche has evolved *genetically innate specialized mechanisms* for assessing male and female physical traits and using this information in adjusting gender roles.

The problem with the upper paths is that it is difficult to find a behavioral trait with zero heritability (Plomin & McClearn, 1993). For a more compete interpretation of how behavior geneticists and evolutionary psychologists think of the genetics of adaptations, consider the bottom pathway. Here, genetic variation has not been eliminated by natural selection. The heritabilities for both paths are nonzero. But again, there are two interpretations. First, as shown in the upper branch of the lower pathway, genetic variation remains and it is related to fitness-enhancing differences between individuals. The science of behavior genetics is based on the notion that such genetic difference provides important information about the functioning of evolved organs.

However, evolutionary psychologists, because of their focus on the evolved design of adaptations, take much less interest in this variation than do behavior geneticists. Nevertheless, they do not claim that genetic differences do not affect adaptation functioning, but argue instead that the effect is indirect. Variation in the protein structure of organs, in which the design of adaptations is instantiated, protects them from the attacks of pathogens, but it has a cost. It produces "minute lesions" in the organs that detract from the implementation of the adaptation's design.

The argument for this interpretation goes as follows (Tooby & Cosmides, 1990). The functioning of most complex adaptations requires the action of genes at many loci. The genetic recombination that occurs during sexual reproduction scrambles genes every generation. If genes were important in the development of an adaptation, this recombination would disrupt its functioning. Hence, this recombination, for the most part, must not affect major design features of adaptations, since if it did, it would disrupt their functioning. Pathogens attack organs at the level of the protein building blocks of organs rather than at the level of the tasks that the organ performs. Hence, scrambling the genotype each generation protects the organs in which the design is instantiated from pathogen attacks.

Both branches of the upper pathway in Figure 10.3 would be unlikely in nature. However, the lower branch of the lower pathway labeled, "Genetic variation remains, but is not directly related to the adaptation's function," could be relatively common in nature. It is the alternative favored by many evolutionary psychologists. This reasoning explains the use of the phrase *innate adaptation* for the genotype of the adaptation shown in Figure 10.2.

Finally, note that if a geneticist computed the realized heritability of the scorpionfly tactics, it would not be zero, as is implied in Figure 10.1. The reason is that a variety of genetic factors, peripheral to the design of the adaptation, may influence its functioning. One is the genetic variation at the protein level that protects scorpionfly organs from pathogen attacks mentioned above. In addition, there may be genetic variation in traits—such as growth rate, metabolic rate, and so forth—that affects how the tactics are deployed, and, hence, their realized heritability.

The human mind grows out of two sources of environmental information. One is information about ancestral environments, the problems they posed for our ancestors and aspects of their solutions that was encoded in genes by natural selection. The other is information from the current environment. Beginning at conception, these sources of information come together to produce the adult human mind. The genetic architecture of the mind is concerned with the organization of the first source of information and how it acquires, manages, and uses information from the current environment to solve problems we encountered in our current ancestral environments. Because of the extent and complexity of the system, it may appear as if the mind is a general-purpose computer more or less independent of its ancestral history. However, a vast hierarchy of interacting developmentally and concurrently contingent genetic predispositions produces this apparent generality.

ADAPTATION FUNCTIONING: THEN AND NOW

Now, let us return to the lower right cell of Table 10.1, "Correctly believing in a considerable degree of genetic involvement in the development and functioning of psychological mechanisms," and Figure 10.2, which explains how ancestral adaptations function in ancestral and current environments. Note that the indicated table cell is headed, "Limits on policy options." The limitations exist because the "innate adaptations" shown in Figure 10.2 are involved in the development of the operational adaptations that actually produce behavior. Table 10.2 indicates something about how this thinking plays out in the moments of evolutionary time where we live.

It provides a classification of how behavioral adaptations function in ancestral and current environments. The "ancestral" dimension of the table is defined in terms of adaptive and maladaptive, where adaptive refers to the ancestral reproductive success of an individual possessing a trait relative to the reproductive success of an individual possessing an alternative trait. The "current" dimension of the table is defined in terms of how a trait contributes to the current health and well-being of an individual and his or her associates. The result is a two-by-two classification that produces true pathologies, pseudopathologies, quasinormal behaviors, and adaptive-culturally variable behaviors.

True pathologies, such as infantile autism, brother-sister incest, or brain damage–caused memory loss, did not contribute to ancestral reproductive success and they do not contribute to current well-being (Crawford & Anderson, 1989). Here, well-being is analogous to the adequacy of an engineering design for dealing with current environmental stress. True pathologies result from the disruption of major adaptations that were, and are, necessary for survival, reproduction, and well-being. Some may be due to unusual rearing patterns of children. For example, some instances of brother-sister incest may be due to the lack of intimate contact between brothers and sisters during their childhoods. Similarly, a cause of child abuse and neglect may be inadequate rearing of the abusers. Finally, note that at the level of the gene, a trait may spread even if it detracts from the well-being of individuals possessing it. A possible example is Huntington's chorea, a serious neurological deterioration caused by a dominant allele. It develops late in life, after most children have been produced. Hence, natural selection has difficulty reducing its frequency.

Pseudopathologies are behaviors that have their origin in adaptations that evolved in response to problems our ancestors encountered, but for one reason or another, are no longer healthy, morally acceptable, or culturally valued (Crawford & Anderson, 1989). For example, the reason why people desire sugar and fat is probably because the taste for sugar and fat motivated our ancestors to do the physical work and take the risks necessary to obtain these vital nutrients. However, we can now obtain them with little physical effort and few risks. As a consequence, some of us consume too much of them, and the result is obesity (Nesse & Williams, 1994). Ancestral females and males may have exchanged sex for resources and protection (Symons, 1979). If this is the case, then modern prostitution may be a distorted and exaggerated form of this exchange, due to some women

Table 10.2 A Classification of Behavior with Respect to Adaptation Functioning in Ancestral and Current Environments

Contribution to Expected Ancestral Fitness	Contribution to Current Health and Well Being	
	No	**Yes**
	True pathologies	Quasinormal behaviors
No	Autism	Freedom of speech
	Brother–sister incest	Close birth spacing
	Phenylketonuria	Adoption of unrelated children
	Schizophrenia	Innocent until proven guilty
	Child abuse and neglect	Equality of sexes
	Korsakoff's syndrome	Exclusive homosexuality
	Down's syndrome	Democratic government
	Plegra	Female infantry
	Scurvy	House husbands
	Brain damage-caused memory loss	Monogamy
	Huntington's chorea	Polyandry
		Communism
	Pseudopathologies	Adaptive culturally variable behaviors
Yes	Taste for sugar and fat-caused obesity	Athletic sports
	Wife abuse	Favoring kin
	Anorexic behavior	Gossip
	Nepotism	Sexual jealousy
	Prostitution	Pornography
	Teenage gangs	Self-deception
	Sexual harassment	Beauty in mate choice
	Infanticide	Courtship behaviors
	Rape	Facial expressions
	Father–stepdaughter marriages	Reciprocal exchanges
		Self-deception
		Polygyny

Source: Modified from Crawford (1998b).

needing resources and protection and some men lacking sexual access to women through normal courtship.

Since pseudopathologies have their basis in evolved adaptations, they may be difficult to eradicate from a society. For example, if obesity has its basis in ancestral adaptations that made sugar and fat taste good enough to motivate our ancestors to do the work and take the risks of obtaining them, then eliminating obesity may be a difficult task. An evolutionary psychologist might predict that eliminating obesity will be more difficult than eliminating smoking, since the former likely has its basis in an evolved specialized adaptation, whereas the latter likely does not. Similarly, if infanticide, prostitution, male pornography, sexual harassment, and wife abuse have their origins in evolved ancestral specialized emotional and motivational adaptations, then completely eliminating them may be difficult. Moreover, strenuous attempts to eliminate them may produce new pseudo-pathologies. For example, if prostitution has its origin in ancestral trading of sex for resources and protection, then legalistic attempts to eliminate it may increase the rate of shoplifting by women, the use of pornography by men, and may even attenuate some of the motivations that enable family life. Attempts to eliminate infanticide by women through coercive laws may lead to an increase in depression and suicide.

Quasinormal behaviors are those that would have been rare or nonexistent in an ancestral environment because of their long-term fitness costs, but that have become socially acceptable to a significant proportion of the population of a particular society (Crawford & Anderson, 1989). The adoption of genetically unrelated children that would have detracted from ancestral fitness is culturally valued in many parts of the world. Late child bearing and close birth spacing, which would have reduced ancestral lifetime reproductive success, are the norm in most modern industrialized cultures. Polyandry, a mating system that is unlikely to have existed in the Pleistocene, is acceptable and encouraged in a few societies (Daly & Wilson, 1983). A variety of circumstances may produce quasinormal behaviors. A new technology may alter some of the emotional consequences of a behavior, resulting in an infrequent behavior becoming more prevalent. For example, birth control may alter the felt emotional consequences of recreational sexual behavior so that widespread recreational sex becomes possible and socially acceptable in a society. Close birth spacing, which would have been detrimental to ancestral women's fitness, may become more common when new technologies and social support mechanisms reduce the fitness cost of closely spaced children.

In general, quasinormal behaviors are not as problematic as either true pathologies or pseudo-pathologies. Nevertheless, there are at least three reasons why quasinormal behaviors may cause problems for individuals exhibiting them and for those with whom they associate (Crawford & Anderson, 1989). First, the environmental conditions producing quasinormal behaviors may produce conflicting or ambiguous inputs to psychological mechanisms, both in the individuals exhibiting them and their associates, resulting in emotional conflicts. A woman who engages in recreational sex may experience emotional conflict because other adaptations related to sexual behavior, such as those involved in the desire for children and long-term intimacy, may be telling her psyche the behavior is too costly.

Second, because the current behavior is a fortuitous effect of an adaptation that evolved to do something else, the cues from the environment producing it may be inadequate to produce a fully functional behavior. Rearing a genetically unrelated, adopted child can be even more stressful than rearing a biological child (Silk, 1990). The reason may be that some of the ancestral cues involved in parental attachment to biological children are absent for an adopted child. Third, no matter how well a quasinormal behavior is accepted in a particular culture, there may be some individuals who do not find it conducive to their well-being and happiness because of its evolutionary novelty. Many of the women in polyandrous societies who do not find husbands, and some of the men who must share wives, may not be as enthusiastic of polyandry as the elders who arrange the marriages are. Grandparents may not be as enthusiastic about their grandchildren being cared for in day care centers as their daughters are.

Finally, societal standards may change across time, moving a particular behavior in and out of the range of acceptability. Fifty years ago, divorce, day care centers, and homosexuality were not as acceptable as they are today in most Western democracies. Twenty years ago, the stock market was not as valued in Russia and China as it is now.

Quasinormal behaviors are among the most important characteristics of all human societies. Yet, they can be a source of trouble and stress. If a society values its quasinormal ideas and institutions such as monogamy, equality of the sexes, democratic government, communism, freedom of speech, the stock market, and innocent until proven guilty, then it must find ways of maintaining them. From the prospective of evolutionary psychology, this might involve designing them to use known psychological adaptations for producing human sociality, such as those mediated by kinship, reciprocity, and mate choice. However, some quasinormal institutions, such as pure communism, open marriage, and complete equality of the sexes in achievement, may be difficult to maintain because of the dearth of evolved psychological mechanisms that can be used to support them, as well as the presence of psychological adaptations that may make them difficult to sustain.

In most cases, adaptations carry out the tasks they were designed to accomplish by natural selection. If they did not, we would be an extinct—or at least an endangered—species. The adaptations producing these activities and behaviors are *adaptive-culturally variable* (Crawford, 1998). They are adaptive because they are currently doing what natural selection designed them to do. They are variable because they do it in a relatively wide variety of environmental circumstances. Our hearts are still pumping blood and our eyes are still seeing. Our mating and parenting systems are still enabling us to find adequate mates and rear our children. Our systems of reciprocal altruism are still enabling us to engage in complex social interactions. However, our hearts are pumping blood at altitudes different from those where we evolved. Our eyes are seeing sights our distant ancestors would not have imagined. Our language adaptation is enabling people in Brazil to speak Portuguese and those in Sweden learn Swedish. Our mildly polygynous mating adaptation has given rise to various types of polygyny in many cultures, and monogamy in others (Daly & Wilson, 1983). Reciprocal systems vary considerably across different cultures, but they are the primary basis of sociality in them all (Alexander, 1987). The list in Table 10.2 could be expanded almost infinitely.

Adaptive-culturally variable behaviors are robust because they are based in deeply evolved systems of cognitive and emotional mechanisms. If some great environmental disaster eliminated one of them—such as spoken language, courtship, or reciprocal exchanges—our evolved predispositions for them would generate new forms within a few generations. Nevertheless, they can produce problems because all adaptations have costs. Gossip, for example, is an important form of communication in all societies (Dunbar, 1996). Yet, it can be a source of conflict. Courtship behaviors are essential for finding mates (Buss, 1994), but they can result in conflict and violence. Marriage is not an easy street. In a fast-moving world, a danger is that social and cultural change can move a behavior from being an adaptive-culturally variable behavior to being a pseudopathology. All of the pseudopathological behaviors listed in Table 10.2 have their basis in adaptive mechanisms. A society must monitor many of them so that their costs do not escalate and make them even more noxious.

RESEARCH METHODOLOGIES

Determining whether a particular behavior or syndrome is a true pathology, a pseudopathology, an adaptive-culturally variable behavior, or a quasinormal behavior is scientifically interesting. Moreover, it may also be of considerable practical significance, as it may help legislators, social planners, and health-care professionals in their work.

Table 10.3 suggests the kinds of information that may be useful in classifying and understanding the behaviors described in Table 10.2. The rows provide hypotheses about several possible examples of the four classes of behavior. Note that the empirical information in the table is not the result of a rigorous review of the literature. The information in the table reflects general psychological hunches about what might be obtained if a comprehensive review were undertaken. Hence, the information in Table 10.3 is primarily of heuristic value.

The first two columns describe the categories from Table 10.2. Columns three, four, and five indicate the information useful for placing a particular behavior into one of the four categories. Some of this information will be difficult to obtain. "Contribution to fitness: then" requires modeling studies based on information on reproductive success in ancient and recent hunter-gatherer hominids. Anderson and Crawford (1992a, 1992b) provide examples of one approach to this task

Table 10.3 Research Strategies for Investigating Evolutionary Significance of Current Behavior

Hypothesized Class of Behavior	Possible Examples	Contribution to Individual Fitness		Current Well-Being	Experimental Studies of Mental Mechanisms	Correlational Studies		Exploring Proximate Biological Mechanisms
		Then	Now			Within Cultures	Across Cultures	
True pathology	• Autism	No	No	No	Yes	Yes	Yes	Yes
	• Huntington's chorea	No	No	No	Yes	Yes	Yes	Yes
	• Brother-sister incest	No	No	No	Yes	Yes	Yes	Yes
	• Korsakoff's syndrome	No	No	No	Yes	Yes	Yes	Yes
Pseudopathology	• Prostitution	Yes	No	No	Yes	Yes	Yes	Yes
	• Wife abuse	Yes	No	No	Yes	Yes	Yes	Yes
	• Teenage gangs	Yes	Yes	Yes	Yes	Yes	Yes	Yes
	• Taste for sugar and fat	Yes	No	No	Yes	Yes	Yes	Yes
Adaptive-culturally variable	• Athletic sports	Yes	No	Yes	Yes	Yes	Yes	Yes
	• Gossip	Yes	Yes	Yes	Yes	Yes	Yes	Yes
	• Facial expressions	Yes	Yes	Yes	Yes	Yes	Yes	Yes
	• Sexual jealousy	Yes	Yes	Yes	Yes	Yes	Yes	Yes
Quasinormal behavior	• True altruism	No	No	Yes	Yes	Yes	Yes	Yes
	• Polyandry	No	Yes	Yes	Yes	Yes	Yes	Yes
	• Equality of sexes	No	No	Yes	Yes	Yes	Yes	Yes
	• Female infantry	No	No	Yes	Yes	Yes	Yes	Yes

for reproduction suppression in women and differential investment in sons and daughters. Other approaches need to be developed.

The last four columns outline the information useful in determining how a behavior is related to putative adaptations. True experiments, requiring random assignment of treatments to individuals, are essential for deriving strong causal conclusions about the relation between environmental contingencies and the way behavioral adaptations respond to them. Cross-cultural studies provide information about how macroenvironmental factors are associated with behaviors, while within-cultural studies provide information on how microenvironmental factors are associated with behaviors. Thus, the information in columns seven and eight provides information on how a putative adaptation responds to environmental conditions. The final column focuses attention on the relation of adaptations to neurological and hormonal processes.

CONCLUSION

The organization of Table 10.1 is based on Pasca's wager about belief in God. Pascal argued that we cannot know if God exists. However, the possibility that he does exist creates a dilemma. If He does exist and we do not believe, the costs of the error, possibly burning in hell forever, are very great. However, if He does not exist and we believe, the costs of the error is rather small. Hence, the most prudent course is to believe in God. Many psychologists apparently engage in a similar type of reasoning concerning evolutionary psychology. That is, they assume that the possible costs suggested for cell 3 of Table 10.1—"**Incorrect decision:** Explanations that fail—missed opportunities"—that might be experienced if evolutionary theory is used to help explain human behavior are very great, but that the costs suggested for cell 2—"**Incorrect Decision:** Inadequate explanations—realization difficult"—are rather small. Hence, the most prudent course is to avoid using evolutionary theory in developing explanations for human behavior. However, there is a problem with Pascal's assumption. It is to assume that the costs of incorrectly believing in God when he does not exist are small. There may, in fact, be very great costs for believing in God when he does not exist. There may also be great costs for believing in a *tabula rasa* that does not exist. This is the risk that those who are unwilling to recognize evolutionary psychology as a valid way of studying and explaining the human mind and the behavior that it produces are willing to take.

As I see it, evolutionary psychology is concerned with the problems and stresses our hominine and primate ancestors encountered in their environments, the psychological adaptations natural selection shaped to deal with these problems and stresses, and the way these adaptations function in the infinitesimal slices of evolutionary time in which we now live. I claim that if it could be shown that natural selection had created the human mind as a *tabula rasa*, then evolutionary theory would be of little or no value in the study of human mind and behavior. I assume that our genes provide information about the ancestral history of our species and contain information about the problems our ancestors encountered and the solutions that natural selection shaped to help deal with them. Evolutionary psychology is concerned with understanding how this information is involved in the development of the specialized mechanisms that produce current behavior. Hence, the central purpose of this chapter is to describe the role that evolutionary psychologists assume ancestral genes and ancestral environments play in the production of current behavior. It begins with a definition of innate developmental organization. It then considers possible social and political outcomes for low and high levels of innate developmental organization paired with different beliefs about these levels. The notion of psychological mechanisms as evolved adaptations is considered in some detail. Then the ways in which evolutionary psychologists claim that genes are involved in the development of adaptations is considered. The chapter concludes with a framework for considering how ancestral adaptations function in current environments and outlines some ways studying them.

REFERENCES

Alexander, R. D. (1979). *Darwinism and human affairs.* Seattle: University of Washington Press.

Alexander, R. D. (1987). *The biology of moral systems.* Hawthorne, NY: Aldine de Gruyter.

Anderson, J. L., & Crawford, C. B. (1992a). Modeling costs and benefits of adolescent weight control as a mechanism for reproduction suppression. *Human Nature, 3,* 299–334.

Anderson, J. L., & Crawford, C. B. (1992b). Modeling costs and benefits of adolescent weight control as a mechanism for reproductive suppression. *Human Nature, 3*(4), 299–334.

Bevc, I., & Silverman, I. (2000). Early separation and sibling incest: A test of the revised Westermarck theory. *Evolution and Human Behavior, 21,* 151–161.

Boas, F. (1966). *Race, language and culture.* New York: Free Press.

Boyd, R., & Silk, J. B. (2006). *How humans evolved* (4th ed.). New York: W. W. Norton.

Boyer, P., & Barrett, C. (2005). Domain specificity and intuitive ontology. In D. Buss (Ed.), *The handbook of evolutionary psychology* (pp. 96–118). Hoboken, NJ: John Wiley & Sons.

Buss, D. (1994). *The evolution of desire: Strategies of human mating.* New York: Basic Books.

Buss, D. (2004). *Evolutionary psychology: The new science of the mind* (2nd ed.). New York: Pearson.

Cavalli-Sforza, L. L. (1977). *Elements of human genetics* (2nd ed.). Menlo Park, CA: W. A. Benjamin.

Cosmides, L. (1989). The logic of social exchange: Has natural selection shaped how humans reason? Studies with the Wason selection task. *Cognition, 31,* 187–276.

Cosmides, L., & Tooby, J. (1992). Cognitive adaptations for social exchange. In J. Barkow, L. Cosmides, & J. Tooby (Eds.), *The adapted mind: Evolutionary psychology and the generation of culture* (pp. 163–228). New York: Oxford University Press.

Crawford, C. (1993). The future of sociobiology: Counting babies or studying proximate mechanisms. *Trends in Evolution and Ecology, 8,* 183–186.

Crawford, C. (1998). Environments and adaptations: Then and now. In C. Crawford & D. Krebs (Eds.), *Handbook of evolutionary psychology. Ideas, issues and applications* (pp. 275–302). Mahwah, NJ: Lawrence Erlbaum.

Crawford, C. (2003). A prolegomenon for a viable evolutionary psychology: The myth and the reality. *Psychological Bulletin, 124,* 854–857.

Crawford, C. (2004). Public policy and personal decisions: The evolutionary context. In C. Crawford & C. Salmon (Eds.), *Evolutionary psychology, public policy and personal decisions* (pp. 3–22). Mahwah, NJ: Lawrence Erlbaum.

Crawford, C. (2007). Reproductive success: Then and now. In S. Gangestad & J. Simpson (Eds.), *The evolution of mind: Fundamental questions and controversies* (pp. 69–77). New York: Guilford Publications.

Crawford, C., & Anderson, J. (1989). Sociobiology: An environmentalist discipline? *American Psychologist, 44,* 1449–1459.

Crespi, B. J. (2001). *Evolution of social behavior. In international encyclopedia of social & behavioral sciences.* New York: Elsevier.

Daly, M., & Wilson, M. (1983). *Sex, evolution, and behavior* (2nd ed.). Boston: PWS Publishers.

Duchaine, B. C. (2000). Developmental prosopagnosia with normal configural processing. *Neuroreport, 11*(1), 79–83.

Dunbar, R. (1996). *Grooming, gossip, and the evolution of language.* London: Faber and Faber.

Eagly, A., & Wood, W. (1999). The origins of sex differences in human behavior: Evolved dispositions versus social roles. *American Psychologist, 54,* 408–423.

Eibl-Eibesfeldt, I. (1989). *Human ethology.* New York: Aldine De Gruyter.

Fiddick, L., Spampinato, M. V., & Grafman, J. (2005). Social contracts and precautions activate different neurological systems: An FMRI investigation of deontic reasoning. *Neuroimage, 28*(4), 778–786.

Gross, M. (1996). Alternative reproductive strategies and tactics: Diversity within sexes. *Trends in Ecology and Evolution, 11,* 92–98.

Kroeber, A. L. (1952). *Nature of culture.* Chicago: University of Chicago Press.

Lieberman, D., Tooby, J., & Cosmides, L. (2003). Does morality have a biological basis: An empirical test of the factors governing moral sentiments relating to incest. *Proceedings of the Royal Society B: Biological Sciences, 270,* 819–826.

Lorenz, K. Z. (1965). *The evolution and modification of behavior.* Chicago: The University of Chicago Press.

Mealey, L. (2000). *Sex differences: Developmental and evolutionary strategies.* San Diego, CA: Academic.

Mill, J. S., & Stillinger, J. (1969). *Autobiography, and other writings.* Boston: Houghton Mifflin.

Nesse, R., & Williams, G. (1994). *Why we get sick: The new science of Darwinian medicine.* New York: Times Books.

Pinker, S. (2002). *The blank slate: The modern denial of human nature.* New York: Viking.

Plomin, R., & McClearn, G. E. (1993). *Nature, nurture, & psychology* (1st ed.). Washington, DC: American Psychological Association.

Shepher, J. (1983). *Incest: A biosocial view.* New York: Academic Press.

Silk, J. B. (1990). Human adoption in evolutionary perspective. *Human Nature, 1,* 25–52.

Singh, D. (1993). Adaptive significance of female physical attractiveness: Role of waist-to-hip ratio. *Journal of Social and Personality Psychology, 65,* 293–307.

Skinner, B. F. (1972). *Beyond freedom and dignity.* Toronto, Ontario, Canada: Bantam Books.

Skinner, B. F. (1976). *Walden two.* New York: MacMillan Publishing Co.

Sober, E., & Wilson, D. S. (1998). *Unto others: The evolution and psychology of unselfish behavior.* Cambridge, MA: Harvard University Press.

Symons, D. (1979). *The evolution of human sexuality.* New York: Oxford.

Symons, D. (1989). A critique of Darwinian anthropology. *Ethology and Sociobiology, 10,* 131–144.

Thornhill, R. (1980). Rape in Panorpa scorpionflies and a general rape hypothesis. *Animal Behavior, 28,* 52–59.

Thornhill, R., & Gangestad, S. (1993). Human facial beauty: Averageness, symmetry, and parasite resistance. *Human Nature, 4,* 237–239.

Tooby, J., & Cosmides, L. (1990). On the universality of human nature and the uniqueness of the individual: The role of genetics and adaptation. *Journal of Personality, 58*(1), 17–67.

Walters, S., & Crawford, C. (1994). The importance of mate attraction for intrasexual competition in men and women. *Ethology and Sociobiology,* 15.

Westermarck, E. A. (1891). *The history of human marriage.* New York: Macmillan.

Williams, G. C. (1966). *Adaptation and natural selection: A critique of some current evolutionary thought.* Princeton, NJ: Princeton University Press.

Wilson, E. O. (1975). *Sociobiology: The new synthesis.* Cambridge, MA: Harvard University Press.

Wittenberger, J. F. (1981). *Animal social behavior.* Boston: Duxbury Press.

Wolf, A. (1995). *Sexual attraction and childhood association: A Chinese brief for Edward Westermarck.* Stanford, CA: Stanford University Press.

Zuckerman, M., Buchsbaum, M. S., & Murphy, D. L. (1980). Sensation seeking and its biological correlates. *Psychological Bulletin, 88,* 187–214.

11

Evolutionary Psychology Research Methods

DAVID P. SCHMITT

EVOLUTIONARY PSYCHOLOGY RESEARCH METHODS

When addressing the specific ways in which an organism's evolutionary past can influence its contemporary nature, biological scientists often invoke the concept of *adaptation* (Amundson, 1996; W. J. Bock, 1980). Although adaptations can be defined in many ways, most biologists consider adaptations to be those attributes of an organism that show evidence of "special design" for the purpose of increasing fitness (M. R. Rose & Lauder, 1996; Williams, 1966). Evidence of special design can come from showing that an attribute is extremely efficient, subtly complex, incredibly specialized, and emerges reliably in all members of a species. Evidence of functionality can come from showing that an attribute enhances fitness and leads to differential reproductive success relative to same-sex conspecifics (or at least would have done so in the ancestral past; see Crawford, 1998).

The general goal of evolutionary biology has been described as the programmatic search for each living organism's basic adaptations to life, or the "adaptationist program" (Mayr, 1983). For some, identifying all the biological adaptations that comprise human nature—the adaptationist program of humanity—is what the science of psychology should be all about (Buss, Haselton, Shackelford, Bleske, & Wakefield, 1998; M. Daly & M. Wilson, 1999; J. Panksepp & J. B. Panksepp, 2000; Tooby & Cosmides, 1992). Most evolutionary psychologists focus their research efforts on identifying human *psychological* adaptations—those features of human thought, emotion, and behavior that show evidence of special design for the purpose of enhancing fitness (G. R. Bock & Cardew, 1997; Thornhill, 1997). The ultimate objective of evolutionary psychology as a science is to reveal the specially designed psychological architecture of human nature, including its evolved computational adaptations, and to understand how these adaptations reliably influence the way contemporary humans think, feel, and behave (Barkow, Cosmides, & Tooby, 1992).

Evolutionary Psychology and Identifying Human Psychological Adaptations

Given the current limitations of evolutionary science as applied to humans, this might seem an exceptionally difficult task. For example, for ethical reasons, evolutionary scientists cannot inactivate or manipulate specific human genes, as they have with some insect species, in hopes of determining each gene's specific adaptive functions (Ridley, 2000). Even if such techniques were viable, most human genes interact in such complex ways with other genes, external environments, and developmental experiences that mapping the precise gene-protein-behavior pathways of all human psychological adaptations is, for the time being, beyond our scientific capability (Ridley, 2003).

One research technique evolutionary psychologists do have available for identifying human psychological adaptations is to use evolutionary *theories* as heuristic guides when looking for adaptations. For example, inclusive fitness theory (Hamilton, 1964) leads evolutionary psychologists to hypothesize certain kinds of familial helping adaptations. Reciprocal altruism theory (Axelrod & Hamilton, 1981; Trivers, 1971) assists evolutionary psychologists in uncovering adaptations of human friendship and coalition formation. Life history theory (Hill, 1993) guides researchers to adaptations for differentially expending effort on various types of relationships over the course of lives, as well as explaining why humans go about surviving and reproducing differently than other species do (Low, 1998). This basic "top-down" approach to identifying psychological adaptations—using theories to generate hypotheses that predict the special adaptive designs of human nature—has been incredibly productive over the last few decades (Buss, 1995, 2004) and continues to qualify evolutionary psychology as a "progressive" scientific paradigm (Coss & Charles, 2004; Ketelaar & Ellis, 2000; Lakatos, 1970). This is true both theoretically (evolutionary psychology continues to generate novel hypotheses and explain a wider and wider range of phenomena) and empirically (many of evolutionary psychology's hypotheses are accumulating continued research support).

Evolutionary psychologists also use "bottom-up" approaches, in which evidence of a psychological adaptation's special design is gathered and is then used to reverse-engineer the adaptive function of a given attribute (Dawkins, 1983; Pinker, 1997). Identifying human psychological adaptations in this manner is aided by the fact that evolutionary psychologists have a reasonably good idea of what adaptations will look like (G. R. Bock & Cardew, 1997; Buss et al., 1998). For example, most evolutionary psychologists expect that human adaptations will display *modularity* (Barrett & Kurzban, 2006; Pinker, 1997; Sperber, this volume). That is, each psychological adaptation should be relatively discrete from all other adaptations; each will have its own particular design with a limited array of functions (cf. Geary, 2000). It is true that adaptations feed into one another, such as when informational output from other adaptations is used in adaptive computations (e.g., Buston & Emlen, 2003). However, in general, psychological adaptations will be designed to accomplish specific tasks in an individual's life that, given a natural developmental environment, will tend to lead to greater survival and reproduction (Tooby & Cosmides, 1992). This idea is not new to psychology (Fodor, 1983), and evidence from neuropsychology and cognitive neuroscience has pointed to discrete mental functions associated with discrete parts of the brain for many years (Baron-Cohen, 1995; Haman, 2005; Hirshfeld & Gelman, 1994; Ponseti, Bosinski, Wolff, Peller, & Jansen, 2006). However, evolutionary psychologists tend to take an extremely design-specific view of the mind, and they argue that most human psychological functioning is decidedly modular in form (Carruthers & Chamberlin, 2000; D. D. Cummins & Allen, 1998; Pinker, 2002).

Of course, this view does not mean that every psychological adaptation has one and only one physical location in the human brain (Pitchford, 2001). Instead, modularity assumes that certain functions of the brain are relatively *domain-specific*. That is, each module of the mind (each psychological adaptation) is designed to accomplish specific goals, not general ones (Gallistel, 1995). This view of the human mind is somewhat controversial, in part, because it runs directly counter to the established social science view that humans have a predominantly domain-general brain (Skinner, 1956), with only a few basic mechanisms that simply learn whatever is taught by local culture (D. D. Cummins & R. Cummins, 1999; Pinker, 2002; Tooby, Cosmides, & Barrett, 2005). There is a substantial amount of evidence that the brain is, in some ways, domain-general (e.g., Geary, 2000; Mithen, 1996). Nevertheless, most evolutionary psychologists assume the mind has numerous mental modules with domain-specific functions, rather than only a few general modules with innumerable functions.

There are other features that help evolutionary psychologists to identify adaptations. Sometimes, these identifying features seem at odds with one another. For example, psychological adaptations are expected to be *universal*, in that all people everywhere share the same basic human nature (see D. E. Brown, 1991, on facultative or conditional adaptations). At the same time, adaptations are expected to be *interactive*, in that it takes exposure to certain environments (such as the skin friction needed to activate our callous-producing adaptations) for the adaptation to become activated and have an impact on psychology (e.g., Gangestad, Haselton, & Buss, 2006). Adaptations will also be *complex*, usually because they are created from previous adaptations from earlier in our species' phylogenetic history (see Andrews, Gangestad, & Matthews, 2002, on exaptation) and because functional trade-offs result in very few "optimal" phenotypic designs (Parker & Maynard Smith, 1990). At the same time, adaptations are expected to be *efficient* and *economical*, in the sense that little that is energetically wasteful is retained in an adaptation's structure over evolutionary time (Williams, 1966).

Thus, there are a lot of helpful clues when looking for evidence of psychological adaptation: "top-down" clues from heuristic theories and "bottom-up" clues from the special design features of functionality, modularity, complexity, and so forth. Still, how do evolutionary psychologists formally evaluate whether a given adaptation exists? What research methods do evolutionary psychologists use to scientifically demonstrate that a particular attribute has special design for the purpose of increasing fitness?

Evolutionary Research Methods for Identifying Psychological Adaptation

Evolutionary psychologists do not typically look at a specific human attribute and reflexively proclaim that it is the result of a biological adaptation (though critics often portray evolutionary psychology as a series of "just so" stories; see Gould, 1991; H. Rose & M. Rose, 2000). Rather, evolutionary psychologists tend to look at an attribute and ask a series of questions about design specificity and fitness. Many times, evolutionary psychologists build a case for a particular adaptation from both the top-down and the bottom-up, using well-reasoned theoretical rationale and multiple pieces of empirical evidence (M. Daly & M. Wilson, 1998; Holcomb, 1998; E. A. Smith, 2000). Although nothing in science is ever "True" with a capital "T" (Ketelaar & Ellis, 2000; Popper, 1959), with an elaborated "nomological network" of evidence (D. T. Campbell & Fiske, 1959; Cronbach & Meehl, 1955), evolutionary psychologists can, just like other psychologists, make scientific arguments for the valid existence of hypothetical constructs (see Schmitt & Pilcher, 2004). In the case of evolutionary psychology, these hypothetical constructs are the psychological adaptations that constitute our common human nature.

Perhaps more than other psychologists, evolutionary psychologists use a wide variety of evidentiary forms, ranging from self-report survey studies and behavioral experiments, to findings in genetics and medical science, to cross-species and cross-cultural comparisons, to ethnographies of foraging societies and theoretical computer modeling (Barkow et al., 1992; Holcomb, 1998; E. A. Smith, 2000). Andrews et al. (2002) listed six basic evolutionary psychology research methods for evaluating evidence of psychological adaptation: (a) phylogenetic comparisons, (b) fitness maximization evidence, (c) hypothesized fitness benefits in the ancestral past, (d) mathematical modeling

Table 11.1 Eight Categories of Research Methods Commonly Used in Evolutionary Psychology

Category 1: "Theoretical" Research Methods	Category 5: Genetic Research Methods
Evolutionary Biology Theories	Behavioral and Population Genetics
Adaptive Problems and Selection Pressures	Molecular Genetics
Computer and Algorithmic Modeling	Experimental Gene Mapping
Game Theory Simulations	Manipulation and Gene Replacement Studies
Artificial Intelligence	Developmental Evolutionary Biology
	Comparative Genetics
Category 2: Psychological Research Methods	
Self-Report Surveys	**Category 6: Phylogenetic Research Methods**
Informed Observer-Reports	Animal Ethology
Field Studies	Comparative Psychology
Field Experiments	Primatology
Experimental Manipulations	Physical Anthropology
Life Outcome Data	Paleontology
Public Documents	
Government Records	**Category 7: Hunter-Gatherer Research Methods**
Physiognomic and Bodily Assessments	Cultural Anthropology
	Ethnography
Category 3: Medical Research Methods	Human Ethology
Fertility and Fecundity Studies	Human Behavioral Ecology
Physical Health and Mortality Risk	Human Sociobiology
Mental Health and Happiness	
Psychiatric Disorders	**Category 8: Cross-Cultural Research Methods**
Nutrition and Exercise	Ethnological Comparisons
Darwinian Medicine	Human Universals and the "Universal People"
	Facultative and Conditional Adaptations
Category 4: Physiological Research Methods	Ecology-Dependent Adaptations
Neuroanatomical Structures	Multilevel Selection
Neurotransmitter Substrates	
Hormonal Substrates	
Pheromonal Mechanisms	
Cognitive Neuroscience	
Brain and Behavior Research	

evidence, (e) the theoretical links between an adaptation and a specific adaptive problem, and (f) empirical evidence of special design (see also Gangestad, this volume; Schmitt & Pilcher, 2004; Simpson & L. Campbell, 2005).

In Table 11.1, a schematic description is presented of eight categories of research methods that evolutionary psychologists use to evaluate evidence of psychological adaptation. This interdisciplinary categorization scheme covers a broad spectrum of evolution-relevant research, with each category representing a traditional subdiscipline within evolutionary science. Often, individual evolutionary researchers utilize only one or two of these eight basic methods, though the best evolutionary science uses more than one method (e.g., M. Daly & M. Wilson, 1998; Profet, 1992). Ultimately, other breakdowns of evolutionary disciplines are viable (e.g., comparative psychology and paleontology could reasonably be placed in different research method categories). However, this categorization has proven useful for formally evaluating the quality of adaptation evidence, as noted later in this chapter (see also Schmitt & Pilcher, 2004).

Theoretical research methods. Evolutionary psychologists frequently start with theories—often from the core principles of evolutionary biology—that heuristically guide their attention toward potential psychological adaptations (see Table 11.1). Nearly all evolutionary psychology is, of course, embedded within the general theory of natural selection (see Alcock, this volume; Darwin, 1859). However, other theories have helped to guide researchers to specific psychological adaptations. Sexual selection theory (Darwin, 1871) has helped guide psychologists to potential mating adaptations in humans (see Miller, 2000; Møller, this volume), as have other theories, such as parental investment theory (Trivers, 1972), parent-offspring conflict theory (Trivers, 1974), strategic pluralism theory (Gangestad & Simpson, 2000), and sexual strategies theory (Buss & Schmitt, 1993).

Inclusive fitness theory (Hamilton, 1964) has led evolutionary psychologists to look for certain familial helping adaptations (Burnstein, Crandall, & Kitayama, 1994; Cronin, 1991; West, this volume). Reciprocal altruism theory (Axelrod & Hamilton, 1981; Trivers, 1971) has assisted in uncovering adaptations of human friendship and coalitions (Axelrod, 1984; Johnson & Price, this volume). Life history theory (Hill, 1993; Kaplan & Gangestad, 2005; Morbeck, 1997) generates hypotheses concerning adaptations that cause people to expend effort on different types of relationships over time, as well as why humans go about surviving and reproducing differently than other species (Lancaster, 1994; Low, 1998; see also Chapter 3 of this book). If a hypothesized adaptation follows directly from an evolutionary biological theory, evolutionary psychologists express more confidence in the adaptation's existence (see Ketelaar & Ellis, 2000).

Other "theoretical" research methods include detailed cost-benefit analyses of adaptive solutions to specific adaptive problems and selection pressures (Buss, 1995; Cosmides & Tooby, 1992, 2004), algorithmic and computer modeling of particular adaptations (Gigerenzer & Selten, 2001; Simao & P. M. Todd, 2002), and game theory simulations of adaptations (Axelrod, 1984; Dugatkin & Reeve, 1998). Within the field of evolutionary psychology, artificial intelligence, neural networks, and theoretical model building have become increasingly important pieces of evidence for psychological adaptation (Grafen, 1991; Kohler & Gumerman, 2000; Tooby & DeVore, 1987).

Many of the research methods in the "Theoretical" section of Table 11.1 are, in practice, heavily empirical (e.g., game theory, modeling, and artificial intelligence) and so should not be considered merely theoretical. Again, other interdisciplinary breakdowns of evolutionary psychology are possible, and Table 11.1 is intended to be a broad—not definitive—schematic representation of evolutionary psychology research methods. As a group, the "theoretical" research methods continue to serve as a useful means for evaluating evidence of human psychological adaptation (G. R. Bock & Cardew, 1997).

Psychological research methods. Evolutionary psychologists use a variety of the research methods commonly used in psychological science (e.g., self-reports surveys, field studies, and experimental manipulations) to investigate whether a human attribute shows special design for the purpose of increasing fitness. For example, in seeking to reveal human psychological adaptations involving human sexuality, evolutionary psychologists have employed self-report surveys asking people about their own mate value (James, 2003; Quinsey, Book, & Lalumiere, 2001; Regan, 1998), mating effort (Giosan, 2006; Rowe, Vazsonyi, & Figueredo, 1997), mating strategies (J. M. Bailey,

Kirk, Zhu, Dunne, & N. G. Martin, 2000; Perusse, 1994; Simpson & Gangestad, 1991), mate preferences (Buss, 1989; Buss, Shackelford, Kirkpatrick, & Larsen, 2001; Graziano, Jenson-Campbell, M. Todd, & Finch, 1997; Sprecher, Sullivan, & Hatfield, 1994), mating desires (Regan & Dreyer, 1999; Schmitt et al., 2003), and personal beliefs and judgments about sexual offers and romantic tactic effectiveness (Cashdan, 1993; Greitemeyer, Hengmith, & P. Fischer, 2005; Walters & Crawford, 1994).

Similarly, evolutionary psychologists use surveys to ask people about their current and past romantic partners (Buss, 1994), their same-sex competitors (Bleske-Rechek & Shackelford, 2001; Speed & Gangestad, 1997), and others that they know relatively well (i.e., informed observations about friends; Bleske-Rechek & Buss, 2001). Evolutionary psychologists ask individuals what they believe people in general are like (Barr, Bryan, & Kenrick, 2002) and what they would personally do under different situations and hypothetical conditions (Kruger & M. L. Fisher, 2005; N. P. Li, M. J. Bailey, Kenrick, & Linsenmeier, 2002). Finally, evolutionary psychologists use cognitive ability tests to evaluate the validity of potential psychological adaptations (e.g., Silverman & Choi, 2006).

Evolutionary psychologists also measure objective behaviors with both field studies and field experiments. For example, evolutionary psychologists have examined people's sexual attitudes and mating behaviors in real-life settings (Kurzban & Weeden, 2005; Perper, 1985), including using confederates who gauge a stranger's reaction to an offer of having casual sex (Clark, 1990; Clark & Hatfield, 1989). Evolutionary psychologists have experimentally manipulated subjects to examine whether attributes such as physical attractiveness, social status, and personal resemblance really have an impact of romantic attraction behavior, mate selection, relationship investment, and self-assessment (Cunningham, 1986; Kenrick, Neuberg, Zierk, & Krones, 1994; Platek, 2002; Roney, 2003; Schmitt, Couden, & M. Baker, 2001; Townsend & Levy, 1990; Townsend & Wasserman, 1998).

Evolutionary psychologists have used research methods involving life outcome data, such as evaluating whether people's self-reported behaviors actually match their objectively recorded public behaviors. For example, evolutionary psychologists have related people's stated sexual preferences with their actual sexual behavior using archival marriage records (Kenrick & Keefe, 1992; Low, 2000), content analysis of personal ads (S. Davis, 1990; Pawlowski & Dunbar, 1999; Wiederman, 1993), mail order bride preferences (Minervini & McAndrew, 2006), and economic statistics on pornography, prostitution, and romance novel consumption (Ellis & Symons, 1990; Malamuth, 1996; M. McGuire & Gruter, 2003; Salmon & Symons, 2003). Other life outcome research methods include analyses of government records and public documents regarding marital violence (M. Daly & M. Wilson, 1988), divorce (Betzig, 1989), child abuse (M. Daly & M. Wilson, 1998), and child support (Shackelford, Weekes-Shackelford, & Schmitt, 2005).

Finally, evolutionary psychologists use research methods involving physiognomic and bodily assessments to investigate evidence of psychological adaptation (e.g., Gallup et al., 2003; Perrett et al., 1999; Rhodes & Zebrowitz, 2002). Psychological adaptations within the realm of human mating appear to be sensitive to finger length ratios (Manning, 2002), shoulder-to-hip and waist-to-hip ratios (Hughes & Gallup, 2003; Singh & Young, 1995), shapes of breasts and buttocks (Low, R. D. Alexander, & Noonan, 1987), location of body tattoos and scarification (Singh & Bronstad, 1997), degrees of facial and bodily symmetry (Gangestad & Thornhill, 2003; Rikowski & Grammer, 1999; Soler et al., 2003), degrees of facial masculinity and neoteny (Johnston, Hagel, Franklin, Fink, & Grammer, 2001; D. Jones, 1995; Mueller & Mazur, 1998), and many of these adaptations are further specially designed to vary across women's ovulatory cycles (Gangestad & Thornhill, 1998; Pillsworth & Haselton, 2006; Regan, 1996).

Using a wide range of classic psychological research methods—self-report surveys, informed-observer reports, field studies and experimental manipulations, life outcome data such as public documents and government records, and physiognomic and bodily measurements—evolutionary psychologists have documented evidence of functionality and "special design" for many human attributes. These specialized attributes, according to evolutionary psychologists, are possible adaptations that reside within the psychological architecture of human nature (G. R. Bock & Cardew, 1997; Buss et al., 1998; Thornhill, 1997).

Medical research methods. In addition to using the standard methods of psychological science, evolutionists often invoke the different research methods of medical science when investigating human adaptations (Stearns, 1998). For example, they sometimes look at the modern fertility, physical health, and mental well-being consequences of certain psychological attributes (R. R. Baker & Bellis, 1995; Faer, Hendriks, Abed, & Figueredo, 2005; Trevathan, E. O. Smith, & McKenna, 1999). These research methods often have applied value in the domain of psychiatric illness (Keller & Nesse, 2006; Murphy, 2005; Troisi, this volume), life satisfaction and happiness (Grinde, 2002; Kanazawa, 2004), and exercise and nutrition (Cordain & Friel, 2005; Eaton, Shostak, & Konner, 1987; Thiessen, 1998).

It is often assumed that morphologies and behaviors that lead to better health and more prolific reproduction today are probably linked, in some way, to our basic evolved psychology (Betzig, 1998; Rhodes & Zebrowitz, 2002; Singh & Young, 1995). However, evolutionary psychologists also acknowledge that many of the mental and physical problems among modern human populations may be due, in part, to fundamental breakdowns of our evolved psychological adaptations, mismatches between modern environments and the ancestral environments in which our psychological adaptations evolved, or extreme activations of normally functional psychological adaptations (Crawford, 1998). Many of these medical research methods within evolutionary psychology have, as a group, been dubbed the emerging field of "Darwinian Medicine" (Nesse & Williams, 1994).

Physiological research methods. Evolutionary psychologists also seek out specific physiological substrates of psychological adaptations (Flinn, Ward, & Noone, 2005), including linking hormones such as testosterone to sexual strategies and mate value (Mazur & Booth, 1998; Udry & B. C. Campbell, 1994). If a highly specialized and fitness-promoting psychological attribute is linked to discrete neuronal structures and neurotransmitter pathways within the brain (H. E. Fisher, Arthur, Mashek, H. Li, & L. L. Brown, 2002; Haman, 2005; Kohl & Francoeur, 1995), to hormone levels in the blood (G. M. Alexander & Sherwin, 1991; Flinn et al., 2005; Penton-Voak & Chen, 2004), or is associated with specialized chemicals used in communication (Kohl & Francoeur, 1995; Thornhill & Gangestad, 1999), and this design-specificity is linked to function, evolutionists can argue more strongly that the phenomenon represents a psychological adaptation (see Baron-Cohen, this volume). Within psychological science, this major research method is sometimes referred to as "cognitive neuroscience" or "brain and behavior" research.

In the domain of human emotion (see Frank, this volume), evolutionary psychologists have shown that many specific emotions—ranging from sadness to joy—are likely psychological adaptations. Physiological research methods have documented that certain emotions are tied to specific facial expressions, patterns of brain activation, neurological structures, and functionality of outcomes (Ekman, 1973; Johnston, 1999; Nesse, 1990; Plutchik, 1980). This includes critical emotions such as fear (I. M. Marks & Nesse, 1994) and its relation to specific phobias (Ohman & Mineka, 2001, 2003), as well as depression and its links to cognitive accuracy and support solicitation (Sloman, Gilbert, & Hasey, 2003; Watson & Andrews, 2002).

Genetic research methods. Evolutionary psychologists sometimes rely on genetics to make a case for human adaptation (see Brown, this volume; Ridley, 2003). Although it is true that most evolutionary psychologists assume that all people share the same basic human nature (Tooby & Cosmides, 1990), evidence from population and quantitative genetics, including pedigree analysis (Pettay, Kruuk, Jokela, & Lumma, 2005), suggests that there are some genetic differences among individuals that may be linked to adaptive variation (see Bouchard & Loehlin, 2001; Cavalli-Sforza & Bodmer, 1999; Maynard Smith, 1998; McGue & Lykken, 1992; D. S. Wilson, 1994).

At the same time, many molecular geneticists are looking at specific genes in hopes of identifying a common human genetic heritage, against which individual genes linked to diseases and to normal adaptive variations in our common genome can be mapped (Comings, Muhleman, Johnson, & MacMurray, 2002; Hamer & Copeland, 1994; Moffitt, Caspi, & Rutter, 2006; Ridley, 2000). Although not always permissible in humans, gene replacement and gene manipulation studies in nonhuman animals can reveal functional details related to human adaptations (Ridley, 2003). The field of evolutionary developmental biology (or "evo-devo") is a quickly emerging subdiscipline in biology and genetics that will be critical to our future understanding of how psychological adaptations emerge and interact with predictable features of the environment over developmental time (see Mealey, 2000; West-Eberhard, 2003). Finally, comparative genetics methods allow us to trace the evolution of specific attributes deep into our ancestral past (S. B. Carroll, 2006; Jensen-Seaman, Deinard, & Kidd, 2001).

Phylogenetic research methods. As schematically portrayed under phylogenetic research methods (see Table 11.1), evolutionary psychologists often rely on cross-species (Alcock, 1993; M. Daly & M. Wilson, 1999), comparative (Gomez, 2004; Greenberg & Haraway, 1998; Hausfater & Hrdy, 1984), and ethological analyses (Hinde, 1982; Tinbergen, 1963) to make arguments of psychological adaptation (see Collard, this volume; Harvey & Purvis, 1991). For example, in comparing several species at the same time, many studies have suggested that humans, as do other animals with promiscuous mating strategies, likely possess specific psychological adaptations involving sperm competition (Møller, 1988; Shackelford & LeBlanc, 2001). This research method, closely related to the subdiscipline of "physical anthropology," has been particularly prominent in comparisons across primate species (de Waal, 1982; Dixson, 1998; Wrangham, 1995), including cross-fostering methods in which chimpanzees are raised by humans (Chalcraft & Gardner, 2005).

Physical anthropologists and evolutionary psychologists also use paleontological and cladistic evidence (Haun, Rapold, Call, Janzen, & Levinson, 2006). If converging lines of evidence suggest that an attribute had a logical development across our historical phylogenetic development (S. Jones, R. Martin, & Pilbeam, 1992; Leakey, 1994), or displays evidence of homology across modern species (especially across primates), this can be used as evidence of adaptation (Fraley, Brumbaugh, & M. J. Marks, 2005; Maestripieri & Roney, 2006; Wrangham, 1993). For example, archeological evidence of prehuman and primate fossils suggests that sex differences in physical size have a long evolutionary history in the human lineage and indicates that many psychological sex differences likely emerged millions of years ago (Gaulin & Boster, 1985; Gaulin & Sailer, 1984). Using cross-species comparisons to examine analogous adaptations is also common (Alcock, 1993; Thornhill & Palmer, 2000; Trivers, 1985; Weingart, Mitchell, Richerson, & Maasen, 1997).

Hunter-gatherer research methods. As noted under "hunter-gatherer" research methods (see Table 11.1), evolutionary psychologists seek out information generated by cultural anthropologists who ethnographically study hunter-gatherer cultures when evaluating human adaptation (e.g., Chagnon, 1992; Hill & Hurtado, 1996; Howell, 1979; Lee, 1979; Marlowe, 2004). Humans have spent most of our species' evolutionary history living a foraging lifestyle as hunters and gatherers (Foley, 1996; O. D. Jones et al., 1992). Our adaptations, therefore, were designed to function in that type of culture (Crawford, 1998). By looking at contemporary cultures that still practice a foraging way of life (Kelly, 1995; Lee & R. Daly, 2000; Marlowe, 2005), and by comparing and contrasting those foraging cultures along with extant data on foraging cultures studied by anthropologists in the past (Broude & Greene, 1980; Ford & Beach, 1951; Korotayev & Kazankov, 2003; Marlowe, 2003; Pasternak, C. Ember, & M. Ember, 1997; Whyte, 1980), evolutionary psychologists can build a portrait (albeit a sketchy one) of *Homo sapiens* distinctive ancestral past and the adaptive selective pressures that resided in it (Foley, 1996; Forsyth, 1993; Tooby & DeVore, 1987).

Such a portrait is referred to by D. E. Brown (1991) as the ethnography of the "Universal People." Thinking of life among the Universal People has served as a useful tool for identifying several potential human psychological adaptations. For example, evolutionary psychologists have explored psychological adaptations regarding fire, learning (Kessler, 2006), music (Graham, 2006), math (Cruz, 2006), and emotional reactions to natural landscapes (M. A. Fischer & Shrout, 2006) and flowers (Haviland-Jones, Rosario, P. Wilson, & T. R. McGuire, 2005), and they have considered the function of all of these potential adaptations within the context of a foraging way of life. In additional to cultural anthropology, many closely related fields study humans in a wide range of "natural" environments (e.g., horticultural, pastoral, and small-scale farming cultures; Henrich et al., 2004) and in so doing, they try to evaluate evidence of psychological adaptation. This basic approach includes many subdisciplines across biology and anthropology, including human ethology (e.g., Eibl-Eibesfeldt, 1989), human behavioral ecology (J. R. Krebs & Davies, 1997; E. A. Smith & Winterhalder, 1992), and human sociobiology (E. O. Wilson, 1975).

Cross-cultural research methods. Finally, evolutionary psychologists frequently employ cross-cultural research methods to ethnologically evaluate evidence of psychological adaptation (e.g., Cunningham, Roberts, Barbee, Druen, & Wu, 1995; Frayser, 1985; Gangestad et al., 2006; R. L. Munroe & R. H. Munroe, 1997). Often, evolutionary psychologists study a range of cultures from foraging to modern industrial nations (Betzig, 1997; Clarke & Low, 2001; Cronk, Chagnon, & Irons, 2000; Smuts, 1995). If a psychological attribute shows up in every culture, or conditionally emerges given exposure to certain predictable ecological stimuli (e.g., Barber, 2002; Belsky, 1999; Gangestad & Buss, 1993; Low, 2000; Pedersen, 1991; Schmitt, 2005), then evolutionists are in a better position to argue for the existence of a psychological adaptation (D. E. Brown, 1991). The possibility of multilevel selection as a force across cultures in human evolution has traditionally served as an important consideration within evolutionary psychology (Boyd & Richerson, 1985; Lumsden & E. O. Wilson, 1981; McAndrew, 2002; Richerson & Boyd, 2005; D. S. Wilson, 2003).

Carrying out the task of identifying all of our psychological adaptations will most certainly be difficult, and it will be fraught with many pitfalls and errors (Mayr, 1983). In the end, whether our evolutionary biology plays a fundamental role in a given psychological attribute will be determined by cross-disciplinary integration in the form of nomological networks of evidence. This basic approach has long been used by traditional psychologists to provide evidence for all kinds of psychological attributes that one cannot visibly see, but which nonetheless exist (Cronbach & Meehl, 1955). Because of the interdisciplinary nature of evolutionary psychology, construct validation techniques—including nomological networks of evidence—may be particularly suited to the task of evaluating whether a given human attribute represents a psychological adaptation.

Formally Evaluating Evidence of Psychological Adaptation

Schmitt and Pilcher (2004) outlined a tentative set of standards for evaluating nomological networks of psychological adaptation evidence. There are two important dimensions along which nomological networks can vary—evidentiary *breadth* and evidentiary *depth*. For example, some nomological networks might include only one research method listed in Table 11.1, whereas others might include evidence across all eight categories of research methods. In practice, extreme breadth has rarely been reached, in part because evolutionary psychology is a relatively young science. Based on traditional norms for evaluating the validity of measuring psychological constructs (Whitley, 1996), one category of adaptation evidence should be considered a "minimal" level of evidentiary breadth. Two or three categories can be considered "moderate" evidentiary breadth. Four or five categories of evidence can be considered "extensive" evidentiary breadth, and six or more categories can be considered "exemplary" evidentiary breadth (Schmitt & Pilcher, 2004).

In addition to breadth, nomological networks can vary in evidentiary depth. It would be problematic, however, to evaluate the depth of evidence by simply totaling the number of supportive research findings within each category of Table 11.1. Research study quality depends on several factors, including whether multiple modes of measurement are used, whether methodological rigor and control are present, and whether sampling biases have been avoided. For example, a single survey study based on a representative national sample within the United States (Sprecher et al., 1994) might be considered of higher quality than dozens of survey studies using convenience samples of college students from around the world (Buss, 1989).

It is probably best to evaluate the depth of a nomological network by looking at the evidence across all categories and making a judgment as to whether the overall depth is minimal (i.e., single studies with one mode of measurement, poor methodological control, and unrepresentative sampling), moderate (i.e., at least two studies, more than one mode of measurement, good levels of control, good sampling techniques), extensive (numerous studies within each category, more than two modes of measurement, high levels of control, high sampling quality), or exemplary (dozens of studies, multiple modes of measurement, highest levels of control, true representative sampling). This nomenclature for describing nomological networks of adaptation evidence is only a tentative guideline and is based on traditional norms for evaluating the validity of psychological constructs (Whitley, 1996).

Pregnancy Sickness as a Psychological Adaptation

One example of a potential psychological adaptation that has received considerable empirical support is pregnancy sickness. Profet (1988, 1992) accumulated a wide range of research evidence and concluded that pregnancy sickness is likely a psychological adaptation. For example, she noted that certain plant foods contain toxins, specifically teratogens, that are not especially harmful to adults, but when pregnant women eat them, they cause birth defects and actually induce abortions. This finding provided a potential adaptive problem and an accompanying selection pressure that may have been theoretically strong enough to have forged a psychological adaptation causing pregnancy sickness. Profet also found in medical science that women who suffer from severe pregnancy sickness—and as a result, consume far less teratogens—tend to have fewer miscarriages and fewer babies with birth defects. This was clear evidence of *functionality*. Profet noted that women with pregnancy sickness do not avoid all foods. They selectively avoid only certain types of foods, especially avoid foods that are bitter or pungent, highly flavored, and novel. These are exactly the foods that normally contain the most teratogens. This was evidence of *special design*. The adaptation was designed to have women specifically avoid only toxin-containing foods.

Profet (1988, 1992) documented that pregnancy sickness typically begins only after the embryo has started forming its major organ systems, about three weeks after conception, exactly when it is most susceptive to the toxins present in the bitter foods. Conversely, pregnancy sickness wanes when the embryo's organs are nearly complete and the absolute need for nutrients grows. Again, the adaptation was showing signs of design-specificity. In her review of the literature on pregnancy sickness, Profet found that women's sense of smell becomes hypersensitive during pregnancy, and then less sensitive thereafter. Profet also laid out a physiological pathway from specific areas of brain to the olfactory system of nose by which pregnancy sickness likely works.

Profet (1988, 1992) also found that pregnancy sickness is probably a cross-cultural universal. Not every pregnant woman experiences vomiting and nausea, but Profet found that most women experience some forms of pregnancy sickness. For example, nearly 100% of pregnant women experience nausea, vomiting, or at least some form of food aversion. Many hunting and gathering cultures in Africa and Oceania practice ritualistic clay eating during pregnancy. The types of clay they have pregnant women eat tend to detoxify the body and lead to less birth defects and abortions.

Profet (1988, 1992) placed pregnancy sickness in a phylogenetic perspective by relating the way humans naturally collect food to the way other animals collect their food. Species in which many different and new types of plants are always being eaten would be at extreme risk for ingesting plant toxins during pregnancy. Humans are experimental omnivores. In our natural foraging habitat we tend to eat new plant foods all of the time. From a cross-species perspective, it would be likely that humans possess pregnancy sickness adaptations.

The nomological network of evidence identified by Profet (1988, 1992) strongly suggested that women possess an evolved psychological adaptation designed to protect their developing child from ingested toxins. It is *functional* in that it solves the problem of avoiding toxins that can hurt a developing fetus. It is *design-specific* in that it emerges at specific times and serves as a solution to only this problem. Of course, the final evidence will come from molecular geneticists finding the genes associated with this adaptation, and developmental evolutionists outlining how experience feeds into this genetic predisposition. At this point, however, the evidence is convincing to many that the pregnancy sickness phenotype is caused by an adaptation residing somewhere in the genotype of human females (see also Flaxman & Sherman, 2000; Huxley, 2000). Using the tentative guidelines described earlier for evaluating the quality of this evidence, the nomological network of pregnancy sickness as a psychological adaptation has both "exemplary" breadth and "exemplary" depth.

Research Methods and Adaptations Across Psychological Science

There are many examples of evolutionary psychologists embedding human psychological adaptations within well-researched nomological networks of evidence (see G. R. Bock & Cardew, 1997; Buss et al., 1998; Cartwright, 2000). Psychologists have used a wide range of the evolutionary research methods outlined in this chapter to investigate adaptations involving crime (M. Daly & M. Wilson, 1988; O. D. Jones, 2005), aggression (Duntely, 2005; Kirkpatrick, Waugh, Valencia, & Webster, 2002; Schaller, this volume), altruism (Burnstein, 2005; Fehr & Fischbacher, 2003; Kenrick, this volume), attachment (Belsky, 1999; Chisholm, 1996), family relations (Barber, 2003; J. N. Davis & M. Daly, 1997; Emlen, 1995; Low, 1989; G. E. Weisfeld & C. C. Weisfeld, 2002), religion (Atran, 2002, this volume; Dennett, 2006; Kirkpatrick, 2005), morality (R. D. Alexander, 1987; D. Krebs, 2005, this volume; Ridley, 1996; Thompson, 1995; Walter, 2006), language (Dunbar, 1996; MacNeilage & P. L. Davis, 2005; Pinker, 1994), culture (Barkow, 1989; Cronk, 1999; Tooby & Cosmides, 1992), literature (J. Carroll, 2005; Gottschall & D. S. Wilson, 2005; Kruger, M. L. Fisher, & Jobling, 2003), aesthetics (Aiken, 1998; J. Carroll, 1995; Thornhill, 1998), creativity (Griskevicius, Cialdini, & Kenrick, 2006; Miller, 2000), memory (Klein, Cosmides, Tooby, & Chance, 2002), and consciousness (Bering & Shackelford, 2004; Carruthers, 2002; Dennett, 1991; Griffin, 1981). These are just some of the areas in which evolutionary psychologists have used their wide range of research methods to confirm that certain psychological attributes show reliable signs of design-specificity and functionality.

At present, the research methods of evolutionary psychology—along with evolutionists' general goal of revealing the specially designed psychological architecture of human nature—are being more and more frequently applied across the traditional subdisciplines of psychology. This includes such subdisciplines as social psychology (Kenrick, Maner, & N. P. Li, 2005; Simpson & Kenrick, 1997), developmental psychology (Bjorklund & Blasi, 2005; Bjorklund & Pellegrini, 2002; Ellis, this volume; G. E. Weisfeld, 1999), personality psychology (Buss, 1997; Figueredo et al., 2005; MacDonald, 1998; D. S. Wilson, 1994), cognitive psychology (Barrett & Kurzban, 2006; Kimura, 1999; P. M. Todd, Hertwig, & Hoffrage, 2005), sensation and perception (M. A. Fischer & Shrout, 2006; Silverman & Choi, 2006), industrial-organizational psychology (Saad & Gill, 2000), political psychology (Crawford & Salmon, 2004; O. D. Jones, 2005; Somit & Peterson, 2003), clinical psychology (Keller & Nesse, 2006; Nesse, 2005), and motivation and emotion (French, Kamil, & Leger, 2001; Haviland-Jones et al., 2005; Johnston, 1999; Nesse, 1990). Ultimately, all of psychological science will benefit from researchers building cross-disciplinary nomological networks of evidence—using biological theories, psychological research, medical science, physiological methods, genetics, phylogenetics, hunter-gatherer studies, and cross-cultural approaches—to seek out, confirm, and integrate our understanding of the psychological adaptations that constitute human nature.

REFERENCES

Aiken, N. E. (1998). *The biological origins of art.* Westport, CT: Praeger.

Alcock, J. (1993). *Animal behavior: An evolutionary approach* (5th ed.). Sunderland, MA: Sinauer.

Alexander, G. M., & Sherwin, B. B. (1991). The association between testosterone, sexual arousal, and selective attention for erotic stimuli in men. *Hormones and Behavior, 25,* 367–381.

Alexander, R. D. (1987). *The biology of moral systems.* Hawthorne, NY: de Gruyter.

Amundson, R. (1996). Historical development of the concept of adaptation. In M. R. Ruse & G. V. Lauder (Eds.), *Adaptation* (pp. 11–53). San Diego, CA: Academic Press.

Andrews, P. W., Gangestad, S. W., & Matthews, D. (2002). Adaptationism: How to carry out an exaptationist program. *Behavioral and Brain Sciences, 25,* 489–553.

Atran, S. (2002). *In gods we trust: The evolutionary landscape of religion.* New York: Oxford University Press.

Axelrod, R. (1984). *The evolution of cooperation.* New York: Basic Books.

Axelrod, R., & Hamilton, W. D. (1981). The evolution of cooperation. *Science, 211,* 1390–1396.

Bailey, J. M., Kirk, K. M., Zhu, G., Dunne, M. P., & Martin, N. G. (2000). Do individual differences in sociosexuality represent genetic or environmentally contingent strategies? Evidence from the Australian twin registry. *Journal of Personality and Social Psychology, 78,* 537–545.

Baker, R. R., & Bellis, M. A. (1995). *Human sperm competition.* London: Chapman & Hall.

Barber, N. (2002). On the relationship between fertility and geographic latitude: A cross-national study. *Cross-Cultural Research, 36,* 3–15.

Barber, N. (2003). Paternal investment prospects and cross-national differences in single parenthood. *Cross-Cultural Research, 37,* 163–177.

Barkow, J. H. (1989). *Darwin, sex, and status: Biological approaches to mind and culture.* Toronto, Ontario, Canada: University of Toronto Press.

Barkow, J. H., Cosmides, L., & Tooby, J. (Eds.). (1992). *The adapted mind: Evolutionary psychology and the generation of culture.* New York: Oxford University Press.

Baron-Cohen, S. (1995). *Mindblindness.* Cambridge, MA: MIT Press.

Barr, A., Bryan, A., & Kenrick, D. T. (2002). Sexual peak: Socially shared cognitions about desire, frequency, and satisfaction in men and women. *Personal Relationships, 9,* 287–299.

Barrett, H. C., & Kurzban, R. (2006). Modularity in cognition: Framing the debate. *Psychological Review, 113,* 628–647.

Belsky, J. (1999). Modern evolutionary theory and patterns of attachment. In J. Cassidy & P. R. Shaver (Eds.), *Handbook of attachment* (pp. 141–161). New York: Guilford.

Bering, J. M., & Shackelford, T. K. (2004). The causal role of consciousness: A conceptual addendum to human evolutionary psychology. *Review of General Psychology, 8,* 227–248.

Betzig, L. (1989). Causes of conjugal dissolution: A cross-cultural study. *Current Anthropology, 30,* 654–676.

Betzig, L. L. (Ed.). (1997). *Human nature: A critical reader.* New York: Oxford University Press.

Betzig, L. L. (1998). Not whether to count babies, but which. In C. B. Crawford & D. Krebs (Eds.), *Handbook of evolutionary psychology: Ideas, issues, and applications* (pp. 265–273). Mahwah, NJ: Lawrence Erlbaum Associates, Inc.

Bjorklund, D. F., & Blasi, C. H. (2005). Evolutionary developmental psychology. In D. M. Buss (Ed.), *The handbook of evolutionary psychology* (pp. 828–850). Hoboken, NJ: John Wiley & Sons.

Bjorklund, D. F., & Pellegrini, A. D. (2002). *The origins of human nature: Evolutionary developmental psychology.* Washington, DC: American Psychological Association.

Bleske-Rechek, A. L., & Buss, D. M. (2001). Opposite-sex friendship: Sex differences and similarities in initiation, selection, and dissolution. *Personality & Social Psychology Bulletin, 27,* 1310–1323.

Bleske-Rechek, A. L., & Shackelford, T. K. (2001). Poaching, promiscuity, and deceit: Combating mating rivalry in same-sex friendships. *Personal Relationships, 8*, 407–424.

Bock, G. R., & Cardew, G. (Eds.). (1997). *Characterizing human psychological adaptations.* West Sussex, U.K.: John Wiley & Sons.

Bock, W. J. (1980). The definition and recognition of biological adaptation. *American Zoologist, 20*, 217–222.

Bouchard, T. J., Jr., & Loehlin, J. C. (2001). Genes, personality and evolution. *Behavior Genetics, 31*, 243–273.

Boyd, R., & Richerson, P. J. (1985). *Culture and the evolutionary process.* Chicago: University of Chicago Press.

Broude, G. J., & Greene, S. J. (1980). Cross-cultural codes on twenty sexual attitudes and practices. In H. Barry III & A. Schlegel (Eds.), *Cross-cultural samples and codes* (pp. 313–333). Pittsburgh, PA: University of Pittsburgh Press.

Brown, D. E. (1991). *Human universals.* New York: McGraw-Hill.

Burnstein, E. (2005). Altruism and genetic relatedness. In D. M. Buss (Ed.), *The handbook of evolutionary psychology* (pp. 528–551). Hoboken, NJ: John Wiley & Sons.

Burnstein, E., Crandall, C., & Kitayama, S. (1994). Some neo-Darwinian rules for altruism: Weighing cues for inclusive fitness as a function of the biological importance of the decision. *Journal of Personality and Social Psychology, 67*, 773–789.

Buss, D. M. (1989). Sex differences in human mate preferences: Evolutionary hypotheses tested in 37 cultures. *Behavioral and Brain Sciences, 12*, 1–49.

Buss, D. M. (1994). *The evolution of desire.* New York: Basic Books.

Buss, D. M. (1995). Evolutionary psychology: A new paradigm for psychological science. *Psychological Inquiry, 6*, 1–30.

Buss, D. M. (1997). Evolutionary foundations of personality. In R. Hogan (Ed.), *Handbook of personality psychology* (pp. 317–344). London: Academic Press.

Buss, D. M. (2004). *Evolutionary psychology: The new science of the mind* (2nd ed.). Boston: Allyn & Bacon.

Buss, D. M., Haselton, M. G., Shackelford, T. K., Bleske, A. L., & Wakefield, J. C. (1998). Adaptations, exaptations, and spandrels. *American Psychologist, 53*, 533–548.

Buss, D. M., & Schmitt, D. P. (1993). Sexual Strategies Theory: An evolutionary perspective on human mating. *Psychological Review, 100*, 204–232.

Buss, D. M., Shackelford, T. K., Kirkpatrick, L. A., & Larsen, R. J. (2001). A half century of mate preferences: The cultural evolution of values. *Journal of Marriage & the Family, 63*, 491–503.

Buston, P. M., & Emlen, S. T. (2003). Cognitive processes underlying human mate choice: The relationship between self-perception and mate preferences in Western society. *Proceedings of the National Academy of Sciences, 100*, 8805–8810.

Campbell, D. T., & Fiske, D. W. (1959). Convergent and discriminant validation by the multitrait-multimethod matrix. *Psychological Bulletin, 56*, 81–105.

Carroll, J. (1995). *Evolution and literary theory.* Columbia: University of Missouri Press.

Carroll, J. (2005). Literature and evolutionary psychology. In D. M. Buss (Ed.), *The handbook of evolutionary psychology* (pp. 931–952). Hoboken, NJ: John Wiley & Sons.

Carroll, S. B. (2006). *The making of the fittest: DNA and the ultimate forensic record of evolution.* New York: W. W. Norton.

Carruthers, P. (2002). The evolution of consciousness. In P. Carruthers & A. Chamberlain (Eds.), *Evolution and the human mind: Modularity, language and meta-cognition* (pp. 254–276). Cambridge, U.K.: Cambridge University Press.

Carruthers, P., & Chamberlin, A. (Eds.). (2000). *Evolution and the human mind: Modularity, language, and meta-cognition.* Cambridge, U.K.: Cambridge University Press.

Cartwright, J. (2000). *Evolution and human behavior.* Cambridge, MA: MIT Press.

Cashdan, E. (1993). Attracting mates: Effects of paternal investment on mate attraction strategies. *Ethology and Sociobiology, 14*, 1–24.

Cavalli-Sforza, L. L., & Bodmer, W. F. (1999). *The genetics of human populations.* Mineola, NY: Dover.

Chagnon, N. A. (1992). *Yanomamö: The last days of Eden.* San Diego, CA: Harcourt Brace Jovanovich.

Chalcraft, V. J., & Gardner, R. A. (2005). Cross-fostered chimpanzees modulate signs of American Sign Language. *Gesture, 5*, 107–119.

Chisholm, J. S. (1996). The evolutionary ecology of attachment organization. *Human Nature, 7,* 1–38.

Clark, R. D. (1990). The impact of AIDS on gender differences in willingness to engage in casual sex. *Journal of Applied Social Psychology, 20,* 771–782.

Clark, R. D., & Hatfield, E. (1989). Gender differences in receptivity to sexual offers. *Journal of Psychology and Human Sexuality, 2,* 39–55.

Clarke, A. L., & Low, B. S. (2001). Testing evolutionary hypotheses with demographic data. *Population and Development Review, 27,* 633–660.

Comings, D. E., Muhleman, D., Johnson, J. P., & MacMurray, J. P. (2002). Parent-daughter transmission of the androgen receptor gene as an explanation of the effect of father absence on age of menarche. *Child Development, 73,* 1046–1051.

Cordain, L., & Friel, J. (2005). *The Paleo diet for athletes: A nutritional formula for peak athletic performance.* Emmaus, PA: Rodale.

Cosmides, L., & Tooby, J. (1992). Cognitive adaptations for social exchange. In J. H. Barkow, L. Cosmides, & J. Tooby (Eds.), *The adapted mind: Evolutionary psychology and the generation of culture* (pp. 163–228). New York: Oxford University Press.

Cosmides, L., & Tooby, J. (2004). Social exchange: The evolutionary design of a neurocognitive system. In M. S. Gazzaniga (Ed.), *The cognitive neurosciences* (Vol. 3, pp. 1295–1308). Cambridge, MA: MIT Press.

Coss, R. G., & Charles, E. P. (2004). The role of evolutionary hypotheses in psychological research: Instincts, affordances, and relic sex differences. *Ecological Psychology, 16,* 199–236.

Crawford, C. B. (1998). Environments and adaptations: Then and now. In C. B. Crawford & D. Krebs (Eds.), *Handbook of evolutionary psychology: Ideas, issues, and applications* (pp. 275–302). Mahwah, NJ: Lawrence Erlbaum Associates, Inc

Crawford, C. B., & Salmon, C. (Eds.). (2004). *Evolutionary psychology, public policy, and personal decisions.* New York: Lawrence Erlbaum Associates, Inc.

Cronbach, L. J., & Meehl, P. E. (1955). Construct validity in psychological tests. *Psychological Bulletin, 52,* 281–302.

Cronin, H. (1991). *The ant and the peacock: Altruism and sexual selection from Darwin to today.* New York: Cambridge University Press.

Cronk, L. (1999). *That complex whole: Culture and the evolution of human behavior.* Boulder, CO: Westview.

Cronk, L., Chagnon, N. A., & Irons, W. (Eds.). (2000). *Adaptation and human behavior: An anthropological perspective.* New York: de Gruyter.

Cruz, H. (2006). Towards a Darwinian approach to mathematics. *Foundations of Science, 11,* 157–196.

Cummins, D. D., & Allen, C. (Eds.). (1998). *The evolution of mind.* New York: Oxford University Press.

Cummins, D. D., & Cummins, R. (1999). Biological preparedness and evolutionary explanation. *Cognition, 73,* B37–B53.

Cunningham, M. R. (1986). Measuring the physical in physical attractiveness: Quasi-experiments on the sociobiology of female facial beauty. *Journal of Personality and Social Psychology, 50,* 925–935.

Cunningham, M. R., Roberts, R., Barbee, A. P., Druen, P. B., & Wu, C. (1995). Their ideas of attractiveness are, on the whole, the same as ours: Consistency and variability in the cross-cultural perception of female attractiveness. *Journal of Personality and Social Psychology, 68,* 261–279.

Daly, M., & Wilson, M. (1988). *Homicide.* New York: de Gruyter.

Daly, M., & Wilson, M. (1998). *The truth about Cinderella: A Darwinian view of parental love.* New Haven, CT: Yale University Press.

Daly, M., & Wilson, M. (1999). Human evolutionary psychology and animal behaviour. *Animal Behaviour, 57,* 509–519.

Darwin, C. (1859). *On the origin of species by means of natural selection, or, preservation of favoured races in the struggle for life.* London: Murray.

Darwin, C. (1871). *The descent of man and selection in relation to sex.* London: Murray.

Davis, J. N., & Daly, M. (1997). Evolutionary theory and the human family. *Quarterly Review of Biology, 72,* 407–435.

Davis, S. (1990). Men as success objects and women as sex objects: A study of personal advertisements. *Sex Roles, 23,* 43–50.

Dawkins, R. (1983). *The extended phenotype: The gene as the unit of selection.* New York: Oxford University Press.

Dennett, C. N. (1991). *Consciousness explained.* Boston: Little Brown.

Dennett, C. N. (2006). *Breaking the spell: Religion as a natural phenomenon.* New York: Viking.

de Waal, F. (1982). *Chimpanzee politics: Sex and power among apes.* Baltimore: Johns Hopkins University Press.

Dixson, A. F. (1998). *Primate sexuality: Comparative studies of the prosimians, monkeys, apes, and human beings.* New York: Oxford University Press.

Dugatkin, L. A., & Reeve, H. K. (Eds.). (1998). *Game theory and animal behaviour.* New York: Oxford University Press.

Dunbar, R. (1996). *Grooming, gossip, and the evolution of language.* Cambridge, MA: Harvard University Press.

Duntely, J. (2005). Adaptations to dangers from humans. In D. M. Buss (Ed.), *The handbook of evolutionary psychology* (pp. 224–249). Hoboken, NJ: John Wiley & Sons.

Eaton, S. B., Shostak, M., & Konner, M. (1987). *The Paleolithic prescription.* New York: Harper & Row.

Eibl-Eibesfeldt, I. (1989). *Human ethology.* New York: de Gruyter.

Ekman, P. (1973). Cross-cultural studies of facial expression. In P. Ekman (Ed.), *Darwin and facial expression: A century of research in review* (pp. 169–222). New York: Academic Press.

Ellis, B. J., & Symons, D. (1990). Sex differences in sexual fantasy: An evolutionary psychological approach. *Journal of Sex Research, 27,* 527–556.

Emlen, S. T. (1995). An evolutionary theory of the family. *Proceedings of the National Academy of Science, 92,* 8092–8099.

Faer, L. M., Hendriks, A., Abed, R. T., & Figueredo, A. J. (2005). The evolutionary psychology of eating disorders: Female competition for mates or for status? *Psychology and Psychotherapy: Theory, Research, and Practice, 78,* 397–415.

Fehr, E., & Fischbacher, U. (2003). The nature of human altruism. *Nature, 425,* 785–791.

Figueredo, A. J., Sefcek, J. A., Vasquez, G., Brumbach, B. H., King, J. E., & Jacobs, W. J. (2005). Evolutionary theories of personality. In D. M. Buss (Ed.), *Handbook of evolutionary psychology* (pp. 851–877). Hoboken, NJ: John Wiley & Sons.

Fischer, M. A., & Shrout, P. E. (2006). Children's liking of landscape paintings as a function of their perceptions of prospect, refuge, and hazard. *Environment and Behavior, 38,* 373–393.

Fisher, H. E., Arthur, A., Mashek, D., Li, H., & Brown, L. L. (2002). Defining brain systems of lust, love, and attachment. *Archives of Sexual Behavior, 31,* 413–419.

Flaxman, S. M., & Sherman, P. W. (2000). Morning sickness: A mechanism for protecting mother and embryo. *Quarterly Review of Biology, 75,* 113–148.

Flinn, M. V., Ward, C. V., & Noone, R. (2005). Hormones and the human family. In D. Buss (Ed.), *Handbook of evolutionary psychology* (pp. 552–580). Hoboken, NJ: John Wiley & Sons.

Fodor, J. A. (1983). *The modularity of the mind.* Cambridge, MA: MIT Press.

Foley, R. (1996). The adaptive legacy of human evolution: A search for the environment of evolutionary adaptedness. *Evolutionary Anthropology, 5,* 194–203.

Ford, C. S., & Beach, F. A. (1951). *Patterns of sexual behavior.* New York: Harper & Row.

Forsyth, A. (1993). *A natural history of sex: The ecology and evolution of mating behavior.* Shelburne, VT: Chapters.

Fraley, R. C., Brumbaugh, C. C., & Marks, M. J. (2005). The evolution and function of adult attachment: A comparative and phylogenetic analysis. *Journal of Personality and Social Psychology, 89,* 731–746.

Frayser, S. (1985). *Varieties of sexual experience: An anthropological perspective.* New Haven, CT: HRAF Press.

French, J. A., Kamil, A. C., & Leger, D. W. (Eds.). (2001). *Evolutionary psychology and motivation.* Lincoln: University of Nebraska Press.

Gallistel, C. R. (1995). The replacement of general-purpose theories with adaptive specializations. In M. Gazzaniga (Ed.), *The cognitive neurosciences* (pp. 1255–1267). Cambridge, MA: MIT Press.

Gallup, G. G., Burch, R. L., Zappieri, M. L., Parvez, R. A., Stockwell, M. L., & Davis, J. A. (2003). The human penis as a semen displacement device. *Evolution and Human Behavior, 24,* 277–289.

Gangestad, S. W., & Buss, D. M. (1993). Pathogen prevalence and human mate preferences. *Ethology and Sociobiology, 14*, 89–96.

Gangestad, S. W., Haselton, M. G., & Buss, D. M. (2006). Evolutionary foundations of cultural variation: Evoked culture and mate preferences. *Psychological Inquiry, 17*, 75–95.

Gangestad, S. W., & Simpson, J. A. (2000). The evolution of human mating: Trade-offs and strategic pluralism. *Behavioral and Brain Sciences, 23*, 573–587.

Gangestad, S. W., & Thornhill, R. (1998). Menstrual cycle variation in women's preferences for the scent of symmetrical men. *Proceedings of the Royal Society of London B, 265*, 927–933.

Gangestad, S. W., & Thornhill, R. (2003). Facial masculinity and fluctuating asymmetry. *Evolution and Human Behavior, 24*, 231–241.

Gaulin, S. J. C., & Boster, J. (1985). Cross-cultural differences in sexual dimorphism: Is there any variance to be explained? *Ethology and Sociobiology, 6*, 219–225.

Gaulin, S. J. C., & Sailer, L. D. (1984). Sexual dimorphism in weight among primates: The relative impact of allometry and sexual selection. *International Journal of Primatology, 5*, 515–535

Geary, D. C. (2000). *Male, female: The evolution of human sex differences.* Washington, DC: American Psychological Association.

Gigerenzer, G., & Selten, R. (Eds.). (2001). *Bounded rationality: The adaptive toolbox.* Cambridge, MA: MIT Press.

Giosan, C. (2006). High-K strategy scale: A measure of the high-K independent criterion of fitness. *Evolutionary Psychology, 4*, 394–405.

Gomez, J. C. (2004). *Apes, monkeys, children and the growth of mind.* Cambridge, MA: Harvard University Press.

Gottschall, J., & Wilson, D. S. (Eds.). (2005). *The literary animal: Evolution and the nature of narrative.* Chicago: Northwestern University Press.

Gould, S. J. (1991). Exaptation: A crucial tool for evolutionary psychology. *Journal of Social Issues, 47*, 43–65.

Grafen, A. (1991). Modeling in behavioral ecology. In J. R. Krebs & N. B. Davies (Eds.), *Behavioural ecology: An evolutionary approach* (3rd ed., pp. 5–31). Oxford, U.K.: Blackwell.

Graham, R. (2006). Evolutionary psychology: A natural selection for music education. *Music Education Research, 8*, 433–437.

Graziano, W. G., Jensen-Campbell, L. A., Todd, M., & Finch, J. F. (1997). Interpersonal attraction from an evolutionary perspective: Women's reactions to dominant and prosocial men. In J. A. Simpson & D. T. Kenrick (Eds.), *Evolutionary social psychology* (pp. 141–167). Mahwah, NJ: Lawrence Erlbaum Associates, Inc..

Greenberg, G., & Haraway, M. M. (Eds.). (1998). *Comparative psychology: A handbook.* New York: Garland.

Greitemeyer, T., Hengmith, S., & Fischer, P. (2005). Sex differences in the willingness to betray and switch romantic partners. *Swiss Journal of Psychology, 64*, 265–272.

Griffin, D. R. (1981). *The question of animal awareness: Evolutionary continuity of animal experience.* New York: Rockefeller University Press.

Grinde, B. (2002). *Darwinian happiness.* Princeton, NJ: Darwin Press.

Griskevicius, V., Cialdini, R. B., & Kenrick, D. T. (2006). Peacocks, Picasso, and parental investment: The effects of romantic motives on creativity. *Journal of Personality and Social Psychology, 91*, 63–76.

Haman, S. (2005). Sex differences in the responses of the human amygdala. *Neuroscientist, 11*, 288–293.

Hamer, D. H., & Copeland, P. (1994). *The science of desire: The search for the gay gene and the biology of behavior.* New York: Simon & Schuster.

Hamilton, W. D. (1964). The genetical evolution of social behavior. *Journal of Theoretical Biology, 7*, 1–52.

Harvey, P. H., & Purvis, A. (1991). Comparative methods for explaining adaptations. *Nature, 20*, 619–624.

Haun, D. B. M., Rapold, C. J., Call, J., Janzen, G., & Levinson, S. C. (2006). Cognitive cladistics and cultural override in Hominid spatial cognition. *Proceedings of the National Academy of Sciences, 103*, 17568–17573.

Hausfater, G., & Hrdy, S. B. (Eds.). (1984). *Infanticide: Comparative and evolutionary perspectives.* New York: de Gruyter.

Haviland-Jones, J., Rosario, H. H., Wilson, P., & McGuire, T. R. (2005). An environmental approach to positive emotions: Flowers. *Evolutionary Psychology, 3*, 104–132.

Henrich, J., Boyd, R., Bowles, S., Camerer, C., Fehr, E., & Gintis, H. (Eds.). (2004). *Foundations of human sociality: Economic experiments and ethnographic evidence from fifteen small-scale societies.* New York: Oxford University Press.

Hill, K. (1993). Life history theory and evolutionary anthropology. *Evolutionary Anthropology, 2,* 78–88.

Hill, K., & Hurtado, M. (1996). *Ache life history.* Hawthorne, NY: de Gruyter.

Hinde, R. A. (1982). *Ethology.* Oxford, U.K.: Oxford University Press.

Hirshfeld, L. A., & Gelman, S. (Eds.). (1994). *Mapping the mind: Domain specificity in cognition and culture.* New York: Cambridge University Press.

Holcomb, H. R. (1998). Testing evolutionary hypotheses. In C. B. Crawford & D. Krebs (Eds.), *Handbook of evolutionary psychology: Ideas, issues, and applications* (pp. 303–334). Mahwah, NJ: Lawrence Erlbaum Associates, Inc.

Howell, N. (1979). *Demography of the Dobe !Kung.* New York: Academic Press.

Hughes, S. M., & Gallup, G. G. (2003). Sex differences in morphological predictors of sexual behavior: Shoulder to hip and waist to hip ratios. *Evolution and Human Behavior, 24,* 173–178.

Huxley, R. R. (2000). Nausea and vomiting in early pregnancy: Its role in placental development. *Obstetrics & Gynecology, 95,* 779–782.

James, J. (2003). *Sociosexuality and self-perceived mate value: A multidimensional approach.* Poster session presented at the 15th annual meeting of Human Behavior and Evolution Society, Lincoln, NE.

Jensen-Seaman, M. I., Deinard, A. S., & Kidd, K. K. (2001). Modern African ape populations as genetic and demographic models of the last common ancestor of humans, chimpanzees, and gorillas. *Journal of Heredity, 92,* 475–480.

Johnston, V. S. (1999). *Why we feel.* Reading, MA: Perseus.

Johnston, V. S., Hagel, R., Franklin, M., Fink, B., & Grammer, K. (2001). Male facial attractiveness: Evidence for hormone-mediated adaptive design. *Evolution and Human Behavior, 22,* 251–267.

Jones, D. (1995). Sexual selection, physical attractiveness, and facial neoteny: Cross-cultural evidence and implications. *Current Anthropology, 36,* 723–748.

Jones, O. D. (2005). Evolutionary psychology and the law. In D. M. Buss (Ed.), *The handbook of evolutionary psychology* (pp. 953–974). Hoboken, NJ: John Wiley & Sons.

Jones, S., Martin, R., & Pilbeam, D. (Eds.). (1992). *The Cambridge encyclopedia of human evolution.* New York: Cambridge University Press.

Kanazawa, S. (2004). Social sciences are branches of biology. *Socio-Economic Review, 2,* 371–390.

Kaplan, H. S., & Gangestad, S. W. (2005). Life history theory and evolutionary psychology. In D. M. Buss (Ed.), *The handbook of evolutionary psychology* (pp. 68–95). Hoboken, NJ: John Wiley & Sons.

Keller, M. C., & Nesse, R. M. (2006). The evolutionary significance of depressive symptoms: Different adverse situations lead to different depressive symptom patterns. *Journal of Personality and Social Psychology, 91,* 316–330.

Kelly, R. L. (1995). *The foraging spectrum.* Washington, DC: Smithsonian Institution Press.

Kenrick, D. T., & Keefe, R. C. (1992). Age preferences in mates reflect sex differences in human reproductive strategies. *Behavioral and Brain Sciences, 15,* 75–133.

Kenrick, D. T., Maner, J. K., & Li, N. P. (2005). Evolutionary social psychology. In D. M. Buss (Ed.), *The handbook of evolutionary psychology* (pp. 803–827). Hoboken, NJ: John Wiley & Sons.

Kenrick, D. T., Neuberg, S. L., Zierk, K. L., & Krones, J. M. (1994). Evolution and social cognition: Contrast effects as a function of sex, dominance, and physical attractiveness. *Personality and Social Psychology Bulletin, 20,* 210–217.

Kessler, D. M. T. (2006). A burning desire: Steps toward an evolutionary psychology of fire burning. *Journal of Culture and Cognition, 6,* 429–451.

Ketelaar, T., & Ellis, B. J. (2000). Are evolutionary explanations unfalsifiable: Evolutionary psychology and the Lakatosian philosophy of science. *Psychological Inquiry, 11,* 1–22.

Kimura, D. (1999). *Sex and cognition.* Cambridge, MA: MIT Press.

Kirkpatrick, L. A. (2005). *Attachment, evolution, and the psychology of religion.* New York: Guilford.

Kirkpatrick, L. A., Waugh, C. E., Valencia, A., & Webster, G. D. (2002). The functional domain specificity of self-esteem and the differential prediction of aggression. *Journal of Personality and Social Psychology, 82,* 756–767.

Klein, S. B., Cosmides, L., Tooby, J., & Chance, S. (2002). Decisions and the evolution of memory: Multiple systems, multiple functions. *Psychological Review, 109,* 306–329.

Kohl, J. V., & Francoeur, R. T. (1995). *The scent of eros: Mysteries of odor in human sexuality.* New York: Continuum.

Kohler, T. A., & Gumerman, G. J. (2000). *Dynamics in human and primate societies.* Oxford, U.K.: Oxford University Press.

Korotayev, A. V., & Kazankov, A. A. (2003). Factors of sexual freedom among foragers in cross-cultural perspective. *Cross-Cultural Research, 37,* 29–61.

Krebs, D. (2005). The evolution of morality. In D. M. Buss (Ed.), *The handbook of evolutionary psychology* (pp. 747–771). Hoboken, NJ: John Wiley & Sons.

Krebs, J. R., & Davies, N. B. (1997). *Behavioural ecology* (4th ed.). Oxford, U.K.: Blackwell.

Kruger, D. J., & Fisher, M. L. (2005). Males identify and respond adaptively to the mating strategies of other men. *Sexualities, Evolution and Gender, 7,* 233–243.

Kruger, D. J., Fisher, M. L., & Jobling, I. (2003). Proper and dark heroes as dads and cads: Alternative mating strategies in British Romantic literature. *Human Nature, 14,* 305–317.

Kurzban, R., & Weeden, J. (2005). Hurry date: Mate preferences in action. *Evolution and Human Behavior, 26,* 227–244.

Lakatos, I. (1970). Falsificationism and the methodology of scientific research programmes. In I. Lakatos & A. Musgrave (Eds.), *Criticism and the growth of knowledge* (pp. 91–196). Cambridge, U.K.: Cambridge University Press.

Lancaster, J. B. (1994). Human sexuality, life histories, and evolutionary ecology. In A. S. Rossi (Ed.), *Sexuality across the life course* (pp. 39–62). Chicago: University of Chicago Press.

Leakey, R. (1994). *The origin of humankind.* London: Weidenfeld & Nicolson.

Lee, R. B. (1979). *The !Kung San: Men, women, and working in a foraging society.* New York: Cambridge University Press.

Lee, R. B., & Daly, R. (Eds.). (2000). *The Cambridge encyclopedia of hunters and gatherers.* Cambridge, U.K.: Cambridge University Press.

Li, N. P., Bailey, J. M., Kenrick, D. T., & Linsenmeier, J. A. (2002). The necessities and luxuries of mate preferences: Testing the tradeoffs. *Journal of Personality and Social Psychology, 82,* 947–955.

Low, B. S. (1989). Cross-cultural patterns in the training of children: An evolutionary perspective. *Journal of Comparative Psychology, 103,* 313–319.

Low, B. S. (1998). The evolution of human life histories. In C. B. Crawford & D. Krebs (Eds.), *Handbook of evolutionary psychology: Ideas, issues, and applications* (pp. 131–161). Mahwah, NJ: Lawrence Erlbaum Associates, Inc.

Low, B. S. (2000). *Why sex matters.* Princeton, NJ: Princeton University Press.

Low, B. S., Alexander, R. D., & Noonan, K. M. (1987). Human hips, breasts and buttocks: Is fat deceptive? *Ethology and Sociobiology, 8,* 249–257.

Lumsden, C. J., & Wilson, E. O. (1981). *Genes, mind, and culture.* Cambridge, MA: Harvard University Press.

MacDonald, K. (1998). Evolution, culture, and the five-factor model. *Journal of Cross-Cultural Psychology, 29,* 119–149.

MacNeilage, P. F., & Davis, P. L. (2005). The evolution of language. In D. M. Buss (Ed.), *The handbook of evolutionary psychology* (pp. 698–723). Hoboken, NJ: John Wiley & Sons.

Maestripieri, D., & Roney, J. R. (2006). Evolutionary developmental psychology: Contributions from comparative research with nonhuman primates. *Developmental Review, 26,* 120–137.

Malamuth, N. M. (1996). Sexually explicit media, gender differences, and evolutionary theory. *Journal of Communication, 46,* 8–31.

Manning, J. T. (2002). *Digit ratio: A pointer to fertility, behavior, and health.* New Brunswick, NJ: Rutgers University Press.

Marks, I. M., & Nesse, R. M. (1994). Fear and fitness: An evolutionary analysis of anxiety disorders. *Ethology & Sociobiology, 15,* 247–261.

Marlowe, F. M. (2003). The mating system of foragers in the standard cross-cultural sample. *Cross-Cultural Research, 37,* 282–306.

Marlowe, F. M. (2004). Mate preferences among Hadza hunter-gatherers. *Human Nature, 15,* 365–376.

Marlowe, F. M. (2005). Hunter-gatherers and human evolution. *Evolutionary Anthropology, 14,* 54–67.

Maynard Smith, J. (1998). *Evolutionary genetics* (2nd ed.). Oxford, U.K.: Oxford University Press.

Mayr, E. (1983). How to carry out the adaptationist program. *American Naturalist, 121*, 324–334.

Mazur, A., & Booth, A. (1998). Testosterone and dominance in men. *Behavioral and Brain Sciences, 21*, 353–397.

McAndrew, F. T. (2002). New evolutionary perspectives on altruism: Multilevel-selection and costly-signaling theories. *Current Directions in Psychological Science, 11*, 79–82.

McGue, M., & Lykken, D. T. (1992). Genetic influence on the risk of divorce. *Psychological Science, 3*, 368–373.

McGuire, M., & Gruter, M. (2003). Prostitution: An evolutionary perspective. In A. Somit & S. Peterson (Eds.), *Human nature and public policy: An evolutionary approach* (pp. 29–40). New York: Palgrave Macmillan.

Mealey, L. (2000). *Sex differences: Developmental and evolutionary strategies.* San Diego, CA: Academic Press.

Miller, G. F. (2000). *The mating mind.* New York: Doubleday.

Minervini, B. P., & McAndrew, F. T. (2006). The mating strategies and mate preferences of mail order brides. *Cross-Cultural Research, 40*, 111–129.

Mithen, S. (1996). *The prehistory of the mind.* London: Thames & Hudson.

Moffitt, T. E., Caspi, A., & Rutter, M. (2006). Measured gene-environment interactions in psychopathology: Concepts, research strategies, and implications for research, intervention, and public understanding of genetics. *Perspectives on Psychological Science, 1*, 5–27.

Møller, A. P. (1988). Ejaculate size, testes size, and sperm competition in primates. *Journal of Human Evolution, 17*, 479–488.

Morbeck, M. E. (1997). Life history, the individual, and evolution. In M. E. Morbeck, A. Galloway, & A. L. Zihlman (Eds.), *The evolving female: A life-history perspective* (pp. 3–14). Princeton, NJ: Princeton University Press.

Mueller, U., & Mazur, A. (1998). Facial dominance in *Homo sapiens* as honest signaling of male quality. *Behavioral Ecology, 8*, 569–579.

Munroe, R. L., & Munroe, R. H. (1997). A comparative anthropological perspective. In J. W. Berry, Y. H. Poortinga, & J. Pandey (Eds.), *Handbook of cross-cultural psychology* (2nd ed., Vol. 1, pp. 171–213). Boston: Allyn & Bacon.

Murphy, D. (2005). Can evolution explain insanity? *Biology and Philosophy, 20*, 745–766.

Nesse, R. M. (1990). Evolutionary explanations of emotions. *Human Nature, 1*, 261–289.

Nesse, R. M. (2005). Evolutionary psychology and mental health. In D. M. Buss (Ed.), *The handbook of evolutionary psychology* (pp. 903–927). Hoboken, NJ: John Wiley & Sons.

Nesse, R. M., & Williams, G. C. (1994). *Why we get sick: The new science of Darwinian medicine.* New York: Times Books.

Ohman, A., & Mineka, S. (2001). Fears, phobias, and preparedness: Toward an evolved module of fear and fear learning. *Psychological Review, 108*, 483–522.

Ohman, A., & Mineka, S. (2003). The malicious serpent: Snakes as a prototypical stimulus for an evolved module of fear. *Current Directions in Psychological Science, 12*, 5–9.

Panskepp, J., & Panskepp, J. B. (2000). The seven sins of evolutionary psychology. *Evolution and Cognition, 6*, 108–131.

Parker, G. A., & Maynard Smith, J. (1990). Optimality theory in evolutionary biology. *Nature, 348*, 27–33.

Pasternak, B., Ember, C., & Ember, M. (1997). *Sex, gender, and kinship: A cross-cultural perspective.* Upper Saddle River, NJ: Prentice Hall.

Pawlowski, R., & Dunbar, R. I. M. (1999). Impact of market value on human mate choice decisions. *Proceedings of the Royal Society B, 266*, 281–285.

Pedersen, F. A. (1991). Secular trends in human sex ratios: Their influence on individual and family behavior. *Human Nature, 2*, 271–291.

Penton-Voak, I. S., & Chen, J. Y. (2004). High salivary testosterone is linked to masculine male facial appearance in humans. *Evolution and Human Behavior, 25*, 229–241.

Perper, T. (1985). *Sex signals: The biology of love.* Philadelphia: ISI Press.

Perrett, D. I., Burt, D. M., Penton-Voak, I. S., Lee, K. J., Rowland, D. A., & Edwards, R. (1999). Symmetry and human facial attractiveness. *Evolution and Human Behavior, 20*, 295–307.

Perusse, D. (1994). Mate choice in modern societies: Testing evolutionary hypotheses with behavioral data. *Human Nature, 5*, 255–278.

Pettay, J. E., Kruuk, L. E. B., Jokela, J., & Lumma, V. (2005). Heritability and genetic constraints of life-history trait evolution in preindustrial cultures. *Proceedings of the National Academy of Sciences, 102*, 2838–2843.

Pillsworth, E. G., & Haselton, M. G. (2006). Male sexual attractiveness predicts differential ovulatory shifts in female extra-pair attraction and male mate retention. *Evolution and Human Behavior, 27*, 247–258.

Pinker, S. (1994). *The language instinct.* New York: Morrow.

Pinker, S. (1997). *How the mind works.* New York: W. W. Norton.

Pinker, S. (2002). *The blank slate.* New York: Viking.

Pitchford, I. (2001). No evolution, no cognition. *Evolution and Cognition, 7*, 39–45.

Platek, S. M. (2002). Unconscious reactions to children's faces: The effects of resemblance. *Evolution and Cognition, 8*, 207–214.

Plutchik, R. (1980). A general psychoevolutionary theory of emotion. In R. Plutchik & H. Kellerman (Eds.), *Emotion: Theory, research, and experience: Theories of emotion* (Vol. 1, pp. 3–24). New York: Academic Press.

Ponseti, J., Bosinski, H. A., Wolff, S., Peller, M., & Jansen, O. (2006). A functional endophenotype for sexual orientation in humans. *Neuroimage, 33*, 825–833.

Popper, K. R. (1959). *The logic of scientific discovery.* New York: Hutchinson Education.

Profet, M. (1988). The evolution of pregnancy sickness as protection to the embryo against Pleistocene teratogens. *Evolutionary Theory, 8*, 177–190.

Profet, M. (1992). Pregnancy sickness as adaptation: A deterrent to maternal ingestion of teratogens. In J. Barkow, L. Cosmides, & J. Tooby (Eds.), *The adapted mind: Evolutionary psychology and the generation of culture* (pp. 327–366). New York: Oxford University Press.

Quinsey, V. L., Book, A., & Lalumiere, M. L. (2001). A factor analysis of traits related to individual differences in anti-social behavior. *Criminal Justice and Behavior, 28*, 522–536.

Regan, P. C. (1996). Rhythms of desire: The association between menstrual cycle phases and female sexual desire. *The Canadian Journal of Human Sexuality, 5*, 145–156.

Regan, P. C. (1998). Minimum mate selection standards as a function of perceived mate value, relationship context, and gender. *Journal of Psychology and Human Sexuality, 10*, 53–73.

Regan, P. C., & Dreyer, C. S. (1999). Lust? Love? Status? Young adults' motives for engaging in casual sex. *Journal of Psychology and Human Sexuality, 11*, 1–24.

Rhodes, G., & Zebrowitz, L. A. (Eds.). (2002). *Facial attractiveness.* Westport, CT: Ablex.

Richerson, P. J., & Boyd, R. (2005). *Not by genes alone: How culture transformed human evolution.* Chicago: University of Chicago Press.

Ridley, M. (1996). *The origins of virtue.* London: Viking.

Ridley, M. (2000). *Genome.* London: Harper Collins.

Ridley, M. (2003). *Nature via nurture.* London: Harper Collins.

Rikowski, A., & Grammer, K. (1999). Human body odor, symmetry, and attractiveness. *Proceedings of the Royal Academy of London B, 266*, 869–874.

Roney, J. R. (2003). Effects of visual exposure to the opposite sex: Cognitive aspects of mate attraction in human males. *Personality and Social Psychology Bulletin, 29*, 393–404.

Rose, H., & Rose, M. (2000). *Alas, poor Darwin: Arguments against evolutionary psychology.* New York: Harmony Books.

Rose, M. R., & Lauder, G. V. (Eds.). (1996). *Adaptation.* San Diego, CA: Academic Press.

Rowe, D. C., Vazsonyi, A. T., & Figueredo, A. J. (1997). Mating effort in adolescence: A conditional or alternative strategy. *Personality and Individual Differences, 23*, 105–115.

Saad, G., & Gill, T. (2000). Applications of evolutionary psychology in marketing. *Psychology and Marketing, 17*, 1005–1034.

Salmon, C., & Symons, D. (2001). *Warrior lovers: Erotic fiction, evolution, and female sexuality.* London: Weidenfeld & Nicolson.

Schmitt, D. P. (2005). Sociosexuality from Argentina to Zimbabwe: A 48-nation study of sex, culture, and strategies of human mating. *Behavioral and Brain Sciences, 28*, 247–275.

Schmitt, D. P., Alcalay, L., Allik, J., Ault, L., Austers, I., Bennett, K. L., et al. (2003). Universal sex differences in the desire for sexual variety: Tests from 52 nations, 6 continents, and 13 islands. *Journal of Personality and Social Psychology, 85*, 85–104.

Schmitt, D. P., Couden, A., & Baker, M. (2001). Sex, temporal context, and romantic desire: An experimental evaluation of Sexual Strategies Theory. *Personality and Social Psychology Bulletin, 27*, 833–847.

Schmitt, D. P., & Pilcher, J. J. (2004). Evaluating evidence of psychological adaptation: How do we know one when we see one? *Psychological Science, 15*, 643–649.

Shackelford, T. K., & LeBlanc, G. J. (2001). Sperm competition in insects, birds, and humans: Insights from a comparative evolutionary perspective. *Evolution and Cognition, 7*, 194–202.

Shackelford, T. K., Weekes-Shackelford, V. A., & Schmitt, D. P. (2005). An evolutionary perspective on why some men refuse or reduce their child support payments. *Basic and Applied Social Psychology, 27*, 297–306.

Silverman, I., & Choi, J. (2006). Non-Euclidean navigational strategies of women: Compensatory response or evolved dimorphism? *Evolutionary Psychology, 4*, 75–84.

Simao, J., & Todd, P. M. (2002). Modeling mate choice in monogamous mating systems with courtship. *Adaptive Behavior, 10*, 113–136.

Simpson, J. A., & Campbell, L. (2005). Methods of evolutionary sciences. In D. M. Buss (Ed.), *The handbook of evolutionary psychology* (pp. 119–144). Hoboken, NJ: John Wiley & Sons.

Simpson, J. A., & Gangestad, S. W. (1991). Individual differences in sociosexuality: Evidence for convergent and discriminant validity. *Journal of Personality and Social Psychology, 60*, 870–883.

Simpson, J. A., & Kenrick, D. T. (Eds.). (1997). *Evolutionary social psychology.* Mahwah, NJ: Lawrence Erlbaum Associates, Inc.

Singh, D., & Bronstad, M. P. (1997). Sex differences in the anatomical location of human body scarification and tattooing as a function of pathogen prevalence. *Evolution and Human Behavior, 18*, 403–416.

Singh, D., & Young, R. K. (1995). Body weight, waist-to-hip ratio, breasts, and hips: Role in judgments of female attractiveness and desirability in relationships. *Ethology and Sociobiology, 16*, 483–507.

Skinner, B. F. (1956). A case history in scientific method. *American Psychologist, 11*, 221–233.

Sloman, L., Gilbert, P., & Hasey, G. (2003). Evolved mechanisms in depression: The role and interaction of attachment and social rank in depression. *Journal of Affective Disorders, 74*, 107–121.

Smith, E. A. (2000). Three styles in the evolutionary analysis of human behavior. In L. Cronk, N. A. Chagnon, & W. Irons (Eds.), *Adaptation and human behavior: An anthropological perspective* (pp. 27–46). New York: de Gruyter.

Smith, E. A., & Winterhalder, B. (Eds.). (1992). *Evolutionary ecology and human behavior.* Hawthorne, NY: de Gruyter.

Smuts, B. B. (1995). The evolutionary origins of patriarchy. *Human Nature, 6*, 1–32.

Soler, C., Nunez, M., Gutierrez, R., Nunez, J., Medina, P., Sancho, M., et al. (2003). Facial attractiveness in men provides clues to semen quality. *Evolution and Human Behavior, 24*, 199–207.

Somit, A., & Peterson, S. (Eds.). (2003). *Human nature and public policy: An evolutionary approach.* New York: Palgrave Macmillan.

Speed, A., & Gangestad, S. W. (1997). Romantic popularity and mate preferences: A peer-nomination study. *Personality and Social Psychology Bulletin, 23*, 928–935.

Sprecher, S., Sullivan, Q., & Hatfield, E. (1994). Mate selection preferences: Gender differences examined in a national sample. *Journal of Personality and Social Psychology, 66*, 1074–1080.

Stearns, S. (Ed.). (1998). *Evolution in health and disease.* Oxford, U.K.: Oxford University Press.

Thiessen, D. (1998). *Survival of the fittest: The Darwinian diet and exercise program.* Austin, TX: Morgan.

Thompson, P. (Ed.). (1995). *Issues in evolutionary ethics.* Albany: State University of New York Press.

Thornhill, R. (1997). The concept of an evolved adaptation. In G. R. Bock & G. Cardew (Eds.), *Characterizing human psychological adaptations* (pp. 4–22). Chichester, U.K.: John Wiley & Sons.

Thornhill, R. (1998). Darwinian aesthetics. In C. B. Crawford & D. Krebs (Eds.), *Handbook of evolutionary psychology: Ideas, issues, and applications* (pp. 543–572). Mahwah, NJ: Lawrence Erlbaum Associates, Inc.

Thornhill, R., & Gangestad, S. W. (1999). The scent of symmetry: A human sex pheromone that signals fitness? *Evolution and Human Behavior, 20*, 175–201.

Thornhill, R., & Palmer, C. T. (2000). *A natural history of rape.* Cambridge, MA: MIT Press.

Tinbergen, N. (1963). On the aims and methods of ethology. *Zeitschrift für Tierpsychologie, 20*, 410–433.

Todd, P. M., Hertwig, R., & Hoffrage, U. (2005). Evolutionary cognitive psychology. In D. M. Buss (Ed.), *The handbook of evolutionary psychology* (pp. 776–802). Hoboken, NJ: John Wiley & Sons.

Tooby, J., & Cosmides, L. (1990). On the universality of human nature and the uniqueness of the individual: The role of genetics and adaptation. *Journal of Personality, 58,* 17–67.

Tooby, J., & Cosmides, L. (1992). The psychological foundations of culture. In J. Barkow, L. Cosmides, & J. Tooby (Eds.), *The adapted mind: Evolutionary psychology and the generation of culture* (pp. 19–136). New York: Oxford University Press.

Tooby, J., Cosmides, L., & Barrett, H. C. (2005). Resolving the debate on innate ideas: Learnability constraints and the evolved interpenetration of motivational and conceptual functions. In P. Carruthers, S. Laurence, & S. Stich (Eds.), *The innate mind: Structure and content* (pp. 305–337). New York: Oxford University Press.

Tooby, J., & DeVore, I. (1987). The reconstruction of hominid behavioral evolution through strategic modeling. In W. G. Kinzey (Ed.), *The evolution of human behavior: Primate models* (pp. 183–237). Albany: State University of New York Press.

Townsend, J. M., & Levy, G. D. (1990). Effects of potential partners' physical attractiveness and socioeconomic status on sexuality and partner selection. *Archives of Sexual Behavior, 19,* 149–164.

Townsend, J. M., & Wasserman, T. (1998). Sexual attractiveness: Sex differences in assessment and criteria. *Evolution and Human Behavior, 19,* 171–191.

Trevathan, W. R., Smith, E. O., & McKenna, J. J. (Eds.). (1999). *Evolutionary medicine.* New York: Oxford University Press.

Trivers, R. L. (1971). The evolution of reciprocal altruism. *Quarterly Review of Biology, 46,* 35–57.

Trivers, R. L. (1972). Parental investment and sexual selection. In B. Campbell (Ed.), *Sexual selection and the descent of man: 1871–1971* (pp. 136–179). Chicago: Aldine.

Trivers, R. L. (1974). Parent-offspring conflict. *American Zoologist, 14,* 249–264.

Trivers, R. L. (1985). *Social evolution.* Palo Alto, CA: Benjamin/Cummings.

Udry, J. R., & Campbell, B. C. (1994). Getting started on sexual behavior. In A. S. Rossi (Ed.), *Sexuality over the life course* (pp. 187–207). Chicago: University of Chicago Press.

Walter, A. (2006). The anti-naturalistic fallacy: Evolutionary moral psychology and the insistence on brute facts. *Evolutionary Psychology, 4,* 33–48.

Walters, S., & Crawford, C. B. (1994). The importance of mate attraction for intrasexual competition in men and women. *Ethology and Sociobiology, 15,* 5–30.

Watson, P. J., & Andrews, P. W. (2002). Toward a revised evolutionary adaptationist analysis of depression: The social navigation hypothesis. *Journal of Affective Disorders, 72,* 1–14.

Weingart, P., Mitchell, S. D., Richerson, P. J., & Maasen, S. (Eds.). (1997). *Human by nature: Between biology and the social sciences.* Mahwah, NJ: Lawrence Erlbaum Associates, Inc.

Weisfeld, G. E. (1999). *Evolutionary principles of human adolescence.* New York: Basic Books/Wayne State University.

Weisfeld, G. E., & Weisfeld, C. C. (2002). Marriage: An evolutionary perspective. *Neuroendocrinology Letters, 23,* 47–54.

West-Eberhard, M. J. (2003). *Developmental plasticity and evolution.* New York: Oxford University Press.

Whitley, B. E. (1996). *Principles of research in behavioral science.* Mountain View, CA: Mayfield.

Whyte, M. K. (1980). Cross-cultural codes dealing with the relative status of women. In H. Barry III & A. Schlegel (Eds.), *Cross-cultural samples and codes* (pp. 335–364). Pittsburgh, PA: University of Pittsburgh Press.

Wiederman, M. W. (1993). Evolved gender differences in mate preferences: Evidence from personal advertisements. *Ethological and Sociobiology, 14,* 331–352.

Williams, G. C. (1966). *Adaptation and natural selection.* Princeton, NJ: Princeton University Press.

Wilson, D. S. (1994). Adaptive genetic variation and human evolutionary psychology. *Ethology and Sociobiology, 15,* 219–235.

Wilson, D. S. (2003). *Darwin's cathedral: Evolution, religion, and the nature of society.* Chicago: University of Chicago Press.

Wilson, E. O. (1975). *Sociobiology: The new synthesis.* Cambridge, MA: Harvard University Press.

Wrangham, R. W. (1993). The evolution of sexuality in chimpanzees and bonobos. *Human Nature, 4,* 47–79.

Wrangham, R. W. (1995). *Demonic males.* Boston: Houghton Mifflin.

Part IV

THE EVOLUTIONARY PSYCHOLOGY OF SEX DIFFERENCES

The three chapters in this section explore evolved sources of differences between the two sexes. The first chapter examines similarities and differences between the qualities that males and females find physically attractive, and it explores their role in signaling fitness. The second chapter examines the role of natural selection and sexual selection in producing differences between males and females, especially with respect to mating behavior. The final chapter in this part examines sex differences in preferences for different forms of erotica.

12

Physical Attractiveness
Signals of Phenotypic Quality and Beyond

GLENN J. SCHEYD,
CHRISTINE E. GARVER-APGAR,
AND STEVEN W. GANGESTAD

Nonhuman animals do not mate randomly. Neither do people. Both men and women strongly prefer mates who exhibit certain qualities. Preferred qualities include physical features. In general, individuals of both sexes prefer mates who look attractive (e.g., Langlois et al., 2000) and smell attractive (Herz & Cahill, 1997).

Why do people care about the visually perceived traits and scents of people with whom they mate? Evolutionary psychologists typically adopt the working hypothesis that traits of one sex that the other sex reliably prefers in mates historically covaried with fitness benefits that mates provide. That is, some traits ancestrally "promised" a flow of fitness benefits from individuals who exhibit them to the individuals with whom they mate. Preferences for those traits were accordingly selected.

This chapter has several aims. First, we discuss theory concerning the kinds of benefits that mates provide and how preferred traits come to indicate those benefits. Second, we review the literature that speaks to attractive physical features and the benefits they promise. Third, we discuss several future directions of research and theory.

THE EVOLUTION OF ATTRACTIVENESS: THEORETICAL CONSIDERATIONS

Attractiveness and Beauty Outcomes of Selection

In broad terms, evolutionary biologists delineate two types of benefits that mates provide: first, *genetic benefits*—those that endow offspring with superior ability to survive and reproduce; second, *nongenetic material benefits* to the perceiver such as food, care for offspring, physical protection, or avoidance of disease. Selection favors attraction to mates who possess qualities that signal the delivery of either category of benefits. Adaptationist researchers have typically hypothesized that many of people's tendencies to find specific features attractive are outcomes of this kind of historical selection (although see our discussion of alternative, sensory bias models in a later section).

Once individuals of one sex prefer particular qualities, the preferences exert selection pressures on the preferred traits. Individuals who possess preferred traits have, as a result, greater reproductive success. Selection, hence, led many individuals to expend energy and time to display favored traits (although see our discussion of nonsignaled attractive traits in a later section). As Charles Darwin (1871) himself recognized, such selection can lead to the evolution of extravagant ornaments, even those detrimental to an animal's viability, provided that they give a sufficient reproductive advantage. (In the eyes of evolution, survival is useful only insofar as it provides more opportunities to spread one's genes.) In turn, selection may exert pressures on perceivers' greater ability to discern truly favored traits.

Sexual Selection and Signaling Theory

Physical traits individuals are selected to find attractive, and which then are enhanced through selection, may be thought of as *signals* of underlying qualities. The coevolution of preferences and preferred traits, then, can be thought of as the evolution of a *signaling system*, which entails that one sex (signalers) possesses signals and the other sex (receivers) possesses psychological (cognitive and motivational) capacities to perceive and act upon (e.g., be attracted to) those signals. In a given species, both sexes may evolve preferences and hence be receivers in signaling systems.

Signals of underlying condition have received the greatest attention from biological signaling theorists. Condition refers to an organism's ability to efficiently extract energy from the environment and convert it into fitness-promoting activities (e.g., Rowe & Houle, 1996). Superior condition has been associated with the concept of health (e.g., Grammer et al., 2003). The concept of health it implies, however, is much broader than simply the absence of disease; it implies greater phenotypic fitness or resourcefulness. In particular circumstances (discussed in the following section), individuals of superior condition may be *more* prone to disease than others may be; "health" is therefore a poor stand-in for biologists' notion of condition.

Individuals in superior condition may make better mates for a variety of reasons: fitter genes to pass on to offspring (e.g., a paucity of mildly harmful mutations; Houle, 1992); greater ability to provide material benefits such as protection or food; greater fertility and ability to reproduce (e.g., more viable sperm in the case of males or greater ability to conceive, gestate, and bear offspring in the case of females); absence of communicable disease. General models of signals of quality do not specify the nature of the benefits.

A signaling system may be said to be at equilibrium when neither the signaling sex nor the receiving sex benefits from a change (i.e., in signal sent or preference exercised) given that the other retains its strategy. For a signal to be a valid indicator of one's quality at equilibrium, a reliable relation between the signaler's quality and the signal strength must persist. Zahavi (1975) introduced the idea that the very costliness of a trait ensures its honesty. He specifically proposed that animals may signal superior quality with a "handicap"—a feature that imposes a cost on the individual. Zahavi did not provide a mathematical optimization model of this process; his argument was purely a verbal one. The process he described is analogous to conspicuous consumption: Individuals who can afford a large handicap must be more viable than individuals who have smaller handicapping traits. Big signalers can afford to "waste" some of their viability and still have residual viability greater than that of small signalers, and this fact renders the handicapping trait an "honest" signal of viability. In this context, a "bigger" signal need not be larger. Rather, the term indicates greater *cost* for individuals, on average, to produce. The cost itself could be due to the signal's size or its complexity, or it can be mediated socially. Developing a formidable-looking phenotype, for example, might attract abundant intrasexual competition and hence be a particularly poor strategy for an organism short on physical prowess.

Grafen (1990) was the first to quantitatively model handicapping. He assumed that all individuals, regardless of quality, obtain the same fitness benefits from a particular level of a signal (although see Getty, 1998). The signal can evolve to display quality, according to this model, when the fitness costs (mortality) associated with developing and maintaining a particular level of the signal are less for individuals of higher quality than for individuals of lower quality. In that instance, the size of the handicap that maximizes net fitness (benefits minus costs) is larger for individuals of higher quality than for individuals of lower quality. The signal "honestly" conveys fitness, then, simply because it is not in the interest of individuals of lower quality to "cheat" and develop a larger signal; the viability costs they would suffer exceed the fertility benefits they would derive from the increased signal size.

Recent developments in honest signaling theory have furthered and revised our understanding of it. Despite the intuitive appeal, systems of mate choice via signals of condition need not imply that the biggest signals are sent by the most viable individuals. For signals to be reliable, higher quality individuals need only higher *efficiency* (i.e., a greater fitness return from a marginal increase in signal investment; Getty, 2002). Modeling has demonstrated that individuals of highest quality may have the same, higher, or lower viability than small signalers at equilibrium, depending on specific parameters of the system. A key parameter is the expense paid by receivers for preferring those with big signals to others. The requisite perceptual development itself is not without cost. More important, however, is the cost of search time. An individual with no preferences for signals of a certain quality would simply accept the first available mate and thereby save the time and effort ordinarily expended in mate search. Individuals with strong preferences for a signal of a certain size may delay mating and hence lose valuable time reproducing. A preference may be very cheap in some species—for example, lekking species in which males collectively gather and display to females, who can assess relative quality with a minimal search time sacrifice. In such species, a few males who "win" the display contest may garner nearly all of the matings, which in turn boosts the intensity with which males capable of sending strong signals will do so, sometimes beyond the point at which high-quality males have reduced their viability to that of their lower quality rivals. Oddly, then, quality and mortality can actually become *positively* correlated in a population, with the highest quality individuals dying, on average, at younger ages than lower quality individuals do (Kokko, Brooks, McNamara, & Houston, 2002). When females pay relatively high costs for their preference in relation to its benefits, the system will not drive signal intensity to be as great (i.e., signals themselves will be less costly at equilibrium), and furthermore, individuals of highest quality are unlikely to invest in signals to the extent that they actually have lower viability than individuals of lower quality. Similarly, the association between quality and parasite load (disease level) can be positive, negative, or negligible, depending on the system (Getty, 2002).

Are Honest Signaling Systems of Quality Ubiquitous?

A model that does not assume an association between signal intensity and quality is the *sensory bias* model (e.g., Kirkpatrick & Ryan, 1991). In this model, one sex has a bias to prefer individuals with particular qualities because that bias has advantages in realms other than mating. For instance, redness may be preferred in features of mates because redness signals ripeness of fruit and a sensory bias to be attracted to redness spills over into domains other than food selection. Fisher (1930) famously described a process whereby a small initial preference ultimately leads to extreme traits and preferences through "runaway" selection. If a particular trait in one sex is preferred in mates due to sensory bias in the other sex, then genes disposing stronger preference for the trait could spread because they become linked with genes predisposing the preferred trait.

Another sensory bias model, the "chase-away" model (Holland & Rice, 1998), assumes that individuals of the choosing sex with a sensory bias nonadaptively applied to mate choice pay a cost for it (e.g., increased search time) and, hence, have lower reproductive success than those who are "resistant" to the bias. Signal resistance will then be selected for in the receiving sex. This, in turn, leads to selection for more intense signals in the other sex, which itself leads to selection for a still higher threshold of resistance. After many generations, the "chase-away" process results in extreme manifestations of the trait.

Kokko, Brooks, Jennions, and Morley (2003) argued that both runaway and chase-away processes due to small initial sensory biases tell incomplete stories. In each case, the signal that evolves is presumed to become increasingly *costly*. As costs increase, individuals of highest quality will be able to produce the signal more efficiently than others will—precisely the condition in which a signal comes to honestly convey quality. Rather than conceptualizing sensory bias or chase-away models as *competitors* of honest signaling models, then, Kokko et al. argue that sensory bias may be the starting point of a process that leads to honest signaling. Honest signals of quality need not initially be uncorrelated with quality, however. Features may covary with quality prior to being signals because individuals of higher quality pay lower marginal costs for them (e.g., in some species, larger individuals or those better able to intrasexually compete may possess higher quality). Preferences for these traits (or natural correlates of them) may then evolve, which further intensifies them by increasing the benefit of investing in the development of these traits.

Genetic Versus Direct Benefits

Honest signaling of quality can evolve either through benefits that directly enhance reproductive success (e.g., food, protection, lack of contagious disease, etc.) or genetic benefits passed on to offspring. In some instances, both may account for the preference. For instance, males in a multimale primate group better able to protect offspring than others may well possess genes associated with quality as well.

In socially monogamous mating systems in which males invest heavily in offspring (e.g., many bird species), direct benefits and indirect benefits may covary negatively. This should particularly be true when females are not *sexually* monogamous and offspring are frequently sired by "extrapair" males (also true of many bird species; e.g., Petrie & Kempenaers, 1999). In such cases, it pays males who are most preferred by females as extrapair mates to invest time and energy into extrapair mating. And because they provide more genetic benefits than males of lower quality, their partners are willing to tolerate lower levels of help at the nest from them. Female preferences may hence depend on whether they are selecting a social partner or an extrapair mate. In collared flycatchers on the island of Gotland, for instance, females have no clear preference for pair bond males having a relatively large forehead patch, an honest signal of quality; smaller patched males feed offspring more than larger patched males (Qvarnström, 1999). When choosing extrapair partners (from whom they only receive genes for offspring), however, females clearly prefer large-patched males.

Multiple Signals

In many species, mate choosers attend to multiple signals, sometimes through different sensory channels (e.g., both olfactory and visual cues). Multiple signals of the same quality may evolve because each adds unique information (e.g., Grafen & Johnstone, 1993). Relatedly, they may be explained through a combination of constrained transmission time and a need to convey abundant information (Endler, 1993).

Mutual Mate Choice

In many species, sexual selection on signals is much greater in one sex than the other. In mammalian species, females are typically a limiting reproductive resource, and hence, males compete through intrasexual competition and signaling for females. Selection on female signaling is much weaker, as males may seldom turn down sexual opportunities with females. In species in which both males and females invest substantially in offspring, however, mutual mate choice whereby both sexes are selected to display desired mate qualities may evolve (e.g., Kokko & Johnstone, 2002). Although the extent to which men have provided material assistance to offspring throughout human evolutionary history is hotly debated (e.g., Hawkes, O'Connell, & Blurton Jones, 2001; Kaplan, Hill, Lancaster, & Hurtado, 2000), mutual mate choice is characteristic of human cultures.

Intrinsic Good Genes and Compatible Genes

The kinds of indicators of genetic benefits discussed thus far are indicators of "intrinsic" good genes: genes that could have benefited the offspring of most if not all individuals (e.g., relative lack of mutation in the genome or genes currently associated with pathogen resistance). Other genetic benefits are "compatible" or "complementary" genes: those that work well with the genes of the mate chooser, but not the genes of all individuals (see J. A. Zeh & D. W. Zeh, 2001). Candidates include genes within the major histocompatibility complex (MHC), a set of genes that control immunological self-/nonself-recognition and are crucial for mounting effective immune responses to pathogens and parasites. MHC loci are highly polymorphic; there are many different variants that individuals could possess at each gene site. Two unrelated individuals, then, are unlikely to possess identical MHC genotypes. Men who possess alleles at MHC loci that differ from women's own MHC alleles may possess a form of compatible genes (e.g., Penn & Potts, 1999). Preferences for MHC-dissimilarity may function to help individuals avoid inbreeding, increase the genetic diversity (heterozygosity) of individual offspring (within-individual diversity), and obtain rare, beneficial alleles. Increasing offspring heterozygosity may help buffer them from multiple pathogens and parasites by increasing the number of foreign cell-surface markers recognized by their immune systems (J. L. Brown, 1997), as MHC alleles are expressed codominantly, with each coding for different cell-surface receptors. Heterozygous mice and salmon are indeed more fit than homozygous mice and salmon, respectively, when pathogens are present (see Neff & Pitcher, 2005). Among offspring of human couples who share MHC alleles, homozygotes are underrepresented, possibly reflecting *in utero* selection against homozygotes (e.g., Hedrick & Black, 1997).

Mice can detect MHC identities in scents of other mice (Yamazaki, Beauchamp, Curran, Baird, & Boyse, 2000) and prefer mates who possess dissimilar MHC genotypes, based on scent (Penn & Potts, 1999). Similar preferences have been found in other species. Later, we discuss evidence for preferences for MHC-compatibility in humans.

Nonsignaling Systems

Features found attractive by members of the opposite sex need not function as signals. In a signaling system, again, the attractive feature has been exaggerated by selection induced by the opposite sex's preferences. In some situations, however, it may not pay individuals to invest additional energy into an attractive trait. Examples may include when individuals choose others for compatible rather than intrinsic good genes. The compatible genes a target individual possesses are compatible with just a subset of potential mates' genes. If that subset can detect these genes based on by-products (e.g., MHC molecules naturally shed by skin cells and detectable by scent), there may be no benefit to broadcasting MHC types through costly signaling.

Similarly, it may rarely pay females to signal when they are fertile in the cycle. Males are sexually selected to perceive when females are fertile and, in most mammalian and many other vertebrate species, do so based on scent, through which they detect by-products of hormone metabolism characteristic of the fertile period. Because males are good at detecting female fertility status based on by-products, females are typically not benefited by costly signaling of fertility status (e.g., Gangestad & Thornhill, 2007).

THE ATTRACTIVENESS OF SEXUALLY DIMORPHIC FEATURES

We now turn to review literature on facial and bodily features that men and women find attractive. A number of these traits are sexually dimorphic features—traits that differ across the sexes (e.g., see Grammer, Fink, Møller, & Thornhill, 2003).

Facial Sexual Dimorphism

Men and women's faces differ in a number of ways. On average, men's chins are longer and broader than women's are. Development of the brow ridge renders men's eyes smaller (as a proportion of total face size) than women's eyes. Women's cheekbones are more gracile, and their lips are fuller. During adolescence, testosterone promotes growth of the lower face (see Swaddle & Reierson, 2002). Estrogens may cap growth of bones during puberty, contributing to sexual dimorphism as well. Despite variation in facial proportions across human groups, sex differences exist wherever they have been examined (e.g., D. Jones & Hill, 1993). We refer to the aggregate differences between men and women's faces as facial masculinity and femininity, respectively.

The Attractiveness of Female Facial Femininity

Highly attractive women's faces are more feminine than average (e.g., Johnston & Franklin, 1993; Perret, May, & Yoshikawa, 1994). This finding has been replicated in a wide variety of groups, including traditional South American groups with little to no exposure to Western standards of beauty (e.g., Ache; D. Jones & Hill, 1993). Men prefer female faces with relatively small chins, large eyes, high cheekbones, and full lips (Cunningham, 1986). Several theories explaining men's attraction to femininity have been offered.

Facial femininity reflects babyness, preferred due to sensory bias. An early theory is that feminine features such as large eyes and small chin reflect "babyness" (see D. Jones, 1995). People may be disposed to respond to babies with care and, hence, be attracted to baby-like features. Ancestral females who exploited this sensory bias may have been advantaged over those who did not.

This theory encounters three major problems. First, some attractive feminine features are not baby-like. Babies have puffy, protruding cheeks (e.g., McArthur & Apatow, 1984), whereas men are attracted to women's gracile, high cheekbones (e.g., Grammer & Atzwanger, 1994). Second, women nurture babies more heavily than men do (e.g., Clutton-Brock, 1991). The sex that could best extract investment by activating a partner's disposition toward parental investment should be men, not women. Third, as noted earlier, even a sensory bias model should expect that, as a trait is driven to be extreme, some individuals should be best able to display it, and hence, it should become correlated with quality (Kokko et al., 2003).

Female facial femininity marks sex appropriateness. The view that attractive displays exaggerate species- or sex-typical traits to foster choice of a species- or sex-appropriate partner was prominent in the first half of the 20th century (see Cronin, 1993). It might also predict women to prefer highly masculine faces, which (as discussed in a later section) is not universally the case. Furthermore, once again, selection due to a bias favoring a trait uncorrelated with quality should ultimately result in the trait becoming a quality cue.

Female facial femininity is a marker of reproductive value. Reproductive value (RV) is the expected residual reproductive success of an individual, generally based on age (Fisher, 1930). RV is maximal when women reach reproductive age and diminishes thereafter. If men ancestrally mated with pair-bonded partners throughout their reproductive careers (e.g., Kaplan et al., 2000), they would have maximized their fecundity by selecting mates with maximal RV (Symons, 1979). As women age, their facial proportions become less feminine, probably due to accumulated exposure to androgens (see Thornhill & Gangestad, 1993). Men's preference for facial femininity, then, could reflect selection for age-based RV. Indeed, male chimpanzees actually prefer relatively old females (Muller, Thompson, & Wrangham, 2006). Unlike humans, chimpanzees do not form long-lasting pair bonds.

RV could account for selection for a preference favoring facial femininity. Again, however, women should have been selected to exaggerate and prolong the period of facial femininity, with some women better able to do so than others, ultimately leading facial femininity to be a cue of quality.

Facial femininity is a marker of female quality or condition. Female femininity may signal reproductive condition and ability to dedicate energy to offspring production. Women's production of estrogen and their fertility status are designed to be sensitive to conditions that affect their ability to carry and lactate for offspring. Women have diminished ovarian function when they do not have fat stored for reproduction (low energy load), do not reliably take in calories that surpass energy expenditure (low energy balance), or incur extreme (very low or high) energetic demands (high energy flux; Ellison, 2003). Extreme instances result in amenorrhea, but normal variation affects the production of ovarian hormones, including estradiol, and thereby ovarian function, such that female fertility varies along a continuum. Energy balance and flux appear to have larger effects than energy status (Lipson & Ellison, 1996). Facial femininity does not change drastically with immediate circumstances, but it could index women's accumulated history of energy balance and flux appropriate for reproduction. That history could reflect lower disease incidence, better development due to favorable levels of parental investment, greater ability to forage effectively, and so forth, direct benefits affecting current reproductive capabilities. It could also promise genetic benefits to offspring.

Evidence pertaining to whether women's facial femininity or attractiveness are associated with current or developmental health is mixed, with some, but not all, studies showing positive associations (for reviews, see Gangestad & Scheyd, 2005; Grammer, Fink, Møller, & Manning, 2005; Langlois et al., 2000; Weeden & Sabini, 2005). No study has examined facial femininity in relation to health in traditional societies exposed to ecological circumstances reasonably similar to ones encountered by ancestral humans, in which childhood mortality rates may typically have been 30–50% (e.g., Hill & Hurtado, 1996) and energy budgets were constrained. Moreover, no one to our knowledge has explored associations between ovarian function and facial femininity. We suspect that preference for female facial femininity has been maintained because of this trait's historical association with both RV and fertility, but the latter link requires additional evidence.

Attractiveness in Relation to Male Facial Masculinity

One might suspect that, just as men find feminine faces attractive, women are attracted to masculine faces. In fact, no consistent preference exists; studies have found a female preference for somewhat masculine faces, preference for feminine faces, and no systematic preference either way (see Gangestad & Scheyd, 2005).

Male facial masculinity nonetheless covaries with certain desired male traits. Across a variety of cultures, men with masculine faces are perceived to be, and probably are (Mueller & A. Mazur, 1997), socially dominant (e.g., Keating, A. Mazur, & Segall, 1981; A. Mazur, J. Mazur, & Keating,

1984). Kung San bushmen, with broad chins and robust bodies, have relatively high reproductive success (Winkler & Kirchengast, 1994). One argument is that testosterone promotes male mating effort, which partly involves male-male competition, and that men's condition affects the extent to which they can effectively dedicate energy to mating effort (analogous to the way in which women's condition affects their ability to dedicate effort to reproduction). Variation in condition therefore gives rise to variation in testosterone metabolism, which, during adolescence, causes variation in facial masculinity. Men with more masculine faces may be tested in male-male competition, a cost that may ensure its honesty as a signal of condition. Indeed, a number of studies have found associations between male facial masculinity and reported health (for a review, see Gangestad & Scheyd, 2005). Male facial masculinity may be weakly associated with current testosterone level (Penton-Voak & Chen, 2004). However, as male testosterone level is a function of several factors, including mating status and paternity (e.g., Burnham et al., 2003), facial masculinity may better index levels during adolescence and early adulthood. If adolescence is characterized by relatively intense male-male competition, facial masculinity may nonetheless reflect condition.

If male facial masculinity predicts condition, why do women not consistently prefer masculine faces? Women may face a trade-off: Though more dominant and fit, masculine men may be less willing to invest exclusively in partners and help care for offspring (Penton-Voak et al., 1999). Hence, just as female collared flycatchers do not particularly prefer males with large forehead patches as social mates, women may not prefer more masculine men as mates. Consistent with this hypothesis, men with feminine faces are perceived to be warmer, more agreeable, and more honest than men with masculine faces are (Fink & Penton-Voak, 2002).

According to this view, attraction to male masculinity should have been shaped by selection to be *conditional*—depend on conditions that affect (or ancestrally would have affected) the relative value of (possibly heritable) condition and paternal investment. A wealth of evidence suggests that it is.

Preference varies with phase of the ovulatory cycle. Women's mate preferences vary across their ovulatory cycles. When normally ovulating women (i.e., those with regular menstrual cycles who are not using hormonal-based contraception) are close to ovulation and, hence, fertile, they are particularly attracted to the scent of symmetrical men, deep, masculine male voices, and more confident, intrasexually competitive men, particularly when they evaluate men as sexual partners (their "sexiness") rather than as long-term mates (for a review, see Gangestad, Thornhill, & Garver-Apgar, 2005). Changes in preferences across the cycle may reflect female design to weight signals of heritable condition more heavily when they are fertile, particularly when selecting a sex partner. Interestingly, then, the face that women most prefer when close to ovulation is more masculine than the face most preferred when they are in the luteal phase (Johnston, Hagel, Franklin, Fink, & Grammer, 2001; Penton-Voak et al., 1999; Penton-Voak & Perrett, 2000). Furthermore, the effect is specific to female attraction to men as sex partners, not long-term social mates (Penton-Voak et al., 1999).

Preference varies as a function of relationship context. The face women find most attractive in short-term mates is more masculine than the face they find most attractive in long-term mates (Penton-Voak et al., 2003).

More attractive women have a stronger preference for masculine faces. Little, D. M. Burt, Penton-Voak, and Perrett (2001) reasoned that attractive women need not trade off male condition and investment as markedly as must unattractive women; masculine men should be more likely to invest in relationships with attractive women. In fact, attractive women more strongly prefer facial masculinity (Little et al., 2001; Penton-Voak et al., 2003).

Preference varies with culture. Penton-Voak, Jacobson, and Trivers (2004) proposed that women's preference for masculinity should have been selected to be sensitive to cues of the relative value of condition (and genetic benefits) and investment of male mates in their local ecologies. In Jamaica, infectious disease is more prevalent and male parental investment less pronounced than in the United Kingdom. They predicted and found that Jamaican women show greater preference for facial masculinity than do British women.

Findings that women's preferences for facial masculinity are conditional constitute design evidence that women's attraction to male faces has been shaped by how male condition and parental investment have traded off.

SEXUALLY DIMORPHIC BODY FEATURES

Female Body Form

In 1993, Singh proposed that, although preferences with respect to female body weights vary cross-culturally, men universally prefer women with a low waist-to-hip ratio (WHR). Women have lower WHRs than men do, largely due to the fact that women tend to store in the hips (as well as breasts) fat that is selectively available for gestation and lactation. It now appears that, across a wide variety of cultures (although see the following section), men do prefer a lower than average WHR (most preferred typically being about .7, compared to a mean in most populations of about .75–.80; e.g., Singh, 1993; Singh & Luis, 1995; Streeter & McBurney, 2003; Tassinary & Hansen, 1998).

The primary benefit of this preference may ancestrally have been the same as a benefit of a preference for feminine faces: Low WHRs reflect a history of energy balance and flux that promotes allocation of energy into reproductive effort. The proximate mechanism may involve estrogens. Indeed, Jasienska, Ziomkiewicz, Ellison, Lipson, and Thune (2004) found that, within a Polish population, women with lower WHRs and larger breasts have greater fertility than other women do, as assessed through precise measurements of estradiol and progesterone. Women's tendency to store fat on the hips and breasts may have evolved as adaptations for creating a low center of gravity appropriate for carrying fetuses and babies and putting fat where it can readily be converted for lactation, respectively (e.g., Pawlowski & Grabarczyk, 2003). As a correlate of fertility, however, it may have evolved as a signal of quality, with mating benefits leading to some exaggeration of the display.

If facial femininity and attractive body shapes signal overlapping qualities, they should covary across women. In fact, however, the correlation is modest (Penton-Voak et al., 2003; Thornhill & Grammer, 1999). WHR and facial femininity contain largely nonredundant information; future research should address their distinct sources of influence.

The universality of a preference for low WHRs has been challenged. Men in a traditional society, the Matsigenka of Peru, have been claimed to largely disregard WHR and generally prefer women viewed as relatively heavy (Yu & Shepard, 1998; see also Marlowe, Apicella, & Reed, 2005, on the Hadza of Tanzania). Sugiyama (2004) found a similar preference for large body size in the Shiwiar of Ecuador. There, as in other foraging societies studied, however, women have higher WHRs (close to .9 on average) than do women in Western populations. Using a sample of figures with variation typical of the Shiwiar and controlling for weight, Sugiyama found that Shiwiar men do prefer smaller WHRs. In foraging societies, female body weight may be a positive predictor of fertility (e.g., Hill & Hurtado, 1996) and obesity may rarely be a health problem (e.g., P. J. Brown & Konner, 1987). Hence, men may use energy status (stored body fat) as a cue of fertility and ability to lactate effectively. In Western cultures, energy status appears to be weakly associated with fecundity (Ellison, 2003) and hence men weigh more heavily indicators of energy balance and flux (e.g., WHR). At the same time, they may prefer women of moderate body mass index (BMI), argued to be a powerful predictor of female body attractiveness in Western samples (e.g., Tovee, Hancock, Mahmoodi, Singleton, & Cornelissen, 2002).

A key question is whether and, if so, how selection has shaped adaptations for male preference for female body shapes or sizes to be conditional and depend on local ecological factors that affect predictors of female fecundity. Sugiyama (2004) has proposed that men do have specialized adaptations for preferring women of high fertility (see also Marlowe & Wetsman, 2001), which have been shaped to be sensitive to local conditions, but the nature of such conditional inputs (e.g., food scarcity, distribution of body types, etc.) remains poorly understood. Cultural transmission processes (e.g., Boyd & Richerson, 1985) may also play important roles, but are not well understood either.

Male Physique

Scant research has addressed female preferences for male body features. Dixson, Halliwell, East, Wignarajah, and Anderson (2003) found that women in both Britain and Sri Lanka prefer lean, muscular body types most, followed by average, and then skinny body types; heavy body types are least preferred. Women also prefer men with broad shoulders, relative to waist or hip size (i.e., a "V-shaped" torso; Franzoi & Herzog, 1987; Horvath, 1981; Hughes & Gallup, 2003; Lindner, Rychman, Gold, & Stone, 1995; Mehrabian & Blum, 1997), and average WHRs (Singh, 1995). To date, these preferences have been studied in few cultures.

A number of benefits might explain these preferences: physical protection, nutritional resources, benefits of male status, and genetic benefits to offspring. Preferences for muscularity, similar to those for facial masculinity, are conditional: Women particularly prefer muscularity in men as short-term (as opposed to long-term) partners (e.g., Buss & Schmitt, 1993), and normally ovulating women are particularly attracted to muscular men as short-term partners when near ovulation (Gangestad et al., 2007). These effects suggest that muscularity partly signals genetic benefits (Frederick & Haselton, 2004).

Testosterone promotes muscle growth (Ellison, 2003). Though sharing some influences, body and facial masculinity may not signal precisely the same traits. Future research should examine the independent influences on these traits.

The 2D:4D

The traits we have discussed thus far are affected by adolescent or adult hormone levels. The ratio of the length of the index finger to the length of the ring finger (the 2D:4D ratio) is a potential footprint of early hormone exposure. Individual differences in digit ratio are established *in utero*. Females reliably have higher 2D:4D than males (though the sex difference is modest). Multiple lines of evidence suggest that perinatal testosterone (negatively) and possibly estrogen (positively) affect the ratio (see McIntyre, 2006, for a review). Thereafter, despite growth of the body and hands, digit ratios are largely stable throughout childhood (e.g., Trivers, Manning, & Jacobson, 2006).

Sexually antagonistic selection is said to operate when the optimum level of a heritable trait exhibits a sex difference, such that either sex or both sexes are prevented from evolving to their ecological optimum as a result of their necessary inheritance of genes from the other sex. Manning et al. (2000) proposed that sexually antagonistic genes affect perinatal hormones. English and Spanish men with low digit ratios have more offspring, as do English, Hungarian, and German women with high digit ratios. Honekopp, Voracek, and Manning (2006) found that male digit ratio negatively correlated with self-reported number of sex partners. Women with high ratios have been found to have higher self-perceived attractiveness (Wade, Shanley, & Imm, 2004; see also Russell, 2006), more regular menses, and longer sexual relationships (Scarbrough & Johnston, 2005). Fink, Manning, Neave, and Grammer (2004) found that facial symmetry is associated with low digit ratios in men but with high digit ratios in women, suggesting not only effects of sexually antagonistic genes but also that digit ratio, like symmetry (discussed below), may be a marker of developmental stability.

(We note that all sexually dimorphic traits—including facial features—likely also partly reflect influences by sexually antagonistic genes.)

Low digit ratios are associated with greater physical fitness (Hönekopp, Manning, & Müller, 2006) and, in both German and Indian men, physical strength (Fink, Thanzami, Seydel, & Manning, 2006). Men with low 2D:4D have also been found to be less agreeable (Luxen & Buunk, 2005) and more physically aggressive (Bailey & Hurd, 2005). Pervasive developmental disorders, more common among males, are also predicted by low digit ratio when sex has been controlled for (Manning, Baron-Cohen, S. Wheelwright, & Sanders, 2001). Women with more male-typical digit ratios outperform their same-sex peers on mental rotation, a task that shows a male advantage (Kempel et al., 2005; Scarbrough & Johnston, 2005), and possess a relatively masculine sex-role identity (Csatho et al., 2003).

Not all findings have been positive. Putz et al. (2004) found virtually no predicted associations with a variety of sexually dimorphic traits thought to be affected by sex hormones (e.g., spatial ability, physical prowess, voice pitch) or measures of mating success. Firman, Simmons, Cummins, and Matson (2003) did not find the digit ratio to predict men's semen qualities.

The digit ratio itself is probably not a major component of attractiveness (though one study did find that hands with sex-typical digit ratios are more attractive than hands with ratios more characteristic of the other sex; Saino, Romano, & Innocenti, 2006). The prenatal hormonal patterns the ratio reflects, however, may affect components of attractiveness. Fink, Neave, and Manning (2003) reported mixed associations between digit ratio and sexually dimorphic body features. Roney and Maestripieri (2004) found that men with low digit ratios were judged to be more physically attractive than men with high ratios in an interaction with an attractive female confederate. By contrast, Neave et al. (2003) did not find that male digit ratio predicts facial attractiveness, but men with low ratios were perceived to be relatively dominant. Interestingly, the shape of men and women's faces may be affected by prenatal hormone levels (Fink et al., 2005), in ways distinct from effects of chromosomal sex. Compared to same-sex counterparts, both men and women with relatively masculine 2D:4D ratios have more "robust" faces—broader jaws, thinner lips, and heavier brow ridges. Additional work on is needed to clarify how perinatal hormones affect attractiveness and other perceived qualities.

OTHER PREFERRED FACIAL TRAITS: AVERAGENESS AND SYMMETRY

Facial Averageness

In 1990, Langlois and Roggman published a highly influential study. They digitized photographs of faces, then created "average" composites of sex-specific sets of them. Raters of both sexes found the averaged faces to be attractive, consistent with earlier speculation by Symons (1979) and suggestive findings by Sir Francis Galton (1878). The finding has been replicated many times, including in China and Japan and among the Ache (D. Jones & Hill, 1993). This preference is not merely because composite faces are symmetrical and have unblemished skin; people find average face shape and morphology attractive (for a review, see Rhodes, 2006). Some faces are more attractive than the averaged faces. Nonetheless, extreme departures from average on even sexually dimorphic traits are not attractive.

Two main hypotheses may explain preference for averageness.

1. A generalized sensory bias favors prototypes. Organisms may show preference for stimuli that are readily processed (e.g., Enquist & Arak, 1994). People may build up cognitive prototypes of distinct categories of stimuli, representations consisting of average features, which can be used to discriminate new instances of the category.

Stimuli that match prototype well may be preferred. Halberstadt and Rhodes (2000, 2003) found that people indeed find averaged instances not only of human faces, but also of dogs, fish, birds, wristwatches, and automobiles, attractive. But they proposed that people have a preference for averageness per se, independent of familiarity, when judging the attractiveness of living organisms, which may reflect a preference for signals of quality.

2. Averageness reflects quality. Departures from average may reflect the effects of genetic mutation, chromosomal abnormality, nongenetic congenital deformation, disease, or other factors affecting quality. Zebrowitz and Rhodes (2004) found that facial averageness predicts pubertal intelligence and adolescent health (the latter for women), but only in the lower half of the averageness distribution. They therefore proposed that averageness (and other purported indicators of condition, e.g., facial masculinity) discriminates average from "bad" genes (or poor condition) but not from "good" genes. In fact, however, this effect may not be robust, as the regression slopes for high and low averageness groups did not significantly differ. Moreover, a plausible alternative is that prediction at the high end of averageness is compromised because some nonaverage features indicative of good condition (e.g., sexually dimorphic features) are preferred. Aggregates of different signals may discriminate condition along a continuum, a possibility to be explored in future research.

Facial Symmetry

Bilateral asymmetry on features that, on average within a population, are symmetrical may reflect perturbations occurring during development due to mutations, pathogens, toxins, and other stresses (e.g., Møller, 1999). Manipulations of symmetry of signals in some (but not all) other species affect attractiveness (see Møller & Thornhill, 1998). And they typically do so in humans as well (for a review, see Rhodes, 2006).

Two empirical questions arise. The first is the size of the effect of symmetry on normal variation of attractiveness. Whereas female femininity and facial averageness reliably account for moderate amounts of variation in attractiveness, symmetry does not (for a review, see Gangestad & Scheyd, 2005). The correlation in most populations is probably in a predicted direction but weak ($r < .2$).

A second question concerns the extent to which facial symmetry per se generates its association with attractiveness. Scheib, Gangestad, and Thornhill (1999) found that both facial and body asymmetry predict male facial attractiveness. But facial symmetry predicted just as well the attractiveness of half-faces, which possess minimal cues of symmetry (see also Penton-Voak et al., 2001). Jaw size and prominent cheekbones covaried with symmetry and were able to account for its association with attractiveness. Men with symmetrical faces may have healthier-looking skin as well (B. C. Jones et al., 2004).

Perhaps ironically, it is not clear that facial symmetry *should* be used as a cue of condition. Single trait asymmetries are very weak indicators of underlying variation in developmental instability (Gangestad & Thornhill, 1999, 2003). Only by aggregating asymmetries of multiple traits can researchers develop reasonably valid measures. Facial asymmetry and broad composites of body asymmetry covary modestly (see Gangestad & Scheyd, 2005). Facial symmetry may weakly tap developmental stability.

Enquist and Johnstone (1997) proposed that symmetry preferences may be a byproduct of generalization effects when individuals are exposed to asymmetrical variants of an object (e.g., faces) that are symmetrical on average. Jansson, Forman, and Enquist (2002) demonstrated that chickens repeatedly exposed to asymmetrical novel stimuli (around a symmetric mean) came to prefer symmetrical stimuli to which they had not previously been exposed. Little and B. C. Jones (2003) demonstrated a greater symmetry preference for faces in normal orientation than for inverted faces, which can be explained by generalization (as people rarely see inverted faces). They also showed a preference for symmetry even in familiar faces, which a prototype (though not a mere familiarity) account may explain. Simmons, Rhodes, Peters, and Koehler (2004) found that, although faces are characterized by directional asymmetries (mean $L > R$ or $R > L$ differences in the population), these asymmetries do not affect attractiveness; rather, deviations around them (*atypical* asymmetries) do—a finding also consistent with either the perceptual bias account or the symmetry-marks-quality explanation.

One finding favoring the symmetry-marks-quality explanation is that, just as attractive women have relatively strong masculinity preferences, they have strong symmetry preferences (Little et al., 2001). Koehler, Rhodes, and Simmons (2002), however, found no evidence that normally ovulating women particularly prefer symmetrical faces—as they prefer masculine faces—when near ovulation.

In sum, we do not yet know the extent to which symmetry drives attractiveness judgments and, to the extent it does, what explains the preference. This is not to say, however, that developmental stability does not covary with physical attractiveness. A number of studies have shown that men's *body* symmetry (aggregated across a number of traits, which gives a reasonably good measure of organism-wide developmental stability) predicts their facial attractiveness (see Gangestad & Thornhill, 1999). And Jasienska, Lipson, Ellison, Thune, and Ziomkiewicz (2006) found that women with greater body symmetry had greater potential fertility (as assessed through hormone profiles). Again, however, the cues of developmental stability that perceivers find attractive need not include facial symmetry per se.

PREFERENCES FOR MHC: COMPATIBILITY AND HETEROZYGOSITY

MHC Compatibility

If individuals gain a selective advantage by mating with individuals dissimilar to themselves at the MHC loci, mate preferences may be sensitive to a potential partner's MHC genotype. In fact, MHC-dissimilar mate preferences have been detected in mice (Penn, 2002; Penn & Potts, 1999), species of birds (Freeman-Gallant, Meguerdichian, N. T. Wheelwright, & Sollecito, 2003), fish (Milinski et al., 2005), and lizards (Olsson et al., 2003). In humans, too, women appear to be particularly attracted to the scent of men who possess MHC alleles dissimilar to their own (Santos, Schinemann, Gabardo, & Bicalho, 2005; Wedekind & Füri, 1997; Wedekind, Seebeck, Bettens, & Paepke, 1995; cf. Thornhill et al. 2003). In two out of three studies, men exhibited a corresponding preference for the scent of MHC-dissimilar women (Thornhill et al., 2003; Wedekind & Füri, 1997; cf. Santos et al., 2005). These preferences, in fact, may affect actual romantic relationships. Compared to other women, women who share MHC alleles with romantic partners, and thereby have partners with incompatible genes, appear to be less sexually responsive to their partners and more likely to have been sexually unfaithful to their partners. They furthermore report particularly enhanced sexual attraction to men other than partners when near ovulation (Garver-Apgar, Gangestad, Thornhill, Miller, & Olp, 2006). Thornhill et al., however, found no evidence that women's preference for the scent of men who possess dissimilar MHC alleles is particularly strong when women are fertile in their cycles.

MHC Heterozygosity

Individuals in some species also prefer the scent of members of the opposite sex who are themselves heterozygous at MHC loci. Preferences for MHC-heterozygosity may serve to increase the genetic diversity of an entire brood, assuming the preference is found either in a species that produces large litters, or for a long-term mate with whom one intends on producing multiple offspring. Increasing within-brood diversity at MHC loci may decrease transmission of contagious diseases among close kin (siblings) if pathogens are adapted to some genotypes better than others are. More generally, it increases the probability that at least some offspring will be well adapted to any potential suite of pathogens in an uncertain environment.

Female mate preferences for MHC-heterozygosity or greater reproductive success of MHC-heterozygotic males have been found in sticklebacks (Reusch, Haber, Aeschlimann, & Milinski, 2001), salmon (Skarstein, Folstad, Liljedal, & Grahn, 2005), and house sparrows (Bonneaud, Chastel, Federici, Westerdahl, & Sorci, 2006). In warblers, females are more likely to obtain extrapair paternity when their social mate has low MHC diversity, and the MHC diversity of the extrapair male is higher than that of the cuckolded male (Richardson, Komdeur, Burke, & von Schantz, 2005). Thornhill et al. (2003) found evidence of such a mechanism acting in humans as well: In their study, women preferred the scent of MHC heterozygous men over homozygous men and did so more during low-fertility times of the cycle. This makes sense given that benefits of heterozygosity are only realized in a long-term partner. Women also appear to find faces of men heterozygous at MHC loci more attractive that faces of men homozygous at MHC loci (Roberts et al., 2005).

THE CONDITIONAL NATURE OF PREFERENCES

As previously noted, preferences may be shaped by selection to be conditional: to depend on particular circumstances that modulate the value of attraction to specific features. This theme has driven a number of recent research programs. At least four types of condition-dependent preferences have been conjectured.

Calibration of preferences to local ecological and socioecological conditions. Despite substantial cross-cultural convergence with respect to standards of beauty such as female facial femininity and averageness, some preferences vary cross-culturally (e.g., female preferences for male facial masculinity, male preferences for female body fat). Do these variations reflect adaptations sensitive to specific ecological inputs that ancestrally affected the value of particular features (e.g., disease prevalence in relation to male facial masculinity; food scarcity in relation to female body mass)? To what extent are variations nonadaptive and maintained through cultural transmission processes?

Calibration of preferences to individual variations within culture. Different individuals may differentially benefit from pursuing particular individuals as mates. Just as Little et al. (2001) proposed that attractive women should have a stronger preference for facial masculinity, Brase and Walker (2004) hypothesized that attractive men should particularly value women with attractive WHRs. More generally, Scheyd (2003) proposed and found evidence that men's own attractiveness affects their weighting of features that are consensually considered attractive. In three samples (including one from a rural village in Dominica, West Indies), unattractive men, relative to attractive men, were less drawn to those women found to be most attractive overall. Men differentially disposed to long-term and short-term mating might also be differentially attracted to signals of RV (youth) and current fertility, respectively (e.g., Scheyd, 2002).

Preferences vary as a function of relationship context. What may be most attractive in a long-term mate may not be what is most attractive in a short-term mate. No work on this issue has yet been done in traditional societies.

Preferences vary as a function of individual circumstances. Until the late 1990s, no one reading the literature would have suspected that women's standards of attraction change across their ovulatory cycles. We now know that they change in many ways. What other immediate life circumstances (e.g., pregnancy, mating status, parental status) affect standards of attraction in ways predicted by adaptationist hypotheses?

CONCLUSION

The topography of the human body is a testament to the power of selection. The vertebrate eye, the bipedal stance, the opposable thumb—each is a product of the benefits it provided—but nowhere is selection pressure greater than where reproduction itself is involved. Long before the evolution of language, there existed already a communication system of profound importance, that of signal production and perception, that provided the framework upon which each component of attractiveness could be set. The ability to discern valid signals of benefits in choosing a mate is a fundamental skill in the adaptive repertoire of a sexually reproducing animal such as *Homo sapiens*, and the nature of signaling systems allows even arbitrary preferences to evolve into those that can incisively evaluate a phenotype for the benefits it promises.

In this light, we have presented physical attractiveness (both visual and olfactory) as the emergent property of this form of signaler-receiver system. We have endeavored, as well, to explore the landscape of phenotypic quality more broadly by discussing the morphological measures of fluctuating asymmetry and digit ratio, for which individual differences exist below the threshold of attractiveness discrimination, but each of which is rapidly generating an empirical literature that testifies to its value as a marker of developmental stability. Research on physical attractiveness conducted from an evolutionary perspective over the past 2 decades has provided us a great many answers and a great many fascinating questions. We look forward to the data of the next 2 decades—the hypotheses they will produce, the debates they will provoke, and the answers they will provide.

REFERENCES

Bailey, A. A., & Hurd, P. L. (2005). Finger length ratio (2D:4D) correlates with physical aggression in men but not in women. *Biological Psychology, 68*, 215–222.

Bonneaud, C., Chastel, O., Federici, P., Westerdahl, H., & Sorci, G. (2006). Complex Mhc-based mate choice in a wild passerine. *Proceedings of the Royal Society of London B, 273*, 1111–1116.

Boyd, R., & Richerson, P. (1985). *Culture and the evolutionary process*. Chicago: University of Chicago Press.

Brase, G. L., & Walker, G. (2004). Male sexual strategies modify ratings of female models with specific waist-to-hip ratios. *Human Nature, 15*, 209–224.

Brown, J. L. (1997). A theory of mate choice based on heterozygosity. *Behavioral Ecology, 8*, 60–65.

Brown, P. J., & Konner, M. (1987). An anthropological perspective on obesity. *Annals of the New York Academy of Sciences, 499*, 29–46.

Burnham, T. C., Chapman, J. F., Gray, P. B., McIntyre, M. H., Lipson, S. F., & Ellison, P. T. (2003). Men in committed, romantic relationships have lower testosterone. *Hormones and Behavior, 44*, 119–122.

Buss, D. M., & Schmitt, D. P. (1993). Sexual strategies theory: A contextual evolutionary analysis of human mating. *Psychological Review, 100*, 204–232.

Clutton-Brock, T. H. (1991). *The evolution of parental care*. Princeton, NJ: Princeton University Press.

Cronin, H. (1993). *The ant and the peacock*. Cambridge, U.K.: Cambridge University Press.

Csatho, A., Osvath, A., Bicsak, E., Karadi, K., Manning, J. T., & Kallai, J. (2003). Sex role identity related to the ratio of second to fourth digit length in women. *Biological Psychology, 62*, 147–156.

Cunningham, M. R. (1986). Measuring the physical in physical attractiveness: Quasi-experiments on the sociobiology of female beauty. *Journal of Personality and Social Psychology, 50*, 925–935.

Darwin, C. (1871). *The descent of man and selection in relation to sex*. London: Murray.

Dixson, A. F., Halliwell, G., East, R., Wignarajah, P., & Anderson, M. J. (2003). Masculine somatotype and hirsuteness as determinants of sexual attractiveness to women. *Archives of Sexual Behavior, 32*, 29–39.

Ellison, P. T. (2003). Energetics and reproductive effort. *American Journal of Human Biology, 15,* 342–351.

Endler, J. A. (1993). Some general comments on the evolution and design of animal communication systems. *Philosophical Transactions of the Royal Society of London B, 340,* 215–225.

Enquist, M., & Arak, A. (1994). Symmetry, evolution, and beauty. *Nature, 372,* 169–172.

Enquist, M., & Johnstone, R. A. (1997). Generalization and the evolution of symmetry preferences. *Proceedings of the Royal Society of London B, 264,* 1345–1348.

Fink, B., Grammer, K., Mitteroecker, P., Gunz, P., Schaefer, K., Bookstein, F. L., et al. (2005). Second to fourth digit ratio and face shape. *Proceedings of the Royal Society of London B, 272,* 1995–2001.

Fink, B., Manning, J. T., Neave, N., & Grammer, K. (2004). Second to fourth digit ratio and facial asymmetry. *Evolution and Human Behavior, 25,* 125–132.

Fink, B., Neave, N., & Manning, J. T. (2003). Second to fourth digit ratio, body mass index, waist-to-hip ratio, and waist-to-chest ratio: Their relationships in heterosexual men and women. *Annals of Human Biology, 30,* 728–738.

Fink, B., & Penton-Voak, I. S. (2002). Evolutionary psychology of facial attractiveness. *Curent Directions in Psychological Science, 11,* 154–158.

Fink, B., Thanzami, V., Seydel, H., & Manning, J. T. (2006). Digit ratio (2D:4D) and hand grip strength in German and Mizos men: Cross-cultural evidence for an organising effect of prenatal testosterone on strength. *American Journal of Human Biology, 18,* 776–782.

Firman, R. C., Simmons, L. W., Cummins, J. M., & Matson, P. L. (2003). Are body fluctuating asymmetry and the ratio of 2nd to 4th digit length reliable predictors of semen quality? *Human Reproduction, 18,* 808–812.

Fisher, R. A. (1930). *The genetical theory of natural selection.* Oxford, U.K.: Clarendon.

Franzoi, S. L., & Herzog, M. E. (1987). Judging physical attractiveness: What body aspects do we use? *Personality and Social Psychology Bulletin, 13,* 19–33.

Frederick, D. A., & Haselton, M. G. (2004). *Is male muscularity a sexually-selected fitness indicator? Evidence from women's preferences for short-term and long-term mates.* Paper presented at the evolutionary preconference of the Society for Personality and Social Psychology, Austin, TX.

Freeman-Gallant, C. R., Meguerdichian, M., Wheelwright, N. T., & Sollecito, S. V. (2003). Social pairing and female mating fidelity predicted by restriction fragment length polymorphism similarity at the major histocompatibility complex in a songbird. *Molecular Ecology, 12,* 3077–3083.

Galton, F. J. (1878). Composite portraits. *Nature, 18,* 97–100.

Gangestad, S. W., & Scheyd, G. J. (2005). The evolution of human physical attractiveness. *Annual Review of Anthropology, 34,* 523–548.

Gangestad, S. W., & Thornhill, R. (1999). Individual differences in developmental precision and fluctuating asymmetry: A model and its implications. *Journal of Evolutionary Biology, 12,* 402–416.

Gangestad, S. W., & Thornhill, R. (2003). Fluctuating asymmetry, developmental instability, and fitness: Toward model-based interpretation. In M. Polak (Ed.), *Developmental instability: Causes and consequences* (pp. 62–80). Cambridge, U.K.: Cambridge University Press.

Gangestad, S. W., & Thornhill, R. (2007). The evolution of social inference processes: The importance of signaling theory. In J. P. Forgas, M. G. Haselton, & W. von Hippel (Eds.), *Evolutionary psychology and social cognition* (pp. 33–48). New York: Psychology Press.

Gangestad, S. W., Thornhill, R., & Garver-Apgar, C. E. (2005). Adaptations to ovulation: Implications for sexual and social behavior. *Current Directions in Psychological Science, 14,* 312–316.

Gangestad, S. W., Garver-Apgar, C. E., Simpson, J. A., & Cousins, A. J. (2007). Changes in women's mate preferences across the ovulatory cycle. *Journal of Personality and Social Psychology, 92,* 151–163.

Garver-Apgar, C. E., Gangestad, S. W., Thornhill, R., Miller, R. D., & Olp, J. (2006). MHC alleles, sexually responsivity, and unfaithfulness in romantic couples. *Psychological Science, 17,* 830–835.

Getty, T. (1998). Handicap signalling: When fecundity and mortality do not add up. *Animal Behaviour, 56,* 127–130.

Getty, T. (2002). Signaling health versus parasites. *American Naturalist, 159,* 363–371.

Grafen, A. (1990). Sexual selection unhandicapped by the Fisher process. *Journal of Theoretical Biology, 144,* 473–516.

Grafen, A., & Johnstone, R. A. (1993). Why we need ESS signaling theory. *Philosophical Transactions of the Royal Society of London B, 340,* 245–250.

Grammer, K., & Atzwanger, K. (1994). Der Lolita-complex: Sexualle attractivität und kindchenschema. In F. Naumann (Ed.), *Kommunikation und humanontogenese* (pp. 77–99). Bielefeld, Germany: Kleine Verlag.

Grammer, K., Fink, B., Møller, A. P., & Manning, J. T. (2005). Physical attractiveness and health: Comment on Weeden and Sabini. *Psychological Bulletin, 131,* 658–661.

Grammer, K., Fink, B., Møller, A. P., & Thornhill, R. (2003). Darwinian aesthetics: Sexual selection and the biology of beauty. *Biological Reviews, 78,* 385–407.

Halberstadt, J., & Rhodes, G. (2000). The attractiveness of nonface averages: Implications for an evolutionary explanation of the attractiveness of average faces. *Psychological Science, 11,* 285–289.

Halberstadt, J., & Rhodes, G. (2003). It's not just average faces that are attractive: Computer-manipulated averageness makes birds, fish, and automobiles attractive. *Psychonomic Bulletin and Review, 10,* 149–156.

Hawkes, K., O'Connell, J. F., & Blurton Jones, N. G. (2001). Hunting and nuclear families—some lessons from the Hadza about men's work. *Current Anthropology, 42,* 681–709.

Hedrick, P. W., & Black, F. L. (1997). HLA and mate selection: No evidence in South Amerindians. *American Journal of Human Genetics, 61,* 505–511.

Herz, R. S., & Cahill, E. D. (1997). Differential use of sensory information in sexual behavior as a function of gender. *Human Nature, 8,* 275–286.

Hill, K., & Hurtado, A. M. (1996). *Ache life history: The ecology and demography of a foraging people.* New York: de Gruyter.

Holland, B., & Rice, W. R. (1998). Chase-away sexual selection: Antagonistic seduction versus resistance. *Evolution, 52,* 1–7.

Hönekopp, J., Manning, J. T., & Müller, C. (2006). Digit ratio (2D:4D) and physical fitness in males and females: Evidence for effects of prenatal androgens on sexually selected traits. *Hormones and Behavior, 49,* 545–549.

Hönekopp, J., Voracek, M., & Manning, J. T. (2006). 2nd to 4th digit ratio (2D:4D) and number of sex partners: Evidence for effects of prenatal testosterone in men. *Psychoendocrinology, 31,* 30–37.

Horvath, T. (1981). Physical attractiveness: The influence of selected torso parameters. *Archives of Sexual Behavior, 10,* 21–24.

Houle, D. (1992). Comparing evolvability and variability of traits. *Genetics, 130,* 195–204.

Hughes, S. M., & Gallup, G. G. (2003). Sex differences in morphological predictors of sexual behavior: Shoulder to hip and waist to hip ratios. *Evolution and Human Behavior, 24,* 173–178.

Jansson, L., Forkman, B., & Enquist, M. (2002). Experimental evidence of receiver bias for symmetry. *Animal Behaviour, 63,* 617–621.

Jasienska, G., Lipson, S. F., Ellison, P. T., Thune, I., & Ziomkiewicz, A. (2006). Symmetrical women have higher potential fertility. *Evolution and Human Behavior, 27,* 390–400.

Jasienska, G., Ziomkiewicz, A., Ellison, P. T., Lipson, S. F., & Thune, I. (2004). Large breasts and narrow waists indicate high reproductive potential in women. *Proceedings of the Royal Society of London B, 271,* 1213–1217.

Johnston, V. S., & Franklin, M. (1993). Is beauty in the eye of the beholder? *Ethology and Sociobiology, 14,* 183–199.

Johnston, V. S., Hagel, R., Franklin, M., Fink, B., & Grammer, K. (2001). Male facial attractiveness: Evidence for hormone mediated adaptive design. *Evolution and Human Behavior, 21,* 251–267.

Jones, B. C., Little, A. C., Feinberg, D. R., Penton-Voak, I. S., Tiddeman, B. P., & Perrett, D. I. (2004). The relationship between shape symmetry and perceived skin condition in male facial attractiveness. *Evolution and Human Behavior, 25,* 24–30.

Jones, D. (1995). Sexual selection, physical attractiveness, and facial neoteny. *Current Anthropology, 36,* 723–748.

Jones, D., & Hill, K. (1993). Criteria of facial attractiveness in five populations. *Human Nature, 4,* 271–296.

Kaplan, H., Hill, K., Lancaster, J., & Hurtado, A. M. (2000). A theory of human life history evolution: Diet, intelligence, and longevity. *Evolutionary Anthropology, 9,* 156–185.

Keating, C. F., Mazur, A., & Segall, M. H. (1981). A cross-cultural exploration of the physiognomy of dominance and happiness. *Ethology and Sociobiology, 2,* 41–48.

Kempel, P., Gohlke, B., Klempau, J., Zinsberger, P., Reuter, M., & Hennig, J. (2005). Second-to-fourth digit length, testosterone and spatial ability. *Intelligence, 33,* 215–230.

Kirkpatrick, M., & Ryan, M. J. (1991). The evolution of mating preferences and the paradox of the lek. *Nature, 350*, 33–38.

Koehler, N., Rhodes, G., & Simmons, L. W. (2002). Are human female preferences for symmetrical male faces enhanced when conception is likely? *Animal Behaviour, 64*, 233–238.

Kokko, H., Brooks, R., Jennions, M. D., & Morley, J. (2003). The evolution of mate choice and mating biases. *Proceedings of the Royal Society of London B, 270*, 653–664.

Kokko, H., Brooks, R., McNamara, J. M., & Houston, A. I. (2002). The sexual selection continuum. *Proceedings of the Royal Society of London B, 269*, 1331–1340.

Kokko, H., & Johnstone, R. A. (2002). Why is mutual mate choice not the norm? Operational sex ratios, sex roles, and the evolution of sexually dimorphic and monomorphic signalling. *Philosophical Transactions of the Royal Society of London B, Biological Sciences, 357*, 319–330.

Langlois, J. H., Kalakanis, L., Rubenstein, A. J., Larson, A., Hallam, M., & Smoot, M. (2000). Maxims or myths of beauty? A meta-analytic and theoretical review. *Psychological Bulletin, 126*, 390–423.

Langlois, J. H., & Roggman, L. A. (1990). Attractive faces are only average. *Psychological Science, 1*, 115–121.

Lindner, M. A., Rychman, R. M., Gold, J. A., & Stone, W. F. (1995). Traditional and nontraditional women and men's perceptions of the personalities and physique of ideal men and women. *Sex Roles, 32*, 675–690.

Lipson, S. F., & Ellison, P. T. (1996). Comparison of salivary steroid profiles in naturally occurring conception and non-conception cycles. *Human Reproduction, 11*, 2090–2096.

Little, A. C., Burt, D. M., Penton-Voak, I. S., & Perrett, D. I. (2001). Self-perceived attractiveness influences human female preferences for sexual dimorphism and symmetry in male faces. *Proceedings of the Royal Society of London B, 268*, 39–44.

Little, A. C., & Jones, B. C. (2003). Evidence against perceptual bias views for symmetry preferences in human faces. *Proceedings of the Royal Society of London B, 270*, 1759–1763.

Luxen, M. F., & Buunk, B. P. (2005). Second-to-fourth digit ratio related to verbal and numerical intelligence and the big five. *Personality and Individual Differences, 39*, 959–966.

Manning, J. T., Barley, L., Walton, J., Lewis-Jones, D. I., Trivers, R. L., Singh, D., et al. (2000). The 2nd:4th digit ratio, sexual dimorphism, population differences and reproductive success: Evidence for sexually antagonistic genes? *Evolution and Human Behavior, 21*, 163–183.

Manning, J. T., Baron-Cohen, S., Wheelwright, S., & Sanders, G. (2001). The 2nd to 4th digit ratio and autism. *Developmental Medicine and Child Neurology, 43*, 160–164.

Marlowe, F., Apicella, C., & Reed, D. (2005). Men's preference for women's profile waist-to-hip ratio in two societies. *Human Behavior and Evolution, 26*, 458–468.

Marlowe, F., & Wetsman, A. (2001). Preferred waist-to-hip ratio and ecology. *Personality and Individual Differences, 30*, 481–489.

Mazur, A., Mazur, J., & Keating, C. F. (1984). Military rank attainment of a West Point class: Effects of cadets' physical features. *American Journal of Sociology, 90*, 125–150.

McArthur, L. Z., & Apatow, K. (1984). Impressions of baby-faced adults. *Social Cognition*, 315–342.

McIntyre, M. H. (2006). The use of digit ratios as markers for perinatal androgen action. *Reproductive Biology and Endocrinology, 4*, 10.

Mehrabian, A., & Blum, J. S. (1997). Physical appearance, attractiveness, and the mediating role of the emotions. *Current Psychology, 16*, 20–42.

Milinski, M., Griffiths, S., Wegner, K. M., Reusch, T. B. H., Haas-Assenbaum, A., & Boehm, T. (2005). Mate choice decisions of stickleback females predictably modified by MHC peptide ligands. *Proceedings of the National Academy of Sciences, USA, 102*, 4414–4418.

Møller, A. P. (1999). Asymmetry as a predictor of growth, fecundity and survival. *Ecology Letters, 2*, 149–156.

Møller, A. P., & Thornhill, R. (1998). Bilateral symmetry and sexual selection: A meta-analysis. *American Naturalist, 151*, 174–192.

Mueller, U., & Mazur, A. (1997). Facial dominance in Homo sapiens as honest signaling of male quality. *Behavioral Ecology, 8*, 569–579.

Muller, M. N., Thompson, M. E., & Wrangham, R. W. (2006). Male chimpanzees prefer mating with old females. *Current Biology, 16*, 2234–2238.

Neave, N., Laing, S., Fink, B., & Manning, J. T. (2003). Second to fourth digit ratio, testosterone, and perceived male dominance. *Proceedings of the Royal Society of London B, 270*, 2167–2172.

Neff, B. D., & Pitcher, T. E. (2005). Genetic quality and sexual selection: An integrated framework for good genes and compatible genes. *Molecular Ecology, 14*, 19–38.

Olsson, M., Madsen, T., Nordby, J., Wapstra, E., Ujvari, B., & Wittsell, H. (2003). Major histocompatibility genes and mate choice in sand lizards. *Proceedings of the Royal Society of London B, 270*, S254–S256.

Pawlowski, B., & Grabarczyk, M. (2003). Center of body mass and the evolution of female body shape. *American Journal of Human Biology, 15*, 144–150.

Penn, D. J. (2002). The scent of genetic compatibility: Sexual selection and the major histocompatibility complex. *Ethology, 108*, 1–21.

Penn, D. J., & Potts, W. K. (1999). The evolution of mating preferences and major histocompatibility complex genes. *The American Naturalist, 153*, 145–164.

Penton-Voak, I. S., & Chen, J. Y. (2004). High salivary testosterone is linked to masculine male facial appearance in humans. *Evolution and Human Behavior, 25*, 229–241.

Penton-Voak, I. S., Jacobson, A., & Trivers, R. (2004). Populational differences in attractiveness judgements of male and female faces: Comparing British and Jamaican samples. *Evolution and Human Behavior, 25*, 355–370.

Penton-Voak, I. S., Jones, B. C., Little, A. C., Baker, S., Tiddeman, B., Burt, D. M., et al. (2001). Symmetry, sexual dimorphism in facial proportions and male facial attractiveness. *Proceedings of the Royal Society of London B, 268*, 1617–1623.

Penton-Voak, I. S., Little, A. C., Jones, B. C., Burt, D. M., Tiddeman, B. P., & Perrett, D. I. (2003). Female condition influences preferences for sexual dimorphism in faces of male humans (*Homo sapiens*). *Journal of Comparative Psychology, 117*, 264–271.

Penton-Voak, I. S., & Perrett, D. I. (2000). Female preference for male faces changes cyclically—further evidence. *Evolution and Human Behavior, 21*, 39–48.

Penton-Voak, I. S., Perrett, D. I., Castles, D., Burt, M., Koyabashi, T., & Murray, L. K. (1999). Female preference for male faces changes cyclically. *Nature, 399*, 741–742.

Perrett, D. I., May, K. A., & Yoshikawa, S. (1994). Facial shape and judgments of female attractiveness. *Nature, 368*, 239–242.

Petrie, M., & Kempenaers, B. (1998). Extra-pair paternity in birds: Explaining variation between species and populations. *Trends in Ecology and Evolution, 13*, 52–58.

Putz, D. A., Gaulin, S. J. C., Sporter, R. J., & McBurney, D. H. (2004). Sex hormones and finger length: What does 2D:4D indicate? *Evolution and Human Behavior, 25*, 182–199.

Qvarnström, A. (1999). Different reproductive tactics in male collared flycatchers signalled by size of secondary sexual character. *Proceedings of the Royal Society of London B, 266*, 2089–2093.

Reusch, T. B. H., Haber, M. A., II, Aeschlimann, P. B., & Milinski, M. (2001). Female sticklebacks count alleles in a strategy of sexual selection explaining MHC polymorphism. *Nature, 414*, 300–302.

Rhodes, G. (2006). The evolutionary psychology of facial beauty. *Annual Review of Psychology, 57*, 199–226.

Richardson, D. S., Komdeur, J., Burke, T., & von Schantz, T. (2005). MHC-based patterns of social and extra-pair mate choice in the Seychelles warbler. *Proceedings of the Royal Society of London B, 272*, 759–767.

Roberts, S. C., Little, A. C., Gosling, L. M., Perrett, D. I., Carter, V., Jones, B. C., et al. (2005). MHC-heterozygosity and human facial attractiveness. *Evolution and Human Behavior, 26*, 213–226.

Roney, J. R., & Maestripieri, D. (2004). Relative digit lengths predict men's behavior and attractiveness during social interactions with women. *Human Nature, 15*, 271–282.

Rowe, L., & Houle, D. (1996). The lex paradox and the capture of genetic variance by condition-dependent traits. *Proceedings of the Royal Society of London B, 263*, 1415–1421.

Russell, D. C. (2006). Raise your hand if you think I am attractive: Second and fourth digit ratio as a predictor of self- and other-ratings of attractiveness. *Personality and Individual Differences, 40*, 997–1005.

Saino, N., Romano, M., & Innocenti, P. (2006). Length of index and ring fingers differentially influence sexual attractiveness of men's and women's hands. *Behavioral Ecology and Sociobiology, 60*, 447–454.

Santos, P. S. C., Schinemann, J. A., Gabardo, J., & Bicalho, M. D. (2005). New evidence that the MHC influences odor perception in humans: A study with 58 southern Brazilian students. *Hormones and Behavior, 47*, 384–388.

Scarbrough, P. S., & Johnston, V. S. (2005). Individual differences in women's facial preferences as a function of digit ratio and mental rotation ability. *Evolution and Human Behavior, 26*, 509–526.

Scheib, J. E., Gangestad, S. W., & Thornhill, R. (1999). Facial attractiveness, symmetry, and cues of good genes. *Proceedings of the Royal Society of London B, 266*, 1318–1321.

Scheyd, G. J. (2002). *Reproductive value, fertility, and age preferences in human mating.* Unpublished master's thesis, University of New Mexico, Albuquerque.

Scheyd, G. J. (2003, June). *Individual differences in attraction: Evidence for a facultative calibration?* Paper presented at the annual meeting of the Human Behavior and Evolution Society, Lincoln, NE.

Simmons, L. W., Rhodes, G., Peters, M., & Koehler. N. (2004). Are human preferences for facial symmetry focused on signals of developmental instability? *Behavioral Ecology, 15*, 864–871.

Singh, D. (1993). Adaptive significance of female physical attractiveness: Role of the waist-to-hip ratio. *Journal of Personality and Social Psychology, 65*, 293–307.

Singh, D. (1995). Female judgment of male attractiveness and desirability for relationships: Role of waist-to-hip ratio and financial status. *Journal of Personality and Social Psychology, 69*, 1089–1101.

Singh, D., & Luis, S. (1995). Ethnic and gender consensus for the effect of the waist-to-hip ratio on judgment of women's attractiveness and desirability for relationships. *Ethology and Sociobiology, 16*, 484–507.

Skarstein, F., Folstad, I., Liljedal, S., & Grahn, M. (2005). MHC and fertilization success in the Artic charr (*Salvenlinus alpinus*). *Behavioral Ecology and Sociobiology, 57*, 374–380.

Streeter, S. A., & McBurney, D. H. (2003). Waist-hip ratio and attractiveness: New evidence and a critique of "a critical test." *Evolution and Human Behavior, 24*, 89–98.

Sugiyama, L. S. (2004). Is beauty in the context-sensitive adaptations of the beholder? Shiwiar use of waist-to-hip ratio in assessments of female mate value. *Evolution and Human Behavior, 25*, 51–62.

Swaddle, J. P., & Reierson, G. W. (2002). Testosterone increases the perceived dominance but not attractiveness of human males. *Proceedings of the Royal Society of London B, 269*, 2285–2289.

Symons, D. (1979). *The evolution of human sexuality.* New York: Oxford University Press.

Tassinary, L. G., & Hansen, K. A. (1998). A critical test of the waist-to-hip-ratio hypothesis of female physical attractiveness. *Psychological Science, 9*, 150–155.

Thornhill, R., & Gangestad, S. W. (1993). Human facial beauty: Averageness, symmetry, and parasite resistance. *Human Nature, 4*, 237–270.

Thornhill, R., Gangestad, S. W., Miller, R. D., Scheyd, G. J., McCollough, J., & Franklin, M. (2003). MHC, symmetry, and body scent attractiveness in men and women. *Behavioral Ecology, 14*, 668–678.

Thornhill, R., & Grammer, K. (1999). The body and face of woman: One ornament that signals quality? *Evolution and Human Behavior, 20*, 105–120.

Tovee, M. J., Hancock, P. J. B., Mahmoodi, S., Singleton, B. R. R., & Cornelissen, P. L. (2002). Human female attractiveness: Waveform analysis of body shape. *Proceedings of the Royal Society of London B, 269*, 2205–2213.

Trivers, R., Manning, J. T., & Jacobson, A. (2006). A longitudinal study of digit ratio (2D:4D) and other finger ratios in Jamaican children. *Hormones and Behavior, 49*, 150–156.

Wade, T. J., Shanley, A., & Imm, M. (2004). Second to fourth digit ratios and individual differences in women's self-perceived attractiveness, self-esteem, and body-esteem. *Personality and Individual Differences, 37*, 799–804.

Wedekind, C., & Füri, S. (1997). Body odor preference in men and women: Do they aim for specific MHC combinations or simply heterozygosity? *Proceedings of the Royal Society of London B, 264*, 1471–1479.

Wedekind, C., Seebeck, T., Bettens, F., & Paepke, A. J. (1995). MHC-dependent mate preferences in humans. *Proceedings of the Royal Society of London B, 260*, 245–249.

Weeden, J., & Sabini, J. (2005). Physical attractiveness and health in Western societies: A review. *Psychological Bulletin, 131*, 635–653.

Winkler, E. M., & Kirchengast, S. (1994). Body dimensions and differential fertility in Kung San males from Namibia. *American Journal of Human Biology, 6*, 203–213.

Yamazaki, K., Beauchamp, G. K., Curran, M., Baird, J., & Boyse, E. A. (2000). Parent-progeny recognition as a function of MHC odortype identity. *Proceedings of the National Academy of Sciences, USA, 97*, 10500–10502.

Yu, D. W., & Shepard, G. H. (1998). Is beauty in the eye of the beholder? *Nature, 396,* 321–322.

Zahavi, A. (1975). Mate selection—A selection for a handicap. *Journal of Theoretetical Biology, 53,* 205–214.

Zebrowitz, L. A., & Rhodes, G. (2004). Sensitivity to "bad genes" and the anomalous face overgeneralization effect: Cue validity, cue utilization, and accuracy in judging intelligence and health. *Journal of Nonverbal Behavior, 28,* 167–185.

Zeh, J. A., & Zeh, D. W. (2001). Reproductive mode and the genetic benefits of polyandry. *Animal Behavior, 61,* 1051–1063.

13

Two Human Natures
How Men and Women Evolved Different Psychologies

ALASTAIR P. C. DAVIES AND TODD K. SHACKELFORD

INTRODUCTION

The bodies of men and women differ from each other, both internally and externally. These anatomical differences across gender, however, are dwarfed by the similarities. The external and internal structures of men's and women's bodies are more similar than dissimilar because evolving men and women overwhelmingly faced similar adaptive problems and so the evolutionary selection pressures on the physical makeup of men and women were overwhelmingly the same. Evolving men and women, however, also faced many different adaptive problems, and therefore, many selection pressures on the human anatomy differed across the sexes. These sex-specific selection pressures have produced numerous external and internal differences in the bodies of men and women. Indeed, these differences are so profound that they allow one to easily identify whether a particular individual is a man or a woman.

Despite the foregoing, there remains significant resistance to the notion that evolution has resulted in profound psychological differences between men and women. In both popular and academic writings, a number of contemporary authors have argued either that men and women are essentially the same psychologically or that any significant psychological differences between the sexes are not evolved but, rather, are socially constructed (e.g., Butler, 1990; Harris, 2003; Hyde, 2005; Thurer, 2005). We believe, however, that, except for those who might be creationists, not one of these authors would contest any of the evolutionary reasoning regarding human bodies laid out in the opening paragraph. Yet precisely the same reasoning necessarily also applies to human brains: Because evolving men and women overwhelmingly faced similar adaptive problems, their psychologies are overwhelmingly the same. Nevertheless, because they also faced many different adaptive problems, numerous differences between the psychologies of men and women are expected to have evolved. Indeed, these psychological sex differences are likely to be so profound that they should give rise to behaviors that allow one to easily identify whether a particular individual is a man or a woman.

In this chapter, we aim to demonstrate that there are profound evolved psychological sex differences in humans. First, we outline how sex or reproductive roles lead to the evolution of anatomical and psychological sex differences. We then outline why these sex roles evolve. Next, we discuss how the psychology of mating is influenced by whether an individual is pursuing a short-term or long-term mate. After this, in the main part of the chapter, we use evolutionary psychological reasoning to identify a number of psychological sex differences among humans that are hypothesized to have evolved within several domains related to mating and present some of the empirical evidence in support of their existence. Next, we outline why many anatomical and psychological traits are shaped by both natural and sexual selection. Finally, we consider a prominent social constructivist account for behavioral sex differences, as formulated by Wood and Eagly (2002), that rejects the notion that humans evolved psychological sex differences and we attempt to show that an evolutionary psychological account of behavioral sex differences is more valid.

NATURAL SELECTION AND SEXUAL SELECTION

Evolution produces adaptations through natural selection and sexual selection. Although these processes are considered distinct, they typically operate on traits simultaneously. Accordingly, although, for simplicity, in the first part of this chapter we consider traits to be the product of either natural selection or sexual selection, we later outline why the evolution of many traits has been shaped by both processes.

Natural selection leads to the evolution of traits that facilitate survival and that directly facilitate reproduction. Since adaptive problems related to survival are similar across men and women, evolutionary reasoning expects traits that facilitate survival to be similar across the sexes. Of such traits, anatomical examples include the heart, liver, and eyes, and psychological examples include fear of predators, fear of heights, and preferences in foods.

The different sex or reproductive roles of men and women, however, mean that they face different adaptive problems in the context of reproduction and mating. Consequently, both natural and sexual selection are expected to produce sex differences in traits within these domains. Sex-differentiated traits related to sex roles that make their ontogenic appearance before the onset of puberty are termed *primary sexual characteristics*. Since they appear before individuals fully enter the mating game, they evolve through natural selection and include such anatomical traits as the genitalia and reproductive organs.

At puberty, however, in order for individuals to successfully fulfill their respective sex roles, there occurs the further development of existing traits, as well as the emergence of additional traits. These sex-specific developments are known as *secondary sexual characteristics*. An anatomical example that has evolved through natural selection is the pubertal widening of the pelvic bone that occurs in girls but not in boys (Geary, 1998). In addition, since individuals fully enter the mating game at puberty, natural selection has resulted in the evolution of psychological traits that become further developed at this stage in the life cycle. These traits are sex-specific mating preferences. They are sex differentiated because they necessarily reflect the fact that sex roles involve intrasexual competition for mates being more intense within one sex and scrupulousness of intersexual selection of mates being greater in the other sex.

Mating preferences drive the process of sexual selection and have, thereby, led to the evolution of additional sex-differentiated traits that make their ontogenic appearance at puberty. This is because sexual selection involves individuals within one sex evolving traits that facilitate the winning of *intrasexual competition* to meet the mate preferences of the opposite sex and so, through *intersexual selection*, to be chosen as mates over same-sex rivals. Anatomical examples of such traits include men's greater body size and muscle mass (Geary, 1998) and women's continually swollen breasts and greater fat deposits around the buttocks, thighs, and hips (Buss, 2004). The psychological traits that have been sexually selected in this way are the sex-specific mating strategies that facilitate the sexes in meeting the mate preferences of the opposite sex.

Moreover, since the reproductive goals of the sexes are often in conflict, sexual selection has led to the evolution of additional sex-specific traits that facilitate the winning of *intersexual competition*, in which individuals within one sex attempt to impede the mating strategies of the opposite sex. A physiological example of such traits is the tendency for the size of the ejaculate deposited by a man into his partner to be directly related to his perception of the likelihood that his partner has recently been sexually unfaithful to him to redu   the probability that his partner will be successful in her attempt to be impregnated by another man (for a review, see Shackelford, Pound, & Goetz, 2005). Sexually selected psychological traits that have evolved in the context of intersexual competition consist of additional sex-specific mating strategies through which one sex attempts to impede the mating strategies of the other.

The foregoing indicates that the different sex roles related to mating led to the evolution of sex-differentiated psychological traits. In the next section, therefore, we outline why there evolved different sex roles in the context of mating.

THE EVOLUTION OF SEX ROLES

Sex roles in the context of mating evolve due to a sex difference in potential reproductive rates (Clutton-Brock & Vincent, 1991), that is, the number of offspring that each sex can possibly produce per unit of time. This is because a sex difference in potential reproductive rates means that there is not a one-to-one operational sex ratio (OSR; Emlen & Oring, 1977); that is, the number of sexually receptive males does not equal the number of sexually receptive females at any one time. As a result, there are a relatively large number of individuals among one sex in competition to mate with a relatively small number of individuals among the other sex. This leads to sex roles in which members of the former sex compete more intensely for mates, and members of the latter sex are more scrupulous in their choice of mates.

A sex difference in potential reproductive rates exists when there is a sex difference in parental investment (Trivers, 1972). Although, across species, maternal investment is typically greater than paternal investment, it can be misleading to use anisogamy as an indicator of the relative amounts of parental investment made by the sexes. This is because despite the fact that males produce the smaller sex cell, they produce them in vastly greater numbers than females do. As a result, parental investment in terms of energy expended in producing sex cells may be greater among males than among females. A more reliable indicator of relative reproductive rates, therefore, is the minimum amounts of parental investment that each sex must contribute toward gestation and nurturing. Specifically, the sex whose minimum contribution toward gestation and nurturing is greater will have the lower potential reproductive rate.

Among humans, as among most species, it is females who necessarily invest more in gestation and nurturing. Once impregnated, women must gestate the child for 9 months and during the period in which modern humans were evolving were obliged to lactate for several years after giving birth (Howell, 1979). During this period of gestation and lactation, evolving women would have remained infertile. In contrast, a man's minimum investment in gestation and nurturing can range from being as little as nothing to being more than that of the woman. Consequently, once a man has successfully mated with one woman, he has the possibility of quickly moving on to successfully mate with another. As a result, in comparison to women, the number of children that men produce is more highly correlated with the number of matings that they secure. Thus, the potential reproductive rate of men is higher than that of women, and typically, the OSR is biased toward men.

Notwithstanding the foregoing, it is important to note that male-biased potential reproductive rates and OSRs indicate only that intrasexual competition is likely to be more intense among men and scrupulousness in mate choice is likely to be greater among women. The possibility of paternal investment leads to the possibility of competition for mates among women and selection of mates by men. First, women will compete among themselves for men who are willing and able to make the most parental investment. Second, in comparison to men who do not parentally invest, those men who do invest will be especially careful to mate with women who are of relatively high quality with respect to such traits as health, fertility, and sexual fidelity (e.g., Johnstone, Reynolds, & Deutsch, 1996).

In sum, sex roles involving a greater intensity of intrasexual competition among men, and a greater scrupulousness of mate choice among women have led to the evolution of psychological sex differences related to mating. The psychology of mating, however, is influenced by whether an individual is pursuing a short-term or long-term mate. Before we delineate a number of psychological sex differences, therefore, we first consider the temporal contexts in which mating takes place.

LONG-TERM AND SHORT-TERM MATINGS

As noted previously, in comparison to that among women, the variance in the amount of investment that men contribute to the raising of children is relatively great. This means that men can choose to pursue either *long-term* matings in which they invest substantially in the raising of their children or *short-term* matings in which any economic investment made by men should be viewed as mating effort or a strategy to gain sexual access, rather than as direct paternal investment.[1] Men can gain reproductive benefits and suffer reproductive costs from both types of matings. It is expected, therefore, that men will have an evolved psychology that enables them to perform a cost-benefit analysis regarding which mating strategy will maximize their reproductive success. As we outline in the following section, such analyses may motivate a *mixed reproductive strategy* in which men pursue both short- and long-term matings.

Even though women are obliged to make a substantial investment toward gestating (if not toward nurturing) their children, it follows that if men are engaging in both short- and long-term matings, then women must also be doing so. Women, therefore, are also expected to have an evolved psychology that allows them to perform cost-benefit analyses regarding which type of mating to pursue. As we outline in the next section, women may also be motivated to attempt to maximize their reproductive success by pursuing a mixed reproductive strategy. We now proceed to delineate the psychological sex differences that evolutionary psychological reasoning suggests have evolved among humans.

PSYCHOLOGICAL SEX DIFFERENCES

Based on the general principles by which natural selection and sexual selection produce adaptations and the potential reproductive rates of men and women, evolutionary psychologists have derived hypotheses regarding the psychological sex differences that are likely to have evolved in humans. In this section, we outline the psychological sex differences that this evolutionary reasoning suggests have evolved within the following domains: readiness to mate and number of sexual partners desired, risk-taking and aggression, economic parental investment, age and physical attractiveness, sexual versus emotional commitment, and sexual versus emotional jealousy.

For all but two of the hypothesized sex differences that we outline, we present empirical evidence in support of their existence. For the two for which we know of no supportive empirical

---

[1] Although, as we later outline, women may direct resources gained through short-term matings toward the raising of their children.

evidence, we offer accounts for why research might have failed to provide such evidence and high-light the value of evolutionary reasoning in informing possible future research.

Readiness to Mate and Number of Sexual Partners Desired

Women's relatively low potential reproductive rate means that, in comparison to men, they gain little reproductive advantage by having multiple short-term mates. In addition, women risk both dying during childbirth and wasting their relatively large minimum parental investment if their child does not survive. Accordingly, women are expected to have evolved a psychology that causes them to be relatively hesitant to mate and choosy in their mate selection. In contrast, men's relatively high potential reproductive rate and low minimum parental investment means that men can increase their reproductive success by having multiple mates. Accordingly, men are expected to have evolved a psychology that causes them to desire numerous, short-term sexual partners. In addition, they are hypothesized to be relatively eager to mate and indiscriminate in their mate selection, as both these traits facilitate the securing of multiple mates.

Numerous studies have provided empirical evidence in support of the evolutionary psycho-logical arguments that there are sex differences in eagerness to mate and number of mates desired. Clark and Hatfield (1989) conducted an experiment in which they found that, when approached by an opposite-sex stranger asking if they would have sex with him or her, no female students consented, whereas 75% of men did. Buss and Schmitt (1993) found that when asked to rate the likelihood that they would have sex with someone that they found attractive after knowing them for various periods, men gave a higher rating for every time period less than 5 years (the greatest length of time considered in the study). This study also found that when asked how many sexual partners they would like to have per various time intervals ranging from one month to life, men gave a higher number than did women for every one.

The foregoing psychological sex differences in eagerness to mate and number of partners desired are also reflected in reported sexual fantasies. Ellis and Symons (1990) and Wilson (1987) found that men have about 2 times as many sexual fantasies as women. They also found that men's sexual fantasies are more likely to include multiple partners, strangers, and the changing of part-ners and that 32% of men but only 8% of women reported having fantasized about more than 1,000 sexual partners in their life.

Paralleling the findings regarding sexual fantasy are those regarding the consumption of erotic media. Pornography typically isolates sex from any emotional context and frequently displays indi-viduals choosing sexual partners indiscriminately. In contrast, romance novels typically portray sex as being embedded in a drawn out, nonsexual, romantic relationship between a particular man and a particular woman. In support of the foregoing hypotheses, the consumers of pornography are overwhelmingly men, whereas the readers of romance novels are overwhelmingly women (Ellis & Symons, 1990; Pound, 1998).

A possible additional source of evidence in favor of the predicted sex differences in eagerness to mate and number of partners desired was suggested by Symons (1979). He argued that if, in comparison to women, men are more eager to have sex and desire more sexual partners, then hetero-sexual men must be prevented from fully living out their sexual desires by the relative sexual con-servatism of women. The sexual behavior of homosexual men, however, should more closely reflect men's mating preferences. In line with this, although heterosexual and homosexual men report no difference in their desire for uncommitted sex, homosexual men report much more success in real-izing this desire. In contrast, the number of actual sexual partners that women report having does not differ across sexual orientation (Bailey, Gaulin, Agyei, & Gladue, 1994).

Men's greater eagerness to engage in sexual relations and greater desire for multiple sexual partners are expected to have produced selection pressure on women to have an evolved psychol-ogy that especially motivates them to use short-term mating tactics that meet these preferences. Indeed, several studies have found that, when attempting to attract short-term mates, women are significantly more likely than men to use and to have success with tactics, which involve indicating their sexual accessibility and the sexually unavailability of rivals (e.g., Buss, 1988a; Buss & Schmitt, 1996; Schmitt & Buss, 2001).

Economic parental investment

The relatively great minimum parental investment of women, in comparison to men, means that a woman's primary reproductive concern is expected to be ensuring that her child reaches reproductive age so that she avoids wasting this investment. Accordingly, women are expected to be especially desirous to secure a long-term mate who is able to invest economically in the raising of her children. This will include not only men who have substantial resources but also those who display high social standing or dominance, as these are typically correlated with resource acquisition.

In reality, however, over evolutionary history, the amount of economic investment that a particular woman's long-term partner typically would have been able to provide would have been highly limited. Accordingly, it is likely that women with long-term mates would have been able to further their reproductive success by also pursuing short-term matings through which they could secure additional resources. Ancestral women without a long-term partner may also have secured resources through short-term matings. Such women may have been unattached because they were able to secure a greater amount of resources from multiple short-term matings than they could extract from any available long-term partner. In addition, they would have avoided the huge risks that, as we outline later, are undertaken by women who are sexually unfaithful to a long-term mate. In ancestral times, as well as today, prostitution may be the least ambiguous means by which women secure resources from men who wish to engage in sex without direct paternal investment.

Ancestral women who pursued short-term matings may have been able to secure meat for their children by exploiting male hunters' desires for sex in which they could avoid direct paternal investment. In modern societies, single and attached women pursuing short-term matings may facilitate the raising of their children by securing gifts such as jewelry and cash. Other modern gifts secured by such women, including flowers and expensive dinners, that cannot be readily invested toward raising children, may be evolutionarily novel means by which men exploit women's evolved desire to secure resources from short-term matings.

Nevertheless, although both men and women may pursue long-term and short-term matings, women's relatively great physiological parental investment means that they are likely to place a greater importance than are men on a person's ability to provide economic resources in the context of both short-term and long-term matings. Greiling and Buss (2000) provided empirical evidence in line with this hypothesized sex difference in the context of short-term sexual affairs. Men and women were presented with a number of potential benefits that individuals in long-term relationships might secure from engaging in a short-term sexual infidelity and were asked to rate the likelihood that the individuals would actually receive them. Results indicated that sexually unfaithful women were perceived as being significantly more likely than men were to receive resources such as money, jewelry, free dinners, and clothing.

In addition, Greiling and Buss (2000) asked men and women to rate the likelihood that several circumstances would motivate individuals in long-term relationships to commit a short-term sexual infidelity. Results indicated that among the circumstances judged likely to motivate a woman to be sexually unfaithful were the inability of her long-term partner to keep a job and meeting a man who had a better economic outlook than her long-term partner did. In contrast, circumstances judged likely to motivate a man to be sexually unfaithful included discovering that his partner is having an affair, and his partner is no longer willing to have sexual relations with him.

There is much empirical evidence in support of the hypothesized sex difference regarding the importance placed on a long-term mate's ability to invest in offspring. In studies in the years 1939, 1956, 1967, and 1988 (Buss, 1989a; Hill, 1945; Hudson & Henz, 1969; Mcginnis, 1958), when American women and men were asked to rate the relative desirability in a marriage partner of 18 traits, women rated "good financial prospect" about 2 times as highly as men did. Similarly, Kenrick, Sadalla, Groth, and Trost (1990) found that when American college students were asked to indicate for each of several qualities, the "minimum percentiles" that they would find acceptable in a marriage partner, women and men respectively indicated the 17th and 40th percentiles for earning capacity. Parallel results were found for earning capacity with respect to partners in a dating, sexual, and steady dating relationship. Convergent evidence outside of college campuses for this mate preference was provided by Wiederman (1993) who found that women taking out personal ads were about 11 times more likely than men were to request a mate with financial resources. Evidence suggesting that these sex differences in desired mate qualities may be universal across humans was provided by Buss (1989a). He found that among individuals from each of the 37 cultures and various political systems spanning six continents that he investigated, women invariably placed a greater importance on the good financial prospects of a marriage partner than men did and, across all cultures, women rated it about 2 times as important as men did.

If women place a greater importance than do men on the amount of resources held by both short-term and long-term mates, then they should also have a greater preference for both short-term and long-term mates with high social status or dominance, as such individuals are better able to secure resources. This hypothesis finds much empirical support. Betzig (1986) found that across a diverse range of 186 societies, high-status men invariably had greater resources, had more wives, and better provided for their children. Numerous studies of Americans have found that women invariably rate such attributes as high social status, high-status profession, prestige, rank, position, power, standing, station, high place, and high level of education as significantly more desirable in both a short- or long-term mate than men do (e.g., Buss & Barnes, 1986; Buss & Schmitt, 1993; Hill, 1945; Langhorne & Secord, 1955a). This sex difference was paralleled in the vast majority of the 37 cultures considered by Buss (1989a). Further, Kenrick and his colleagues (1993) asked men and women what would be the minimum percentile at which a person would have to be along different mate qualities, before they would consider the person as partner for a single date, steady dating, a one-night stand, and marriage. Across all relationship types, women required a potential mate to be at a higher percentile for social status than men did.

Langhorne and Secord (1955b) found that among 5,000 American undergraduates, women desired far more than men did mates who showed ambition and industriousness—qualities shown to facilitate the securing of higher salaries and occupational status (Jencks, 1979; Kyl-Heku & Buss, 1996; Willerman, 1979). Further, across the overwhelming majority of the 37 cultures investigated by Buss (1989a), women but not men rated these two qualities between important and indispensable in both a short-term and long-term mate.

Further evidence in support of the argument that a mate's social status is of greater importance to women than it is to men was provided by Kenrick, Neuberg, Zierk, and Krones (1994) using contrast effects. Among men and women in long-term relationships who were shown pictures of opposite sex individuals who were described as being socially dominant, women subsequently reported a greater reduction in their commitment to their current partner than men did.

Other findings suggest that these preferences are evolved, and not due to women being excluded from the economic arena and positions of power. Thus, Buss (1989b) found a positive correlation between women's income and the importance they placed on a partner's income, and Townsend (1989) found that a sample of women who expected their future employment to provide them with a relatively high salary and social status placed a high importance on earning potential in their mate choice.

The greater importance placed by women than by men on a partner's ability to provide economic parental investment means that women are also expected to have an evolved psychology that causes them to place a greater importance on a partner's willingness to do so. La Cerra (1994) provided empirical support for this hypothesized sex difference through a study in which women and men were asked to rate the relative attractiveness of an individual of the opposite sex posing in a variety of contexts in slide images. La Cerra found that women rated the man in the slides as increasingly attractive the greater the degree to which the slide depicted the man as interacting positively with a young child. In contrast, men rated the woman in the slides as equally attractive across all contexts. As we outline later, convergent evidence for this hypothesized sex difference in the importance placed on a mate's willingness to provide resources is also provided by studies investigating sex differences in the importance placed on a mate's emotional commitment.

Women's relatively great preference for short- and long-term mates who are able to economically invest in their offspring, is additionally expected to have produced sexual selection pressure for men to have an evolved psychology that especially motivates them to use mating tactics that meet these preferences. In accordance with this, several studies have found that, when attempting to attract either short-term or long-term mates and to retain long-term mates (by definition, one does not retain short-term mates), men are more likely than women are to use and to have success with tactics that involve displaying their own resources, ambitiousness, and physical and social dominance, or derogating rivals along these attributes (e.g., Buss & Dedden, 1990; Buss & Schmitt, 1993, 1996).

Risk-Taking and Aggression in Intrasexual Competition

Men's greater potential reproductive rate means that the variance in reproductive success among men is greater than that among women. Thus, in comparison to women, intrasexual competition offers men greater reproductive gains from winning and a greater likelihood of total reproductive failure from losing. These circumstances are likely to have produced sexual selection pressures for men to evolve a psychology that makes them more willing than women to undertake risks (Daly & Wilson, 2001).

There is a wealth of empirical evidence in support of this hypothesized sex difference regarding risk-taking. Numerous studies indicate that rates of death in accidents are much higher among men than they are among women (e.g., Holinger, 1987; Wilson & Daly, 1997) and that men are more likely than women are to expose themselves to dangers in recreational activities (e.g., Lyng, 1990) and substance abuse (e.g., Irwin, Igra, Eyre, & Millstein, 1997). Similarly, Wilson, Daly, and Gordon (1998) found that the level of pollution in a job location did not affect men's job choice but was an important negative influence on women's job choice, suggesting that men are less sensitive to health dangers posed by the environment. Paralleling these findings, studies indicate that men are less conscientious than women are in monitoring their health and undertake less preventative health care (e.g., Woodwell, 1997).

It is worth noting that although the form or context of risk-taking engaged in by men today may sometimes be evolutionarily novel, it is often related to the securing of resources, as in the previous example of selecting a job location. Other examples of modern day risk-taking that appear to be unrelated to intrasexual competition may involve activities, such as roller-coaster rides, that were designed to exploit or parasitize the predisposition for risk-taking that evolved in the context of intrasexual competition. Even the engagement in these activities, however, may allow men to display their disregard for danger to male rivals or potential mates.

If, indeed, it is a sex difference in the intensity of sexual selection pressures in the context of intrasexual competition for mates that has lead to the sex difference in risk-taking, then the difference should be most pronounced at the stage in the life cycle when the sex difference in the intensity of sexual selection pressures is greatest. This stage is young adulthood because it is then that individuals enter the mating game. Failure to get ahead early on in the game in accruing the attributes preferred in a mate by women, is likely to have left a man in the EEA unable catch up with his rivals (especially as life expectancy then was relatively low), greatly limiting his sexual access to women.

In line with this hypothesis, numerous studies have found that, across a wide range of activities, young men, in particular, are motivated by competition and willing to incur hazards (e.g., Bell &

Bell, 1993; Gove, 1985). Further, demographics indicate that the magnitude of the sex difference regarding men's greater likelihood of dying because of factors correlated with attitudes toward risk, such as accident, suicide, and homicide (Daly & Wilson, 1988; Holinger, 1987), reaches its zenith during young adulthood. Indeed, it is at this stage in the life cycle that the sex difference regarding men's greater tendency for "sensation-seeking," as measured by preferences for exciting, hazardous activities in general, is greatest (Zuckerman, 1994).

If women prefer as mates those men who have relatively high status, it follows that another indication that men's greater risk-taking evolved in the context of intrasexual competition for mates would be provided if it is motivated by a greater desire to gain or avoid losing social status. This would be indicated by men undertaking greater risks in the presence of an audience. In accordance with this argument, several studies indicate that young male drivers take greater risks in the presence of peers than when alone (e.g., Chen, Baker, Braver, & Li, 2000). The strategy for winning intrasexual competition that, perhaps, entails the greatest risk is the use of physical aggression. Accordingly, if the sex difference in the intensity of intrasexual competition for mates has resulted in men evolving a psychology that causes them to be greater risk-takers than women, then men should be more inclined than women to engage in physical aggression against same-sex rivals to gain status and resources. Several lines of evidence provide support for this. For instance, studies of same-sex bullying among schoolchildren in the United States and Finland both found bullying among boys to be more likely to involve the expropriation of possessions (Ahmad & Smith, 1994; Bjorkqvist, Lagerspetz, & Kaukiainen, 1992). In addition, a man's employment status (along with his marital status) is the major modulator of the likelihood of him becoming involved in a male-male, nonrelative homicide (Daly & Wilson, 2001; Wilson & Daly, 1985).

Further, although male-male, nonrelative homicides are most commonly classified in police reports as arising from "trivial altercations" (Daly & Wilson, 1988), evidence, such as the fact that these reports frequently implicate the presence of an audience in their escalation, suggests that underlying the inconsequential issue being disputed, lies an evolutionarily nontrivial contest over social dominance or status (Daly & Wilson, 1988; Polk, 1994; Wilson & Daly, 1985). Moreover, studies of tribal cultures have found there to be a high correlation between a man's social status and his warriorship or the number of men from other tribes that he has killed (Chagnon, 1983, 1988; Patton, 1997).

Homicides involving same-sex, unrelated adults constitute one of most clear indicators of the use of aggression in intrasexual competition. Daly and Wilson (1988) compiled statistics of same-sex, nonrelative homicides from all 35 of the studies that provided such data at the time. The studies investigated a broad range of cultures, ranging from Pittsburg in the United States to the Kung San of Botswana. Within every single study, the number of nonrelative homicides that were male-male far exceeded those that were female-female. Furthermore, other studies have shown this sex difference to peak dramatically during young adulthood (Daly & Wilson, 1990; Wilson & Daly, 1993). The hypothesis that these male-male, nonrelative homicides are motivated by a greater intensity among men than among women of intrasexual competition for mates is supported by the fact that (along with employment status) the major modulator of a man's likelihood of becoming involved in such a homicide is his marital status (Daly & Wilson, 2001; Wilson & Daly, 1985).

Sex differences in both the type and rate of same-sex bullying also indicate a sex difference in the tendency to use aggression that has evolved due to a sex difference in the intensity of intrasexual competition. Ahmad and Smith (1994) found that among American high school students, 36% of boys but only 9% of girls reported being physically hurt by a same-sex bully. Paralleling these findings, Bjorkqvist, Lagerspetz, and Kaukiainen (1992) found that among Finnish 15-year-olds, boys were 3 times more likely than girls were to have engaged in direct physical aggression against individuals of the same sex.

It is warfare, however, that constitutes perhaps the most destructive example of the sex difference in aggression in the context of intrasexual competition. Ethnographies reveal coalitional warfare almost universal across human cultures, pursued almost exclusively by men, and directed overwhelmingly against other men (e.g., Alexander, 1979; Chagnon, 1988; Keeley, 1996; Tooby & Cosmides, 1988; Wrangham & Peterson, 1996). Moreover, in support of the evolutionary psychological hypothesis that men's greater tendency to engage in high-risk, aggressive behavior is due to men having been subject to more intense sexual selection pressures in the context of intrasexual competition for mates, there is both anecdotal and empirical evidence indicating that men are motivated to form aggressive coalitions, whether they are war parties or gangs, in order to gain social status, material resources, and territory, as well as direct sexual access to women (Chagnon, 1988; Keeley, 1996; Palmer & Tilley, 1995).

Age and physical attractiveness. Pursuing a mixed reproductive strategy is also expected to offer reproductive advantages for men. Since the viability of a child is best ensured through biparental investment, it follows that while continuing to pursue multiple short-term mates, a man should also be motivated to have at least one long-term mate and to invest in the raising of any children that they produce together. In this way, men can increase their reproductive success by best ensuring the viability of some of their offspring, while possibly producing other viable offspring in which they do not invest.

Ancestral men are likely to have increased their inclusive fitness by investing in the children of a long-term partner even if the woman and her relatives had sufficient resources of their own with which to ensure the viability of a child. This is because the process of evolution is essentially competitive in the sense that it operates by selecting or filtering individuals according to their fitness *relative* to that of others, not according to some absolute level of fitness. Thus, children who received a greater amount of economic parental investment than other children did are also likely to have had relatively greater fitness and reproductive success.

In the context of both long- and short-term mating, because men's fertility exhibits far less variability over the life span than women's fertility does, men are expected to place a greater emphasis on fertility than are women. Since women between the onset of puberty and their mid- to late-20s are most fertile, men are expected to prefer relatively young mates. In addition, as relative youth is indicated by such physical features as skin that is unwrinkled and not sagging, and hair that is not gray, men are expected to find women who possess such features as especially attractive and to be especially desirous of them as mates. This preference not only best ensures that men's long-term mate is fertile, but it also enables them to best exploit the relatively great reproductive advantage that they gain from having multiple short-term mates. Accordingly, men are expected to place great importance on youth and physical attractiveness in both types of mates.

Evolutionary reasoning also suggests the expected preferences of women regarding the physical attractiveness of a mate. Thus, although a woman's primary goal is to secure the economic investment from a long-term mate that will ensure the survival of her children, another reproductive benefit that women require from a mate is "good" genes. Having "superior" genes may mean that her children have relatively greater survival chances because they are better able to repel parasitic infections and withstand environmental perturbations (e.g., Gangestad, Thornhill, & Yeo, 1994; Grammer & Thornhill, 1994). Moreover, as "good" genes are indicated by a person's physical appearance, such as symmetrical body and facial features, high cheekbones, and a prominent chin (e.g., Barber, 1995; Hume & Montgomerie, 1999), children with superior genes may also have relatively greater reproductive chances because they are more attractive than other individuals (Fisher, 1958; Gangestad & Buss, 1993). It follows that, if her long-term mate is able and willing to provide substantial resources but is genetically inferior to other men, a woman may attempt to secure good genes through a short-term mating in which the attribute on which she is likely to place the greatest importance will be physical attractiveness.

The foregoing suggests that when choosing a long-term mate, women may be willing to relax their standards regarding genetic quality in return for greater economic investment. However, when choosing a short-term mate from whom they do not expect to secure resources, women may put a premium on genetic quality.

Although men are expected to emphasize physical attractiveness when attempting to secure a short-term mate, setting their standards too high will limit the number of short-term mates that they are likely to attain. In contrast, women gain little reproductive benefit from having multiple mates. It follows that when their primary requirement in a short-term mate is "good" genes, women are expected to place a greater importance on the physical attractiveness of a short-term mate than are men. In a long-term mate, however, as fertility is most important for men, and resources are most important for women, men are expected to value physical attractiveness more than are women.

Despite the greater importance that women are hypothesized to place on physical attractiveness in a short-term mate, men are expected to place a greater importance on youth in both long- and short-term mates than are women. In other words, men are expected to prefer mates who are relatively younger than those preferred by women. This is because men's fertility is relatively stable across the life span, and so a man's physical attractiveness in the eyes of women will not be so highly correlated with youth. It is also because in both short- and long-term mates, women, more than men, value the ability to provide economic parental investment and it typically takes an individual a large number of years after puberty to accumulate resources or to attain the high social status or dominance that facilitates doing so.

Numerous studies have provided empirical support for the foregoing hypothesized sex differences regarding the importance placed on a mate's physical attractiveness and the preferred age of a mate, across short-term and long-term mating. First, there is much empirical evidence in support of the notion that men place a greater importance than do women on the physical appearance of a long-term mate. All the aforementioned studies between 1939 and 1988 that found that women place a far greater importance on the financial prospects of a potential spouse than do men also found that men reliably place a far greater importance on the physical attractiveness of a potential spouse than do women (Buss, 1989a; Hill, 1945; Hudson & Henz, 1969; Mcginnis, 1958). Further, the aforementioned study by Kenrick et al. (1994) using contrast effects, also found that among men and women in long-term relationships who were shown pictures of nude, highly attractive, opposite-sex individuals, men subsequently reported a significantly greater reduction than did women in the amount of love that they expressed for their current partner. In addition, Wiederman (1993) found that in personal ads in North America, an explicit request for physical attractiveness in a long-term mate was made about 3 times as often by men as by women. This sex difference is paralleled across cultures. Thus, in all of the 37 cultures considered by Buss (1989a), men placed a greater importance on a marriage partner's physical attractiveness than did women, and in all but 3 of the cultures, this difference was significant.

These findings of sex differences regarding the importance placed on physical attractiveness in the context of long-term mating are in contrast to those in the context of short-term mating. Thus, as predicted by the foregoing evolutionary psychological reasoning, the aforementioned study by Kenrick et al. (1993) found that for, and only for, the relationship type "one night-stand," women required a potential mate to be at a higher percentile than did men along the mate attribute "attractiveness." Several other studies have found that women place a premium on a short-term mate's physical attractiveness (e.g., Buss & Schmitt, 1993; Gangestad & Simpson, 1990). Several sources have found evidence in accordance with the foregoing predicted sex difference in mate preferences regarding age. The aforementioned studies into mate preferences between 1939 and 1988 found that among American college students, men desire mates who are younger than they are, whereas women desire mates who are older than they are (Buss, 1989a; Hill, 1945; Hudson & Henze, 1969; Mcginnis, 1958). Further, Buss found that, on average, across the 37 cultures studied, women preferred men who were about 3 years older than they were, whereas men preferred women who were about 3 years younger than they were. Similarly, Kenrick and Keefe (1992) found that in personal ads, as men age, they request women who are increasingly younger than they are, whereas, as women age, they request men whose ages more or less match their own. Several studies have also found that, in comparison to women, men are especially attracted to individuals who possess the aforementioned features indicating relative youth (e.g., Henss, 1992; Jackson, 1992). These mate preferences regarding age are reflected in actual mating behavior. Thus, across the world, grooms are, on average, 3 years older than brides are (Buss & Schmitt, 1993).

Men's greater preference than women's for physical attractiveness in a long-term mate is hypothesized to have resulted in women evolving a psychology that especially motivates them to use long-term mating strategies that facilitate them in meeting this preference. In line with this, Buss (1988b) found that when attempting to retain a long-term mate, women were judged more likely than men to use and to have success with tactics involving appearance enhancement.

Women's greater preference than men's for physical attractiveness in a short-term mate is expected to have produced sexual selection pressures for men to be more likely than women to use and to have success with short-term mating strategies that involve displaying one's own physical attractiveness and derogating that of same-sex rivals. We, however, know of no studies that support this reasoning. In contrast, to the best of our knowledge, studies indicate that it is mostly women, not men, who use and have success with such short-term strategies (e.g., Buss & Schmitt, 1996). We offer two interrelated accounts for these findings. One is that due to the relatively great variability of women's fertility across the life cycle, physical attractiveness in a short-term mate is also highly important to men. Second, as outlined in a foregoing section, as well as "good genes" (indicated by physical attractiveness), women may also seek to secure economic resources from a short-term mate, thus requiring men to use a short-term mating strategy other than that outlined in the preceding paragraph. Consequently, if studies fail to investigate short-term matings in which women are seeking "good genes," then, due to the high importance that men invariably place on physical attractiveness in a short-term mate, such studies are unlikely to find men being more likely to use and have success with short-term tactics involving displaying one's own physical attractiveness and derogating that of rivals. This suggests, therefore, that future research into short-term mating strategies should specify or identify the reproductive benefits that the pursued sex seeks to secure from a short-term mate and that the pursuing sex believes are sought by the pursued.

Sexual versus emotional commitment The sex difference in the type of parental investment made indicates that there are likely to have evolved additional sex differences in the context of long-term relationships. As women are internally fertilized, men can never be entirely sure that the child to whom their long-term mate gives birth is their own. It follows that, perhaps, the greatest threat to the reproductive success of a man is unknowingly directing his economic investment toward children to whom he is not genetically related because they are the result of his long-term mate being impregnated by another man. A man cuckolded, thus, not only directly furthers the reproductive success of rivals, but also has fewer resources both to invest in children to whom he *is* genetically related and with which to attract short-term mates. This leads to the expectation that men will have evolved a psychology that causes them to prefer as long-term mates women who indicate that they are not sexually promiscuous and are likely to be sexually faithful to them.

In contrast, perhaps the greatest threat to the reproductive success of a woman is her physiological investment in a child going to waste if the child dies as a result of her long-term mate's withdrawal of his economic investment and his redirecting of it toward another woman. This leads to the expectation that, as a high level of emotional commitment from a mate is a reliable indicator of a willingness to continually provide resources, women will have evolved a psychology that causes them to prefer as long-term mates, men who indicate that they are emotionally attached to them.

Empirical evidence in support of the hypothesized sex difference in preferences for long-term mates has been provided by several studies. For instance, Buss (1989a) found that within all 37 of the cultures he considered, men placed a greater importance on the chastity or virginity of a potential marriage partner than did women, and within 23 of the cultures, this difference was significant. In addition, Ellis and Symons (1990) found that, whereas men's sexual fantasies are typically based on pure lust and sexual gratification, such that they are highly visual, with a focus on bodily parts and sexual positions, women's sexual fantasies typically are based on romantic commitment. Thus, women are substantially more likely than are men to focus on the emotional and personality attributes of the partner in their fantasies and to fantasize about a current romantic partner.

Additional sex differences regarding long-term mating tactics are expected to have evolved because of the selection pressures created by the sex difference regarding the preference for sexual versus romantic commitment. Thus, men's preference for long-term mates who are sexually faithful leads to the expectation that women will have evolved a psychology that, when they are attempting to attract long-term mates, causes them to be more likely than men to use and have success with mating tactics that involve displaying their own sexual fidelity and impugning rivals as being sexually promiscuous.

Several studies have provided empirical support for this hypothesis (e.g., Buss, 1988a, 1994; Buss & Dedden, 1990; Buss & Schmitt, 1996). In addition, when attempting to retain a long-term mate, the findings of several studies have indicated that women are more likely than men to use and to have success with the tactic of threatening to be sexually unfaithful (e.g., Buss, 1988b; Buss & Dedden, 1990; Buss & Schmitt, 1996); presumably because a partner's sexual fidelity is especially important to men, and so the threat of losing it especially heightens a man's appreciation of his current mate.

These strategies of women in the context of intrasexual rivalry are also evidenced in bullying. Thus, the aforementioned studies of same-sex bullying among schoolchildren in the United States and Finland both found bullying among girls to be more likely to involve pejorative name-calling and the spreading of rumors labeling rivals as sexually promiscuous (Ahmad & Smith, 1994; Bjorkqvist, Lagerspetz, & Kaukiainen, 1992). Further, the finding that such bullying exists among girls in high school but not those in middle school, indicates that it emerges when girls enter the mating game and so is a form of intrafemale competition for mates (Ahmad & Smith, 1994).

In contrast, due to women's preference for long-term mates who are emotionally faithful to them, it is expected that men will have an evolved psychology that, when they are attempting to attract long-term mates, causes them to be especially likely to engage in mating tactics that involve displaying their own emotional fidelity or commitment and impugning rivals as being unlikely to offer such a commitment. Although, now we know of no empirical evidence that speaks to this hypothesis, the aforementioned findings of La Cerra (1994) regarding women's preferences for men interacting with a child, suggest that men might be successful in attracting long-term mates by displaying a potential for being good fathers.[2]

In line with this, Alastair P. C. Davies recalls that a photograph of a hunky male model holding a baby became a sales phenomenon among women in England in the 1980s. Several years later, having hit upon hard times, the male model sold his story to a tabloid newspaper and told how being in that photograph had enabled him to sleep with over 3,000 women. Several further years later, a TV channel interviewed some of the women who had bought the photograph, dated the model, and slept with the model. These women related how, at the time, they had believed that the model would make the ideal husband and father. However, when they later read the tabloid story of what a philanderer he had been, they felt that they had been terribly deceived and, in anger, had immediately destroyed the photograph that they had bought! This anecdote also suggests that men may be successful in securing short-term matings by successfully deceiving women into believing that they have strong paternal inclinations.

Sexual versus emotional jealousy When a partner in a long-term relationship commits either a sexual or emotional infidelity, he or she is pursuing a mating strategy by which to increase

---

[2] We thank the editors for this suggestion.

his or her own reproductive success at the expense of the reproductive success of the other partner. This creates intersexual competition and, therefore, sexual selection pressures for the evolution of sex-differentiated psychological traits that facilitate individuals within one sex in impeding attempts by the other sex to commit a romantic or sexual infidelity.

Since men and women differ in whether romantic or sexual infidelity poses the greater threat to their respective reproductive successes, it is expected that there will be divergent sexual selection pressures across the sexes regarding the evolution of psychological traits to prevent romantic infidelity. As a mate's sexual infidelity poses the greater threat to the reproductive success of a man, men are expected to have evolved a psychology that makes them especially motivated to prevent their partners from being sexually unfaithful. Accordingly, men are hypothesized to be especially likely to experience sexual jealousy, such that they become especially distressed by signs, or actual instances, of their long-term mate being sexually unfaithful to them. In contrast, as a mate's emotional infidelity poses the greater threat to the reproductive success of a woman, women are expected to have evolved a psychology that makes them especially motivated to prevent their partners from being emotionally unfaithful. Thus, women are hypothesized to be especially likely to experience emotional jealousy, in which they feel especially distressed by signs, or actual instances, of their long-term partner forming an emotional attachment to another woman.

This hypothesized sex difference in romantic jealousy has received empirical support from numerous studies. Thus, Buss, Larsen, Westen, and Semmelroth (1992) found that among a sample of American college students, 83% of women but only 40% of men reported that they would find a long-term partner becoming emotionally involved with someone else more distressing than the individual having sexual intercourse with someone else. In contrast, 60% of men but only 17% of women reported that they would find a partner's sexual infidelity more upsetting. These self-report findings were paralleled in measures of both physiological arousal and brow muscle contraction. Thus, when asked to imagine the two types of infidelities, greater responses in terms of pulse rate, skin conductance, and frowning were reliably displayed by men to the scenario involving a sexual infidelity and by women to the scenario involving an emotional infidelity. These sex differences in the level of distress felt in response to a sexual and an emotional infidelity have found empirical support from numerous other studies, across a broad range of cultures (e.g., Buss et al., 1999; Buunk, Angleitner, Obaid, & Buss, 1996; Sagarin, Becker, Guadagno, Nicastle, & Millevoi, 2003).

A large and disturbing psychological sex difference that results from romantic jealousy is in the motivation to kill a spouse or partner. Police reports indicate that a large proportion of spousal homicides in the United States are motivated by jealousy, and of such homicides, an overwhelming number are committed by men (Daly & Wilson, 1988). These patterns regarding spousal homicide are paralleled across cultures (Daly & Wilson, 1988).[3]

One way by which a man can reduce his risk of being cuckolded as a result of his partner's sexual infidelity is to reduce the likelihood of his partner's lover fertilizing her egg by placing his sperm in competition with that of his partner's lover (Birkhead & Parker, 1997). This suggests an additional psychological sex difference, for it is expected that men (but clearly not women) will have evolved a psychology that motivates them to create sperm competition for this purpose. In accordance with this, Shackelford et al. (2002) found that the greater the likelihood that a man's partner had been sexually unfaithful, as indicated by the amount of time that the couple had spent apart, the more attractive he found her and the more eager he was to copulate with her. The fact that this finding was independent of the amount of time since the couple's last copulation indicates that men

---

[3] The finding that wives who leave their husbands are significantly more likely to be killed by their estranged husbands than are wives who do not, appears contradictory to the notion that men's violence against their wives is motivated by a desire to prevent cuckoldry. Wilson and Daly (1996), however, suggest that a man is only likely to be successful in scaring any partner that he might have into being sexually faithful, if he occasionally evidences that he will actually follow through with his threats of violence.

have a psychology that motivates them to place their sperm in competition with that of a possible lover of their partner, as soon as possible after the partner's suspected sexual infidelity. A literary example of the psychological effect that the threat of cuckoldry may have on men can be found in the novel *Fear of Flying* by Erica Jong (1973). In it, the narrator, Isadora Wing, relates that, when her husband caught her *in flagrante delicto* with another man, the husband was overcome with the urge to have mad, passionate sex with her.

Although, up to this point, we have considered anatomical and psychological traits to be the product of either natural selection or sexual selection, the evolution of many traits has been shaped by both processes. In the next section, therefore, we outline why traits are subject to both forces and illustrate this through examples of anatomical and psychological traits.

THE DUAL ACTION OF NATURAL AND SEXUAL SELECTION ON TRAITS

Although natural selection and sexual selection are considered to be distinct processes, they typically operate on traits simultaneously. Accordingly, both forces shape the evolution of many traits. An interesting illustration of the notion that traits may be subject to both natural and sexual selection is provided by the *handicap principle* (Zahavi, 1975). According to this principle, the evolution of some traits may involve natural selection for survival being opposed by sexual selection for attracting mates. Specifically, such traits evolve precisely because they reduce the survival chances of their possessors, for they signal to the opposite sex that in order to be able support the traits, their possessors must be of relatively high genetic quality. These traits are handicaps because they are energetically costly to grow and to maintain and they make their possessors more susceptible to predation. They are hypothesized to include large and elaborate anatomical features, such as the peacock's tail, as well as elaborate physical maneuvers. The size and elaborateness of handicapping traits will increase only up to the point at which reproductive benefits associated with attracting mates are outweighed by reproductive costs associated with reduced survival chances.

Although they may not be examples of the handicap principle, we shall use the traits of risk-taking and aggression to illustrate how numerous human psychological traits are likely to have been shaped by both natural and sexual selection. It is almost certain that sex differences in risk-taking and aggression are the product of sexual selection because they facilitate the winning of intramale competition, and are likely to have been further supported by intersexual selection, for those women who found them attractive would have benefited from having aggressive, risk-takers as mates. They are also likely to have been supported by natural selection, as aggressiveness and risk-taking are likely to have advantaged men in the context of hunting. At the point, however, at which increases in the sex differences in aggressiveness and risk-taking meant that the reproductive benefits that men accrued in the context of intramale competition, intersexual selection and hunting began to be outweighed by the reproductive costs associated with an increased risk of death, natural selection would have opposed any further increases in sex differences along them.

The sex differences outlined in the foregoing are those that evolutionary psychological principles suggest have evolved. As we stated in the introduction to this chapter, however, social constructivist perspectives suggest that any observed psychological or behavioral sex differences are not evolved but are products of social norms. Prominent among such perspectives is Wood and Eagly's (2002) *biosocial theory*. In the next section, therefore, we outline this theory and suggest why an evolutionary psychological account of behavioral sex differences has greater explanatory power.

Wood and Eagly's (2002) *biosocial theory* is fundamentally an extended and more detailed version of the *social role theory* outlined by them in an article in 1999 (Eagly & Wood, 1999). Accordingly, as there are no inconsistencies across the two theories, they can be considered as the same theory. We, therefore, treat them as such in the critique that follows.

WOOD AND EAGLY'S (2002) BIOSOCIAL THEORY

Wood and Eagly's (2002) biosocial theory posits that behavioral sex differences emerge from an interaction between distal biological and contextual factors. The biological factors are evolved sex-specific anatomical attributes, especially the greater speed, upper-body strength, and size of men, as well as behaviors related to them, especially women's reproductive activities of childbearing and nursing. Wood and Eagly consider these biological attributes to be *essentialist*, such that they are stable across societies. The contextual factors consist of the social, economic, technological, and ecological forces to which people are subject. The interaction of these ultimate biological and social factors either facilitates or hinders each sex in performing specific tasks, resulting in one sex being more efficient than the other at performing them. Sex-differentiated behavior in a society, therefore, emerges as men and women each assume the tasks or roles that they can most efficiently perform. Wood and Eagly stated, "[W]e develop a biosocial theory of sex differences and similarities that blends essentialist and social constructionist perspectives" (p. 701). As such, they reject both the essentialist assumption that humans have stable sex-differentiated psychological dispositions and the strict social constructivist assumption that biology plays no role in producing general patterns of sex differences.

According to the biosocial theory, from the division of labor into sex-specific social roles arise certain proximal processes that lead to sex-differentiated behavior. One of these processes consists of gender roles such that the psychological traits necessary for the performance of the sex-specific labor become stereotypic of each sex. These gender roles guide social behavior by way of mediating processes, among which are several socialization processes, such as reinforcement, observational learning, and role modeling. Biological proximal processes also guide and facilitate sex-differentiated behavior. Most notable among these are hormonal changes that occur in response to or anticipation of the demands associated with the performance of social roles, such as the rise in males' testosterone levels in anticipation of engaging in competition.

Friedman, Bleske, and Scheyd (2000) argued that by allowing the evolution of physical but not of psychological sex differences, Eagly and Wood (1999) made a dualistic distinction between mind and body. In response, Wood and Eagly (2000) stated,

> On the contrary, ours is an interactionist perspective in which psychological and physical sex-linked attributes are repeatedly constructed or emergent in response to the evolved attributes of the species, the developmental experiences of each sex, and the situated activity of men and women in society. (pp. 1062–1063)

Wood and Eagly's response explains that their theory does not hold that there cannot be an interface or interplay between mind and body. The response, however, in no way addresses the dualistic issue put forward in Friedman et al.'s critique: How is it possible that divergent selection pressures across the sexes shaped the formation of the human body but that the formation of the human brain evaded these same divergent selection pressures?

Eagly and Wood (1999) stated,

> [A]n implicit assumption of our approach is that social change emerges, not from individuals' tendencies to maximize their inclusive fitness, but instead from their efforts to maximize their personal benefits and minimize their personal costs in their social and ecological settings. (p. 421)

The difficulty with this approach, however, is that if the psychology for the maximization of utilities does not maximize inclusive fitness, then it would be selected against in favor of one that does. Moreover, in contrast to terms such as personal costs and benefits in the biosocial account, the meaning of the terms "reproductive benefits," "reproductive costs," and "inclusive fitness" used in evolutionary psychological accounts and how they are to be measured have been precisely defined elsewhere (e.g., Williams, 1966). We contend, therefore, that the evolutionary psychological model for the origin of behavioral sex differences is superior to the biosocial model in terms of preciseness and explanatory power. In addition, in contradiction of the biosocial model but in accordance with the evolutionary psychological model, neuropsychological evidence strongly indicates the existence of sex differences in the design and functioning of the human brain (see Kimura & Watson, this volume).

CONCLUSION

For scientists weighing the empirical evidence, the theory of evolution is the only theory in the game with respect to accounting for how we humans came to exist. Moreover, while by no means all human traits evolved through the process of either natural selection or sexual selection (Gould & Lewontin, 1979), the empirical evidence argues irrefutably that an overwhelming proportion of the anatomical and psychological traits that enable us to successfully function on this planet did evolve through one of these processes (Buss, Haselton, Shackelford, Bleske, & Wakefield, 1998). The acceptance of the foregoing means that since it is a biological fact that the sexes have differing reproductive roles, it follows that, in areas related to reproduction and mating, men and women will have faced divergent selection pressures.

Our goal in this chapter has been to demonstrate that from both a theoretical and an empirical standpoint, it is not reasonable to contend that our bodies were subject to these divergent selection pressures but that our brains escaped them. We hope, thereby, to have convincingly argued that the sexes are just as clearly differentiated by their thoughts and behaviors as they are by their anatomies and, thus, that if one accepts that brains as well as bodies evolved, then one must also accept that sex differences evolved in both.

REFERENCES

Ahmad, Y., & Smith, P. K. (1994). Bullying in schools and the issue of sex differences. In J. Archer (Ed.), *Male violence* (pp. 70–83). London: Routledge.

Alexander, R. D. (1979). *Darwinism and human affairs*. Seattle: University of Washington Press.

Bailey, J. M., Gaulin, S. Agyei, Y., & Gladue, B. (1994). Effects of gender and sexual orientation on evolutionarily relevant aspects of human mating psychology. *Journal of Personality & Social Psychology*, 66, 1081–1093.

Barber, N. (1995). The evolutionary psychology of physical attractiveness: Sexual selection and human morphology. *Ethology and Sociobiology*, 16, 395–424.

Bell, N. J., & Bell, R. W. (1993). *Adolescent risk taking*. Newbury Park, CA: Sage.

Betzig, L. L. (1986). *Despotism and differential reproduction. A Darwinian view of history*. Hawthorne, NY: Aldine.

Birkhead, T. R., & Parker, G. A. (1997). Sperm competition and mating systems. In J. R. Krebs & N. B. Davies (Eds.), *Behavioral ecology*. Oxford, U.K.: Blackwell Science.

Bjorkqvist, K., Lagerspetz, K. M. J., & Kaukiainen, A. (1992). Do girls manipulate and boys fight? Developmental trends in regard to direct and indirect aggression. *Aggression Behavior*, 18, 117–127.

Buss, D. M. (1988a). The evolution of human intrasexual competition: Tactics of mate attraction. *Journal of Personality & Social Psychology*, 54, 616–628.

Buss, D. M. (1988b). From vigilance to violence: Tactics of mate retention in American undergraduates. *Ethology & Sociobiology*, 9, 291–317.

Buss, D. M. (1989a). Sex differences in human mate preferences: Evolutionary hypotheses tested in 37 cultures. *Behavioral and Brain Sciences*, 12, 1–49.

Buss, D. M. (1989b). Toward an evolutionary psychology of human mating. *Behavioral and Brain Sciences*, 12, 39–49.

Buss, D. M. (1994). *The evolution of desire*. New York: Basic Books.

Buss, D. M. (2004). *Evolutionary psychology* (2nd ed.). Boston: Allyn & Bacon.

Buss, D. M., & Barnes, M. F. (1986). Preferences in human mate selection. *Journal of Personality & Social Psychology, 50,* 559–570.

Buss, D. M., & Dedden, L. A. (1990). Derogation of competitors. *Journal of Social & Personal Relationships, 7,* 395–422.

Buss, D. M., Haselton, M. G., Shackelford, T. K., Bleske, A. L., & Wakefield, J. C. (1998). Adaptations, exaptations, and spandrels. *American Psychologist, 53,* 533–548.

Buss, D. M., Larsen, R. J., Westen, D., & Semmelroth, J. (1992). Sex differences in jealousy: Evolution, physiology, and psychology. *Psychological Science, 3,* 251–255.

Buss, D. M., & Schmitt, D. P. (1993). Sexual strategies theory: A contextual evolutionary analysis of human mating. *Psychological Review, 100,* 204–232.

Buss, D. M., & Schmitt, D. P. (1996). Strategic self-promotion and competitor derogation: Sex and context effects on the perceived effectiveness of mate attraction tactics. *Journal of Personality and Social Psychology, 70,* 1185–1204.

Buss, D. M., Shackelford, T. K., Kirkpatrick, L. A., Chloe, J., Hasegawa, M., Hasegawa, T., et al. (1999). Jealousy and beliefs about infidelity: Tests of competing hypotheses in the United States, Korea, and Japan. *Personal Relationships, 6,* 125–150.

Butler, J. (1990). *Gender trouble: Feminism and the subversion of identity.* London: Routledge.

Buunk, B. P., Angleitner, A., Obaid, V., & Buss, D. M. (1996). Sex differences in jealousy in evolutionary and cultural perspective: Tests from the Netherlands, Germany, and the United States. *Psychological Science, 7,* 359–363.

Chagnon, N. A. (1983). *Yanomamo: The fierce people* (3rd ed.). New York: Holt, Rinehart, & Winston.

Chagnon, N. A. (1988). Life histories, blood revenge and warfare in a tribal population. *Science, 239,* 985–992.

Chen, L. H., Baker, S. P., Braver, E. R., & Li, G. (2000). Carrying passengers as a risk factor for crashes fatal to 16- and 17-year-old drivers. *Journal of the American Medical Association, 283,* 1578–1582.

Clark, R. D. & Hatfield, E. (1989). Gender differences in receptivity to sexual offers. *Journal of Psychology and Human Sexuality, 2,* 39–55.

Clutton-Brock, T. H., & Vincent A. C. J. (1991) Sexual selection and the potential reproductive rates of males and females. *Nature, 351,* 58–60.

Daly, M., & Wilson, M. (1988). *Homicide.* Hawthorne, NY: Aldine de Gruyter.

Daly, M., & Wilson, M. (1990). Killing the competition. *Human Nature, 1,* 83–109.

Daly, M., & Wilson, M. (2001). Risk-taking, intra-sexual competition, and homicide. *Nebraska Symposium on Motivation, 47,* 1–36.

Eagly, A. H., & Wood, W. (1999). The origins of sex differences in human behavior: Evolved dispositions versus social roles. *American Psychologist, 54,* 408–423.

Ellis, B., & Symons, D. (1990) Sex differences in sexual fantasy: An evolutionary psychological approach. *Journal of Sex Research, 27,* 527–555.

Emlen, S. T., & Oring, L. W. (1977). Ecology, sexual selection, and the evolution of mating systems. *Science, 197,* 215–223.

Fisher, R. A. (1958). *The genetical theory of natural selection* (2nd ed.). New York: Dover.

Friedman, B. X., Bleske, A. L., & Scheyd, G. J. (2000). Incompatible with evolutionary theorizing. *American Psychologist, 55,* 1059–1060.

Gangestad. S. W., & Buss, D. M. (1993). Pathogen presence and human mate preferences. *Ethology and Sociobiology, 14,* 89–96.

Gangestad, S. W., & Simpson, J. A. (1990). Toward an evolutionary history of female sociosexual variation. *Journal of Personality, 58,* 69–96.

Gangestad, S. W., Thornhill, R., & Yeo, R. A. (1994). Facial attractiveness, developmental stability, and fluctuating asymmetry. *Ethology and Sociobiology, 15,* 73–85.

Geary, D. C. (1998). Male, female: The evolution of human sex differences. Washington, D.C.: American Psychological Association.

Gove, W. R. (1985). The effect of age and gender on deviant behavior: A biopsychosocial perspective. In A. S. Rossi (Ed.), *Gender and the life course* (pp. 115–144). New York: Aldine.

Gould, S. J., & Lewontin, R. C. (1979). The spandrels of San Marco and the Panglossian paradigm: A critique of the adaptionist programme. *Proceedings of the Royal Society of London, 205,* 581–598.

Grammer, K., & Thornhill, R. (1994). Human (Homo sapiens) facial attractiveness and sexual selection: The role of symmetry and averageness. *Journal of Comparative Psychology, 108,* 233–242.

Greiling, H., & Buss, D. M. (2000). Women's sexual strategies: The hidden dimension of extra-pair mating. *Personality and Individual Differences, 28,* 929–963.

Harris, C. R. (2003). A review of sex differences in sexual jealousy, including self-report data, psychophysiological responses, interpersonal violence, and morbid jealousy. *Personality and Social Psychology Review, 7,* 102–128.

Henss, R. (1992). *Perceiving age and attractiveness in facial photographs.* Unpublished manuscript, Psychologisches Institut, University of Saarland, Germany.

Hill, R. (1945). Campus values in male selection. *Journal of Home Economics, 37,* 554–558.

Howell, N. (1979). *Demography of the Dobe !Kung.* New York: Academic.

Holinger, P. C. (1987). *Violent deaths in the United States.* New York: Guilford Press.

Hyde, J. S. (2005). The gender similarities hypothesis. *American Psychologist, 60,* 581–592.

Hudson, J. W., & Henz, L. F. (1969). Campus values in mate selection: A replication. *Journal of Marriage and the Family, 31,* 772–775.

Hume, D., & Montgomerie, R. (1999, June). *Facial attractiveness and symmetry in humans.* Paper presented at the Annual Conference of the Human Behavior and Evolution Society, Salt Lake City, UT.

Irwin, C. E., Igra, V., Eyre, S., & Millstein, S. (1997). Risk-taking behavior in adolescents: The paradigm. *Annals of the New York Academy of Sciences, 817,* 1–35.

Jackson, L. A. (1992). *Physical appearance and gender. Sociobiological and sociocultural perspectives.* Albany, NY: SUNY Press

Jencks, C. (1979). *Who gets ahead? The determinants of economic success in America.* New York: Basic Books.

Johnstone, R. A., Reynolds, J. D., & Deutsch, J. C. (1996). Mutual mate choice and sex differences in choosiness. *Evolution, 50,* 1382–1391.

Jong, E. (1973). *Fear of flying.* New York: New American Library.

Keeley, L. H. (1996). *War before civilization.* Oxford, U.K.: Oxford University Press.

Kenrick, D. T., & Keefe, R. C. (1992). Age preferences in mates reflect sex differences in reproductive strategies. *Behavioral and Brain Sciences, 15,* 75–133.

Kenrick, D. T., Sadalla, E. K., Groth, G., & Trost, M. R. (1990). Evolution, traits and the stages of human courtship: Qualifying the parental investment model. *Journal of Personality, 58,* 97–116.

Kenrick, D. T., Groth, G. E., Trost, M. R., & Sadalla, E. K. (1993). Integrating evolutionary and social exchange perspectives on relationship: Effects of gender, self-appraisal, and involvement level on mate selection criteria. *Journal of Personality and Social Psychology, 64,* 951–969.

Kenrick, D. T., Neuberg, S. L., Zierk, K. L., & Krones, J. M. (1994). Evolution and social cognition: Contrast effects as a function of sex, dominance, and physical attractiveness. *Personality and Social Psychology Bulletin, 20,* 210–217.

Kyl-Heku, L. M., & Buss, D. M. (1996). Tactics as units of analysis in personality psychology: An illustration using tactics of hierarchy negotiation. *Personality and Individual Differences, 21,* 497–517.

La Cerra, M. M. (1994). *Evolved mate preferences in women: Psychological adaptations for assessing a man's willingness to invest offspring.* Unpublished doctoral dissertation, Department of Psychology, University of California, Santa Barbara.

Langhorne, M. C., & Secord, P. F. (1955a). Attractive faces are only average. *Psychological Science, 1,* 115–121.

Langhorne, M. C., & Secord, P. F. (1955b). Variations in marital needs with age, sex, marital status, and regional composition. *Journal of Social Psychology, 41,* 19–37.

Lyng, S. (1990). Edgework: A social psychological analysis of voluntary risk taking. *American Journal of Sociology, 95,* 851–856.

Mcginnis, R. (1958). Campus values in mate selection. *Social Forces, 35,* 368–373.

Palmer, C. T., & Tilley, C. F. (1995). Sexual access to females as a motivation for joining gangs: An evolutionary approach. *The Journal of Sex Research, 32,* 213–217.

Patton, J. Q. (1997, June). *Are warriors altruistic? Reciprocal altruism and war in the Ecuadorian Amazon.* Paper presented at the Ninth Annual Conference of the Human Behavior and Evolution Society, University of Arizona, Tucson, AZ.

Polk, K. (1994). *When men kill.* Cambridge, U.K.: Cambridge University Press.

Pound, N. (1998, July 8–12). *Polyandry in contemporary pornography.* Paper presented at the Tenth Annual Conference of the Human Behavior and Evolution Society. University of California, Davis.

Sagarin, B. J., Becker, D. V., Guadagno, R. E., Nicastle, L. D., & Millevoi, A. (2003). Sex differences (and similarities) in jealousy: The moderating influence of infidelity experience and sexual orientation of the infidelity. *Evolution and Human Behavior, 24,* 17–23.

Schmitt, D. P., & Buss, D. M. (2001). Human mate poaching: Tactics and temptations for infiltrating existing relationships. *Journal of Personality and Social Psychology, 80,* 894–917.

Shackelford, T. K., LeBlanc, G. J., Weekes-Shackelford, V. A., Bleske-Rechek, A. L., Euler, H. A. et al. (2002). Psychological adaptation to human sperm competition. *Evolution and Human Behavior, 23,* 123–138.

Shackelford, T. K., Pound, N., & Goetz, A. T. (2005). Psychological and physiological adaptations to sperm competition in humans. *Review of General Psychology, 9,* 228–248.

Symons, D. (1979). *The evolution of human sexuality.* New York: Oxford University Press.

Thurer, S. L. (2005). *The end of gender: A psychological autopsy.* New York: Routledge.

Tooby, J., & Cosmides, L. (1988). *The evolution of war and its cognitive foundations.* Institute for Evolutionary Studies, Technical Report #88-1.

Townsend, J. (1989). Mate selection criteria: A pilot study. *Ethology & Sociobiology, 10,* 241–253.

Trivers, R. L. (1972). Parental investment and sexual selection. In B. Campbell (Ed.), *Sexual selection and the descent of man* (pp. 136–179). Chicago: Aldine.

Wiederman, M. W. (1993). Evolved gender differences in mate preferences: Evidence from personal advertisements. *Ethology and Sociobiology, 14,* 331–352.

Willerman, L. (1979). *The psychology of individual and group differences.* San Francisco: Freeman.

Williams, G. C. (1966). *Adaptation and natural selection.* Princeton, NJ: Princeton University Press.

Wilson, G. D. (1987). Male-female differences in sexual activity, enjoyment and fantasies. *Personality and Individual Differences, 8,* 125–126.

Wilson, M., & Daly, M. (1985). Competitiveness, risk-taking and violence: The young male syndrome. *Ethology & Sociobiology, 6,* 59–73.

Wilson, M., & Daly, M. (1993). Lethal confrontational violence among young men. In N. J. Bell & R. W. Bell (Eds.), *Adolescent risk taking* (pp. 84–106). Newbury Park, CA: Sage.

Wilson, M., & Daly, M. (1996). Male sexual proprietariness and violence against wives. *Current Directions in Psychological Science, 5,* 2–7.

Wilson, M., & Daly, M. (1997). Life expectancy, economic inequality, homicide and reproductive timing in Chicago neighbourhoods. *British Medical Journal, 314,* 1271–1274.

Wilson, M., Daly, M., & Gordon, S. (1998). The evolved psychological apparatus of human decision making is one source of environmental problems. In T. Caro (Ed.), *Behavioral ecology and conservation biology* (pp. 501–523). New York: Oxford University Press.

Wood, W., & Eagly, A. H. (2000). Once again, the origins of sex differences. *American Psychologist, 55,* 1062–1063.

Wood, W., & Eagly, A. H. (2002). A cross-cultural analysis of the behavior of women and men: Implications for the origins of sex differences. *Psychological Bulletin, 128,* 699–727.

Woodwell, D. A. (1997). National ambulatory medical care survey: 1995 summary. National Center for Health Statistics (Centers for Disease Control & Prevention, Atlanta). *Advance Data, 286,* 1–28.

Wrangham, R., & Peterson, D. (1996). *Demonic males.* Boston: Houghton Mifflin.

Zahavi, A. (1975). Mate selection—A selection for a handicap. *Journal of Theoretical Biology, 53,* 205–214.

Zuckerman, M. (1994). *Behavioral expressions and biosocial bases of sensation seeking.* Cambridge, U.K.: Cambridge University Press.

14

Heroes and Hos
Reflections of Male and Female Sexual Natures

CATHERINE SALMON

For evolutionary psychologists, it goes almost without saying that male and female sexual psychologies are different in a variety of ways. While social psychologists, feminists, and other popular writers (e.g., Hyde, 2005; Mackinnon, 1989; Wood & Eagly, 2002) have suggested that either psychological differences between the sexes do not exist or, if they do, they are socially constructed, evolutionarily minded folk have pointed out that the adaptive problems that faced ancestral men and women were different (for a very different evolutionary psychology friendly feminist perspective on sex differences, see Paglia, 1990, 1994). If men and women faced different problems, it would be logical to assume that the solutions (their adaptations) to those problems were different as well—designed to solve their somewhat different agendas.

This chapter is focused on outlining the advantages of using unobtrusive measures in the study of human sexual psychology and the way in which studies of pornography and romance novels illuminate our understanding of the differences between our evolved male and female sexual natures.

UNOBTRUSIVE MEASURES

Researchers have used a variety of methodologies in their attempts to illuminate human nature, all of which have advantages and disadvantages. Some researchers have employed questionnaires and surveys, which may sometimes introduce a foreign element into the feature the study is designed to measure. As a result, they may not illicit a typical response. Others have used observational studies and experiments. Perhaps one of the most novel methods is to combine questionnaire studies with unobtrusive measures. Unobtrusive measures are research methods that do not require the cooperation of respondents and do not themselves contribute to the response (Salmon & Symons, 2001;

Webb, Campbell, Schwartz, & Sechrest, 1966). Daly and Wilson (1988, 1998) used unobtrusive measures in their studies of homicide. They used police statistics on child abuse and homicide to illuminate the psychology of parental love (or discriminative parental solicitude), drawing attention to variables (e.g., offspring quality, step relationship, etc.) that influence parental investment in offspring.

Another example of the use of unobtrusive measures is Devendra Singh's (1993, 1994) work on the relationships between waist-to-hip ratio (WHR) and attractiveness. Singh (and others) have suggested that in the EEA (the ancestral environment in which human adaptations evolved), selection favored those males who were preferentially sexually aroused by visually detected characteristics of female bodies that were reliable indicators of female mate value. WHR provides reliable information about health, age, hormonal status, parity, and fecundity. Consequently, we would expect human males to have evolved psychological mechanisms specialized to extract and process this very useful information (Singh, 1993). Since female mate value varies inversely with WHR, all else being equal, female sexual attractiveness is also expected to vary inversely with WHR. Singh (1993, 1994) tested this hypothesis using both unobtrusive measures and experimental data.

Singh (1993) concluded, based on analyses of the measurements of Playboy centerfold models and Miss American contest winners over the last 30 to 60 years, that

> a narrow waist set against full hips (WHR in the .68–.72 range) has been a consistent feature of female attractiveness, whereas other bodily features, such as bustline, overall body weight, or physique, have been assigned varying degrees of importance over the years. (p. 296)

A final example of the use of unobtrusive measures pertains to the potential wealth of information about human nature to be found in free markets (Saad, 2006; Saad & Gill, 2000). Free markets clearly adapt products to our preferences through cycles of market research, consumer feedback, and economic competition. Consequently, such products are a window into our natural preferences, our basic human desires. Evolutionarily inspired examinations of our food and taste preferences illustrate that the success of the fast food industry is not due simply to successful marketing techniques, powerful though they may be, but to our evolved preference for foods high in fat and sugar. Over most of our species' history, such nutrients have been essential to our dietary health (and still are, but not in the quantities currently consumed); they required significant physical labor to obtain (Eaton, Eaton, & Konner, 1997; Nesse & Williams, 1994; Rozin, 1976). Since people who were highly motivated to seek out such foods (i.e., people with a taste for sugar and fat) were more successful than those who were less highly motivated, they left more children who shared their taste preferences. All humans alive today are the descendents of fat and sugar fanciers, which is why foods high in fat and sugar are so difficult to resist (and why low-fat, low-sugar foods often seem rather unappealing).

In this chapter, I will focus on the use of unobtrusive measures associated with mass-market erotica and view it in the light of evolved preferences and free markets. The production of male-oriented pornography and female-oriented romance novels are multibillion dollar, worldwide industries whose products have been shaped in free markets by the cumulative choices made by millions of men and women who have expressed their erotic preferences through their consumer choices. The reason why these products are successful and appealing to their consumers is that they tap into basic human nature, or more exactly, different male and female sexual psychologies. While fast food chains are successful because they provide products that take advantage of our human dietary preferences, producers of romance and pornography become successful by tapping into our sexual preferences. The essential features of porn and romance are integral components of our male and female sexual natures.

Commercial pornography exists in almost every industrialized society and in many developing societies as well. Worldwide sales of sexually explicit magazines, books, and videos bring in approximately $56 million annually (Morais, 1999). Sexually explicit videos are stocked by two thirds of American video rental stores (U.S. Department of Justice, 1986) and in 1998, Americans rented nearly 7 million "adult" videotapes (Morais, 1999), while 8,948 hard-core videos hit the U.S. market. The expansion of the porn industry has been accompanied by success stories that have become almost mythical in nature. The film *Deep Throat,* highlighting the art of fellatio in 1972, cost about $25,000 to produce and became an instant classic, generating more than $100 million in profit (Cook, 1978). Estimated revenues in the United States range from $35 million for Vivid Video (which makes around 90 feature-length movies per year) to $318 million for Playboy Enterprises (including adult television, video, and publishing). The success of the online DVD rental company Netflix (which does not carry hard-core films) has spurred the creation of online rental companies specializing in the rental of porn such as www.sugardvd.com and www.bushdvd.com.

In *The Jaguar and the Anteater*, Bernard Arcand (1991) wrote that it is "essential to know whether there is such a thing as a pornography consumed exclusively by women, and whether it is fundamentally different from that preferred by men" (p. 49). The answer is yes there is, and it is the much maligned romance novel.

Romance novels make up close to 35% of mass-market paperback sales in the United States, generating annual revenues of around $2 billion. In the last year, over 2,000 romances were published in North America, where more than 50 million women are regular readers of romance novels. Harlequin Enterprises, one of the largest publishers of romances, boasts annual worldwide sales of close to 200 million books, a testament to the enormous appeal of these narratives to women everywhere.

Real-life heterosexual interactions unavoidably involve compromise. As a result, they blur the differences between male and female sexual desires and dispositions. Erotica, aimed at either a male or a female audience, has to please only one sex at a time.

One way in which erotica can enlighten us about human sexual psychology is to compare those products that achieve commercial success to those that do not. Sales figures, reader recommendations, and royalty checks provide reliable information about women's psychology. Best-selling romance novels, for example, almost never feature sensitive, new-age heroes, because female readers prefer fantasies of powerful, self-assured men who ultimately are tamed only by their love for the heroine. The popularity of Russell Crowe's character Maximus in the motion picture *Gladiator* is but one example of how appealing strong heroes are. Romance writers who have experimented with gentle, sensitive heroes have not been rewarded in the marketplace. Within the last decade, there was an attempt to market a line of sensitive new-age guy romances. It was not a commercial success. Those romances that incorporate classic elements are the ones that readers consistently place on best seller lists (Krentz, 1992).

Another way to utilize unobtrusive measures is to attempt to identify the essential components of erotic genres. For example, a common characteristic of pornographic videos is attempted humor (e.g., *The Postman Always Comes Twice*, etc.); but humor is *not* an essential ingredient. Many thousands of humorless porn videos are commercially successful. In contrast, impersonal sex *is* an essential ingredient of porn videos. This approach will be explored in the next section.

THE WORLD OF PORNOGRAPHY FOR MEN

As written narratives and color photographs cannot match the visual and auditory realism of film, movies are the preferred media for modern day male consumers of sexually explicit material. Analyses of contemporary pornographic movies reveal a narrow range of themes and content.

The utopian male fantasy realm depicted in pornography, dubbed "pornotopia" by historian Steven Marcus, varies little across time and space. Pornographic artifacts exist from many ancient cultures, from the sculptures and wall paintings that decorated the brothels of the city of Pompeii to Renaissance sculptures and frescos (Bullough & Bullough, 1995; Paglia, 1990). There is little, other than the medium, to distinguish them in nature or design from modern magazines such as *Playboy* and *Penthouse* or the typical modern pornographic movie. In pornotopia, the nature of sex is lust and physical gratification, devoid of courtship, commitment, durable relationships, or mating effort. It is a fantasy world in which women are instantly aroused, eagerly have sex with strangers, and always experience orgasm. Where else would a guy be joined in an elevator by several beautiful strangers who drag him to the floor for some oral sex? Porn videos contain little to no plot development, concentrating on the sex acts themselves and emphasizing the display of attractive female bodies, especially close-ups of sexually aroused facial expressions, breasts, and genitals. Most porn videos focus almost entirely on sex, routinely including lesbianism, group sex, anal intercourse, oral-genital contact, as well as visible ejaculation or money shots (Hebditch & Anning, 1988). Nonsexual interpersonal behavior is pretty much nonexistent. A content analysis of 50 random films revealed fellatio to be the act engaged in most frequently, followed by vaginal intercourse, and cunnilingus (Brosius, Weaver, & Staab, 1993). Sex scenes typically culminate with a male ejaculating on a female's body, the infamous external cum shot. The domination of male-oriented erotica by film, and increasingly, the Internet, attests to the deeply visual nature of male sexuality. For the most part, men are sexually aroused by "objectified" visual stimuli. As a result, porn does not require the existence of a point-of-view character to be effective, and scenes of a woman masturbating alone, or engaging in sexual activity with another woman, are ubiquitous. The male viewer can create his own role in the fantasy, his own scene of sexual interaction with the aroused woman. The female stars, decorating the DVD cases to entice men to buy or rent, manifest cues of high mate value. They are young and physically attractive. Pornotopia, in summary, is a world in which men have easy access to low-cost, impersonal sex with an endless succession of lustful, beautiful, orgasmic women. It is an optimal fantasy world of the male short-term mating strategy.

In fact, this is as true for pornography targeted to a gay male audience as that aimed at a heterosexual audience. In fact, gay and straight male porn are essentially identical, differing only in the sex of the actors and the attractiveness of the male actors (gay porn requiring more attractiveness on the part of men than straight porn for a male audience). A content analysis of gay and straight male porn revealed no significant differences in terms of the activities engaged in (with vaginal and anal sex acts grouped together for obvious reasons) except that in the homosexual audience movies, there were more acts of sexual intercourse that took place in a face-to-face position (Satava, 2006). Some have also pointed out that impersonal sex that characterizes male fantasy in heterosexual porn and is also characteristic of homosexual porn is not very different from the real-life sexual relations of many gay men (Bailey, Gaulin, Agyei, & Gladue, 1994; Mahay, Laumann, & Michaels, 2000; Symons, 1979).

The Ho

As previously mentioned, female porn stars display cues of high mate value in terms of fertility and their sexual behavior signals the opportunity for low-cost mating. An examination of some of the most popular (in terms of earning, number of movies made, sold, and rented) female stars such as Crissy Moran, Kendra Jade, Jesse Jane, and Jenna Jameson reveal a particular pattern of facial and bodily characteristics. All are beautiful women, but they have a particular type of beauty. Hair color is relatively unimportant—blondes and brunettes are both in the top ranks—, but all of them have faces characterized by big bright eyes, shiny long hair, and pouty, full lips. All of these are traits linked to female attractiveness and, in particular, health and fertility (Etcoff, 1999; Grammer, Fink, Thornhill, Juette, & Runzal, 2002; Hinsz, Matz, & Patience, 2001; Symons, 1995). They all have large but firm breasts and tiny waists; the average proportions are 36D-24-34 (for somewhat different measurements, see Voracek & Fisher, in press). Such measurements are very close to the ideal WHR of 0.7 and display the bodily and facial characteristics that have been pointed out in various research studies as indicators of health, fertility, and youth (Singh & Young, 1995; Sugiyama, 2005; Symons, 1979, 1995).

The Romance Novel

Although some have referred to the romance novel as, with some justification, "women's pornography," its essential nature is quite the opposite of male-oriented porn. The goal of a romance novel's heroine is never sex as an end in itself. Even less so is it about impersonal sex with strangers. At the heart of a romance novel's plot is a love story in which the heroine overcomes all barriers to find, win the heart of, and ultimately form a permanent union with the one man who is right for her. This is as true for the modern, contemporary romance as for the equally popular historical romances. It is also one reason why romance serials do not feature the same heroine, as there are endless iterations of James Bond, Max Brand, or other male-oriented adventurers; each romance must end with the establishment of a permanent union. That is the goal of the fantasy. Unlike male-oriented porn, one essential feature of the romance is the existence of a point-of-view (POV) character with whom the reader subjectively identifies. The main POV character is typically the heroine, though the POV can shift back and forth between heroine and hero.

There is a great deal of variation in the extent to which sexual activity is depicted in romances, from fade to black to highly explicit descriptions. Although the description of sexual activities is common in romances, it is not an essential component. When sex is described, it contributes to the plot without dominating it. The hero finds in his heroine a rewarding focus for his passion. It binds him to her, ensuring his future fidelity. Sex scenes often focus on the heroine's control of the hero, not her sexual submissiveness. Sexual activity is described subjectively as opposed to objectively; the primary focus is the heroine's emotions, rather than her physical responses or some visual imagery. The emotional focus of a romance is on love, commitment, and domesticity. Its final goal is the creation of a perfect union with the heroine's ideal mate, one who is strong yet nurturing (Radway, 1984). As one novelist writes, "It was as if their souls yearned toward each other, and in a flash of glory, merged and became one" (Barlow, 1986, p. 401).

The Romance Hero

The characteristic features of the heroes of successful romance novels can illuminate our understanding of the psychology of female mate choice. Interestingly, successful romances almost never feature gentle, sensitive new-age men. As part of her dissertation, anthropologist April Gorry (1999) analyzed every description of the heroes of 45 different romances. Each of the novels she sampled had been independently nominated for excellence by at least three romance readers or writers. In almost all of the romances analyzed, the hero was older than the heroine. The average was by 7 years. The heroes were always described as being taller than the heroine, and the adjectives used to describe the physical features of heroes were most often muscular, handsome, strong, large, tanned, masculine, and energetic. Such terms focus on desirable qualities from the perspective of looking for good genetic quality in a mate as well as the ability to provide for and protect (Buss & Schmitt, 1993; Pawlowski & Koziel, 2002).

Gorry's (1999) heroes also displayed cues of what she called physical and social "competence." They were described as sexually bold, calm, confident, and impulsive. In a majority of romances, the hero's intelligence was remarked upon, though some lacked any formal education.

The most consistently articulated characteristics of heroes were those that dealt with their feelings for the heroines: their sexual desire for them; their declarations of love; that they want her more than any other woman; that she is the only women for whom they have felt such love; that they are consumed with thoughts of her and are sexually jealous and proprietary of her; and that they treat her gently and want to protect her. A list of the universal features of romantic love would contain all of these feelings.

The successful romance hero's essential characteristics consist of those concentrated primarily upon his physical appearance, physical and social competence, and intense love for the heroine. As Amanda Quick (1990) writes, the heroine is "[d]rawn to his masculine strength and the glitter of desire that burned in his emerald eyes" (p. 126). His physique typically follows the ideal inverted triangle with physical strength and muscle development in the upper body that has been shown to significantly contribute to male attractiveness to women (Franzoi & Hertzog, 1987; Maisey, Vale, Cornelissen, & Tovee, 1999). In contrast to his physical form, being rich and of high social status, while more common among romance heroes than among men in general, are not essential characteristics of the hero. In Gorry's (1999) research, heroes had high social status or a prestigious occupation about 50% of the time. It is worth keeping in mind, while pondering the psychological adaptations of female mate choice, that money, social classes, and formal education did not exist for the majority of early human evolutionary history. It is not necessary for successful romance novel heroes to be rich or aristocratic. What is necessary is for them to consistently possess characteristics that would have made them highly desirable mates during the course of human evolutionary history. They are tall, strong, good looking, vigorous, intelligent, self-assured, capable, and "dangerous" men whose love for the heroine guarantees that she and her children will be the beneficiaries of these highly desirable qualities.

Romance writer Robyn Donald (1992) summed up these aspects of the hero and his appeal very nicely when she wrote,

> To be the only much-loved mate of such a man would have distinct survival value for both the woman and her children. A romantic hero may have a character that is less than perfect, but he must be shown to have the capacity to love and a basic human sense of responsibility and compassion. He is an authoritative figure; he takes charge in an emergency with the knowledge that what he is doing is the best that can be done under those particular circumstances. He is successful. (p.83)

In the end, the world of the romance, "romantopia," is a utopian, sexual female counterfantasy to pornotopia. While the actresses in porn exhibit a sexual nature that is suspiciously malelike, romance novels transform masculinity to align with female preferences. They are tales of the search for a long-term mate, a quality as opposed to quantity strategy. As such, the essential components of porn and romance novels indicate the existence of profound and enduring differences between male and female mating psychologies.

WHY THE BIG DIFFERENCE BETWEEN EROTICA FOR MEN AND WOMEN?

One might wonder how it is possible for male and female sexual psychologies to be as dramatically different as studies of commercial erotica imply. Particularly in light of the belief that over the course of human evolutionary history most successful reproduction occurred within marriages, and most marriages were monogamous partnerships.

The answer can be found in the qualitative differences in the adaptive problems faced by ancestral men and women in the mating domain. Despite the likelihood that the typical parental investments of men and women did not differ significantly, men and women did differ dramatically in their minimum possible investments (Buss, 1989; Hinde, 1984; Symons, 1979). If a man fathered a child and contributed no parental investment (just mating effort), he could have reproduced at almost no cost. Even if such opportunities were relatively rare in ancestral human populations, taking advantage of them when they did occur was adaptive enough that males evolved a sexual psychology that makes low-cost sex with novel women exciting to imagine and to engage in (Gangestad & Simpson, 2000). This motivates men to seek out such sexual opportunities. As a result, males are quick to consent to sex with new partners and are easily attracted to new females (Buss & Schmitt, 1993). Pornotopia is a short-term mating strategy fantasy realm, made possible by evolutionarily novel technology, in which impersonal sex with a progression of high-mate-value women is the norm rather than the rare exception.

In contrast, ancestral females would gain nothing and risk much from impersonal sex with random strangers or seeking sexual variety for its own sake. There were substantial benefits to choosing their mates carefully (Symons, 1979; Wright & Reise, 1997). The romance novel is a tale of female mate choice in which the heroine's time and effort is rewarded by finding and marrying a man who epitomizes the physical, psychological, and social characteristics that translated into high male mate value over the span of human evolutionary history. In the end, the romance is a story of one woman's search for the highest quality long-term mate. In other words, the sexually explicit material most frequently consumed by males reflects the main components of the short-term aspects of male sexual strategies, whereas the sexually explicit material most frequently consumed by women reflects the primary aspects of long-term female sexual strategies (Malamuth, 1996).

Personal sexual fantasies reflect the same sex differences as commercial erotica. "In fantasy one can imagine anything one likes, however unrealistic, without experiencing embarrassment or rejection or societal and legal restrictions" (Leitenberg & Henning, 1995, p. 469). Female sexual fantasies are more likely than male fantasies to contain familiar partners and to include descriptions of context, setting, and feelings associated with the sexual encounter. Female sexual fantasies are more contextual, emotive, intimate, and passive, while male sexual fantasies are more ubiquitous, frequent, visual, specifically sexual, promiscuous, and active (Ellis & Symons, 1990). Sex differences in commercial erotica, expectedly, are a mirror of the sex differences in personal sexual fantasies.

One might wonder why there no commercial erotic genre that combines the essential components of pornotopia and romantopia. From a business perspective, such a genre would double the potential customers and perhaps the potential profit. In the end, women are sexual as well as romantic creatures, as capable of being physically aroused by hard-core sex scenes as they are likely to melt at a good romance. In addition, the evidence from romance novels would seem to suggest that women, like men, prefer erotica in which the sexual partners are new to each other rather than members of a long-term relationship. The process of careful mate choice and establishing long-term mateships were problems faced by both sexes, not just females, throughout our ancestral past.

In fact, many commercially successful romantic comedies and romantic adventures do appeal to both sexes, and men and women alike can enjoy the literary works of Jane Austen or a movie like *Sense and Sensibility* or *Mr. and Mrs. Smith*. But the wide-ranging appeal of such novels and films is gained at the cost of failing to represent many of pornotopia's and romantopia's essential components. One could conceive of a film genre that brought together a majority of the essentials of romantopia, pornotopia, and mainstream commercial cinema. There could be romantic adventures with complex plots, great dialogue, captivating characters, top of the line acting, beautiful stars, happy endings, and hard-core sex scenes.

But even if it were possible to produce such films, they would not do away with the markets for porn and romances, because some of the essential aspects of pornotopia and romantopia are mutually exclusive. Perhaps most obvious, impersonal sex, the heart of pornotopic fantasy, is incompatible with romantopia. The so-called plot of a porn film is seldom more than a loosely connected sequence of sex scenes, each typically ending with an external ejaculation. A porn film has as many climaxes as it does scenes, but a romance novel has only one climax. It occurs when the hero and heroine proclaim their mutual love. Figure 14.1 provides a clear demonstration of this incompatibility. It is hard to imagine any adult DVD titles or romance novel titles appearing on the other list.

Successful porn video rental titles	Successful romance novels
Jenna's Provovateur	Lord of Scoundrels
Fetish Fanatic 4	Mr. Perfect
Weapons of Ass Destruction	Ravished
Britney Rears 3	Dreaming Of You
Barely Legal 63	Outlander
Cum Stained Casting Couch 6	All Through The Night
Crack Her Jack 6	Sea Swept
Teagan's Juice	It Had To Be You
The Sex Whisperer	A Kingdom of Dreams
All You Can Eat 3	Flowers From The Storm

Figure 14.1 Successful porn videos for men and romance novels for women. Their titles provide a stark illustration of the differences between erotica produced for men and women. The porn titles were taken from the AVN monthly top DVD rentals list while the romance titles were taken from the All About Romance 2004 top 100 readers poll.

FINAL THOUGHTS

The stark differences between the worlds of pornotopia and romantopia are an illustration of how different our male and female sexual natures can be. In "Warrior Lovers," Salmon and Symons (2001) wrote that "to encounter erotica designed to appeal to the opposite sex is to gaze into the abyss that separates the sexes" (p. 4).

While many men and women meet, fall in love, marry, have children, and perhaps stay married for long periods, sex differences in our sexual fantasies and our preferred erotic genres suggest that the different adaptive problems faced by men and women in our ancestral past have shaped our sexual psychologies in significantly different ways. Both men and women may follow long- and short-term mating strategies. Sometimes the focus may be on one strategy, sometimes the other, and sometimes both may be pursued. But the differences in the erotic material people prefer suggest that the reproductive benefits to males of being easily visually aroused and having a preference for variety (or novel women) have been substantial as have the benefits to women of being choosy and looking carefully for their "heroes." Makers of mass-market pornography and romance capitalize on these essential features of our male and female sexual natures.

REFERENCES

Arcand, B. (1991). *The jaguar and the anteater: Pornography and the modern world.* New York: McClelland & Stewart.

Bailey, J. M., Gaulin, S., Agyei, Y., & Gladue, B. A. (1994). Effects of gender and sexual orientation on evolutionarily relevant aspects of human mating psychology. *Journal of Personality and Social Psychology, 66*, 1081–1093.

Barlow, L. (1986). *Fires of destiny.* New York: Onyx.

Brosius, H. B., Weaver, J. B., & Staab, J. F. (1993). Exploring the social and sexual "reality" of contemporary pornography. *Journal of Sex Research, 30*, 161–170.

Bullough, V. L., & Bullough, B. (1995). *Sexual attitudes: Myths and realities.* New York: Prometheus Books.

Buss, D. M. (1989). Sex differences in human mate preferences: Evolutionary hypotheses tested in 37 cultures. *Behavioral and Brain Sciences, 12,* 1–49.

Buss, D. M., & Schmitt, D. P. (1993). Sexual strategies theory: An evolutionary perspective on human mating. *Psychological Review, 100,* 204–232.

Cook, J. (1978, September 18). The X-rated economy. *Forbes,* 81–92.

Daly, M., & Wilson, M. (1988). *Homicide.* Hawthorne, NY: Aldine de Gruyter.

Daly, M., & Wilson, M. (1998). *The truth about Cinderella: A Darwinian view of parental love.* London: Weidenfeld & Nicolson.

Donald, R. (1992). Mean, moody, and magnificent: The hero in romance literature. In J. Krentz (Ed.), *Dangerous men and adventurous women: Writers on the appeal of the romance* (pp. 81–84). Philadelphia: University of Pennsylvania Press.

Eaton, S. B., Eaton III, S. B., & Konner, M. J. (1997). Paleolithic nutrition revisited: A twelve-year retrospective on its nature and implications. *European Journal of Clinical Nutrition, 51,* 207–216.

Ellis, B. J., & Symons, D. (1990). Sex differences in sexual fantasy: An evolutionary psychological approach. *Journal of Sex Research, 27,* 527–555.

Etcoff, N. (1999). *Survival of the prettiest.* New York: Doubleday.

Franzoi, S. L., & Hertzog, M. E. (1987). Judging physical attractiveness: What body aspects do we use? *Personality and Social Psychology Bulletin, 13,* 19–33.

Gangestad, S. W., & Simpson, J. A. (2000). The evolution of human mating: Trade-offs and strategic pluralism. *Behavioral and Brain Sciences, 23,* 573–644.

Gorry, A. (1999). *Leaving home for romance: Tourist women's adventures abroad.* Unpublished doctoral thesis, University of California at Santa Barbara.

Grammer, K., Fink, B., Thornhill, R., Juette, A., & Runzal, G. (2002). Female faces and bodies: N-dimensional feature space and attractiveness. In G. Rhodes & L. A. Zebrowitz (Eds.), *Facial attractiveness: Evolutionary, cognitive, and social perspectives* (pp. 91–126). Westport, CT: Greenwood.

Hebditch, D., & Anning, N. (1998). *Porn gold: Inside the pornography business.* London: Faber & Faber.

Hinde, R. A. (1984). Why do the sexes behave differently in close relationships? *Journal of Social and Personal Relationships, 1,* 471–501.

Hinsz, V. B., Matz, D. C., & Patience, R. A. (2001). Does women's hair signal reproductive potential? *Journal of Experimental Social Psychology, 37,* 166–172.

Hyde, J. S. (2005). The gender similarities hypothesis. *American Psychologist, 60,* 581–592.

Krentz, J. A. (1992). Trying to tame the romance: Critics and correctness. In J. Krentz (Ed.), *Dangerous men and adventurous women: Writers on the appeal of the romance* (pp. 107–114). Philadelphia: University of Pennsylvania Press.

Leitenberg, H., & Henning, K. (1995). Sexual fantasy. *Psychological Bulletin, 117,* 469–496.

MacKinnnon, C. (1989). Toward a feminist theory of the state. Cambridge, MA: Harvard University Press.

Mahay, J., Laumann, E. O., & Michaels, S. (2000). Race, gender, and class in sexual scripts. In E. O. Laumann & R. T. Michael (Eds.), *Sex, love, and health in America: Private choices and public policies.* Chicago: University of Chicago Press.

Maisey, D. S., Vale, E. L. E., Cornelissen, P. L., & Tovee, M. J. (1999). Characteristics of male attractiveness for women. *The Lancet, 353,* 1500.

Malamuth, N. M. (1996). Sexually explicit media, gender differences, and evolutionary theory. *Journal of Communications, 46,* 8–31.

Morais, R. C. (1999). Porn goes public. *Forbes, 163,* 214–221.

Nesse, R. M., & Williams, G. C. (1994). *Why we get sick.* New York: Random House.

Paglia, C. (1990). *Sexual personae: Art and decadence from Nefertiti to Emily Dickinson.* New Haven, CT: Yale University Press.

Paglia, C. (1994). *Vamps and tramps: New essays.* New York: Vintage.

Pawlowski, B., & Koziel, S. (2002). The impact of traits offered in personal advertisements on response rates. *Evolution and Human Behavior, 23,* 139–149.

Quick, A. (1990). *Seduction.* New York: Bantam Books.

Radway, J. (1984). *Reading the romance: Women, patriarchy, and popular literature.* Chapel Hill: University of North Carolina Press.

Rozin, P. (1976). The selection of food by rats, humans, and other animals. In J. Rosenblatt, R. A. Hinde, & E. Shaw (Eds.), *Advances in the study of behavior* (Vol. 6, pp. 21–76). New York: Academic Press.

Saad, G. (2006). Applying evolutionary psychology in understanding the Darwinian roots of consumption phenomena. *Managerial and Decision Economics, 27*, 189–201.

Saad, G., & Gill, T. (2000). Applications of evolutionary psychology in marketing. *Psychology and Marketing, 17*, 1005–1034.

Salmon, C. and Symons, D. (2001). *Warrior lovers: Erotic fiction, evolution and female sexuality.* London: Weidenfeld & Nicolson.

Satava, K. (2006). A content analysis of heterosexual and homosexual pornography focused on depictions of the submissive/dominant relationship. Unpublished senior thesis, University of Redlands, Redlands, CA.

Singh, D. (1993). Adaptive significance of waist-to-hip ratio and female physical attractiveness. *Journal of Personality and Social Psychology, 65*, 298–307.

Singh, D. (1994). Is thin really beautiful and good? Relationship between waist-to-hip ratio (WHR) and female attractiveness. *Personality and Individual Differences, 16*, 465–481.

Singh, D., & Young, R. K. (1995). Body weight, waist-to-hip ratio, breasts, and hips: Role in judgments of female attractiveness and desirability for relationships. *Ethology and Sociobiology, 16*, 483–507.

Sugiyama, L. S. (2005). Physical attractiveness in adaptationist perspective. In D. Buss (Ed.), *The handbook of evolutionary psychology* (pp. 292–344). Hoboken, NJ: Wiley & Sons.

Symons, D. (1979). *The evolution of human sexuality.* New York: Oxford University Press.

Symons, D. (1995). Beauty is in the adaptations of the beholder: The evolutionary psychology of human female sexual attractiveness. In P. R. Abramson & S. D. Pinkerton (Eds.), *Sexual nature, sexual culture* (pp. 80–118). Chicago: University of Chicago Press.

U.S. Department of Justice. (1986). *Attorney general's commission on pornography: Final report.* Washington, DC: U.S. Government Printing Office.

Voracek, M., & Fisher, M. (in press). Success is all in the measures: Androgynousness, curvaceousness, and starring frequencies in adult media actresses. *Archives of Sexual Behavior.*

Webb, E., Campbell, D. T., Schwartz, R., & Sechrest, L. (1966). *Unobtrusive measures: Non-reactive research in the social sciences.* Chicago: Rand McNally.

Wood, W., & Eagly, A. H. (2002). A cross-cultural analysis of the behavior of women and men: Implications for the origins of sex differences. *Psychological Bulletin, 128*, 699–727.

Wright, T. M., & Reise, S. P. (1997). Personality and unrestricted sexual behavior: Correlations of sociosexuality in Caucasian and Asian college students. *Journal of Research in Personality, 31*, 166–192.

Part V
THE EVOLUTIONARY PSYCHOLOGY OF PROSOCIAL BEHAVIOR

It is ironic that although most people view evolution as a process that selects selfish traits, evolutionary theory has gone further than any other theory to explain why animals behave in prosocial ways. The chapters in this section discuss advances in the evolutionary psychology of cooperation, helping, altruism, and morality. Evolutionary theorists do not always agree with one another. An important controversy is explicated in chapters 16 and 17.

15

How Selfish by Nature?

DENNIS KREBS

The idea that all animals, including humans, are selfish by nature has a long history in theology, philosophy, and the social sciences. It appears to have been endorsed by scholars who are in the best position to evaluate it—evolutionary biologists. In *Descent of Man*, Charles Darwin (1874) wrote,

> It is extremely doubtful whether the offspring of the most sympathetic and benevolent parents, or of those which were the most faithful to their comrades, would be reared in greater number than the children of selfish and treacherous parents of the same tribe. He who was ready to sacrifice his life ..., rather than betray his comrades, would often leave no offspring to inherit his noble nature. (p. 163)

Following the publication of *Descent of Man*, Thomas Huxley (1893) considered the moral implications of Darwin's theory of evolution and concluded that if "brought before the tribunal of ethics, [nature] might well stand condemned" (p. 59). More than a century later, Williams (1989) evaluated Huxley's (1893) conclusions in light of refinements in the theory of evolution and found it "indecisive and disappointing" (p. 180). After considering the evidence, Williams (1989) reached the following decisive conclusion:

> There is no encouragement for any belief that an organism can be designed for any purpose other than the most effective pursuit of ... self-interest (p. 197). Nothing resembling the Golden Rule or other widely preached ethical principles seems to be operating in living nature. It could scarcely be otherwise, when evolution is guided by a force that maximizes genetic selfishness. (p. 195)

In his highly influential book, *The Selfish Gene*, Dawkins (1989) popularized William's position:

> I think "nature red in tooth and claw" sums up our modern understanding of natural selection admirably ... If you look at the way natural selection works, it seems to follow that anything that has evolved by natural selection should be selfish ... Be warned that if you wish, as I do, to build a

society in which individuals cooperate generously and unselfishly toward a common good, you can expect little help from biological nature. (pp. 2–4)

In this chapter, I will evaluate the idea that the process of natural selection has rendered all beings selfish by nature and find it wanting. I will begin by spelling out the logic that has induced evolutionary theorists to conclude that all evolved behavioral dispositions are selfish, then go on to argue that because the genetically selfish dispositions favored by natural selection do not equate to biologically or psychologically selfish dispositions, the latter can evolve. In the remainder of the chapter, I will review evidence suggesting that both selfish and unselfish dispositions have evolved in a variety of social species, including our own.

THE SELFISHNESS OF EVOLVED DISPOSITIONS

The reason why evolutionary theorists hold that all evolved behavioral dispositions are selfish is because they define selfishness in terms of behaviors that enhance animals' fitness relative to, or at the expense of, the fitness of other animals. As expressed by Sober and D. S. Wilson (2000), "By definition altruists have lower fitness than the selfish individuals with whom they interact. It therefore seems inevitable that natural selection should eliminate altruistic behaviour, just as it eliminates other traits that diminish an individual's fitness" (p. 186). (Sober & D. S. Wilson also argue that altruistic traits can evolve through group selection.)

The ultimate measure of fitness lies in the propagation of genes. Dawkins (1989) suggested that it is appropriate to label genes that are selected and transported to future generations selfish, because, in an environment with a limited carrying capacity, such genes increase their welfare, or frequency, at the expense of the welfare, or frequency, of their alleles. As expressed by Nesse (2000),

> It is correct beyond question that genes shape brains that induce individuals to do whatever best gets copies of those genes into future generations. This principle follows from the logic of how natural selection works, and is not an empirical issue. When this is combined with our intuitive notion that altruism consists of costly acts that benefit others, and genes are seen as the ultimate currency, then altruism [seems] impossible. (p. 228)

As defined by evolutionary biologists, a disposition or trait qualifies as *genetically selfish* when it induces those who possess it to behave in ways that have the consequence of increasing the number of replicas of their genes in the population. Genetic selfishness equates to success at genetic replication.

Although it may be appropriate to define all evolved behavioral dispositions as genetically selfish, it is important to recognize the constraints on this definition. First, it pertains only to the environment in which the dispositions were selected, in a post hoc manner (see Crawford, this volume; Gangestad, this volume). In a book called *Mean Genes*, Burnham and Phelan (2000) review evidence demonstrating that mechanisms governing hunger, thrill seeking, greed, and sexual relations that were fitness enhancing (and therefore genetically selfish) in the environments in which they were selected now dispose people to behave in fitness-reducing (i.e., genetically unselfish) ways in current environments. Troisi (this volume) explains how maladaptive behaviors and disorders such as obesity, drug addition, and alcoholism originate from a mismatch between modern environments and the environments in which the mechanisms that give rise to them were selected (for a more detailed account of the evolution or maladaptations, see Crespi, 2000).

Second, the genetic selfishness of social dispositions may vary with their frequency in the population (Axelrod, 1988; Maynard-Smith, 1982). The same disposition could be genetically selfish in one social environment and genetically unselfish in another social environment. For example, the disposition to reciprocate could pay off genetically in an environment replete with reciprocators, but prove genetically costly (genetically altruistic) in an environment replete with cheaters.

Third, evolved mechanisms that, on balance, enhance the fitness of those who inherit them may be designed in adaptively imperfect ways, which may induce individuals to emit some genetically unselfish behaviors. Simon (1990) has argued that the adaptive benefits of susceptibility to social influence ("docility") outweigh the genetic costs of the altruistic acts that the mechanisms occasionally produce. An important implication of this argument is that members of groups may be manipulated into behaving altruistically (William, 1989). Williams has suggested that cognitive mechanisms that enable people to reap adaptive benefits from reason may incidentally induce them to derive moral judgments that dispose them to behave in fitness-reducing ways.

Finally, it is important to note that genetic forms of selfishness do not necessarily pertain to the physical welfare of individuals; they pertain to the effect of individuals' behavior on the number of replicas of their genes they contribute to future generations. Following Dawkins (1989), it is appropriate to view genes as entities that use individuals as vehicles to propagate themselves.

BIOLOGICAL SELFISHNESS

One of the biggest obstacles to scholars' abilities to determine whether humans and other animals are selfish by nature is the pervasive tendency for people to use the word *selfishness* to refer to quite different phenomena. Those who take different sides on the issue often engage in futile debates in which they use the word selfish in quite different ways, while assuming that they are talking about the same thing. Little is gained by arguing that one's preferred definition of selfishness is the only valid definition. It is more constructive to acknowledge that there are different forms of selfishness than to examine the relations among them. To this end, I believe it is useful to distinguish between genetic selfishness and another form of selfishness with which it is often confused—a form that I will label *biological selfishness*.

Evolutionary theorists define selfish behaviors as those that "confer a fitness benefit on the actor, while placing a fitness cost on the recipient" (Kurland & Gaulin, 2005, p. 448), which they contrast with (a) altruistic behaviors, which confer a fitness benefit on the recipient at a cost to the actor and (b) cooperative behaviors, which purvey "mutual fitness benefits for both actors" (p. 448). Ultimately, fitness is defined in terms of the propagation of genes. However, as indicated in the quote from *Descent of Man* at the beginning of this chapter, fitness also may be defined in terms of survival and reproductive success. In these terms, a disposition, trait, or behavior is *biologically selfish* when it enhances the biological welfare (i.e., the survival and reproductive success) of actors at the expense of the biological welfare of recipients.

Biologically selfish and unselfish forms of conduct are similar to their genetic counterparts in that they usually help individuals get replicas of their traits into future generations. However, the two forms of selfishness differ in terms of what is replicated and of the types of costs and benefits that they bestow. The costs and benefits of genetically selfish behaviors are defined in terms of the effect of actors' actions on the number of *replicas of their genes* they contribute to future generations relative to the number of alleles of these genes contributed by others. In contrast, the costs and benefits of biologically selfish and unselfish forms of conduct are defined in terms of the effect of actors' actions on the probability that they (the *individuals*—the vehicles—carrying the genes) will survive and produce other individuals (vehicles) like them (i.e., who share some of their traits).

Although evolutionary theorists might argue that it is misguided to attend to the survival and reproductive success of individuals because, in the end, all that counts is the fate of the genes that they transport, distinguishing between biological and genetic forms of selfishness is helpful in explicating the nature of selfishness and exploring its implications for human nature. Indeed, it is helpful to distinguish between the kinds of biologically selfish dispositions that enhance survival and the kinds that enhance reproductive success. Survival affects evolution only as a prerequisite for reproduction and other means of genetic propagation (see Scheyd, Garver-Apgar, & Gangstad, this volume). Reproductive selfishness is more closely related to genetic selfishness than survival selfishness is. However, behaviors that enhance individuals' survival seem more selfish than those that enhance individuals' reproductive success. Characterizing mating and offspring-supporting behaviors as selfish is neither as connotatively comfortable nor as theoretically appropriate as characterizing survival behaviors as selfish. When individuals seek to foster their own survival, they benefit themselves, but when they seek to foster their reproductive success, they bestow biological benefits on the most direct recipients of their reproductive behaviors—their mates and offspring.[1]

PSYCHOLOGICAL SELFISHNESS

Laypeople rarely use the word "selfish" in the way in which evolutionary biologists use it in their disciplines. When people characterize a behavior, disposition, or person as selfish, they mean, "[D]eficient in consideration for others, concerned chiefly with one's own profit or pleasure" (*The Oxford Dictionary of Current English*, 1987); "seeking or concentrating on one's own advantage, pleasure, or well-being without regard for others" (*Funk & Wagnalls Standard Dictionary*, 1980); "regarding one's own interest chiefly or solely" (*Webster's New Twentieth Century Dictionary of the English Language Unabridged*, 1964); or "concerned only to satisfy one's own desires and prepared to sacrifice the feelings and needs etc. of others to do so" (*The New Lexicon Webster's Encyclopedic Dictionary of the English Language,* 1988). Note the implicit association between selfishness and immorality in these definitions. Most people believe that it is right to show consideration for others, and wrong for people to sacrifice others' feelings and needs to satisfy their own desires. People define altruism, which is commonly considered good, as the opposite of selfishness.

In this paper, I will define psychological selfishness and psychological altruism in the way in which it is implicitly defined by most laypeople, and explicitly defined by the psychologists and philosophers who have considered the concept most extensively, Batson (1991) and Sober and D. S. Wilson (2000), in terms of the motives that are reflected in the proximate terminal goals (ends) that individuals seek to achieve. A motive or desire is *psychologically selfish* when its aim (terminal goal) is to benefit the actor, especially by increasing his or her "profit," "pleasure," "well-being," and "advantage," without regard for others. By implication, a behavior is psychologically altruistic when its terminal goal is to benefit a recipient, as an end in itself (rather than as a means of benefiting the actor).

Many researchers, especially economists and social exchange theorists, define selfishness, altruism, and fairness in terms of how people choose to distribute material resources. Selfishness is defined operationally as taking more than one's share; altruism is defined as giving more than one's share; and fairness and equity are defined as giving people what they deserve. As discussed in other chapters of this volume (e.g., Gintis, Bowles, Boyd, & Fehr, this volume; Johnson Price, & Takezawa, this volume; Kenrick & Sundie, this volume), a great deal of recent research has challenged the classic "homo economicus" conception of human nature by demonstrating that people often refrain from making instrumental self-serving "rational choices" when they allocate resources, opting instead to distribute resources in more equitable ways (see also Lerner, 2003; Miller, 1999).

I will accommodate to economic definitions of selfishness and altruism when I review relevant research later in this chapter, evaluating it on its own terms. However, it is important to recognize that economic definitions fail to meet the criteria of selfishness and altruism employed by Batson (1991) and Sober and D. S. Wilson (1998) because they fail to establish that the choices in question reflect the terminal goals that those who make them are attempting to achieve. Although studies that employ economic definitions of selfishness and altruism may control such terminal goals as currying favor and making a good impression (e.g., by permitting participants to make only one choice, by using strangers as recipients, and by making choices anonymous; see Gintis et al., this

---

[1] On the other side of the coin, evolutionary biologists such as A. Zahavi and A. Zahavi (1997) have labeled dispositions to sacrifice one's prospects of surviving in order to optimize one's prospects of reproducing "altruistic."

volume; Johnson et al., this volume), they rarely attempt to establish that participants are not making fair and altruistic choices in order, for example, to make themselves feel good; that is, participants are not, in effect, sacrificing their profits in order to increase their pleasure.

Psychological selfishness and unselfishness differ from their evolutionary (genetic and biological) counterparts in two related ways. First, psychological forms of selfishness and altruism are defined in terms of the *motivational states* individuals are in, as reflected in the kinds of goals that they pursue. In contrast, evolutionary forms of selfishness and altruism are defined in terms of the ultimate *effects* they have on animals' *fitness*, relative to the fitness of other animals affected by the behaviors (recipients). When we ask whether a behavior is psychologically selfish, we are asking how the proximate mechanisms that generate it are designed. When we ask whether a behavior is biologically or genetically selfish, we are asking about its effects on the biological or genetic success of those who emit it. It follows that psychological selfishness and unselfishness pertain to the nature of the *vehicles* created by natural selection (and the mechanisms and adaptations the vehicles contain), whereas biological and genetic forms of selfness and unselfishness pertain to what ultimately happens to the vehicles as they pursue their proximate goals—whether they survive, produce offspring, and propagate their genes.

Defined strictly, actual effects and consequences of any kind—even profit, pleasure, advantage, and well-being—are irrelevant to psychological selfishness and altruism, except as goals. A psychologically altruistic act could end up benefiting people and making them feel good, and a psychologically selfish act could end up harming people and making them feel bad. To quote Batson (1998), "[T]he pleasure obtained [from a psychologically altruistic behavior] can be a consequence of reaching [the] goal [of benefiting another rather than oneself] without being the goal itself" (p. 300). The behaviors directed at achieving psychologically selfish goals remain psychologically selfish even when they fail to produce the desired results. Behaviors that stem from psychologically selfish motives could end up harming actors and benefiting recipients, and behaviors that stem from psychologically altruistic motives could end up benefiting actors and harming recipients. For example, a coward who fled from battle might be killed, yet distract the enemy to the benefit of his comrades, and a hero who tried to rescue his comrades, but failed, might win a medal of honor.

The second way in which psychological and evolutionary forms of selfishness differ pertains to the types of interests individuals (attempt to) advance. Whereas the interests that evolutionarily selfish behaviors promote are restricted to biological and genetic interests, the interests that psychologically selfish behaviors are directed at promoting are defined more broadly in terms of anything that individuals believe will benefit them. As indicated in dictionary definitions, psychologically selfish behaviors are aimed at accruing such physical, material, and psychological benefits as "profit," "pleasure," "well-being," and "advantage." Whether the benefits that people seek for themselves end up enhancing their biological and genetic welfare is an open question.

To classify a behavior or form of conduct as psychologically selfish or altruistic, we must decipher the motivational state of the individuals emitting it. This could be accomplished directly by assessing their physiological or neurological reactions, or indirectly by identifying the terminal goals that they are trying to achieve. Deciphering individuals' motivational states is a very difficult undertaking because actors may be in more than one motivational state at the same time and because they may use the same behavior to achieve more than one goal. For example, individuals could be motivated to bestow benefits on both themselves and others. In addition, individuals may use unselfish behaviors to achieve selfish goals (and vice versa). For example, as I will discuss more fully later, individuals may help others instrumentally, as a means of achieving the terminal goal of gaining recipients' approval, impressing observers, relieving vicariously experienced distress, or elevating their self-esteem. In many contexts, it is difficult to identify the terminal goal of a behavior or choice. You observe one individual helping another; is the helper trying to enhance the welfare of the recipient as an end in itself, or is the helper using the seemingly altruistic behavior instrumentally to achieve some selfish goal? If you scratch an altruist, will you see a hypocrite bleed?

POSSIBLE RELATIONS AMONG GENETIC, BIOLOGICAL, AND PSYCHOLOGICAL FORMS OF SELFISHNESS AND UNSELFISHNESS

As outlined in Figure 15.1, there are eight possible relations among psychological, biological, and genetic forms of selfishness and unselfishness. There is a pervasive tendency to assume that, if an evolved disposition is genetically selfish (or unselfish), it also is biologically and psychologically selfish (or unselfish). This tendency is understandable on conceptual and theoretical grounds. Conceptually, it is natural to assume that selfish is selfish. It seems incongruent or contradictory to characterize the same behavior as both selfish and unselfish. Theoretically, there are good reasons to expect natural selection to produce a correspondence among the different forms of selfishness. We would expect a positive relation between biologically and genetically selfish behaviors because the most direct way for members of sexually reproducing species to propagate their genes is to survive and maximize the number of offspring they contribute to future generations. In addition, as implied in the quotation from *Descent of Man* at the beginning of this paper, it makes sense to expect animals that are psychologically disposed to benefit themselves without regard for others to fare better biologically (and genetically) than animals that are motivated to help others without regard for their own welfare.

The expected correspondences notwithstanding, the three forms of selfishness (and unselfishness) need not *necessarily* be related (Batson, 2000; Dawkins, 1989; Nesse, 2000; Sober & D. S. Wilson, 2000). To quote Sober and D. S. Wilson (1998)

> The automatic assumption that individualism in evolutionary biology and egoism in the social sciences must reinforce each other is as common as it is mistaken. More care is needed to connect the behaviors that evolved … with the psychological mechanisms that evolved to motivate those behaviors. (p. 205)

Whether individuals who seek to obtain benefits for themselves without regard for others fare better biologically and contribute more copies of their genes to future generations than those who behave in less psychologically selfish ways is an open question. They might, or they might not. Certainly, nothing in the process of natural selection dictates that individuals who are motivated to behave in psychologically selfish ways will prevail in the struggle for existence and reproduction.

On the other side of the coin, there is no logical inconsistency in the assertion that behaving in psychologically unselfish ways may pay off biologically and genetically in the end. Cooperative

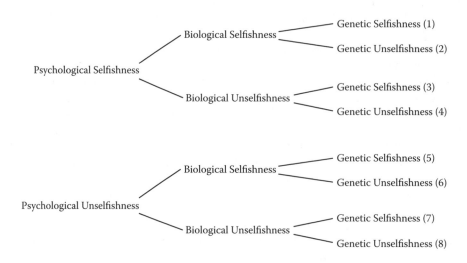

Figure 15.1 Possible relations between genetic, biological, and psychological forms of selfishness.

individuals motivated to benefit both themselves and others, and altruistic individuals motivated to help others as an end in itself, could end up being more likely to survive, to produce offspring, and to propagate their genes than individuals who were motivated to help themselves at the expense of others.[2]

Finally, biologically selfish dispositions need not necessarily be genetically selfish. As Dawkins (1989) has explained, "[T]here are special circumstances in which a gene can achieve its own selfish goals by fostering a limited form of altruism at the level of individual animals" (p. 6). Individuals can propagate their genes by sacrificing their survival and reproductive interests for the sake of those who possess copies of their genes.

Conclusions

We can safely conclude that the assertion that all evolved dispositions are selfish is at best valid—or more exactly, true by definition—with respect to genetic forms of selfishness in the types of environment in which they were selected. Changes in environments can render dispositions that were genetically selfish when they were selected genetically unselfish (i.e., maladaptive) when emitted by descendants of those in whom they originated. Because biologically and psychologically unselfish dispositions may be genetically selfish, they can evolve. Genetic benefits trump biological benefits and psychological motives in the evolution of social behavior.

Establishing that animals need not necessarily be selfish by nature does not equate to establishing that they are not, in fact, selfish by nature. Establishing that mechanisms that dispose animals to behave in biologically and psychologically unselfish ways *can* evolve does not equate to establishing that they *have* evolved. It raises a question. What kinds of mental mechanisms enabled the ancestors of humans and members of other social species to solve the adaptive problems they encountered and to propagate their genes most effectively in the social and physical environments in which the mechanisms evolved—mechanisms that enabled or motivated them to benefit themselves at the expense of others, mechanisms that enabled or motivated them to benefit both themselves and others, or mechanisms that enabled or motivated them to benefit others at their own expense. I believe that the answer to these questions is "all of the above mechanisms," depending on the conditions. I turn now to a consideration of the evidence relevant to first, the evolution of biologically selfish and unselfish dispositions, then to the evolution of psychologically selfish and unselfish dispositions.

THE EVOLUTION OF BIOLOGICALLY SELFISH AND UNSELFISH DISPOSITIONS

The Selection of Dispositions to Behave in Biologically Selfish Ways

There is no denying the potential in biologically selfish dispositions to help animals propagate their genes. In support of his case for the evolution of selfishness and his case against the evolution of morality, Williams (1989) offered "obvious examples of the pursuit of self-interest as practiced in

---

[2] Indeed, psychologically unselfish dispositions could also maximize individuals' net *psychological* gains. For example, individuals who were motivated to enhance the profit and pleasure of others without consideration for their own profit and pleasure could, over the long run, end up experiencing more *net* profit and pleasure than individuals who possessed more psychologically selfish dispositions. As demonstrated by Rachlin (2002), and others, individuals who make immediately unselfish choices may end up with greater net benefits than those who make immediately selfish choices, because the long-term benefits of moderation and cooperation may exceed those of short-sighted selfishness. Even though the long-term psychological benefits may reinforce the strategies or dispositions that give rise to the unselfish choices, the reinforcement does not render the motivational states or immediate goals of those invoking them psychologically selfish, as long as the individuals who invoke or are guided by them are not motivated to help others as a means of enhancing their own personal welfare when they make the choices in question.

the biological cosmos," noting that, "I will need no theoretical subtleties to show their gross selfishness and moral unacceptability" (p. 197). Included in these examples were tendencies for offspring to attempt to obtain more than their share of resources from parents, for males to rape females, and for females to cuckold males: "Recent accounts of reproductive behavior in wild animals are tales of sexual intrigue full of deception, desertion, double-dealing, and sometimes lethal violence" (p. 198). In addition, Williams argued, "[T]he killing of other members of the same species is a frequent phenomenon in a wide variety of forms and contexts" (p. 202). Clearly, humans also behave in the morally repugnant ways described by Williams.

When Williams (1989) adduced evidence that animals behave in ways that seem both psychologically selfish and morally repugnant to support his contention that all evolved dispositions are genetically selfish, he performed a little slight of hand. There are three problems with this tactic. First, even if the morally unacceptable forms of conduct he described were biologically and genetically selfish in the environments in which they were selected, they may not be biologically or genetically selfish in modern environments. Whether individuals who are disposed to take more than their share, steal, cheat, assault, rape, cuckold their mates, and murder members of their groups are more likely than those who behave in more morally acceptable ways to survive, produce more offspring, and propagate their genes is an open question. Behaviors that people consider selfish and morally repugnant—suicide, sloth, and uncontrolled aggression, for example—could diminish individuals' chances of surviving and reproducing (and therefore qualify as biologically unselfish).

Second, some biologically selfish behaviors are morally acceptable. Consider the often-cited mating behaviors of scorpion flies, for example. Although male scorpion flies may resort to rape, they also may foster their reproductive success by giving gifts to potential mates. When they work, both tactics are biologically selfish. Or consider prudential and temperate behaviors such as working hard, delaying gratification, and consuming resources in an optimally healthy manner. Even though these types of behavior may increase the survival and reproductive success of those who emit them relative to (therefore at a cost to) the survival and reproductive success of other members of their groups, they do not seem selfish or morally repugnant. Finally, evidence that some evolved dispositions are biologically selfish does not establish that all evolved dispositions are biologically selfish. Biologically unselfish dispositions could have evolved as well.

The Selection of Dispositions to Behave in Biologically Cooperative Ways

There is no question that cooperative dispositions have evolved in a wide array of social species (Dugatkin, 1997). There is compelling evidence that animals are disposed to coordinate their efforts to solve adaptive problems (mutualism), to exchange goods and services (reciprocity), and to invest in members of their groups (long-term social investments). Let us consider each form of cooperation in turn.

Mutualism. Members of many social species join forces and coordinate their efforts to accomplish such tasks as mating, caring for offspring, increasing status, grooming, hunting large game, attacking competing groups, defending territory, and protecting their groups (for reviews, see Alcock, 2004; Kurland & Gaulin, 2005). The magnitude of mutualism in the human species is unprecedented in the animal kingdom. It takes thousands of people coordinating their efforts to create a city or to build a dam. Although the biological benefits that those who join forces extend to others may be incidental by-products of efforts to enhance their own biological welfare, this does not render their efforts biologically selfish as long as they have the consequence of increasing the survival and reproductive success of others as well as themselves.

Social exchange. More than three decades ago, Trivers (1971) explained how dispositions to reciprocate could evolve through gains in trade, and he offered evidence that they have evolved in a selection of species. The title of Trivers' (1971) seminal piece on the evolution of reciprocity is

"The Evolution of Reciprocal Altruism." Clearly, Trivers was not using the word altruism to refer to biological or genetic forms of altruism. The point of Trivers' paper was to explain how dispositions to exchange goods and services could pay off biologically and genetically under some conditions. Although particular acts of giving and repaying could be viewed as (temporarily) biologically altruistic if they enhanced the biological welfare of recipients at a cost to the biological welfare of donors, these acts become biologically cooperative when recipients reciprocate. "Reciprocal altruism" is a form of biological cooperation.

It is well-established that dispositions to reciprocate evolved in relatively small groups through individual selection in the way described by Trivers (1971). There is, however, considerable controversy about whether the forms of cooperation displayed by humans living in large groups can be accounted for by selection at the level of individuals. On one side, theorists such as Johnson et al. (this volume) argue that reciprocity can evolve in large groups if those who are disposed to cooperate interact selectively with other cooperators. On the other side, theorists such as Richerson and Boyd (2005) and Gintis et al. (this volume) argue that it is not possible to account for the kind of large-scale cooperation displayed by humans without appealing to gene-culture coevolution.

Social investments. Enhancing the biological welfare of mates may help individuals increase their reproductive success because they need them in order to reproduce. In addition, it may be in the adaptive interest of mates to join forces to preserve their mutual biological interests in their offspring. Inasmuch as the biological benefits that members of pair bonds reap are dependent on the welfare of their partners, it may be in their biological interest to foster the welfare of their partners over long periods in order to foster their own ultimate reproductive success (Ellis, 1998).

It also may pay off biologically for members of groups to form long-term, mutually supportive relationships with individuals other than their mates. Several investigators have pointed out that exchanges among friends rarely conform to the principles of concrete reciprocity (Clark & Mills, 1993; Janicki, 2004; Nesse, 2001; Shackelford & Buss, 1996; Tooby & Cosmides, 1996). People do not keep track of every favor they do for their friends, and people are disposed to help their friends when their friends are in need, without expectation of immediate repayment. Tooby and Cosmides have argued that it could be in individuals' ultimate biological interest to contribute to the biological welfare of their friends over long periods if such acts increased the probability that their friends would contribute to their biological welfare when it was in serious jeopardy. In effect, it could pay for people to invest in their friends as insurance policies to foster their long-term security.

In a recent paper, S. L. Brown and M. Brown (2006) reviewed evidence demonstrating that humans are disposed to form affectively laden social bonds with members of their groups, which dispose them support them over long periods, at costs to themselves. S. L. Brown and M. Brown argued that these mechanisms were selected because it is in the ultimate genetic interest of individuals to form relationships with, and feel motivated to support, those on whom their fitness is dependent, whether offspring, parents, mates, friends, or members of one's in-group. Although S. L. Brown and M. Brown consider such social support "altruistic" because at a phenotypic level it involves costs to donors and benefits to recipients, it would qualify as biologically altruistic only if it ended up enhancing the survival and reproductive success of recipients at a cost to the survival and reproductive success of donors. Although this is plausible with respect to social support for kin, as discussed in the following section, it is not plausible with respect to social support for nonkin, because the biological costs suffered by individuals who help nonkin tend to be outweighed by the biological benefits of sustaining relationships with them, or even simply having them around. As explained by Flack and de Waal (2000),

> Inasmuch as every member [of a group] benefits from a unified, cooperative group, one expects them to care about the society they live in, and to make an effort to improve and strengthen it similar to the way the spider repairs her web, and the beaver maintains the integrity of his dam. Each and every

individual has a stake in the quality of the social environment on which its survival depends. In trying to improve this quality for their own purposes, they help many of their group mates at the same time. (p. 95)

More generally, Laland, Odling-Smee, and Feldman (2000) have suggested that organisms should be prepared to cooperate with other organisms when the other organisms niche construct in ways that increase their fitness.

In conclusion, there is no question that biologically cooperative dispositions have evolved in humans and other social species. Individuals may increase their chances of surviving and reproducing by joining forces with others to achieve biologically beneficial goals, by initiating and sustaining the exchange of biologically beneficial goods and services, and by investing in those on whom their fitness is dependent. Some behaviors that appear to be altruistic, because they bestow physical and material benefits on others without any immediate return, turn out to be biologically cooperative, because they enhance the biological welfare of both donors and recipients.

The Selection of Dispositions to Behave in Biologically Altruistic Ways

Members of virtually all mammalian species are disposed to help their offspring at costs to themselves. The prolonged dependency of human infants has led to the selection of mechanisms that dispose parents to invest a great deal in their offspring (Flinn & Low, 1986; J. B. Lancaster & C. S. Lancaster, 1987; MacDonald, 1997). Although parental investment is most appropriately classified as biologically cooperative because helping one's offspring contributes to one's own reproductive success as well as to the reproductive success of the recipients—one's offspring—, it seems altruistic when assessed in terms of the willingness of parents to sacrifice their survival interests (most extremely, their lives) for the sake of their offspring. The significance of parental investment is easy to overlook. It provides clear and pervasive proof that dispositions to sacrifice one's own physical and material welfare for the sake of other individuals have evolved in many species.

Kin selection of biologically altruistic dispositions. In an insight that had a profound effect on our understanding of the evolution of altruism, Hamilton (1964) explained that dispositions to help others could evolve if the fitness costs of the behaviors were less than the fitness benefits they bestowed on recipients, weighted by their degree of relatedness ($c < rb$). In effect, Hamilton's rule explicates the "if" conditions built into an evolved strategy. Helping kin (other than offspring) qualifies as biologically altruistic when it reduces actors' survival and reproductive success relative to the survival and reproductive success of recipients.

There is no question that biological forms of altruism can evolve through kin selection, and there is a great deal of evidence that biologically altruistic dispositions have evolved through this process in many species (Kurkland & Gaulin, 2005; Sachs, Mueller, Wilcox, & Bull, 2004; West, this volume). Ethnographic and experimental research on humans has revealed strong positive correlations between degree of relatedness and the probability of engaging in a variety of helping behaviors, including—indeed especially—those that are very costly and life threatening to the helper (Burnstein, 2005; Kurkland & Gaulin, 2005). There is, however, some question about the extent to which such biologically altruistic dispositions can be evoked by nonkin.

The expansion of kin-selected altruism. To help one's kin, one must be able to distinguish them from nonkin, and to accomplish this, animals must rely on kin recognition cues such as familiarity, proximity, and phenotypic similarity (Johnson et al., this volume; Porter, 1987). Early imprinting-like familiarity and facial resemblance appear to constitute especially important cues in humans (Burstein, 2005). There is evidence that nonkin who emit such cues—either incidentally or as a form of manipulation—are able to activate kin-selected altruistic dispositions, thus expanding the range of recipients. The more imprecise the mechanisms of kin recognition are, the more we would expect them to misfire in modern environments, the larger the circle of recipients we would expect to activate them, and the more biologically (and genetically) altruistic we would expect the behaviors to be (cf. Johnson et al., this volume; Krebs, 1998).

Although we would expect natural selection to refine kin-recognition mechanisms in ways that decrease fitness-reducing mistakes, the process of refinement would take time. Some theorists (e.g., Johnson et al., this volume; Trivers, 2004) argue that the kin-recognition mechanisms inherited by contemporary humans dispose them to help a large array of nonkin. Theorists such as Gintis et al. (this volume) are skeptical.

Even if animals possessed kin-recognition mechanisms that were perfectly precise, the best most mammals could do is direct their altruism toward recipients who had a 50% probability of sharing their genes. If the process mediating kin selection of altruism involves individuals fostering the fitness of other individuals who possess copies of their genes, why limit it to kin? It would be more efficient for individuals to be able to detect the presence in other individuals of the genes that dispose them to behave altruistically and direct their altruism toward them, whatever their degree of relatedness. Any phenotypic quality that enabled altruistic individuals to identify other individuals who possessed copies of the genes that disposed them to behave altruistically could mediate the evolution of selectively altruistic dispositions.[3]

Phenotypic manifestations of altruism may supply a more reliable indicator of altruistic dispositions than kinship does. The strategy "if you are disposed to help others, select as recipients of your altruism those who also are disposed to help others" could evolve if there were a reliable relation between the shared genes and shared dispositions in question. As with the evolution of strategies that induce cooperators to cooperate with cooperators, the key to the evolution of such strategies is discrimination in favor of those who adopt similar strategies and possess similar genes.

Group-level selection of biologically altruistic dispositions. Sober and D. S. Wilson (1998) have explained how, in certain conditions, altruistic strategies can evolve through selection at the level of groups. These theorists make the plausible assumption that groups of altruists fare better than groups of selfish individualists, just as pairs of cooperators fare better than pairs of defectors in prisoner's dilemma games. Sober and D. S. Wilson explain how, if groups of altruists were sufficiently large, if the between-group variance in altruism were greater than the within-group variance, and if groups integrated at optimal points in time, the proportion of altruistic genes in the population could increase even though it decreased within all subgroups that make up the population. Although Sober and D. S. Wilson acknowledge that the conditions necessary for between-group selection for altruism to outpace within-group selection for selfishness may be rare in the animal kingdom, they argue that these conditions might well have existed in the human species, augmented by cultural evolution (see also Gintis et al., this volume). Altruistic behaviors that stem from mechanisms designed by group selection qualify as genetically altruistic when they are directed toward selfish members of one's group.

THE EVOLUTION OF PSYCHOLOGICALLY SELFISH AND UNSELFISH DISPOSITIONS

Having adduced evidence that animals that are disposed to behave in biologically selfish ways also may be disposed to behave in biologically cooperative and altruistic ways, I turn to a different ques-

---

[3] It is theoretically possible for a gene to be selected that enabled animals to recognize replicas of itself in others and disposed them to behave altruistically toward those who carried them (the Green Beard Effect); however, most theorists agree that there are significant obstacles to the evolution of such genes (Dawkins, 1989; Kurkland & Gaulin, 2005).

tion, pertaining to the ways in which the mechanisms that give rise to social behaviors are designed. I ask whether mechanisms have evolved that dispose individuals (a) to seek to benefit themselves without regard for others, (b) to seek to benefit both themselves and others, and (c) to seek to benefit others as an end in itself. In contrast to biological questions about the consequences of social behaviors, psychological questions pertain to the nature of the motivational states generated by evolved mechanisms and the types of goals they induce people to pursue.

The Selection of Psychologically Selfish Dispositions

If people were asked to give examples of psychologically selfish behaviors, they probably would list the kinds of behaviors described by Williams (1989) as evidence of the "triumph of selfishness"—behaviors that stem from motivational states such as those that define the seven deadly sins (i.e., wrath, lust, gluttony, envy, sloth, pride, and greed). There is no denying that humans and other animals are sometimes driven by morally repugnant motives that induce them to seek to benefit themselves without consideration for others. However, there is more to human nature (and to the nature of other animals) than dispositions to behave in nasty and brutish ways. Although there are contexts in which individuals who seek to maximize their benefits without regard for others fare better biologically and genetically than those who behave in less psychologically selfish ways, the adaptive potential in short-sighted, unrestrained, and unconditional selfishness is limited in several ways.

Adaptive Limitations of Short-Sighted Selfishness

The unmitigated pursuit of pleasure may be dangerous to one's heath. For example, gluttony and the unconstrained consumption of alcohol and drugs may jeopardize people's survival and reproductive success (Burnham & Phelan, 2000; Crawford, this volume). Unrestrained promiscuity may jeopardize animals' reproductive success (see Gangestad, this volume; Lack, 1954). Individuals who resist the temptation to maximize their pleasure without consideration for others may fare better biologically than those who behave in self-indulgent and hedonistic ways.

An important limitation of selfish behaviors—especially those that people consider morally repugnant—is that they tend to evoke costly reactions from others. Two animals bent on maximizing their profit by taking more than their share of resources or by exploiting one another could end up in a conflict that diminished their survival and reproductive success—an outcome that is modeled in prisoner's dilemma games in which two players making selfish choices gain fewer points than two players making cooperative choices (Axelrod & Hamilton, 1981). In addition, animals that try to maximize their benefits at the expense of others may provoke their intended victims and other members of their groups to punish them—by refusing to help them when they are in need (Nowack & Sigmund, 1998), by inflicting physical and material sanctions on them (Gintis et al., this volume), by turning others against them, and by ostracizing them from their group (Alexander, 1987).

More indirectly, selfish motives to maximize one's benefits without regard for others may destroy beneficial relationships, undermine coalitions, and diminish the welfare of one's group as a whole, thereby jeopardizing the social environment that one needs to survive and reproduce. In contrast, less selfish motives to help one's friends and other members of one's group may help preserve valuable resources, and therefore pay off physically, materially, biologically, and genetically in the end.

Further, it is important to remember that the evolutionary consequences of motivational states, decision-making strategies, and forms of conduct are a function of the net genetic costs and benefits to the actor and to everyone else affected by the actor's behavior, including those with the same genes. Although we would expect psychologically selfish motives to be selected when they induced individuals to behave in ways that helped them propagate their genes at the expense of those who possessed alleles of their genes, we would not necessarily expect them to be selected when they induced individuals to behave in ways that jeopardized the genetic success of those who possessed copies of their genes.

The adaptive limitations of psychologically selfish forms of conduct open the door for the selection of dispositions to behave in psychologically unselfish ways. Although the biological benefits that animals behaving in biologically cooperative and altruistic ways bestow on others could be by-products of their desire to benefit themselves, this is neither the only, nor the most plausible, possibility. If we assume animals that benefit themselves biologically are motivated to benefit themselves, why not assume animals that benefit others are motivated to achieve this goal?

In conclusion, although psychologically selfish forms of conduct may be adaptive in some conditions, they are limited in other conditions. For this reason, we would expect the mechanisms regulating selfish (and unselfish) forms of conduct to be designed in terms of "if-then" types of decision rules. The key to understanding human nature and the nature of other animals lies in deciphering the design of these mechanisms, mapping the ways in which they are shaped during development, and identifying the internal and external stimuli that activate them in everyday life.

The Selection of Psychologically Cooperative Dispositions

Cooperative social exchanges may produce three beneficial consequences: benefiting actors, benefiting recipients, and benefiting the partnership or group involved in the exchange. Identifying the motives of those involved in cooperative exchanges is challenging because individuals may employ seemingly altruistic and cooperative tactics to achieve selfish goals. Although those who engage in social exchanges may sometimes—perhaps even often—seek to maximize their net gains without regard for others, there is evidence that they also may be motivated (a) to maximize the joint gains of their partners and themselves, (b) to repay those who have helped them, and (c) to foster fair outcomes, as ends in themselves.

Seeking to Maximize Mutual Benefits

If people were driven by selfish motives, we would expect them to try to obtain as much as possible for themselves and to give as little as possible in return, either on individual exchanges or over the long run. However, many studies have found that in some contexts individuals choose to take less than they could for themselves in order to maximize the net benefits of everyone involved in the exchange, even when they engage in such behaviors anonymously and never expect to see their exchange partners again. As one example, Fehr and Gächter (2002) found that when game players were given an opportunity to contribute some of their winnings anonymously to a common pool that was doubled by the experimenter and shared equally among members of their group regardless of their contributions, players tended to contribute approximately half of their earnings, even though they could have maximized their gains by contributing nothing (for additional examples, see Gintis et al., this volume; Johnson et al., this volume).

Those who seek to maximize joint gains rather than their own gains may be driven either by the desire to be fair, which I will discuss in the following section, or by the desire to enhance the welfare of a unit with which they identify. Social psychologists have found that people are disposed to identify with those with whom they have formed social bonds, view themselves in terms of units that contain both themselves and others—whether it be a partnership, a team, or an in-group—and feel motivated to promote the welfare of the unit, as an end in itself (A. Aron & E. N. Aron, 1986; Cialdini et al., 1976; Richerson & Boyd, 2001; Schaller & Neuberg, this volume; Tajfel & Turner, 1985). In such cases, people view their outcomes in terms of how "we" fare against "them," instead of how "I" fare against "you." Although the motivation that drives people to help the groups with which they identify could be considered selfish (a) because the individuals view themselves in terms of their groups and seek to benefit this aspect of their sense of self or (b) because they are motivated to help their groups in order to foster their own welfare, studies have found that members of groups often choose to uphold the interests of their groups at a cost to themselves (see Gintis et al., this volume; Johnson et al., this volume).

Seeking to Reciprocate

Social psychologists have concluded that receiving assistance from others may evoke two qualitatively different affective reactions—feelings of indebtedness and a sense of gratitude. Feeling indebted is unpleasant. It motivates people to pay others back as a means of reducing aversive arousal (Greenberg, 1980). In contrast, feelings of gratitude are pleasant. They motivate people to help not only those who benefited them but also third parties (McCullough, Kilpatrick, Emmons, & Larson, 2001). Helping behaviors that stem from feelings of gratitude would qualify as psychologically unselfish if their terminal goal were to benefit recipients, or to benefit third parties, even if the behaviors had the incidental effect of increasing recipients' or observers' desire to proffer additional assistance to those who expressed gratitude.

If those who engage in reciprocal exchanges were motivated to maximize their own gains, we would expect them to be more concerned about being paid back than about paying back, and we might expect them to overestimate the value of the goods they give to others and underestimate the value of the goods they receive in return. However, studies on social exchange between friends have found the opposite. For example, Janicki (2004) found that participants underestimated the costs of giving to their friends and overestimated the value of the benefits they received. In addition, they reported feeling more upset when they failed to pay their friends back than they did when their friends failed to pay them back.

Seeking to Foster Fair Outcomes

When people reciprocate, they are, in effect, making things even—balancing the scales. More generally, justice involves ensuring that people get what they deserve. Social psychologists have attempted to determine whether people possess a "justice motive" that disposes them to promote equity and fairness, as an end in itself, even when it is costly for them to do so. Many studies have found that people who are given the choice between maximizing their own immediate gains and distributing resources in a fair and equitable manner opt for the latter (Greenberg & Cohen, 1982). The question is are people motivated to uphold justice as an end in itself or are they motivated to use justice instrumentally as a "tool of self-interest" (Lerner, 2003, p. 388). Research on equity, retribution, and third-party punishment suggests that people may be intrinsically motivated to uphold justice.

Seeking equity. Research aimed at identifying the motives that induce individuals to promote equitable outcomes has produced mixed results. Compare, for example, studies by Adams (1963) and Rivera and Tedeschi (1976). Adams found that workers performed better when they were paid more than they deserved and concluded that the workers were motivated to bring about a fair outcome rather than to maximize their own gains. In contrast, Rivera and Tedeschi found that although workers who publicly evaluated payments that they and others received after doing the same amount of work reported feeling more pleased with fair outcomes than with outcomes that favored them, workers who evaluated the payments in private, when hooked up to a lie detector, said they felt happier when they received more than their share.

In a recent paper, Lerner (2003) offered an explanation for the inconsistencies in the findings on research on equity and justice. Lerner adduced evidence that when people are faced with

> high impact contexts: those situations involving serious deprivation, suffering, loss of esteem, humiliation, or significant amounts of desired resources … the awareness of an injustice can elicit several emotions: anger, guilt, shame, disgust, contempt, sadness … [and that] people are impelled to act on those emotions and are motivated to eliminate or rectify the injustice. (p. 394)

In contrast, in low-impact contexts in which people have the opportunity to reflect before passing judgment or making a decision, they may behave in more rationally self-serving ways. Note that in contrast to cognitive-developmental theorists, such as Gibbs (2006), who argue that justice-upholding behaviors stem from uniquely human, sophisticated forms of moral reasoning, the data that Lerner (2003) adduces suggest that justice-upholding behaviors are the product of phylogenetically primitive affective reactions shared by humans and other animals (cf. Frank, this volume; Haidt, 2001; Krebs, 2007; Krebs & Denton, 2005).

Seeking retribution. An important implication of the idea that people are motivated to uphold justice is that they will be motivated to redress injustices. We know that people feel angry and indignant when others exploit them and that they may seek to get even. The immediate aim of vengeful behavior may be to hurt the exploiters or to repair a damaged reputation, which seems psychologically selfish. However, retribution also could be a means to a less selfish end, namely restoring balance and upholding justice by evening the score.

Seeking to punish wrongdoers. Researchers have adduced an impressive array of experimental and naturalistic evidence that people possess an other regarding "predisposition to cooperate with others, and to punish those who violate the norms of cooperation, at personal cost, even when it is implausible to expect that these costs will be repaid" (Gintis, Bowles, Boyd, & Fehr, 2003, p. 153)—a phenomenon Gintis et al. call "strong reciprocity." For example, game theorists have found that in ultimatum games in which one player decides how to divide a pot of money and another decides whether to accept the division or to return all the money, players reject unfair offers (which punishes the player making the offer) even though it costs them to do so (see Gintis et al., this volume, for additional examples). Consistent with these findings, Lerner (1982) found that participants chose to forgo opportunities to make money in order to punish an individual who had abused their (fictitious) partner. As pointed out by Gintis (in press), such behaviors defy rational choice theory only if we assume that people's preferences are narrowly self-regarding. It is rational to behave fairly if one's goal is to be fair.

The Selection of Psychologically Altruistic Dispositions

If natural selection designed mechanisms equipped to generate psychologically altruistic motives, the mechanisms that dispose animals to help their offspring and other kin seem like the most promising candidates. Although animals may enhance their inclusive fitness by helping their kin, they are not aware of this ultimate goal, nor do they seek to pursue it as an end in itself. Animals, in effect, do not say to themselves, "I will try to maximize the number of genes I contribute to future generations by helping those who possess copies of my genes." Although animals may sometimes feel good about helping their kin, Sober and D. S. Wilson (1998) have argued that it would have been more efficient for natural selection to have designed a psychological system that motivates animals directly to help their kin than to design a psychological system that motivates them help their kin in order to maximize their pleasure. Animals may be willing to suffer significant pain and even death to assist their kin.

Although psychologically altruistic motivational states could be generated in humans from higher order cognitive processes such as moral reasoning, altruistic states could not be generated by these processes in other animals, because they do not possess them. In humans and in other animals, psychologically altruistic motives appear to stem primarily from mental mechanisms that give rise to affective states such as those we call love, loyalty, sympathy, empathy, and so on. As implied in the earlier discussion of biological altruism, after a psychological system that motivates individuals to help their kin evolved, it could have been activated by those who resemble kin. In support of this possibility, studies have found that humans are disposed to empathize with, feel loyalty to, and love those whom they view as similar to them, those with whom they grew up, those with whom they identify, those with whom they have formed affectionate bonds, and so on (Batson, 1991; Decety, 2005; Fischer, 2004; Richerson & Boyd, 2001).

It is well-established that individuals are disposed to help those who evoke affective states such as love and empathy (Batson, 1998). Psychologists have attempted to determine the nature of the motives generated by these affective states. Do these affective states dispose individuals to help others as an end in itself, or do they dispose individuals to help others as a means to other ends, such as promoting their long-term interests or making themselves feel good? This question has been addressed most extensively with respect to the motivational state generated by empathy.

Empathically Induced Altruistic Motives

Batson (1991) and his collaborators hypothesized that empathy triggers an altruistic motivational state that induces people to want to help those with whom they empathize, as an end in itself, as opposed to wanting to help them instrumentally in order to achieve egoistic goals. To test the "empathy-altruism hypothesis," Batson and his colleagues designed more than two dozen experiments, some of them quite ingenious, in which they induced groups of participants to empathize with victims (e.g., by inducing them to take their perspective or by leading them to believe they were similar to them), then provided them with ways of achieving a variety of egoistic goals in less costly ways than by helping the victims (see Batson, 1991, 1998 for references to specific studies).

Consider some examples. To determine whether those who empathize with others help them in order to gain social approval or to avoid disapproval, Batson and his colleagues compared the amount of helping in public and private conditions. To determine whether high-empathy participants help in order to reduce their own vicariously experienced aversive arousal, Batson and his colleagues offered them an opportunity to reduce their arousal by terminating their exposure to the victim or by leaving the experiment. To determine whether empathizing people help in order to avoid self-censure, Batson and his colleagues offered them personally and socially acceptable reasons and justifications for not helping. To determine whether those in empathic states help in order to feel good about themselves, Batson and his colleagues, assessed the mood of participants after they learned that third parties helped victims. Without exception, the studies conducted by Batson and his colleagues supported the empathy-altruism hypothesis.

Batson and his colleagues challenged skeptics to demonstrate that those who empathize with others will choose to pursue self-serving goals rather than to help victims when given the opportunity or that they will help victims only when this option provides the most effective way of achieving self-serving goals. Researchers such as Cialdini et al. (1987) and Schaller and Cialdini (1988) claim to have met this challenge, adducing evidence that people help distressed victims with whom they empathize in order to relieve the negative state of sadness that they experience, but Batson and his colleagues (e.g., Batson et al., 1989) have disputed their conclusions (see also Dovidio, Allen, & Schroeder, 1990). Although Batson and his colleagues have been remarkably successful at rejecting hypotheses pertaining to the most plausible sources of selfishness, no one will ever be able to prove that empathically aroused people are not motivated to achieve some subtle selfish goal not assessed by the experimenter.

CONCLUSION

What, then, is the answer to the question addressed in this chapter: How selfish are humans and other animals by nature? The answer implied by my analysis of the nature of selfishness and the evolution of social dispositions is, more or less, depending on the type of selfishness in question and the extent to which individuals are exposed to the conditions in which it is activated. All dispositions that help individuals propagate their genes are genetically selfish by definition. However, individuals may inherit dispositions that, though genetically selfish in the environments in which they were selected, may misfire in modern environments, produce unselfish by-products, and give rise to maladaptive, genetically unselfish behaviors.

Because natural selection tends to design animals to behave in ways that foster their survival and reproductive success, most evolved dispositions are biologically selfish. However, dispositions to behave in cooperative ways that foster others' biological success in addition to one's own also have evolved in many social species. Cooperative dispositions probably played a pivotal role in the evolution of the human species (Leakey & Lewin, 1977; Tooby & DeVore, 1987). In addition, the evidence strongly suggests that biologically altruistic dispositions have evolved through kin selection, perhaps augmented by selection at the level of groups; and that these dispositions may be activated by nonkin.

When it comes to questions about human nature, people are rarely concerned about biological and genetic forms of selfishness. What they want to know is whether humans and other animals are naturally disposed to advance their own profit, pleasure, well-being, and advantage without consideration for others. That people are disposed to behave in ways that propagate their genes and foster their biological welfare is only tangentially relevant to this question. What is relevant is how the mechanisms that dispose people to behave in fitness-enhancing ways are designed, and how people go about achieving fitness-enhancing goals. The evidence establishes unequivocally that, in conducive conditions, people are motivated (a) to divide resources in fair and equitable ways, even when they could take more than their share without adverse physical, material, or social costs; (b) to reciprocate, even when they end up giving more than they receive; (c) to punish those who violate norms of fairness, at a cost to themselves; and (d) to help their relatives, friends, and in-group members over long periods without tangible compensation. The evidence also clearly establishes that in conducive conditions, people are disposed to suffer considerable pain, and even death, in order to help those for whom they care and with whom they empathize.

It remains unclear whether people who sacrifice their interests for the sake of others are driven by the desire to achieve internally rewarding goals such as allaying their sadness, making themselves feel good about themselves, upholding their values, and behaving in ways that are consistent with their identity; but with regard to judgments about human nature, does it really matter? Although there is theoretical and practical value in mapping the motivational states and identifying the terminal goals that drive prosocial and altruistic behaviors, establishing that people help others in order to uphold their identity or their values would not detract significantly from the nobleness of human nature. Even if, on a strict definition, such motives turned out to be psychologically selfish, virtually no one would consider those who are driven by them selfish in any morally deficient way.

REFERENCES

Adams, J. S. (1963). Toward an understanding of inequity. *Journal of Abnormal and Social Psychology, 67,* 422–436.

Alcock, J. (2004). *Animal behavior: An evolutionary approach* (8th ed.). Sunderland, MA: Sinauer Associates.

Alexander, R. D. (1987). *The biology of moral systems.* New York: Aldine de Gruyter.

Aron, A., & Aron, E. N. (1986). *Love and the expansion of self: Understanding attraction and satisfaction.* New York: Hemisphere.

Axelrod, R. (1988). The further evolution of cooperation. *Science, 242,* 1385–1389.

Axelrod, R., & Hamilton, W. D. (1981). The evolution of cooperation. *Science, 211,* 1390–1396.

Batson, C. D. (1991). *The altruism question: Toward a social-psychological answer.* Hillsdale, NJ: Erlbaum.

Batson, C. D. (1998). Altruism and prosocial behavior. In D. T. Gilbert, S. T. Fiske, & G. Lindzey (Eds.), *The handbook of social psychology* (4th ed., pp. 282–315). Boston: McGraw-Hill.

Batson, C. D. (2000). Unto others: A service … and a disservice. *Journal of Consciousness Studies, 7,* 207–210.

Brown, S. L., & Brown, M. (2006). Selective investment theory: Recasting the functional significance of close relationships. *Psychological Inquiry, 17*, 30–59.

Burnham, T., & Phelan, J. (2000). *Mean genes*. New York: Perseus Publishing.

Burnstein, E. (2005). Altruism and genetic relatedness. In D. Buss (Ed.), *The handbook of evolutionary psychology* (pp. 528–551). Hoboken, NJ: John Wiley & Sons.

Cialdini, R. B., Borden, R. J., Thorne, A., Walker, M. R., Freeman, S., & Sloan, L. R. (1976). Three (football) field studies. *Journal of Personality and Social Psychology, 34*, 366–375.

Cialdini, R. B., Schaller, M., Houlihan, D., Arps, J., Fultz, J., & Beaman, A. L. (1987). Empathy-based helping: Is it selflessly or selfishly motivated? *Journal of Personality and Social Psychology, 52*, 749–758.

Clark, M. S., & Mills, J. (1993). The difference between communal and exchange relationships: What it is and is not. *Personality and Social Psychology Bulletin, 19*, 684–691.

Crespi, B. J. (2000). The evolution of maladaptation. *Heredity, 84*, 623–629.

Darwin, C. (1874). *The descent of man and selection in relation to sex*. New York: Rand, McNally & Company.

Dawkins, R. (1989). *The selfish gene* (2nd ed.). Oxford, U.K.: Oxford University Press.

Decety, J. (2005). Perspective taking as the royal avenue to empathy. In B. F. Malle & S. D. Hodges (Eds.), *Other minds: How humans bridge the divide between self and others* (pp. 143–157). New York: Guilford Press.

Dovidio, J. F., Allen, J. L., & Schroeder, D. A. (1990). The specificity of empathy induced helping: Evidence for altruistic motivation. *Journal of Personality and Social Psychology, 59*, 249–260.

Dugatkin, L. A. (1997). *Cooperation among animals: An evolutionary perspective*. New York: Oxford University Press.

Ellis, B. J. (1998). The partner-specific investment inventory: An evolutionary approach to individual differences in investment. *Journal of Personality, 66*, 383–442.

Fehr, E., & Gächter, S. (2002). Altruistic punishment in humans. *Nature, 415*, 137–140.

Fisher, H. (2004). *Why we love: The nature and chemistry of romantic love*. New York: Henry Holt.

Flack, J. C., & de Waal, F. B. M. (2000). 'Any animal whatever': Darwinian building blocks of morality in monkeys and apes. *Journal of Consciousness Studies, 7*, 1–29.

Flinn, M. V., & Low, B. S. (1986). Resource distribution, social competition, and mating patterns in human societies. In D. I. Rubenstein & R. W. Wrangham (Eds.), *Ecological aspects of social evolution: Birds and mammals* (pp. 217–243). Princeton, NJ: Princeton University Press.

Funk & Wagnalls standard dictionary (1980). New York; Lippincott & Crowell.

Gibbs, J. C. (2006). Ideals, pragmatics, and morality: Comment on Krebs and Denton. *Psychological Review, 15*, 668–671.

Gintis, H. (in press). A framework for the unification of the behavioral sciences. *Behavioral and Brain Sciences*.

Gintis, H., Bowles, S., Boyd, R., & Fehr, E. (2003). Explaining altruistic behavior in humans. *Evolution and Human Behavior, 24*, 153–172.

Greenberg, J. (1980). A theory of indebtedness. In K. Gergen, M. S. Greenberg, & R. H. Willis (Eds.), *Social exchange: Advances in theory and research*. New York: Plenum.

Greenberg, J., & Cohen, R. L. (1982). *Equity and justice in social behavior*. New York: Academic Press.

Haidt, J. (2001). The emotional dog and its rational tail: A social intuitionist approach to moral judgment. *Psychological Review, 108*, 814–834.

Hamilton, W. D. (1964). The evolution of social behavior. *Journal of Theoretical Biology, 7*, 1–52.

Huxley, T. H. (1893). *Evolution and ethics: The second Romanes Lecture*. London: Macmillan.

Janicki, M. (2004). Beyond sociobiology: A kinder and gentler evolutionary view of human nature. In C. Crawford & C. Salmon (Eds.), *Evolutionary psychology: Public policy and personal decisions* (pp. 51–72). Mahwah, NJ: Erlbaum.

Krebs, D. L. (1998). The evolution of moral behavior. In C. Crawford & D. L. Krebs (Eds.), *Handbook of evolutionary psychology: Ideas, issues, and applications* (pp. 337–368). Hillsdale, NJ: Erlbaum.

Krebs, D. L. (2007). The origin of justice. In J. Duntley & T. K. Shackelford (Eds.), *Evolutionary forensic psychology*. Oxford, U.K.: Oxford University Press.

Krebs, D. L., & Denton, K. (2005). Toward a more pragmatic approach to morality: A critical evaluation of Kohlberg's model. *Psychological Review, 112*, 629–649.

Kurland, J. A., & Gaulin, S. J. C. (2005). Cooperation and conflict among kin. In D. Buss (Ed.), *The handbook of evolutionary psychology* (pp. 447–482). Hoboken, NJ: John Wiley & Sons.

Lack, D. (1954). *The natural regulation of animal numbers*. Oxford, U.K.: Oxford University Press.

Laland, K. N., Odling-Smee, F. L., & Feldman, M. (2000). Group selection: A niche construction perspective. *Journal of Consciousness Studies, 7,* 221–223.

Lancaster, J. B., & Lancaster, C. S. (1987). The watershed: Change in parental-investment and family-formation strategies in the course of human evolution. In J. B. Lancaster, J. Altmann, A. S. Rossi, & L. R. Sherrod (Eds.), *Parenting across the life span: Biosocial dimensions* (pp. 187–205). New York: Aldine de Gruyter.

Leakey, R. E., & Lewin, R. (1977). *Origins*. New York: Dutton.

Lerner, M. J. (1982). Justice motive in human relations and the economic model of man. In V. Derlega & J. Grzelak (Eds.), *Cooperation and helping behavior* (pp. 249–277). New York: Academic Press.

Lerner, M. L. (2003). The justice motive: Where social psychologists found it, how they lost it, and why they may not find it again. *Personality and Social Psychology Review, 7,* 388–399.

MacDonald, K. (1997). Life history theory and human reproductive behavior: Environmental/contextual influences and heritable variation. *Human Nature, 8,* 327–359.

Maynard-Smith (1982). *Evolution and the theory of games*. Cambridge, U.K.: Cambridge University Press.

McCullough, M. E., Kilpatrick, S, D., Emmons, R. A., & Larson, D. B. (2001). Is gratitude a moral affect? *Psychological Bulletin, 127,* 249–266.

Miller, D. T. (1999). The norm of self interest. *American Psychologist, 54,* 1053–1060.

Nesse, R. M. (2000). How selfish genes shape moral passions. In L. D. Katz (Ed.), *Evolutionary origins of morality: Cross-disciplinary perspectives* (pp. 227–231). Thorverton, U.K.: Imprint Academic.

Nesse, R. M. (Ed.). (2001). *Evolution and the capacity for commitment*. New York: Russell Sage Foundation.

Nowak, M. A., & Sigmund, K. (1998). Evolution of indirect reciprocity by image scoring. *Nature, 393,* 573–577.

Porter, R. H. (1987). Kin recognition: Functions and mediating mechanisms. In C. B. Crawford & D. L. Krebs (Eds.), *Sociobiology and psychology: Ideas, issues and applications* (pp. 175–205). Hillsdale, NJ: Erlbaum.

Rachlin, H. (2002). Altruism and selfishness. *Behavioral and Brain Sciences, 25,* 239– 250.

Richerson, P. J., & Boyd, R. (2001). The evolution of subjective commitment: A tribal instincts hypothesis. In R. Nesse (Ed.) *Evolution and the capacity for commitment* (pp. 186–219). New York: Russell Sage Foundation.

Richerson, P. J., & Boyd, R. (2005). *Not by genes alone: How culture transformed human evolution*. Chicago: University of Chicago Press.

Rivera, A. N., & Tedeschi, J. T. (1976). Public versus private reactions to positive inequity. *Journal of Personality and Social Psychology, 34,* 895–900.

Sachs, J. L., Mueller, U. G., Wilcox, T. P., & Bull, J. J. (2004). The evolution of cooperation. *Quarterly Review of Biology, 79,* 135–160.

Schaller, M., & Cialdini, R. B. (1988). The economics of empathic helping: Support for a mood management motive. *Journal of Experimental Social Psychology, 24,* 163–181.

Shackelford, T. K., & Buss, D. M. (1996). Betrayal in mateships, friendships, and coalitions. *Personality and Social Psychology Bulletin, 22,* 1151–1164

Simon, H. (1990). A mechanism for social selection of successful altruism. *Science, 250,* 1665–1668.

Sober, E., & Wilson, D. S. (1998). *Unto others: The evolution and psychology of unselfish behavior*. Cambridge, MA: Harvard University Press.

Sober, E., & Wilson, D. S. (2000). Summary of "Unto others: The evolution and psychology of unselfish behavior." *Journal of Consciousness Studies, 7,* 185–206.

Tajfel, H., & Turner, J. C. (1985). The social identity theory of intergroup behavior. In S. Worchel & W. G. Austin (Eds.), *Psychology of intergroup relations* (pp. 7–24). Chicago: Nelson-Hall.

The new Lexicon Webster's encyclopedic dictionary of the English language. Canadian editon. (1988). New York: Lexicon Publishing.

The Oxford dictionary of current English. (1987). Oxford, U.K.: Oxford University Press.

Tooby, J., & Cosmides, L. (1996). Friendship and the banker's paradox: Other pathways to the evolution of adaptations for altruism. *Proceedings of the British Academy, 88,* 119–143.

Tooby, J., & Devore, I. (1987). The reconstruction of hominid behavioral evolution through strategic modeling. In W. G. Kinzey (Ed.), *The evolution of human behavior: Primate models* (pp. 183–237). Albany, NY: SUNY Press.

Trivers, R. L. (1971). The evolution of reciprocal altruism. *Quarterly Review of Biology, 46*, 35–57.

Trivers, R. L. (2004). Mutual benefits at all levels of life. *Science*, 964–965.

Webster's new twentieth century dictionary of the English language unabridged, 2nd edition. (1964). New York: Prentice Hall.

Williams, G. C. (1989). A sociobiological expansion of *"Evolution and Ethics."* In Evolution and ethics (pp. 179–214). Princeton, NJ: Princeton University Press.

Zahavi, A., & Zahavi, A. (1997). *The handicap principle.* New York: Oxford University.

16

Gene-Culture Coevolution and the Emergence of Altruistic Behavior in Humans

HERBERT GINTIS, SAMUEL BOWLES,
ROBERT BOYD, AND ERNST FEHR

INTRODUCTION

The stunning evolutionary success of *Homo sapiens* over the last 10,000 years has been based on our species' capacity to sustain widespread cooperation among individuals who are not close genealogical kin. In this chapter, we will argue that the behavioral basis for cooperation is a set of predispositions for prosocial behavior that may be generally termed *altruistic*: Humans are predisposed to behave in ways that sometimes subordinate personal material gain on behalf of increasing the well-being of other group members, including those who are not close genealogical kin. Moreover, humans have a predisposition to punish selfish group members at a cost to themselves, even where no personal material long-run gain is forthcoming. Finally, humans have a predisposition to follow such *moral rules* as behaving honestly, truthfully, fairly, and charitably. These behavioral characteristics, unique to our species but with important precursors in other primates, explain the ubiquity and efficacy of cooperation in humans (Gintis, Bowles, Boyd, & Fehr, 2005).

The evolutionary dynamic underlying human sociality is *gene-culture coevolution*, in which not only does human culture obey its own evolutionary dynamic parallel to genetic evolution but it serves as sufficiently powerful environmental context of human evolution that human genetic evolution is itself the product of prior stages of cultural evolution. Prominent examples of the effect of culture on genes include the evolution of human vocal (Wind, 1990) and even musical (Morley, 2002) capacities. In addition, such human emotions as empathy and shame are uniquely human adaptations to biocultural systems that reward prosocial and penalize antisocial behavior (Bowles & Gintis, 2004).

The theory and evidence supporting the previously mentioned assertions has been amassed only over the past two decades, and social science has not yet fully caught up with these findings. Even many evolutionary psychologists continue to espouse the "genes-eye" view of evolution that served as the received wisdom in evolutionary biology from the mid-20th century until recently. According to this view, social behavior in any species can be explained either as the result of *kin selection*, which involves benefiting close genealogical kin at personal cost, or *reciprocal altruism,* which involves helping someone who will return the favor in the future (Hamilton, 1964; Williams, 1966; Trivers, 1971; Chapter 17 of this volume). In this view, altruism cannot exist.

Richard Dawkins (1976, 1989), for instance, in his justly renowned book, *The Selfish Gene,* asserted that we must "try to *teach* generosity and altruism, because we are born selfish" (p. xx). R. D. Alexander, the great 20th century evolutionary ethicist, even denied that altruistic culture could overcome selfish genes. In *The Biology of Moral Systems*, Alexander (1979) claims, "[E]thics, morality, human conduct, and the human psyche are to be understood only if societies are seen as collections of individuals seeking their own self-interest" (p. 3). Similarly, in his book on the origins of humanity, Ghiselin (1974), a leading figure in the biology of human behavior, claims, "No hint of genuine charity ameliorates our vision of society, once sentimentalism has been laid aside. What passes for cooperation turns out to be a mixture of opportunism and exploitation... Scratch an altruist, and watch a hypocrite bleed" (p. 247).

So unshakable among many biologists is the belief that true altruism is biologically impossible that until recently (and in some evolutionary psychology circles, still) the mere mention of altruistic motivation provokes ridicule. Indeed, some biologists *define* altruism to mean sacrificing inclusive fitness, in which case of course altruism could not evolve. But, this is a serious error. Of course, a gene that promotes self-sacrifice will die out unless those helped carry the mutant gene, or its spread is otherwise promoted. But, altruistic behavior can be observed and documented in the laboratory and so it must have evolved. As such, altruistic behavior must be fitness enhancing. Our task is to determine how and why.

In a population without structured social interactions of individuals, behaviors of the type found in our experiments and depicted in our models could not have evolved. However, gene-culture coevolutionary models support cooperative behavior among individuals who are not close genealogical kin (Cavalli-Sforza & Feldman, 1973; Bowles, Choi, & Hopfensitz, 2003; Henrich & Boyd, 2001; Gintis, 2003; Richerson & Boyd, 2004). These models, some of which are discussed in the following sections, are not vulnerable to the classic critiques of group selection by Williams (1966), Dawkins (1976), Maynard Smith (1976), Rogers (1990), and others.

An alternative account of altruistic behavior is that in our hunter-gatherer ancestral environment, helping and punishing behaviors were not altruistic, but rather were individually fitness maximizing, as they allowed individuals to develop a reputation for being both willing to cooperate and committed to retaliating against those who betray their trust. In the contemporary environment, so the argument goes, such behavior persists in situations where it is altruistic, but these situations would rarely have arisen in our hunter-gatherer past, where anonymous, one-shot interactions were supposedly extremely rare. According to this view, altruistic behavior is a maladaptation rather than an adaptation. We think this alternative is unlikely, and address the issues in a later section. This analysis is related to our argument in the section called "Gene-Culture Coevolution" that, through gene-culture coevolution, our species developed a whole range of social emotions, including shame, guilt, pride, and honor, that both promoted individual well-being and a high level of social cooperation. The remainder of the chapter is devoted to a deeper analysis of social emotions.

EXPERIMENTAL GAME THEORY

General evolutionary principles suggest that individual decision making can be modeled as maximizing a preference function subject to informational and material constraints. Natural selection leads the content of preferences to reflect biological fitness, at least in the typical environment in which these preferences were evolutionarily selected. The resulting model is called *the rational actor model* in economics, but we will generally refer to this more descriptively as the beliefs, preferences, and constraints (BPC) model. Beliefs in this model refer to the way the organism forms internal representations of its environment that are relevant to its maximizing behavior. As such, any organism that has a brain can be said to have "beliefs."

The analysis of biological systems includes one concept that does not occur in the nonliving world and is not analytically represented in physics or chemistry. This is the notion of a *strategic interaction*, in which the behavior of agents is derived by assuming that each is choosing a *best response*, given its BPC system, to the actions of other agents. The study of systems in which agents choose best responses and in which such responses evolve dynamically is called *evolutionary game theory*. Experimental game theory assumes the BPC model of choice and subjects individuals to strategic settings such that their behavior reveals their underlying preferences and beliefs. This controlled experimental process allows us to adjudicate between contrasting models of human motivation. In the next few sections, we will apply this framework to the study of human altruism.

CHARACTER VIRTUES AND HUMAN NATURE

A particularly clear example of altruistic behavior is reported by Gneezy (2005), who studied 450 undergraduate participants paired off to play some game of the following form. There are two players who never see each other (anonymity), and they interact exactly once (one shot). Player 1, whom we will call the Advisor, is shown the contents of two envelopes, labeled *A* and *B*. Each envelope has two compartments, the first containing money to be given to the Advisor, and the other to be given to Player 2. We will call Player 2 the Chooser, because this player gets to choose which of the two envelopes will be distributed to the two players. The catch, however, is that the Chooser is not permitted to see the contents of the envelopes. Rather, the Advisor, who did see the contents, was required to advise the Chooser which envelope to pick.

The games all begin with the experimenter showing both players the two envelopes, and asserting that one of the envelopes is better for the Advisor and the other is better for the Chooser. The Advisor is then permitted to inspect the contents of the two envelopes and say to the Chooser either "*A* will earn you more money than *B*," or "*B* will earn you more money than *A*." The Chooser then picks either *A* or *B*, and the game is over.

Suppose both players are self-regarding, each caring only about how much money he earns from the transaction. Suppose also that both players believe their partner is self-regarding. The Chooser will then reason that the Advisor will say whatever induces him, the Chooser, to choose the envelope that gives him, the Chooser, the lesser amount of money. Therefore, nothing the Advisor says should be believed, and the Chooser should just make a random pick between the two envelopes. The Advisor can anticipate the Chooser's reasoning and will pick randomly which envelope to advise the Chooser to pick. Economists call the Advisor's message "cheap talk" because it costs nothing to give, but is worth nothing to either party.

By contrast, suppose the Chooser believes that the Advisor places a positive value on transmitting honest messages and so will be predisposed to follow whatever advice he is given, and suppose the Advisor does value honesty and believes that the Chooser believes that he values honesty and, hence, will follow the Advisor's suggestion. Then, the Advisor will weight the financial gain from lying against the cost of lying, and unless the gain is sufficiently large, he will tell the truth, the Chooser will believe him, and the Chooser will get his preferred payoff.

Gneezy (2005) implemented this experiment as series of three games with the previously mentioned structure (his detailed protocols were slightly different). The first game, which we will write *A = (6, 5), B = (5, 6)*, pays the Advisor 6 and the Chooser 5 if the Chooser picks *A*, and the reverse if the Chooser picks *B*. The second game, *A = (6, 5), B = (5, 15)* pays the Advisor 6 and the Chooser

5 if the Chooser picks *A*, but pays the Advisor 5 and the Chooser 15 if the Chooser picks *B*. The third game, *A = (15, 5), B = (5, 15)* pays the Advisor 15 and the Chooser 5 if the Chooser picks *A*, but pays the Advisor 15 and the Chooser 5 if the Chooser picks *B*.

Before having the subjects play any of the games, he attempted to determine whether Advisors believed that their advice would be followed. For, if they did not believe this, then it would be a mistake to interpret their giving advice favorable to Choosers to the Advisor's honesty. Gneezy (2005) elicited truthful beliefs from Advisors by promising to pay an additional sum of money at the end of the session to each Advisor who correctly predicted whether his advice would be followed. He found that 82% of Advisors expected their advice to be followed. In fact, the Advisors were remarkably accurate, since the actual percent was 78%.

The most honesty was elicited in game 2, where *A = (5, 15), B = (6, 5)*, so lying was very costly to the Chooser and the gain to lying for the Advisor was small. In this game, a full 83% of Advisors were honest. In game 1, where *A = (5, 6)* and *B = (6, 5)*, so the cost of lying to the Chooser was small and equal to the gain to the Advisor, 64% of the Advisors were honest. In other words, subjects were loathe to lie, but considerably more so when it was costly to their partner. In game three, where *A = (5, 15)* and *B = (15, 5)*, so the gain from lying was large for the Advisor, and equal to the loss to the Chooser, only 48% of the Advisors were honest. This shows that many subjects are willing to sacrifice material gain to avoid lying in a one-shot, anonymous interaction, their willingness to lie increasing with an increased cost of truth telling to themselves, and decreasing with an increase in their partner's cost of begin deceived.

ALTRUISTIC PUNISHMENT: THE ULTIMATUM GAME

In the ultimatum game, under conditions of anonymity, two players are shown a sum of money, say $10. One of the players, called the "proposer," is instructed to offer any number of dollars, from $1 to $10, to the second player, who is called the "responder." The proposer can make only one offer. The responder, again under conditions of anonymity, can either accept or reject this offer. If the responder accepts the offer, the money is shared accordingly. If the responder rejects the offer, both players receive nothing.

Since the game is played only once and the players do not know each other's identities, a self-regarding responder will accept any positive amount of money. Knowing this, a self-regarding proposer will offer the minimum possible amount, $1, and this will be accepted. However, when actually played, the self-regarding outcome is never attained and never even approximated. In fact, as many replications of this experiment have documented, under varying conditions and with varying amounts of money, proposers routinely offer respondents very substantial amounts (50% of the total generally being the modal offer), and respondents frequently reject offers below 30% (Camerer & Thaler, 1995; Güth & Tietz, 1990; Roth, Prasnikar, Okuno-Fujiwara, & Zamir, 1991).

The ultimatum game has been played around the world but mostly with university students. We find a great deal of individual variability. For instance, in all of the previously mentioned experiments a significant fraction of subjects (typically, about a quarter) behave in a self-regarding manner. But among student subjects, average performance is strikingly uniform from country to country.

To expand the diversity of cultural and economic circumstances of experimental subjects, Henrich et al. (2005) undertook large cross-cultural study of behavior in various games including the ultimatum game and the public goods game. Working in 12 countries on four continents, 12 experienced field researchers, recruited subjects from 15 small-scale societies exhibiting a wide variety of economic and cultural conditions. These societies consisted of 3 foraging groups (the Hadza of East Africa, the Au and Gnau of Papua New Guinea, and the Lamalera of Indonesia), 6 slash-and-burn horticulturists (the Aché, Machiguenga, Quichua, and Achuar of South America and the Tsimané and Orma of East Africa), 4 nomadic herding groups (the Turguud, Mongols, and Kazakhs of Central Asia and the Sangu of East Africa) and 2 sedentary, small-scale agricultural societies (the Mapuche of South America and Zimbabwe farmers in Africa). We can summarize our results as follows:

- The canonical model of self-regarding behavior is not supported in any society studied. In the ultimatum game, for example, in all societies, respondents, proposers, or both behaved in a reciprocal manner.
- There is considerably more behavioral variability across groups than had been found in previous cross-cultural research. While mean ultimatum game offers in experiments with student subjects are typically between 43% and 48%, the mean offers from proposers in our sample ranged from 26% to 58%. While modal ultimatum game offers are consistently 50% among university students, sample modes with these data ranged from 15% to 50%. In some groups, rejections were extremely rare, even in the presence of very low offers, while in others, rejection rates were substantial, including frequent rejections of hyperfair offers (i.e., offers above 50%). By contrast, the most common behavior for the Machiguenga was to offer zero. The mean offer was 22%. The Aché and Tsimané distributions resemble American distributions, but with very low rejection rates. The Orma and Huinca (non-Mapuche Chileans living among the Mapuche) have modal offers near the center of the distribution.
- Differences among societies in "market integration" and "cooperation in production" explain a substantial portion of the behavioral variation between groups: the higher the degree of market integration and the higher the payoffs to cooperation, the greater the level of cooperation and sharing in experimental games. The societies were rank-ordered in five categories—"market integration" (how often do people buy and sell or work for a wage), "cooperation in production" (is production collective or individual), plus "anonymity" (how prevalent are anonymous roles and transactions), "privacy" (how easily can people keep their activities secret), and "complexity" (how much centralized decision making occurs above the level of the household). Using statistical regression analysis, only the first two characteristics, market integration and cooperation in production, were significant, and they together accounted for 66% of the variation among societies in mean ultimatum game offers.
- Individual-level economic and demographic variables did not explain behavior either within or across groups.
- The nature and degree of cooperation and punishment in the experiments was generally consistent with economic patterns of everyday life in these societies. In a number of cases the parallels between experimental game play and the structure of daily life were quite striking.

This relationship was not lost on the subjects themselves. Here are some examples:

- The Orma immediately recognized that the public goods game was similar to the harambee, a locally initiated contribution that households make when a community decides to construct a road or school. They dubbed the experiment "the harambee game" and gave generously (mean 58% with 25% maximal contributors).
- Among the Au and Gnau, many proposers offered more than half the pie, and many of these "hyperfair" offers were rejected. This reflects the Melanesian culture of status seeking through gift giving. Making a large gift is a bid for social dominance in everyday life in these societies, and rejecting the gift is a rejection of being subordinate.
- Among the whale hunting Lamalera, 63% of the proposers in the ultimatum game divided the pie equally, and most of those who did not offered more than 50% (the mean offer was

57%). In real life, a large catch—always the product of cooperation among many individual whalers—is meticulously divided into predesignated parts and carefully distributed among the members of the community.

- Among the Aché, 79% of proposers offered either 40% or 50%, and 16% offered more than 50%, with no rejected offers. In daily life, the Aché regularly share meat, which is being distributed equally among all other households, irrespective of which hunter made the kill. The Hadza, unlike the Aché, made low offers and had high rejection rates in the ultimatum game. This reflects the tendency of these small-scale foragers to share meat, but with a high level of conflict and frequent attempts of hunters to hide their catch from the group.
- Both the Machiguenga and Tsimané made low ultimatum game offers, and there were virtually no rejections. These groups exhibit little cooperation, exchange or sharing beyond the family unit. Ethnographically, both show little fear of social sanctions and care little about "public opinion."
- The Mapuche's social relations are characterized by mutual suspicion, envy, and fear of being envied. This pattern is consistent with the Mapuche's postgame interviews in the ultimatum game. Mapuche proposers rarely claimed that their offers were influenced by fairness, but rather by a fear of rejection. Even proposers who made hyperfair offers claimed that they feared rare spiteful responders, who would be willing to reject even 50-50 offers.

THE PUBLIC GOODS GAME

A typical public goods game consists of a number of rounds, say 10. The subjects are told the total number of rounds, as well as all other aspects of the game. The subjects are paid their winnings in real money at the end of the session. In each round, each subject is grouped with several other subjects, say 3 others, under conditions of strict anonymity. Each subject is then given a certain number of "points," say 20, redeemable at the end of the experimental session for real money. Each subject then places some fraction of his points in a "common account," and the remainder in the subject's "private account." The experimenter then tells the subjects how many points were contributed to the common account and adds to the private account of each subject some fraction, say 40%, of the total amount in the common account. So if a subject contributes his whole 20 points to the common account, each of the 4 group members will receive 8 points at the end of the round. In effect, by putting the whole endowment into the common account, a player loses 12 points but the other 3 group members gain in total 24 $(= 8 \times 3)$ points. The players keep whatever is in their private account at the end of the round.

A self-regarding player will contribute nothing to the common account. However, in fact, only a fraction of subjects conform to the self-regarding model. Subjects begin by contributing on average about half of their endowment to the public account. The level of contributions decays over the course of the 10 rounds, until in the final rounds most players are behaving in a self-regarding manner (Dawes & Thaler, 1988; Ledyard, 1995). In a metastudy of 12 public goods experiments, Fehr and Schmidt (1999) found that in the early rounds, average and median contribution levels ranged from 40% to 60% of the endowment, but in the final period, 73% of all individuals $(N = 1042)$ contributed nothing, and many of the remaining players contributed close to zero. These results are not compatible with the self-interested actor model, which predicts zero contribution on all rounds, though they might be predicted by a reciprocal altruism model, since the chance to reciprocate declines as the end of the experiment approaches. However, this, in fact, is not the explanation of moderate but deteriorating levels of cooperation in the public goods game.

The explanation of the decay of cooperation offered by subjects when debriefed after the experiment is that cooperative subjects became angry at others who contributed less than themselves, and retaliated against free-riding, low contributors in the only way available to them—by lowering their own contributions (Andreoni, 1995; Ostrom, Gardner, & Walker, 1994). Moreover, in the beginning of the game, some self-regarding players contribute in order to induce the reciprocators to contribute in later rounds. Toward the end of the game, though, there is less personal gain from this inducement, so the self-regarding players stop contributing as well.

Experimental evidence supports this interpretation. When subjects are allowed to punish non-contributors, they do so at a cost to themselves. For instance, Fehr and Gächter (2000) set up an experimental situation in which the possibility of strategic punishment was removed. They used 6 and 10 round public goods games with groups of size 4, and with costly punishment allowed at the end of each round, employing 3 different methods of assigning members to groups. There were sufficient subjects to run between 10 and 18 groups simultaneously. Under the *Partner* treatment, the 4 subjects remained in the same group for all 10 periods. Under the *Stranger* treatment, the subjects were randomly reassigned after each round. Finally, under the *Perfect Stranger* treatment the subjects were randomly reassigned and assured that they would never meet the same subject more than once. Subjects earned an average of about $35 for an experimental session.

Fehr and Gächter (2000) performed their experiment for 10 rounds with punishment and 10 rounds without (for additional experimental results and their analysis, see Bowles & Gintis, 2002; Fehr & Gächter, 2002). They found that when costly punishment is permitted, cooperation does not deteriorate, and in the Partner game, despite strict anonymity, cooperation increases to almost full cooperation, even on the final round. When punishment is not permitted, however, the same subjects experience the deterioration of cooperation found in previous public goods games. The contrast in cooperation rates between the Partner and the two Stranger treatments is worth noting, because the strength of punishment is roughly the same across all treatments. This suggests that the credibility of the punishment threat is greater in the Partner treatment because, in this treatment, the punished subjects are certain that once they have been punished in previous rounds, the punishing subjects are in their group. The prosociality impact of reciprocators on cooperation is thus more strongly manifested, the more coherent and permanent the group in question.

ALTRUISTIC THIRD-PARTY PUNISHMENT

Prosocial behavior in human society occurs not only because those directly helped and harmed by an individual's actions are likely to reciprocate in kind but also because there are general *social norms* that foster prosocial behavior and many people are willing to bestow favors on someone who conforms to social norms and to punish someone who does not, even if they are not personally helped or hurt by the individual's actions. In everyday life, third parties who are not the beneficiaries of an individual's prosocial act will help the individual and his family in times of need, will preferentially trade favors with the individual, and otherwise, will reward the individual in ways that are not costly but are nonetheless of great benefit to the cooperator. Similarly, third parties who have not been personally harmed by the selfish behavior of an individual will refuse aid even when it is not costly to do so and will shun the offender and approve of the offender's ostracism from beneficial group activities, again at low cost to the third party but highly costly to the offender.

It is hard to conceive of human societies operating at a high level of efficiency in the absence of such third-party reward and punishment. Yet, self-regarding actors will never engage in such behavior if it is at all costly. An experiment conducted by Fehr and Fischbacher (2004) addresses this question by conducting a series of third-party punishment experiments using prisoner's dilemma and dictator games. The experimenters implemented four experimental treatments, in each of which subjects were grouped into threes. In each group, in stage one, subject A played a prisoner's dilemma or dictator game with subject B as the recipient, and subject C was an outsider whose payoff was not affected by A's decision. Then, in stage two, subject C was endowed with 50 points and allowed to deduct points from subject A, such that every 3 points deducted from A's score cost C 1 point. In the first treatment (TP-DG), the game was the dictator game, in which A was endowed with 100 points, and could give 0, 10, 20, 30, 40, or 50 points to B, who had no endowment.

The second treatment (TP-PD) was the same, except that the game was the prisoner's dilemma. Subjects A and B were each endowed with 10 points, and each could either keep the 10 points or transfer the 10 points to the other subject, in which case it was tripled by the experimenter. Thus, if both cooperated, each earned 30 points, and if both defected, each earned 10 points. If one cooperated and one defected, however, the cooperator earned 0 points and the defector 40 points. In the second stage, C was given an endowment of 40 points and was allowed to deduct points from A and/or B, just as in the TP-DG treatment.

To compare the relative strengths of second- and third-party punishment in the dictator game, the experimenters implemented a third treatment, S&P-DG. In this treatment, subjects were randomly assigned to player A and player B, and A-B pairs were randomly formed. In the first stage of this treatment, each A was endowed with 100 points, each B with no points, and the As played the dictator game as before. In the second stage of each treatment, each player was given an additional 50 points, and the B players were permitted to deduct points from A players on the same terms as in the first two treatments. S&P-DG also had two conditions. In the S condition, a B player could only punish his *own* dictator, whereas in the T condition, a B player could only punish an A player *from another pair*, to which he was randomly assigned by the experimenters. In the T condition, each B player was informed of the behavior of the A player to which he was assigned.

To compare the relative strengths of second- and third-party punishment in the prisoner's dilemma, the experimenters implemented a fourth treatment, S&P-PG. This was similar to the S&P-DG treatment, except that now they played a prisoner's dilemma.[1]

In the first two treatments, since subjects were randomly assigned to positions A, B, and C, the obvious fairness norm is that all should have equal payoffs (an *equality norm*). For instance, if A gave 50 points to B and C deducted no points from A, each subject would end up with 50 points. In the dictator game treatment (TP-DG), 60% of third parties (Cs) punish dictators (As) who give less than 50% of the endowment to recipients (Bs). Statistical analysis (ordinary least squares regression) showed that for every point an A kept for him- or herself above the 50-50 split, he or she was punished an average 0.28 points by Cs, leading to a total punishment of $3 \times 0.28 = 0.84$ points. Thus, a dictator who kept the whole 100 points would have $0.84 \times 50 = 42$ points deducted by Cs, leaving a meager gain of 8 points over equal sharing.

The results for the prisoner's dilemma treatment (TP-PD) were similar, with an interesting twist. If one partner in the A-B pair defected and the other cooperated, the defector would have on average 10.05 points deducted by Cs, but if both defected, the punished player lost only an average of 1.75 points. This shows that third parties (Cs) care not only about the intentions of defectors but also about how much harm they caused and/or how unfair they turned out to be. Overall, 45.8% of third parties punished defectors whose partners cooperated, whereas only 20.8% of third parties punished defectors whose partners defected.

Turning to the third treatment (T&SP-DG), second-party sanctions of selfish dictators are found to be considerably stronger than third-party sanctions, although both were highly significant. On average, in the first condition, where recipients could punish their own dictators, they imposed a deduction of 1.36 points for each point the dictator kept above the 50-50 split, whereas they imposed a deduction of only 0.62 points per point kept on third-party dictators. In the final treatment (T&SP-PD), defectors are severely punished by both second and third parties, but second-party punishment is again found to be much more severe than third-party punishment is. Thus, cooperating subjects

---

[1] It is worth repeating that the experimenters never use value-laden terms such as *punish,* but rather neutral terms, such as *deduct points.*

deducted on average 8.4 points from a defecting partner, but only 3.09 points from a defecting third party.

This study confirms the general principle that punishing norm violators is very common but not universal, and individuals are prone to be more harsh in punishing those who hurt them personally, as opposed to violating a social norm that hurts others than themselves.

THE EVOLUTIONARY STABILITY OF STRONG RECIPROCITY

By *strong reciprocity* we mean the propensity for individuals to cooperate in a collective endeavor and to punish noncooperators when this option is available, even when they can derive no net material gain from this behavior. Gintis (2000b) developed an analytical model showing that under plausible conditions strong reciprocity can emerge from reciprocal altruism. The paper models cooperation as a repeated *n*-person public goods game in which, under normal conditions, if agents are sufficiently forward looking, cooperation can be sustained by the threat of ostracism (Fudenberg & Maskin, 1986; Gintis, 2000a). However, when the group is threatened with extinction or dispersal, say through war, pestilence, or famine, cooperation is most needed for survival. During such critical periods, which were common in the evolutionary history of our species, future gains from cooperation become very uncertain, since the probability that the group will dissolve becomes high. The threat of ostracism then carries little weight, and cooperation cannot be maintained if agents are self-regarding. Thus, precisely when a group is most in need of prosocial behavior, cooperation based on reciprocal altruism will collapse.

But a small number of strong reciprocators, who punish defectors whether or not it is in their long-term interest, can dramatically improve the survival chances of human groups. Moreover, among species that live in groups and recognizing individuals, humans are unique in their capacity to formulate and communicate rules of behavior and to inflict heavy punishment at low cost to the punisher (Bingham, 1999), as a result of their superior tool-making and hunting abilities (Darlington, 1975; Fifer, 1987; Goodall, 1964; Isaac, 1987; Plooij, 1978). Under these conditions, strong reciprocators can invade a population of self-regarding types. This is because even if strong reciprocators form a small fraction of the population, at least occasionally they will form a sufficient fraction of a group that cooperation can be maintained in bad times. Such a group will then outcompete other self-interested groups, and the fraction of strong reciprocators will grow. This will continue until an equilibrium fraction of strong reciprocators is attained.

This model highlights a key adaptive feature of strong reciprocity—its independence from the probability of future interactions—but it presumes that reciprocal altruism explains cooperation in normal times, when the probability of future interactions is high. However, reciprocal altruism does not work well in large groups (Boyd & Richerson, 1988; Choi, 2002; Joshi, 1987; Taylor, 1976). This is because when one withdraws cooperation in retaliation for the defection of a single group member, one inflicts punishment on all members, defector and cooperators alike. The only evolutionarily stable strategy in the *n*-person public goods game is to cooperate as long as all others cooperate and to defect otherwise. For any payoff-monotonic dynamic, the basin of attraction of this equilibrium becomes very small as group size rises, so the formation of groups with a sufficient number of conditional cooperators is very unlikely, and as a result, such an outcome may be easily disrupted by idiosyncratic play, imperfect information about the play of others, or other stochastic events. As a result, if group size is large, such equilibrium is unlikely to be arrived at over reasonable historical time scales. Moreover, the only equilibrium is a "knife-edge" that collapses if just one member deviates.

Another influential model of cooperation among self-regarding agents relies upon *reputation* effects in a repeated game setting. For instance, in *standing models* (Boyd, 1989; Panchanathan & Boyd, 2003; Sugden, 1986) individuals who are "in good standing" in the community cooperate with others who are in good standing. If an individual fails to cooperate with someone who is in good standing, he or she falls into "bad standing," and individuals in good standing will not cooperate with him or her. Such models are less sensitive to errors but require that each individual know the standing of each other individual, updating with a high degree of accuracy in each period. This is plausible for small groups but not for larger groups in which each individual observes only a small fraction of the total number of interactions among group members in each period.

In sum, strategies supporting contingent cooperation in large groups have to achieve two competing *desiderata*. To be stable when common, they must be intolerant of defection. But, to increase when rare, there must be a substantial chance that groups with enough reciprocators can form; otherwise, they cannot be evolutionarily stable, as defectors will prosper. As groups increase in size, this becomes geometrically more difficult.

To inject more realism in an evolutionary model of strong reciprocity, Henrich and Boyd (2001) developed a model in which norms for cooperation and punishment are acquired via payoff-biased transmission (imitate the successful) and conformist transmission (imitate high-frequency behavior). They show that if two stages of punishment are permitted, then an arbitrarily small amount of conformist transmission will stabilize cooperative behavior by stabilizing punishment. They then explain how, once cooperation is stabilized in one group, it may spread through a multigroup population via cultural group selection. Once cooperation is prevalent, they show how prosocial genes favoring cooperation and punishment may invade in the wake of cultural group selection, for instance, because such genes decrease an individual's chance of suffering costly punishment.

This analysis reveals a deep asymmetry between altruistic cooperation and altruistic punishment, explored further in Boyd, Gintis, Bowles, and Richerson (2003), who show that altruistic punishment allows cooperation in quite larger groups because the payoff disadvantage of altruistic cooperators relative to defectors is independent of the frequency of defectors in the population, while the cost disadvantage of those engaged in altruistic punishment declines as defectors become rare. Thus, when altruistic punishers are common, selection pressures operating against them are weak. The fact that punishers experience only a small disadvantage when defectors are rare means that weak within-group evolutionary forces, such as conformist transmission, can stabilize punishment and allow cooperation to persist. Computer simulations show that selection among groups leads to the evolution of altruistic punishment when it could not maintain altruistic cooperation.

GENE-CULTURE COEVOLUTION

If group selection is part of the explanation of the evolutionary success of cooperative individual behaviors, then it is likely that group-level characteristics, such as relatively small group size, limited migration, or frequent intergroup conflicts, that enhance group selection pressures coevolved with cooperative behaviors. Thus, group-level characteristics and individual behaviors may have synergistic effects. This being the case, cooperation is based in part on the distinctive capacities of humans to construct cultural forms that reduce phenotypic variation within groups, thus heightening the relative importance of between-group competition and, hence, allowing individually costly but in-group-beneficial behaviors to coevolve with these supporting environments through a process of interdemic group selection.

The idea that the suppression of within-group competition may be a strong influence on evolutionary dynamics has been widely recognized in eusocial insects and other species. Boehm (1982) and Eibl-Eibesfeldt (1982) first applied this reasoning to human evolution, exploring the role of culturally transmitted practices that reduce phenotypic variation within groups. Examples of such practices are leveling institutions, such as monogamy and food sharing among individuals who are not close genealogical kin, namely those that reduce within-group differences in reproductive fitness or material well-being. By reducing within-group differences in individual success, such structures may have attenuated within-group genetic or cultural selection operating against individually costly but group-beneficial practices, thus giving advantages in intergroup contests to the groups that adopt the practices. Group-level institutions, thus, are constructed environments capable of imparting distinctive direction and pace to the process of biological evolution and cultural change. Hence, the evolutionary success of social institutions that reduce phenotypic variation within groups may be explained by the fact that they retard selection pressures working against in-group beneficial individual traits and the fact that high frequencies of bearers of these traits reduces the likelihood of group extinctions. We have modeled an evolutionary dynamic along these lines, exploring the possibility that intergroup contests play a decisive role in group-level selection. Our models assume that genetically and culturally transmitted individual behaviors, as well as culturally transmitted group-level characteristics, are subject to selection (Bowles, 2001; Bowles et al., 2003). We show that intergroup conflicts may explain the evolutionary success of both (a) altruistic forms of human sociality toward those who are not close genealogical kin and (b) group-level institutional structures such as food sharing and monogamy, which have emerged and diffused repeatedly in a wide variety of ecologies during the course of human history. In-group-beneficial behaviors may evolve if (a) they inflict sufficient costs on out-group individuals and (b) group-level institutions limit the individual costs of these behaviors and thereby attenuate within-group selection against these behaviors.

Our simulations show that if group-level institutions implementing resource sharing or non-random pairing among group members are permitted to evolve, group-beneficial individual traits coevolve along with these institutions, even where the latter impose significant costs on the groups adopting them. These results hold for specifications in which cooperative individual behaviors and social institutions are initially absent in the population. In the absence of these group-level institutions, however, group-beneficial traits evolve only when intergroup conflicts are very frequent, groups are small, and migration rates are low. Thus, the evolutionary success of cooperative behaviors during the last few hundred thousand years of human evolution existence may have been a consequence of distinctive human capacities in social institution building (Boyd & Richerson, 2004).

IS STRONG RECIPROCITY AND ADAPTATION?

Some behavioral scientists have suggested that the behavior we have described in this chapter was individually fitness maximizing in our hunter-gatherer past, when anonymity and one-shot interactions were, so they say, virtually nonexistent (Johnson, Stopka, & Knights, 2003; Trivers, 2004). The human brain, they note, is not a general-purpose information processor, but rather a set of interacting modular systems adapted to solving the particular problems faced by our species in its evolutionary history. Since the anonymous, nonrepeated interactions characteristic of experimental games were not a significant part of our evolutionary history, we could not expect subjects in experimental games to behave in a fitness-maximizing manner when confronted with them. Rather, we would expect subjects to confuse the experimental environment in more evolutionarily familiar terms as a nonanonymous and repeated interaction and to maximize fitness with respect to this reinterpreted environment. This critique, even if correct, would not lessen the importance of strong reciprocity in contemporary societies, to the extent that modern life leads individuals to face the frequent anonymous, nonrepeated interactions that are characteristic of modern societies with advanced trade, communication and transportation technologies. Thus, even if strong reciprocity were not an adaptation, it could nevertheless be an important factor in explaining human cooperation today.

But we do not believe that this critique is correct. In fact, humans are well capable of distinguishing individuals with whom they are likely to have many future interactions from others with whom future interactions are less likely. Indeed, human subjects cooperate much more if they expect frequent future interactions than if future interactions are rare (Gächter & Falk, 2002; Keser & van Winden, 2000).

This human capacity to react differentially to one-shot interactions, to repeated interactions, and to profit from anonymity is likely to have arisen from the importance of such distinctions in our evolutionary history. In every hunter-gatherer and other small-scale society today there is ano-nymity, there are one shots, and people adjust their behavior according to whether they believe they can or cannot avoid reputational effects. Consider, for instance, food hiding, extramarital affairs, shirking while hunting, avoiding injury in warfare when no one is looking, and the like. There is no sense in which these behaviors are particularly "modern." Indeed, the reason why the human cheater-detector module is so prominent in humans is because people are tempted to cheat when they think they are not being watched and have been so tempted since the origins of our species.

Humans with fine-tuned behavioral repertoires depending on whether they face close genealog-ical kin and repeated or one-time interactors and on whether they can or cannot gain an individual reputation probably had an evolutionary advantage in our ancestral environment. The likely reason for this advantage is that humans faced many interactions where the probability of future interac-tions was sufficiently low to make defection worthwhile (Gintis, 2000b; Manson & Wrangham, 1991). Humans are similarly capable of recognizing when their actions are hidden from view and profiting from such situations.

None of this is to deny that strong reciprocity, especially when exhibited in a laboratory setting, may well be maladaptive in contemporary society. However, the whole issue of whether a human trait is adaptive or maladaptive in contemporary society is of little importance in understanding human behavior. Contraception is widespread and is doubtless "maladaptive." It nevertheless has emerged as an important part of the human repertoire and is central to explaining why human population growth has generally ceased among groups with high consumption levels and low death rates—a situation that in any other species would entail rapid exponential growth. Similarly, it is "maladaptive" to expend resources supporting one's hometown sports team, becoming sexually aroused watching a film, or even helping one's aged, postreproductive parents. Indeed, promoting global warming and ecological destruction is maladaptive behavior that may well lead to a sharp reduction in the human population in coming years. It is a short step to conclude that the status of strong reciprocity as "maladaptive" adds little to our understanding of the phenomenon.

DID STRONG RECIPROCITY EVOLVE THROUGH GROUP SELECTION OR INDIVIDUAL SELECTION?

Our explanation of the evolution of altruism depends heavily on the notion of gene-culture coevolu-tion. Specifically, early human culture itself was an environmental force affecting individual fitness in a way that promoted such prosocial traits as strong reciprocity, shame, and empathy. This obser-vation, we must stress, in no way conflicts with the notion that if a gene has an inclusive fitness of less that unity, the behavior it supports cannot evolve. Rather, it suggests that the inclusive fitness of a gene depends on the social environment within which it is expressed. Group-level and individual-level fitness analyses are merely alternative ways of "fitness book keeping," and which one we wish to deploy depends on the particular question we are asking. In particular, any fitness measurement in terms of group-level categories can be reorganized using individual-level categories, and indeed, any individual-level fitness measurement can be written in gene-level terms. Ultimately, a behavior can grow only if its effects include an increase in the expected number of genes in the population involved in the behavior, and the "level of selection" represents only an accounting framework that is more or less conducive to the effective modeling of the phenomenon.

If the description of the environment relevant to measuring the fitness of a gene does not depend on interactions with other genes, the gene-centered accounting framework is appropriate. Suppose, however, that a number of genes act in concert to produce a phenotypic effect. Then, the complex of genes itself is part of the environment under which the fitness of each gene is measured. This complex of genes (which may be localized at the level of the individual, or at a lower level, such oxygen transport or signal transmission systems) may be best analyzed at a higher level than that of the single gene.

In species that produce complex environments (e.g., beaver dams and bee hives), these environments themselves modulate the fitness of individual genes and gene complexes, so are best analyzed at the level of the social group, as suggested in niche-construction theory. Gene-culture coevolutionary theory, which applies almost exclusively to our species, is a form of niche-construction theory in which cultural rules more than genetically encoded social interactions serve to modulate the fitness of various genes and gene complexes. Gene-culture coevolution is thus a form of group selection, although the whole analysis of genetic fitness even in this case, in principal, can be carried out at the level of the individual gene, with the social context being brought in as fitness relevant. In considering the place of group selection in the evolution of human altruism, it is important to distinguish between "hard" and "soft" group selection. The former assumes that the altruist is disadvantaged as compared with his or her nonaltruist group mates, but that altruists as a whole have superior population-level fitness because groups with many altruists have higher mean fitness than groups with few altruists. This form of "hard" (between- vs. within-group) selection, exemplified by the use of Price's (between- vs. within-group) selection, exemplified by the use of Price's famous equation, probably is important in the case of humans, especially because human culture reduces the within-group variance of fitness and increases the between-group variance, hence speeding up group-level selection.

However, hard group selection is not necessary for our analysis of altruism. The second, less demanding, form is "soft" group selection, in which altruists are not less fit within the group, but groups with a high fraction of altruists do better than groups with a lower fraction. The forms of altruism documented by behavioral game theory could have evolved by a soft group-selection mechanism alone. For instance, suppose social rules in a particular society favor giving gifts to the families of men honored for bravery and killed in battle. Suppose these gifts enhance the survival chances of a man's offspring or enhance their value as a mate. The altruism of individuals in this case can spread through weak group selection, leading to more and more human groups following this rule. This is surely group selection but, of course, could just as easily be accounted for as individual selection, or even gene selection, as long as the role of social rules in affecting fitness is kept in mind. The special importance of altruistic behavior for humans doubtlessly lies in the action of gene-culture coevolution, which provides an evolutionary framework considerably more powerful in engendering prosocial behaviors than the purely genetic reasoning that served as the basis for an earlier generation's critique of altruistic models.

PSYCHOLOGICAL AND BEHAVIORAL ASPECTS OF ALTRUISM: PROSOCIAL EMOTIONS AND STRONG RECIPROCITY

Prosocial emotions are physiological and psychological reactions that induce agents to engage in cooperative behaviors as we have previously defined them. The prosocial emotions include some such as shame, guilt, empathy, and sensitivity to social sanction that induce agents to undertake constructive social interactions and others such as the desire to punish norm violators that reduce free riding when the prosocial emotions fail to induce sufficiently cooperative behavior in some fraction of members of the social group (Frank, 1987; Hirshleifer, 1987).

Without the prosocial emotions, we would all be sociopaths, and human society would not exist, however strong the institutions of contract, governmental law enforcement, and reputation. Sociopaths have no mental deficit except that their capacity to experience shame, guilt, empathy, and remorse is severely attenuated or absent. They comprise 3% to 4% of the male population in the United States (Mealey, 1995) but account for approximately 20% of the United States' prison population and between 33% and 80% of the population of chronic criminal offenders.

Prosocial emotions are responsible for the host of civil and caring acts that enrich our daily lives and render living, working, shopping, and traveling among strangers feasible and pleasant. Moreover, representative government, civil liberties, due process, women's rights, respect for minorities, to name a few of the key institutions without which human dignity would be impossible in the modern world, were brought about by people involved in collective action, pursuing not only their personal ends, but also a vision for all of humanity. Our freedoms and our comforts alike are based on the emotional dispositions of generations past. While we think the evidence that prosocial emotions account for important forms of human cooperation is strong, there is no universally accepted model of how emotions combine with more cognitive processes to affect behaviors. Nor is there much agreement on how best to represent the prosocial emotions that support cooperative behaviors, although Bowles and Gintis (2002) is one attempt in this direction.

THE INTERNALIZATION OF NORMS

An *internal norm* is a pattern of behavior enforced in part by internal sanctions, including shame and guilt as outlined in the previous section. People follow internal norms when they value certain behaviors for their own sake, in addition to, or despite, the effects these behaviors have on personal fitness and/or perceived well-being. The ability to internalize norms is nearly universal among humans. While widely studied in the sociology and social psychology literature (socialization theory), it has been virtually ignored outside these fields (but see Caporael, Dawes, Orbell, & van de Kragt, 1989; Simon, 1990).

Socialization models have been strongly criticized for suggesting that people adopt norms independent of their perceived payoffs. In fact, people do not always blindly follow the norms that have been inculcated in them, but at least at times treat compliance as a strategic choice (Gintis, 1975). The "oversocialized" model of the individual presented in the sociology literature can be counteracted by adding a phenotypic copying process reflecting the fact that agents shift from lower to higher payoff strategies (Gintis, 2003).

All successful cultures foster internal norms that enhance personal fitness, such as future orientation, good personal hygiene, positive work habits, and control of emotions. Cultures also universally promote altruistic norms that subordinate the individual to group welfare, fostering such behaviors as bravery, honesty, fairness, willingness to cooperate, and empathy with the distress of others.

Given that most cultures promote cooperative behaviors, and if we accept the sociological notion that individuals internalize the norms that are passed to them by parents and other influential elders, it becomes easy to explain human cooperation. If even a fraction of society internalized the norms of cooperation and punished free riders and other norm violators, a high degree of cooperation can be maintained in the end. The puzzles are two: Why do we internalize norms, and why do cultures promote cooperative behaviors?

In Gintis (2003), we provide an evolutionary model in which the capacity to internalize norms develops because this capacity enhances individual fitness in a world in which social behavior has become too complex and multifaceted to be fruitfully evaluated piecemeal through individual rational assessment. Internalization moves norms from constraints that one can treat instrumentally toward maximizing well-being, to norms that are then valued as ends rather than means. It is not difficult to show that if an internal norm is fitness enhancing, then for plausible patterns of socialization, the allele for internalization of norms is evolutionarily stable.

We may then use this framework to model Herbert Simon's (1990) explanation of altruism. Simon suggested that altruistic norms could "hitchhike" on the general tendency of internal norms to be fitness enhancing. However, Simon provided no formal model of this process and his ideas have been widely ignored. This paper shows that Simon's insight can be analytically modeled and is valid under plausible conditions. A straightforward gene-culture coevolution argument then explains why fitness-reducing internal norms are likely to be prosocial as opposed to socially harmful: Groups with prosocial internal norms will outcompete groups with antisocial or socially neutral internal norms.

CONCLUSION

Contemporary behavioral theory is the legacy of several major contributions (Dawkins, 1989; Hamilton, 1964; Maynard Smith, 1982; Tooby & Cosmides, 1992; Trivers, 1971; Williams, 1966; Wilson, 1975), all of which assumed the relations between those who are not close genealogical kin could be modeled using self-regarding actors. It is not surprising, then, that the most successful research in behavioral theory has been in the area of the family, kinship, and sexual relations, while the attempts to deal with the more complex interactions characteristic of social group behavior have been less persuasive. To address this situation, we believe that more attention should be paid to (a) the origin and nature of social emotions (e.g., guilt, shame, empathy, ethnic identity, and ethnic hatred), (b) the coevolution of genes and culture in human social history, (c) the role of group structure and group conflict in human evolution, and (d) integrating sociobiological insights into mainstream social sciences.

REFERENCES

Alexander, R. D. (1979). *Biology and human affairs.* Seattle: University of Washington Press.

Andreoni, J. (1995). Cooperation in public goods experiments: Kindness or confusion. *American Economic Review, 85*, 891–904.

Bingham, P. M. (1999). Human uniqueness: A general theory. *Quarterly Review of Biology, 74*, 133–169.

Boehm, C. (1982). The evolutionary development of morality as an effect of dominance behavior and conflict interference. *Journal of Social and Biological Structures, 5*, 413–421.

Bowles, S. (2001). Individual interactions, group conflicts, and the evolution of preferences. In S. N. Durlauf & H. P. Young (Eds.), *Social dynamics* (pp. 155–190). Cambridge, MA: MIT Press.

Bowles, S., & Gintis, H. (2002). Homo reciprocans. *Nature, 415*, 125–128.

Bowles, S., & Gintis, H. (2004). The origins of human cooperation. In P. Hammerstein (Ed.), *Genetic and cultural origins of cooperation.* Cambridge, MA: The MIT Press.

Bowles, S., Choi, J., & Hopfensitz, A. (2003). The co-evolution of individual behaviors and social institutions. *Journal of Theoretical Biology, 223*, 135–147.

Boyd, R. (1989). Mistakes allow evolutionary stability in the repeated prisoner's dilemma game. *Journal of Theoretical Biology, 136*, 47–56.

Boyd, R., Gintis, H., Bowles, S., & Richerson, P. J. (2003). Evolution of altruistic punishment. *Proceedings of the National Academy of Sciences, 100*, 3531–3535.

Boyd, R., & Richerson, P. J. (1988). The evolution of reciprocity in sizable groups. *Journal of Theoretical Biology, 132*, 337–356.

Boyd, R., & Richerson, P. J. (2004). *The nature of cultures.* Chicago: University of Chicago Press.

Camerer, C., & Thaler, R. (1995). Ultimatums, dictators, and manners. *Journal of Economic Perspectives, 9*, 209–219.

Caporael, L., Dawes, R., Orbell, J., & van de Kragt, J. C. (1989). Selfishness examined: Cooperation in the absence of egoistic incentives. *Behavioral and Brain Science, 12*, 683–738.

Cavalli-Sforza, L., & Feldman, M. W. (1973). Models for cultural inheritance: Within group variation. *Theoretical Population Biology, 42*, 42–55.

Choi, J.-K. (2002). *Three essays on the evolution of cooperation.* Boston: University of Massachusetts.

Darlington, P. J. (1975). Group selection, altruism, reinforcement and throwing in human evolution. *Proceedings of the National Academy of Sciences, 72*, 3748–52.

Dawes, R. M., & Thaler, R. (1988). Cooperation. *Journal of Economic Perspectives, 2*, 187–197.

Dawkins, R. (1976). *The selfish gene.* Oxford, U.K.: Oxford University Press.

Dawkins, R. (1989). *The selfish gene* (2nd ed.). Oxford, U.K.: Oxford University Press.

Eibl-Eibesfeldt, I. (1982). Warfare, man's indoctrinability and group selection. *Journal of Comparative Ethnology, 60*, 177–198.

Fehr, E., & Fischbacher, U. (2004). Third party punishment and social norms. *Evolution & Human Behavior, 25*, 63–87.

Fehr, E., & Gächter, S. (2000). Cooperation and punishment. *American Economic Review, 90*, 980–994.

Fehr, E., & Gächter, S. (2002). Altruistic punishment in humans. *Nature, 415*, 137–140.

Fehr, E., & Schmidt, K. M. (1999). A theory of fairness, competition, and cooperation. *Quarterly Journal of Economics, 114*, 817–868.

Fifer, F. C. (1987). The adoption of bipedalism by the hominids: A new hypothesis. *Human Evolution, 2*, 135–47.

Frank, R. H. (1987). If *Homo economicus* could choose his own utility function, would he want one with a conscience? *American Economic Review, 77*, 593–604.

Fudenberg, D. & Maskin, E. (1986). The folk theorem in repeated games with discounting or with incomplete information. *Econometrica, 54*, 533–554.

Gächter, S., & Falk, A. (2002). Reputation and reciprocity: Consequences for the labour relation. *Scandinavian Journal of Economics, 104*, 1–26.

Ghiselin, M. T. (1974). *The economy of nature and the evolution of sex.* Berkeley: University of California Press.

Gintis, H. (1975). Welfare economics and individual development: A reply to Talcott Parsons. *Quarterly Journal of Economics, 89*, 291–302.

Gintis, H. (2000a). *Game theory evolving.* Princeton, NJ: Princeton University Press.

Gintis, H. (2000b). Strong reciprocity and human sociality. *Journal of Theoretical Biology, 206*, 169–179.

Gintis, H. (2003).The hitchhiker's guide to altruism: Genes, culture, and the internalization of norms. *Journal of Theoretical Biology, 220*, 407–418.

Gintis, H., Bowles, S., Boyd, R., & Fehr, E. (2005). *Moral sentiments and material interests: On the foundations of cooperation in economic life.* Cambridge, MA: The MIT Press.

Gneezy, U. (2005). Deception: The role of consequences. *American Economic Review, 95*, 384–394.

Goodall, J. (1964). Tool-using and aimed throwing in a community of free-living chimpanzees. *Nature, 201*, 1264–1266.

Güth, W., & Tietz, R. (1990). Ultimatum bargaining behavior: A survey and comparison of experimental results. *Journal of Economic Psychology, 11*, 417–449.

Hamilton, W. D. (1964). The genetical evolution of social behavior I & II. *Journal of Theoretical Biology, 7*, 1–16, 17–52.

Henrich, J., & Boyd, R. (2001). Why people punish defectors: Weak conformist transmission can stabilize costly enforcement of norms in cooperative dilemmas. *Journal of Theoretical Biology, 208*, 79–89.

Henrich, J., Boyd, R., Bowles, S., Camerer, C., Fehr, E., Gintis, H., et al. (2005). Economic man in cross-cultural perspective: Behavioral experiments in 15 small-scale societies. *Behavioral and Brain Sciences, 28*(6), 795–815.

Hirshleifer, J. (1987). Economics from a biological viewpoint, in Barney, J. B., & Ouchi, W. G. (Eds.), *Organizational economics* (pp. 319–371). San Francisco: Jossey-Bass .

Isaac, B. (1987). Throwing and human evolution. *African Archeological Review, 5*, 3–17.

Johnson, D. P., Stopka, P., & Knights, S. (2003). The puzzle of human cooperation. *Nature, 421*, 911–912.

Joshi, N. V. (1987). Evolution of cooperation by reciprocation within structured demes. *Journal of Genetics, 66*, 69–84.

Keser, C., & van Winden, F. (2000). Conditional cooperation and voluntary contributions to public goods. *Scandinavian Journal of Economics, 102*, 23–39.

Ledyard, J. O. (1995). Public goods: A survey of experimental research. In J. H. Kagel & A. E. Roth (Eds.), *The handbook of experimental economics* (pp. 111–194). Princeton, NJ: Princeton University Press.

Manson, J. H., & Wrangham, R. W. (1991). Intergroup aggression in chimpanzees. *Current Anthropology, 32*, 369–390.

Maynard Smith, J. (1976). Sexual selection and the handicap principle. *Journal of Theoretical Biology, 57*, 239–242.

Maynard Smith, J. (1982). *Evolution and the theory of games.* Cambridge, U.K.: Cambridge University Press.

Mealey, L. (1995). The sociobiology of sociopathy. *Behavioral and Brain Sciences, 18*, 523–541.

Morley, I. (2002). Evolution of the physiological and neurological capacities for music. *Cambridge Archaeological Journal, 12*, 195–216.

Ostrom, E., Gardner, R., & Walker, J. (1994). *Rules, games, and common-pool resources.* Ann Arbor: University of Michigan Press.

Panchanathan, K., & Boyd, R. (2003). A tale of two defectors: The importance of standing for evolution of indirect reciprocity. *Journal of Theoretical Biology, 224*, 115–126.

Plooij, F. X. (1978). Tool-using during chimpanzees' bushpig hunt. *Carnivore, 1*, 103–106.

Richerson, P. J., & Boyd, R. (2004). *Not by genes alone.* Chicago: University of Chicago Press,.

Rogers, A. R. (1990). Group selection by selective emigration: The effects of migration and kin structure. *American Naturalist, 135*, 398–413.

Roth, A. E., Prasnikar, V., Okuno-Fujiwara, M., & Zamir, S. (1991). Bargaining and market behavior in Jerusalem, Ljubljana, Pittsburgh, and Tokyo: An experimental study. *American Economic Review, 81*, 1068–1095.

Simon, H. (1990). A mechanism for social selection and successful altruism. *Science, 250*, 1665–1668.

Sugden, R. (1986). *The economics of rights, co-operation and welfare.* Oxford, U.K.: Basil Blackwell.

Taylor, M. (1976). *Anarchy and cooperation.* London: John Wiley and Sons.

Tooby, J., & Cosmides, L. (1992). The psychological foundations of culture. In J. H. Barkow, L. Cosmides, & J. Tooby (Eds.), *The adapted mind: Evolutionary psychology and the generation of culture* (pp. 19–136). New York: Oxford University Press.

Trivers, R. L. (1971). The evolution of reciprocal altruism. *Quarterly Review of Biology, 46*, 35—57.

Trivers, R. (2004). Mutual benefits at all levels of life. *Science, 304*, 964–965.

Williams, G. C. (1966). *Adaptation and natural selection: A critique of some current evolutionary thought.* Princeton, NJ: Princeton University Press.

Wilson, E. O. (1975). *Sociobiology: The new synthesis.* Cambridge, MA: Harvard University Press.

Wind, J. (1990). The evolutionary history of the human speech organs. In J. Wind, A. Jonker, R. Allot, & L. Rolfe (Eds.), *Studies in language origins* (pp. 173–197). Amsterdam: Benjamins.

17

Renaissance of the Individual
Reciprocity, Positive Assortment, and the Puzzle of Human Cooperation

DOMINIC D. P. JOHNSON,
MICHAEL E. PRICE, AND
MASANORI TAKEZAWA

At the end of all our journeying, we will arrive at the original place and know it for the first time.

—T. S. Eliot

When recognized, adaptation should be attributed to no higher a level of organization than is demanded by the evidence.

—G. C. Williams

Cooperation determines the success or failure of human interactions ranging from everyday social exchange, to global trade, environmental management, and international conflict. Yet, strangely enough, this fundamental aspect of human behavior remains poorly understood and a topic of great debate spanning several disciplines. Since the mid-1960s, cooperation was widely understood as promoting the inclusive fitness of the individual cooperator. However, in the past few years, researchers have asserted that the unprecedented extent of cooperation among human groups of nonkin (e.g., in collective actions) lies beyond the explanatory power of individual-level theories. These researchers argue that this unusual level of cooperation demands a special, higher level explanation such as

331

biological or cultural group selection. While humans are indeed unusually cooperative, we outline evidence suggesting that cooperation is best explained not in terms of group-level adaptation, but rather by applying, extending, and synthesizing existing theories of individual-level adaptation. Specifically, we contend that (1) most humans are "conditional reciprocators," who cooperate to whatever extent their interaction partners do (a Triversian *reciprocity* model) and (2) cooperators can achieve "positive assortment" and, thus, outcompete free riders, by preferentially interacting with other cooperators (a Hamiltonian *positive assortment* model). Previous models have tended to examine Triversian and Hamiltonian processes in isolation, yet the synergistic effects between them may account for the evolution and maintenance of collective action. In this chapter, we present (1) an overview of evolutionary accounts of human cooperation and how they have changed over time, (2) a *theoretical* model demonstrating how a strategy for continuous (as opposed to binary) reciprocity in sizable groups could replicate successfully in a population of competing strategies, and (3) *empirical* evidence from several different disciplines which suggests that most people do in fact act as positively assorting reciprocators in group interactions. Group selection is possible in theory but remains unnecessary to explain the diversity and prevalence of human cooperation. As we argue, the current focus on group selection stems from an erroneous fork along the road of research on human cooperation, traceable to a specific influential model of reciprocity by Robert Boyd and Pete Richerson in 1988. Our initial exploration of the alternative path suggests there are fruitful avenues for a much improved understanding of human cooperation.

DARWIN'S PUZZLE

Charles Darwin worried that his entire theory of evolution by natural selection might be blown out of the water by a phenomenon apparently prevalent in nature: altruism. If evolution proceeded through the survival of the fittest individuals, then why would bees, for example, evolve to engage in suicidal stinging behavior in defense of their colonies? Biologists after Darwin did not worry about this too much because they tended to see evolution as working for "the good of the species" or "the good of the group," a self-regulating machine in which altruism made perfect sense in the continuation of a greater cause. Only later was this perception revealed to be fatally flawed. As biologists stripped away the veiled mechanisms of DNA and genetic replication and recombination, whose effects Darwin predicted without knowing the cause, it became clear that traits that benefited the species as a whole would quickly disappear from the gene pool. Since genetic information is passed directly only from parents to offspring, any strategy so foolish as to sacrifice itself for unrelated others will die a quick death. Rejection of the good of the group argument, however, brought biologists back to the original puzzle: how can altruism evolve? Sadly for Darwin, this problem, which vexed him so much, was not solved until long after his death. But since the 1960s, the foundation of the gene as the unit of selection, and the predominance of individual-level adaptationism paved the way for a new understanding of altruism/cooperation via four specific theories described in the following section: kin selection (and genic self-favoritism in general), reciprocal altruism, indirect reciprocity, and costly signaling.

Kin Selection (and Genic Self-Favoritism in General)

In 1964, W. D. Hamilton published his famous insight that cooperation could evolve via kin selection. Since a gene for altruism could spread by promoting the replication of copies of itself contained in other individuals, and because close genetic kin will be relatively likely to carry copies of the same gene for altruism, promoting the survival and reproduction of one's relatives promotes the survival and reproduction of one's own genes (for more on kinship and social behavior, see West et al., this volume). This simple idea went on to revolutionize biology and anthropology (Chagnon & Irons, 1979; E. O. Wilson, 1975, 2000). Hamilton's insight is more profound than is often realized, because his theory of kin selection is actually just one (albeit very important) application of his more general theory of "genic self-favoritism." The more general theory can in principle explain altruism not only among close genetic kin, but also among nonkin, as long as they (1) share the same gene(s) for altruism and (2) are able to interact preferentially with each other. Dawkins' (1976) famous example of genic self-favoritism among nonkin imagined a gene that produced a recognizable phenotypic label (a green beard) in its bearers, as well as a motivation to cooperate with others who have green beards. Although regarded by many as implausible during the time at which Hamilton's ideas were being disseminated, apparent examples of green-beard altruism have recently surfaced in the literature (Haig, 1996; Keller, 2002; Keller & Ross, 1998; Queller, Ponte, Bozzaro, & Strassmann, 2003; Sinervo et al., 2006).

Reciprocal Altruism

A few years after Hamilton published his theory, Robert Trivers (1971) showed that cooperation could also evolve if a cooperative act by a donor toward a beneficiary were reciprocated by the beneficiary at a later time. Such mutually beneficial reciprocal altruism, in theory, could evolve in the complete absence of the genic self-favoritism described by Hamilton's kin selection—indeed, even between different species. Trivers' ideas were later supported in formal modeling by Axelrod and Hamilton (1981) and, like kin selection, dramatically altered the research agendas and understanding of animal and human interactions in biology, anthropology, and the social sciences (see Trivers, 2006).

Indirect Reciprocity

Richard Alexander (1987) later extended the logic of Trivers' reciprocal altruism by noting that altruistic acts may advertise a propensity to cooperate and, via a process of "indirect reciprocity," attract future cooperation *from third parties*. Third parties may acquire information about an individual's cooperativeness either via direct observation of a reciprocal exchange, or by acquiring reputational information about an individual's past history of cooperative behavior. Like Trivers' theory, Alexander's ideas eventually found support from formal models (Nowak & Sigmund, 1998; Panchanathan & Boyd, 2004), as well as experimental evidence that people cooperate more when their interaction history is publicly advertised (Nowak & Sigmund, 2005; Wedekind & Milinski, 2000).

Costly Signaling

Alexander (1987) and Trivers (1971) both focused on what kinds of benefits might be supplied and acquired by altruists, and both identified cooperative acts themselves as the primary benefit: Altruistic donors receive more altruistic donations, via direct and indirect reciprocity, because others prefer them as cooperative partners. Amotz Zahavi (1975, 1995), however, pointed out that the return benefit acquired by altruists need not be altruism per se. Altruism could be a "costly signal" that is used to advertise an attractive genetic quality that is only incidentally related to altruism itself (the logic being that only most fit individuals can afford to help others on top of the demands of their own survival). Such signaling may be rewarded by forms of fitness benefit other than altruism, such as increased mating opportunities (Gintis, Smith, & Bowles, 2001; Zahavi, 1995).

Kin selection (and to a lesser extent genic self-favoritism in general), reciprocal altruism, indirect reciprocity and costly signaling have since routinely been used to explain formerly puzzling examples of animal cooperation in a wide diversity of nonhuman species and contexts (for a review, see Dugatkin, 1997; Gadagkar, 2001; Wilson, 2000). More than a century after Darwin, the first puzzle of cooperation has largely been solved.

THE NEW PUZZLE OF COOPERATION

By contrast with cooperation among nonhuman animals, cooperation *among humans* is still relatively poorly understood. Although people do increase cooperation when the four "traditional" theories of cooperation—kin selection, reciprocal altruism, indirect reciprocity, and costly signaling—predict that we should do so, we nevertheless continue to cooperate even when these theories would seem to predict otherwise (Fehr & Fischbacher, 2003; Gintis, 2003). The key evidence for this puzzling behavior comes from controlled experimental studies demonstrating that subjects cooperate even when experimenters have tried to carefully eliminate any possible self-interested incentives to cooperate. For example, even in games in which reputational gains are impossible because all players are anonymous and in which reciprocity is impossible because all interactions are one-shot, subjects continue to behave cooperatively to some extent—not as much as they do when reputation and reciprocity are permitted, but to a significant extent nevertheless. In the words of Fehr and Gächter (2002), "[P]eople frequently cooperate with genetically unrelated strangers, often in large groups, with people they will never meet again, and when reputation gains are small or absent," leaving human cooperation as an "evolutionary puzzle" (p. 137). A growing experimental literature agrees that, when asked to play simple games that are designed to represent everyday social dilemmas, people from both modern and preindustrial societies around the globe cooperate to a greater extent than can be accounted for by traditional theories of cooperation—a phenomenon dubbed "strong reciprocity" (Fehr & Fischbacher, 2003; Gintis, 2000; Henrich et al., 2004). So far, no one has come up with a consensus explanation for this apparent excess of cooperation.

In recent years, two camps have arisen that explain human cooperation in different ways. Both camps agree on the empirical evidence that, in laboratory situations, humans exhibit a propensity to engage in voluntary and costly cooperation and punishment of defectors. The debate is not *if* people do this but *why*. The first camp, the *group*-level adaptationist camp, believes that the traditional theories of cooperation—which are based on individual-level adaptation—*cannot* explain human cooperation. From this, they deduce that human cooperation must serve group purposes. They therefore resort to some form of biological or cultural group selection as a possible explanation (Boyd, Gintis, Bowles, & Richerson, 2003; Fehr & Fischbacher, 2003; Gintis, 2000). The second camp, the *individual*-level adaptationist camp, believes that the traditional theories based on individual-level adaptation *can* explain human cooperation. They maintain that the experimental economic evidence is being interpreted wrongly and that, with an alternative perspective, individual-level theories can explain human cooperation after all (Burnham & Johnson, 2005; Hagen & Hammerstein, 2006; Johnson, Stopka, & Knights, 2003; Price, Cosmides, & Tooby, 2002).

The divergence between the group- and individual-level camps is so significant for theoretical understanding, as well as practical applications, that it is essential to try and work through the arguments and resolve the differences. In doing so, we must differentiate the two general ways in which the camps disagree: First, they disagree about the interpretation of the experimental data; second, they disagree about the theoretical grounds for suggesting that human cooperation evolved via individual-level adaptation. These two aspects of disagreement are discussed in turn in the following section.

First Disagreement: Do the Experimental Data Refute Individual-Level Adaptationist Theories of Human Cooperation?

As previously noted, subjects in experimental games continue to engage in costly cooperation and punishment even when game designers have attempted to eliminate incentives that should elicit such behavior (according to individual-level adaptationist theories). Group-level adaptationists regard these results as evidence that cooperative behavior must be generated by adaptations that evolved to serve the interests of biological or cultural groups. From the individual-level perspective, however, a big problem remains: Even if subjects consciously understand and believe that there are no personal consequences of their actions—for example, that the game is anonymous and they can do what they like with impunity the semiautonomous psychological mechanisms that regulate their cooperative behavior may remain alert and sensitive to cues of social exchange. Subjects cannot simply *switch off* the psychological mechanisms that guide our behavior in everyday social exchanges—they cannot leave their brains at the laboratory door (Trivers, 2004, 2006; Vogel, 2004). The experimental evidence, in fact, does suggest that subliminal cues of social exchange—for example, the presence of stylized eye spots on the wallpaper of computer screens or of a robotic head with human-like eyes in experimental laboratories—*do* increase levels of cooperation (Bateson, Nettle, & Roberts, 2006; Burnham & Hare, in press; Burnham, 2003; Haley & Fessler, 2005).

A major problem with the group-level adaptationist interpretation is that it confuses ultimate and proximate causes of behavior (Tinbergen, 1968; see Table 17.1) . They expect that if psychological mechanisms evolved as individual-level adaptations, then these mechanisms should function adaptively as such in every environment (focusing exclusively on the "ultimate" explanation). However, they overlook the fact that these semiautonomous mechanisms are capable only of responding to informational cues that would have been present in the environments to which they are adapted (which redirects our attention toward "proximate" explanations). Our psychology simply fails to optimize behavior in evolutionarily novel circumstances (e.g., laboratory experiments or big cities), and better reflects the constraints of the environments in which our psychological mechanisms for cooperation evolved, environments characterized by small groups of extended kin, few strangers, strong hierarchies, and lasting reputations (Barkow, Cosmides, & Tooby, 1992; T. Burnham & Johnson, 2005; Hagen & Hammerstein, 2006; Johnson et al., 2003). Of course, thinking human beings are perfectly able to *adjust* their cooperation to situations in which these social contexts are at stake, but if even part of our response is subconscious, then we continue to behave *as if* they are at stake even where they are not.

A further problem with the group-level adaptationist interpretation revolves around the significance and ecological validity of one-shot encounters, which are often central to laboratory demonstrations of costly cooperation behavior (Hagen & Hammerstein, 2006). Group-level adaptationists like to argue that one-shot interactions were common or important in our evolutionary history, because this would imply that humans have adapted to deal with them. If so, there is not necessarily any mismatch between cooperative behavior in one-shot experimental games and our evolved psychological mechanisms. This would, they argue, rule out the possibility that people "mistake" one-shot experimental encounters for repeated encounters (behaving *as if* in an ongoing reciprocal exchange). Instead, they should recognize a one-shot encounter for what it is and withhold cooperation. This line of reasoning has spawned a considerable debate over how common such one-shot encounters were in human evolutionary history.

Table 17.1 Tinbergen's Four Causes of Behavior

Cause	Description	Relevance for Cooperation?	Possible Tests
Ultimate	The behavior's evolutionary function (e.g., building nests to protect eggs)	What is the adaptive significance of cooperation?	Experiments that identify the contexts and payoffs associated with cooperation
Proximate	The behavior's immediate trigger (e.g., hormones)	What are the psychological motives behind cooperation?	Experiments that elicit subconscious triggers of cooperation
Ontological	The behavior's developmental or learned components (e.g., observing or imitating parents)	How does childhood development and learning influence cooperation?	Experiments with children of different ages; comparative studies of communities with different teaching methods
Phylogenetic	The behavior's distribution among closely related species and common ancestors	What are the differences and similarities between human and primate/other animals' cooperation?	Cross-species comparisons of cooperation behavior

However, this argument has run into a number of problems. Firstly, encountering a stranger does not necessarily represent a one-off encounter. A single meeting may (1) actually *cause* an increased probability of positive or negative encounters in the future (Hagen & Hammerstein, 2006) or (2) *contain* multiple mini-reciprocal exchanges operating over seconds or minutes, which could make the difference between offering a banana to make a new friend or threatening violence and getting killed (Trivers, 2004). Secondly, being told that games are a one-shot encounter may fail to cause the games to be recognized as such by experimental subjects, given that they are usually consciously or unconsciously aware that they are playing with fellow students or villagers (Hagen & Hammerstein, 2006). Finally, a hunter-gatherer's one-shot encounter implies by definition an interaction with a *nongroup* member and, thus, would hardly be expected to elicit prosocial behaviors that are held to evolve for *within-group* cooperation in competition with other groups (Hagen & Hammerstein, 2006). At best, the significance of one-shot encounters can be interpreted both ways. At worst, it is a meaningless distraction from the central issue, especially given that we will never know what the frequency of one-shot encounters really was in our evolutionary past.

Regardless of how rare or common such circumstances may have been in our ancestors' lives, it is reasonable to doubt that these circumstances are realistically recreated in experimental laboratories that are crowded with other people (who, anonymous or not, visible or not, are nevertheless present), who are playing some sort of interaction game *with you* (and, therefore, have an explicit interest in your actions), and in which your behavior is being recorded by computers and scrutinized by scientists. The techniques that experimenters use to create an impression of anonymity (e.g., telling subjects that the experiment is anonymous, or implementing a double-blind methodology) may not represent valid cues of anonymity to subjects' semiautonomous psychological mechanisms for cooperation.

Second Disagreement: Could Selection Have Favored Individual-Level Adaptations for Cooperation in Humans?

The different interpretations of the experimental data just described are influenced by different theoretical orientations: Only the individual-level adaptationists, and not the group-level adaptationists, believe that individual-level adaptations were predominant in the natural selection of cooperation behavior in humans. To understand the source of these differences of opinion, it is first necessary to consider what is special about human cooperation. Both the individual- and group-level adaptationists agree that to an extent that is apparently unique among animals, humans cooperate in large groups of unrelated individuals to produce shared resources (hereafter, "collective actions"). In considering why many scientists consider human cooperation to be an evolutionary puzzle, it is important to remember that it is this *specific kind* of interaction—collective actions—that they consider puzzling. Simpler kinds of cooperative interactions, for example dyadic exchange, are relatively easy to explain via conventional models of direct or indirect reciprocity (Axelrod & Hamilton, 1981; Nowak & Sigmund, 1998; Panchanathan & Boyd, 2004).

The special structure of collective actions requires special models to explain how cooperators avoid being exploited to extinction by free riders. Formal modelers are yet to demonstrate that the individual-level adaptive strategies that allow cooperation to evolve in simple dyadic contexts, such as direct and indirect reciprocal strategies, can promote the evolution of cooperation in collective actions (although the potential to do so is great; Nowak & Sigmund, 2005). Further, one very influential model (Boyd & Richerson, 1988) suggests explicitly that collective action *cannot* evolve via reciprocity. On the other hand, group-level adaptationists have produced several models demonstrating that collective action *could* evolve via biological or cultural group selection (Boyd et al., 2003; Gintis, 2000, 2003). At this point, therefore, the group-level adaptationists seem to wield a theoretical advantage over the individual-level adaptationists in the extent to which they have expressed their theories formally.

That being the case, it remains essential to explore individual-level theories to the full (and this has simply not been done). If we trace the history of the literature on human cooperation, we can see that some wrong turns were made in the path that led to the current popularity of group selection. By exploring the untrodden paths, we find that cooperation may in fact be explicable in terms of individual-level theories, with a high degree of parsimony with experimental data. There are three primary reasons why such a "renaissance of the individual" is likely to improve our comprehension of human cooperation: (1) Group selection models are generally not parsimonious as biological adaptationist explanations, (2) existing individual-level theories can be extended and synthesized to produce successful formal models of collective action, and (3) behavioral data from real-life collective actions are better predicted by individual-level rather than group-level models. Each of these arguments is developed in detail in the following sections.

GROUP SELECTION VERSUS PARSIMONY

Once ridiculed as a wrong-headed misunderstanding of how selection works (Williams, 1966, 1992), group selection has enjoyed a resurgence of interest since the 1980s (Wilson, 2001; Wilson & Sober, 1994), and has attracted particular attention in studies of human cooperation (Boyd et al., 2003; Gintis, 2000; Sober & Wilson, 1998; Wilson, 2002). Three things have changed to make this possible. First, there was a realization that, in purely theoretical terms, group selection might work after all (Wilson, in press). Second, there was a realization that the selection of *cultural* traits, rather than genes alone, may be driven by group selection (Boyd & Richerson, 1985; Richerson & Boyd, 2004). The evolution of cultural traits was, of course, seen as particularly relevant to our own culturally rich species, where innovations in one group can lead to advantages over other groups. The third change was the general realization that group selection need not compete directly with the often opposing selective forces working at the individual level (Sober & Wilson, 1998). Rather a process of multilevel selection is envisaged, in which group traits may come to the fore at certain times. This new work on group selection raises the opportunity to explain a number of otherwise puzzling traits by invoking their benefit in terms of the good of the group.

Darwin himself mused on the possibility of group selection (partly for want of an alternative explanation for altruism). Without any knowledge of DNA, the idea seemed perfectly plausible and conformed to the logic of natural selection. Especially with respect to humans, he saw that, in principle, human groups that shared certain traits that favored the in-group may spread at the expense of more selfish groups who were less able to work together. This, he thought, might represent an evolutionary origin for the development of human morality (Darwin, 1871).

It is crucial to remember, however, that we need only invoke mechanisms that are sufficient to explain the puzzle at hand. Group selection may or may not explain human cooperation. But before it is invoked, are we certain that individual-level adaptationism cannot explain human cooperation? The principle of Occam's razor advises us to be sure that the simpler explanations can be ruled out before going on to more complex and controversial explanations that contain more assumptions (as group selection does). George Williams (1966) took this parsimonious approach when he stated, in the opening words of *Adaptation and Natural Selection*, "[W]hen recognized, adaptation should be attributed to no higher a level of organization than is demanded by the evidence" (p. v). In other words, our evolutionary accounts will more likely be correct if we thoroughly attempt to explain adaptation in terms of lower level selective processes, before we resort to higher level explanations.

BACK TO SQUARE ONE: AN INDIVIDUAL-LEVEL ADAPTATIONIST EXPLANATION OF COOPERATION IN GROUPS

As previously noted, cooperation between two individuals is relatively easy to explain via reciprocity, the real problem is explaining the evolution of *n*-player collective actions. In such groups, cooperation can quickly break down because while there may be an attractive reward if everyone cooperates, cheats can do better than cooperators by withholding their contributions while nevertheless benefiting from the public good (Olson, 1965; Ostrom, 1990). For example, a cheat can fail to pay taxes and still drive on public roads. More formally, in a group of n members, one's cost of contributing c creates a public good, with a total benefit mc that is shared equally by all members (where m is some positive number). One can contribute productively when $m > 1$; however, if $n > m > 1$, then one can profit more individually by contributing nothing, and free riding on the contributions of comembers.

How can cooperators in collective actions harvest the benefits of their production, without allowing free riders to exploit them to extinction? The solution to this problem, in general, is to cooperate preferentially with other cooperators instead of with free riders and, thus, to exclude free riders from the benefits of production. This principle of preferential cooperation among cooperators is a basic law of adaptive cooperation, and it underlies the evolutionary success of Trivers' (1971) reciprocal altruism, which allows cooperators to sustain interactions only with other cooperators while avoiding benefiting free riders. This principle also explains the adaptiveness of Alexander's (1987) indirect reciprocity and Hamilton's (1964) genic self-favoritism among nonkin, both of which allow cooperators to preferentially assort with other cooperators and exclude free riders from the circle of mutual cooperation, that is, to engage in *positive assortment*.

Given the adaptive potential of reciprocity and positive assortment, why have they been regarded by many researchers as inadequate explanations for collective action? In the case of positive assortment, the argument is not about whether systems requiring cooperators to identify and assort with each other could in principle allow collective action to evolve; rather, it is about whether such systems could (1) survive invasions by deceptive individuals posing as cooperators (the *deception problem*) and (2) involve a mechanism for efficiently ostracizing free riders who wanted to remain in a group of cooperators (the *ostracization problem*).

The deception problem arises because in a system of positive assortment, cooperators must have some means of recognizing other cooperators, in order to interact with them preferentially. Cooperators, therefore, must display some phenotypic label that identifies them as cooperators. If this label can be easily faked and displayed by noncooperators, then the system will be vulnerable to deception: Mutations that produce the label of cooperativeness but do not produce the cooperative behavior itself, will acquire the benefits of cooperation without paying the costs and, thus, will exploit honest label displayers to extinction. The deception problem will be more serious in a system involving a label that is more arbitrary and less intrinsically indicative of cooperative behavior itself, e.g., Dawkins' (1976) "green beard". The solution to this problem would be for cooperators to rely on a label that is a maximally nonarbitrary and difficult-to-fake signal of cooperativeness, ideally convincing displays of altruistic behavior itself (Dawkins, 1976; Price, 2006).

The seriousness of the ostracization problem in a system of positive assortment will depend heavily on the scale and type of collective action. For instance, it may be very costly in a large, complex society to maintain an institution that excludes nontaxpayers from driving on public roads. On the other hand, in a small village in which neighbors often help repair one another's homes, an individual who refuses to help can be ostracized relatively easily: When his home needs repairing, his neighbors can refuse to help him.

The Fork in the Road

The rejection of positive assortment as an evolutionary explanation of collective action has been based mainly on casually formulated and informally defended assumptions about the abilities of cooperators to identify one another and to ostracize free riders. Reciprocal altruism, on the other hand, has been rejected somewhat more rigorously. This rejection can in fact be traced back to a specific influential publication, "The Evolution of Reciprocity in Sizable Groups" (Boyd & Richerson, 1988), which concluded that reciprocity could allow for the evolution of only very small collective actions and that it is an inadequate explanation for the large-scale collective actions in which humans interact. Boyd and Richerson's (1988) paper was an important "fork in the road" that led many researchers to veer away from individual-level adaptationist accounts of human cooperation. Since Boyd and Richerson, the tendency has been for evolutionary modelers to simply note that reciprocity does not apply directly to collective action contexts and to proceed to explore alternative explanations instead—alternatives that do not invoke Trivers' theory (Brandt, Hauert, & Sigmund, 2003; Fehr, 2004; Henrich, 2004; Panchanathan & Boyd, 2004), and which often depend on group selection (Boyd et al., 2003; Fehr & Fischbacher, 2003; Gintis, 2000). Given the influential role that Boyd and Richerson have had in rejecting individual-level adaptationist accounts of collective action, it is worth revisiting this publication and examining its conclusions in some detail (see also Trivers, 2006).

First, let us assume that there is a population with two strategies, R (reciprocator) and F (free rider). Boyd and Richerson (1988) defined reciprocity, R, in the collective action as a strategy which cooperates as long as all the other $n - 1$ group members cooperate, but stops cooperation immediately if one or more group members free ride. (The tolerance of R, i.e., the number of comembers who must cooperate in order for R to cooperate, can vary in Boyd and Richerson's model, but for now we will assume that this value is $n - 1$). This means that R continues cooperating only when all its comembers are also Rs. In a mixed group with R and F, R cooperates in the first round and then stops cooperating from the second round. Rs are exploited in such mixed groups but only in the first round. When R is in a group consisting only of other Rs, it can enjoy the benefit of sustained mutual cooperation. Thus, whether R can avoid extinction and increase its share (i.e., its relative proportion) in a population depends on how likely R is to find itself in a group consisting of only Rs.

Second, let us assume that multiple groups of n individuals are randomly formed and members play a game of public goods (i.e., they interact in a collective action where $n > m > 1$, as described previously) in each group for a certain number of rounds. This process of random matching is a standard assumption in most evolutionary game theoretical models of cooperation. As there are only two strategies in this population, group composition simply follows a binomial process. In principle, if the average payoff to R exceeds that of F, R can evolve and increase its share in the population. According to Boyd and Richerson (1988), "[R]eciprocity is likely to evolve only when reciprocating groups are quite small" (p. 352) simply because it is very challenging for Rs to form groups of only Rs, even when R is common in the population. For example, consider a population with 80% of Rs and 20% of Fs, and in which groups of 3 members are randomly formed. The probability of a group consisting of 3 Rs is 0.8^3 (= 0.512). If group size increases to 20, however, this probability quickly decreases to 0.012. As group size gets larger, this probability decreases exponentially, and it becomes increasingly difficult for R to reap the benefits of mutual cooperation. Thus, Boyd and Richerson conclude, "[T]he conditions that allow the evolution of reciprocal altruism become extremely restrictive as group size increases" (p. 337).

If R gets more tolerant by continuing to cooperate even when more of its comembers free ride, for instance, if it cooperates as long as $n - 2$ of its comembers cooperate (instead of $n - 1$, as with the previous example), then R will have more opportunities to benefit from mutual cooperation. However, the more tolerant R becomes, the more F can exploit the cooperation enabled by R's tolerance, and Boyd and Richerson (1988) show that increasing R's tolerance does not allow R to overcome F. And while positive assortment can increase the probability that R will find itself in groups that include other Rs and that exclude F, Boyd and Richerson show that even with the help of very strong positive assortment, R's evolution still quickly becomes difficult as group size increases.

Boyd and Richerson (1988, p. 352) suggest that collective actions involving 3 individuals could evolve relatively easily even with low positive assortment (i.e., the probability that a reciprocator's comember will also be a reciprocator is modified and increased by a parameter $r = 1/32$, which is comparable to Hamilton's kin coefficient), and with few (i.e., about 10) repeated interactions. However, in collective actions involving 16 individuals, even with high positive assortment

(r = 1/4), an unrealistically high number of interactions (about 10 million) would be required in order for reciprocity to evolve. Critically, subsequent publications stated that the Boyd and Richerson model shows that reciprocity could evolve in collective actions of "about 10" (Henrich, 2004, p. 10) or "a handful of" (Boyd et al., 2003, p. 3531) participants. These authors note that human collective actions are often much larger than this and, therefore, conclude that such cooperation cannot be explained in terms of reciprocal altruism. There are, however, a number of problems with this rejection of reciprocity as an explanation for large-scale cooperation, to which we now turn.

Proximate Causation

First, even if psychological mechanisms for reciprocity did evolve in small groups, they could still produce reciprocity in larger ones. Hunter-gatherer bands typically consist of about 7–8 male and female full-time foragers (Kelly, 1995, p. 213), and the average sex-segregated foraging group may involve only 3–5 members. If reciprocators in these groups followed a scalable decision rule similar to "contribute to the observed (or expected) extent of the average co-participant," then they might have been motivated to reciprocate in larger groups as well (the larger the group, the larger the denominator used to calculate the average contribution). Even if selection against such a strategy would occur in modern environments characterized by large collective actions, it could be that when people in industrialized societies participate in large-scale cooperation (e.g., vote in elections, fight in wars), they are motivated by proximate adaptations that evolved by promoting reciprocity in much smaller groups.

Replacing Binary Reciprocity with Continuous Reciprocity

The previous argument about proximate causation is not a direct criticism of Boyd and Richerson's (1988) model, but simply raises the question of whether reciprocity should be rejected as an explanation of collective action, based on the results of a single theoretical model. In this section, we provide a more fundamental criticism of Boyd and Richerson's rejection of reciprocity by pointing out and reexamining one typical error that theoreticians tend to commit. Boyd and Richerson's model explored only a binary reciprocal strategy that contributes either all (1.0) or nothing (0.0) to the public good. However, a more realistic model would allow for *continuous* reciprocity, that is, for contributions that can vary continuously between 0.0 and 1.0. Binarization of individual behavior is a simplification of a more complex reality that may sometimes be necessary for making a model tractable. Further, the difference between a binary and continuous reciprocal strategy may seem so insignificant that one may be tempted to conclude that Boyd and Richerson's simplification is acceptable. However, in the following section, we show that if Boyd and Richerson had looked at continuous rather than binary reciprocity, then they may have reached a quite different conclusion about the adaptiveness of reciprocity in sizable groups (and the subsequent history of research on human cooperation might have been quite different, too).

Consider a new strategy, *CR*, that contributes in round t as a function of the average contribution made by the $n - 1$ other group members in round $t - 1$ (i.e., in the previous round). Takezawa and Price (2006) consider a single variant of *CR* that simply matches the average comember contribution from the previous round, and their model is in all other respects identical to the model presented in Boyd and Richerson (1988). Figure 17.1 shows the minimum proportion of reciprocal strategies (*R* and *CR*) that is necessary for reciprocators to spread at the expense of *F*. *R*'s share in a population needs to be very high—above 80%—when group size is 50. This value must be high, regardless of the value of several other parameters in the model, such as the efficiency of cooperation (marginal per capita return, or *MPCR*—a value that is higher in groups that produce more resources for a given level of effort), and regardless of the length of the interaction (*w*; Figure 17.1a). In contrast, *CR* can increase its share against *F* even when its initial proportion in the population is relatively low, and especially when cooperation is very efficient. For example when *MPCR* = 0.95, *CR* can evolve even when its initial share is only 5% of a population. Figure 17.1b indicates a case

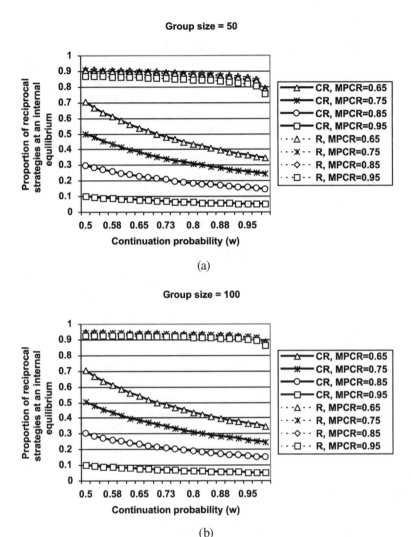

(a)

(b)

Figure 17.1a–b The minimum proportion of reciprocal strategies (*R* or *CR*) necessary to invade a population of free riders (*F*).

where group size is 100, and continues to show a similar pattern: *CR* can evolve even when it is rare, as long as cooperation is efficient.

Next we will consider a third cooperative strategy, the unconditional cooperator, *C*. This strategy contributes fully in every round, regardless of how its comembers behave. The bad news for *C* is that in a population consisting of only *C* and *F*, even a single *F* can invade and take over, because there is nothing that *C* can do to defend itself from being exploited to extinction. The bad news for *R*, however, is that when *F* is absent in a population, *C* will not be exploited and so can receive the same payoff as *R*. If *C* is rare and it invades a population of *CR*, stochastic processes such as mutation may increase the share of *C*. As the proportion of *C* increases, however, *F* may be able to invade the population by exploiting *C*, which may result in the extinction of both *C* and *CR*. It is therefore important to check the robustness of *CR*, assuming that there are three strategies in a population—*F, C,* and *CR*.

In numerical computer simulations, we varied the proportions of the three strategies F, C, and CR, and found that the system evolved toward a mixture of C and CR in most combinations of proportions of the three strategies. Figure 17.2a is called a ternary plot. Any one point within this equilateral triangle represents the relative proportions of the three strategies in a population, which sum to 100%. Each base (or side) of the triangle represents a minimum proportion of 0% of a given strategy, while the point opposite represents a maximum proportion of 100% of that strategy. For instance, if a point is near the bottom-right corner, it means that a population is dominated by CR. Any proportion between these limits, for all three strategies, can thus be simultaneously represented by a single point within the triangle. For example if the point is somewhere along the perimeter between the top corner and bottom-right corner, it means that only two strategies, CR and F, exist in a population (and C is absent). The arrow at each point indicates the *direction* in which the system is evolving, for instance an arrow pointing toward the bottom-right corner indicates that the system is evolving toward domination by CR. The length of the arrow indicates the *strength* of evolution in that direction. Finally, the line that bisects the triangle divides it into the area in which the system evolves toward a C-CR mixture and that which evolves toward a pure equilibrium of F. In Figure 17.2a, the C-CR area is much larger than the F area. Roughly speaking, the cooperative strategies C and CR can evolve as long as the proportion of CR is larger than 5–6% under the parameter combination $MPCR = 0.95$, $w = 0.7$, group size = 100. Very similar results are found even when group size is increased to 500 (Figure 17.2b). Figure 17.2c shows a ternary plot where CR is replaced by Boyd and Richerson's (1988) binary reciprocal strategy R, and shows that the area leading to the evolution of cooperation is much smaller than when reciprocity is continuous.

Why did replacing binary reciprocity with continuous reciprocity generate such a dramatic difference? Consider a group of five individuals. As we discussed in the previous section, R can gain the benefits of mutual cooperation only when all four of its comembers are also R. Just one F in the group induces the collapse of cooperation. On the other hand, when four CR and one F exist in a group, CR still can enjoy some degree of mutual cooperation (Table 17.2a). When the number of F increases, for instance to three, CR stops cooperating very quickly and can avoid being exploited by F (Table 17.2b). The power of CR is in its capacity to quickly reduce cooperation when there are too many Fs among its comembers, while maintaining a moderately high level of cooperation when there are fewer Fs.

Some Notes on Interpretation of the Model Results

Although quite different conclusions can be drawn from a model of continuous as opposed to binary reciprocity, one must be careful in interpreting these results. First, the area favoring the evolution of cooperative strategies in the ternary plot gets smaller quickly as the efficiency of cooperation, $MPCR$, goes down (see also Figure 17.1). The $MPCR$ value of 0.95, which is used in Figure 17.2, is very high compared to the values used in many public goods game experiments, which are usually around 0.40 (though note that we used the *same* MPCR value when comparing our CR model with Boyd and Richerson's R model). Unless evidence is provided that collective actions in human ancestral environments were very efficient, it should not be concluded that our model is sufficient for explaining the evolution of large-scale cooperation. Second, even when cooperation is very efficient, at least 5–6% of the population needs to mutate into CR at the same time in order for CR to overcome domination by F. If stochastic forces are sufficient to make such a multiple mutation realistic, the system starts to drift and may oscillate between an equilibrium of all F or a mixture of C-CR, in which case one must examine in which equilibrium, F or C-CR, the system spends more time.

Despite these issues, it is noteworthy that this model challenges Boyd and Richerson's (1988) argument that reciprocity cannot explain the evolution of cooperation, and does not rely on any exotic assumptions such as group extinctions (Boyd et al., 2003; Gintis, 2000) or cultural group selection (Boyd & Richerson, 1985; Henrich, 2004).

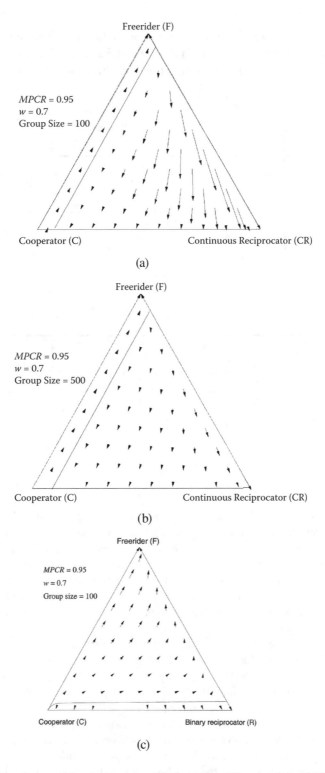

Figure 17.2a–c Dynamics of unconditional cooperators (*C*), free riders (*F*) and reciprocal (*CR*) strategies, for continuous reciprocity under two sets of parameter values (a and b), and when reciprocity is binary instead of continuous as in Boyd and Richerson's (1988) original model (c).

Table 17.2a–b Transition of the Amount of Contributions by Continuous Reciprocators across Six Rounds When There Are: (a) Four Continuous Reciprocators and One Free Rider and (b) Two Continuous Reciprocators and Three Free Riders

(a)

	Rounds					
	1	2	3	4	5	6
CR	1	0.75	0.56	0.42	0.32	0.24
CR	1	0.75	0.56	0.42	0.32	0.24
CR	1	0.75	0.56	0.42	0.32	0.24
CR	1	0.75	0.56	0.42	0.32	0.24
F	0	0	0	0	0	0

(b)

	Rounds					
	1	2	3	4	5	6
CR	1	0.25	0.06	0.02	<0.01	<0.01
CR	1	0.25	0.06	0.02	<0.01	<0.01
F	0	0	0	0	0	0
F	0	0	0	0	0	0
F	0	0	0	0	0	0

Rethinking Positive Assortment

As previously demonstrated, a single rather simple adjustment to Boyd and Richerson's (1988) model—changing the reciprocity strategy from binary to continuous—produces a dramatically different result. Compared to the binary strategy, continuous reciprocity is much better at replicating when it is rare in a population. Further, reciprocity's enhanced adaptiveness is achieved even without assuming any higher a level of positive assortment among reciprocators than assumed in the original model. When reciprocators are allowed to positively assort, *synergy* between the two behaviors may further enhance reciprocity's ability to evolve in groups. The effect found in our model, therefore, may be on the conservative side.

The fact that positive assortment can interact synergistically with other cooperative strategies points to another problem that has plagued models of the evolution of cooperation—*population structure* (or lack thereof). While reciprocity may not survive in populations that intermix randomly, as in Boyd and Richerson (1988), if individuals can *choose* their interaction partners and preferentially cooperate with them, then reciprocity can survive even in large populations. Models that assume *random mixing* of interactions are misleading because they artificially exaggerate the effective population size. Even in a big city like New York, one tends to interact with a small subset of the same people every day—family, colleagues, bosses, friends, and so forth. In real life, choosing interaction partners means that the likelihood of meeting again remains high over time, because individual A will *seek out* individual B and vice versa. Unless one forces them to rely on bumping into each other at some random location in New York each time, A can simply go and find B (e.g., go and knock on their door).

Another potentially misleading assumption is that the population is mixed up so that individuals must find each other at all. Most human groups have a number of *structural features* that ensure interactions are *constrained* to certain dyads and groups and not others (over and above any effects of preference). These include: spatial structure (one is more likely to interact with neighbors or people one passes regularly), hierarchies (one is more likely to interact with certain ranks within the hierarchy and not others), peer groups (one is more likely to interact with members who have similar characteristics), and activities (one is more likely to interact with groups formed for specific reasons, e.g., hunting parties, warrior groups, etc., which do not constitute the whole population).

The dynamics of positive assortment are absolutely crucial to constructing realistic models of human social behavior *and* to understanding the paths not taken in the cooperation literature. Low levels of positive assortment can drastically increase cooperation, as shown in many spatial prisoner's dilemma games (Axelrod, 1997; Nowak, May, & Sigmund, 1995; Hammond & Axelrod, 2006; Nowak, 2006), as well as accelerate the spread of norms within structured networks, rendering group selection models "neither justified nor necessary. Such behaviors can emerge from individual-based models, simply involving rewards to individuals who belong to groups" (Ehrlich & Levin, 2005, p. 946; see also Durrett & Levin, 2005; Nakamaru & Levin, 2004).

To sum up, previous models have assumed that people reciprocate according to an all or nothing binary rule, and that people either are not allowed to choose who they interact with at all, or they have to rely on chance. Both are clearly inaccurate descriptions of human social behavior. Allowing people to reciprocate continuously, and allowing them to choose who they interact with, is far more realistic and, crucially, leads to radically different predictions about whether or not cooperation in groups could evolve via individual-level adaptation.

WHERE DOES THE EVIDENCE POINT? SUPPORT FOR THE INDIVIDUAL-LEVEL ADAPTATIONIST VIEW

We argued previously that human collective action could in theory be the product of individual-level adaptation, if evolution favored reciprocity in collective actions and/or positive assortment among cooperators. As well as exploring such theoretical issues, another avenue of inquiry is to assess whether existing models accurately describe how people actually behave in real life. Does the empirical evidence point toward group selection, or do members of cooperative groups behave as predicted by the individual-level theories just discussed? We address these questions in this section, for each of several topics in turn.

Conditional Cooperation in Public Good Games

A standard finding of experimental collective actions (public good games), is that the majority of subjects are "conditional" cooperators, that is, they cooperate more when they perceive that coplayers are more willing to cooperate (Fischbacher, Gächter, & Fehr, 2001; Kurzban & Houser, 2005; Ledyard, 1995), and less when they believe that coplayers are free riding (Fehr & Gächter, 2000; Kurzban, et al., 2001). "Conditional cooperation" in these games, then, is essentially a term for reciprocity between a player and multiple coplayers. Anthropologists have long considered reciprocity to be a cross-cultural universal (Brown, 1991; Gouldner, 1960), and conditional cooperation in collective actions may be similarly universal. Existing cross-cultural data on this point are scant but supportive: In a public good game conducted among the Mapuche of southern Chile, players' contribution amounts were best predicted by their beliefs about how much coplayers would contribute (Henrich & Smith, 2004). Research on the neurological basis of reciprocity may provide clues about the proximate motivations behind conditional cooperation in public good games. In one fMRI study, reciprocity was associated with consistent activation in brain areas that have been linked with reward processing (Rilling et al., 2002). This suggests that reciprocity has deeply engrained biological roots.

Consistent with our previous model that represents reciprocity as a continuous rather than binary strategy, cooperators in public good games apparently strive to match the average coplayer contribution. Experimental studies (Fischbacher et al., 2001; Kurzban & Houser, 2005) suggest that one half to two thirds of public good game subjects engage in a reciprocal strategy whereby their contributions correlate positively with the average observed or expected cosubject contribution. Another study (Croson, 1999) found that players' contributions were better predicted by their expectations about the mean coplayer contribution than by their expectations about the minimum or maximum coplayer contribution. Further, players' contributions were predicted not just by the *mean expected* coplayer contribution but by the *actual mean* coplayer contribution; in other words, players' expectations tended to be accurate. Another public good study (Keser & van Winden, 2000) found that subjects tended to increase contributions after discovering that they had been contributing less than the average coplayer, decrease contributions after discovering that they had been contributing above the average and maintain contribution levels after discovering that they had been matching the average.

Signaling Cooperativeness Initially and the Decay of Cooperativeness Over Repeated Rounds

Evidence just reviewed suggests that public good game subjects tend to match expected coplayer contributions. But what if subjects are interacting for the first time, and lack information on which to base expectations about coplayer contributions? In that case, conditional cooperators would need to be biased toward initial cooperativeness, in order to signal their cooperativeness to each other and, perhaps, prime the interaction with a high initial average contribution. Thus, when interactants have no information about each other's cooperativeness, they should be biased toward cooperativeness at the start of the interaction (analogous to the optimal strategy in iterated prisoner's dilemma, Axelrod, 1984). All else equal, they should then continue to cooperate to the extent that they perceive cointeractors to be reciprocating. And indeed, a standard finding of anonymous public good games, in which players have no information about coplayer cooperativeness at the start of the game, is that cooperative behavior follows the pattern described previously. Contributing is highest at the outset of the game and, then, decays gradually over time, as players receive information that some coplayers are free riding (Ledyard, 1995; Masclet, Noussair, Tucker, & Villeval, 2003). This gradual decay apparently occurs because higher contributors in initial rounds down-ratchet their contributions as the game progresses, in order to match the average expected coplayer contribution, which dwindles constantly due to a persistent minority of free riders (Fischbacher et al., 2001; Kurzban et al., 2001).

Mutual Monitoring

If people cooperate to the extent to which they expect coparticipants to reciprocate, then they must continually monitor coparticipants in order to assess their level of reciprocation. Evidence indicates that cross-culturally, successful collective actions involve mutual monitoring efforts by participants (Erasmus, 1977; Ostrom, 1990). Interactants appear to monitor one another not just constantly but accurately. In a Shuar hunter-horticulturalist village, *perceptions* of covillagers' engagement in provillage altruism correlated positively with covillagers' *actual* engagement in specific altruistic activities (Price, 2003). In a sugarcane cultivating workgroup in this same society, perceptions of coworker cooperativeness (attendance record and physical effort in work sessions) correlated positively with more objective measures of this cooperativeness (Price, 2006). Moreover, participants accurately distinguished "intentional" low contributors (those who could have contributed highly but chose not to) from "unintentional" low contributors (those physically *unable* to contribute highly). Experimental studies provide additional evidence that people are cognitively adapted for mutual monitoring. Cross-culturally, subjects detect violators of social contracts quickly and easily: Both Western and Amazonian Shiwiar subjects are better at solving a logic problem when the problem is presented in terms of detecting a cheater in a social exchange (Cosmides & Tooby, 1992; Sugiyama, Tooby, & Cosmides, 2002). A brain-injured patient showed selective impairment in this cheater-detection ability (Stone, Cosmides, Tooby, Kroll, & Knight, 2002), suggesting that the ability is enabled by a specialized cognitive mechanism. As Martin Nowak and Karl Sigmund (2005) recently concluded, "The moralistic assessment of the other members in the population, even if they are observed only at a distance, provides a powerful tool for channelling support towards those who collaborate, and an incentive to join group efforts" (p. 1296).

Positive Assortment Via Partner Choice

Experimental evidence suggests that both cooperators and free riders choose partners whom they expect will cooperate more. When subjects are allowed partner choice, cooperators attempt to interact with other cooperators and to avoid free riders, while free riders attempt to avoid being avoided. In a study that allowed subjects to join the public good game group of their choosing, Ehrhart and Keser (1999) observed a continual flight of the more cooperative subjects away from the less cooperative ones, as the more cooperative subjects attempted to form groups with each other, and the less cooperative subjects attempted to join groups of cooperators in order to free ride. In another public good game study, players were informed of coplayers' contribution histories and were allowed to form cooperative groups based on mutual partner preference. The highest contributors chose to cooperate with each other and proceeded to interact more productively than less cooperative coplayers did (Page, Putterman, & Unel, 2005). Similarly, when Sheldon, Sheldon and Osbaldiston (2000) allowed subjects to form groups with the comembers of their choosing, they found that relatively prosocial individuals tended to cluster together and cooperate relatively productively. Preferential interaction with expected cooperators has also been elicited experimentally in the form of indirect reciprocity: Experimental subjects will cooperate more with people whom they have observed cooperating with others (Barclay, 2004; Milinski, Semmann, & Krambeck, 2002; Nowak & Sigmund, 2005; Wedekind & Milinski, 2000) and whom they may therefore expect would cooperate with them. Further, the finding that cooperation flourishes in environments characterized by high levels of "trust," that is, environments in which people expect others to cooperate, has been reported consistently in the literature of organizational behavior and other fields (Dirks & Ferrin, 2001; Jones & George, 1998; Kramer, 1999; Ostrom, 2003).

Reputation

Humans universally acquire reputations based on their cooperativeness (Alexander, 1987; Panchanathan & Boyd, 2003; Trivers, 1971). Numerous studies suggest a correlation between cooperativeness and goodness of reputation in small scale societies, with reputations being based on, for example, how much people provision resources such as food (Gurven, Allen-Arave, Hill, & Hurtado, 2000; Hawkes, 1993), military service (Chagnon, 1988; Meggitt, 1977), and labor in group work projects (Price, 2003, 2006). An altruism-reputation correlation was also reported in a study of a large western business firm, in which employees' social status was positively related to their perceived generosity (Flynn, 2003). Further, experimental results suggest that people cooperate more when they can acquire a reputation (Barclay, 2004; Milinski et al., 2002). The importance of reputation effects for sustaining cooperation has also been noted in fields outside of experimental economics, such as transaction cost economics (Demsetz, 1993; Williamson, 1996). The selection of cooperative partners may be enabled by psychological mechanisms for remembering potential interactants based on their reputations. When subjects were shown photographs of people and given various kinds of information about them and then asked several days later which of them they remembered, subjects displayed enhanced memory for those who had been portrayed as cheaters in cooperative interactions (Mealey, Daood, Krage, 1996; Oda, 1997). Further, compared to neutral faces, faces of people who have intentionally cooperated or defected in a prisoner's dilemma game are remembered better and elicit more activity within a neural system associated with social cognition (Singer, Kiebel, Winston, Dolan, & Frith, 2004).

The previous examples assume that assessment of others' cooperativeness would be based on information about others' actual past engagement in cooperative behavior. However, cooperativeness also seems to be assessed via information gathered during verbal communication and face-to-face interaction. Subjects cooperate more when they have been given opportunities for such interaction (for a review, see Ostrom, 2003), perhaps because they can discuss their intentions (Ostrom, Walker, & Gardner, 1992), and make inferences about coplayer dispositions (Frank, Gilovich, & Regan, 1993), facial expressions and features (Brown & Moore, 2002; W. Brown, Palameta, Moore, 2003; Eckel & Wilson, 2003; Yamagishi, Tanida, Mashima, Shimoma, & Kanazawa, 2003), or other verbal and nonverbal indicators of cooperative intent (Bochet, Page, & Putterman, in press; Brown et al., 2003).

CONCLUSIONS

The mainstream literature on the evolution of cooperation has recently tended toward a group-selectionist view. However, as we have demonstrated in this chapter, progress in understanding human cooperation requires not the abandonment of individual-level adaptationist theories, but rather the extension and synthesis of these theories. The group selectionist paradigm faces significant theoretical and empirical challenges (Burnham & Johnson, 2005; Hagen & Hammerstein, 2006; Haley & Fessler, 2005; Price et al., 2002), while individual-level theories appear to be superior at predicting how collective action participants actually behave. There is good evidence that humans (and perhaps some animals, Stevens & Hauser, 2004) behave as reciprocators and engage in positive assortment. Both behaviors are predicted directly by the individual-level theories and the model described above but *not* by theories of biological and cultural group selection.

The important challenge facing students of human cooperation in the future is to identify the key factors that influence variation in human cooperative behavior and to design experiments that expose the evolved psychological mechanisms that regulate this behavior. Another challenge remains for the group-selectionists: to provide *any* empirical evidence for their favored view of cooperation. A considerable and growing body of empirical work has begun to reveal genetically selfish motives— serving the interests of individuals rather than groups—underlying so-called "strong reciprocity" (Bateson et al., 2006; Burnham & Hare, in press; Burnham, 2003; Haley & Fessler, 2005; Kurzban, DeScioli, & O'Brien, 2007). It will be interesting to see if the group selectionists can maintain the direction of their march (to which they have already committed themselves theoretically) against the rising tide of empirical evidence for individual-level adaptations for cooperation.

It is ironic that one of the most basic and everyday features of human nature—cooperation—is so poorly understood by behavioral scientists, despite a plethora of great minds working on and discussing the problem in the pages of the world's leading science journals. What is more, it is urgent that the problem is resolved. If we cannot agree on even the basic origins and motives of human cooperation, how can we hope to promote it in our rapidly globalizing world of environmental devastation, genocide, terrorism, poverty, and war? The mainstream literature has, we believe, been led astray largely because early models presented an erroneous "fork in the road," which caused the majority of theorists to discount the power of reciprocity to explain human cooperation in groups and to rush headlong into group selection. As Robert Frost might have advised us, where those two roads diverge, we would now be wise to explore the one less travelled.

REFERENCES

Alexander, R. D. (1987). *The biology of moral systems.* Aldine, NY: Hawthorne.

Axelrod, R. (1984). *The evolution of cooperation.* London: Penguin.

Axelrod, R. (1997). *The complexity of cooperation: Agent-based models of competition and collaboration.* Princeton, NJ: Princeton University Press.

Axelrod, R., & Hamilton, W. D. (1981). The evolution of cooperation. *Science, 211,* 1390–1396.

Barclay, P. (2004). Trustworthiness and competitive altruism can also solve the "tragedy of the commons." *Evolution and Human Behavior, 25,* 209–220.

Barkow, J. H., Cosmides, L., & Tooby, J. (Eds.). (1992). *The adapted mind: Evolutionary psychology and the generation of culture.* Oxford, U.K.: Oxford University Press.

Bateson, M., Nettle, D., & Roberts, G. (2006). Cues of being watched enhance cooperation in a real-world setting. *Biology Letters, 2,* 412–414.

Bochet, O., Page, T., & Putterman, L. (2006). Communication and punishment in voluntary contribution experiments. *Journal of Economic Behavior and Organization, 60*(1), 11–26.

Boyd, R., Gintis, H., Bowles, S., & Richerson, P. J. (2003). The evolution of altruistic punishment. *Proceedings of the National Academy of Sciences, 100,* 3531–3535.

Boyd, R., & Richerson, P. J. (1985). *Culture and the evolutionary process.* Chicago: University of Chicago Press.

Boyd, R., & Richerson, P. J. (1988). The evolution of reciprocity in sizable groups. *Journal of Theoretical Biology, 132,* 337–356.

Brandt, H., Hauert, C., & Sigmund, K. (2003). Cooperation, punishment and reputation in spatial games. *Proceedings of the Royal Society, London B, 270,* 1099–1104.

Brown, D. E. (1991). *Human universals.* New York: McGraw-Hill.

Brown, W. M., & Moore, C. (2002). Smile asymmetries and reputation as reliable indicators of likelihood to cooperate: An evolutionary analysis. *Advances in Psychology Research, 11,* 59–78.

Brown, W. M., Palameta, B., & Moore, C. (2003). Are there nonverbal cues to commitment? An exploratory study using the zero-acquaintance video presentation paradigm. *Evolutionary Psychology, 1,* 42–69.

Burnham, T. C., & Hare, B. (in press). Engineering cooperation: Does involuntary neural activation increase public goods contributions? *Human Nature.*

Burnham, T. C., & Johnson, D. D. P. (2005). The biological and evolutionary logic of human cooperation. *Analyse & Kritik, 27*(1), 113–135.

Burnham, T. C. (2003). Engineering altruism: A theoretical and experimental investigation of anonymity and gift giving. *Journal of Economic Behavior and Organization, 50*(1), 133–144.

Chagnon, N. A. (1988). Life histories, blood revenge, and warfare in a tribal population. *Science, 239,* 985–992.

Chagnon, N. A., & Irons, W. (Eds.). (1979). *Evolutionary biology & human social behaviour: An anthropological perspective.* North Scituate, MA: Duxburg Press.

Cosmides, L., & Tooby, J. (1992). Cognitive adaptations for social exchange. In J. H. Barkow, L. Cosmides, & J. Tooby (Eds.), *The adapted mind: Evolutionary psychology and the generation of culture* (pp. 163–228). New York: Oxford University Press.

Croson, R. T. A. (1999). *Contributions to public goods: Altruism or reciprocity?* Philadelphia: Wharton School of Business, University of Pennsylvania.

Darwin, C. (1871). *The descent of man.* New York: Penguin Classics.

Dawkins, R. (1976). *The selfish gene.* Oxford, U.K.: Oxford University Press.

Demsetz, H. (1993). The theory of the firm revisited. In O. E. Williamson & S. G. Winter (Eds.), *The nature of the firm: Origins, evolution and development* (pp. 159–178). New York: Oxford University Press.

Dirks, K. T., & Ferrin, D. L. (2001). The role of trust in organizational settings. *Organization Science, 12,* 450–467.

Dugatkin, L. A. (1997). *Cooperation in animals.* Oxford, U.K.: Oxford University Press.

Durrett, R., & Levin, S. A. (2005). Can stable social groups be maintained by homophilous imitation alone? *Journal of Economic Behavior and Organization, 57*(3), 267–286.

Eckel, C. C., & Wilson, R. K. (2003). The human face of game theory: Trust and reciprocity in sequential games. In E. Ostrom & J. Walker (Eds.), *Trust and reciprocity: Interdisciplinary lessons from experimental research* (pp. 245–274). New York: Sage.

Ehrhart, K., & Keser, C. (1999). *Mobility and cooperation: On the run* (pp. 99s–24). Montreal, Quebec, Canada: CIRANO.

Ehrlich, P., & Levin, S. (2005). The evolution of norms. *PLoS Biology, 3*(6), e194.

Erasmus, C. J. (1977). *In search of the common good*. New York: The Free Press.

Fehr, E. (2004). Don't lose your reputation. *Nature, 432*, 449–450.

Fehr, E., & Fischbacher, U. (2003). The nature of human altruism. *Nature, 425*, 785–791.

Fehr, E., & Gächter, S. (2000). Cooperation and punishment in public goods experiments. *American Economic Review, 90*, 980–994.

Fehr, E., & Gächter, S. (2002). Altruistic punishment in humans. *Nature, 415*, 137–140.

Fischbacher, U., Gächter, S., & Fehr, E. (2001). Are people conditionally cooperative? Evidence from a public goods experiment. *Economics Letters, 71*, 397–404.

Flynn, F. J. (2003). How much should I give and how often? The effects of generosity and frequency of favor exchange on social status and productivity. *Academy of Management Journal, 46*, 539–553.

Frank, R. H., Gilovich, T., & Regan, D. T. (1993). The evolution of one-shot cooperation: An experiment. *Ethology and Sociobiology, 14*, 247–256.

Gadagkar, R. (2001). *Survival strategies: Cooperation and conflict in animal societies*. Cambridge, MA: Harvard University Press.

Gintis, H. (2000). Strong reciprocity and human sociality. *Journal of Theoretical Biology, 206*, 169–179.

Gintis, H. (2003). Solving the puzzle of prosociality. *Rationality and Society, 15*, 155–187.

Gintis, H., Smith, E., & Bowles, S. (2001). Costly signalling and cooperation. *Journal of Theoretical Biology, 213*, 103–119.

Gouldner, A. W. (1960). The norm of reciprocity: A preliminary statement. *American Sociological Review, 25*, 161–178.

Gurven, M., Allen-Arave, W., Hill, K., & Hurtado, A. M. (2000). 'It's a wonderful life': Signaling generosity among the Ache of Paraguay. *Evolution and Human Behavior, 21*, 263–282.

Hagen, E. H., & Hammerstein, P. (2006). Game theory and human evolution: A critique of some recent interpretations of experimental games. *Theoretical Population Biology, 69*, 339–348.

Haig, D. (1996). Gestational drive and the green-bearded placenta. *Proceedings of the National Academy of Sciences, 93*, 6547–6551.

Haley, K., & Fessler, D. (2005). Nobody's watching? Subtle cues affect generosity in an anonymous economic game. *Evolution and Human Behavior, 26*, 245–256.

Hamilton, W. D. (1964). The genetical evolution of social behaviour, I & II. *Journal of Theoretical Biology, 7*, 1–52.

Hammond, R. A., & Axelrod, R. (2006). The evolution of ethnocentrism. *Journal of Conflict Resolution, 50*(6), 926–936.

Hawkes, K. (1993). Why hunter-gatherers work—An ancient version of the problem of public goods. *Current Anthropology, 34*, 341–361.

Henrich, J. (2004). Cultural group selection, coevolutionary processes and large-scale cooperation. *Journal of Economic Behavior & Organization, 53*, 3–35.

Henrich, J., Boyd, R., Bowles, S., Camerer, C., Fehr, E., & Gintis, H. (Eds.). (2004). *Foundations of human sociality: Economic experiments and ethnographic evidence from fifteen small-scale societies*. Oxford, U.K.: Oxford University Press.

Henrich, J., & Smith, N. (2004). Comparative experimental evidence from machiguenga, mapuche, huinca & American populations. In J. Henrich, R. Boyd, S. Bowles, C. Camerer, E. Fehr, & H. Gintis (Eds.), *Foundations of human sociality: Economic experiments and ethnographic evidence from fifteen small-scale societies* (pp. 125–167). Oxford, U.K.: Oxford University Press.

Johnson, D. D. P., Stopka, P., & Knights, S. (2003). The puzzle of human cooperation. *Nature, 421*, 911–912.

Jones, G. R., & George, J. M. (1998). The experience and evolution of trust: Implications for cooperation and teamwork. *Academy of Management Review, 23*, 531–546.

Keller, L. (2002). Marsupial sperm pairing: A case of 'sticky' green beards? *Trends in Ecology and Evolution, 17*, 113.

Keller, L., & Ross, K. G. (1998). Selfish genes: A green beard in the red fire ant. *Nature, 394*, 573–575.

Kelly, R. L. (1995). *The foraging spectrum: Diversity in hunter-gatherer lifeways*. Washington, DC: Smithsonian Institution Press.

Keser, C., & van Winden, F. (2000). Conditional cooperation and voluntary contributions to public goods. *Scandinavian Journal of Economics, 102*, 23–29.

Kramer, R. M. (1999). Trust and distrust in organizations: Emerging perspectives, enduring questions. *Annual Review of Psychology, 50*, 569–598.

Kurzban, R., DeScioli, P., & O;Brien, E. (2007). Audience effects on moralistic punishment. *Evolution and Human Behavior, 28*, 75–84.

Kurzban, R., & Houser, D. (2005). Experiments investigating cooperative types in humans: A complement to evolutionary theory and simulations. *PNAS, 102*(5), 1803–1807.

Kurzban, R., McCabe, K., Smith, V. L., & Wilson, B. J. (2001). Incremental commitment and reciprocity in a real time public goods game. *Personality and Social Psychology Bulletin, 27*, 1662–1673.

Ledyard, J. O. (1995). Public goods: A survey of experimental research. In J. H. Kagel & A. E. Roth (Eds.), *The handbook of experimental economics* (pp. 111–194). Princeton, NJ: Princeton University Press.

Masclet, D., Noussair, C., Tucker, S., & Villeval, M. (2003). Monetary and nonmonetary punishment in the voluntary contributions mechanism. *American Economic Review, 93*, 366–380.

Mealey, L., Daood, C., & Krage, M. (1996). Enhanced memory for faces of cheaters. *Ethology and Sociobiology, 17*, 119–128.

Meggitt, M. (1977). *Blood is their argument*. Palo Alto, CA: Mayfield.

Milinski, M., Semmann, D., & Krambeck, H. (2002). Reputation helps solve the "tragedy of the commons." *Nature, 415*, 424–426.

Nakamaru, M., & Levin, S. A. (2004). Spread of two linked social norms on complex interaction networks. *Journal of Theoretical Biology, 230*, 57–64.

Nowak, M. A. (2006). Five rules for the evolution of cooperation. *Science, 314*, 1560–1563.

Nowak, M. A., May, R. M., & Sigmund, K. (1995, June). The arithmetics of mutual help. *Scientific American, 272*, 50–55.

Nowak, M. A., & Sigmund, K. (1998). Evolution of indirect reciprocity by image scoring. *Nature, 393*, 573–577.

Nowak, M. A., & Sigmund, K. (2005). Evolution of indirect reciprocity. *Nature, 437*, 1291–1298.

Oda, R. (1997). Biased face recognition in the prisoner's dilemma games. *Evolution and Human Behavior, 18*, 309–315.

Olson, M. (1965). *The logic of collective action: Public goods and the theory of groups*. Cambridge, MA: Harvard University Press.

Ostrom, E. (1990). *Governing the commons: The evolution of institutions for collective action*. Cambridge, U.K.: Cambridge University Press.

Ostrom, E. (2003). Toward a behavioral theory linking trust, reciprocity and reputation. In E. Ostrom & J. Walker (Eds.), *Trust and reciprocity: Interdisciplinary lessons from experimental research* (pp. 19–79). New York: Sage.

Ostrom, E., Walker, J., & Gardner, R. (1992). Covenants with and without a sword: Self governance is possible. *American Political Science Review, 86*, 404–417.

Page, T., Putterman, L., & Unel, B. (2005). Voluntary association in public goods experiments: Reciprocity, mimicry and efficiency. *The Economic Journal, 115*, 1032–1053.

Panchanathan, K., & Boyd, R. (2003). A tale of two defectors: The importance of standing for the evolution of indirect reciprocity. *Journal of Theoretical Biology, 224*, 115–126.

Panchanathan, K., & Boyd, R. (2004). Indirect reciprocity can stabilize cooperation without the second-order free rider problem. *Nature, 432*, 499–502.

Price, M. E. (2003). Pro-community altruism and social status in a Shuar village. *Human Nature, 14*, 191–208.

Price, M. E. (2006). Monitoring, reputation, and 'greenbeard' reciprocity in a shuar work team. *Journal of Organizational Behavior, 27*, 201–219.

Price, M. E., Cosmides, L., & Tooby, J. (2002). Punitive sentiment as an anti-free rider psychological device. *Evolution and Human Behavior, 23*, 203–231.

Queller, D. C., Ponte, E., Bozzaro, S., & Strassmann, J. E. (2003). Single-gene greenbeard effects in the social amoeba *dictyostelium discoideum*. *Science, 299*, 105–106.

Richerson, P. J., & Boyd, R. (2004). *Not by genes alone: How culture transformed human evolution*. Chicago: University of Chicago Press.

Rilling, J. K., Gutman, D. A., Zeh, T. R., Pagnoni, G., Berns, G. S., & Kilts, C. D. (2002). A neural basis for social cooperation. *Neuron, 35*, 395–405.

Sheldon, K. M., Sheldon, M. S., & Osbaldiston, R. (2000). Prosocial values and group-assortation within an n-person prisoner's dilemma. *Human Nature, 11*, 387–404.

Sinervo, B., Chaine, A., Clobert, J., Calsbeek, R., Hazard, L., Lancaster, L., et al. (2006). Self-recognition, color signals, and cycles of greenbeard mutualism and altruism. *Proceedings of the National Academy of Sciences, 103*, 7372–7377.

Singer, T., Kiebel, S. J., Winston, J. S., Dolan, R. J., & Frith, C. D. (2004). Brain responses to the acquired moral status of faces. *Neuron, 41*, 653–662.

Sober, E., & Wilson, D. S. (1998). *Unto others: The evolution and psychology of unselfish behaviour.* Cambridge, MA: Harvard University Press.

Stevens, J. R., & Hauser, M. D. (2004). Why be nice? Psychological constraints on the evolution of cooperation. *Trends in Cognitive Sciences, 8*, 60–65.

Stone, V. E., Cosmides, L., Tooby, J., Kroll, N., & Knight, R. T. (2002). Selective impairment of reasoning about social exchange in a patient with bilateral limbic system damage. *Proceedings of the National Academy of Sciences, 99*, 11531–11536.

Sugiyama, L. S., Tooby, J. T., & Cosmides, L. (2002). Cross-cultural evidence of cognitive adaptations for social exchange among the Shiwiar of Ecuadorian Amazonia. *Proceedings of the National Academy of Sciences, 99*, 11537–11542.

Takezawa, M., & Price, M. E. (2006, September). *Revisiting "the evolution of reciprocity in sizable groups."* Paper presented at the 4th CEFOM Symposium 21 International "Cultural and Adaptive Bases of Human Sociality," International House of Japan, Tokyo.

Tinbergen, N. (1968). On war and peace in animals and man: An ethologist's approach to the biology of aggression. *Science, 160*, 1411–1418.

Trivers, R. L. (1971). The evolution of reciprocal altruism. *Quarterly Review of Biology, 46*, 35–57.

Trivers, R. L. (2004). Mutual benefits at all levels of life. *Science, 304*, 964–965.

Trivers, R. L. (2006). Reciprocal altruism: 30 years later. In P. M. Kappeler & C. P. van Schaik (Eds.), *Cooperation in primates and humans: Mechanisms and evolution.* New York: Springer.

Vogel, G. (2004). The evolution of the golden rule. *Science, 303*, 1128–1131.

Wedekind, C., & Milinski, M. (2000). Cooperation through image scoring in humans. *Science, 288*, 850–852.

Williams, G. C. (1966). *Adaptation and natural selection.* Princeton, NJ: Princeton University Press.

Williams, G. C. (1992). *Natural selection: Domains, levels and challenges.* Oxford, U.K.: Oxford University Press.

Williamson, O. E. (1996). *The mechanisms of governance.* New York: Oxford University Press.

Wilson, D. S. (2001). Evolutionary biology: Struggling to escape exclusively individual selection. *Quarterly Review of Biology, 76*(2), 199–205.

Wilson, D. S. (2002). *Darwin's cathedral: Evolution, religion, and the nature of society.* Chicago: University of Chicago Press.

Wilson, D. S. (2006). Human groups as adaptive units: Toward a permanent consensus. In P. Carruthers, S. Laurence, & S. Stich (Eds.), *The innate mind: Culture and cognition.* (pp. 78–90). Oxford, U.K.: Oxford University Press.

Wilson, D. S., & Sober, E. (1994). Reintroducing group selection to the human behavioural sciences. *Behavioral and Brain Sciences, 17*(4), 585–654.

Wilson, E. O. (1975). *Sociobiology: The new synthesis.* Cambridge, MA: Belknap Press.

Wilson, E. O. (2000). *Sociobiology: The new synthesis, Twenty-fifth anniversary addition.* Cambridge, MA: Belknap Press.

Yamagishi, T., Tanida, S., Mashima, R., Shimoma, E., & Kanazawa, S. (2003). You can judge a book by its cover: Evidence that cheaters may look different from cooperators. *Evolution and Human Behavior, 24*, 290–301.

Zahavi, A. (1975). Mate selection—A selection for a handicap. *Journal of Theoretical Biology, 53*, 205–214.

Zahavi, A. (1995). Altruism as handicap: The limitations of kin selection and reciprocity. *Journal of Avian Biology, 26*, 1–3.

18

Cooperation and Conflict between Kith, Kin, and Strangers
Game Theory by Domains

DOUGLAS T. KENRICK,
JILL M. SUNDIE, AND
ROBERT KURZBAN

Perhaps the majority of meaningful social interactions involve opportunities for cooperation juxtaposed with dangers of conflict. Brutus and Caesar, Jung and Freud, Lennon and McCartney all had famously productive friendships preceding their infamously nasty splits. Even the closest of relationships—those involving family members—are occasionally staging grounds for marital spats, sibling rivalries, and parent-offspring conflicts (Trivers, 1974). There are numerous historical instances of rulers, such as Edward IV of England and Selim I, Sultan of the Ottoman Empire, who ordered the executions of their own brothers. And even informal interactions between casual friends, such as an invitation to dinner or a party, involve various trade-offs, and may require deciding between a mini-betrayal and a minor self-sacrifice. Do you stick with your commitment to go to a distant coworker's birthday dinner or skip it when a better friend invites you out? More generally, how do people come to decisions about prioritizing their own immediate interests or those of their acquaintances, friends, or families?

Although evolutionary models are also premised on the harsh economic realities of a gene-centered view of behavioral decision making, advances in evolutionary research have contributed to our redefinition of what motivates "economic man." Most evolutionary models of social relationships presume that self-interest intrinsically incorporates the interests of other people via factors such as inclusive fitness and reciprocity (Buunk & Schaufeli, 1999; Kurland & Gaulin, 2005; Maynard-Smith, 1982). Evolutionary theorists have also recently been considering other recurring factors that modulate self-interest in social contexts, such as punishments and reputation costs for those who cheat on social contracts. It would be a great mistake to regard *Homo economicus* as dead (Aktipis & Kurzban, 2004). Instead, he has been dressed in more epistemologically presentable attire. Many modern evolution-informed economic models presume that people behave—with very important exceptions (e.g., Burnham & Phelan, 2000; Hagen & Hammerstein, 2006)—in ways that serve their proximate ability to survive and succeed and, ultimately, reproduce (but see Symons, 1992).

Evolutionary psychologists have elucidated the fitness consequences of a number of the decision-rules humans use to navigate social contexts, personal relationships, and the distribution of their scarce resources. While some of these rules are applied in navigating through group contexts, others are directed toward specific targets: evaluating the attractiveness of a potential mate, deciding whether one's current partner requires higher levels of mate-guarding, or dealing with a business associate who has just cheated you. To the extent that such individual decision-rules can be quantified, a game theoretic framework may provide a useful method of examining the effects of these decision-rules on strategic behavior within such human dyadic interactions. One appealing feature of game theory analyses is the ability to quantify trade-offs, self-presentations, negotiations, and plays and counter-plays of everyday life in the real world. By incorporating evolved decision rules and biases into a game theoretic framework, it may be possible to simultaneously make game theory more realistic and make evolutionary models more quantitatively precise.

Our ancestors interacted most frequently and most intimately with kin and other individuals who we would today call in-laws. Beyond that, our ancestors had the remainder of their meaningful social interactions with people they expected to see again and on whom they might very well have depended for reciprocal benefits. Both of these generalizations continue to be true of most people in the world today, and even North Americans and Europeans still have most of their meaningful interactions with either close kin or members of long-term reciprocal alliances. To accomplish important tasks that humans everywhere need to accomplish, people need other people. And reciprocal relationships still help pool risks even in some modern environments where the odds of starving to death or being attacked by predators are lower than they were in the ancestral past.

MODULARITY AND SOLUTIONS TO RECURRING SOCIAL PROBLEMS

Evolutionary theorists generally presume that the brain solves problems by executing problem-specific psychological mechanisms that were shaped by the processes of natural selection (e.g., Cosmides & Tooby, 1992; Gigerenzer & Selten, 2001). This view challenges traditional models that attempt to explain the range of human thought and behavior with the application of one or two broad and unqualified domain-general principles (such as "repeat behavior that led previously to rewards" or "maximize reproductive fitness"). The modularity assumption posits that selection processes lead to the development of efficient, specialized solutions to recurrent problems faced by organisms living in specialized niches (for a recent review, see Barrett & Kurzban, 2006). It has been argued that these specialized solutions to complex problems can be simultaneously relatively quick and fairly accurate (Gigerenzer, Todd, & the ABC Research Group, 1999).

Supporting the validity of the modularity assumption, broad-ranging evidence indicates that learning and cognition operate according to different rules and employ different neural architectures and mental subroutines to process and respond to information about words, faces, tastes, potential physical threats, and so on (Kenrick, Sadalla, & Keefe, 1998; Sherry & Schacter, 1987). Because our human ancestors were social animals who lived in small groups, decision-rules for behaviors promoting mutually beneficial social relationships would have been an important subset of the design features passed on to generations of modern humans. Selection should have favored traits that assisted in regulating cooperative behavior—striking a balance between the desire to maximize one's own benefits in the present and the need to incur costs to stay in the good graces of the other group members, thereby capitalizing on future potential benefits.

We, and other researchers, have suggested elsewhere that humans universally confront persistent problems in a set of broad social domains (e.g., Bugental, 2000; Buss, 2003; Gigerenzer, 1997; Kenrick, Li, & Butner, 2003; Sundie, Cialdini, Griskevicius, & Kenrick, 2006). The particular framework we adopt here considers six key domains of social life: forming coalitions, gaining and maintaining status, protecting oneself and valued others from threats, finding mates, maintaining romantic bonds, and caring for offspring. Our ancestors would have had to solve a set of problems within each of these domains in order to survive and reproduce. Modern humans face similar social challenges. Pursuit of such goals requires cleverly negotiating a relevant set of social relationships that naturally oscillate between cooperation and conflict, as the other parties in those relationships simultaneously pursue their own objectives.

The kinds of recurring conflict and cooperation individuals experience in their social relationships vary systematically depending on the social domain within which one is exchanging scarce resources. For example, parents caring for their children do not expect reciprocation of benefits in the same way as do friends exchanging gifts, and the rules of exchange between men and women during courtship likely differ from those between higher and lower status individuals in a social network (Clark & Mills, 1979; Fiske, 1992; Foa & Foa, 1980; Kenrick & Trost, 1989). Coalitional behaviors are more likely among kin, or individuals who have a history of sharing resources with one another—two decision rules based on well-established principles of kin selection and reciprocal altruism (Burnstein, Crandall, & Kitayama, 1994; Van Vugt & Van Lange, 2006). Evolutionary psychologists presume that such psychological mechanisms or decision-rules, though heritable, are also quite sensitive to environmental input (Kenrick, Neuberg, Zierk, & Krones, 1994; Öhman & Mineka, 2001). Many decision-rules can be conceptualized as "if-then" statements, where environmental input plays a fundamental role in determining which decision-path is chosen.

Evolutionary researchers have made significant progress in understanding human behavior through their search for various adaptive decision rules. Some of these mechanisms have been outlined in primarily qualitative terms (Kenrick, Li, et al., 2003; Kenrick, Maner, & Li, 2005; Sundie et al., 2006). We suggest next that it is possible to begin converting the qualitatively different decision-rules into more precise quantitative estimates (see also Bergstrom, 1995 and Van Lange, 1999). Those quantitative estimates can then be integrated into the study of strategic behavior using a game theoretic framework. We will consider how qualitative decision-rules may be converted into quantitative weights, which will increase in precision as research continues to illuminate the specifics of the underlying decision biases.

RECASTING THE CLASSIC PRISONER'S DILEMMA

The prisoner's dilemma is one of game theory's simplest and most widely known frameworks for analyzing strategic behavior (Rapaport & Chammah, 1965; Van Vugt & Van Lange, 2006). As depicted in Figure 18.1, the dilemma arises from a payoff structure in which, in the one-shot version, each player's best choice is to defect on his or her partner, resulting in lower benefits than each would have had if instead they had both cooperated. As depicted in the leftmost grid in Figure 18.1, the payoffs include the temptation to defect (T), a reward for cooperating if both do (R), a punishment for mutual defection (P), and a sucker's pay-off for cooperating when the partner defects (S). The prisoner's dilemma requires that $T > R > P > S$.[1] This game is one in which the Nash equilibrium (a situation in which no player can gain by changing strategy) is not Pareto optimal (such optimality requires that no player can be made better off without decreasing another player's welfare). When each player yields to the temptation to defect, their joint social welfare is lower than it would be if both cooperated. The basic logic of such models has been expanded to encompass repeated rounds of play between multiple players to help understand broader dilemmas that may contribute

---

[1] An additional constraint, $T + S < 2R$, may also be imposed.

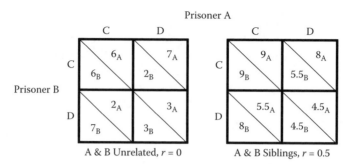

Figure 18.1 Using a standard set of payoffs in the prisoner's dilemma game played defection is the dominant strategy. The same payoffs in game played by siblings, incorporating their Hamilton's *r* of .5, lead to mutual cooperation. In the figure on the right, the payoffs become prisoner A's own plus half of his brother's.

to key social problems, including overpopulation, environmental destruction, and international conflict (e.g., Axelrod, 1984).

In this chapter, we exclusively focus on strategic behavior at the individual level, as it plays out between pairs of individuals in very different types of social relationships. In this way we can explore how evolved decision-rules change payoffs of various strategies depending on the nature of the relationship between the two individuals and the specific social context in which an interaction occurs. Applying principles grounded in evolutionary biology, we will reconsider how the outcomes of simple strategic games can change when evolved decision constraints are quantified and incorporated into the payoffs individuals face. We will consider, for example, how one's own payoffs change when inclusive fitness between the players is incorporated into the game theoretic framework.

We will reexamine this basic payoff structure as it applies in six central domains of social interaction. We will suggest that payoff structures leading to the prisoner's dilemma in interactions between strangers get transformed by decision-biases that change the psychological game when individuals interact with kin, unrelated coalition members, members of out-groups, potential mates, existing mates, and people above and below them in status hierarchies (for related ideas, see Kelley & Thibaut, 1978; Van Lange, 1999). Those transformations are qualitatively and quantitatively different within each of these relationship types and are further influenced by evolutionarily relevant variables such as the decision-maker's sex and phase of life-history.

HOW DOMAIN-SPECIFIC BIASES MIGHT ALTER COOPERATIVE TRADE-OFFS

In the previous section, we argued that human beings are equipped with qualitatively different decision-rules for thinking about their relationships within the different domains. Many of the decisions people make in their interactions with friends, relatives, acquaintances, and strangers are intrinsically linked to cooperation and conflict. Does a man give a quarter to the demanding beggar or tell him to get a job? Does a woman bang on the ceiling to get her musician neighbor to lower the volume on his bass guitar, or does she put in earplugs? Does a young man pick up the tab at the restaurant for the fifth time in a row, or ask his dating partner whether she is familiar with the concept of turn-taking? Does a wife clean the kitchen uncomplainingly, or initiate a possible marital spat about the distribution of domestic labor? Does a mother yield to her daughter's loud lobbying for a sugary treat at the market, or say "no" and risk the possibility that the situation will escalate into an embarrassingly full-blown public tantrum? To the extent that our ancestors confronted analogous interactions, one might expect that we have inherited inclinations to make these decisions in ways that kept costly conflicts to a minimum and to choose conflict over cooperation only when the estimated probabilistic benefits outweighed estimated costs. Obviously, the benefits and costs to self and other are very different in different relationships because our interests align differently with strangers, unrelated neighbors, dating partners, spouses, and blood relatives. In what follows, we consider the specific kinds of resources exchanged and some important constraints on the relative value of those resources within each social domain.

ALLIANCE FORMATION

Mutual help and sympathy are among the most powerful weapons, as they are also certainly the most noble incentives, which can be employed in fighting the battle of life. (Arabella B. Buckley, 1892, p. 301)

For most of human evolutionary history, our ancestors lived in small, highly interdependent groups (Sedikides & Skowronski, 1997). By cooperating with others, they accomplished things they could not have hoped to accomplish individually. Simply pooling unreliable resources (such as meat yielded from a hunt) with other group members, some researchers argue, could have provided insurance against starvation (Hill & Hurtado, 1996), translating ultimately into reproductive success.

There are, however, costs as well as benefits to cooperating with others: it takes time and resources to help others, and others may be motivated to take a little more than they give in return. Alliance members also directly and indirectly compete with one another for food, status, mates, and other resources (Alcock, 1993; Hill & Hurtado, 1996). How much to cooperate, and with whom, is influenced by two very powerful evolutionary principles: inclusive fitness and reciprocity. The trade-offs involved in cooperation are more favorable with other people who share our genes and with people who have established long-term mutually beneficial patterns of sharing with us.

Cooperating With Kin

From an inclusive fitness perspective (Hamilton, 1964), it should be expected that there are psychological mechanisms in place that, everything else equal, cause people to be more inclined to deliver benefits to kin than nonkin. Conversely, if your relatives exact costs on you, there are also indirect costs to them. Research with species ranging from ground squirrels to humans suggests lower thresholds for engaging in various types of cooperative behavior among neighbors who are closely related (e.g., Burnstein et al., 1994; Essock-Vitale & McGuire, 1985; Sherman, 1981).

A consideration of inclusive fitness provides the clearest and simplest example of how a prisoner's dilemma can be transformed by evolutionarily important factors. Two brothers share roughly half of their genes,[2] hence (from the gene's perspective), 100 units of benefit to one brother are worth 50 units of benefit to the other. If one takes this into account in considering the classic trade-off between cooperation and conflict depicted in Figure 18.1, cooperation becomes the dominant strategy.

This is true for brothers across a wide range of payoffs, but not all. For some payoffs (and degrees of relatedness), defection will still be the dominant strategy. The example of royal family members killing their competitors for the throne vividly illustrates that not all is cooperative within families. It is possible to precisely specify "zones" where cooperation would be a dominant strategy for brothers, but not strangers (Kenrick, Sanabria, Sundie, & Killeen, 2006).

Just as "zones of cooperation" can be calculated for brothers, they can be calculated for other relatives by incorporating appropriately different weights for grandchildren (.25 instead of .50), cousins (.125), and so on (Burnstein et al., 1994). Additional ecological precision could be added to such models by taking into account other life-history and ecological factors. For example, being

---

[2] Brothers shared approximately 50% of the genes that are free to vary within the human population.

willing to take a loss in an interaction with a sibling should theoretically be more likely if that sibling is in his or her late teens or early twenties (at the beginning of the reproductive years) compared to a sibling who is relatively younger or past reproductive age. The number of siblings would theoretically be relevant as well: A 2-year-old in a two-child family is, from a reproductive exchange perspective, worth more than the same child in a ten-child family because of the opportunity costs associated with investing in one individual when the possibility of investing in others is present. Similarly, a sibling who is in good health and who is highly attractive might also elicit less competitive rivalry than one who does not manifest cues to high reproductive potential (cf. Kurland & Gaulin, 2005).

Dyadic Alliances With Nonkin

Whereas cooperation is less contingent on past history of reciprocation among close kin, collaboration between less related individuals is linked to a history of reciprocal sharing (e.g., Essock-Vitale & McGuire, 1985; Fiske, 1992; Trivers, 1971). According to the principle of reciprocal altruism, our ancestors would have benefited from cooperating with others to the extent those others were likely to reciprocate (e.g., Axelrod & Hamilton, 1981; Trivers, 1971). If one expects to see another group member repeatedly, and one has reason to believe that this individual is trustworthy, then cooperation on any given interaction is less chancy than it would be with a stranger.

As in the case of kinship, membership in a dyadic reciprocal alliance ought to be associated with cognitive mechanisms designed, where possible, to keep the two interactants in the cooperate/ cooperate cell. Yielding to the temptation to defect by betraying another individual can undermine a long-term productive reciprocal relationship (Frank, 1988). Indeed, there is evidence that people are quite sensitive to violations of social contracts (Cosmides & Tooby, 1989, 1992). Further, there is evidence that people will occasionally be willing to take additional losses to punish defectors (Gintis, Bowles, Boyd, & Fehr, 2003). While taking losses to punish defectors might not seem advisable in a one-shot prisoner's dilemma with a stranger, it is easier to justify over the longer term (Hagen & Hammerstein, 2006). Those who are willing to punish cheaters are establishing a reputation that can serve to reduce the probability that others will try to exploit them in the future (Frank, 1988; Kurzban, DeScioli, & O'Brien, 2007).

A person's thresholds for cooperation and conflict are also likely to be influenced by group size, one's number of alternative alliance partners, and their relative frequency of interaction. For example, members of a large group may feel they have a larger pool to draw close alliance partners from. They could therefore afford to be more selective in choosing alliance partners, and more strict in enforcing the rules of exchange. However, the tolerance for free-riding may be higher when fewer good alternatives are accessible. For example, if a person has just moved to a new neighborhood, or joined a new group, he or she may be less demanding in his or her interactions with alliance partners. These are all factors that one could, in principle, quantify (i.e., counting the number of alternative partners available, the number of those regarded as members of one's inner circle, and the psychological proximity of any given alliance partner).

STATUS

Social status is a key factor in human social groups (D. E. Brown, 1989; Cummins, 1998; Eibl-Eibesfeldt, 1989; Henrich & Gil-White, 2001). Around the world, "dominant" versus "submissive" is one of the two primary dimensions on which people evaluate others (Wiggins & Broughton, 1985). Even in face-to-face interactions between complete strangers, relative status differences emerge quickly and spontaneously (Fisek & Ofshe, 1970). As Henrich and Gil-White (2001) have argued, "status" as used by social scientists is usefully separable into dominance, coercive power over others, prestige, and respect for an individual, often because of his or her skills or accomplishments.

For both sexes, there are adaptive advantages to holding high prestige and status within one's group, as both potentially increase access to resources and play important roles in the formation and maintenance of alliances. These advantages, in turn, can be leveraged to enhance one's reproductive success. Of course, striving for prestige and dominance brings concurrent costs. Establishing dominance through antagonistic encounters may be physically risky or even life threatening. Striving for prestige also requires investment of scarce resources such as the time and energy to master skills, gain knowledge, and so forth. Maintaining one's current level of status, once it is acquired, involves ongoing costs such as investing energy in competition with new challengers and eliciting resentment in underlings who do not enjoy the same benefits of status.

There is a sex-based asymmetry in the returns to status because women have a stronger preference for status when choosing mates than men do (Li & Kenrick, 2006). Dominant men, for example, can offer relatively greater protection and access to resources—both useful when caring for offspring. Consequently, males are, compared to females, more motivated to seek high levels of prestige and dominance (Hill & Hurtado, 1996; see also Sidanius & Kurzban, 2003). Men are also more likely than women to monitor their relative status within the group (Gutierres, Kenrick, & Partch, 1999). In interactions with peers, coming out on the losing side of any exchange may translate into a loss of one's perceived dominance within the group, and such losses should be of more concern and consequence for males. This might lead to systematic differences in how potential losses are weighted in decision making, with men weighting this factor more strongly than women. This pattern of results would be consistent with research indicating that males respond more aggressively when a "loss of face" is at stake (e.g., Wilson & Daly, 1985).

Like dominance, prestige can influence many different types of social interactions because high-prestige individuals can exchange their knowledge, skills, and so forth for different types of resources, both physical and social (Fiske, 1992; Haslam, 1997; Henrich & Gil-White, 2001). As Henrich and Gil-White (2001) explore in some detail, low-status individuals might be likely to defer to high-prestige individuals in many of the social "games" that are played by virtue of the benefits, either direct or as a result of externalities, generated by high-prestige people (Levine & Kurzban, 2006; Tooby & Cosmides, 1996). People of low prestige might be willing to endure costs that are difficult, but perhaps not impossible, to quantify to obtain the benefits of association with high-prestige individuals.

SELF-PROTECTION AND GROUPS

As with other primate species (Wrangham, 1987), ancestral humans frequently confronted threats from members of other groups (Baer & McEachron, 1982). Additionally, intragroup competition over status and material resources led to recurrent threats from in-group members among humans and other primate species (Daly & Wilson, 1988). Such threats often lead people to respond aggressively (e.g., Berkowitz, 1993; Dodge, Price, Bachorowski, & Newman, 1990). In addition to increasing aggressive behavior, threats also enhance affiliative motivation (Geary & Flinn, 2002; Griskevicius, Goldstein, Mortensen, Cialdini, & Kenrick, 2006; Taylor et al., 2000; Wisman & Koole, 2003). There is safety in numbers, and a threat-induced affiliation motivation can lead to the formation of larger groups (Diamond, 1997; Kenrick et al., 2003).[3] Because males were more likely to be involved in direct conflicts with other groups, men might be expected to more easily and spontaneously band together under external threat (Sidanius & Pratto, 1999; Tiger, 1969; Van Vugt & De Cremer, in press).

---

[3] We ignore here the vast literature and complications surrounding cooperation in groups (e.g., Boyd & Richerson, 2006) as it is far beyond the scope of this chapter. We simply note here that humans form groups that engage in conflict, and that this social reality can alter payoff structures in decision making in important ways.

Very generally, because coordinated, cooperative, intergroup conflict is historically (Keegan, 1993) and probably phylogenetically (Boehm, 1992) a largely male phenomenon, one might expect male "coalitional psychology" (Kurzban, Tooby, & Cosmides, 2001) and its concomitant in-group bias to be more easily activated and of greater strength than the analogous psychology in women. Consistent with this logic, Van Vugt and his colleagues (2007) found that competition with an outside group led men (more than women) to contribute in a public goods task. Conversely, we would expect that men would also be more likely to disfavor out-group members in cooperative decisions.

Depending on the availability of resources, the outcomes of out-group members may be either orthogonal to one's own (when resources are abundant) or opposed (when there is competition over scarce resources). Social psychologists have long observed that intergroup hostilities increase as resources get scarce (Hepworth & West, 1988; Hovland & Sears, 1940). Because members of powerful groups might be more likely to severely punish defections during economically harsh times, the effects of limited resources might act differently on members of numerically or politically dominant or nondominant groups. One might expect that members of dominant groups, but not members of weaker minorities, are more likely to defect on the out-group in such times. When groups are more equated in power and/or numbers, iterated interactions ought to be more likely to follow a tit-for-tat rule, especially when resources are scarce.

MATE SELECTION

Because *Homo sapiens* is a sexually reproducing species, a key task is to find a mate. Human beings have only a small number of offspring in whom they invest considerable resources; hence there is a strong evolutionary incentive to make those decisions carefully. According to the logic of parental investment theory (Trivers, 1972), human females are presumed to be generally more selective than males because females' reproductive capacities are inherently more limited. Abundant research supports this reasoning (e.g., Buss, 1989; Kenrick, Sadalla, Groth, & Trost, 1990; Kenrick, Groth, Trost, & Sadalla, 1993; Li & Kenrick, 2006; Schmitt, 2005).

Although human males are in principle capable of having a large number of offspring at low cost, most human mating occurs within the context of long-term committed relationships in which the male contributes substantial resources to his offspring. As a consequence, males are also selective, particularly if the relationship is expected to involve long-term commitment (Kenrick et al., 1990; Li & Kenrick, 2006). The two sexes, on average, contribute somewhat different resources to their offspring: females contribute relatively more physiological resources through gestation and nursing, while males contribute by providing food, protection, and so on. There are life-history differences in the ability to provide these resources, with young postpubescent females being relatively highest in reproductive resources, but males peaking in their ability to provide indirect resources much later in life. As a consequence, women tend to emphasize resource potential in choosing men as partners, and therefore choose relatively older partners, whereas males tend to place relatively more emphasis on cues to fertility and health, and to tend to prefer females in the years of peak fertility (Kenrick & Keefe, 1992; Kenrick, Gabrielidis, Keefe, & Cornelius, 1996).

During early phases of mate selection, females have potentially more to lose from choosing a partner who will not remain committed. Consistently, females have relatively higher thresholds for trusting a man's commitment than the reverse (Haselton & Buss, 2000). These considerations would lead us to expect that men and women will make different trade-offs during courtship. Men seeking long-term relationships should be willing, if not eager, to display their inclination toward sharing resources with their mate, in the interest of securing a high-quality mate for that type of reproductive relationship (see Miller, 2000, for an extended discussion). Women, on the other hand, ought to be more reticent to chance resource loss, and more willing to test the limits or a male's inclination to suffer losses on her behalf, since this willingness to share may serve as a signal of relationship commitment (Haselton & Buss, 2000).

Because mating can be usefully construed as a market (e.g., Waynforth & Dunbar, 1995), men's decisions to expend resources might be mediated by a potential partner's relative mate quality and, conversely, women's mate quality might regulate expectations regarding men's willingness to expend resources. In short, high-quality women can expect to fetch a high price on the mating market (e.g., Todd, 1997). Decision making in this domain would also be expected to vary with life-history changes in reproductive value. In the early reproductive years, the average female's reproductive value will outweigh the average male's. This equalizes later, and then reverses as the average female's reproductive value more rapidly declines (Kenrick & Keefe, 1992). Hence, young men might be willing to provision the largest percentage of their resource base to a potential long-term romantic partner. As men age, and their absolute level of resources increases, that same level of provisioning to a romantic partner would become relatively less costly.

This type of strategizing might also be affected by other factors. A man's willingness to expend resources on a female might follow an inverted U-shaped distribution, such that he is unwilling to expend resources on females he regards as below him in mate value, and perhaps also reticent to take resource risks on women who are clearly out of his range. In short, men can be expected to have adaptations that reflect a payoff structure in which maximizing one's return is not simply investing in the best possible mate, but investing where the marginal return is highest. Models of mate selection and signaling should reflect the importance of the marginal, rather than absolute, return on investments.

MATE RETENTION

Human infants are initially completely helpless, and young children are also dependent on their parents for protection, food, information, and other resources. Hence, their chance of survival is improved when resources are provisioned by both parents (Geary, 1998; Hrdy, 1999). Cross-culturally, a recurring feature of human social organization is cooperative relationships in which both parents contribute to the offspring's welfare (D. E. Brown, 1989). Thus, beyond merely attracting a mate, a key adaptive problem for both sexes is to maintain mating bonds with desirable partners (Buss & Schmitt, 1993; Flinn, 1988; Gangestad & Simpson, 2000).

Individuals involved in long-term mating relationships enter into what Clark and Mills (1979) term communal, as opposed to exchange, relations: They are more likely to share with one another without continuous explicit assessment of relative costs and benefits (Fiske, 1992; Tooby & Cosmides, 1996). For example, although a pair of college roommates might keep track of who owns which containers of milk and cereal, such detailed accounting is not (usually) found in (smoothly functioning) marriages. Long-term relationships, in this sense, cause a confluence of interests such that the welfare of one individual is, by virtue of this confluence, of benefit to the other individual (S. L. Brown & R. M. Brown, 2006; Fiske, 1992; see Tooby & Cosmides, 1996, for an extended discussion).

This confluence of interests should have profound effects on an individual trying to balance his or her own costs and benefits against those of another individual. This analysis can transform payoffs in a way similar to that described in Figure 18.2. However, mating relationships are not permanent in the same way that blood relationships are, and the degree of confluence of interests varies across mated couples in a number of ways. For example, the existence of shared children is perhaps the single strongest case of a confluence of interests. If you and I share a child, we both have an interest in that child's success. Hence, I have an interest in your continued well-being and ability to invest. Of course, these calculations can be complicated by other variables. For example, if you have other children by other partners, or other mating opportunities, then this diminishes the overlap in our interests, and should attenuate my willingness to sacrifice for you.

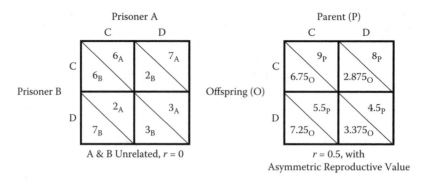

Figure 18.2 A parent and child ($r = .5$) playing the prisoner's dilemma where the parent has 25% remaining reproductive value and the child has 100% remaining reproductive value. The child's payoffs are his own plus .125 times the parent's payoffs, and the parent's payoffs are his own, plus .5 times the child's. The dominant strategy for the parent is to cooperate, while the dominant strategy for the child is to defect.

In short, whereas coincident interests are a potentially powerful force in altering computations of costs versus benefits to self and others, opportunity costs should also figure prominently in evolved psychology. To the extent that one's investment in other relationships might yield a larger marginal return, one should expect that investment should be diverted toward these higher return social opportunities. Individuals may decide to terminate a given mateship depending on factors such as existence of offspring, the availability of resources to each parent within and outside the relationship, presence and quality of same-sex interlopers on the social horizon, and the sex ratio in the local mating pool (Guttentag & Secord, 1983; Kenrick & Trost, 1987). This, in turn, should be something to which our evolved psychology should be acutely attuned, and designed to prevent. Indeed, people experience notoriously high levels of anger and jealousy when their partners terminate a courtship (Buss, 2000; Kenrick & Sheets, 1994). These emotions probably serve several functions, not the least of which is to regain a mate who is either desirable or particularly valuable because he or she is the parent of one's offspring (there is only one person with a similar fitness interest in one's offspring as oneself—the other parent). Well-designed affective and behavioral regulation systems should take these factors into account and motivate action to remain in relationships with those who share one's (genetic) interests.

PARENTAL CARE

As just noted, human social life is not governed by one overarching principle, such as "maximize one's number of offspring" (Symons, 1992). However, reproductive fitness is clearly enhanced when one expends resources to further the welfare of one's own offspring and the offspring of one's close genetic relatives. Because both men and women face inherent constraints on reproduction, the trade-offs involved in allocating scarce resources across all available genetic outlets differ depending on factors such as life-history stage and the age range of individuals involved; investment in one genetic outlet cannot be invested in another outlet, including potential future offspring (Trivers, 1972). For example, a child produced by a young parent is, in essence, in competition with that parent's yet-to-be-born offspring for resources. If a child is born to a parent approaching the end of his or her reproductive lifespan, on the other hand, all else equal, there are fewer opportunity costs for the investment in that offspring, making present investment more likely.

Parents and children are as related as full siblings ($r = .5$). However, parents tend to invest more in their children than their siblings for several reasons. For example, the marginal benefit to young individuals is likely to be greater than the marginal benefit of investment to adults, and children have greater remaining reproductive value relative to full siblings, particularly if those siblings are older and have other access to resources. As Kurland and Gaulin (2005) note:

> Due to senescence, older individuals are less efficient at converting resources into offspring. Moreover, benefits passed to younger individuals tend to exert their effects over a longer part of the life span. Thus, aid is expected to flow from older to younger individuals because the two differ in reproductive value (the age-specific expectation of future offspring; Fisher, 1958). (p. 458)

More formally, child and parent might weigh benefits delivered to the other at .5 (their genetic relatedness), but discount them according to the other's remaining reproductive value. This can transform different kinds of strategic interactions because of the differential discounting of benefits (see Figure 18.2).

In addition to remaining reproductive value, the opportunity cost of investing in any given offspring is tempered by paternity certainty. Fathers and their kin are potentially subject to the opportunity costs of mistakenly investing in a child who is not their genetic relative. Based on a review of literature on paternal certainty, Kurland and Gaulin (2005) estimate that the average rate of paternity certainty in the general population is 90%. Of course, if a man's partner displays cues that lead him to further doubt paternity, the expected discount in investment in that child may be even greater.

In addition, the fact that men can produce offspring much later in their life history leads to another asymmetry. Once past their reproductive span, women have no opportunity costs associated with future direct offspring. Men, on the other hand, who have the possibility of future offspring during most of their life span, essentially always have opportunity costs associated with investing in current offspring, including potential investment in finding an additional mate and investing in additional descendants. Very broadly, this leads to the prediction that women's psychology will be designed to invest in offspring relatively more than in men's.

Parents' willingness to invest resources in a given child should be mediated by the existence of other children and, further, parents and children are expected not to agree about the allocation of benefits across children (Trivers, 1974). Even though a child and her (full) sibling are, like the child and her parent, related to one another by $r = .5$, there is a conflict of interest regarding a parent's investment in a given child. As Trivers (1974) observed, the parent will be, all else equal, generally motivated to invest similarly in multiple children, each of whom is related 50%. However, the child is related to herself 100%, so she should be motivated to demand more than an equal share of the parents' resources, because any resources diverted to siblings are subject to an r-discounted self-benefit.

Along the same lines, because people toward the end of their lives have limited possibilities for reproduction, their opportunity cost with respect to future potential offspring approaches zero. Investment in descendants—children and grandchildren—can still enhance reproductive fitness by increasing the likelihood that those descendants' genes will be passed on to future generations. The mechanisms designed to deliver these benefits should take into account the array of alternatives (children, grandchildren) and their point in their life history, all in the interest of maximizing marginal benefits (multiplied by r, as always).

These systems should also be sensitive to parental uncertainty, an issue discussed at length by DeKay (1998; see also Laham, Gonsalkorale, & von Hippel, 2005). For a mother's mother, there are no uncertain genetic links to her grandchildren in this line, and several studies have indicated that mother's mothers are in fact the grandparents who invest most in such offspring. The father's father, on the other hand, has two uncertain links, and paternal grandfathers are generally the least investing grandparents. However, Laham et al. (2005) found that the reduction in investment by paternally linked grandparents is modified by the existence of other grandchildren. If a paternal grandmother has grandchildren by both her daughter and her son, her investment in the son's offspring is reduced.

If, however, she only has sons, then she invests relatively more in those grandchildren, presumably because there is no competition for her investment that would yield a higher marginal payoff.

DISCUSSION

Perhaps the main take-home message of our arguments is that many variables should be expected to act as inputs to decision-making systems designed to take advantage of opportunities for cooperation and to navigate the potential costs of conflicts—and each of these inputs should have an effect on downstream decision making. Careful attention to the principles of kin selection theory, opportunity costs, and ideas drawn from an understanding of how to achieve success in markets should direct investigations in domains such as friendship, protecting oneself from enemies, seeking status, searching for mates, trying to keep an existing mate, and interacting with one's offspring. The design of the decision-making apparatus in each domain can be predicted to include features that incorporate relevant variables such as individuals' sex and life-history phase, mate value, the density and sex of other players, and the distribution of resources.

The prisoner's dilemma, used here as an example, is almost certainly not the modal payoff structure in human social interactions. For each domain, it is important to develop formal structures that model the interaction in question. In mating, the prisoner's dilemma is not nearly as relevant as market mechanisms, and ideas drawn from the relevant areas of economics can be fruitfully applied in this area (Kurzban & Weeden, 2005; Todd, 1997). Behavioral game theorists have developed any number of other games, each of which might be more or less well suited to understanding a particular set of real-life circumstances (e.g., Barash, 2003; Camerer, 2003).

S. L. Brown and R. M. Brown (2006) have suggested the interesting concept of "fitness interdependence" to describe the extent to which two individuals are affected by one another's outcomes, and would therefore be expected to act altruistically toward one another (see also Fiske, 1992; Tooby & Cosmides, 1996). Although there are likely to be distinct psychological systems designed to interact with friends as opposed to relatives, it makes some sense to consider how the different mediating variables are ultimately transformed into a decision-weight that encompasses one's valuation of the other's outcomes. Identifying the particular inputs that affect decision making with kin, friends, potential mates, and so forth should be a focus of future work. Specifically, formalizing the variables—such as life-history variables—that are likely to influence these decisions is an important direction for theoretical development.

In this chapter, we have focused on dyadic interactions. We have considered a number of factors related to players external to a given dyad, such as the existence of additional siblings. When considering individual decisions, those other genetic relatives can be construed as opportunity costs for the investment of scarce resources. These costs may be factored into the net cost/benefit computations associated with the calculation of a single decisional outcome. Of course, dyadic partners make their decisions in complex social networks. How you treat neighbor A may affect how your neighbor B treats you, and how you in turn treat neighbor C, and so on (e.g., Levine & Kurzban, 2006). Game theorists have begun to consider how individual decisions unfold in complex social networks (e.g., Nowak & May, 1992; Nowak & Sigmund, 2004). These group-level dynamics are also likely to unfold in different ways as a function of the decision-rules used in different social domains (Kenrick, et al., 2003; Kenrick & Sundie, 2007). And, different decision-rules favor the emergence of different social geometries across the different social domains.

It bears reiterating the straightforward point that models are not meant to replace empirical data collection, but to assist in theory building. Models and empirical data collection can, and should, be mutually informative; with models helping to spell out the implications of theoretical assumptions, and empirical data helping to make the models more ecologically valid. Some of our reasoning in this chapter is based on existing empirical findings, but much of our speculation remains to be empirically tested.

ACKNOWLEDGMENTS

The authors thank Bram Buunk, Dennis Krebs, and Mark Schaller for their comments on an earlier draft of this chapter.

REFERENCES

Aktipis, C. A., & Kurzban, R. (2004). Is *Homo economicus* extinct? Vernon Smith, Daniel Kahneman and the evolutionary perspective. In R. Koppl (Ed.), *Advances in Austrian economics* (Vol. 7, pp. 135–153). Amsterdam: Elsevier.

Alcock, J. (1993). *Animal behavior: An evolutionary approach* (5th ed.). Sunderland, MA: Sinauer.

Axelrod, R. (1984). *The evolution of cooperation*. New York: Basic Books.

Axelrod, R., & Hamilton, W. D. (1981). The evolution of cooperation. *Science, 211*, 1390–1396.

Baer, D., & McEachron, D. L. (1982). A review of selected sociobiological principles: Application to hominid evolution I: The development of group social structures. *Journal of Social and Biological Structures, 5*, 69–90.

Barash, D. P. (2003). *The survival game: How game theory explains the biology of cooperation and competition*. New York: Times Books.

Barrett, H. C., & Kurzban, R. (2006). Modularity in cognition: Framing the debate. *Psychological Review, 113*, 628–647.

Bergstrom, T. C. (1995). On the evolution of altruistic ethical rules for siblings. *American Economic Review, 85*, 58–81.

Berkowitz, L. (1993). *Aggression*. New York: McGraw-Hill.

Boehm, C. (1992). Segmentary warfare and management of conflict: A comparison of East African chimpanzees and patrilineal-patrilocal humans. In A. Harcourt & F. B. M. de Waal (Eds.), *Coalitions and alliances in humans and other animals* (pp. 137–173). Oxford, U.K.: Oxford University Press.

Boyd, R., & Richerson, P. J. (2006). Solving the puzzle of human cooperation. In S. C. Levinson & J. Pierre (Eds.), *Evolution and culture: A Fyssen Foundation symposium* (pp. 105–132). Cambridge, MA: MIT Press.

Brown, D. E. (1989). *Human universals*. New York: McGraw-Hill.

Brown, S. L., & Brown, R. M. (2006). Selective investment theory: Recasting the functional significance of close relationships. *Psychological Inquiry, 17*, 1–29.

Buckley, A. B. (1892). *Life and her children: Gimpses of animal life*. New York: D. Appleton and Company.

Bugental, D. B. (2000). Acquisition of the algorithms of social life: A domain-based approach. *Psychological Bulletin, 126*, 187–219.

Burnham, T., & Phelan, J. (2000). *Mean genes: From sex to money to food, taming our primal instincts*. Cambridge, MA: Perseus.

Burnstein, E., Crandall, C., & Kitayama, S. (1994). Some neo-Darwinian decision rules for altruism: Weighing cues for inclusive fitness as a function of the biological importance of the decision. *Journal of Personality and Social Psychology, 67*, 773–389.

Buss, D. M. (1989). Sex differences in human mate preferences: Evolutionary hypotheses tested in 37 cultures. *Behavioral and Brain Sciences, 12*, 1–49.

Buss, D. M. (2000). *Jealousy: The dangerous passion*. New York: Free Press.

Buss, D. M. (2003). *Evolutionary psychology: The new science of mind*. Boston: Allyn & Bacon.

Buss, D. M., & Schmitt, D. P. (1993). Sexual strategies theory: An evolutionary perspective on human mating. *Psychological Review, 100*, 204–232.

Buunk, B. P., & Schaufeli, W. B. (1999). Reciprocity in interpersonal relationships: An evolutionary perspective on its importance for health and well-being. In W. Stroebe & M. Hewstone (Eds.), *European review of social psychology* (Vol. 10, pp. 259–291). London: John Wiley & Sons.

Camerer, C. F. (2003). Behavioral game theory: Experiments in strategic interaction. New York: Russell Sage Foundation.

Clark, M. S., & Mills, J. (1979). Interpersonal attraction in exchange and communal relationships. *Journal of Personality & Social Psychology, 37,* 12–24.

Cosmides, L., & Tooby, J. (1989). Evolutionary psychology and the generation of culture, Part II. Case study: A computational theory of social exchange. *Ethology & Sociobiology, 10,* 51–97.

Cosmides, L., & Tooby, J. (1992). Cognitive adaptations for social exchange. In J. Barkow, L. Cosmides, & J. Tooby (Eds.), *The adapted mind: Evolutionary psychology and the generation of culture* (pp. 163–228). New York: Oxford University Press.

Cummins, D. D. (1998). Social norms and other minds: The evolutionary roots of higher cognition. In D. D. Cummins & C. Allen (Eds.), *The evolution of mind* (pp. 30–50). New York: Oxford University Press.

Daly, M., & Wilson, M. (1988). *Homicide.* New York: Aldine deGruyter.

DeKay, T. (1998). *An evolutionary-computational approach to social cognition: Grandparental investment as a test case.* Unpublished doctoral dissertation, University of Michigan.

Diamond, J. (1997). *Guns, germs, and steel: The fates of human societies.* New York: Norton.

Dodge, K. A., Price, J. M., Bachorowski, J. A., & Newman, J. P. (1990). Hostile attributional biases in severely aggressive adolescents. *Journal of Abnormal Psychology, 99,* 385–392.

Eibl-Eibesfeldt, I. (1989). *Human ethology.* New York: Aldine deGruyter.

Essock-Vitale, S. M., & McGuire, M. T. (1985). Women's lives viewed from an evolutionary perspective. II. Patterns of helping. *Ethology and Sociobiology, 6,* 155–173.

Fisek, M. H., & Ofshe, R. (1970). The process of status evolution. *Sociometry, 33,* 327–346.

Fiske, A. P. (1992). The four elementary forms of sociality: Framework for a unified theory of social relations. *Psychological Review, 99,* 689–723.

Fisher, R. A. (1958). *The genetical theory of natural selection* (2nd ed.). New York: Dover.

Flinn, M. (1988). Mate guarding in a Caribbean village. *Ethology and Sociobiology, 9,* 1–28.

Foa, E. B., & Foa, U. G. (1980). Resource theory: Interpersonal behavior as exchange. In K. J. Gergen, M. S. Greenberg, & R. H. Willis (Eds.), *Social exchange: Advances in theory and research* (pp. 77–94). New York: Plenum Press.

Frank, R. (1988). *Passions within reason: The strategic role of the emotions.* New York: Norton.

Gangestad, S. W., & Simpson, J. A. (2000). The evolution of human mating: Trade-offs and strategic pluralism. *Behavioral and Brain Sciences, 23,* 573–644.

Geary, D. C. (1998). *Male, female: The evolution of human sex differences.* Washington, DC: American Psychological Association.

Geary, D. C., & Flinn, M. V. (2002). Sex differences in behavioral and hormonal response to social threat: Commentary on Taylor et al. (2000). *Psychological Review, 109,* 745–750.

Gigerenzer, G. (1997). The modularity of social intelligence. In A. Whiten & R. W. Byrne (Eds.), *Machiavellian intelligence II* (pp. 264–288). Cambridge, U.K.: Cambridge University Press.

Gigerenzer, G., & Selten, R. (2001). *Bounded rationality.* Cambridge, MA: MIT Press.

Gigerenzer, G., Todd, P. M., & the ABC Research Group (Eds.). (1999). *Simple heuristics that make us smart.* London: Oxford University Press.

Gintis, H., Bowles, S., Boyd, R., & Fehr, E. (2003). Explaining altruistic behavior in humans. *Evolution and Human Behavior, 24,* 153–172.

Griskevicius, V., Goldstein, N., Mortensen, C., Cialdini, R. B., & Kenrick, D. T. (2006). Going along versus going alone: When fundamental motives facilitate strategic (non)conformity. *Journal of Personality & Social Psychology, 91,* 281–294.

Gutierres, S. E., Kenrick, D. T., & Partch, J. J. (1999). Beauty, dominance, and the mating game: Contrast effects in self-assessment reflect gender differences in mate selection. *Personality and Social Psychology Bulletin, 25,* 1126–1134.

Guttentag, M., & Secord, P. F. (1983). *Too many women? The sex ratio question.* Beverly Hills, CA: Sage Publications.

Hagen, E. H., & Hammerstein, P. (2006). Game theory and human evolution: A critique of some recent interpretations of experimental games. *Theoretical Population Biology, 69,* 339–348.

Hamilton, W. D. (1964). The genetical evolution of social behavior. *Journal of Theoretical Biology, 7,* 1–52.

Haselton, M., & Buss, D. (2000). Error management theory: A new perspective on biases in cross-sex mind reading. *Journal of Personality and Social Psychology, 78,* 81–91.

Haslam, N. (1997). Four grammars for primate social relations. In J. A. Simpson & D. T. Kenrick (Eds.), *Evolutionary social psychology* (pp. 297–316). Mahwah, NJ: Erlbaum.

Henrich, J., & Gil-White, F. J. (2001). The evolution of prestige: Freely conferred status as a mechanism for enhancing the benefits of cultural transmission. *Evolution and Human Behavior, 22,* 165–196.

Hepworth, J. T., & West, S. G. (1988). Lynching and the economy: A time-series reanalysis of Hovland and Sears (1940). *Journal of Personality and Social Psychology, 55,* 239–247.

Hill, K., & Hurtado, A. M. (1996). *Ache life history.* Hawthorne, NY: Aldine deGruyter.

Hovland, C. I., & Sears, R. (1940). Minor studies in aggression: VI. Correlation of lynchings with economic indices. *Journal of Psychology, 9,* 301–310.

Hrdy, S. B. (1999). *Mother Nature: A history of mothers, infants, and natural selection.* New York: Pantheon.

Keegan, J. (1993). *A history of warfare.* New York: Alfred A. Knopf.

Kelley, H. H., & Thibaut, J. W. (1978). *Interpersonal relations: A theory of interdependence.* New York: Wiley.

Kenrick, D. T., Gabrielidis, C., Keefe, R. C., & Cornelius, J. (1996). Adolescent's age preferences for dating partners: Support for an evolutionary model of life-history strategies. *Child Development, 67,* 1499–1511.

Kenrick, D. T., Groth, G. R., Trost, M. R., & Sadalla, E. K. (1993). Integrating evolutionary and social exchange perspectives on relationships: Effects of gender, self-appraisal, and involvement level on mate selection criteria. *Journal of Personality & Social Psychology, 64,* 951–969.

Kenrick, D. T., & Keefe, R. C. (1992). Age preferences in mates reflect sex differences in reproductive strategies. *Behavioral and Brain Sciences, 15,* 75–133.

Kenrick, D. T., Li, N. P., & Butner, J. (2003). Dynamical evolutionary psychology: Individual decision rules and emergent social norms. *Psychological Review, 110,* 3–28.

Kenrick, D. T., Maner, J., & Li, N. P. (2005). Evolutionary social psychology. In D. M. Buss (Ed.), *Handbook of evolutionary psychology* (pp. 803–827). New York: Wiley.

Kenrick, D. T., Neuberg, S. L., Zierk, K., & Krones, J. (1994). Evolution and social cognition: Contrast effects as a function of sex, dominance, and physical attractiveness. *Personality & Social Psychology Bulletin, 20,* 210–217.

Kenrick, D. T., Sadalla, E. K., Groth, G., & Trost, M. R. (1990). Evolution, traits, and the stages of human courtship: Qualifying the parental investment model. *Journal of Personality, 53,* 97–116.

Kenrick, D. T., Sadalla, E. K., & Keefe, R. C. (1998). Evolutionary cognitive psychology: The missing heart of modern cognitive science. In C. Crawford & D. L. Krebs (Eds.), *Handbook of evolutionary psychology* (pp. 485–514). Hillsdale, NJ: Erlbaum.

Kenrick, D. T., Sanabria, F., Sundie, J. M., & Killeen, P. R. (2006). *When dilemmas disappear: How fitness interdependencies transform strategic games.* Unpublished manuscript.

Kenrick, D. T., & Sheets, V. (1994). Homicidal fantasies. *Ethology and Sociobiology, 14,* 231–246.

Kenrick, D. T., & Sundie, J. M. (2007). Dynamical evolutionary psychology and mathematical modeling: Quantifying the implications of qualitative biases. In S. W. Gangestad & J. A. Simpson (Eds.), *The evolution of mind: Fundamental questions and controversies.* (pp. 137–144). New York: Guilford Press.

Kenrick, D. T., & Trost, M. R. (1987). A biosocial model of relationship formation. In K. Kelley (Ed.), *Females, males and sexuality: Theories and research* (pp. 59–100). Albany, NY: SUNY Press.

Kenrick, D. T., & Trost, M. R. (1989). A reproductive exchange model of heterosexual relationships: Putting proximate economics in ultimate perspective. In C. Hendrick (Ed.), *Review of personality & social psychology* (Vol. 10, pp. 92–118). Newbury Park, CA: Sage.

Kurland, J. A., & Gaulin, S. (2005). Cooperation and conflict among kin. In D. M. Buss (Ed.), *Handbook of evolutionary psychology* (pp. 447–482). New York: Wiley.

Kurzban, R., DeScioli, P., & O'Brien, E. (2007). Audience effects on moralistic punishment. *Evolution and Human Behavior. 28,* 75–84.

Kurzban, R., Tooby, J., & Cosmides, L. (2001). Can race be erased? Coalitional computation and social categorization. *Proceedings of the National Academy of Sciences, 98,* 15387–15392.

Kurzban, R., & Weeden, J. (2005). HurryDate: Mate preferences in action. *Evolution and Human Behavior, 26,* 227–244.

Laham, S. M., Gonsalkorale, K., & von Hippel, W. (2005). Darwinian grandparenting: Preferential investment in more certain kin. *Personality & Social Psychology Bulletin, 31,* 63–72.

Levine, S. S., & Kurzban, R. (2006). Explaining clustering within and between organizations: Towards an evolutionary theory of cascading benefits. *Managerial and Decision Economics, 27,* 173–187.

Li, N. P., & Kenrick, D. T. (2006). Sex similarities and differences in preferences for short-term mates: What, whether, and why. *Journal of Personality & Social Psychology, 90,* 468–489.

Maynard-Smith, J. (1982). *Evolution and the theory of games.* Cambridge, U.K.: Cambridge University Press.

Miller, G. F. (2000). *The mating mind: How sexual choice shaped the evolution of human nature.* New York: Doubleday.

Nowak, M. A., & May, R. M. (1992). Evolutionary games and spatial chaos. *Nature, 359,* 826–829.

Nowak, M. A., & Sigmund, K. (2004). Evolutionary dynamics of biological games. *Science, 303,* 793–799.

Öhman, A., & Mineka, S. (2001). Fears, phobias, and preparedness: Toward an evolved module of fear and fear learning. *Psychological Review, 108,* 483–522.

Rapaport, A., & Chammah, A. M. (1965). *Prisoner's dilemma.* Ann Arbor: University of Michigan Press.

Schmitt, D. P. (2005). Sociosexuality from Argentina to Zimbabwe: A 48-nation study of sex, culture, and strategies of human mating. *Behavioral & Brain Sciences, 28,* 247–311.

Sedikides, C., & Skowronski, J. J. (1997). The symbolic self in evolutionary context. *Personality and Social Psychology Review, 1,* 80–102.

Sherman, P. W. (1981). Kinship, demography, and Belding's ground squirrel nepotism. *Behavioral Ecology and Sociobiology, 8,* 251–259.

Sherry, D. F., & Schacter, D. L. (1987). The evolution of multiple memory systems. *Psychological Review, 94,* 439–454.

Sidanius, J., & Kurzban, R. (2003). Evolutionary approaches to political psychology. In D. O. Sears, L. Huddy, & R. Jervis (Eds.), *Handbook of political psychology* (pp. 146–181). Oxford: Oxford University Press.

Sidanius, J., & Pratto, F. (1999). *Social dominance: An intergroup theory of social hierarchy and oppression.* New York: Cambridge University Press.

Sundie, J. M., Cialdini, R. B., Griskevicius, V., & Kenrick, D. T. (2006). Evolutionary social influence. In M. Schaller, J. Simpson, & D. T. Kenrick (Eds.), *Evolution and social psychology* (pp. 287–316). New York: Psychology Press.

Symons, D. (1992). On the use and misuse of Darwinism in the study of human behavior. In J. Barkow, L. Cosmides, & J. Tooby (Eds.), *The adapted mind: Evolutionary psychology and the generation of culture* (pp. 137–159). Oxford, U.K.: Oxford University Press.

Taylor, S. E., Klein, L. C., Lewis, B. P., Gruenwald, T. L., Gurung, R. A. R., & Updegraff, J. A. (2000). Biobehavioral responses to stress in females: Tend-and-befriend, not fight-or-flight. *Psychological Review, 107,* 411–429.

Tiger, L. (1969). *Men in groups.* New York: Random House.

Todd, P. M. (1997). Searching for the next best mate. In R. Conte, R. Hegselmann, & P. Terna (Eds.), *Simulating social phenomena* (pp. 419–436). Berlin, Germany: Springer-Verlag.

Tooby, J., & Cosmides, L. (1996). Friendship and the banker's paradox: Other pathways to the evolution of adaptations for altruism. *Proceedings of the British Academy, 88,* 119–143.

Trivers, R. L. (1971). The evolution of reciprocal altruism. *Quarterly Review of Biology, 46,* 35–37.

Trivers, R. L. (1972). Parental investment and sexual selection. In B. Campbell (Ed.), *Sexual selection and the descent of man, 1871–1971* (pp. 136–179). Chicago: Aldine.

Trivers, R. L. (1974). Parent-offspring conflict. *American Zoologist, 14,* 249–264.

Van Lange, P. (1999). The pursuit of joint outcomes and equality in outcomes: An integrative model of social value orientation. *Journal of Personality and Social Psychology, 77,* 337–349.

Van Vugt, M., De Cremer, D., & Janssen, D. P. (2007). Gender differences in the influence of intergroup competition on intragroup cooperation. *Psychological Science, 18,* 19–23.

Van Vugt, M., & Van Lange, P. A. M. (2006). The altruism puzzle: Psychological adaptations for prosocial behavior. In M. Schaller, J. A. Simpson, & D. T. Kenrick (Eds.), *Evolution and social psychology* (pp. 237–261). New York: Psychology Press.

Waynforth, D., & Dunbar, R. I. M. (1995). Conditional mate choice strategies in humans: Evidence from lonely hearts advertisements. *Behaviour, 132,* 755–779.

Wiggins, J. S., & Broughton, R. (1985). The interpersonal circle: A structural model for the integration of personality research. In R. Hogan & W. H. Jones (Eds.), *Perspectives in personality* (Vol. 1, pp. 1–48). Greenwich, CT: JAI Press.

Wilson, M., & Daly, M. (1985). Competitiveness, risk taking, and violence: The young male syndrome. *Ethology and Sociobiology, 6,* 59–73

Wisman, A., & Koole, S. L. (2003). Hiding in the crowd: Can mortality salience promote affiliation with others who oppose one's worldviews? *Journal of Personality & Social Psychology, 84,* 511–526.

Wrangham, R. (1987). The significance of African apes for reconstructing human social Evolution. In W. G. Kinzey (Ed.), *The evolution of human behavior: Primate models* (pp. 51–71). Albany, NY: SUNY Press.

19

On the Evolution of Moral Sentiments

ROBERT H. FRANK

Moral sentiments such as sympathy motivate people to engage in costly behaviors, often for no other reason than that the behaviors feel "good" or "right." When asked why they leave tips even after dining at restaurants they never expect to visit again, for example, people often respond that they do not want to feel responsible for the server's disappointment at not having received the expected reward for good service.

That people are guided by moral sentiments in such ways is a good thing from the perspective of society as a whole. However, it poses a profound challenge when viewed within Darwin's framework of evolution by natural selection. In the Darwinian framework, the selection pressures that molded the nervous system were much like those that molded eyes and muscles. Unless a specific feature assists the organism in its struggle to acquire the resources needed to survive and rear offspring, it will not be favored. Thus, in Darwinian terms, the notion that a person might feel motivated to pass up an opportunity for gain when there is no possibility of penalty is an anomaly of the first order.

Tipping on the road is just one of a long list of behaviors that are anomalous in this way. We donate anonymously to charity, we return lost wallets to their owners with the cash intact, we vote in presidential elections, and some of us risk our lives to save strangers in distress. Each of these behaviors promotes the larger interests of society. But how could the moral sentiments that motivate individuals have been forged in the crucible of natural selection, which accords primacy to individual material payoffs? In this chapter, I summarize my attempts in earlier work to answer this question (see, e.g., Frank, 1987, 1988, 2004a, 2004b, 2005; see Hirshleifer, 1987, for a closely related argument).

THE MYSTERY OF COOPERATION IN ONE-SHOT SOCIAL DILEMMAS

One of Darwin's central insights was that traits and behavioral tendencies are selected primarily for their effect on the reproductive fitness of individuals, not for how they affect the welfare of larger groups. For example, a mutation coding for larger antlers in male elk will be favored by natural selection because males carrying it are more likely to prevail in contests for access to females. However, when all males have larger antlers than before, no male enjoys greater access. And since larger antlers also make it more difficult to escape from predators, this mutation is clearly disadvantageous for male elk as a group.

Individual reproductive fitness is an increasing function not only of access to mates but also of control over material resources. That simple fact gives rise to the Darwinian presumption that all behavior is ultimately selfish. After all, individuals whose nervous systems prompted them to exploit all available opportunities for material gain should on that account be more likely than others to survive and reproduce.

Every one-shot social dilemma entails a conflict between the individual and group. In the case of tipping on the road, the best attainable outcome for the group as a whole occurs when servers provide good service and receive the prescribed tip. The tip, after all, is sufficient to compensate for the extra effort that good service requires, and the value of good service to diners generally exceeds the cost of the tip. Yet, the dominant strategy for any selfish diner is to refrain from tipping on the road. The dilemma arises because the tip comes at the end of the meal, so the server cannot alter the level of service already provided. Nor can he or she credibly threaten to retaliate by withholding good service in the future, since these particular diners will not return.

The upshot is that if diners routinely failed to tip on the road, servers in restaurants patronized mostly by out-of-town diners would eventually cease providing good service. Yet, courteous service persists in such restaurants, where observed tipping rates are essentially the same as in other restaurants (Bodvarsson & Gibson, 1994).

Moral sentiments that motivate people to tip on the road turn Darwin's fundamental insight on its head. In any one instance, the impulse to tip on the road reduces the material payoffs to the individual diner. However, because this impulse leads to pervasive tipping on the road, it leads to a better outcome for both diners and servers as a group. The question before us, then, is how impulses that promote the interests of groups at the apparent expense of individual interests could have survived the ruthless pressures of natural selection.

A SIMPLE THOUGHT EXPERIMENT

The following simple thought experiment provides a convenient framework for sketching the essence of my argument:

> You are the owner of successful local business. After careful study, you conclude that an outlet of your business would thrive in a similar city located 200 miles away. You cannot manage the outlet yourself, and the limitations of external auditing and control mechanisms will prevent you from knowing whether a hired manager has cheated you. If you could hire an honest manager, you could pay her $100,000 (twice the going rate) and still expect a net gain of $100,000 by opening the outlet. The difficulty is that any manager you hire will face powerful incentives to cheat. By managing dishonestly, she could augment her own return by $40,000, in which case you would lose $100,000 on the venture. In that event, you would have no recourse, since there would be no way to know, much less prove, that your manager had cheated you. Would you open the branch outlet?

Before you respond, let us review how conventional Darwinian analysis would portray this decision. The information given in the thought experiment is summarized in the decision tree shown in Figure 19.1. At point A, you must decide whether to open the outlet. If you do not (that is, if you take

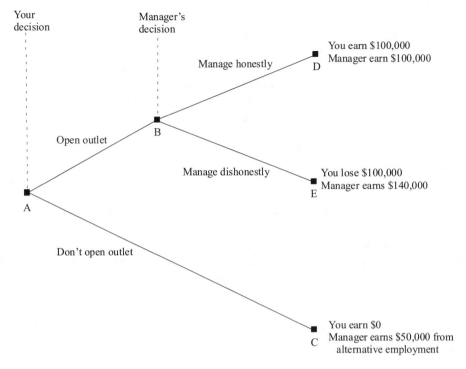

Figure 19.1 Decision tree for the outlet problem.

the bottom branch of the decision tree at A), the scenario ends at C. You neither gain nor lose any money, and the managerial candidate you failed to hire earns the going rate of $50,000 in alternative employment. If you choose instead to open the outlet (taking the top branch of the decision tree at A), the manager you hire must then decide at B whether to manage honestly. If she does so (taking the top branch at B), the scenario ends at D. You and the manager both earn $100,000 from the venture. However, if the manager takes the bottom branch at B, the scenario ends at E. By managing dishonestly, she earns $140,000 while you suffer a loss of $100,000.

The default assumption in Darwinian analysis is that you will open the outlet in the distant city only if you can reasonably expect to make money by doing so. Your task is thus to predict how the manager you hire would evaluate the choices confronting her at B. Darwinian theory conventionally assumes narrow self-interest on the part of individuals interacting with nonkin. Such a manager would choose the bottom branch at B, since that would net her a pay-off higher by $40,000 than the amount she would receive on the top branch. And because that choice results in a loss of $100,000 for you, your best bet would be not to open the outlet. After all, your pay-off at C on the bottom branch from A ($0) is better than your predicted payoff if you choose the top at A and hire a self-interested manager (–$100,000).

As just described, the outlet decision problem constitutes what the economist Thomas Schelling (1960) has called a commitment problem. If you assume that potential managers are self-interested in the narrow sense, you will not open the outlet, and this is a worse outcome for both you and the manager than if you had opened the outlet and the manager had run it honestly. If a managerial candidate could somehow commit herself to behave honestly, she would clearly want to do so.

My essential claim in *Passion Within Reason* and other earlier works was that moral sentiments like the ones described by Adam Smith (1795/1966) and David Hume (1759/1978) could be favored by natural selection, provided that certain conditions were met. In the context of the decision problem just described, the key requirement is that owners be able to identify a candidate who would manage honestly with at least a statistical threshold level of reliability. Suppose, for example, that as the owner confronting the outlet decision problem, a managerial candidate whom you believe to be honest is in fact honest with probability 0.7. Referring to the payoffs summarized in Figure 19.1, we then see that if you open the outlet, your expected payoff will be (0.7)($100,000) + (0.3)(–$100,000) = $40,000. In this example, if owners could distinguish honest individuals from dishonest ones with 70% accuracy, they would open branch outlets that would be profitable 70% of the time. An honest managerial candidate's expected payoff would be (0.7)($100,000) + (0.3)($50,000) = $85,000, while a dishonest candidate's expected payoff would be (0.7)($50,000) + (0.3)($140,000) = $77,000. Therefore, it is clear that if sufficiently accurate predictions of honest behavior could be made, someone who was predisposed not to cheat in such circumstances could survive the pressures of natural selection.

Can you think of a specific individual (not related to you by blood or marriage) who you feel at least 70% sure would manage your outlet honestly if he or she happened to be available for the assignment? Faced with this question, most people say yes. If you agree, then you accept the central premise of my argument.

The argument in brief is that a moral sentiment that moved people to incur avoidable costs can be favored by natural selection for its capacity to help solve one-shot social dilemmas, provided it satisfies two constraints: (1) those who experience the emotion in a given setting must choose differently, on the average, from those who do not; and (2) at least some people must be capable of making statistically reliable assessments of the extent to which at least some of their prospective interaction partners are influenced by the emotion.

In the specific case of sympathy, the moral sentiment emphasized most heavily by Smith (1795/1966) and Hume (1759/1978), abundant empirical evidence suggests that these requirements are met (Sally, 2000). When two people enjoy a strong sympathetic bond with one another, they seem to realize it. And, they are likely to behave cooperatively toward one another, even though they could earn more by behaving noncooperatively in situations that entail no chance of detection and punishment.

But how do you know whether someone feels sympathy for your interests? Darwin (1872/1965) wrote of the hard-wired link between emotional states in the brain and various details of involuntary facial expression and body language. Consider the crude drawing in Figure 19.2.

This drawing shows only a few details, yet people in every culture recognize even this simple abstraction as an expression of sadness, distress, sympathy, or some other closely related emotion. Most people cannot produce this expression on command (Ekman, 1985). (Sit in front of a mirror and try it!) Yet the muscles of the human face create the expression spontaneously when the relevant emotion is experienced (Darwin, 1872/1965). Suppose you stub your toe painfully, leading an acquaintance who witnesses your injury to manifest that expression immediately. Such a person is more likely to be a trustworthy trading partner than someone who reacted to the same incident without expression.

Simple facial expressions, of course, are not the only clues on which we rely, or even the most important ones. Typically, we construct character judgments over extended periods on the basis of a host of other subtle signals, many of which enter only subconscious awareness (for an extended discussion, see Sally, 2000). Based on these impressions, we choose among potential trading partners those we feel are most likely to weigh not just their own interests when deciding what to do, but our own interests as well.

MIMICRY AND A SIGNAL'S PROBLEMATIC FIRST STEP

Opportunistic individuals have an obvious incentive to mimic whatever signs we employ for identifying reliable trading partners. Selection pressure should therefore favor capacities for deception, and examples of such capacities clearly abound in human interaction. If signals of emotional

Figure 19.2 The characteristic expression of sadness, distress, or sympathy.

commitment could be mimicked perfectly and without cost, these signals would eventually cease to be useful. Over time, natural selection would mold false signals into perfect replicas of real ones, driving the capacity for signaling commitment to extinction.

But the mere observation that costless, perfect mimicry would render a signal useless does not rule out the possibility of an equilibrium that entails strategic signaling. Natural selection might be good at building a copy of a useful signal, but it might also be good at modifying an existing signal to evade mimicry. And, because the original signal often has a substantial head start in this process, it may be a difficult target. At the very least, it is a moving one. Whether attempts to mimic it could keep pace simply cannot be settled on a priori grounds.

The signal in question might also be one that others simply cannot mimic. Long, brightly colored tail feathers, for example, are thought to signal robust health in peacocks, and hence to explain why peahens exhibit a strong preference for males with such displays. Why don't males in poor health just mimic the colorful displays of their rivals? Because they cannot. The observed preference of peahens is thought to be a stable equilibrium because unhealthy males simply cannot muster the physiological resources needed to support bright displays.

Mimicry is not the only problem that must be surmounted in explaining how individuals might credibly signal their intentions to potential rivals. An even more fundamental obstacle is that natural selection cannot be forward looking. It cannot recognize, for example, that a series of mutations might eventually produce an individual able to signal its capacity to solve one-shot social dilemmas, and then favor the first costly step to that end, even though it yields no immediate benefit. It is this first step that constitutes the hurdle, because the initial appearance of a signal would have no meaning to external observers. It would thus entail costs, but no benefits. And the Darwinian rule is that a mutation must offer an *immediate* surplus of benefits over costs, or else be consigned to the evolutionary scrap heap.

How do signals ever originate, then? Essentially by accident, according to the derivation principle developed by Niko Tinbergen (1952). The constraint imposed by this principle is clearly illustrated by the example of the dung beetle. The insect gets its name because it escapes from predators by virtue of its resemblance to the fragments of dung on which it feeds. Biologists argue, however, that this advantage cannot explain how this beetle came to resemble a fragment of dung in the first place. The problem is that if we start with a species whose individuals bear not the slightest resemblance to a dung fragment, a minor mutation in the direction of a dung-like appearance would not have been of any use, since, as Stephen Jay Gould (1977, p. 104) asks, "Can there be any edge in looking 5 percent like a turd?" A mutation toward dung-like appearance will enhance fitness only if the individual's appearance *already* happened to be similar enough to a dung fragment for the mutation to have fooled the most myopic potential predator.

Thus, the initial path toward near resemblance must have been essentially a matter of chance—the result of mutations that were favored for other reasons and just happened to produce a dung-like appearance in the process. Once the resemblance crosses the recognition threshold by chance, however, natural selection can be expected to fine-tune the resemblance, in the same ruthlessly effective way it fine-tunes other useful traits.

Essentially the same logic should apply to the emergence of an observable signal of a moral emotion such as sympathy. If the *only* behavioral effect of having sympathy were to motivate cooperation in one-shot social dilemmas, the first mutants with a small measure of this emotion would have enjoyed no advantage, even if their mutation happened to be accompanied by an observable signal. By virtue of its novelty, no one would have known what the signal meant, so it could not have facilitated selective interaction among sympathetic individuals. And, since an undiscriminating tendency to cooperate entails costs, natural selection should have worked against sympathy, for the reasons just described.

If sympathy and other moral emotions were favored by natural selection in their earliest stages, they must therefore have conferred some other benefit. For example, perhaps a mutant with the capacity for sympathy was a more effective parent, which might have compensated for the initial costs of an indiscriminately sympathetic posture toward unrelated individuals. However, because people are able to discriminate between kin and nonkin, it seems unlikely that sympathy selected for just this purpose could sustain cooperation with unrelated partners in one-shot social dilemmas.

A more promising possibility is that emotions like sympathy may function as self-control devices. In a world populated by the rational, self-interested individuals assumed by economists, self-control problems would not exist. Such individuals would discount future costs and benefits at a constant exponential rate, which means that any choice that would seem best right now would also seem best in hindsight. Extensive evidence summarized by George Ainslie (1992), however, suggests that all creatures, animal and human, tend to discount future rewards not exponentially but hyperbolically. As Ainslie explains, hyperbolic discounting implies a temporary preference for "the poorer but earlier of two goals, when the poorer goal is close at hand" (pp. frontispiece). Seated before a bowl of salted cashews, for example, people often eat too many, and then later express sincere regret at having spoiled their dinners.

A similar problem confronts people who interact in a sequence of repeated social dilemmas. In such situations, Rapport and Chammah (1965), Axelrod (1984), and others have demonstrated the remarkable effectiveness of the tit-for-tat strategy—in which you cooperate in the first interaction, then in each successive interaction mimic whatever your partner did in the immediately preceding one. Note, however, that implementation of tit-for-tat entails an inherent self-control problem. By cooperating in the current round, the tit-for-tat player must incur a present cost in order to receive a potentially much larger benefit in the future. In contrast, a player who defects in the current round receives a benefit immediately, whereas the costs of that action are both delayed and uncertain. Thus, someone might realize he would come out ahead in the long run if he cooperated in the current interaction, yet find himself unable to resist the temptation to reap the immediate gains from defecting.

A person who is sympathetic toward potential trading partners is, by virtue of that concern, less likely than others to yield to temptation in the current interaction. Such a person would still find the gains from defecting attractive, but their allure would be mitigated by the prospect of the immediate aversive psychological reaction that would be triggered by defecting. For this reason, persons who experience sympathetic bonds with their trading partners would find it easier than others to implement the tit-for-tat strategy in repeated social dilemmas. To the extent that the ability to execute tit-for-tat enhances fitness, people who experienced sympathy would have fared better than those who did not, even if no observable signal of sympathy were generally recognized.[1]

But given that external markers of sympathy exist, there is every reason to expect natural selection to have refined them for signaling purposes once they become recognized. We know, for example, that individual differences in emotional responsiveness are at least weakly heritable (Bruell, 1970). If selective trustworthiness is advantageous and observable, natural selection should favor individual variants that are both more trustworthy and better able to communicate that fact to others.

Consideration of how signals of moral sentiments are likely to have emerged suggests that the difficulties confronting opportunists who attempt to mimic them may be even more formidable than might appear. Thus, if an emotion was originally selected for reasons independent of its observable symptoms, the problem confronting mimics is that by the time observable manifestations of the emotion first play any strategic signaling role, they already have a long evolutionary history. The complex and multidimensional links between specific emotions and facial expressions, eye movements, the pitch and timbre of the voice, body language, and a host of other observable details were well entrenched long before those observable markers could have begun to function as strategic signals. This is problematic because complex signals are more difficult to mimic than simple ones.

Recall that in the case of a dung beetle, a small initial mutation was unlikely to fool even the most nearsighted predator unless the beetle already happened by chance to look almost like a fragment of dung. Similarly, a small mutation in an individual in whom sympathy is not already present is unlikely to make that person more likely to be mistaken for a sympathetic person unless he or she already happened, purely by accident, to appear almost sympathetic.

Although the brain is a marvelously flexible organ, nothing in our theoretical understanding of how it functions suggests that it ought to be able to summon the complex suite of observable manifestations normally associated with an emotion when the emotion itself is not present. Skilled actors are prized for their ability to convey the emotions called for by their scripts. However, they must rehearse to perform convincingly. In everyday interactions, rehearsal is difficult, because emotional cues often arise unpredictably in real time.

In any event, the claim that specific emotions are accompanied by characteristic observable signals is not in dispute. As Charles Darwin observed and as has since been confirmed by numerous other investigators, emotional states within the brain produce characteristic suites of autonomous nervous system responses that are visible to external observers (see, e.g., Darwin, 1872/1965; Ekman, Friesen, & Ancoli, 1980; Ekman & Rosenberg, 1997; Fernandez-Dols, Sanchez, Carrera, & Ruiz-Belda, 1997). Evidence suggests that people rely on such cues when they interact with others

---

[1] Similar reasoning applies in the case of commitment problems that entail deterrence. It will often be prudent to exact revenge against an aggressor, even at considerable personal cost, when doing so would help create a reputation that will deter future aggression. Self-interested rational persons with perfect self-control would always seek revenge whenever the future reputational gains outweighed the current costs of taking action. As before, however, the gains from a tough reputation come only in the future while the costs of vengeance-seeking come now. A person may know full well that it pays to be tough, yet still be tempted to avoid the current costs of a tough response. Thus an angry person may be more likely to behave prudently than a merely prudent person who feels no anger. See Frank, 1988, chapter 3.

in social dilemmas (see Sally, 2000). Evidence also supports the claim that people are reasonably accurate in their predictions about who is likely to defect in such dilemmas. Tom Gilovich, Dennis Regan, and I (1993) found, for example, that subjects of only brief acquaintance were able to identify defectors in one-shot prisoners' dilemma games with better than twice chance accuracy.

I do not claim that character judgments are always well founded. Even close friends sometimes disappoint. Indeed, I have argued in earlier work that even if we grant the existence of reliable signals of emotional commitment, the resulting equilibrium must entail a mixed population of cooperators and defectors (Frank, 1987). In any population consisting only of cooperators, no one would be vigilant, and opportunities would thus abound for defectors. In a mixed population, cooperators can survive only by being sufficiently vigilant and skilled in their efforts to avoid good mimics. In short, mimicry is important. However, it does not always preclude strategic signaling.

CONCLUDING REMARKS

Selfishness of the sort predicted by conventional Darwinian models is in abundant supply. Yet the prospects for sustaining cooperation are not as bleak as many seem to think. Many people are willing to set aside self-interest to promote the common good.

The question of how moral sentiments that promote such behavior could have survived the ruthless pressures of natural selection has long occupied scholars in the Darwinian tradition. I have argued that the key to answering this question is to recognize that although moral sentiments promote group interests, there are also plausible conditions under which individuals who are motivated by them might enjoy advantages sufficient to offset their costs.

Thus, even if the moral emotions were unobservable by others (and hence unable to facilitate cooperation in one-shot dilemmas), they could still help people muster the patience required to reap the benefits of cooperation in repeated social dilemmas. However, if others recognize you to be a trustworthy person, there are all sorts of additional ways in which you become more valuable. If you are in business, your boss is likely to have a firm opinion about whether you would be the sort of person to manage a branch outlet honestly. It would be strongly in your interest for him or her to think that you would be. And, the best way to get your boss to think that, it appears, is to actually be an honest person.

REFERENCES

Ainslie, G. (1992). *Picoeconomics*, New York: Cambridge University Press.

Axelrod, R. (1984). *The evolution of cooperation*. New York: Basic Books.

Bodvarsson, O. B., & Gibson, W. A. (1994). Gratuities and customer appraisal of service: Evidence from Minnesota restaurants. *Journal of Socioeconomics, 23*, 287–302.

Bruell, J. (1970). Heritability of emotional behavior. In P. Black (Ed.), *Physiological correlates of emotion*. New York: Academic Press.

Darwin, C. (1872/1965). *The expression of emotions in man and animals*. Chicago: University of Chicago Press. (Original work published 1872)

Ekman, P. (1985). *Telling lies*. New York: W. W. Norton.

Ekman, P., Friesen, W.V., & Ancoli, S. (1980). Facial signs of emotional experience. *Journal of Personality and Social Psychology, 39*, 1125–1134.

Ekman, P., & Rosenberg, E. (Eds.). (1997). *What the face reveals: Basic and applied studies of spontaneous expression using the facial action coding system (FACS)*. New York: Oxford University Press.

Fernandez-Dols, J. M., Sanchez, F., Carrera, P., & Ruiz-Belda, M. A. (1997). Are spontaneous expressions and emotions linked? An experimental test of coherence. *Journal of Nonverbal Behavior, 23*, 163–177.

Frank, R. H. (1987, September). If *Homo economicus* could choose his own utility function, would he want one with a conscience? *American Economic Review, 77*, 593–604.

Frank, R. H. (1988). *Passions within reason*. New York: W. W. Norton.

Frank, R. H. (2004a). *What price the moral high ground?* Princeton, NJ: Princeton University Press.

Frank, R. H. (2004b). In defense of sincerity detection. *Rationality and Society, 16*(3), 287–305.

Frank, R. H. (2005, December). Altruists with green beards: Still kicking? *Analyse & Kritik, 27*(1), 85–96.

Frank, R. H., Gilovich, T., & Regan, D. (1993, July). The evolution of one-shot cooperation. *Ethology and Sociobiology, 14,* 247–256.

Gould, S. J. (1977). *Ever since Darwin*. New York: W. W. Norton.

Hirshleifer, J. (1987). On the emotions as guarantors of threats and promises. In J. Dupre (Ed.). *The latest on the best: Essays in evolution and optimality* (pp. 307–326). Cambridge, MA: MIT Press.

Hume, D. (1978). *A treatise of human nature*. Oxford, U.K.: Oxford University Press. (Original work published 1740)

Rapoport, A., & Chammah, A. (1965). *Prisoner's dilemma*. Ann Arbor: University of Michigan Press.

Sally, D. (2000). A general theory of sympathy, mind-reading, and social interaction, with an application to the prisoners' dilemma. *Social Science Information, 39*(4), 567–634.

Schelling, T. C. (1960). *The strategy of conflict*. New York: Oxford University Press.

Smith, A. (1966). *The theory of moral sentiments*. New York: Kelley. (Original work published 1759)

Tinbergen, N. (1952). Derived activities: their causation, biological significance, and emancipation during evolution. *Quarterly Review of Biology, 27,* 1–32.

Part VI
THE EVOLUTIONARY PSYCHOLOGY OF ANTISOCIAL BEHAVIOR AND PSYCHOPATHOLOGY

The chapters in this section examine four issues. The first chapter examines theory and research that indicates that stepchildren are, on average, treated less well than biological offspring are. The authors ask why critiques of the "Cinderella effect" have been so heated and irrational. The second chapter examines the evolved sources of prejudice and conflict between groups. The third and fourth chapters offer evolutionary explanations for two types of brain mechanisms—those that pertain to social intelligence and those that pertain to mechanical intelligence—and use these explanations to account for sex differences in cognitive functioning and pathological conditions such as autism and paranoid psychosis. The final chapter in this section explains how a Darwinian perspective gives rise to a radically different view of mental illness from those harbored by most practitioners.

20

Is the "Cinderella Effect" Controversial?
A Case Study of Evolution-Minded Research and Critiques Thereof

MARTIN DALY AND MARGO WILSON

Skepticism is a useful faculty for any scientist, and one that the social sciences afford their practitioners abundant opportunities to exercise. However, the work of evolutionary psychologists has elicited more than its share of skepticism, for reasons that seem to have little to do with the quality of either the theorizing that motivated the researchers' hypotheses or their evidence. An example is provided by critical reactions to our own research on the "Cinderella effect."

The phenomenon at issue is parental discrimination against stepchildren, relative to how parents treat their birth children. It is manifest both in reduced levels of investment in stepchildren and in elevated rates of mistreatment, up to the extreme of lethal abuse. Given the ubiquity of abused stepchildren in folklore and the pervasive negative stereotyping of stepparents (e.g., Fine, 1986), any child-abuse researcher might have wondered whether steprelationship is a genuine risk factor, but in fact, those whose imaginations were uninformed by Darwinism never thought to ask. We conducted the first comparison of abuse rates in stepfamilies versus intact birth families, and the difference turned out to be large (Wilson, Daly, & Weghorst, 1980).

Abundant confirmatory research has followed, such that the disproportionate victimization of stepchildren is now the most extensively documented generalization in the family violence literature. The establishment of this epidemiological fact has of course raised further questions, such as what explains variability in the magnitude of Cinderella effects between maltreatment types and locales, and whether the individual-level predictors of abuse are the same for fathers, mothers, stepfathers, and stepmothers. Unfortunately, progress on these important issues has been hindered

383

by a relentless distraction: the manufacture of "controversy" about whether Cinderella effects exist at all. We suspect that the reason for this nay-saying resides largely, though not entirely, in antipathy to the Darwinian worldview and/or its application to the study of *Homo sapiens*, but before getting into that, we should explain our rationale for investigating this issue and review some relevant evidence.

Why would a Darwinian hypothesize that stepchildren might be discriminated against? Hamilton's (1964) inclusive fitness theory suggests that the social inclinations of organisms can be understood as "nepotistic": because natural selection favors that which promotes the proliferation of a focal individual's genes in competition with their alleles, it favors actions that contribute to the production, well-being, and eventual reproduction of the actor's genetic relatives. If the psychological underpinnings of parental care have evolved by natural selection, we may thus anticipate that parental feeling and action will not typically be elicited by just any conspecific juvenile. Instead, care-providing animals may be expected to care selectively for young who are (a) their own genetic offspring, and (b) able to convert that care into improved prospects for survival and reproduction. This is the kernel of the theory of *discriminative parental solicitude*, which (notwithstanding some interesting twists and *caveats*) has been abundantly verified in a broad range of care-giving species (Clutton-Brock, 1991; Daly & Wilson, 1980, 1988a, 1995).

From an evolutionary perspective, care of young other than the caretaker's own requires explanation. In nonhuman animals, such adoptions can usually be understood as failures of discrimination, either because encounters with unrelated conspecific young were not regular features of the species' environment of evolutionary adaptedness ("EEA"; e.g., Birkhead, 1978) or because that EEA was characterized by an "evolutionary arms race" between discriminative parents and those (of the same or other species) who could gain fitness by overcoming parents' evolved defenses and parasitizing their efforts (e.g., Davies & Brooke, 1991; Yom-Tov, 1980).

Even before Hamilton, astute animal behaviorists had twigged both the Darwinian rationale for expecting parents to care selectively for their own young and the idea that exceptions to this rule warrant EEA-based explanations. Here, for example, is Lack (1943) on the subject:

> The comparative failure of the gull to recognize its eggs and the robin to recognize its young is related to the ways of life of the two species. There is considerable survival value to the robin but none to the gull in detecting egg-substitutes, since the robin is parasitized by the cuckoo, but in nature strange egg-like objects are unlikely to get into the gull's nest, and it does not usually matter if they do. On the other hand, while owing to the territorial system young robins rarely come into contact with the young of another pair, this frequently happens to young gulls in the crowded gullery, hence there is considerable survival value to the gull but not the robin in distinguishing its own young. (pp. 92–93)[1]

In the human case, adoption by unrelated persons is a recent cultural invention rather than a recurrent aspect of ancestral environments, and it was probably not a significant feature of the human EEA (see Silk, 1990). However, stepparenting is cross-culturally ubiquitous and almost certainly ancient. It is furthermore not peculiar to human beings, and its distribution in the animal kingdom suggests a reason for its existence: helping raise a new mate's young of prior unions is a component of "mating effort" in species in which suitable mates are scarce and couples often stay together for more than a single breeding attempt (Rohwer, Herron, & Daly, 1999). Thus, pseudoparental care of a predecessor's offspring can be favored by selection.

However, although stepparental investment is not, after all, an evolutionary anomaly, a stepchild must rarely have been as valuable to a stepparent's expected fitness as a child of one's own

---

[1] Lack was clearly aware that the issue is not the literal "survival" of the behaving organism, but the persistence of the trait (parental discrimination in this case) and its heritable basis over generations. "Survival value" is, in this passage, a euphemism for selective advantage.

would be, and we may therefore anticipate that stepparents will not, in general, feel such whole-hearted, self-sacrificial love for their wards as genetic parents so often do. It is on these grounds that we hypothesized, many years ago, that all sorts of abuse and exploitation would occur at higher rates in steprelationships than in genetic parent-child relationships, and that differences between family types would persist when possible confounds such as socio-economic status were controlled (Daly & Wilson, 1980, 1998). Note that this is a "by-product" hypothesis: discriminative parental solicitude is the hypothesized adaptation, not child abuse. It is implausible that abusing or killing stepchildren would have promoted assailants' fitness in the human EEA, but a general preference for their own offspring surely would have.

THE EVIDENCE

Fatal batterings of small children exhibit differences of the greatest magnitude: in several countries, stepparents beat very young children to death at per capita rates more than 100 times higher than do genetic parents. The most thorough analyses are from Canada, where data in a national archive of all homicides known to police indicate that children under 5 years of age were beaten to death by their putative genetic fathers at a rate of 2.6 deaths per million child-years at risk (residing with their fathers) in 1974–1990, while the corresponding rate for stepfathers was over 120 times higher at 321.6 (Daly & Wilson, 2001). Note that because few small children *have* stepfathers, this rate differential does not, in itself, convey anything about the absolute numbers of victims; what these rates represent are 74 fatal batterings by genetic fathers in 28.3 million child-years at risk, and 55 by stepfathers in 0.17 million child-years at risk.

Fully comparable estimates have not been made elsewhere, but it is clear that this immense risk differential is not peculiar to Canada. In England and Wales, for example, 117 children under 5 years of age were beaten to death by putative genetic fathers and 103 by stepfathers in 1977–1990 (Daly & Wilson, 1994); as in Canada, fewer than 1% of age-matched British children dwelt with stepfathers and over 90% with putative genetic fathers, and so, as in Canada, the difference in per capita rates of such fatal assaults is well over 100-fold. Australian data indicate an even larger Cinderella effect. Wallace (1986) reported that perpetrators of fatal baby battering in New South Wales in 1968–1981 included 11 putative genetic fathers and 18 stepfathers, although the victims' median age was only 12 months. Strang (1996) reported that comparable cases for the entire country in 1989–1993 included 11 children killed by putative genetic fathers and 12 by stepfathers, and the median victim in these cases was even younger. For both samples, less than 0.5% of a random sample of same-age children from the general population would be expected to have had a stepfather, according to *Australian Family Characteristics Survey* data, and the estimated relative risk from stepfathers versus genetic fathers exceeds 300-fold.

There are no high-quality national data on fatal batterings in the United States, but the available evidence implies a similar situation. Weekes-Shackelford and Shackelford (2004) used the FBI's *Supplemetary Homicide Reports* (SHR) to estimate that stepfathers beat children under 5 years old to death at a rate of 55.9 per million children at risk per annum versus 5.6 by genetic fathers. A 10-fold risk differential, albeit substantial, is surprisingly low in light of the Canadian, British and Australian data, but the true figure is surely much higher. The SHR database restricts the stepparent code to persons in registered marriages, whereas genetic fathers are coded as "fathers" regardless of marital status, so the comparison is one of married stepfathers versus married *plus* unmarried genetic fathers; moreover, 13 boys under 5 years of age who were beaten to death by adult men were miscoded in the SHR as their killers' stepfathers rather than stepsons and were therefore omitted from the estimates. Most importantly, there is direct evidence that Weekes-Shackelford and Shackelford's 10-fold estimate of excess risk is low. Wilson et al. (1980) analyzed child-abuse data from jurisdictions representing about half the U.S. population, and found 279 cases of "fatal physical abuse" (a broader category than lethal battering) in 1976; 43% of the victims (whose median age was under 2 years) dwelt with stepparents, and these data in combination with population surveys suggest that young stepchildren incurred such mortality at about 100 times the rate for those living with two genetic parents (Daly & Wilson, 1988b). Other more localized studies likewise imply a very large Cinderella effect among murdered U.S. toddlers (e.g., Hicks & Gaughan, 1995; Lucas et al., 2002; Lyman et al., 2003; Stiffman, Schnitzer, Adam, Kruse, & Ewigman, 2002).

Swedish data indicate a smaller, but substantial, Cinderella effect for parental homicides *in toto* (i.e., not just fatal batterings). Temrin, Buchmayer, and Enquist (2000) initially reported that there was no excess risk to Swedish stepchildren, but this conclusion was based on an analytical error: rates were estimated relative to a population at large that was much older than the victims were. When the analysis was done correctly, toddlers were found to have been killed by genetic parents at a rate of 3.8 per million coresiding parent-child dyads per annum, while the corresponding rate for stepparents was 31.7 (Daly & Wilson, 2001). Because these estimates include all parental and stepparental killings, many of which have different typologies and risk factors than fatal batterings, they are not strictly comparable to the Canadian, British, and Australian numbers previously discussed, but they suggest that the magnitude of Cinderella effects may vary considerably across countries (see also Temrin, Nordlund, & Sterner, 2004).

How and why Cinderella effects vary in magnitude are important questions that can only be answered by cross-national research that differentiates homicide typologies. A fatal battering is very different, for example, from a murder-suicide by a depressed parent, who may construe killing her children as a "rescue," and both Canadian and British stepparents are overrepresented as killers to a much lesser extent in murder-suicides and family massacres than in fatal batterings (Daly & Wilson, 1994; Wilson, Daly, & Daniele, 1995). In regard to the specific case of Sweden, Daly and Wilson (2001, p. 294) speculate that "it may well be the case that the modern Swedish welfare state provides a social climate in which stepparents do not experience, and thus do not resent, heavy pseudoparental obligation." Whether social policy indeed has such effects on rates of family violence is a crucial question for future research.

Evidence for Cinderella effects in nonlethal abuse is even more extensive. One kind of evidence comes from case data collected by child protection agencies, in which stepfamily households and stepparent perpetrators are greatly overrepresented relative to their prevalence in the population at large (e.g., Craissati & McClurg, 1996; Creighton, 1985; Creighton & Noyes, 1989; Cyr, Wright, McDuff, & Perron, 2002; Daly & Wilson, 1985; Gordon, 1989; Gordon & Creighton, 1988; Klevens, Bayón, & Sierra, 2000; Rodney, 1999; Sirles & Franke, 1989; Trocmé et al., 2001; Wilson et al., 1980). Another source of evidence is victimization surveys, from which comparisons can be made between the responses of those who live or formerly lived with stepparents and those raised by genetic parents; the former routinely report much higher rates of both physical and sexual abuse (e.g., Kim & Ko, 1990; Russell, 1984; Sariola & Uutela, 1996). Surveys of runaway youth combine the features of the criterion case study and the victimization survey, and provide further evidence: a very large proportion of runaway and homeless adolescents report that they have fled stepfamilies in which they were subject to abuse (e.g., Powers, Eckenrode, & Jaklitsch, 1990; Tyler & Cauce, 2002).

Are Cinderella Effects By-Products of Other Risk Factors Associated With Stepparenthood?

The fact that stepparents abuse and kill children at much higher *per capita* rates than genetic parents does not necessarily implicate the steprelationship as a causal factor. It could instead be correlated (confounded) with some other factor of more direct relevance. One obvious possibility is socioeconomic status: perhaps the stresses of poverty make the poor especially likely both to abuse their children and to divorce and remarry, making steprelationship an incidental correlate of abuse. This initially plausible hypothesis has been tested and rejected with respect to Cinderella effects in Canada and the United States, where poverty is indeed a risk factor for child maltreatment but is weakly or not at all associated with steprelationship, with the result that having a stepparent and being poor are more or less independent, additive predictors of the risk that a child will be abused (Daly & Wilson, 1985; Wilson & Daly, 1987; Wilson, Daly, & Weghorst, 1980).

Other confound hypotheses that have been tested and rejected are that differences between stepparent and genetic parent families might be by-products of differences in parental age or family size; such differences are in fact small and make negligible contributions to Cinderella effects (e.g., Daly & Wilson, 1985). A final confound hypothesis is that the effect is a by-product of the traits of those who become stepparents: in principle, the population of remarried adults might include disproportionate numbers of violent people, elevating victimization rates for those living in remarriages regardless of relationship. However, although those who become stepparents may indeed be atypical of parents in general, one fact speaks against the idea that this could account for Cinderella effects: abusive stepparents typically spare their own children. In a U.S. study of abusive families, for example, only the stepchildren were abused in every 1 of 10 households containing both stepchildren and children of the current marital union (Lightcap, Kurland, & Burgess, 1982); similarly, in Canada, only the stepchildren were abused in 9 of 10 such families in one study (Daly & Wilson, 1985), and in 19 of 22 in another (Rodney, 1999). This tendency for stepchildren to be targeted is especially striking in light of two additional facts: (1) when child abuse is detected, it is often found that all children in the home have been victimized, and (2) an abused stepchild is almost always the eldest child in the home, whereas the general (albeit slight) tendency in genetic-children-only families is for the youngest to be the most frequent victims (Rodney, 1999).

Stepfathers or "Mothers' Boyfriends"?

Here and in our research papers, we call coresiding partners of genetic parents "stepparents" regardless of marital registration. This raises the question of whether Cinderella effects are due primarily, or even solely, to abuse by *de facto* stepparents. The answer is that such effects are large regardless of marital registration.

Both registered-marriage stepfathers and *de facto* stepfathers (also called "common-law stepfathers," "mothers' boyfriends," "cohabitees," and, in older literature, "paramours") are overrepresented as abusers in many of the studies previously cited. Weekes-Shackelford and Shackelford (2004) analyzed U.S. homicides using a database that restricts "stepparent" to persons in registered marriages and found large Cinderella effects even though the comparison group of "parents" included both the married and the unmarried. Creighton and Noyes (1989) estimated rates of child abuse by married stepfathers versus mothers' cohabitees in Britain, and actually found the former to be significantly higher than the latter, a unique result that is likely to prove exceptional.

The most thorough examination of the simultaneous relevance of steprelationship and marital registration is that conducted by Daly and Wilson (2001) with respect to fatal batterings in Canada. What they found was that both steprelationship and common-law status were strong predictors of homicide risk, and that neither variable's influence could be explained away as an artifact of the other's. In other words, stepfathers were greatly overrepresented as killers within both registered and *de facto* unions considered separately, and *de facto* fathers were greatly overrepresented within both genetic and stepfathers considered separately.

Stepparents or Stepfathers?

Many of the analyses previously discussed contrast stepfathers versus (putative) genetic fathers, but this cannot be taken to mean that excess risk of abuse derives only from male stepparents. Stepmothers are often omitted from the data presentation only because small children reside with them so infrequently that in all but the largest databases, the cases are few and any estimate of abuse rates would have very wide confidence intervals.

Although the evidence on this point is limited, it is consistent in indicating that excess risk from stepmothers (relative to genetic mothers) is roughly on the same order as excess risk from stepfathers (relative to genetic fathers). In an interview study of Korean schoolchildren, for example, Kim and Ko (1990) reported identical rates of child beating in stepmother and stepfather households, both far in excess of the rate in two-genetic-parent homes. More substantial evidence comes from large child-abuse databases such as those analyzed by Daly and Wilson (1981) and Creighton and Noyes (1989). Both studies included large numbers of stepmother cases and provided evidence that rates of physical abuse in stepmother and stepfather households are roughly similar and far in excess of those in two-genetic-parent households. Stepmothers are also substantially and significantly more likely to kill young children than genetic mothers according to the analyses of U.S. data by Weekes-Shackelford and Shackelford (2004), despite the facts that (1) as with stepfathers, the code "stepmother" was restricted to those in registered marriages, and (2) the genetic mother cases included neonaticides, a distinct category of homicides that is sometimes quite numerous. Finally, stepmother households tend to be even more extremely overrepresented than stepfather households among adolescent runaways who say they are fleeing abusive homes.

Mundane (Nonabusive) Discrimination Against Stepchildren

It is important to stress that although stepchildren incur elevated rates of abuse and homicide, these dire outcomes are by no means typical. Many, perhaps most, stepparents make positive contributions to the well-being of their stepchildren, and most stepparents and stepchildren evaluate their relationships at least somewhat positively. Nevertheless, steprelationships are difficult, and those who make it their business to help stepfamilies in distress are unanimous in cautioning that it is a mistake to expect that a stepparent-stepchild relationship is, or will with time become, psychologically equivalent to a birthparent-child relationship (e.g., Johnson, 1980; Turnbull & Turnbull, 1983). Research tells the same story. Duberman (1975), for example, interviewed a select sample of well-established, "successful," middle-class, registered-marriage U.S. stepfamilies, and reported that only 53% of the stepfathers and 25% of the stepmothers felt able to say that they had any "parental feeling" (much less love) for their stepchildren. There are literally hundreds of self-help manuals for stepfamily members, with a single focus: how to cope with the characteristic conflicts of stepfamily life.

To an evolutionist, these facts are unsurprising. Becoming a stepparent may be a tolerable price to pay for a desired mate, but how much will then be invested in stepchildren remains negotiable. The extent to which a couple's combined resources will be devoted to such children is therefore likely to be a source of persistent conflict, an expectation that is abundantly confirmed by studies of marital discord (see Daly & Wilson, 1996; Wilson & Daly, 2001, 2004). Children of former unions enter into (re)marriage negotiations as costs, not benefits (e.g., White & Booth, 1985), and their presence reduces the custodial parent's value on the marriage market. Moreover, children of former unions increase the marital-duration-specific probability of divorce, whereas children of the present union reduce it (Becker, Landes, & Michael, 1977; Hall & Zhao, 1995). Having children of former unions also elevates the risk that wives will be assaulted (Daly, Singh & Wilson, 1993) and killed (Campbell et al., 2003; Daly, Wiseman & Wilson, 1997).

In light of the theoretical ideas that we espoused at the beginning of this review and facts like those reviewed above, we long ago proposed that violence against stepchildren is best understood as the atypical and extreme "tip of the iceberg" of a more ubiquitous discrimination (Daly & Wilson, 1980). Recent research in diverse disciplines has now confirmed this proposal. Econometric analyses of large data bases such as the U.S. *Panel Study of Income Dynamics* provide one sort of evidence: controlling for family income, stepchildren receive reduced investment in the form of support for higher education, routine medical and dental care, and even food (e.g., Case, Lin, & McLanahan, 2000; Case & Paxson, 2001; Zvoch, 1999). Surveys that ask directly about parental support tell the same story: according to both the parents and the children, stepparents withhold investment relative to genetic parents (e.g., Anderson, Kaplan, Lam & Lancaster, 1999; Anderson, Kaplan, & Lancaster, 1999; White, 1994). Also of interest in this context is Ferri's (1984) finding that both the mothers and the stepfathers in British stepfamilies express low aspirations for the children's education, lower even than those of single mothers of lesser means.

Other evidence comes from anthropological studies using observational sampling methods. In one study of Trinidadian villagers, Flinn (1988) found that stepfathers spent significantly less time with their children than genetic fathers, and that a significantly higher proportion of their interactions were "agonistic." In another such study of Hadza hunter-gatherers in Tanzania, Marlowe (1999) reported that although stepfathers baby sit their stepchildren, they are unlike genetic fathers in their behavior toward them; for example, they never play with them. Stepchildren also suffer elevated rates of accidental injury, both lethal and nonlethal, apparently because they are less assiduously monitored and protected (e.g., Fergusson, Fleming, & O'Neil, 1972; Tooley, Karakis, Stokes, & Ozanne-Smith, 2006; Wadsworth et al., 1983), and they suffer elevated mortality in general (e.g., Hill & Kaplan, 1988; Voland, 1988).

In view of all these factors, it is no surprise that stepchildren find their home lives stressful. Many studies have reported that they leave home at a substantially younger age than children from intact birth families (e.g., Aquilino, 1991; Davis & Daly, 1997; Kiernan, 1992; White & Booth, 1985), and not only do they leave earlier, but they are also far more likely to cite family conflict as the reason (Kiernan, 1992). More direct evidence of the stress associated with being a stepchild comes from a remarkable long-term study of child health in Dominica, where stepchildren exhibit reduced growth (Flinn, Leone, & Quinlan, 1999) and have chronically higher circulating levels of the stress hormone cortisol (Flinn & England, 1995; Flinn, Quinlan, Decker, Turner, & England, 1996) than their age mates living with only their genetic parents under similar material circumstances in the same village.

THE CONTROVERSY

Despite the immense body of consistent evidence, dismissals of the Cinderella effect persist, even in refereed journals. Three published studies, in particular, have been packaged by their authors as failures to replicate our results, and despite obvious flaws, each of the three has been enthusiastically cited by skeptics.

In the first of the three, Gelles and Harrop (1991) estimated rates at which U.S. stepparents and genetic parents assault children on the basis of disclosures to telephone interviewers, who called and asked respondents a series of questions such as whether they had slapped certain family members (considered one by one) within the last year, had punched them, had used a knife or gun on them, and so forth, when they had a disagreement or were angry with them. Unsurprisingly, the 117 stepparents who agreed to be interviewed were no more likely to say they had assaulted children under their care than were genetic parents. Never questioning the validity of such data, Gelles and Harrop assert that because their study was based on a "large nationally representative sample," it constitutes the first test of differential abuse rates "that has met the normal standards of social scientific evidence." Sadly, this may be so, but there are obvious grounds for doubting whether (1) self-selection for interview was unbiased with respect to the relevant behavior, and (2) the telephone interviewees spoke the truth. In the latter regard, it is noteworthy that in another interview study, U.S. stepparents *did* admit to striking the children substantially more often than genetic parents when the question was framed with a defensible rationale of discipline rather than with respect to being angry (Hashima & Amato, 1994).

The second alleged counterdemonstration is a paper by Malkin and Lamb (1994), who analyzed data on U.S. child-abuse reports and concluded that "biological parents were more rather than less likely than nonbiological parents to abuse severely and to kill rather than cause major physical injuries to their children" (p. 129). Curiously, however, these authors presented only cross-tabulations within the abuse cases (hence the convoluted and confusing double "rather than" construction quoted above), and made no estimates of abuse *rates* at the hands of stepparents or genetic parents. The analyses entailed no failure to replicate prior findings because no prior paper had ever presented such an (uninformative) analysis. In fact, in the data archive that Malkin and Lamb analyzed, *every* form of abuse was perpetrated at massively higher rates by stepparents than by genetic parents, and yet this study has been repeatedly cited as proving the converse.

The third alleged failure to replicate was provided by Temrin, Buchmayer, & Enquist (2000) who analyzed Swedish national data on child homicide victimization and summarized their findings as follows: "In contrast to the Canadian data, children in Sweden living with a step-parent were not at an increased risk compared with children living together with two parents to whom they were genetically related. In addition, there were no other indications that step-parents are overrepresented as offenders" (abstract). As we have already mentioned, however, Temrin and his collaborators computed their homicide rates without regard to the fact that the proportion of children who reside with a stepparent is near zero at birth and increases steadily with age, and their erroneous affirmation of the null hypothesis derives from this oversight. Their data, like Malkin and Lamb's (1994), actually exhibit a large Cinderella effect (Daly & Wilson, 2001).

Documentation of a local exception to the Cinderella effect could be illuminating, but these studies deliver much less than that. Remarkably, however, their authors claim to have delivered much more: Each of the three studies was touted not simply as a local null result, showing that the Cinderella effect is of limited generality, but as reason to doubt that it exists at all, anywhere. Gelles and Harrop (1991) assert that all prior studies are biased by their reliance on "official report data," and that only their telephone survey can be considered free of bias. Malkin and Lamb (1994) subtitle their paper "a test of sociobiological theory" (needless to say, the "theory" fails the "test"); maintain that their results constitute a failure to replicate ours (they do not); and conclude vaguely that our findings might result from some unspecified artifact. Temrin and colleagues (2000) subtitle their paper "new data contradict evolutionary predictions," and write "Daly & Wilson have found an overrepresentation of stepfathers in studies of child abuse in North America. Confounding variables are, however, at hand and have not been thoroughly investigated" (p. 945). The intent is clearly to instill doubt that steprelationship has been persuasively linked to child abuse anywhere, but although we are glad to agree that hypotheses about possible confounds should be investigated more "thoroughly," Temrin et al.'s remarks are deceptive: They present no evidence of confounds (merely suggesting that psychiatric illness and drug abuse might be prevalent in stepfamilies); neglect to mention that the obvious confound hypotheses were tested and rejected in papers that they cite; and ignore the fact that confounds with family type cannot explain why abusive stepparents usually spare their own children selectively, as previously discussed.

The structure of these arguments appears to be motivated by something other than a humble search for the truth. Gelles and Harrop's passionate defense of their survey data is understandable when one realizes that Gelles's stature as a leading family violence researcher was built on such surveys and that their validity was already under attack from other quarters, especially feminists (see Dobash, Dobash, Wilson, & Daly, 1992). However, the Malkin and Lamb (1994) and Temrin and colleagues subtitles and discussion sections suggest another agenda: these authors evidently believe that a sociobiological or evolutionary approach provides a unique, falsifiable prediction that can be pitted against alternatives such as "culture." In reality, of course, culture is not an alternative to evolution, and there is no single privileged "evolutionary prediction" in a case such as this. If the data were actually to contradict some *particular* model of the evolved human psyche, what would be required is a *better* model of the evolved human psyche.

Could Cinderella Effects Be Artifacts of Biased Reporting?

Gelles and Harrop (1991) raise one point that deserves serious consideration: to what extent might Cinderella effects be artifacts of biased detection or recording, such that stepparental abuse is more likely than comparable acts by genetic parents to end up in official records? It is precisely this issue that initially led us to shift focus from child abuse in general to lethal abuse, on the presumption that the most extreme cases should be relatively immune to such biases, and our general finding has been that the overrepresentation of stepparents as perpetrators is actually higher in child homicide cases than in nonlethal abuse cases, just the opposite of what one would expect if Cinderella effects were mere artifacts of biased recording.

Gelles (1991) has conceded that the Cinderella effect is real and large in the case of homicide, while clinging to the view that his telephone survey data are valid and that Cinderella effects in nonlethal abuse must therefore be artifacts of biased reporting. More recently, this idea has been taken up and extended even to lethal abuse by a philosopher, David Buller (2005a, 2005b), as part of a vehement, mendacious general attack on evolutionary psychology that has garnered considerable attention, much of it positive. According to Buller (2005b, p. 282; emphasis in original), "*all* of the evidence cited in support" of Cinderella effects can be explained as being products of a reporting bias, and he argues his case at length. What the papers Buller cites in support of this conjecture actually contain is very different from what he says; however, before going into those details, it is first worth noting how big this imagined bias would have to be.

Recall that Daly and Wilson (2001) estimated rates of fatal batterings of Canadian children under 5 years of age in 1974–1990 at 2.6 deaths per million child-years at risk for those residing with and killed by their (presumed) genetic fathers versus 321.6 per million child-years at risk for those residing with and killed by stepfathers. The latter rate is more than 120 times higher than the former. To give Buller's argument its best chance, suppose for the moment that stepfathers were always caught whereas genetic fathers often got away with murder. Even so, for the true rate of fatal batterings by genetic fathers to equal that for stepfathers, there would have to have been more than 500 undiscovered paternal murders each year in addition to the annual average of four that were detected. It's time for a reality check—there aren't even enough dead children! According to Canadian Vital Statistics, fewer than 400 children under 5 years of age died annually in 1974–1990 from *any* cause other than disease and congenital abnormality (i.e., homicides plus accidental injuries plus unknown causes). Thus, Buller's fantasy requires that in each of the 17 years, all accidental and unknown-cause deaths, plus more than 100 others that were attributed to specific diseases or congenital conditions, were actually successfully covered-up paternal beatings.

In regard to nonlethal abuse, the hypothesis that recording biases might explain Cinderella effects is again untenable, notwithstanding the fact that such abuse must often go undetected. The principle evidence justifying this conclusion comes from victimization surveys, which consistently reveal large differences in the experiences of persons raised in stepfamilies versus two-genetic-parent families. Consider just three examples published in the journal *Child Abuse & Neglect*. Russell (1984) surveyed a representative sample of San Francisco women and reported that 17% of those who said that a stepfather had been their primary father figure before age 14 also said they had been sexually abused by him by that age, whereas the comparable figure for women raised by their fathers was 2%; Kim and Ko (1990) reported that 40% of surveyed Korean primary schoolchildren living with one genetic and one stepparent reported receiving severe beatings, compared to 7% of those living with two genetic parents; and Sariola and Uutela (1996) reported that 3.7% of 15-year-old Finnish schoolgirls currently living with a stepfather affirmed on a questionnaire that he had abused them sexually, compared to 0.2% of those living with their genetic fathers. These estimates do not depend on anyone other than the victims themselves detecting and recording the abuse, so Buller's conjecture that stereotypes induce professionals to expect abuse in stepfamilies and to overlook it in genetic-parent families is irrelevant. One can, of course, resort to further speculation and propose that responses to victimization surveys are also biased against stepparents, but a modest bias will not suffice: in order to equalize the highly disparate rates, it would have to be the case that the vast majority of stepchildren who claim to have been abused are lying, or the vast majority of those who are actually abused by their genetic parents are lying when they deny it, or both. There is no evidence-based rationale for giving credence to such an insulting blanket dismissal of the validity of victims' reports.

Is there in fact *any* evidence for the existence of detection biases against stepparents? In an effort to show that there is, Buller misrepresents the findings of several U.S. *Child Fatality Review Panels* that have addressed "underascertainment" of child-abuse mortality. What all these Review Panels have reported is that when childhood deaths that were not clearly disease related were reviewed to see if there was an element of parental maltreatment or serious negligence in the precipitating events, the number of maltreatment-related deaths was approximately doubled over what one would have inferred from the causes of death recorded by coroners and/or pursued as criminal matters. This underascertainment is serious, but it falls far short of the level required by Buller's argument. More importantly, Buller fails to remark that the studies he cites all provide additional confirmation of the existence of very large Cinderella effects, after the *Child Fatality Review Panels* had done their work and the underascertainment had been rectified.

The first such paper that Buller (2005a, pp. 403–406) discusses at length is the report (Ewigman, Kivlahan, & Land, 1993) of a Missouri *Child Fatality Review Panel* that reexamined all 384 cases in which a child under 5 years of age died of external causes in 1983–1986. Only 58 of the deaths had been called homicides on the death certificate, and yet the panel concluded that 121 were definite maltreatment fatalities; this much Buller gets right. What he fails to mention is that the Missouri team proceeded to address the question of who actually killed these children in a subsequent case-control study (Stiffman et al., 2002): after review of all injury-related deaths had identified the fatal maltreatment cases, the identified killers included 15 stepfathers (married and *de facto*; plus two noncoresiding mothers' boyfriends) and 11 putative genetic fathers. Comparing the maltreatment cases to natural deaths (the case controls), 22% of the former dwelt with stepfathers versus 4% of the latter (still, interestingly, more than would be expected on the basis of the living arrangements of Missouri children). The authors cite our prior results, and emphasize that theirs' are fully supportive. We know that Buller did not overlook this second report, because he cites it, and one could hardly read it and fail to notice its documentation of a large Cinderella effect, since the authors consider it their main finding—the abstract's "Results" and "Conclusions" mention nothing else. It takes considerable chutzpah to cite this *Child Fatality Review Panel's* work in support of a denial of Cinderella effects, while neglecting to mention that further documentation of such effects, after death review and using a novel case-control methodology, was the Panel's primary empirical finding.

Buller (2005a) similarly miscites a North Carolina study (Herman-Giddens et al., 1999), stressing that it, like the Missouri study, uncovered many more "child-abuse homicides" than had been recorded as such in official statistics, while neglecting to mention that the findings again exhibit a very large Cinderella effect after child fatality review. However, the paper that Buller (2005a, 2005b) most stresses is a Colorado study by Crume, DiGiuseppi, Byers, Sirotnak, and Garrett (2002), which is unique among these *Child Fatality Review Panel* investigations in that it presents explicit comparisons between maltreatment-related deaths that were initially ascertained as such and those that were added as a result of the review process. Buller (2005a, p. 409) asserts that this study "found that a case of fatal maltreatment is more than eight times more likely to be recorded as such if perpetrated by a (commonlaw) stepfather than if perpetrated by a genetic parent," a claim that is wildly at odds with the actual data. For one thing, "(commonlaw) stepfathers" were not in fact distinguished from neighbors, clergymen, strangers, and other unrelated persons in the data presented, nor, according to a personal communication from the paper's senior author, can they be distinguished retrospectively. Moreover, what Crume et al. (2002) actually report is this: only 43% of 152 maltreatment deaths that the review panel attributed to "parents" were initially recorded as such, compared to 47% of 36 deemed to have been committed by "other relatives (including stepparents)," and 86% of 51 deemed to have been committed by "other unrelated (including boyfriend)." In other words, the initial ascertainment rate for the category including stepparents was scarcely different from that for "parents," and the initial ascertainment rate for the category including mothers' "boyfriends" was exactly two (not "more than eight") times higher than that for "parents."[2] Buller (2005a, p. 409) concludes triumphantly that "the degree of diagnostic bias exposed by Crume and her colleagues is more than sufficient to account for the greater abuse by stepfathers in official case reports." In fact, it would be nowhere near sufficient to account for the 100-fold and greater Cinderella effects that have been documented in child maltreatment deaths, even if Crume et al. actually had "exposed" an 8-fold reporting bias, which they did not.

The simple truth is that no one knows whether there is even a slight reporting bias against step-parents in child-abuse records, and there are reasons to suspect that such biases as do exist might even run the other way. One reason for suspecting this derives from studies of sexual-abuse allegations that were later substantiated by medical examination and/or perpetrator confession: it turns out that girls who disclosed such abuse to their mothers were most likely to be disbelieved, and their allegations therefore ignored, if the abuser was a stepfather. In a U.S. study, Sirles and Franke (1989) reported that 86% of girls who disclosed paternal abuse to their mothers were believed, as were 92% of those abused by other relatives, but only 56% of those abused by stepfathers. A subsequent Canadian study (Cyr et al., 2002) produced almost identical results: 90% of girls who disclosed paternal abuse to their mothers were believed, as were 86% of those abused by a brother, but only 61% of those abused by stepfathers. The samples were large and the differences highly significant in both cases. What these data suggest is that, at least in cases of sexual abuse, maltreatment by genetic fathers may actually be more likely to find its way into official records than maltreatment by stepfathers.

Like other researchers, we had long been inclined to suppose that reporting biases with respect to physical abuse probably operate against stepfathers, thinking along the following lines:

> Suppose that you lived next door to a child who exhibited recurrent, suspicious bruising, and that you (like everyone else) were familiar with the stereotype of step-parental cruelty. Isn't it possible that your likelihood of assuming the worst and calling a child protection agency might be affected by knowing that the man in the house was a stepparent? (Daly & Wilson, 1998, p. 27)

However, we may have been wrong in this intuition. An ambitious Canadian study of 135,573 investigations of child-abuse allegations (Trocmé et al., 2002) suggests that reporting biases may actually operate against genetic fathers instead. After investigation, the allegations were classified as substantiated, suspected but unconfirmed, or "unsubstantiated" (conclusively disconfirmed). Disconfirmed allegations were not rare, constituting 43% of physical-abuse reports and 40% for sexual abuse; about 10% of disconfirmed allegations were judged to be "malicious" (knowingly false), and about 90% to be "honest mistakes." For present purposes, the most striking result of this massive national study is that reports of abuse by genetic fathers were significantly more likely to turn out to be false than reports against stepfathers: 43% of 19,486 allegations of physical or sexual abuse by "biological fathers" were disconfirmed by investigation (and 35% substantiated), compared to 34% of 5,667 allegations against stepfathers disconfirmed (and 39% substantiated).

These results suggest that when third parties suspect abuse on the basis of shaky evidence, they are more willing to blow the whistle if the suspected perpetrator is a genetic father than a stepfather. However, could it really be the case that reporting is biased against genetic fathers in this way? A possible reason why this might be so is that child welfare workers and teachers may "bend over backwards" in response to the steady stream of materials exhorting them to not succumb to "the

---

[2] Where the "more than eight times more likely" claim comes from is misinterpretation of an "odds ratio": 86% versus 43% is translated into "odds" of 86:14 versus 43:57, and then divided thus: [(86/14)/(43/57)] = 8.1. Crume et al. do indeed translate such ratios into statements of relative "likelihood," but this does violence to the ordinary English meaning of "x times more likely"; to see the absurdity of this use of "likely," consider that if 100% of stepfather homicides were detected versus "only" 99.99% of those by genetic fathers, then by Buller's logic, the former would be *infinitely* more likely" to be detected. Buller deceptively uses the phrase "8 times more likely" to create the illusion that a 2-fold difference in rates of recording could account for an 8-fold difference in incidence rates.

myth of the cruel stepparent." That, of course, is speculation. What can be said with confidence is this:

1.   that no one knows whether a reporting bias against stepparents even exists;
2.   that Buller grossly misrepresents the research that he cites to support his claim that such a bias not only exists but is large; and
3.   that even if a reporting bias were as large as Buller fantasizes, it would not be nearly large enough to explain observed Cinderella effects, which are often more than an order of magnitude greater still.

Scholarship and Civility

Buller provides an extreme example in his apparently willful distortions of the evidence that he cites. However, it is not unusual for evolutionary psychology's critics to heap scorn on a caricature of the field or its findings, and it often appears that those who do so have never troubled to read the material they are trashing. In a wide-ranging attack, for example, Lickliter and Honeycutt (2003, p. 870) wrote

> A second threat to validity [of evolutionary psychology] stems from a wealth of counterfactual observations. As a case in point, Daly and Wilson (1988, 1999) claimed that humans (and other species) possess a cognitive module to love and protect genetic offspring and that during humans' evolutionary history it was likely adaptive for men to engage in infanticide of the offspring of their mate(s) that were not their biological offspring. In support of this thesis, Daly and Wilson (1988) presented evidence that children who grow up in a household with a stepfather are at greater risk of abuse than those raised with their biological father. To their credit, Daly and Wilson (1999) acknowledged that their hypothesis has difficulty explaining why a majority of stepfathers do not abuse their children, but they ignored other potentially counterfactual evidence such as the lesser levels of abuse in families that adopt children.

Nothing in this paragraph is accurate except for the fact of excess abuse risk in stepchildren. The claims that Lickliter and Honeycutt attribute to us are not merely things we have never said, but explicit opposites of what we wrote in the works they are purportedly citing. We have consistently rejected, not advocated, the hypothesis that selection favored steppaternal infanticide during human evolution. In the short book that Lickliter and Honeycutt cite as "Daly & Wilson (1999)" (originally 1998), what we had to say about this hypothesis was this (p. 37):

> Human beings are not like langurs and lions. We know that "sexually selected infanticide" is not a human adaptation because men, unlike male langurs and lions, do not routinely, efficiently dispose of their predecessors' young. Stepfathers are very much more likely to inflict non-lethal abuse than to kill, and such abuse is obviously not a "well-designed" means to hasten the production of one's own children nor even to reduce the costs of step-parental investment. Child abuse must therefore be considered a non-adaptive or maladaptive byproduct of the evolved psyche's functional organization, rather than an adaptation in its own right. Moreover, because of the complex social life of the human animal, which includes reputations and retribution, those who assault or kill children flirt with disaster. All told, we see little reason to imagine that the average reproductive benefits of killing stepchildren would ever have outweighed the average costs enough to select for specifically infanticidal inclinations. (pp. 37–38)

It is galling to be accused of advocating a hypothesis that one has carefully dissected and dismissed, but it is almost more galling to be given left-handed "credit" for something equally fantastic, namely for having "acknowledged that [our] hypothesis has difficulty explaining why a majority of stepfathers do not abuse their children." We have "acknowledged" nothing of the sort, since we have never entertained any hypothesis that would generate such a prediction. We hypothesized that steprelationship might be a risk factor for family violence as a by-product of parental adaptations, and this hypothesis has been abundantly confirmed. With identical logic, Lickliter and Honeycutt might complain that the hypothesis that smoking is a risk factor for lung cancer "has difficulty explaining" why most smokers do not get the disease. And of course, the accusation that we "ignored other potentially counterfactual evidence such as the lesser levels of abuse in families that adopt children" is also false (see Daly & Wilson, 1998, pp. 45–46).

How is it that one can write one thing, and yet be cited as having asserted its opposite? Lickliter and Honeycutt's approving citation of H. Rose and S. Rose (2000), two tireless opponents of evolutionary psychology who are utterly unconcerned with accuracy, provides a hint, for it turns out that the paragraph that we have quoted is a minimal paraphrase therefrom. The Roses' slanders evidently fit Lickliter and Honeycutt's prejudices so well that they felt no need to check whether they were true. The presumption seems to be that the evolutionary psychological slant on a given topic is a predictable "it's innate; it's adaptive," and there is a community that buys into this presumption and feeds off one another. In a column purporting to debunk the notion "that human behavior is the Stone Age artifact that evolutionary psychology claims," a Wall Street Journal columnist smugly demands, "Why, if child abuse by stepfathers is such a great evolutionary strategy, do many more stepdads love and care for their stepchildren than abuse them?" (Begley, 2005), apparently without pausing to wonder whether anyone had ever suggested that child abuse is a "great evolutionary strategy."

Unfortunately, it is not just newspaper columnists who are so sure that they know what evolutionary psychologists must have said that they need not read their actual words before attacking. Two book reviews of Daly and Wilson (1998) by academic biologists provide further examples. Evolutionary biologist Deborah Charlesworth (1999, p. 987) patronizingly scolds us for equating homicide by human stepfathers with infanticide by male lions: "The differences between lion and human social systems, and even between the social lives of lions and other members of the cat tribe, are large, and we cannot pick out only the similarities." Apparently, she did not read as far as page 37 (quoted above) before writing her review. Neurobiologist Steven Rose (1999) snorts derisively that "The fact that stepfamilies are more likely to be poor" is explanation enough for the excess violence in stepfamilies "but somehow they [i.e. we] can't see the obvious." On page 28 of the work under review, we, too, described as "obvious" the hypothesis that poverty might be a relevant confound, and then explained the evidence that poverty is not in fact confounded with steprelationship and is an orthoginal risk factor. But like Charlesworth, Rose does not seem to have actually read the (very short) book he is ostensibly reviewing.

As we have discussed above, many of our critics have tried (not always honestly) to make some sort of evidence-based case against the reality of the Cinderella effect. But, most of the biologists who have taken pot shots accept that the phenomenon must be real and have different fish to fry. In addition to attributing hypotheses to us that we have explicitly refuted, both Steven and Hilary Rose have tried in several writings to convince their readers that excess risk to stepchildren was well known before our research and that we have provided nothing but an implausible post hoc explanation for it. In a similar vein, geneticist Steve Jones harrumphs:

> The way sociobiology rediscovers the blindingly obvious and then packages it as scientific breakthrough makes me laugh. The great biological "discovery" … is that stepmothers (sic) kill their children more than mothers do. OK, it is good to get the data, but is anybody surprised? You can go back to the middle ages and find that is already known. (quoted in Patel, 1999)

In sum, some critics believe that the Cinderella effect is "blindingly obvious," others that it is non-existent, but they are united in their indignation about a simple-minded evolutionary approach that exists in their own imaginations and in the diatribes they write for what Robert Wright (personal communication) calls "the anti-ev-psych market niche."

From the perspective of two researchers on the receiving ends of these attacks, a disturbing and sometimes perplexing element has been their incivility. Our critics do not merely question our theoretical arguments or our data. Indeed, we have seen no critique, measured or otherwise, of our rationale for hypothesizing that parents will not love their stepchildren as they do their genetic children, and our attackers have paid scarcely more attention to our empirical findings. They are not just skeptical, they are angry, and we are still not entirely sure what they are angry about.

Some of evolutionary psychology's detractors apparently believe that it denies agency and undermines personal responsibility, as witness the frequent accusations of "determinism" and the characterization of efforts to understand the roots of antisocial behavior as efforts to excuse it. But why should this brand of moralistic aggression target evolutionary psychology in particular, rather than psychological science in general? It was not, after all, some raving Darwinian who maintained that his science had rendered "freedom and dignity" obsolete; it was B. F. Skinner (1971). When the attackers are biologists, perhaps evolutionary psychology stands alone in their gun sights because they are scarcely aware that psychology is a science whose practitioners are quietly and steadily eroding the domain of an unfettered human will. Biologists like Rose, Jones, Stephen Jay Gould, and Richard Lewontin apparently dislike the idea that human beings can and should be studied within the same Darwinian framework that applies to other creatures, for their contempt for evolution-minded research on *Homo sapiens* is Catholic in its targets.

The charge of "determinism" is so philosophically naive that one must suspect that it is a rhetorical tactic of these biologists rather than a sincere accusation. A more important source of their ire may be suspicions that evolutionary psychology is a smoke screen for a reactionary political agenda. Subscribers to such a conspiracy theory were unabashed during the "sociobiology debate" of the 1970s (Segerstråle, 2000), and critics like the Roses beat this drum ceaselessly. It even surfaces in denials of the Cinderella effect. Writing in the journal that is circulated to more clinical psychologists than any other, for example, Silverstein and Auerbach (1999) cite the Malkin and Lamb (1994) study previously discussed, as well as reporting that the absolute numbers (sic) of abusive stepfathers and genetic fathers are about equal in one small sample, and conclude that they have debunked "the neoconservative contention that stepfathers or mothers' boyfriends abuse children more frequently than biological fathers (and mothers)" (p. 402)!

That these writers can see no difference between epidemiological generalizations and political positions is alarming, but it would be foolhardy to deny that political preferences influence the issues that social scientists elect to pursue and sometimes color the interpretation of results. What is transparently false is the notion that evolutionary psychology has some sort of right-wing political agenda or is even especially compatible therewith (Pinker, 2002; Segerstråle, 2000). When its practitioners feel moved to political advocacy, they are at least as likely to invoke their field's theories and findings in support of politically progressive causes as the reverse. Tooby and Cosmides (1990) argue forcefully that an evolutionary psychological view of human nature is antithetical to racism, for example, and Trivers (1981) sees the same perspective as a force against authoritarianism and sexism. We interpret some of our own research (Daly, Wilson & Vasdev, 2001: Wilson & Daly, 1997) as supportive of egalitarian, redistributive policies. But the science itself (unlike its attackers) is politically neutral.

Our experience with angry and uncivil critics is not unusual, and some of the sneers directed at the enterprise of evolutionary psychology are astounding in their breadth (see, e.g., quotes in Hagen, 2005). It is not clear whether evolutionary psychologists will be able to counter the popular caricatures of our discipline, which feed on themselves as well as on the public's ignorance, and it can be disheartening when this antipathy comes from other Darwinians, as it surprisingly often does. However, it is important not to lose sight of the fact that we have more allies than enemies in evolutionary biology. In our view, perhaps the most effective thing that evolutionary psychologists can do, both to counter misrepresentations of our field and to foster its continuing development, is to assist our colleagues in other life sciences in their battle to ensure that children are given a genuine biological education from an early age.

REFERENCES

Anderson, K. G., Kaplan, H., Lam, D., & Lancaster, J. (1999b). Paternal care by genetic fathers and stepfathers II: Reports by Xhosa high school students. *Evolution & Human Behavior, 20*, 433–451.

Anderson, K. G., Kaplan, H., & Lancaster, J. (1999a). Paternal care by genetic fathers and stepfathers I: Reports from Albuquerque men. *Evolution & Human Behavior, 20*, 405–431.

Aquilino, W. S. (1991). Family structure and home leaving: A further specification of the relationship. *Journal of Marriage & the Family, 52*, 405–419.

Becker, G. S., Landes, E. M., & Michael, R. T. (1977). An economic analysis of marital instability. *Journal of Political Economy, 85*, 1141–1187.

Begley, S. (2005, April 29). Evolutionary psych may not help explain our behavior after all. *Wall Street Journal*, p. B1.

Birkhead, T. R. (1978). Behavioural adaptations to high-density nesting in the common guillemot, *Uria aalge*. *Animal Behaviour, 26*, 321–331.

Buller, D. J. (2005a). *Adapting minds*. Cambridge, MA: MIT Press.

Buller, D. J. (2005b). Evolutionary psychology: The emperor's new paradigm. *Trends in Cognitive Sciences, 9*, 277–283.

Campbell, J. C., et al. (2003). Risk factors for femicide in abusive relationships: Results from a multisite case control study. *American Journal of Public Health, 93*, 1089–1097.

Case, A., Lin, I.-F., & McLanahan, S. (2000). How hungry is the selfish gene? *Economic Journal, 110*, 781–804.

Case, A., & Paxson, C. (2001). Mothers and others: Who invests in children's health? *Journal of Health Economics, 20*, 301–328.

Charlesworth, D. (1999). Four little books about evolution. *Evolution, 53*, 985–987.

Clutton-Brock, T. H. (1991). *The evolution of parental care*. Princeton, NJ: Princeton University Press.

Craissati, J., & McClurg, G. (1996). The challenge project: Perpetrators of child sexual abuse in south east London. *Child Abuse & Neglect, 20*, 1067–1077.

Creighton, S. J. (1985). An epidemiological study of abused children and their families in the United Kingdom between 1977 and 1982. *Child Abuse & Neglect, 9*, 441–448.

Creighton, S. J., & Noyes, S. (1989). *Child abuse trends in England and Wales 1983–1987*. London: National Society for the Prevention of Cruelty to Children.

Crume, T. L., DiGiuseppi, C., Byers, T., Sirotnak, A. P., & Garrett, C. J. (2002). Underascertainment of child maltreatment fatalities by death certificates, 1990–1998. *Pediatrics, 110*(2), e18. (DOI: 10.1542/peds110.2.e18)

Cyr, M., Wright, J., McDuff, P., & Perron, A. (2002). Intrafamilial sexual abuse: Brother-sister incest does not differ from father-daughter and stepfather-stepdaughter incest. *Child Abuse & Neglect, 26*, 957–973.

Daly, M., Singh, L. S., & Wilson, M. I. (1993). Children fathered by previous partners: A risk factor for violence against women. *Canadian Journal of Public Health, 84*, 209–210.

Daly, M., & Wilson, M. I. (1980). Discriminative parental solicitude: A biological perspective. *Journal of Marriage & the Family, 42*, 277–288.

Daly, M., & Wilson, M. I. (1981). Abuse and neglect of children in evolutionary perspective. In R. D. Alexander & D. W. Tinkle (Eds.), *Natural selection and social behavior* (pp. 405–416). New York: Chiron.

Daly, M., & Wilson, M. I. (1985). Child abuse and other risks of not living with both parents. *Ethology & Sociobiology, 6*, 197–210.

Daly, M., & Wilson, M. I. (1988a). The Darwinian psychology of discriminative parental solicitude. *Nebraska Symposium on Motivation, 35*, 91–144.

Daly, M., & Wilson, M. I. (1988b). *Homicide*. New York: Aldine de Gruyter.

Daly, M., & Wilson, M. I. (1994). Some differential attributes of lethal assaults on small children by stepfathers versus genetic fathers. *Ethology & Sociobiology, 15*, 207–217.

Daly, M., & Wilson, M. I. (1995). Discriminative parental solicitude and the relevance of evolutionary models to the analysis of motivational systems. In M. Gazzaniga (Ed.), *The cognitive neurosciences* (pp. 1269–1286). Cambridge, MA: MIT Press.

Daly, M., & Wilson, M. I. (1996). Evolutionary psychology and marital conflict: The relevance of stepchildren. In D. M. Buss & N. Malamuth (Eds.), *Sex, power, conflict: Feminist and evolutionary perspectives* (pp. 9–28). New York: Oxford University Press.

Daly, M., & Wilson, M. I. (1998). *The truth about Cinderella.* London: Weidenfeld & Nicolson.

Daly, M., & Wilson, M. I. (2001). An assessment of some proposed exceptions to the phenomenon of nepotistic discrimination against stepchildren. *Annales Zoologici Fennici, 38,* 287–296.

Daly, M., Wilson, M. I., & Vasdev, S. (2001). Income inequality and homicide rates in Canada and the United States. *Canadian Journal of Criminology, 43,* 219–236.

Daly, M., Wiseman, K. A., & Wilson, M. I. (1997). Women with children sired by previous partners incur excess risk of uxoricide. *Homicide Studies, 1,* 61–71.

Davies, N. B., & Brooke, M. (1991). Coevolution of the cuckoo and its hosts. *Scientific American, 264,* 92–98.

Davis, J. N., & Daly, M. (1997). Evolutionary theory and the human family. *Quarterly Review of Biology, 72,* 407–435.

Dobash, R. P., Dobash, R. E., Wilson, M. I., & Daly, M. (1992). The myth of sexual symmetry in marital violence. *Social Problems, 39,* 71–91.

Duberman, L. (1975). *The reconstituted family: A study of remarried couples and their children.* Chicago: Nelson-Hall.

Ewigman, B., Kivlahan, C., & Land, G. (1993). The Missouri child fatality study: Underreporting of maltreatment fatalities among children younger than five years of age, 1983 through 1986. *Pediatrics, 91,* 330–337.

Fergusson, D. M., Fleming, J., & O'Neill, D. P. (1972). *Child abuse in New Zealand.* Wellington: Government of New Zealand Printer.

Ferri, E. (1984). *Stepchildren: A national study.* Windsor, U.K.: NFER-Meslon.

Fine, M. A. (1986). Perceptions of stepparents: Variation in stereotypes as a function of current family structure. *Journal of Marriage & the Family,* 48, 537–543.

Flinn, M. V. (1988). Step and genetic parent/offspring relationships in a Caribbean village. *Ethology & Sociobiology,* 9, 335–369.

Flinn, M. V., & England, B. G. (1995). Family environment and childhood stress. *Current Anthropology, 36,* 854–866.

Flinn, M. V., Leone, D. V., & Quinlan, R. J. (1999). Growth and fluctuating asymmetry of stepchildren. *Evolution & Human Behavior, 20,* 465–479.

Flinn, M. V., Quinlan, R. J., Decker, S. A., Turner, M. T., & England, B. G. (1996). Male-female differences in effects of parental absence on glucocorticoid stress response. *Human Nature, 7,* 125–162.

Gelles, R. J. (1991). Physical violence, child abuse, and child homicide: A continuum of violence, or distinct behaviors? *Human Nature, 2,* 59–72.

Gelles, R. J., & Harrop, J. W. (1991). The risk of abusive violence among children with nongenetic caretakers. *Family Relations, 40,* 78–83.

Gordon, M. (1989). The family environment of sexual abuse: A comparison of natal and stepfather abuse. *Child Abuse & Neglect, 13,* 121–130.

Gordon, M., & Creighton, S. J. (1988). Natal and nonnatal fathers as sexual abusers in the United Kingdom: A comparative analysis. *Journal of Marriage & the Family, 50,* 99–105.

Hagen, E. (2005). Controversial issues in evolutionary psychology. In D. M. Buss (Ed.), *The handbook of evolutionary psychology* (pp. 145–173). New York: Wiley.

Hall, D. R., & Zhao, J. Z. (1995). Cohabitation and divorce in Canada: Testing the selectivity hypothesis. *Journal of Marriage & the Family, 57,* 421–427.

Hashima, P. Y., & Amato, P. R. (1994). Poverty, social support, and parental behavior. *Child Development, 65,* 394–403.

Herman-Giddens, M. E., Brown, G., Verbiest, S., Carlson, P. J., Hooten, E. G., Howell, E., et al. (1999). Underascertainment of child abuse mortality in the United States. *Journal of the American Medical Association, 281,* 463–467.

Hicks, R. A., & Gaughan, D. C. (1995). Understanding fatal child abuse. *Child Abuse & Neglect, 19,* 855–863.

Hill, K., & Kaplan, H. (1988). Tradeoffs in male and female reproductive strategies among the Ache, part 2. In L. L. Betzig, M. Borgerhoff Mulder, & P. Turke (Eds.), *Human reproductive behavior: A Darwinian perspective* (pp. 291–305). Cambridge, U.K.: Cambridge University Press.

Johnson, H. C. (1980). Working with stepfamilies: Principles of practice. *Social Work, 25,* 304–308.

Kiernan, K. (1992). The impact of family disruption in childhood on transitions made in young adult life. *Population Studies, 46,* 218–234.

Kim, K., & Ko, B. (1990). An incidence survey of battered children in two elementary schools of Seoul. *Child Abuse & Neglect, 14,* 273–276.

Klevens, J., Bayón, M. C., & Sierra, M. (2000). Risk factors and context of men who physically abuse in Bogotá, Colombia. *Child Abuse & Neglect, 24,* 323–332.

Lack, D. (1943). *The life of the robin.* London: Witherby.

Lickliter, R., & Honeycutt, H. (2003). Developmental dynamics and contemporary evolutionary psychology: Status quo or irreconcilable views? Reply to Bjorklund (2003), Krebs (2003), Buss and Reeve (2003), Crawford (2003), and Tooby et al. (2003). *Psychological Bulletin, 129,* 866–872.

Lightcap, J. L., Kurland, J. A., & Burgess, R. L. (1982). Child abuse: A test of some ideas from evolutionary theory. *Ethology & Sociobiology, 3,* 61–67.

Lucas, D. R., Wezner, K. C., Milner, J. S., McCanne, T. R., Harris, I. N., Monroe-Posey, C., et al. (2002). Victim, perpetrator, family, and incident characteristics of infant and child homicide in the US Air Force. *Child Abuse & Neglect, 26,* 167–186.

Lyman, J. M., McGwin, G., Malone, D. E., Taylor, A. J., Brissie, R. M., Davis, G., et al. (2003). Epidemiology of child homicide in Jefferson County, Alabama. *Child Abuse & Neglect, 27,* 1063–1073.

Malkin, C. M., & Lamb, M. E. (1994). Child maltreatment: A test of sociobiological theory. *Journal of Comparative Family Studies, 25,* 121–134.

Marlowe, F. (1999). Showoffs or providers? The parenting effort of Hadza men. *Evolution & Human Behavior, 20,* 391–404.

Patel, K. (1999, September). Aping Darwin. *The Times Higher Education Supplement, 10,* 24.

Pinker, S. (2002). *The blank slate: The modern denial of human nature.* New York: Viking Penguin.

Powers, J. L., Eckenrode, J., & Jaklitsch, B. (1990). Maltreatment among runaway and homeless youth. *Child Abuse & Neglect, 14,* 87–98.

Rodney, J. (1999). *Household composition and the risk of child sexual and physical abuse.* Unpublished bachelor's thesis, McMaster University, Hamilton, Onario, Canada.

Rohwer, S., Herron, J. C., & Daly, M. (1999). Stepparental behavior as mating effort in birds and other animals. *Evolution & Human Behavior, 20,* 367–390.

Rose, H., & Rose, S. (2000). *Alas, poor Darwin: Arguments against evolutionary psychology.* New York: Harmony Books.

Rose, S. (1999). Evolutionary psychology: Biology impoverished. *Interdisciplinary Science Reviews, 24,* 175–178.

Russell, D. E. H. (1984). The prevalence and seriousness of incestuous abuse: Stepfathers vs. biological fathers. *Child Abuse & Neglect, 8,* 15–22.

Sariola, H., & Uutela, A. (1996). The prevalence and context of incest abuse in Finland. *Child Abuse & Neglect, 20,* 843–850.

Segerstråle, U. (2000). *Defenders of the truth: The battle for science in the sociobiology debate and beyond.* Oxford, U.K.: Oxford University Press.

Silk, J. B. (1990). Human adoption in evolutionary perspective. *Human Nature, 1,* 25–52.

Silverstein, L. B., & Auerbach, C. F. (1999). Deconstructing the essential father. *American Psychologist, 54,* 397–407.

Sirles, E. A., & Franke, P. J. (1989). Factors influencing mothers' reactions to intrafamily sexual abuse. *Child Abuse & Neglect, 13,* 131–139.

Skinner, B. F. (1971). *Beyond freedom and dignity.* New York: A. A. Knopf

Stiffman, M. N., Schnitzer, P. G., Adam, P., Kruse, R. L., & Ewigman, B. G. (2002). Household composition and risk of fatal child maltreatment. *Pediatrics, 109,* 615–621.

Strang, H. (1996). *Children as victims of homicide.* Trends and issues in crime and criminal justice (No. 53). Canberra, Australia: Australian Institute of Criminology.

Temrin, H., Buchmayer, S., & Enquist, M. (2000). Stepparents and infanticide: New data contradict evolutionary predictions. *Proceedings of the Royal Society of London B, 267,* 943–945.

Temrin, H., Nordlund, J., & Sterner, S. (2004). Are stepchildren overrepresented as victims of lethal parental violence in Sweden? *Proceedings of the Royal Society of London B, 271,* S124–S126.

Tooley, G. A., Karakis, M., Stokes, M., & Ozanne-Smith, J. (2006). Generalising the Cinderella Effect to unintentional childhood fatalities. *Evolution & Human Behavior, 27,* 224–230.

Trocmé, N. et al. (2000). Canadian incidence study of reported child abuse and neglect. Ottawa, Canada: Public Health Agency of Canada. Retrieved Month, August 16, 2007, http://www.phac-aspc.gc.ca/publicat/cisfr-ecirf/index.html

Trivers, R. L. (1981). Sociobiology and politics. In E. White (Ed.), *Sociobiology and human politics* (pp. 1–44). Lexington, MA: Heath.

Turnbull, S. K., & Turnbull, J. M. (1983). To dream the impossible dream: An agenda for discussion with stepparents. *Family Relations, 32,* 227–230.

Tyler, K. A., & Cauce, A. M. (2002). Perpetrators of early physical and sexual abuse among homeless and runaway adolescents. *Child Abuse & Neglect, 26,* 1261–1274.

Voland, E. (1988). Differential infant and child mortality in evolutionary perspective: Data from 17th to 19th century Ostfriesland. In L. L. Betzig, M. Borgerhoff Mulder, & P. Turke (Eds.), *Human reproductive behaviour: A Darwinian perspective* (pp. 253–261). Cambridge, U.K.: Cambridge University Press.

Wadsworth, J., Burnell, I., Taylor, B., & Butler, N. (1983). Family type and accidents in preschool children. *Journal of Epidemiology & Community Health, 37,* 100–104.

Wallace, A. (1986). *Homicide: The social reality.* Sydney, New South Wales, Canada: New South Wales Bureau of Crime Statistics & Research.

Weekes-Shackelford, V. A., & Shackelford, T. K. (2004). Methods of filicide: Stepparents and genetic parents kill differently. *Violence & Victims, 19,* 75–81.

White, L. (1994). Stepfamilies over the life course: Social support. In A. Booth & J. Dunn (Eds.), *Stepfamilies. Who benefits? Who does not?* (pp. 109–137). Hillsdale, NJ: Lawrence Erlbaum.

White, L. K., & Booth, A. (1985). The quality and stability of remarriages: The role of stepchildren. *American Sociological Review, 50,* 689–698.

Wilson, M. I., & Daly, M. (1987). Risk of maltreatment of children living with stepparents. In R. J. Gelles & J. B. Lancaster (Eds.), *Child abuse and neglect: Biosocial dimensions* (pp. 215–232). NY: Aldine de Gruyter.

Wilson, M. I., & Daly, M. (1997). Life expectancy, economic inequality, homicide, and reproductive timing in Chicago neighbourhoods. *British Medical Journal, 314,* 1271–1274.

Wilson, M. I., & Daly, M. (2001). The evolutionary psychology of couple conflict in registered versus de facto marital unions. In A. Booth, A. C. Crouter, & M. Clements (Eds.), *Couples in conflict* (pp. 3–26). Mahwah, NJ: Lawrence Erlbaum.

Wilson, M. I., & Daly, M. (2004). Marital cooperation and conflict. In C. Crawford & C. Salmon (Eds.), *Evolutionary psychology, public policy, and personal decisions* (pp. 197–215). Mahwah, NJ: Lawrence Erlbaum.

Wilson, M. I., Daly, M., & Daniele, A. (1995). Familicide: The killing of spouse and children. *Aggressive Behavior, 21,* 275–291.

Wilson, M. I., Daly, M., & Weghorst, S. J. (1980). Household composition and the risk of child abuse and neglect. *Journal of Biosocial Science, 12,* 333–340.

Yom-Tov, Y. (1980). Intraspecific nest parasitism in birds. *Biological Reviews, 55,* 93–108.

Zvoch, K. (1999). Family type and investment in education: A comparison of genetic and stepparent families. *Evolution & Human Behavior, 20,* 453–464.

21

Intergroup Prejudices and Intergroup Conflicts

MARK SCHALLER
AND STEVEN L. NEUBERG

Group stereotypes. Ethnic prejudices. Wars. These are substantial social problems, and they attract the attention of many social scientists, including psychologists who study social cognition and behavior. That's good. But in order to grapple intelligently and realistically with these problems, it is important to consider not just the insights of the social sciences but the biological sciences as well. The roots of modern prejudices and intergroup conflicts can be found in the ecological circumstances within which our species evolved and in the psychological processes that emerged as adaptations to those circumstances. Inquiry into these evolved psychological processes helps us understand intergroup stereotypes and prejudices, and how these contribute to various forms of discrimination as well as to full-blown intergroup conflict. An evolutionary analysis also yields novel insights into the circumstances under which these prejudices may be exaggerated or inhibited. These insights may prove useful in the development of interventions that might actually help alleviate intergroup discrimination and conflict in the modern world.

AN EVOLUTIONARY PERSPECTIVE ON THREATS AND PREJUDICES

Wars do not just happen; they result from actions taken by individual people. More generally, any act of intergroup discrimination is either directly or indirectly the product of the psychological processes that govern individuals' attitudes, decisions, and behavior. If we want to understand the roots of intergroup conflict, we first need to understand the specific thoughts and feelings that are aroused in intergroup contexts. Here is where an evolutionary approach to psychology comes in handy.

A rigorous evolutionary approach to social psychology typically entails a four-step process: (1) The specification of plausible fitness-relevant "problems" recurrently posed by ancestral social environments; (2) the employment of an evolutionary cost-benefit analysis to deduce plausible psychological adaptations that would have helped "solve" those problems; (3) the deduction of hypotheses specifying exactly how these alleged adaptations govern cognition, emotion, and behavior in contemporary human environments; and (4) the use of empirical data to test these hypotheses.

This general strategy of inquiry has been enormously successful in the study of human social cognition (Schaller, Park, & Kenrick, 2007). Within that broad sphere of inquiry, this strategy has also yielded many novel insights about the psychological bases of stereotypes, prejudices, and various forms of behavioral discrimination. Many of these insights result from programs of research that connect specific kinds of ancestral threats to specific kinds of contemporary prejudices (Kurzban & Leary, 2001; Neuberg & Cottrell, 2006).

There are a variety of distinct kinds of enduring fitness-relevant threats posed by the presence of specific people. A person might be angry and seek to do you harm. A person might exploit your generosity and never reciprocate. A person might be infected with some disease-causing parasite and infect you, too. Humans evolved to be sensitive to cues indicating that particular people might pose threats such as these. For instance, we are hypervigilant to facial expressions signaling anger and are highly adept at identifying individuals with a history of exploitive nonreciprocation (E. Fox, Russo, Bowles, Dutton, 2001; Mealey, Daood, & Krage, 1996). The perception of threat-connoting cues automatically triggers aversive cognitions and emotions. For instance, when we perceive someone marked by symptoms signaling the possible presence of parasites (e.g., hacking coughs, open sores) disease-connoting cognitions are quickly activated into working memory and we feel disgusted (Curtis, Aunger, & Rabie, 2004; Schaller & Duncan, 2007).

Specific threats are best evaded by engaging in specific behavioral responses, and these behavioral responses are facilitated by specific emotions and cognitions. The implication is that each specific kind of social threat (and the specific set of cues signaling that threat) is likely to arouse a specific suite of emotional and cognitive responses. The perception of a face marked by open sores is likely to inspire disgust and disease-connoting cognitions, whereas the perception of an angry face is likely to inspire fear and specific cognitions consistent with a fearful response. Thus, each specific threat is associated with a unique "prejudice syndrome" characterized by a functionally specific suite of emotional, cognitive, and behavioral responses (Cottrell & Neuberg, 2005; Neuberg & Cottrell, 2006).

Our goal in this chapter is to discuss some intergroup threats and their implications for our understanding of contemporary stereotypes, prejudices, and intergroup conflict. We focus first, and most extensively, on a set of psychological processes that may have evolved as a means of facilitating adaptive behavioral responses to actual intergroup aggression during ancestral times. A close consideration of these processes helps us understand why intergroup conflict is such a tragically enduring part of human life. It helps us to predict the circumstances under which intergroup conflict is especially likely to be triggered and sustained. It also provides some useful insights into circumstances that may help promote peacemaking instead.

We then discuss two additional, conceptually distinct sets of psychological processes that likely evolved to help our distant ancestors manage some of the threats commonly arising within their social groups, but that also have significant implications for intergroup relations. A consideration of these processes implicates at least two additional forms that intergroup discrimination may take, and leads to specific predictions about circumstances under which these forms of discrimination may be especially likely, or unlikely, to emerge.

THE NATURE OF GROUP AND INTERGROUP RELATIONS DURING ANCESTRAL TIMES

A vast amount of human evolutionary history occurred during times in which our species and its precursors lived as hunter-gatherers. Anthropological, archeological, and zoological evidence suggests that individuals lived in and identified with relatively small subsistence groups. These subsistence groups served as a fundamental unit of social interaction. Within more recent evolutionary history, it appears that a superordinate kind of group coalition may have become relevant as well—a tribal coalition consisting of multiple, geographically proximal, mutually cooperative subsistence groups. Group life provided individuals with significant fitness-relevant opportunities and benefits. For instance, it offered efficient means for finding mates and raising offspring, enabled individuals to more effectively exploit natural resources necessary for survival, and provided a powerful buffer against predators (including those posed by other human groups; see Kurzban & Neuberg, 2005). Group life also had its costs, however, and likely introduced a variety of fitness-relevant problems related to managing intragroup effectiveness and the risks posed by living in immediate proximity to others. Psychological adaptations designed to reduce these risks would have included, for instance, specific inclinations to stigmatize in-group members who violate norms of social exchange and to avoid those who carry infectious diseases (e.g., Cosmides, 1989; Neuberg & Cottrell, 2006; Schaller & Duncan, 2007).

Individuals were also likely attuned to the threat of injury posed by individuals from other coalitional groups—from out-groups. Although the vast majority of social interactions historically occurred within groups, some intergroup interactions are likely to have occurred as well. Many different kinds of evidence indicate that, historically, intergroup interactions were marked by hostility and violence.

Other Primate Populations

It is likely that some of the basic psychological processes pertaining to intergroup behavior emerged long ago, before the emergence of *Homo sapiens*. Consequently, inferences about the social structures of relevant ancestral populations may be informed by observations of other primate populations that share the same evolutionary history. Although there is variability in the nature of the intergroup interactions of different primate species (see Smuts, Cheney, Seyfarth, Wrangham, & Struhsaker, 1986), there are a number of cross-species regularities that allow reasonably confident conclusions about common ancestors (Wrangham, 1987).

Within most primate species, groups are territorial to some degree, and relations between those groups tend to be hostile. Evidence of intergroup hostility is readily apparent from observations of chimpanzees. Dugatkin (1997, p. 132) summarizes the nature of between-group encounters among chimpanzees as follows: "Such encounters on occasion can be friendly, and even solicited... but most often they are not." Raids into another group's territory often result in bloodshed, and the cumulative impact of this sort of violence can, on occasion, result in the total destruction of a group (Goodall, 1986). Among chimpanzees and other primates, intergroup aggression has a distinctly more violent character than aggression within groups (e.g., Goodall, 1986; Southwick, Siddiqi, Farooqui, & Pal, 1974). Goodall observed that out-group victims "are treated more as though they were prey animals" (p. 532), and concluded that chimpanzee aggression against out-group members is "prompted by what appears to be an inherent dislike or 'hatred' of strangers" (p. 331).

Within this context, it is worth noting a sex difference we shall revisit later. Among the primate species most closely related to human beings, intergroup hostilities involve males more than females (Carpenter, 1974; Cheney, 1986; Wilson & Wrangham, 2003). Male chimpanzees range more widely than females (Hasegawa, 1990), and "patrol groups" that travel to territorial boundaries—and so are especially likely to encounter patrolling members of other communities—tend to be comprised entirely or primarily of males (Goodall, 1986). The "inherent dislike" of strangers noted by Goodall will thus have more opportunities for expression in males (and against males). In contrast, when reproductive possibilities are limited, female chimpanzees may approach other communities and, if sexually receptive at the time of contact, may be accepted by that group's males; given this possibility of migration and acceptance, it would make sense that female chimpanzees possess the potential for out-group tolerance in addition to dislike. In all, several pressures would seem to logically contribute to the tendency for male chimpanzees to be especially hostile toward out-group members, and toward out-group males in particular (Goodall, 1986; Wilson & Wrangham, 2003).

CONTEMPORARY HUMAN HUNTER-GATHERER POPULATIONS

Just as with different primate species, there is much variation across different human hunter-gatherer societies in different geographical regions (Kelly, 1995). Nonetheless, there are commonalities across otherwise diverse populations, and these commonalities offer clues to group structures and intergroup behavior in our prehistoric past.

Human hunter-gatherer societies tend to be territorial (Eibl-Eibesfeldt, 1974; Kelly, 1995; Robarchek, 1990). Kelly (1995, p. 185) observed that within all hunter-gatherer societies individuals "have specific use rights or statuses as members of a group or band that connect them with a particular area," and concluded that, "upon reconsideration of ethnographic evidence, we see that no society has a laissez-faire attitude toward spatial boundaries." Individuals seeking to cross another group's territory engage in carefully articulated rituals of permission seeking to do so. Unsolicited trespasses onto out-group territory can be dangerous. For instance, Lebzelter (1934, p. 21) observed of the !Kung "bushmen" of Africa that, "Every armed man is considered as an enemy. The Bushman must not enter other tribal territory, except unarmed. When a Bushman is sent as a messenger to another farm, the mutual hostility will not permit him to leave the path that is recognized as some kind of neutral zone" (translated by Eibl-Eibesfeldt, 1974).

Given these group structures, relations with in-group members are quite different from relations with out-group members. For instance, of the Semai Senoi of Malaysia, Robarchek (1990, p. 66) observed that, "The only source of nurturance and support, the only place where a person can feel secure, is in the band." The anthropological literature on war offers many examples of chronically hostile intergroup relations among hunter-gatherers (Ferguson, 1984; Haas, 1990). The risk of injury and death at the hands of out-group members can be so high in some cases that day-to-day life is marked by chronic vigilance and war readiness in case of attack (Carneiro, 1990). Chronic concern about intergroup hostility is observed even among peoples for whom actual intergroup violence is rare. Intergroup relations between different tribal groups in the Upper Xingu basin in Brazil are famously peaceful, but the potential danger posed by other tribal groups is extremely salient. Gregor (1990, p. 114) concluded that it is exactly this concern with intergroup hostility that maintains the peace: "The Xingu peace relies heavily on institutions that separate the tribes and preoccupy villagers with thoughts of death and violence."

The actual dangers posed by out-group members differs somewhat depending upon the sex of the out-group member. As with nonhuman primates, raiding parties organized for the purposes of penetrating another group's territory are most likely to be comprised of men, so hostilities between such parties is primarily restricted to men (Chagnon, 1988).

ADAPTIVE FEATURES OF INTERGROUP COGNITION AND EMOTION

Given the dangerous nature of intergroup interactions during vast stretches of human evolutionary history, it is plausible that certain kinds of psychological mechanisms have evolved that helped protect individuals from that danger. These would be mechanisms that promoted behavioral avoidance of unexpected intergroup interactions or, when avoidance was impossible, promoted caution within the context of an ongoing intergroup interaction.

What psychological mechanisms would be necessary to promote avoidance and caution in regard to out-group members? At minimum, mechanisms that allow individuals to quickly and efficiently distinguish between in-group and out-group members would have been necessary. There is abundant evidence that people are extraordinarily adept at this kind of social categorization. Some forms of social categorization are effortful, but distinguishing between "us" and "them" apparently is not. Just as we cannot help but to categorize individuals as male or female, we also cannot help but to identify an individual as belonging to a coalitional in-group or out-group (Brewer, 1988; R. Fox, 1992; Kurzban, Tooby, & Cosmides, 2001).

Merely categorizing an individual as an out-group member is not sufficient to promote avoidance. There must also be some cognitive association linking that out-group, and its members, with some specific connotative or affective information that promotes behavioral avoidance. In short, it requires the activation of some sort of negative stereotype or negative emotional state. However, not just any negative stereotype or negative emotional state promotes avoidance. Some negative emotions, such as anger, promote incaution and behavioral approach. And certain kinds of specific negative stereotypes ("People from Group X are ignorant") may also fail to strongly dissuade contact. Our evolutionary analysis suggests that fitness advantages may have accrued to individuals for whom out-groups and out-group members automatically triggered specific emotional states (such as fear) and specific kinds of stereotypical trait information (traits connoting danger and threat) that compel behavioral avoidance and caution (Cottrell & Neuberg, 2005; Neuberg & Cottrell, 2006). Just as people appear to be biologically prepared to learn to associate fear with evolutionarily relevant nonhuman predators, such as snakes (Öhman & Mineka, 2001), people may also be biologically prepared to learn to associate fear (and danger-relevant stereotypes) with coalitional out-group members. Once these implicit associations are acquired, they may be triggered quite readily upon the perception of out-groups and/or out-group members.

Costs, Benefits, and Functional Flexibility

If we left it at that, we would not have much more to write about. To assert that there exist deep evolutionary roots for the human tendency to fear out-groups, and to hold danger-connoting stereotypes about them, is not really news. Nor does such an assertion by itself provide much useful insight into ways in which stereotypes, prejudices, and intergroup conflicts might be attenuated. What makes this conceptual perspective scientifically interesting and practically useful, however, is the evolutionary cost/benefit analysis that is necessarily a part of it.

Any evolved defense mechanism evolved specifically because it offered fitness-enhancing benefits to the individuals who have those mechanisms, relative to individuals who do not. However, the actual activation and deployment of those mechanisms entails costs as well. The immune system offers a good illustration. The immune system is adaptive: you are much better off having an immune system than not. However, the immune system also imposes costs whenever it is actually triggered by an invasive pathogen. When activated, human immunological responses consume substantial metabolic resources, often to such an extent that individuals are temporarily debilitated. The same is true of psychological defense systems. It is certainly adaptive to have the capacity to experience fear, because that capacity serves to prevent contact with things that might just kill us. However, an actual fearful response consumes metabolic resources. And by diverting resources toward behavioral withdrawal, it temporarily prevents individuals from engaging in other forms of potentially fitness-enhancing behavior (e.g., food acquisition, procreation). Consequently, psychological defense mechanisms, such as fear, are functionally flexible: they are activated differentially (and with different levels of magnitude) depending on the presence of information signaling whether the potential benefit of a defensive response is likely to outweigh the costs associated with that response. If additional information indicates that individuals are highly vulnerable to danger, this signals a greater benefit/cost ratio and is more likely to result in a fearful response. However, if additional information indicates that one is relatively invulnerable to danger, the benefit/cost ratio is drastically reduced, and a fearful response is less likely to occur. Consider, for example, the acoustic startle reflex—the tendency for sudden loud noises to automatically elicit a fearful startle response. When people are in the dark—an ecological condition that heuristically signals greater vulnerability—the acoustic startle response occurs more strongly (Grillon, Pellowski, Merikangas, & Davis, 1997).

This evolutionary logic of functional flexibility has clear implications for the activation of group stereotypes and prejudices (Schaller, Park, & Faulkner, 2003; Schaller, Park, & Kenrick, 2007). Although there may be some default inclination to perceive out-groups as dangerous, this implicit inclination is likely to vary depending on the extent to which individuals perceive themselves to be vulnerable to that danger. If for whatever reason an individual feels highly vulnerable to harm (whether that perception is realistic or fantastic, and whether it is a chronic attitude or a fleeting concern), then that individual is especially likely to demonize out-groups—to fear them, to perceive them to be stereotypically dangerous, and to feel justified in preemptively acting aggressively toward them. On the other hand, if an individual feels relatively invulnerable to harm, intergroup cognitions and behaviors are likely to be more generous.

The logic of functional flexibility also implies that important sex differences in stereotyping, prejudice, and discrimination may exist. If, like the chimpanzee males just discussed, human males have been more vulnerable than females to the threat of intergroup violence, it suggests that men especially may have benefited from a cautious approach to intergroup contact. If so, men may be more likely to exhibit a default tendency toward viewing out-groups as stereotypically dangerous and to behaving in aggressive ways when viewing themselves to have a relative advantage. Moreover, the prejudicial responses of men (compared to those of women) may be especially sensitive to vulnerability-connoting cues.

IMPLICATIONS FOR CONTEMPORARY STEREOTYPES, PREJUDICES, AND CONFLICTS

Variation in the Acquisition and Activation of Fearful Intergroup Cognitions

The preceding evolutionary analysis implies three general hypotheses: (1) People have an implicit tendency to fear out-groups and out-group members and to stereotypically associate them with danger-connoting characteristics; (2) this implicit tendency is exaggerated when individuals perceive themselves to be especially vulnerable to harm, and it is attenuated when individuals perceive themselves to be relatively invulnerable; and (3) these tendencies are likely to be especially strong among men. Evidence of various kinds supports all three of these hypotheses.

One manifestation of the alleged inclination to fear out-group members occurs in the associative learning process through which individuals acquire specific stereotypes and prejudices in the first place. People find it easier to learn (and harder to unlearn) aversive responses to out-group faces (e.g., Olsson, Ebert, Banaji, & Phelps, 2005).

Once learned, these danger-connoting stereotypic associations and fearful responses may be activated any time one perceptually encounters an out-group member. Empirical evidence of this tendency shows up not only in self-report data, but also in physiological measures. People show heightened levels of threat-relevant physiological reactions in the presence of unfamiliar out-group members (Blascovich, Mendes, Hunter, Lickel, & Kowai-Bell, 2001; Phelps, et al. 2000), and those who show the greatest amygdala activity—an indicator of a fearful response—when viewing out-group faces also possess more negative cognitive associations with the out-group. These findings suggest that individuals have a highly automatized tendency to perceive out-groups as sources of potential danger, and that this perceived danger is linked to prejudicial cognitions.

Even though people may be biologically prepared to associate out-group members with danger, this tendency is malleable. Biological preparedness implies the operation of a learning process and, as Öhman (2005, p. 713) notes, "what is learned can be unlearned." Among people with a history of forming interpersonal relationships across group boundaries, there is a reduced tendency to learn a conditioned aversive response to out-group faces (Olsson et al., 2005).

More generally, and consistent with the principle of functional flexibility, there is abundant evidence that danger-connoting stereotypes and prejudices are more or less likely to be activated into working memory depending on individuals' perceptions of their own vulnerability. For instance, one set of studies revealed that danger-connoting stereotypic traits of Blacks were more strongly activated into working memory among non-Black individuals who (a) chronically believed that the world was a dangerous place and (b) were in the dark (Schaller, Park, & Mueller, 2003). In another study, the same variables predicted Canadians' prejudicial beliefs about Canada and Iraq: Canadians who were chronically worried about danger and who were in the dark were especially likely to perceive their countrymen as trustworthy and to perceive Iraqis as untrustworthy (Schaller, Park, & Faulkner, 2003). It is worth noting that these effects were specific to danger-relevant prejudices; no effects whatsoever were found on highly evaluative but danger-irrelevant belief items (e.g., beliefs about intelligence).

When a danger-connoting stereotype about an out-group is activated into working memory, it not only influences judgments of the entire out-group, but also influences inferences about individual out-group members. Maner et al. (2005) found that when perceivers felt personally vulnerable to danger—after watching scenes from a frightening movie—they were especially likely to erroneously perceive anger (but not other emotions) in the faces of out-group members (but not in-group members). This perception of anger—an expression that signals dangerousness and hostile intent—occurred even though the target faces were not actually displaying any real emotional signals whatsoever.

This highlights an important point: the effects we have described, and describe next, do not require that a group or group member targeted for prejudice and danger-connoting cognitions *actually* pose a realistic threat. Rather, they merely need to possess a characteristic that has been probabilistically associated with the threat. Large, rapidly approaching men from an unfamiliar group may indeed pose authentic dangers—and likely did in ancestral times—but a particular man so described on the street in a strange city may merely be running past you to catch a bus. Nonetheless, the evolved cognitive system is conservative, and fitness considerations suggest stereotypes and prejudices are likely to err toward characterizing out-groups and their members as dangerous (e.g., Haselton & Nettle, 2006; Nesse, 2005; R. Fox, 1992). Thus, even though the fearful perceivers in the Maner at al. (2005) study were looking at out-group faces with objectively *neutral* expressions, they nonetheless saw them as expressing anger: the skin color of the faces activated thoughts of dangerousness, and so perceivers "saw" danger in the form of anger on the faces. We will see other forthcoming examples of the irrational—but, from an evolutionary perspective, predictable, and protective—nature of prejudicial cognitions.

What about sex differences in these sorts of intergroup cognitions? Consistent with the implications of the evolutionary cost/benefit analysis, there is empirical evidence that men are more likely than women to respond aversively to out-groups. Across many studies, men report higher levels of racism and ethnocentrism than women and are more likely to show in-group favoritism in ratings of ad hoc coalitional groups (e.g., Gerard & Hoyt, 1974; Sidanius, Cling, & Pratto, 1991; Watts, 1996). In addition, in several of the studies previously reviewed here, the prejudicial responses of men showed a greater sensitivity to the presence of vulnerability cues. For instance, in one study reported by Schaller, Park, and Mueller (2003), men showed a stronger interactive effect of chronic vulnerability and ambient darkness on the activation of danger-relevant Black stereotypes. There was a similar sex difference in the study that examined Canadians' beliefs about Iraqi untrustworthiness (Schaller, Park, & Faulkner, 2003). Several other lines of research also indicate that, compared to women, men perceive more threat within intergroup contexts and are more responsive to that threat in a variety of different ways (Pemberton, Insko, & Schopler, 1996; Van Vugt, De Cremer, & Janssen, 2007). The pattern emerging in these findings suggests that while danger-avoidant intergroup cognitions are triggered across both sexes, they are likely to be triggered especially strongly in men.

Instigation and Persistence of Intergroup Conflict

Our analysis thus far indicates that, because the human brain evolved in a social ecology marked by real intergroup conflict, there emerged a set of psychological mechanisms that dispose individuals to distrust out-groups and their members—to reflexively perceive them as threatening, even in the absence of any explicit evidence of real threat. This can have terrible consequences because, like a self-fulfilling prophecy, these perceptions may precipitate conflict where none existed in the first place. The perception of threat instigates competitive behavior in mixed-motive experimental games (Insko & Schopler, 1998; Kelley & Stahelski, 1970). It contributes to acts of real-world aggression such as bullying and gang violence (Decker & Van Winkle, 1996; Dodge, 1980). It is a causal factor in small-scale tribal conflicts, as well as in large-scale civil and international wars (Bar-Tal, 2001; Chagnon, 1992; Chirot, 2001; Eidelson & Eidelson, 2003; Robarchek, 1990; Vasquez, 1992).

If stereotypic perceptions of threat precipitate intergroup conflict, and if these perceptions of threat are themselves amplified when individuals feel vulnerable to some sort of peril, the implication is that intergroup conflict is more likely to be precipitated (and sustained) under conditions in which individuals, for whatever reason, feel vulnerable.

Several lines of research are consistent with this perspective. One line of work has examined the impact that ruminations about death and mortality have on conflict-relevant political attitudes and actions. Americans for whom death and mortality are salient are more inclined to vote for a militaristic, conflict-oriented political leader (Cohen, Ogilvie, Solomon, Greenberg, & Pyszczynski, 2005; Landau et al., 2004). Among Americans with conservative political leanings, mortality salience leads individuals to be more supportive of extreme military measures (e.g., the use of nuclear and chemical weapons) and preemptive military attacks against perceived threats to national security (Pyszczynski et al., 2006). These kinds of findings are not peculiar to Americans: Iranians for whom mortality is salient are more likely to endorse martyrdom attacks (e.g., suicide bombings) against nations perceived to be threats (Pyszczynski et al., 2006).

Another line of research has examined how the perceived minority status of one's in-group may lead to conflict-sustaining political attitudes. If, as the cliché suggests, there is safety in numbers, then there is vulnerability in being outnumbered. Consistent with this intuitive notion is evidence from several species—including humans—that when individuals are in a relatively smaller group, they are more hypervigilant to potential dangers from outside the group (e.g., Roberts, 1996; Wirtz & Wawra, 1986). Thus, the very perception of being in a numerical minority group may arouse feelings of vulnerability to danger. This is important because, within many regions marked by persistent intergroup conflict, the members of every warring group may legitimately perceive their own group to be the outnumbered minority. Jews greatly outnumber Arabs within Israel but, within the Middle East more broadly, Arabs greatly outnumber Jews. Sinhalese greatly outnumber Tamils within Sri Lanka but, within southern Asia more broadly, Tamils greatly outnumber Sinhalese. These "double-minority" situations provide a geographical context that may lead all parties to feel they are outnumbered and therefore vulnerable, and that may be especially conducive to intractable conflict.

These double-minority situations also provide a unique opportunity to experimentally test whether conflict-sustaining attitudes are promoted by a "we are the outnumbered group" mindset. Schaller and Abeysinghe (2006) conducted such a study in Sri Lanka, during a fragile ceasefire in the civil war between the Sri Lankan government and Tamil rebellion forces. The participants were Sinhalese students. An experimental manipulation was introduced in the form of a geography task that temporarily made salient either just the island nation of Sri Lanka (within which Sinhalese outnumber Tamils), or a broader region of south Asia (within which Sinhalese are outnumbered by Tamils). Following the manipulation, stereotypes and conflict-relevant attitudes were assessed. Results revealed that when participants focused on the broader geographical region (and thus were inclined to think of their in-group as the outnumbered minority), their stereotypic perceptions of

Tamils were more demonizing, and their conflict-relevant attitudes were less conciliatory. Particularly notable was the fact that individuals who adopted the vulnerability-connoting minority mindset were less supportive of ongoing attempts to negotiate an end to the civil war. Those who adopted the mindset of the majority group, however, tended to perceive the Tamil out-group in less fearful way, and were more supportive of the peace process.

ADDITIONAL THREATS, ADDITIONAL PREJUDICES, ADDITIONAL IMPLICATIONS

Our discussion thus far has focused on one particular kind of evolutionarily important intergroup threat and its implications for contemporary intergroup prejudice. However, this is not the only kind of threat associated with out-group members, nor is the resulting prejudice the only form of prejudice directed toward out-group members.

The Threat of Parasite Transmission

We alluded earlier to the fitness threat posed by carriers of pathogenic parasites. As a result of this threat, it is been suggested that there evolved a sort of "behavioral immune system"—a suite of psychological processes that serve as a first line of immunological defense by promoting avoidance of potentially harmful parasites and their carriers (Schaller, 2006; Schaller & Duncan, 2007). This behavioral immune system is triggered by the perception of specific kinds of features indicating that another individual might already be infected. When any such feature is perceived, there ensues the automatic activation of specific emotions and cognitions (e.g., disgust; inferences about disease-connoting traits) that facilitate functional behavioral reactions. This system, like many evolved defense systems, tends to be hypersensitive, erring on the side of false-positive errors rather than false-negative errors. The result is that disease-avoidant responses may be triggered by the perception of people who are perfectly healthy but who just happen to appear, at some superficial level, not quite normal. It seems likely that this set of mechanisms evolved primarily in response to disease threats that existed within an individual's own social group (i.e., an already infected in-group member). And a growing body of evidence indicates that disease-avoidant responses are triggered by the perception of ostensible in-group members who appear morphologically anomalous is some way (e.g., disfigured or disabled or grossly obese; Park, Faulkner, & Schaller, 2003; Schaller & Duncan, 2007). Even so, because of their adaptive hypersensitivity, these processes may also be triggered by the perception of out-group members—especially those who are perceived to be "foreign"—with predictable consequences for intergroup prejudice and discrimination.

There are at least two plausible reasons why a subjective sense of foreignness might serve as a crude cue connoting a heightened risk of parasite transmission. One reason is that contact with individuals from previously unencountered populations is associated with an increased risk of contracting contagious diseases to which one has no acquired immunity. A second reason is that foreign peoples may be unaware of, and thus more likely to violate, local customs (such as those pertaining to food preparation and personal hygiene) that serve as barriers to the transmission of disease. When we infer that another person is fundamentally foreign in some way, it may trigger a concern that the person poses a threat to our physical health.

Consistent with this reasoning, people sometimes display disgust when speaking about ethnic out-groups (Schiefenhövel, 1997) and a greater sensitivity to disgust is associated with higher levels of both ethnocentrism and xenophobia (Navarrete & Fessler, 2006). That last result is consistent with the notion of functional flexibility—the implication that foreign-seeming peoples will inspire more negative responses when perceivers feel more vulnerable to the transmission of pathogenic parasites. Faulkner, Schaller, Park, and Duncan (2004) conducted a series of studies showing that individuals who were chronically more concerned about their vulnerability to disease also tended to have stronger anti-immigrant attitudes—but only toward immigrants from subjectively foreign locations. There was no such effect on attitudes toward culturally familiar immigrant populations. A conceptually identical conclusion emerged from two experiments (also reported by Faulkner et al., 2004) in which participants were randomly assigned to see a slide show that made salient either the threat of parasite transmission or, in a control condition, the threat of disease-irrelevant dangers (e.g., electrocution). Results revealed more strongly xenophobic attitudes after parasites were made salient. For instance, in one of these experiments, Canadian participants were told about a government program designed to recruit new immigrants to Canada, and then indicated how much of the budget should be spent to recruit immigrants from various nations that had been prerated as either culturally familiar (e.g., Taiwan, Poland) or unfamiliar (e.g., Mongolia, Brazil). Participants who had seen the control slide show allocated roughly equal amounts of money to recruit immigrants from both familiar and unfamiliar places; but those for whom parasite transmission had been made salient were much more likely to allocate money to recruit immigrants from familiar rather than unfamiliar places.

These underlying psychological processes may be implicated in various modern forms of intergroup aggression, such as "ethnic cleansing" and genocide. The horrible effectiveness of Nazi propaganda to inspire the genocidal complicity of ordinary citizens may have resulted, in part, from the fact that this propaganda abounded with text and images that cast Jews explicitly as parasites and vectors of disease (Suedfeld & Schaller, 2002).

Threats to the Efficiency of Group Processes

The presence of foreign peoples may also trigger an additional set of psychological processes that protect groups (and the individual group members whose reproductive fitness depends nontrivially on group-level outcomes) against threats to the efficiency of group processes.

Group living is enormously beneficial to individual-level reproductive fitness, and this fact has many social psychological implications (Brewer & Caporael, 2006; Campbell, 1982; Neuberg, Smith, & Asher, 2000). However, the benefits of group living depend, in part, on the efficiency of within-group interactions and group processes. Any individual who disrupts those interactions, interferes with those processes, or otherwise undermines the efficiency of group living may pose an indirect threat to the reproductive fitness of other group members.

There are a variety of specific kinds of within-group interactions and processes, of course, each of which may have somewhat distinct fitness implications. Some interactions may be devoted to the exchange of consumable resources; other interactions may be devoted to the assortment of mates; still other interactions may be devoted to the education and socialization of children; and so on. However, what virtually all such interactions require, in order to be accomplished most efficiently, is that the individuals involved have similar goals and follow similar normative rules as to the means through which those goals might be achieved. When the collection of individuals disagrees on the basic goals of childhood education, for instance, then it becomes very different to accomplish any single educational goal in an efficient manner. At an even more basic level, it is very difficult to accomplish any group-level task if the individuals within the group fail to speak the same language.

For this reason, any person who acts in a manner inconsistent with normative standards may be implicitly viewed by others as a threat to the integrity of the group (Neuberg et al., 2000). Subjectively foreign individuals—who necessarily imply some deviation from local population norms— are likely to be viewed as such a threat and to inspire a specific form of prejudice.

The affective response associated with this form of prejudice is not likely to be fear, nor is it likely to be the sort of core physical disgust associated with parasite-avoidance mechanisms. Rather, it is likely to be contempt—a combination of moral disgust and anger. The stereotypical trait inferences that accompany this prejudice are not likely to connote hostility or disease, but rather to connote a sort of moral wrongness. Behaviorally, this process is likely to manifest in much the same way that the parasite-avoidance process manifests—in discriminatory actions designed to keep foreign-seeming peoples at a distance. Failing that, group members are likely to marginalize or otherwise exclude these people from access to the institutionalized mechanisms—such as teaching in grade-school classrooms and gaining political office—through which groups socialize their members and accomplish their tasks.

FINAL THOUGHTS

A full understanding of intergroup prejudice and intergroup conflict requires a consideration of the socioecological circumstances in which our ancestors evolved and the problems they faced. From the evolutionary perspective, humans possess a set of adaptations designed by natural selection to address the kinds of threats they have long encountered as social animals. Each prejudice syndrome—comprised of a suite of emotional responses, cognitions, and behavioral inclinations—has been designed to deal with a particular threat. Different groups may elicit qualitatively different prejudices, depending on the threats they are perceived to pose. And some groups—such as populations perceived to be subjectively foreign—will elicit multiple forms of prejudice, because they are perceived to pose multiple forms of threat. These prejudice syndromes can be triggered by superficial features of out-group members that signal "threat" even when the actual threat may be nonexistent. This is especially likely to occur when, for whatever reason, individuals feel vulnerable to that threat. As a consequence—because the perception of threat inspires predictably hostile reactions—these psychological mechanisms forged in our evolutionary past have implications for intergroup conflict in the present.

Some people, especially those with a limited education in biology, tend to view evolutionary explanations of this sort with some dismay. They assume that if some phenomenon has roots in ancient evolutionary processes, then the phenomenon must be inevitable—and that is a depressing conclusion, especially when applied to social problems. This assumption is wrong, however, and the more accurate conclusion is much more optimistic. Many of the psychological processes that contribute to intergroup prejudices and conflicts may indeed have roots in our species' evolutionary history, and it is precisely *because* of this evolutionary history that these processes are highly flexible and responsive to features of the immediate context. This insight has useful implications for the practical problem of reducing inappropriate prejudices.

First, just as specific forms of intergroup discrimination and conflict may be enhanced in contexts that promote feelings of vulnerability, they may also be attenuated in contexts that promote feelings of safety and security. Objective assessments of (in)vulnerability are perhaps less important than subjective assessments. For instance, regardless of individuals' actual vulnerability to disease transmission, they may not easily tolerate the proximity of seemingly foreign peoples unless they feel subjectively invulnerable. Similarly, the actual size of groups within a conflict may matter less than individuals' subjective perceptions of the extent to which their group might be outnumbered by out-group members. Interventions that attend closely to these sorts of perceptions and attempt to constructively alter these perceptions may be especially successful at reducing intergroup hostilities and conflicts.

A second important practical implication results from the modularity implicit in the evolutionary perspective and its more specific corollary that there exists no single intergroup prejudice. Rather, there exist multiple, psychologically distinct prejudices, each of which is implicated by a different kind of threat. Each form of prejudice is triggered by a different set of cues; each is defined by different suite of emotional, cognitive, and behavioral responses; and each is moderated by a different set of variables. Consequently, no single intervention is likely to inhibit all forms of intergroup prejudice; there is no silver bullet. The fight against intergroup prejudices and intergroup conflicts will almost certainly require a multipronged approach, in which multiple intervention strategies are each devised to address specific prejudice syndromes.

The application of evolutionary principles to intergroup relations is still a young endeavor, yet it is already bearing fruit. The evolutionary approach has illuminated aspects of prejudice that have been long ignored. It has generated a host of novel predictions, empirical discoveries, and implications that may be applied productively to contemporary social problems. These insights are not just interesting; they are important.

REFERENCES

Bar-Tal, D. (2001). Why does fear override hope in societies engulfed by intractable conflict, as it does in the Israeli society. *Political Psychology, 22*, 601–627.

Blascovich, J., Mendes, W. B., Hunter, S. B., Lickel, B., & Kowai-Bell, N. (2001). Perceiver threat in social interactions with stigmatized others. *Journal of Personality and Social Psychology, 80*, 253–267.

Brewer, M. B. (1988). A dual process model of impression formation. In T. K. Srull & R. S. Wyer, Jr. (Eds.), *Advances in social cognition* (Vol. 1, pp. 1–36). Mahwah, NJ: Lawrence Erlbaum.

Brewer, M. B., & Caporael, L. (2006). An evolutionary perspective on social identity: Revisiting groups. In M. Schaller, J. A. Simpson, & D. T. Kenrick (Eds.), *Evolution and social psychology* (pp. 143–161). New York: Psychology Press.

Campbell, D. T. (1982). Legal and primary-group social controls. *Journal of Social and Biological Structures, 5*, 431–438.

Carneiro, R. L. (1990). Chiefdom-level warfare as exemplified in Fiji and the Cauca Valley. In J. Haas (Ed.), *The anthropology of war* (pp. 190–211). New York: Cambridge University Press.

Carpenter, C. R. (1974). Aggressive behavioral systems. In R. L. Holloway (Ed.), *Primate aggression, territoriality, and xenophobia* (pp. 459–496). New York: Academic Press.

Chagnon, N. A. (1988). Life histories, blood revenge, and warfare in a tribal population. *Science, 239*, 985–992.

Chagnon, N. A. (1992). *Yanomamö: The last days of Eden.* New York: Harcourt Brace.

Cheney, D. L. (1986). Interactions and relationships between groups. In B. B. Smuts, D. L. Cheney, R. M. Seyfarth, R. W. Wrangham, & T. T. Struhsaker, T. T. (Eds.), *Primate societies* (pp. 267–281). Chicago: University of Chicago Press.

Chirot, D. (2001). Introduction. In D. Chirot & M. E. P. Seligman (Eds.), *Ethnopolitical warfare: Causes, consequences, and possible solutions* (pp. 3–26). Washington: American Psychological Association.

Cohen, F., Ogilvie, D. M., Solomon, S., Greenberg, J., & Pyszczynski, T. (2005). American roulette: The effect of reminders of death on support for George W. Bush in the 2004 presidential election. *Analysis of Social Issues and Public Policy, 5*, 177–187.

Cosmides, L. (1989). The logic of social exchange: Has natural selection shaped how humans reason? *Cognition, 31*, 187–276.

Cottrell, C. A., & Neuberg, S. L. (2005). Different emotional reactions to different groups: A sociofuntional threat-based approach to "prejudice." *Journal of Personality and Social Psychology, 88*, 770–789.

Curtis, V., Aunger, R., & Rabie, T. (2004). Evidence that disgust evolved to protect from risk of disease. *Proceedings of the Royal Society of London B, 271*, S131–S133.

Decker, S. H., & Van Winkle, B. (1996). *Life in the gang.* New York: Cambridge University Press.

Dodge, K. A. (1980). Social cognition and children's aggressive behavior. *Child Development, 51*, 162–170.

Dugatkin, L. A. (1997). *Cooperation among animals: An evolutionary perspective.* New York: Oxford University Press.

Eibl-Eibesfeldt, I. (1974). The myth of the aggression-free hunter and gatherer society. In R. L. Holloway (Ed.), *Primate aggression, territoriality, and xenophobia* (pp. 435–457). New York: Academic Press.

Eidelson, R. J., & Eidelson, J. I. (2003). Dangerous ideas: Five beliefs that propel groups toward conflict. *American Psychologist, 58*, 192.

Faulkner, J., Schaller, M., Park, J. H., & Duncan, L. A. (2004). Evolved disease-avoidance mechanisms and contemporary xenophobic attitudes. *Group Processes and Intergroup Behavior, 7*, 333–353.

Ferguson, R. B. (1984). *Warfare, culture, and environment.* Orlando, FL: Academic Press.

Fox, E., Russo, R., Bowles, R., & Dutton, K. (2001). Do threatening stimuli draw or hold visual attention in subclinical anxiety? *Journal of Experimental Psychology: General, 130*, 681–700.

Fox, R. (1992). Prejudice and the unfinished mind: A new look at an old failing. *Psychological Inquiry, 3*, 137–152.

Gerard, H. B., & Hoyt, M. F. (1974). Distinctiveness of social categorization and attitude toward in-group members. *Journal of Personality and Social Psychology, 29*, 836–842.

Goodall, J. (1986). *The chimpanzees of Gombe*. Cambridge, MA: Belknap Press.

Gregor T. (1990). Uneasy peace: Intertribal relations in Brazil's Upper Xingu. In J. Haas (Ed.), *The anthropology of war* (pp. 105–124). New York: Cambridge University Press.

Grillon, C., Pellowski, M., Merikangas, K. R., & Davis, M. (1997). Darkness facilitates acoustic startle reflex in humans. *Biological Psychiatry, 42*, 453–460.

Haas, J. (1990). *The anthropology of war*. New York: Cambridge University Press.

Hasegawa, T. (1990). Sex differences in ranging patterns. In T. Nishida (Ed.), *The chimpanzees of the Mahale mountains* (pp. 99–114). Tokyo: University of Tokyo Press.

Haselton, M. G., & Nettle, D. (2006). The paranoid optimist: An integrative evolutionary model of cognitive biases. *Personality and Social Psychology Review, 10*, 47–66.

Insko, C. A., & Schopler, J. (1998). Differential distrust of groups and individuals. In C. Sedikides, J. Schopler, & C. A. Insko (Eds.), *Intergroup cognition and intergroup behavior* (pp. 75–107). Mahwah, NJ: Lawrence Erlbaum Associates.

Kelley, H. H., & Stahelski, A. J. (1970). Social interaction basis of cooperators' and competitors' beliefs about others. *Journal of Personality and Social Psychology, 16*, 66–91.

Kelly, R. L. (1995). *The foraging spectrum: Diversity in hunter-gatherer lifeways*. Washington, DC: Smithsonian Institution Press.

Kurzban, R., & Leary, M. R. (2001). Evolutionary origins of stigmatization: The functions of social exclusion. *Psychological Bulletin, 127*, 187–208.

Kurzban, R., & Neuberg, S. L. (2005). Managing in-group and out-group relationships. In D. Buss (Ed.), *Handbook of evolutionary psychology* (pp. 653–675). New York: John Wiley & Sons.

Kurzban, R., Tooby, J., & Cosmides, L. (2001). Can race be erased? Coalitional computation and social categorization. *Proceedings of the National Academy of Sciences, 98*, 15387–15392.

Landau, M. J., Solomon, S., Greenberg, J., Cohen, F., Pyszczynski, T., et al. (2004). Deliver us from evil: The effects of mortality salience and reminders of 9/11 on support for President George W. Bush. *Personality and Social Psychology Bulletin, 30*, 1136–1150.

Lebzelter, V. (1934). *Eingeborenenkulturen von Süd- und Südwestafrika*. Leipzig, Germany: Hiersemann.

Maner, J. K., Kenrick, D. T., Becker, D. V., Robertson, T., Hofer, B., Neuberg, S. L., et al. (2005). Functional projection: How fundamental social motives can bias interpersonal perception. *Journal of Personality and Social Psychology, 88*, 63–78.

Mealey, L., Daood, C., & Krage, M. (1996). Enhanced memory for faces of cheaters. *Ethology and Sociobiology, 17*, 119–28.

Navarrete, C. D., & Fessler, D. M. T. (2006). Disease avoidance and ethnocentrism: The effects of disease vulnerability and disgust sensitivity on intergroup attitudes. *Evolution and Human Behavior, 27*, 270–282.

Nesse, R. M. (2005). Natural selection and the regulation of defenses: A signal detection analysis of the smoke detector principle. *Evolution and Human Behavior, 26*, 88–105.

Neuberg, S. L., & Cottrell, C. A. (2006). Evolutionary bases of prejudices. In M. Schaller, J. A. Simpson, & D. T. Kenrick (Eds.), *Evolution and social psychology* (pp. 163–187). Psychology Press: New York.

Neuberg, S. L., Smith, D. M., & Asher, T. (2000). Why people stigmatize: Toward a biocultural framework. In T. Heatherton, R. Kleck, J. G. Hull, & M. Hebl (Eds.), *The social psychology of stigma* (pp. 31–61). New York: Guilford.

Öhman, A. (2005). Conditioned fear of a face: A prelude to ethnic enmity? *Science, 309*, 711–713.

Öhman, A., & Mineka, S. (2001). Fear, phobia, and preparedness: Toward an evolved module of fear and fear learning. *Psychological Review, 108*, 483–522.

Olsson, A., Ebert, J. P., Banaji, M. R., & Phelps, E. A. (2005). The role of social groups in the persistence of learned fear. *Science, 309*, 785–787.

Park, J. H., Faulkner, J., & Schaller, M. (2003). Evolved disease-avoidance processes and contemporary anti-social behavior: Prejudicial attitudes and avoidance of people with physical disabilities. *Journal of Nonverbal Behavior, 27,* 65–87.

Pemberton, M. B., Insko, C. A., & Schopler, J. (1996). Memory for and experience of differential competitive behavior of individuals and groups. *Journal of Personality and Social Psychology, 71,* 953–966.

Phelps, E. A., O'Conner, K. J., Cunningham, W. A., Funayama, E. S., Gatenby, J. C., Gore, J. C., et al. (2000). Performance on indirect measures of race evaluation predicts amygdala activation. *Journal of Cognitive Neuroscience, 12,* 729–738.

Pyszczynski, T., Abdollahi, A., Solomon, S., Greenberg, J., Cohen, F., & Weise, D. (2006). Mortality salience, martyrdom, and military might: The Great Satan versus the Axis of Evil. *Personality and Social Psychology Bulletin, 32,* 525–537.

Robarchek, C. (1990). Motivations and material causes: On the explanation of conflict and war. In J. Haas (Ed.), *The anthropology of war* (pp. 56–76). Cambridge, U.K.: Cambridge University Press.

Roberts, G. (1996). Why individual vigilance declines as group size increases. *Animal Behaviour, 51,* 1077–1086.

Schaller, M. (2006). Parasites, behavioral defenses, and the social psychological mechanisms through which cultures are evoked. *Psychological Inquiry, 17,* 96–101.

Schaller, M., & Abeysinghe, A. M. N. D. (2006). Geographical frame of reference and dangerous intergroup attitudes: A double-minority study in Sri Lanka. *Political Psychology, 27,* 615–631.

Schaller, M., & Duncan, L. A. (2007). The behavioral immune system: Its evolution and social psychological implications. In J. P. Forgas, M. G. Haselton, & W. von Hippel (Eds.), *Evolution and the social mind: Evolutionary psychology and social cognition.* (pp. 293–307). New York: Psychology Press.

Schaller, M., Park, J. H., & Faulkner, J. (2003). Prehistoric dangers and contemporary prejudices. *European Review of Social Psychology, 14,* 105–137.

Schaller, M., Park, J. H., & Kenrick, D. T. (2007). Human evolution and social cognition. In R. I. M. Dunbar & L. Barrett (Eds.), *Oxford handbook of evolutionary psychology* (pp. 491–504). Oxford, U.K.: Oxford University Press.

Schaller, M., Park, J. H., & Mueller, A. (2003). Fear of the dark: Interactive effects of beliefs about danger and ambient darkness on ethnic stereotypes. *Personality and Social Psychology Bulletin, 29,* 637–649.

Schiefenhövel, W. (1997). Good tastes and bad tastes: Preferences and aversions as biological principles. In H. MacBeth (Ed.), *Food preferences and taste* (pp. 55–64). Providence, RI: Berghahn.

Sidanius, J., Cling, B. J., & Pratto, F. (1991). Ranking and linking behavior as a function of sex and gender: An exploration of alternative explanations. *Journal of Social Issues, 47,* 131–149.

Smuts, B. B., Cheney, D. L., Seyfarth, R. M., Wrangham, R. W., & Struhsaker, T. T. (1986). *Primate societies.* Chicago: University of Chicago Press.

Southwick, C. H., Siddiqi, M. F., Farooqui, M. Y., & Pal, B. C. (1974). Xenophobia among free-ranging rhesus groups in India. In R. L. Holloway (Ed.), *Primate aggression, territoriality, and xenophobia* (pp. 185–212). New York: Academic Press.

Suedfeld, P., & Schaller, M. (2002). Authoritarianism and the Holocaust: Some cognitive and affective implications. In L. S. Newman & R. Erber (Eds.), *What social psychology can tell us about the Holocaust: Understanding perpetrator behavior* (pp. 68–90). Oxford, U.K.: Oxford University Press.

Van Vugt, M., De Cremer, D., & Janssen, D. (2007). Gender differences in cooperation and competition: The male warrior hypothesis. *Psychological Science, 18,* 19–23.

Vasquez, J. A. (1992). The steps to war: Toward a scientific explanation of Correlates of War findings. In J. A. Vasquez & M. T. Henehan (Eds.), *The scientific study of peace and war: A text reader.* New York: Lexington Books.

Watts, M. W. (1996). Political xenophobia in the transition from socialism: Threat, racism, and ideology among East German youth. *Political Psychology, 17,* 97–126.

Wrangham, R. W. (1987). The significance of African apes for reconstructing human social evolution. In W. G. Kinzey (Ed.), *The evolution of human behavior: Primate models* (pp. 51–71). Albany, NY: SUNY Press.

Wilson, M. L., & Wrangham, R. W. (2003). Intergroup relations in chimpanzees. *Annual Review of Anthropology, 32,* 363–392.

Wirtz, P., & Wawra, M. (1986). Vigilance and group size in *Homo sapiens. Ethology, 71,* 283–286.

22

The Evolution of Brain Mechanisms for Social Behavior

SIMON BARON-COHEN

In this chapter, I discuss the evolution of two cognitive processes, empathizing and systemizing, and their relevance to the evolution and development of social behavior.

EMPATHIZING

Empathizing is the drive to identify another person's emotions and thoughts and to respond to these with an appropriate emotion (Davis, 1994). Empathy is a skill (or a set of skills). As with any other skill, we all vary in it. In the same way that we can think about why someone is talented, average, or even disabled in these other areas, we can also think about individual differences in empathy.

In 1994, I proposed a model to specify the neurocognitive mechanisms that comprise the "mind-reading system" (Baron-Cohen, 1994, 1995). *Mind reading* is defined as the ability to interpret one's own or another agent's actions as driven by mental states. The model was proposed in order to explain (a) ontogenesis of a theory of mind and (b) neurocognitive dissociations that are seen in children with or without autism. The model is shown in Figure 22.1 and contains four components: (a) ID or the intentionality detector; (b) EDD or the eye direction detector; (c) SAM or the shared attention mechanism; and finally, (d) ToMM or the theory of mind mechanism.

ID and EDD build "dyadic" representations of simple mental states. ID automatically interprets or represents an agent's self-propelled movement as a desire or goal-directed movement, a sign of its agency, or an entity with volition (Premack, 1990). For example, ID interprets an animate-like moving shape as "it wants x," or "it has goal y." EDD automatically interprets or represents eye-like stimuli as "looking at me" or "looking at something else." That is, EDD picks out that an entity with

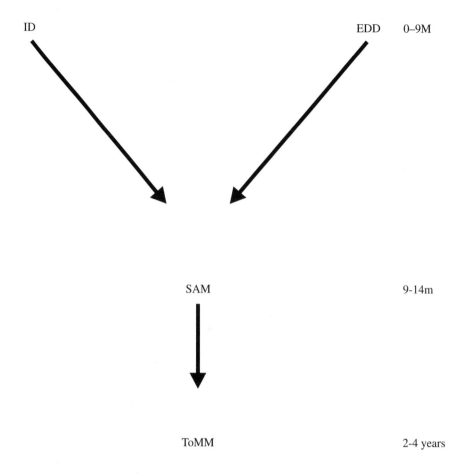

Figure 22.1 Baron-Cohen's (1994) model of the mind-reading system.

eyes can perceive. Both ID and EDD are developmentally prior to the other two mechanisms and are active early in infancy.

SAM is developmentally more advanced, and it comes on line at the end of the first year of life. SAM automatically interprets or represents if the self and another agent are (or are not) perceiving the same event. SAM does this by building "triadic" representations. For example, where ID can build the dyadic representation "Mother wants the cup" and where EDD can build the dyadic representation "Mother sees the cup," SAM can build the triadic representation "Mother sees that I see the cup." As is apparent, triadic representations involve embedding or recursion. (A dyadic representation—"I see a cup"—is embedded within another dyadic representation—"Mum sees the cup"—to produce this triadic representation.) SAM takes its input from ID and EDD, and triadic representations are made out of dyadic representations. SAM typically functions from 9–14 months of age and allows "joint attention" behaviors such as protodeclarative pointing and gaze monitoring (Scaife & Bruner, 1975).

ToMM allows an epistemic mental states to be represented (e.g., "Mother thinks this cup contains water" or "Mother pretends this cup contains water"), and it integrates the full set of mental state concepts (including emotions) into a theory. ToMM develops between 2 and 4 years of age and allows pretend play (Leslie, 1987), understanding of false belief (Wimmer & Perner, 1983), and understanding of the relationships between mental states (Wellman, 1990). An example of the latter is the seeing-leads-to-knowing principle (Pratt & Bryant, 1990), where the typical 3-year-old can infer that, if someone has seen an event, then they will know about it.

The model shows the ontogenesis if a theory of mind in the first 4 years of life and justifies the existence of four components based on developmental competence and neuropsychological dissociation. In terms of developmental competence, joint attention does not appear possible until 9–14 months of age, and joint attention appears to be a necessary but not sufficient condition for understanding epistemic mental states (Baron-Cohen, 1991; Baron-Cohen & Swettenham, 1996). There appears to be a developmental lag between acquiring SAM and ToMM, suggesting that these two mechanisms are dissociable. In terms of neuropsychological dissociation, congenitally blind children can ultimately develop joint (auditory or tactile) attention, using the amodal ID rather than the visual EDD route. Children with autism appear able to represent the dyadic mental states of seeing and wanting but show delays in shared attention (Baron-Cohen, 1989b) and in understanding false belief (Baron-Cohen, 1989a; Baron-Cohen, Leslie, & U. Frith, 1985)—that is, in acquiring SAM and ultimately ToMM. This specific developmental delay suggests that SAM is dissociable from EDD.

The 1994 model of the mind-reading system was revised in 2005 because of certain omissions and too narrow of a focus. The key omission is that information about affective states, available to the infant perceptual system, has no dedicated neurocognitive mechanism. In Figure 22.2, the revised model (Baron-Cohen, 2005) is shown, and it now includes a new fifth component: TED or the emotion detector. A particular problem for any account of the distinction between autism and psychopathy is the fact that the concept of mind reading (or theory of mind) makes no reference to the affective state in the observer triggered by recognition of another's mental state. For this reason, the revised model no longer focuses on "mind reading" but rather focuses on "empathizing," and also includes a new sixth component: TESS or the empathizing system. Where the 1994 mind-reading system was a model of a passive observer (all of the components had simple decoding functions), the 2005 empathizing system is a model of an observer impelled toward action (because an emotion is triggered in the observer, which typically motivates the observer to respond to the other person).

Like the other infancy perceptual input mechanisms of ID and EDD, the new component of TED can build dyadic representations of a special kind, namely, it can represent affective states. An example would be "Mother—is unhappy" or even "Mother—is angry—with me." Formally, we can describe this as agent affective state proposition. We know that infants can represent affective states from as early as 3 months of age (Walker, 1982). As with ID, TED is amodal, in that affective information can be picked up from facial expression, or vocal intonation, "motherese" being a particularly rich source of the latter (Field, 1979). Another's affective state is presumably also detectable from their touch (e.g., tense vs. relaxed), which implies that congenitally blind infants should find affective information accessible through both auditory and tactile modalities. TED allows the detection of the basic emotions (Ekman & Friesen, 1969). The development of TED is probably aided by simple imitation that is typical of infants (e.g., imitating caregiver's expressions) which in itself would facilitate emotional contagion (Meltzoff & Decety, 2003).

When SAM becomes available at 9–14 months of age, it can receive inputs from any of the three infancy mechanisms—ID, EDD, or TED. Here, I focus on how a dyadic representation of an affective state can be converted into a triadic representation by SAM. An example would be that the dyadic representation "Mother is unhappy" can be converted into a triadic representation "I am unhappy that Mother is unhappy," "Mother is unhappy that I am unhappy," and so forth. Again, as

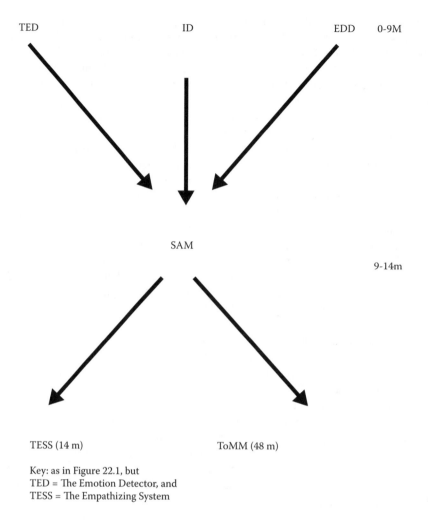

Figure 22.2 Baron-Cohen's (2005) model of empathizing.

with perceptual or volitional states, SAM's triadic representations of affective states have this special embedded, or recursive, property.

ToMM is of major importance in allowing the child to represent the full range of mental states, including epistemic ones (e.g., false belief) and is important in allowing the child to pull mentalistic knowledge into a useful theory with which to predict behavior (Baron-Cohen, 1995; Wellman, 1990). But TESS allows more than behavioral explanation and prediction (itself a powerful achievement). TESS allows an empathic reaction to another's emotional state. This, however, is not to say that these two modules do not interact. Knowledge of mental states of others made possible by TOMM could certainly influence the way in which an emotion is processed and/or expressed by TESS. TESS also allows for sympathy. This element of TESS gives it the adaptive benefit of ensuring that organisms feel a drive to help each other.

Before leaving this revision of the model, it is worth discussing why the need for this has arisen. First, emotional states are an important class of mental states to detect in others, and yet, the earlier model focused on only volitional, perceptual, informational, and epistemic states. Second, when it comes to pathology, it would appear that in autism TED may function, although its onset may be delayed (Baron-Cohen, Spitz, & Cross, 1993; Baron-Cohen, Wheelwright, & Jolliffe, 1997; Hobson, 1986), at least in terms of detecting basic emotions. Even high-functioning people with autism or Asperger Syndrome have difficulties both in ToMM (when measured with mental-age appropriate tests; Baron-Cohen, Jolliffe, Mortimore, & Robertson, 1997; Baron-Cohen, Wheelwright, Hill, Raste, & Plumb, 2001; Happe, 1994) and TESS (Attwood, 1997; Baron-Cohen, O'Riordan, Jones, Stone, & Plaisted, 1999; Baron-Cohen, Richler, Bisarya, Gurunathan, & Wheelwright, 2003; Baron-Cohen & Wheelwright, 2004; Baron-Cohen, Wheelwright, Stone, & Rutherford, 1999). I return to discuss autism further later in the chapter. But even at this point, this suggests TED and TESS may be fractionated.

In contrast, the psychiatric condition of psychopathy may entail an intact TED and ToMM, alongside an impaired TESS. The psychopath (or sociopath) can represent that you are in pain or that you believe he is the gasman, thereby gaining access to your house or your credit card. The psychopath can go on to hurt you or cheat you without having the appropriate affective reaction to your affective state. In other words, he or she does not care about your affective state (Blair, Jones, Clark, & Smith, 1997; Mealey, 1995). Lack of guilt or shame or compassion in the presence of another's distress are diagnostic of psychopathy (Cleckley, 1977; Hare, Hakstian, Ralph, Forth-Adelle, & Al, 1990). Separating TESS and ToMM thus allows a functional distinction to be drawn between the neurocognitive causes of autism and psychopathy.

DEVELOPMENTAL DISSOCIATIONS

Developmentally, one can also distinguish TED from TESS. We know that at 3 months of age, infants can discriminate facial and vocal expressions of emotion (Trevarthen, 1989; Walker, 1982) but that it is not until about 14 months that they can respond with appropriate affect (e.g., a facial expression of concern) to another's apparent pain (Yirmiya, Kasari, Sigman, & Mundy, 1989) or show "social referencing." Clearly, this account is skeletal in not specifying how many emotions TED is capable of recognizing. Our recent survey of emotions identities that there are 412 discrete emotion concepts that the adult English language user recognizes (Baron-Cohen, Wheelwright, Hill, & Golan, 2007). How many of these are recognized in the first year of life is not clear. It is also not clear exactly how empathizing changes during the second year of life. We have assumed the same mechanism that enables social referencing at 14 months old also allows sympathy and the growth of empathy across development. This is the most parsimonious model, though it may be that future research will justify further mechanisms that affect the development of empathy.

SEX DIFFERENCES IN EMPATHIZING—A CLUE
TO ITS EVOLUTIONARY ORIGINS?

Many studies converge on the conclusion that there is a female superiority in empathizing. These are reviewed here:

1. *Sharing and turn taking.* On average, girls show more concern for fairness, while boys share less. In one study, boys showed 50 times more competition, while girls showed 20 times more turn taking (Charlesworth & Dzur, 1987).
2. *Rough and tumble play or "rough housing" (e.g., wrestling, mock fighting, etc.).* Boys show more of this than girls do. Although there is a playful component, it can hurt or be intrusive, so it needs lower empathizing to carry it out (Maccoby, 1999).
3. *Responding empathically to the distress of other people.* Girls from 1 year old show greater concern through more sad looks, sympathetic vocalizations, and comforting. More women than men also report frequently sharing the emotional distress of their

friends. Women also show more comforting, even of strangers, than men do (Hoffman, 1977).

4. *Using a "theory of mind."* By 3 years old, little girls are already ahead of boys in their abilities to infer what people might be thinking or intending (Happe, 1995). This sex difference appears in some but not all studies (Charman, Ruffman, & Clements, 2002).

5. *Sensitivity to facial expressions.* Women are better at decoding nonverbal communication, picking up subtle nuances from tone of voice or facial expression, or judging a person's character (Hall, 1978).

6. *Questionnaires measuring empathy.* Many of these find that women score higher than men do (Davis, 1994).

7. *Values in relationships.* More women value the development of altruistic, reciprocal relationships, which by definition require empathizing. In contrast, more men value power, politics, and competition (Ahlgren & Johnson, 1979). Girls are more likely to endorse cooperative items on a questionnaire and to rate the establishment of intimacy as more important than the establishment of dominance. Boys are more likely than girls to endorse competitive items and to rate social status as more important than intimacy (Knight, Fabes, & Higgins, 1989).

8. *Disorders of empathy.* Disorders of empathy (e.g., psychopathic personality disorder, or conduct disorder) are far more common among males (Blair, 1995; Dodge, 1980).

9. *Aggression, even in normal quantities, can only occur with reduced empathizing.* Here again, there is a clear sex difference. Males tend to show far more "direct" aggression (e.g., pushing, hitting, punching, etc.), while females tend to show more "indirect" (or "relational," covert) aggression (e.g., gossip, exclusion, bitchy remarks, etc.). Direct aggression may require an even lower level of empathy than indirect aggression. Indirect aggression needs better mind-reading skills than does direct aggression, because its impact is strategic (Crick & Grotpeter, 1995).

10. *Murder is the ultimate example of a lack of empathy.* Daly and Wilson (1988) analyzed homicide records dating back over 700 years, from a range of different societies. They found that "male-on-male" homicide was 30–40 times more frequent than "female-on-female" homicide.

11. *Establishing a "dominance hierarchy."* Males are quicker to establish these. This in part may reflect their lower empathizing skills, often because a hierarchy is established by one person pushing others around to become the leader (Strayer, 1980).

12. *Language style.* Girls' speech is more cooperative, reciprocal, and collaborative. In concrete terms, this is also reflected in girls being able to keep a conversational exchange with a partner going for longer. When girls disagree, they are more likely to express their different opinion sensitively, in the form of a question, rather than an assertion. Boys' talk is more "single-voiced discourse" (the speaker presents their own perspective alone). The female speech style is more "double-voiced discourse" (girls spend more time negotiating with the other person, trying to take the other person's wishes into account; Smith, 1985).

13. *Talk about emotions.* Women's conversation involves much more talk about feelings, while men's conversation with each other tends to be more object or activity focused (Tannen, 1991).

14. *Parenting style.* Fathers are less likely than mothers are to hold their infant in a face-to-face position. Mothers are more likely to follow through the child's choice of topic in play, while fathers are more likely to impose their own topic. And mothers fine-tune their speech more often to match what the child can understand (Power, 1985).

15. *Face preference and eye contact*. From birth, females look longer at faces, particularly at people's eyes, and males are more likely to look at inanimate objects (Connellan, Baron-Cohen, Wheelwright, Ba'tki, & Ahluwalia, 2001).

16. *Finally, females have also been shown to have better language ability than males have.* It seems likely that good empathizing would promote language development (Baron-Cohen, Baldwin, & Crowson, 1997) and vice versa, so these may not be independent.

NATURAL SELECTION OF GOOD EMPATHY AMONG FEMALES?

Why might this sex difference in empathy exist? One possibility is that it reflects natural selection of empathy among females over human evolution. If one considers that good empathizing would have led to better caregiving, then since caregiving can be assumed to have been primarily a female activity until very recent history, those mothers who had better empathy would have succeeded in tuning into their infant offspring's preverbal emotional and physical needs better, which may have led to a higher likelihood of the infant surviving to an age to reproduce. Hence, good empathy in the mother would have promoted her inclusive fitness.

A second explanation is that females with better empathy might have found it easier to socialize—chat, gossip, and network—with other females, thereby being more successful in creating social support for themselves while engaged in being a caregiver to their infant. Social support from other females is also likely to buffer mothers from the range of life events (e.g., illness, poverty, loss, physical attack, etc.) that might otherwise threaten her ability to care for her offspring and, so, increase the likelihood of her infant surviving to the age of reproduction, thereby increasing her inclusive fitness.

Having spent some time discussing empathizing, I want to now turn to a very different cognitive process, systemizing, because of the evidence for this being stronger in males.

SYSTEMIZING

Systemizing is a new concept. By a "system," I mean something that takes inputs and deliver outputs. To systemize, one uses "if-then" (correlation) rules. The brain zooms in on a detail or parameter of the system and observes how this varies. That is, it treats a feature of a particular object or event as a variable. Alternately, a person actively, or systematically, manipulates a given variable. One notes the effect(s) of operating on one single input in terms of its effects elsewhere in the system (the output). If I do *x*, *a* changes to *b*. If *z* occurs, *p* changes to *q*. Systemizing, therefore, requires an exact eye for detail.

Systemizing involves observation of *input-operation-output* relationships, leading to the identification of laws to predict that event *x* will occur with probability *p* (Baron-Cohen, 2002). Some systems are 100% lawful (e.g., an electrical light switch or a mathematical formula). Systems that are 100% lawful have zero variance or only 1 degree of freedom and, therefore, can be 100% predicted (and controlled). A computer might be an example of a 90% lawful system: The variance is wider, or there are more degrees of freedom. The social world may be only 10% lawful. This is why systemizing the social world is of little predictive value.

Systemizing involves 5 phases: Phase 1 is *analysis*: Single observations of input and output are recorded in a standardized manner at the lowest level of detail. Phase 2 is *operation*: An operation is performed on the input and the change to the output is noted. Phase 3 is *repetition*: The same operation is repeated to test if the same pattern between input and output is obtained. Phase 4 is *law derivation*: A law is formulated of the form if *X* (operation) occurs, *A* (input) changes to *B*. Phase 5 is *confirmation/disconfirmation*: If the same pattern of input-operation-output holds true for all

Table 22.1 Main Types of Analyzable Systems

- **Technical** systems (e.g., a computer, a musical instrument, a hammer)
- **Natural** systems (e.g., a tide, a weather front, a plant)
- **Abstract** systems (e.g., mathematics, a computer program, syntax)
- **Social** systems (e.g., a political election, a legal system, a business)
- **Organizable** systems (e.g., a taxonomy, a collection, a library)
- **Motoric** systems (e.g., a sports technique, a performance, a musical technique)

instances, the law is retained. If a single instance does not fit the law, phases 2–5 are repeated, leading to modification of the law or a new law.

Systemizing nonagentive changes are effective because these are *simple* changes: The systems are at least moderately lawful, with narrow variance (or limited degrees of freedom). Agentive change is less suited to systemizing because the changes in the system are *complex* (wide variance or many degrees of freedom).

There are at least six kinds of systems that the human brain can analyze or construct, as shown in Table 22.1. Systemizing works for phenomena that are ultimately lawful, finite, and deterministic. The explanation is exact, and its truth value is testable. Systemizing is of almost no use for predicting moment-to-moment changes in a person's behavior. To predict human behavior, empathizing is required. Systemizing and empathizing are wholly different kinds of processes.

SEX DIFFERENCES IN SYSTEMIZING

What Is the Evidence for a Stronger Drive to Systemize in Males?

1. *Toy preferences.* Boys are more interested than girls in toy vehicles, weapons, building blocks, and mechanical toys, all of which are open to being "systemized" (Jennings, 1977).

2. *Adult occupational choices.* Some occupations are almost entirely male. These include metalworking, weapon making, manufacture of musical instruments, and the construction industries, such as boat building. The focus of these occupations is on creating systems (Geary, 1998).

3. *Math, physics, and engineering.* All of these disciplines require high systemizing and are largely male dominated. The Scholastic Aptitude Math Test (SAT-M) is the mathematics part of the test administered nationally to college applicants in the United States. Males on average score 50 points higher than females on this test (Benbow, 1988). Considering only individuals who score above 700, the sex ratio is 13:1 (men to women; Geary, 1996).

4. *Constructional abilities.* On average men score higher than women in an assembly task in which people are asked to put together a three-dimensional (3-D) mechanical apparatus. Boys are also better at constructing block buildings from two-dimensional (2-D) blueprints. Lego bricks can be combined and recombined into an infinite number of systems. Boys show more interest than girls do in playing with Lego. Boys as young as 3 years of age are also faster at copying 3-D models of outsized Lego pieces. Older boys, from the age of 9 years, are better than girls are at imagining what a 3-D object will look like if it is laid out flat. Boys are also better at constructing a 3-D structure from just an aerial and frontal view in a picture (Kimura, 1999).

5. *The water level task.* Originally devised by the Swiss child psychologist Jean Piaget, the water level task involves a bottle that is tipped at an angle. Individuals are asked to predict the water level if the water level will be horizontal or aligned with the angle of the bottle. Women more often draw the water level aligned with the tilt of the bottle and not horizontal, as is correct (Wittig & Allen, 1984).

6. *The rod and frame test.* If a person's judgment of vertical is influenced by the tilt of the frame, he or she is said to be "field dependent"; that is, their judgment is easily swayed by extraneous input in the surrounding context. If they are not influenced by the tilt of the frame, they are said to be "field independent." Most studies indicate that females are more field dependent; that is, women are relatively more distracted by contextual cues, and they tend not to consider each variable within a system separately. They are more likely than men to state erroneously that a rod is upright if it is aligned with its frame (Witkin et al., 1954).

7. *Good attention to relevant detail.* This is a general feature of systemizing and is clearly a necessary part of it. Attention to relevant detail is superior in males. One measure of this is the embedded figures test. On average, males are quicker and more accurate in locating a target object from a larger, complex pattern (Elliot, 1961). Males, on average, are also better at detecting a particular feature (static or moving) than women are (D. Voyer, S. Voyer, & Bryden, 1995).

8. *The mental rotation test.* This test provides another example in which males are quicker and more accurate. This test involves systemizing because it is necessary to treat each feature in a display as a variable that can be transformed (e.g., rotated) and then predict the output or how it will appear after transformation (Collins & Kimura, 1997).

9. *Reading maps.* This is another everyday test of systemizing, because features from 3-D input must be transformed to a 2-D representation. In general, boys perform at a higher level than girls do in map reading. Men can also learn a route by looking at a map in fewer trials than women can, and they are more successful at correctly recalling detail about direction and distance. This observation suggests that men treat features in the map as variables that can be transformed into three dimensions. When children are asked to make a map of an area that they have visited only once, boys' maps have a more accurate layout of the features in the environment. More of the girls' maps make serious errors in the location of important landmarks. Boys tend to emphasize routes or roads, whereas girls tend to emphasize specific landmarks (e.g., the corner shop, the park, etc.). These strategies of using directional cues versus using landmark cues have been widely studied. The directional strategy represents an approach to understanding space as a geometric system. Similarly, the focus on roads or routes is an example of considering space in terms of another system, in this case a transportation system (Galea & Kimura, 1993).

10. *Motoric systems.* When people are asked to throw or catch moving objects (target directed tasks), such as playing darts or intercepting balls flung from a launcher, males tend to perform better than females. In addition, on average men are more accurate than women in their ability to judge which of two moving objects is traveling faster (Schiff & Oldak, 1990).

11. *Organizable systems.* People in the Aguaruna tribe of northern Peru were asked to classify 100 or more examples of local specimens into related species. Men's classification systems included more subcategories (i.e., they introduced greater differentiation) and were more consistent among individuals. Interestingly, the criteria that the Aguaruna men used to decide which animals belonged together more closely resembled the taxonomic criteria used by Western (mostly male) biologists (Atran, 1994). Classification

and organization involves systemizing because categories are predictive. With more fine-grained categories, a system will provide more accurate predictions.

12.   *The systemizing quotient.* This questionnaire has been tested among adults in the general population. It includes 40 items that ask about a subject's level of interest in a range of different systems that exist in the environment, including technical, abstract, and natural systems. Males score higher than females on this measure (Baron-Cohen et al., 2003).

13.   *Mechanics.* The Physical Prediction Questionnaire (PPQ) is based on an established method for selecting applicants to study engineering. The task involves predicting which direction levers will move when an internal mechanism of cogwheels and pulleys is engaged. Men score significantly higher on this test, compared with women (Lawson, Baron-Cohen, & Wheelwright, 2004).

Evolutionary accounts for the male advantage in systemizing include the argument that males were primarily involved in hunting and tracking of prey, and that a male who was a good systemizer would have had greater success in both using and making tools for hunting, or navigating space to explore far afield, Both could have affected a male's reproductive success. Secondly, a good systemizer would have been better placed to acquire wealth or status through being expert in making things, and wealth/status is correlated with reproductive success because of sexual selection.

Some might argue that socialization may have caused these sex differences in both empathizing and systemizing. Although evidence exists for differential socialization contributing to sex differences, this is unlikely to be a sufficient explanation. Connellan and colleagues (2001) showed that, among one-day-old babies, boys look longer at a mechanical mobile, which is a system with predictable laws of motion, than at a person's face, an object that is next to impossible to systemize. One-day-old girls show the opposite profile. These sex differences are therefore present very early in life. This raises the possibility that, while culture and socialization may partly determine the development of a male brain with a stronger interest in systems or a female brain with a stronger interest in empathy, biology may also partly determine this. There is ample evidence to support both cultural determinism and biological determinism (Eagly, 1987; Gouchie & Kimura, 1991). For example, the amount of time a one-year-old child maintains eye contact is inversely related to the prenatal level of testosterone (Lutchmaya, Baron-Cohen, & Raggatt, 2002). The evidence for the role of fetal testosterone (FT) is reviewed next and more extensively elsewhere (Baron-Cohen, 2003).

FETAL TESTOSTERONE AS AN ORGANIZER OF BRAIN DEVELOPMENT AND SEXUAL DIMORPHISM

Both male and female fetuses produce some testosterone. In males, the main source is the testes. Females are exposed to small amounts of testosterone from the fetal adrenal glands and from the maternal adrenals, ovaries, and fat. Testosterone can be measured in amniotic fluid collected during midtrimester amniocentesis. Testosterone is thought to enter the amniotic fluid via diffusion through the fetus' skin in early pregnancy and later from fetal urination. Although the exact correlation between testosterone levels in the fetal serum and the amniotic fluid is unknown, the maximal sex difference in amniotic testosterone between males and females occurs between weeks 12 and 18, closely paralleling peak serum levels. In animal models, the general critical period for sexual differentiation of the brain usually occurs when sex differences in serum testosterone are highest. Therefore, this is likely an important period for sexual differentiation of the human brain as well. This is supported by the study that found that only prenatal androgen exposure in the 2nd trimester related to adult gendered behavior and by the study that found a relationship between gendered play and testosterone in maternal blood during pregnancy at a mean gestational age of 16 weeks.

The amniocentesis design has several strengths. As with the measurement of testosterone in maternal blood, it involves quantitative measures of hormone levels and measures normal variability. For example, Addenbrooke's Hospital, which analyzes amniocentesis samples from six hospitals in East Anglia, United Kingdom, processes approximately 1,000 samples a year. Amniocentesis takes place in midgestation, which is thought to be an important period for sexual differentiation of the human brain and, unlike studies using maternal blood, testosterone exposure can be measured in both boys and girls. A significant limitation of research using this method is that a truly random sample cannot be collected, since one can include in a study only those individuals who have decided/been advised to have an amniocentesis due to late maternal age or other factors that increase the risk of fetal abnormality. In the following section, I review the results of a longitudinal study examining the relationship between amniotic testosterone, social development, and other traits.

The Cambridge Fetal Testosterone Project

At Cambridge University, we have been following up a group of approximately 100 children whose fetal testosterone level had been measured in amniotic fluid. Their mothers had undergone amniocentesis in the Cambridge region between June 1996 and June 1997 and had given birth to the healthy singleton infants between December 1996 and December 1997. The children were first seen at 12 months of age when the infants and parents were filmed and the amount of eye contact made by the infant to the parent was recorded. Eye contact is of major importance in normal social development. Infants as young as 2 months of age spend more time looking at the eye region of the face than any other part of the face. This may also be relevant to autism, which is defined by marked social impairment, including abnormal eye contact. Girls made significantly more eye contact than boys did. The amount of eye contact varied quadratically with amniotic testosterone level when data from both sexes was examined together and when the data for the boys was examined alone. This suggests that testosterone may shape the neural mechanisms underlying social development.

The children were next followed up 18 and 24 months after birth and their vocabulary size was assessed using the Oxford Communicative Development Inventory. Girls were found to have a significantly larger vocabulary than boys did at both ages. This replicates previous findings of a female advantage in language ability but reveals this sex difference at the earliest point of development. Additionally, amniotic testosterone was an inverse predictor of vocabulary size when data from both sexes was examined together but not within sex. The lack of a significant correlation between testosterone and vocabulary within each sex may reflect the relatively small sample size. However, the significant correlation between testosterone and vocabulary when the sexes were combined suggests testosterone might be involved in shaping the neural mechanisms underlying communicative development.

The children were next followed up at 48 months. Their mothers completed the Children's Communication Checklist, a questionnaire assessing language, quality of social relationships and restricted interests. Amniotic testosterone was negatively correlated to quality of social relationships and directly correlated with restricted interests, taking into account sex differences. Testosterone was also positively correlated with restricted interests when boys were examined separately. These findings implicate testosterone in both social development and attentional focus. Causal interpretations are, of course, unjustified from these correlational studies, but the results suggest that high levels of fetal testosterone could produce a behavioral profile of lower empathy alongside stronger systemizing. (Full details of this study are available in Simon Baron-Cohen's *Prenatal Testosterone in Mind,* MIT Press, 2005.)

Table 22.2 The Main Brain Types

Profile	Shorthand Equation	Type of Brain
Individuals in whom empathizing is more developed than systemizing	E > S	Type E: more common in females
Individuals in whom systemizing is more developed than empathizing	S > E	Type S: more common in males
Individuals in whom systemizing and empathizing are both equally developed	S = E	"balanced" or Type B
Individuals in whom systemizing is hyper-developed while empathizing is hypo-developed	S > > E	Extreme Type S: the extreme male brain; more common in people with an autism spectrum condition
Individuals who have hyper-developed empathizing skills, while their systemizing is hypo-developed	E > > S	Extreme Type E: the extreme female brain (postulated)

BRAIN TYPES

We all have both systemizing and empathizing skills. One can envisage five broad types of brain, as Table 22.2 shows. The evidence reviewed here suggests that not all men have the male brain and not all women have the female brain. Expressed differently, some women have the male brain, and some men have the female brain. My claim here is only that *more* males than females have a brain of type S, and *more* females than males have a brain of type E. Data relevant to this claim is summarized elsewhere (Goldenfeld, Baron-Cohen, & Wheelwright, 2005).

AUTISM: HYPER-SYSTEMIZING ALONGSIDE IMPAIRED EMPATHIZING?

The autistic spectrum comprises four subgroups: Asperger Syndrome (AS; Asperger, 1944; U. Frith, 1991) and high-, medium-, and low-functioning autism (Kanner, 1943). They all share the phenotype of social difficulties and obsessional interests (American Psychiatric Association [APA], 1994). In AS, the individual has normal or above average IQ and has no language delay. In the three autism subgroups, there is invariably some degree of language delay, and the level of functioning is indexed by overall IQ. These four subgroups are known as autism spectrum conditions (ASC).

In terms of causes, the consensus is that ASC have a genetic etiology (Bailey et al., 1995), which leads to altered brain development (Baron-Cohen, Ring, et al., 1999; Courchesne, 2002; C. Frith & U. Frith, 1999; Happe et al., 1996) affecting social and communication development and leading to the presence of unusual narrow interests and extreme repetitive behavior (APA, 1994). I have already reviewed some evidence for empathy impairments in ASC (but for an extensive review, see Baron-Cohen, 1995). In the next section, I review evidence for hyper-systemizing in autism and in first-degree relatives of people with autism. Such findings are then discussed for their significance for the evolution of systemizing in the general population.

THE SYSTEMIZING MECHANISM

The hyper-systemizing theory of ASC posits that all human brains have a systemizing mechanism (SM), and this is set at different levels in different individuals. In people with ASC, the SM is set too high. The SM is like a volume control. Evidence suggests that within the general population, there are eight degrees of systemizing.

Level 1. Such individuals have little or no drive to systemize, and consequently, they can cope with rapid, unlawful change. Their SM is set so low that that they hardly notice if the input is structured or not. While this would not interfere with their ability to socialize, it would lead to a lack of precision over detail when dealing with structured information. We can think of this as *hypo-systemizing.* Such a person would be able to cope with agentive change easily but may be challenged when dealing with highly lawful, nonagentive systems.

Levels 2 and 3. Most people have *some* interest in lawful, nonagentive systems, and there are sex differences in this. More females in the general population have the SM set at Level 2, and more males have it set at Level 3 (see the evidence for sex differences reviewed earlier).

Level 4. Level 4 corresponds to individuals who systemize at a higher level than average. There is some evidence that above average systemizers have more autistic traits. Thus, scientists (who by definition have the SM set above average) score higher than nonscientists on the Autism Spectrum Quotient (AQ). Mathematicians score highest of all scientists on the AQ (Baron-Cohen, Wheelwright, Skinner, Martin, & Clubley, 2001). Parents of children with ASC also have their SM set higher than average (Baron-Cohen & Hammer, 1997; Happe, Briskman, & U. Frith, 2001) and have been described as having the "broader phenotype" of autism. At Level 4, one would expect a person to be talented at understanding systems with moderate variance or lawfulness.

Level 5. People with AS have their SM set at Level 5: The person can easily systemize lawful systems such as calendars or train timetables (Hermelin, 2002). Experimental evidence for hypersystemizing in AS includes the following: (a) People with AS score higher than average on the Systemizing Quotient (SQ; Baron-Cohen et al., 2003); (b) people with AS perform at a normal or high level on tests of intuitive physics or geometric analysis (Baron-Cohen, Wheelwright, Scahill, Lawson, & Spong, 2001; Jolliffe & Baron-Cohen, 1997; Lawson et al., 2004; Shah & U. Frith, 1983); (c) people with AS can achieve extremely high levels in domains such as mathematics, physics, or computer science (Baron-Cohen, Wheelwright, Stone, et al., 1999c); and (d) people with AS have an "exact mind" when it comes to art (Myers, Baron-Cohen, & Wheelwright, 2004) and show superior attention to detail (O'Riordan, Plaisted, Driver, & Baron-Cohen, 2001; Plaisted, O'Riordan, & Baron-Cohen, 1998).

Levels 6–8. In people with high-functioning autism (HFA), the SM is set at Level 6; in those with medium-functioning autism (MFA), it is at Level 7; and in low-functioning autism (LFA), it is at the maximum setting (Level 8). Thus, people with HFA try to socialize or empathize by "hacking" (i.e., systemizing; Happe, 1996), and on the picture-sequencing task, they perform above average on sequences that contain temporal or physical-causal information (Baron-Cohen, Leslie, & U. Frith, 1986). People with MFA perform above average on the false photograph task (Leslie & Thaiss, 1992). In LFA, their obsessions cluster in the domain of systems, such as watching electric fans go round (Baron-Cohen & Wheelwright, 1999); and given a set of colored counters, they show extreme "pattern imposition" (U. Frith, 1970).

The evidence for systemizing being part of the phenotype for ASC includes the following: Fathers and grandfathers of children with ASC are twice as likely to work in the occupation of engineering (a clear example of a systemizing occupation), compared to men in the general population (Baron-Cohen, Wheelwright, Stott, Bolton, & Goodyer, 1997). The implication is that these fathers and grandfathers have their SM set higher than average (Level 4). Students in the natural sciences (engineering, mathematics, and physics) have a higher number of relatives with autism than do students in the humanities (Baron-Cohen et al., 1998). Mathematicians have a higher rate of AS compared to the general population, and so do their siblings (Baron-Cohen, Wheelwright, Burtenshaw, & Hobson, 2006).

The evidence that autism could be the genetic result of having *two* high systemizers as parents (assortative mating) includes the following: (a) Both mothers *and* fathers of children with AS have been found to be strong in systemizing on the embedded figures test (Baron-Cohen & Hammer, 1997); (b) both mothers and fathers of children with autism or AS have elevated rates of systemizing occupations among their fathers (Baron-Cohen, Wheelwright, Stott, et al., 1997); and (c) both mothers and fathers of children with autism show hyper-masculinized patterns of brain activity during a systemizing task (Baron-Cohen et al., 2006). Whether the current high rates of ASC simply reflect better recognition, growth of services, and widening of diagnostic categories to include AS, or also reflect the increased likelihood of two high systemizers have children, is a question for future research.

It is important to stress that the term *assortative mating* here may not be entirely accurate. What the available evidence allows us to conclude is that parents of children with an ASC share a common psychological trait: hyper-systemizing. How they came to share this is not at all clear. Assortative mating would imply that the two parents were attracted to and chose their partners based on this common psychological trait. While this may be the case (e.g., each may have been impressed by the remarkable mind of the other, displayed as excellent attention to detail and in depth knowledge of how a system works), it is equally possible that the two individuals formed a couple because of some other factor (e.g., proximity, due to both of them working in a field that required good systemizing; availability, due to both of them being single because those with higher levels of empathy had already formed couples; awareness levels, due to both of them being relatively oblivious of the eccentricities of the other because of their lower levels of social awareness; or immunity to convention, due to both of them being less interested in what others in the social group might think about their partner choice). Future research will need to test these alternatives against each other. The important point for the transmission and mixing of the genes related to systemizing is that through whatever means, mating of such couples (which cannot be random) may have increased the likelihood of having a child with an ASC.

CONCLUSIONS

This chapter has reviewed the development of neurocognitive mechanisms underpinning two key psychological processes: empathizing and systemizing. These show strong sex differences and, therefore, might reflect natural selection operating differently on the two sexes. Also reviewed is the evidence that individuals on the autistic spectrum, which has a genetic basis, have degrees of empathizing difficulties alongside hyper-systemizing. According to the hyper-systemizing theory, ASC are the result of a normative SM—the function of which is to serve as a change-predicting mechanism—being set too high. While ASCs are disabling in the social world, hyper-systemizing can lead to talent in areas that are systemizable. In this sense, it is likely that the genes for increased systemizing have made remarkable contributions to human history (Fitzgerald, 2000, 2002; James, 2003). Finally, the assortative mating theory proposes that the cause of ASC is the genetic combination of having two strong systemizers as parents. This theory remains to be fully tested, but if confirmed, may help explain why the genes that can cause social disability have also been maintained in the gene pool, as they confer all the fitness advantages that strong systemizing can bring on the first-degree relatives of people with such conditions.

ACKNOWLEDGEMENTS

I am grateful for the support of the MRC and the Nancy Lurie-Marks Family Foundation during this work. Portions of this paper are taken from elsewhere (Baron-Cohen, 2005, 2006; Knickmeyer & Baron-Cohen, 2006).

REFERENCES

Ahlgren, A., & Johnson, D. W. (1979). Sex differences in cooperative and competitive attitudes from the 2nd to the 12th grades. *Developmental Psychology, 15*, 45–49.

American Psychiatric Association. (1994). *DSM-IV diagnostic and statistical manual of mental disorders* (4th ed.). Washington, DC: Author.

Asperger, H. (1944). Die "autistischen psychopathen" im kindesalter [English Translation]. *Archiv fur Psychiatrie und Nervenkrankheiten, 117*, 76–136.

Atran, S. (1994). Core domains versus scientific theories: Evidence from systematics and Itza-Maya folkbiology. In L. A. Hirschfeld & S. A. Gelman (Eds.), *Mapping the mind: Domain specificity in cognition and culture.* New York: Cambridge University Press.

Attwood, T. (1997). *Asperger's syndrome.* London: Jessica Kingsley.

Bailey, A., Le Couteur, A., Gottesman, I., Bolton, P., Simmonoff, E., Yuzda, E., et al. (1995). Autism as a strongly genetic disorder: Evidence from a British twin study. *Psychological Medicine, 25*, 63–77.

Baron-Cohen, S. (1989a). The autistic child's theory of mind: A case of specific developmental delay. *Journal of Child Psychology and Psychiatry, 30*, 285–298.

Baron-Cohen, S. (1989b). Perceptual role taking and protodeclarative pointing in autism. *British Journal of Developmental Psychology, 7*, 113–127.

Baron-Cohen, S. (1991). Precursors to a theory of mind: Understanding attention in others. In A. Whiten (Ed.), *Natural theories of mind.* Oxford, U.K.: Basil Blackwell.

Baron-Cohen, S. (1994). The mindreading system: New directions for research. *Current Psychology of Cognition, 13*, 724–750.

Baron-Cohen, S. (1995). *Mindblindness: An essay on autism and theory of mind.* Boston: MIT Press/Bradford Books.

Baron-Cohen, S. (2002). The extreme male brain theory of autism. *Trends in Cognitive Science, 6*, 248–254.

Baron-Cohen, S. (2003). *The essential difference: Men, women and the extreme male brain.* London: Penguin.

Baron-Cohen, S. (2005). The empathizing system: A revision of the 1994 model of the Mindreading System. In B. Ellis & D. Bjorklund (Eds.), *Origins of the social mind.* New York: Guilford.

Baron-Cohen, S. (2006). The hyper-systemizing, assortative mating theory of autism. *Neuropsychopharmacology and Biological Psychiatry, 30*, 865–872.

Baron-Cohen, S., Baldwin, D., & Crowson, M. (1997). Do children with autism use the Speaker's Direction of Gaze (SDG) strategy to crack the code of language? *Child Development, 68*, 48–57.

Baron-Cohen, S., Bolton, P., Wheelwright, S., Short, L., Mead, G., Smith, A., et al. (1998). Does autism occur more often in families of physicists, engineers, and mathematicians? *Autism, 2*, 296–301.

Baron-Cohen, S., & Hammer, J. (1997). Parents of children with Asperger syndrome: What is the cognitive phenotype? *Journal of Cognitive Neuroscience, 9*, 548–554.

Baron-Cohen, S., Jolliffe, T., Mortimore, C., & Robertson, M. (1997). Another advanced test of theory of mind: Evidence from very high functioning adults with autism or Asperger syndrome. *Journal of Child Psychology and Psychiatry, 38*, 813–822.

Baron-Cohen, S., Leslie, A. M., & Frith, U. (1985). Does the autistic child have a 'theory of mind'? *Cognition, 21*, 37–46.

Baron-Cohen, S., Leslie, A. M., & Frith, U. (1986). Mechanical, behavioural and intentional understanding of picture stories in autistic children. *British Journal of Developmental Psychology, 4*, 113–125.

Baron-Cohen, S., O'Riordan, M., Jones, R., Stone, V., & Plaisted, K. (1999). A new test of social sensitivity: Detection of faux pas in normal children and children with Asperger syndrome. *Journal of Autism and Developmental Disorders, 29*, 407–418.

Baron-Cohen, S., Richler, J., Bisarya, D., Gurunathan, N., & Wheelwright, S. (2003). The systemising quotient (SQ): An investigation of adults with Asperger syndrome or high functioning autism and normal sex differences. *Philosophical Transactions of the Royal Society, 358*, 361–374.

Baron-Cohen, S., Ring, H., Wheelwright, S., Bullmore, E. T., Brammer, M. J., Simmons, A., et al. (1999). Social intelligence in the normal and autistic brain: An fMRI study. *European Journal of Neuroscience, 11*, 1891–1898.

Baron-Cohen, S., Spitz, A., & Cross, P. (1993). Can children with autism recognize surprise? *Cognition and Emotion, 7*, 507–516.

Baron-Cohen, S., & Swettenham, J. (1996). The relationship between SAM and ToMM: The lock and key hypothesis. In P. Carruthers & P. Smith (Eds.), *Theories of theories of mind*. Cambridge, U.K.: Cambridge University Press.

Baron-Cohen, S., & Wheelwright, S. (1999). Obsessions in children with autism or Asperger syndrome: A content analysis in terms of core domains of cognition. *British Journal of Psychiatry, 175*, 484–490.

Baron-Cohen, S., & Wheelwright, S. (2004). The Empathy Quotient (EQ). An investigation of adults with Asperger syndrome or high functioning autism, and normal sex differences. *Journal of Autism and Developmental Disorders, 34*, 163–175.

Baron-Cohen, S., Wheelwright, S., Burtenshaw, A., & Hobson, E. (in press). Mathematical talent is genetically linked to autism. *Human Nature*.

Baron-Cohen, S., Wheelwright, S., Hill, J., & Golan, O. (2007). A new taxonomy of human emotions. *Israeli Journal of Psychiatry*. Manuscript submitted for publication.

Baron-Cohen, S., Wheelwright, S., Hill, J., Raste, Y., & Plumb, I. (2001). The "Reading the mind in the eyes" test revised version: A study with normal adults, and adults with Asperger syndrome or high-functioning autism. *Journal of Child Psychology and Psychiatry, 42*, 241–252.

Baron-Cohen, S., Wheelwright, S., & Jolliffe, T. (1997). Is there a "language of the eyes"? Evidence from normal adults and adults with autism or Asperger syndrome. *Visual Cognition, 4*, 311–331.

Baron-Cohen, S., Wheelwright, S., Scahill, V., Lawson, J., & Spong, A. (2001). Are intuitive physics and intuitive psychology independent? *Journal of Developmental and Learning Disorders, 5*, 47–78.

Baron-Cohen, S., Wheelwright, S., Skinner, R., Martin, J., & Clubley, E. (2001). The autism spectrum quotient (AQ): Evidence from Asperger syndrome/high functioning autism, males and females, scientists and mathematicians. *Journal of Autism and Developmental Disorders, 31*, 5–17.

Baron-Cohen, S., Wheelwright, S., Stone, V., & Rutherford, M. (1999). A mathematician, a physicist, and a computer scientist with Asperger syndrome: Performance on folk psychology and folk physics test. *Neurocase, 5*, 475–483.

Baron-Cohen, S., Wheelwright, S., Stott, C., Bolton, P., & Goodyer, I. (1997). Is there a link between engineering and autism? *Autism: An International Journal of Research and Practice, 1*, 153–163.

Baron-Cohen, S., Wheelwright, S., Willams, S. H. R., Bullmore, E. T., Gregory, L., & Chitnis, X. (2006). Parents of children with autism: An fMRI study. *Brain and Cognition, 61*, 78–95.

Benbow, C. P. (1988). Sex differences in mathematical reasoning ability in intellectually talented preadolescents: Their nature, effects and possible causes. *Behavioural and Brain Sciences, 11*, 169–232.

Blair, R. J. (1995). A cognitive developmental approach to morality: Investigating the psychopath. *Cognition, 57*, 1–29.

Blair, R. J., Jones, L., Clark, F., & Smith, M. (1997). The psychopathic individual: A lack of responsiveness to distress cues? *Psychophysiology, 34*, 192–198.

Charlesworth, W. R., & Dzur, C. (1987). Gender comparisons of preschoolers' behavior and resource utilization in group problem-solving. *Child Development, 58*, 191–200.

Charman, T., Ruffman, T., & Clements, W. (2002). Is there a gender difference in false belief development. *Social Development, 11*, 1–10.

Cleckley, H. M. (1977). *The mask of sanity: An attempt to clarify some issues about the so-called psychopathic personality*, St Louis, MO: Mosby.

Collins, D. W., & Kimura, D. (1997). A large sex difference on a two-dimensional mental rotation task. *Behavioral Neuroscience, 111*, 845–849.

Connellan, J., Baron-Cohen, S., Wheelwright, S., Ba'tki, A., & Ahluwalia, J. (2001). Sex differences in human neonatal social perception. *Infant Behavior and Development, 23*, 113–118.

Courchesne, E. (2002). Abnormal early brain development in autism. *Molecular Psychiatry, 7*, 21–23.

Crick, N. R., & Grotpeter, J. K. (1995). Relational aggression, gender, and social-psychological adjustment. *Child Development, 66,* 710–722.

Daly, M., & Wilson, M. (1988). *Homicide.* New York: Aldine de Gruyter.

Davis, M. H. (1994). *Empathy: A social psychological approach.* Boulder, CO: Westview Press.

Dodge, K. (1980). Social cognition and children's aggressive behavior. *Child Development, 51,* 162–170.

Eagly, A. H. (1987). *Sex differences in social behavior: A social-role interpretation.* Hillsdale, NJ: Erlbaum.

Ekman, P., & Friesen, W. (1969). The repertoire of non-verbal behavior: Categories, origins, usage, and coding. *Semiotica, 1,* 49–98.

Elliot, R. (1961). Interrelationship among measures of field dependence, ability, and personality traits. *Journal of Abnormal and Social Psychology, 63,* 27–36.

Field, T. (1979). Visual and cardiac responses to animate and inanimate faces by term and preterm infants. *Child Development, 50,* 188–194.

Fitzgerald, M. (2000). Did Ludwig Wittgenstein have Asperger's syndrome? *European Child and Adolescent Psychiatry, 9,* 61–65.

Fitzgerald, M. (2002). Did Ramanujan have Asperger's disorder or Asperger's syndrome? *Journal of Medical Biography, 10,* 167–169.

Frith, C., & Frith, U. (1999). Interacting minds—A biological basis. *Science, 286,* 1692–1695.

Frith, U. (1970). Studies in pattern detection in normal and autistic children. II. Reproduction and production of color sequences. *Journal of Experimental Child Psychology, 10,* 120–35.

Frith, U. (1991). *Autism and Asperger's syndrome.* Cambridge, U.K.: Cambridge University Press.

Galea, L. A. M., & Kimura, D. (1993). Sex differences in route learning. *Personality & Individual Differences, 14,* 53–65.

Geary, D. C. (1996). Sexual selection and sex differences in mathematical abilities. *Behavioural and Brain Sciences, 19,* 229–284.

Geary, D. C. (1998). *Male, female: The evolution of human sex differences.* Washington, DC: American Psychological Association.

Goldenfeld, N., Baron-Cohen, S., & Wheelwright, S. (2005). Empathizing and systemizing in males, females and autism. *International Journal of Clinical Neuropsychiatry, 2,* 338–345.

Gouchie, C., & Kimura, D. (1991). The relationship between testosterone levels and cognitive ability patterns. *Psychoneuroendocrinology, 16,* 323–334.

Hall, J. A. (1978). Gender effects in decoding nonverbal cues. *Psychological Bulletin, 85.*

Happe, F. (1994). An advanced test of theory of mind: Understanding of story characters' thoughts and feelings by able autistic, mentally handicapped, and normal children and adults. *Journal of Autism and Development Disorders, 24,* 129–154.

Happe, F. (1995). The role of age and verbal ability in the theory of mind task performance of subjects with autism. *Child Development, 66,* 843–855.

Happe, F. (1996). *Autism.* London: UCL Press.

Happe, F., Briskman, J., & Frith, U. (2001). Exploring the cognitive phenotype of autism: Weak "central coherence" in parents and siblings of children with autism: I. Experimental tests. *Journal of Child Psychology and Psychiatry, 42,* 299–308.

Happe, F., Ehlers, S., Fletcher, P., Frith, U., Johansson, M., Gillberg, C., et al. (1996). Theory of mind in the brain. Evidence from a PET scan study of Asperger syndrome. *NeuroReport, 8,* 197–201.

Hare, R. D., Hakstian, T. J., Ralph, A., Forth-Adelle, E., & Al, E. (1990). The revised psychopathy checklist: Reliability and factor structure. *Psychological Assessment, 2,* 338–341.

Hermelin, B. (2002). *Bright splinters of the mind: A personal story of research with autistic savants.* London: Jessica Kingsley.

Hobson, R. P. (1986). The autistic child's appraisal of expressions of emotion. *Journal of Child Psychology and Psychiatry, 27,* 321–342.

Hoffman, M. L. (1977). Sex differences in empathy and related behaviors. *Psychological Bulletin, 84,* 712–722.

James, I. (2003). Singular scientists. *Journal of the Royal Society of Medicine, 96,* 36–39.

Jennings, K. D. (1977). People versus object orientation in preschool children: Do sex differences really occur? *Journal of Genetic Psychology, 131,* 65–73.

Jolliffe, T., & Baron-Cohen, S. (1997). Are people with autism or Asperger's syndrome faster than normal on the embedded figures task? *Journal Child Psychology and Psychiatry, 38,* 527–534.

Kanner, L. (1943). Autistic disturbance of affective contact. *Nervous Child, 2,* 217–250.

Kimura, D. (1999). *Sex and Cognition,* Cambridge, MA; MIT Press.

Knight, G. P., Fabes, R. A., & Higgins, D. A. (1989). Gender differences in the cooperative, competitive, and individualistic social values of children. *Motivation and Emotion, 13,* 125–141.

Lawson, J., Baron-Cohen, S., & Wheelwright, S. (2004). Empathising and systemising in adults with and without Asperger syndrome. *Journal of Autism and Developmental Disorders, 34,* 301–310.

Leslie, A. M. (1987). Pretence and representation: The origins of "theory of mind." *Psychological Review, 94,* 412–426.

Leslie, A. M., & Thaiss, L. (1992). Domain specificity in conceptual development: Evidence from autism. *Cognition, 43,* 225–251.

Lutchmaya, S., Baron-Cohen, S., & Raggatt, P. (2002). Foetal testosterone and eye contact in 12 month old infants. *Infant Behavior Development, 25,* 327–335.

Maccoby, E. (1999). *The two sexes: Growing up apart, coming together.* Cambridge, MA: Harvard University Press.

Mealey, L. (1995). The sociobiology of sociopathy: An integrated evolutionary model. *Behavioral and Brain Sciences, 18,* 523–599.

Meltzoff, A. N., & Decety, J. (2003). What imitation tells us about social cognition: A rapprochement between developmental psychology and cognitive neuroscience. *Philosophical Transactions of the Royal Society, 358,* 491–500.

Myers, P., Baron-Cohen, S., & Wheelwright, S. (2004). *An exact mind.* London: Jessica Kingsley.

O'Riordan, M., Plaisted, K., Driver, J., & Baron-Cohen, S. (2001). Superior visual search in autism. *Journal of Experimental Psychology: Human Perception and Performance, 27,* 719–730.

Plaisted, K., O'Riordan, M., & Baron-Cohen, S. (1998). Enhanced visual search for a conjunctive target in autism: A research note. *Journal of Child Psychology and Psychiatry, 39,* 777–783.

Power, T. G. (1985). Mother- and father-infant play: A developmental analysis. *Child Development, 56,* 1514–1524.

Pratt, C., & Bryant, P. (1990). Young children understand that looking leads to knowing (so long as they are looking into a single barrel). *Child Development, 61,* 973–983.

Premack, D. (1990). The infant's theory of self-propelled objects. *Cognition, 36,* 1–16.

Scaife, M., & Bruner, J. (1975). The capacity for joint visual attention in the infant. *Nature, 253,* 265–266.

Schiff, W., & Oldak, R. (1990). Accuracy of judging time to arrival: Effects of modality, trajectory and gender. *Journal of Experimental Psychology, Human Perception and Performance, 16,* 303–316.

Shah, A., & Frith, U. (1983). An islet of ability in autism: A research note. *Journal of Child Psychology and Psychiatry, 24,* 613–620.

Smith, P. M. (1985). *Language, the sexes and society.* Oxford, U.K.: Basil Blackwell.

Strayer, F. F. (1980). Child ethology and the study of preschool soical relations. In H. C. Foot, A. J. Chapman, & J. R. Smith (Eds.), *Friendship and social relations in children.* New York: John Wiley.

Tannen, D. (1991). *You just don't understand: Women and men in conversation.* London: Virago.

Trevarthen, C. (1989). The relation of autism to normal socio-cultural development: The case for a primary disorder in regulation of cognitive growth by emotions. In G. Lelord, J. Muk, & M. Petit (Eds.), *Autisme er troubles du developpment global de l'enfant* [English translation]. Paris: Expansion Scientifique Francaise.

Voyer, D., Voyer, S., & Bryden, M. (1995). Magnitude of sex differences in spatial abilities: A meta-analysis and consideration of critical variables. *Psychological Bulletin, 117,* 250–270.

Walker, A. S. (1982). Intermodal perception of expressive behaviours by human infants. *Journal of Experimental Child Psychology, 33,* 514–535.

Wellman, H. (1990). *Children's theories of mind,* Cambridge, MA: Bradford/MIT Press.

Wimmer, H., & Perner, J. (1983). Beliefs about beliefs: Representation and constraining function of wrong beliefs in young children's understanding of deception. *Cognition, 13,* 103–128.

Witkin, H. A., Lewis, H. B., Hertzman, M., Machover, K., Bretnall Meissner, P., & Wapner, S. (1954). *Personality through perception.* New York: Harper & Brothers.

Wittig, M. A., & Allen, M. J. (1984). Measurement of adult performance on Piaget's water horizontality task. *Intelligence, 8,* 305–313.

Yirmiya, N., Kasari, C., Sigman, M., & Mundy, P. (1989). Facial expressions of affect in autistic, mentally retarded, and normal children. *Journal of Child Psychology and Psychiatry, 30,* 725–735.

23

An Evolutionary Theory of Mind and Mental Illness:
Genetic Conflict and the Mentalistic Continuum

CHRISTOPHER BADCOCK

Although theories about the mind are as old as philosophy—and probably older—modern scientific, evolutionary theories of the mind date from only very recently. In 1978, Premack and Woodruff posed the question does the chimpanzee have a theory of mind? However, such a theory of mind— particularly on the part of a chimpanzee—is clearly not something explicit or even something that most people could formulate as a set of propositions if asked to do so and, so, is emphatically not a theory in the same sense in which the general theory of relativity is. The philosopher A. J. Ayer (1910–1989), for example, who has been posthumously diagnosed with an autistic disorder, once remarked that none of his philosophical preoccupations had given him as much trouble as the problem of our knowledge of other minds (Fitzgerald, 2005, p. 141). Indeed, a principal symptom of autism is so-called *mind-blindness*: deficits in theory of mind that manifest themselves as insensitivity to other people's feelings; difficulty in interpreting others' intentions, beliefs, and knowledge; and failure to anticipate the reactions that other people will have to your own behavior. Autistics also typically have difficulty dealing with misunderstandings and are often unable to practice, detect, or understand deception. The result is that their behavior often seems bizarre, callous, or childish to others (Baron-Cohen, 1995; Baron-Cohen & Howlin, 1993).

A critical assessment of such mind-blindness is the so-called *false belief* or *Sally-Anne test.* A child is shown two dolls, Sally and Anne, each of which has a toy box. The child sees that Sally has a toy in her box, but Anne does not. Now the child is asked to imagine that Sally leaves the room, and while she is absent, Anne takes Sally's toy out of Sally's box, puts it into her own box, and shuts it again. Now Sally returns. The crucial question is where does Sally think her toy is now? The majority of 4-year-old children can appreciate Sally's false belief that her toy is still in her box despite the fact that they personally know that it is not, but autistic children even considerably older typically reply that Sally now thinks that her toy is in Anne's box. Such reactions are taken to indicate that those who fail the test are answering based on their own knowledge and seem unable to appreciate others' ignorance because they lack the ability to understand another person's different state of mind (Baron-Cohen, Leslie, & Frith, 1985; Wimmer & Perner, 1983).

MENTALISTIC AND MECHANISTIC COGNITION

Mentalism was a term that was originally used to describe stage acts in which the performer appeared to be able to read other people's thoughts—a feat that was also called "mind reading." However, mentalism is also used in philosophy and psychology to describe the belief that the mind is real and that our subjective experience of it provides valid insights for these disciplines. As such, it stands in opposition to what might be called *antimentalism*—the denial of the reality of the mind as a serious subject for scientific investigation by behaviorist psychologists, ethologists, and neo-Darwinians (Badcock, 2004b). Alternatively, mentalism can be understood as the primary deficit associated with autistic mind-blindness. Indeed, to this extent mentalism can be seen as equivalent to "mind reading," "folk psychology," "mentalizing" (Frith, 2003), or "mindness" (Llinás, 2001). Effectively it asserts the contrary of antimentalism: that mental phenomena are real and worthy of study by science and enables a person to do what autistics symptomatically cannot—to understand your own and others' behavior in mental terms.

One of the most revealing illustrations of this is provided by the way in which people use mentalistic terminology in talking or thinking about objects, abstractions, or other nonhuman phenomena as if they were nevertheless mental agents, such as describing a wayward object as *having a mind of its own*. Other examples from everyday life would be saying that a car *did not want to start*, that *nature knows best*, or that something you ate *did not agree with you*. Clearly, *wanting*, *knowing*, and *agreeing* are all mental acts and properly speaking can be attributed to only human minds. But despite this limitation, normal human beings find it more or less impossible not to speak and to think in this way. Indeed, what Donald Hebb (1946) described as "a thorough-going attempt to avoid anthropomorphic description in the study of temperament" in chimpanzees at the Yerkes laboratories was eventually abandoned after 2 years with the realization that "[a]ll that resulted was an almost endless series of specific acts in which no order or meaning could be found" (p. 88). On the other hand, Hebb confessed that by the use of "anthropomorphic concepts of emotion and attitude one could quickly and easily describe the peculiarities of individual animals" and concluded that such mentalistic terminology was justified to the extent that "it provides *an intelligible and practical guide to behaviour*" (p. 88).

The fact that you can try—albeit with great difficulty—to avoid mentalistic thinking in relation to animals, objects, or other nonhuman phenomena and that the sciences have made a distinct virtue of doing so suggests that mentalistic cognition is not the only option. Indeed, an indication that mentalism is only one mode of cognition comes from the remarkable finding that some autistics who fail tests of false belief like those mentioned just now nevertheless show cognitive skills far above the average in more mechanistic applications, such as calendar calculation, music, mathematics, or rote memorization (Treffert, 2000, 2001; Treffert & Christensen, 2005). In a previous contribution to a volume preceding this one, I suggested that human beings had evolved a second, parallel system of cognition to mentalism: what you might call *mechanistic cognition*. At its simplest, you could see mechanistic cognition as an adaptation to the physical, material environment and mentalism as a parallel one to the human, psychological one. In both cases, intuitions of causality, agency, and meaning are found, but each is appropriate to a different universe of experience: subjective, psychological, particular, and personal in one case, objective, universal, physical, and impersonal in the other (Badcock, 2004b).

ATTENTION, INTENTION, AND CENTRAL COHERENCE

Eyes are often called "the windows of the soul," and detection of another person's direction of gaze and shifts of attention have been described as "the linchpin of social cognition" (Langdon, Corner, McLarena, Coltheart, & Ward, 2006) and provide a possible evolutionary origin of mentalism (Badcock, 2004b). It has been proposed that young children first experience the "meeting of minds," which epitomizes mentalism when they shift their attention to join that of someone else as indicated by the other person's direction of gaze (Baron-Cohen, 1995, pp. 38–58). In other words, where the eyes lead, the mind follows, and as the mind-blindness of autism might suggest, autistics are notoriously poor at monitoring, interpreting, and returning gaze (Asperger, 1991; Frith, 2003, p. 105).

Direction of gaze also often reveals the current state of an organism's attention: In other words, it reveals its probable current awareness. Furthermore, this can betray more than merely the direction in which it is looking, or even the exact target of its concern. Direction of gaze can also show much about an organism's state of mind. A fixed, unblinking stare at an object can reveal a high level of concern, such as when a predator is stalking prey, or prey being stalked have seen the predator and are apprehensively monitoring it. By contrast, an unfocused, drifting direction of gaze that wanders over a large area can indicate a relaxed, unconcerned frame of mind—for example, on the part of prey that have not yet spotted a predator. Yet again, a probing, restless scanning of an area can reveal that the organism is searching for something in a state of anxiety or anticipation, as when prey know that a predator is near by but cannot tell exactly where it is or when a predator has temporarily lost its prey but knows it to be in the immediate vicinity.

Such examples as these show what a short step it is to go from monitoring an organism's attention to beginning to detect and even predict its *intention*: in other words, extrapolating from its current awareness to its next likely action. Furthermore, these examples also suggest the probable evolutionary forces that might have been at work in bringing about such a development. A prey animal that correctly anticipated the next move of a predator, for example, in predicting where and when the predator would pounce, could easily owe its life to that ability. Such a development is an obvious candidate for so-called *arms-race evolutionary escalation*: a situation in which better prediction of predators' intentions on the part of prey leads to predators having to become more resourceful in outwitting such anticipation, which leads to prey having to become even better at predicting intention, and so on, in principle ad infinitum—and in practice until both sides have become very good at monitoring and detecting the other's intentions.

Recently, brain scanning has suggested that in order to predict others' behavior we probably put ourselves in their shoes and unconsciously run through the same processes in our own minds as they do in theirs. So-called *mirror neurones* are known to be excited in parts of the cortex involved with the action when someone sees someone else performing an act and deficits in corresponding areas might explain some aspects of autistic mind-blindness (Chenga, Tzengb, De cetye, Imadaf, & Hsieh, 2006). A subcircuit known as the *ventral premotor cortex* appears to be involved with predicting others' behavior, while another area called the *dorsal premotor cortex* plans the actual execution of it. Some of the brain regions involved in prediction have been found to be abnormal in the brains of people with autism, suggesting where autistics' difficulties with understanding others' intentions and predicting their behavior may be found (Ramani & Miall, 2004). Indeed, there is evidence that not only are autistic children poor at detecting, interpreting, and predicting the intentions of others but that they also fail to conceptualize their own intentions as such (Frith & Happé, 1999).

Yet another autistic deficit is found in *shared attention mechanism*. Autistic people typically do not become involved in group conversations or activities because they usually fail to understand the element of collective psychological activity that is inevitably involved (Leekam & Moore, 2001). One autistic reports that she noticed

> a kind of electricity that goes on between people … I have observed that when several people are together and having a good time, their speech and laughter follow a rhythm. They will all laugh together and then talk quietly until the next laughing cycle. I have always had a hard time fitting in with this rhythm, and I usually interrupt conversations without realizing my mistake. The problem is that I can't follow the rhythm. (Grandin, 1995, pp. 91–92)

Following considerations like these, it has been suggested that autistics may have deficits in four particular mental modules: eye direction detection; intentionality detection; shared attention mechanism; and finally, theory of mind mechanism (Baron-Cohen, 1995).

However, other authorities have described autism in terms of its symptomatic bottom-up, detail-focused, field-independent style of cognition: something otherwise described as a deficit in *central coherence*. The latter term describes a top-down, field-dependent, holistic approach to perception vividly illustrated by language, where words owe their specific meanings to their place within the larger whole of an utterance. Examples would be homonyms such as *they're, their*, or *there*, which sound exactly the same but whose meaning is normally clear to listeners thanks to their context. But autistics will typically read sentences such as "He took a bow from his violin case" with exactly the same pronunciation of *bow* as in "He took a bow and everybody clapped" or will speak of "a big *tear* in her dress" in exactly the same way as if it were a "big *tear* in her eye" (Snowling & Frith, 1986).

An example from visual perception is provided by the Ebbinghaus illusion (Figure 23.1). In reality, both central black circles are exactly the same size, but they seem different because of the size contrast of the surrounding figures. Francesca Happé (1999a) found that autistics are less prone to this illusion, presumably because they go from specific to general and are more field independent than others and so are less likely to be fooled by the surrounding circles. According to a model proposed by Happé, central coherence/field dependence (or the lack of it) can be found in visual, verbal, auditory, and other domains and varies from strong to weak in the normal population, with autistics showing a similar range, but being biased toward the less centrally coherent/more field-independent extreme. She also suggests that normal mentalizing relies on field dependence and, in particular, on the ability to place things in their context and relate them to their proper background. Indeed, brain imaging reveals that autistics solve embedded figure tasks using regions involved in object perception, whereas in normal controls the approach is more global and involves the use of working memory much more (Koenig, Tsatsanis, & Volkmar, 2001). Children who score high on

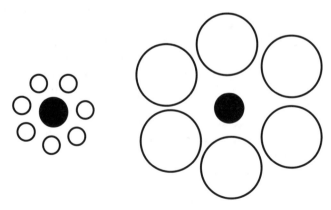

Figure 23.1 The Ebbinghaus illusion.

field independence in cognitive tests also score low on social competence: For example, in 1,276 children 3 to 5 years old, those who were more field independent showed more nonsocial play. Happé (1999b) concludes, "[I]ndividuals with weak central coherence and detail-focused processing are less successful in putting together the information necessary for sensitive social inference" (p. 215). Uta Frith (2003) comments, "Field-dependent people are easily swayed by others' opinion and tend to take on the prevailing views of their group; field-independent people are unaffected by current crazes and don't care so much about other people's opinion" (p. 153).

THE EVOLUTIONARY GENETICS OF MENTALISM

Although there is good evidence that autism—and therefore by implication, mentalism—has a predominantly genetic basis, it does not appear to be a classical Mendelian one. In other words, the deficits (and occasional compensations) listed previously cannot be attributed to recessive or dominant gene effects, and although there is a clear sex bias in the incidence of autism (which affects more males than females), classical sex chromosome gene linkage cannot explain it on its own. However, a possible alternative has recently been suggested to such Mendelian explanations which directs attention to the *expression* of genes, rather than their inheritance (Badcock & Crespi, 2006; Crespi, in press; Crespi & Badcock, in press).

Although a child inherits half its DNA from each parent, we now know that certain genes are only expressed if they come from one rather than the other parent. *IGF2* codes for a growth hormone (insulin-like growth factor 2) and is only normally expressed from the father's gene. If the mother's *IGF2* gene is also expressed Beckwith-Wiedemann syndrome results. Beckwith-Wiedemann babies are 1.5 times normal birth weight and show excessive growth during adolescence along with other overgrowth symptoms, such as tumors. Normally the mother's copy of the *IGF2* gene is silenced, or *imprinted*, but if both copies of this gene are silenced, the result is the opposite: the pre- and postnatal growth retardation of Silver-Russell syndrome (Crespi & Badcock, in press).

The underlying evolutionary logic of this reflects the contrasting costs and benefits of growth to the mother as opposed to the father. Although the mother's genes in her children benefit from their growth to exactly the same extent as the father's, only the mother pays the cost. In the tangible terms of a child's birth weight, the mother's contribution is billions of times greater than the father's is, which is only a single sperm. Intangible costs are much the same: In modern sub-Saharan Africa, a woman has a 1 in 21 lifetime risk of death from pregnancy, childbirth, or abortion (Potts & Short, 1999). Although the risk for a Western woman is about 1 in 10,000, the risk for men everywhere and throughout history has been precisely zero. However you look at it, a mother's obligatory biological investment in her offspring exceeds that of the father by staggeringly large orders of magnitude. As a result, paternally active imprinted genes favor growth much more than maternally active ones and are particularly strongly expressed in the placenta—an organ primarily designed to extract resources from the mother. Indeed, an abnormal conceptus with a double set of paternal genes without any genes whatsoever from the mother results in a massive proliferation of the placenta without any associated fetus (Haig, 1993).

After birth and discarding of the placenta, more imprinted genes are expressed in the brain than in any other single organ. Given that the brain—and the neocortex in particular—is the seat of the mind and the adaptation to which we owe our dominance as a species, it is otherwise inexplicable that evolution should disable second, backup copies of key genes that are expressed there by means of imprinting—particularly since both parents' genes are expressed in the most primitive part of the brain: the brain stem. In chimeric mice, cells with only maternal genes are found in large numbers in the neocortex and forebrain but very few are found in the lower brain—especially in the hypothalamus. This is true both of mature, fully grown mice but even more so of fetuses, where there is a complete absence of maternal cells from the hypothalamus. In both cases, mother-only cells are found to be particularly clustered in the frontal lobes of the cortex. Father-only cells, by contrast, are the exact opposite: These are found in the hypothalamus and lower brain, but not in the cerebral cortex. The few that are found in the forebrain tissue of embryos do not proliferate and are subsequently eliminated (Allen et al., 1995).

In human beings, the hypothalamus is concerned with basic drives and appetites such as hunger, thirst, sex, and aggression, and with emotional responses such as pleasure, pain, and anxiety. The hypothalamus also regulates the production of pituitary growth hormones, which along with adrenal, thyroid, and sex hormones, either directly or indirectly control growth. The pituitary is sometimes called "the master endocrine gland" of the body but is itself under the control of the hypothalamus, both neurologically and chemically. Neurologically, the posterior pituitary is just a part of the hypothalamus that protrudes from the brain and is not a gland in its own right (Thomson, 1985). Indeed, from this point of view, you could see the hypothalamus as performing a role in the body analogous to that of *IGF2* in the genome. Like *IGF2*, the hypothalamus is concerned with growth and consumption of resources and, again like it, mammalian mothers appear to place imprints on the genes that build it, just as they do the *IGF2* gene. Presumably, this is because imprinting limbic brain genes limits the growth that would result if the genes for building the limbic brain from both parents were expressed. Cells in the embryonic hypothalamus are critical for later development, and the sizes of its cell populations in the fetus could provide a prediction of subsequent neurohormonal activity during later life (Deacon, 1990). In other words, imprinted genes that control the growth of nerve cells in the development of the fetal brain could indirectly determine body size: According to this way of looking at it, fathers would want more, but mothers would want less. Indeed, to this extent you could see the limbic system effectively as the individual's *paternal brain* by contrast to the neocortex, which—at least with the evidence from the chimeric mice in mind—you might correspondingly call the *maternal brain*.

Evidence that imprinted genes play a conflicting role in human behavior is suggested by two pediatric disorders: Angelman and Prader-Willi syndromes. In both cases, there is abnormal expression of imprinted genes in a region of chromosome 15. In Angelman, there is more paternal and/or less maternal gene expression, but in Prader-Willi, it is the opposite—more maternal and/or less paternal genes are expressed. Whereas Angelman children feature prolonged suckling, frequent crying, hyperactivity and sleeplessness—every mother's worst fear—, Prader-Willi cases are characterized by poor suckling, weak crying, inactivity and sleepiness—much more like the ideal baby. At the very least, Angelman and Prader-Willi syndromes graphically illustrate the potentially contradictory effects of imprinted genes: Failures can result in everything or nothing, with the normal something poised precariously in between. Furthermore, the balance appears to be shifted in the direction that you would expect: More paternal/less maternal gene expression makes for a more demanding baby, whereas the converse has the opposite result. (Admittedly, Prader-Willi children, although poor sucklers at first, become indiscriminate and uncontrollable foragers for food and become obese as a result.) But even this can be seen to fit in with maternal genetic self-interest because such traits make children more independent of the mother's resources (principally breast milk) and more likely to survive periods of prolonged neglect by her thanks to their fat reserves (Haig & Wharton, 2003).

Angelman children show severe retardation, little or no language, and tend to be diagnosed as autistic. Prader-Willi cases with two copies of chromosome 15 from their mother (and none from the father) are usually diagnosed psychotic in adulthood and show less severe retardation. Indeed "exceptional skill at jigsaw puzzles" is listed as a diagnostic feature. A striking finding is that schizophrenics have less cancer than normal despite the fact that they smoke much more. As the tumors often found associated with Beckwith-Wiedemann syndrome suggest, the reason for this could be that paternally expressed imprinted genes tend to promote the development of cancer (which is another form of overgrowth), while many maternally expressed genes act as tumor suppressors and reduce cancer risk (Crespi & Badcock, in press).

HYPER-MENTALISM AND PSYCHOSIS

As we have seen, autistics characteristically lack mentalistic skills, such as monitoring gaze and interpreting intention. However, it is a striking fact that you find the opposite in paranoid schizophrenia. For example, paranoiacs notoriously overinterpret direction of gaze to the extent that they think they are being watched or spied on. Recent laboratory experiments have found that schizophrenics are abnormally responsive to the direction of others' gaze. Indeed, the social deficits seen in schizophrenia could be the outcome of such an oversensitivity—particularly in preventing them making accurate inferences about what another person is likely to be thinking (Langdon et al., 2006).

When you say someone is "being paranoid," you mean that they are overinterpreting someone else's behavior, words, or expressions. Paranoid schizophrenia is one of the major subtypes of the disorder, and paranoid schizophrenics symptomatically take mental interpretation to bizarre and pathological lengths (American Psychiatric Association [APA], 2000). They also overinterpret intention but do so in two completely different ways. Other people's intentions toward you can be positive or negative, and it is interesting that although most paranoid psychotics overinterpret negative intention in characteristic symptoms of delusions of persecution, others (particularly women) overinterpret positive intentions to the extent of believing that others are in love or are infatuated with them (so-called *erotomania*). But in both cases, the delusions are founded on overinterpretation of what are often trifling details or very minor grains of truth which then become enormously amplified out of all proportion to reality. The evolutionary psychiatrist Randolph Nesse (2004) notes, "[T]hose who have worked with schizophrenics know the eerie feeling of being with someone whose intuitions are acutely tuned to the subtlest unintentional cues, even while the person is incapable of accurate empathic understanding" (p. 863). Furthermore, there are grounds for believing that such subjective impressions are, by no means, inaccurate. Experiments on schizophrenics' mind-reading abilities have seldom been carried out and might be open to question in relation to the often very effective drug therapies to which such patients nowadays are normally subjected. Nevertheless, at least one carefully controlled study suggests that paranoid patients even when on medication are demonstrably better than normal controls in interpreting nonverbal cues—at least where the resulting expressions are genuine and where the situation is one of expectation of an electric shock. With simulated expressions, normal subjects performed better than paranoid ones, but as the experimenter points out, this is just what you would expect if you thought that paranoiacs have a special sensitivity to nonverbal cues (LaRusso, 1978).

Again, autistics' typical failure to understand shared attention in groups is countered by paranoid delusions of conspiracy, which vastly exaggerate it. And where many autistics have a diminished sense of personal agency and identity, psychotics often become megalomanic and subject to delusions of grandeur. Whereas autistics are often mistakenly thought to be deaf thanks to their mentalistic deficits, one of the most common features of paranoid schizophrenia is hearing imagined voices. And while autistics tend to be literal and to find deception difficult, psychotics characteristically suffer from severe delusional thinking and bizarre self-deception. Indeed, there is evidence that schizophrenics and others with milder schizotypical tendencies also have impaired visual-spatial and arithmetic abilities relative to their verbal abilities. Furthermore, there is evidence that carriers of a genetic tendency to psychosis in their near relatives show impairments in verbal memory and in visual and spatial skills. Indeed, a separate study concludes that a relative superiority of verbal to spatial skills—or what I would call mentalistic to mechanistic cognition—represents a cognitive asymmetry characteristic of schizophrenia (Kravariti et al., 2006; Toulopoulou et al., 2006).

Autism is a disorder with an early onset because the affected child never matures mentalistically. Schizophrenic psychosis, on the other hand, is much more of an adult-onset disorder because a person needs to acquire normal mentalism before they can become pathologically overmentalistic.

Indeed, in a previous publication, I suggested that such excessive mentalizing might be described as *hyper-mentalism*, while autistic mind-blindness could be correspondingly described as *hypo-mentalism* (Badcock, 2004b).

Another way of describing this tendency to mentalize to excess is what has been called *magical ideation*. The magical ideation scale developed at the University of Wisconsin presents a questionnaire asking the respondent to agree or disagree with a list of statements. These range from what you might call commonplace superstition (e.g., "Horoscopes are right too often for it to be a coincidence"), to some with a distinctly delusional tone, themselves ranging from the erotomanic (e.g., "I sometimes had the passing thought that strangers are in love with me"), to the more conventionally paranoid (e.g., "I have sometimes sensed an evil presence around me"). Also included are many sentiments endorsed by conventional religions (e.g., "I have wondered whether the spirits of the dead can influence the living"), belief in the paranormal (e.g., "I think I could learn to read other people's minds if I wanted to"), or even science fiction (e.g., "The government refuses to tell us the truth about flying saucers"; Eckblad & L. J. Chapman, 1983). Students who scored high on the scale also showed more psychotic symptoms than students with lower scores did, and in a study of psychiatric patients, those with schizophrenia had a higher magical ideation score than nonschizophrenic patients or normal controls. A longitudinal study of 7,800 students revealed that those who scored high on magical ideation in college showed more symptoms of so-called *schizotypal personality* and other schizophrenia-related disorders a decade later and reported more psychotic experiences than others did. The number of people who had developed some form of psychosis 10 years later was significantly greater in the group that had scored high on magical ideation (L. J. Chapman, J. P. Chapman, Kwapil, Eckblad, & Zinser, 1994).

Indeed, you could see religion along with magic and superstitious thinking in general as the normal, socially acceptable expression of hyper-mentalism in human culture. Magic invites credulity for miracles and mental intervention in the form of the belief that prayers, rituals, or spells can affect physical reality and bring about the fulfillment of wishes. Superstition is based on the belief that things are not what they seem, and that behind apparent chance events or manifest appearances lurks a deeper, more significant reality that can be interpreted with typical mentalistic terms such as intention, meaning, guilt, or justice. Fundamental to all religion, magic, and mentally elaborated superstition is the belief that purely mental factors—believers would say "spiritual," "supernatural," or "extrasensory"—represent a different, higher or parallel reality to the purely physical, tangible, and mundane. All such thinking goes beyond the immediate appearance of the physical world and attributes souls, spirits, essences, or other mental realities to the universe. In magic and superstition, there is always an occult but mentally perceived truth beyond the immediately obvious perceptions of the senses.

Religion applies mentalistic thinking to the world and maintains that beyond immediate appearances life has a moral and ethical dimension often represented in divine judgment and retribution in an afterlife, heaven, or hell. As a result, reality as a whole—and not just social reality—becomes peopled with mental agents who can be influenced in ways analogous to those in which ordinary humans can be through supplication (prayer), flattery (praise), generosity (sacrifice), apology (confession), restitution (penance), or personal visitation (pilgrimage) and through the good offices of influential intermediaries (saints, angels, and other deities). Accommodation for deities is provided in temples, and entertainment added in the form of sacred music, dramas, and processions. Indeed, some religions even claim to have quasi-legal, mutually binding contracts with their deity, such as the Old and New Covenants of Judaism and Christianity respectively—and several regard God as the author of their sacred book and guarantor of their claims to territorial sovereignty and racial integrity. In this way, all manner of personal and collective fears, failings, and frustrations beyond the remedy of mere mortals can be redressed, and a mentalistic adaptation could be seen as the foundation for the evolution of religion—something that previously caused Darwinism much difficulty, but that now seems natural and obvious in terms of the concept of hyper-mentalism. In a vast extension of mentalistic thinking that inflated it far beyond its original, human, interpersonal, and social dimension, magical ideation filled the explanatory void left by early humans' deficits in a more mechanistic understanding of nature by peopling the universe at large with mental agencies of all kinds.

But of course, none of this explains why hyper-mentalism exists in the first place. Surely, nature would not have endowed human beings with so bizarre a tendency as that seen in magical ideation in particular and in paranoid thinking in general. Nevertheless, there is a very good reason why we should not be surprised at the existence of hyper-mentalism. According to David Hume in his *Natural History of Religion*, there is a

> universal tendency among mankind to conceive all beings like themselves, and to transfer to every object, those qualities, with which they are familiarly acquainted, and of which they are intimately conscious. We find human faces in the moon, armies in the clouds; and by a natural propensity, if not corrected by experience and reflection, ascribe malice or good-will to every thing, that hurts or pleases us. Hence ... trees, mountains and streams are personified, and the inanimate parts of nature acquire sentiment and passion. (Guthrie, 1993, p. 69)

But the question remains of why human beings should so compulsively and routinely mentalize nature. A more recent suggestion is that "We see apparent people everywhere because it is vital to see actual people wherever they may be" (p. viii), and not just people—"it is better for a hiker to mistake a boulder for a bear than to mistake a bear for a boulder" (pp. 5–6). In other words, to the extent that hyper-mentalism means attributing human-like minds to objects or organisms that in reality lack them, it is entirely normal, and the occasional false alarms, so to speak, are more than compensated for by the importance of not missing a real occurrence.

> [W]hen we see something as alive and humanlike, we can take precautions. If we see it as alive we can, for example, stalk it or flee. If we see it as humanlike, we can try to establish a social relationship. If it turns out not to be alive or humanlike we usually lose little by having thought it was. This practice thus yields more in occasional big successes than it costs in frequent little failures. In short, ... "better safe than sorry." (p. 5)

Exactly the same reasoning explains other pathological mental states such as anxiety attacks or phobias. In these cases too, the better safe than sorry principle applies and explains why, even though there may be so many false alarms, the fear/phobia system is nevertheless more useful if set for too much sensitivity than it would be if set for too little. For some individuals at the extreme end of the sensitivity distribution this may mean chronic, disabling anxiety or irrational phobias, and much the same could be true of mentalism. It may be that paranoiacs, for example, represent only the extreme end of a normal distribution, with everyone having some tendency to overmentalize in some situations but few taking it to such lengths as psychotics do. Hyper-mentalism, in other words, like anxiety or phobias, may be a naturally selected tendency that would only become pathological in cases where it far exceeded its normal bounds. And if anyone wanted to know why natural selection should have endowed human beings with such supernumerary mentalism, so to speak, they have only to consider the plight of autistics to see what happens to those without enough of it.

Dyslexia describes difficulty in learning to read despite adequate intelligence and opportunity and is found in about 1 in 20 primary-school age children, with a prevalence in boys about 4 times that in girls. As many as 70–80 per cent of schizophrenics were found to exhibit a significant number of dyslexic language traits in one study, and the neuroanatomical and cognitive correlates of dyslexia are similar to those found in both schizophrenia and schizotypal personality disorder (Crespi & Badcock, in press). *Hyperlexia* is essentially the opposite of dyslexia. The term describes the spontaneous and precocious mastery of reading in children, usually before the age of 3, and in conjunction with impairments of verbal communication. Hyperlexics typically can read more or less anything but cannot necessarily understand what they are reading. Hyperlexia is a rare condition, found almost exclusively in conjunction with autism and typically in autistic savants. Indeed, to the extent that reading words is a purely mechanistic skill now performed by computers but understanding what they mean is a mentalistic one only fully developed in normal human beings, you could see hyperlexia as representing an extreme of the pattern of preserved mechanistic but impaired mentalistic cognition often seen in autism as a whole. And as this association would lead you to expect, hyperlexic children show enhanced visual-spatial abilities like those typically found associated with autism (Crespi & Badcock, in press). In other words, whereas autistics are sometimes hyperlexic, schizophrenics are more likely to be dyslexic: another diametrically opposed set of symptoms to add to the list (see Table 23.1; Crespi & Badcock, in press).

The association of dyslexia with schizophrenia and hyperlexia with autism, along with all the other symptoms listed here, provides striking support for the hypothesis that psychosis and autism represent opposite disorders arrayed on a continuous mentalistic spectrum. Like autism, dyslexia is a highly heritable trait, and genome scans have provided strong evidence for the involvement of sites on chromosomes 2, 6, 7, 13, and 18. Dyslexia has also been noted in three of four children from the same family with a maternal duplication of the Prader-Willi/Angelman region of chromosome 15 mentioned earlier. The striking antithesis between the symptoms of autism and psychosis set out in Table 23.1 recalls the case of Prader-Willi and Angelman syndromes and suggests the possibility that something similar may underlie both (Crespi & Badcock, in press). However, because a large number of genes on many different chromosomes appear to be involved and because the variations in gene expression related to parent of origin can vary from gene to gene and tissue to tissue in the same individual, the range of variation of symptoms in autism and psychosis can be expected to be much greater than in Prader-Willi and Angelman syndromes, explaining why the antithetical features listed in Table 23.1—which is by no means exhaustive—are usually only found in some cases.

Again, autism is common in Rett, Turner's, and Fragile X syndromes, in Tuberous Sclerosis, and in the children of older fathers. It can also be environmentally induced by prenatal valproic acid, thalidomide, or viral infection, and other factors which have been proposed include poisoning by mercury or PCBs (polychlorinated biphenyls) and perhaps—most controversially of all—the MMR (measles, mumps and rubella) vaccination. Nevertheless, all of these could conceivably have an impact on imprinting in individual cases, making them proximate, rather than ultimate causes of the condition.

Table 23.1 Diametrically Different Symptoms in Autism and Psychosis

Autism	Psychosis
Gaze-monitoring deficits	Delusions of being watched/spied on
Intentionality deficits	Erotomania/delusions of persecution
Shared attention deficits	Delusions of conspiracy
Theory of mind deficits	Magical ideation/delusions of reference
Deficit in sense of personal agency	Megalomania/delusions of grandeur
Literalness/inability to deceive	Delusional self-deception
Audio/verbal deficits	Audio/verbal hallucinations
Early onset	Adult onset
Visual/spatial skills	Visual/spatial deficits
Some hyperlexic	Some dyslexic

MENTALISM AND THE MOTHER

To summarize the argument so far, you could say that maternal and paternal genes expressed within the brain could be seen as engaged in the same conflict in relation to the mind as that seen in the body in relation to growth in general and to *IGF2* in particular. Indeed, following the precedent of Angelman and Prader-Willi syndromes, you might account for the mental deficits in autism by noting that mentalism could be seen as having evolved to benefit females more than males.

There is certainly good evidence that women are generally more mentalistic than men are. Experiments with babies only a day old show that from birth girls attend more to social stimuli, such as faces and voices than do boys, who have a preference to attend more to nonsocial, spatial stimuli, such as mobiles or traffic (Baron-Cohen, 2005). Most girls develop language earlier than most boys, and higher levels of the male hormone testosterone are generally associated with lower verbal ability (van Goozen, Cohen-Ketennis, Gooren, Frijda, & van de Poll, 1995). Indeed, by 18 months there can be a huge difference between boys and girls, with some children still not yet speaking and others with vocabularies of up to 600 words (Baron-Cohen, 2005). Women on average perform better at verbal tasks than men do. For example, they can generally name twice as many synonyms for a word than the average man can, and women can usually generate longer lists of words beginning with the same letter. Normally girls develop social skills sooner than boys and studies suggest average female superiority in language skills, social judgment, empathy, and cooperation. Women exceed men in facial expressiveness, interpretative skill, gazing, smiling, and expressiveness of body language, and on measures of anxiety, trust, tender-mindedness, and gregariousness (Hall, 1984). According to one authority, these differences are invariant across ages, educational levels, and nations (Feingold, 1994). Universally—and as the theory of the hyper-mentalistic nature of religion sketched out just now would predict—women are more religious than men (at least where men allow them to be; Stark, 2002), and the brain-imaging study of mirror neurones I mentioned earlier revealed not only that autistics have deficits here but that women generally show a more marked mirror-neurone response, perhaps explaining their greater ability to empathize with others (Chenga et al., 2006).

There is also evidence from brain imaging that women generally have greater ability to inhibit their behavior than men have (Gur, Gunning-Dixon, Bilker, & Gur, 2002), and it has been suggested,

> Because of women's greater involvement in childbearing ... it would have been to their selective advantage to inhibit behaviors that would conflict with the best interests of children. ... The single interpretation that best describes the research findings across a wide range of tasks is that women have greater inhibitory abilities than men on most tasks involving sexual, social, emotional and some behavioral content. (Bjorklund & Kipp, 1996, p. 167)

In other words, mentalism, social sensitivity, and an ability to inhibit antisocial behavior are all found particularly well developed in women, and make sense in terms of the evolutionary logic of a woman's genetic investment. Because the mother's genes are equally present in all of her offspring, her genetic self-interest is best served by cooperation and family unity. Any net benefit from social behavior among her offspring is also a benefit to the ultimate reproductive success of the mother's genes invested in them. Consequently, mothers are selected to favor at least twice as much altruism among siblings than siblings themselves are selected to favor (because siblings, unlike the mother, will discount their willingness to make sacrifices for one another by their degree of relatedness; Trivers, 1974).

Thanks to gestation and lactation, the mother is the prime nurturer, and so it serves her interests to be able to nurture, educate, and instruct her children—for example, to teach them their mother tongue and then use it to program their thinking in ways she approves. By these means, the mother can indoctrinate, condition, and socialize her offspring in behavior that is likely to benefit her equitable genetic investment in all of them. Here mentalism might be particularly useful in influencing a child's social interaction with its siblings, peers, and parents. This would make a child much more likely to see things from its mother's point of view—particularly to see them in a family context—and perhaps less likely to act impulsively on the promptings of its paternal brain (Badcock, 2000, pp. 262–268; see also Badcock, 2004a). Indeed, there is evidence that when what I am calling maternal brain centers are activated in dreaming (the forebrain and neocortex), aggressive impulses are inhibited and cooperative and prosocial ones expressed. However, when paternal brain centers such as the hypothalamus and amygdalas are active in dreams, aggressive impulses on the part of the dreamer emerge, just as the conflict theory of imprinting would predict (McNamara, McLaren, Smith, Brown, & Stickgold, 2005).

Again, a major function of mentalism in everyday life is to manage and manipulate other people, and very often, mentalism can be an alternative to more physical means. In raising their own children, it could have paid ancestral women to use mentalistic measures whenever possible for this reason alone. This is because making or preventing a child do something merely by a word, look, or gesture—by mentalistic means, in other words—is not merely energetically less costly than physically intervening but is much less dangerous (not to mention more efficient because such expressions can often be directed to more than one recipient simultaneously). Manhandling a child always carries the danger of inflicting injury, however slight, and in really serious confrontations verbal and emotional substitutes for physical contact could prevent otherwise potentially severe injury. Fearsome but purely mental expressions of maternal wishes could nevertheless be very effective, especially with younger children, and so selection may have favored mothers who could substitute verbal, emotional, and gestural expressions for more directly physical ones. And even though such substitutions may have had only marginal and minimal effects, natural selection, relentlessly working over the millennia, would gradually preserve them if there overall effect were (on average and all other things being equal) to promote the survival of the genes responsible for them.

Indeed, children too would have benefited to the extent that a child is physically smaller and weaker than its mother is. Lacking an ability to influence its parent by more direct physical means, children who could use mentalistic ploys such as facial, emotional, and verbal expressions might also have marginally promoted their own survival and reproductive success if the effect of that was to secure them more parental investment or avoid risk of injury. Tears, temper tantrums, and cries of distress, in other words, could be as effective in their own way on a child's parent as any kind of physical compulsion that one person could use against another. To this extent, both mothers and children may have had converging evolutionary interests in avoiding mindless violence and substituting the purely mental conflicts, which are now so deeply woven into the fabric of family life that psychotherapists have been able to make a vocation of trying to unravel them.

The father, on the other hand, need make no obligatory biological contribution to his offspring beyond a single sperm, and other children of the same mother need not share his genes: *Mother's baby—father's? Maybe!* As a result, the father's genes build parts of the brain that tend to motivate self-interested, instinctual, and nonsocial behavior (parts of what I called earlier the paternal brain, e.g., the hypothalamus), and the father's genetic self-interest is not necessarily served by his child seeing things its mother's way—for example, in making sacrifices for siblings to which its paternal genes may not be related in any way whatsoever. According to the view advanced here, autism could be the consequence of the failure of the maternal brain in this respect, and the impulsiveness, compulsiveness, and contrariness of autistics the inevitable result of the paternal brain's corresponding success. The striking social deficits seen in autism would certainly fit the idea that paternal genetic self-interest underlies the disorder because autistic children seem perversely committed to doing things their own way and in their own time. If they can learn at all, they usually refuse to do so in the way adults think they should, and certainly pose a severe challenge to any caregiver (who in our evolutionary past would predominantly have been the mother and her relatives). Certainly, the reduced empathy, uncooperativeness and insistence of routine seen in autism hardly contribute to easy parenting. And as you would predict if autism was indeed caused by enhanced expression of the father's genes, studies suggest that autistics—and males in particular—are heavier than normal at birth, suggesting that they are indeed predisposed to consume more than usual of the mother's resources (Y. Sugie, H. Sugie, Fukuda, & Ito, 2005). Again, there is evidence that autistics by contrast to psychotics show early brain growth during gestation at the expense of the mother (Crespi & Badcock, in press).

MALES AND MECHANISTIC MENTALITY

If a centrally coherent, contextual style of thought benefits the mother's genetic self-interest in making her children more likely to see things from her point of view, the contrasting field-independent, bottom-up way of looking at things might be seen as fitting in with the more individualistic, self-concerned view of the child's paternal genome. However, it might also chime with social and cognitive differences characteristic of men—and all fathers are men, of course.

If we take the issue of social behavior first, there is overwhelming evidence, not simply that men are less sociable than we have seen women to be, but that they also account for much more antisocial behavior. For example, in a study of 35 societies worldwide, a man was found to be 20 times more likely to be murdered by another man than a woman was by another woman (and this study excluded war and other such conflicts). In the United States, men commit 86% of simple assaults, 87% of aggravated assaults, and 88% of murders—and such figures are typical. On the contrary, "[C]ompetition is far more violent among men than among women in every human society for which information exists" (Daly & Wilson, 1988, p. 161). Reduced frontal brain volume is associated with antisocial and psychopathic behavior, which are much more common in men, and claims have been made that temporal and frontal lobe brain volumes are larger in women (Gur et al., 2002). In any event, reduced volume in these areas suggests inferior abilities where prosocial and self-inhibitory behavior is concerned, and the same frontal lobe region appears to be implicated in central coherence, perhaps explaining male deficits in all of these associated traits (Cohen, 2002).

Where purely cognitive differences between the sexes are concerned, autism again suggests important insights. *Asperger's syndrome* describes so-called high-functioning autistics that show little if any deficits in language or overall IQ. Although Asperger's subjects have obvious deficits in many ways and have often been described as clumsy and uncoordinated in their actions, they are often notably better than average at performing spatial tasks, such as doing jigsaw puzzles. Unlike normal children or those with general intellectual impairment, whose performance on different cognitive tests tends to be similar, autistic children often show a more uneven pattern. Perhaps because of their mentalistic deficits, autistic children tend to do worst on subtests that demand a high degree of communicative competence and/or social intelligence, such as comprehension tests, which demand an ability to interpret the often implicit meanings, intentions, and understandings conveyed in a passage of writing. However, autistic children in general, and those diagnosed with Asperger's syndrome in particular, do best—and sometimes better than normal children—at tests of spatial ability, such as the block design test (Frith, 2003, pp. 139–141). Indeed, if extraordinary facility with doing things like jigsaw puzzles is included (Frith, 2003, p. 151), the majority of people with autism would be classed as showing some specific talent (Happé, 1999, p. 216).

The contrast between the false belief and false photo tests is a telling illustration of the finding that autism may have compensations, as well as deficits. As we have seen, an autistic child who sees an object moved without the knowledge of another person does not usually appreciate that other's ignorance of its new position—a clear mentalistic deficit (the Sally-Anne situation described earlier). However, autistic children of similar age who see an object moved after they have photographed it usually predict where it will appear in the resulting photograph correctly. This can be seen as a compensating mechanistic competence to the extent that it involves a correct understanding of the optics of photography (Baron-Cohen, 2000).

Findings like these are important, not only because they suggest that there may indeed be pluses as well as minuses associated with autism as Asperger himself clearly believed, but also because they tie in with what is already known about normal differences between the sexes where issues like language, social skills, and spatial ability are concerned. Male superiority is normally found in mathematical reasoning, especially geometry and logic. Indeed, at the highest level male mathematicians outnumber female 13 to 1. Men also normally excel in embedded and rotated figure tasks (Baron-Cohen, 2002; Kimura, 2000). Interestingly in this respect, female-to-male transsexuals who receive testosterone injections in preparation for their sex-change operations have been reported to show large increases in rotational ability (van Goozen, Cohen-Ketennis, Gooren, Frijda, & van de Poll, 1995). Another recent finding that may have a similar explanation is the fact that women carrying male fetuses improve their performance on difficult cognitive tasks involving working memory and spatial ability but not on any other tests. Although the factor responsible could not be determined and is unlikely to have been fetal testosterone, some other similar product of the fetus/placenta is almost certainly the cause (Vanston & Watson, 2005). By contrast, *androgen deprivation* is a male sex hormone-reducing therapy sometimes used to treat prostate cancer in men. Subjects given cognitive tests after therapy showed slightly improved verbal fluency but reduced ability to recall images, suggesting that their skills in these respects had been shifted toward the female pole of cognitive ability (Salminen, 2005).

Males are generally superior in most (but not all) spatial skills, and in target-directed motor skills, irrespective of practice. Where navigation is concerned, recent experiments found that men travel about 20% further in virtual mazes than women do. Furthermore, women take approximately 30% longer to orientate themselves and are more likely than men are to be wrong when they do. Out of an equal number of males and females using a virtual maze for real life navigation, only 1 of 17 subjects who got completely lost was male (Charles, 2001). One possible explanation is that male and female brains simply do not work the same way in such situations. Brain imaging recently demonstrated that, on exiting a virtual 3-D maze, women activate the right parietal cortex and right prefrontal cortex, whereas men trigger the left hippocampus alone (Gron et al., 2000).

In general, men—but not boys—seem to navigate preferentially by vector (i.e., directions and distances), whereas women—but not girls—normally prefer to use landmarks (Motluk, 2002). In the case of geography, boys always win the National Geography Bee, which tests American children in grades four to eight on their knowledge of places around the world (Liben, 1995), and male college students can locate almost twice as many countries on an unlabelled map of the world as female students can (Cross, 1987). The average man does better than the average woman on most—but not all—tests of mechanical skill, notwithstanding the fact that women generally appear to be more dexterous than men appear (Dabbs & Dabbs, 2000).

Standard psychometric tests—so-called IQ tests—usually exclude any items that show large sex differences simply because they are designed to test populations of both sexes. The result, of course, is that sex differences in cognition are systematically ignored or underestimated by such measures (Kimura, 2000, p. 69). However, some special aptitude tests are exceptions, and these show a very marked superiority in male performance where mechanical skills are concerned. For example, U.S. Air Force aptitude tests for mechanical comprehension show that the average male performance exceeds that of 80% of females (Browne, 2001, p. 92), and in the top 10% of mechanical reasoning ability, males outnumber females by approximately 8 to 1 (Browne, 2006, p. 146).

Certainly, where spatial skills are concerned, there is good reason to think that ancestral males' hunting activities would have powerfully selected for a tendency to navigate by vector, rather than by landmark, as women we have just seen characteristically do. The reason is that vegetarian food of the kind typically collected by women in primal hunter-gatherer societies is indeed often best located by reference to fixed landmarks, whereas game that is being pursued by hunters can take off in any direction and may well dictate a novel, cross-country return to base, rather than one using well-known paths. Such cross-country navigation demands exactly the kind of spatial sense at which men excel, and studies of women's greater ability to remember the location of objects closer to home also fits the predictions from the hunter-gatherer model (Silverman & Eals, 1992). Again, tool-making and missile-throwing ability would certainly have benefited primeval males more than females in most instances, and such skills would probably have been critically involved with males' success in conflicts both with other males and in hunting. At the very least, this would explain why mechanical, manual, and throwing skills all seem to be aspects of male cognitive proficiency today—not to mention why they are also found in connection with superior blind-navigating ability and geographical expertise.

THE X FACTOR IN PSYCHOSIS

Another factor influencing the incidence of autism in relation to sex is the discovery that a gene on one of a woman's X chromosomes is protective. Genes are grouped together on chromosomes, and human beings have 46 of them: 23 from each parent, one of which is a *sex chromosome*. Female mammals get a so-called X sex chromosome from each parent (they are XX), but males receive an X from the mother and a Y from the father (making them XY). Unfortunately for them, the X men receive from their mother does not carry the gene that protects against autism, partly explaining why so many more males than females are autistic (Badcock, 2000, pp. 253–260; Skuse, 2000).

In the case of abnormal females with three complete copies of the X chromosome—so-called *X-trisomy*—increased rates of schizophrenia have been reported. Imaging studies show that XXX females exhibit three features of brain anatomy characteristic of schizophrenia: reduced brain volume and enlarged ventricles; reduced asymmetry of the prefrontal and temporal lobes; and a reduction in amygdala size. The smaller brains, reduced asymmetries, and smaller amygdala of X-trisomy females suggest that their increased X chromosome gene dosages results in a brain anatomically skewed toward a more female type (Crespi & Badcock, in press).

Klinefelter syndrome is caused by the presence of an additional X chromosome along with an existing X and Y (as in a normal male), so sufferers are XXY. This syndrome also involves a four- to tenfold increase in liability to psychosis. Psychosis in Klinefelter syndrome normally involves a relatively high incidence of auditory hallucinations and paranoia like that found in female psychotics, along with the later age of onset, which is also typical of the disorder in women. As in X-trisomy, Klinefelter syndrome patients exhibit aspects of brain anatomy similar to those in schizophrenia, including smaller whole-brain volume, reduced or reversed asymmetry of the prefrontal and temporal lobes, and reduced volume of the amygdala. X-trisomy and Klinefelter syndrome involve parallel effects on brain anatomy and liability to psychosis, which are presumably due in both cases to the extra X chromosome. Thus, in both XXX and XXY, the presence of an additional X results in brain features similar to those found in schizophrenia, and notably increased vulnerability to psychosis (Crespi & Badcock, in press).

In other words, the presence of an additional X chromosome makes its bearer more female in brain structure and cognition (as well as being less prone to autism). According to this theory, the differences between male and females in brain anatomy and cognition tend to parallel the differences between normal individuals and those exhibiting full-blown psychosis or milder psychotic tendencies. We have already seen that Prader-Willi syndrome is caused by enhanced maternal and/or reduced paternal gene expression, whereas Angelman is the other way around: reduced maternal and/or enhanced paternal gene expression. If so, autism and psychosis may be similar: Although the two disorders have until now seemed unrelated, genetically, they may be the outcome of oppositely expressed genes, as the diametrically different pattern of symptoms listed in Table 23.1 suggests. Certainly, this possibility is supported by the variant of Prader-Willi syndrome mentioned earlier in which two copies of the mother's chromosome 15 are present, without one from the father (so-called *uniparental disomy* or *UPD*). Quite apart from any link with dyslexia, and by contrast to the variant of the syndrome in which paternal genes are deleted, the majority of maternal UPD cases become psychotic in adulthood, implicating the duplication of this maternal part of the individual's genome as the likely explanation (Soni et al., 2006). Indeed, at the time of writing this was the only example known of such a direct relationship between a specific genetic abnormality and psychotic illness (Boer et al., 2002; Whittington et al., 2001).

The finding of high rates of psychosis in Prader-Willi syndrome with maternal UPD supports the suggestion that psychosis may result from the excessive expression of maternal genes, and/or reduced expression of paternal genes. Moreover, Prader-Willi maternal UPD cases exhibit less severe impairments in social behavior than those with deletion of paternal genes (Veltman et al., 2004; Whittington & Holland, 2004). Prader-Willi syndrome maternal UPD also involves stronger disruptions in visual-spatial abilities, as indicated by mathematical and 3-D visualization performance, and these patients lack the notably enhanced skill in doing jigsaw puzzles found in many cases of paternal deletion (Whittington et al., 2004). Taken together, these findings suggest that Prader-Willi maternal UPD cases exhibit better social and language functioning than deletion cases, but worse visual-spatial ability. This is a pattern consistent with increased effects from maternally expressed imprinted genes which as we saw earlier can be expected to favor language and social skills—what you might term *mentalistic* ones.

While whole brain size is reduced in schizophrenia because of reductions in grey matter (neurones) and reduced and altered white matter (nerve fibers), brain size in autism is increased during early development thanks to a striking growth spurt between birth and age 4, an acceleration driven mainly by increases in white matter volume. However, after about age 4, brain growth in autism levels off, so that adult brain size is not notably increased on average. Remarkably, a recent study of Asperger's syndrome showed that grey matter volume did not decrease with age between 15 and 50 as it does substantially in normal individuals. These findings suggest that autism and schizophrenia exhibit divergent patterns of grey matter loss, with little to no loss in autism, moderate loss in normal development, and high rates of loss in schizophrenia (Crespi & Badcock, in press; see Figure 23.2).

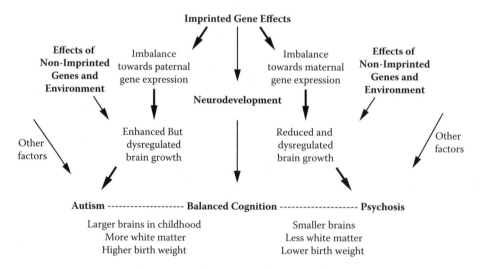

Figure 23.2 The balance of the mentalistic continuum as the outcome of genetic and other factors (modified from Crespi & Badcock, in press).

At the time of writing, the genetic causes of both autism and psychosis remain unknown. However, this chapter has outlined a new theory that potentially can account for most of the findings relating to both—not to mention providing an evolutionary rationale for two types of mental illness, which up to now have seemed inexplicable from a Darwinian point of view. Finally, it can also give a new insight into normality because, as Figure 23.1 clearly indicates, what we take for sanity represents a midpoint between the extremes of autistic hypo-mentalism and psychotic hyper-mentalism thanks to a balanced expression of maternal, paternal, and sex chromosome genes (and absence of other disturbing factors). Mental illness, in other words, is not some qualitatively different, alien condition, but a quantitatively extreme expression of tendencies that exist in all of us and enable us to achieve what is perhaps most distinctive of our species: an ability to understand other people's minds and mental states.

ACKNOWLEDGMENT

The author is indebted to Bernard Crespi for some of the material and many of the insights presented here.

REFERENCES

Allen, N. D., Logan, K., Lally, G., Drage, J. D., Norris, M. L., & Keverne, B. (1995). Distribution of parthenogenetic cells in the mouse brain and their influence on brain development and behavior. *Proceedings of the National Academy of Sciences, USA, 92*(11/95), 10782–10786.

American Psychiatric Association. (2000). *Diagnostic and statistical manual of mental disorders* (4th ed., Rev. ed.). Washington, DC: Author.

Asperger, H. (1991). "Autistic psychopathy" in childhood (U. Frith, Trans.). In U. Frith (Ed.), *Autism and Asperger syndrome* (pp. 37–92). Cambridge, U.K.: Cambridge University Press.

Badcock, C. R. (2000). *Evolutionary psychology: A critical introduction*. Cambridge, U.K.: Polity Press.

Badcock, C. R. (2004a). Emotion versus reason as a genetic conflict. In D. Evans & P. Cruse (Eds.), *Emotion, evolution, and rationality* (pp. 207–222). Oxford, U.K.: Oxford University Press.

Badcock, C. R. (2004b). Mentalism and mechanism: The twin modes of human cognition. In C. Crawford & C. Salmon (Eds.), *Human nature and social values: Implications of evolutionary psychology for public policy* (pp. 99–116). Mahwah, NJ: Lawrence Erlbaum Associates.

Badcock, C. R., & Crespi, B. (2006). Imbalanced genomic imprinting in brain development: An evolutionary basis for the etiology of autism. *Journal of Evolutionary Biology, 19*(4), 1007–1032.

Baron-Cohen, S. (1995). *Mindblindness: An essay on autism and theory of mind*. Cambridge, MA: MIT Press.

Baron-Cohen, S. (2000). Autism: Deficits in folk psychology exist alongside superiority in folk physics. In S. Baron-Cohen, H. Tager-Flusberg, & D. J. Cohen (Eds.), *Understanding other minds* (pp. 73–82). Oxford, U.K.: Oxford University Press.

Baron-Cohen, S. (2002). The extreme male brain theory of autism. *Trends in Cognitive Science, 6*(6), 248–254.

Baron-Cohen, S. (2005). *The assortative mating theory*. Retrieved April 6, 2005, from http://www.edge.org/documents/archive/edge158.html

Baron-Cohen, S., & Howlin, P. (1993). The theory of mind deficit in autism: Some questions for teaching and diagnosis. In S. Baron-Cohen, H. Tager-Flusberg, & D. J. Cohen (Eds.), *Understanding other minds* (pp. 466–480). Oxford, U.K.: Oxford University Press.

Baron-Cohen, S., Leslie, A. M., & Frith, U. (1985). Does the autistic child have a "theory of mind"? *Cognition, 21*, 37–46.

Bjorklund, D. F., & Kipp, K. (1996). Parental investment theory and gender differences in the evolution of inhibition mechanisms. *Psychological Bulletin, 120*(2), 163–188.

Boer, H., Holland, A. J., Whittington, J. E., Butler, J., Webb, T., & Clarke, D. (2002). Psychotic illness in people with Prader Willi syndrome due to chromosome 15 maternal uniparental disomy. *Lancet, 359*, 135–136.

Browne, K. R. (2001). Women at war: An evolutionary perspective. *Buffalo Law Review, 49*(1), 51–247.

Browne, K. R. (2006). Evolved sex differences and occupational segregation. *Journal of Organizational Behavior, 27*, 143–162.

Chapman, L. J., Chapman, J. P., Kwapil, T. R., Eckblad, M., & Zinser, M. C. (1994). Putatively psychosis prone subjects ten years later. *Journal of Abnormal Psychology, 103*, 171–183.

Charles, J. (2001, June 28). In a virtual maze, men are smart rats. *New York Times*, http://query.nytimes.com/gst/fullpage.html?res=9D00EFDA1F30F93BA15755C0A9679C8B63.

Chenga, Y.-W., Tzengb, O. J. L., De cetye, J., Imadaf, T., & Hsieh, J.-C. (2006). Gender divergences in the human mirror system: A magnetoencephalography study. *Neuroreport, 7*(11), 1115–1119.

Cohen, H. (2002). Frontline comment. *The Scientist, 16*(20), 7.

Crespi, B. (in press). Genomic imprinting in the evolution and development of psychosis and autism. *Biological Reviews*.

Crespi, B., & Badcock, C. (in press). Psychosis and autism as diametrical disorders of the social brain. *Behavioral and Brain Sciences*.

Cross, J. A. (1987). Factors associated with students' place location knowledge. *Journal of Geography, 86*, 59–63.

Dabbs, J. M., & Dabbs, M. G. (2000). *Heroes, rogues and lovers: Testosterone and behavior.* New York: McGraw-Hill.

Daly, M., & Wilson, M. (1988). *Homicide.* New York: Aldine de Gruyter.

Deacon, T. W. (1990). Problems of ontogeny and phylogeny in brain-size evolution. *International Journal of Primatology, 11*(3), 237–282.

Eckblad, M., & Chapman, L. J. (1983). Magical ideation as an indicator of schizotypy. *Journal of Consulting and Clinical Psychology, 51*, 215–225.

Feingold, A. (1994). Gender differences in personality: A meta-analysis. *Psychological Bulletin, 116*, 429–456.

Fitzgerald, M. (2005). *The genesis of artistic creativity: Asperger's syndrome and the arts.* London: Jessica Kingsley Publishers.

Frith, U. (2003). *Autism: Explaining the enigma* (2nd ed.). Oxford, U.K.: Blackwell.

Frith, U., & Happé, F. (1999). Theory of mind and self-consciousness: What is it like to be autistic? *Mind and Language, 14*, 23–32.

Grandin, T. (1995). *Thinking in pictures and other reports from my life with autism.* New York: Vintage Books.

Grön, G., et al. (2000). Brain activation during human navigation: Gender-different neural networks as substrate of performance. *Nature Neuroscience, 3*, 404–408.

Gur, R. C., Gunning-Dixon, F., Bilker, W. B., & Gur, R. E. (2002). Sex difference in temporo-limbic and frontal brain volumes of healthy adults. *Journal of the Cerebral Cortex, 12*, 998.

Guthrie, S. (1993). *Faces in the clouds: A new theory of religion.* Oxford, U.K.: Oxford University Press.

Haig, D. (1993). Genetic conflicts in human pregnancy. *Quarterly Review Of Biology, 68*(4), 495–532.

Haig, D., & Wharton, R. (2003). Prader-Willi syndrome and the evolution of human childhood. *American Journal of Human Biology, 15*, 320–329.

Hall, J. (1984). *Nonverbal sex differences.* Baltimore: Johns Hopkins.

Happé, F. (1999a). Autism: Cognitive deficit or cognitive style? *Trends in Cognitive Sciences, 3*(6), 216–222.

Happé, F. (1996b). Parts and wholes, meaning and minds: Central coherence and its relation to theory of mind. In S. Baron-Cohen, H. Tager-Flusberg, & D. J. Cohen (Eds.), *Understanding other minds* (pp. 203–221). Oxford: Oxford University Press.

Happé, F. (2001). Social and non-social development in autism: Where are the links? In J. A. Burack, C. Charman, N. Yirmiya, & P. R. Zelazo (Eds.), *The development of autism: Perspectives from theory and research* (pp. 237–253). Mahwah, NJ: Lawrence Erlbaum Associates.

Hebb, D. (1946). Emotion in man and animal. *Psychological Review, 53*, 88–106.

Kimura, D. (2000). *Sex and cognition.* Cambridge, MA: MIT Press.

Koenig, K., Tsatsanis, K. D., & Volkmar, F. R. (2001). Neurobiology and genetics of autism: A developmental perspective. In J. A. Burack, C. Charman, N. Yirmiya, & P. R. Zelazo (Eds.), *The development of autism: Perspectives from theory and research* (pp. 81–101). Mahwah, NJ: Lawrence Erlbaum Associates.

Kravariti, E., Toulopoulou, T., Mapua-Filbey, F., Shultze, W., Sham, P., Murray, R. M., et al. (2006). Intellectual asymmetry and genetic liability in first-degree relatives of probands with schizophrenia. *British Journal of Psychiatry, 188,* 186–187.

Langdon, R., Corner, T., McLarena, J., Coltheart, M., & Ward, P. B. (2006). Attentional orienting triggered by gaze in schizophrenia. *Neuropsychologia, 44,* 417–429.

LaRusso, L. (1978). Sensitivity of paranoid patients to nonverbal cues. *Journal of Abnormal Psychology, 87*(5), 463–471.

Leekam, S., & Moore, C. (2001). The development of attention and joint attention in children with autism. In J. A. Burack, C. Charman, N. Yirmiya, & P. R. Zelazo (Eds.), *The development of autism: Perspectives from theory and research* (pp. 105–129). Mahwah, NJ: Lawrence Erlbaum Associates.

Liben, L. (1995). Psychology meets geography: Exploring the gender gap on the National Geography Bee. *Psychological Science Agenda, 8,* 8–9.

Llinás, R. R. (2001). *I of the vortex.* Cambridge, MA: MIT Press.

McNamara, P., McLaren, D., Smith, D., Brown, A., & Stickgold, R. (2005). A "Jekyll and Hyde" within: Aggressive versus friendly interactions in REM and non-REM dreams. *Psychological Science, 16*(2), 130–136.

Motluk, A. (2002, August 24). You're holding the map upside-down. *New Scientist,* 21.

Nesse, R. M. (2004). Cliff-edged fitness functions and the persistence of schizophrenia. *Behavioral and Brain Sciences, 27,* 862–863.

Potts, M., & Short, R. (1999). *Ever since Eve: The evolution of human sexuality.* Cambridge, U.K.: Cambridge University Press.

Premack, D., & Woodruff, G. (1978). Does the chimpanzee have a theory of mind? *Behavioral and Brain Sciences, 1*(4), 515–526.

Ramani, N., & Miall, R. C. (2004). A system in the human brain for predicting the actions of others. *Nature Neuroscience, 7*(1), 85–90.

Salminen, E. (2005, March 5). Men's trouble. *New Scientist,* 20.

Silverman, I., & Eals, M. (1992). Sex differences in spatial abilities: Evolutionary theory and data. In J. Barkow, L. Cosmides, & J. Tooby (Eds.), *The adapted mind: Evolutionary psychology and the generation of culture* (pp. 533–549). Oxford, U.K.: Oxford University Press.

Skuse, D. H. (2000). Imprinting, the X-chromosome, and the male brain: Explaining sex differences in the liability to autism. *Pediatric Research, 47*(1), 9–16.

Snowling, M., & Frith, U. (1986). Comprehension of "hyperlexic" readers. *Journal of Experimental Child Psychology, 42,* 392–415.

Soni, S., Whittington, J., Holland, A. J., Webb, T., Maina, E. N., Boer, H., et al. (2006). An investigation into psychiatric illness in Prader-Willi syndrome: Evidence for a genetic basis for psychosis.

Stark, R. (2002). Physiology and faith: Addressing the universal gender difference in religious commitment. *Journal for the Scientific Study of Religion, 41*(3), 495–507.

Sugie, Y., Sugie, H., Fukuda, T., & Ito, M. (2005). Neonatal factors in infants with autistic disorder and typically developing infants. *Autism, 9*(5), 487–494.

Thomson, R. F. (1985). *The brain: An introduction to neuroscience.* New York: W. H. Freeman.

Toulopoulou, T., Mapua-Filbey, F., Quraishi, S., Kravariti, E., Morris, R. G., McDonald, C., et al. (2006). Cognitive performance in presumed obligate carriers for psychosis. *British Journal of Psychiatry, 187,* 284–285.

Treffert, D. A. (2000). *Extraordinary people: Understanding Savant syndrome.* Lincoln, NE: iUniverse. com.

Treffert, D. A. (2001). Savant syndrome: "Special faculties" extraordinaire. *Psychiatry Times,* 20–21.

Treffert, D. A., & Christensen, D. D. (2005, December). Inside the mind of a Savant. *Scientific American, 293,* 88–91.

Trivers, R. (1974). Parent-offspring conflict. *American Zoologist, 14,* 249–264.

van Goozen, S. H. M., Cohen-Ketennis, P., Gooren, L. J. G., Frijda, N. H., & van de Poll, N., E. (1995). Activating effects of androgens on cognitive performance: Causal evidence in a group of female-to-male transsexuals. *Neuropsychologica, 32,* 1153–1157.

Vanston, C. M., & Watson, N. V. (2005). Selective and persistent effect of foetal sex on cognition in pregnant women. *Neuroreport, 16*(7), 779–782.

Veltman, M. W., Thompson, R. J., Roberts, S. E., Thomas, N. S., Whittington, J., & Bolton, P. F. (2004). Prader-Willi syndrome—A study comparing deletion and uniparental disomy cases with reference to autism spectrum disorders. *European Child & Adolescent Psychiatry, 13*(1), 42–50.

Whittington, J. E., & Holland, T. (2004). *Prader-Willi syndrome: Development and manifestations.* Cambridge, U.K.: Cambridge University Press.

Whittington, J. E., Holland, A. J., Webb, T., Butler, J., Clarke, D., & Boer, H. (2001). Population prevalence and estimated birth incidence and mortality rate for people with Prader-Willi syndrome in one U.K. Health Region. *Journal of Medical Genetics, 38,* 792–798.

Whittington, J. E., Holland, A., Webb, T., Butler, J., Clarke, D., & Boer, H. (2004). Cognitive abilities and genotype in a population-based sample of people with Prader-Willi syndrome. *Journal of Intellectual Disability Research: JIDR, 48*(2), 172–187.

Wimmer, H., & Perner, J. (1983). Beliefs about beliefs: Representation and constraining function of wrong beliefs in young children's understanding of deception. *Cognition, 13,* 103–128.

24

Psychopathology and Mental Illness

ALFONSO TROISI

INTRODUCTION

The aim of this chapter is to argue that evolutionary theory can and should serve as the general theoretical framework for explaining and treating mental disorders. As currently understood, mental illness has relatively little to do with the view that human mind and behavior are products of evolutionary processes and that some psychological and behavioral traits may be adaptive while others are not. Instead, psychiatry is deeply immersed in activities such as the description of signs and symptoms, the classification of disorders, the identification of pathogenetic mechanisms, and the development of new therapeutic strategies. It is not that these activities are unimportant; rather, there is a price to pay when they monopolize psychiatric research and clinical practice to the exclusion of a theory dealing with why people behave as they do (McGuire & Troisi, 1998).

The chapter is divided into three parts. First, I will summarize some basic points that distinguish Darwinian psychiatry (defined as the evolutionary study of mental disorders) from prevailing psychiatric thinking and that reflect the most original contributions of evolutionary theory to psychopathology (Table 24.1). This section reviews the concepts of adaptation, function, ultimate causation, proximate mechanisms, novel environments, short-term biological goals, and trait variation as they apply to the study of mental disorders.

The central part of the chapter illustrates how the application of sexual selection theory and life history theory (two middle-level evolutionary theories) can shed light on different aspects of psychiatric disorders, including sex differences in prevalence rates, vulnerability to stressful events, and origin of deviant personality profiles. In discussing these issues, I will take an approach that largely differs from that of most previous work in the field of Darwinian psychiatry. Instead of referring to the superordinate theory of inclusive fitness, I will use the principles and concepts derived from two middle-level theories. The aim is twofold: (a) to convince the reader that the potential contribution

Table 24.1. Major Theoretical Differences between Mainstream Psychiatry and Darwinian Psychiatry

	Mainstream Psychiatry	Darwinian Psychiatry
Reference framework	Functional biology	Evolutionary biology
Causes	Proximate	Ultimate
Approach to variation	Typological thinking	Populational thinking
Criterion of morbidity	Somatic lesion	Dysfunctional consequences
Aim of therapy	Fix the broken machine	Restore functional capacities

of evolutionary thinking to psychopathology is not limited to a generic discussion of the adaptive/maladaptive nature of psychiatric syndromes; and (b) to show how the complexity of modern evolutionary models translates into specific hypotheses about psychopathology. In addition, I will not take the approach that accepts psychiatry's current classification system and attempts to accommodate evolutionary reasoning and data within this theoretical framework. This approach, which has been tried for decades without much success, would require a systematic review of disorders (e.g., schizophrenia, mood disorders, anxiety disorders, etc.) and would give conceptual priority to prevailing psychiatric thinking and secondary priority to evolutionary models. The approach I will take reverses the relationship between evolutionary biology and psychiatry and uses evolutionary theories, not psychiatric syndromes, as the starting point for the analysis.

Finally, I will conclude with a brief discussion of some methodological problems that complicate the integration of the evolutionary approach into clinical psychiatry and that require more consideration than they have so far received.

BASIC POINTS

The Concept of Mental Disorder

It may come as a surprise to those unfamiliar with the current controversies among mental health professionals that one of the most important contributions that evolutionary theory can offer psychiatry is the definition of its field of study. Psychiatry lacks a formal definition of what constitutes a mental disorder, and the failure to set a valid distinction between mental health and mental illness has largely undermined its scientific credibility.

For example, the use of official diagnostic criteria to quantify the prevalence rates of psychiatric disorders in the U.S. general population has produced implausibly high figures: one out of every two persons would suffer from a mental disorder during his or her lifetime (Kessler et al., 1994). According to many, the most basic problem with current criteria of psychiatric diagnosis is that they fail to distinguish mental disorders from "problems in living"—that is, the vast array of problematic but nondisordered human conditions that reflect "the aches and pains of normal life" (Frances, 1998, p. 119). In other words, current methods of psychiatric diagnosis would be overinclusive and would produce a high number of false positive. Defining a mental disorder involves specifying the features of human experiences that demarcate where normality shades into pathology. This is not an easy task. It can be accomplished on the basis of value judgments and cultural prejudices, but this is not what we expect from a scientific approach to the problem. On the other hand, each of the scientific criteria of morbidity (i.e., statistical deviance, suffering, and lesion) that have been used for centuries in the rest of medicine has its important limitations when applied to psychiatry (Kendell, 1975).

Traditional critiques of the criterion of statistical deviance have stressed the risk of labeling as diseases socially ostracized behaviors. In addition, there are disorders that are extremely frequent or normal in the statistical sense, yet abnormal for an individual from a clinical viewpoint. There are also many behavioral profiles that are statistically deviant and undesirable, but are not disorders (e.g., criminality or extreme shyness). There are also major problems with the idea that suffering is an essential criterion for diagnosing mental disorder. In some psychiatric disorders, patients do not complain of emotional suffering (e.g., antisocial personality disorder and hypomania). Even more compelling is the objection that people often experience painful emotions (e.g., anxiety and depression) even though they have no psychiatric diagnosis. Loss of a loved one, poverty, and social ostracism may induce an intensity of mental suffering comparable to that of some psychiatric disorders. Finally, the apparently "strong" criterion of morbidity based on the demonstration of somatic lesion is, in fact, not so strong. Ascertaining the pathological nature of a somatic change is relatively straightforward as long as one is concerned with a departure from a recognized and standard pattern. The problem is that it is not always apparent where normal variation ends and pathology begins. For example, subjects who are in the early romantic phase of a love relationship are not different from patients with obsessive compulsive disorder in terms of density of the platelet serotonin transporter, which proves to be significantly lower than in the normal controls (Marazziti, Akiskal, Rossi, & Cassano, 1999). Thus, the objectivity of the criterion of lesion is only apparent. Defining lesion is as difficult as defining disease, and the risk of circular reasoning is always present.

According to Darwinian psychiatry, the validity of the conventional criteria of morbidity is dependent on their association with functional impairment. Statistical deviance, suffering, and somatic lesion are frequent correlates of mental disorders, but in absence of dysfunctional consequences, none of these criteria is sufficient for considering a psychological or behavioral condition as a psychiatric disorder (Troisi & McGuire, 2002). However, this approach to identifying mental disorders requires that the adaptive functions of mental mechanisms be known before claims of dysfunctions can be made. Psychiatry's difficulty in defining mental disorder derives from its difficulty in defining mental health. To identify what has gone wrong with the individual's mental and behavioral functioning, one should have a detailed idea of how the individual functions or would function when nothing is going wrong. In this regard, evolutionary psychology has much to offer psychiatry.

The evolutionary concept of mental health builds from two basic ideas: (a) The capacity to achieve biological goals is the best single attribute that characterizes mental health, and (b) the assessment of functional capacities cannot be properly made without consideration of the environment in which the individual lives. These two ideas reflect a concept of mental health that is both functional and ecological (Troisi & McGuire, 1998). During the course of evolutionary history, natural selection favored those psychological and behavioral traits that served a specific function more efficiently than available alternative traits did. Therefore, an evolutionary account of the human mind and behavior is an account of how psychological and behavioral traits function as adaptations and how they vary across persons. In an evolutionary context, individuals can be viewed as a mosaic of evolved traits employing a variety of strategies to achieve biological goals. The term *strategy* refers to a cluster of coevolved anatomical, physiological, psychological, and behavioral traits designed by natural selection to enhance inclusive fitness. When we say that a trait is functional or adaptive, we mean that it enhances the inclusive fitness of the individual. In current environments, the ancestral-fitness consequences of evolved strategies may no longer be realized. Nevertheless, the capacity to achieve short-term biological goals remains a valid measure of mental health because it is an indication that the individual possesses those optimal functional capacities that, in the ancestral environment, promoted biological adaptation. The study of interactions between individuals and their environments (the ecological perspective) is essential to evaluate the efficiency of functional capacities. Optimal functional capacities are sets of coevolved traits that are (or were) best suited to increasing inclusive fitness in specific environments. No trait is adaptive in all environments. The same trait can be highly adaptive in one environment and minimally adaptive in another.

The preceding discussion underscores two important points: (a) The evolutionary concept of mental health is consequence-oriented—what makes a condition pathological are its consequences, not its causes or correlates—and (b) the degree of efficiency of functional capacities is dependent on features of the environment. Adverse environments can compromise the efficiency of optimal capacities, just as favorable environments can offset or mitigate the inefficiency of suboptimal capacities. In conclusion, the evolutionary view of mental health places functional capacities and biological adaptation at the core of attempts to define mental disorder. As a result, issues of statistical deviance, emotional suffering, and organic lesion are de-emphasized and the issue of functional impairment moves to the center stage. Using the evolutionary perspective does not resolve all of the quandaries that mental health professionals face when trying to provide a formal definition of mental disorder. However, it does take an important step toward clarifying why current methods of psychiatric diagnosis are criticizable and how clinicians can improve the identification of true mental disorders (Crawford & Salmon, 2002).

Novel Environments and the Function of Emotions

Environment is a crucial variable in psychiatry. Clinicians interviewing patients routinely pose questions regarding early experiences and current environmental conditions, and theoretical models trying to explain the origin of mental disorders invariably include environmental variables among the causal factors. However, the environment psychiatry cares about is not necessarily the environment where *Homo sapiens* has evolved as species.

A number of evolutionary psychologists have argued that the last period of intense selection for many of the present-day traits of human beings occurred during a period referred to as the "environment of evolutionary adaptedness" (EEA; Tooby & Cosmides, 1990). Scholars differ on the exact dates of the EEA, but most agree that it was sometime between 50,000 and 10,000 years ago. This view holds that *Homo sapiens* largely ceased to evolve genetically, morphologically, or psychologically following EEA. Thus, in many respects, human beings no longer live in the environment for which they were adapted.

Because the modern world is so different from the ancestral environment, some medical and psychiatric disorders could result from novel aspects of our physical and social environment (the so-called "mismatch hypothesis"). Among medical disorders, obesity is a good example of a clinical condition caused in part by the mismatch between current environment and traits selected in the EEA. In the ancestral environment, high-calorie foods were rarely available, and the selective power of famine favored the evolution of eating habits appropriate to starvation—that is, seeking out and devouring any available high-calorie food. In addition, carriers of genes encoding efficient mechanisms of energy extraction and storage from dietary sources had an advantage during times of food shortage. In present-day affluent societies, the individuals who carry these genes are now being exposed to sedentary lifestyles and fat-rich diets. Therefore, obesity can be viewed as the maladaptive outcome of a lack of fit of "Stone Age genes" with new nutritional patterns and lifestyle changes (Eaton & Eaton, 2000).

Among psychiatric disorders, substance abuse and addiction are particularly good examples of maladaptive conditions resulting from the mismatch between modern environment and evolved psychological traits (Troisi, 2001b). Even though their use dates back to prehistoric times, drugs of abuse are a novelty in evolutionary terms. These chemical agents have in common the capacity to stimulate brain pathways that have evolved to guide the execution of adaptive behaviors (Koob & Le Moal, 2001).

Human beings, like all other organisms, have been designed by natural selection to strive for the achievement of specific goals or experiences, such as acquiring resources, making friends, developing social support networks, having high status, attracting a mate, and establishing intimate relationships. In the ancestral environment, the achievement of these goals correlated consistently with a gene-transmitting advantage (i.e., increased fitness). The achievement of adaptive goals often depends on a long chain of events and requires the implementation of complex behavioral strategies. In each animal species, a variety of psychobiological mechanisms ensure the correct execution of each step of these behavioral strategies. In species characterized by a highly stereotyped behavioral repertoire, the implementation of adaptive behaviors can occur through a coordinated sequence of "fixed action patterns," without any correlates in terms of emotional experience. However, in species characterized by greater behavioral plasticity and flexibility, natural selection has favored the evolution of brain reward systems as a means to guide behavioral choices and to address the individual toward the achievement of biological goals: "Pleasure is nature's way of telling the brain that it is experiencing stimuli that are useful" (Panksepp, 1998).

In humans, brain reward systems and the positive emotions originating from their stimulation play a central role in controlling the correct execution of adaptive behaviors. The capacity to experience mental pleasure and mental pain helps the individual to pursue goals relevant to biological adaptation and to avoid maladaptive situations. In other words, emotions have evolved to provide information about costs and benefits of past, present, and future behavior (Nesse, 2004). Under minimally adaptive circumstances, individuals experience mental suffering (e.g., depression) that functions as a warning system that one's goal-seeking efforts are failing. Unpleasant emotions mold subsequent behavior by reducing the likelihood that one will behave in the same way again. Conversely, pleasant emotions associated with adaptive behavior are experienced as beneficial and increase the probability that one will engage in similar behavior in the future. In this context, it is clear why mental pleasure and adaptive behavior are so strictly associated.

Under natural conditions, brain reward systems were activated when (and only when) the individual was pursuing or achieving a goal relevant to biological adaptation. In contrast, drugs of abuse directly interact with specific receptors in the brain that normally help mediate feelings of satisfaction and pleasure associated with the execution of adaptive behaviors. Direct chemical stimulation of these receptors creates a signal in the brain that indicates, falsely, the achievement of biological goals (Nesse & Berridge, 1997). The individual who uses drugs no longer needs the presence of natural rewards to experience the positive emotions that, under normal conditions, are the psychic reflections of doing the "right thing" biologically. The behavior of some drug addicts resembles that of rats implanted with electrodes located in the septal area and allowed to self-stimulate through lever pressing. These animals stop drinking, eating, and mounting estrous females because they continuously engage in bar pressing to receive electrical stimulation in the brain reward systems.

Despite the attractiveness of the mismatch hypothesis for explaining the existence of some mental disorders, many questions remain unanswered. While there is no doubt that many features of the physical and social environment have changed more rapidly than the species genome, some features that are particularly relevant in terms of adaptation may be more similar than not; for example, the number of persons with whom one regularly interacts may now differ minimally from thousands of years ago. In addition, the mismatch hypothesis often implies the existence of a uniform EEA, whereas current anthropological and archeological thinking holds that there were many different EEAs (Chisholm, 1996). Finally, there is also the possibility that *Homo sapiens* is still undergoing genetic change and that the current version of our own species may have significantly different adaptive capacities from those of our ancestors even 20,000 years ago. Consider, for example, that the ability to digest lactose as an adult has evolved as an adaptation to dairying in groups that have been keeping cattle for less than 10,000 years (Mace, 2000). All these points could apply to mental disorders.

The Evolutionary Origin of Symptoms

In current medical thinking, the prevailing metaphor is that of the body as a machine that the doctor is called upon to fix when it breaks; the doctor's role is that of an engineer who uses therapeutic technology in the service of patients' health and well-being. Based on the metaphor of the broken machine, the signs and symptoms of disease are just epiphenomena that reflect the underlying pathological process. For example, the excess production of thyroid hormone in hyperthyroidism is viewed as an instance of somatic dysfunction, and the associated signs and symptoms are viewed as direct consequences (epiphenomena) of excess thyroid production.

In their book *Why We Get Sick*, Nesse and Williams (1994) showed that many manifestations of disease are not epiphenomena of a broken machine, but sophisticated adaptations. Using their classification, symptoms can be divided into two broad categories: (a) symptoms as defects in the body's mechanisms and (b) symptoms as useful defenses. For example, seizures, jaundice, coma, and paralysis have apparently no adaptive function and arise from defects in the organism. Many other manifestations of disease, however, are defenses. Vomiting eliminates toxins from the stomach. The low iron levels associated with chronic infection limit the growth of pathogens. Coughing clears foreign matter from the respiratory tract. Considering that the modern therapeutic armamentarium includes many drugs capable of suppressing symptoms (the so-called symptomatic or palliative therapy), the distinction between defects and defenses is not only interesting for theoretical reasons, but is also of paramount practical importance.

To understand why the concept of adaptive manifestations of disease does not come easily to clinical medicine, we must turn to Ernst Mayr, an evolutionary biologist who participated in the "modern synthesis" of the 1930s and 1940s that emerged as neo-Darwinism. One of his most important contributions to the philosophy of biology is the distinction between functional biology and evolutionary biology (Mayr, 1982). These two currents of biological thought are distinguished by the questions they raise. Functional biology deals with the mechanisms controlling the functionality of organic elements, from molecules to individuals. The questions a functional biologist asks are *proximate* questions and are preceded by *how*: How does brain serotonin regulate mood? How do neurons communicate? How does maternal influenza increase the risk of schizophrenia? Evolutionary biology, the second current, focuses on the phylogenetic history and adaptive significance of biological traits. The questions an evolutionary biologist asks are *ultimate* questions and are preceded by *why*: Why is facial symmetry attractive? Why are women more empathic than men are? Why have the genes for Alzheimer disease not been eliminated by natural selection?

Traditionally, medicine is included within the realm of functional biology. Therefore, when clinicians speak of the cause of a disease or symptom, they mean the proximate events that set in motion the dysfunctional processes we call pathogenesis. However, this analysis omits ultimate causes, those evolutionary forces that lead to or away from conditions that favor or prevent the advent of proximate cause (Childs, 1999). The engineering mentality is drawn only to the immediate reasons for illness and to what needs fixing, but a deeper understanding of a manifestation of disease, including the discovery of its possible adaptive significance, can be attained only by taking into account those evolutionary factors that made the proximate causes possible.

Empirical evidence for the existence of symptoms as defenses is abundant in the field of infectious diseases, where the adaptive functions of fever, nausea, vomiting, cough, diarrhea, fatigue, and iron withholding have been repeatedly demonstrated. Data on psychiatric symptoms are much more limited. However, Keller and Nesse (2006) have recently introduced and tested a new framework for understanding the evolutionary origin of depressive symptoms. Their hypothesis (called the "situation-symptom congruence [SCC]" hypothesis) predicts that if different depressive symptoms serve different functions, then different events that precipitate a depressive episode should give rise to different symptom patterns that increase the ability to cope with the adaptive challenges specific to each situation. Thus, for example, crying should be especially prominent when social bonds are threatened, lacking, or lost; decreased ability to experience positive emotions when the environment is unpropitious; and pessimism, when future efforts are unlikely to succeed. These predictions are based on the different adaptive functions that each of these depressive symptoms serves in the regulation of behavior and psychological processes. Crying elicits comforting behaviors and strengthens social bonds; positive emotions facilitate approach behavior and increase risk-taking; and pessimism withdraws the individual from current and potential goals. The SSC hypothesis was tested by asking 445 participants to identify depressive symptoms that followed a recent adverse situation. Guilt, rumination, fatigue, and pessimism were prominent following failed efforts; crying, sadness, and desire for social support were prominent following social losses. These significant differences were replicated in an experiment in which 113 students were randomly assigned to visualize a major failure or the death of a loved one.

The findings reported above have two important implications. First, much that seems abnormal about the functioning of the brain and body is not abnormal at all. Second, an evolutionary approach to symptoms and diseases can stimulate the formulation of testable and useful hypotheses in medicine and psychiatry.

SEXUAL SELECTION AND PSYCHIATRIC DISORDERS

As originally formulated by Darwin, sexual selection theory explained the evolution of unusual secondary sex characters that reduce their bearers' survival, but increase their success in reproduction. In its modern formulation, the theory of sexual selection explains the physiological and behavioral mechanisms that have evolved to ensure preferential access to mates. The relevance of sexual selection theory to human behavior lies in its capacity to explain the evolutionary origin of sex differences in psychology, mating strategies, and response to social events. These differences are in part the result of different adaptive problems recurrently faced by the sexes over the course of human evolutionary history (Buss & Schmitt, 1993).

Psychiatry has largely ignored the importance of sexual selection theory to understand sex differences in psychopathology. Although, in the last two decades, a growing number of clinical studies have analyzed how the epidemiology, etiology, pathogenesis, clinical picture, and therapeutic outcome of a variety of psychiatric disorders differ in women and men, the questions explored by these studies have been invariably formulated in terms of proximate causation. In contrast, the application of sexual selection theory to the study of mental disorders aims at exploring the ultimate causation of sex differences and may serve as a source of original predictions and explanations about the relationship between gender and psychopathology. Three examples are provided below.

The Epidemiology of Sexual Disorders

Differences in gender ratios are common in both medical and psychiatric disorders. However, for most psychiatric disorders (e.g., mood and anxiety disorders), the magnitude of these gender differences is small and varies across social classes and cultures. This is not the case for paraphilias. The paraphilias consist of recurrent, intensely sexually arousing fantasies, sexual urges, or sexual behaviors that involve either nonhuman objects (fetishism), prepubescent children (pedophilia), or nonconsenting persons (exhibitionism, voyeurism, and frotteurism). In the past, these conditions were indicated with the terms *inversions*, *perversions*, or *deviance*. Men are vastly overrepresented among individuals diagnosed with a paraphilia, and some clinicians doubt the existence of true female paraphiliacs. Although many explanatory hypotheses have been advanced in the psychiatric literature, the reasons for this dramatic gender difference in the prevalence rates remain unknown.

According to an evolutionary psychological perspective, paraphilias may be viewed as a by-product of the male adaptation to become aroused by a variety of sexual stimuli and to engage in a mating strategy oriented toward promiscuity and casual sex (Troisi, 2003). Evolutionary theory predicts that the relative parental investment of the sexes in their offspring is associated with different mating strategies in males and females. Individuals of the sex that invests more in offspring should be more discriminative in their sexual interactions, because the costs of making a poor mate choice are greater for the highest investing sex. In *Homo sapiens*, as in many other mammal species, because of physiological and behavioral constraints (i.e., internal fertilization, pregnancy, lactation), the higher-investing sex is the female sex. Therefore, evolutionary psychology predicts that, compared to men, women should be more discriminative in their sexual preferences and less promiscuous (Gangestad & Simpson, 2000).

Many aspects of male sexual psychology and behavior reflect such a propensity toward a scarcely discriminative mating strategy, including frequency of sexual thoughts, fantasies, and spontaneous arousal; desired frequency of sex; frequency of masturbation; desired number of sex partners; enjoyment of many types of sexual practices; and sacrificing resources to obtain sex (Okami & Shackelford, 2001). On average, compared to women, men have a lower threshold for sexual arousal, and their vulnerability to paraphilias is likely be the maladaptive by-product of the adaptive capacity to be quickly aroused by a variety of sexual stimuli not to miss many profitable, low-cost opportunities to reproduce. A frequent misperception is that paraphiliacs commit deviant sexual acts because avenues to appropriate sexual behavior are blocked by a lack of appropriate sexual arousal. The history of most sex offenders, however, reveals that they have always had adequate nondeviant sexual arousal and that their paraphilic behavior often coexists with appropriate sexual behavior with adult partners. Yet, in many cases, paraphiliacs with appropriate nonparaphiliac sexual arousal lack appropriate social skills. They may experience sexual arousal to possible appropriate partners, but may lack the social skills to initiate and maintain conversations, show interest and concern, and interact without anxiety. These clinical observations suggest that, in many cases, the pathogenic process leading to the development of a paraphilia is best described as the generalization of a strong sexual interest to inappropriate stimuli in individuals with suboptimal social skills rather than the obsessive fixation of insufficient sexual energies upon substitute objects. The fact that sexual selection set loose limits to male sexual arousal explains why such a process occurs much more frequently in men than in women (Figure 24.1).

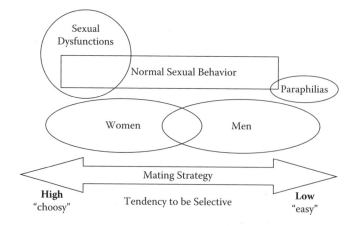

Figure 24.1 An evolutionary model of sexual disorders based on sex differences in mating strategies. Paraphilias are viewed as a by-product of the male adaptation to engage in a scarcely discriminative mating strategy. Sexual dysfunctions are viewed as an extreme variant of the female adaptation to engage in a highly discriminative mating strategy. Different dimensions of the areas depicting paraphilias and sexual dysfunctions reflect different prevalence rates for the two groups of disorders. The big area of overlapping between sexual dysfunctions and female normal sexual behavior indicates that these conditions often reflect adaptive responses to difficult or adverse circumstances. The small area of overlapping between paraphilias and male normal sexual behavior denotes the pathological nature of these conditions.

A word of caution is needed here. The etiology of sexual disorders is complex and involves a variety of organic, psychological, and cultural factors whose relative importance varies for each individual case. Accordingly, the origin of paraphilias cannot be reduced to evolved sex differences in mating strategies. These differences are universal in the human species and have been observed across a wide range of cultures (Schmitt, 2003). Yet, only a minority of men is affected by paraphilias. Evolutionary predispositions represent just a risk factor that interacts with a variety of other variables (physiological, developmental, relational, and cultural) in determining the occurrence of a paraphilia in the single individual.

A major insight of modern evolutionary theory is that adaptations are compromises constrained by a variety of factors with their pros and cons. Women are at low risk for paraphilias because sexual selection has made them more discriminative in their sexual preferences and more dependent upon reproductively functional stimuli in their patterns of arousal than men. However, these protective factors turn into risk factors when we look at the prevalence rates of other kinds of sexual disorders. Clinical data show that women are more vulnerable to those sexual disorders that, according to current psychiatric diagnostic systems, are classified as sexual dysfunctions. The essential feature of sexual dysfunctions is inhibition in one or more of the phases of the sexual response, including disturbance in the subjective sense of pleasure or desire or disturbance in the objective performance. Women's sexual dysfunctions include sexual desire disorders (hypoactive sexual desire and sexual aversion), sexual arousal disorders (lack of lubrication or swelling response), orgasm disorders (anorgasmia), and sexual pain disorders (dyspareunia and vaginismus). In population surveys, some 30–35% of women have reported a lack of sexual desire during the previous 1–12 months (Laumann, Paik, & Rosen, 1999). Figures for the prevalence of dyspareunia and vaginismus are equally impressive. A population-based assessment of 5,000 women identified about 16% reporting histories of unexplained chronic, burning vulvar pain lasting longer than 3 months. The overall cumulative incidence of those who reported inability to have sexual intercourse because of the pain was 10% (Harlow & Stewart, 2003).

How can we explain these remarkably high prevalence rates? According to an evolutionary psychological perspective, many cases of women's sexual dysfunctions are extreme variants of a mating strategy involving greater voluntary control over mate choice, accurate assessment of the quality of potential mates, and a tendency toward sexual restraint. Clinical data showing the importance of contextual and interpersonal factors in the etiology of women's sexual dysfunctions are in accord with the evolutionary hypothesis. In a recent national probability sample of American women 20–65 years of age, their emotional relationship with the partner during sexual activity and general emotional well-being were the two strongest predictors of absence of distress about sex. Feeling emotionally close to their partner during sexual activity decreased the odds of "slight distress" by 33% and "marked distress" by 43%; in other words, the stronger the emotional intimacy with the partner, the lower the probability of sexual dysfunction (Bancroft, Loftus, & Long, 2003).

The highly contextual nature of women's sexuality reflects a "choosy" and discriminative mating strategy that places a greater premium on the quality of the partner and on the relationship with him. The woman who has poor emotional intimacy with her partner or is attempting to be sexual without the required context and needed specific stimuli (e.g., man's status, maturity, resources, or genetic quality) is reacting normally by not becoming aroused, being desirous, or experiencing any orgasm. In evolutionary terms, there is nothing wrong with her sex response system, per se. However, such an interpretation of the epidemiological data is at variance with the current medical model that views women's sexual problems as dysfunctions as opposed to a normal response to difficult or adverse circumstances (Basson, 2005). The use of an evolutionary perspective can help clinicians to pay appropriate attention to evolved sex differences in sexual psychology and to avoid transposing to women the pattern of male sex response.

The Impact of Reproductive-Related Trauma

Clinical psychiatrists have long noted that failing to reach a goal is an especially potent elicitor of emotional travail and negative affect. From an evolutionary psychological perspective, stressful events are associated with a subjective experience of mental pain because emotions function as a source of information about goal achievement (Nesse, 2000). Negative affect (e.g., anxiety and depression) has evolved as an emotional indicator that biological goals have not been or are not being achieved, that is, that one's fitness has been or is being compromised. Since reproductive success is one of the most important biological goals, reproductive-related trauma is expected to trigger intense emotional distress and increase the risk for psychiatric disorders. Clinical data confirm that reproductive-related trauma is a major cause of anxiety and depression but also show that men and women have a different vulnerability to reproductive failure.

Consider infertility. Clinical studies have consistently demonstrated that men and women react differently to infertility. McEwan, Costello, and Taylor (1987) studied psychological adjustment to the threat of being unable to bear children among 62 women and 45 men. They found that approximately 37% of women and 1% of men in infertile marriages showed psychological disturbance. In a study aimed at evaluating sex differences in psychosocial responses of 449 first-admission couples in a fertility clinic, Wright et al. (1991) found that infertile women showed higher distress than their partners on a global measure of psychiatric symptoms, and on subscales of anxiety, depression, hostility, and cognitive disturbances. A recent prospective study (Verhaak, Smeenk, van Minnen, Kremer, & Kraaimaat, 2005) on emotional adjustment before and after fertility treatment cycles in infertile couples found that women showed an increase of both anxiety and depression after unsuccessful treatment and a decrease after successful treatment. Men showed no change in anxiety and depression either after successful or after unsuccessful treatment. In the 6 months after unsuccessful treatment, women showed no recovery and more than 20% of them showed symptoms of anxiety and/or depression. The percentages of male partners who scored above the threshold for clinically relevant forms of anxiety and depression varied from 0% to 2%. In addition to increasing [e] the risk of anxiety and/or depression, infertility may adversely affect several areas of functioning, including satisfaction with life, avoidance of friends with children, control over life, general self-esteem, and self-esteem about sexuality. For all these infertility-related concerns, the impact is greater in women (Anderson, Sharpe, Rattray, & Irvine, 2003).

Why are men apparently less vulnerable to the emotional impact of infertility? The answer lies in the fact that fertilization occurs internally with women and not men. Men can never be certain that their putative children are their genetic children. Women, in contrast, are always certain that they are the genetic parent of their offspring. Because men cannot be certain of paternity, natural selection has not favored the evolution of strong emotional responses to infertility among males. Rather, men are expected to value more indirect clues of fecundity, such as control of resources and sexual success, that, in the ancestral environment, were likely to correlate with reproductive success. In other words, the male emotional brain has been selected to monitor the first steps of the complex chain of events leading to successful reproduction, paying less attention to the subsequent ones. Interestingly, reproductive failure other than infertility produces similar sex-specific reactions. Among parents who have lost a child through sudden infant death syndrome, neonatal death, or stillbirth, 25–30% of mothers had clinically significant levels of depression, whereas the rate among fathers was 4–10% (Vance et al., 1991).

The evolutionary psychology of female reproductive behavior is also relevant to a better understanding of the psychiatric conditions that are associated with pregnancy and motherhood. In modern societies, many women experience depressive symptoms during pregnancy and at postpartum. Depending on the criteria used to diagnose depressive illness, prevalence estimates range from 10% to 85% (Nonacs & Cohen, 2000). Why is mood disturbance so frequent during pregnancy and the postpartum period? Answering this question is facilitated by considering the natural selective factors that have linked maternal emotional responses with the optimization of parental investment.

In a low-fertility species like *Homo sapiens*, each child-rearing episode consumes a major proportion of the mother's lifetime reproductive effort. Consider, for example, that in natural-fertility populations living primarily by foraging, a woman who survives until menopause is likely to give birth to no more than five children in her lifetime and to nurse each of them for several years (Mace, 2000). Such findings suggest that the optimal allocation of reproductive effort and the minimization of the risks of wasting parental investment were critical problems for ancestral human females. Because of these problems, the emotional mechanisms regulating maternal mood have evolved to be especially sensitive to the conditions that, in the ancestral environment, correlated with poor survival prospects for offspring. Considering that evolution has not had sufficient time to change our emotional reactions, it is likely that present-day mothers are sensitive to the same conditions that were stressful for ancestral mothers, and that being involved in child care in disadvantageous circumstances is still a major contributing factor for the onset of prenatal and postnatal depression. Clinical evidence is in line with these evolutionary hypotheses. Several studies have demonstrated that risk factors for depression during gestation and the postpartum period include teenage pregnancy; undesired pregnancy; being unmarried, separated, or divorced; marital conflict; feeling unloved by one's husband; limited support from kin; poverty; and birth of a high-risk or premature infant. Today, thanks to legalized forms of social support and medical technology, these conditions do not necessarily imply poor survival prospects for young children. However, in the ancestral environment, the probability of successfully rearing a child without the assistance of a permanent male partner and collateral kin was very low. This explains why the conditions listed above are still so stressful for present-day mothers.

The Impact of Interpersonal Stressful Life Events

Although the most numerous evolved sex differences are likely to be found in the field of sexuality and reproduction, the influence of sexual selection on human psychology and behavior is not limited to these domains. Social behavior is another important area where the different selective pressures that appear to have confronted males and females during human evolution have determined the emergence of specific sex differences.

Two of the most widely replicated findings for clinical depression are its greater prevalence in women after adolescence and its causal association with stressful life events. When these findings are considered together, it may be asked if an increased vulnerability to stressful life events in women could account for the sex difference in rates of depression. Women's increased vulnerability to stressful life events could be general or specific. It is possible that women actually experience any type of negative event as more stressful, being more likely to develop depression as a result. Alternatively, only specific events may impact more on women.

An evolutionary psychological approach favors the latter hypothesis (Troisi, 2001a). When a life event interferes with achieving a biological goal, its harmful impact will depend primarily on the importance of the goal to an individual, and the importance attached to the same biological goals differs in men and women. Sexual selection theory provides an ultimate explanation for the origin of these evolved sex differences in commitment to goals and predicts that the "perceived stressfulness" of the same stressful life events should be different for men and women. Following this line of reasoning, in the previous section, we have examined the impact of reproductive-related trauma. Here, we focus on sex differences in coping with interpersonal stressful events.

Human population genetic data support the argument that, during hominid evolution, males tended to stay in their birth group and females tended to migrate to the group of their mate. Women emigrating into these groups formed social support networks with nonkin based on reciprocal altruism. This web of relationships was based on day-to-day contact with a small number of individuals, required high investment, and involved a more subtle form of competition compared to male-on-male aggression and male stable dominance hierarchies. This set the stage for the evolution of numerous sex differences in social behavior and cognition, which have been documented by hundreds of studies. On average, compared to men, women (a) invest more time and energy in developing social support networks and in learning about the personality, history, and preferences of other people in their life; (b) show greater emotional dependency on enduring relationships; (c) are better at decoding nonverbal communication, picking up subtle nuances from tone of voice or facial expression; (d) value intimacy and the development of altruistic, reciprocal relationships more important than social status; (e) have a greater ability to infer what people might be thinking or intending; (f) show greater concern for the distress of other people; (g) share more intensely the emotional suffering of their friends; and (h) show more comforting, even of strangers. These sex differences in social behavior and cognition are consistent both over time and across cultures. Female superiority in empathizing would not only facilitate development of stable social relationships, garner social support, and increase sensitivity to the needs of others (all of which are important for child rearing), but it would also be adaptive in negotiating the more subtle competition that develops among girls and women (Baron-Cohen, 2005).

Darwinian psychiatry predicts that women's greater inclination to develop social support networks and their greater capacity to empathize should translate into a greater vulnerability to life events with negative interpersonal consequences. The evidence for this is quite good.

Comparing the results of interview-based assessments of stressful life events in male and female depressed adolescents, Cyranowski, Frank, Young, and Shear (2000) found that 71% of the females, but only 14% of the males, reported one or more interpersonal negative events during the six months prior to onset. In a large study of twin pairs, Kendler, Thornton, and Prescott (2001) found consistent sex differences in the depressogenic effects of three categories of stressful life events. Men were more sensitive to the effects of divorce or separation and work problems; women were more sensitive to the effects of problems getting along with individuals in their proximal network (i.e., the subject's spouse, child, parent, co-twin, or nontwin sibling). In a community-based sample of 1,024 men and 1,800 women, Maciejewski, Prigerson, and Mazure (2001) analyzed sex-differences in event-related risk for major depression and found that women were at greater risk for depression associated with distant, interpersonal losses (i.e., death of a close friend or relative). Vathera et al. (2006) studied sex differences in health after stressful life events in the family among 6,095 male and 21,217 female public sector employees in Finland. They found that exposure to stressful events was associated with a greater increase in sickness absence and a longer recovery period among women than among men. For the women, death or illness in the family was also associated with self-reported health problems irrespective of the time lag between the event and the measurement of health, whereas for the men, this association was found only in the first months after the event.

Overall, the consistency of the data showing that women are more vulnerable than men are to interpersonal stressful life events is impressive. The explanation based on sexual selection theory is not only heuristic for the epidemiologist who aims at developing theoretical models linking stressful life events with depression, but is also useful for the clinician who has the task of assessing the severity and the pathogenic impact of the stressful event in the individual patient.

LIFE HISTORY THEORY AND PSYCHIATRIC DISORDERS

A hallmark of modern evolutionary models is the capacity to integrate explanations focusing on species-typical patterns with explanations focusing on individual differences that diverge from these modal patterns. Such an appreciation for individual differences dates back to Darwin, who, in his seminal work *The Origin of Species*, understood that a new species buds off from an existing one when within-species variation becomes so extreme that individual differences turn into species differences (Insel, 2006). Evolutionary biologists are aware that variation in natural populations is widespread at every level, from gross morphology to DNA sequences, and that such a variation is the fuel for evolution.

The approach of medicine and psychiatry to individual differences is substantially different. In ordinary medical usage, the word *normal* has two meanings: (a) "that which is common" and (b) "that which is compatible with health." The fact that the two meanings are often confused reflects the tendency to equate statistical normality with biological normality. The origin of this way of thinking dates back to the Platonic and Aristotelian notion of the "ideal" or "type" to which actual organisms are imperfect approximations (Mayr, 1982). According to typological thinking, homogeneity in a population is the natural state, and variation is the result of some sort of interference. When this way of thinking is applied to clinical practice, most somatic and psychological traits are assumed to fall into a normal distribution, with most of the cases in the middle and a few at the extremes. These extremes, which constitute only a small percentage of the total population, are arbitrarily lopped off and labeled "abnormal" or "pathological" and the far larger percentage clustering around the middle is arbitrarily called "normal." The definition of disease as "a quantitative deviation from the normal" exemplifies the conventional medical approach to individual differences. Of course, in medicine, statistical abnormality is not the only criterion of morbidity. Other independent criteria, such impaired function and presence of organic lesion, are commonly applied before deciding that a statistically deviant feature is a manifestation of disease. However, the relevant point here is that both medicine and psychiatry largely subscribe to the pre-Darwinian way of thought that attributes no adaptive significance to individual differences and that ignores the possibility that within-species variation is actively maintained by natural selection.

Rejecting typological thinking, Darwinian psychiatry suggests that it may prove useful to think about individual differences in human behavior in terms of adaptive, within-species variation, including those deviant behavioral profiles that are currently defined as psychiatric disorders. The driving force behind this approach to individual differences is life history theory, one of the major middle-level evolutionary theories. Traditionally, life history theory deals with how individuals optimally allocate somatic versus reproductive effort, given current life circumstances, and it explains why life history features (e.g., rate of growth, time to sexual maturity, degree of parental investment) vary across species (Stearns, 1992). However, more recently, life history theory has emerged as a major perspective to explain the existence of alternative strategies within species.

The term *alternative strategies* refers to the presence of two or more discrete behavioral variants among adults of one sex and one population when those variants serve the same functional end, such as more than one way of foraging, or attracting mates, or nesting (Brockmann, 2001). Often discrete behavioral variants are associated with specific morphological, physiological, and life history characters. Alternative strategies may evolve as genetically based programs and may be maintained within a population because the environment is heterogeneous and what works in one ecological niche does not necessarily do as well as in another. A second account of alternative strategies emphasizes their "frequency-dependent" origins. A given strategy is only advantageous if it is displayed by no more than a certain proportion of the population. If the variant strategy becomes too common, its advantages are reduced, and the proportion of individuals enacting it declines, but when an alternative strategy becomes less common, its characteristics become more advantageous, and the proportion of individuals enacting it increases. This is considered a "balanced polymorphism."

Fish and amphibians provide excellent examples of alternative strategies. In coho salmons (*Oncorhynchus kisutch*), some males have exaggerated snouts and enlarged teeth, and they fight for access to the spawning females. Other males lack secondary sexual characters and are relatively cryptic on the breeding grounds. Instead of fighting, they attempt to gain access to females by sneaking (Gross, 1996). In North American bullfrogs (*Rana catesbiana*), the largest males win the best territories and attract females by croaking. Small, young males are not strong enough to defend a territory, so they behave as satellites, sitting silently near a calling male, and attempting to intercept and mate with any females the calling male attracts. The satellite males are not very successful but they make the best of a bad job by parasitizing the largest calling males because they do not have a better chance of getting a female when they are small (Krebs & Davis, 1987).

Not unreasonably, the reader may wonder what all of this has to do with human psychiatric disorders. The answer develops along two points. First, alternative strategies do also exist in our close relatives, the nonhuman primates, and there is no reason to assume that they do not exist in humans. Second, if alternative strategies exist in humans, they are likely to be mistaken for psychiatric disorders because deviant behavioral profiles are often associated with abnormal physiological features (Troisi, 2005). The latter point is well illustrated by alternative mating strategies of male mandrills and orangutans.

In mandrills, there are two morphological and behavioral variants of adult males that differ in terms of secondary sexual adornments and reproductive strategies (Setchell & Dixson, 2001). "Fatted" males have highly developed sex skin coloration, large testes, high plasma testosterone levels, and fat rumps, whereas "nonfatted" males have paler sex skin, smaller testes, lower plasma testosterone, and slimmer rumps. While "fatted" males mate-guard fertile females, less developed males remain in the periphery of the group and mate sneakily with females. Similar intermale differences have been observed in orangutans (Maggioncalda, Czekala, & Sapolsky, 2000). In the presence of many dominant males, adolescent male orangutans undergo a developmental arrest: they become fertile but do not develop fully adult secondary sexual features, such as cheek flanges, laryngeal sac, beard and mustache, large body size, and a musky odor. Developmental arrest is associated with a distinct hormonal profile (Maggioncalda, Sapolsky, Czekala, 1999). Arrested males lack levels of luteinizing hormone (LH), testosterone, and dihydrotestosterone (DHT) necessary for development of secondary sexual traits. However, they have sufficient testicular steroids, LH, and follicle stimulating hormone (FSH) to fully develop primary sexual function and fertility. Like in mandrills, the two morphological variants of male orangutans use different mating strategies. Developed males are frequently involved in male-male aggression, are attractive to females and typically consort with them, and may sire many offspring over a relatively short period of time. In contrast, being inconspicuous and less attractive to females, arrested males adopt a low-cost, low-benefit reproductive strategy based on sneaky matings and forced copulations. In the short period, the reproductive success of "nonfatted" male mandrills and arrested male orangutans is lower than that of fully developed males. However, there are advantages associated with the use of the "sneak and rape" mating strategy. While the "combat and consort" strategy imposes costs on dominant males in terms of metabolic energy and exposure to intermale aggression, the suppression of secondary sexual traits allows subordinate males to minimize aggression and injury from dominant, fully mature males, while still being able to sire.

How would an endocrinologist or a clinical psychiatrist evaluate the health status of nonfatted male mandrills and arrested male orangutans? In all probability, they would agree that these individuals are sick because they not only display deviant behavioral patterns, but also have abnormal hormonal profiles. In the rest of medicine, since the end of the 19th century, the presence of somatic lesion is the primary criterion for defining morbidity. For many years, this was not possible in psychiatry because the demonstration of the organic bases of mental disorders remained elusive. Thanks to the impressive advances of neurosciences, the situation is changing rapidly. Today, psychiatrists look at neurobiological research as the "oracle" that can provide the definitive solution to longstanding debates about the morbid status of a variety of human behaviors that are statistically deviant and socially disliked. Given such a theoretical background, it is easy to imagine that an evolved alternative strategy could be erroneously labeled as a psychiatric disorder if brain imaging or molecular genetic studies show that it is associated with abnormal somatic changes. This is likely to be the case for primary psychopathy, a subtype of antisocial personality disorder.

Antisocial personality disorder is a pervasive pattern of disregard for the rights of others associated with distinctive emotional and behavioral features. Individuals with this personality disorder are frequently deceitful and manipulative in order to gain personal profit. Even though they may display a glib, superficial charm, these subjects lack empathy and tend to be callous, cynical, and contemptuous of the feelings, rights, and suffering of others. Finally, they display a reckless disregard for their personal safety and are free of symptoms of anxiety. Also, the physiological and neurobiological profiles of individuals with antisocial personality appear to be abnormal in the statistical sense. Compared to control subjects, they are more likely to show orienting responses to novel stimuli, to show less physiological arousal in response to threats of pain or punishment and more tolerance of actual pain or punishment, and to have a lower resting heart rate (Raine, 2002). These distinctive physiological responses reflect reduced noradrenergic functioning and a fearless, stimulation-seeking temperament. A recent study employing magnetic resonance imaging (MRI) has suggested that the low autonomic stress reactivity and the emotional deficits of psychopathic antisocial individuals may be caused by abnormalities of the corpus callosum (Raine et al., 2003).

Although antisocial personality is classified as a mental disorder in current nosographic systems, some investigators have conceptualized a variant known as "primary psychopathy" (Skeem, Poythress, Edens, Lilienfeld, & Cale, 2003) as an alternative strategy because a number of psychological and behavioral traits typical of primary psychopaths meet the requirements of "special design" (Williams, 1966) and could well have contributed to reproductive and survival success in the ancestral environment (Book & Quinsey, 2004; Harpending & Sobus, 1987; Mealy, 1995). Reasonable assumptions are that approximately 50% of the persons who could meet the criteria for this disorder go through life undiagnosed and undetected, and they are successful by evolutionary criteria (McGuire & Troisi, 1998). For example, in a sample of male offenders, Lalumiere, Harris, and Rice (2001) found a positive correlation between the Psychopathic Checklist-Revised (PCL-R) score, physical attractiveness, and the number of children. In addition, psychopathic offenders scored lower than nonpsychopathic offenders did on fluctuating asymmetry, a reliable measure of past developmental perturbations.

During our recent evolutionary history, it seems likely that there has been strong selection for cooperation based on reciprocity. To deal with the adaptive challenges posed by the ancestral environment, our ancestors developed a strong propensity to share resources (e.g., food, tools, and knowledge) and to help the sick, the wounded, and the very young. Selection for cooperation and altruism is expected to generate cheating. In a society made up primarily of cooperators, genes for cheaters can enter the population and remain, provided that, under specific circumstances, the benefits of cheating outweigh the costs. As long as selective pressures for cooperative strategies coexist with counterpressures for cheating, a mixture of phenotypes will result, such that some sort of statistical equilibrium will be approached. Antisocial personality should thus be expected to be maintained as a low-level, frequency-dependent alternative strategy. Data concerning both the heritability of antisocial personality (Slutske, 2001) and its prevalence in the general population (Skilling, Quinsey, & Craig, 2001) are consistent with the hypothesis of frequency-dependent selection. In an evolutionary context, primary psychopathy might thus represent a high-risk strategy of social defection associated with resource acquisition and reproduction.

Interestingly, many different aspects of the psychology and physiology of individuals with antisocial personality that are currently viewed as defective or abnormal traits can be reinterpreted as complex adaptations that have evolved to allow the successful use of a cheating strategy. Sociopaths are characterized by a lack of the social emotions (such as love, shame, guilt, empathy, and remorse) in the absence of any other cognitive or mental deficit. Persons with this disorder are capable of accurately assessing the costs and benefits of short-term social interactions, accurately reading others' behavior rules, utilizing self-monitoring information to alter their strategies, and successfully disguising their intentions. Therefore, their limited capacity to experience social emotions is puzzling, considering that such a capacity is preserved even in patients suffering from a variety of severe psychopathologies. The lack of social emotions in individuals with antisocial personality becomes understandable considering the evolutionary function of these emotions. Social emotions play a central role as "commitment devices." Feeling certain emotions commits an individual to act in certain ways. We know from the work of social psychologists that there is a strict relationship between positive emotions such as sympathy and love and altruistic behavior: We are more altruistic toward those we like. On the other hand, negative social emotions experienced before or after defection (anxiety vs. guilt and remorse) discourage the use of exploitative and manipulative strategies in social interactions. Not feeling these emotions, individuals with antisocial personality may act where others are constrained from doing so: "Without love to commit them to cooperation, anxiety to prevent defection, or guilt to inspire repentance, they will remain free to continually play for the short-term benefit" (Mealy, 1995, p. 536).

Based on the medical model of disease with its emphasis on the concept of lesion, one is tempted to conclude that the organic correlates of antisocial personality definitely demonstrate its morbid nature. However, these statistically deviant biological features could simply represent a complex set of adaptations evolved to favor the use of a high-risk strategy of social defection. If the lack of social emotions prevents experiencing feelings that naturally inhibit the acting out of exploitative and aggressive impulses, so the lack of fear in response to aversive events and the incapacity to form conditioned associations between antisocial behavior and the consequent punishment allow primary sociopaths to persist in using a cheating strategy oriented toward short-term benefits.

LIMITATIONS

Evolutionary psychology has much to offer psychiatry. The issues treated in this chapter are only a small fraction of the large body of knowledge that psychiatry could profitably obtain from the evolutionary studies of human psychological processes. Yet, some methodological problems complicate the integration of the evolutionary psychological approach into clinical psychiatry. Three of these problems are briefly discussed next. In my opinion, none of them is intrinsically unsolvable, but each problem requires more consideration than it has so far received.

Lax Adaptationism

In evolutionary biology, the adaptationist program is a research strategy that seeks to identify adaptations and the specific selective forces that drove their evolution in past environments. Although everyone agrees that organisms have adaptations, adaptationism as a research strategy has not enjoyed consensual affection within evolutionary biology (Andrews, Gangestad, & Matthews, 2002). In the 1970s, it became the target of attacks by paleontologist Stephen Jay Gould and geneticist Richard Lewontin, who argued that adaptive explanations given for most human behavioral and cognitive traits were analogous to Rudyard Kipling's "just-so" stories. In effect, adaptive stories are easy to create and hard to falsify, and the risk of using inappropriate or insufficient standards of evidence for identifying adaptations and their functions is always present in the evolutionary study of human behavior.

Such a risk is even higher when the trait (or the complex of traits) for which an adaptive hypothesis is being advanced is a psychiatric syndrome. From an evolutionary perspective, the existence of psychopathology is perplexing. How can Darwin's theory of natural selection explain the persistence of psychopathology that places individuals at a reproductive disadvantage? In order to resolve the paradox of common and heritable mental disorders, many evolutionary psychiatrists have endorsed a lax version of the adaptationist program. They have picked a disorder out from current nosologies and invented an adaptive explanation for its existence. The search for a hidden genetic advantage to mental disorders has certainly produced ingenious hypotheses. Genes for schizophrenia might have made certain individuals more charismatic and shamanistic. Distractible, risk-taking individuals who are currently diagnosed as having attention deficit/hyperactivity disorder (ADHD) might have had a competitive advantage in dangerous environment where survival would depend on being "response-ready." Anorexia nervosa might have evolved as a strategy for conserving reproductive resources in environments in which males are perceived as scarce and female competition for males is perceived to be intense. Although intriguing, these adaptationist hypotheses remain unproven. The unfortunate result is that clinicians are skeptical of the validity and utility of evolutionary psychiatry and believe that the preferred activities of evolutionary psychiatrists are storytelling and the invention of outlandish explanations to elucidate the selection pressures that forged psychopathological traits (Dubrovsky, 2002; McCrone, 2003).

Although the search for possible adaptive functions of psychiatric syndromes is an important counterbalance to the prevailing assumption that statistical deviance or subjective distress equal to mental disorder (Troisi, 2006), the application of the evolutionary theory to psychopathology does not necessarily consist in finding hidden adaptive benefits for each clinical condition. For example, Keller and Miller (2006) have argued against those evolutionary thinkers who assume that adaptive forces are the only possible explanations for common and heritable mental disorders and have convincingly suggested that the apparent evolutionary paradox of the existence of these disorders can be resolved by recognizing the enormous mutational target size of human behaviors. In their book *Darwinian Psychiatry*, McGuire and Troisi (1998) repeatedly acknowledged the maladaptive nature of the great majority of clinical conditions and employed the evolutionary analysis to define the suboptimal traits associated with psychiatric syndromes, not to speculate about their unknown adaptive benefits.

The development of strict and falsifiable criteria for identifying possible adaptive aspects of psychiatric disorders is a major task for evolutionary psychiatry over the coming years. The development of these criteria should build on two crucial points. First, psychiatric syndromes as described in current classification systems are a weak starting point for the search of adaptive explanations. Individual symptoms, endophenotypes, and behavior systems are better targets for evolutionary analysis (Troisi & D'Amato, 2005). Second, evolutionary studies should take into account the findings that are emerging from behavioral genomics and that show the importance of polymorphisms, pleiotropic effects (i.e., genes having multiple phenotypic expressions), oligogenic transmission (i.e., a small number of genes of moderate effect), and polygenic transmission (i.e., many genes of small effect) for the evolution of psychological and behavioral traits (Plomin, 2002).

Neglect of Behavior Analysis

A major theoretical point that differentiates evolutionary psychology from other evolutionary disciplines such as sociobiology, behavioral ecology, Darwinian anthropology, and human ethology is the relative importance attributed to psychological mechanisms as opposed to behavior. Evolutionary psychologists argue that behavior itself does not contribute to fitness and that the psychological mechanisms that produce behavior should be the focus of evolutionary analysis. Interestingly, such an emphasis on psychological processes to the detriment of behavioral analysis is in line with prevailing psychiatric thinking. Such a concordance is potentially dangerous because it could immunize psychiatry against the critiques that stress its weakness in assessing the actual behavior of persons with mental disorders.

The clinical phenomenology of psychiatric disorders includes both subjective psychological experiences and objective behavioral changes. Nevertheless, the diagnostic process in psychiatry is based almost exclusively on the evaluation of the psychological symptoms as voiced by the patient with virtually no use of direct observation of behavior. Behavioral changes, if taken into account, are assessed primarily through indirect reports (by the patients themselves or by other informants). The weakness of such an approach to behavioral assessment has several negative consequences for psychiatric research and clinical practice.

In psychiatric research, while almost all the physiological data about a patient are measured to at least one decimal point on parametric scales, the behavior of the patient is given only ordinal ratings. It is difficult to estimate to what extent the findings of biological studies are confounded or invalidated by the fact that they are generally based on correlations between accurate neurobiological measurements and crude behavioral ratings, sometimes of the type "better/worse" or "much/less." Another negative consequence of psychiatry's neglect for direct observation of behavior is the difficulty of integrating animal and human data about the effects of drugs on behavior. Not knowing how an animal feels or what its mental experiences might be restricts animal researchers to inferences based on observable behavior. In contrast, clinicians rely primarily on psychometric assessment to evaluate the effects of drugs on patients' behavior. Such a difference between the methods employed in human and animal studies is a major obstacle for the development of valid animal models of psychiatric disorders. If the clinical phenomenology of mental illnesses could be reformulated in behavioral terms, the same, or similar, definitions could then be applied to the development of animal models, and analogs for specific behaviors might then become more feasible.

Finally, the weakness of behavioral assessment in psychiatry has negative implications for clinical practice as well. While concentrating mainly on the analysis of verbal communication, most psychiatrists tend to neglect patients' nonverbal signals because they are not trained in capturing and interpreting them. Consequently, a great deal of information is lost or misinterpreted. Several studies have shown that the objective and quantitative recording of patients' behavior may sometimes yield different results from those obtained using rating scales or structured interviews (Troisi, 1999). These findings cast doubt on the validity of routine psychiatric assessments and suggest caution in basing important clinical decisions (e.g., when to discharge a patient or whether to increase drug dosage) exclusively on patients' reports of their symptoms.

Considering the severity of the methodological limitations described above, it would be an unforgivable error to miss the opportunity of importing into clinical psychiatry the theoretical framework developed by evolutionary disciplines such as sociobiology, behavioral ecology, and human ethology for studying behavior. For example, human ethology has developed distinctive and powerful methods for observing and measuring behavior. The ethological approach involves direct observation, coding, and analysis of specific nonverbal behaviors in naturalistic settings. Rigorous description is combined with a theoretical emphasis on those behaviors that are most closely related to adaptive functioning. The behavior patterns that are observed occur as a part of the individual's interaction with the natural environment, allowing an understanding of the relationship of specific behaviors to the capacity of dealing with real-life situations. In conclusion, when arguing for the integration of an evolutionary approach into psychiatry, it is best to leave disciplinary disputes apart and keep an open mind about selection favoring psychological capacities rather than behavior.

Therapeutic Irrelevance

As a branch of medicine, psychiatry has as its main objective the treatment of mental disorders. Yet, therapy has not been a major focus of research and discussion in evolutionary psychiatry. Almost certainly, this is the most important reason that can explain why the evolutionary approach has had so little impact on clinical psychiatry (Troisi & McGuire, 2006). When evolutionary psychiatrists suggest ultimate explanations of vulnerability to psychopathology based on phenomena such as evolutionary trade-offs (different traits are adaptive in different environments), genome lag (evolved traits may be out of step with modern environments), and historical constraints (how a trait has evolved may result in particular susceptibility to disease), certainly they are offering a deeper understanding of the origin of psychiatric disorders. But let us be practical. When patients with schizophrenia or severe depression arrive at the hospital, all that matters is to relieve their symptoms. It is, then, proximate causes that are at the center of therapeutic intervention, and remote causes are just that: remote. In a recent paper, Nesse (2005) has acknowledged that, at present, there are no evolutionary-based treatments for mental disorders and has concluded that evolutionary biology's main contribution to psychiatry is that of offering a theoretical framework for integrating findings from the many disciplines that study and treat persons labeled as suffering from mental disorders. However, this is not enough for clinical psychiatrists: "Unless evolutionary explanations are tied directly to genetic and physiological knowledge of why some people get sick in certain ways while others do not, they are too vague and general to be useful in medicine" (Guze, 1992, p. 92).

Should we agree with the above reflections and be pessimistic about the therapeutic relevance of Darwinian psychiatry? If we embrace the engineering mentality that conceptualizes successful treatment as the reversal of immediate reasons for illness, the answer is a disappointing, "Yes." It is highly improbable that evolutionary studies will lead to the discovery of a drug to eliminate cognitive deficits of persons with schizophrenia or a prenatal kit to switch off the susceptibility genes for autism. Yet, if we accept a broader concept of the aims of therapeutic interventions, the answer is more optimistic. According to an alternative view of medicine, the aim of therapy is not only to reverse the pathogenesis (i.e., proximate mechanisms) of illness, but also to restore the congruence between a patient's individuality and the conditions of the environment (Childs, 1999). If therapy is conceived of in these terms, the therapeutic relevance of Darwinian psychiatry emerges clearly (McGuire & Troisi, 1998).

According to Darwinian psychiatry, assessment of treatment efficacy should focus primarily on functional capacities and person-environment interactions. Like mentally healthy people, individuals with psychiatric symptoms act to optimize the achievement of short-term goals and their behavior reflects interactions between their strategies, their functional capacities, and environmental contingencies. It follows that an accurate assessment of functional capacities is essential to the development of valid and useful outcome measures. Therapeutic interventions that focus primarily on signs and symptoms and the putative mechanisms for their production (e.g., neurochemical imbalance), and only secondarily on function, limit themselves to relieve only one aspect of the clinical picture. For example, drug-induced remission of delusions and hallucinations in a person with schizophrenia cannot be considered a successful treatment if that person continues to be impaired in work, family, and social functioning. Therapy should primarily aim at improving the patient's chances of achieving short-term biological goals. Depending on the features of the patient and the factors that cause the symptoms, the therapeutic strategy will include different interventions. Persons with intact functional capacities who experience dysfunctional states could be helped to identify the environmental and personal constraints that interfere with achieving short-term goals. Therapy should facilitate: (1) the refinement of the capacities to assess cost-benefit outcomes; (2) the development of revised models of the social environment; and (3) the improvement of capacities to selectively enact behaviors associated with goal achievement.

For suboptimal functional capacities that are due to individual differences, therapy should attempt either to refine traits or to foster the use of alternative capacities that improve the likelihood of achieving high-priority goals. Altering minimally adaptive capacities is sometimes extremely difficult, however. If the patient is not able to develop and execute novel behavioral strategies, environmental change is usually essential to ensure lasting improvement. Said differently, persons with suboptimal functional capacities should be advised to actively search for environments in which they are most likely to achieve high-priority goals.

Theoretically, symptoms that are attempts to adapt should not be treated, unless symptomatic therapy does not interfere with the restoration of normal functioning of evolved behavioral systems. In practice, attempts to treat these symptoms are justified if symptomatic therapy is the only feasible option. However, the mere elimination of adaptive symptoms should always be a second-choice therapeutic option because, in the long run, it is likely to be less effective than a therapy aimed at promoting the optimal functioning of evolved behavioral systems. Clinical psychiatrists should be aware that (a) clinical manifestations reflecting defensive responses should be distinguished from those that are caused by the direct action of etiological agents (symptoms as defects), and (b) treatment of adaptive symptoms should be avoided if there is the possibility to treat successfully the causes that impede the achievement of short-term goals and that are therefore responsible for the origin of the symptoms.

REFERENCES

Anderson, K. M., Sharpe, M., Rattray A., & Irvine, D. S. (2003). Distress and concerns in couples referred to a specialist infertility clinic. *Journal of Psychosomatic Research, 54*, 353–355.

Andrews, P. W., Gangestad, S.W., & Matthews, D. (2002). Adaptationism—How to carry out an exaptationist program. *Behavioral and Brain Science, 25*, 489–553.

Bancroft, J., Loftus, J., & Long, J. S. (2003). Distress about sex: A national survey of women in heterosexual relationships. *Archives of Sexual Behavior, 32*, 193–208.

Baron-Cohen, S. (2005). The empathizing system: A revision of the 1994 model of the mindreading system. In B. J. Ellis & D. F. Bjorklund (Eds.), *Origins of social mind. Evolutionary psychology and child development* (pp. 468–492). New York: Guilford.

Basson, R. (2005). Women's sexual dysfunction: Revised and expanded definition. *Canadian Medical Association Journal, 172*, 1327–1333.

Book, A., & Quinsey, V. L. (2004). Psychopaths: Cheaters or warrior-hawks? *Personality and Individual Differences, 36*, 3–45.

Brockmann, H. J. (2001). The evolution of alternative strategies and tactics. *Advances in the Study of Behavior, 30*, 1–51.

Buss, D. M., & Schmitt, D. P. (1993). Sexual strategies theory: An evolutionary perspective on human mating. *Psychological Review, 100*, 204–232.

Childs, B. (1999). Genetic medicine. In *A logic of disease*. Baltimore: The John Hopkins University Press.

Chisholm, J. (1996). The evolutionary ecology of attachment organization. *Human Nature, 7*, 1–38.

Crawford, C., & Salmon, C. (2002). Psychopathology or adaptation? Genetic and evolutionary perspectives on individual differences and psychopathology. *Neuroendocrinol Letters 23*(Suppl. 4), 39–45.

Cyranowski, J. M., Frank, E., Young, E., & Shear, K. (2000). Adolescent onset of the gender difference in lifetime rates of major depression. A theoretical model. *Archives of General Psychiatry, 57*, 21–27.

Dubrovsky, B. (2002). Evolutionary psychiatry. Adaptationist and nonadaptationist conceptualizations. *Progress in Neuro-Psychopharmacology and Biological Psychiatry 26*, 1–19.

Eaton, S. B., & Eaton, S. B., III. (2000). Paleolithic vs. modern diets: Selected pathophysiological implications. *European Journal of Nutrition, 39*, 67–70.

Frances, A. (1998). Problems in defining clinical significance in epidemiological studies. *Archives of General Psychiatry, 55*, 119.

Gangestad, S. W., & Simpson, J. A. (2000). The evolution of human mating: Trade-offs and strategic pluralism. *Behavioral and Brain Sciences, 23*, 573–644.

Gross, M. R. (1996). Alternative reproductive strategies and tactics: Diversity within sexes. *Trends in Ecology & Evolution, 11*, 92–97.

Guze, S. B. (1992). *Why psychiatry is a branch of medicine*. New York: Oxford University Press.

Harlow, B. L., & Stewart, E. G. (2003). A population-based assessment of chronic unexplained vulvar pain: Have we underestimated the prevalence of vulvodynia? *Journal of the American Medical Women's Association, 58*, 82–88.

Harpending, H., & Sobus, J. (1987). Sociopathy as an adaptation. *Ethology and Sociobiology, 8*(Suppl. 3), 63s–72s.

Insel, T. R. (2006). From species differences to individual differences. *Molecular Psychiatry, 11*, 424.

Keller, M. C., & Miller, G. (2006). Resolving the paradox of common, harmful, heritable mental disorders: Which evolutionary genetic models work best? *Behavioral and Brain Sciences, 29*, 385–404.

Keller, M. C., Nesse, R. M. (2006). The evolutionary significance of depressive symptoms: Different adverse situations lead to different depressive symptom patterns. *Journal of Personality and Social Psychology, 91*, 316–330.

Kendell, R. E. (1975). *The role of diagnosis in psychiatry*. Oxford, U.K.: Blackwell.

Kendler, K. S., Thornton, L. M., & Prescott, C. A. (2001). Gender differences in the rates of exposure to stressful life events and sensitivity to their depressogenic effects. *American Journal of Psychiatry, 158,* 587–593.

Kessler, R. C., McGonagle, K. A., Zhao, S., Nelson, C. B., Hughes, M., Eshleman, S., et al. (1994). Lifetime and 12–month prevalence of DSM-III-R psychiatric disorders in the United States. *Archives of General Psychiatry, 51,* 8–19.

Koob, G. F., & Le Moal, M. (2001). Drug addiction, dysregulation of reward, and allostasis. *Neuropsychopharmacology, 24,* 97–129.

Krebs, J. R., & Davis, N. B. (1987). *An introduction to behavioural ecology* (2nd ed.). Oxford, U.K.: Blackwell.

Lalumiere, M. L., Harris, G. T., & Rice, M. E. (2001). Psychopathy and developmental instability. *Evolution and Human Behavior, 22,* 75–92.

Laumann, E. O., Paik, A., & Rosen, R. C. (1999). Sexual dysfunction in the United States: Prevalence and predictors. *Journal of the American Medical Association, 281,* 537–544.

Mace, R. (2000). Evolutionary ecology of human life history. *Animal Behaviour, 59,* 1–10.

Maciejewski, P. K., Prigerson, H. G., & Mazure, C. M. (2001). Sex differences in event-related risk for major depression. *Psychological Medicine, 31,* 593–604.

Maggioncalda, A. N., Sapolsky, R. M., & Czekala, N. M. (1999). Reproductive hormone profiles in captive male orangutans: Implications for understanding developmental arrest. *American Journal of Physical Anthropology, 109,* 19–32.

Maggioncalda, A. N., Czekala, N. M., & Sapolsky, R. M. (2000). Growth hormone and thyroid stimulating hormone concentrations in captive male orangutans: Implications for understanding developmental arrest. *American Journal of Primatology, 50,* 67–76.

Marazziti, D., Akiskal, H. S., Rossi, A., & Cassano, G. B. (1999). Alteration of the platelet serotonin transporter in romantic love. *Psychological Medicine, 29,* 741–745.

Mayr, E. (1982). *The growth of biological thought.* Cambridge, MA: Harvard University Press.

McCrone, J. (2003) Darwinian medicine. *Lancet Neurology, 2,* 516.

McEwan, K. L., Costello, C. G., & Taylor, P. J. (1987). Adjustment to infertility. *Journal of Abnormal Psychology, 96,* 108–116.

McGuire, M. T., & Troisi, A. (1998). *Darwinian psychiatry.* New York: Oxford University Press.

Mealy, L. (1995). The sociobiology of sociopathy: An integrated evolutionary model. *Behavioral and Brain Sciences, 18,* 523–599.

Nesse, R. M. (2000). Is depression an adaptation? *Archives of General Psychiatry, 57,* 14–20.

Nesse, R. M. (2004). Natural selection and the elusiveness of happiness. *Philosophical Transactions of the Royal Society of London, Series B, Biological Sciences 359,* 1333–1347.

Nesse, R. M. (2005). Evolutionary psychology and mental health. In D. Buss (Ed.), *Handbook of evolutionary psychology* (pp. 903–927). Hoboken, NJ: Wiley.

Nesse, R. M., & Berridge, K. C. (1997). Psychoactive drug use in evolutionary perspective. *Science, 278,* 63–66.

Nesse, R. M., & Williams, G. C. (1994). *Why we get sick: The new science of Darwinian medicine.* New York: Random House.

Nonacs, R., & Cohen, L. S. (2000). Postpartum psychiatric syndromes. In B. J. Sadock & V. A. Sadock (Eds.), *Kaplan & Sadock's comprehensive textbook of psychiatry* (VII ed., Vol. 1., pp. 1276–1283). Philadelphia: Lippincott Williams & Wilkins.

Okami, P., & Shackelford, T. K. (2001). Human sex differences in sexual psychology and behavior. *Annual Review of Sex Research, 12,* 186–241.

Panksepp, J. (1998). *Affective neuroscience: The foundations of human and animal emotions.* New York: Oxford University Press.

Plomin, R. (2002). Individual differences research in a postgenomic era. *Personality and Individual Differences, 33,* 909–920.

Raine, A. (2002). Biosocial studies of antisocial and violent behavior in children and adults: A review. *Journal of Abnormal Child Psychology, 30,* 311–326.

Raine, A., Lencz, T., Taylor, K., Hellige, J. B., Bihrle, S., Lacasse, L., et al. (2003). Corpus callosum abnormalities in psychopathic antisocial individuals. *Archives of General Psychiatry, 60,* 1134–1142.

Schmitt, D. P. (2003). Universal sex differences in the desire for sexual variety: Tests from 52 nations, 6 continents, and 13 islands. *Journal Personality and Social Psychology, 85,* 85–104.

Setchell, J. M., & Dixson, A. F. (2001). Arrested development of secondary sexual adornments in subordinate adult male mandrills (Mandrillus sphinx). *American Journal Physical Anthropology, 115,* 245–252.

Skeem, J. L., Poythress, N., Edens, J. F., Lilienfeld, S. O., & Cale, E. M. (2003). Psychopatic personality or personalities? Exploring potential variants of psychopathy and their implications for risk assessment. *Aggression and Violent Behavior, 8,* 513–546.

Skilling, T. A., Quinsey, V. L., & Craig, W. (2001). Evidence of a taxon underlying serious antisocial behavior in boys. *Criminal Justice and Behavior, 28,* 450–470.

Slutske, W. S. (2001). The genetics of antisocial behavior. *Current Psychiatry Reports, 3,* 158–162.

Stearns, S. C. (1992). *The evolution of life histories.* Oxford, U.K.: Oxford University Press.

Tooby, J., & Cosmides, L. (1990). On the universality of human nature and the uniqueness of the individual: The role of genetics and adaptation. *Journal of Personality, 58,* 17–67.

Troisi, A. (1999). Ethological research in clinical psychiatry: The study of nonverbal behavior during interviews. *Neuroscience & Biobehavioral Reviews, 23*(7), 905–913.

Troisi, A. (2001a). Gender differences in vulnerability to social stress: A Darwinian perspective. *Physiology & Behavior, 73,* 443–449.

Troisi, A. (2001b). Harmful effects of substance abuse: A Darwinian perspective. *Functional Neurology, 16*(Suppl. 4), 237–243.

Troisi, A. (2003). Sexual disorders in the context of Darwinian psychiatry. *Journal of Endocrinological Investigation, 26*(Suppl. 3), 54–57.

Troisi, A. (2005). The concept of alternative strategies and its relevance to psychiatry and clinical psychology. *Neuroscience & Biobehavioral Reviews, 29*(1), 159–168.

Troisi, A. (2006). Adaptationism and medicalization: The Scylla and Charybdis of Darwinian psychiatry. *Behavioral and Brain Sciences, 29,* 422–423.

Troisi, A., & D'Amato, F. R. (2005). Deficits in affiliative reward: An endophenotype for psychiatric disorders? *Behavioral and Brain Sciences, 28,* 345–366.

Troisi, A., & McGuire, M. T. (1998). Evolution and mental health. In H. S. Friedman (Ed), *Encyclopedia of mental health* (Vol. 2, pp. 173–181). San Diego, CA: Academic Press.

Troisi, A., & McGuire, M. T. (2002). Darwinian psychiatry and the concept of mental disorder. *Neuroendocrinology Letters, 23*(Suppl. 4), 31–38.

Troisi, A., & McGuire, M. T. (2006). Darwinian psychiatry: It's time to focus on clinical questions. *Clinical Neuropsychiatry, 3,* 85–86.

Vance, J. C., Foster, W. J., Najman, J. M., Embelton, G., Thearle, M. J., & Hodgen, F. M. (1991). Early parental responses to sudden infant death, stillbirth or neonatal death. *Medical Journal Australia, 155,* 292–297.

Vathera, J., Kivimaki, M., Vaananen, A., Linna, A., Pentti, J., Helenius, H., et al. (2006). Sex differences in health effects of family death or illness: Are women more vulnerable than men? *Psychosomatic Medicine, 68,* 283–291.

Verhaak, C. M., Smeenk, J. M. J., van Minnen, A., Kremer, J. A. M., & Kraaimaat, F. W. (2005). A longitudinal, prospective study on emotional adjustment before, during and after consecutive fertility treatment cycles. *Human Reproduction, 20,* 2253–2260.

Williams, G. C. (1966). *Adaptation and natural selection.* Princeton, NJ: Princeton University Press.

Wright, J., Duchesne, C., Sabourin, S., Bissonnette, F., Benoit, J., & Girard, Y. (1991). Psychosocial distress and infertility: Men and women respond differently. *Fertility and Sterility, 55,* 100–108.

Part *VII*
EXPLORING THE EXPLANATORY POWER OF EVOLUTIONARY PSYCHOLOGY

Religion is the source of some of the most extreme forms of prosocial and antisocial behavior. Can evolutionary psychology account for phenomena such as religion? Because religion is universal, we might suspect that it stems from specific evolved adaptations that serve specific adaptive functions. However, because of its functional diversity including contrary functions it is difficult to see how it could have evolved through natural selection. The ability to account for religion within the paradigm of evolutionary psychology would indicate great strides in applying evolutionary theory to human behavior.

25

The Evolutionary Psychology of Religion

SCOTT ATRAN

INTRODUCTION: RELIGION AS AN EVOLUTIONARY BY-PRODUCT

Explaining religion is a serious problem for any evolutionary account of human thought and society. All known human societies—past or present—bear the very substantial costs of religion's material, emotional, and cognitive commitments to factually impossible, counterintuitive worlds. From an evolutionary standpoint, the reasons for why religion should not exist are patent: Religion is materially expensive and it is unrelentingly counterfactual and even counterintuitive. Religious practice is costly in terms of material sacrifice (at least one's prayer time), emotional expenditure (inciting fears and hopes), and cognitive effort (maintaining both factual and counterintuitive networks of beliefs).

Summing up the anthropological literature on religious offerings, Raymond Firth (1963) concludes, "[S]acrifice is giving something up at a cost ... 'Afford it or not,' the attitude seems to be" (pp. 13–16). That is why "sacrifice of wild animals which can be regarded as the free gift of nature is rarely allowable or efficient" (Robertson Smith, 1894, p. 466). As Bill Gates (as cited in

Keillor, 1999) aptly surmised, "Just in terms of allocation of time resources, religion is not very efficient. There's a lot more I could be doing on a Sunday morning".[1]

Functionalist arguments, including adaptationist accounts, usually attempt to offset the apparent functional disadvantages of religion with even greater functional advantages. There are many different and even contrary explanations for why religion exists in terms of beneficial functions served. These include functions of social (e.g., bolstering group solidarity, group competition), economic (e.g., sustaining public goods, surplus production), political (e.g., mass opiate, rebellion's stimulant), intellectual (e.g., explain mysteries, encourage credulity), health and well-being (e.g., increase life expectancy, accept death), and emotional (e.g., terrorizing, allaying anxiety) utility. Many of these functions have obtained in one cultural context or another, yet all also have been true of cultural phenomena besides religion.

Such descriptions of religion often insightfully help to explain how and why given religious beliefs and practices help to provide competitive advantages over other sorts of ideologies and behaviors for cultural survival. Still, these accounts provide little explanatory insight into cognitive selection factors responsible for the ease of acquisition of religious concepts by children or for the facility with which religious practices and beliefs are transmitted across individuals. They have little to say about which beliefs and practices—all things being equal—are most likely to recur in different cultures and most disposed to cultural variation and elaboration. None predicts the cognitive peculiarities of religion, such as

- why do *agent* concepts predominate in religion;
- why are *supernatural-agent* concepts culturally universal;
- why are some supernatural agent concepts *inherently better* candidates for cultural selection than others;
- why is it necessary, and how it is possible, to *validate* belief in supernatural agent concepts that are logically and factually inscrutable; and
- how is it possible to prevent people from deciding that the existing moral order is simply wrong or *arbitrary* and from *defecting* from the social consensus through denial, dismissal, or *deception*?

This argument does not entail that religious beliefs and practices cannot perform social functions or that the successful performance of such functions does not contribute to the survival and

---

[1] In sum, religious sacrifice generally runs counter to calculations of immediate utility, such that future promises are not discounted in favor of present rewards. In some cases, sacrifice is extreme. Although such cases tend to be rare, they are often held by society as religiously ideal—for example, sacrificing one's own life or nearest kin. Researchers sometimes take such cases as prima facie evidence of "true" (nonkin) social altruism (Kuper, 1996; Rappaport, 1999), or group selection, wherein individual fitness decreases so that overall group fitness can increase (relative to the overall fitness of other, competing groups; Sober & Wilson, 1998; Wilson, 2002). But this may be an illusion. Consider suicide terrorism (Atran, 2003). The "Oath to Jihad" taken by recruits to Harkat al-Ansar, a Pakistani-based ally of Al-Qaeda, affirms that by their sacrifice they help secure the future of their "family" of fictive kin: "Each [martyr] has a special place—among them are brothers, just as there are sons and those even more dear." In religiously inspired suicide terrorism, these sentiments are purposely manipulated by organizational leaders and trainers to the advantage of the manipulating elites rather than the individual (much as the fast food or soft drink industries manipulate innate desires for naturally scarce commodities like fatty foods and sugar to ends that reduce personal fitness but benefit the manipulating institution). No "group selection" is involved for the sake of the cultural "superorganism" (Wilson, 2002; cf. Kroeber, 1923/1963)—like a bee for its hive—only cognitive and emotional manipulation of some individuals by others. In evolutionary terms, quest for status and dignity may represent proximate means to the ultimate end of gaining resources, but as with other proximate means (e.g., passionate love) may become emotionally manipulated ends in themselves (Tooby & Cosmides, 1992).

spread of religious traditions. Indeed, there is substantial evidence that religious beliefs and practices often alleviate potentially dysfunctional stress and anxiety (Ben-Amos, 1994; Worthington, Kurusu, McCullough, & Sandage, 1996) and maintain social cohesion in the face of real or perceived conflict (Allport, 1956; Pyszczynski, Greenberg, & Solomon, 1999). It does imply that social functions are not phylogenetically responsible for the cognitive structure and cultural recurrence of religion.

The claim is that religion is not an evolutionary adaptation per se, but a recurring cultural by-product of the complex evolutionary landscape that sets cognitive, emotional, and material conditions for ordinary human interactions (Atran, 2002; Boyer, 2001; Kirkpatrick, 1999; Pinker, 2004; Pyysiäinen, 2001). Religion exploits ordinary cognitive processes to passionately display costly devotion to counterintuitive worlds governed by supernatural agents. The conceptual foundations of religion are intuitively given by task-specific panhuman cognitive domains, including folk mechanics, folk biology, and folk psychology. Core religious beliefs minimally violate ordinary notions about how the world is, with all of its inescapable problems, thus enabling people to imagine minimally impossible supernatural worlds that solve existential problems, including death and deception.

THE SUPERNATURAL AGENT: HAIR-TRIGGERED FOLK PSYCHOLOGY

Religions invariably center on supernatural *agent* concepts, such as gods, goblins, angels, ancestor spirits, jinns, and so forth. Granted, nondeistic "theologies," such as Buddhism and Taoism, doctrinally eschew personifying the supernatural or animating nature with supernatural causes. Nevertheless, common folk who espouse these faiths routinely entertain belief in an array of gods and spirits that behave counterintuitively in ways that are inscrutable to factual or logical reasoning.[2] Even Buddhist monks ritually ward off malevolent deities by invoking benevolent ones and conceive altered states of nature as awesome.[3]

Mundane *agent* concepts are central players in what cognitive and developmental psychologists refer to as folk psychology and theory of mind. A reasonable speculation is that agency evolved hair-triggered in humans to respond automatically under conditions of uncertainty to potential threats (and opportunities) by intelligent predators (and protectors). From this evolutionary perspective, agency is a sort of "innate releasing mechanism" (Tinbergen, 1951) whose original evolutionary domain encompasses animate objects but which inadvertently extends to moving dots on computer

---

[2] Although the Buddha and the buddhas are not regarded as gods, Buddhists clearly conceive of them as "counterintuitive agents" (Pyysiäinen, 2003). In Sri Lanka, Sinhalese relics of the Buddha have miraculous powers. In India, China, Japan, Thailand, and Vietnam, there are magic mountains and forests associated with the Buddha; and the literature and folklore of every Buddhist tradition recount amazing events surrounding the Buddha and the buddhas.

[3] Experiments with adults in the United States (Barrett & Keil, 1996) and India (Barrett, 1998) illustrate the gap between theological doctrine and actual psychological processing of religious concepts. When asked to describe their deities, subjects in both cultures produced abstract and consensual theological descriptions of gods as being able to do anything, to anticipate and react to everything at once, to always know the right thing to do, and to dispense entirely with perceptual information and calculation. When asked to respond to narratives about these same gods, the same subjects described the deities as being in only one place at a time, puzzling over alternative courses of action, and looking for evidence in order to decide what to do (e.g., to first save Johnny, who's praying for help because his foot is stuck in a river in the United States and the water is rapidly rising, or to first save little Mary, whom he has seen fall on railroad tracks in Australia where a train is fast approaching).

screens, voices in the wind, faces in clouds, and virtually any complex design or uncertain situation of unknown origin (Guthrie, 1993; Hume, 1757/1956).[4]

Experiments show that children and adults spontaneously interpret the contingent movements of dots and geometrical forms on a screen as interacting agents with distinct goals and internal motivations for reaching those goals (P. Bloom & Veres, 1999; Csibra, Gergely, Biró, Koós, & Brockbank, 1999; Heider & Simmel, 1944; D. Premack & A. Premack, 1995). Such a biologically prepared, or "modular," processing program would provide a rapid and economical reaction to a wide—but not unlimited—range of stimuli that would have been statistically associated with the presence of agents in ancestral environments. Mistakes, or "false positives," would usually carry little cost, whereas a true response could provide the margin of survival (Geary & Huffman, 2002; Seligman, 1971).

Our brains may be trip wired to spot lurkers (and to seek protectors) where conditions of uncertainty prevail (e.g., when startled, at night, in unfamiliar places, during sudden catastrophe, in the face of solitude, illness, prospects of death, etc.). Plausibly, the most dangerous and deceptive predator for the genus *Homo* since the Late Pleistocene has been *Homo* itself, which may have engaged in a spiraling behavioral and cognitive arms race of individual and group conflicts (Alexander, 1989). Given the constant menace of enemies within and without, concealment, deception, and the ability to generate and recognize false beliefs in others would favor survival. In potentially dangerous or uncertain circumstances, it would be best to anticipate and fear the worst of all likely possibilities: presence of a deviously intelligent predator.

From an evolutionary perspective, it is better to be safe than sorry regarding the detection of agency under conditions of uncertainty. This cognitive proclivity would favor emergence of malevolent deities in all cultures, just as a countervailing Darwinian propensity to attach to protective caregivers would favor apparition of benevolent deities. Thus, for the Carajá Indians of Central Brazil, intimidating or unsure regions of the local ecology are religiously avoided:

> The earth and underworld are inhabited by supernaturals.... There are two kinds. Many are amiable and beautiful beings who have friendly relations with humans ... others are ugly and dangerous monsters who cannot be placated. Their woods are avoided and nobody fishes in their pools. (Lipkind, 1940, p. 249)

Similar descriptions of supernaturals appear in ethnographic reports throughout the Americas, Africa, Eurasia, and Oceania (Atran, 2002).

In addition, humans *conceptually create* information to mimic and manipulate conditions in ancestral environments that originally produced and triggered evolved cognitive and emotional dispositions (Sperber, 1996). Humans habitually "fool" their own innate releasing programs, as when people become sexually aroused by make-up (which artificially highlights sexually appealing attributes), fabricated perfumes or undulating lines drawn on paper or dots arranged on a computer

---

[4] When triggered by a certain range of stimuli, an innate releasing mechanism "automatically" unleashes a sequence of behaviors that were naturally selected to accomplish some adaptive task in an ancestral environment. Consider food-catching behavior in frogs. When a flying insect moves across the frog's field of vision, bug-detector cells are activated in the frog's brain. Once activated, these cells in turn massively fire others in a chain reaction that usually results in the frog shooting out its tongue to catch the insect. The bug detector is primed to respond to any small dark object that suddenly enters the visual field. For each natural domain, there is a proper domain and (possibly empty) actual domain (Sperber, 1996). A proper domain is information that is the device's naturally selected function to process. The actual domain is any information in the organism's environment that satisfies the device's input conditions whether or not the information is functionally relevant to ancestral task demands—that is, whether it also belongs to its proper domain. If flying insects belong to the proper domain of frog's food-catching device, then small wads of black paper dangling on a string belong to the actual domain.

screen, that is, pornographic pictures.[5] Indeed, much of human culture—for better or worse—can be arguably attributed to focused stimulations and manipulations of our species' innate proclivities. Such manipulations can serve cultural ends far removed from the ancestral adaptive tasks that originally gave rise to those cognitive and emotional faculties triggered, although manipulations for religion often centrally involve the collective engagement of existential desires (e.g., wanting security) and anxieties (e.g., fearing death).

Recently, numbers of devout American Catholics eyed the image of Mother Theresa in a cinnamon bun sold in a Tennessee shop. Latinos in Houston prayed before a vision of the Virgin of Guadalupe, whereas Anglos saw only the dried ice cream on a pavement. Cuban exiles in Miami spotted the Virgin in windows, curtains, and television afterimages as long as there was hope of keeping young Elian Gonzalez from returning to godless Cuba. And on 9/11, newspapers showed photos of smoke billowing from one of the World Trade Center towers that "[seem] to bring into focus the face of the Evil One, with beard and horns and malignant expression, symbolizing to many the hideous nature of the deed that wreaked horror and terror upon an unsuspecting city" ("Bedeviling: Did Satan rear his ugly face," 2001). In such cases, there is culturally conditioned emotional priming in anticipation of agency. This priming, in turn, amplifies the information value of otherwise doubtful, poor, and fragmentary agency-relevant stimuli. This enables the stimuli (e.g., cloud formations, pastry, and ice cream conformations) to achieve the minimal threshold for triggering hyperactive facial recognition and body-movement recognition schemata that humans possess.

In sum, supernatural agents are readily conjured up perhaps because natural selection has trip wired cognitive schema for agency detection in the face of uncertainty. Uncertainty is omnipresent, and so too the hair triggering of an agency-detection mechanism that readily promotes supernatural interpretation and is susceptible to various forms of cultural manipulation. Cultural manipulation of this modular mechanism and priming facilitate and direct the process. Because the phenomena created readily activate intuitively given modular processes, they are more likely to survive transmission from mind to mind under a wide range of different environments and learning conditions than entities and information that are harder to process (Atran, 1990; Boyer, 1994). As a result, they are more likely to become enduring aspects of human cultures, such as belief in the supernatural.

"Minimally counterintuitive" worlds allow supernatural agents to resolve existential dilemmas. Supernatural agents, like ghosts and the Abrahamic Deity and Devil are much like human agents, psychologically (e.g., belief, desire, promise, inference, decision, emotion, etc.) and biologically (e.g., sight, hearing, feel, taste, smell, coordination, etc.), but lack material substance and some associated physical constraints. As we shall see in the next section, these imaginary worlds are close enough to factual, everyday worlds to be perceptually compelling and conceptually tractable, but also surprising enough to capture attention, prime memory and so "contagiously" spread from mind to mind.

CULTURAL SURVIVAL: MEMORY EXPERIMENTS WITH COUNTERINTUITIVE BELIEFS

Many factors are important in determining the extent to which ideas achieve a cultural level of distribution. Some are ecological, including the rate of prior exposure to an idea in a population,

---

[5] An example from ethology offers a parallel. Many bird species have nests parasitized by other species. Thus, the cuckoo deposits eggs in passerine nests, tricking the foster parents into incubating and feeding the cuckoo's young. Nestling European cuckoos often dwarf their host parents (Hamilton & Orians, 1965): "The young cuckoo, with its huge gape and loud begging call, has evidently evolved in exaggerated form the stimuli which elicit the feeding response of parent passerine birds…. This, like lipstick in the courtship of mankind, demonstrates successful exploitation by means of a 'super-stimulus'" (Lack, 1968). Late nestling cuckoos have evolved perceptible signals to manipulate the passerine nervous system by initiating and then arresting or interrupting normal processing. In this way, cuckoos are able to subvert and co-opt the passerine's modularized survival mechanisms.

physical as well as social facilitators and barriers to communication and imitation, and institutional structures that reinforce or suppress an idea. Of all cognitive factors, however, mnemonic power may be the single most important one at any age (Sperber, 1996). In oral traditions that characterize most of human cultures throughout history, an idea that is not memorable cannot be transmitted and cannot achieve cultural success (Rubin, 1995). Moreover, even if two ideas pass a minimal test of memorability, a more memorable idea has a transmission advantage over a less memorable one (all else being equal). This advantage, even if small at the start, accumulates from generation to generation of transmission leading to massive differences in cultural success at the end.

One of the earliest accounts of memorability and the transmission of counterintuitive cultural narratives was Bartlett's (1932) classic study of "the war of the ghosts." Bartlett examined the ways by which British university students remembered and then transmitted a Native American folktale. Over successive retellings of the story, some culturally unfamiliar items or events were dropped. Perhaps Bartlett's most striking finding was that the very notion of the ghosts—so central to the story—was gradually eliminated from the retellings, suggesting that counterintuitive elements are at a cognitive disadvantage. Bartlett reasoned that items inconsistent with students' cultural expectations were harder to represent and recall, hence less likely to be transmitted than items consistent with expectations.

In recent years, though, there has been growing theoretical and empirical work to suggest that minimally counterintuitive concepts are cognitively optimal; that is, they enjoy a cognitive advantage in memory and transmission in communication. Religious beliefs are counterintuitive because they violate what studies in cognitive anthropology and developmental psychology indicate are universal expectations about the world's everyday structure, including such basic categories of "intuitive ontology" (i.e., the ordinary ontology of the everyday world that is built into the language learner's semantic system) as person, animal, plant, and substance (Atran, 1989). They are generally inconsistent with fact-based knowledge, though not randomly. Beliefs about invisible creatures who transform themselves at will or who perceive events that are distant in time or space flatly contradict factual assumptions about physical, biological, and psychological phenomena (Atran & Sperber, 1991). Consequently, these beliefs more likely will be retained and transmitted in a population than random departures from common sense, and thus, they will become part of the group's culture. Insofar as category violations shake basic notions of ontology, they are attention arresting, hence memorable. But only if the resultant impossible worlds remain bridged to the everyday world can information be stored, evoked, and transmitted. As a result, religious concepts need little in the way of overt cultural representation or instruction to be learned and transmitted. A few fragmentary narrative descriptions or episodes suffice to mobilize an enormously rich network of implicit background beliefs (Boyer, 1994, 2001).

Basic conceptual modules—naturally selected cognitive faculties—are activated by stimuli that fall into a few intuitive knowledge domains, including folk mechanics (inert object boundaries and movements), folk biology (species configurations and relationships), and folk psychology (interactive and goal-directed behavior). Ordinary ontological categories are generated when conceptual modules are activated. Among the universal categories of ordinary ontology are person, animal, plant, and substance. The relationship between conceptual modules and ontological categories is represented as a matrix in Table 25.1. Changing the intuitive relationship expressed in any cell generates what Pascal Boyer (2001) calls a "minimal counterintuition." For example, switching the cell (– folk psychology, substance) to (+ folk psychology, substance) yields a thinking talisman, whereas

Table 25.1 Mundane Relations between Naturally Selected Conceptual Domains and Universal Categories of Ordinary Ontology

ONTOLOGICAL CATEGORIES	Conceptual Domains (and Associated Properties)				
	Folk Mechanics	Folk Biology		Folk Psychology	
	(Inert)	(Vegetative)	(Animate)	(Psycho-physical, e.g., hunger, thirst, etc.)	(Epistemic, e.g., believe, know, etc.)
PERSON	+	+	+	+	+
ANIMAL	+	+	+	+	–
PLANT	+	+	–	–	–
SUBSTANCE	+	–	–	–	–

Note: Changing the relation in any one cell (+ to –, or – to +) yields a minimal, supernatural counterintuition.

switching (+ folk psychology, person) to (– folk psychology, person) yields an unthinking zombie (cf. Barrett, 2000).[6]

In one series of experiments, Barrett and Nyhoff (2001) asked participants to remember and retell Native American folk tales containing natural as well as nonnatural events or objects. Content analysis showed that participants remembered 92% of minimally counterintuitive items, but only 71% of intuitive items.[7] These results, contrary to the findings in Bartlett's classic experiments, seem to indicate that minimally counterintuitive beliefs are better recalled and transmitted than intuitive ones.

Importantly, the effect of counterintuitiveness on recall is not linear. Too many ontological violations render a concept too counterintuitive to be comprehensible and memorable. Boyer and Ramble (2001) demonstrated that concepts with too many violations were recalled less well than those that were minimally counterintuitive. These results were observed immediately after exposure, as well as after a 3-month delay, in cultural samples as diverse as the Midwestern United States, France, Gabon, and Nepal. Consistent with the idea that this memory advantage is related to cultural success, a review of anthropological literature indicates that religious concepts with too many ontological violations are rather rare (Boyer, 1994).

---

[6] These are general, but not exclusive, conditions on supernatural beings and events. Intervening perceptual, contextual or psycho-thematic factors, however, can change the odds. Thus, certain natural substances—mountains, seas, clouds, sun, moon, planets—are associated with perceptions of great size or distance, and with conceptions of grandeur and continuous or recurring duration. They are, as Freud surmised, psychologically privileged objects for focusing the thoughts and emotions evoked by existential anxieties like death and eternity. Violation of fundamental social norms also readily lends itself to religious interpretation (e.g., ritual incest, fratricide, status reversal). Finally, supernatural agent concepts tend to be emotionally powerful because they trigger evolutionary survival templates. This also makes them attention arresting and memorable. For example, an all-knowing blood-thirsty deity is a better candidate for cultural survival than a do-nothing deity is, however omniscient.

[7] Barrett and Nyhof (2001) list as common items "a being that can see or hear things that are not too far away," "a species that will die if it doesn't get enough nourishment or if it is severely damaged," and "an object that is easy to see under normal lighting conditions" (p. 79). Such items fall so far below ordinary expectations that communication should carry some new or salient information that Barrett and Nyhof report "common items were remembered so poorly relative to other items.... In some instances of retelling these items, participants tried to make the common property sound exciting or unusual" (pp. 82–83). In other words, some subjects tried to meet minimum conditions of relevance (Sperber & Wilson, 1995). For the most part, common items failed these minimum standards for successful communication.

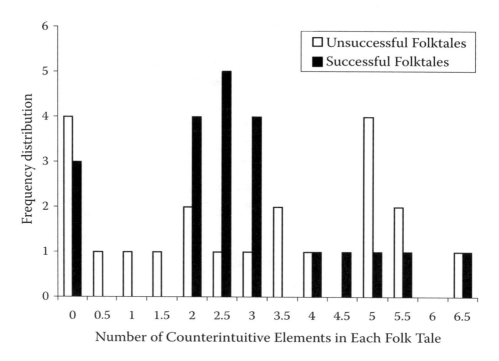

Figure 25.1 Frequency distribution of counterintuitive elements contained in samples of culturally successful and unsuccessful folktales.

Although suggestive, these studies leave several issues unresolved. For one, why do minimally counterintuitive concepts not occupy most of the narrative structure of religions, folktales, and myths? Even casual perusal of culturally successful materials, like the Bible, Hindu *Veda,* or Maya *Popul Vuh,* suggests that counterintuitive concepts and occurrences are a minority. The Bible is a succession of mundane events—walking, eating, sleeping, dreaming, copulating, dying, marrying, fighting, and suffering storms and drought—interspersed with a few counterintuitive occurrences, such as miracles and appearances of supernatural agents like God, angels, and ghosts. One possible explanation for this is that counterintuitive ideas are transmitted in narrative structures. To the extent that narratives with too many counterintuitive elements are at a cognitive disadvantage, cognitive selection at the narrative level would favor minimally counterintuitive narrative structures.

In one study that tested this hypothesis, Norenzayan, Atran, Faulkner, and Schaller (2006; Atran & Norenzayan, 2004) analyzed folktales possessing many of the counterintuitive aspects of religious stories. They examined (a) the cognitive structure of Grimm Brothers' folktales and (b) the relative cultural success of each tale measured in terms of stable patterns of retention of story elements over time. The hypothesized nonlinear relation between the frequency of counterintuitive elements and cultural success was confirmed (Figure 25.1).[8] Minimally counterintuitive folktales (containing 2–3 supernatural events or objects) constituted 76.5% of culturally successful sample, whereas stories with fewer counterintuitive elements (scores < 2), and with excessive numbers of

---

[8] In Figure 25.1, the *y*-axis is the frequency distribution of culturally successful and unsuccessful folktales. The *x*-axis is the number of counterintuitives in each folktale. The number of counterintuitives for some folktales is expressed as a fraction (1.5, 2.5, etc.). This is because when the two raters who counted disagreed, their ratings were averaged. Successful tales clustered within the range of 2–3 counterintuitives; unsuccessful tales had a flat distribution.

counterintuitive elements (scores > 3) constituted only 30% and 33% of the culturally successful sample, respectively. Overall, minimal counterintuitiveness predicted cultural success of folktales accurately 75% of the time. Perceived memorability and ease of transmission, but not other features of the folktale (e.g., whether the tale contains a moral lesson, interest value to children) partly mediated the relationship between minimal counterintuitiveness and cultural success. While results indicate that cultural success is a nonlinear (inverted U-shaped) function of the number of counterintuitive elements, success was not predicted by unusual narrative elements that are otherwise intuitive.

If memorability is the critical variable that mediates the effect of minimal counterintuitiveness on cultural success, then minimally counterintuitive knowledge structures should enjoy superior memory in the long run. To test this hypothesis more directly, in a related study Atran and Norenzayan (2004) examined the short- and long-term memorability of knowledge structures that systematically varied in the proportion of counterintuitive elements. Their methodology differed from prior studies by employing "basic level" concepts (e.g., thirsty door) that are cognitively privileged (Rosch, Mervis, Grey, Johnson, & Boyes-Braem, 1976) and are most commonly found in supernatural narratives. Participants were not cued to expect unusual events or transmit interesting stories to others. Instead, a standard memory paradigm was used to measure recall.

The study examined the memorability of intuitive (INT) and minimally counterintuitive (MCI) beliefs and belief sets over a period of a week. Two-word statements that represented INT and MCI items were generated. Each statement consisted of a concept and one property that modified it. INT statements were created by using a property that was appropriate to the ontological category (e.g., closing door). MCI statements were created by modifying the concept by a property that was transferred from *another* ontological category (e.g., thirsty door). This procedure explicitly operationalizes minimal counterintuitiveness as the transfer of a property associated with the core conceptual domains of folk physics, folk biology, folk psychology, from an appropriate ontological category of person, animal, plant, and substance, to an inappropriate one. For example, a "thirsty door" transfers a folk-biological property (thirst) from its proper category (animal) to an improper category (inert object/substance).

U.S. students rated these beliefs on degree of supernaturalness using a 6-point Likert scale, with MCI beliefs significantly more likely to be associated with supernaturalness than INT beliefs. Although no differences were found in immediate recall, after 1-week delay minimally counterintuitive knowledge structures led to superior recall relative to all intuitive or maximally counterintuitive structures,[9] replicating the curvilinear function found in the folktale analysis. With Yukatek Maya speakers, minimally counterintuitive beliefs were again more resilient than intuitive ones. A follow-up study revealed no reliable differences between the Yukatek recall pattern after 1 week and after 3 months (Atran & Norenzayan, 2004), indicating a cultural stabilization of the recall pattern.

In brief, minimally counterintuitive beliefs, as long as they come in small proportions, help people remember and presumably transmit the intuitive statements. A small proportion of minimally counterintuitive beliefs give the story a mnemonic advantage over stories with no counterintuitive beliefs or with far too many counterintuitive beliefs, just like moderately spiced-up dishes, have a cultural advantage over bland or far too spicy dishes. This dual aspect of supernatural beliefs and belief sets—commonsensical and counterintuitive—renders them intuitively compelling yet fantastic, eminently recognizable but surprising. Such beliefs grab attention, activate intuition, and

---

[9] Maximally counterintuitive statements (MXCI) were created by modifying a concept with two properties taken from another ontological category (e.g., squinting wilting brick). To control for memory differences on two-word items versus three-word items, for each MXCI statement, a matching statement was generated, only one of the properties being counterintuitive (e.g., chattering climbing pig).

mobilize inference in ways that greatly facilitate their mnemonic retention, social transmission, cultural selection, and historical survival (cf. Atran, 2001).

METAREPRESENTING COUNTERINTUITIVE WORLDS: A THEORY OF MIND EXPERIMENT

If counterintuitive beliefs arise by violating innately-given expectations about how the world is built, how can we possibly bypass our own hard wiring to form counterintuitive religious beliefs? The answer is that we do not entirely bypass commonsense understanding but conceptually parasitize it to transcend it. This occurs through the cognitive process of metarepresentation.

Humans have a metarepresentational ability to form representations of representations. This allows people to understand a drawing or picture of someone or something as a drawing or picture and not the real thing. It lets us imagine fiction and gives us an ability to think about being in different situations and deciding which are best for the purposes at hand, without our having to actually live through (or die in) the situations we imagine. It affords us the capacity to model the world in different ways and to change the world conscientiously by entertaining new models that we invent, evaluate, and implement. It enables us to become aware of our experienced past and imagined future as past or future events that are distinct from the present that we represent to ourselves and, so, permits us to reflect on our own existence. It allows people to comprehend and interact with one another's minds.

Metarepresentation also lets people retain half-understood ideas, as when children come to terms with the world in similar ways when they hear a new word. By embedding half-baked (quasi-propositional) ideas in other factual and commonsense beliefs, these ideas can simmer through personal and cultural belief systems and change them (Atran & Sperber, 1991; Sperber, 1985). A half-understood word or idea is initially retained metarepresentationally, as standing in for other ideas we already have in mind. Supernatural ideas always remain metarepresentational.

After Dennett (1978), most researchers in folk psychology, or "theory of mind," maintain that attribution of mental states, such as belief and desire, to other persons requires metarepresentational reasoning about false beliefs. Not before the child can understand that other people's beliefs are *only* representations—and not just recordings of the way things are—can the child entertain and assess other people's representations as veridical or fictional, truly informative or deceptive, exact or exaggerated, worth changing one's own mind for or ignoring. Only then can the child appreciate that God thinks differently from most people, in that only God's beliefs are always true.

In one of the few studies to replicate findings on "theory of mind" in a small-scale society (cf. Avis & P. Harris, 1991), Knight, Sousa, Barrett, and Atran (2004) showed 48 Yukatek-speaking children (26 boys and 22 girls) a tortilla container and told them, "Usually tortillas are inside this box, but I ate them and put these shorts inside." They asked each child in random order what a person, God, the sun (k'in), principal forest spirits (yumil k'ax'ob', "Masters of the Forest"), and other minor spirits (chiichi') would think was in the box. As with American children (Barrett, Richert, & Driesenga, 2001), the youngest Yukatek (4 years old) overwhelmingly attribute true beliefs to both God and people in equal measure. After age 5, the children attribute mostly false beliefs to people but continue to attribute mostly true beliefs to God. Thus, 33% of the 4-year-olds said that people would think tortillas were in the container versus 77% of 7-year-olds. In contrast, no significant correlation was detected between answers for God and age.

Collapsing over ages, Yukatek children attribute true beliefs according to a hierarchy of human and divine minds, one in which humans and minor spirits are seen as easier to deceive. Mental states of humans were perceived as different from those of God, and those of Masters of the Forest and the Sun God. God is seen as all-knowing and local religious entities fall somewhere in the middle (Figure 25.2). Lowland Maya believe God and forest spirits to be powerful, knowledgeable

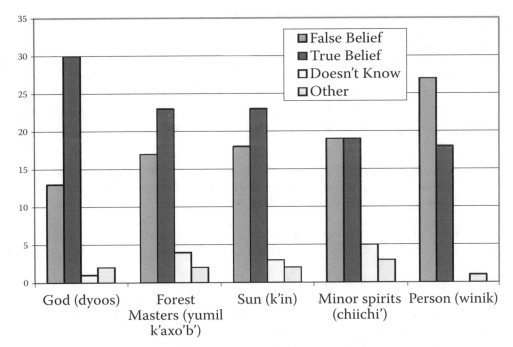

Figure 25.2 What is in the container? Yukatek Maya Children's Responses to False Belief Task.

agents that punish people who overexploit forest species. For adults, such beliefs have measurable behavioral consequences for biodiversity, forest sustainability, and so forth (Atran, Medin, & Ross, 2005; Atran et al., 2002). In brief, from an early age people may reliably attribute to supernaturals cognitive properties that are *different* from parents and other people.

In brief, human metarepresentational abilities, which are intimately bound to fully developed cognitions of agency and intention, also allow people to entertain, recognize, and evaluate the differences between true and false beliefs. Given the ever-present menace of enemies within and without, concealment, deception and the ability to both generate and recognize false beliefs in others would favor survival. But because human representations of agency and intention include representations of false belief and deception, human society is forever under threat of moral defection. If some better ideology is likely to be available somewhere down the line, then reasoning by backward induction, there is no more justified reason to accept the current ideology than convenience.

As it happens, the very same metacognitive aptitude that initiates this problem also provides a resolution through metarepresentation of minimally counterintuitive worlds. Invoking supernatural agents who may have true beliefs that people ordinarily lack creates the arational conditions for people to commit steadfastly to one another in a moral order that goes beyond apparent reason and self-conscious interest. In the limiting case, an omniscient and omnipotent agent (e.g., the supreme deity of the Abrahamic religions) can ultimately detect and punish cheaters, defectors, and free riders no matter how devious (Dennett, 1997; Frank, 1988).

EXISTENTIAL ANXIETY: AN EXPERIMENT ON WHAT MOTIVATES RELIGIOUS BELIEF

If supernatural agents are cognitively salient and possess hidden knowledge and powers, then they can be invoked to ease existential anxieties such as death and deception that forever threaten human life everywhere. To test this, Norenzayan, Hansen, and Atran (2005, as cited in Atran & Norenzayan,

2004) built on a study by Cahill, Prins, Weber, and McGaugh (1994) dealing with the effects of adrenaline (adrenergic activation) on memory.

The hypothesis was that existential anxieties (particularly death) not only deeply affect how people remember events but also their propensity to interpret events in terms of supernatural agency. Each of three groups of college students were primed with one of three different stories (Table 25.2): Cahill et al.'s (1994) uneventful story (neutral prime), Cahill et al.'s stressful story (death prime), and another uneventful story whose event-structure matched the other two stories but which included a prayer scene (religious prime). Afterwards, each group of subjects read a *New York Times* article (Nagourney, 2001) whose lead ran

> Researchers at Columbia University, expressing surprise at their own findings, are reporting that women at an in vitro fertilization clinic in Korea had a higher pregnancy rate when, unknown to the patients, total strangers were asked to pray for their success.

The article was given under the guise of a story about "media portrayals of scientific studies." Finally, students rated strength of their belief in God and the power of supernatural intervention (prayer) on a 9-point scale.

Results show that strength of belief in God's existence and in the efficacy of supernatural intervention (Figure 25.3) are reliably stronger after exposure to the death prime than either to the neutral or religious prime (no significant differences between either uneventful story). This effect held even after controlling for religious background and prior degree of religious identification. In a cross-cultural follow-up, 75 Yukatek-speaking Maya villagers were tested, using stories matched for event structure but modified to fit Maya cultural circumstances. They were also asked to recall the priming events. Altran and Norenzayan (2004) found no differences among primes for belief in the existence of God and spirits (near ceiling in this very religious society). However, subjects' belief in efficacy of prayer for invoking the deities was significantly greater with the death prime than with religious or neutral primes. Awareness of death more strongly motivates religiosity than mere exposure to emotionally nonstressful religious scenes, such as praying. This supports the claim that emotionally eruptive existential anxieties motivate supernatural beliefs.[10]

According to terror management theory (TMT), cultural worldview is a principal buffer against the terror of death. TMT experiments show that thoughts of death function to get people to reinforce their cultural (including religious) worldview and derogate alien worldviews (Greenberg et al., 1990; Pyszczynski et al., 1999). On this view, then, awareness of death should enhance belief in a worldview-consistent deity, but diminish belief in a worldview-threatening deity. An alternative view is that the need for belief in supernatural agency overrides worldview defense needs for death-aware subjects.

To test these competing views, Norenzayan and Hansen (2006) told 73 American undergraduates that the prayer groups described previously in the first experiment were Buddhists in Taiwan, Korea, and Japan. Supernatural belief was measured either shortly after the primes or after a significant delay between the primes and the belief measures. When the primes were recently activated, as expected there was a stronger belief in the power of Buddhist prayer in the death prime than in the control prime. Remarkably, death-primed subjects who previously self-identified as strong believers in Christianity were *more* likely to believe in the power of Buddhist prayer. In the neutral (control) condition, there was no correlation between Christian identification and belief in Buddhist

---

[10] In control conditions, equally anxiety-provoking scenarios (e.g., visit to the dentist where dental pain is experienced) did not lead to stronger supernatural belief. Moreover, whenever stronger anxiety was found in the mortality salience condition, controlling for self-reported anxiety (measured on the PANAS scale) failed to eliminate the effect (Norenzayan & Hansen, 2006).

Table 25.2 Three Stories with Matching Events Used to Prime Feelings of Religiosity: Neutral (Uneventful), Death (Stressful), Religious (Prayer Scene)

	Neutral	Death	Religious
1	A mother and her son are leaving home in the morning.	A mother and her son are leaving home in the morning.	A mother and her son are leaving home in the morning.
2	She is taking him to visit his father's workplace.	She is taking him to visit his father's workplace.	She is taking him to visit his father's workplace.
3	The father is a laboratory technician at Victory Memorial Hospital.	The father is a laboratory technician at Victory Memorial Hospital.	The father is a laboratory technician at Victory Memorial Hospital.
4	They check before crossing a busy road.	They check before crossing a busy road.	They check before crossing a busy road.
5	While walking along, the boy sees some wrecked cars in a junk yard, which he finds interesting.	While crossing the road, the boy is caught in a terrible accident, which critically injures him.	While walking along, the boy sees a well-dressed man stop by a homeless woman, falling on his knees before her, weeping.
6	At the hospital, the staff are preparing for a practice disaster drill, which the boy will watch.	At the hospital, the staff prepares the emergency room, to which the boy is rushed.	At the hospital, the boy's father shows him around his lab. The boy listens politely, but his thoughts are elsewhere.
7	An image from a brain scan machine used in the drill attracts the boy's interest.	An image from a brain scan machine used in a trauma situation shows severe bleeding in the boy's brain.	An image from a brain scan that he sees reminds him of something in the homeless woman's face.
8	All morning long, a surgical team practices the disaster drill procedures.	All morning long, a surgical team struggles to save the boy's life.	On his way around the hospital, the boy glances into the hospital's chapel, where he sees the well-dressed man sitting alone.
9	Make-up artists are able to create realistic-looking injuries on actors for the drill.	Specialized surgeons are able to reattach the boy's severed feet, but cannot stop his internal hemorrhaging.	With elbows on his knees, and his head in his hands, the man moves his lips silently. The boy wants to sit beside him, but his father leads him away.
10	After the drill, while the father watches the boy, the mother leaves to phone her other child's preschool.	After the surgery, while the father stays by the dead boy, the mother leaves to phone her other child's preschool.	After a brief tour of the hospital, while the father watches the boy, the mother leaves to phone her other child's preschool.
11	Running a little late, she phones the preschool to tell them she will soon pick up her child.	Barely able to talk, she phones the preschool to tell them she will soon pick up her child.	Running a little late, she phones the preschool to tell them she will soon pick up her child.
12	Heading to pick up her child, she hails a taxi at the number nine bus stop.	Heading to pick up her child, she hails a taxi at the number nine bus stop.	Heading to pick up her child, she hails a taxi at the number nine bus stop.

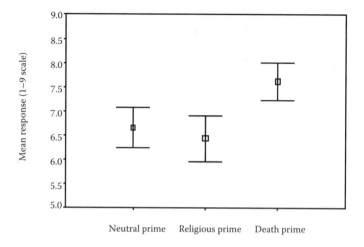

Figure 25.3 Strength of belief in supernatural power after priming (neutral, religious, or death) and then reading a newspaper article about effects of prayer on pregnancy (vertical bars represent margin of error at $p = .05$).

prayer[11] Given a choice between supernatural belief versus rejecting an alien worldview (Buddhism), Christians chose the former. This finding is difficult to explain in terms of bolstering a proprietary cultural worldview.

There was no evidence for differences in recall of priming events after subjects rated strength of belief in God and the efficacy of supernatural intervention. With this in mind, note that uncontrollable arousal mediated by adrenergic activation (e.g., subjects chronically exposed to death scenes) can lead to posttraumatic stress syndrome if there is no lessening of terror and arousal within hours; however, adrenergic blockers (e.g., propranolol, guanfacine, and possibly antidepressants) can interrupt neuronal imprinting for long-term symptoms, as can cognitive-behavioral therapy (Marmar as cited in McReady, 2002, p. 9). A plausible hypothesis is that heightened expression of religiosity following exposure to death scenes that provoke existential anxieties may also serve this blocking function. It remains to test the further claim that existential anxieties not only spur supernatural belief, but also these beliefs, in turn, are affectively validated by assuaging the very emotions that motivate belief in the supernatural.

SACRED VALUES IN DECISION MAKING AND THE LIMITS OF REASON

Religious behavior often seems to be motivated by sacred values (SVs)—that is, values which a moral community treats as possessing transcendental significance that precludes comparisons or trade-offs with instrumental values of *realpolitik* or the marketplace. As Immanuel Kant (1788/1997) framed it, virtuous religious behavior is its own reward and attempts to base it on utility nullifies its moral worth. Instrumental decision making (or "rational choice") involves strict cost-benefit calculations regarding goals and entails abandoning or adjusting goals if costs for realizing them are too high. A sacred value is a value that incorporates moral and ethical beliefs independently of, or all out of proportion to, its prospect of success (Weber, 1978, p. 24). To say that sacred values are protected from trade-offs with instrumental (e.g., economic) values does not mean that they are immune from all material considerations. Devotion to some core values may represent universal

---

[11] Under control conditions, the Christian subjects are unwilling to believe in Buddha or shamanic spirits, and they believe in God far more than they believe in Buddha or spirits.

responses to long-term evolutionary strategies that go beyond short-term individual calculations of self-interest yet advance individual interests in the aggregate and long run. This may include devotion to children (parents sacrifice for their genes to live on), to community (members forego present interests for the promise of cooperation), or even to a sense of fairness (people refuse free payouts to signal the "injustice" of others receiving more) (Atran, Axelrod, & Davis, 2007).

Political scientists and economists acknowledge the role of religious values in coordinating groups for economic, social, and political activities, and in providing people with immunity that goes with action in large numbers (Schelling, 1963). From a rational-choice perspective, such values operate instrumentally to form convergent trust among masses of people with disparate interests and preferences (Hardin, 1995), thus reducing "transaction costs" that would otherwise be needed to mobilize them (Fukuyama, 1995). Others (Horowitz, 1984; Varshney, 2003) grant the instrumental value of "ethnicity"—and values rooted in other ascriptive (birth-based) identities such as religion and language—but ask, "[W]hy would ethnicity be the basis for mobilization at all" (Varshney, 2003). And why does the mobilization of these values energize the most enduring and intractable conflicts between groups (Cohen, 2002)? This suggests that noninstrumental values possess inherent qualities that instrumental values may lack (e.g., passion, obligation), and that these two sorts of values can interact in intricate ways. (Of course, one can always recast noninstrumental values in instrumental terms, just as one can always frame any perceptual or conceptual relationship in terms of "similarity"; but the issue is whether in doing so explanatory power to predict further judgments and decisions is helped or hindered.)[12]

Identifying how universal proclivities for holding to sacred values play out in different cultures and compete for people's affections is surely a first step in learning how to prevent differences between those values from spiraling into mortal conflict between societies. All religions and many quasi-religious ideologies that make claims about the laws of history or universal missions to reform humanity are based on sacred values. Such values are linked to emotions that underpin feelings of cultural identity and trust. These emotion-laden sentiments are amplified into moral obligations to strike out against perceived opponents no matter the cost (c.f. Skitka & Mullen, 2002) when conditions of relative deprivation get to a point at which some members of a group see no acceptable alternative within their society's framework of sacred values. Such sentiments are characteristic of emotionally driven commitments, such as heartfelt romantic love and uncontrollable vengeance, which are apparently arational and may have emerged under through natural selection to override rational calculations when confronted with seemingly insurmountable obstacles to the attainment of deep-seated needs (Frank, 1988).

High cost personal sacrifices to (nonkin) others in society seem to be typically motivated by, and framed in terms of, sacred values. This includes Jihadi conceptions of martyrdom, which also involves moral commitment to kill infidels for the sake of God (cf. Hoffman & McCormack, 2004). One review finds, "[O]nly a minority of human violence can be understood as rational, instrumental behavior aimed at securing or protecting material rewards" (Baumeister, Smart, & Boden, 1996, p. 5). Historically, religiously motivated violence tends to underpin the most intractable and enduring conflicts within and between cultures (Allport, 1956) and civilizations (Huntington, 1997). In religiously inspired terrorism, these sentiments are manipulated by organizational leaders, and by

---

[12]Psychologists have recently developed controlled ways of testing ideas about allied notions of "protected values" and "taboo trade-offs" (Fiske & Tetlock, 1997; cf. Heinrich et al., 2001). Tetlock (2000) describe a protected value as "any value that a moral community implicitly or explicitly treats as possessing infinite or transcendental significance that precludes comparisons, tradeoffs ... with bounded or secular values." Despite more than a decade of research on protected values and decision making, knowledge of their influence is quite limited. Clearly, protected values have a privileged link to moral outrage and other emotions (Baron & Spranca, 1997), especially when a person holding a sacred value is offered a secular value or trade-off such as selling one's child or selling futures betting on acts of terrorism (Medin, Schwartz, Blok, & Birnbaum, 1999; Tetlock, 2003).

the group dynamics of peer pressure, mostly for the organization's benefit at the expense of the individual (Atran, 2003; Atran & Stern, 2005). In times of crisis, of course, every society routinely calls upon some of its own people to sacrifice their lives for the general good of the community as a whole. One important difference is that for militant jihadis, crisis is constant and unabating, and extreme sacrifice is necessary as long as there are nonbelievers (*kuffar*) in the world.

To some extent, organizations that sponsor suicide terrorism are indeed motivated by instrumental rationality to fight policies they abhor. Al-Qaeda deputy Ayman Al-Zawahiri argues in his "testament," *Knights Under the Prophet's Banner*, "[T]he method of martyrdom operations [i]s the most successful way of inflicting damage against the opponent and the least costly to the mujahidin in casualties" (Al-Zawahiri, 2001). Jihadi leaders point to sacrifice of their "best and brightest" as signals of costly commitment to their community, which increases the organization's political market share (see Sosis & Alcorta, 2003, on the evolutionary underpinnings of costly signaling behavior for sacred values). In September 2004, Sheikh Hamed Al-Betawi (personal communication, 2004), a spiritual leader of Hamas, said,

> Our people do not own airplanes and tanks, only human bombs. Those who undertake martyrdom actions are not hopeless or poor, but are the best of our people, educated, successful. They are intelligent, advanced combat techniques for fighting enemy occupation.

Recent studies reliably show that the majority of Hamas suicide bombers are college educated, without criminal records, socially well adjusted, and economically better off than the surrounding Palestinian population (M. Bloom, 2005). Similar patterns hold for Al-Qaeda militants (Sageman, 2004).

Our research team (including psychologists Jremy Ginges and Douglas Medin, and political scientist Khalil Shikaki) recently conducted studies indicating that instrumental approaches to resolving political disputes are suboptimal when protagonists transform the issues or resources under dispute into sacred values. We found that emotional outrage and support for violent opposition to compromise over sacred values is (a) not mitigated by offering instrumental incentives to compromise but (b) is decreased when the adversary makes instrumentally irrelevant compromises over their own sacred values.

In a survey of Jewish Israelis living in the West Bank and Gaza (*settlers*, N = 601) conducted in August 2005, days before Israel's withdrawal from Gaza, we randomly presented participants with one of several hypothetical peace deals (see Ginges, Atran, Medin, & Shikaki, 2007). All involved Israeli withdrawal from 99% of the West Bank and Gaza in exchange for peace. We identified a subset of participants (46%) who had transformed land into an essential value; they believed that it was never permissible for the Jewish people to "give up" part of the "Land of Israel" no matter how extreme the circumstance. For these participants, all deals thus involved a "taboo" trade-off. Some deals involved an added instrumental incentive, such as money or the promise of a life free of violence ("taboo +"), while in other deals Palestinians also made a "taboo" trade-off over one of their own sacred values in a manner that neither added instrumental value to Israel nor detracted from the taboo nature of the deal being considered ("tragic"). From a rational perspective, the taboo + deal is improved relative to the taboo deal, and thus, violent opposition to the tragic deal should be weaker. However, we observed the following order of support for violence: taboo + > taboo > tragic (see Figure 25.4a); where those evaluating the tragic deal showed less support for violent opposition than the other two conditions. An analysis of intensity of emotional outrage again found that taboo + > taboo > tragic (see Figure 25.4c); those evaluating the tragic deal were least likely to report anger or disgust at the prospect of the deal being signed.

These results were replicated in a survey of Palestinian refugees (N = 535) in Gaza and the West Bank conducted in late December 2005, one month before Hamas was elected to power. In this experiment, hypothetical peace deals (see supporting online materials for Ginges et al., 2007)

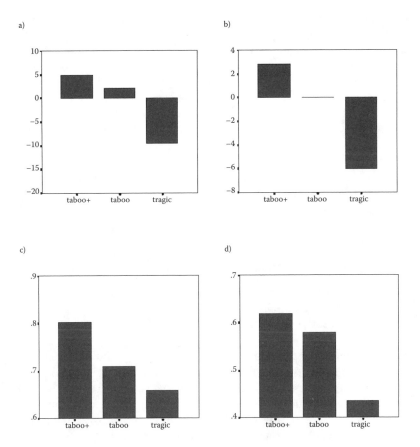

Figure 25.4 Predictions of the percentage of the population who would use violence to oppose: a peace deal perceived to violate a sacred value ("taboo" condition), the taboo deal plus an added instrumental incentive ("taboo +"), or the taboo deal plus a sacred value concession without instrumental value, from the adversary ("tragic") for (a) Israeli settlers (linear trend $F[1,195] = 5.698$, $P = .018$) and (b) Palestinian refugees ($F[1, 384] = 7.201$, $P = .008$). Parallel results obtained for emotional reactions by (c) settlers reporting "anger" or "disgust" at an Israeli leader who would agree to the trade-off being evaluated ($F[1, 260] = 4.436$, $P = .036$), and (d) refugees reporting "joy" at hearing of a suicide bombing according to the type of trade-off being evaluated ($F[1, 418] = 7.48$, $P = .007$). The trend of emotional intensity and support for violence in each case, taboo + > taboo > tragic, could not be predicted by an instrumental rationality account of human behavior.

all violated the Palestinian "right of return," a key issue in the conflict (Shamir & Shikaki, 2005). For the 80% of participants who believed this was an essential value, we once more observed that for violent opposition the order between conditions was taboo + > taboo > tragic, where those evaluating a "tragic" deal showed lowest support for violent opposition (see Figure 25.4b). Further, the same order was found for two measures ostensibly unrelated to the experiment: (a) The belief that Islam condones suicide attacks, and (b) reports of joy at hearing of a suicide attack (for evidence of for joy as a neurophysiological correlate of revenge, see de Quervain et al., 2004). Compared to refugees who had earlier evaluated a taboo or taboo + deal, those who had evaluated a tragic deal believed less that Islam condoned suicide attacks and were less likely to report feeling of joy at hearing of a suicide attack (see Figure 25.4d). In neither the settler nor the refugee study did participants responding to the "tragic" deals regard these deals as more implementable than participants evaluating taboo or taboo + deals did.

These experiments, as well as direct studies with political leaders (Atran et al., 2007), reveal that in political disputes where sources of conflict are cultural, such as the Israeli-Palestinian conflict or emerging clashes between the Muslim and Judeo-Christian world, violent opposition to compromise solutions may be exacerbated rather than decreased by insisting on instrumentally driven trade-offs, while noninstrumental symbolic compromises may reduce support for violence (Atran, 2006). Ongoing pilot studies show similar tendencies among Christian fundamentalists who consider abortion and gay marriage to violate sacred values.

In sum, while study of judgment and decision making has greatly advanced (for reviews, see Kahneman, 2003; Markman & Medin, 2002), much more is known about decision-making facets of economic behavior than about morally motivated behavior, especially religiously motivated social and political behavior. I hope this will change, given the critical importance of religious values in human judgment and decision making and given their crucial involvement in personal well-being, cultural survival, and political conflict.

CONCLUSION: RELIGION IS HUMANKIND'S PROVISIONAL EVOLUTIONARY DESTINY

Ever since Edward Gibbon's (1776–1788/1845) *Decline and Fall of the Roman Empire*, scientists and secularly minded scholars have been predicting, or at least advocating, the ultimate demise of religion (Russell, 1927/2004). But, if anything, religious fervor is increasing across parts of the world, including in the United States, the world's most economically powerful and scientifically advanced society. An underlying reason is that science treats humans and intentions only as incidental elements in the universe, whereas for religion they are central. Science is not particularly well suited to deal with people's existential anxieties, including death, deception, sudden catastrophe, loneliness, or longing for love or justice. It is not particularly suited to dealing with problems of human existence that have no enduring logical or factual solution, such as avoiding death, overcoming loneliness, finding love, or ensuring justice. Science cannot tell us what we ought to do or what ought to be; it can tell us only what we can do and what is. Religion thrives because it addresses our deepest emotional yearnings and society's foundational moral needs. No society has ever lasted more than a few generations without a moral foundation that is considered true without question but which is not rationally justified.

Even brilliant scientists and philosophers often have no clue how to deal with the basic irrationality of human life and society other than to insist against all reason and evidence that things ought to be rational and evidence based. Of late, the antireligion crusade has picked up steam with *Letter to a Christian Nation* by neuroscientist Sam Harris (2006), *Breaking the Spell* by philosopher Dan Dennett (2006), and *The God Delusion* by biologist Richard Dawkins (2006). I praise Dawkins' clarity, I rejoice in Dennett's call to study religion scientifically as a natural phenomena, and I admire S. Harris's keen polemical skill. Yet, I think these thinkers are all arrogantly out of their depth. These "neo-atheist" authors chiefly use highly selective analogy, anecdote, personal sentiment, and rash generalization to argue their missions, rather than any appreciable scientific research. It may be just as absurd to hold that science can replace religion or that reason can eradicate war as it is to believe that science or reason can annul "romantic love." Science may one day tell us what the physiological correlates of love are, and we may already know a bit about how irrational professions of unlimited love convince partners that love endures beyond limited fitness calculations; however, even people in the know will probably continue to irrationally profess eternal love to the subjects of their desire (or get spurned if they whisper only physiology and fitness in their honey's ear). So, too, is religion likely to survive scientific knowledge of religion?

In the competition for moral allegiance, secular ideologies are at a disadvantage (reasoning by backward induction): If a better ideology might be available down the line, then there is no better reason to accept the current ideology than convenience. And if people come to believe that all apparent commitment is self-interested convenience—or, worse, self-interested manipulation of others—, then commitment withers and dies. In times of vulnerability and stress, the pursuit of self-preservation is likely to take precedence over the pursuit of the public good, as the great Arab historian Ibn Khaldûn (1377/1958) noted centuries ago. Religion passionately rouses hearts and minds to break out of this viciously rational cycle of self-interest to adopt group interests that can benefit individuals in the end. In the narrowest case, a couple bound by devotion more easily overcomes personal difficulties; in the broadest case, a shared faith in an omniscient and omnipotent agent (the supreme being of Abrahamic religions) weakens the every-man-for-himself mentality.

Science, therefore, will not likely ever replace religion in the lives of most people or in any society that hopes to survive for very long. But science can help us understand how religions are structured in and across individual minds and societies—or, equivalently for our purposes, brains, and cultures—and also, in a strictly material sense, why religions endure. Recent advances in cognitive science, a branch of psychology with roots also in evolutionary biology, focus on religion, in general, and awareness of the supernatural, in particular, as a converging by-product of several cognitive and emotional mechanisms that evolved under natural selection for mundane adaptive tasks.

As human beings routinely interact, they naturally tend to exploit these by-products to solve inescapable, existential problems that have no apparent worldly solution, such as the inevitability of death and the ever-present threat of deception by others. Religion involves costly and hard-to-fake commitment to a counterintuitive world of supernatural agents that master such existential anxieties. The greater one's display of costly commitment to that factually absurd world—as in Abraham's willingness to sacrifice his beloved son for nothing palpable save faith in a "voice" demanding the killing—the greater society's trust in that person's ability and will to help out others with their inescapable problems (Kierkegaard, 1843/1955).[13]

All of this is not to say that *the* function of religion and the supernatural is to promise resolution of all outstanding existential anxieties anymore than *the* function of religion and the supernatural is to neutralize moral relativity and establish social order, to give meaning to an otherwise arbitrary existence, to explain the unobservable origins of things, and so on. Religion has no evolutionary functions per se. Rather, existential anxieties and moral sentiments constitute—by virtue of evolution—ineluctable elements of the human condition; and the cognitive invention, cultural selection, and historical survival of religious beliefs in the supernatural owes, in part, to success in accommodating these elements. Other factors in religion's persistence as humankind's provisional evolutionary destiny involve naturally selected elements of human cognition. These include the inherent susceptibility of religious beliefs to modularized (e.g., innate, universal, and domain-specific) conceptual processing systems, such as folk psychology, that favor survival and recurrence of the supernatural within and across minds and societies.

REFERENCES

Al- Betawi, H. (2004, September). Personal communication, Nablus, West Bank.
Al-Zawahiri, A. (2001, December, 2). *Knight's under the prophet's banner.* (Translated Al-Sharq, Al-Awsat), London. Retrieved October 14, 2004, from http://www.fas.org/irp/world/para/ayman_bk.html
Alexander, R. (1989). Evolution of the human psyche. In P. Mellars, & C. Stringer (Eds.), *The human revolution* (pp. 455–513). Edinburgh, U.K.: The University of Edinburgh Press.
Allport, G. (1956). *The nature of prejudice.* Cambridge, MA: Harvard University Press.
Atran, S. (1989). Basic conceptual domains. *Mind and Language, 4,* 7–16.

---

[13]The outlines of the factually preposterous world a person is committed to must be shared by a significant part of society, lest the person be considered a deviant psychopath or sociopath (e.g., lest Abraham's willingness to sacrifice his beloved son Isaac be considered attempted murder or child abuse).

Atran, S. (1990). *Cognitive foundations of natural history: Towards an anthropology of science.* Cambridge, U.K.: Cambridge University Press.

Atran, S. (2001). The trouble with memes: Inference versus imitation in cultural creation. *Human Nature, 12,* 351–381.

Atran, S. (2002). *In gods we trust.* New York: Oxford University Press.

Atran, S. (2003). Genesis of suicide terrorism. *Science, 299,* 1534–1539.

Atran, S. (2006, April). *Global network terrorism.* Retrieved August 11, 2007, from http://www.au.af.mil/au/awc/awcgate/whitehouse/atrannsc-042806.pdf#search=%22atran%20nsc%22

Atran, S., Axelrod, R., & Davis, R. (2007). Social Science: Sacred barriers to conflict resolution. *Science, 317*(5841), 1039–1040.

Atran, S., Medin, D., & Ross, N. (2005). The cultural mind: Ecological decision making and cultural modeling within and across populations. *Psychological Review, 112,* 744–776.

Atran, S., Medin, D., Ross, N., Lynch, E., Vapnarsky, V., Ucan Ek', E., et al. (2002). Folkecology, cultural epidemiology, and the spirit of the commons: A garden experiment in the Maya Lowlands, 1991–2001. *Current Anthropology, 43,* 421–450.

Atran, S., & Norenzayan, A. (2004). Religion's evolutionary landscape: Counterintuition, commitment, compassion, communion. *Behavioral and Brain Sciences, 27,* 713–770.

Atran, S., & Sperber, D. (1991). Learning without teaching: Its place in culture. In L. Tolchinsky-Landsmann (Ed.), *Culture, schooling and psychological development* (pp. 39–55). Norwood NJ: Ablex.

Atran, S., & Stern, J. (2005). Small groups find fatal purpose through the web. *Nature, 436,* 620.

Avis, J., & Harris, P. (1991). Belief-desire reasoning among Baka children. *Child Development, 62,* 460–467.

Baron, J., & Spranca, M. (1997). Protected values. *Organizational Behavior and Human Decision Processes, 70,* 1–16.

Barrett, J. (1998). Cognitive constraints on Hindu concepts of the divine. *Journal for Scientific Study of Religion, 37,* 608–619.

Barrett, J. (2000). Exploring the natural foundations of religion. *Trends in Cognitive Science, 4,* 29–34.

Barrett, J., & Keil, F. (1996). Conceptualizing a non-natural entity. *Cognitive Psychology, 31,* 219–247.

Barrett, J., & Nyhof, M. (2001). Spreading nonnatural concepts. *Journal of Cognition and Culture, 1,* 69–100.

Barrett, J., Richert, R., & Driesenga, A. (2001). God beliefs versus mother's: The development of nonhuman agent concepts. *Child Development, 72,* 50–65.

Bartlett, F. (1932). *Remembering.* Cambridge, U.K.: Cambridge University Press.

Baumeister, R., Smart, L., & Boden, J. (1996). Relation of threatened egotism to violence and aggression. *Psychological Review, 103,* 5–23.

Bedeviling: Did Satan rear his ugly face? (2001, September 14). *Philadelphia Daily News.*

Ben-Amos, P. G. (1994). The promise of greatness: Women and power in an Edo spirit possession cult. In D. T. Blakely, W. E. A. van Beek, & D. L. Thomson (Eds.), *Religion in Africa. Experience and Expression* (pp. 118–134). London: James Currey.

Bloom, M. (2005). *Dying to kill: The allure of suicide terrorism.* New York: Columbia University Press.

Bloom, P., & Veres, C. (1999). The perceived intentionality of groups. *Cognition, 71,* B1–B9.

Boyer, P. (1994). *The naturalness of religious ideas.* Berkeley: University of California Press.

Boyer, P. (2001). *Religion explained.* New York: Basic Books.

Boyer, P., & Ramble, C. (2001). Cognitive templates for religious concepts. *Cognitive Science, 25,* 535–564.

Cahill, L., Prins, B., Weber, M., & McGaugh, J. (1994). Beta-adrenergic activation and memory for emotional events. *Nature, 371,* 702–704.

Cohen, S. (2002). India, Pakistan, and Kashmir. *Journal of Strategic Studies, 25,* 32–60.

Csibra, G., Gergely, G., Bíró, S., Koós, O., & Brockbank, M. (1999). Goal attribution without agency cues. *Cognition, 72,* 237–267.

Dawkins, R. (2006). *The God delusion.* Boston: Houghton Mifflin.

Dennett, D. (1978). Response to Premack and Woodruff: Does the chimpanzee have a theory of mind? *Behavioral and Brain Sciences, 4,* 568–570.

Dennett, D. (1997). Appraising grace: What evolutionary good is God? *The Sciences, 37,* 39–44.

Dennett, D. (2006). *Breaking the spell: Religion as a natural phenomenon.* New York: Viking.

de Quervain, D. J.-F., Fischbacher, U., Treyer, V., Schellhammer, M., Schnyder, U., Buck, A., et al. (2004). The neural basis of altruistic punishment. *Science, 305,* 1254–1258.

Fiske, A., & Tetlock, P. (1997). Taboo trade-offs: Reactions to transactions that transgress the spheres of justice. *Political Psychology, 18,* 255–297.

Firth, R. (1963). Offering and sacrifice. *Journal of the Royal Anthropological Institute, 93,* 12–24.

Frank, R. (1988). *Passions within reason.* New York: W. W. Norton.

Fukuyama, F. (1995). *Trust.* New York: Free Press.

Geary, D., & Huffman, K. (2002). Brain and cognitive evolution. *Psychological Bulletin, 128,* 667–698.

Gibbon, E. (1845). *Decline and fall of the Roman Empire.* London: International Book Co. (Original work published 1776–1788)

Greenberg, J., Pyszczynski, T., Solomon, S., Rosenblatt, A., Veeder, M., Kirkland, S., et al. (1990). Evidence for terror management theory II. *Journal of Personality and Social Psychology, 58,* 308–318.

Guthrie, S. (1993). *Faces in the clouds: A new theory of religion.* New York: Oxford University Press.

Hardin, R. (1995). *One for all: The logic of group conflict.* Princeton, NJ: Princeton University Press.

Hamilton, W., & Orians, G. (1965). Evolution of brood parasitism in altricial birds. *Condor, 67,* 361–382.

Harris, S. (2006). *Letter to a Christian nation.* New York: Knopf.

Heider, F., & Simmel, S. (1944). An experimental study of apparent behavior. *American Journal of Psychology, 57,* 243–259.

Henrich, J., Boyd, R., Bowles, S., Camerer, C., Fehr, E., & Gintis, H. (2001). In search of *Homo economicus*: Behavioral experiments in 15 small-scale societies. *American Economic Review, 91,* 73–78.

Hoffman, B., & McCormick, G. (2004). Terrorism, signaling, and suicide attack. *Studies in Conflict & Terrorism, 27,* 243–281.

Horowitz, D. (1984). *Ethnic groups in conflict.* Berkeley: University of California Press.

Hume, D. (1757/1956). *The natural history of religion.* Stanford, CA: Stanford University Press. (Original work published 1757)

Huntington, S. (1997). *The clash of civilizations.* New York: Simon and Schuster.

Kahneman, D. (2003). Maps of bounded rationality: Psychology for behavioral economics. *American Economic Review, 93,* 1449–1475.

Kant, I. (1997). *Critique of practical reason.* Cambridge, U.K.: Cambridge University Press. (Original work published 1788)

Keillor, G. (1999, June 14). Faith at the speed of light. *Time.*

Khaldûn, I. (1958). *The Muqaddimah* (Vols. 1–3). London: Routledge & Kegan Paul. (Original work published 1377)

Kierkegaard, S. (1955). *Fear and trembling and the sickness unto death.* New York: Doubleday. (Original work published 1843)

Kirkpatrick, L. (1999). Toward an evolutionary psychology of religion and personality. *Journal of Personality, 67,* 921–952.

Knight, N., Sousa, P., Barrett, J., & Atran, S. (2004). Children's attributions of beliefs to humans and God: Cross-cultural evidence. *Cognitive Science, 28,* 117–126.

Kroeber, A. L. (1963). *Anthropology: Culture patterns and processes.* New York: Harcourt, Brace and World. (Original work published 1923)

Kuper, A. (1996). *The chosen primate.* Cambridge, MA: Harvard University Press.

Lack, D. (1968). *Ecological adaptations for breeding in birds.* London: Methuen.

Lipkind, W. (1940). Carajá cosmography. *The Journal of American Folk-Lore, 53,* 248–251.

Markman, A. B., & Medin, D. L. (2002). *Decision making.* In D. L. Medin, & H. Pashler (Eds.), *Steven's handbook of experimental psychology. Volume 2 (3rd ed),* New York: J. Wiley and Sons.

McReady, N. (2002, February). Adrenergic blockers shortly after trauma can block PTSD. *Clinical Psychiatry News,* 9.

Medin, D., Schwartz, H., Blok, S., & Birnbaum, L. (1999). The semantic side of decision making. *Psychonomic Bulletin and Review, 6,* 562–569.

Norenzayan, A., Atran, S., Faulkner, J., & Schaller, M. (2006). Memory and mystery: Cultural selection of minimally counterintuitive narratives. *Cognitive Science, 30,* 1–23.

Norenzayan, A., & Hansen, I. (2006) Belief in supernatural agents in the face of death. *Personality and Social Psychology Bulletin, 32,* 174–187.

Pinker, S. (2004, October). *The evolutionary psychology of religion* [Electronic version]. Paper presented at the annual meeting of the Freedom from Religion Foundation, Madison, WI.

Premack, D., & Premack, A. (1995). Origins of human social competence. In M. Gazzaniga (Ed.), *The cognitive neurosciences* (pp. xiv, 1447). Cambridge, MA: MIT Press.

Pyszczynski, T., Greenberg, J., & Solomon, S. (1999). A dual process model of defense against conscious and unconscious death-related thoughts: An extension of terror management theory. *Psychological Review, 106,* 835–845.

Pyysiäinen, I. (2001). *How religion works.* Leiden, South Holland, The Netherlands: Brill.

Pyysiäinen, I. (2003). Buddhism, religion, and the concept of 'God." *Numen, 50,* 147–171.

Rappaport, R. (1999). *Ritual and religion in the making of humanity.* New York: Cambridge University Press.

Robertson Smith, W. (1894). *Lectures on the religion of the Semites.* London: A. & C. Black.

Rosch, E., Mervis, C., Grey, W., Johnson, D., & Boyes-Braem, P. (1976). Basic objects in natural categories. *Cognitive Psychology, 8,* 382–439.

Rubin, D. (1995). *Memory in oral traditions.* New York: Oxford University Press.

Russell, B. (2004). *Why I am not a Christian: And other essays on religion and related subjects.* London: Routledge. (Original work published 1927)

Sageman, M. (2004). *Understanding terror networks.* Philadelphia: University of Pennsylvania Press.

Schelling, T. (1963). *The strategy of conflict.* New York: Oxford University Press.

Seligman, S. (1971). Phobias and preparedness. *Behavioral Therapy, 2,* 307–320.

Shamir, J., & Shikaki, K. (2005). Public opinion in the Israeli-Palestinian two-level game. *Journal of Peace Research, 42,* 311–328.

Skitka, L., & Mullen, E. (2002). The dark side of moral conviction. *Analyses of Social Issues and Public Policy, 2,* 35–41.

Sober, E., & Wilson, D. S (1998). *Unto others.* Cambridge, MA: Harvard University Press.

Sosis, R., & Alcorta, C. (2003). Signaling, solidarity, and the sacred: The evolution of religious behavior. *Evolutionary Anthropology, 12,* 264–274.

Sperber, D. (1985). Anthropology and psychology. *Man, 20,* 73–89.

Sperber, D. (1996). *Explaining culture.* Oxford, U.K.: Blackwell.

Tetlock, P. (2000). Coping with trade-offs: Psychological constraints and political implications. In S. Lupia, M. McCubbins, & S. Popkin (Eds.), *Political reasoning and choice.* Berkeley: University of California Press.

Tetlock, P. (2003). Thinking the unthinkable: Sacred values and taboo cognitions. *Trends in Cognitive Sciences, 7,* 320–324.

Tinbergen, N. (1951). *The study of instinct.* London: Oxford University Press.

Tooby, J., & Cosmides, L. (1992). The psychological foundations of culture. In J. Barkow, L. Cosmides, & J. Tooby (Eds.), *The adapted mind* (pp. 19–136). New York: Oxford University Press.

Varshney, A. (2003). Nationalism, ethnic conflict and rationality. *Perspectives on Politics, 1,* 85–99.

Weber, M. (1978). *Economy and society* (C. Wittich & G. Roth, Eds.). Berkeley: University of California Press.

Wilson, D. S. (2002). *Darwin's cathedral.* Chicago: University of Chicago Press.

Worthington, E., Kurusu, T., McCullough, M., & Sandage, S. (1996). Empirical research on religion and psychotherapeutic processes of outcomes. *Psychological Bulletin, 19,* 448–487.

Author Index

A

Alcock, John, 25–43, 219
   alliance formation, 357
   animal behavior, 226, 309, 365
   mutualism, 300
   phylogenetic research methods, 222
Alexander, G. M., 226
Alexander, Richard, 18, 42, 43, 88, 110, 147, 198, 212, 220, 226, 232, 277, 309, 327, 349, 397, 495
   adaptationism, 36
   altruism, 16, 314, 333
   indirect reciprocity, 338
   intergroup competition, 11
   parent-offspring conflict, 101
   parental manipulation, 139
   physiological research, 221
   primary basis of sociality, 210
   reciprocal altruism, 333
   research methods, 225
   selfishness, 304, 314
   sexual selection, 79, 86
Allal, Nadine, 16, 47–63, 68
Andreoni, J., 16, 18, 319, 327
Andrews, P. W., 15, 18, 166, 170, 194, 226, 236, 472
   adaptationism, 468
   complex adaptations, 217
   Dupré vs., 167
   exapted learning mechanism, 164
   research, 217, 221
Aristotle, 2
Aron, A., 305, 309
Aron, E. N., 305, 309
Aron, S., 102, 112
Atran, Scott, 225, 226, 477–495
   organization systems, 423
Axelrod, R., 89, 226, 309, 336, 345, 349, 350, 365, 376, 378, 496
   cooperation, 304
   dyadic alliances with nonkin, 358
   game theory simulation of adaptations, 219
   parasite virulence, 73
   prisoner's dilemma, 355–356
   reciprocal altruism, 216, 219, 333
   selfishness, 294, 304

B

Badcock, Christopher, 433–449
   antimentalism, 434
   autism vs. psychoses, 445
   dyslexia and schizophrenia, 441
   genes as tumor suppressors, 438
   genomic imprinting, 103, 141
   incidence of autism, 447
   mentalism, 435, 439–440
   schizophrenia and, 448
   Silver-Russell syndrome and, 437
   visual-spatial abilities in autism, 442
   X-trisomy, 447
Bailey, A. A., 249, 253
Bailey, J. M., 121, 131, 219, 226, 232, 265, 277, 288
Bailey, S. M., 55, 64
Baillargeon, R., 6, 18
Baldwin, James Mark, 5
Baron-Cohen, Simon, 141, 147, 216, 415–429, 429–430, 431, 432, 449, 472
   attention, 435
   brain development, 426
   cognitive differences between males and females, 446
   digit ratios, 249
   empathizing model, 418
   mind reading, 415–416
   mindblindness, 185
   sex differences, 424, 443, 446
   theory of mind, 142, 177, 436
Barrett, C., 212
Barrett, H. Clark, 15, 173–184, 185, 236, 365
   modularity, 216, 354
   research, 225, 226
Barrett, J., 479, 483, 486, 496, 497
Barrett, L., 414
Bateson, M., 177, 183, 185, 335, 348, 349
Bateson, P., 6, 18, 61, 65

499

Batson, C. D., 298, 308, 309
Belsky, J., 12, 18, 223, 225, 226
Betzig, L. L., 16, 21, 179, 185
    conjugal dissolution, 226
    despotism, 277
    research, 220, 221, 223
Birkhead, T. R., 84, 88, 274, 277, 384, 397
Bjorklund, D. F., 12, 139, 145, 147, 148, 226, 429, 449, 472
    evolutionary development psychology, 142
    on female inhibitory abilities, 443
    research, 225
Bleske-Rechek, 217, 228, 229, 279, 280, 282
    same-sex competitors, 222
    sex differences, 278
Boas, Franz, 7, 193, 194, 212
Bock, G. R., 215, 216, 219, 221, 225, 227, 235
Bock, W. J., 215, 227
Boomsma, J. J., 102, 110, 113
Bourhis, R. Y., 16, 20
Bowlby, John, 18, 125, 131, 141, 147
    attachment, 11–12
Bowles, Samuel, 231, 307, 310, 313–327, 328, 349, 350,
        366, 497
    cooperation, 334
    dyadic alliances with nonkin, 358
    facial expressions, 402
    family violence, 97, 110
    mating, 333
    resource allocation, 296
Boyd, Robert, 18, 45, 169, 212, 253, 296, 305, 313–327,
        327, 329, 333
    adaptations, 199
    altruism, 16
    as evolutionary modeler, 339
    binary reciprocal strategy, 340, 342
    coevolutionary models, 314
    cooperation, 301, 334, 336
    cultural transmission, 248
    evolutionary psychology, 223
    gene-culture coevolution, 314301
    group selection, 337
    model, 340
    reciprocity, 321, 338, 339
    strong reciprocity, 307, 322
Brown, A., 451
Brown, D. E., 217, 223, 227, 345, 349, 358, 361, 365
Brown, E. R., 93, 110
Brown, G., 398
Brown, J. L., 26, 32, 43, 93, 96, 110, 243, 253
Brown, L. L., 221, 229
Brown, M., 301, 310
Brown, P. J., 247, 253
Brown, R. M., 361, 364
Brown, S. L., 301, 310, 361, 364, 365
Brown, W. L., 45
Brown, William M., 117, 119–131, 132, 348, 349
Browne, K. R., 446, 450
Buller, David, 42, 43, 175, 187, 399
    Cinderella effect, 393–396
Burnham, T. C., 18, 185, 253, 310, 365

altruism, 16, 349
cooperation, 334, 335, 349
face recognition, 183
facial cues, 177
fitness enhancing mechanisms, 294
male-male competition, 246
reproductive success, 304, 354
strong reciprocity, 348
Burt, A., 131, 132, 149
    genomic imprinting, 139
    kin selection, 103
    selfish gene, 121
Burt, D., 233, 246, 256, 257
Buss, David M., 17, 18–19, 20, 43, 141, 147, 228, 229, 291,
        313, 357, 367
    developmental dynamics approach, 145
    error management, 368
    evolution of desire, 214
    homicide as adaptation, 14–15
    jealousy, 367
    mate retention, 363
    mating strategies, 200, 206, 229, 362, 474
    natural selection, 28
    reciprocity, 303
    research methods, 221, 222, 225, 226, 227
    sexual selection, 86, 88, 194, 250, 255, 461

C

Caceres, M., 41, 45
Cardew, G., 215, 216, 219, 221, 225, 227, 235
Chapuisat, M., 102, 110, 113
Chisholm, J. S., 139, 147, 228, 472
    EEA, 457
    infant attachment, 12, 19
    life history theory, 16
    research, 225
Cialdini, R. B., 230, 305, 310, 311, 366, 368
    approach to problems, 355
    empathy and altruism, 308
    research, 225
    self-protection and groups, 359
Cling, B. J., 407, 414
Cosmides, Leda, 10, 18, 19, 20, 21, 43, 45, 88, 112, 147,
        149, 170, 171, 172, 185, 187, 188, 213, 214, 226,
        228, 231, 234, 236, 280, 311, 329, 349, 351, 352,
        366, 367, 368, 412, 413, 451, 474, 478, 498
    adaptation, 216
        cost-benefit analyses of research, 217
        innate, 206
        research methods, 221, 225
    aggression, 270
    coalitional psychology, 360, 405
    concrete reciprocity, 301
    decision-making adaptations, 199
    detecting cheaters, 181, 198, 347
    EEA, 42, 456
    fitness interdependence, 364
    genomic imprinting, 139

individual-level adaptationism, 334
infectious diseases, 404
information processing cognitive-experimental
    perspective, 13
innate adaptation, 206
intragenomic conflict, 139, 140
kin discrimination, 96
mate retention, 361
mechanisms of evolutionary psychology, 173
prestige, 359
racism, 396
reciprocal altruism, 181
sex-specific transmission of organelles, 77
sibling incest, 198
social contract theory, 13, 181, 358
task analysis, 163
Westermarck's hypothesis, 179
Crawford, Charles, 1–18, 5, 17, 19, 25–43, 44, 123, 131,
    147, 170, 191–212, 213, 214, 215, 220, 221, 226,
    228, 235, 236, 304, 310, 311, 367, 399, 400,
    449, 472
    adaptations, 164, 191, 204
        design and, 166
        psychological, 163
    adaptive-culturally variable, 210
    evolutionary psychology vs. sociobiology, 28, 142–143
    gene interaction, 123
    hunter-gatherer culture, 222
    innate information-processing mechanisms, 205
    kin interactions, 179
    political psychology, 225
    pseudopathologies, 156, 207
    psychiatric diagnoses, 456
    psychological adaptations, 163
    quasinormal behaviors, 209
    reproduction suppression, 211
Creighton, S. J., 388, 397, 398
    Cinderella effect, 386, 387
Crespi, B. J., 33, 44, 132, 213, 450
    among microorganisms, 109, 110
    cognitive development, 126
    cooperation, 104, 110
    genomic imprinting, 103, 110
    maladaptation, 294, 319
    mentalism, 437
    psychoses, 447
    selection, 200
Cunningham, M. R., 220, 223, 228, 244, 253

D

Daly, Martin, 21, 58, 64, 88, 90, 110, 139, 148, 172, 186,
    195, 213, 217, 228, 232, 278, 280, 287, 366, 369,
    383–397, 398, 400, 431, 450
    aggression, 359
    book reviews, 395
    child abuse, 19, 220
    Cinderella effect, 383–397
    competition, 86, 269, 359, 445

decision-making, 90
discriminative parental solicitude, 148
domestic violence, 280
family violence, 97, 110, 220
gene interaction, 139
homicide, 19, 64, 97, 110, 148, 186, 228, 269, 274, 280,
    282, 366, 368
marital violence, 20
mating, 384
mortality, 87
parental solicitude, 139
polyandry, 209
psychological adaptation, 215
research methods, 14, 219, 222, 225
risk taking, 26, 86, 268, 278
self-protection, 359–360
sex differences in risk taking, 86
sexually proprietary behavior, 14
stepparenthood, 58, 179, 383, 385, 386, 393
training, 14
Darwin, Charles, 1–11, 19, 26, 27, 28, 29, 30, 32, 33, 37,
    38, 39, 44, 71, 75, 78, 88, 109, 138, 148, 153,
    170, 219, 228, 242, 255, 293, 310, 332, 349, 374,
    377, 378
    adaptationists and, 37
    central insights, 372
    framework, 371
    group selection, 337
    influence on nonpsychologists, 4–6
    insights, 2–4
    parental care, 384
    reciprocal altruism and, 333
    rediscovering, 8–11
    sexual selection, 4
Darwin, Erasmus, 2
Davies, Alastair P. C., 261–277
Davies, N. B., 102, 106, 111, 112, 223, 230, 232, 277, 384,
    398
Dawkins, Richard, 10, 19, 25, 44, 92, 110, 132, 148, 229,
    293, 310, 327, 328, 349, 496
    antireligious crusade, 333
    blueprint metaphor for DNA, 119
    evolution of genes, 303
    gene competition, 32
    gene labeling, 294
    gene replication, 145
    genes as catalysts, 120
    genic self-favoritism, 333
    green beard effect, 303
    group selection, 107, 314
    individuals as vehicles for genes, 295
    kin selection, 32
    outlaw gene, 118
    progress in evolution, 35
    psychological adaptations, 216
    selfishness, 121, 298, 314
De Cremer, D., 359, 368, 407, 414
Dedden, L. A., 15, 19, 270, 275, 280
Dennett, Dan, 19, 44, 225, 229, 496
    adaptation, 37

antireligion crusade, 496
attribution of mental states, 486
gene frequencies, 5
supernatural agents, 487
Depew, D. J., 5, 6, 19
DeVore, I., 20, 223, 236, 312
cooperation, 309
psychological adaptation, 219
Draper, P., 12, 18
Dugatkin, L. A., 229, 310, 349, 412
cooperation, 300, 333
intergroup hostility, 403
research, 219
Dunbar, R. I. M., 19, 57, 64, 65, 67, 68, 213, 233, 368, 414
gossip, 210
group conflict, 15
mating, 361
parental investment, 60
research, 220, 225

E

Eagly, Alice H., 19, 206, 213, 278, 280, 290
biological and cultural determinism, 424
biosocial theory, 276–277
genetic involvement in human behavior, 193
natural selection, 192
sex differences, 17, 262, 281
Eberhard, W. G., 139, 140, 148
Egeth, M., 143, 145
Eibl-Eibesfeldt, Irenäus, 193, 194, 213, 229, 328, 366, 412
hunter-gatherer societies, 404
research, 223
status, 358
within-group competition, 322
Ekman, Paul, 4, 19, 221, 229, 374, 377, 378, 431
Ellis, B., 16, 19, 429, 472
reproductive success, 301
sexual differences, 278, 289
sexual fantasies, 265, 272, 287
Ellison, P. T., 50, 56, 57, 61, 62, 65, 66, 245, 253, 254, 255, 256
body symmetry, 251
fecundity, 247
female body form, 247
muscle growth, 248

F

Faulkner, J., 406, 407, 409, 410, 412, 414, 484, 497
Fehr, Ernest, 107, 110, 229, 231, 305, 313–327, 328, 339, 350, 366, 497
altruism, 310
altruistic punishment, 310
cooperation, 334, 345
dyadic alliances with nonkin, 358
research, 225
selfishness, 296

strong reciprocity, 307
Fessler, D. M. T., 177, 183, 186, 335, 348, 350
Fink, B., 231, 245, 246, 248, 249, 254, 255, 257, 289
female attractiveness, 284
low digit ratios and physical fitness, 249
research, 220
sexually dimorphic features, 244
Fischbacher, U., 110, 229, 328, 334, 346, 350, 497
altruistic third-party punishment, 319
cooperation, 107, 334, 345, 346
group selection, 339
research, 225
Flaxman, S. M., 225, 229
Fox, E., 402, 413
Fox, J. R., 179, 186
Fox, R., 112, 405, 407, 413
Frank, Robert H., 221, 328, 350, 358, 371–378, 379, 487, 491
Frank, S. A., 93, 94, 101, 111, 113
comparative statics, 100
cooperation, 107
group selection, 106
Freud, Sigmund, 138, 148, 353, 483

G

Gächter, S., 305, 310, 319, 328
conditional cooperation, 345
cooperation, 323, 334
Gallup, G. G., 188, 220, 229, 231
body features, 248
parental investment, 180
sex differences, 255
Galton, Francis J., 7, 20, 251, 256
Gangestad, Steven W., 18, 20, 88, 153–170, 170, 171, 172, 213, 214, 226, 230, 231, 235, 241–253, 254, 258, 278, 289, 366, 367, 472
adaptations, 217, 468
body asymmetry, 198
life history theory, 16
mating, 219–220, 361
parasite-mediated mortality, 86, 270
physical attractiveness, 271
research, 220, 221, 223
sex differences, 460
sexual psychologies, 286, 460
strategic pluralism theory, 219
Garber, J., 16, 19
Gardner, Andy, 91–109, 111, 113, 114
Gardner, R., 222, 227, 319, 329, 351
Garver-Apgar, Christine E., 86, 88, 165, 170, 241–253, 254, 295
Gaulin, S. J. C., 28, 43, 232, 259, 279, 290, 355
cooperation, 313, 369
female-female competition, 57, 65
kin interactions, 181, 365
kin selection, 304
paternal certainty, 365
pornography, 286

selfishness, 297
sex differences, 224
sexual partners, 267
Geary, D. C., 42, 148, 217, 230, 278, 366, 431, 480, 497
domain cognitive modules, 140
evolutionary development psychology, 142
modularity, 216
offspring's survival, 361
sex differences, 44
sexual characteristics, 262, 263
threat-induced affiliation, 359
Gerard, H. B., 407, 413
Geschwind, D. H., 41, 45
Gigerenzer, G., 186, 230, 366
computer modeling of adaptations, 219
natural selection, 354
Wason task, 182
Gintis, Herbert, 231, 296, 301, 303, 305, 307, 310,
313–327, 328, 342, 349, 350, 366, 497
cooperation, 333, 334, 337
dyadic alliances with nonkin, 358
group selection, 334, 336, 339
Gluckman, P. D., 55, 61, 65
Goodman, D., 9, 20
Gould, Stephen Jay, 11, 35, 41, 43, 44, 132, 148, 155, 156,
170, 230, 279, 376, 379, 396
attack on adaptationism, 36, 37, 154, 167, 217, 468
brain evolution, 128
definition of adaptation, 37
exaptation, 37, 157–158, 169
historical legacy of evolution, 40
Hox genes story, 40
natural selection, 32, 35, 36
ontology recapitulates phylogeny, 138, 167
spandrels, 38, 157
Gouldner, A. W., 345, 350
Grafen, A., 99, 111, 122, 132, 230, 254
coefficient of relatedness, 94
fitness-maximizing, 92
group selection, 104, 106
Hamilton's rule, 99
handicapping model, 241
kin discrimination, 96
multiple signals, 242
research, 219
Grammer, K., 16, 248, 254, 255, 258, 284, 289
facial attractiveness, 231, 244
genes and survival, 270
health and superior condition, 240
research, 220
Griffin, Ashleigh S., 49, 65, 91–109, 111, 114
Griffin, D. R., 225, 230
Gumerman, G. J., 219, 232, 233

H

Hagen, E. H., 25, 41, 44, 352, 368
human cooperation, 336, 360
issues in evolutionary psychology, 398, 400

sexual selection, 31, 42
Haig, D., 65, 66, 121, 133, 141, 148, 333, 350, 438, 450
abortion, 52
adaptation, 156
birth weight, 53
genes as catalysts, 120
genetic conflict in human pregnancy, 83, 89, 170
genomic imprinting, 124, 132, 140
intragenomic conflict, 123
intrapersonal conflict, 128
intrapersonal reciprocity, 128
intrauterine growth, 52
kinship, 103, 111, 123
parent-offspring conflict, 123
placental genes in placenta, 437
Halberstadt, J., 250, 255
Haley, K. J., 177, 183, 186, 335, 348, 350
Hamilton, William Donald, 20, 32, 44, 66, 89, 111–112,
132, 133, 145, 148, 186, 187, 226, 230, 309, 310,
328, 349, 350, 357, 365, 366, 497
adaptive altruism, 10
aging, 60
altruistic behavior, 9
behavioral theory, 327
genes as catalysts, 120, 130
host resistance to parasites, 73, 80
inclusion fitness theory, 93, 107, 139, 216, 219, 384
kin coefficient, 94, 339
kinship theory, 10, 91, 92, 108, 302
laws of genetics, 117–119
mating types, 74
natural selection at gene level, 178
new group selection, 106
parasite resistance genes, 80
parent-offspring conflict, 10, 101–102
parental investment, 10
population genetics, 123
positive assortment model, 338
prosopagnosia, 176
reciprocal altruism, 10, 107, 216, 219, 314, 358
selfishness, 304
water level task, 423
Hammerstein, P., 336, 352, 360
Hanson, M. A., 55, 61, 65
Harlow, B. L., 461, 472
Harlow, Harry, 12, 20, 125, 133
Haselton, M. G., 227, 230, 254, 277, 278, 366, 413, 414
cognitive mechanisms, 175
female mate selection, 360
genetic benefits, 248
modularity, 174
prejudice, 407
research, 215, 217, 220
Henrich, J., 223, 231, 328, 339, 340, 342, 350, 367, 497
cooperation, 345
social interactions, 314
status, 358
strong reciprocity, 332, 334
ultimatum game, 316
Herman-Giddens, M. E., 55, 66, 392, 398

Hill, K., 48, 50, 55, 66, 69, 187, 243, 255, 399
    childhood mortality, 245
    facial proportions, 244
    female mortality, 59
    fertility and body weight, 247
    food sharing, 179
    infanticide, 56, 58
    life history theory, 16, 216, 219, 231
    research, 222
Hofstadter, M. C., 6, 20
Houser, D., 345, 346, 351
Hoyt, M. F., 407, 413
Hurst, L. D., 75, 89, 121, 133
    multiple sexes, 74
    mutation, 76, 126
Hurtado, A. M., 20, 48, 66, 231, 255, 350, 359, 367
    alliance formation, 357
    female mortality, 59, 245
    fertility and obesity, 247
    infanticide, 56, 58
    life history theory, 16, 50
    mate selection, 243
    optimal age and size at maturity, 55
    research, 222
Huxley, L., 3, 20
Huxley, R. R., 225, 231
Huxley, T. H., 310
Huxley, Thomas, 293

I

Insko, C. A., 407, 408, 413, 414

J

James, I., 428, 431
James, J., 219, 231
James, William, 5
Janssen, D. P., 368, 407, 414
Jasienska, G., 57, 62, 66, 247, 251, 255
Johnson, Dominic D. P., 16, 228, 328, 331–348, 349, 350

K

Kant, Immanuel, 2, 20, 490, 497
Kaplan, H. S., 219, 245, 255, 397, 399
    food sharing, 179
    intergenerational transfer, 60
    life history theory, 16, 20, 50, 66, 219
    stepparenthood, 388, 389
Keller, L., 106, 108, 110, 112, 113, 131, 133
    cooperation, 107
    green-beard altruism, 333, 350
    group selection, 102
    sex ratio, 102
Keller, M. C., 221, 225, 231, 458, 469, 471, 472
Kelley, H. H., 356, 367, 408, 413

Kenrick, Douglas T., 28, 45, 222, 234, 355–371, 414, 415, 416
    aggression, 361
    altruism, 227
    cooperation, 359
    developmental dynamics approach, 145
    functionality flexibility, 408
    interaction with peers, 361
    mate selection, 362–363
    modularity assumption, 356, 357
    research methods, 227
    selfishness, 298
    sex differences, 233
    sex ratio, 102
    sexual peak, 228
    sexual selection, 269, 273, 281, 361
    sociobiology, 36
Kirkpatrick, L. A., 220, 225, 227, 231
Koella, J., 49, 55, 64, 68
Kohler, T. A., 219, 232
Kokko, H., 112, 241, 256
    cooperation, 107
    sensory bias, 242
    sexual selection, 243
Krebs, Dennis, 16, 131, 143, 148, 149, 170, 171, 213, 231, 232, 235, 293–309, 310, 311, 367
    research, 225, 226
Krebs, J. R., 106, 111, 112, 223, 230, 232, 277, 466, 473
Kuhn, T. S., 17, 20
Kurzban, Robert, 184, 185, 345, 353–364, 365, 367, 368
    altruism, 16
    ancestral threats and contemporary prejudices, 402
    coalitional psychology, 405, 413
    cognitive psychology, 225
    cooperation, 345
    facial cues, 177, 183
    mating behavior, 220, 232
    modularity, 174, 216, 226, 365
    stigmatization, 20, 413
    strong reciprocity, 348, 351

L

Lack, David, 9, 20, 112, 171, 399, 497
    clutch size analyses, 159
    selective advantage, 384
    stimulation of innate releasing mechanism, 480–481
Lamarck, J.-B., 2, 138, 148
Lancaster, C. S., 311
Lancaster, J. B., 20, 219, 232, 243, 255
    life theory history, 16
    parental investment, 302, 311, 397
    stepparenthood, 388, 400
Lancaster, L., 352
Larsen, R. J., 15, 19, 222, 229, 276, 280
Leary, M. R., 16, 20, 402, 413
Ledyard, J. O., 318, 328, 345, 346, 351
Lewontin, Richard, 11, 44
    adaptationism and, 36, 154, 161, 167, 170, 279, 468

Darwinian framework and, 396
natural selection, 277
spandrels, 37, 38, 157
Li, N. P., 255, 355, 368
Lopreato, J., 29, 36, 45
Lorenz, Konrad, 8, 20, 192, 193, 213
Low, B. S., 84, 89, 216, 219, 220, 232

M

MacDonald, K. B., 139, 140, 147, 148, 311
research, 225, 232
selection of dispositions, 302
Mace, Ruth, 16, 47–63, 453
adaptation, 457
grandmother presence, 56
orphanhood, 58
Mandler, J. M., 6, 20
Maner, J. K., 225, 231
Manning, J. T., 253, 254, 255, 256, 257, 258
digit ratios, 248, 249
Marlowe, F. M., 222, 232, 247, 248, 256, 399
Matthews, D., 15, 18, 164, 170, 226, 468, 472
Maynard Smith, J., 128, 131, 164, 232, 327, 353
animal conflict, 133
ESS approaches, 123
game theory, 133, 368
group selection, 106, 107, 112, 314
kin selection, 93
models of evolution, 112, 159
optimality theory, 171, 233
research, 222
selfishness, 294
sexual selection, 328
Mayr, Ernest, 32, 41, 45, 151, 475
adaptationism, 217, 225, 235
functional *vs.* evolutionary biology, 460
gene interactions, 33
second Darwinian revolution, 155, 173
synthetic theory, 145
McBurney, D. H., 28, 43, 44, 249, 259, 260
Mead, Margaret, 8, 20
Mehdiabadi, N. J., 102, 112
Mendel, Gregor, 6, 7, 20, 138, 153
Millikan, R., 157, 171
Mineka, S., 165, 171, 182, 187, 221, 233, 355, 368, 405, 406, 413
Møller, Anders Pape, 71–87, 89
Mueller, U. G., 102, 107, 112, 113, 233, 256, 311
kin selection, 302
male facial masculinity, 245
prejudices, 407
research, 220
sex differences, 407
Mulder, Borgerhoff, 167, 168, 170, 399, 400

N

Nesse, Randolph M., 213, 231, 233, 282, 289, 311, 451, 457, 472
drugs and disease resistance, 198
goal achievements, 462
obesity, 207
prejudice, 407, 413
psychoses, 439, 458, 470
reciprocity, 301
research, 221, 225
selfishness, 294, 298
Nettle, P., 55, 67, 130, 134, 185, 349, 413
cooperation, 335
danger connoting cognitions, 407
prosocial behavior, 177
Neuberg, Steven L., 231, 279, 305, 355, 367, 401–412, 413
mate's social status, 267

O

Ober, C., 52, 67, 180, 186, 187
Öhman, A., 165, 171, 182, 187, 221, 233, 355, 368, 405, 406, 413
Oldham, M. C., 41, 45
Oldham, N. J., 110
Oyama, S., 144, 148, 149
development systems theory, 142–143

P

Park, J. H., 407, 409, 412, 414
parasite transmission, 409
prejudices, 406
social recognition, 402
Passera, L., 102, 112
Pellegrini, A. D., 12, 140, 145, 147, 225
Pemberton, J. M., 111, 407, 414
Penton-Voak, I. S., 233, 247, 254, 255, 256, 257
facial symmetry, 250
male facial masculinity, 246
mate selection, 246
research, 221
Perdeck, A. C., 8, 20
Perreault, S., 16, 20
Petrie, M., 78, 89, 90, 257
Petrie, R., 16, 18
Piaget, Jean, 6, 20, 149, 432
stage theories, 138
water level task, 423
Pillsworth, E. G., 220, 234
Pinker, Steven, 41, 218, 401
genetic involvement in behavior, 195
language and learning, 167, 183, 189, 215
political preferences, 398
religion, 481, 500
research, 227, 236
sexual culture, 292

Plomin, R., 194, 206, 213, 469, 473
Pratto, F., 359, 368, 407, 414
Preuss, T. M., 41, 45
Price, George R., 111, 113, 133, 325
Price, J. M., 359, 366
Price, Michael E., 123, 219, 296, 331–348, 351, 352

R

Reeve, H. K., 45, 112, 113, 143, 147, 149, 168, 170, 171,
        173, 229, 231, 399, 401
    adaptation, 37
    adaptiveness, 167, 169
    developmental dynamics approach, 145
    fitness tokens, 168
    game theory simulations of adaptation, 219
    group selection, 106
    sex ratio, 102
Regan, D. T., 348, 350, 378, 379
Regan, P. C., 219, 220, 234
Reilly, P., 7, 20
Reznick, J. S., 6, 20
Rhodes, G., 220, 221, 234, 249, 250, 251, 255, 256, 257,
        258, 259, 289
Richerson, Pete J., 18, 169, 171, 227, 234, 236, 253, 305,
        313–327, 327, 329, 349, 351, 365
    altruism, 16
    as evolutionary modeler, 339
    binary reciprocal strategy, 340, 342
    coevolutionary models, 314
    cooperation, 301, 334, 336
    cultural transmission, 248
    evolutionary psychology, 223
    gene-culture coevolution, 314301
    group selection, 337
    model, 340
    reciprocity, 321, 338, 339
    research, 222, 223
    strong reciprocity, 307, 322
Ridley, M., 132, 216, 234
    cooperative gene, 134
    Mendelian inheritance, 118, 119, 121
    research methods, 221, 222, 225
    virtue, 234
Rikowski, A., 220, 234
Roberts, G., 177, 185, 335, 349, 408, 414
Roberts, R., 223, 228
Roberts, S. C., 252, 257
Rosset, H., 102, 113

S

Salmon, Catherine, 1–18, 162, 195, 213, 228, 234,
        281–288, 400, 449
    erotic fiction, 288
    mental disorders, 456, 472
    political psychology, 225

research methods, 220, 225, 281
Schaller, Mark, 401–412, 413, 414, 484, 497
Scheyd, Glenn J., 241–255, 258, 276, 278, 295
Schmitt, David P., 15, 19, 280, 282, 288, 461, 463, 474, 476
    hypothetical constructs, 219
    male physique, 250
    mate retention, 363–364
    mate selection, 362, 370
    research methods, 217–228
    romance hero, 287
    sex differences, 267, 273, 274
    sex selection, 270
    sexual fidelity, 275
    sexual strategies, 255, 274, 291, 367
Schopler, J., 407, 408, 413, 414
Semmelroth, J., 15, 19, 276, 280
Shackelford, Todd K., 19, 228, 229, 237, 261–277, 280,
        282, 312, 313, 402, 475
    casual role of consciousness, 228
    child abuse, 387, 389, 390
    intersexual competition, 265
    mating strategy, 460
    reciprocity, 303
    research methods, 222, 224, 228
    sexual fidelity, 276
Shepher, J., 96, 113, 179, 188, 191, 198, 213
Sherman, P. W., 45, 88, 113, 171, 229, 368
    adaptation, 37, 167
    cooperation, 357
    fitness tokens, 168
    kin selection, 93
    polygyny, 79
    pregnancy sickness phenotype, 225
Sidanius, J., 359, 368, 407, 414
Simpson, J. A., 16, 20, 170, 171, 172, 213, 230, 235, 254,
        278, 289, 366, 367, 368, 412, 413, 472
    life history theory, 16
    mating, 219–220, 361
    physical attractiveness, 271
    research, 225
    sex differences, 460
    sexual psychologies, 286, 460
    strategic pluralism theory, 219
Singh, Devendra, 55, 221, 235, 256, 284, 290
    female physical attractiveness, 68, 213, 258
    waist-to-hip ratio, 198, 220, 248, 282, 2147
Singh, L. S., 388, 397
Sober, E., 32, 45, 171, 213, 294, 311, 352, 478, 498
    adaptativeness vs. adaptation, 156, 225
    altruism, 294, 307
    group selection, 294, 303, 337, 352
    natural selection, 200, 307
    selfishness, 298
Spencer, H. G., 61, 65
Spencer, Herbert, 5, 6
Sperber, D., 15, 181, 188, 480, 482, 483, 496, 498
    functional specialization, 174
    metarepresentation, 486
    mnemonic power, 482
    modularity, 184, 216

Stearns, Stephen C., 16, 47–63, 50, 55, 121
  life history, 50, 139, 145, 465
  microevolution, 49
  research, 221
Steinberg, J., 12, 18
Sugiyama, L. S., 14, 20, 188, 290, 352
  female body size, 247, 284
  sex differences, 248
  social contract, 182, 347
Surbey, Michele K., 137–147, 149
Symons, Donald, 176, 193, 203, 286, 354
  analyses for establishing adaptation, 166
  behavior pattern adaptations, 199
  facial averageness, 249
  female attractiveness, 284
  homosexual porn, 284
  mate selection, 245, 287
  parental care, 362
  pseudopathologies, 207
  research methods, 220, 281
  sexual fantasies, 265, 272–273, 287

T

Takezawa, Masanori, 296, 331–348, 352
Tanese, R., 73, 89
Thornhill, R., 83, 86, 88, 89, 170, 171, 172, 214, 221, 230,
    244, 246, 247, 250, 254, 255
  adaptation, 160–161, 166
    phylogenetic data for, 169
  cost-benefit structure, 200
  empirical evidence for ELM, 165
  evolved adaptation, 235
  female facial femininity, 245, 258
  fluctuating body asymmetry, 198, 254
  male-male competition, 196
  mate preferences, 251
  mating strategies, 196
  on Darwin, 235
  research, 215, 221, 222, 225
  sexual conflict over fertilization, 84
Tinbergen, Niko, 8, 20, 45, 122, 235, 352, 379, 498
  causes of behavior, 335
  derivation principle, 376
  ethological analyses, 222
  supernatural agency, 479
Tooby, John, 10, 18, 19, 20, 21, 43, 45, 88, 112, 147, 149,
    171, 172, 182, 185, 188, 193, 195, 213, 214, 226,
    228, 234, 236, 280, 311, 312, 329, 349, 351, 352,
    366, 367, 368, 399, 413, 451, 474, 498
  adaptations, 199, 206, 215, 219
  authoritarianism, 396
  behavior, defined, 13
  cheater-detection ability, 347
  coalitional psychology, 360, 405
  cognitive-experimental perspective, 13
  concrete reciprocity, 301
  cooperative dispositions, 309
  decision-making adaptations, 199
  detectors of cheaters on social obligations, 198
  EEA, 456
  foundations of evolutionary psychology, 25, 139
  genomic imprinting, 140
  human nature, 221
  individual-level theories, 334
  intragenomic conflict, 140
  kin discrimination, 96
  natural selection, 354
  parent-specific expression, 140
  prestige, 358
  racism, 396
  reciprocal altruism, 181
  sex-specific transmission of organelles, 77
  sexism, 396
  sibling incest, 198
  social contracts, 13–14, 180, 358
  specialized information processing, 199
  task analysis, 163
  Westmarck's hypothesis and, 179
Trivers, Robert, 20, 52, 65, 85, 107, 110, 114, 132, 134,
    149, 188, 222, 236, 258, 259, 260, 280, 312,
    329, 334, 352, 368, 400, 451
  altruism-reputation correlation, 347
  authoritarianism, 396
  cooperation, 107, 122
  costly signaling, 333
  digit ratios, 250
  genes as catalysts, 120, 141
  Hamilton's rule, 10
  intragenomic conflicts, 121, 123
  kin selection, 103, 303
  longevity, gender variations in, 86
  mating success, male vs. female, 86
  parent-offspring conflict, 56, 101, 123, 353
  parental investment, 10, 75, 87, 125, 127, 219, 360, 363
  polygyny, 55, 57
  preference and culture, 249
  racism, 396
  reciprocal altruism, 11, 181, 216, 301, 314, 333, 338
  theories, 10
Troisi, Alfonso, 453–472
Turke, P., 16, 21, 179, 185, 399, 408

U

Udry, J. R., 55, 68, 221, 236

V

Van Vugt, M., 355, 359, 360, 368, 407, 414
Vargo, E. L., 102, 112
von Frisch, K., 8, 21
Vrba, E. S., 44, 155, 170
  adaptation, 37, 156, 158
  exaptation, 37, 157, 158, 169

W

Wallace, A., 385, 400
Walters, S., 192, 214, 220, 236
Watts, E. S., 54, 69
Watts, M. W., 407, 414
Weisfeld, C. C., 139, 149, 225, 239
Weisfeld, G. E., 96, 114, 139, 149, 225, 236
Weismann, A., 5, 145, 149
West, Stuart A., 16, 49, 65, 90, 91–109, 110, 111, 114
    sex ratio, 86
West-Eberhard, M. J., 122, 184, 222, 236
Westen, D., 15, 19, 276, 280
Wharton, R., 111, 133, 450
    genomic imprinting, 103
    inclusive fitness, 124
    kinship, 125
    parent-offspring conflict, 438
Williams, George C., 69, 90, 114, 129, 135, 149, 213, 214,
        280, 289, 312, 329, 331
    adaptation, 191
        economics of, 217
        exaptation vs., 159, 161
        reasoning and, 295
    age-specific selection, 60
    altruism, 9–10
    arguments of design, 163
    atomizing traits, 167
    design, 215
    drugs and resistance to infection, 198
    eating habits, 282
    evolutionary biology, challenges of, 129
    eye, evolution of, 40
    gene interaction, 32–33, 120, 139, 155, 200
    group selection, 106, 130, 314, 337
    killing instincts, 300
    manifestation of disease, 458
    medical research, 221
    morality, 293, 299
    natural selection, 31
        effect of, 154, 159
    on Thomas Huxley, 293
    pseudopathologies, 207
    psychologically selfish behavior, 304
    psychopathology, 467
    reciprocal altruism, 314
    reproductive costs, 276–277
    sibling competition, 73
    speciation, 35
Wilson, B. J., 349
Wilson, D. S., 45, 106, 130, 134, 213, 222, 223, 230, 294,
        311, 352, 478, 498
    adaptive genetic variation, 236
    altruism, 294, 307
    group selection, 114, 294, 303, 337
    natural selection, 200, 307
    research, 222, 223, 225
    selfishness, 298

Wilson, E. O., 11, 21, 45, 194, 214, 215, 232, 329, 352
    eusociality, 108, 114
    kin selection, 332
        as key to altruism, 114
    social behavior, 28, 149, 194
Wilson, G. D., 265, 280
Wilson, K. D., 176, 186
Wilson, M. I., 397–398
Wilson, M. L., 414
Wilson, Margo, 21, 139, 195, 213, 217, 228, 232, 278, 280,
        366, 369, 398, 400, 431, 450
    aggression, 359
    book reviews, 395
    child abuse, 19, 220
    Cinderella effect, 383–397
    competition, 86, 269, 359, 445
    decision-making, 90
    discriminative parental solicitude, 148
    domestic violence, 280
    family violence, 97, 110, 220
    gene interaction, 139
    homicide, 19, 64, 97, 110, 148, 186, 228, 269, 274, 280,
        282, 366, 368
    marital violence, 20
    mating, 384
    mortality, 87
    parental solicitude, 139
    polyandry, 209
    psychological adaptation, 215
    research methods, 14, 219, 222, 225
    risk taking, 26, 86, 268, 278
    self-protection, 359–360
    sex differences in risk taking, 86
    sexually proprietary behavior, 14
    stepparenthood, 58, 179, 383, 385, 386, 393
    training, 14
Wilson, P., 223, 230
Wilson, R. A., 186
Wilson, R. K., 349
Wood, J. W., 57, 59, 69
Wood, M. J., 96, 113
Wood, W., 19, 206, 213, 278, 280, 290
    biosocial theory, 276–277
    natural selection, 192
    sex differences, 17, 262, 281
Wrangham, R. W., 270, 310
    age and reproductive value, 245
    aggression, 328, 403
    evolution of sexuality, 236
    intragroup competition, 359
    mate selection, 245, 280
    reciprocity, 324
    research, 222
Wynne-Edwards, V. C., 21, 45, 114, 194
    group selection, 9, 33, 104–106

Y

Young, A. J., 110
Young, A. W., 176, 189
Young, E., 464, 472
Young, R. K., 220, 221, 235, 284, 290

Z

Zebrowitz, L. A., 220, 221, 234, 250, 259, 289
Zuckerman, M., 204, 214, 269, 280

Subject Index

A

Actual domain, 175, 480
Adaptation(s), 37
  algorithmic and computer modeling, 219
  by-products, 10, 157, 385, 495
    of atresia, 59
    Cinderella effects as, 386–387
    deleterious, 58
    of hormonal metabolism, 243
    incidental, 300
    maladaptive, 43, 460
    nonfunctional, 160, 161
    polyovulation, 56
    of sexual evolution, 71
    spandrels as, 38
    unselfish, 309
  complex, 206, 217, 467
  concept of, 156, 204, 213
  constraints on, 38–40
  cost benefit analyses, 219
  decision-making, 199
  defined, 37, 156
  design and, 166
  economical, 217
  efficient, 217
  exaptation *vs.*, 159, 161
  game theory simulations, 219
  innate, 206
  interactive, 217
  kin discrimination, 163
  learning mechanisms as, 164
  psychological, 163, 191, 215, 219
    evidence of, 219, 223–224
    pregnancy sickness as, 224–225
    research methods for identifying, 217–224
    universal, 217
  research, 217–224
  secondary, 158
  traits that qualify as, 36
Adaptationism, 36–37
  attacks on, 36, 37, 154, 167, 468
  criticism of, 37–38

  evolutionary biology and, 468
  individual-level, 334
Adaptive altruism, 32
Adaptive-culturally variable, 210
Adaptive eusociality, 26
Adaptive genetic variation, 236
Adult survival, developmental determinants of, 61
Age-specific selection, 60
Aggression, 8, 54, 101, 264, 268–270, 420, 438
  direct *vs.* indirect, 420
  in early life, 8
  gender differences, 204, 269, 420
  indirect *vs.* direct, 277, 420
  information processing mechanisms, 192
  intergroup, 328, 402, 410
  intermale, 466
  kin selection and, 91, 109
  male-male, 466
  moralistic, 396
  play and, 12
  real-world, 408
  relational, 431
  research, 225
  testosterone and, 62
  uncontrolled, 300
Aging, 60–61
Alliance formation, 357–358
Altruism, 9–10, 16, 314
  adaptive, 32
  defined, 108, 296
  hunter-gatherer and, 314
  kin selection and, 110, 114, 302, 314
  reciprocal, 107, 214, 299, 314, 331, 333, 356
    biological, 301
    defined, 181, 314
    evolution of, 10–11, 134, 188, 236, 301, 312, 339
Altruistic third-party punishment, 319–321
Androgen deprivation, 446
Angelman syndrome, 103, 132, 134, 442
Anisogamy, 87
Anorexia, 469
Antimentalism, 434
Antireligion crusade, 494

Arguments of design, 161
Arms-race evolutionary escalation, 435
Asperger's syndrome, 429, 431, 445, 448, 450
Assortative mating, 428, 429, 449
Atomizing traits, 167
Atresia, 51
Attachment theory, 11–12. *See also* Parental attachment
Attention deficit/hypersensitivity disorder, 469
    approaches to investigation, 123
    central tenet of, 56
    as key foundation of evolutionary psychology, 122
Authoritarianism, 396
Autism, 103, 110, 207, 208, 211, 415, 426–428
    abnormal eye contact, 425
    brain size, 448
    central coherence and, 436
    compensations, 445
    emotional detection, 418
    gender and, 381, 425, 437, 447
    genetic origins, 437, 471
    high-functioning, 427
    hyper-systemizing in, 426
    hyperlexia and, 442
    impairment theory of mind and, 142
    low-functioning, 427
    medium functioning, 427
    neurocognitive causes, 419
    pathology, 417
    protection against, 447
    psychopathy *vs.*, 417, 439, 448
    psychosis *vs.*, 439, 442, 445, 447
    schizophrenic psychosis *vs.*, 439, 448
    shared attention mechanism in, 435
    spectrum conditions, 426
    spectrum quotient, 427, 430
    symptom, 433
    theory of mind mechanism, 419
    visual-spatial abilities in, 442

B

Bacteria, 109
Baldwin Effect, 5, 6
Baron-Cohen's model for mind reading, 416
Beckwith-Wiedemann syndrome, 437, 438
Behavior
    antisocial, 445
    causes of, 41–42, 335
    defined, 13
    evolutionary *vs.* sociocultural explanations, 41–42
    inhibition, male *vs.* female, 443
    psychopathic, 445
    social, 28, 149, 194
        brain mechanisms for, 415–432
    sociocultural *vs.* evolutionary explanations, 41–42
    spiteful, 93
Behaviorism, 6, 138, 194
Best response, 315
Bet-hedging, 58

Binary reciprocity, 340
Biosocial theory, 275, 276–277
Birth defects, 52
Birth size, 53–54
Birth weight, adult survival and, 61
Brain, 216
    amygdala, 444
    analyzable systems, 422
    anatomy, 204
        schizophrenia and, 441
    in autism, 448
    beliefs and, 315
    cerebral cortex, 438
    damage
        cheater-detection ability and, 347
        memory loss and, 207, 208
        prosopagnosia following, 176
        social contract reasoning and, 182
    domain-specific functions, 216
    dorsal premotor cortex, 435
    emotional states in, 374, 376
    evolution, 128, 408, 415–432
    female, 424, 426
    flexibility, 377
    forebrain, 437, 438
    formation, 276
    frontal volume, antisocial behavior and, 445
    gender differences, 277
    gene interaction, 443
    genes and development of, 294
    hypothalamus, 62, 125, 141, 437, 438, 444
    limbic system, 141
        genes of, 438
    male, 424, 426
    maternal, 438, 444
    mechanisms, 381
        for social behavior, 415–432
    mirror neurones, 435
    modules, 354 (*See also* Module(s))
    neocortex, 437
    paternal, 438, 444
    primitive part, 437
    reward systems, 457
    scan, 183, 435
    schizophrenic, 441, 447
    as set of interacting modular systems, 323
    sexual differentiation, 424
    size, 87
    types, 426–428
    ventral premotor cortex, 435
Bride-price, 57
By-products, 10, 157, 385, 495
    of atresia, 59
    Cinderella effects as, 386–387
    deleterious, 58
    of hormonal metabolism, 243
    incidental, 300
    maladaptive, 43, 460
    nonfunctional, 160, 161
    polyovulation, 56

of sexual evolution, 71
spandrels as, 38
unselfish, 309

C

Cambridge fetal testosterone project, 425
Cancer, 438
Cardiovascular disease, 61, 156
Central coherence, 431, 436–437, 445, 450
Cheater-detection ability, 181, 198, 347
Cheaters, 92, 108
Child abuse, 19, 208, 220, 282, 385, 387
    cause, 207
    database analysis, 388
    as evolutionary strategy, 395
    household composition, 21
    investigation of allegations, 393
    journal, 391, 397, 399, 400
    mortality, 392, 398, 399
    in New Zealand, 398
    in North America, 390
    research, 220, 383, 385, 388
    risk, 87
    in South Korea, 391
    stepparenthood and, 14, 387, 393, 395
    in U. K., 397
    in U. S., 389, 398
Children
    abuse of (*See* Child abuse)
    birth defects, 52
    birth weight, 53
    closely spaced, 209
    depression, 12
    egocentricity, 141
    emotion signals, 126
    emotional signals and intragenomic conflict, 126
    genetic inheritance, 118
    growth rate, 54
    intuitive physics, 165
    kinship detection, 179
    learning, 165, 178
    maternal deprivation, 12
    mutations, 51
    nutrition, 61
    parental investment, 29, 56, 57
    Piaget's theory, 6
    same-sex bullying, 273
    stepparental discrimination, 388–389
    unusual rearing patterns, 207
Cinderella effect, 16, 340
    biased reporting, 390–394
    controversy, 389–397
    critiques of, 383–400
    evidence, 385–389
    mothers' boyfriend and, 387–388
    stepparenthood and, 386–387
    varying magnitude, 386
Coalitional psychology, 269–270, 355, 360, 403, 405

Cognition
    development, 126
    intergroup, 407
    mechanisms, 175
    mechanistic, 434, 439
    sex differences in, 446, 464
Cognitive-experimental perspective, 13
Competition, 2, 359
    cooperation and, 105, 111, 114, 336
    economic, 282
    female-female, 57, 75, 273
    gender difference, 445
    genes and, 32
    group, 310, 478
    Hamilton's rule and, 114
    intergroup, 11, 34, 104, 322
    intersexual, 4, 263, 264
    intragroup, 359
    intrasexual, 4, 15, 214, 236, 241, 243, 262, 264,
        268–270
    killing of, 278, 280
    kin selection, 104
    male-male, 55, 75, 78, 86, 196, 197, 198, 204, 246, 275
    for mates, 76, 229, 273, 469
    for moral allegiance, 494
    physiology and, 55
    repression and, 111
    reproductive, 28, 31, 112
    resources and, 360
    sibling, 73, 93
    social, 310
    sperm, 71, 72, 77, 82, 84–85, 226, 233, 235, 274
    unconscious, 43
Concrete reciprocity, 301
Concurrently contingent tactics, 196
Conflict(s)
    group, 327, 480, 497
    intergroup, 360, 401–412
        evolutionary success and, 323
        frequent, 322
        instigation and persistence, 408–409
        roots, 401
    intragenomic, 139, 140
        asymmetry and, 124
        autosomes and, 121
        cytoplasmic inheritance and, 88, 147
        defined, 140
        emotional signals in young children and, 126
        persistence following birth, 125
        related asymmetries and, 121, 123
    kin selection and, 49
    marital, 19
    parent-offspring
        approaches to investigation, 123
        central tenet of, 56
        as key foundation of evolutionary psychology, 122
    sexual, 83, 84, 85
        male-female interactions and, 87
    sibling, 102–103
Continuous reciprocity, 340

Cooperation, 309
    competition and, 105, 111, 114, 336
    defined, 108
    evolution of, 344
    as evolutionary puzzle, 334
    kin selection and, 92, 107
    models, 321
    reciprocal altruism as form of biological, 301
    sex differences in, 110, 429
    within-group, 336
Cost benefit structure, 200
Costly-signaling, 233, 332, 333
    broadcasting MHC types through, 245
    evolutionary underpinnings, 492

D

Darwinian psychiatry
    defined, 453
    mainstream psychiatry vs., 454
    social support networks and, 464
    therapeutic relevance, 471
    typological thinking and, 465
Deception problem, 338
Decision-making, 90, 199
Depression, 209, 455
    cognitive accuracy and, 221
    event-related risk for, 464
    during gestation, 463
    postnatal, 463
    prenatal, 463
    in reproductive-related trauma, 462
    severe, 470
    stress and, 463
    support solicitation and, 221
    theoretical, 472
Design, 215
Developmental determinants of adult survival, 61
Developmental dynamics approach, 143
Developmental Systems Theory, 128, 142–146
Diabetes, 54, 61, 156
    gestational, 52
Digit ratios, 248
    high, 248
    low, 248
    as markers for perinatal androgen action, 258
    physical fitness and, 259
    sex-typical, 249
Direct fitness, 93, 100, 108
Discriminative parental solicitude, 19, 139, 148, 282, 384, 397, 398
Disease, 458
Domain-specific information processing, 13, 140, 216
    modules, 141
Domestic violence, 97, 110, 280
Drugs, resistance to infection and, 198
Dyadic alliances with nonkin, 358
Dyslexia, 187, 441–442, 448

E

Eating habits, 282
EEA. See Environment of evolutionary adaptedness (EEA)
ELM. See Exapted learning mechanism (ELM)
Embryo, 51
Emotional infidelity, 13, 273–274
Environment of evolutionary adaptedness (EEA), 15, 25, 456
    rejection, 42
Environmentalism, 8
Erotomania, 439, 442
Eugenics, 7
Eusociality, 26, 108, 114
Evolution
    historical legacy of, 40
    models, 112
Evolutionary biology, 223, 298, 356, 396, 495
    adaptation in, 37, 156
    adaptationism and, 468
    as branch of evolutionary psychology, 43
    challenges, 129
    core principles, 219
    functional biology vs., 458
    goal, 215
    psychiatry and, 454
    subfield, 154
    theoretical tool in, 159
Evolutionary developmental psychology, 142
Evolutionary psychology, 13–18
    assumptions, 13
    current issues, 15–16
    evolutionary biology as branch of, 43
    foundations, 25, 122, 139
    key foundations, 122
    marital conflict, 19
    mechanisms, 173–174
    modules, 174 (See also Module(s))
    psychiatry and, 468, 469
    questions concerning, 25–43
    sociobiology vs., 122, 139, 469
    suspicions of, 16–17
Evolutionary thinking
    heralds of modern, 11–12
    pre-Darwin, 1–2
Evolved function, incidental effect vs., 31–32
Exaptation, 37, 157–158, 167
    adaptation vs., 159, 161
    primary, 158
    usefulness of, 158
Exapted learning mechanism (ELM), 164
Eye, evolution of, 40

F

Facial averageness, 249–250
Facial cues, 177, 183, 335
False-belief
    gender difference in development of, 430
    metarepresentational reasoning about, 486

recognizing, 480, 487
test, 433
   false photo *vs.*, 445
understanding of, 417
Family violence, 97, 110, 220
Fitness interdependence, 364
Fitness tokens, 168
Food sharing, 92, 185, 187, 323
  genetic kinship and, 179, 322
Fragile X syndrome, 442
Function(s)
  alternative concept, 156
  ancestral adaptations, 15
  behavior and, 8
  brain, 12, 13, 216
  cross-cultural, 4
  of crying, 37, 45
  evolved, 42
    incidental effect *vs.*, 31
  immune, 62
  invariant, 6
  postreproductive period, 47
  psychological, 216
  sexual jealousy, 15
  of social exclusion, 20
  of traits, 154, 156
  unaltered, traits *vs.*, 37
Functional specialization, 174

G

Game theory, 229
  appealing features, 354
  evolutionary, 315
  human face of, 349
  prisoner's dilemma as framework for, 355
  simulations, 218, 219
Gametes, 51
Gene(s)
  as atom of selection, 130
  as catalysts, 120, 130
  evolution of, 303
  individuals as vehicles for, 295
  labeling, 294
  outlaw, 118
  replication, 145
  selfish, 121
  as tumor suppressors, 438
Gene-culture coevolution, 301, 313, 322–323
  models, 314
Gene interaction, 32–33, 120, 123, 139, 155, 200
Genetic determinism, 17, 129
Genic self-favoritism, 333
Genomic imprinting, 66, 110, 111, 123–126, 131, 132, 133, 134, 139, 141, 148, 149
  breakdown, 103
  conflict theory, 123
  defined, 83, 103, 140
  imbalanced, 110

kin selection theory and, 103, 123
  in mammals, 148
  sexual conflict and, 83
  significance, 139
Germ line, 145
Gossip, 208, 210, 211
Grandparents, 209, 363
Green beard effect, 303, 333, 338
Group conflict, 327, 480, 497. *See also* Intergroup
    conflict(s)
Group selection, 33, 104–106, 114, 130, 294, 303, 314, 337
  individual reproductive success *vs.*, 31–32
  parsimony *vs.*, 337
Growth patterns, human, 54–55

H

Hamilton's inequality, 99
Hamilton's rule, 10, 97, 302
  alternate way of writing, 92
  defined, 108
  quantitative, 99–100
Handicap principle, 80, 275, 312, 328
Homicide, 19, 64, 97, 110, 186, 228, 269, 366, 369
Homosexual pornography, 284
Hox genes, 40
Human nature, 221
Hunter-gatherer(s), 169
  altruism and, 314
  bands, 340
  culture, 222
  current environments, 203
  early, 2
  female infanticide and, 58
  Hadza, 389
  life-histories, 55
  model, predictions from, 447
  research, 218, 222–223
  territorial nature, 404
Hyper-mentalism, 440, 441, 449
Hyperlexia, 441–442
Hypo-mentalism, 440, 449
Hypothalamus, 62, 125
  functions, 438
  paternal control, 141, 437, 444
Hypothetical constructs, 217

I

Incidental effects, 38, 157
Inclusive fitness, 32, 93, 107, 139, 216, 219, 384. *See also*
    Kin selection
Indirect fitness, 93, 100
  benefit, 9
  defined, 108
Indirect reciprocity, 11, 107, 333, 338, 347
  adaptiveness, 338
  evolution, 311, 329, 351

Indirect selection, 32. *See also* Kin selection
Individual-level theories, 334
Infanticide, 56, 58, 208, 209, 230, 394, 400
Infectious diseases, 403
Infidelity, 13, 15, 266, 273–274
Information processing cognitive-experimental
    perspective, 13
Innate adaptation, 206
Innate genetic developmental organization, 192
Innate information-processing mechanisms, 205,
    480–481
Instinct theory, 6
Intention, 435, 439
Intergenerational transfer, 60
Intergroup cognitions, 404–406
    sex differences in, 407
Intergroup competition, 11
Intergroup conflict(s), 360, 401–412
    evolutionary success and, 323
    frequent, 322
    instigation and persistence, 408–409
    roots, 401
Internal norm, 326
Intersexual competition, 263
Intersexual selection, 263
Intragenomic conflict, 139, 140
    asymmetry and, 124
    autosomes and, 121
    cytoplasmic inheritance and, 88, 147
    defined, 140
    emotional signals in young children and, 126
    persistence following birth, 125
    related asymmetries and, 121, 123
Intragroup competition, 359
Intrapersonal conflict, 128
Intrapersonal reciprocity, 128
Intrasexual competition, 262, 268–270
Intrauterine growth, 52–53

J

Jealousy, 18, 365
    sex differences in, 19, 274, 279
    sexual, 15, 208
        emotional *vs.*, 264, 273–275
    termination of courtship and, 362

K

Killing instincts, 300
Kin coefficient, 339
Kin discrimination, 98–100
    across species, 108
    adaptations, 163
    defined, 108
    limited dispersal and, 103–104
Kin interactions, 179
Kin recognition, 112, 303, 311

learned cues, 113
major histocompatability complex and, 110
mechanisms, 179, 180, 303
by olfactory cues, 188
phenotype-matching-based mechanism, 180
psychological mechanism, 179
test of alternative hypotheses for, 112
Kin selection, 65, 123, 314, 332–333
    alternative, 107
    altruism and, 110, 114, 302, 314
    basic principles, 91
    coefficient of relatedness, 94
    competition, 104
    conflict and, 49, 183
    cooperation and, 92, 107
    defined, 108
    development of theory, 92
    effect, 32
    example of, 108
    generality, 93
    genomic imprinting and, 103, 123
    implications of, 69
    as key to altruism, 114
    limitations, 352
    by limited dispersal, 109
    misunderstandings about, 110
    models, 107, 113
    mutualisms and, 109
    natural selections and, 109
    population and, 113
    predictions using methodology of, 94
    results, 95
    sibling conflict and, 102–103
    testing, 99–101, 110
        with comparative statics, 100–101
        using Hamilton's rules, 99–100
Klinefelter's syndrome, 447

L

Lack effect, 9
Lamarckian theory, 5, 6
Learning mechanisms, as adaptations, 164
Leptin, 62
Life history theory, 12, 47–63
    adaptations and, 203, 216
    comparative evidence, 48–49
    constructing evolutionary explanation of, 49–51
    fertility and, 56
    focus, 16
    postulate, 144
    psychiatric disorders and, 464–468
    reproductive value of parents and, 75
Life span, 60–61, 311, 363
    long, 47
    male fertility, 271
    maximum, 48
    mortality rates and, 63
    reproductive, 59, 270

Limited dispersal, 98–99
    kin discrimination and, 103–104
    kin selection and, 109
Long-term matings, 264
Longevity, 20
    coevolution of intelligence and, 66, 257
    number of children and, 60
    reproduction and, 61, 67
    sex differences in, 61, 84, 86

M

Macroevolution, 49
Magical ideation, 440–441, 441, 442, 450
Marital conflict, 19
Mate retention, 18, 19, 88, 234, 361–362
Mate selection, 245, 287, 368
    campus values in, 279
    early, 360
    female, 265, 360
    models, 361
    natural selection designed, 191
    sexual differences in, 279
    standards, 234
Maternal brain, 438, 444
Maternity, mortality and, 60
Mating, 361
    assortative, 428, 429, 449
    strategies, parental investment and, 459–461
    success, male vs. female, 86
Mechanistic cognition, 434, 439
Medical research, 221
Menopause, 58–60, 64, 65, 66, 67, 68, 463
Mentalism, 434, 435, 439–440
Metarepresentation, 486
Microevolution, 49
Microorganisms, 109
Mind-blindedness, 433, 434, 440
Mind reading, 379, 434, 439
    cross sex, 366
    defined, 415
    model, 416, 417
Mixed reproduction strategy, 264, 270
Mnemonic power, 482
Module(s), 13, 41, 131, 139, 482
    activation, 482
    cognitive, 140, 174
    domain-specific cognitive, 140
    interaction, 174, 184
    number of, 217
Morality, 293, 299, 313
Mortality
    child abuse, 392, 398, 399
    maternity and, 60
Mosaic brain evolution, 128
Mutual benefit, defined, 108
Mutual monitoring, 346–347
Mutualism, 109, 110, 114, 300, 352

N

Natural selection, 29–30, 31, 32, 35, 36, 262–263, 307,
    354. See also Selection
    dual action of sexual selection and, 275
    effect of, 154, 159
    evolution of psychological traits, 262
    evolutionary progress and, 35–36
    at gene level, 178
    logic, 34
    sexual selection vs., 30–31, 78
        traits and, 275

O

Ontology recapitulates phylogeny, 138
Optimality, 171, 217
Organelles, sex-specific transmission of, 77
Ostracization problem, 338
Outlaw gene, 118

P

Parent-offspring conflict, 10, 101–102, 139, 143, 353, 451
    approaches to investigation, 123
    central tenet of, 56
    as key foundation of evolutionary psychology, 122
Parent-specific expression, 140
Parental attachment
    biological vs. adopted children, 209
    REM sleep and, 125
    research, 225
Parental investment, 363, 444, 448, 465
    bias, 87
    change in, 311
    classification of, 302
    defined, 75
    determinants, 55
    differential, 85
    economic, 10, 266–268, 270, 271
    examples, 125
    factors affecting, 282
    gender and, 263
    grandparental, 363
    intergenerational transfer, 60
    logic of, 360
    male vs. female, 75, 286
    mating strategies and, 459–461
    measuring, 57
    optimization, 463
    predicting, 459
    sex biasing, 57
    significance, 302
    stepparental, 384, 394
Parental manipulation, 68, 139
Parliament of the mind, 141
Parsimony, selection group vs., 337
Paternal brain, 438, 444

Personal ads, 220, 267, 271
Physical Prediction Questionnaire, 424
Physiological research, 221
Political psychology, 225
Polyandry, 209
Polygyny, 55, 208
    fertility and, 66
    forms, 195, 210
    inheritance of wealth and, 66
    multimale, 79
    single-male, 79
    threshold, offspring quality and, 90
    types, 195, 210
Population structure, 344
Pornography, 208, 265, 283–286
    consumers, 265
    economic statistics, 220
    female, 282, 283, 285
    gay male, 284
    gender differences in interest, 286–287
    male, 208–209
    ubiquity, 282
Pornotopia, 286
    defined, 283–284
    romantopia and, 286, 287
Positive assortment, 338
    model, 332
    ostracization and, 338
    rejection of, 338
    rethinking, 344–345
    via partner choice, 347
Prader-Willi syndrome, 111, 133, 442, 450, 451, 452
    etiology, 447
    gene expression, 438
    genomic imprinting and, 103
    maternal UPD, 448
    psychosis in, 448
    variant, 447
Preadaptation, 158
Prejudices, 401–402, 406–409
    affective response and, 410
    ancestral threats and, 402
    associative learning and, 406
    danger-relevant, 407
    functional flexibility and, 406
    psychological bases, 402
    sex differences in, 406
    syndrome, 402
Prestige, 267, 358–359, 367
Primary sexual characteristics, 262
Prisoner's dilemma, 355–356
Proper domain, 175, 480
Prosocial emotions, 325
Prosopagnosia, 176
Pseudopathologies, 156, 207
Psychiatric disorders
    diagnoses, 456
    life history theory and, 464–468
    sexual selection and, 459–464

Psychiatry
    Darwinian
        defined, 453
        mainstream psychiatry vs., 454
        social support networks and, 464
        therapeutic relevance, 471
        typological thinking and, 465
    environment and, 456
    evolutionary, 469
    mainstream vs. Darwinian, 454
    objective, 470
    sexual selection theory and, 459
Psychological adaptations, 163
    evidence, 219
        evaluating, 223–224
        pregnancy sickness as, 224–225
        research methods for identifying, 217–224
        universal, 217
Psychologically selfish behavior, 304
Psychopathology, 466
Puberty, 54
    bone growth in, 244
    onset, 262, 270
    reproductive investment after, 55–60
    risk taking during, 86
    testosterone effects of late, 62
Public goods game, 108, 318–319

Q

Quasinormal behaviors, 209

R

Racism, 396
Random mixing, 344
Rational actor model, 315
Realpolitik, 490
Reciprocal altruism, 107, 216, 301, 333, 358
    defined, 181, 314
    evolution of, 10–11, 134, 188, 236
    as form of biological cooperation, 301
    model, 318
    rejection of, 338
    social interactions and, 210, 219
    war and, 280
Reciprocity, 314, 333, 348
    binary, 340
    concrete, 301
    continuous, 340
    indirect, 11, 107, 333, 338, 347
        adaptiveness, 338
        evolution, 311, 329, 351
    reward processing and, 346
    strong, 107, 307, 321, 334, 348
        adaptation and, 323–324
        adaptive feature, 321
        defined, 321

evolution of, 324–325
    evolutionary model, 322
    evolutionary stability, 321–322
    prosocial emotions and, 325–326
    Triversian model, 332
Relatedness, 108
Reproduction suppression, 211
Reproductive costs, 276–277
Reputation, 175, 347–348
    altruism and, 347
    effects, 321, 324, 377
    reciprocity and, 328, 334
    repairing damaged, 307
    social contracts and, 354
Research methods, 15, 215–236
    across psychological sciences, 225–226
    cross-cultural, 218, 223
    genetic, 218, 221–222
    hunter-gatherer, 218, 222–223
    for indentifying psychological adaptation, 217–224
    medical, 218, 221
    phylogenetic, 218, 222
    physiological, 218, 221
    psychological, 218, 219–221
    theoretical, 218, 219
    usefulness, 211
Rett syndrome, 442
Risk minimization, 58
Risk-taking, 268–270, 468–470
    adolescent, 279, 280
    positive emotions and, 459
    sex differences in, 86, 275

S

Sally-Anne test, 433, 445
Scala naturae, 35
Schizophrenia, 447, 470, 471
    autism vs., 439, 448
    brain anatomy and, 441
    cancer and, 438
    cognitive asymmetry, 439
    dyslexia and, 441
    genes, 468
    magical ideation and, 440
    maternal influenza and, 458
    mind-reading ability, 439
    paranoid, 439
    X-factor in, 447
Schizotypal personality, 440, 441
Secondary sexual characteristics, 262
Selection
    age-specific, 60
    arena, 51
    by-products, 10, 157, 385, 495
        of atresia, 59
        Cinderella effects as, 386–387
        deleterious, 58
        of hormonal metabolism, 243

incidental, 300
        maladaptive, 43, 460
        nonfunctional, 160, 161
        polyovulation, 56
        of sexual evolution, 71
        spandrels as, 38
        unselfish, 309
    gene as atom of, 130
    group, 33, 104–106, 114, 130, 294, 303, 314, 337
        individual reproductive success vs., 31–32
        parsimony vs., 337
    kin, 65, 123, 314, 332–333
        alternative, 107
        altruism and, 110, 114, 302, 314
        basic principles, 91
        coefficient of relatedness, 94
        competition, 104
        conflict and, 49, 183
        cooperation and, 92, 107
        defined, 108
        development of theory, 92
        effect, 32
        example of, 108
        generality, 93
        genomic imprinting and, 103, 123
        implications of, 69
        as key to altruism, 114
        limitations, 352
        by limited dispersal, 109
        misunderstandings about, 110
        models, 107, 113
        mutualisms and, 109
        natural selections and, 109
        population and, 113
        predictions using methodology of, 94
        results, 95
        sibling conflict and, 102–103
        testing, 99–101, 110
            with comparative statics, 100–101
            using Hamilton's rules, 99–100
    mate, 245, 287, 368
        campus values in, 279
        early, 360
        female, 265, 360
        models, 361
        natural selection designed, 191
        sexual differences in, 279
        standards, 234
    natural, 29–30, 31, 32, 35, 36, 262–263, 307, 354
        dual action of sexual selection and, 275
        effect of, 154, 159
        evolutionary progress and, 35–36
        at gene level, 178
        logic, 34
        sexual selection vs., 30–31, 78
            traits and, 275
    pressures operating on ancestors, 42–43
    sexual, 4, 77–79, 86, 262–263, 268, 272, 465
        basis for, 71
        benefits, 89

brain size and, 87
defined, 77
dual action of natural selection and, 275
effects, 30, 55
evolution, 72
females *vs.* males, 75
genetic compatibility and, 83
handicap principle and, 328
intensity of, 75
methods, 4
mutation rate and, 73, 76–77
mutual, 75
natural selection *vs.*, 30–31, 78
origins, 30
parasite-mediated, 82
pathogen prevalence and, 86, 88
psychiatric disorders and, 459–464
role, 16
sex differences in intensity of, 75, 77
signaling theory and, 240–241
sperm competition, 87
traits and, 275
stabilizing, 35
unit, 32–35
Self-protection, 359
Selfish gene, 121
Selfishness, 121, 304, 314
defined, 108
forms of, 298–299
Sensory bias, 243
Sex allocation, 88, 110, 113
hormonal basis, 86
Sex differences
in aggressiveness, 269, 275
behavioral, 262, 275
biosocial theory, 276
in cognition, 446, 464
in cooperation, 110, 429
cross-cultural evidence, 15
in depressogenic effects, 464
in eagerness to mate, 265
in economic parental investment, 266–268
in empathizing, 424, 431
in emphasis on age and physical attractiveness,
    270–272
essential nature of, 12
evaluating, 462
evolutionary origins, 459, 463
feminist perspective, 281
in intergroup cognitions, 407
in intrasexual aggression, 268–270
in jealousy, 19, 274, 279
in life history, 204
in longevity, 61, 84, 86
in mathematical ability, 430, 431
in mating strategies, 88, 192, 227, 279, 460
in morphological predictors of
    sexual behavior, 231
in morphological predictors of sexual behavior, 231
nonverbal, 450

in number of partners, 265–266
origins, 213, 459
physical, 222
psychological, 17, 222, 264–275
in readiness to mate, 265–266
research, 425, 429
in responses of amygdala, 230
in risk taking, 86, 275
in romantic jealousy, 274
in route learning, 431
in sexual fantasy, 229, 265, 278, 289
in sexual selection, 75
in sexual *vs.* emotional commitment, 272–273
in sexual *vs.* emotional jealousy, 273–275
in social behavior, 431, 464
in social perception, 430
in spatial abilities, 432, 446, 451
in systemizing, 424
Sex ratio, 85–86, 102, 422
manipulation, 57, 85, 102
maternal influence on, 57, 93
one-to-one operational, 263
optimal, 85
primary, 86
secondary, 86
sexual conflict and, 83
tertiary, 86
theory, 85
Sex roles, 263–264
Sex-specific transmission of organelles, 77
Sexism, 396
Sexual behavior, morphological predictors of, 231
Sexual characteristics, 262
Sexual competition, 87
Sexual conflict, 83, 84, 85
male-female interactions and, 87
Sexual disorders, 459–461
Sexual fantasies, 265, 272–273, 287. *See also* Pornography
sex differences in, 229, 265, 278, 289
Sexual fidelity, 264, 273
Sexual infidelity, 15, 274
short-term, 266
Sexual selection, 4, 77–79, 86, 262–263, 268, 272, 465
basis for, 71
benefits, 89
brain size and, 87
defined, 77
dual action of natural selection and, 275
effects, 30, 55
evolution, 72
females *vs.* males, 75
genetic compatibility and, 83
handicap principle and, 328
intensity of, 75
methods, 4
mutation rate and, 73, 76–77
mutual, 75
natural selection *vs.*, 30–31, 78
origins, 30
parasite-mediated, 82

pathogen prevalence and, 86, 88
psychiatric disorders and, 459–464
role, 16
sex differences in intensity of, 75, 77
signaling theory and, 240–241
sperm competition, 87
traits and, 275
Sexual signals, 79–80
Sexual strategies, 14, 144, 219
    explanations, 192
    female *vs.* male, 287
    testosterone and, 221
Sexually proprietary behavior, 14
Short-term matings, 264
Sibling competition, 73
Sibling conflict, 102–103
Sibling incest, 185, 186, 210
    moral judgments about, 179
    predicted attitudes toward, 179
    third-party reactions to, 179, 198
Silver-Russell syndrome, 437
Social behavior, 28, 149, 194
    primary basis of, 210
Social contract, 13, 183, 192, 358
    testing, 14
    violation, 358
Social institution building, 323
Social role theory, 275
Sociobiology, 28
    critics, 36
    evolutionary psychology *vs.*, 122, 139, 469
    natural selection and, 43
    study group, 11
Spandrels, 38, 157
Specialized information processing, 199
Speciation, 35
Spite, 108
Spontaneous abortion, 52
Stabilizing selection, 35
Standard Social Science Model, 7
Standing models, 321
Status, 168, 211, 358–359
    adult, 54
    conceptual, of biological adaptations, 154
    employment, 269
    energy, 245, 247
    fertility, 244
    gaining and maintaining, 355
    health, 466
    hierarchies, 356
    hormonal, 282
    increasing, 300, 317
    male, benefits of, 248
    marital, 269, 385
    mating, 246, 253
    minority, 408
    nutritional, 61
    occupational, 267
    social, 220, 267, 286
    strong reciprocity and, 324

Stepchildren, 381
Stepparenthood, 58, 179
    child abuse and, 14, 387, 393, 395
    Cinderella effect and, 386–387
    parental investment, 384, 394
Stigmatization, 20, 413
Strategic interaction, 315
Strategic pluralism, 20, 219, 230
Strong reciprocity, 107, 307, 334, 348
    adaptation and, 323–324
    adaptive feature, 321
    defined, 321
    evolution of, 324–325
    evolutionary model, 322
    evolutionary stability, 321–322
    prosocial emotions and, 325–326
Supernatural agent, 479
Synergy, 344
Synthetic theory, 145
Systemizing
    phases, 421
        analysis, 421
        confirmation/disconfirmation, 421
        law derivation, 421
        operation, 421
        repetition, 421
    sex differences in, 422–424

T

Task analysis, 163
Theory of mind mechanism, 416
Threats, 401–402
    to efficiency of group processes, 410–411
    of parasite transmission, 409–410
Tragedy of Commons, 108
Trivers-Hare hypothesis, 110
Triversian reciprocity model, 332
Tuberous sclerosis, 442
Turner's syndrome, 442

U

Ultimatum game, 316–318
Uniparental disomy (UPD), 448, 450, 452
UPD. *See* Uniparental disomy (UPD)

W

Wason's selection task, 14, 170, 181, 182, 185, 213
Westermarck's hypothesis, 179

X

X-trisomy, 447